Footpri

Charlie Godfrey-Fau

1 Minack Theatre
Open-air theatre carved out of the cliff with the sea for a backdrop

2 Tate St Ives
Arty enclave in the deep southwest

3 Eden Project
Ground-breaking transformation from claypit into biodome

4 South West Coast Path
Stunning long distance footpath right round the peninsula

5 Croyde Bay
Top surfing beach away from the crowds

6 Dartmoor
Last wilderness in the south, bleak granite moorland

7 Quantocks
Somerset cider hills, heather-clad with glimpses of the sea

8 Salisbury Plain
Stone circles and standing stones, not least Stonehenge

9 Wye Valley
Dramatic winding gorges full of canoes

10 Cotswolds
Honeystone towns dotted among cosy green hills

11 Oxford
Dreaming academic spires on the River Thames

12 London
Irresistible, sensational, essential. The capital

England Highlights

See colour maps at back of book

13 Seven Sisters Country Park
Superb undulating white chalk cliffs overlooking the Channel

14 Suffolk Coast
Eerie marshes, lost towns and delicious smoked fish

15 Cambridge
Water-backed old colleges and fenland

16 National Space Centre
Dynamic exhibition on the exploration of space

17 Imperial War Museum of the North
Stunning architecture modelled on a broken teapot

18 Peak District
Mysterious caves, wonderful walks and tumbling rivers

19 Yorkshire Dales
Hills, valleys and dry stone walls

20 Wastwater
The quietest and most secluded of the lovely lakes

21 Robin Hood's Bay
Sweeping cliffs high above the beach

22 Newcastle Gateshead
Urban regeneration watched over by the Angel of the North

23 Dunstanburgh
Dramatic castle perched on a headland

Contents

The South

The Southwest

East Anglia

East Midlands

West Midlands

Northwest

Yorkshire

The white cliffs of Dover: "There is a cliff, whose high and bending head looks fearfully on the confined deep" King Lear, *Shakespeare.*

The North

Background

Footnotes

Inside front cover

Inside back cover

Bigger and better

The Great Court at the British Museum illuminates world cultures like never before with its latticework roof and 3312 unique panes of glass making it the largest covered square in Europe.

A foot in the door

England is an oddball. So many people have lived in the place so close together for so long that it's become a seedbed for eccentricities. Just look at the painstaking attention to detail in its carefully recreated one-thirtieth scale model villages, its matchstick ships, bicycle museums and teddy bear factories.

Quite apart from the choked up roads, crummy railways and the exorbitant cost of everything, what usually amazes both English people and visitors to the country is the variety of things going on. Everywhere you look there's something being organized: DJ-driven clubnights, art show openings, village fêtes and game fairs, car boot sales, antiques road shows, book markets, guided walks and talks. England may be a very busy country, but it's not all about such frenzied activity. There are settled and peaceful pleasures to be found up and down the land as well. Perhaps it's the fact that the sea is never more than a couple of hours' drive away that makes it seem so restful. The gentleness of England has often been remarked upon: the soft rains, low rolling hills, clouded skies and, oh yes… the manners of the people. Hard to fathom that – especially after a lager-fuelled Saturday night out in almost any small town or large city, but then, if you're lucky, there's always an easy Sunday morning afterwards.

The briskness with which brutality flares up and subsides here has shocked visitors and puzzled historians for centuries. That said, England is changing very rapidly in many respects. For every story of manufacturing decline, loss of Empire and urban blight, there's one of reinvigorated city centres, vibrant arts scenes and coffee bar culture. With its multicultural mix, steady nerve and mongrel talent, its weight of history, European values and Americanized culture, England often seems to be on the verge of collapsing on itself. That's what makes it such an exciting country to visit. Catch it while it lasts.

10 There'll always be an England?

With much of the government in London being Scottish and the Welsh increasingly directing their own affairs, England's sense of itself seems much less secure than before the collapse of the British Empire. In fact the different English regions, especially Cornwall, the Northeast and Northwest have all expressed strong interest in self-government, seeing Westminster as being remote and too wrapped up in London and the Southeast. At the same time, the nation's urban renaissance and increasing multi-cultural diversity is impossible to underestimate. It's hard to exaggerate the importance of the rebirth of the Midlands, Manchester, Leeds, Sheffield, Liverpool and Newcastle as exciting, optimistic places to live after such a terrible 20th century: unemployment and deprivation have been the lot of millions in these parts for more than three generations. The phenomenon has also widened the most obvious gulf in English society – that between city and country. While metropolitan areas have received serious government attention, the countryside has been forced to cope with BSE

Winter Gardens, Sheffield

This 70m long wooden-framed glasshouse was part of the £120 million scheme to regenerate Sheffield's city centre.

and foot and mouth disease. Their different agendas have been crystalized by government plans to ban fox hunting – an issue which has united the land-owning gentry and the rural poor – and incidentally re-opened the debate about how England regards itself.

Home is where the art is...

England has traditionally thought of itself as fashionably philistine, more interested in the horses, dogs, fighting and football than any of the gentler arts. Even the works of Shakespeare were passed on to posterity thanks only to the goodwill of a couple of friends after his death. England is still fanatical about football and all the rest, but has also relatively recently found that, suitably packaged, the arts, entertainment and architecture are also well worth a look. The media, the National Lottery and the advertising guru Charles Saatchi have all been big players in this cultural turnaround. Perhaps as a result the whole project already looks suspiciously shallow – merely an extension of the global cult of celebrity – but even so, it remains the most promising arena for England to argue with itself.

Lacock

Immaculately-preserved 13th-century Lacock, both feudal village and the birthplace of photography. Here William Fox Talbot discovered the principle of photographic negatives.

1

2

4

5

7

8

10

11

1 *Astonishing stones at Stonehenge, the centre of one of the most ancient civilizations on the planet. Was it a temple to the sun or perhaps an astronomical clock?* ▸▸ *See page 285.*

2 *Big Ben, telling the capital when it's time to leave work and head off into the rush hour.* ▸▸ *See page 78.*

3 *The red pantile roofs of Robin Hood's Bay stack up on the precipitous Yorkshire coast.* ▸▸ *See page 710.*

4 *Relaxing Manchester-style. Cafés and bars are abuzz with music in this northern metropolis.* ▸▸ *See page 621.*

5 *Hadrian's Wall, now symbol of a nation's strength or insecurity?* ▸▸ *See page 784.*

6 *Canal barges in Stratford-upon-Avon's marina.* ▸▸ *See page 561.*

7 *Stop in for a cider in Salcombe, Devon.* ▸▸ *See page 403.*

8 *Make straw while the sun shines. Harvest time in the rolling southern home counties landscape.* ▸▸ *See page 143.*

9 *Replica of the Sanctuary Knocker on the north door of Durham Cathedral, a towering Norman achievment.* ▸▸ *See page 798.*

10 *That's the way not to do it: social commentary Punch and Judy style.* ▸▸ *See page 712.*

11 *Where shepherds watch their flocks. Sheepfolds in North Yorkshire.* ▸▸ *See page 700.*

12 *Follow royal example and be silly by the seaside in Brighton, like generations before you.* ▸▸ *See page 198.*

Countryside dalliance

Only a few hours' drive from all this urban regeneration is some of England's most traditional and beautifully conserved countryside: the Cotswold and Malvern hills, the Peak District, Yorkshire Dales and Northumberland National Park. As well as providing ample walking space, these places and many others like the Wye Valley, the Norfolk Broads, South Downs and the Shropshire hills, are where any number of different outdoor activity cravings are indulged: paragliding, windsurfing, horse riding, potholing, rock climbing, mountain biking and fishing. The English want to have their cake and eat it: feel the big city buzz as well as the refreshing thrill of the great outdoors. With any luck they should succeed, and already the chance to combine the best bits of both town and countryside makes visiting the country much more pleasurable.

Northern exposure and southern comfort

As fundamental as the urban-rural split is the north-south divide, and though less obvious and economically unfair than it has been under previous governments, it's still visible. Broadly speaking, the north is less expensive, more hilly, and rougher round the edges. York, a medieval walled city and cathedral with a Viking past, is the ancient capital of this end of the country, a job it once shared with Durham, with an even more extraordinary cathedral. Come the Industrial Revolution and the growth of the manufacturing cities and mining towns, the mountainous Lake District's picture-postcard serenity came into its own as a place to unwind, and Blackpool pleasure beach

Heddon Valley, a carpet of late summer heather on the north Devon coast.

A frozen winter's day beside the River Waveney at Gillingham in Norfolk.

boomed. They're both still very popular tourist destinations. Further north, beyond Hadrian's Wall, the boundary of the Roman Empire, the wild wastes of Northumberland have long been border country disputed with Scotland. The south, on the other hand, is generally richer, less industrialized and more touristy. London is the big influence of course, but Winchester was once the centre of the area, with wonderful medieval buildings still standing to show for it. Just to its north, Stonehenge on Salisbury Plain stands testament to a much older Bronze Age civilization. To the west, England heads down to the sea and the setting sun.

The coast with the most

England's coastline is one of its prime natural assets. While north Norfolk, Northumberland, Beachy Head and Robin Hood's Bay all have their charms, it's the southwest of the country that has long been most appreciated. Beyond the cider orchards of Somerset and the heather-clad Quantock hills, the beaches of Devon and Cornwall call surfers, optimistic sunbathers and the bucket and spade brigade every summer. Studded with tiny fishing villages beneath cliffs and headlands, the coast dips in and out of the Atlantic willy-nilly all the way to Land's End. The mild climate has been capitalized upon by the Eden Project, a vast high-tech greenhouse in an abandoned clay pit, while the quality of the light has drawn artists to St Ives. From the Isle of Purbeck to Exmouth, including the strange shingle bank of Chesil Beach, has been designated a World Natural Heritage Site. Swanage, on the tip of the peninsula of Poole harbour, is the start of the South West Coast Path, the longest and one of the most popular long-distance footpaths in the country.

A haunted landscape – not least by Sir Arthur Conan Doyle's slavering Hound of the Baskervilles – Dartmoor is England's last great wilderness.

A walk on the mild side

England's footpaths are the most delightful way to see its countryside. Clearly marked on Ordnance Survey maps, along with countless other points of interest, they mean that walking is always an option. It's a good thing, because England is a country best appreciated on foot or horseback. As well as the long-distance tracks that follow well-trodden routes, some stretching back to the Iron Age, such as the Ridgeway, the whole country is criss-crossed by smaller rights of way, perfect for an afternoon's stroll. They are a great treasure, preserving access for all to scenery that might otherwise be hidden away in private hands. Combined with a mild climate, long summer evenings and gentle landscape, they have made walking, riding and fishing the most popular outdoor activities in the nation. Whichever part of the country you choose to discover, the chances are that some of the most memorable will be the times when you have just stopped walking and stared.

Indefinable Englands

Like football, England is a game of two halves, the North and the South. Then again it's like six games of tennis: the Southeast, East Anglia, Southwest, Midlands, Northeast and Northwest. Or countless overs of cricket. Distinct regions of the country can be multiplied almost without end. Continuously celebrated and supported in sporting fixtures of all kinds, local pride rewards the visitor with an astonishing array of different histories and cultures across each county. It's just one of the characteristics that makes any notion of 'England' so joyously difficult to define.

Essentials

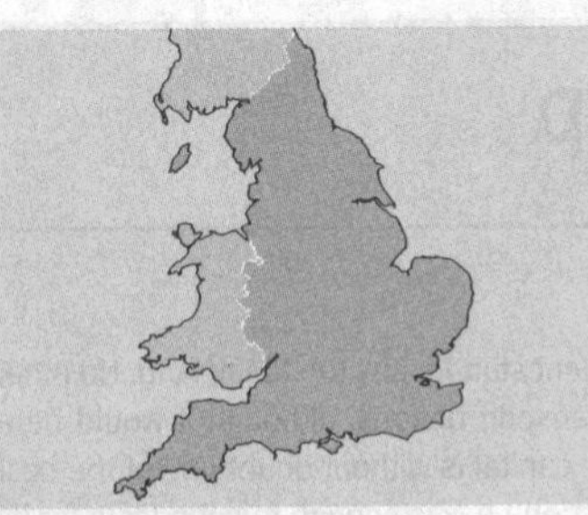

Footprint features

Planning your trip

Where to go

London is the most obvious and likely convenient start for any trip to England. No other city has anything like the range of onward transport options, although it would be a shame to make use of them immediately. The capital is without doubt one of the best things about the UK. Despite its size, even just one day is enough to get a taste for its energy and to see some of the major sights: the river, British Museum, and Covent Garden are all within walking distance of each other. That said, London is superficially very different from much of the rest of the country. Whatever your first impressions of the city, any conclusions you might draw here about England and the English are likely to change quickly as soon as you get beyond the M25 London Orbital Motorway.

One week trip

With only a few days or a week to spare, you might find it best to limit your exploration of the country to destinations within easy reach of London, depending on how you define 'easy'. Getting around England by car, train or bus (see page 37) can be an expensive, time-consuming and frustrating business. If you're thinking of hiring a car, try to avoid the centre of the capital. Every morning and evening the city still holds traffic in a vice-like grip, parking is next to impossible and the centre of the city is subject to a daily £5 congestion charge. However you choose to travel, several places within 2 hour's train ride are all a treat: **Oxford**, **Brighton**, **Cambridge**, **Bath**, **Windsor**, **Stratford-upon-Avon** and **Canterbury** should be somewhere near the top of any list. Each are likely to appeal for different reasons and present many options for exploring the regions around.

With limited time it's only really necessary to see one of the ancient university towns, Oxford or Cambridge. Northwest of Heathrow, **Oxford** is the more 'real', although its old stone colleges and museums are still an extraordinary sight, and a visit here could conveniently lead on to either **Stratford** or **Bath** (see below) or up the **Thames Valley** for walks in the honeystone Cotswold hills. Close to Stansted airport, **Cambridge** is more 'picturesque', with an equal number of old college buildings. It can also make a convenient base for a trip to the **East Anglian coast**, either in Suffolk or lazy Norfolk.

Windsor is the closest tourist hotspot to the capital and it's not hard to see why: it has a fairy tale old castle inhabited by a proper Queen surrounded by miles of amazing parkland and Eton College on the River Thames. It's really only good for a day trip from the capital, unless you want to stay for the gourmet delights of the **Thames Valley**.

A short hop from Gatwick airport, **Brighton** is the full-on clubbing capital of the south, squatting on its pebbly beach with a famous pier and a glut of designer restaurants and bars. Walk off the hangover on the **South Downs** nearby or head into **The Weald** and **Tunbridge Wells** on your way back to compare Brighton with another once-fashionable Royal spa town.

Bath really wins the prize in that category though, 2 hours' drive west of London down the M4. Architecturally it's the most elegant 18th-century town in England, with a hot spring still bubbling into Roman baths at its heart. From Bath, the **Cotswolds**, **Salisbury Cathedral** and the mystical heart of England at **Glastonbury** are all within easy reach, as is the business end of the West Country, **Bristol**.

Stratford-upon-Avon is a must of course for Shakespeare wallahs, but it's also close to very English places in the Midlands like **Warwick Castle**, **Leamington Spa** and the UK's thriving second city, **Birmingham**.

The medieval wonderland that is **York** could also well be seen in a week along with London, but the north really demands a more leisurely pace.

Two week trip

With two weeks to spare, a trip either northwards to **Yorkshire, the Peaks** or the **Lake District**; or westwards to **Devon** and **Cornwall** becomes an option. Delightful northbound itineraries could include: **Cambridge** and the medieval cathedral cities of **Norwich, Lincoln** and **York**, even **Durham** too; **Oxford, Stratford-upon-Avon** and then either the **Peak District** or **Yorkshire Dales** for superb walking country; or **Stamford** for its Georgian townscape and extraordinary churches, followed by **Lincoln, York** and the **North Yorkshire Moors.**

If seeing as much as of the country as possible on your visit isn't a pressing priority, a couple of weeks could just as happily be spent by setting up base in **Harrogate, Ripon** or **York** or anywhere round about, and exploring the **Dales and Moors**. Or head straight for the **Lake District** (especially if you can avoid June-August) for superb walks among lakes and hills. Either way it would still be a shame to miss out on a couple of nights – cultural or otherwise – in one of the large northern cities: **Leeds** for student life, or **Manchester** for nightlife.

Westward itineraries could include **Bath** and then either the 'Jurassic' **Dorset** coast and **Isle of Purbeck** via **Salisbury**; or the romantic wooded **Exmoor coast** and **Hartland**; or even the ruggedly beautiful **North Cornish Coast** around **Tintagel** and the **Eden Project** biodomes near St Austell. Again, finding a base in Hartland or **Dartmoor** and exploring the coast round about is likely to be just as rewarding as pushing on for more.

Three to four week trip

With three to four weeks at your disposal, England's your oyster. In fact if it's oysters you're after, **Whitstable** or the Essex coast are the places to start looking. There's superb seafood too on the **Isles of Scilly,** a surprisingly untouristy archipelago even further west than Cornwall, with a balmy climate that can make a refreshing change after Cornish wet weather. **Herefordshire** and **Shropshire,** on the border with Wales, are still just about off the beaten track, although the charms of Ludlow and Church Stretton have been drawing in gastrophiles and hillwalkers for some time.

Statistically it actually rains least in the east of the country, although it's likely to be some time before the wetlands of the **Norfolk Broads** dry out. That news won't disappoint the small navy of boating enthusiasts that embarks here each summer. The Broads can easily be combined with a trip along the delightful **North Norfolk coast.** As well as Whitstable, the **North Kent Coast** harbours some surprising destinations with an old-fashioned, delapidated air and bracing sea breezes.

At the other end of the country, in the far north, **Northumberland** and its neighbour **Newcastle upon Tyne** could hardly be more different from each other: one furnishes mile upon mile of unspoilt beaches, ruined castles on headlands and **Hadrian's Wall**; the other a serious night out on the tiles after enjoying the renovated Tyneside development.

With unlimited mileage, the dinky delights of the **New Forest**, with its ponies, and the **Isle of Wight**, England in miniature, are both worth exploring. In the Midlands, **Birmingham** is generally underrated and misunderstood. It's a surprisingly green metropolis on the spine of the country, keeping lively multicultural company with **Leicester** and the clubnight nirvana of **Nottingham** and **Sheffield**.

When to go

The high season in the English countryside runs from April until October, when most attractions are open and summer festivities are organized in almost every town and village. School holidays (most of July and August) are even busier, when the most popular tourist destinations – the Lakes, Devon and Cornwall, the Cotswolds and Stratford-upon-Avon – are really best avoided altogether. The best accommodation anywhere in the countryside must be booked well in advance for the summer months.

London and the major cities don't really have a tourist season as such, which makes them an excellent alternative in the autumn and winter months (September-March). That said, many of England's seaside hotspots are also best appreciated once the weather's turned nasty or even in clear winter sunlight, if you're lucky.

Climate

The English temperate climate is notoriously unpredictable. Bright, sunny mornings can turn into a downpour in the time it takes to butter your toast. Predicting the weather is not an exact science and tables of statistics are most likely a waste of time. Very generally, the west side of the country receives more rain than the east, and the east coast gets more sunshine. The west is also milder in the winter because of the relatively warm waters of the Gulf Stream. Winters in the north can be pretty harsh, especially in the mountains, making hiking conditions treacherous. Generally speaking, May to September are the warmest months (in particular July and August), but you can expect rain at any time of the year, even in high summer. So, you'll need to come prepared, and remember the old hikers' adage that there's no such thing as bad weather, only inadequate clothing.

Tours and tour operators

There are many companies offering general interest or special interest tours of England. Travel agents will have details, or you can check the small advertisements in the travel sections of newspapers, or visit the **British Tourist Authority** at www.visitbritain.com, for a list of operators.

General sightseeing tours

A recommended British company with a very wide range of tours aimed at the more mature traveller is **Saga Holidays**, Saga Building, Middelburg Sq, Folkestone, Kent CT20 1AZ, T0800-300500. Saga also operates in the USA, 222 Berkeley St, Boston, MA 02116; and in Australia, Level 1, 10-14 Paul St, Milsons Point, Sydney 2061, and is on the web at www.sagaholidays.com.

USA

Abercrombie & Kent, T1-800-3237308, www.abercrombiekent.com.
Cross-Culture, 52 High Point Dr, Amherst MA01002-1224, T800-4911148, www.crosscultureinc.com.
Especially Britain, T1-800-8690538, www.expresspages.com/e/especiallybritain.
Sterling Tours, T1-800-7274359, www.sterlingtours.com.

Australia and New Zealand

Adventure Specialists, 69 Liverpool St, Sydney, T02-92612927, www.totaltravel.com.
Adventure Travel Company, 164 Parnell Rd, Parnell, East Auckland, T09-3799755. New Zealand agents for Peregrine Adventures.
Peregrine Adventures, 258 Lonsdale St, Melbourne, T03-96638611, www.peregrine.net.au; also branches in Brisbane, Sydney, Adelaide and Perth.

Backpackers and adventure tours

There are many companies catering for any number of special interest holidays in London for students and young people, seniors and veterans, disabled travellers, gays and lesbians, singles, couples or families. A wide range of themes includes antiques, historic houses, theatre and the arts, boats, barges and canals, murder and mystery, religious, movies and garden tours. Finally, a good resource for finding bus tours, walking and cycling tours and adventure tours is www.uktrail.com, a site designed for budget and adventure travellers, which also has information on accommodation.
Compass Holidays, T01242-250642, www.compass-holidays.com, offer a variety of cycling holidays in the UK for a range of

abilities. Prices available on request.
Exodus Travels, T020-8772 3882, www.exodus.co.uk. A London-based company offering a wide variety of specialist holidays.
Karibuni, T0118-9618 577, www.karibuni.co.uk, offer weekend adventure tours including skiing, watersports, walking, climbing and lots more from around £50 to £175. They can also arrange custom tours for groups.
Road Trip, T0845-200 6791, www.roadtrip.co.uk, who have a variety of weekly tours from 5 to nine days for around £130.
Stray Travel, T020-7373 7737, www.straytravel.com, who offer hop-on, hop-off tours around the country from £34 for a day to £159 for 6 days.

British tourism offices overseas

VisitBritain are an excellent excellent source of information for visitors to England. More information can be obtained from their website (www.visitbritain.com), or from the offices listed below:

Australia Level 2, 15 Blue St, North Sydney NSW 2060, T02-90214400, F02-90214499.
Austria C/o The British Council, Shenke str 4, 1010 Vienna, T00 80 007 007 007, F01/5 332 616 85.
Belgium Louizalaan 140, 2 de verdiping, 1050 Brussels, T2-6463510, F2-6463986.
Canada 5915 Airport Rd, Suite 120, Mississauga, Ontario, L4V 1T1, T905-4051720, F905- 4051835.
Denmark Møntergade 3, 1116 Copenhagen K, T70-215011, F33-140136.
France 5th Floor, 22 Ave Franklin Roosevelt, 75008 Paris, T01-58365050, F01-58365051.
Germany Hackescher Markt 1, 10178 Berlin, T03-03157190, F03-031571910.
Ireland 18-19 College Green, Dublin 2, T1-6708000, F1-6708244.
Italy Corso Magenta 32, 20123 Milano, T02 88 08 151, F02 7201 0086.
Netherlands Aurora Gebouw (5e), Stadhouderskade 2, 1054 ES Amsterdam, T020 689 0002, F020 689 0003.
New Zealand Level 17, NZI House, 151 Queen St, Auckland 1, T09-3031446, F09-3776965.
South Africa Lancaster Gate, Hyde Park, Sandton 2196, Johannesburg, T011-3250342.
Switzerland Badenerstr 21, 8004 Zurich, T08 44/007 007, F043/3 22 20 01.
UK 1 Regent St, London, SW1Y 4XT.
USA 551 Fifth Av, Suite 701, New York, NY 10176-0799, T212-986-2266, F212-986-1188.

Finding out more

A good way to find out more before your trip is to contact the **British Tourist Authority** (BTA) in your home country, or write (or email) direct to the head office of the **English Tourist Board** (ETB). The BTA and ETB can provide a wealth of free literature and information such as maps, city guides, events calendars and accommodation brochures. Travellers with special needs should also contact their nearest BTA office.

Useful websites

Several useful websites give more information about England:
www.visitbritain.com (maintained by the BTA),
www.britainusa.com,
www.travelengland.org.uk,
www.touristinformation.co.uk,
www.aboutbritain.com
www.britannia.com.
www.bbc.co.uk, excellent resource on arts, sport and other events,
www.gayscape.com,
www.londontheatre.co.uk
www.timeout.com.

Language

The official language is English, which is spoken throughout the country (with a wide variety of accents). In parts of the largest cities, non-European languages such as Bengali, Urdu, Turkish and Arabic are also common.

Disabled travellers

For travellers with disabilities, visiting England independently can be a difficult business. While most theatres, cinemas and modern tourist attractions are accessible to wheelchairs, accommodation is more problematic. Many large, new hotels do have disabled suites, but will charge more, and most B&Bs, guesthouses and smaller hotels are not designed to cater for people with disabilities. Public transport is just as bad, though newer buses have lower steps for easier access and some train services now accommodate wheelchair users in comfort. Taxis, as opposed to minicabs, all carry wheelchair ramps, and if a driver says he or she can't take a wheelchair, it's because they're too lazy to fetch the ramp.

Wheelchair users and blind or partially sighted people are automatically given 30-50% discount on train fares, and those with other disabilities are eligible for the **Disabled Person's Railcard**, see page 38, which costs £14 per year and gives a third off most tickets. There are no reductions on buses, however.

If you are disabled you should contact the travel officer of your national support organization. They can provide literature or put you in touch with travel agents specializing in tours for the disabled.

Contacts

Artsline, T020-7388 2227, www.dircon.co.uk/artsline, has detailed information and publications on arts, attractions and entertainment for disabled people in London.

Can Be Done, T020-8907 2400, www.canbedone.co.uk, will arrange holidays for disabled visitors in a range of accommodation to suit individual requirements.

The Holiday Care Service, 2nd floor, Imperial Building, Victoria Rd, Horley, Surrey RH6 7PZ, T01293-774535, provides free lists of accessible accommodation and travel in the UK. In London, tour operator

The Royal Association for Disability and Rehabilitation (RADAR), Unit 12, City Forum, 250 City Rd, London, EC1V 8AF, T020-7250 3222, www.radar.org.uk, is a good source of advice and information, and produces an annual guide on travelling in the UK (£7.50 including P&P).

The Royal National Institute for the Blind, T020-7388 1266, publishes a *Hotel Guide Book* for blind and partially sighted people. They also have maps for the blind of London and other cities.

Gay and lesbian travellers

Homosexuality may be the English vice, but unfortunately in some parts of the country it's still the love that dare not speak its name. Gay couples are not guaranteed a warm reception in too many rural areas, especially in the north. It's not all doom, gloom and prejudice though. Outside London, Brighton made a name for itself with its gay scene and many coastal resorts have tried the same trick: Bournemouth, Newquay, and Blackpool among them. Manchester prides itself on its gay nightlife, and in fact all the major cities at least display a tolerant attitude. Almost every university town has its own scene too.

Contacts

www.whatsonwhen.com, for a good selection of gay events and venues.

www.queenscene.com, information on clubs, gay groups, accommodation, events, HIV/AIDS and cultural and ethical issues.

Other good sites include:
www.gaybritain.co.uk
www.gaypride.co.uk
www.gaytravel.co.uk
www.rainbownetwork.com

Student travellers

The explosion in English higher education since the 1990s means that student visitors will find themselves far from alone. All the northern cities in particular have embraced student culture with both arms, as have Nottingham, Birmingham and Bristol. By comparison, smaller towns like Oxford and Cambridge inevitably seem stuffy and overcrowded, a bit like Exeter. London's student scene is centred on Bloomsbury but percolates throughout the city. Leamington Spa jumps every weekend with student acitivity from nearby Warwick University. Newcastle is in the process of re-inventing itself (once again) as the most happening place to be a student in the country.

There are various official youth/student ID cards available. The most useful is the **International Student ID Card (ISIC)**. For £6 the ISIC card gains you access to a series of discounts, including most forms of local transport, up to 30% off international air fares, cheap or free admission to museums, theatres and other attractions, and cheap meals in some restaurants. There's also free or discounted internet access, and a website where you can check the latest student travel deals (www.usitworld.com). You'll also receive the ISIC handbook, which ensures you get the most out of services available. ISIC cards are available at student travel centres, such as **STA Travel** ⓘ *86 Old Brompton Rd, London, SW7 3LH, T020-7361 6161, www.statravel.co.uk*; and **Trailfinders** ⓘ *194 Kensington High St, London, W8 6FT, T020-7938 3939, www.trailfinders.co.uk*. US and Canadian citizens are also entitled to emergency medical coverage, and there's a 24-hour hotline to call in the event of medical, legal or financial emergencies.

If you're aged under 26 but not a student, you can apply for a **Federation of International Youth Travel Organisations** (FIYTO) card, or a **Euro 26 Card**, which give you much the same discounts. If you're 25 or younger you can qualify for a **Go-25 Card**, which gives you the same benefits as an ISIC card. These discount cards are also issued by student travel agencies and hostelling organizations (see page 41).

Studying in England

If you want to study in England you must first prove you can support and accommodate yourself without working and without recourse to public support. Your studies should take up at least 15 hours a week for a minimum of 6 months. Once you are studying, you are allowed to do 20 hours of casual work per week in the term time and you can work full-time during the holidays. In **North America** full-time students can obtain temporary work or study permits through the **Council of International Education Exchange** (CIEE) ⓘ *205 E 42nd St, New York, NY 10017, T212-8222600, www.ciee.org*. For more details, contact your nearest British embassy, consulate or high commission, or the **Foreign and Commonwealth Office** ⓘ *London, T020-7270 1500*.

Travelling with children

Flying

Inform the airline in advance that you're travelling with a baby or toddler, and check out the facilities when booking as these vary with each aircraft. **British Airways** now has a special seat for under 2s; check which aircraft have been fitted with them when booking. Pushchairs can be taken on as hand luggage or stored in the hold. Skycots are available on long-haul flights. Take snacks and toys for in-flight entertainment, and remember that swallowing food or drinks during take-off and landing will help prevent ear problems. **www.babygoes2.com** is a useful website.

Eating out

Eating out with children can be a frustrating experience, and some establishments are downright unhelpful, others, on the other hand, are happy to help with high chairs and kids' menus. In major towns and cities Italian restaurants are often more child-friendly. In more remote areas, however, most people are helpful and friendly.

Women travellers

Travelling in England is neither easier nor more difficult for women than it is for men. Generally speaking, people are friendly and courteous and even lone women travellers should experience nothing unpleasant. In the main cities and larger towns, the usual precautions need to be taken and you should avoid walking in quiet, unlit streets and parks at night.

Working in England

Citizens of **European Union** (EU) countries can live and work in Britain freely without a visa, but **non-EU residents** need a permit to work legally. This can be difficult to obtain without the backing of an established company or employer in the UK. Also, visitors from Commonwealth countries who are aged between 17 and 27 may apply for a working holiday-maker's visa which permits them to stay in the UK for up to 2 years and work on a casual basis (ie non-career orientated). These certificates are only available from British embassies and consulates abroad, and you must have proof of a valid return or onward ticket, as well as means of support during your stay. **Commonwealth** citizens with a parent or grandparent born in the UK can apply for a **Certificate of Entitlement to the Right of Abode**, allowing them to work in Britain.

An option for citizens of some non-commonwealth countries is to visit on an 'au pair' placement in order to learn English by living with an English-speaking family for a maximum of 2 years. Au pairs must be aged between 17 and 27, and come from one of the following countries: Andorra, Bosnia-Herzegovina, Croatia, Cyprus, Czech Republic, The Faroes, Greenland, Hungary, Macedonia, Malta, Monaco, San Marino, Slovak Republic, Slovenia, Switzerland or Turkey. This can be a good way to learn English, but check out the precise conditions of your placement before taking it up.

Before you travel

Visas

Visa regulations are subject to change, so it is essential that you check with your local British embassy, high commission or consulate before leaving home (see nxt page). Everyone needs a passport to enter Britain. Citizens of Australia, Canada, New Zealand, South Africa or the USA do not need a visa and can stay for up to 6 months, providing they have a return ticket and sufficient funds to cover their stay. Citizens of most European countries do not need a visa and can generally stay for up to 3 months. However, citizens of Albania, Bosnia, Bulgaria, Macedonia, Romania, Slovakia, Yugoslavia, all former Soviet republics (other than the Baltic states) and most other countries require a visa from the commission or consular office in the country of application.

The **Foreign Office's** website (www.fco.gov.uk) provides details of British immigration and visa requirements. Also the **Immigration Advisory Service** (IAS) ⓘ *County Ho, 190 Great Dover St, London SE1 4YB, T020-73576917, www.vois.org.uk*, offers free and confidential advice to anyone applying for entry clearance into the UK.

For visa extensions once in England, contact the Home Office, Immigration and Nationality Department, Lunar House, Wellesley Rd, Croydon, London CR9, T020-86860688, before your existing visa expires. Citizens of Australia, Canada, New Zealand, South Africa or the USA wishing to stay longer than 6 months will need an **Entry Clearance Certificate** from the British High Commission in their country. For more details, contact your nearest British embassy, consulate or high commission, or the Foreign and Commonwealth Office in London, T020-72701500.

British embassies abroad

Australia High Commission: Commonwealth Av, Yarralumla, Canberra, ACT 2600, T02-62706666, www.uk.emb.gov.au.
Canada High Commission: 80 Elgin St, Ottowa, K1P 5K7, T613-2371530, www.britain-in-canada.org.
France 9 Av Hoche, 8e, Paris, T01-42663810, www.amb-grandebretagne.fr.
Germany Wilhelmstrasse 70-71, 10117 Berlin, T030-20457-0, www.britischebotschaft.de.
Ireland 29 Merrion Rd, Ballsbridge, Dublin 4, T01-2053700, www.britishembassy.ie.
Israel 192 Hayarkon St, Tel Aviv, T3-7251222, www.britemb.org.il.
Netherlands Koningslaan 44, 1075AE Amsterdam, T20-6764343, www.britain.nl.
New Zealand High Commission: 44 Hill St, Wellington, T04-4726049, www.britain.org.nz.
South Africa High Commission: 91 Parliament St, Cape Town 8001, T21-4617220, www.britain.org.za.
USA 3100 Massachusetts Av NW, Washington DC 20008, T1-202-588 7800, www.britain-info.org, regional consulates in 12 other cities.

Customs and duty free

For more information on British import regulations, contact **HM Customs and Excise** ⓘ *Dorset Ho, Stamford St, London, SE1 9PJ, T020-79283344, www.hmce.gov.uk.*

Britain is an island, and customs officials are fiercely protective about keeping out unwanted diseases such as rabies. They take their jobs very seriously, and it's not a good idea to make jokes if they ask you about the contents of your bags.

There are various import restrictions, most of which should not affect the average tourist. It is difficult to bring pets into Britain, and tight quarantine restrictions apply (with some exemptions for dogs and cats travelling from Europe). For more information on bringing a pet, contact the **Department of Environment, Food and Rural Affairs** ⓘ *Nobel Ho, 17 Smith Sq, London SW1P 3JR, T020-72386000, www.defra.gov.uk/animalh/quarantine.*

Visitors from EU countries do not have to make a declaration to customs on entry into the UK. The limits for duty-paid goods from within the EU are 800 cigarettes, or 1kg of tobacco, 10 litres of spirits, 20 litres of fortified wine, 90 litres of wine and 110 litres of beer. There is no longer any duty-free shopping. Visitors from non-EU countries are allowed to import 200 cigarettes, or 250g of tobacco, 2 litres of wine, and 2 litres of fortified wine or 1 litre of spirits.

Vaccinations

No vaccinations are required to enter the UK. See also the Health section, page 52.

What to take

Your main problem is going to be the weather, which is very unpredictable – it's not uncommon to experience heavy rain and hot sunshine in the same afternoon. You should pack layered clothing, therefore, and bring a lightweight waterproof jacket and warm sweater whatever the time of year. Light clothes are sufficient for the summer. You'll be able to find everything else you could possibly need in any English city, so you can pack light and buy stuff as you go along.

A sleeping bag is useful in hostels. A sleeping sheet with a pillow cover is needed for staying in **Youth Hostel Association** (YHA) hostels to save you the cost of having to hire one. A padlock can also be handy for locking your bag if it has to be stored in a hostel for any length of time. Other useful items include an alarm clock (for those early ferry departures), an adapter plug for electrical appliances, a Swiss army knife (not in your aeroplane carry-on) and some string.

Insurance

Insurance is not very exciting but is crucial if things go seriously wrong. A good insurance policy should cover you in case of theft, loss of possessions or money (often including cash), the cost of any medical and dental treatment, cancellation of flights, delays in travel arrangements, accidents, missed departures, lost baggage, lost passport, and personal liability and legal expenses.

There's nearly always small print: some policies exclude 'dangerous activities' such as scuba diving, skiing, horse riding or even trekking. Older travellers should note that some companies won't cover people over 65 years old, or may charge high premiums. Not all policies cover ambulance, helicopter rescue or emergency flights home. Find out if your policy pays medical expenses direct to the hospital or doctor, or if you have to pay and then claim the money back later. If the latter applies, make sure you keep all records. Whatever your policy, if you are unfortunate enough to have something stolen, make sure you get a copy of the police report, as you will need this to substantiate your claim.

Before shopping around for prices, check whether your credit card and home insurance companies already offer overseas travel within your policy. If not, a good place to start is **STA Travel** ⓘ *www.sta-travel.com*. Travellers from North America can try **Travel Guard** ⓘ *T1-800-8261300*, *www.noelgroup.com*; **Access America** ⓘ *T1-800-2848300*; **Travel Insurance Services** ⓘ *T1-800-9371387* and **Travel Assistance International** ⓘ *T1-800-8212828*. From Australia try www.travelinsurance.com.au.

Money

Currency

The British currency is the pound sterling (£), divided into 100 pence (p). Coins come in denominations of 1p, 2p, 5p, 10p, 20p, 50p, £1 and £2. The main notes (bills) are £5, £10, £20 (£50 are not widely used and may be difficult to change).

Banks and bureaux de change

Branches of the main High Street banks – **Barclays, HSBC, Lloyds TSB, NatWest, Royal Bank of Scotland** and **Bank of Scotland** – are easily found throughout England. Bank opening hours are Monday-Friday from 0930 to 1600 or 1700. Some larger branches may open later on Thursdays and on Saturday mornings. Banks tend to offer similar exchange rates and are usually the best places to change money and cheques. Outside banking hours you'll have to use a **bureau de change**, which can be easily found at the airports and train stations and in larger cities. **Thomas Cook** and other major travel agents also operate bureaux de change with reasonable rates. Avoid changing money or cheques in hotels, as the rates are usually poor. Main post offices and branches of Marks and Spencer will change cash without charging commission.

Credit cards and ATMs

Most hotels, shops and restaurants accept the major credit cards Access/MasterCard, Visa and Amex), though some places may charge for using them. Some smaller establishments such as B&Bs may only accept cash. Visa card and Access/MasterCard holders can use all major High Street banks (**Barclays, HSBC, Lloyds TSB, NatWest, Royal Bank of Scotland** and **Bank of Scotland**). Amex card holders can use the **HSBC**, the **Royal Bank of Scotland** and any other bank or building society displaying the 'Link' symbol. The Cirrus symbol is accepted in most ATMs (cashpoints). Note that your bank may charge you for using a foreign ATM, and many card companies charge high interest rates for cash withdrawals.

Travellers' cheques

The safest way to carry money is in travellers' cheques. These are available for a small commission from all major banks. **American Express** (Amex), **Visa** and **Thomas Cook** cheques are widely accepted and are the most commonly issued by banks. You'll normally have to pay commission again when you cash each cheque. This will usually be 1%, or a flat rate. No commission is payable on Amex cheques cashed at Amex offices. Make sure you keep a record of the cheque numbers and the cheques you've cashed separate from the cheques themselves, so that you can get a full refund of all uncashed cheques should you lose them. It's best to bring sterling cheques to avoid changing currencies twice. Also note that in Britain travellers' cheques are rarely accepted outside banks, so you'll need to cash them in advance and keep a good supply of ready cash.

Money transfers

If you need money urgently, the quickest way to have it sent to you is to have it wired to the nearest agent via **Western Union** (T0800-833833) or **Moneygram** (T0800-89718971). Charges are on a sliding scale, and it will cost proportionately less to wire out more money. Money can also be wired by **Thomas Cook** or **American Express**, though this may take a day or two, or transferred via a bank draft, but this can take up to a week.

Taxes

Most goods in Britain are subject to a **Value Added Tax** (VAT) of 17.5%, with the major exception of books and food. VAT is usually already included in the advertised price of goods. Visitors from non-EU countries can save money through the Retail Export Scheme, which allows a refund of VAT on goods that will be taken out of the country. Note that not all shops participate in the scheme and that VAT cannot be reclaimed on hotel bills or other services.

Cost of living/travelling

The average salary in England is £25,000. There's a huge disparity, however, between the standard of living of, say, a salaried professional in London and a casual labourer in the north of England. Once everyone has been taken into account, the average household income is actually much lower. Most people spend around a third of their income on rent and transport. Weekly grocery shopping costs around £60, a pint of beer costs £2.50, a meal for two costs £40 and a paperback costs around £8.

 England can be an expensive place to visit, and London and the south in particular can eat heavily into your budget. The minimum daily budget if you're staying in hostels or cheap B&Bs, cooking your own meals and doing minimal travelling will be around £30 per person per day. Those staying in slightly more upmarket B&Bs or guest houses, eating out at pubs or modest restaurants and visiting tourist attractions, such as castles or museums, can expect to pay around £60 per person per day. Single travellers will have to pay more than half the cost of a double room in most places and should budget on spending around 60% of what a couple would spend. In order to enjoy your trip to the full then you'll need at least £70 per day, without being extravagant.

Getting there

Air

The majority of visitors to England fly to London, which has five airports. The largest of these, **Heathrow**, is the busiest airport in the world with direct flights to most major cities on all continents. There are also good air links to all parts of the British Isles. London is one of the best places in the world to get good deals on flights, so it may be worth planning onward travel once you've arrived.

More and more people are turning to budget airlines, which offer a variety of routes throughout **Europe**. Note, however, that the main hubs in London (Stansted and Luton) are not near the city itself and will require some extra overland travel. Direct flights from Europe also arrive at **Birmingham**, **Bristol**, **Leeds**, **Liverpool**, **Manchester**, **Newcastle**, **Newquay**, **Plymouth** and **Southampton** airports.

Buying a ticket

There are a mind-boggling number of outlets for buying your plane ticket and finding the best deal can be a confusing business. Fares will depend on the season. Ticket prices are highest from around early June to mid-September, which is the tourist high season. Fares drop in the months either side of the peak season – mid-September to early November and mid-April to early June. They are cheapest in the low season, from November to April, although prices tend to rise sharply over Christmas and the New Year. It's also worth noting that flying at the weekend is normally more expensive. It is always worth spending a bit of time researching the various options available and starting early, as some of the cheapest tickets have to be bought months in advance and the most popular flights sell out early.

One of the best ways of finding a good deal is to use the internet. There are a number of sites where you can check out prices and even book tickets. You can search in the travel sections of your web browser or try the sites of the discount travel companies and agents and the budget airlines listed in this section. Also worth trying are: **www.expedia.com, lastminute.com, e-bookers.com, cheapflights.co.uk, deckchair.com, flynow.com, dialaflight.co.uk, opodo.com** and **travelocity.com.**

Cheap flight tickets fall into two categories; official and unofficial. Official tickets are called budget fares, Apex, Super-Apex, advance-purchase tickets, or whatever a particular airline chooses to call them. Unofficial tickets are discounted or consolidated tickets which are released by airlines through selected travel agents. They are not sold directly by airlines. Discounted tickets are usually as low or lower than the official budget-price tickets. Return tickets are usually a lot cheaper than buying two one-way tickets. London is ideally situated for a round-the-world itinerary and Round-the-World (RTW) tickets can be a real bargain, with prices ranging from between £500 and £1500.

The cheapest flights usually arrive and leave from London's Luton or Stansted airports. They are often subject to rigid restrictions but the savings can make the extra effort worthwhile. Cheaper tickets usually have to be bought at least a week in advance, apply to only a few mid-week flights and must include a Saturday night stay. They are also non-refundable, or only partly refundable, and non-transferable. A standard flexible and refundable fare can be as much as two or three times a budget fare.

When trying to find the best deal, make sure you check the route, the duration of the journey, stopovers, any travel restrictions such as minimum and maximum periods away, and cancellation penalties. Many cheap flights are sold by small agencies, most of whom are reliable, but there may be some risks with buying tickets at low prices. Avoid paying too much money in advance, and you could check with the airline directly to make sure you have a reservation. You may be safer choosing a better-known travel agent, such as **STA**, which has offices world-wide, or **Trailfinders** in the UK, or **Council Travel** in the USA. These and other reputable discount companies and agents are listed above.

Those wishing to fly on to other parts of Britain should note that it may be cheaper if you use an Airpass or Europass bought in your own country. These are offered by **British Airways** and **British Midlands** and are valid only with an international scheduled flight ticket. You can also try specialist agencies such as **STA** who offer **Domestic Air Passes** on **British Airways** and **British Midlands** flights to full-time students and travellers under 26 years old. These give substantial discounts on flights from **Heathrow** and **Gatwick** to specified destinations in England, Scotland, Northern Ireland and Jersey, in the Channel Islands. Flights work out at between £28 and £32 each, with a minimum of four flights per person. Alternatively, there is a growing number of low-cost airlines which offer cheap air tickets on the Internet and on back pages of weekend national newspapers.

All tickets are subject to taxes (£10-20 depending on route), insurance charge (around £6) and passenger service charge, which varies according to airport. This adds up quickly – for economy-fare flights within the UK and from EU countries expect additions of £20-30. For inter-continental flights, this will rise to around £60-70.

Flights from Europe

In addition to regular flights operated by the major national carriers, the surge in budget airline routes means that you can fly from practically anywhere in Europe to anywhere in England. The budget airlines specialise in routes to provincial and smaller cities, and it's always worth checking what the onward transport arrangements are, since airports are often a long way from town. The flight consolidator www.opodo.com can often offer good rates, but it's worth noting that flight consolidators do not include budget airline fares. Fares for a return ticket can range from around €15 to €300 on a scheduled flight.

Flights from North America

There are regular non-stop flights to **London** from many US and Canadian cities, including Atlanta, Boston, Calgary, Chicago, Dallas, Denver, Houston, Las Vegas, Los Angeles, Montreal, New York, Philadelphia, San Francisco, Toronto, Vancouver and Washington DC, and many more connections to other cities. Transatlantic carriers are listed above.

Non-stop flights are available from **New York** to **Manchester** with **Pakistan International Airlines** and **British European**, and to **Birmingham** with **British European** and **Continental Airlines**, for much the same prices as fares to London. **British Midland** also offers service between **Chicago** and **Manchester**: www.flybmi.com.

For low-season **Apex** fares expect to pay around US$200-450 from **New York** and other East Coast cities, and around US$300-600 from the West Coast. Prices rise to around US$500-800 from **New York** and US$400-900 from the West Coast in the summer months. Low-season **Apex** fares from **Toronto** and **Montreal** cost around CAN$600-700, and from **Vancouver** around CAN$800-900, rising to $750-950 and $950-1150 respectively during the summer.

Flights from Australia and New Zealand

The cheapest scheduled flights to London from Australia or New Zealand are via Asia with **Gulf Air, Royal Brunei** or **Thai Airways**. They charge A$1300-1500 in low season and up to A$1800 in high season, and involve a transfer en route. Flights via Africa start at around $2000 and are yet more expensive via North America. Flights to and from Perth via Africa or Asia are a few hundred dollars cheaper.

The cheapest scheduled flights from New Zealand are with **Korean Air, Thai Airways** or **JAL**, all of whom fly via their home cities for around NZ$2000-2300. The most direct route is via North America with **United Airlines**, via Chicago or Los Angeles. Fares range from around NZ$2800 in low season to NZ$3200 in high season.

Connecting service from London to other English airports is available on a number of airlines, including **British Airways, Qantas** and many of the budget airlines. **Emirates** flies to Birmingham and Manchester from Sydney via Dubai, and Manchester is also served via Singapore on **Singapore Airlines**.

A Round-the-World (RTW) ticket may work out just as cheap as, or cheaper than, a return ticket. Good deals are offered by **Qantas/British Airways**.

Flights from Africa

British Airways, Virgin Atlantic and **South African Airways** all offer non-stop service to London from Johannesburg and Cape Town for between ZAR 5000-10,000 according to season. Many other European airlines, such as **Lufthansa** or Air France, offer connecting service at competitive rates via their capital cities.

Budget airlines in Europe

Budget airlines offer no frills: no meals, no reserved seating, little flexibility, and heavy baggage restrictions. On the plus side, you can sometimes travel for as little as €5. Check terms and airport location carefully before booking. Websites include: **www.ryanair.com**; **www.flybe.com**; **www.easyjet.com**; **www.flybmi.com** and **www.virginexpress.com**.

Airlines flying from North America

Air Canada, T1-800-7763000, www.aircanada.ca.
Air India, www.airindia.com.
American Airlines, T1-800-4337300, www.americanair.com.
British Airways, T1-800-2479297, www.britishairways.com.
British European, www.flybe.com.
Continental Airlines, T1-800-2310856, www.flycontinental.com.
Delta Airlines, T1-800-2414141, www.delta-air.com.
Icelandair, T1-800-2235500, www.icelandair.com.
Northwest Airlines, T1-800-4474747, www.nwa.com.
Pakistan International Airlines, www.fly-pia.com.
United Airlines, T1-800-5382929, www.ual.com.
Virgin Atlantic Airways, T1-800-8628621, www.fly.virgin.com.

Discount travel agents in North America

Air Brokers International, 323 Geary St, Suite 411, San Francisco, CA94102, T1-800-8833273, www.airbrokers.com. Consolidator and specialist in RTW and Circle Pacific tickets.
Council Travel, 205 E 42nd St, New York, NY 10017, T1-888-COUNCIL, www.counciltravel.com. Budget agency with branches in many other US cities.
Discount Airfares Worldwide On-Line, www.etn.nl/discount.htm. A hub of consolidator and discount agent links.
STA Travel, 5900 Wiltshire Blvd, Suite 2110, Los Angeles, CA 90036, T1-800-7770112, www.sta-travel.com. Discount student/youth travel discount company with branches in New York, San Francisco, Boston, Miami, Chicago, Seattle and Washington DC.
Travel CUTS, 187 College St, Toronto, ON M5T 1P7, T1-800-6672887, www.travelcuts.com.

Specialist in student discount fares, IDs and other travel services. Branches in other Canadian cities.
Online agents such www.expedia.com, www.travelocity.com or www.orbitz.com.

Airlines flying from Australia and New Zealand

Air France, T02-93211030 (Sydney), www.airfrance.com.
Air New Zealand, T09-3573000, www.airnz.co.nz.
British Airways, T02-92583200 (Sydney); T09-3568690 (Auckland), www.british-airways.com.
Cathay Pacific, T02-99315500 (Sydney), www.cathaypacific.com.
Gulf Air, T02-92442199 (Sydney); www.gulfairco.com.
Emirates, T02-92909700 (Sydney); www.emirates.com.
Japanese Airlines (JAL), T02-92721111 (Sydney); T09-3799906 (Auckland).
Korean Air, Australia, T02-9262 6000 (Sydney); T09-3073687 (Auckland).
Qantas, T13-1313 (Australia), T0800 808 767 (New Zealand); www.qantas.com.au.
Singapore Airlines, T02-93500100 (Sydney); T09-3793209 (Auckland), www.singaporeair.com.
South African Airways, T02-92234448 (Sydney), www.saa.co.za.
Thai Airways, T02-92511922 (Sydney); T09-3773886 (Auckland), www.thaiair.com.
United Airlines, T02-92924111 (Sydney); T09-3793800 (Auckland), www.ual.com.
Virgin Atlantic, Australia, T02-93526199, www.flyvirgin.com.

Discount travel agents in Australia and New Zealand

Flight Centres, 82 Elizabeth St, Sydney, T13-1600; 205 Queen St, Auckland, T09-3096171. Also branches in other towns and cities.
STA Travel, www.statravel.com.au, in Australia: 855 George St, Sydney, T02-92121255. In New Zealand: 229 Queen St, Auckland, T64-9309 9723, also in major towns and campuses around both countries.
Travel.com.au, 80 Clarence St, Sydney, T02-92901500, www.travel.com.au.

Rail

Since 1994, when the Channel Tunnel finally linked Britain to continental Europe, **Eurostar** ⓘ *T0990-186186, www.eurostar.com*, has been operating high-speed trains to **London Waterloo** from **Paris** (3 hours) and **Brussels** (2 hours 40 minutes) via **Lille** (2 hours). Standard-class tickets to Paris and Brussels range from £70 for a weekend day return to £300 for a fully flexible mid-week return. There are substantial discounts for children (4-11 years) and for passengers who are under 26 years on the day of travel. It is worth keeping an eye open for special offers, especially in the low season.

All other rail connections will involve some kind of ferry crossing (see below). For full details on rail services available, contact your national railway or **Rail Europe** at www.raileurope.com for information on routes, timetables, fares and discount passes.

Road

If you're driving from continental Europe you can take the **Eurotunnel Shuttle Service** ⓘ *T0800-969992, www.eurotunnel.com, for bookings, call T08705-353535*, a freight train which runs 24 hours a day, 365 days a year, and takes you and your car from Calais to Folkestone in 35-45 minutes. Fares are per carload, and range from £135 one way to £270 return depending on the time of year or how far in advance you book. Foot passengers cannot cross on the Shuttle.

Sea

Ferry

Ferries operate along 33 routes to England, arriving at Ramsgate, Dover, Newhaven, Portsmouth, Bournemouth and Plymouth (south coast), Harwich, Hull and Tynemouth (east coast) and Liverpool, Fishguard and Holyhead (west coast and Wales), as follows.

From France Dieppe to Newhaven, Calais to Dover, Dunkerque to Dover, Caen to Portsmouth, Cherbourg to Portsmouth or Bournemouth, Le Havre to Portsmouth, St Malo to Portsmouth, Bournemouth or Plymouth and Roscoff to Plymouth.

From Belgium, Holland and Germany Oostende to Dover or Ramsgate, Zeebrugge to Dover or Hull, Rotterdam to Hull, Hoek van Holland to Harwich, Amsterdam to Tynemouth and Hamburg to Harwich. From Scandinavia: Bergen to Tynemouth, Gothenburg to Tynemouth, Haugesund to Tynemouth, Stavanger to Tynemouth, Kristiansand to Tynemouth, Esjberg to Harwich. From Spain: Santander to Plymouth and Bilbao to Portsmouth.

From Ireland and the Isle of Man From Dublin to Liverpool, Larne to Liverpool, Belfast to Liverpool, Douglas to Liverpool, Dun Laoghaire (Dublin) to Holyhead, Wales and Rosslare to Fishguard, Wales.

Prices vary according to season. A foot passenger travelling in low season from **Calais** to **Dover** could pay as little as €10, whereas a couple taking a car to Bilbao could pay up to €1200 return. You can check prices on one of the many online booking agent websites: **www.cheapferry.com**, **www.ferry-to-france.co.uk**, **www.ferrycrossings-uk.co.uk** or **www.ferrysavers.com**, or by contacting major route operators direct: **P&O Stena Line**, T0870-6000600, www.posl.com (Spain, France, Irish Sea & North Sea routes), **Brittany Ferries**, T0990-360360, T+33-299-828-080 in France, T+34-942-360-611 in Spain, www.brittanyferries.com, (Spain and western France to south coast), **Fjord Line**, www.fjordline.com, (North Sea routes from Scandinavia).

Touching down

Airport information

Most visitors arrive in England via one of London's five airports: Heathrow, Gatwick, Stansted, City or Luton. Long-haul flights also land at Manchester and Birmingham. Other common points of entry include the ports of Dover and Holyhead (in Wales) and by car at Folkestone via *Le Shuttle*. Those arriving by budget airline at one of England's other regional airports (Bristol, Leeds, Liverpool, Newcastle, Newquay, Plymouth or Southampton) should check arrival information via the airline's website.

London Heathrow Airport

London Heathrow Airport ⓘ *(LHR), Hounslow, Middlesex, TW6 1JH, T0870-0000123*, is the world's busiest international airport and it has four terminals, so when leaving London, it's important to check which terminal to go to before setting out for the airport.

Transport for London and British Rail have travel information points in Terminals 1, 2 and 4. Bus and coach sales/information desks are located in all four terminals. There are hotel reservations desks in the arrivals area of each terminal (a booking fee is charged).

For general enquiries, passengers with special needs should contact **Call Centre**, T0870-0000123. For further help or advice concerning travel arrangements call **Heathrow Travelcare** T020-8745 7495.

Touching down

Electricity The current in Britain is 240V AC. Plugs have three square pins and adaptors are widely available.
Emergencies For police, fire brigade, ambulance and mountain rescue or coastguard, dial 999.
Laundry Most towns have coin-operated launderettes. The average cost for a wash and tumble dry is about £3. A service wash, where someone will do your washing for you, costs around £4-5. In more remote areas, you'll have to relyon hostel and campsite facilities.
Time Greenwich Mean Time (GMT) is used from late October to late March, after which time the clocks go forward an hour to British Summer Time (BST). GMT is five hours ahead of US Eastern Time and 10 hours behind Australian Eastern Standard Time.
Toilets Public toilets are found at all train and bus stations and motorway service stations. They may charge 20p, but are generally clean, with disabled and baby-changing facilities. Those in town centres are often pretty grim.
Weights and measures Imperial and metric systems are both currently in use. Distances on roads are measured in miles and yards, drinks are poured in pints and gills, but generally, nowadays, the metric system is used elsewhere.

By train The airport is on the **London Underground** Piccadilly Line, which runs trains every 5-9 minutes to the centre of London and beyond, with an approximate journey time of 50 minutes. There are two stations: one serving Terminals 1, 2, and 3; the other for Terminal 4. The first train from central London arrives at Terminal 4 at 0629 (0749 on Sunday) and the last arrives at 0107 (0008 on Sunday). Allow a further 5 minutes to reach the station for Terminals 1, 2 and 3. Details of timetables and fares are available on T020-7222 1234 (24 hours). **Heathrow Express** ⓘ *T0845-6001515, www.heathrowmexpress.co. uk*, non-stop train to and from Paddington Station in central London. The journey takes 15 minutes to Terminals 1, 2 and 3, and 20 minutes to Terminal 4. Trains depart every 15 minutes between 0510 and 2340, 365 days a year. There is plenty of luggage space and wheelchairs and pushchairs are catered for. Some airlines have check-in facilities at Paddington. Tickets cost £12 (single), £22 (return). A £2 premium is charged for tickets purchased on board the train. Discounted fares are available and tickets purchased via the website are also cheaper. Children (0-15 years) travel free when accompanied by an adult.

For more on UK airports, visit www.baa.co.uk. Coaches leave from Heathrow and Gatwick to other cities in the UK. www.britbus.com.

By bus An **Airlinks'**, T0990-747777, 'Hotel Hoppa' shuttle service serves most major hotels near the airport. **Airbus A2**, T020-8400 6655, runs every 30 minutes throughout the day to and from a number of stops in central London. During the night, the N97 bus connects Heathrow with central London. **National Express**, T08705-808080, coaches run from Victoria Coach Station every 30 minutes. Airlinks also operates frequent coach services between Heathrow, Gatwick, Luton, Stansted and other airports.

By car/taxi Heathrow is 16 miles west of London at Junctions 3 and 4 on the M4 motorway. A taxi from Heathrow Airport to central London takes approximately 1 hour and should cost around £40. There are taxi desks in the Arrivals area of all four terminals (Terminal 1, T020-8745 7487; Terminal 2, T020-8745 5408; Terminal 3, T020-8745 4655; Terminal 4, T020-8745 7302).

London Gatwick Airport

London Gatwick Airport ⓘ *(LGW), Gatwick, West Sussex, RH6 0JH, T0870-0002468.* London's second airport 28 miles south of the capital, has two terminals, North and

South, with all the usual facilities including car hire, currency exchange, 24-hour banking, Flight Shops (T08000-747787), Hotel Reservations Desks (T01293-504549) and a **Travel Shop** in the South Terminal (T01293-506783). There are many help points for passengers with special needs and free wheelchair assistance or help with baggage to reach check-in.

By train All trains arrive at the **South Terminal** where there is a fast link to the North Terminal. A number of airlines offer check-in facilities at London's Victoria Station. The fastest service is the non-stop 30-minute **Gatwick Express,** T0990-301530, which runs to and from London Victoria every 15 minutes during the day, and hourly throughout the night. Standard tickets cost £10.50 single and £20 return; first-class and cheap-day returns are available. **Thameslink** rail services run from King's Cross, Farringdon, Blackfriars and London Bridge stations. For further information call **National Rail Enquiries,** T08457-484950.

By bus **Airbus A5** operates hourly to/from Victoria Coach Station. For further information call the Airport Travel Line, T0990-747777.

By car Gatwick is at Crawley, off Junction 9 on the M23 motorway, about an hour's drive from central London. A taxi to central London for up to 4 people costs around £75.

London City Airport

London City Airport ⓘ *(LCY) Royal Dock, London E16 2PX, T020-7646 0000*, is 6 miles (15 minutes' drive) east of the City of London. Continually updated flight information is available at www.londoncityairport.com/index.wml.

By train, car and bus Take the **Jubilee line** or **Docklands Light Railway** (DLR) to Canning Town for a connecting shuttle bus service. A taxi into central London will cost around £20. An Airbus shuttle service also runs every 10 minutes to and from Liverpool Street via Canary Wharf Underground and DLR stations until around 2130. London sightseeing bus services are also available from the airport.

London Luton Airport

London Luton Airport ⓘ *(LTN), Luton, Beds, LU2 9LU, T01582-405100*. Luton airport, about 30 miles north of central London, deals particularly with flights operated by budget airlines. All the usual facilities are available plus fax, internet, a children's play area and an airport chapel. There is also a **Skyline Travel Shop**, T01582-726454.

By train Regular **Thameslink** trains leave from London Bridge, Blackfriars, Farringdon and King's Cross stations to Luton Airport Parkway station; a free shuttle bus service operates between the station and the airport terminal. The Thameslink station at King's Cross is about 100 yards east of the main station, along the Pentonville Road.

By bus **Green Line** coaches run to and from Victoria Coach Station, Hyde Park Corner, Marble Arch, George Street and Baker Street in central London.

By car The airport is southeast of Luton, 2 miles off the M1 at Junction 10. The 30-mile journey into London will take around 50 minutes, and costs around £55 by taxi. Two companies operate from outside the terminal.

Stansted Airport

Stansted Airport ⓘ *(STN) Stansted, CM24 1RW, T08700-000303, 35 miles northeast of London (near Cambridge)*, is another budget airline hub. Terminal facilities include car hire, ATMs, 24-hour currency exchange, shops, restaurants and bars. There's a **Book and Go Travel Shop,** T08700-102015, a hotel reservations desk, T01279-661220, and **AAS Assistance,** T01279-663213, for passengers with special needs and also for left luggage.

By train **Stansted Express,** T0845-8500150, runs trains every 15 minutes from London's Liverpool Street Station to the main terminal building. The journey takes 45 minutes and costs £13 single and £23 open return.

By bus **Airbus A6** runs every hour from Victoria Coach Station, Hyde Park Corner, Marble Arch and Baker Street. **Airbus A7** runs an hourly service from Victoria Coach

Station, Embankment and Aldgate. The journey takes around 1 hour 30 minutes. **Jetlink**, T08705-747777, operates a frequent service between London's main airports.

By car The airport is north of London by Junction 8 of the M11. The 35-mile journey to/from central London takes around an hour to 1 hour 30 minutes depending on traffic.

Manchester Airport

Manchester International Airport (MAN) ⓘ *T0161-4893000, www.manchesterairport.co.uk*. The airport has three terminals with all the usual facilities, and is located south of the city centre, at Junction 5 of the M56.

By train, bus and car The airport is well-served by public transport, with trains to and from Manchester Piccadilly as well as direct and connecting services from all over the north of England. **National Express**, T08705-808080, runs from Terminals 1 and 2 on routes covering the whole of the UK. A taxi into the city centre should cost around £15.

Birmingham International Airport

Birmingham International Airport (BHX) ⓘ *T0121-7675511, www.bhx.co.uk*. Birmingham airport is 8 miles east of the city centre at Junction 6 on the M42, and has two terminals with standard facilities.

By train, bus and car A taxi into the centre should cost around £12. Several trains per hour run the 10 minute journey into the city centre, and other connections across England and Wales can be made by rail or coach, with **National Express**, T08705-808080. There are no local bus services at night.

The Channel Tunnel and Channel Ports

Most visitors arriving by sea will generally already have onward rail or coach tickets to London or other English cities, but for those who haven't organised onward travel, the port at Dover is served by regular trains to London and other cities, and by **National Express**, T08705-808080, coaches (for an idea of prices, see Getting Around, page 39). If arriving by car, you will proceed through customs and have two choices for getting to London: the M2 and M20 motorways. It takes around 1 hour 30 minutes to get to central London, 70 miles to the north. Don't forget to drive on the left.

Visitors arriving by **Eurostar** arrive at **Waterloo International Station** in central London, which has direct connections to London Underground and bus services. If you're putting your car on the shuttle, you'll emerge at the Folkestone terminal, where you proceed through customs before driving onto the M20, which links London to the coast. It takes around 1 hour 30 minutes to get to London.

Other English sea ports

Like the Channel ports, all sea ports in England are connected to the main road network, and are served by rail and coach services (see Getting around page 37). If you're arriving late at night, check in advance whether a connection will be available. Most arrivals at Holyhead and Fishguard are served by direct onward connections to Liverpool, London and other major cities. Services from other ports vary – check what is available in advance when booking your sea passage (see Getting there page 32).

Tourist information

Most cities and towns that you're likely to visit in England have a local tourist information centre (TIC), which can give you information on local attractions, restaurants and accommodation (including handling bookings – generally for a small fee) and help with general visitors' enquiries, such as where to find an internet café. Many sell books, local guides, maps and souvenirs, and some have free street plans and leaflets describing local walks. In general, however, tourist offices tend to cater to those interested in taking tours or day trips, and are less useful if you're on a tight budget, in which case youth hostels can provide much the same information. » *See individual town information sections for lists of local TICs.*

Museums, art galleries and stately homes

Over 300 stately homes, gardens and countryside areas, are cared for by the **National Trust (NT)** ⓘ *36 Queen Anne's Gate, London SW1H 9AS, T0870-609 5380, www.nationaltrust.org.uk*. National Trust properties are indicated in this guide '(NT)', and entry charges and opening hours are given for each property. **Youth Hostel Association (YHA)** and **Hostelling International (HI)** members and student-card holders get 50% discount on NT admission charges.) If you're going to be visiting several sights during your stay, then it's worth taking annual membership, which costs £28, £12 if you're aged under 26 and £47 for a family, or investing in a National Trust Touring Pass for 7 days at £15 per adult, £25 per couple and £30 per family, or for 14 days at £19.50, £32.50 and £39 respectively. Both give free access to all National Trust properties. A similar organization is **English Heritage** ⓘ *23 Savile Row, London W1S 2ET, T020-79733000, www.english-heritage.org.uk*, which manages hundreds of ancient monuments and other sights around England, including Stonehenge, and focuses on restoration and preservation. Membership includes free admission to sites, and advance information on events, and costs from £31.50 per adult to £58.50 per family. There's also an **Overseas Visitors' Pass**, which costs £13.50 for a week per adult and includes entry to many but not all properties. **English Nature** ⓘ *Northminster Ho, Peterborough PE1 1UA, T01733-455000, www.english-nature.org.uk*, is concerned with restoring and conserving the English countryside, and can give information on walks and events in the countryside.

Many other historic buildings are owned by local authorities, and admission is cheap, or in many cases free. Most municipal **art galleries** and **museums** are free, as well as most state-owned museums, particularly those in London and other large cities. Most fee-paying attractions give a discount or concession for senior citizens, the unemployed, full-time students and children under 16 (those under five are admitted free in most places). Proof of age or status must be shown. For other properties, admission charges are usually between £4 and £8.

Local customs and laws

In general, customs and laws are the same as you would encounter in any other western country. Informal clothing is acceptable throughout England, except at special events that specify a dress code (such as Glyndebourne Opera). If you are planning to work in England, business clothes may be appropriate. Visitors may find the English to be reserved, and, as in most countries, politeness is appreciated.

Tipping

Tipping in England is at the customer's discretion. In a restaurant you should leave a tip of 10-15% if you are satisfied with the service. If the bill already includes a service charge, you needn't add a further tip. Tipping is not normal in pubs or bars. Taxi drivers expect a tip, usually of around 10%. As in most other countries, porters, bellboys and waiters in more upmarket hotels rely on tips to supplement their meagre wages.

Prohibitions

If you use mace or pepper spray for self defence at home, you should note that both are illegal in the UK, and if you are caught carrying or using them, you may be arrested. Marijuana is illegal, as are all the usual drugs. However, under a recently introduced pilot policy, police in some parts of London (eg Lambeth) can turn a blind eye to possession of small amounts of cannabis.

How big is your footprint?

Whether you're travelling in Europe or in the developing world, it's important to remember that you have an impact on the places you visit. While you're letting your hair down, don't forget to treat the country you are visiting with respect. Please don't drop litter, in the countryside or in cities, and this means cigarette ends too. Respect ancient monuments, buildings and sites of religious importance. Before taking a photograph, ask yourself whether it's appropriate, and always ask permission before photographing people. Leave shells, wild flowers, birds' eggs and historical artefacts where they are – collecting rare birds' eggs is illegal, and removing other wildlife and heritage is irresponsible. And respect others who want to enjoy the peace, solitude and tranquillity of a place by keeping noise to a minimum.

Of course, most of these things are about manners, not about tourism. But don't doubt for a moment that if you're a visitor, even the smallest contravention of good manners will be noticed, remembered and resented.

Responsible tourism

Sustainable or eco-tourism has been described as, "...ethical, considerate or informed tourism where visitors can enjoy the natural, historical and social heritage of an area without causing adverse environmental, socio-economic or cultural impacts that compromise the long-term ability of that area and its people to provide a recreational resource for future generations and an income for themselves..."

Many parts of England are areas of outstanding natural beauty, and home to both wildlife and people who make their living from the land. Please behave responsibly in the countryside, and around ancient monuments. For more information on what action is being taken throughout UK or across the world to control the negative aspects of tourism on the environment and traditional cultures, contact **Tourism Concern** ① *277-281 Holloway Rd, London, T020-77533330, www.tourismconcern.org.uk.*

Safety

Generally speaking, England is a safe place to visit. English cities have their fair share of crime, but much of it is drug-related and confined to the more deprived peripheral areas. You should take heed of the usual advice and avoid wandering alone around unlit city centre streets, parks and lonely railway stations. Trust your instincts, and if in doubt, pay for a taxi. (See Women travellers, page 24.) Your main problem is going to be remembering to look right, not left, when crossing the road.

Getting around

Compared to the rest of Western Europe, public transport in England is generally poor and can be expensive. Rail, in particular, is expensive and notoriously unreliable. Coach travel is cheaper but much slower, and is further hampered by serious traffic problems around London, Manchester and Birmingham. Some areas, such as the Cotswolds, Peak or Lake District, are poorly served by public transport of any kind, and if you plan to spend much time in rural areas, it may be worth hiring a car, especially if you are travelling as a couple or group. A useful website for all national public transport information is **www.pti.org.uk**.

Air

England is a small country, and air travel isn't strictly necessary to get around. However, with the railways in disarray and traffic a problem around the cities, some of the cheap fares offered by budget airlines may be very attractive. There are good connections between **London** and all the regional airports, although travel from region to region without coming through London is more difficult and expensive.

Services between English cities are operated by many of these budget airlines and by **British Airways** ① *T0845-7733377, www.british-airways.com*. Bear in mind the time and money it will take you to get to the airport (including check in times) when deciding whether flying is really going to be a better deal.

Rail

There are three main companies operating frequent rail services between London and other towns and cities in England: **GNER** ① *T0845-7225225, www.gner.co.uk*, leave from London King's Cross and run up the east coast to the East Midlands, Yorkshire and northeast England; **Virgin Trains** ① *T0845-7222333, www.virgin.com*, operate a cross-country and a west coast service from London Euston to the Midlands, and the northwest. Trains to the west of England are run by **First Great Western** ① *T0845-7000125, www.great-western-trains.co.uk*, from Paddington Station in London. Local operators manage routes between cities in the north and Midlands.

Discount railcards

There are a variety of railcards which give discounts on fares for certain groups. Cards are valid for 1 year and most are available from main stations. You need two passport photos and proof of age or status.

A **Young Person's Railcard** is for those aged 16-25 or full-time students in the UK. It costs £18 and gives 33% discount on most train tickets and some ferry services. The **Senior Citizen's Railcard** is for those aged over 60. Same price and discount as above. The **Disabled Person's Railcard**, costs £14 and gives 33% discount to a disabled person and one other. Pick up application forms from stations and send it to: Disabled Person's Railcard Office, PO Box 1YT, Newcastle upon Tyne, NE99 1YT. It may take up to 21 days to process, so apply in advance. **Family Railcard**, costs £20 and gives 33% discount on most tickets (20% on others) for up to four adults travelling together, and 81% discount for up to four children.

Fares

To describe the system of rail ticket pricing as complicated is a huge understatement. There are many and various discounted fares, but restrictions are often prohibitive, which explains the long queues and delays at ticket counters in railway stations. Moreover, each rail company has devised its own catchy names for its discounted tickets, presumably because market research shows that travelling on a Virgin Value ticket is more pleasurable than travelling on a 14-day Apex return. Confused? Don't be: the cheapest tickets must be booked at least 2 weeks in advance, and are only accepted on certain non-peak time trains. Next cheapest are tickets that are booked at least 7 days in advance, with some restrictions at weekends and peak times. Everything else is a full-price ticket, unless you're using a railcard (see page 38). All discount tickets should be booked as quickly as possible because they get sold out weeks in advance. Seat reservations may cost an extra £1 and are very much worth getting – ask when you buy whether a seat is included in the price you are paying. And what is that price? Well, a standard return ticket from London to Manchester (operator: Virgin) costs £175, a saver (book 7 days in advance) costs £50, and a Virgin Value ticket (book 14 days in advance) costs £20. So be sure to book early.

To help you navigate the vagaries of the railways, enlist the help of **National Rail Enquiries**, T0845-7484950, www.nationalrail.co.uk, who will provide advice on routes, timetables, fares and connections. Better still, visit **www.chester-le-track.co.uk**. You can also book tickets and consult timetables online at **www.thetrainline.com**. For details of various discount rail passes and rail services within the United Kingdom, see page 38.

Road

Bus

This is the generally the cheapest form of travel in the UK. Road links between major cities are excellent and a number of companies offer express coach services day and night. The main operator, **National Express** ⓘ *T08705-808080, www.nationalexpress.com*, operates out of **Victoria Coach Station** in **London**, and has a nationwide network with over 1000 destinations. Tickets can be bought at bus stations or from a huge number of agents throughout the country. Sample return fares if booked in advance: London to Manchester (6 hours) £23, London to Brighton (2 hours) £14.

Bus travel passes

Full-time students or those aged under 25 or over 50, can buy a Coach Card for £9 which is valid for 1 year and gets you a 20-30% discount on all fares. Children normally travel for half price, but with a **Family Card** costing £15, two children travel free with two adults. The **Tourist Trail Pass** offers unlimited travel on all National Express services throughout Britain. Passes cost from £49 for 2 days' travel out of 3 up to £190 for 15 days' travel out of 30. They can be bought from major travel agents, at Gatwick and Heathrow airports, as well as from bus stations.

In **North America** these passes are available from **British Travel International** ⓘ *T1-800-3276097, www.britishtravel.com*, or from **US National Express** ⓘ T502-2981395.

Car

Visitors from Continental Europe may be shocked by the levels of congestion on English roads. This is particularly heavy on the M25 which encircles London, the M6 around Birmingham and the M62 around Manchester. The M4 and M5 motorways to the West Country can also become choked at weekends and bank holidays and the roads around Cornwall often resemble a glorified car park during the summer.

To drive in the UK you must have a current driving licence. Although foreign nationals may use their own licence for 1 year, international driving permits, available from your country of origin, may be required for some rentals, especially if your own licence is not in English. Visitors importing their own vehicle should also have their vehicle registration or ownership document. Make sure you're adequately insured. In all of the UK you drive on the left. Speed limits are (unless otherwise indicated) 30 miles per hour (mph) in built-up areas, 70 mph on motorways and dual carriageways and 60 mph on most other roads.

> *Rules and regulations www.dvla.gov.uk has details on every aspect of driving in the UK.*

Organizations

England has two main motoring organizations, which can help with route planning, traffic advice, insurance and breakdown cover. These are: The **Automobile Association (AA)** ⓘ *T0800-444999, emergency number T0800-887766, www.theaa.co.uk.* 1 year's membership starts at £43. The **Royal Automobile Club (RAC)** ⓘ *T0800-550550, emergency number T08000-828282, www.rac.co.uk.* 1 year's membership starts at £39. Both have cover for emergency assistance. They also provide many other services, including an agreement for free assistance with many overseas motoring organizations – check to see if your organization is included. You can still call the emergency numbers if you're not a member, but you'll have to a pay a large fee.

Vehicle hire

Car hire is expensive in England and you may be better off making arrangements in your home country for a fly/drive deal through one of the main multi-national companies: The minimum you can expect to pay is around £150 per week for a small car. Always check and compare conditions, such as mileage limitations, excess payable in the case of an accident, etc. Small, local hire companies often offer better deals than the larger multi-nationals. Most companies prefer payment with a credit card – some insist on it – otherwise you'll have to leave a large deposit (£100 or more). You need to have had a full driver's licence for at least 1 year and to be aged between 21 (25 for some companies) and 70. Motorcycle hire is expensive, ranging from around £200 up to £350 per week.

Bicycle

Cycling is becoming increasingly popular in England, and it's a pleasant if slightly hazardous way to see the country. Although conditions for cyclists are improving, with a growing network of cycle lanes in cities, most other roads do not have designated cycle paths, and cyclists are not allowed on motorways. You can load your bike onto trains, though some restrictions apply during rush hour. Consult **www.ctc.org.uk** for information on routes, restrictions and facilities. **www.cycling.uk.net** is another good cycling information station with links to other useful sites.

Maps

You'll find a good selection of maps of England in most book shops and at the main tourist offices. **Road atlases** can be bought at service stations. The best of these are the large-format ones produced by the **AA, Collins** and **Ordnance Survey,** which cover all of Britain at a scale of around 3 miles to 1 inch and include plans of the major towns and cities. The **Michelin** and **Bartholomew** fold-out maps are also excellent, as are the official regional tourist maps published by **Estate Publications.**

The best detailed maps for walking are the **Ordnance Survey** maps. These are available at different scales. The **Landranger** series at 1:50,000 (11/4 inches to a mile) covers the whole of Britain and is good for most walkers. The new **Explorer** and **Outdoor Leisure** series are 1:25,000 and offer better value for walkers and cyclists. An excellent source of maps is **Stanfords** ⓘ *12-14 Longacre, London WC2E 9LP.*

Sleeping

Accommodation in England is plentiful, although unfortunately much of it is either very expensive or very shabby. **Hotels** range from world-class luxury, not just in London but especially also along the M4 corridor as well as in or around most major cities, for which you can expect to pay at least £250 a night, to delapidated concerns with dodgy plumbing and threadbare carpets are especially prevalent in the traditional tourist hotspots. For the privilege of staying at one of these places you can still expect to pay at least £50 a night for a double room. Most of the more salubrious hotels, the ones that can afford to pay the cleaner but may not offer full room service, are likely to cost between £80-£160 for a double room for a night. Generally it's still true to say that guests paying over £100 a night can expect a superior level of comfort and service: from well-sprung mattresses to fluffy bathtowels and flowers in the room.

See inside the front cover for a guide to the hotel price codes used in this book.

Guesthouses occupy the middle ground between hotels and Bed & Breakfasts. The quality of accommodation in guesthouses varies wildly: some provide exceptional value for the money in houses of great character; others have seen much better days. They can usually charge anything from £50-£100 for the night, sometimes quoting initially for half-board (dinner, bed and breakfast). Most have a restaurant and bar, which may or may not be open to non-residents.

Bed & Breakfasts (B&Bs) are something of an English speciality. As their name suggests, they usually offer fairly staightforward accommodation in a private home, with a heart-stopping breakfast fry-up thrown in. In the south of England, many are run by empty-nesters with beautiful period houses and gardens; elsewhere, the best of them tend to be on working farms. Again, their standards are extremely variable, but they're unlikely to cost much more than £60 for the room for the night, some as little as £40 – depending on their location as much as the quality they offer – and some hosts can really bring their area to life. Many hotels, guesthouses and B&Bs offer discounts for stays of more than one night, weekend deals, and high and low season prices. They can be booked through Tourist Information Centres (TICs). Some TICs charge a booking fee.

Budget accommodation is offered by basic backpackers hostels and YMCAs in the cities and tourist hotspots, campsites and youth hostels run by the **Youth Hostel Association** ⓘ *Trevelyan House, Dimple Rd, Matlock, DE4 3YH, T01629-592600, or customer services T0870-870 8808, www.yha.org.uk*, in most major cities, the national parks and other areas of beauty. A bed in a dormitory usually costs less than £15 a night. Some **TICs** and a large number of private organizations keep lists of **self-catering** options on their books. Two of the more interesting are **The Landmark Trust** ⓘ *Shottisbrooke, Maidenhead, Berks, SL6 3SW, T01628-825925, www.landmarktrust.co.uk*, who rent out renovated historic landmark buildings, at a price, and **The National Trust** ⓘ *36 Queen Anne's Gate, London, SW1H 9AS, T0870-6095380, brochure line T0870-4584411, www.nationaltrustcottages.co.uk*, who provide a wide variety of different accommodation on their estates. A reputable agent for self-catering cottages around the country is **English Country Cottages** ⓘ *Springmill, Earby, Barnoldswick, Lancs, BB94 0AA, T01282-841785, www.countrycottages.co.uk*.

Youth Hostel Associations

Australia Australian Youth Hostels Association, 422 Kent St, Sydney, T02-92611111, www.yha.org.au.
Canada Hostelling International Canada, Room 400, 205 Catherine St, Ottowa, ON K2P 1C3, T800-6635777, www.hihostels.ca.
England and Wales Youth Hostel Association (YHA), Trevelyan House, 8 St Stephen's Hill, St Albans, Herts AL1 2DY, T01727-855215, www.yha/england/wales/org.uk.
France Auberges de Jeunesse, 7 Rue Pajol, 75018 Paris, T1-44 898727, www.fuaj.org.
Germany DJH Die Jugendherbergen, Hauptverband, Postfach 1455, 32704 Detmold, T5231-74010, www.jugendherberge.de.
Ireland An Oige, 61 Muntjoy St, Dublin 7, T01-8304555, www.irelandyha.org.
New Zealand Youth Hostels Association of New Zealand, PO Box 436, Christchurch 1, T03-379970, www.yha.org.nz.
USA Hostelling International-American Youth Hostels (HI-AYH), 733 15th St NW, Suite 840, PO Box 37613, Washington DC 20005, T202-7836161, www.hiayh.org.

If your country is not listed, consult **www.youtrek.com**, which has excellent information on hostelling all over the world.

Eating

Food

Only a decade or so ago, few would have thought to come to England for haute cuisine. Since the 1980s, though, the English have been determinedly shrugging off their reputation for over-boiled cabbage and watery beef. Now cookery shows are the most popular on TV after the Soaps, and thanks in part to the wave of celebrity chefs they have created, visitors can expect a generally high standard of competence in restaurant kitchens across the land. The sheer variety of different menus can be bewildering. Gourmets are particularly well-catered for, at around £80 a head, in London and the South. Slightly less fussy eaters won't be disappointed just about everywhere else, while towns like Ludlow, Padstow, and Whitstable have carved reputations for themselves almost solely on the strength of their cuisine.

See inside front cover for a guide to eating price categories used in this book.

So what exactly are you likely to end up eating in England? Some things seem to stay the same: the full **English breakfast** (a selection of fried eggs, bacon, sausages, tomatoes, mushrooms, beans, black pudding and even kidneys) is still going strong, despite not being exactly what celebrity cook Nigella Lawson would describe as 'temple food'. Other breakfast fortes are kippers (although the best are from Scotland), scrambled eggs and boiled eggs with toasted soldiers.

For much of the working population, at **lunchtime**, the **sandwich** is King and comes in all shapes and sizes: from fashionable breads and prosciutto in London to *Mother's Pride* white and reconstituted ham in pubs. That said, **pub food** has also been transformed in recent years, and now many of them offer ambitious lunchtime and supper menus. Watch out for extensive use of the microwave, though, especially in pubs that offer food all day. Meal times are still quite strictly observed by the catering industry: generally about 1200-1430 for lunch and 1830-2130 for supper. Most restaurants also offer something for lunch, usually a cheaper and lighter version of their supper menu. It may not be the healthiest time to eat, but the evening meal has become the main meal in England. In the north it's still known as 'tea', while in the south the same word refers to an English institution on a par with breakfast. (Oddly enough most 'tearooms' are not open at 'teatime', which is generally around 1630.) The ceremony ranges from a cup of tea and a biscuit to platefuls of cucumber sandwiches, cakes and of course its tour de force, the **cream tea**. These achieve their apotheosis in the southwest, where the quality of the fresh clotted cream served up with warm scones and jam can be exceptional, although they're widely available throughout the countryside.

The **evening meal** has also experienced a revolution in the quality of its ingredients and preparation in recent years. Menus from all over the world are on offer in all the major cities (**curry** has been declared the new national dish) while in the countryside the freshest local produce, much of it organic, can create memorable dining experiences. Most parts of the country still boast regional specialities, from the dubious delights of the **Cornish pasty** to succulent **Colchester oysters**. Seek out some of the finest beef, lamb, duck or game in the world, generally served with roast potatoes (or chips of course), broccoli, peas or carrots, and possibly even some **Yorkshire Pudding** (roasted batter to soak up the gravy). Other English specialities are absolutely fresh seafood, especially oysters, winkles, and crabs, as well as fish from the sea – often bass, mullet and sole, and from the farm – trout and salmon mainly. For a much cheaper supper, **Fish'n'Chip** shops can still be found in most small towns, especially in the north. They usually have restricted 'frying times' (lunch and supper again) and the fish served with fat chips tends to be battered and deep-fried cod, sole, plaice or rock. Approach with caution.

Drink

Drinking is a national hobby and sometimes a dangerous one at that. **Real ale** – flat, brown beer known as bitter, made with hops – is the national drink, but now struggles to maintain its market share in the face of fierce competition from continental lagers and alcopops. Many small independent breweries are still up and running though, as well as microbreweries attached to individual pubs. **Cider** (fermented apple juice) is also experiencing a resurgence of interest. English **wine** is also proving surprisingly resilient: generally it compares favourably with German varieties and many vineyards now offer continental-style sampling sessions.

The **pub** is still the traditional place to enjoy a drink: the best are usually 'freehouses' (not tied to a brewery) and feature real log or coal fires in winter, flower-filled gardens for the summer (even in cities occasionally) and most importantly, thriving local custom. In the countryside, many also offer characterful accommodation, and hence may call themselves an 'inn'. Pubs are prey to the same market forces as any other business, though, and many a delightful local has recently succumbed to exorbitant property prices (in the south mainly) or to the bland makeover favoured by the large chains.

Entertainment

England enjoys one of the most vibrant arts and entertainment scenes in Europe. London is often accused of soaking up all the talent in the performance arts, although a trip to Bristol, Birmingham, Manchester, Newcastle or Leeds will quickly prove that the regions are alive and kicking. All these cities play host on a regular basis to world-class theatre, music and dance, and plenty of smaller towns and villages have also made a name for themselves with their festivals and events (see below). Again, it's the sheer variety of what's on offer that impresses most and much of it of a very high standard. Think Huddersfield for contemporary world music, Cheltenham for modern literature, York for early music, Aldeburgh for more music, or Brighton for just about everything.

Nightlife in the regions is wide awake too, although thankfully still only in the major towns and cities. Every Thursday to Saturday most of the Midlands, Sheffield and Tyneside get mad, bad and dangerous to know, usually but not always very enjoyably so, with an astonishing array of restaurants, bars, pubs and nightclubs. Manchester, Leeds and Liverpool have practically turned their ailing fortunes around simply on the strengh of their music scene and party atmosphere alone.

Festivals and events

Festival time is when the normally repressed English shake off the yolk of inhibition and let rip. Summer in England is punctuated by an astonishing number of festivals – many of them centuries-old – ranging from the quaint to the dangerously eccentric. Every town, village and hamlet has its own tradition, some involving months of careful planning and preparation of costumes and choreography, others requiring simply a worrying desire to make a complete and utter fool of oneself. A particular feature of the English summer is the music festival. During the months of July and August the country moves to the beat of a thousand rock bands and dance DJs, proving that there's more to life than Glastonbury. As well as those listed here, there are also several major sporting events worthy of note, and these are covered under Sports and special interest on page 47.

Festivals

January

New Year's Day Parade, 1 Jan. Big family event, formerly known as the Lord Mayor's Parade. www.londonparade.co.uk.

February

Cheltenham Folk Festival, early Feb. Features top UK and international folk acts. T01242-227979 (box office), www.cheltenhamfestivals.co.uk.

April

Boat Race, first weekend in Apr. The 149-year-old race between Oxford and Cambridge Universities held on the Thames. www.theboatrace.org.

Flora London Marathon, mid Apr. The most famous 26 miles in the country. Televised live. www.london-marathon.co.uk.

May

May Day, 1 May. Celebrated up and down the land. Highlights include the choir of Magdalen College in Oxford singing in the new May dawn from the top of their chapel tower, Morris Dancers strutting their stuff atop a huge, erect chalk penis at Cerne Abbas in Doset, and hobby horses rampaging through the streets of Minehead in Somerset.

Bath International Music Festival, from the 3rd Fri in May for 2 weeks. Highly acclaimed festival of mainly classical and jazz music. www.bathmusicfest.org.uk.

Bath Literature Festival, beginning of May. 9 days of meeting and greeting the great and the good of English literature. www.bathlitfest.org.uk.

Brighton Festival, 1st 2 weeks in May. Over 300 events including music, theatre, dance, book fair and various outdoor performances. Tickets: T01273-709709; information www.brighton-festival.org.uk.

Chard Festival of Women in Music, end of May. Oestrogen-fuelled frenzy of jazz, classical and contemporary music. T01460-66115, www.chardfestival.org.uk.

Chelsea Flower Show, mid to late May. Horticultural heaven. www.rhs.org.uk.

Cheltenham International Jazz Festival, 1st week in May. One of the largest jazz festivals in the UK. T01242-227979 (box office), www.cheltenhamfestivals.co.uk.

Hay-on-Wye Festival, end of May and beginning of Jun. An internationally renowned book fair and the UK's most prestigious literary event. www.hayfestival.co.uk.

Leicester Early Music Festival, series of concerts in May and Jun. T0116-2709984, www.earylmusicleicester.co.uk.

Norwich Festival, beginning of May. Music, dance, comedy and visual arts. T01603-766400, www.n-joy.org.uk.

Salisbury Festival, late May to mid Jun. 2 weeks of music, dance and theatre, preceded by Salisbury Live, 3 days of live performances.

June

Aldeburgh Festival, 2 weeks from the second Fri in Jun. Legendary music festival showcasing new classical works. Founded in 1948 by Benjamin Britten. T01728-687110, www.aldeburgh.co.uk.

Cambridge Strawberry Fair, 1st Sat in Jun. Free festival held over 1 day, with live bands, street performers and markets. www.strawberryfair.org.uk.

City of London Festival, late Jun to early Jul. Arts and cultural events. www.colf.org.

Glastonbury Festival, last weekend in Jun, at Pilton, near Glastonbury. The UK's biggest and best music festival. 2004 will feature Paul McCartney and Oasis as headliners, www.glastonburyfestivals.co.uk. See also p364.

Hebden Bridge Arts Festival, late Jun-early Jul. Music, theatre, exhibitions and street events. T01422-842684, www.hebdenbridge.co.uk.

Leicester International Music Festival, mid-late Jun. A feast of classical music concerts held at various venues across the city. T0116-2473043, www.musicfestival.co.uk.

Lichfield International Arts Festival, first 2 weeks in Jul. Classical and jazz festival. www.lichfieldfestival.org.

London International Festival of Theatre (LIFT), biennial summer festival of all things dramatic; www.liftfest.org.

London's Lufthansa Festival of Baroque Music, early Jun. Been a long time since you Baroque'n'rolled? www.lufthansafestival.org.uk.

Ludlow Festival, late Jun-mid Jul. Music, exhibitions, talks and a programme of open-air Shakespeare. T01584-872150, www.ludlowfestival.co.uk.

Meltdown, held over last 2 weeks in Jun at the Royal Festival Hall in London. Each a different musical celebrity organizes the event. Past curators have included Nick Cave and David Bowie. T020-7960 4242.

Spitalfields Festival, mid to late Jun. Early classical and world music playing on the Huegenot heritage of this London district. T020-7377 1362, www.spitalfields.org.uk.

Wimbledon, 2 weeks of tennis, tears and tantrums in southwest in London.

July

Cheltenham International Festival of Music, beginning of Jul. Excellent programme of classical concerts. At the same time is the Fringe Festival, which features jazz, folk and world music, as well as comedy, theatre and dance. T01242-227979 (box office), www.cheltenhamfestivals.co.uk.

Greenwich and Docklands International Festival, early to mid Jul. The capital's largest multi-artform festivals. T0870-6082000, www.festival.org.

Henley Royal Regatta, first week in Jul. Large gathering of hooray Henrys and Henriettas horsing around on the River Thames. T01491-572153, www.hrr.co.uk.

Larmer Tree Festival, mid Jul, at Larmer Tree Gardens, Cranborne Chase near Shaftsbury. 4 days of pop and rock acts such as Van Morrison. T01725-552300, www.larmertree.co.uk.

Merseyside International Street Festival, late Jul to early Aug. Free festival of dance, drama, music and street performers. www.brouhaha.uk.com.

Warwick Folk Festival, late Jul. Big, important fold event held in the grounds of beautiful Warwick Castle. T01926-614932.

WOMAD, late Jul in Reading. The UK's leading world music event. www.womad.org.

York Early Music Festival, early Jul. England's top early music festival. T01904-658338, www. yorkearlymusic.org.

August

Bishopstock Blues Festival. The top blues festival in the country, held in Exeter. T01392-875220, www.bishopstock.co.uk.

Cambridge Folk Festival. Not as well-known as other music festivals but no less significant, and not strictly folk music. T01223-457245, www.cam-folkfest.co.uk.

Carling Weekend. Last weekend in Aug. Top rock acts featured at Reading (www.readingfestival.com) and Leeds (www.leedsfestival.com).

Notting Hill Carnival. Aug Bank Holiday weekend. Largest street festival in Europe. Starts with the Children's Day Parade on Sun, followed by the main parade on Mon. T020-7229 3819. See also page 109.

Ross-on-Wye International Festival. 10 days of music, dance, comedy, poetry and various other cultural events. T01989-565760, www.festival.org.uk.

V2004. Mid month at Hylands Park in Chelmsford and Weston Park in Stafford. Has featured the likes of Coldplay and the Red Hot Chilli Peppers. T0870-1202002, www.vfestival.com.

September

Artsfest. The UK's biggest free arts festival, held on the streets of Birmingham. T0121-2481300, www.artsfest.org.uk.

October

Bristol Poetry Festival. Early in the month. Lots of rhyming couplets and low-flying iambic pentameters. www.poetrycan.demon.co.uk.

Canterbury Festival, last 2 weeks in Oct. Smorgasbord of drama, music, dance, literary talks, films and visual arts. T01227-378188, www.canterburyfestival.co.uk.

Cheltenham Festival of Literature, mid Oct. The largest of its kind in Europe. Also a taster for what's to come at the Spring Weekend in early Apr. T01242-227979 (box office), www.cheltenhamfestivals.co.uk.

November

Guy Fawkes Night, 5 Nov. Bonfires are lit and fireworks set off in every town and village in the country. The main event is in the small Sussex town of Lewes, see page 196).

Public holidays

1 Jan New Year's Day.
Mar/Apr Easter Good Friday and Easter Monday.
May May Day Bank Holiday (1 Mon in May).
May Spring Bank Holiday (last Mon in May).
Aug Bank Holiday (last Mon in Aug).
Dec Christmas Day (25 Dec); and Boxing Day (26 Dec).

Ten of the most bizarre festivals

Abbots Bromley Horn Dance, mid September, Abbots Bromley, near Rugeley, Staffs. One of the oldest rituals still held in England. The dance consists of six men carrying reindeer horns around the surrounding villages, accompanied by a hobby horse (a 'mock' horse used as a fertility symbol in the 17th century), a fool, a Robin Hood figure and a Maid Marion.

British and World Marbles Championship, every Good Friday, Greyhound Public House, Tinlsey Green, West Sussex. This popular kids' playground game is played for real by a bunch of hopelessly nostalgic middle-aged men. T01403-730602, marbelam@ hotmail.com

Cooper's Hill Cheese Rolling, late May, Brockworth, Gloucs. Involves rolling a 7lb round of Double Gloucester Cheese down a very steep hill with hundreds of human lemmings in hot pursuit. It's said to derive from an ancient fertility rite. For details contact Gloucester Tourist Board, T01452-421188.

Egremont Crab Fair and Sports, mid September, Egremont, Cumbria. Local fair with some unusual events such as pipe-smoking contests and a gurning competition, which involves competitive face pulling and facial contortions. T01946-821554.

International Bognor Birdman, mid August, Bognor Regis. £25,000 is awarded to the contestant who can fly the longest distance over 100 m after leaping off Bognor pier. T01903-737500, birdman@arun.gov.uk

Robert Dover's Games and Scuttlebrook Wake, at the end of May, in Chipping Campden. The lovely Cotswold town has celebrating Spring with a series of ancient and games since 1612. Known as the Cotswold Olympic Games, they include the distinctly unorthodox shin-kicking. Contact the local tourist office: T01386-841206.

Royal Shrovetide Football, early March, Ashbourne, Derby. Not so much a game of football as a combination of rugby, mud wrestling and a full-scale riot. Apparently murder and carrying the ball in a motorized vehicle are forbidden – but only just. The game starts at 1400 and must finish by midnight. T01335-343666.

Tewkesbury Medieval Festival, mid July, in Tewkesbury, Gloucs. Around 800 brave souls dress up in medieval garb and fight it out in a re-enactment of the Battle of Tewkesbury. Contact the sinister- sounding Companion of the Black Bear, T01386-871908.

Viking Festival, second week in February, in York. York, or Jorvik, was once a Viking stronghold and every year an epic battle is fought between the Vikings and their enemies, the Saxons. T01904-643211.

World Toe Wrestling Championships, third week in June, in Wetton in the Peak District. Many an ankle has been broken during this strange sporting event. The locals take it very seriously, none more so than reigning champion Alan "Nasty" Nash. www.dcfg.fsnet.co.uk

Shopping

Shopping in England is expensive when compared with the rest of Europe and the US. Even so, the variety of different opportunities makes browsing a real treat, even in some of the smallest villages. Although the brand names of the big retail chains may come to seem familiar in town centres and High Streets up and down the country, independent retailers are still just about holding out in pockets around them, especially in the north of England. Many small towns, like Louth, Frome, Wareham and Penrith, still support a large number of traditional grocers, butchers and bakers as well as more offbeat shops.

In London and the major tourist centres the souvenir merchandising continues apace, but it's often given an entertaining local twist. Sugary sweets are a favourite, from Brighton Rock to Kendal Mint Cake, as well as knitwear, headgear, pottery, gnomes, dolls, trolls and of course, tea towels. Speciality local and organic foods can be found at farmer's markets throughout the country.

Sport and special interest

Cricket

If one sport sums up the English mentality then it must be cricket. Two teams will battle it out for four of five days and then at the end, having had to spend most of the time watching from the pavilion as the rain pours down, settle for a draw. During the days of the empire the English took cricket to the natives and gave them a sound thrashing while imparting the finer points of gentlemanly sportsmanship. These days, however, the chickens have come home to roost and the former colonies of Australia, India, Pakistan and the West Indies beat England at their own game with almost monotonous regularity. Those wishing to experience the esoteric pleasures of the game should try to secure a ticket for one of the five-day international Test matches which are played in the middle of the cricket season (April-September). These are played at **Lord's** and **The Oval**, both in London, **Edgbaston** (Birmingham), **Trent Bridge** (Nottingham), **Old Trafford** (Manchester, not to be confused with Manchester United's home ground) and **Headingly** (Leeds) and the atmosphere more than compensates for the inevitable lack of comprehension at what's going on. Running concurrently with these is a series of one-day internationals which are far more fun for the uninitiated. Tickets for internationals are very hard to come by. If you can't get a ticket, and don't fancy watching on TV, then you can witness the zen-like atmosphere of a county cricket match, which takes place over four days, from the comfort of a deckchair. There are also one-day competitions, namely the **Benson & Hedges Cup** and **Natwest Trophy** – both knockout competitions – and the CGU National league. Ticket prices for **international Test matches** range from £15 to £40 for one day. One-day international cost £20-50, while county games cost less than £10. **Contacts** For details of forthcoming Tests and county fixture, contact the **England and Wales Cricket Board (ECB)** ① *Lord's Cricket Ground, St John's Wood, London NW8 8QN, T020-7432 1200.*

Cycling

Cycling in England can be a hazardous business. Too many motorists are downright aggressive towards cyclists and though the wearing of helmets is not yet compulsory, you are strongly advised to protect yourself against the dangers of urban traffic. As well as having to contend with psychopathic drivers, cities themselves are not particularly cycle-friendly, very few have proper cycle routes and there's the added problem of security. If you want to explore the country by bike it's best to stick to rural backroads, especially unclassified roads and country lanes, which are not numbered but are signposted and marked on OS maps. The only problem with more remote areas is the scarcity of spare parts should something go wrong with your machine. There are also forest trails and dedicated routes along canal towpaths and disused railway tracks. These are part of the expanding National Cycle Network which is covered by the *Official Guide to the National Network* (£9.99), published by the charity SUSTRANS. There is also a series of demanding long-distance routes. Details and maps are available from the **Cyclists' Touring Club** (CTC). The wilder and more remote areas are popular with off-road mountain bikers but as it is also walking country cyclists should stick to tracks where a right to cycle exists. These tracks are marked on maps as **Bridleways**, **BOAT**s (Byways Open To All Traffic) or **RUPF**s (Roads Used as Public Footpaths). Cyclists should also be considerate towards walkers.

You can cut down on the amount of pedalling you have to do by transporting your bike by train. Bikes can be taken free on most local rail services on a first come-first served basis, and only outside morning and evening rush hours (0730-0930 and 1600-1900). On long-distance routes you'll have to make a reservation at least 24 hours in advance and pay a small charge. Space is limited on trains so it's a good idea to book as far in advance as possible. Bus and coach companies will not carry bikes, unless they are dismantled and boxed. Details are available on the CTC website.

Bike rental is available at cycle shops in most large towns and cities and tourist centres. Expect to pay from around £10-20 per day, with discounts for longer periods, plus a refundable deposit. There are cycle shops in most large towns, and smaller towns and villages in popular tourist areas. Addresses and phone numbers are given under the transport sections of individual towns in this book. **Contacts Cyclists' Touring Club (CTC)** ⓘ *Cotterell Ho, 69 Meadrow, Godalming, Surrey, GU7 3HS, T01483-417217, www.ctc.org.uk*. The largest cycling organization in the UK, providing a wide range of services and information on transport, cycle hire and routes, from day rides to longer tours. **SUSTRANS** ⓘ *T0117-9290888, www.sustrans.co.uk.*

Football

Football is the undisputed king of English sport. The passion generated by the game is unmatched – not only in any other national sport but also in almost any other walk of life. Anyone with more than just a passing interest should certainly endeavour to catch a game while they're here. Though the national team have under-achieved for many years (since 1966 in fact) the top club sides have recovered from the 5-year ban imposed by **UEFA** in the wake of the Heysel Stadium tragedy and begun to impose themselves on the latter stages of European competition. **Manchester United** in particular are now regarded as one of the big players on the European stage, winning the Champions League in 1999. Man U have dominated the domestic scene for the past decade, although **Arsenal** have challenged their superiority in recent years, winning the league and **FA Cup** double in the season 2001-02 and looking favourites to repeat the feat in 2003-04. Despite having several of the French national side, however, Arsenal have so far failed to make a major impact in Europe. While Manchester and north London may be the centres of footballing excellence, in terms of passion, the cities of Liverpool and Newcastle cannot be matched. **Newcastle United** have also recently found some good form, and their home, St James Park, is probably the number one place in the country to watch a football match for atmosphere as well as quality.

The 92 English league clubs are split into four divisions: the 20-club **Barclaycard Premiership** is the top division, followed by Nationwide divisions one, two and three, all of 24 teams each. The English football season runs from mid-August to early May, ending with the **FA Cup final** (which is currently held in Wales until a new national stadium is built). Most matches are played on Saturday, at 1500, and there are also midweek games (mostly on Wednesdays) and some games on Sunday afternoons and Monday evenings. Ticket prices range from £20 and upwards for Premiership games, to £15 and less for the lower divisions.

Horse racing

There are two types of horse race in England: **steeplechasing** is run over fences between August and April while the **flat racing** season runs from April to October. It's not too much of a generalisation to say that the two types of racing mirrors the British class divide. While steeplechasing attracts a broad-based following, flat racing is very much an upper-class event, with strong royal connections. The late Queen Mother was often seen at the racetrack – and not averse to the occasional flutter. The most precious jewel in the flat racing crown is **Royal Ascot**, held over a week in mid-June. Part equestrian event, part fashion parade for the nation's blue bloods, Ascot's preening self-importance reaches its zenith on **Ladies Day**, with breathtaking displays of millinery madness. The other major events in the flat racing calendar are **Derby Day**, held on the first Saturday in June at Epsom in Surrey; the **1000 Guineas** and **2000 Guineas** (both run at Newmarket); and the **St Leger** (at Doncaster).

For information on clubs and fixtures, visit www.thefa.com.

The biggest day in the steeplechasing season, and indeed in the entire British horse racing calendar, is the **Grand National**, run over improbably high fences at Liverpool's Aintree racecourse on the first Saturday in April. Everyone, but everyone in the country puts at least a couple of quid on their own favourite and the BBC devotes its entire sports coverage to this famous day. Another great day out in the steeplechasing season is the **Cheltenham Gold Cup** in mid-March. Tickets for these main events range from £50-60 and upwards. You can buy tickets online at www.londonticketshop.co.uk. **Betting** is an intrinsic part of horse racing, of course, though the complexities of betting odds are too detailed to go into here. Bets can be placed with racetrack book-makers, though the majority of the nation's gamblers prefer to watch the race on TV in their local 'bookies'.

Rugby

The 'hard game' is actually two distinct games: **Rugby Union** and **Rugby League**. While the latter (13-a-side) variety is of working-class origins and largely played in the northern towns and cities of England, the former (15-a-side) variety originates from the country's fee-paying public schools, hence the name – Rugby. To the uninitiated, a game of rugby can resemble a cross between mud wrestling and a re-enactment of the Battle of Culloden, played by nightclub bouncers. In reality, though, it is a very tactical game with a complex set of rules. Rugby Union has a broader geographical appeal but is still very much the preserve of the four-wheel-drive-owning middle classes, despite the recent upgrade to professionalism. For example, on an international day at Twickenham, the home of English rugby, in southwest London, it is said that the combined income of the spectators would be greater than the GDP of most African countries. But though 'rugger' lags behind football and cricket in terms of mass appeal it has, in recent years, been earning plenty of column inches in the sports pages, mainly thanks to the success of the national side. England now dominate the annual Six Nations Championship (comprising England, Scotland, Wales, Ireland, France and Italy) and even won the World Cup in 2003, competing against the might of the southern hemisphere nations, such as New Zealand (the All Blacks), Australia (the Wallabies) and South Africa (the Springboks). Each year at least one of the southern hemisphere sides tour the UK and though hard to come by, tickets are well worth seeking out. Contact the **Rugby Football Union** (RFU) for details: www.rfu.com. There is also a national league, the Zurich Premiership, where you can watch many of the Six Nations players week-in-week-out, and finding tickets is never a problem. More popular are the Heineken Cup matches which feature the best sides from Britain, Ireland, France and Italy and which are usually shown on TV.

Surfing

England may not be top of your list when you're thinking of that perfect break, but surfing is becoming increasingly popular across the UK, and there are some great waves to be found, especially in **Cornwall** and along the northeast coast, from **Scarborough** to **Berwick-upon-Tweed**. (If you're planning a serious surf trip, you should also consider travelling to the far north of Scotland, where the waves are on a par with Hawaii.) Even in England, you'll be wondering about water temperatures: expect 5-7°C in winter and 15-18°C in summer, with the west coast slightly warmer than the east. Wherever you surf, you'll need a wetsuit and, depending on how tough you are, boots, gloves and hat. Generally, the best surf is to be found in late summer/early Autumn.

Most surf spots in England are beach breaks, and there are hundreds of remote and scenic beaches to choose from. The better-known ones are on Cornwall's north coast, including **Fistral**, and other beaches around **Newquay**, **Polzeath** and **Perranporth**. To find a break and get information on facilities including board rental, accommodation, tide charts and surf reports, try www.surf-uk.org.uk, www.britsurf.co.uk. Don't expect there to be a surf shop just because the waves are good – many breaks have no facilities at all, and it's wise to check in advance. If you're renting, always check whether the shop rents fibreglass boards – some shops in popular beaches cater mainly to tourists and only rent out the less breakable foam kind, and the only place to get the real thing may be the nearest town. Please note that many breaks are unsuitable for inexperienced surfers, because of strong currents, rocks and other hazards. Another consideration is water pollution, which can be a problem in some areas. If you're planning an extended stay, get in touch with the excellent environmental campaign group **Surfers Against Sewage** ① *T01872-553001, www.sas.co.uk.*

For more detailed information about surfing throughout the UK, look out for Footprint Surfing Europe.

Tennis

Tennis is a minority sport in Britain, but for 2 weeks of the summer everyone becomes an expert on the game. This is **Wimbledon** fortnight, held during the last week in June and first week in July, when Union Jacks are brought of storage and waved furiously every time a British player bravely goes down in straight sets to the latest whizz-kid from Guatemala, Angorra or Outer Mongolia. The well-mannered suburb of southwest London is home to the **All England Lawn Tennis and Croquet Club**, which hosts the only 'Grand Slam' tennis tournament played on grass. All the world's top players compete, though many are not so keen on this alien playing surface, and many more even less keen on the notoriously fickle weather, which often means that games have to be played in fits and starts over several days. This is particularly harsh on the hordes of eager tennis fans who have queued since dawn in the hope of securing a precious ticket. But despite the vagaries of the British climate, the inflated prices of strawberries and cream, the constant threat of spontaneous outbreaks of singing on Centre Court by pop has-beens and the occasional ungentlemanly antics of Johnny Foreigner, Wimbledon fortnight is a magical time when the nation unites behind the dream of seeing a Brit lift the men's or women's singles trophy. **Contacts** For ticket details Wimbledon visit www.wimbledon.com and for information on other tennis tournaments try www.lta.org.uk.

Walking

Walking is popular in England and there's a wide variety of walking terrain, from the gentle, rolling downs of the south to the more hardcore rocky peaks of the north. Some of the most popular areas are in the National Parks. The **Lake District** offers the toughest challenge, with proper mountains but also the greatest rewards. Next in terms of popularity are the **Yorkshire Dales** and the **Peak District**, while Northumbria offers a couple of excellent routes in **Hadrian's Wall** and the **Coast Walk.**

There is a network of **long-distance paths** (LDPs) carefully prepared to provide ideal walking conditions together with sufficient places for accommodation and supplies en route. These walks can be attempted in full or sampled in part by less experienced walkers. Area tourist boards and local tourist offices can provide information and advice for their own particular sections. These include the 259-mile **Pennine Way,** from Edale to Kirk Yetholm (in Scotland) and the **Coast to Coast Walk,** from St Bees in the west to Robin Hood's Bay in the east. Walking in the south of England is altogether gentler, and the likelihood of good weather greater. The three main routes are the *South Downs Way*, **Cotswold Way** and the **South West Coast Path,** which at 630 miles travels around the entire Cornish peninsula and offers some amazing scenery.

Countryside Code

While in the countryside please follow the Countryside Code:

- Enjoy the countryside and respect its life and work
- Guard against all risk of fire
- Fasten all gates
- Keep your dogs under close control
- Keep to public paths across farmland
- Use gates and stiles to cross fences, hedges and walls
- Leave livestock, crops and machinery alone
- Take your litter home
- Help to keep all water clean
- Protect wildlife, plants and trees
- Take special care on country roads
- Make no unnecessary noise

The best time for hiking in the mountains is usually from May to September, though in the more low-lying parts, April and October should also be safe. July and August are the busiest times, though only the most popular routes get really crowded. Another problem during these months are midges. May to mid-June is probably the most pleasant time overall, as the weather can often be fine and the midges have yet to appear. September is also a good time, though it can be a lot colder.

The country is covered by the excellent series of **maps** published by **Ordnance Survey** (OS). The most detailed are the **Outdoor Leisure** series which covers areas such as national parks at a scale of 1:25,000, but the **Landranger** series (1:50,000) which covers the entire country, is detailed enough for most walks. OS maps can be found at tourist offices and also at outdoor shops, which are usually staffed by experienced climbers and walkers who can give good advice about the right equipment.

Many of the hills are straightforward climbs, but many also entail a high level of fitness and experience, and all require proper clothing. Visitors should be aware of the need for caution and safety preparations when walking or climbing in the mountains, especially in the **Lake District**. The nature of British weather is such that a fine sunny day can turn into driving rain or snow in a matter of minutes. Remember that a blizzard can be raging on the summit when the car park at the foot of the mountain is bathed in sunshine. It is essential to get an up-to-date weather forecast before setting off on any walk or climb.

Whatever the time of year, or conditions when you set off, you should always carry or wear essential items of clothing. A basic list for summer conditions would be: boots with a good tread and ankle support and a thick pair of socks; waterproof jacket and trousers, even on a sunny day; hat and gloves are important if the weather turns bad; warm trousers should be worn or carried, tracksuit bottoms are okay if you also have waterproof trousers; spare woolly jumper or fleece jacket will provide an extra layer; map and compass are essential to carry and to know how to use. Other essentials are food and drink, a simple first aid kit, a whistle and a torch. A small 25-30 litre rucksack should be adequate for carrying the above items. Also remember to leave details of your route and expected time of return with someone, and remember to inform them on your return. In the winter extra warm clothing is needed, as well as an ice axe and crampons (and the ability to use them) for the higher peaks. The skills required for moving over ice or snow should be practised with an experienced and qualified mountain guide/instructor.

Rights of way A right of way allows you to cross private land. There are three main types: a **footpath** is for walkers only, while **bridleways** and **byways** can be used by cyclists and horse riders.

Useful contacts There are a number of organizations that can help with suggested routes, maps or people to get in touch with. The biggest is the **Ramblers' Association** ⓘ *T020-7339 8500, www.ramblers.org.uk*, which has resources in different languages. Other good sources of information are **www.walkingbritain.co.uk** and the **British Tourist Authority** web site www.visitbritain.com/walking.

Please refer to the Countryside Code when walking (see box, page 51), and remember that the countryside is a working home to farmers and others making their living from the land.

Health

No vaccinations are required for entry into Britain. Citizens of **EU countries** are entitled to free medical treatment at National Health Service hospitals on production of an E111 form. Also, Australia, New Zealand and several other non-EU European countries have reciprocal health-care arrangements with Britain.
Citizens of other countries will have to pay for all medical services, except accident and emergency care given at Accident and Emergency (A&E) Units at most (but not all) National Health hospitals. Health insurance is therefore strongly advised for citizens of non-EU countries.

Medical emergency: dial 999 or 112 (both free) for an ambulance.

Pharmacists can dispense only a limited range of drugs without a doctor's prescription. Most are open for normal shop hours, though some are open late, especially in larger towns. Local newspapers will carry lists of which are open late.

Doctors' surgeries are usually open from around 0830-0900 till 1730-1800. Outside surgery hours you can go to the casualty department of the local hospital for complaints requiring urgent attention. For the address of the nearest hospital or doctors' surgery, T0800-665544. ➤➤ *See individual town directory sections for hospital and medical services listings.*

Keeping in touch

Communications

Internet

Many **hotels** and **hostels** offer internet access to their guests, and **cybercafés** are springing up all over the place (these are listed in the directory sections of individual towns in the main travelling section of this book). Email works out much, much cheaper than phoning home, and is also useful for booking hotels and tours and for checking out information. However, some internet cafés are expensive, so enquire to whether they operate a discount card scheme. In the absence of any internet cafés listed under a particular town listing, try the **public library** for internet access or ask at the tourist office.

Post

Most post offices are open Monday-Friday 0900-1730 and Saturday 0900-1230 or 1300. Many smaller sub-post offices operate out of a shop. Some rural offices may close on Wednesday afternoon. **Stamps** can be bought at post offices or from newsagents and supermarkets. It will be no surprise to you that England operates a class system in its post: a first-class letter or postcard to anywhere in the UK costs 28p and should arrive the following day, while second-class costs 20p and takes between 2 and 4 days. Airmail letters and postcards to Europe cost 38p. Airmail letters and postcards to the rest of the world cost 68p. If sending valuables, ask about the Recorded Delivery service, and if you are sending large parcels, ask about surface mail. For more information about Royal Mail postal services, call T0845-740740 or see www.royalmail.com.

Telephone

Telephone operator, T100; **International operator,** T155; **national directory enquiries,** T11 88 88 (calls to this number cost 20p); **overseas directory enquiries,** T153. Any number prefixed by 0800 or 0500 is free to the caller. Note that many cell phones from the USA/Canada/Latin America will not work in the UK.

Most **public payphones** are operated by **British Telecom** (BT) and can be found throughout the country, though many of the traditional red ones have been removed. *BT* payphones take either coins (20p, 50p, £1 and occasionally £2) or phonecards, which are available at newsagents, post offices and supermarkets displaying the *BT* logo. These cards come in denominations of £3, £5, £10 and £20. Some payphones also accept credit cards (Delta, Visa and Diners Club). For most countries (including Europe, USA and Canada) calls are cheapest between 1800 and 0800 Monday-Friday and all day Saturday and Sunday. For Australia and New Zealand it's cheapest to call from 1430 to 1930 and from midnight to 0700 every day. To call **England** from overseas, dial 011 from **USA** and **Canada,** 0011 from **Australia** and 00 from **New Zealand**, followed by 44, then the area code minus the first zero, then the number. To call **overseas** from **England** dial 00 followed by the country code and the number (minus the first zero). Country codes include: **Australia** 61; **France** 33; **Ireland** 353; **New Zealand** 64; **South Africa** 27; **USA** and **Canada** 1. Most phone boxes display a list of international dialling codes.

STD codes are included in all telephone numbers listed in this book.

Media

Newspapers

Newspapers are published nationally, with all the main daily and Sunday newspapers widely available throughout the UK. Some, (e.g. The Guardian and many tabloid newspapers) publish regional editions. There is a huge variety of national newspapers and competition between them is fierce. The national dailies are divided into two distinct camps; the tabloids, which are more downmarket; and the broadsheets, which are generally of a higher standard. Foreign visitors may find the broadsheets easier to understand as they tend to use less slang than the tabloids. The broadsheets include *The Times* and *The Daily Telegraph*, which are politically conservative, and *The Guardian* and *The Independent*, which have more of a liberal/left-wing leaning. There's also the distinctively coloured and very serious *Financial Times*, which focuses on business and finance. The Saturday editions of these papers carry their own listings guides with useful reviews of movies, clubs, restaurants, theatre, etc. The broadsheets' Sunday versions are huge and would take most of your holiday to read thoroughly. They include the *Independent on Sunday, Sunday Times, Sunday Telegraph* and the *Observer* (the Sunday edition of *The Guardian*).

The list of tabloids (known also as redtops) comprises *The Sun* and *The Mirror* which are the most popular and provide celebrity gossip and extensive sports coverage, the *Daily Mail* and *Daily Express* which are right-wing and aimed directly at 'Middle England'. The tabloids have their own Sunday versions, these include the notorious *News of the World*; the *Sunday Mirror, Sunday People* and *Sunday Sport.*

Regional and **local newspapers** are published throughout, and are on sale in newsagents alongside the national papers. Many regions also deliver free local papers, which are concerned with community news and gossip. **Foreign newspapers** and **magazines**, including the *Die Zeit*, *Le Monde*, *El Pais*, *USA Today* and *The New York Times* are available in larger newsagents, at airports and in railway stations.

Magazines

If you've got any kind of social conscience, then you should buy *The Big Issue*, which is sold exclusively on the streets by the homeless and which offers an overview of some of the issues affecting England's inner cities. There are thousands of magazines available: racing, cars, fish, women's interest, history, aeroplanes, money, sex, films, cookery, ponies – whatever your interest, there's a magazine to serve it. Some particularly common or popular ones include *NME* for music news and reviews, *Marie-Claire*, for a slightly more intelligent slant on women's interests, *FHM*, for men who like scantily-clad women but can't reach the top shelf, or the *New Statesman* and *The Spectator*, which offer political comment from the left and right respectively. If you have a long train journey ahead of you, check out such gems as *Private Eye* (political satire), *The Lady* (for the more mature female) and *The Chap* (for the last word on sartorial elegance). Most magazines are available across the country. *Time*, *Newsweek*, international editions of *Cosmopolitan*, *Vogue* etc, and other foreign magazines are widely available in large cities.

Television

There are five main television channels in the UK; the publicly funded *BBC1* and *BBC2*, and the independent commercial stations *ITV*, *Channel 4* and *Channel 5*. The BBC and ITV both offer regional programming, some of which is aimed at local special interest. The paucity of channels is more than made up for by the generally high standard of programming, especially in news, documentaries and drama. There are plenty of imported US shows, game shows and reality TV as well, but if you want to get a sense of what England is about, one evening watching TV during your trip is a good way of getting it. If, however, the terrestrial channels can't satisfy you, you can approach one of the various digital cable companies, such as **Sky Digital**, which currently has 170 channels, and **ONdigital**. Packages include movie channels such as *FilmFour*, *Sky Movies* and the *Movie Channel*, as well as sports-only channels like *Sky Sports*, which also show sports from around the world (such as American or Aussie Rules Football). Most upmarket hotels will have at least some of these channels on the TV in your room. The five main terrestrial channels are now supplemented by equally popular digital channels, such as *BBC3*, for drama and British comedy and *BBC4* for an excellent selection of culture, arts, science, history and business. *Channel 4* also have *E4*, for popular culture and the *ITV* have *ITV2*, often featuring extended versions of their terrestrial programmes.

Radio

The BBC network also broadcasts several radio channels, most of which are based in London. These include: *Radio 1* aimed at a young audience; *Radio 2* targeting a more mature audience; *Radio 3* which plays mostly classical music; *Radio 4* which is talk-based and features arts, drama and current affairs; and *Radio 5 Live* which is a mix of sport and news. In addition, the BBC broadcasts on local and regional affairs, through a network of local radio stations.

There are a large number **commercial** radio stations including *Jazz FM* (102.2), *Virgin FM* (1215AM, rock), *Classic FM* (99.9-101.9FM), and hundreds of local radio stations (try *XFM* on 104.9 FM in London), which can all be found at the touch of a dial. If you happen to be near a digital radio the choice extends even further, with channels dedicated to everything from sport to books.

London

Footprint features

Introduction

London is more of a great big jumble than a wild urban jungle. Like the British weather, it has difficulty making up its mind whether it's coming or going. The city is a hotch-potch, an anonymous sprawl riddled with diversity and character. First impressions are likely to be decidely mixed: the capital of the UK is the largest and apparently least English city in England. Despite itself, London makes the rest of the country feel small.

Traditionally it's been perceived by 'the regions' to be bloated and corrupt, an evil metropolis squatting at the mouth of the Thames, daily sucking in and spewing out all the talent, energy and traffic within a 50-mile radius. Not a pretty sight, you might think. Dilapidated and shambolic, the city wheezed into the 21st century freighted with some shiny new millennium projects – Tate Modern, the London Eye, the Millennium Bridge – and all the old problems: overcrowded accommodation, unreliable transport and alarming prices. The good news is that, finally, there seems to be a determination to do something about it: all the major museums are free; the cross-London rail link is in development; and the city centre congestion charge is having a radical and very desirable effect. London still rejects any attempt to make it conform to expectations. With its ethnic mix, street markets and multinational business, its political pragmatism and creative chaos, London remains one of the most global, engaging and invigorating places on the planet.

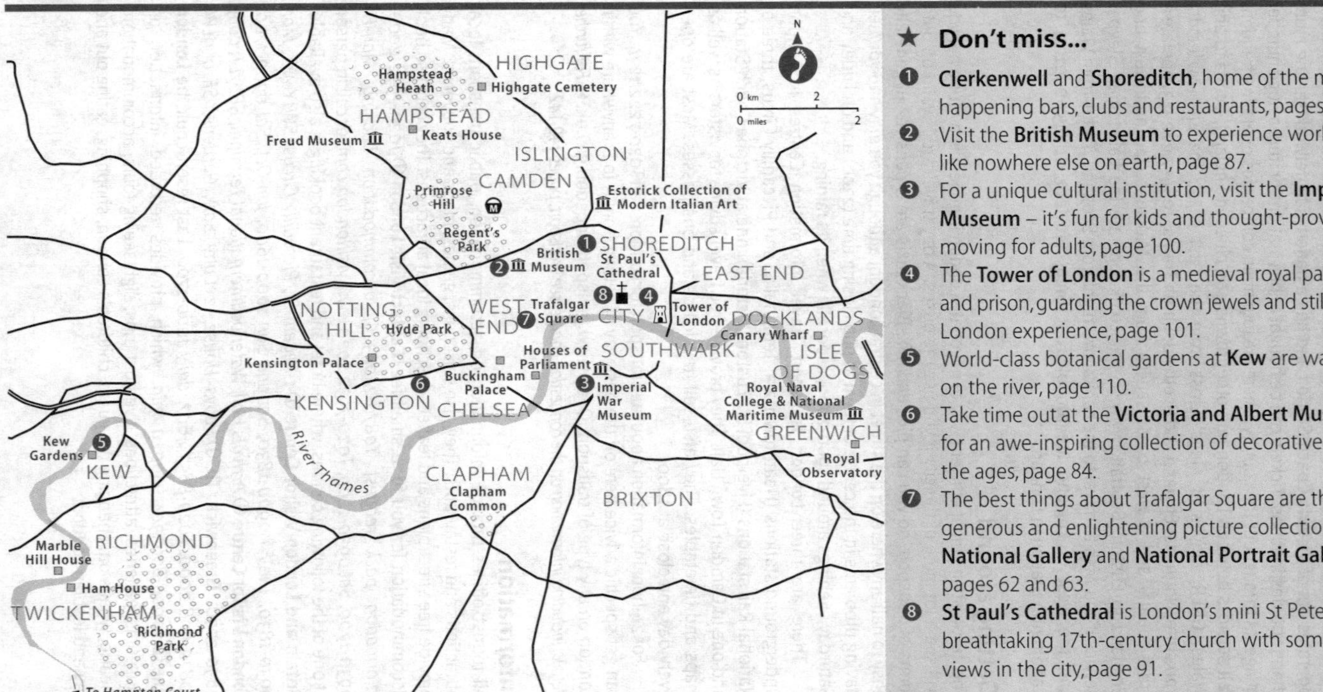

★ Don't miss...

1. **Clerkenwell** and **Shoreditch**, home of the most happening bars, clubs and restaurants, pages 89 and 102.
2. Visit the **British Museum** to experience world cultures like nowhere else on earth, page 87.
3. For a unique cultural institution, visit the **Imperial War Museum** – it's fun for kids and thought-provoking and moving for adults, page 100.
4. The **Tower of London** is a medieval royal palace, fortress and prison, guarding the crown jewels and still an essential London experience, page 101.
5. World-class botanical gardens at **Kew** are way out west on the river, page 110.
6. Take time out at the **Victoria and Albert Museum (V&A)** for an awe-inspiring collection of decorative arts down the ages, page 84.
7. The best things about Trafalgar Square are the superbly generous and enlightening picture collections at the **National Gallery** and **National Portrait Gallery**, pages 62 and 63.
8. **St Paul's Cathedral** is London's mini St Peter's – a breathtaking 17th-century church with some of the best views in the city, page 91.

Ins and outs

Getting there

The main **coach** operator, **National Express**, T08705-808080, www.gobycoach.com, operates out of **Victoria Coach Station** and has a nationwide network serving more than 1000 destinations. Tickets can be bought at bus stations or from a huge number of agents throughout the country. There are four main companies operating frequent **rail** services between London and other towns and cities in England, Scotland and Wales: **GNER**, arrives at Kings' Cross from the east coast, the East Midlands, Yorkshire, Northeast England and Scotland; **Virgin Trains**, T08457-222333, operate a cross-country and a west coast service from the Midlands, the northwest and Scotland to Euston. **Scotrail**, www.scotrail.co.uk, operate the Caledonian Sleeper service if you wish to travel to the capital overnight from Scotland. **Trains** from Wales and the west of England are run by **First Great Western**, T08457-000125, to Paddington Station in London.

Getting around

The quickest and most efficient way to negotiate London is generally by Tube but you will see a lot more of the city if you use the buses. A day travelcard is valid on both forms of transport, so you can pick and mix. Black taxis are expensive but generally easy to hail anywhere on the street in central London, although you may find yourself having problems in the centre of town at pub closing time (2300) and on Friday and Saturday evenings around 1900-2000, especally when its raining.

There are three **London Transport Travel Information Centres** in London underground stations (Heathrow 1,2,3, Terminal 4, and Piccadilly Circus, three at National Rail stations (Liverpool St, Euston, Victoria), one at Victoria Coach Station and one in Camden Town Hall. They provide free travel advice for vistors as well as maps and timetables. They also sell travelcards and bus passes. Most are open every day and close at 1800.

For 24-hour information about all Transport for London, call T020-7222 1234. You can get specific advice here on the best way of getting from A to B anywhere within London on any type of transport. Or try www.transportforlondon.gov.uk. ⏩ *For further details, including information on the congestion charge, see Transport, pages 140-142.*

Information

All tourist offices provide information on accommodation, public transport, local attractions and restaurants. They also sell books, guides, maps and souvenirs. Many provide free street plans and leaflets describing local attractions. They can also book accommodation for you for a small fee. **Contact Visit London** ⓘ *T020-7932 2000, information pack request T0870-2404326, accommodation booking Mon-Fri 0930-1700, Sat 0930-1200, T020-7932 2020 www.visitlondon.com*, or call in person at one of the following centres, where hotel and restaurant booking is also available: **Britain and London Visitor Centre** ⓘ *1 Regent St, Piccadilly Circus, SW1Y 4XT, Mon 0930-1830, Tue-Fri 0900-1830, Sat and Sun 1000-1600, Jun-Oct, Sat 0900-1700.* **London Visitor Centre** ⓘ *Arrivals Hall, Waterloo International Terminal, SE1 7LT, daily 0830-2230.* **Greenwich TIC** ⓘ *Pepys House, 2 Cutty Sark Gardens, SE10 9LW, T0870-608 2000, F020-8853 4607, daily 1000-1700.* Last resort could be **London Line** ⓘ *T0906-8663344, 60p a min*, which provides recorded information on museums, galleries, attractions, riverboat trips, sightseeing tours, accommodation, theatre, what's on, changing the guard, children's London, shopping, eating out and gay and lesbian London.

24 hours in London

Seeing much of London in a day is really only for the brave, although with sensible shoes and some stamina it can certainly be attempted. Try the following as a suggested tour.

Start the day with a coffee from one of the outlets near the Embankment tube. Take a croissant into the **Victoria Gardens** and sit among the statuary. Stroll across Hungerford Footbridge (the right hand side of the railway is best for views of the London Eye and Houses of Parliament) and then turn left for a 20-minute walk along the **South Bank**. Pass beneath Waterloo Bridge and the Royal National Theatre to be at **Tate Modern** on Bankside when it opens at 1000. Here you can see some modern and contemporary art in a converted power station and the morning sun catching the dome of **St Paul's Cathedral** across the river.

After digesting as much of the artwork as you like, head for lunch in **Soho** by taking the tube from Southwark northwards on the Jubilee Line to Green Park and walking east down Piccadilly to the Circus. If you want to see the outside of **Buckingham Palace** make a detour across Green Park itself before heading down Piccadilly. After a leisurely lunch in Soho, somewhere like *Maison Bertaux* perhaps, or a browse around the shops, walk east across Tottenham Court Rd to the **British Museum** (about 20-minutes again). Spend the afternoon wondering at some of the things in the finest museum in the country.

Head out to **Clerkenwell** for supper, a well-deserved steak at *Smith's* perhaps, and then dance the night away at *Fabric* or another of the area's clubs. Stumble out again at daybreak and get yourself a hearty breakfast and pint of Guinness in the *Cock Tavern* in **Smithfield Market**, after which you should feel sufficiently restored to remember where your hotel was and what time your train left for Bristol.

History

Londinium

The Romans are popularly believed to have established the first settlement where the City now lies, but prehistorians have uncovered evidence of habitation in this part of the Thames Valley dating back half a million years. However, it was the Romans who first established the town of Londinium as a major trading port, a role it has played for almost two millennia. Despite distractions in further-flung regions of Britannia, such as the Scots spilling over the northern border or the Druids in Anglesey, and the city being razed to the ground by Boudicca, Queen of the Iceni, in AD 61, Roman London flourished in the second and third centuries. Londinium was the fifth largest city in the Western Empire, and its reputation earned it the honorific title of 'Augusta'. Over the next 150 years, however, its prosperity declined with that of the Empire as a whole.

Mart of many nations

The Saxons left Roman London abandoned for almost 200 years, and little record remains of the city until about the time of the first building of St Paul's in 604. By the mid-eighth century, however, the Venerable Bede could describe London as "the mart of many nations resorting to it by land and sea". In the late 11th century, William the Conqueror, having announced his arrival by burning Southwark, granted privileges to the citizens of the City, being especially careful to keep the merchants sweet, but he was nonetheless wary enough of their independent streak to build three forts within the city walls – Montfichet's Tower, Baynard's Castle, and The White Tower, now the Tower of London. Wealth and poverty lived cheek by jowl, a feature of London throughout the centuries. The Peasants' Revolt of 1381, led by Wat Tyler from Kent and Jack Straw from Essex, involved up to 60,000 people laying waste to much of London in pursuit of airing their grievances to the king. Aided by the many city apprentices who joined the crowd, they dragged the Archbishop of Canterbury out of the Tower and beheaded him.

Tudor palaces and Stuart barricades

Despite the explosions of violence, poor public health, and the virulent plagues, by the end of the 15th century when the Tudors came to power the population was almost 50,000 and growing. The Tudors liked their palaces. Henry VIII, the most ostentatious, had about fifty residences spread throughout the country, most around the capital. Whitehall, Greenwich, Hampton Court and Richmond all found royal favour, each enhanced to display the magnificence of monarchy. Theatres also opened up, notably the Globe and the Rose in Southwark. London Bridge itself was a fragile but magnificent sight. Rebuilt in stone in the 13th century, houses and shops clung to its edges, often arching over the road itself. During the Civil War, London sided with Parliament and Cromwell, forcing King Charles I to raise his army from Nottingham. Barricades were erected on all major roads in and out of the capital, and forts, batteries and ramparts built around the city. Eventually, one cold January morning in 1649, Charles walked out of Banqueting House in Whitehall to be beheaded. The puritanical nature of Cromwell's rule, however, meant that following the restoration of the monarchy in 1660, his exhumed and rotting head remained on a spike on Westminster Hall for 25 long years.

Fire and Wrenaissance

Over the next decade London suffered first with the plague of 1665 and then in the flames of the Great Fire in 1666: over 80 churches, 44 livery halls, and 13,000 houses were destroyed, and although only six people were reported dead, thousands were made homeless, settling in tented villages in the fields and meadows north of the city. The fire did, however, provide the opportunity for the city to be rebuilt, Sir Christopher Wren, the great architect of his time, devoting his energy to overseeing the construction of more than 50 churches, his signature piece being a further incarnation of St Paul's Cathedral, towering over the city with a splendour befitting the world's first Protestant cathedral.

Hub of the British Empire

By the end of the 18th century, London had grown significantly, reaching a population of almost one million. Putney, Westminster and Blackfriars became the first bridges over the Thames since the Roman settlers built the stilted wooden affair across to Southwark. Buckingham Palace became one of George III favoured residences, although it was only later under Queen Victoria that it became established as the monarch's primary London residence. By the time Victoria came to the throne in 1837, London was at the centre of an Empire spanning one-fifth of the globe, its spoils contributing wealth and employment to the capital at its heart. By far the greatest transformation to the city's landscape was brought about by the transport revolution, particularly the arrival of the railways. In 1836 the first railway in London ran between the *Bricklayer's Arms* in Southwark and Deptford. Over the next 20 years stations and large termini began cropping up across the city. In 1863 the Metropolitan Line, the world's first underground line, opened, ferrying a mixture of excited and sceptical Londoners across the city under the New Road from Paddington to Farringdon Road. Mile upon mile of Victorian terraces went up to accommodate the growing population of commuters.

Cradle of revolution

London also became a haven for radical thinkers and activists from abroad. Karl Marx lived in poverty in Soho (although aided by Freidrich Engels, a resident of Camden), plodding to the Reading Room at the British Museum to work on his potboiler, *Das Kapital*. Mahatma Gandhi and Mohammed Ali Jinnah both studied law here towards the end of the century; Jawarharlal Nehru (also a student at Harrow and Cambridge) completed the trinity when he studied at the bar at Inner Temple in 1910. Revolutionaries studied or worked here before returning to their homeland to act out their destiny. Sun Yat Sen (China), Marcus Garvey (West Indies), Michael Collins (Ireland) and Lenin (Russia) could all be found here in the early years of the 20th century; Ho Chi Minh washed up dishes at the Carlton Hotel before doing much the same to American forces in his native Vietnam some 60 years later.

The Blitz

"Britain's finest hour", as Churchill called it, began on Black Saturday, 7 September 1940. A raid of 400 bombers signalled the start of a bombardment that was to kill 20,000 Londoners, leave another 25,000 injured, and at its most intense, run for 57 consecutive days. Londoners' reaction was mixed – some were hysterical, but many were defiant. They continued to go to work, stumbling across debris en route if necessary, and a Mass Observation survey held in the winter of the Blitz recorded more Londoners to be depressed by the weather than by the bombing. By the end of the war, there were 1½ million Londoners who simply didn't have a home anymore.

Rationing and recovery

New towns such as Basildon, Stevenage and Harlow sprung up beyond the Green Belt as London raised itself from the ashes. The Olympics at Wembley in 1948, the Festival of Britain in 1951 and the Coronation of Queen Elizabeth II two years later all lent some sparkle to a time made lean by rationing. Also London suffered a particularly acute year of smog in 1952, causing up to 4000 deaths in associated illnesses. But theatres and cinemas were buoyant, football matches were well attended, and jazz was heard in the pubs and clubs of Soho.

Immigration and inner city expansion

Heathrow and Gatwick both opened in the 1950s, and by 1956 the dockyards were dealing with up to 1000 ships a week. A skilled labour shortage prompted the likes of London Transport and the health service to seek employees from abroad. The 492 Jamaicans who disembarked from the *Empire Windrush* in 1948 had been broadly welcomed, but as economic pressures intensified and the West Indian population grew, local relations became strained. In the 1960s many of Britain's colonies achieved independence, and were free to seek other markets. London's trade with the Commonwealth halved. Dockyards such as The East India and St Katharine closed, often in the wake of union struggles that protected the workers' rights in the short term, but lost them their jobs in the long term. The laxness of planning authorities allowed over 400 tower blocks to be built across the city, a transformation of London's skyline comparable with that achieved by Wren but hardly as picturesque.

Style capital

Meanwhile, in 1966, *Time* magazine confidently reported that London "swings, it is the scene". From the tentative appearance of the first coffee bar in Soho in 1953, and the bistros and the Mary Quant boutique in Chelsea, London was becoming the music and fashion capital of the world. Thirty years later, in 1996, another American publication, *Newsweek*, announced that London was "the world's coolest city", a claim that for many was as ignorant as it was meaningless. Paradoxically, perhaps, a 1991 a survey revealed that 48% of Londoners wanted to leave the city, at a time when tourism was booming (25 million tourists visited in 1990). The Conservative government squeezed through one further election, and then limped to sleaze-ridden defeat in 1997, as New Labour swept to victory on a wave of optimism.

Central London

Trafalgar Square → *Tube: Charing Cross*

Trafalgar Square is the centre of London, avoided by Londoners if at all possible. It's the lynch pin of the West End's tourist triangle between Piccadilly Circus and Leicester Square. But it's the breadth of Whitehall approaching from Westminster and the south that explains the prominence of the square in London's geography. This is where the administrative offices of government meet the people, and the monarch comes too, with The Mall marching straight up from Buckingham Palace into the southwest corner through Admiralty Arch. It has recently undergone an impressive makeover, with a pedestrianised north side in front of the National Gallery.

Nelson's Column

The square itself, hardly very beautiful, well-designed, or even square, does at least have a focal point in Nelson's Column. Admiral Horatio Nelson is just about the only military commander ever to have been truly taken to heart by the British people. Even so, it took 40 years after he was mortally wounded while defeating Napoleon's navy at Trafalgar before his Column was finally erected. In a fit of patriotic fervour in 1843, two days after the anniversary of the battle, 14 people ate a dizzy supper of rump steak on the top. Then the statue of the one-armed hero, three times life size and sporting his eye-patch and three-cornered hat, was hoisted into position on his granite Corinthian column, facing southwest so that he could review the fleet in Portsmouth. Around the base the bronze relief sculptures were cast from captured French cannons, celebrating his sea victories at Copenhagen, the Nile, and Cape St Vincent, as well as Trafalgar.

Church of St Martin-in-the-Fields

ⓘ *T020-7766, Mon-Fri 0745-1800, Sat 0845-1800, Sun 0745-1930.*
The oldest of the buildings surrounding the square is the Church of St Martin-in-the-Fields. Like St Mary-le-Strand nearby, but on a larger scale, it's a fusion of classical and Baroque by James Gibbs, dating from 1722-26. The interior is less remarkable, although beautifully proportioned, and includes a font from the original medieval church. There's a tourist market in the churchyard at the back, near where notables such as Joshua Reynolds, Hogarth, and Charles II's mistress Nell Gwynne are buried. Concerts are also given here and there's an excellent café in the crypt.

National Gallery

ⓘ *T020-7747 2885, www.nationalgallery.org.uk, daily 1000-1800, Wed 1000-2100, free.*
Stretching along the north side of the square, and easily its most unmissable attraction, is the National Gallery, housing more than 2000 Western European paintings dating from the 13th century to 1900. The collection began with the purchase by the government in 1824 of 38 paintings from the financier John Julius Angerstein. Originally housed in Pall Mall, the present building was purpose built and completed by 1838. Artificial lighting, to extend the winter opening hours, was introduced in 1935. The Sainsbury Wing, specially designed to house the earliest paintings, was finished in 1991. Today the gallery is pushed to cope with about five million visitors a year. Although it may not possess as many masterpieces as the Louvre, the Prado or the Hermitage, it glories in a selection of outstanding work from all the great schools of European painting down the ages.

On the ground floor the 16 rooms of the **Sainsbury Wing** house paintings from 1260-1510 broadly arranged in chronological order. In the first room, the most significant exceptions are two masterpieces of the early Renaissance by Leonardo da Vinci. In a special alcove of its own, behind his *Virgin of the Rocks*, is the gallery's most fragile and precious possession, a charcoal and chalk cartoon on paper of *The Virgin and Child with St Anne and St John the Baptist*. Carefully restored after being attacked by a maniac with a shotgun in the 80s, the dim lighting establishes a suitably devotional mood. Most of the pictures in this wing have religious and devout themes, with a strong Italian and Dutch emphasis. Painted at a time when all western nations were under the Pope, they would look best in flickering candlelight. The other most significant works are those of Giotto, Jan van Eyck, Pierro della Franscesca, Botticelli, and Raphael.

Erika Langmuir's 'Companion Guide' to the collection is an excellent investment.

Leaving the Sainsbury Wing, the High Renaissance begins in the **West Wing** (paintings from 1510-1600), in the main body of the gallery, starting with the Wohl Room and three outstanding Titian's, *Bacchus and Ariadne, Noli Me Tangere* and the possible self-portrait *Portrait of a Man*. In the same wing, *The Entombment* and *The Manchester Madonna* are both exceptionally rare things, paintings by Michelangelo, both unfinished. Look out too for Tintoretto's dynamic *Saint George and the Dragon* and Holbein's *Christina of Denmark*.

The **North Wing** (paintings from 1600-1700), comprising the back rooms of the gallery, houses 17th-century paintings, with a stronger emphasis on landscapes and especially rich in the Spanish and Dutch schools, including Velázquez's extraordinary play on the nature of 'looking', *The Rokeby Venus*. The first room includes two remarkable paintings by Claude Lorrain, *Seaport with the Embarkation of the Queen of Sheba* and *Landscape with the Marriage of Isaac and Rebekah*. Thanks to a clause in Turner's will, that superlative 19th-century British painter's *Sun Rising through Vapour* and *Dido Building Carthage* hang alongside those of his hero. This wing is also home to the collection's wonderful array of Rubens, Poussin and also Rembrandt paintings.

Unsurprisingly, the most crowded part of the gallery is often the **East Wing** (paintings from 1700-1900), where the collection of works by Van Gogh, Gauguin, Cézanne, Degas, Monet and Renoir draw in admirers of the Impressionists and post-Impressionists. The 18th-century British landscapes and portraits are also well-represented, with some beautiful family portraits by Gainsborough and Stubbs, and also several works, including *The Haywain*, by John Constable. Goya's lively portrait of the Duke of Wellington is also worth seeking out, as is William Hogarth's irresistible and satirical *Marriage Settlement*. No visit to the gallery is complete without a look at Turner's shimmering *Rain, Steam and Speed*.

National Portrait Gallery

ⓘ *Charing Cross Rd, T020-7306 0055, information ext 216, recorded information T020-7312 2463, www.npg.org.uk, Mon-Wed, Sat, Sun 1000-1800, Thu and Fri 1000-2100. Free. Lectures: Tue 1500 and Thu 1310, Sat and Sun 1330 PR 1500, free. Thu 1900, admission charge. Fri music nights 1830, free. IT Gallery does print outs; black and white free, colour postcard £5.50, colour A4 £17.50.*

Tucked away behind the National Gallery, the National Portrait Gallery is a shrine to British history pictured in the portraits of those who have shaped it. A six-year lottery-funded project has resulted in the excellent new **Ondaatje Wing**, opened in May 2000. Directly beyond the old main entrance, visitors arrive in a soaring lobby, ready to be whisked up an escalator to the earliest pictures in the collection.

It might come as a disappointment that there are no medieval works here, the earliest being an impressive portrait of Henry VII, but the new **Tudor Galleries** more than make up for their absence. Modelled on an Elizabethan Long Room, they include the only portrait of Shakespeare known to have been taken from life, Holbein's Henry

Central London

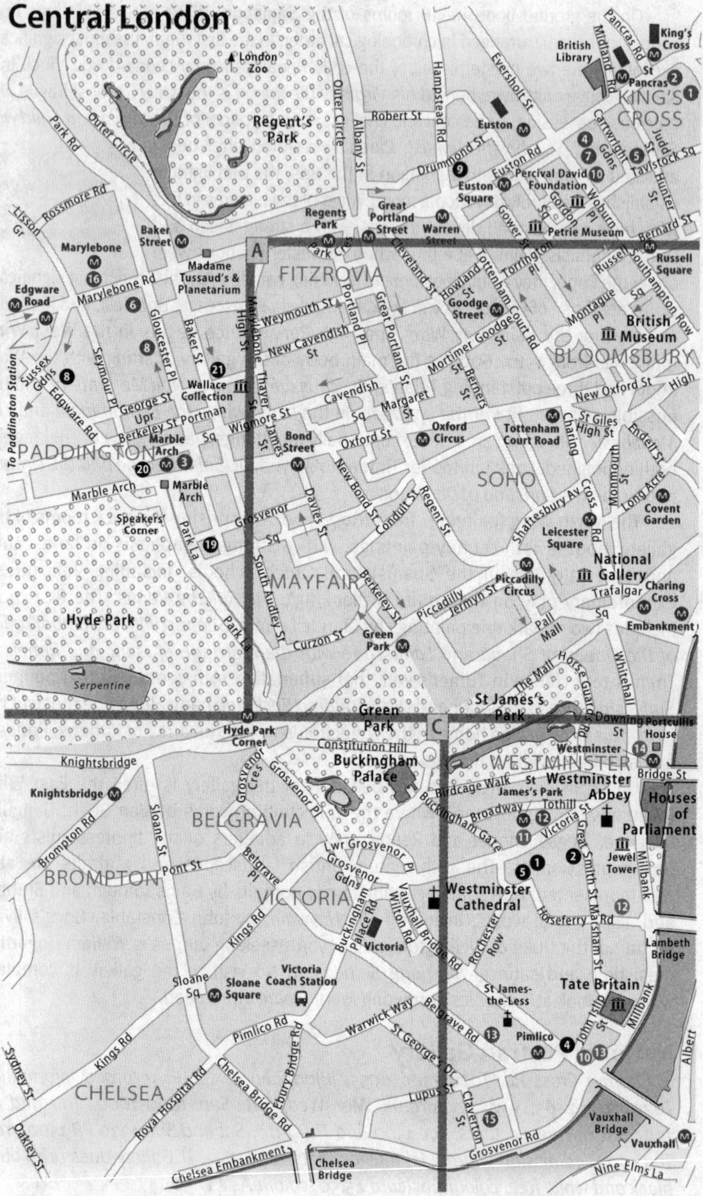

Sleeping
- Ashlee House 1
- Butler's Wharf Residence 14
- Carlton 2
- Cumberland 3
- Dolphin Square 15
- Euston Travel Inn Capital 4
- Generator 5
- Georgian House 6
- Harlingford 7
- Hart House 8
- Landmark 16
- London Marriott County Hall & London County Hall Travel Inn Capital 9
- Mentone 10
- Novotel London Tower Bridge 11
- Sanctuary House 12
- Victoria Inn 13

Eating
- Bagel Express 1
- Cinnamon Club 2
- Defune 21
- Delfina Studio Café 18

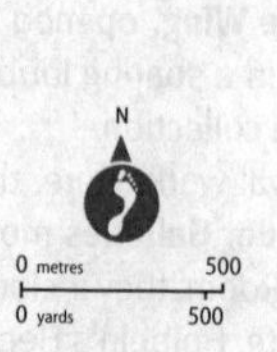

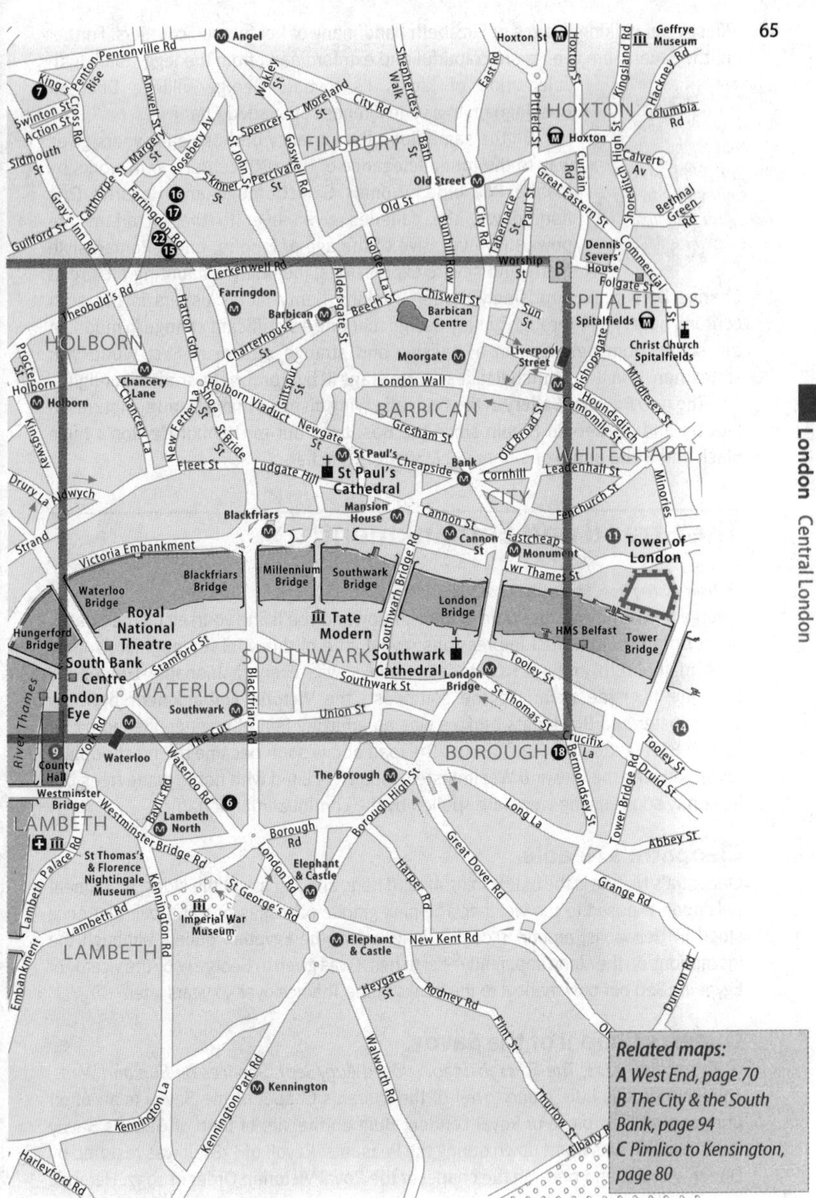

Diwana Bhel Poori House **3**
Eagle **15**
JR Jenkins Café **4**
La Gavroche **19**
Laughing Halibut **5**
Little Bay **22**
Locanda Locatelli **20**
Masters Super Fish **6**
Moro **16**

Paolina **7**
Patogh **8**
Ravi Shankar **9**
Quality Chop House **17**
Relish, the Sandwich Shop **10**

Pubs & bars
Albert Tavern **11**
Marquis of Granby **12**
Morpeth Arms **13**
Red Lion **14**

 VIII, several striking images of Elizabeth I and many of her famous courtiers. Further on, the Stuarts are even more colourful and extraordinary: from the leggy full-length celebration of James I's toyboy, George Villiers, Duke of Buckingham to a vivid likeness of a jaded Charles II.

The gallery runs a series of lectures, opens late on Thu and Fri, and has a restaurant and bar with great views over the old roofs of the National Gallery towards Big Ben.

On the same floor, the vibrancy of those early years gives way to the formal elegance of the 18th century, with works by Joshua Reynolds, Thomas Gainsborough and Hogarth. One floor down, the galleries given over to the Victorians are powerfully evocative of the age of Empire, full of Roman-style busts and severe expressions, including a haunting picture of Charles Darwin. A surprisingly modern-looking Henry James ushers in the 20th century, a wavy see-through gallery design marking a significant change in mood. In the small room before it, in a massive and strange picture of First World War statesmen, Winston Churchill takes centre stage lit by a prophetic shaft of sunlight.

The new **Balcony Gallery** in the Ondaatje Wing displays images and sculptures of movers and shakers in Britain since the 60s. Look out for Helmut Newton's huge black and white photo of former PM Margaret Thatcher.

The Strand and Embankment

→ *Tube: Charing Cross, Embankment and Temple (closed Sun)*

Emerge from Charing Cross train or tube station and you'll find yourself on the Strand. Apart from its width, first impressions reveal little of this vital thoroughfare's glory days in the 18th and 19th centuries, when it was every fashionable Londoner's favourite riverside prom. To the southeast, the **Victoria Embankment** between Westminster and Blackfriars bridges was an amazing feat of engineering led by Sir Joseph Bazalgette in the late 1860s. The road above soon became the most popular route between the City and Westminster. Today it is lined with noble plane trees but its sunny south-facing views are spoiled by the continual roar of traffic.

Cleopatra's Needle

Cleopatra's Needle is the oldest thing around here, and just about the oldest monument in London exposed to the weather. The pink granite obelisk is one of a pair that once stood in Heliopolis, around 1500 BC, long before the Egyptian queen, although the inscriptions on the stone apparently refer to her. It was given to George IV by the viceroy of Egypt in 1820 but only made it to the banks of the Thames over 50 years later.

Queen's Chapel of the Savoy

ⓘ *T020-7836 7221, Tue-Fri 1130-1530, (closed Aug/Sep). Services on Sun and Wed.*

The incongruous little stone tower of the Queen's Chapel of the Savoy is an often unremarked little piece of Royal London. Built on the site of John of Gaunt's Savoy Palace, which was burnt down during the Peasants' Revolt of 1381, it was restored by Queen Victoria and became the chapel of the Royal Victorian Order in 1937. Heraldic copper plaques mark the pews of the different knights in the splendid late-Gothic interior, its flat ceiling decorated with the Royal Arms above the monarch's seat at the west end. The BBC broadcast its first daily radio programmes in 1922 from the building over the road, moving to Broadcasting House 10 years later.

Somerset House

Further east along the Strand, on the right, stands Somerset House. It was designed by Sir William Chambers in 1776 for George III's Naval office, with the wings on the Strand purpose-built for the fledgling Royal Academy of Arts (which was founded in 1768 but moved to Piccadilly in 1837), the Royal Society, and the Society of

Antiquaries. Appropriately enough, since 1990, this northern wing has been occupied by the **Courtauld Institute and Gallery** ⓘ *T020-7848 2526, www.courtauld.ac.uk, daily 1000-1800, £5, children free, concessions £4, joint ticket with Gilbert Collection or Hermitage Rooms £8, concessions £7, or all 3 £12, concessions £10, free on Mon 1000-1400 except bank holidays*. Ascending the winding stairway, apparently designed to inspire the terror that the time considered necessary to the appreciation of the Sublime, the 11 rooms afford a delightful potted introduction to Western art; from early Dutch through the Renaissance in Italy and Northern Europe, via Rubens, to the Baroque, 18th-century British portraiture and the post-Impressionists.

In 2000 the southern buildings were opened up to display Arthur Gilbert's collection in what is London's latest museum of decorative art and Hermitage Rooms, providing access for the first time to the river frontage. Described as the single most generous gift ever made to the nation, the **Gilbert Collection** ⓘ *T020-7240 9400, daily 1000-1800 (last entry 1715), £5, students and children free, OAPs £4, disabled and helpers £2 (joint ticket with Courtauld Gallery £7, OAPs £5)*, includes gold and silverware, precious snuff boxes and peculiar Roman micromosaics.

A fairly recent addition to the collections at Somerset House are the contents of the **Hermitage Rooms** ⓘ *T020-7845 4630, daily 1000-1800 (last admission 1715), £6, concession £4, children free*, designed to exhibit changing selections of artefacts from the great St Petersburg museum. The five rooms have been decorated in the Imperial style of the Winter Palace, with replica chandeliers, gilded chairs and marquetry floors and include, amongst changing exhibitions, a live feed to St Petersburg, looking across Palace Square, and a video taking you on a tour of the Hermitage itself.

The great central courtyard of Somerset House has been rechristened the **Edmond J Safra Fountain Court** ⓘ *the fountains operate from 1000-2300, with short displays on the hr and ½ hr, and main displays at 1300, 1800, and 2200, for details on ice skating in the courtyard in winter,* *see page 138*, and blessed with a diverting but controversial computer-operated fountain. In December and January, it becomes an open-air ice rink.

Leicester Square and around → *Tube: Leicester Sq*

Leicester Square always gets bad press, written off as a charmless tourist-trap rife with pickpockets, bagsnatchers and buskers. The criticisms are still justified – not too many of the businesses round here expect to see the same face twice – but since the square's pedestrianization and then refurbishment in the early 90s it has provided a focal point for the entertainment scene in the West End. The two main draws are the cinemas, not only the blockbusting first-run multiscreens surrounding the square, but also places like the cult rep the *Prince Charles*, or the fashionable Curzon Soho, and the nightclubs, like the *Wag*, *Sound* and *Limelight*. And then there's the *Comedy Store*, the place that set many comedians on the road to stardom in the 70s. Just north of the square lies **Chinatown**, not really the home of London's Chinese community, more like its market place, and only consisting of a couple of streets of restaurants, but still an area with one of the most distinctive cultural identities in the capital. It squeezes into a little niche between the square itself, **Shaftesbury Avenue**, the high street of 'Theatreland', and **Charing Cross Road**, the bookseller's favourite address.

Soho → *Tube: Leicester Sq or Tottenham Court Rd for east, Oxford Circus for west, Piccadilly Circus both*

Soho has always been the West End at its least respectable and most lively, and now it's the only part of central London that really comes close to keeping the same hours

Sex and clubs and rock 'n' roll

Soho has long been associated with sex and vice. Central London's notorious one-square-mile district was home to some 300 prostitutes in the 1950s and when they moved elsewhere in the 60s, Soho turned to other methods, such as 'clipping' (which involves getting the customer to pay before sending them to a fictitious address and then disappearing). Around this time, the number of strip clubs and drinking clubs increased dramatically. The most famous, Raymond Revuebar, is still doing business, though most have now closed.

From the late 60s Soho became the centre of the porn industry. While pornographic magazines were shipped over from the continent in Danish Bacon lorries, the Obscene Publications Squad (OPS) was being bribed to turn a blind eye. But in 1972 a new commissioner of the Metropolitan Police was appointed to clean up Soho and the OPS was suspended. In the early 80s new legislation requiring all sex shops to be licensed came into effect.

Soho was also one of the centres of British bohemia as well as the culinary capital of Britain. Its drinking clubs are still famous: The Colony Room, on Dean Street, has always been a favourite haunt of hard-drinking British artists, from Francis Bacon to Damien Hirst, and the Groucho, once the epitome of Thatcherite excess, still serves the inflated egos of medialand.

Soho also has mighty impressive music credentials. Ronnie Scott's was the first outlet in the capital for modern jazz, while the Marquee (now closed) played host to the Yardbirds and the Rolling Stones. Its dance clubs, such as The Wag and Beat Route were at the cutting edge of late 70s/early 80s music and its most famous late-night coffee bar, Bar Italia on Frith Street, still gives homeward-bound clubbers the coolest of caffeine kicks.

as New York. Long considered to be shifty and disreputable, this small well-defined area south of Oxford Street, east of Regent Street, west of the Charing Cross Road and north of Shaftesbury Avenue has more character (and characters) per square yard than all those big names put together. That's mainly because people still actually live here and are proud of the place.

Shopfronts, restaurant windows, doorways, alleys and, most important of all, other people, are the sights of Soho, all packed so close together that somewhere somehow here you can reasonably expect to find your heart's desire.

Running south down to Shaftesbury Avenue from Soho Square, roughly parallel to the Charing Cross Road, are **Greek Street** and **Frith Street**. The **Frith Street Gallery** ⓘ *T020-7494 1550, 59-60 Frith St, W1*, picks up on their tone by putting on shows of cutting-edge contemporary art. The length of **Dean Street** lies one block further west. Even though each is crowded with highly individual shops, restaurants and bars, these three streets and the alleyways between them are so similar in atmosphere and appearance that they can easily baffle the inexperienced Soho partygoer.

Just before reaching Shaftesbury Avenue they all cross **Old Compton Street**, the area's unofficial high street. A recent attempt to pedestrianize this main drag failed due to problems policing the late-night hordes. The street has also become the main artery of the gay scene, while its junction with Greek Street and Moor Street must be one of the most characteristic and crowded spots in the area.

Brewer Street continues the thrust of Old Compton Street westwards, heading into the newly branded 'West Soho'. Just along here on the right, a seedy little passage called Walker's Court leads through into **Berwick Street**, home to the West End's one and only pukka **fruit 'n' veg market**.

The west side of Soho is generally more seedy and money-grabbing than boho high Soho. Nearer Regent Street, around **Carnaby Street**, it also becomes even more fashion-conscious, especially along Newburgh Street. Carnaby Street itself, a by-word for anything groovy in the 60s, has begun to reclaim some of the cachet that it let slip in the 1980s after becoming a tourist trap trading on its heyday.

Covent Garden → *Tube: Covent Garden, Charing Cross*

Covent Garden has been attracting traders, entertainers, their customers and audiences for at least 300 years but it only became a respectable tourist hotspot about 30 years ago, a fairly successful transformation of one of the oldest meeting places in the West End into one of the youngest. Thankfully it's still largely free of the depressing tat peddled to visitors around Leicester Square.

Sandwiched between the Charing Cross Road, Bloomsbury, the Strand and Holborn, the area is almost as well defined as Soho. The focal point is still what was once London's largest and most famous fruit 'n' veg market before it moved out to Nine Elms in 1974. Now an impressive piazza, it still bears a faint flavour of those bustling times thanks to its converted Victorian covered market and the crowds that flock here day and night to shop, eat, drink and enjoy a pleasant place away from all the traffic. North of Long Acre, what were once narrow streets of warehouses and slums have experienced a boom in youth-orientated shops and bars, led by long-established crowd-pullers like the Donmar Warehouse theatre and Neals Yard wholefood hippy enclave.

To the east of the piazza, the **Royal Opera House** has reopened to great acclaim following great controversy after its multi-million pound redevelopment. Open to the general public throughout the day, it includes a terrace overlooking the piazza while the refurbished Floral Hall provides a soaring space to enjoy a coffee or light meal.

The west side is dominated by the classical portico of **St Paul's Church** ⓘ *T020-7836 5221, Mon-Fri 0930-1630, wwwactorschurch.org*, a 17th-century box designed by Inigo Jones that has long been known as the actors' church thanks to the plaques inside commemorating bygone stars of the stage and screen. The portico on the piazza forms the backdrop to regular street theatre events of widely varying quality throughout the year.

On the south side, the **Jubilee Market** is another covered market with a much lower-rent selection of clothing and jewellery stalls as well as some reasonable snack stops. Things improve here on Mondays when an antiques market sets up shop and at weekends when craftworkers arrive with their wares.

London Transport Museum

ⓘ *T020-7379 6344, www.ltmuseum.co.uk, Mon-Thu, Sat, Sun 1000-1800, Fri 1100-1800 (last entry 1715), £5.95, concessions £4.50, free for under-16s.*

Next door in the old flower market in the southeast corner of the piazza, the London Transport Museum is an excellent place to take the kids for free. As well as a host of antique carriages, trams, buses and tube trains, many of which can be boarded and explored, the great glass-roofed hall contains a formidable battery of hands-on exhibits, push-button panels and a cunning labyrinth of aerial walkways.

West End

London Central London

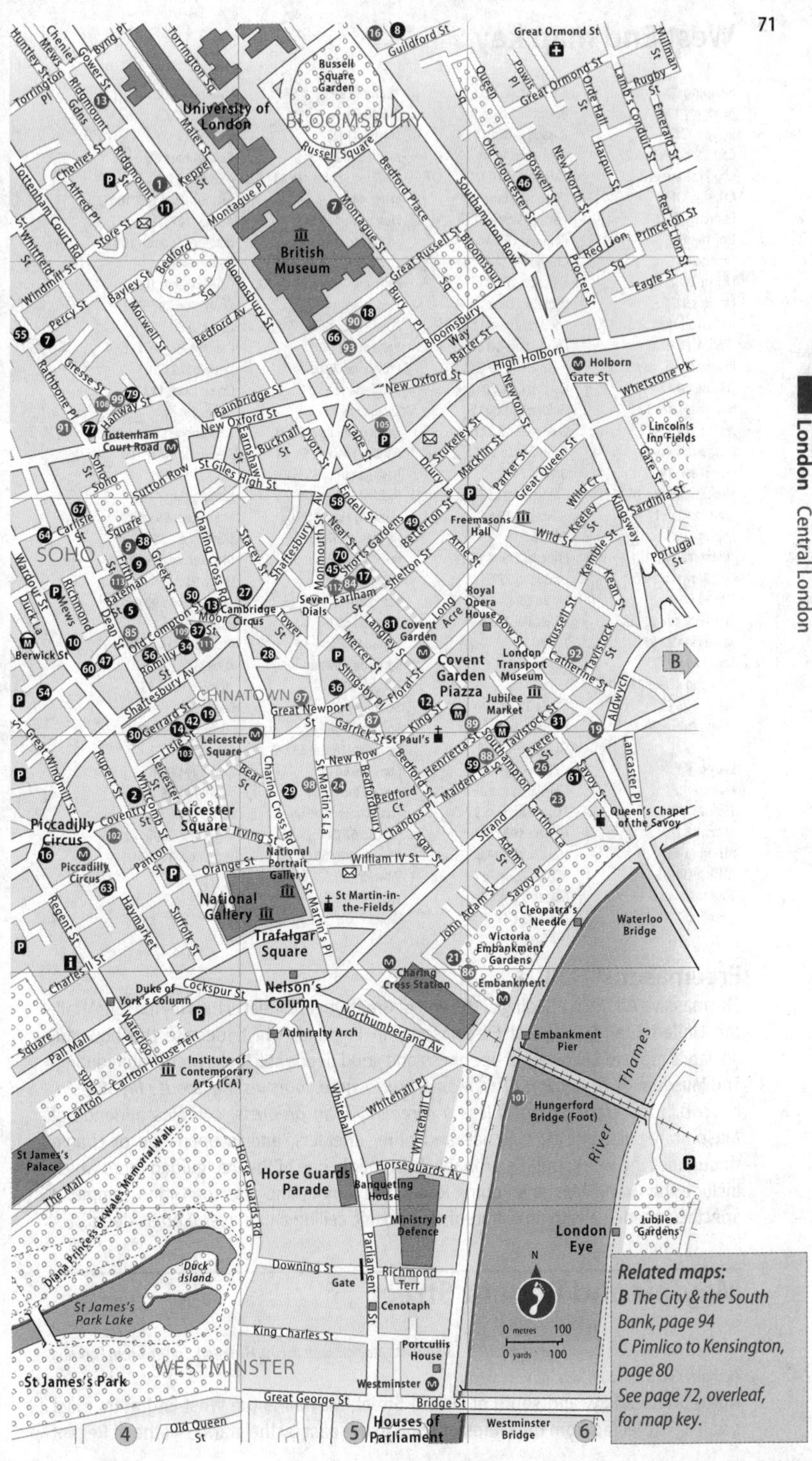

Related maps:
B The City & the South Bank, page 94
C Pimlico to Kensington, page 80
See page 72, overleaf, for map key.

West End map key

Sleeping
Academy **1** *A4*
Brown's **2** *D2*
Carr Saunders Hall **27** *A3*
Charlotte Street **3** *B3*
Claridge's **4** *C1*
Connaught **5** *D1*
Dorchester **6** *E1*
Grange Blooms **7** *A5*
Hallam **8** *A2*
Hazlitt's **9** *C4*
Indian Student YMCA **11** *A3*
International Student's House **10** *A2*
Ivanhoe Suites **12** *B1*
Jesmond **13** *A4*
London Hilton Park Lane **14** *E1*
Meridien Russell **16** *A5*
Metropolitan **17** *E1*
Millennium Britannia **18** *D1*
One Aldwych **19** *C6*
Ritz **20** *E2*
Royal Adelphi **21** *D5*
Sanderson **22** *B3*
Savoy **23** *D6*
St Martin's Lane **24** *D5*
Stafford **25** *E3*
Strand Palace **26** *D6*

Eating
@venue **1** *E3*
1997 **2** *D4*
Al Duca **3** *D3*
Al Hamra **4** *E2*
Alastair Little **5** *C4*
Back to Basics **6** *A3*
Bam-Bou **7** *B4*
Bar Centrale **8** *A5*
Bar Italia **9** *C4*
Busaba Eathai **10** *C4*
Café Deco **11** *A4*
Café Pacifico **81** *C5*
Calabash at the Africa Centre **12** *C5*
Centrale **13** *C4*
Chisou **74** *C2*
Criterion **16** *D4*
Eagle Bar Diner **77** *B4*
Food for Thought **17** *C5*
Forum Café **18** *B5*
Fung Shing **19** *C4*
Garden Café **20** *C3*
Golden Eagle **21** *B1*
Golden Hind **22** *B1*
Greenhouse **23** *E1*
Greens **24** *E3*
Guinea Grill **25** *D2*
Hakkasan **79** *B4*
Ibla **26** *A1*
Imperial China **14** *C4*
Incognito **27** *C5*
Ivy **28** *C5*
J Sheekey **29** *D5*
Jen **30** *C4*
Joe Allen **31** *C6*
Kaya **32** *D2*
Kerala **33** *B2*
Kettners **34** *C4*
La Madeleine **35** *D3*
La Trouvaille **75** *C3*
Le Palais du Jardín **36** *C5*
Maison Bertaux **37** *C4*
Manzi's **103** *D4*
Mar I Terra **104** *D3*
Masala Zone **76** *C3*
Milfred's Wholefood Café **38** *C4*
Mirabelle **39** *E2*
Mô **40** *D3*
Momo **41** *D3*
Mr Kong **42** *C4*
Mulligan's of Mayfair **43** *D3*
Nanis **44** *B3*
Neal's Yard Bakery & Tearoom **45** *C5*
October Gallery Café **46** *A6*
Patisserie Valerie **47** *C4, B1*
Pied-à-Terre **48** *B3*
Poetry Society **49** *C5*
Pollo **50** *C4*
Providores **73** *B1*
Purple Sage **51** *B1*
Quaglino's **52** *E3*
Quiet Revolution **53** *A1*
Randall & Aubin **54** *C4*
Rasa Samudra **55** *B4*
Richard Corrigan at Lindsay House **56** *C4*
RK Stanley **57** *B3*
Rock & Sole Plaice **58** *C5*
Rules **59** *D6*
Sardo **80** *A3*
Satsuma **60** *C4*
Shumi **82** *E3*
Simpson's-in-the-Strand **61** *D6*
Sketch **83** *C3*
Sotheby's Café **62** *C2*
Spaghetti House **63** *D4*
Star Café **64** *C4*
Sugar Club **65** *D3*
Thai Garden Café **66** *B5*
Toucan **67** *C4*
Veeraswamy **68** *D3*
Villandry **69** *A2*
Wolseley **15** *E3*
World Food Café **70** *C5*
Yoshino **71** *D3*
Zilli Fish **72** *C3*

Pubs & bars
AKA **105** *B5*
Atlantic Bar & Grill **106** *D3*
Audley **107** *D1*
Bradley's Spanish **108** *B4*
Bünker **84** *C5*
Café Bohème **109** *C4*
Champion **78** *B3*
Che **110** *E3*
Coach & Horses **111** *C4*
Detroit **112** *C5*
Dog & Duck **113** *C4*
Duke of York (Rathbone St) **114** *B3*
French House **85** *C4*
Gordon's **86** *E5*
Lamb & Flag **87** *C5*
Maple Leaf **88** *D6*
Market Café **89** *C6*
Museum Tavern **90** *B5*
Office **91** *B4*
Opera Tavern **92** *C6*
Plough **93** *B5*
Propaganda **94** *B3*
Red Lion (Crown Pass) **95** *E3*
Red Lion (Waverton St) **96** *E1*
Saint **97** *C5*
Salisbury **98** *D5*
Sevilla Mia **99** *B4*
Social **100** *B3*
Tattershall Castle **101** *E6*
Tiger Tiger **102** *D4*

Freemasons' Hall

The massive Art Deco building at the end of Great Queen Street is the Freemasons' Hall, the United Grand Lodge of Freemasonry in England, which despite the powerful society's repeated avowals of openness and good deeds still looks pretty intimidating. The **Museum** ① *T020-7831 9811, Mon-Fri 1000-1700, tours lasting about 1 hr, Mon-Fri, at 1100, 1200, 1400, 1500 unless a ceremony is in progress*, contains all kinds of Masonic regalia, clocks, watches and other artefacts, and is open free of charge throughout the week, but it's probably best to join one of the free guided tours which include the Grand Master's Robing Room, the Shrine, and also the Grand Temple, a spectacular edifice with an extraordinary mosaic ceiling and massive brass doors.

Mayfair and Regent Street

→ *Tube: Marble Arch, Bond St and Oxford Circus for North Mayfair, west to east. Hyde Park Corner, Green Park and Piccadilly Circus for South Mayfair, west to east*

North of Piccadilly, and south of Oxford Street, Mayfair is the West End at its most swanky. Protected from the chaos of Soho to the east by the grand swathe of Regent

Street, it still earns its place as the last and most expensive stop on the Monopoly board by boasting the capital's most luxurious hotels, the hautest couture and cuisine, and some of its wealthiest residents. Unbelievably, people of more modest means do still live here, although the daytime and early evening population consists largely of itinerant office workers, business people and tourists.

Lavish and louche, Mayfair smells of money and the area's traditional exclusivity has ensured that there's little of the usual 'see and do' variety. At weekends the wide streets can be almost deserted. But recently Mayfair is supposed to have become less stuffy and more fashionable: although superficially little seems to have changed, digging a bit deeper behind those imposing façades is likely to unearth some stylish and affordable surprises. Window-shopping in the Arcades and **New Bond Street**, inspecting the objets d'art up for auction at Sotheby's, getting measured for a suit in **Savile Row,** wondering at contemporary artwork in **Cork Street**, sipping lime cordials in luxury hotel bars, listening for nightingales in Berkeley Square, or just taking a quiet stroll around the Duke of Westminster's several hundred acre estate (he still owns much of the area, including the land beneath the American Embassy): all these cost next to nothing.

Piccadilly and St James's → *Tube: Piccadilly Circus, Green Park, Hyde Park Corner*

Piccadilly Circus and around

Piccadilly Circus, the heart of the West End, is usually so relentlessly busy that it's not a particularly pleasant place to linger, but thousands do, gathering around the endearing little monument representing the Angel of Christian Charity but persistently taken to be the God of Love, **'Eros'**. Erected in 1893 in memory of the stern philanthropist Lord Shaftesbury, who did much to help abolish child labour, the winged boy with his bow was so unpopular that the sculptor Sir Arthur Gilbert went into retirement. Nowadays it is dwarfed by the neon-lit logos of Macdonalds, Nescafé and Coca Cola on the north side. Opposite them is the grand façade of *The Criterion Restaurant*. To its right, there's a strikingly beautiful view down Lower Regent Street past the Duke of York's Column and over the trees of St James's Park towards the Victoria Tower of the Palace of Westminster.

To the left of the *Criterion*, Coventry Street, is a tasteless stretch of tourist-tat retailers and 'have a nice day' diners, epitomised by the **Pepsi Trocadero** ⓘ*T09068-881100, Mon-Thu 1000-2400, Fri-Sat 1000-0100*, six floors of noisy high-tech entertainment and bottom-drawer commercialism.

Along Piccadilly

Progressing westwards for about a mile to Hyde Park Corner, Piccadilly itself is a top-class, frantic and congested strip of extraordinary shops, world-class hotels, green space and fine architecture.

One of the most beautiful church interiors in London is on the left a few hundred yards down from Piccadilly Circus, at 197 Piccadilly. **St James's Piccadilly** ⓘ *T020-7734 4511, daily 0800-1900, café T020-7437 9419, daily 0830-1900, antique market Tue 1000-1730, craft market T020-7437 7688, Wed-Sat 1000-1730*, known as the 'visitors' church', was its architect Christopher Wren's personal favourite. Completed in 1684, the church sustained severe bomb damage in the Second World War and needed extensive restoration. The interior retains its delightful balance and poise, best appreciated in bright daylight, and includes a spectacular limewood altar-screen carved by Grinling Gibbons in the 17th century, who may also have been responsible for the font here in which William Blake was baptized.

Royal Academy of Arts

ⓘ *T020-7300 8000. Mon-Thu, Sun 1000-1800, Fri, Sat 1000-2200. Admission to exhibitions varies.*

Burlington House, on the opposite side of Piccadilly, has been the home since 1869 of the Royal Academy of Arts. Under the directorship of Norman Rosenthal, the Academy has determinedly cast off an increasingly fusty image by mounting popular attention-grabbing exhibitions of contemporary British art, with titles like 'Sensation' and 'Apocalypse'. Guided tours of the permanent collection, which includes works by Reynolds, Turner, Constable and Stanley Spencer, are given Tuesday-Friday at 1300 and are free (be there on time).

Hyde Park Corner

Piccadilly continues downhill to Hyde Park Corner, past the Inigo Jones-designed Devonshire Gates into Green Park. They were removed from Devonshire House, one of the grand houses that once lined the length of Piccadilly's north side. Hyde Park Corner itself terrifies drivers and pedestrians alike.

The main reason to come here and not hurry through is a visit to **Apsley House** ⓘ *T020-7499 5676, www.apsleyhouse.org.uk, Tue-Sun 1100-1700, £4.50, £3 concessions free for under-18s, guided tours on request, £30 for groups of up to 25 people*, the house that Arthur Wellesley, the Duke of Wellington, bought off his brother after Waterloo. It stands on the north side of Hyde Park corner, by the entrance to Park Lane. Known as No 1 London, for being the first house in the West End on the road from Knightsbridge, it's now **The Wellington Museum**, a dignified monument to the man and the post-Napoleonic era in Britain. It was restored in Louis XIV style, and refurbished throughout in its original colour scheme in 1995.

Green Park

ⓘ *T020-7930 1793. Dawn-dusk daily.* Laid out by Henry VIII, the 53-acre park's name is self-explanatory enough, kept free of formal flower beds out of respect for the lepers from the Hospital of St James's buried beneath. More fancifully, Charles II is supposed to have picked a flower here to give to the next beautiful woman he saw. Queen Katharine was so furious that she banned flowers from the park for good. Nowadays the plane trees, crocuses, daffodils and deck chairs make it a charming spot to wile away an afternoon in the spring.

St James's

St James's is the land that time forgot, pretty much stuck in a fantasy of the English past, peddling classy airs and graces as though they had never lost influence, or even political favour. Even so, it's well worth exploring for its peculiar air of self-conscious restraint and an awareness that its prestige lies largely in pandering to the mega rich. The layout of its streets little changed since the 17th century, it has preserved a more intimate scale than Mayfair, although the grandeur of its aspirations are forcefully expressed in **St James's Square** and along **Pall Mall**. Above all, this is the part of London that enshrines the idea of the English gentleman. Parallel to Piccadilly, off St James's Street to the left, **Jermyn Street** sets the tone for the shops that cater for the area's clubbable gents.

At the bottom of St James's Street, where it turns sharp left into Pall Mall, two fully armed redcoats in their bearskin busbies stand or stomp about like clockwork beneath the red-brick Tudor gatehouse of **St James's Palace**. Now used as offices for various Royals including Prince Charles, the palace is closed to visitors, although the **Chapel Royal** inside is open for Sunday services from October until Good Friday.

How to act like a Londoner on the tube

After the incredibly annoying London Underground tannoy warning of 'Mind the Gap', which is repeated ad nauseum by equally annoying tourists, should be added, 'and do not, under any circumstances, talk to, or even look at, the natives'.

Visitors please take note: that broadsheet newspaper is not for reading. It is the London tube traveller's shield against the outside world. London can be a tough place, full of highly undesirable and dangerous people, and those precious few millimetres of newsprint is all that stands between the London commuter and the excrutiating pain and social embarrassment of human interaction with a perfect stranger in a crowded place.

So, please, dear visitor, be sensitive. Do not engage your neighbour in conversation – even if it's to tell them their hair's on fire – and do not attempt to read their newspaper. This can result in a severe bout of tut-tutting or, worse still, a filthy look. Just head straight for the nearest seat, open your copy of the *Financial Times*, and ignore everything and everyone around you – especially if it's someone asking if this tube stops at Buckingham Palace.

The Mall

Here you enter Toytown. This is Royal London, with its processional road, its smart soldiers on parade, and in the distance, safe in her palace, its very own Queen. The Mall is an imposing public space, lined with trees and flagstaffs, its pink tarmac matching the forecourt of Buckingham Palace, that comes into its own for ceremonies like Trooping the Colour. Just beyond, **St James's Park**, work of the indefatigable John Nash and the finest and most carefully laid out of the Royal parks, is the Palace's front garden.

At the bottom of the steps on the left, the **Institute of Contemporary Arts** ⓘ *(ICA), 12 Carlton House Terr, T020-7930 3647, www.ica.org.uk, galleries T020-7930 6844, daily 1200-1930, £1.50, £2.50 Sat-Sun, day membership £1.50 Mon-Fri, £2.50 Sat-Sun*, was founded in 1948 by the anarchist Herbert Read. Nash's stately Georgian terrace seems an incongruous setting for the radical film, theatre, dance and art shown here.

Buckingham Palace

ⓘ *T020-7930 4832; tickets in advance by credit card on T020-7321 2233, 7766 7300, or by post to The Visitor Office, Buckingham Palace, London, SW1A 1AA, www.royal.gov.uk, 0930-1630 Aug and Sep. Ticket Office in Green Park near The Mall, for tickets on the day, 0900-1600. £12.50, concessions £10.50, children £6.50. Changing of the Guard at 1130 daily Apr 1 to the end of Jul; alternate days the rest of the year.*

At the opposite end of The Mall from Admiralty Arch stands the Victoria Memorial, a white marble monument topped with a winged figure of Victory, now best serving as a vantage point from which to view the Changing of the Guard on the forecourt of Buckingham Palace.

In 1993 the Queen opened the doors of the palace for the first time to raise money for the restoration of the fire-damaged Windsor Castle. A maximum of 250 visitors are admitted every 15 minutes, in a fairly successful attempt to avoid overcrowding (or perhaps for fear of a rebellion) on a one-way route around 14 state rooms, with the recent addition of the Ballroom, shepherded by 200 extra staff in navy blue and red uniforms who are generally friendly and well informed.

Entering via the Ambassador's entrance on the south side of the Palace, first impressions are of a place not much more opulent than many West End theatres. Emerging into Nash's central quadrangle of beautifully warm sandstone does create an impression though. 'It ain't much but it's home' was one American woman's wry comment, but then it ain't really 'home' at all. The glossy official brochure (the only floorplan available) emphasizes that this is a working palace, although even if the Royal Standard happens to be flying, indicating that Her Majesty is in residence, there's little chance of bumping into her. The Ballroom supper room contains an exhibition on the coronation itself and the gardens are also open.

The **Queen's Gallery** ⓘ *Mon-Sat 1000-1630, £6.50, £5 concessions, £3 under-16s*, houses the Queen's collection of Old Masters and portraiture, an extraordinary hoard founded by Charles II, whichhas recently been re-hung in purpose-built new galleries.

If you've still got a stomach for all things Royal, next door to the Palace are the **Royal Mews** ⓘ *T020-7930 4832, Feb-Oct daily 1100-1515, Aug-Sep Mon-Thu 1000-1515, last admission 30 mins before closing, £5, £4 concessions, children £2.50*, where all the Queen's stately transport is kept, including her gilded State coach and her Windsor grey horses. If anything the array of splendid carriages gives a better value and more atmospheric insight into the pageant of British sovereignty than the Palace itself.

Oxford Street and Marble Arch

→ *Tube: Tottenham Court Rd, Oxford Circus, Bond St, Marble Arch*

'Don't stop, shop!' could be Oxford Street's strapline, but then there's not much worth seeing here anyway. Emerging from Tottenham Court Road tube station at the east end of the street brings you out beneath the unmistakable honeycomb of the Centrepoint tower. Walking west you have to squeeze along the street's busiest, scruffiest and most second-rate stretch. **Hanway Street**, just up on the right, a curious little alley of private drinking clubs, secondhand record shops and Spanish bars and restaurants, doubles back to Tottenham Court Road as if it lacked the courage of its northward convictions. Apart from a few good shops there's nothing remarkable until the horrendously busy crossroad of **Oxford Circus**. Any of the roads off left lead into Soho; those to the right into Fitzrovia. Beyond Oxford Circus, Oxford Street begins to acquire the dignity the capital's High Street deserves.

Further on to the left, **Dering Street** has become an exciting enclave for some of the city's leading dealers in contemporary art. The presence of these artworld impresarios is perhaps explained by their proximity to the silly money of **New Bond Street**, the next street off to the left.

Apart from the great early 20th-century Ionic block of **Selfridges**, a sight in itself, the last sight Oxford Street has to offer is **Marble Arch**. Designed by John Nash in 1827 to stand in front of Buckingham Palace, it wasn't quite grand enough and was moved to this site 25 years later and eventually stranded in the middle of a hectic roundabout. Nearby, on Sundays, **Speaker's Corner** has been providing a spot for any budding orator to let off steam since the middle of the 19th century. Nowadays the soap boxes are dominated by religious extremists and speakers with more passion than eloquence, but some draw surprisingly large and attentive crowds.

Westminster and Whitehall

→ *Tube: Charing Cross or Embankment for the top of Whitehall nearest Trafalgar Sq. Westminster for Big Ben and Parliament Sq, and St James's for Victoria St, the Abbey and the streets beyond*

The seat of central government power in the Kingdom is an administrative beehive and one of the few parts of London that achieves any architectural cohesion.

Parliament Square, especially viewed from the Broad Sanctuary by Westminster Abbey, manages to present a stirring picture of common purpose with its array of skybound Gothic towers. And Whitehall too makes a decent stab at Venetian grandeur as it connects Parliament with Trafalgar Square. And even though there are easily enough places to see and things to do around here to occupy at least a whole day, the impression is very much one of being kept at arm's length. Even the river hardly gets a look in. Surprisingly though, plenty of people do live here, especially in the streets beyond Westminster Abbey between Millbank and Victoria Street, which are really the only place for a drink in an interesting pub or decent meal day or night.

Westminster Abbey

ⓘ Information and tours T020-7654 4834. Mon-Fri 0930-1645 (last admission 1545), Sat 0930-1445 (last admission 1345). £6; £4 concessions; £4 under-16s; under-11's free with adult. Sun services 0800 (Holy Communion) 1000 (Matins), 1115 (Sung Eucharist), 1500 (Evensong), 1745 (Organ recital), 1830 (Evening service). Weekday services 0730 (Matins, 0900 Sat and bank holidays), 0800 (Holy Communion), 1230 (Holy Communion, except Sat), 1700 (Evensong, 1500 Sat). Chapter House, Pyx Chamber and Museum: summer 1000-1700 daily. Main Cloister open same hours as Abbey. Free (from Dean's Yard). Little Cloister and College Garden: Tue-Thu summer 1030-1800, winter 1030-1600. Free. Buses 3, 11, 12, 24, 53, 77a, 88, 159 and 211 all pass Westminster Abbey.

A surprisingly small church for one of such enormous significance in the Anglican faith and British state (especially for its monarchy), Westminster Abbey's charm lies in its age. Sadly it has inevitably become a well-managed tourist trap. That said, despite the milling crowds clutching the fairly patronizing audio guide and bossy 'free' floorplans, it remains a sacred building and anyone wishing to pray here (or join in a service on Sunday when the Abbey is closed to tourists) is allowed to do so free of charge. And there's also plenty worth seeing for the money.

One of the better approaches to the exterior is from St James's Park tube, a short walk down Broadway and Tothill, to the west front with its twin Hawksmoor towers of 1745, the most recent additions to what from here is clearly a very tall and thin old building. Walking clockwise round to the visitors' entrance, it's easy to understand how the Abbey's architecture could be described as 'the perfect governmental report on French Gothic': it does look like a tight and proper place, lacking the majesty of some other cathedrals in England or France and all the more appropriate for that, especially in comparison to the flamboyant neo-Gothic of the Houses of Parliament across the way.

Once inside it's another story: the length and especially the height (over 100 ft) of the Nave are awe-inspiring. On the tourist route round from the north entrance, this impressive view is left until the end, the tour beginning in the oldest part of the main building, the central Crossing built in the 13th century. Visitors then turn sharp right to skirt the Sanctuary of the High Altar (where sovereigns are crowned) and the founder St Edward the Confessor's Chapel, past the tombs of Edward I and Henry III, to look at the **Coronation Chair**. Made to order for the 'Hammer of the Scots', Edward I, and used to crown every English monarch except three since 1308, the old wooden chair's most obvious feature now is the empty space below the seat purpose-built for the Stone of Destiny. (The sandstone coronation block of Scottish monarchs since the ninth century is now back home in its native land and on display in Edinburgh Castle.) Beyond is **Henry VII's Chapel** (or Lady Chapel), dating from the early 16th century, an extraordinary medieval pageant of flags, stalls, and tombs below a wonderful vaulted stone roof of cobweb intricacy. On either side of this chapel are the hushed tombs of Elizabeth I and Mary Queen of Scots.

Heading back towards the Crossing, the tour passes **Poet's Corner**, decorated with sculptures and monuments to Shakespeare, Chaucer and other poets and actors, as well as scientists, architects, historians and other worthies.

Then it's out into the fresh air of the Cloisters of the 11th-century monastery, past the Chapter House, Pyx Chamber and Museum. In the octagonal **Chapter House**, where the House of Commons sat from the mid-14th-16th centuries, the medieval wall paintings of the Last Judgement and the Apocalypse, and remarkable tiled floor, decorated with griffins, lions, and mythical beasts, have a faded splendour. The dark little **Pyx Chamber** was the monastery's strong room and is the oldest building on site. And the **museum** in the monks' Common Room contains some weird Royal funeral effigies from the Middle Ages as well as a more recent and peculiar one of the Duke of Buckingham.

These three less busy rooms are well worth the small extra charge.

The **Little Cloisters** are reached through an old whitewashed stone tunnel off the main Cloisters, giving a striking view of the Victoria Tower of the Houses of Parliament. After time spent in the peace of the **College Garden** beyond (where concerts are sometimes given at lunchtimes on Thursdays in July and August), the busy tour route back in the main cloisters may seem like a distant memory. It returns though into the Abbey at the 14th-century part of that great Nave near the tombs of the Unknown Soldier and Sir Winston Churchill and ends outside the west front by the Abbey Bookshop.

Jewel Tower

T020-7222 2219. Summer 1000-1800; Oct 1000-1800 (last admission 1730) or dusk if earlier; winter 1000-1600 (last admission 1530). £2, concessions £1.50, £1 under-16s.

Opposite the gardens, on Abingdon Street over the road from the Houses of Parliament and often overlooked, stands the little Jewel Tower, one of the last vestiges of the medieval Palace of Westminster. Surrounded by a dry moat, and emphatically not where the crown jewels are kept, this was a fortified wardrobe for Edward III built in 1365 and now contains a small exhibition on Parliament Past and Present along with a few other interesting things, including, in the ground floor shop, a rusted Rhineland sword of about AD 800 dug up in Victoria Tower Gardens.

Houses of Parliament

Commons Information Line T020-7219 4272; Lords Information Line T020-7219 3107; www.parliament.uk. Parliament usually in session mid-Oct to Christmas, Jan to Easter, Jun and Jul: Mon 1430-2200, Tue-Thu 1130-1900, Thu until 1800 approximately. Guided historical tours (0870-9063773 roughly every 15 mins from 0915-1630 £7, £5 concessions) of both houses are available (either book in advance or queue up outside).

The exhibition in the Jewel Tower just might stoke up an appetite to see Parliament doing its thing over the road in the **Palace of Westminster**, better known as the Houses of Parliament. The government of England has met on this spot since the reign of Edward III, when the King and his court of barons and bishops would meet in St Stephen's Chapel. The chapel and surrounding palace were almost completely razed to the ground by fire in 1834, resulting in the building of the golden Gothic glory in use today.

Its most famous feature is **Big Ben**, the clock tower overlooking Westminster Bridge. The clock strikes the hour on the 13-ton bell that gives the tower its name, and which can be heard up to 4½ miles away.

The oldest part of the building though is **Westminster Hall**, which survived the fire, behind the statue of the victor in the Civil War, Lord Protector Oliver Cromwell. The interior of the Hall with its great hammer-beam roof and the beautifully decorated **St Stephen's Crypt** can only be seen on a guided tour.

A recently retired guide at the Houses of Parliament, who took visitors to the top and back, is reckoned to have climbed the equivalent of 76 Mount Everests.

When Parliament is in session the public are admitted (after a thorough security check) to the 'Strangers' Galleries' of either House through St Stephen's Gate, just beyond Cromwell's statue. Generally it's easier and quicker gaining access to the **House of Lords**, a very grand and gilded debating chamber with its benches of red morocco. In front of the thrones is the woolsack, a cushioned ottoman for the land's senior judge the Lord Chancellor. By contrast, the **House of Commons** seems very small and businesslike, its green leather benches looking quite tatty. The Government sit to the Speaker's right and the Opposition to his left with the front benches reserved for Cabinet Ministers and shadow-Ministers.

Parliament in session is indicated by a light on Big Ben and a Union Jack flying from the Victoria Tower.

Apart from during Prime Minister's Question Time on Wednesdays at 1500, which can only be seen on application to your MP or embassy, both houses are often half-empty or half-asleep.

Whitehall

ⓘ *Details of Foreign Office visits on www.fco.gov.uk.*

Back by Westminster tube, on the left **Portcullis House** contains brand new and very expensive offices for MPs opposite the Houses of Parliament, the latest in the series of palatial government buildings that make up Whitehall. In the middle of the road, where Parliament Street becomes Whitehall, stands the **Cenotaph**, a simple block of Portland Stone designed rapidly by Lutyens for the peace celebrations in July 1919; it has become the focus for national remembrance of the dead of the two World Wars. A service is held annually on the Sunday nearest November 11, the date of the Armistice in 1918.

Just further down on the left, in **Downing Street**, beyond the notorious gates installed by Margaret Thatcher in the 80s, number 10 is the deceptively small-looking home and offices of the Prime Minister.

Whitehall then continues its wide progress up to Trafalgar Square, lined with the offices of the Cabinet and the Treasury, and the Scottish Office. Opposite stands the massive **Ministry of Defence** (MOD), towering over a little statue of Sir Water Raleigh and big statues of Field Marshalls Montgomery (of Alamein) and Slim.

On the corner of Horse Guards Avenue and Whitehall stands the last survivor from the original Whitehall Palace, Inigo Jones's **Banqueting House** ⓘ *T020-7930 4179, www.hrp.org.uk, 1000-1700 (last entry 1630) Mon-Sat, £4, concessions £3.* Completed in 1622, the building is the only Government property on Whitehall that welcomes uninvited visitors (although it, too, occasionally closes for private receptions). A visit includes an introductory 15-minute historical video in the cellars where James I used to drown his sorrows, followed by a 20-minute audio guide to the splendidly proportioned Banqueting Hall itself. Apart from its historical associations, the main attraction is the ceiling, decorated with nine canvasses by Rubens.

Across the road another Palladian edifice built a century later, **Horse Guards**, is the HQ of the Household Division. The **Changing of the Queen's Life Guard** takes place here Monday-Saturday 1100, Sunday 1000, with the guard parading dismounted at 1600 daily, amid a strong smell of horse dung.

Victoria, Belgravia and Pimlico → *Tube: Victoria, Pimlico, Vauxhall*

The grandeur of Belgravia's Eaton Square continues the line of Chelsea's King's Road up to the back door of Buckingham Palace, crossed before it gets there by the Belgrave Road striding up through Pimlico from the river to end in some style at Belgrave Square. Both seem to be doing their best to bypass and ignore the chaotic junction of Victoria and Grosvenor Gardens. Instead, one of central London's most bustling travel hubs has to make do with the lacklustre Vauxhall Bridge Road for company and is left to find its own short and unassuming way to Westminster down Victoria Street.

Pimlico to Kensington

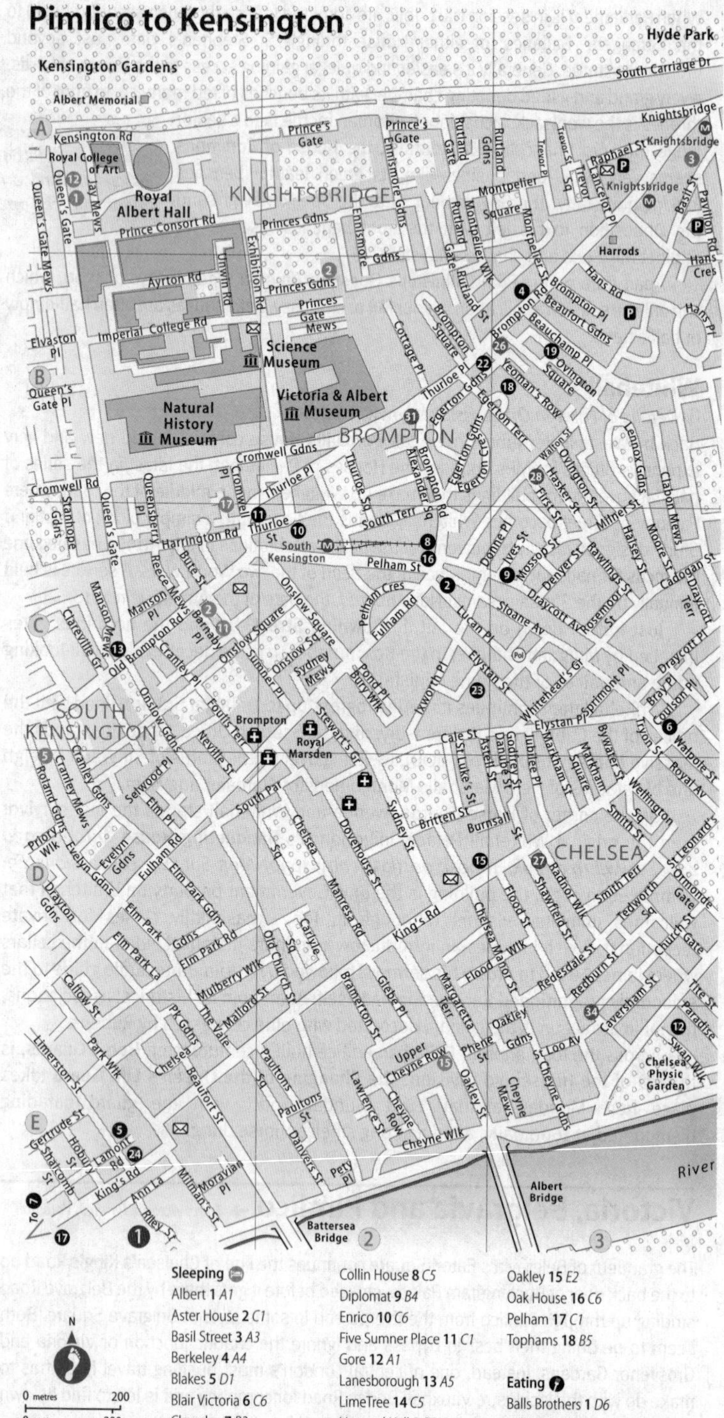

Sleeping

Albert 1 *A1*
Aster House 2 *C1*
Basil Street 3 *A3*
Berkeley 4 *A4*
Blakes 5 *D1*
Blair Victoria 6 *C6*
Claverley 7 *B3*
Collin House 8 *C5*
Diplomat 9 *B4*
Enrico 10 *C6*
Five Sumner Place 11 *C1*
Gore 12 *A1*
Lanesborough 13 *A5*
LimeTree 14 *C5*
Linstead Hall 2 *B2*
Oakley 15 *E2*
Oak House 16 *C6*
Pelham 17 *C1*
Tophams 18 *B5*

Eating

Balls Brothers 1 *D6*
Bibendum 2 *C2*

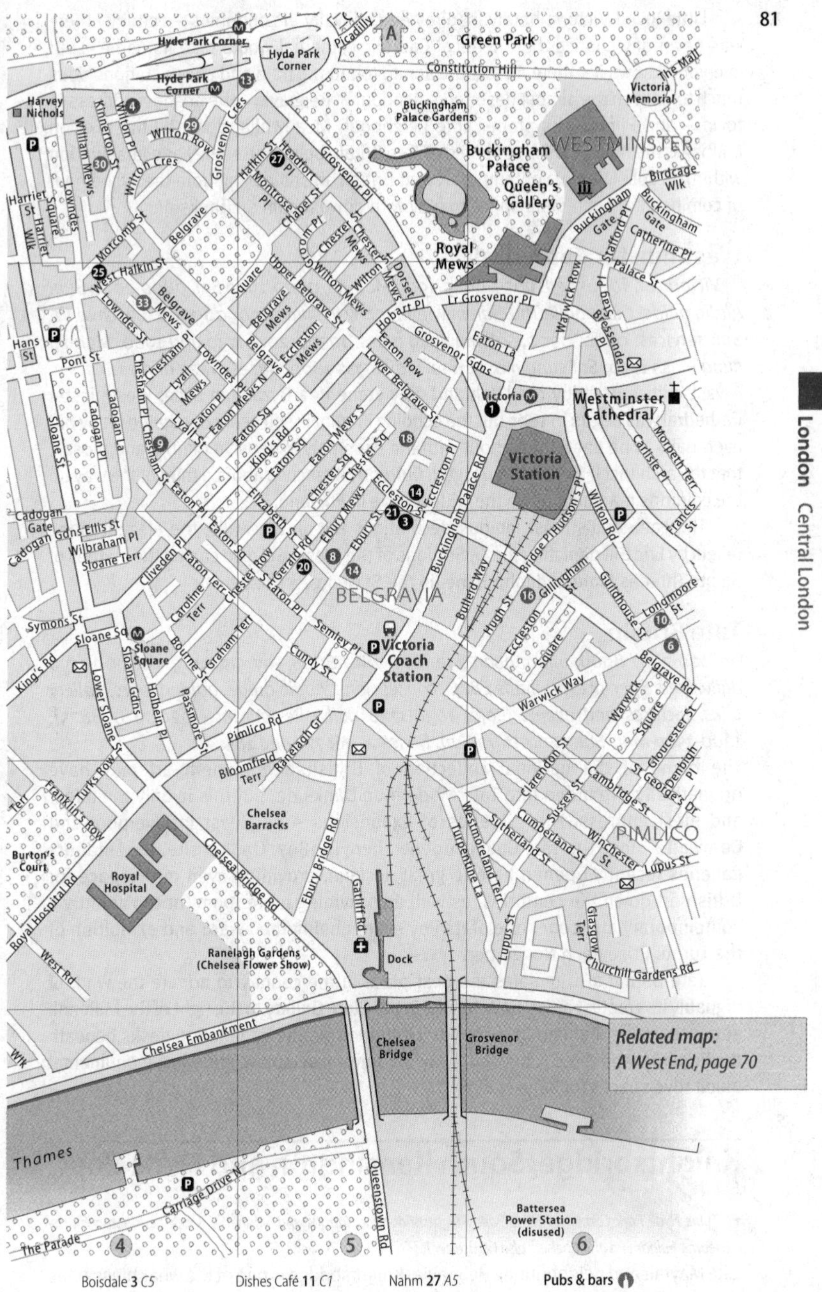

Boisdale **3** *C5*
Café Monpelliano **4** *B3*
Chelsea Bun **5** *E1*
Chelsea Kitchen **6** *C3*
Chutney Mary **7** *E1*
Collection **8** *C2*
Daphne's **9** *C3*
Daquise **10** *C2*
Dishes Café **11** *C1*
Gordon Ramsay **12** *E3*
Il Falconiere **13** *C1*
Jenny Lo's Teahouse **14** *B5*
King's Road Café **15** *D2*
La Brasserie **16** *C2*
Mona Lisa **17** *E1*
Monza **18** *B3*
Nahm **27** *A5*
O Fado **19** *B3*
Oliveto **20** *C5*
Olivo **21** *C5*
Patisserie Valerie **22** *B2*
Pellicano **23** *C2*
Yama **24** *E1*
Zafferano **25** *B4*

Pubs & bars

Bunch of Grapes **26** *B3*
Enterprise **28** *B3*
Grenadier **29** *A4*
Nag's Head **30** *A4*
Oratory **31** *B2*
Star Tavern **33** *B4*
Surprise **34** *E3*

Little-loved Victoria hardly inspires much loyalty in Londoners – certainly there was never any chance that the local Catholic cathedral would take its name – but everyone knows it's there. In fact the scrum round the train and coach stations does much to enliven the almost deserted splendour of Belgravia – the poshest address in town – and Pimlico, its proper little neighbour. Meanwhile, down by the river on Millbank, the heavy classical portico of Tate Britain belies the energy and imagination within, its collection of contemporary and British art still reeling from the excitement of coming into much more space to play with downstream on Bankside.

Westminster Cathedral

ⓘ *Victoria St, T020-7798 9055. 0645-1900 Mon-Fri, 0800-1900 Sat, 0800-2000 Sun. Audio guide. Campanile Thu-Sun in winter, daily in summer 0900-1700. £2, child £1. Sun services: 0800, 0900, solemn sung mass, 1030, 1200, 1730 and 1900. Mon-Fri sung mass 1730, Sat sung mass 1030, vigil mass 1800. Buses 11, 24 and 211.*

A vast edifice of stripy red brick and grey stone in a Byzantine style, Westminster Cathedral was begun in 1895 but the echoing interior is still being decorated bit by bit, eventually to be lined throughout with the extremely expensive marble and mosaic that the architect JF Bentley envisaged. Currently it reaches about a third of the way up the columns marching down the widest nave in England.

The cathedral's most famous decorations are on the walls, the elegant stone reliefs by Eric Gill depicting the 14 Stations of the Cross. Gill also carved the statues of Saints Thomas More and John Fisher in the St George's Chapel.

Tate Britain

ⓘ *T020-7887 8000, information line T020-7887 8008, www.tate.org.uk. 1000-1750 daily. Free. Special exhibitions £8, £5 concessions. Audio guide, guided tours, gallery talks, lectures and events. Café: 1030-1730 daily. Restaurant (T020-7887 8825): 1200-1500 Mon-Sat, 1200-1600 Sun. Buses 2, 36, 77a and 185.*

The home of the national collection of British and modern art may have dramatically expanded into Tate Modern on Bankside, but this is only the latest and most impressive of a series of expansions – not least in Liverpool and Cornwall – since the Tate Gallery opened here in 1897. On this site, the Lindbury galleries recently opened here to great acclaim, providing even more space for British art down the centuries, as well as providing more room for the country's contemporary art scene, one of its key events being the award and exhibition of the Turner Prize each November.

Tate Britain also remains the best place in the country to admire the work of arguably its greatest artist, JMW Turner, in the **Clore Gallery** to the right of the Millbank entrance. Straight ahead from the front entrance are the information desks beneath the Rotunda, and directly beyond these the **Duveen sculpture galleries**, monumental meditative spaces for large works.

Knightsbridge, South Kensington and Hyde Park

➔ *Tube: Hyde Park Corner for Hyde Park; Knightsbridge for Harrods and Sloane St; South Kensington for the museums, Fulham Rd and Chelsea; also Gloucester Rd*

Like Mayfair and neighbouring Belgravia, Knightsbridge is one of the wealthiest areas in central London. South Kensington next door, favoured by cosmopolitan jet-setters, wayward little rich girls and anyone dressed up and on the pull, has a noticeable Middle Eastern, Far Eastern and American flavour with some distinct French, Italian and Polish ingredients.

Harrods' Hall of Fame

Harrods is hard to miss: well signposted at Knightsbridge tube, its famous terracotta building, picked out like a fairground at night, has dominated the Brompton Road for almost a hundred years. Founded half a century earlier by Charles Harrod, his small perfume and cosmetics store became the largest general shop in the world, boasting the first escalator in London and employing thousands of staff. Its seven floors remain a sumptuous five-star shopping experience, featuring the marble chiller cabinets of the legendary Food Halls, acres of designerwear and an alarmingly tidy toy shop.

Since the 1980s though it has become almost as famous for the notoriety of its current owner, Mohammed Al Fayed. A controversial character who loves the limelight, he has stamped his personality all over the store, sadly all the more so since the death of his son Dodi with Princess Diana. Whatever they may be looking to purchase upstairs, most visitors don't want to miss the Diana and Dodi Memorial in the basement at the foot of one of the Egyptian escalators. Portrait photos of the tragic pair are sentimentally enshrined on a sort of funereal ivy-bedecked wishing-well, a fairly second-rate exhibition of the window dresser's art sandwiched between the Harrods marketing shop and the lost property department. Its most macabre feature is an actual wine glass supposedly in use on that fateful night at the Paris Ritz. As everybody knows, the couple were killed in a car accident pursued by paparazzi, making it all the more ironic that this is the only part of the whole store where photography is permitted.

Amid the fashion labels, deluxe hotels, expensive restaurants and private clubs of Knightsbridge stand three tremendous exceptions: the Victoria and Albert (V&A), Natural History, and Science museums each deserve at least a day of anyone and everyone's time. To the south, Chelsea merges seamlessly with South Ken via Brompton and the Fulham Road. At the top of Exhibition Road, the delightful green acres of **Kensington Gardens** and **Hyde Park** harbour grand or whimsical memorials and the world-famous little **Serpentine Gallery**.

Hyde Park and Kensington Gardens

The wide open stretch of grass between **Park Lane** and the Serpentine often seems deserted, even in summer, except during the regular open-air concerts, demonstrations and Royal occasions. The *Lido* (T020-7298 2100), the more attractive of the two café-restaurants in the park, is a good place to hire a boat on the **Serpentine Lake**. The *Lido* can be reached across the bridge that divides the Serpentine from the Long Water and hence Hyde Park from Kensington Gardens. The path in Hyde Park along the north side of the Long Water, past the **Henry Moore Arch**, ends up among the fish ponds and fountains of the Italian Gardens at Lancaster Gate. Look out here for the classical arch known as **Queen Anne's Alcove**, designed by Wren.

Over the Long Bridge though, towards the *Lido*, is Kensington Gardens' prize asset, the **Serpentine Gallery** ⓘ *T020-7402 6075, www.serpentinegallery.org.uk, daily 1000-1800, free*. The quiet gallery was completely refurbished in 1998, confirming a reputation steadily acquired since its opening in 1970 for being one of London's most exciting small spaces for international contemporary art, charmingly at odds with its dinky situation.

Tree-filled Kensington Gardens spread out behind the gallery, criss-crossed with signposted paths leading to the Round Pond, the Peter Pan statue beside Long Water, and the Broad Walk in front of Kensington Palace. The latest suggested route is the seven-mile **Diana Princess of Wales Memorial Walk** ⓘ *To20-7298 2000, or call into the Old Police House information centre*, through four of central London's Royal parks.

Albert Hall

Beyond the gallery on the right looms the Gothic spire and canopy of the **Albert Memorial**, designed by Sir George Gilbert Scott and finished in 1872. Much against his own wishes, Victoria's far-from-pompous consort is surrounded by an excess of ardently imperialist statuary and fancy stonework recently renovated at huge expense. Across the road is his much more fitting memorial, the great domed oval of the Royal Albert Hall. Next up on Exhibition Road, however, is the first of the area's main events in the form of the Science Museum and on the Cromwell Road next door to it the Natural History Museum.

Science Museum

ⓘ *Exhibition Rd, To20-7942 4455; booking and information To870-8704868; www.sciencemuseum.org.uk, 1000-1800 daily. Free, charges for combinations of IMAX and Virtual Voyage (£2.50 extra) or all the South Ken museums. Screenings in IMAX Cinema (£6.95 including museum): at 1045 (Sat, Sun only), 1145, 1245, 1345, 1445, 1545, 1645 daily. Free 20-min guided tours on the hr every hr, as well as one 50-min tour of the whole museum usually at 1400. Buses 14, 70 and 74.*

The Science Museum prides itself on being one of the most forward-thinking, interactive and accessible museums in the country, a claim that has recently been enhanced with the opening of the new Wellcome Wing: four floors dedicated to displaying cutting-edge science and technology incorporating an IMAX cinema and the first Virtual Voyage simulator in Europe. With origins similar to the V&A's (see below), the emphasis here has always been on education. One of the best things about the Science Museum is that guidebooks or guided tours are hardly necessary: most of the exhibits either speak for themselves or are thoroughly labelled. In the basement is Launch Pad, a very popular hands-on gallery of educational scientific games.

Natural History Museum

ⓘ *To20-7942 5000, www.nhm.ac.uk. Mon-Sat 1000-1750, Sun 1100-1750. Free. Buses 14, 70 and 74.*

Behind the Science Museum, on Cromwell Road, stands the extraordinary old orange and blue terracotta building of the Natural History Museum. Until 1963 part of the British Museum, and since then also gobbling up the Geological Museum, this is a serious academic research institution that has become seriously fun-packed. Divided into Life Galleries and Earth Galleries, it tells the history of our animated planet with a not entirely successful combination of venerable artefacts and playschool attractions. Occasionally it feels as if the museum had been entrusted to an over-excited and over-budget biology teacher. Even so, it never disappoints children, and adults are sure to learn something about the natural world whether they want to or not.

Victoria and Albert Museum

ⓘ *To20-7942 2000, information To20-7942 8090, www.vam.ac.uk. Daily 1000-1745, last Wed and Fri of each month 1000-2200. Free. Buses 14, 70 and 74.*

The Victoria and Albert Museum, or the V&A, is one of the world's greatest museums. Surprisingly, considering its grand façade on Cromwell Road, it wears that greatness lightly. Originally founded in 1857 with the intention of educating the populace in the appreciation of decorative art and design it exhibited superb examples of what could be achieved in that field: the object lesson equivalent to the exemplary lives held up for emulation at the National Portrait Gallery (see page 63).

Never a narrowly nationalistic enterprise, its remarkable collection was gathered like the British Museum's from all corners of the globe. The overall impression it makes though is much more human and domestic. Many of the objects on display around its seven-miles-worth of galleries would once have decorated or been in everyday use in people's homes – very wealthy and powerful people's homes for the most part – as well as in magnificent places of worship. And most are nothing like as ancient and remote as the antiquities in the BM. On making first acquaintance with the V&A, instead of trying to see as much as possible with a limited amount of time, wander slowly around it in the certain knowledge that you'll find a rewarding number of amazing things.

Chelsea

It's easy to see why Hillary and Bill Clinton named their daughter Chelsea: the name has a pleasant sound and a familiar ring in certain social circles. As far as London is concerned, it means a very comfortable part of town with an impeccable bohemian pedigree, occasionally displaying bursts of street cred. Its High Street, the **King's Road**, became one of the pivots of 'swinging London' in the 1960s and outraged middle England again a decade later by spawning the Sex Pistols, the shock troops of punk rock.

Nowadays much quieter and more expensive, freighted with designer boutiques and the sleek Chelsea boys and babes they attract, the well-heeled King's Road treads its well-worn path between the Fulham Road and the river, threading its way through a district characterized by smart residential squares and quaint cobbled mews. The most interesting streets to explore lie on its south side, towards the river, along Royal Hospital Road and the Chelsea Embankment up to the Albert Bridge. Apart from the Royal Hospital itself, very grand almshouses from another era for retired soldiers, this pretty area conceals the peaceful delights of the **Chelsea Physic Garden** ⓘ *T020-7352 5646, www.chelseaphysicgarden.co.uk, Apr-Oct, 1200-1700 Wed, 1400-1800 Sun (as well as daily throughout the Chelsea Flower Show and Chelsea Festival), admission £5, £3 under-16s.* Further down the King's Road, around the World's End, Chelsea loosens up a little to become fertile browsing ground for offbeat fashions and better-value restaurants.

Marylebone and Regent's Park

➔ *Tube: Bond St for Marylebone La and the Wallace Collection. Baker St for Madame Tussaud's. Oxford Circus for Portland Pl and Regent's Park or Great Portland St for the Park. Camden Town for the Zoo and Regent's Park*

A discreet Georgian and Victorian backwater just to the north of the busiest street in the West End, much to its own surprise Marylebone has recently become almost fashionable. Marylebone Lane twists up from Oxford Street, and broadens out to become Marylebone High Street, still refusing to follow a straight path up to the traffic jam on the massive Marylebone Road.

Marylebone's hidden treasure, the **Wallace Collection** ⓘ *T020-7935 0687, www.the-wallace-collection.org.uk, 1000-1700 Mon-Sat, 1200-1700 Sun, free (£3 donation requested), restaurant and bookshop, buses 2, 13, 30, 74, 82, 113, 139, 189, 274,* containing 18th-century French paintings in Hertford House, has had a centennial overhaul courtesy of the National Lottery Heritage Fund. Along with the Wigmore Hall, one of London's most endearing venues for chamber music and

Flower power

Organized by the Royal Horticultural Society, the Chelsea Flower Show is the country's most prestigious celebration of the art of gardening, taking place in the grounds of the Royal Hospital every year in the last week of May. The public are normally only admitted to the spectacular displays of model gardens, flower arrangements and trade stands on the last Thursday and Friday of the week. Open 0800-2000, T0870-9063781 or First Call T01293-433956. Admission £10-£27 depending on the time of day.

song, the Wallace Collection continues to conjure the ghost of 19th-century and Edwardian London. In many of the streets and mews around, it doesn't take much imagination to hear the clatter of carriage wheels carrying Sherlock Holmes back to his Baker Street home after his latest adventure.

The crowds imitating the traffic as they queue outside **Madame Tussaud's** ⓘ *T0870-400 3000, www.madame-tussauds.com, Mon-Fri 0930-1730, Sat and Sun 0930-1800, 1000-1730 bookable in 30 min timeslots, admission to Tussaud's and Planetarium, £21.99 before 1400, £20.99 after 1400, £14 after 1700, children £16 before 1400, under-5s free*, might have been a familiar sight to him, and popularity of Madame Tussaud's continues unabated. It's been a surefire hit with tourists since shortly after the French Revolution when the aristocratic French woman exhibited the waxwork portraits of some of her friends who had lost their heads. In those days it may have been understandable, when people had little chance to see what the rich and famous looked like. Nowadays it's more baffling.

It's difficult to say what Mr Holmes would have made of the story of space exploration at the revamped **Planetarium** ⓘ *T0870-400 3000, see above for combined entry tickets with Madame Tussaud's, 1030-1700 first show summer 1030 daily, winter weekends 1030, weekdays 1230, not bookable in advance, £3, concessions and under 16s £2, not recommended for under-5s*. Movie music and projections onto the darkened roof of the dome whizz through the history of the cosmos in an attempt to explain astronomy. The refurbished exhibition has been made more interactive but even so, it's probably still only worth seeing if visiting the much more famous Madame Tussaud's next door.

Regent's Park, just to the north, is still the most delightful place in central London to escape the crush of the West End. And if hell has become other people, here's the chance to get close to some of the protected wildlife in **London Zoo** ⓘ *T020-7722 3333, www.londonzoo.co.uk, daily 1000-1730 summer, 1000-1630 winter (last admission 1hr before closing), £12, £9 under-16s, £10.20 concession, buses 274 from Camden Town or Baker St.*

Euston, St Pancras and King's Cross

→ *Tube: King's Cross, St Pancras, Euston Sq, Warren St*

Most people hurry through King's Cross on the Underground without even surfacing – the area has a reputation for prostitution, drugs and street crime. That said, with the arrival of the Eurostar terminal at St Pancras, this long-neglected and rundown district may get the transformation it deserves. Even the unlovely Euston Road has cleaned up its act in recent years. The opening of the state-of-the-art **British Library** here represented the first bold public statement of government confidence in an area that now looks set to boom. Meanwhile on Friday and Saturday nights the

Scala and the marshalling yards north of the stations are still a Mecca for clubbers, injecting a welcome dose of wide-eyed and healthy nightlife into one of the city's most desolate backyards.

British Library

ⓘ *96 Euston Rd, NW1,T020-7412 7332, www.bl.uk, 0900-1800 Mon, Wed, Thu, Fri, 0930-2000 Tue; 0930-1700 Sat; 1100-1700 Sun. Free.*

Back by the neo-Gothic palace of **St Pancras Station** over Midland Road, stands the British Library. Whatever people have made of the exterior, with its straight lines of plain red brick and dark green trim offset by its Victorian neighbour, the interior has provoked few complaints. Acres of white stone and careful attention to details, such as the handrails, the spacing of the steps and the diffusion of light, all combine to make the building a joy to use. Anyone engaged in research can apply for free membership to gain access to the reading rooms and some 18 million volumes, while the two permanent exhibitions (that can be seen without a pass) are worth a visit.

The **Treasures Gallery** is a beautiful and carefully explained display of precious books and manuscripts: the illuminated Lindisfarne Gospel from around 700AD; a copy of the Magna Carta of 1215; the Sherborne Missal – the only painted book in England to have survived the Reformation; Shakespeare's First Folio from 1623; and many other manuscripts of great authors.

Bloomsbury and Fitzrovia

➔ *Tube: Tottenham Court Rd for southwest Bloomsbury, including the British Museum. Russell Sq for eastern Bloomsbury. Goodge St for Fitzrovia and Warren St for northern Fitzrovia*

Bloomsbury is the academic heart of London, the home of the acronym, full of august institutions better known as SOAS, UCL, RADA and ULU than by their full names, most of them part of the sprawling University of London. North of High Holborn, south of the Euston Road and west of Judd Street, its long straight streets of Georgian and Victorian brick can be gloomy in winter, but in bright sunshine the area's severe little squares with their flower-and tree-filled gardens are a delight. Then again it's no coincidence that this is also the place to find three of the city's most rewarding museums. The revitalized and monumental **British Museum** obviously, but also the serene beauty of the Chinese ceramics in the **Percival David Foundation** and the intriguing collection of ancient Egyptian artefacts in the **Petrie Museum**.

The student population ensures that the area is packed with reasonable places to eat and sleep, surrounded by lively pubs and excellent bookshops. To the west, over Tottenham Court Road, that ugly northbound arm of Oxford Street, Fitzrovia is the name that has been given to the blocks south of Fitzroy Square from here to Portland Place. Something like an upmarket version of Soho, on Charlotte Street and Goodge Street, it even achieves some of its southern neighbour's media buzz.

British Museum

ⓘ *T020-7323 8000; information T020-7323 8299; disabled information T020-7636 7384; minicom T020-7323 8920. Museum 1000-1730 Sat-Wed, 1000-2030 Thu, Fri (late view of main floor galleries, Egypt and Ancient Near East galleries and special exhibitions only). Free (donations appreciated); prices of temporary exhibitions vary. Great Court 0900-2300 Thu-Sat, 0900-1800 Sun-Wed (Also the Reading Room, T020-7323 8162, www.thebritishmuseum.ac.uk. Guided tours: Highlights tour (90 mins) £8, £5 concessions 1030, 1300, 1500 daily; Free tours: Spotlight (1315, 20 mins) and EyeOpener Gallery tours daily (1100-1530 on the hr and ½ hr). Buses 1, 8, 10, 19, 24, 25, 29, 38, 55, 59, 68, 73, 91, 98, 134, 168, 188 and 242.*

Most people visit Bloomsbury for the British Museum. With its new slogan 'illuminating world cultures', it now comes closer to that ideal in spectacular style. Architect Norman Foster's redevelopment of the central Great Court replaced the roof with a latticework glass canopy, turning the museum's long-hidden central quadrangle into the largest covered square in Europe.

From beneath the front portico on Great Russell Street little seems different. Through the tall front doors though, visitors pass straight into a vast creamy space to be confronted by the Reading Room, freshly clad in white stone like a huge post box in the middle of the indoor square. The overall impression of light and space the new design creates is generous and magnificent.

The Great Court On entering the Great Court from the south, the information desk is on the left and the box office for special exhibitions and audio guides on the right, the places to pick up floorplans and get your bearings. Within the square itself there are two cafés, two shops and, up the wide staircases round the outside of the reading room, a temporary exhibition area and a restaurant. 12 sculptures are set around the place at ground level making up the Great Court Concourse Gallery, introducing the museum's collections.

Reading Room Straight ahead as you enter is the little door into the Reading Room. Designed by Robert Smirke in 1823, the Round Reading Room was first opened in 1857 and its original colour scheme of light blue, cream and gold leaf has now been restored. A host of famous thinkers, writers, politicians and idlers have studied, mused or snoozed beneath the lofty dome at one of the 35 long tables fanning out from the central enquiry desk.

Once the pride of the British Library (now in new premises at St Pancras) and only for the use of card-holders, anyone can now soak up the room's resonant atmosphere and imagine the likes of Marx (presumed to have sat near row L), Lenin, Shaw, Carlyle, Elgar or Yeats hunched over their books. The reopening as the British Museum Reading Room includes: an exhibition on the Reading Room's history, with sample books by famous and infamous readers; the use of the Paul Hamlyn Library of reference books relevant to the museum's collection, and of colour and black and white photocopiers (coin or smart card); and the Walter and Leonore Annenberg Centre, 50 computer terminals comprising COMPASS (Collections Multimedia Public Access System) where you can plan a visit to the museum, take a virtual tour, find information on artefacts, or print out images (with smart cards, £2 from Central Enquiry Desk).

Around the museum A first visit to the British Museum galleries is likely to both inspire and bewilder. That said, the new developments mean that the arrangement of millions of objects of every shape, size, and age laid out for inspection in over 90 rooms now seems much more straightforward.

The main part of the museum is on the ground floor in the **west wing**, through the left-hand wall of the Great Court after entering from the main southern entrance. The galleries stretching the length of this wing are devoted to Ancient Egyptian sculpture, the Ancient Near East (including art from the palaces of Nimrud and Nineveh, and Assyrian sculpture), and Ancient Greece (including the sculptures from the Parthenon, the Nereid Monument and the Mausoleum of Halikarnassos). These collections also spill downstairs onto the lower floors of this wing.

On the right-hand side of the Great Court is the **east wing**, once the wonderful old King's Library, now a temporary exhibition space, likely to be devoted to the ethnographic collection that used to be in the Museum of Mankind.

Straight ahead past the Reading Room leads into the **north wing**, another temporary exhibition space and rooms devoted to artefacts from China, Southeast Asia, India and the Americas, with the African collection newly housed on the lower floors.

On the **upper floors**, above the galleries in the west wing – best reached up the south stairs on the left just before entering the Great Court from the front entrance – are more objects from Ancient Greece and also from the Roman Empire. Straight ahead at the top of these stairs leads into the rooms in the east wing devoted to Europe from the Middle Ages to modern times. Beyond these, on the upper floors of the east wing, can be found Roman Britain, Prehistory, and more monuments and treasures from the Ancient Near East which continue round into the north wing, also home to the museum's extraordinary collection of early Egyptian funerary objects – including mummies – as well as the Korean and Japanese collections.

It would be quite impossible to see everything in one day: apart from the guided and audio tours, it's well worth finding out from the Information desk when and where the free 50-minute 'EyeOpener' Gallery Talks are taking place (the first usually at about 1100 and the last at about 1500). Every day many of the museum's main areas are covered, with enthusiastic and well-informed volunteers describing the contents of a particular room in fascinating detail.

The Petrie Museum of Egyptian Archaeology ⓘ *Malet Pl, off Torrington St, T020-7679 2000 (ext 2884), www.petrie.uccl.ac.uk, Tue-Fri 1300-1700, Sat 1000-1300, free (donations appreciated)*, is a hidden gem, bound to delight anyone whose appetite for all things Ancient Egyptian has been whetted by the British Museum. Donated by Sir Flinders Petrie to University College London (UCL) in 1933, this old-fashioned academic museum is a glass-cased treasure trove of amulets, beads, ornaments, instruments and decorative art.

The **Percival David Foundation of Chinese Art** ⓘ *in the southeastern corner of Gordon Sq (No 53), T020-7387 3909, www.pdfmuseum.org.uk, Mon-Fri 1030-1700, free (donations appreciated), under-14s must be accompanied by an adult*, consists of a series of quiet, serene rooms containing a large collection of exquisite Chinese ceramics from the 10th-18th centuries. Ming, Qing, Song and Tang vases, dishes, pots, incense burners and water droppers, many of the items were previously owned by Chinese emperors. The cumulative effect of such an absorbing wealth of fine detail is memorable.

Holborn and Clerkenwell

→ *Tube: Holborn, Chancery La for Lincoln's Inn Fields; Temple for Fleet St, Farringdon or Barbican for Clerkenwell*

East of the West End and west of the City, Holborn falls between two stools, long colonized by lawyers, the press and intermediaries of all kinds. Twenty years ago though, the journos moved out east to Wapping and Docklands and the buzz of the latest news being churned on Fleet Street has died down. The district is now dominated by the atmosphere of the ancient Inns of Court, neat and officious places founded on discretion and class-ridden legal traditions: don't be caught pronouncing the silent L – for litigation – in Holborn. It's pronounced *Ho-bon*. That said, the quiet lawns, secret alleyways and collegiate architecture of the barristers' stamping grounds are peaceful havens for outsiders to explore, and **Lincoln's Inn Fields** houses two of the city's most unusual museums, the **Hunterian Museum of the Royal College of Surgeons** and the spellbinding curiosity of the **John Soane's Museum**.

Over the same period Clerkenwell, on the other hand, northeast of the City and Holborn beyond the Gray's Inn Road, has become one of the most vibrant and creative parts of London, the fashionable home of design consultancies, independent media groups and sassy restaurants. Although it's beginning to look as though the party might already be over, with some tenants feeling the pinch of City property prices, the old streets north of **Smithfield Market** are still a top place to paint the town red.

Hunterian Museum of the Royal College of Surgeons

On the south side of **Lincoln's Inn Fields**, the largest square in London, at 35-43, is the Hunterian Museum of the Royal College of Surgeons. In the 18th century John Hunter amassed a huge collection of pathological specimens, human and animal, in the course of his anatomical studies. With the addition of thousands more in the 19th century, the museum once held a world-beating variety of pickled parts and dissected exhibits. Call for details T020-7869 6560.

Sir John Soane's Museum

ⓘ T020-7405 2107, www.soane.org. Tue-Sat 1000-1700, first Tue of month also 1800-2100 by candlelight in winter. Free. Guided tour on Sat at 1430, £3, concessions free.

On the opposite side of the square, at 12-14, Sir John Soane's Museum is a remarkable memorial to the imagination of one of Georgian London's greatest architects. Most famous for designing the Bank of England, Sir John Soane left his treasured project of a lifetime to the nation on his death in 1837. The eight or so rooms in No 13 that can now be seen are a purpose-built showcase for his highly idiosyncratic and eclectic collection of antiquities, artworks and objets d'art. At its most atmospheric (although often also most crowded) during the late openings on the first Tuesday of every month (candlelit in winter), an hour spent here is usually enough to persuade most people that they need to come again with more time.

Smithfield Market

Clerkenwell is one of the more exciting parts of London to wander around, not simply because of the clutch of new shops, restaurants, clubs and bars that have opened up here in the last decade, but also because it's an old part of town still visibly in a state of fashionable flux. A good place to start is in the south of the area around Smithfield Market, London's meat distribution centre. Unlike the other wholesale fish and fruit and veg markets at Billingsgate and Covent Garden, the market has managed to cling on to its ancient site in the city centre. Especially late at night and at dawn, when the area round about is partying hard or fast asleep, the comings and goings of huge articulated and refrigerated lorries unloading endless fresh carcasses into its grand late 19th-century building can take on a surreal quality. Try a pint of Guinness and a fry-up breakfast in *The Cock Tavern*, T020-7248 2918, at 6am to complete the Smithfield experience.

The City

→ St Paul's for the Cathedral, or Museum of London and the west end of the City, Barbican for the Museum of London. Bank or Monument for the rest of the City.

The City is where London began, and judging from the harried look of its working population, it ain't over yet. Nowhere is the contrast stronger between weekday and weekend, or even between lunch and supper. During the week thousands storm into the Square Mile to deal with billions of other people's money, fortunes are made or broken with a few megabytes in massive offices, and then come Saturday it all might never have happened: the place is left to the coach parties and tourists, a gigantic modern ghost town sprinkled with empty little churches. The grand exception is **St Paul's Cathedral**, its great stone interior always echoing with sightseers or worshippers, its dome one of the most beautiful, symbolic landmarks in London and a spectacular view point. Some idea of what has being going down as well as up all around its prime position over the centuries can be discovered at the **Museum of London**, while next door the **Barbican Centre** provides another cultural oasis for live performances of a high standard.

66 99 The City is where London began, and judging from the harried look of its working population, it ain't over yet...

St Paul's Cathedral

ⓘ T020-7236 4128, www.stpauls.co.uk. 0830-1600 Mon-Sat. £7 including Cathedral Crypt and Galleries, £3 under-16s, concessions £6, family £17. Guided tours 1100, 1130, 1330, 1400 Mon-Sat. £2.50, £2 concessions and under-16s. Audio guide £3.50. Organ recitals 1700 Sun. Free. Buses: 4, 11, 15, 17, 23, 26, 76, 100, 172.

At least the fifth church on the site, St Paul's was started in 1675, took about 35 years to complete and was paid for with taxes raised on coal and wine coming into the Port of London. Hemmed in on all sides over the centuries, Wren's relatively colossal church still inspires awe and wonder.

The current redevelopment of Paternoster Square hopes to open up new views of the place, reflecting its Portland stone in plate-glass office blocks, while the Millennium Bridge now provides a neat approach from the riverside and Tate Modern. Wren had originally hoped to build a church in the form of a Greek cross, but this plan, and his desire to top it with a dome rather than a steeple, were vetoed. Instead he settled on the more traditional Latin cross for the ground plan, and then carried on the building work in such secrecy that no one could complain before his vision, including the dome, was substantially in place. The final result is a kind of mini version of St Peter's in Rome, much less flamboyantly decorated, and one of the most successful Classical interpretations of Gothic in the world.

Twenty-two wide steps lead up to the West Front, looking down Ludgate Hill, with its double portico containing a bas-relief depicting the conversion of the tax-collector Paul. At the apex stands St Paul himself, the patron saint of the City of London, with St Peter on his right and St James on his left. Behind is the Great Dome, invisibly supported with reinforced concrete and a chain of steel after it was discovered that Wren's builders had skimped on the use of solid stone for the supporting columns.

Inside, the massive nave of the Cathedral is wonderfully vast and bare. In fact most of the decoration was only added in the late 19th and early 20th centuries, and not very well at that. It's definitely well worth climbing up the long, gentle, wide wooden spiral staircase to the **Whispering Gallery**, around the base of the inner dome, decorated with statues of Early Church Fathers and painted scenes from the life of St Paul. People press their ears to the wall here hoping to catch what their friends are whispering on the other side. Unfortunately the hubbub from far below often drowns out the famous effect.

> *! Unlike Westminster Abbey, there's room in the Cathedral for visitors not to be so strictly regimented.*

Several steep and narrow flights of stone steps with regular resting places then lead up to the **Stone Gallery** outside, where the views through the balustrade are quite spectacular. In order to look west from here though it's necessary to brave the extraordinary series of vertiginous cast-iron spiral stairways heading up to the **Golden Gallery**. The tremendous wrap-around open-air views from the cramped little balcony up here easily rival those from the London Eye.

Back in the main body of the Cathedral, unmissable sights include the **choir** carved by Grinling Gibbons; **Henry Moore's sculpture** of *Mother and Child* in the north choir aisle; the copy of Holman Hunt's *The Light of the World* in the north transept; a display on the firewatch that saved the building during the Blitz; and the **American Memorial Chapel** at the very east end of the church in the apse, consecrated to the memory of over 28,000 US servicemen based in Britain who died in the Second World War.

Blood and guts

The blood and entrails of the livestock slaughtered in the streets of Smithfield ran in the streets' gutters, and rogue bulls sought sanctuary in the houses of the shops around – hence the phrase 'bull in a china shop'.

But it wasn't only animals who were butchered at Smithfield Market. Until the gallows moved west to Tyburn (modern Marble Arch), this was also a place of execution. Burnings, roastings and boilings were visited on witches and heretics in front of enthusiastic crowds, and Wat Tyler, leader of the Peasants' Revolt of 1381, was stabbed here before being beheaded in front of St Bartholomew's Hospital.

Old Bailey

ⓘ *T020-7248 3277. 1030-1300, 1400-1630 Mon-Fri. No under-14s.*

West of St Paul's, on Newgate Street, stands the Old Bailey, or Central Criminal Court, topped by its copper dome and famous statue of Justice balancing a sword and a pair of scales, on the site of the notoriously brutal Newgate Prison. The prison was finally pulled down in 1902 after countless people had literally rotted away there, forcing the judges to stop their noses with scented posies. Much of the front of the new building used stones from the old prison. Nowadays the famous British justice system can be seen in action from the public galleries of 18 modern courtrooms.

Museum of London

ⓘ *T020-7600 3699, events T020-7814 5777, www.museumoflondon.org.uk. Mon-Sat 1000-1750, Sun 1200-1750. Free. Café: Mon-Sat 1000-1730, Sun 1130-1730.*

Bang in the middle of a busy roundabout, at 150 London Wall, on the site of a Roman fort, is the excellent, purpose-built Museum of London. Opened in 1976, it has a refreshing visual approach to the social history of the city, illustrating the daily lives led here down the ages with a combination of genuine artefacts, reconstructions and canny design.

It really gets into its stride with Roman London, featuring a reconstruction of a wealthy Roman's house and the museum's most exciting recent addition: a cache of 43 gold coins dating from AD65-170 discovered in a hole in the floor of Plantation House, just off Eastcheap. The Dark Age and Saxon galleries are inevitably quite scant in artefacts, but the Medieval and Tudor galleries beyond make up the deficit with carvings, astonishing jewellery, armour and more coins set amid excellent scale models of how a few important buildings may have looked before that defining event in the city's history, the disastrous Great Fire. Downstairs the story of the city's rebuilding, expansion and growth up to the 20th century continues around the Garden court and the sumptuously decorated Lord Mayor's Coach, still used annually for the Lord Mayor's Show.

Barbican Centre

ⓘ *T020-7638 8891; enquiries T020-7638 4141. 1000-1800 Mon, Tue, Thu-Sat; 1000-2000 Wed; 1200-1800 Sun. £7; £4 under-16s.*

Close by the Museum between Aldersgate and London Wall rears the immense, famously disorientating and surprisingly popular 70s housing complex called the Barbican, one of the City's very few residential enclaves. Somewhere in here it's usually an enjoyable challenge looking for the Barbican Centre, with its vibrant galleries, cinemas, music halls and theatres. Be sure to allow plenty of 'ticket time'.

Bank of England and Royal Exchange

ⓘ Bank of England: T020-7601 5545, Mon-Fri, 1000-1700, free. Royal Exchange: Mon-Wed, Fri 1000-1800, Thu 1000-1900.

The Bank of England occupies the entire north side between Prince's Street, Lothbury, Threadneedle Street (hence its nickname 'the old lady of Threadneedle Street') and Bartholomew Lane where visitors are welcomed free of charge into the museum. The centrepiece is a reconstruction of Sir John Soane's original stock office, with six other rooms telling the history of the Bank since 1694 entertainingly enough, including a couple of real gold bars and a pyramid of replicas. There's also the opportunity to chance your arm with a 3 minute spot of simulated foreign exchange trading. Here the Great Motivator gets all the respect it deserves. Opposite the Bank, the 19th-century Royal Exchange building stands on the site of London's original 'bourse', founded by Sir Thomas Gresham in 1565. The fine quadrangle at its heart now provides shop space for a wide variety of super-luxury retailers and a few quirky one-offs.

Leadenhall Market

Heading east from Bank, Cornhill leads up to Gracechurch Street. Tucked away to the left off Gracechurch Street is the Leadenhall Market, a superb Victorian cast-iron covered market. Not really a street market any more, it now houses some fine food shops and cafés that are always packed at lunchtimes. North and east from here towards Liverpool Street the City really means business. Beyond the gleaming **Lloyd's Building** and the former Nat West tower, behind Liverpool Street Station, stands the enormous **Broadgate Centre**. In its massive scale, snappy shops and American confidence it makes interesting comparison with the quaint old Leadenhall Market. Nearby on St Mary Axe, what seems to look like a giant glass artillery shell (affectionately been named 'the gherkin') is in fact the offices of the insurance company Swiss Re, designed by Sir Norman Foster.

Bankside and Southwark

Over the last 10 years the south bank of the river between Blackfriars and Tower Bridge has been transformed. The conversion of the old Bankside Power Station into a world class modern art gallery at **Tate Modern** is the latest and most spectacular confirmation of the area's new-found success, but it joins a wide variety of other attractions that are already well established. An unforgettable walk downstream from the gallery passes **Shakespeare's Globe**, the **Golden Hinde**, **Borough Market**, **Southwark Cathedral** and, beyond London Bridge, the **Old Operating Theatre** and **HMS Belfast**. Further 'inland' to the south, Southwark and the Borough have rediscovered some of the energy that has always characterized their long history, with thriving markets, pubs, cafés and streetlife. That said, neither has entirely shaken off its reputation for being the gateway to south London's bandit country.

Tate Modern

ⓘ T020-7887 8000; ticket bookings T020-7887 8888; information T020-7887 8008.www.tate.org.uk/modern. Sun-Thu 1000-1800; Fri and Sat 1000-2200. Free (charges for special exhibitions). Southwark or Blackfriars tube Buses 45, 63, 100, 381.

Heading east along the south bank of the river, the Queen's Walk passes beneath Blackfriars Bridge and enters Bankside. And there stands Tate Modern, one of the most spectacular and popular new additions to London in years. Opened in May 2000, the converted Bankside Power Station now houses the Tate's collection of international modern art from 1900 to the present. An extraordinary great solid box of brick with a single free-standing square chimney front centre, the power station was designed by Sir Giles Gilbert Scott to be a striking landmark, responding

The City & the South Bank

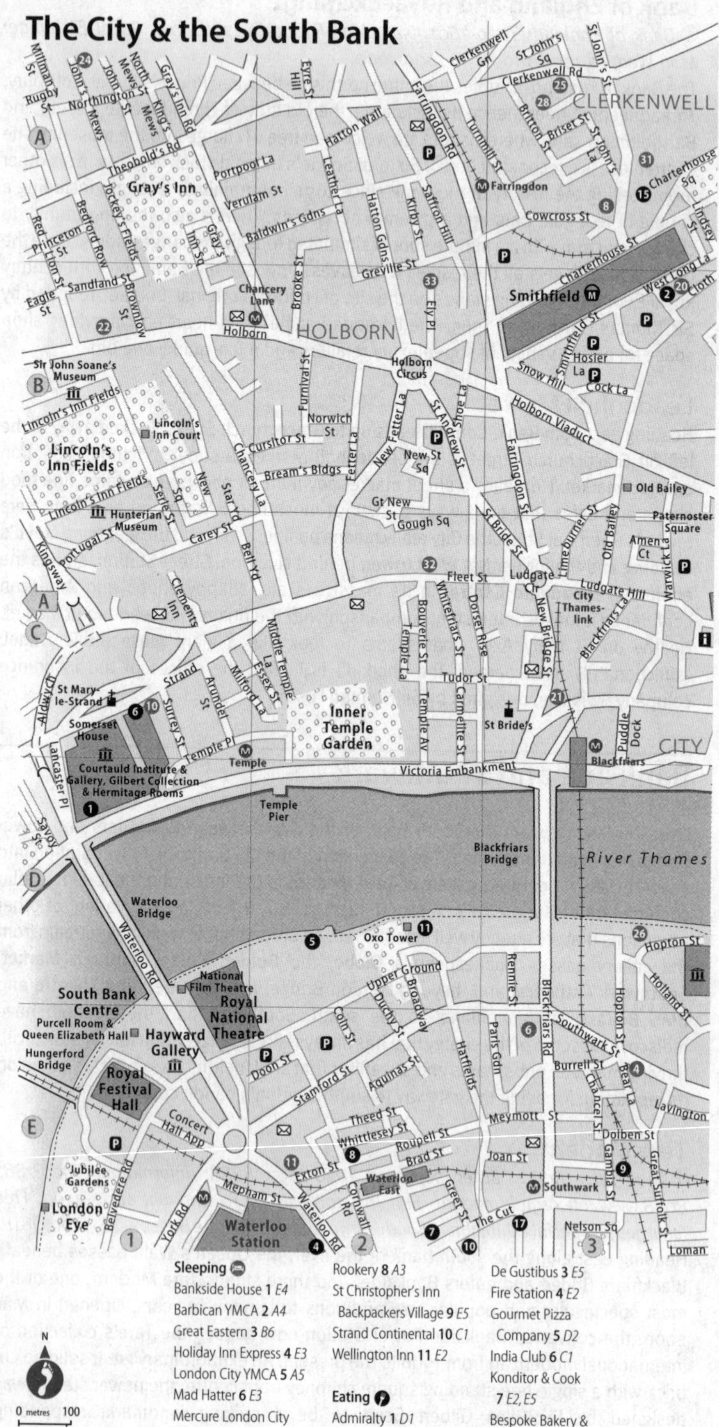

Sleeping
Bankside House 1 *E4*
Barbican YMCA 2 *A4*
Great Eastern 3 *B6*
Holiday Inn Express 4 *E3*
London City YMCA 5 *A5*
Mad Hatter 6 *E3*
Mercure London City
Rookery 8 *A3*
St Christopher's Inn Backpackers Village 9 *E5*
Strand Continental 10 *C1*
Wellington Inn 11 *E2*

Eating
Admiralty 1 *D1*
Bespoke Bakery &
De Gustibus 3 *E5*
Fire Station 4 *E2*
Gourmet Pizza Company 5 *D2*
India Club 6 *C1*
Konditor & Cook 7 *E2, E5*

Mar I Terra 9 *E3*
Mesón Don Felipe 10 *E2*
Oxo Tower 11 *D2*
Place Below 12 *C4*
Prism 13 *C6*
Spiazzo Café 14 *E6*
St John 15 *A3*
Sweetings 16 *C5*

Pubs & bars
Anchor Bankside 18 *D5*
Ball's Brothers 19 *C4*
Barley Mow 20 *B3*
Black Friar 21 *C3*
Cittie of York 22 *B1*
Counting House 23 *C6*
Duke of York
Dust 25 *A3*
Founders Arms 26 *D3*
George Inn 27 *E5*
Jerusalem Tavern 28 *A3*
Twentyfour 29 *B6*
Vertigo 30 *B6*
Vic Naylor's 31 *A3*
Ye Olde Cheshire
Ye Olde Mitre
Tavern *B2* 33

architecturally to its position across the river from St Paul's Cathedral. The building was begun in 1937 but didn't start generating electricity until 1963. Decommissioned in 1986, it was left desolate and empty for a decade. Swiss architects Herzog and de Meuron were finally appointed to adapt the building to its new role. Typically, the praise for their work has not been entirely unqualified but the hype surrounding the project as a whole now seems to be completely justified.

The main entrance is through the west, right-hand side of the building (turn right, away from the river, just beyond the riverside pub the *Founder's Arms*). A wide sloping ramp of brick leads down into the immense Turbine Hall, an astonishing space for artworks on a grand scale. In here, towering up through seven storeys on the north side of the building facing the river, linked by central escalators and stairways, are the galleries themselves, standing proud as illuminated boxes of light.

In a much-publicized break with traditional historical and chronological hangings, the collection is permanently arranged around four themes suggested by the four genres of fine art laid down by the French Academy in the 17th century: Still Life, Landscape, the Nude and History.

On **level 3**, Still Life/Object/Real Life covers the contents of the 14 exhibition spaces on the east side of the building, while Landscape/Matter/Environment covers those on the west side. **Level 4** is taken up with temporary exhibitions (admission charged), while on **level 5**, the Nude/Action/Body galleries are on the east side, and History/Memory/Society on the west. Under these headings the galleries are devoted to selections from the collection that are changed every six months or so, arranged as monographs to single artists, such as Bruce Nauman, Joseph Beuys, or Stanley Spencer, or under themes like *The Intelligent Object*, *Inner Worlds* and *Transfiguration*. The method is designed to ensure that the gallery as a whole can respond to changing currents in contemporary art as well as commenting on how the traditional subjects of artistic activity have been interpreted throughout the modern era.

Because of the mission and layout of the gallery, it's impossible to say exactly what can be seen or heard where and when, but a visit to the website in the Clore Study Room on level 1 enables the location of specific works or of artists room by room. The collection (which even in this vast building cannot be permanently on display in its entirety) contains examples of work by most of the big names of 20th-century art, from Duchamp, Matisse and Picasso through to Bacon, Beuys and Warhol, whose pieces are likely to be found in striking juxtaposition to those of lesser-known or more contemporary artists.

Gallery tours From the Turbine Hall information desk and also on level 3, **hand-held audio tours** (£1) in several languages are available, including the **Collection Tour**, with illuminating commentaries by artists and curators explaining the galleries' themes (each room also has an explanatory panel), specific works and artists. Free audio points are also available in some of the rooms and **free guided tours** leave from level 2 at 1030, 1130, 1430, and 1530, from near Damien Hirst's *Forms without life* – a clinical MDF cabinet full of exotic pristine seashells – and the Starr Auditorium, which incorporates a cinema showing free films throughout the day and special seasons by art directors in the evenings.

Overall, the gallery's popularity is the strongest testament to its success in making modern art accessible: each of the rooms provokes different atmospheres, but few the hushed reverence traditionally associated with art galleries. The place has an industrial impersonality, and yet comfortable armchairs and sofas overlook the Turbine Hall on several of the levels; on level 4, the espresso bar has an outside terrace, while the Reading Points on level 5 provide another chill-out zone with great views and some relevant reading matter. And then there are the views: the East Room on level 7 hosts special events and gives an impressive panoramic view over the thatched circular roof of the Globe Theatre towards the City. Eventually the power station's central chimney will also become an observation tower, with two lifts taking visitors up 93 m for a 360 degree view of London. Of the three shops, the one on the ground floor is the largest, those at the north entrance and on level 4 the quietest, each stocking stacks of Tate merchandising (including desk tidies, shoulder bags, umbrellas and rainjackets), postcards and books on modern art.

Around Tate Modern

Opposite Tate Modern, the new **Millennium Bridge** – a footbridge designed by architect Norman Foster with the sculptor Anthony Caro and engineered by Ove Arup – arcs gracefully over the river to St Paul's. Unfortunately when it opened in the summer of 2000 its experimental design caused an alarming wobble. Some thought it an exciting feature of the new crossing – the *London Evening Standard* even launched a campaign to 'Save the Wobble' – but safety concerns prevailed and the engineers were called back at enormous expense to stop the swaying.

Globe Theatre

ⓘ *T020-7902 1500, www.shakespeares-globe.org. May-Sep, 0900-1200 daily; Oct-Apr, 1000-1700 daily. The theatre's balustraded balconies and gorgeously decorated stage can be viewed throughout the year on guided tours £7.50; £5 child; £6 concession. Cheap standing room for 'groundlings' is usually available. Southwark or Blackfriars tube.*

A short walk downstream brings you to Bankside pier and Shakespeare's Globe Theatre. The brainchild of American film-maker Sam Wanamaker, who sadly didn't live to see its completion, this sweet little open-air Elizabethan playhouse – Shakespeare's 'wooden O' – reconstructed using original techniques and materials, has been an enormous success: under the inspired directorship of Mark Rylance, its summer season of four productions played in rep, some in period dress, often sells out well in advance.

Vinopolis, City of Wine

ⓘ *1 Bank End, T0870-2414040; wine tastings T020-7940 8322; www.vinopolis.co.uk. Mon, Fri, Sat 1200-2100, Tue, Wed, Thur, Sun 1200-1800 (last entry 1600). £12.50; child £5 ; OAPs £11.50; £1 discount if booked in advance.*

Continuing the walk along the riverbank towards London Bridge takes you past the historic and frequently overcrowded *Anchor* pub and into one of the most evocative and distinctive parts of Bankside, hidden away beneath giant road and railway arches. On the corner here, at 1 Bank End, is another new attraction, Vinopolis, City of Wine, an expensive, gimmicky and fairly superficial celebration of all things vinificatory. A visit should at least succeed in giving you a thirst for the stuff itself though, and the ticket price includes five free tastings and a gin cocktail.

Next door Majestic Wine sell the stuff at bargain prices by the box.

Southwark Cathedral

ⓘ *Montague Close, T020-7367 6700, www.dswark.org. 0900-1800 daily (closing times vary on religious holidays). Three services each day throughout the week. Free (donations appreciated). London Bridge train and tube stations.*

Nearby, in Montague Close, is Southwark Cathedral, a beautiful place of worship dating back to the seventh century. It may be small in comparison to other cathedrals in the country, but its place in the heart of a crowded inner-city community makes it distinctive. Both the new London Bridge and the railway nearly ploughed straight over it. The tower was completed in the late 17th century, still standing over the fourth nave that was constructed for the church in the late 19th century, and refurbishment still continues.

Inside, notable monuments include the tomb of John Gower, a friend of Chaucer's and like him one of the fathers of English poetry; a monument to Shakespeare; and a rare wooden effigy of an unknown 13th-century knight. In the north transept, which dates from the same era, a chapel has been dedicated to John Harvard, founder of the American university, who was baptized here in 1607.

Borough market

Nestling beneath the cathedral, Borough Market is a wholesale fruit 'n' veg market that has probably been trading near this spot since the Middle Ages and certainly on this spot since the middle of the 18th century. Nowadays it shelters beneath a great cast-iron Victorian canopy but like other old buildings around here is under threat from the proposed widening of the railway viaduct above. The market itself caters mainly to the restaurant trade and other fruit 'n' veg stallholders, and is at its busiest at dawn, although there are some interesting one-offs. ▸▸ *See also shopping, on page 134.*

London Bridge

From the market, steps lead up onto London Bridge. Built 1967-72, this is the third stone bridge called London Bridge to have crossed the river near this point. The first, a little further downstream, stood for over 600 years, crowded with houses, a chapel in the middle, and almost damming the river with its 19 arches. For several centuries it was the only bridge in London, and Southwark's position at its southern end, beyond the jurisdiction of the City fathers, was responsible for the area's importance to trade, as well as its heavy drinking, gambling, prostitution and lawlessness. The approach from the south was dominated by the famous drawbridge and gate once adorned with an array of traitors' heads pickled in tar and stuck on stakes.

London Dungeon

ⓘ *28-34 Tooley St, T020-7403 7221, www.thedungeons.com. Oct-Mar, 1000-1730 (last admission 1630) daily; Apr-Sep 1000-2000 (last admission 1730) daily (late night openings Jul and Aug). £12.95, under 10s £8.95, 10-14s £9.95, concessions £11.25.*

Not too far away, the blood and guts theme continues, but in a much less authentic way, at the London Dungeon. Waxwork animatronic models, reconstructed instruments of torture, and sensationalist light effects on a variety of 'dark rides' are intended to scare the living daylights out of visitors. Themes include the Jack the Ripper Experience, Judgement Day and most recently, the Great Fire of London. Children enjoy it, judging from the attraction's enduring popularity, but adults are likely to be less impressed. Very small kids, however, may find this too scary.

South Bank and Waterloo → *Tube: Westminster, Waterloo*

Londoners have finally rediscoverered their river and the South Bank is booming. As architecture critic Ian Nairn noted back in the 60s, the area is "a real skeleton key. London is bent around the Thames: however much the north bank might wish to forget it, the south holds the centre of gravity." That's never been more true than now. On the map, this is the centre of the city.

The 18th-century obelisk in St George's Circus, Lambeth, records the fact that this is the only spot exactly one mile from Westminster, Fleet Street (once the home of 'the fourth estate'), and the City. Even so, it comes as some surprise that the riverside walk marketed as the **Millennium Mile**, from County Hall to London Bridge, has become a

The second London Bridge, built 1823-31, was sold and shipped 10,000 miles to Long Beach, California, where it was then trucked to and rebuilt in Lake Havasu City, Arizona.

must for every visitor with more than a day to spend. Only 10 years ago the faceless grey blocks of the **South Bank Centre** and the **National Theatre** were accused of being a dirty, graffiti-stained and inaccessible ghetto for culture vultures. Nowadays, especially on sunny summer weekends, the riverside teems with people from all over the world enjoying breezy traffic-free views of the Thames.

London Eye

ⓘ *T0870-5000 600, www.ba-londoneye.com. Jan-Apr, Oct-Dec daily 0930-2000, May, Sept Mon-Thu 0930-2000, Fri-Sun 0930-2100; Jun, Mon-Thu 0930-2100, Fri-Sun 0930-2200; Jul-Aug daily 0930-2200. £11, concessions £10, children £5.50, under-5s free (advance booking available on the web or on the phone, prices subject to change). The ticket hall for the Eye is in County Hall. Buses: 12, 26, 53, 59, 68, 76, 159, 168, 176, 188, 211.*

The vast spoked white wheel of the London Eye beside Westminster Bridge has already become one of the most welcome additions to the London skyline in years. Well over 100 m in diameter, the largest structure of its kind in the world, it's visible from unexpected places all around the city.

The half-hour 'flight' in one of its surprisingly roomy glass 'capsules', moving at a quarter-metre a second, provides superb 25-mile views over the city, and is neither vertiginous nor at all boring. On a clear day you can see all of London and beyond, including Guildford Cathedral, Windsor Castle and the river flowing out into the North Sea. If the weather is less fine, and there's no banking on it if you've booked in advance (or even stood in the queue for an hour), you're at least guaranteed the peculiar sensation of looking down on the top of Big Ben and overlooking Nelson on his column.

County Hall

Built just before the First World War for the London County Council, the fate of this magisterial building, which became the seat of the left-wing Greater London Council (GLC), is one of London's odder ironies. Since the GLC's abolition by Margaret Thatcher in the mid-80s, London's town hall has been thrown open to the people by its Japanese owners as a hotch-potch leisure and tourist development. It now houses the London Aquarium, a Macdonald's, a Namco videogame arcade, a 24-hr health club, and a Chinese restaurant, as well as a five-star Marriot Hotel and a budget Travel Inn. The new kid in the block is the **Saatchi Gallery** ⓘ *T020-7823 2363, Sun-Thu 1000-1800, Fri, Sat 1000-2200, £8.50, children £6.50*, which houses advertising guru Charles Saatchi's contemporary art collection. Probably the single most famous exhibit is Damien Hirst's pickled shark, entitled 'The Physical Impossibility of Death in the Mind of Someone Living' but it's the sheer variety and accessibility of the sculptures (mainly) and also paintings that makes a visit here wonderfully provoking. Next door, appropriately enough, is the **Dalí Universe** at the **County Hall Gallery** ⓘ *T020-7620 2720, daily 1000-1730, £8.50, concessions £7.50, children £4.95*, devoted to the famous 20th-century Spanish surrealist Salvador Dali, far from publicity-shy himself. The darkened rooms feature more than 500 works, including drawings and sculptures, and the opportunity to buy one to take home.

Underneath these galleries is the **London Aquarium** ⓘ *T020-7967 8000, www.londonaquarium.co.uk, daily 1000-1800 (last admission 1700), £8.75, children £5.25*, which consists of three darkened floors of aquaria designed around two huge tanks, Atlantic and Pacific, home to small sharks, stingrays and conger eels among others. The favourite attractions for children of all ages are the open-top 'touch pools' downstairs: a rock pool alive with crabs and anemones, and the beach pool full of thornback rays. On the way out, there's a display on the threat mankind's activities pose to the marine environment.

The South Bank Centre

ⓘ *T020-7928 3144, www.sbc.org.uk. Mon, Thu-Sun 1000-1800, Tue, Wed 1000-2000. Admission prices vary according to exhibitions. Buses 26, 59, 68, 76, 168, 176, 188.*

Downstream from County Hall and Jubilee Gardens, just beyond the redesigned Hungerford railway and footbridge, stands the South Bank Centre (SBC). The largest arts complex of its kind in Europe, it grew up around the **Royal Festival Hall**, the centrepiece of the Festival of Britain. Apart from the main concert hall, the Grade I listed building also houses an exhibition space, a good bookshop, the Poetry Library, and the high-class *People's Palace* restaurant. Nearby, connected by concrete terraces overlooking the river, are more concert halls, the **Purcell Room** and **Queen Elizabeth Hall** (see page 132), as well as the cutting-edge **Hayward Gallery**.

Opened in 1968 and one of the few remaining examples of 'brutalist' architecture in London. The cantilevered tower of neon tubes on its roof, a kinetic sculpture controlled by the windspeed, has become a familiar, very 70s landmark. This is the place to come for major state-subsidized temporary exhibitions of contemporary art. They tend to focus on four main areas: single artists, historical themes or artistic movements, other cultures, and contemporary art.

Royal National Theatre and National Film Theatre

Next up on the riverside, beneath the arches of Waterloo Bridge, is the **National Film Theatre**, T020-7928 3535. Its restaurant and bar have become one of chattering London's favourite meeting places. Major relocation of the cinema to Jubilee Gardens is planned in the near future, although it will hopefully still be possible to take some refreshment, and shelter from the weather, beneath the bridge.

Next door is the **Royal National Theatre**. The foundation stone was laid for the Festival in 1951, but architect Denys Lasdun's terraced concrete ziggurat didn't open until 1976, the new home for the National Theatre Company. Its grey blocks suit its position next to Waterloo Bridge, although Lasdun apparently hoped they would turn interesting shades of green once lichen and algae had bloomed on the textured walls. Air pollution has so far put paid to the desired effect. Theatre Square is an open-air performance space for street entertainers and occasional showcase events.

Florence Nightingale Museum

ⓘ *T020-7620 0374, www.florence-nightingale.co.uk. 1000-1600 Mon-Fri, 1130-1530 Sat and Sun. £4.80, £3.80 concessions.*

The Florence Nightingale Museum is located in St Thomas' Hospital, at 2 Lambeth Palace Road, where the 'lady with the lamp' opened the world's first nursing school in 1860. The Hospital had recently relocated to its present site in order to be nearer to the new Waterloo Station. The small exhibition includes a 20-minute video on her life and displays explaining her experiences in the Crimean War, her influence in the British Army and the primitive hospital conditions of her era. A fuller understanding of her life is provided by the 20-minute tours Mon-Fri at 1400.

Imperial War Museum

ⓘ *T020-7416 5320, www.iwm.org.uk. Daily 1000-1800. Free. Tube Lambeth North.*

Heading away from the river down Lambeth Road brings you to The Imperial War Museum, founded in 1917 to record the British Empire's involvement in the First World War. Since then it has dedicated itself to the history and consequences of all 20th-century warfare. The bronze cast of the Kalachakra Mandala, associated with world peace, is a good object of contemplation in juxtaposition with the grand entrance to the museum, guarded by a pair of the largest naval guns ever built.

On the ground floor you'll find an even more fearsome collection of military hardware, all quiet, cleaned up and cut away for easy viewing: tanks, mini-subs, aeroplanes and more peculiar equipment like the little observer's pod that was dangled beneath zeppelins hidden in the clouds. A reconstructed First World War trench, 'The Trench Experience', is genuinely unpleasant, although thankfully nothing like as awful as the original must have been. A large exhibition on the Holocaust puts the whole bloody business in perspective.

The Tower and around

ⓘ T0870 751 5177, www.tower-of-london.org.uk. Mar-Oct Mon-Sat 0900-1700, Sun 1000-1700; Nov-Feb Mon, Sun 1000-1600, Tue-Sat 0900-1600. £13.50, children £9. Free Yeoman Warder tours (1hr) every 30 mins from 0925, (Sun, Mon from 1000), last tour 1530. Tower Hill tube or Tower Gateway DLR.

Londoners traditionally dislike the **Tower of London** dismissing it as a tourist trap. In fact it's less a trap than a treat, making an enormous effort to elucidate its wealth of historical associations and bring the old buildings to life for their two and a half million or so visitors each year. Inevitably the gate pressure means that the castle and its grim story come across a bit like a sanitized medieval theme park, but the central place it occupies in the Royal heritage and history of Britain and its capital is impossible to deny. Outside Tower Hill tube a viewing platform overlooks The Tower of London, a classic photo-opportunity for an overall picture of the layout of the fortification and its many towers, with **Tower Bridge**, the distinctive shape of **City Hall** and the river in the background. In the middle stands the original fortress, the White Tower, one of the first, largest and most complete Norman keeps in the country, surrounded at a respectful distance by smaller buildings erected over the last 900 years.

With some justification, the Tower claims to be several tourist attractions in one and for clarity's sake divides itself into seven colour-coded areas, each taking a suggested 20 or 30 minutes to see: the Western Entrance and Water Lane, the Medieval Palace, the Wall Walk, the Crown Jewels, Tower Green, the White Tower, and the Fusiliers' Museum.

East London

→ Tube: Old St for Hoxton and Shoreditch, Aldgate East for Whitechapel and Brick Lane

The East End has long been forced to make the best of a bad lot. North and east of the wealth in the City of London, there's little room here for complacency about cheery cockneys weathering the worst of it with their colourful rhyming slang and robust attitude to a fair deal. That said, the small area round Shoreditch, Hoxton Square, Spitalfields and Whitechapel has changed considerably in recent years, now attracting a large number of outsiders and boasting the most vibrant nightlife in the city beyond Soho. The spectacular boom in late-night clubs, bars and restaurants here has made the area one of the most exciting after-work destinations in town later in the week. In Docklands, where once the masts of tall ships dominated the skyline, the massive obelisk of Canary Wharf now towers over gleaming office blocks and swish apartments, winking across lots of landlocked riverwater. Even so, the peculiar history of the place makes it an intriguing destination and the views from Island Gardens are compensation enough for the architectural eyesores. Across the river, Greenwich rewards the journey east with a convenient cluster of top attractions, most especially the National Maritime Museum, but also the Royal Observatory, and the 18th-century grandeur of the Royal Naval College. *▸▸ For Sleeping, Eating and other listings, see pages 111-142.*

East End

Hoxton Square

Hoxton Square was the epicentre of **Shoreditch's** rebirth as the most happening place in the East End. The square itself is a gloomy little spot but then that adds to its offbeat appeal. Art dealer Jay Jopling opened a second tiny space here called *White Cube*² and confirmed its art cult appeal. By contrast **Hoxton Market** next door has had a thorough makeover, now a smart pedestrianized area, and not to be confused with **Hoxton Street Market** further up the eponymous street on Saturdays, one of the most welcoming and laid-back of London's local street markets. Halfway down is Hoxton Hall, the last surviving Victorian music hall, with a fashionable programming policy.

Geffrye Museum

ⓘ T020-7739 9893; recorded information T020-7739 8543; www.geffrye-museum.org.uk. Tue-Sat 1000-1700, Sun 1200-1700. Free.

On Kingsland Road, the 18th-century almshouses of the Ironmongers' Company have housed the Geffrye Museum since 1913. A beautifully laid out history of furniture and interior design is told here, a series of period rooms along the front of the old building decorated as they might have been at various times between 1600 and the late Victorian age. Most of the furniture and fittings here are original.

Spitalfields

Southbound Shoreditch High Street heads into the City via Bishopsgate. Off to the left just before Liverpool Street Station stands the green cast-iron and brick spectacle of the old **Spitalfields Market**. The wholesale fruit 'n' veg market here was closed down in 1992, and since then the building has been the subject of local concern about its future, a campaign being rallied under the acronym SMUT. It now looks as if half will inevitably soon be replaced by a new development, while the Victorian eastern part will be preserved. Catch the ramshackle whole while you can, at its best during the Farmers' and Crafts Market on Sundays.

Behind Spitalfields Market, on Commercial Street, rears the huge Hawksmoor creation of **Christ Church Spitalfields** ⓘ *T020-7247 7202, Mon-Fri 1300-1500 and 1030 for Sun services*. The full restoration of the exterior of this striking local landmark was completed in late 2000. Every year the Spitalfields Festival of Music take place here in June and during the two weeks before Christmas. For information T020-7377 0287, with concerts of mainly Baroque music, as well as some by new composers.

Beyond the church the mid-18th-century streets like Fournier and Princelet running towards the aptly named Brick Lane are some of the most atmospheric and evocative in London. Still gaslit at night, the old brick terraces adapted for weavers have not yet been over-restored, while a few have been converted into galleries and shops. Most are still private homes in various states of genteel dilapidation or refined refurbishment.

Dennis Severs' House

ⓘ T020-7247 4013, www.dennisseversshouse.co.uk. 'The Experience' on first and third Sun of month 1400-1700 (£8) and the Mon after 1200-1400 (£5), and 'Silent Night' by candlelight every Mon evening (£12) or by appointment.

The desire to slip back into the past was taken to an artistic extreme by the late Dennis Severs, who ran an eccentric 'living museum' nearby at his home, No 18 Folgate Street. His life's work, a painstaking recreation of period décor from the mid-18th century to early 20th can now be explored on 'The Experience', where visitors are encouraged to reassess their attitudes to their own thoughts and feelings about past, present and future in the mysterious light of Dennis Severs'

Popney rhyming slang

Fancy a Britney Spears? And then maybe a Sinead O'Connor afterwards on the way home from the tube station? No, this is not some bizarre new karaoke game, but an updated version of the world famous cockney rhyming slang. Londoners are now using pop stars' names to substitute the old favourites, such as dog and bone (phone), apples and pears (stairs) and saucepan lids (kids).

Some of the best (and cleanest) include: Barry White – fright; Ricky Martin – side parting; Tina Turner – nice little earner; Ronan Keating – central heating; Slim Shady – old lady; Jarvis Cocker – off your rocker; Thom Yorke – leg of pork; Mel C – cup of tea. And Posh and Becks? We'll leave you to work that one out for yourselves!

obsessive attention to detail. Certainly one of the oddest visitor attractions in London, the current caretakers discourage anyone not prepared to enter into the spirit of their friend's vision.

Brick Lane

Running roughly parallel to Commerical Street, Brick Lane is the main artery of 'Bangla Town', famous for its Bengali and Bangladeshi curry houses and warehouses, and also for the extraordinary market held at its top end every Sunday morning. The curry houses still draw people in during the week and the old Truman Brewery building has been successfully converted into the fashionable *Vibe Bar* as well as a cutting-edge performance and contemporary art space.

Bethnal Green Museum of Childhood

ⓘ *T020-8983 5200. Recorded information T020-8980 2415, www.vam.ac.uk, next to Bethnal Green tube station. 1000-1745 Mon-Thu, Sat, Sun. Free.*

Bethnal Green Museum of Childhood is a delightful offshoot of the V&A housing an extensive, superior and priceless collection of antique doll's houses, old puppets, model trains and just about anything else that has been manufactured in the last few centuries to keep nippers amused.

Next door to Aldgate East tube station is the old **Whitechapel Library,** 77 Whitechapel High Street, E1, and also, at No 80-82, the **Whitechapel Art Gallery** ⓘ *T020-7522 7888, recorded information T020-7522 7878, 1100-1800 Tue, Wed, Fri-Sun, 1100-2100 Thu, free,* one of London's most innovative and exciting public spaces for contemporary art, opened in 1901. Its art nouveau façade belies the radical edge to many of its shows.

Docklands → *Tube: Shadwell (East London line) and Canary Wharf*

The Docklands are a pristine and ultimately bland extension to the teeming money-driven office life of the City of London. The **Museum of Docklands** hopes to entice more visitors into the area. Arriving on the DLR at Canary Wharf, or emerging from Norman Foster's fairly awe-inspiring new station for the Jubilee line, it's impossible to miss the **Canary Wharf Tower** ⓘ *1 Canada Sq, E14*, the beacon at the heart of Docklands.

A little to the north, the new **Museum in Docklands** ⓘ *Warehouse No 1, West India Quay, Hertsmere Rd, E14, T020-7001 9800, daily 1000-1800, £3*, takes the themes of River, Port and People to tell the story of the area from salty seafarers via desolation to corporate hospitality. The full history of Docklands is covered in some depth at this outpost of the Museum of London, going some way towards recapturing some of the area's exciting past with Sailor Town, a recreation of a local 19th-century street.

Nearer the tip of the Isle of Dogs, the **Island History Trust** ⓘ *197 East Ferry Rd, E14, T020-7987 6041, Tue, Wed 1330-1630, free*, hold at least 5000 photos depicting the Isle of Dogs in the 20th century. Along with the new museum, a visit here is a must to fully appreciate the changes, good and bad, the area has undergone in recent times.

Nestling at the tip of the Isle of Dogs, **Island Gardens** is a small park that makes an ideal place to sit and admire the view of maritime Greenwich and the Cutty Sark. Look over your shoulder, and you're back in the 21st century, Canary Wharf still oddly close though, more than a mile away. From Island Gardens, the Greenwich foot tunnel, constructed in 1902 for the West India dockers, sneaks under the river and back in time.

Greenwich

As well as being the home of Greenwich Mean Time, the area's ancient Royal and naval associations made it seem an appropriate spot to wave goodbye to the lost Empire of the 20th century and welcome in the era of 'New Britain'. Unfortunately the future of the Millennium Dome still hangs in the balance. A fairly short river trip from Westminster past many of London's most famous sights, the town itself is also pleasant to explore, with a variety of salty sights.

Cutty Sark

ⓘ *T020-8858 3445, www.cuttysark.org.uk. Daily 1000-1700 (last admission 1630). £3.95, £2.95 concession.*

Appropriately enough, visitors to Greenwich arriving by boat land next to the *Cutty Sark*, the only surviving tea clipper, built in 1869 on the Clyde, and named after the skimpy nightie on a dancing witch in Robert Burns' poem, she made her last commercial voyage in 1922, and was dry-docked in Greenwich in 1954. Two decks can be explored, including the Captain's cabin, as well as a collection of figureheads from other tall ships.

Royal Naval College

ⓘ *Daily 1000-1700 (last admission 1615). Free. Guided tours £9/£5 concessions T020-8269 4744, www.greenwichfoundation.org.uk.*

The College represents English architecture at its grandest and most formal. Three of the most celebrated 18th-century British architects had a hand in the design – Wren, Hawksmoor and Vanbrugh – and its twin domes and columns still make a stunning picture when seen from Island Gardens, the river or from the hills of Greenwich Park.

Now part of Greenwich University, visitors can wander its riverside quads and see the Painted Hall, beneath the southwestern cupola, an extraordinary room, busy with murals beneath a magnificent ceiling, all painted by Thornhill over a period of 19 years.

Queen's House

ⓘ *T020-8858 4422; information T020-8312 6565. Daily 1000-1700. Free.*

The Queen's House was the first truly Renaissance house constructed in England, now standing bang in the middle of the National Maritime Museum. It contains a portrait gallery of old sea captains and other mariner types but nothing could diminish the beauty of the architecture: the Great Hall is a perfect cube, while the 'tulip staircase' named after the designs on its bannisters is beautiful too. Look out for **Canaletto**'s view of the Royal Hospital and Greenwich from the Isle of Dogs, little changed today.

National Maritime Museum

ⓘ *T020-8858 4422; recorded information T020-8312 6565, www.nmm.ac.uk. Free. Daily 1000-1700.*

A covered colonnade connects Queen's House on either side to the large National Maritime Museum, with its three levels pretty much doing justice to their enthralling subject, the sea. In a bold move the museum was transformed in early 1999 by the completion of architect Rick Mather's extraordinary £21 million glass roof over the central Neptune Court, manufactured by the company that built the Eiffel Tower.

Royal Observatory

ⓘ *T020-8858 4422, information T020-8312 6565. Daily 1000-1700. Free.*

A steep walk up the hill through the park behind the Museum leads to the Royal Observatory. Most prominent of the buildings is **Flamsteed House** which looks and sounds like something out of Harry Potter but is in fact the 17th-century home of the Astronomer Royal.

North London

North of Euston, St Pancras and King's Cross, Camden is the spigot around which north London spins. And a strange mixed-up place it is too, with its music, markets and self-aware media-savvy folk. The Chalk Farm Road carries Camden High Street on northwest past the genteel slopes of Primrose Hill, a chi-chi celebrity hideout, towards the heights of Hampstead, a London high point. An affluent town astride the hills to the north, it competes in both elevation, social status and antique authenticity with the neighbouring hilltop village of Highgate. Although no longer the liberal, bohemian enclaves they once were, both remain strongly associated with their literary and cultural heritage. Both places are also deservedly famous for the 800 or so acres of rolling grassland, meadows and woodland of Hampstead Heath that divides them. To the east, sitting on a low hilltop northwest of the City, Islington likes to think of itself – with some justification – as the left-wing Notting Hill of north London. Its transformation over the last 20 years into the fashionable stamping ground of the liberal middle classes has not always been entirely happy, but it is now more confident than ever, credited with nurturing the politics of the current Labour government. ▸▸ *For Sleeping, Eating and other listings, see pages 111-142.*

Camden → *Tube: Camden Town which becomes one-way into the area on Sat and Sun.*

The **markets** are Camden Town's main attraction, the city's weekly street festival, and the reason most people come to Camden in the first place. The 'market' (although markets would be more accurate), has ballooned from lowly beginnings into a series of stalls occupying any vacant space on the High Street between Camden Town tube and Camden Lock every Saturday and Sunday. **Camden Market** ⓘ *High St, daily 0900-1730*, and the **Electric Ballroom** ⓘ *High St, 0900-1730 Sun*, and the High Street itself, with its outsize shop signs, are a pop kids' Mecca, awash with cheap leather jackets, brashly sloganed T-shirts and hectic drinking holes.

In recent years though, **Camden Lock Market** ⓘ *daily 1000-1800, Tue-Sat indoor stalls; T020-7284 2084, www.camdenlockmarket.com*, on Camden Lock Place, off Chalk Farm Road, with its array of more interesting clothes, jewellery, books and handicraft, and **Stables Market** ⓘ *off Chalk Farm Rd at the junction with Hartland Road, T020-7485 5511*, with its furniture and bric-a-brac, have provided satisfying browsing. The **Canal Market** runs off Chalk Farm Road, just over the bridge from the High Street on the right, with a mish-mash of stalls inside and out. If

A bit of rough

Camden Town has long had an attraction for artists and bohemian types, due to its rough and ready image and the availability of cheap housing and spacious commercial premises. The reason Camden was cheap was the large Irish immigrant population, who had something of an undesirable reputation for drunk and disorderly behaviour. The old saying, 'Camden Town for the rough lie down' is a reference to their supposed habit of sleeping in the streets after the pubs closed and the fighting stopped.

none of these tickles your fancy you can always plump for plain old fruit 'n' veg at the market on **Inverness Street**.

Camden Lock

By the High Road stand many of the original Grand Union buildings alongside the huge new Suffolk Wharf shop, restaurant and office development under construction. Walk along the towpath for a minute and you'll see the kind of mix of old and new, rich and poor, public and private that London specializes in. Ridiculously expensive waterside condos back onto dilapidated railway bridges, and the area's gentrification doesn't stop the odd shopping trolley disfiguring the canal.

Primrose Hill

A few minutes walk from the High Street, or best reached directly over the railway bridge from Chalk Farm tube, the pretty village here could hardly be more different from its raving eastern neighbour. The hill itself affords magnificent vistas over central London and Essex and Kent beyond. The London Eye in the distance makes a striking addition to one of the city's greatest views, which was much marred in the 60s by a series of thoughtless housing projects.

Hampstead and Highgate

There's a distinctive 'villagey' feel to Hampstead. From Hampstead tube, Heath Street heads sharply uphill towards Hampstead Heath, an oasis of uncultivated land where it is easy to forget the urban mayhem as one wanders leafy avenues, open fields and shaded woods. Spectacular views of London can be found from the top of Parliament Hill, which is also a great place to fly kites. Highgate is often seen as the poor relation, but its famous cemetery and village atmosphere make it a rewarding destination on the more attractive eastern side of the Heath.

Keats House

ⓘ *Wentworth Pl, Keats Grove, NW3, T020-7435 2062, www.cityoflondon.gov.uk/keats. Apr-Oct 1200-1700 Tue-Sun; Nov-Mar 1200-1600 Tue-Sun. £3, £1.50 concessions, under-16s free but donations gratefully accepted.*

This is the little Regency house and garden where Keats penned his most famous poem, *Ode to a Nightingale*, under a plum tree while staying there in 1819. The house was saved and opened to the public in the 1920s largely thanks to the poet's American fans while in the garden a mulberry tree survives from the romantic's day.

The Freud Museum

ⓘ *20 Maresfield Gardens, T020-7435 2002. Wed-Sun 1200-1700. £5, £2 concessions.*
Here, is the Arts and Crafts house where the great psychoanalyst spent the last years of his life. The house has been preserved for posterity, now including a reconstruction of his study and consulting room, complete with the famous couch, and a number of antiquities testifying to Freud's interest in the ancient world.

Highgate Cemetery

ⓘ *T020-8340 1834. Eastern cemetery: 1000-1600 Mon-Fri, 1100-1600 Sat, Sun. Western cemetery: Oct-Feb Sat, Sun tours at 1100, 1200, 1300, 1400, 1500, Mar-Oct weekdays also at 1400, tours cost £4.*
Highgate Cemetery, most famous for being the burial place of **Karl Marx**, in the more modern eastern part of the cemetery; on its western side is also one of London's most extraordinary burial grounds. The western part is the most overgrown and now carefully protected by a society of friends who offer informative guided tours taking in the remarkable Egyptian catacombs, famous graves, monuments and an abundance of wild flowers. Both parts are sometimes closed to the public during funerals.

Islington → *Tube: Angel for southern end of Upper St, Highbury and Islington for northern end*

Islington rewards visitors not with its sights but with a welcoming attitude, a wide array of ethnic restaurants, old pubs and fashionable bars, a thriving theatre and music scene, and two excellent small markets. The antique shops in **Camden Passage** have long been a major draw, while **Chapel Market** is a thriving local street market and increasingly hot nightspot. Friday and Saturday night excitement in Islington can be just as mad, bad and dangerous-to-know as anywhere in the West End – which is quite an achievement in itself.

On the right, just beyond the *Duke of York* pub, the High Street ends up in Camden Passage, running parallel to Upper Street for a short distance, lined with antique shops and restaurants and hosting a bric-a-brac market on Wednesdays.

Further along Upper Street, the 18th-century tower of **St Mary's** survived the Second World War bombing and now stands opposite the *King's Head Theatre Pub*, where Dan Crawford almost single-handedly established North London's fringe theatre scene.

> *Most of the action in Islington takes place on Upper St and around, including Chapel Market.*

Past Islington Town Hall on the right, the imposing presence of Cubitt's **Union Chapel** ⓘ *T020-7226 3750, recorded information line T020-7226 1686*, dominates the east side of the street. Formerly a Congregational chapel containing a fragment of the rock on which the Pilgrim Fathers landed, it has been semi-converted into a performance venue for all manner of different events, including a flamenco club, theatre, art shows and music in its echoing auditorium and studio theatre.

Estorick Collection of Modern Italian Art

ⓘ *T020-7704 9522, www.estorickcollection.com, Wed-Sat 1100-1800, Sun 1200-1700, £3.50, £2.50 concession.*
East of Upper Street lies Canonbury, best appreciated by a visit to the Estorick Collection of Modern Italian Art, at 39 Canonbury Square (entrance on Canonbury Road), not least for a good opportunity to take a look inside a fine Georgian house and enjoy some good food from the café indoors or out. The intriguing permanent collection of Italian art here, featuring an especially strong selection of Futurist work, is often complemented by eye-catching contemporary exhibitions.

West London

West of Hyde Park, Notting Hill basks in celebrity status, even if it is sometimes for all the wrong reasons. One of London's original and now more successful gentrified multicultural districts, its sloping terraces may not be the most attractive in town but the fashionable types patrolling its boutiques, galleries, cafés and bars probably are. Most famously, once a year at the Carnival on the last weekend of August, these spectacularly cool media darlings give way to the wildest and most uninhibited street party in Europe. Just to the east, in the west end of Kensington Gardens, stands the explanation for the persistence of the area's cachet, Kensington Palace, former home of Princess Diana and still the second most important Royal residence in London after Buckingham Palace. Way out southwest, on the river, a visit to Kew or Richmond from central London is likely take up a whole day, but with fine weather the two-hour riverboat or half-hour train journey will be well rewarded. The varying seasonal delights of the Royal Botanical Gardens at Kew are world famous, while the town of Richmond with its tree-lined riverside walk, views from the hill and rolling deer park are the most rural places within easy reach of the city. Further up river, Hampton Court is the most beautiful and engaging of the Royal palaces in London. It set the standard for grand houses along the river and is best seen at sunset, when its mellow red Tudor brick glows with warmth and the riverside gardens take on an other-worldly quality. ▸▸ *For Sleeping, Eating and other listings, see pages 111-142.*

Notting Hill and Kensington High Street

Notting Hill Gate tube station straddles the street at the point where Kensington Church Street dips south to High Street Kensington and Pembridge Road heads north to the Portobello Road, Ladbroke Grove and Westbourne Grove. **Portobello Road Market** continues to pull in the punters every Saturday for its antiques, groovy secondhand clothes and bric-a-brac. The Portobello Road gradually goes downmarket as it approaches the Westway flyover. This is the end to look for most of Notting Hill's more happening retailers and restaurants. Bear in mind that it's less of a walk from Ladbroke Grove tube.

Sandwiched between the slopes of Holland Park and South Kensington, Kensington itself is a quieter, more residential and family-friendly continuation of Knightsbridge west of Museumland.

Kensington Palace

ⓘ *T020-7937 9561, www.royal.gov.uk. Daily Nov-Feb 1000-1600 (last admission 1500); Mar-Oct 1000-1800 (last admission 1700). £10.50, concession £8, under 16's £7, under 5's free. Price includes audio guide.*

Queen Victoria's birthplace is one of the most significant and evocative of the Royal palaces, unfortunately all the more so since the death of Princess Diana, who lived here after her separation from Prince Charles.

The Palace itself has been open to the public for at least a century, the 20 or so rooms on the one and a half hour audio-guided tour including the antique-stuffed King's State Apartments, William Kent's *trompe l'oeil* ceilings and staircases, a considerable selection of old master paintings from the Royal Collection in the Long Gallery and some fine views over the lakes and gardens. Also on display is the Royal Ceremonial Dress Collection, which now rather ghoulishly contains some of the dresses that Diana wore on state occasions, as well as the gilded pageantry of the [illegible] century. The Queen Victoria dress collection looks very restrained in

The party's over?

Since 1966, the Notting Hill Carnival has been on the last weekend of August, on the Sunday and Bank Holiday Monday. Traditionally Sunday is a marginally quieter day for children, while Monday is the main event. What began as a small celebration of Afro-Caribbean culture has exploded into a full-blooded European carnival attracting millions from across the globe, taking place just about everywhere south of Kensal Rise, around Westbourne Park and Ladbroke Grove and north of Notting Hill tube. Thumping DJ-driven sound systems, spectacular floats and steel bands and several live music and performance stages jostle for position with countless food stalls, market traders, dancers and street performers, as well as impossible numbers of sightseers.

Unfortunately several Carnivals of recent years have resulted in isolated incidents of violence and even murder, forcing local residents and the Greater London Assembly to reassess the future of the event. Many accuse the organizers of losing touch with the Carnival's community roots and allowing the weekend to become just another excuse for a massive Euro rave in unpoliceable circumstances. Some have suggested that the event be moved out of the area altogether and into Hyde Park, and despite what have generally been considered the happiest carnivals in recent years, its future still hangs in the balance.

comparison. As the Palace is keen to point out, everything that can be seen is the genuine article. What any of it really represents is more of a mystery.

Richmond, Kew and Hampton Court

Here in the buckle of Surrey's stockbroker belt, the English dream of house and garden – *rus in urbe* – reaches its most complete expression. As well as the more obvious attractions such as Kew Gardens, Richmond Hill and Hampton Court, many of the area's other old mansions are also worth travelling to find, especially the early 17th-century **Ham House**, just over the river by foot ferry from Marble Hill House.

Richmond Park

Europe's largest city park and a former Royal hunting ground dating from the 13th century, Richmond Park is a popular attraction due largely to its freely roaming deer and the historic attraction of the panorama over Surrey, the river and London (especially from **King Henry VIII's Mound,** the highest point in the park).

Marble Hill House

ⓘ *T020-8892 5115. Apr-Oct, Wed-Sun 1000-1800. £3.50. Reached most easily from St Margaret's train station.*

North of the river, on Richmond Road in Twickenham, a rare survivor of the string of grand villas which once lined the Thames, **Marble Hill House** was built in the 1720s for Henrietta Howard, mistress of George II. Regally decorated and perfectly proportioned, this handsome Palladian mansion, refreshing in its authenticity, also possesses examples of early Georgian painting and furniture.

Ham House

ⓘ *T020-8940 1950. Apr-Oct, Mon-Wed, Sat, Sun 1300-1700. £5.*
Maybe because of its slightly disjointed position away from the rest of Richmond's box of delights, but easily reached by the foot ferry from the end of Orleans Road, **Ham House** is often overlooked by visitors to the area. It's a shame really as it's also one of the most appealing of the local estates with original 17th-century artwork (including Van Dyck) and furniture, the ornate extravagance of the Great Staircase, and an enchanting garden with statutory tearoom.

Kew Gardens

ⓘ *T020-8940 1171, www.kew.org.uk. Feb-Oct Daily 0930-1800, last admission 1730, Nov-Jan 0930-1615, last admission 1545. £7.50, concessions £5.50, children free.*
In an area rich in parkland, gorgeous scenery, antique architecture and oodles of stereotypical English charm – somewhat disturbed by the airliners roaring overhead every 2 minutes into Heathrow – the Royal Botanical Gardens (Kew Gardens for short) are the jewel in the crown. Originally founded as a pleasure garden in the grounds of what became Kew Palace by Prince Frederick, the ill-fated heir to George II, in 1731, Kew has evolved into a 300-acre site containing more than 33,000 species grown in plantations, borders and glasshouses and is a world-renowned centre for horticultural research.

Hampton Court Palace

ⓘ *T020-8781 9500, advance booking T0870-753 7777 recorded information T0870-752 7777 switchboard T0870-751 5175 www.hrp.org.uk. Oct 28-Mar 24 1015-1630 Mon, 0930-1630 Tue-Sun (last admission 1545), Mar 24-Oct 27 1015-1800 Mon, 0930-1800 Tue-Sun (last admission 1715). £11.50, concessions £8.50, children £7.50, under 5's free, Privy Garden only £2, £1.50 under-16s. Maze only £2.50, £1.50 under-16s. Self-service cafeteria in the grounds and coffee shop in the Palace.*
Like the Tower of London, Hampton Court Palace is run by Historic Royal Palaces and bears some of that company's hallmarks: lively costumed tours, clarity in the signposting, and division into different themed areas of interest. Unlike the Tower though, the history of the Palace and its presentation to the public focuses mainly on two particular reigns: Henry VIII (1509-1547) and his many wives, and William and Mary (1689-1702) who until Mary's death in 1694 were unique in sharing the monarchy. What particularly marks it out as a visitor attraction is the variety of this history on display, from the late-medieval architecture of Henry VIII's court to the Georgian splendour of the Cumberland Suite.

Six different routes around the interior take in Henry VIII's State Apartments, the Tudor Kitchens, the Wolsey Rooms and Renaissance Picture Gallery, the King's Apartments (William's), the Queen's State Apartments (Mary's) and the Georgian Rooms (decorated by George II – 1727-1760 – the last monarch to use the Palace).

South London

In the long-established rivalry between north and south London, the south often comes off worst. That said, the 80s club dance craze was passionately embraced from the Elephant and Castle to Brixton and beyond. And much of the spirit of those years lives on in the vibrant pubs, bars and clubs of the area. The best reason for taking a trip to Brixton or Clapham is to enjoy some slices of 'real' London life: the clubs, venues, market and bars of multicultural Brixton; the wide common, cafés and pubs of Clapham. ▸▸ *For Sleeping, Eating and other listings, see pages 111-142.*

Brixton

Electric Avenue was one of the first streets in London to be supplied with electricity, and is nowadays the pulsating centre of ethnic Brixton. Dingy and verging on the dilapidated, the energy which emanates from **Brixton Market** represents the heart of this lively multicultural town at its effervescent best.

Nearby is the **Black Cultural Archives** ⓘ *378 Coldharbour La, SW9, T020-7738 4591, www.aambh.org.uk. Mon-Fri 1300-1600 or by appointment, free.* With frequent temporary exhibitions, the Archives is a good information point on black issues and a mouthpiece for Brixton's strong Afro-Caribbean cultural awareness.

Clapham

Clapham Common is a picturesque stretch of commonly owned land which makes a pleasant walking ground at weekends when families and footballers are usually out in force. The long terrace of Georgian townhouses on the north side dates from around 1720 and includes the former residences of Captain Cook and Charles Barry (architect of the Houses of Parliament).

Holy Trinity Church, Clapham Common North Side, T020-7627 0941, was originally built in 1776 and partially rebuilt after the Second World War. Holy Trinity is the former headquarters of the zealously Anglican 'Clapham Sect' led by notable anti-slavery campaigner William Wilberforce. The fountain on the common donated by the local temperance society is an appropriately dry testament to their local influence.

Sleeping

Accommodation in London has always been expensive. That said, fierce competition has meant that even the smartest hotels have been forced to do deals in recent years, especially during the slacker months (Jan to Mar, Oct and Nov). London's very grand hotels are almost all in Mayfair, Knightsbridge and Belgravia, with a sprinkling east towards the City. The most central areas with a large selection of less expensive rooms are on the fringes of these districts, in Victoria, Earls Court, Bayswater and Bloomsbury. Many are cheaper at weekends and most mid-range hotels include breakfast in the price, although it's worth checking. Be sure to book well ahead, especially for the Youth Hostels and other budget options.

Central London

The Strand and Embankment

p66, map p64

L **One Aldwych**, 1 Aldwych, WC2, T020-7300 1000, www.onealdwych.co.uk. Award-winning modern designer hotel with 105 rooms, complete with an extensive art collection, huge swimming pool and plenty of subtle and not-so-subtle style notes.

L **The Savoy**, Strand, WC2, T020-7836 4343, www.savoy-group.co.uk. Opened by Richard D'Oyly Carte in 1889, it retains a reputation for grandeur and traditional British style.

A **Strand Palace**, Strand, WC2, T0870-4008702. Newly refurbished but rather impersonal rooms (all 784 of them), in a good position near Covent Garden though.

B **Royal Adelphi**, 21 Villiers St, WC2, T020-7930 8764, F7930 8735. Very central, small hotel with 47 rooms, not much changed since the 60s.

D **Strand Continental**, 142 Strand, WC2, T020-7836 4880. Very basic, cash-only Indian hotel with running hot and cold water in 24 bedrooms. Shared bathrooms. Above the *India Club* restaurant.

Leicester Square and around

p67, map p70

L **St Martin's Lane**, 45 St Martin's La, WC2, T0800-634 5500, F7300 5501. Ian Schrager's media favourite, designed by minimalist Philippe Starck, with restaurant doing classic French and modern European on side, the awesome *Light Bar* and the *Seabar* for seafood.

B Manzi's, 1-2 Leicester St, WC2, T020-7734 0224, F7437 4864, www.manzis.co.uk. 15 smallish, clean, en suite rooms, 70 years old, above the famous fish restaurant, popular with business travellers as well as tourists.

Soho *p67, map p70*

L Hazlitt's, 6 Frith St, W1, T020-7434 1771, www.hazlittshotel.com. 23 period rooms, in memory of the great essayist, many people's favourite London hotel.

L Sanderson, 50 Berners St, W1, T020-7300 9500, F7300 1400. 150 rooms. The latest in the ultra-modern Philippe Starck-designed chain that includes the *St Martin's La Hotel*. Ultra-chic *Spoon Plus* restaurant, *Purple Bar* for residents only, and *Lobby Bar* open to the public until 0100 nightly.

Mayfair and Regent Street

p72, map p70

L Brown's, 30-34 Albemarle St, W1, T020-7493 6020, www.brownshotel.com. Founded by Byron's butler, this Raffles International hotel is the most popular place to take sumptuous English teas in calm, tinkling comfort. A family hotel with impeccable service and bags of character.

L Claridge's, Brook St, W1, T020-7629 8860, www.savoy-group.com. Mayfair's most cosmopolitan hotel, restored to its 1920s glamour. The bar has won design awards.

L The Connaught, Carlos Pl, W1, T020-7499 7070, www.savoy-group.com. The famous restaurant has recently been refurbished in red. A quiet country-house atmosphere prevails.

L The Dorchester, 54 Park La, W1, T020-7629 8888, www.dorchesterhotel.com. Owned by the Sultan of Brunei, has been refurbished in dazzling style and is now a strong contender for the title of London's finest hotel.

L The London Hilton, 22 Park La, W1, T020-7493 8000, www.hilton.com. A towering hive of activity, with 4 different restaurants and everything an international jet-setter might require. Spectacular views from the top rooms and *Windows* bar.

L The Metropolitan, Old Park La, W1, T020-7447 1000, www.metropolitan.co.uk. Probably still the most fashionable 5-star hotel in London. Not for wallflowers, although you could always do like Jennifer Lopez who booked the whole floor for her privacy.

L Millennium Britannia Hotel, Grosvenor Sq, T020-7629 9400. Luxury hotel with impeccable service right opposite the embattled American embassy.

Piccadilly and St James's

p73, map p70

L The Ritz, 150 Piccadilly, W1J, T020-7493 8181, F7493 2687. 131 rooms. One of the world's most famous hotels. Tea in Italian Garden for £27.

L The Stafford, St James's Pl, SW1, T020-7493 0111, F7493 7121. Converted Carriage House apartments. Expensive restaurant with classic English menu, American bar festooned with hats and baseball helmets, a convivial spot.

Oxford Street and Marble Arch

p76, map p70

A Cumberland Hotel, Marble Arch, W1, T0870-400 8701, F020-7724 4621. Built around Marble Arch tube, busy shopping centre on ground floor at reception. Huge Forte/Meridien place with hundreds of clean, well-appointed rooms.

C The Ivanhoe Suites, 1b St Christopher's Pl, W1, T020-7935 1047, F7722 0435. 7 rooms, very clean, must book about a week in advance.

Westminster and Whitehall

p76, map p64

A Sanctuary House Hotel, 33 Tothill St, SW1, T020-7799 4044, F7799 3657. 34 clean rooms above a Fuller's Ale and Pie House, cheaper at weekends. Breakfast not included.

Victoria, Belgravia and Pimlico

p79, map p80

L The Berkeley Hotel, Wilton Pl, SW1, T020-7235 6000, www.savoy-group.co.uk. 168 rooms. Home of the superlative French cuisine of *Tante Claire* (T020-7823 2003) amid one of the last words in genteel jet-set accommodation.

L Dolphin Square Hotel, Chichester St, SW1 T020-7834 3800, www.dolphinsquare hotel.co.uk. At the lower end of this bracket, a large, comfortable and relatively informal hideaway near the river with its own gardens, swimming pool and fine-dining restaurant Allium.

L The Lanesborough, Hyde Park Corner, SW1, T020-7259 5599, F7259 5606. 95 rooms. Once the St George's Hospital although you'd never know it, now done up in restrained Regency style incorporating the discreet pleasures of the *Library Bar*.
A Lime Tree Hotel, 135 Ebury St, SW1, T020-7730 8191. Small neat and very popular little B&B.
A Tophams, 28 Ebury St, SW1, T020-7730 8147, F7823 5966. Charming small country-house style hotel, family-run with friendly service.
B Collin House, 104 Ebury St, SW1, T/F020-7730 8031. Small, clean hotel at surprisingly reasonable rates considering its location.
C The Blair Victoria Hotel, 78-84 Warwick Way, SW1, T020-7828 8603, sales@blairvictoria 50 rooms. A good example of the area's countless small hotels, rated for its warm welcome and efficient service.
C Enrico Hotel, 79 Warwick Way, SW1, T020-7834 9538, F7233 9995. 26 rooms. Tiny and basic but still good value.
C The Victoria Inn, 65-67 Belgrave Rd, SW1, T020-7834 6721, www.victoriainn.co.uk. 43 rooms. No-nonsense place on the busy Belgrave Rd.
D Oak House, 29 Hugh St, SW1, T020-7834 7151. 6 rooms, beside Victoria Station. More than 5 days bookable (no advance booking for 1 or 2 nights only). Tea and coffee provided.

Knightsbridge, South Kensington and Hyde Park *p82, map p80*

L Blakes, 33 Roland Gdns, SW7, T020-7370 6701, www.smallchichotels.com. 50 rooms. Celebrity and honeymooner favourite without self-consiousness, a place to be pampered, private, recherché and cramped. Each room is different.
L The Gore, 189 Queen's Gate, SW7, T020-7584 6601, www.gorehotel.com. 53 rooms. Wood-panelled, family-run and with that certain something for special occasions. No restaurant.
L Pelham Hotel, 15 Cromwell Pl, SW7, T020-7589 8288, www.firmdale.com. 50 rooms. Genuinely warm and effortlessly gracious staff, a decent rival to *Blakes* with untrendy but delicately tasteful rooms, 2 lobbies and nestling spots just for visitors.
A Aster House, 3 Sumner Pl, SW7, T020-7581 5888, www.asterhouse.com. 14 rooms. Sweet little place with a garden and conservatory.
A Diplomat, 2 Chesham St, SW1, T020-7235 1544, www.btinternet.com/~diplomat.hotel. 26 rooms. Beautiful staircase, old building, near *Harrods*.
A Five Sumner Place, 5 Sumner Pl, SW7, T020-7584 7586, www.sumnerplace.com. Another cosy, chintzy and award-winning hideaway.
D Linstead Hall on Imperial College Campus (Accommodation Link), Watts Way, Prince's Gdns, SW7, T020-7594 9507, www.imperialcollege-accommodationlink.co.uk. More student rooms.
E Albert Hotel, 191 Queen's Gate, SW7, T020-7584 3019. Student halls let in the summer holiday, 70 beds, 10-bed dorms £15 a night, all including breakfast. Book well ahead.

Chelsea *p85, map p80*

A The Claverley, 13-14 Beaufort Gardens, Knightsbridge, SW3, T020-7589 8541, www.claverleyhotel.co.uk. Comfortable and classy small hotel.
C Oakley Hotel, 73 Oakley St, SW3, T020-7352 5599, F7727 1190. Small, clean, friendly and excellent value on the approach to Albert Bridge (£49 including breakfast with shared bathrooms, £59 with en suite bedroom).

Marylebone and Regent's Park *p85, map p70*

L Landmark Hotel, 222 Marylebone Rd, NW1 T020-7631 8000, F7631 8033 www.landmark london.co.uk. 299 rooms, about 100 years old, refurbished, individually furnished rooms.
B Georgian House Hotel, 87 Gloucester Pl, W1, T020-7935 2211/7486 3151, F7486 7535. 19 rooms with bathroom.
B Hart House Hotel, 51 Gloucester Pl, Portman Sq, W1, T020-7935 2288, reservations@harthouse.co.uk. 15 spacious rooms with shower in an

For an explanation of the sleeping and eating price codes used in this guide, see the inside front cover. Other relevant information is provided in the Essentials chapter, page 40.

attractively converted townhouse. Book at least 2 weeks in advance.

C Hallam Hotel, 12 Hallam St, Portland Pl, W1, T020-7580 1166, F7323 4527. A genteel townhouse with 25 rooms.

D Carr Saunders Hall, 18 Fitzroy St, W1, T020-7580 6338. LSE hall of residence just beneath Telecom Tower. 10 twin rooms available during Easter and summer holidays. Book as early as possible.

D Indian Student YMCA, 41 Fitzroy St, WC1, T020-7387 0411. Anyone can stay. 109 rooms, dinner and breakfast included in an Indian canteen.

D International Students House, 229 Great Portland St, W1, T020-7631 8300, F7631 8315. Not necessary to be a student, 275 rooms, open to public throughout, but very full at all other times. Restaurant with international food in the basement, refurbished bar open late to residents. Laundry, cyber-café, microwave.

Euston, St Pancras and King's Cross *p86, p148*

C The Carlton Hotel, Birkenhead St, WC1, T020-7916 9697. 32 clean rooms in what was once a NatWest bank.

C Euston Travel Inn Capital, 1 Duke's Rd, WC1, T0870-2383301, www.travelinn.co.uk. 220 rooms. Clean, safe, modern and impersonal chain.

D-E Ashlee House, 261-265 Gray's Inn Rd, WC1, T020-7833 9400. Clean, secure and bright budget hostel. Twin room £50, dormitory £15.

E The Generator, 37 Tavistock Pl, WC1, T020-7388 7666. 217 funky cell-like bunk rooms £23 per person, 8-bed dormitories £15 a night, busy bar in an old police station.

Bloomsbury and Fitzrovia
p87, map p70

L Charlotte Street Hotel, 15-17 Charlotte St, W1, T020-7907 4000, F7806 2002. Super-fashionable, with 52 rooms, restaurant and bar *Oscar*. Popular with film people.

A Academy, 21 Gower St, WC1, T020-7631 4115, www.etontownhouse.com. Georgian townhouse, library and conservatory, charming staff, with breakfast, bar open to non-residents.

A Grange Blooms, 7 Montague St, WC1, T020-7323 1717, F7636 6498. Behind the British Museum, 18th-century house and furniture to match, walled garden.

A Hotel Meridien Russell, Russell Sq, WC1, T020-7837 6470, T020-7837 2357, www.principalhotels.co.uk. 336 rooms, not including breakfast. Extraordinary Edwardian bar.

B Harlingford, 61-63 Cartwright Gdns, WC1, T020-7387 1551. 43 rooms, refurbished old house.

B Mentone Hotel, 54-56 Cartwright Gdns, WC1, T020-7387 3927, F7388 4671. En suite bathrooms, tastefully decorated, family-run hotel.

C The Jesmond, 63 Gower St, WC1, T020-7636 3199, www.jesmondhotel.org.uk. 16 rooms. Excellent value small hotel, with a garden.

Holborn and Clerkenwell
p89, map p94

A The Rookery, Peter's La, Cowcross St, EC1, T020-7336 0931, www.rookeryhotel.com. Renovated old-fashioned hotel in an antique building with a crow's nest of a penthouse.

The City *p90, map p94*

L Great Eastern Hotel, Liverpool St, EC2, T020-7618 5000, www.great-eastern-hotel.co.uk. 267 rooms. Sir Terence Conran's first hotel, right on top of Liverpool St Station, with an excellent restaurant and tranquil bars.

D Barbican YMCA, 2 Fann St, EC2, T020-7628 0697, F7638 2420. Admin@barbican.ymca.org.uk. Single and double rooms for 240 people, £52 including breakfast.

D London City YMCA, 8 Errol St, EC1, T020-7628 8832, F7628 4080. Breakfast included. 4 twin rooms only. 101 capacity.

Bankside and Southwark *p93, map p94*

A Mercure London City Bankside Hotel, 75-79 Southwark St, SE1, T020-7902 0800, F020-7902 0810. Newish '3-star deluxe', 144 rooms part of the Novotel chain, £12 breakfast, mainly corporate custom, halfway down Southwark St.

B Holiday Inn Express, 103-109 Southwark St, SE1, T020-7401 2525. Continental breakfast included. 88 rooms all en suite, internet access, small bar, book weeks in advance.

C Bankside House, 24 Sumner St, SE1, T020-7633 9877. LSE hall of residence behind Tate Modern, beds in 4-bed rooms for £55 double including breakfast, own shower, 30 Jun-21 Sep only, book as early as possible.

F St Christopher's Inn Backpackers Village, 161-163, 121 and 57 Borough High St, SE1, T020-7407 1856. 160 beds; £15 beds in 4 12-bed dorms, internet access, laundry, sauna £1 a day, no kitchen, book a week in advance for weekends. Sweaty discos downstairs on Fri and Sat, about £5 admission.

South Bank and Waterloo *p98, map p94*

L London Marriot County Hall Hotel, T020-7928 5200. 5-star, 200 rooms, majority with river views, from £245 excluding VAT, up to £750 for the Westminster suite. *County Hall Restaurant*, cocktail area, *Leader's Bar*, open to the public.

A Novotel London Tower Bridge, 10 Pepys St, EC3, T020-7265 6000, F7265 6060. Fairly new, 203 rooms, *Pepys Bar*, garden brasserie and fitness centre.

B The Mad Hatter, 3-7 Stamford St, SE1, T020-7401 9222, Madhatter@fullers.demon.co.uk. Bright new rooms above a Fuller's pub, largish,double-glazed against noise from the busy road junction outside.

C London County Hall Travel Inn Capital, Belvedere Rd, SE1, T0870-2383300. www.travelinn.com. 313 rooms, basic, secure and central.

C Wellington Inn, 81-83 Waterloo Rd, SE1, T020-7928 6083, F7928 6084. Small, clean rooms above a busy refurbished pub. Quite noisy, right next to the railway, but very convenient location. 4 double rooms, 2 twins and 6 singles. Booking at least 2 weeks ahead is advisable. Good for singles and business travellers. Breakfast not included.

D Butler's Wharf Residence, Gainsford St, SE1, T020-7407 7164. For self-catering flats next to Design Museum, another LSE property, approx £22.50 per person per night, each flat for 6/7 people, own room, not right on the river, needs booking well in advance.

East London

East End *p102*

B Holiday Inn Express London-City, 275 Old St, EC1, T020-7300 4300, www.hiexpress.com. Over 200 rooms. Functional and efficient branch of the hotel chain.

F Lea Valley Campsite, Sewardstone Rd, E4, T020-8529 5689. Apr-Oct only. £5.75 per person per night, £2.30 for electricity.

Docklands *p103*

L The Four Season's Hotel, Canary Wharf, 46 Westferry Circus, E14, T020-7510 1999, F7510 1998. Giant space-age structure for the wheeler-dealers of Canary Wharf. In-room facilities include multiline telephones and CD players, in-house hydrotherapy centre and fitness suite. Doubles range from £260 to £310, but the presidential suite is on offer for £1500 if sir is feeling opulent.

A The International Hotel, *Brittania Group*, 163 Marsh Wall, E14, T020-7515 1551. Clean and modern with superb views of the tower and waterfront. 3 restaurants and in-house gym and swimming pool.

C Ibis, Isle of Dogs, Prestons Rd, E14, T0207-517 1100. Standard chain fare. Near Canary Wharf and shopping complex.

D Travelodge Docklands, Coriander Av, E14, T020-7531 9705. Not as spicy as the address suggests but good budget chain accommodation.

D Urban Learning Foundation, 56 East India Dock Rd, E14, T020-7987 0033. Single beds only in shared self-catering flats. £22.50 per person per night. Bargain for the area.

North London

Camden *p105*

C The Camden Lock Hotel, 89 Chalk Farm Rd, NW1, T020-7267 3912. Despite looking like a motel somewhere off a motorway in the Midlands, this is a safe, clean bet for those wishing to stay in the middle of Camden.

C Ibis, 3 Cardington St, NW1, T020-7388 7777. Cheap(ish) and cheerful branch of the budget chain convenient for the delights of Camden High Rd.

Hampstead and Highgate *p106*

A The House Hotel, 2 Rosslyn Hill, NW3, T020-7431 3873, F7433 1775. 27 rooms. Refurbished small hotel at the foot of Rosslyn Hill opposite the Royal Free Hospital.

B La Gaffe, 107-111 Heath St, NW3, T020-7435 8965, www.lagaffe.co.uk. A small family-run hotel offering cosy rooms in a period house with its own locally favoured Italian restaurant. AA and RAC graded.

West London

Notting Hill and Kensington High Street *p108*

L Miller's Residence, 111a Westbourne Grove, W2, T020-7243 1024, www.millersuk.com. Popular with the likes of Hugh Grant and very English country house in style, with antique candle holders and log fires. There are just 8 individually furnished rooms, from £170-250 including a free cocktail bar.

L The Royal Garden Hotel, 2-24 Kensington High St, W8, T020-7937 8000. This huge modern monstrosity next to Diana's old Kensington Palace is a popular international stopover with all the usual business facilities, as well as spectacular views from the bar on the 10th floor.

A The Abbey Court Hotel, 20 Pembridge Gdns, W11, T020-7221 7518, F792 0858. The cleanest and most luxurious of this street packed with modest hotels. The breakfast is served ad lib in the conservatory in its quiet garden. Breakfast included in price.

A K-West, Richmond Way, W14, F020-7674 1050, www.k-west.co.uk. 224 rrooms, 4-star. £158 for a standard room. Refurbished hotel near Shepherd's Bush. Spa, sauna and gym.

A Portobello Hotel, 22 Stanley Gdns, W11, T020-7727 2777, www.portobello-hotel.demon.co.uk. Internationally trendy hotel to the stars. Johnny Depp and Kate Moss allegedly bathed in champagne here.

C London Visitors Hotel, 42-44 Holland Rd, W14, T020-7602 1282, F7602 0736, reservations T020-7603 9060. Big double-fronted, cheap hotel. Round corner from Olympia and nearby Holland Park.

Earl's Court

In Earl's Court, Barkston Gdns, very close to the tube, has a long row of perfectly pleasant hotels, all of which seem individual but clean and welcoming.

B Albany Hotel, 4-12 Barkston Gdns, SW5, T020-7370 6116, albany@realco.co.uk. Rooms for 1-4 people.

B Barkston Gdns Hotel, 34-44 Barkston Gdns, SW5, T020-7373 7851. Less fancy, and more businesslike, offers conference facilities. Breakfast extra (Continental £6.25, English £8.50).

B The Burns Hotel, 18-26 Barkston Gdns, SW5, T020-7373 3151. Price excludes breakfast (English £8.75 per person/Continental £5.75 per person) The biggest and briskest of the row.

C Henley House Hotel, 30 Barkston Gdns, SW5, T020-7370 4111, henleyhse@ aol.com. With bookshelves and tartan sofas, this hotel appeals to the olde-worlde visitor. More individual and charming than the rest of the row.

C Maranton House Hotel, 14 Barkston Gdns, SW5, T020-7373 5782, F7244 9543. Single, double and triple rooms available. Breakfast included.

C Merlyn Court Hotel, 2 Barkston Gdns, SW5, T020-7370 1640. Possibly the cheapest out of the row of hotels. Non-smoking, no TV.

D The Court Hotel, 194-196 Earl's Court Rd, SW5, T020-7373 0027, F7912 8500. Right beside the tube station tucked above the newsagents, this must be the bargain of the century. Frequented by Ozzie backpackers, offering 15 rooms with TV, a kitchen and a microwave to share. £35 a double.

Bayswater, Paddington and Little Venice

L The Colonnade, 2 Warrington Cres, Little Venice, W9, T020-7286 1052, www.theetoncollection.com. 43 rooms. Bar and restaurant.

L The Hempel, 31-35 Craven Hill Gdns, W2, T020-7298 9000, www.the-hempel.co.uk. 41 rooms, 6 apartments. The smartest hotel in the area is still this elegant extravagance designed by the Queen Bee of designer hotels – former model Anouska Hempel aka Lady Weinberger.

L Royal Lancaster Hotel, Lancaster Terr, W2, T020-7262 6737, www.royallancaster.com. Nipa Thai restaurant doing an authentic menu. 416 rooms.
B Columbia Hotel, 95-99 Lancaster Gate, W2, T020-7402 0021, www.columbia hotel.co.uk. Grand-looking hotel just off the Bayswater Rd, popular with visiting rockers and musos and hence often a very lively post-gig late bar. £83 a double including VAT and breakfast.
C Lancaster Hall Hotel, 35 Craven Terr, W2, T020-7723 9276, www.lancaster-hotel.co.uk. 103 rooms. Tucked away, this large, concrete block is surprisingly quiet in the heart of Bayswater backstreets, between the hub of Queensway and Paddington, only a stone's throw from Lancester Gate entrance to the park. Very pleasant despite its 60s concrete exterior and being a corporate favourite.
D-E Dean Court Hotel, 57 Inverness Terr, W2, T020-7229 2961, F7727 1190. Australian-managed. 3-4 to a room, £15 a night, £75 a week, including breakfast. Single sex. Double £45. Dorm room only bookable 2 nights.

Eating

Central London

Trafalgar Square *p62, map p64*

££ The Café in the Crypt under St Martin-in-the-Fields, Trafalgar Sq, T020-7839 4342. Closes at 1930 daily but is an atmospheric location to enjoy some reasonably priced salads, hot soups and meals served canteen style to the strains of classical music.
££ Portrait Rooftop Restaurant, on the top floor of the National Portrait Gallery, T020-7312 2490. Open 1000-1715 Mon-Wed and at the weekends, and from 1000 until 2200 with last orders at 2015 on Thu and Fri. Run by Corrigan-Searcey's, doing a fine modern British menu, but the views are really what people come for.

The Strand and Embankment *p66, map p64*

£££ Simpsons-in-the-Strand,100 Strand, WC2, T020-7836 9112. Can be relied upon to provide good old-fashioned English food in a formal, upper-crust environment any day for lunch and dinner.
££ The Admiralty, Somerset House, T020-7845 4646. The French regional cooking here deserves high praise and a few hiccups in the standard of the service have been ironed out, making booking for one of the 62 covers essential. The 3-course pre-theatre menu available 1800-1900 is £17.50.
£ India Club, 143 Strand, WC2, T020-7836 0650. Open Mon-Sat 1200-1430, 1800-2250. A world apart from the area's many funky cafés and fast-food joints, this is a characterful place to eat cheaply around here. Pay up to £10 for old-style curries at formica tables on linoleum floors with yellow walls. A very Indian institution, since 1950. It also has the unusual advantage (in central London) of being unlicensed: take your own booze and they won't even charge you 'corkage'.

Leicester Square and around *p67, map p70*

£££ J Sheekey, 28-32 St Martin's Court, WC2, T020-7240 2565. A name that has long been associated with fish, and has now been given a sympathetic overhaul by the people responsible for *The Ivy* and *Le Caprice*. Now it's the most stylish place around for top-quality seafood, fairly traditional and exclusive.
£££ Manzi's, 1/2 Leicester St, WC2, T020-7734 0224. Has been around for years, drawing in a generally sedate crowd of regulars, often an elder statesman or 2, who come for its old-fashioned Italian service and traditional ways with fish.
££ Fung Shing, 15 Lisle St, WC2, T020-7437 1539, www.ipi.co.uk/funshing. Has a good reputation for its seafood and Cantonese cooking. It was one of the first restaurants in London to serve up Chinese haute cuisine and standards remain high.
££ Imperial China, White Bear Yard, 25a Lisle St, WC2, T020-7734 3388. Another large restaurant, hidden away in the tranquility of its own courtyard off Lisle St, does very good dim sum until 1700 as well as good value Cantonese dishes.

£ 1997, 19 Wardour St, W1, T020-7734 2868, named after the year of Hong Kong's handover, is open 24 hrs for consistently good-value Cantonese cooking.
£ Jen, 7 Gerrard St, W1, T020-7287 8193, is a newcomer that has successfully cut a dash.
£ Mr Kong, 21 Lisle St, WC2, T020-7437 7923, does some excellent Mandarin dishes and is open until 0300.
£ Spaghetti House, 66 Haymarket, SW1, T020-7839 3641, is part of a chain but still good value for the area. Open all day until 2330 Fri and Sat, 2300 other nights, Sun 2230.

Soho *p67, map p70*
£££ Alastair Little, 49 Frith St, W1, T020-7734 5183, the trailblazer of Anglo-Italian cooking, continues to come up with the freshest of well-prepared goods.
£££ Richard Corrigan at Lindsay House, 21 Romilly St, W1, T020-7439 0450, makes similar waves with his modern British menu. The 18th-century atmosphere of his Soho townhouse may be a little precious but creates an appreciative mood.
£££ The Sugar Club, 21 Warwick St, W1, T020-7437 7776. The most fun and fashionable smart eaterie in Soho where a dressed-up crowd flock here for New Zealand-Asian fusion food in a see-and-be-seen setting.
££ La Trouvaille, 12a Newburgh St, W1, T020-7287 8488. Does a terrific set lunch at £20 for 3 courses, a supremely competent small restaurant bursting with Gallic flair.
££ Masala Zone, 9 Marshall St, W1, T020-7287 9966. Busy and bustling Indian restuarant specialising in street food from Mumbai and recipes from southwest India, serving food all day.
££ Mar i Terra, 17 Air St, W1, T020-7734 1992. Dinky new branch of the Waterloo Spanish restaurant. Its toothsome menu is served up in a bright little place close to Piccadilly Circus.
££ Randall and Aubin, 16 Brewer St, W1, T020-7287 4447. For fish in a bistro style.
££ Zilli Fish, 36-40 Brewer St, W1, T020-7734 8649. Popular fish restaurant at the higher end of this price bracket.
£ Busaba Eathai, 106-110 Wardour St, W1, T020-7255 8686, a newish 'Thai casual dining room' with large windows onto Wardour St, open 1200-2330.
£ Centrale, 16 Moor St, W1, T020-7437 5513, last orders at 2130. An old-school Italian fast-food joint.
£ Kettners, 29 Romilly St, W1, T020-7734 6112, no booking is required and the savoury flatbreads are still exceptional value given the faded grandeur of the décor.
£ Mildred's Wholefood Café, 58 Greek St, W1, T020-7494 1634, which is licensed, clean, non-smoking and vegetarian.
£ Pollo, 20 Old Compton St, W1, T020-7734 5917, last orders at 2330. Popular Italian fast-food joint serving up great portions of comfort food.
£ Satsuma, 56 Wardour St, W1, T020-7437 8338 is a well-established Japanese doing fine ramen soups and bento boxes.
£ Toucan, 19 Carlisle St, W1, T020-7437 4123, does filling platefuls of good-quality Irish nosh.

Cafés and sandwich bars
£ Bar Italia, 22 Frith St, T020-7437 4520, open 24 hrs daily (except Mon). Football and coffee crazy and still as hip as ever.
£ The Garden Café, 4 Newburgh St, W1, T020-7494 0044, is a sweet place that comes into its own when the sun shines, with its quirky little back garden.
£ Maison Bertaux, 28 Greek St, W1. A popular French fancy.
£ Star Café, 22 Great Chapel St, W1, T020-7437 8778, its check tablecloths presided over by the same family since 1936.

Covent Garden *p69, map p64*
£££ Incognito, 117 Shaftesbury Av, WC2, T020-7836 8866, is Nico Landenis' highly acclaimed venture, doing a modern French menu in a discreet and sophisticated style.
£££ The Ivy, 1 West St, WC2, T020-7836 4751. Wood panelling, stained glass, modern art, superb service and Italianate brasserie food have made the tables here the most sought after in London. Long popular with thespians and wealthy families treating themselves, the well-deserved hype has ensured that booking weeks in advance is often the only way of enjoying a meal here in the evenings. Lunchtimes are often booked solid too, but it's well worth having a go.

£££ Rules, 35 Maiden La, WC2, T020-7836 5314, is one of the oldest English restaurants in Britain and now something of a tourist trap, but nonetheless a highly atmospheric Victorian venue for some classic recipes majoring on game.

££ Café Pacifico, 5 Langley St, Covent Garden, T020-7379 7728. Busy and cheerful Mexican restaurant wioth great margueritas at the bar while you wait for your table.

££ Calabash at the Africa Centre, 38 King St, WC2, T020-7836 1976, is probably one of the best African restaurants in London, in a cosy basement which also hosts excellent African live music in a laid-back atmosphere that's not too expensive either.

££ Joe Allen, 13 Exeter St, WC2, T020-7836 0651, is quite hard to find but definitely worth the effort. The American menu served up in this traditional basement diner never fails to please a host of theatre-going regulars as well as tourists in the know and it's open late throughout the week.

££ Le Palais du Jardin, 136 Long Acre, WC2, T020-7379 5353, is a popular brasserie, but often very loud and busy.

£ Food For Thought, 31 Neal St, WC2, T020-7836 0239, is a very good-value vegetarian.

£ The Rock and Sole Plaice, 47 Endell St, WC2, T020-7836 3785, does famously good fish and chips.

Cafés and sandwich bars

£ Neal's Yard Bakery and Tearoom, 6 Neal's Yard, WC2, T020-7836 5199, a good destination for a healthy vegetarian lunch.

£ Poetry Society, 22 Betterton St, WC2, T020-7420 9880, they have an endearing little bar and wholefood café here, run by reliable poem-promoters.

£ World Food Café, Neal's Yard Dining Room, 1st floor, 14 Neal's Yard, WC2, T020-7379 0298 with a self-explanatory name and basic décor.

Mayfair and Regent Street

p72, map p70

£££ Le Gavroche, 43 upper Brook St, W1, T020-7408 0881. A subterranean gourmet's lair that usually needs booking well in advance for some superbly accomplished French haute cuisine. A great place to treat yourself.

£££ The Greenhouse, 27a Hay's Mews, W1, T020-7499 3331, does a very good-value (and very busy) set lunch at £20 for 2 courses Mon to Fri. Evenings in the country cottage-style basement are more expensive but the modern British cuisine is worth it.

£££ The Mirabelle, 56 Curzon St, W1, T020-7499 4636. Marco Pierre White re-opened this classic Mayfair restaurant in the 90s to rave reviews. Everything here justifies the average £90 tab for 2, from the impeccable service to the presentation of top-notch Frenchified food.

££ Al Hamra, 31-33 Shepherd Market, W1, T020-7493 1954, serves good Lebanese food in an attractive room and there are tables outside for those who want to observe the street life of this strange little corner of London.

££ Chisou, 4 Princes St, T020-7629 3931. One of the best Japanese restaurants in the west end, just off Regent's St. Check out the presentation of their humble spinach salad for an idea of care in the kitchen, served up in a cheerful and efficient atmosphere.

££ Momo, 25 Heddon St, W1, T020-7434 4040, a justifiably much-hyped North African dining experience with a distinctly metropolitan approach to taking reservations. Next door, *Mô*, is a Moroccan snack bar run by the same people.

££ The Guinea Grill, 30 Bruton Pl, W1, T020-7499 1210, is tucked away behind the Fuller's pub of the same name and is famous for its steak and kidney pies. Cordial service, good food and a pleasant ambience have been keeping a wide cross-section of diners coming back for more since the 1950s.

££ Kaya, 42 Albemarle St, W1, T020-7499 0622, is the finest Korean restaurant in London. It specializes in table-barbecues and traditional dishes from the region of Seoul.

££ Mulligan's of Mayfair, 13 Cork St, T020-7409 1370. Attached to a very good pub and offers interesting dishes with an Irish twist in a woody, masculine basement that gets lively in the evenings. Last orders at 2130 though.

££ Sketch, 9 Conduit St, T0870-777 4488. Run by the same people as *Momo* and it must be ne of the most hyped and theatrical new restaurants to open in the city for a while. It's a heaving complex of bars and restaurants, which certainly need to be booked.

££ **Veeraswamy**, Victory House, 99 Regent St (entrance on Swallow St), T020-7734 1401, www.realindianfood.com. Claims to be the first Indian restaurant in London and the quality of the food certainly demonstrates their years of experience.
££ **Yoshino**, 3 Piccadilly Pl, W1, T020-7287 6622. For some of the most authentic Japanese dining in town. Tucked away in a corner off Piccadilly and designed by cult architect Rick Mather, the restaurant used only to print its menu in Japanese. Now there's an English translation but the food and service are still as genuine as ever.
£ **La Madeleine**, 5 Vigo St, W1, T020-7734 8353, is open until 2000 every day, a real French patisserie with a brightly lit back area for good omelettes, pasta, quiches, and grills.
£ **Sotheby's Café**, 34-35 New Bond St, W1, T020-7293 5077, a fairly expensive but very English and genteel establishment for the taking of tea in the old auction house. Last orders are at 1645 and it's closed at weekends.

Piccadilly and St James's *p73, map p70*
£££ **@venue**, 7/9 St James's St, SW1, T020-7321 2111, is where the huge glass frontage only narrowly denies punters a view of the Conservative party's favourite club, the Carlton. The spacious minimalist design easily soaks up the buzz of bankers young and old.
£££ **The Criterion**, 224 Piccadilly, W1, T020-7930 0488, is a grand and beautiful setting for some typically assured Marco Pierre White recipes. The interior of this old dance hall is a symphony in wood and gold, the prices are surprisingly reasonable and the atmosphere quite laid back considering the sumptuousness of the surroundings.
£££ **Greens**, 36 Duke St, SW1, T020-7930 4566, has long been one of the English gent's favourite haunts, serving up fresh fish and traditional British food in a congenial, clubby atmosphere.
£££ **Quaglino's**, 16 Bury St, SW1, T020-7930 6767. Terence Conran's atmospheric overhaul here has proved to be one of his most successful and reasonably priced brasserie-style ventures. Even a drink or light meal at the bar has a sense of occasion thanks to the efficient staff, late opening hrs (until 0100) and the glamour of the dramatically lit subterranean interior.
£££ **The Wolseley**, 160 Piccadilly, W1, T020-7499 6996. In the splendid setting of the old Barclays bank on the corner of Piccadilly and Arlington St, this restaurant is run by the same people as *The Ivy*. Smart dining in the shadow of *The Ritz* that needs to be booked well in advance.
££ **Al Duca**, 4-5 Duke of York St, SW1, T020-7839 3090, is a trendy hangout where Milan meets New York in the glass and wood décor and the modern Italian menu.
££ **Red Room**, Waterstone's, lower ground floor, 203 Piccadilly, T020-7851 2464, an attractive and chic restaurant run by Searcey's Corrigan, who are also responsible for the brasserie at the Barbican, the new National Portrait Gallery restaurant, Lindsay House and the catering at the Royal Opera House. On the fifth floor, the *Studio Lounge* is an excellent, fairly expensive bar and brasserie with great views south towards Parliament and the London Eye.
££ **Shumi**, 23 St James's St, SW1, T020-7747 9380. Swish, minimalist place that has caused quite a stir with its Italian-Japanese menu.
£ **The ICA Café**, The Mall, SW1, T020-7930 8619 (£1.50 day membership required), offers imaginative meals, several vegetarian, that are exceptional value at about £2.50 each.

Oxford Street and Marble Arch *p76, map p70*
£ **Rasa W1**, 6 Dering St, W1, T020-7629 1346, is an excellent Keralan restaurant. It's not particularly cheap, but some truly superb south Indian vegetarian dishes are served up in a strictly non-smoking and cheerful environment.

Cafés and sandwich bars
£ **Borders Café**, 2nd floor, 203 Oxford St, W1, T020-7292 1600, open Mon-Sat 0800-2230, Sun 1200-1730, is a licensed café in the bookshop that makes a useful haven from the frantic street outside which can be observed from above through large plate-glass windows.

£ Nanis, 12 Winsley St, W1, T020-7255 1928, open Mon-Fri 0530-1730, Sat 0800-1700, is a long-established, bright and cheerful Italian sandwich bar and snack stop that opens very early in the morning and represents good value for the area. There are others at 36 Albemarle St, W1, T020-7493 0821, and 8-10 Wigmore St, W1, T020-7580 7936.

Westminster and Whitehall
p76, map p64

£££ The Cinnamon Club, The Old Westminster Library, Great Smith St, SW1, T020-7517 9898, is a smart 200-seat Indian restaurant in the shell of the old library opposite Little Smith St.

Cafés and sandwich bars
Strutton Ground is lined with sandwich shops and cafés catering for the local office workers, many only open Mon-Fri. Here there's a **Bagel Express** and also **The Laughing Halibut**, Strutton Ground, T020-7799 2844 (open 1115-2000), for some perfectly decent fish and chips to eat in or take away.

Victoria, Belgravia and Pimlico
p79, map p80

£££ Balls Brothers, 50-52 Buckingham Palace Rd, SW1, T020-7828 4111, is a busy traditional wine bar and brasserie.

£££ Boisdale, 15 Eccleston St, SW1, T020-7730 6922, is one of London's very few specifically Scottish restaurants (although with a French twist) and its old-school whisky and cigar room at the back beyond the courtyard is a treat. Recently it has also opened up another small bar, christened the *Macdonald Bar*, open Mon-Sat until 0100, at the back of the main green, red and tartan restaurant. The whole creaking complex can become impossibly busy with shirt-sleeved bonhomie but then again it is a cheerful place.

£££ Nahm, in the Halkin Hotel, 5 Halkin St, SW1, T020-7333 1234. Probably the most sophisticated Vietnamese restaurant in the capital, a Michelin-starred dining experience in the chic *Halkin Hotel*.

££ Oliveto, 49 Elizabeth St, SW1, T020-7730 0074. A swish spot in Belgravia for some top-class and reasonably priced pizzas and pasta.

££ Olivo, 21 Eccleston St, SW1, T020-7730 2505, (closed for lunch at weekends). For a wider variety of Sardinian dishes, in *Oliveto*'s more grown-up sibling.

£ Jenny Lo's Teahouse, 14 Eccleston St, SW1, T020-7823 6331, open Mon-Fri 1130-1500, 1800-2200, Sat 1200-1500, 1800-1000, an excellent Chinese noodle bar (eat in or takeaway) run by the daughter of celebrity chef Ken Lo. Marginally more expensive than some elsewhere that have followed in its wake, the quality of the ingredients and fine vegetarian options keep it a cut above.

Cafés and sandwich bars
JR Jenkins Café, 10a Vauxhall Bridge Rd, SW1, T020-7821 8849 (closes 1530, Mon-Fri only) is a tiny bog-standard café for full-sized hot meals and teas.

Relish, the Sandwich Shop, 8 John Islip St, T020-7828 0628 (closes 1530, Mon-Fri only) make very good fresh sandwiches much appreciated by local office workers.

Knightsbridge, South Kensington and Hyde Park *p82, map p80*

£££ Bibendum, 81 Fulham Rd, SW3, T020-7581 5817, Conran's great big gastrodome above a stylish oyster and champagne bar, on the first floor of the old Michelin building.

£££ The Collection, 264 Brompton Rd, SW3, T020-7225 1212, is a DJ-driven music bar and restaurant approached by a corridor catwalk, the sort of place where Posh might have met Becks, choosing confidently from the global menu.

£££ Zafferano, 15 Lowndes St, SW1, T020-7235 5800, is easily the best value (it only just scrapes into this bracket), not at all intimidating and worth every penny. It's often fully booked though.

££ La Brasserie, 272 Brompton Rd, SW3, T020-7581 3089, a proper Parisian all-day nosherie that shows up some of its chain competitors, best for an evening rendezvous at the bar or a sit down with your shopping for a late brunch or high tea.

££ Monza, 6 Yeoman's Row, SW3, T020-7591 0210, has a casual and home-baked Italian atmosphere that belies the quality of the food.

££ O Fado, 45-50 Beauchamp Pl, SW3, T020-7589 3002, is an old Portuguese restaurant with bags of character, never afraid to let the joint start jumping to live music.
£ Daquise, 20 Thurloe St, SW7, T020-7589 6117, a perennially fading but stubborn survivor, a Polish restaurant that sums up the spirit of old South Ken.
£ Il Falconiere, 84 Old Brompton Rd, SW7, T020-7589 2401, is a bargain for a traditional family-style Italian meal at a leisurely pace.

Cafés and sandwich bars

Café Monpelliano, 144 Brompton Rd, SW3, T020-7225 2926. A busy, bustling Knightsbridge Italian institution.
Dishes Café, 23 Cromwell Pl, SW7, T020-7584 8839, next to South Ken tube, for gourmet sandwiches, jacket potatoes and hot meals.
Fifth Floor Café, Harvey Nichols, Knightsbridge, T020-7235 5000 (see above), not cheap but then that's not the point.
Patisserie Valerie, 215 Brompton Rd, SW3, T020-7823 9971. Delicious and sophisticated.

Chelsea *p85, map p80*

£££ Daphne's, 112 Draycott Avenue, SW3, T020-7584 6883. Glamour-pusses, jet-setters and flashy businessmen have long enjoyed basking in the brisk Italian atmosphere here.
£££ Gordon Ramsay, 68 Royal Hospital Rd, SW3, T020-7352 4441, run and named after the famously bad-tempered celebrity chef. Formerly called *Tante Claire*, this is the most celebrated gourmet and Michelin-starred restaurant in Chelsea.
££ Chutney Mary, 535 King's Rd, SW10, T020-7351 3113 is a top-quality Indian restaurant in grand surroundings, just off Lots Rd.
££ Pellicano, 19 Elystan St, SW3, T020-7589 3718, is a minimalist place to enjoy some very good modern Italian food with a Sardinian accent.
££ Vama, 438 King's Rd, SW10, T020-7351 4118, another less expensive and less formal modern Indian restaurant, specializes in food from the northwestern frontier, on the corner of Limerston St.
£ Chelsea Bun, 9a Limerston St, SW10, T020-7352 3635, is another Chelsea institution, almost but not quite as popular as its 19th-century namesake, offering over 200 different straightforward meals like pasta or filled baked potatoes.
£ The Chelsea Kitchen, 98 King's Rd, SW3, T020-7589 1330, once a branch of the Stockpot chain and still doing basic meals at rock-bottom prices for this part of London.
£ Kings Road Café, T020-7351 6645; open 1000-1730 daily, in the branch of *Habitat*, 208 King's Rd, where the ingredients of the mainly Italian dishes are usually absolutely fresh.

Cafés and sandwich bars

Coffee and sandwich chains proliferate on the King's Rd, but near the World's End, **Mona Lisa**, 417 King's Rd, SW1, T020-7376 5447, is a very friendly one-off, run by Italians (surprise, surprise) doing good-value hot meals and snacks.

Marylebone and Regent's Park

p85, map p70

£££ Defune 34 George St, W1 T020-7935 8311. A wonderfully lit and cavernous basement and some very good softshell crab. One of the better Japanese restaurants in the area.
£££ Locanda Locatelli, 8 Seymour St, W1 T020-7935 9088. Designed by the same team as the bar at Claridges, with superb fish dishes a forte. Booking ahead is advisable.
£££ Ibla, 89 Marylebone High St, W1, T020-7224 3799, is a fine modern Milanese restaurant in the rooms vacated by Villandry, that belie the superb quality of their French way with the freshest ingredients.
£££ The Providores, 109 Marylebone High St, W1 T020-7935 6175. Busy, cheerful little tapas bar on the ground floor and some very fine Iberian-New Zealand recipes and excellent wines served upstairs with a smile.
£££ Villandry now occupies minimalist premises further east at 170 Great Portland St, W1, T020-7631 3131, still doing top-notch French cuisine.
££ Purple Sage, 90 Wigmore St, W1, T020-7486 1912, is a laid-back place doing modern British cuisine, with set menus focusing on game and fish in season alongside Italian staples.
£ The Golden Eagle, 59 Marylebone La, T020-7935 3228, does scrummy O'Keiths sausages at lunchtimes.

£ The Golden Hind, 73 Marylebone La, W1, T020-7486 3644, is an old-school eat-in or takeaway fish and chip shop done up in a timeless style but perhaps more expensive than you might expect.
£ Kerala, 15 Great Castle St, W1, T020-7580 2125, is a busy south Indian restaurant near Oxford Circus.
£ Patogh, 8 Crawford Pl, W1, T020-7262 4015. For unfussy and unlicensed (BYOB) Persian food.

Cafés and sandwich bars

Patisserie Valerie, 105 Marylebone High St, T020-7935 6240, an excellent outpost of the patisserie française, less arty but more sophisticated than the one in Soho.
The Quiet Revolution, 62 Weymouth St, W1, T020-7487 5683, specialize in 100 % organic soups and delicious stews for about £5 to eat in or take away.

Euston, St Pancras and King's Cross *p86, p148*

Not a hot destination for gourmets, King's Cross is surrounded by fast-food joints and dodgy cafés. Euston doesn't fare much better, although behind the station Drummond St is a famous destination for fans of bargain vegetarian south Indian food.
£ Diwana Bhel Poori House, 121 Drummond St, NW1, T020-7387 5556, is basic and also unlicensed, so diners can bring their own booze.
£ Ravi Shankar, 133-135 Drummond St, NW1, T020-7388 6458, is mellow and comfortable.

Cafés and sandwich bars

Again, the area is packed with places catering badly for the passing trade. Exceptions are the cafés in the *British Library* and
Paolina, 181 King's Cross Rd, WC1, T020-7278 8176, a BYOB Thai café that is a reliable bargain, only open for lunch and supper.

Bloomsbury and Fitzrovia

p87, map p70

Bloomsbury's largely academic and student population don't really encourage gourmet dining options whereas Fitzrovia's advertising execs and their clients certainly do.
£££ Bam-Bou, 1 Percy St, W1, T020-7323 9130, is one of their favourite places, a modern Southeast Asian restaurant with an airy wooden interior and high-style quotient.
£££ Hakkasan, 8 Hanway Pl, W1 T020-7907 1888. Must be the funkiest basement Chinese in the capital, with its blue-lit stylish décor and a Michelin star for the food. Expensive but worth it.
£££ Pied-à-terre, 34 Charlotte St, W1, T020-7636 1178 (closed Sun), is a small Michelin-starred French restaurant expert at nouvelle cuisine.
££ Back To Basics, 21a Foley St, W1, T020-7436 2181 (closed Sat, Sun), is another good destination for seafood, a cheerful restaurant at the lower end of this bracket.
££ Rasa Samudra, 5 Charlotte St, W1, T020-7637 0222 (closed Sun), is the latest and most laid-back branch of the excellent and expanding Rasa chain, distinguished from the others by doing seafood alongside the famously fragrant vegetarian south Indian dishes and having a smoking section.
£ Eagle Bar Diner, 3-5 Rathbone Pl, W1 T020-7637 1418. Fairly pricey but pretty cool cod-American diner doing big burgers and chips by day and excellent cocktails by night.
£ RK Stanley, 6 Little Portland St, W1, T020-7462 0099 (open until 2400 Mon-Sat), are very good purveyors of fine sausages and real ale in a stylish modern British take on American diner-style eating and drinking.
£ Thai Garden Café, 32 Museum St, WC1, T020-7323 1494, does healthy Thai food but you can also enjoy spectacular cakes in the takeaway shop out front.
£ Sardo, 45 Grafton Way, W1 T020-7387 2521. Reasonably priced and very popular little Sardinian restaurant.

Cafés and sandwich bars

Bar Centrale, 4 Bernard St, WC1, T020-7278 5249, is a very popular 70s-style Italian café/sandwich shop, with a restaurant next door, doing a wide range of fillings and breads.
Cafe Deco 43 Store St, WC1, T020-7323 4501, has an interesting range of Italian sandwiches and home-made pasta.
The Forum Café, 62 Great Russell St, WC1, T020-7404 1878, is right opposite the British Museum, doing a wide variety of high-quality sandwiches, salads and hot snacks.

Holborn and Clerkenwell *p89, map p94*

£££ Club Gascon, 57 West Smithfield, EC1, T020-7796 0600, specializes in the regional produce of Gascony, foie gras of course, exquisite (and expensive) gastronomic delights served plate by plate in a gentle, slightly fey and appreciative atmosphere.

£££ Moro, 34-36 Exmouth Market, EC1, T020-7833 8336, is a large modern Spanish restaurant that has been wowing the area's hipsters, shakers and movers for some time with its artful way with super fresh ingredients. It's been so successful that one of its main suppliers, Brindisa Spanish Food Importers, have opened up a deli next door.

££ The Eagle, 159 Farringdon Rd, T020-7837 1353, was one of the first pubs to go gastro, cooking up excellent modern European food right behind the bar.

££ The Quality Chop House, 92-94 Farringdon Rd, T020-7837 5093, is a long-standing cod-working-class diner doing very good (but quite expensive) basic British fare, including fish and chips.

££ St John, 26 St John St, T020-7251 0848. Offal and freshly baked bread are served up in an old smokery celebrating 'nose to tail' eating.

£ Little Bay, 171 Faringdon Rd, EC1, T020-7278 1234. Very good value little place with a no-nonsense approach to good European food all day every day, main courses about £5 before 1900 and not much more than that until 2300.

Cafés and sandwich bars

Café Kick, 43 Exmouth Market, EC1, T020-7837 8077, is as much a bar as a café, a shrine to table football that does a huge variety of different coffees and decent food.

October Gallery Café, 24 Old Gloucester St, T020-7242 7367, in summer, the secret garden comes into its own at lunchtimes.

The City *p90, map p94*

£££ Aurora, T020-7618 7000, on the ground floor of the *Great Eastern Hotel* at Liverpool St Station, and similar in its prices and modern European cooking to the *Orrery* in Marylebone.

£££ Prism, 147 Leadenhall St, EC3, T020-7256 3888, is a Harvey Nichol's venture in the City, where accomplished brasserie-style food can be enjoyed in chic designer surroundings.

£ Pizza Express, 125 Alban Gate, London Wall, T020-7600 8880 (open 1130-2300 Mon-Fri, 1200-2100 Sat, 1200-2000 Sun), beneath Chase Manhattan Bank, and also at their new branch nearer Finsbury Circus, 150 London Wall Buildings. Reliable savoury Italian flatbreads can be had at weekends.

£ The Place Below, St Mary-le-Bow, Cheapside, EC2, T020-7329 0789 (open 0730-1430 Mon-Fri), in the crypt of the church on Cheapside. Bargain vegetarian breakfasts and lunches.

£ Sweetings, 39 Queen Victoria St, T020-7248 3062 (open 1130-1500 Mon-Fri), is a City institution, a very down-to-earth fish restaurant.

Bankside and Southwark *p93, map p94*

££ Delfina Studio Café, 50 Bermondsey St, SE1, T020-7357 0244, open for lunch only, closed weekends. The name belies the quality of the food but declares the place's affiliation to one of the first of the wave of fashionable galleries still opening up in Bermondsey. Booking is advisable for some imaginative British dishes using top-quality ingredients.

££ The Tate Cafés on levels 2 and 7 of the Tate Modern, T020-7401 5020, are open throughout the week for lunch (expect to queue) and in the evenings on Fri and Sat, last orders at 2130 but open until 2300, both offering excellent brasserie-style modern European food, sandwiches and snacks. Tables cannot be reserved, so it's best to arrive not much later than 1830 to guarantee a window seat in the evenings. The one on level 7 has the extraordinary views and a full wine list, while the one on level 2 is bigger, has more buzz and a smoking area. Both are at the lower end of this price bracket.

£ Mar i Terra, Gambia St, tucked away off Union St, a short walk from Tate Modern, T020-7928 7628, open 1200-2330, closed Sun, is a good authentic Catalan tapas bar and restaurant. The food is great value and prepared from the finest ingredients direct from Spain, served up in a jolly atmosphere.

For an explanation of the sleeping and eating price codes used in this guide, see the inside front cover. Other relevant information is provided in the Essentials chapter, page 40.

Cafés and sandwich bars

De Gustibus, on Borough High St, T020-7407 3625, opposite London Bridge tube, is the place to go for high-quality sandwiches, featuring a choice of 19 varieties of bread, also hot food and soups.
Konditor and Cook, 10 Stoney St, SE1, T020-7407 5100, is the local branch of the exceptional Waterloo outfit, the home of luxury cakes, sandwiches, biscuits, teas and top-notch natural ingredients.
Spiazzo Café, Unit 3, 21/27 St Thomas St, SE1, T020-7403 6996, is a reliable Italian café/sandwich bar, with home-made pasta and fresh baguettes, popular with workers at Guy's Hospital opposite.

South Bank and Waterloo *p98, map p94*

£££ Oxo Tower Restaurant, 8th Floor, Oxo Tower Wharf, Barge House St, SE1, T020-7803 3888. It's a busy, costly, corporate favourite run by Harvey Nichol's Fifth-Floor team doing excellent modern European food with the best views on the river from just beneath the Oxo Tower.
£££ The People's Palace, Level 3, Royal Festival Hall, SE1, T020-7928 9999, F020-7928 2355, also has superb views onto the river through the huge plate-glass windows of the Festival Hall. Solicitous staff serve upmarket French food in the spacious Soviet-style dining room.
££ The Fire Station, 150 Waterloo Rd, SE1, T020-7620 2226. Service can be erratic, and the large bar area at the front sometimes gets very loud, but the reliable food is excellent value. More casual, but with a varied and interesting global menu.
££ Four Regions, County Hall, SE1, T020-7928 0988, is a relatively expensive but unusually grand Chinese restaurant with tremendous views of floodlit Big Ben.
££ Mesón Don Felipe, The Cut, T020-7928 3237. For some high-quality tapas in a very lively atmosphere (tables are bookable before 0830, it's always packed after that), complete with live Spanish guitar.
£ Gourmet Pizza Company, Gabriel's Wharf, 56 Upper Ground, SE1, T020-7928 3188, which is right on the river.
£ Masters Super Fish, 191 Waterloo Rd, T020-7928 6924. For top-quality fish and chips, possibly the best in London.
£ Tas, 33 The Cut, SE1, T020-7928 1444. Fixed-price mezes in this Turkish restaurant with decent main courses. Friendly staff and cheerful, modern décor set *Tas* apart.

Cafés and sandwich bars

Bespoke Bakery and Fine Food Shop, at 22 Cornwall Rd, SE1, T020-7261 0456, make some of London's most superb pastries and cakes as well as sandwiches and soup.
Delirium, 19 Lower Marsh, T020-7928 4700, is a gourmet sandwich bar.
Konditor and Cook café next to the Young Vic Theatre on The Cut is a stylish place for patisserie and people-watching.

Pubs, bars and clubs

Central London

The Strand and Embankment *p66, map p64*

Gordon's, 47 Villiers St, WC2, T020-7930 1408, is a subterranean wine-bar at the bottom of Villiers St. Exceptional wines can be enjoyed in the candlelit gloom of its convivial vaults. It also does fairly expensive salad bar-style food.
The Tattershall Castle, T020-7839 6548, is a pub-ship that does bar food with a barbecue on deck through Jul and Aug. There are good views of the Eye from its position just upstream of Hungerford Bridge.

Leicester Square and around *p67, map p70*

Salvador and Amanda, 8 Great Newport St, WC2, T020-7240 1551, is open until 0200 during the week and 0300 Fri and Sat, a subterranean designer dive bar with a good range of cocktails and a Pan Pacific menu (modern British with an Asian twist).
The Salisbury, 90 St Martin's La, WC2, T020-7836 5863. Classic West End boozer, its gleaming Victorian interior fully renovated and as popular as ever (sometimes too popular), especially with tourists, theatregoers and thesps, darling.

Tiger Tiger, 29 Haymarket, SW1, T020-7930 1885, a huge place decorated in a weird mock-North African style that's quite fun.

Soho *p67, map p70*

Atlantic Bar and Grill, 20 Glasshouse St, W1, T020-7734 4888. Book a table at the restaurant if you want guaranteed entry, although it's often not that fussy. The louche comfort of *Dick's Bar* remains the main attraction.

Café Bohème, 13-17 Old Compton St, W1, T020-7734 0623, open 24 hrs Fri and Sat, admission £3 after 2200, £4 after 2300 Fri, Sat (last orders for alcohol 0230 daily) was one of the bars that led the way for late-night Soho, a relaxed, continental-style brasserie on a busy corner with a top-notch restaurant attached. Expect to queue if arriving late.

The Coach and Horses, 29 Greek St, W1, T020-7437 5920, has long established itself as the archetypal Soho boozer, thanks to its famously rude landlord and alcoholic regulars like the late Jeffrey Bernard. It's still a refreshingly unpretentious place for a plain pint and a very old-style ham sandwich.

Dog and Duck, 18 Bateman St, W1, T020-7494 0697, a busy little corner pub on 2 floors pumping very good beer. The film industry's favourite old-fashioned pub.

French House, 49 Dean St, W1, T020-7437 2799, formerly the *Yorkminster*, where the wine is very good and beer served in halves only.

Propaganda, 201 Wardour St, W1, T020-7434 3820, is a new designer style bar with a cutting-edge music policy.

Covent Garden *p69, map p64*

AKA, 18 West Central St, WC2 T020-7836 0110, next door to *The End* nightclub (see p129), open Thu-Sat until 0300, after 2230 admission £5, has live music and DJs, one big split-level floor with a restaurant, the latest in cool.

Bünker, 41 Earlham St, WC2, T020-7240 0606, is another underground venue, more airily done out in stainless steel and pale wood where beer is brewed on the premises and there's a separate dining area for food at reasonable prices.

Detroit, 35 Earlham St, WC2, T020-7240 2662, open until 2400 Mon-Sat, has much more character, a subterranean warren of alcoves, excellent cocktails and decent food.

Lamb and Flag, 33 Rose St, WC2, T020-7497 9504, best approached down a tiny covered alley off Floral St, but its warm and woody interior and front courtyard can become impossibly busy.

The Maple Leaf, 41 Maiden La, WC2, T020-7240 2843 is one of London's few Canadian pubs.

Market Café, 21 The Piazza, WC2, T020-7836 2137, open until 0200 Mon-Sat, in the southwest corner with a small terrace overlooking the courtyard in front of St Paul's.

The Opera Tavern, 23 Catherine St, WC2, T020-7379 9832, with its grand Victorian interior, pays respect to the Royal Opera House.

Speakeasy at Christopher's, 18 Wellington St, WC2, T020-7240 4222, stays open a little later than most pubs, an American-style basement bar with good-value cocktails.

Mayfair and Regent Street *p72, map p70*

Unsurprisingly Mayfair boasts some of the best hotel bars in the country, let alone London. None of them are cheap but some deserve the extra spend, especially these few that are outstanding:

Audley 41-43 Mount St, W1, T020-7499 1843, harks back to Mayfair's grand old days and indulge tourist expectations. Its historic and palatial dark red and wood décor is reminiscent of a rather run-down gentleman's club.

The Red Lion, tucked away at 1 Waverton St, W1, T020-7499 1307, famously feels more like a country pub than many pubs in the country, with its snug set of panelled rooms and high-backed wooden benches. No music and an expensive but high-quality restaurant in the back room.

Trader Vic's at the *Hilton Hotel*, Park La, W1, T020-7493 8000, with its South Island Beach bar theme and glamorous oriental waitresses, is an old-timer that still delivers a kick with its famous hot rum cocktails served in shiver-me-timbers skull mugs. Good Chinese oven-roast food too.

Piccadilly and St James's *p73, map p70*

Che, 23 St James's St, SW1, T020-7747 9380, with its sunken cigar club at the back and ground-floor bar stands out. It's a popular rendezvous for boozy businessmen but nothing like as bad as that makes it sound.

The ICA Bar, The Mall, SW1, T020-7930 2402. £1.50 day membership required, open Mon until 2300, Tue-Sat until 0100, Sun until 2230. A lively late-night hang-out for the arts brigade.
The Red Lion, 23 Crown Passage, SW1, T020-7930 4141, is a bog-standard British boozer that seems to have landed in St James's from some remote provincial outpost a long time ago, and the area would be much poorer without its reassuring cosiness, as welcoming to dogs and old men as suits and bohos. Closed Sun.

Westminster and Whitehall

p76, map p64

Albert Tavern, 52 Victoria St, SW1, T020-7222 5577, all creamy walls and etched glass.
Marquis of Granby, 41 Romney St, SW1, T020-7227 0941 (closed Sat and Sun), the closest watering hole to Conservative HQ in Smith Sq.
Red Lion, 48 Parliament St, SW1, T020-7930 5826. Popular with government pen-pushers.

Victoria, Belgravia and Pimlico

p79, map p80

Certain pubs tucked away in Belgravia stand out for their traditional atmosphere, interesting clientele and affable bar staff:
The Grenadier, 18 Wilton Row, SW1, T020-7235 3074, has honest-to-goodness old-soldiering associations and is often understandably overcrowded.
Morpeth Arms, 58 Millbank, SW1, T020-7834 6442, is quite touristy but has some outside seating on pleasant Ponsonby Pl.
The Nag's Head, 53 Kinnerton St, SW1, T020-7235 1135, is a freehouse with excellent beers, the largest and most rambling of the threesome.
The Star Tavern, 6 Belgrave Mews West, SW1, T020-7235 3019, is a rewarding find, a cosy wood-panelled place for some reasonable food, through an arch in its own little mews.

Knightsbridge, South Kensington and Hyde Park *p82, map p80*

Many of the area's old locals have been converted into restaurants or private houses, leaving the remainder to the tourists and language students. However, there are some notable exceptions:
Bunch of Grapes, 207 Brompton Rd, SW3, T020-7589 4944. A popular watering hole with a certain Victorian cosiness element.
The Enterprise, 35 Walton St, SW3, T020-7584 3148, has been turned into a swanky gastrobar with a considerable reputation for the quality of its expensive food.
Oratory, 232 Brompton Rd, SW3, T020-7584 3493, an unpretentious wine bar in an old building with seats outside and amazing toilets located in the bowels of the Brompton Oratory itself, very convenient for the VandA.
Paxton's Head, 153 Knightsbridge, SW1, T020-7589 6627, full of Edwardian splendour.

Chelsea *p85, map p80*

The loudest and busiest drinking establishments are on the King's Rd, at places like the: **Chelsea Potter**, but it's the genial popularity of those tucked away in the side streets that marks the area out as ideal territory for an enjoyable crawl.
The Surprise, 6 Christchurch Terr, T020-7349 1821, a roomy place with bare floorboards, large tables and pleasant atmosphere.

Bloomsbury and Fitzrovia *p87, map p70*

Bradley's Spanish Bar, 42-44 Hanway St, W1, T020-7636 0359, open daily until 2300, tapas until 2200, is a tiny place, a media boho favourite, with a basement dive bar and excellent jukebox on the ground floor.
Champion, 12-13 Wells St, W1, T020-7323 1228, its tiled and stained-glass interior an antique homage to winning sportsmen of all kinds.
The Duke of York, 47 Rathbone St, W1, T020-7636 7065, is a cosy little Greene King pub on the corner of the chi-chi shopping mews of Charlotte Pl.
Office, 3-5 Rathbone Pl, W1, T020-7636 1598 (open Mon-Fri 1200-0300, Sat 2130-0400; admission charged Wed £2 after 2230, Thu £5 after 2230, Fri £4 after 2230, Sat £5 after 2130, £7 after 2200 and £9 after 2300) is another large basement bar, funkily lit and always jumping late in the week.

Plough, 27 Museum St, WC1, T020-7636 7964, is larger and often less packed than the famous *Museum Tavern* at the end of the street. It too has a refurbished Victorian interior and serves reasonable food throughout the day.
Sevilla Mia, 22 Hanway St, W1, T020-7637 3756, (open Mon-Sat 1900-0100, Sun 1900-2400) is a scruffy, cosy little basement tapas bar that often has live Spanish guitar music.
The Social, 5 Little Portland St, W1, T020-7636 4992 (open Mon-Sat 1200-2400, Sun 1700-2300) is an industrialized music bar serving food upstairs, hardcore sounds and demon cocktails in the basement, popular with twenty-somethings on pre-club warm-ups.

Holborn and Clerkenwell *p89, map p94*

The Cittie of York, 22 High Holborn, WC1, T020-7242 7670, famous for its extra long bar, cubby holes for lawyers and crude wallpaintings of famous tipplers.
Duke of York, 7 Roger St, WC1, T020-7242 7230, near the Dickens' House Museum, does good real ales, has tables outside and serves up scrummy but expensive food.
Dust, 27 Clerkenwell Rd, EC1, T020-7490 5120, open until 0200 Fri, Sat, midnight on Thu, a music bar with bare wooden floorboards, basic furnishings, loud music and hip drinks.
The Jerusalem Tavern, 55 Britton St, T0200-7490 4281, the sole London outlet for St Peter's Ale from Bungay in Suffolk, full of scruffy wood-panelled Georgian charm.
Vic Naylor's, 38-40 St John St, EC1, T020-7608 2181, open until midnight Mon-Thu, till 0100 Fri and Sat, was used as the location for Sting's bar in Guy Ritchie's hit movie *Lock, Stock and Two Smoking Barrels*.
Ye Olde Cheshire Cheese, 145 Fleet St, EC4, T020-7353 6170. Ideal for secret drinking in its warren of historic wooden rooms.
Ye Olde Mitre Tavern, Ely Court, Ely Pl, EC1, T020-7405 4751, tucked away up a tiny alleyway. The last word in cosy and quaint.

The City *p90, map p94*

Ball's Brothers, 6-8 Cheapside, EC2, T020-7248 2708 (open 1130-2130 Mon-Fri). Fine wines in a genteel atmosphere as well as outside seating with views of St Paul's are the strong points here.
The Barley Mow, 50 Long La, EC1, T020-7606 6591 (open 1100-2300 Mon-Fri) is a surprisingly laid-back Hogshead pub pulling some good real ales
Black Friar, 74 Queen Victoria St, EC4, T020-7236 5474 (open Sat 1200-1500). Famous for its extraordinary carved interior and outdoor drinking area near Blackfriars Bridge.
Counting House, 50 Cornhill, EC3, T020-7283 7123 (open 1100-2300 Mon-Fri), a loud and busy Fuller's outfit in a former bank. Another pub with exceptionally grand décor.
Prism, 147 Leadenhall St, EC3, T020-7256 3888 (open 1200-2300 Mon-Fri) has expensive bottled beers and is a sophisticated place to enjoy some top-quality bar snacks.
Twentyfour, Level 24, Tower 42, 25 Old Broad St, EC2, T020-7877 2424 (1200-2300 Mon-Fri), with wide views over the City and elegant cocktails from half way up the old Nat West tower, but not at all cheap.
Vertigo, Level 42, Tower 42, 25 Old Broad St, T020-7877 7742 (1200-1500, 1700-2300 Mon-Fri), which does fine champagne and seafood, also at City prices. For even wider views from the top of the old Nat West tower.

Bankside and Southwark *p93, map p94*

Anchor Bankside, 34 Park St, SE1, T020-7407 1577, is almost too famous for its own good, a much older, very busy warren of rooms, very touristy but also with a riverside terrace tucked beneath the railway line into Cannon St.
Founders Arms, 52 Hopton St, SE1, T020-7928 1899, is an excellent Young's pub that must be laughing all the way to the bank since the opening of Tate Modern. That said, its combination of large riverside terrace with outside seating and efficient, friendly service of decent food all day and everyday deserves to be a success.
The George Inn, 77 Borough High St, SE1, T020-7407 2056, is London's last remaining coaching inn, its galleried design the inspiration for Elizabethan theatres, and now a convivial low-ceilinged series of rooms much enjoyed by both local office workers and tourists.

Nightclubs

Time Out magazine rounds up a pretty comprehensive weekly list of nightlife events, and flyers for one-offs litter fashionable stamping grounds like Exmouth Market and Hoxton Sq. Clubs aren't the only places to hear good dance music and DJs. Bars have become increasingly popular since London relaxed its entertainment licensing laws. Across London there are dozens of bars which now open until 0100 or 0200 and feature DJs and club music. Without a doubt the best place to experience this thriving bar culture is in Shoreditch, just east of central London.

333, 333 Old St, EC1, T020-7739 5949, Fri 2200-0500, Sat 2200-0500, Sun £5 before 2300, £10 after. This is perhaps the quintessential Old St clubbing experience.

Bagley's Studios, King's Cross Goods Yard, off York Way, N1, T020-7278 2777. One of the most popular, long-running clubs around.

Cargo, Rivington St, EC2, T020-7739 3440, www.cargo-london.co.uk. Popular club based in the Old St area.

The Cross, The Arches, 27-131 King's Cross Goods Yard, off York Way, N1, T020-7837 0828, www.the-cross.co.uk. For all your loud and house garage needs.

Dragon Bar, Leonard St, EC1, T020-7490 7110. Ideal surroundings for trendy young things.

Electricity Show Room, 39a Hoxton Sq, N1, T020-7739 6934. A small fashionable bar merely mins away from Old St tube station.

The End, 18 West Central St, WC2, T020-7419 9199, one of the best designed and run clubs in the capital. For black American music like hip hop and R'n'B there are a number of excellent long-running club nights.

Fabric, 77a Charterhouse St, T020-7336 8898. In the supercool Clerkenwell area of East London. The purpose-built club has 3 different dance areas and a sound system with speakers situated under the floor. London's most fashionable super club without a doubt.

Fridge, Town Hall Pde, Brixton Hill, SW2, T020-77326 5100. Banging trance and techno is the staple of Brixton's largest club, though it also hosts several popular gay nights. Admission is generally between £8 and £12.

The Ministry Of Sound,103 Gaunt St, SE1, T020-7378 6528. One of London's biggest and most famous nightclubs is just south of the river Thames in London's Elephant and Castle district. The Ministry was Britain's first ever purpose-built 'super club' and has built itself into a multinational business and the biggest dance brand name in the world. The club itself remains as popular as ever.

Woody's41-43 Woodfield Rd, W9, T020-7266 3030, www.woodysclub.com. Features young mixed crowds and a party atmosphere

Entertainment

Cinemas

Like Londoners themselves, cinemas come in every conceivable shape and size. There are small, sweaty booths at the back of seedy bookshops, and seats for nearly 2000 at the **Odeon Leicester Sq**. Expect to pay £6-10 for screenings in the West End; less before 1700. It's a good idea to book by credit card for the first weekend of a film's release. There's often a small handling fee when booking by phone.

More challenging experiences are to be found in London's excellent network of repertory cinemas which specialize in themes, seasons, festivals, and retrospectives. They aren't grouped in one nicely accessible square, but then they aren't miles away either. The atmosphere is more interesting, the buildings are more unusual and they tend to come with bookshops, superior café-bars, often a restaurant, and always a better class of audience. For more information about the **London Film Festival**, phone T020-7928 3232, or visit www.lff.org.uk, www.bfi.org.uk.

The user-friendly picture palaces with state-of-the-art sound systems and satisfyingly chunky screens congregate around Soho and the West End. Here the latest blockbusters do battle with the best of the independents. For most visitors, Leicester Sq satisfies all their needs with 3 **Odeon Cinemas**, T0870-5050007; **Warner Village West End**, T020-7437 3484 and **Empire**, T020-7437 1234 all showcasing the crop of current releases. Seats are pricier here than at local cinemas but the rumbling special effects look, sound, and feel better simply because of the scale and sophistication of the equipment. Cinemas like these hardly vary from one continent to another.

Barbican Centre, Silk St, EC2, T020-7638 8891, www.barbican.org.uk. With 3 screens offering the latest independent, art-house and blockbuster film releases.

The British Film Institute IMAX cinema/theatre 1 Charlie Chaplin Walk, South Bank, SE1, T020-7902 1234, www.bfi.org.uk/showing/imax. Quite tricky to reach, as it's marooned in the middle of a busy roundabout at Waterloo station. It's best approached from Belvedere Rd through a tunnel studded with blue stars. The screen here virtually inspires vertigo.

The Curzon Mayfair, 38 Curzon St, W1, T020-7465 8865. Probably the most comfortable cinema in London and not as expensive as you might expect for such cosseting. It generally shows middle to highbrow mainstream movies on its 1 screen.

Curzon Soho, 93-107 Shaftesbury Avenue, T020-7734 2255. Normally showcases the most recent big arthouse releases.

The Electric Cinema, Portobello Rd, T020-7229 8688. The lovely old art deco cinema on the Portobello Rd has been fully restored once again, redesigned by the team responsible for hip restaurant *192*.

The Everyman Hampstead, 1 Hollybush Vale, Hampstead, NW3, T020-7431 1777. Famous independent local cinema repeatedly saved from extinction by passionate local support. Offers a mix of mainstream and repertory films in a recently refurbished beautifully luxurious space. Standard, deluxe and 'love seats' available. Bar for drinks. Sat morning kids' club.

Institute of Contemporary Arts (known locally as the ICA), Nash House, The Mall, SW1, T020-7930 6393 for recorded information, T020-7930 3647 for credit card bookings, www.ica.org.uk. Is the place for very rare or independent films. Here you will also find cutting-edge epics projected on to screens that put one in mind of bed sheets. Size does matter. But one can go over the top.

The National Film Theatre (NFT), Belvedere Rd, South Bank, T020-7928 3535. Continues to fulfull its role as London's flagship repertory cinema, showing a truly international selection of rare, first-run and classic films. In any given week it's not unusual for the NFT's 3 auditoria to screen over 30 different movies; even more in Nov when the London Film Festival comes to town.

Notting Hill Coronet, Notting Hill Gate, W11, T020-7727 6705. One of the prettiest and architecturally most interesting local cinemas in London.

Renoir, Brunswick Centre, Brunswick Sq, WC1, T020-7837 8402. Usually foreign films, 4 screenings a day on 2 screens, excellent café and bar.

Ritzys, Brixton Oval, Coldharbour La, SW2, information T020-7737 2121; booking: T020-7733 2229. Classy 5-screen cinema offering the best of both arthouse and mainstream and something of a Brixton institution.

Screen on Baker St, 96 Baker St, NW1, T020-7935 2772. 2 screens showing first-runs from the artier side of the celluloid spectrum.

Music

Rock, jazz, and folk

If London really is the most cosmopolitan city in Europe, it shows clearly in the bewildering array of live music it has to offer. Central London presents rich pickings for the discerning live music fanatic.

The soulless, expensive and unatmospheric **Wembley Arena** apart, the live north London scene is largely centred around 3 areas – Camden Town, Kentish Town and Highbury and Islington. The Camden scene was especially potent throughout the early 80s and 90s when it gained its reputation as the hang-out of the likes of Madness and then a decade later as the creative centre of the Britpop explosion. Camden has retained its reputation and is still a hotbed of fresh and undiscovered talent, though still mainly of the Indie variety.

The 12 Bar Club, Denmark Pl, Denmark St, WC2, T020-7916 6989, tickets T020-7209 2248, presents a fusion of country, folk and funk in intimate and friendly surroundings, and a bar extension and new restaurant out front can only enhance a club whose reputation has soared in recent years making it one of London's finest.

The 100 Club, 100 Oxford St, W1, T020-7636 0933, www. the100club.co.uk. Open Mon-Thu 1930-2400, Fri 1200-1500, 2030-0200, Sat 1930-100, Sun 1930-2330. Admission £7-10. Free lunchtime jazz 1130-1500 in summer. This club is another venue with a healthy record in the music annals having staged the birth of British punk in 1976.

The Africa Centre, 38 King St, WC2, T020-7836 1973, 2130-0300, Fri-Sat, £6-8. Resembles an ill-equipped youth club on first entry, though the bona fide African bands who play most Fri are top notch.

Astoria, 157 Charing Cross Rd, T020-7434 9562. Arguably the most eminent and varied venue, despite the lack of any aesthetic value whatsoever.

Borderline, Manette St, T020-7395 0777. A club of the more intimate variety, and the bands are generally new and unheard of.

Brixton Academy, 211 Stockwell Rd, SW9. Box Office: T020-7771 2000. An old Victorian hall has a capacity that attracts the biggest of artists while not appearing over-large, and in any case it is invariably full.

Cecil Sharp House, 2 Regent's Park Rd, NW1, T020-7485 2206, open at 1900, nights vary, £3-6. Undiluted and traditional, the *Cecil Sharp* is a leader in the otherwise under-represented field of folk music and involves nigh-on mandatory audience participation.

The Jazz Café, 3 Parkway, NW1, T020-7916 6060. Presents an eclectic mix of world, funk and folk music, as well as its jazz staple, and the acts are always of a decent standard. It often pulls in the big names and the atmosphere is relaxed and enjoyable.

Kentish Town Forum, 9-17 Highgate Rd, NW5, T020-7344 0044. Undoubtedly one of the best venues in London.

Ronnie Scott's, 47 Frith St, W1, T020-7439 0747, opens at 2030, admission Mon-Thu £15, Fri and Sat £20, and often needs to be booked at least a fortnight in advance. The Mecca of the central jazz scene, still boasts some of the finest jazz in the metropolis. A night out here isn't cheap, though the quality of the music remains strong and no visiting jazz enthusiast can seriously miss paying the place a visit.

Shepherd's Bush Empire, Shepherd's Bush Green, W12, T020-7771 2000, box office open Mon-Fri 1000-1800, Sat 1200-1800. Admission £5-20. The Empire bears a strong similarity to the Brixton Academy and the Forum not only in terms of exterior and décor but also in the strength and range of what's on.

Underworld, 174 Camden High St, NW1, T020-74821932. A wide selection of mainstream and more underground rock sounds. It is one of the (comparatively) larger Camden venues, and its appearance fits its name.

The University of London Union (ULU for short), Manning Hall, Malet St, WC1, T020-7664 2000. Open 2030-2300, nights vary. Admission £5-10. Offers quality indie stock to a predominantly student audience. As the name suggests its primary role is as a student bar.

Vibe Bar, Truman's Brewery, Brick La, E1, T020-7377 2899, an East End venue for occasional live bands, and regular sound system sessions.

Classical and opera

One of the best places in Europe to hear classical music, London boasts at least 4 world class orchestras and numerous notable ensembles. The **London Symphony Orchestra**, based at the notoriously difficult-to-find **Barbican Centre**, the Barbican Hall, T020-7638 8891, www.barbican.org.uk, is arguably the pick of the bunch, though it is closely followed by the **Philharmonia** and the **London Philharmonic Orchestra** (both resident at the South Bank Centre), as well as the itinerant and slightly weaker **Royal Philharmonic Orchestra**. In addition, there are a number of venues, large and small, which hold regular concerts by internationally renowned musicians, local artists and students.

London Coliseum, St Martin's La, T020-7632 8300, www.eno.org. The Coliseum, likes to think of itself (without necessarily being so) as the antithesis of the ROH. Housing the English National Opera, its programme tends to be more ambitious, tickets are cheaper and the music is sung in English. Recently re-opened after millions of pounds worth of refurbishment.

Royal Albert Hall, Kensington Gore, SW7, T020-7589 8212. Is home to the world-famous Sir Henry Wood Promenade Concerts (Proms for short), the annual classical feast running from Jul-Sep with music ranging from the well-loved to the new and cutting-edge. Seats can be booked in advance, but to truly sample the essence of the season try slumming it with one of the dirt-cheap Arena standing tickets. But it is a grand setting for just about any and every type of entertainment spectacular from high to lowbrow.

Royal Opera House, Bow St, WC2, T020-7240 1200, box office/information T020-7304 4000, www.royaloperahouse.org. Despite the Royal Opera House's rather stuffy and conservative reputation, the old place appears to have loosened up a touch since its long-awaited refurbishment. Prices remain exorbitant (up to £115), though there are seats available in the gods for under £20. There is also a restaurant and bar in which to while away the day, and tours are available for the curious.

South Bank Centre, T020-7960 4242, is really 3 venues in one: The massive **Royal Festival Hall** holds large-scale symphonic orchestral and choral concerts. The slightly smaller **Queen Elizabeth Hall**. And smaller still the **Purcell Room** sticks to chamber music, though the QEH can also stage opera.

Wigmore Hall, 36 Wigmore St, W1, T020-7935 2141, www.wigmore-hall.org.uk. One of London's premier small concert halls, purpose-built in 1901 by the piano-maker Bechstein, stages a huge variety of world-class performances of chamber music and song, lunchtimes at 1300 and evenings at 1930 Mon-Sat, 1600 and 1900 Sun, and popular hour-long coffee concerts at 1130 on Sun, tickets £8-30.

Theatre

The best place to discover the latest on what's just opened where are the reviews and listings in *Time Out*, available weekly in central London on Tue.

The phenomenal vitality of the theatre in London continues to amaze Londoners and visitors alike. From record-breaking blockbusting to the tiniest two-handers in the back rooms of pubs, almost every day of the year except Sun, the city gears up for an astonishing variety of stage performances on a scale unmatched anywhere else on the planet.

The heart of all this activity is still very much the West End, where about 40 venerable old theatres put on a surprisingly diverse range of shows. Long criticized for pandering to the bottom denominator with a numbing array of tacky musicals, the competition for audiences has become so fierce that producers are now often much more adventurous. Many of the smaller theatres and production houses categorized by *Time Out* as 'Off West End' are the places to take the pulse of current theatre practice, generally staging more challenging work. A very small selection of the city's major players are listed below.

Meanwhile the Fringe embraces anything and everything from large scale touring productions at the Bloomsbury Theatre to obscure one-offs mounted above a pub in north Clapham.

The official half-price ticket booth is on the south side of Leicester Sq. Run by the **Society of London Theatre (SOLT)**, T020-7557 6700, it offers discounted tickets, first-come-first- served so there's usually a queue

Donmar Warehouse, 41 Earlham St, WC2, T020-7369 1732. The most innovative, fashionable and exciting small-scale theatre in the West End, where Sam *American Beauty* Mendes still directs occasional productions, as well as welcoming top-class touring companies. Seats are usually at a premium and need to be booked well in advance.

Garrick Theatre, Charing Cross Rd, WC2, T020-7494 5085. Also built in 1889, famous for a long run of *No Sex Please We're British*, and Stephen Daldry's striking production of JB Priestley's *An Inspector Calls*.

Gielgud Theatre, T020-7494 5065. Built in 1906, now usually shows straight plays, casting as the name suggests (was called *The Globe*).
Globe Theatre, see p97.
Haymarket Theatre Royal, Haymarket, SW1, T020-7930 8800. There's been a theatre on this site since 1720, famous for staging Oscar Wilde's *Ideal Husband* and in 1914 the first London production of Ibsen's *Ghosts*.
The London Palladium, Argyll St, W1, T020-7494 5400, a vast entertainment house since 1910 that now specializes in musical spectaculars.
Lyric Shaftesbury, T020-7494 5045. Built in 1888, famous in the 50s for staging plays by TS Eliot and later Alan Bennett, now tends towards West End dramas and star vehicles.
Old Vic, The Cut, SE1, T020-7928 7616. Built in 1817 as Royal Coburg Theatre, and later known as the 'Bucket of Blood' because of the cheap melodramas staged here, the *Old Victoria* theatre was taken over for 25 years from 1912 by Lilian Baylis, the founder of Sadler's Wells. In 1962, it became the birthplace of the National Theatre Company under the directorship of Laurence Olivier. More recently, following sympathetic restoration by Canadian Ed Mirvish, the theatre was home to Sir Peter Hall's own company, unfortunately a short-lived experiment. It narrowly avoided being turned into a lap-dancing venue and is now run by a board of affectionate trustees headed up by Kevin Spacey.
Palace Theatre, T020-7434 0909. Built as an opera house in 1888, staged the *Sound of Music* in the 60s, *Jesus Christ Superstar* in the 70s, and, since 1985, *Les Miserables*.
Queen's Theatre, T020-7494 5040. Built as twin to *The Globe*, now stages a wide mix of classics, musicals and new plays.
The Royal Court Theatre, Sloane Sq, SW1, T020-7565 5000, most famous for starting the 'kitchen sink' school of drama under George Devine in the 50s with plays like Osborne's *Look Back in Anger* (although it had already carved out a reputation for radicalism by staging the first productions of many of GB Shaw's plays). It has recently been fully refurbished and still pursues an adventurous policy of commissioning new writing. The refurbishment includes an atmospheric and happening restaurant and bar in the basement (T020-7565 5061).
The Royal Court Theatre Upstairs stages experimental small-scale work (same box office as main theatre).
Royal National Theatre, South Bank, T020-7452 3000. The foundation stone was laid in 1951, but Denys Lasdun's terraced concrete ziggurat only opened in 1976, the new home for the National Theatre Company under the directorship of Peter Hall. It has 3 stages: the *Olivier*, the largest, with an open stage, steeply raked auditorium, and massive revolve. For some productions, the theatre has been brilliantly converted into a vast theatre in the round. The *Lyttelton*, slightly smaller, is the most traditional, with the option of a proscenium arch. The *Cottesloe*, round the side, is a much more intimate studio theatre for experimental productions.
Sadler's Wells and **Lilian Baylis Theatre**, Rosebery Av, EC1, T020-7863 8000, (nearest tube Angel Islington). Superb state-of-the-art new North London base for large scale dance and opera, and a smaller studio space for adventurous new work, both sadly struggling financially.
The Soho Theatre and Writer's Centre, 21 Dean St, W1, T020-7478 0100, is an excellent brand new base for new playwriting in the West End.
Theatre Royal Drury Lane, Catherine St, WC2, T020-7494 5000. One of London's oldest theatres, founded in 1663, managed by David Garrick in the 18th century, and rebuilt in the early 19th century after 2 disastrous fires. Now usually stages large-scale musicals. Enjoyable backstage tours, which involve actors encouraging audience participation, tell the history of the theatre. Taking about 1 hr, they are at 1230, 1415, 1645 on Mon, Tue, Thu and Fri, and at 1100 and 1300 on Wed, Sat matinee days. £7.50 per person, bookable on box office number.
Young Vic, 66 The Cut, SE1, T020-7928 6363. The best middle-scale experimental theatre in the country.

Shopping

If you can't buy it in London, you can't buy it anywhere. The difficulty is knowing where to begin... A very broad summary of shopping areas in London might look something like this: **Oxford St** for department stores and High St names; **Tottenham Court Rd** for computers and electronics; **Charing Cross Rd** and **Bloomsbury** for books new and secondhand; **Covent Garden** for clothes, specialist foods and gifts; **Bond St** for high fashion and expensive jewellery; **Knightsbridge** for more high fashion and *Harrods*; and **Chelsea** or **Notting Hill** for one-offs and independents. Listed below are some decent starting points for a shopping expedition.

Books

Borders Books Music and Café, 203-207 Oxford St, W1, T020-7292 1600. Mon-Sat until 2300 and on Sun until 1800. London's first book megastore, which holds a huge stock of books and music, and there's a decent café on the second floor with big windows overlooking the street. Charing Cross Rd north of Cambridge Circus has several large shops for new books.
Foyles, 113-119 Charing Cross Rd, T020-7437 5660. 1000-2000 and also open Sun. There's an inimitable, rambling and extraordinary range of new titles on 4 floors. Every fairly recently published book could well be here somewhere, but it may take some finding.
Hatchard's, 187 Piccadilly, T020-7439 9921, 0930-1830 Mon-Sat, 1200-1800 Sun, is now owned by the same company as *Waterstone's*, retains an independent choice of titles along with its old-fashioned woody and winding layout.
Waterstone's, 203 Piccadilly, T020-7851 2400. 1000-2200 Mon-Sat, 1200-1800 Sun. The biggest bookshop in London is which also claims to be the largest bookstore in Europe, this conversion of the old Simpson's store is a bright, inspiring place to wander around, with a café, restaurant or bar to take the book of your choice.

Specialist bookshops

A Moroni and Son, 68 Old Compton St, T020-7437 2847, is a large international newsagent, open until 2000 or 2100 Thu, Fri.
Cinema Bookshop, 13-14 Great Russell St, T020-7637 0206, has a vast range of new and out-of-print books on the movies.
Daunt's Books for Travellers, 83 Marylebone High St, T020-7224 2295, is one of London's most charming travel bookshops, its galleried space stacked with just about every conceivable new title to do with travel as well as carrying an excellent stock of secondhand.
European Bookshop, 5 Warwick St, Soho, T020-7734 5259, has a wide range of European language books.
Gay's the Word, 66 Marchmont St, T020-7278 7654, is one of London's premier gay and lesbian bookshops.
Grant and Cutler, 55-57 Great Marlborough St, T020-7734 2012, is one of the most famous foreign-language bookshops in the city.
Mysteries, 9-11 Monmouth St, T020-7240 3688, stocks titles on anything New Age.
Samuel French's Theatre Bookshop, 52 Fitzroy St, T020-7387 9373, is the destination par excellence for theatrical bibliophiles, and stocks just about every new play in print.
Stanfords, 12-14 Long Acre, T020-7632 8920 or T020-7836 1321, map makers and sellers since 1900, with a comprehensive stock of maps, travel guides and travel literature.

Secondhand and rare books

Charing Cross Rd and Bloomsbury are the best places in London to rummage around for out-of-print, remaindered or secondhand books.
Any Amount of Books, 62 Charing Cross Rd, T020-7836 3697, is a rambling treasure trove of battered secondhand.
G Heywood Hill, 10 Curzon St, T020-7629 0647, a long-established upper-crust bookseller, has a good stock of rare and secondhand books, knowledgeable staff and charming premises.
Henry Pordes Books, T020-7836 9031, is another good general secondhand, specializing in art, literature and cinema.

The Museum Bookshop, 36 Great Russell St, T020-7580 4086, is a charming and scruffy establishment, stocking new and out-of-print books, with archaeology, ancient history, and conservation as strong points.
Unsworths, 12 Bloomsbury St, T020-7436 9836 (open until Mon-Sat 2000, Sun until 1900) is very popular with students for secondhand and remaindered humanities titles.

Clothing

Head for **West Soho** for the latest street fashions, at shops like:
Beau Monde, 43 Lexington St, W1, T020-7734 6563.
Jones, 13 Floral St, T020-7240 8312, is a post-industrialized place for their own-label menswear as well as styles by Miu Miu, and Helmut Lang.
Plum, 79 Berwick St, T020-7734 0812, for skateboard stuff, and jeans.

In **Covent Garden**, most of the big designers have congregated on Floral St:
Question Air, 38 Floral St, T020-7836 822 stocks eccentric female fashione lines by the likes of Shiren Guild, Issey Miyake, and Ghost.
Stephen Jones Millinery, 36 Great Queen St, T020-7242 0770, has an excellent array of extraordinary designer hats for every occasion.

Most of the more affordable fashion shops can be found on the streets north of Long Acre, especially on Neal St, Earlham St and in Shorts Gardens. On Neal St the shops are a little more upmarket:
O'Neill, 9-15 Neal St, T020-7836 7686, bring surfing and skiing chic off the boards and pistes and on to the streets.

Crossing Neal St, Shorts Gardens continues the preoccupation with own-label urban style:
Boxfresh, 2 Shorts Gardens, T020-7240 4742.

All along **Old** and **New Bond streets**, many of the big names' shops are attractions in themselves:
Gucci, 33 Old Bond St, T020-7235. Chances are that if you don't know what these kind of shops are stocking, you won't want to afford them.
Prada,15 Old Bond St, T020-7647 5000, has a gallery-style store.
Versace, at 34-36 Old Bond St, T020-7499 1862, is a massive over-the-top, three-storey shopping palace.

Generally speaking the high fashion outlets and designer jewellery concerns around Knightsbridge are less concentrated but even more numerous than in Mayfair. On **Sloane St** can be found the likes of: *Chanel*, *Dior*, *D&G*, *Armani*, *Gucci*, *Hermes*, *Valentino* and *Starewski*.

Marginally more affordable and youth-orientated are the shops on **Brompton Rd** like:
The Library, 268 Brompton Rd, T020-7589 6569, kind of Issy Miyake meets gay combat gear.
Whistles, 303 Brompton Rd, T020-7823 9134, for own-label and left-field women's designerwear.

Beauchamp Pl (pronounced *Beecham*) is also lined with upmarket boutiques, including the world-famous women's lingerie designer **Janet Reger**, 2 Beauchamp Pl, T020-7584 9360.

In **Chelsea**, shops worth investigating might include:
Daisy and Tom, 181 King's Rd, T020-7352 5000, stocking tasteful toys and clothes for little Jeremies and Lucindas.
R Soles, 109a King's Rd, T020-7351 5520, for their way-out selection of cowboy boots and 'western' footwear.
The World's End Shop, 430 Kings Rd, T020-7352 6551, the turquoise number with the clock going backwards, once Vivienne Westwood's shop *Sex* is still hers, now stocking a wide variety of her designer clothes.

Secondhand and discounted designer clothes

Monmouth St in Covent Garden is the place to go for secondhand and discounted designer clothes, sometimes at bargain prices:
Cenci, 31 Monmouth St, WC2, T020-7836 1400, have long been peddling an affordable profusion of secondhand Italian styles.
The Loft, 35 Monmouth St, WC2, T020-7240 3807, a good first stop.
Pop Boutique, 6 Monmouth St, WC2, T020-7497 5262. For more retro fashions.

Department stores

Harrods, 87-135 Brompton Rd, Knightsbridge, T020-7730 1234, www.harrods.com, Mon-Sat 1000-1900. The smartest and most famous department store in the city, possibly the world, not just for its palatial food hall but for any kind of consumer durable. Their stock is still admirable too but considering the mark-up is generally better left on the peg or shelf where it always looks as if it belongs. Service goes out of the window during the Sales every Jan and Jul, when the initial scrum beggars belief.

Harvey Nichols, 109-125 Knightsbridge, T020-7235 5000, www.harveynichols.com, Mon, Tue, Sat 1000-1900 on Wed, Thu, Fri til 2000, Sun 1200-1800. Knightsbridge's shrine to haute couture is Harvey Nicks for short to the darlings that would simply die if this department store closed down. It too has unseemly sales every Jan and Jul.

John Lewis, 278-306 Oxford St, T020-7629 7711, has long been proudly claiming to be 'never knowingly undersold': if you find something here on sale for less elsewhere, they'll refund the difference.

Marks and Spencer, 458 Oxford St, T020-7935 7954. M&S still sets a nationwide benchmark for affordable high-quality clothes and food.

Selfridges, 400 Oxford St, T020-7629 1234. It has customer services that are legendary and several hectic floors of the latest fashions. On the ground floor, beyond the inevitable perfumery (in pole position because it makes more money per sq ft than any other department), you'll find fashion accessories, wines and spirits, jewellery, toiletries, a cigar shop and menswear. At the back, the food hall is an extraordinary gastrodome of fresh and potted delicacies, including an oyster bar.

Food and drink

Cadenheads Whisky Shop, 3 Russell St, T020-7379 4640, a connoisseur of the finest malts and blends.

Carluccios, 28a Neal St, T020-7240 1487. A supremely elegant and expensive Italian deli, with a restaurant for fungiphiles next door: The *Neal St Restaurant*, 26 Neal St, T020-7836 8368.

Fortnum and Mason, 181 Piccadilly, T020-7734 8040. 1000-1830 Mon-Sat www.fortnumandmason.co.uk, even just for a glimpse of its theatrical way with shelf-stacking. Most famous for its own-label tea and fabulous food hall, it also sells traditional menswear, as well as china and cookware, and antiques on the 4th floor. On the same floor, *St James's Restaurant* is the place for full English teas while the Patio restaurant on the mezzanine at the back of the ground floor has a less formal atmosphere and a champagne and oyster bar.

Neal's Yard Dairy, 19 Shorts Gardens, T020-7379 7646, for its exceptional range of home-grown British and Irish cheeses.

Portwine, 24 Earlham St, T020-7836 2353, an old-fashioned shop with a wide assortment of pies, sausages and other meaty fare.

Gifts

Covent Garden is a good destination for gift-shopping:

Benjamin Pollock's Toy Shop, 44 The Market, T020-7379 7866, specializes in traditional wooden toys, as well as toy theatres, pop-up books and other essentials for an old-fashioned childhood.

The Kite Store, 48 Neal St, T020-7836 1666, has long been famous for its comprehensive stock of anything that flies high or low.

On Show, 19 Shorts Gardens, WC2, T020-7379 4454, is an Aladdin's cave of gifts from around the world, including bonsai trees, oriental lamps and Romanian shawls. The shops in the old Apple Market itself, in the central covered market of the Piazza, also make for good browsing, although many are fairly expensive.

Jewellery

Agatha, 4 South Molton St, T020-7495 2779, is the local branch of the famous French chain, for less expensive designer jewellery.

Asprey and Garrard, 167 New Bond St, T020-7493 6767, is slightly more affordable, with stationery.

Cartier 175-176 New Bond St, T020-7493 6962. Dazzling rocks in a classic environment.

Electrum Gallery, 21 South Molton St, T020-7629 6325, curates a wide selection of

international contemporary jewellery makers including big names like Wendy Ramshaw, Gerda Flöckinger, and Tone Vigeland.
Tiffany and Co, 25 Old Bond St, T020-7409 2790. Old-fashioned interior with high prices.

Markets

Those who love rooting around for a bargain won't be disappointed by London's markets. Everyone has their own favourite, but here are a few of the best:
Borough Market, Southwark St, 020-7407 1002. Daily wholesale fruit and veg market with specialist and organic food retailers on Fri and Sat 0800-1800.
Brick Lane, E1, Sun 0700-1300. Mainly second-hand, including clothes, bric-a-brac, books, records and some furniture.
Camden Market, Camden High St, NW1, Sat and Sun 0900-1700. Everything under the sun, with an accent on techno-clubby gear and retro clothing.
Greenwich, SE5, Sun 0900-1700. Retro clothes, bric-a-brac, antiques, more for the retro purists than Camden.
Portobello Road, Notting Hill, W11. Fri and Sat 0800-1800. Antiques at the beginning, then retro clothes, records, junk and books. Prices drop as you head into Golborne Rd.
Spitalfields Market, Commercial St, E1. Open Sun 1100-1500. Clothes, books, paintings, organic food, jewellery, antiques, bric-a-brac.

Miscellaneous

Anything Left-Handed, 57 Brewer St, T020-7437 3910, selling exactly what its name suggests.
Bliss Chemist, 5-6 Marble Arch, T020-7723 6116, is a late-night pharmacy open until midnight throughout the year.
Hamleys 188-196 Regent St, T020-7494 2000, still leads the way for toy shops the world over but can become nightmarishly busy. Its famous window displays highlight aspects of its staggering stock, none of which comes cheap.
Smythsons, 40 New Bond St, T020-7629 8558, are the last word in traditional British bespoke stationery and writing accessories.
Sotheby's at 34-35 New Bond St, T020-7293 5000. One of London's busiest and grandest auction houses. It has been bringing the gavel down on rare and expensive objets d'art since 1744. It's open for valuations from 0900-1630 Mon-Fri, or you can pick up a catalogue (from £10) and view the current sale. Call in advance to find out what's going... going..., before it's gone. There's also a good bookshop (T020-7293 5856, 0930-1730, sometimes Sun if there's a sale), and a café.
Vintage Magazine Store, 39-43 Brewer St, T020-7439 8525. Also stocks a wide range of old movie posters and postcards.

Music

HMV in the Trocadero, 18 Coventry St, T020-7439 0447 and 150 Oxford St, T020-7631 3423. Open until 2400 Mon-Sat, 1100-1800 Sun. A large branch of the chain store, stocking everything from classical to hip-hop. Marginally more hip that the *Virgin Megastore* and easier to find your way around.
Rough Trade Shop, 130 Talbot Rd, London, W11 1JA, T020 7229 8541. An independent record store that's well worth the visit for anything indie or interesting including their own independent 'Rough Trade' label.
Virgin Megastore,14-16 Oxford St, T020-7631 1234, sets the tone for this stretch of the street with 4 loud floors selling every multimedia music format you could wish for, as well as miniscooters, merchandising and computer games.

Sports

Blacks 10/11 Holborn, T020-7401 5681, is a large branch of the outdoors shop.
Field and Trek, 105 Baker St, T020-7224 0049, was the first and largest branch in London of the expert mountaineering and hill walking chain. Northwest of the Marylebone Rd, in Lisson Grove, Church St has one of London's lesser-known but still lively fruit 'n' veg and clothes markets, at its best on Sat.
JJB Sports, 301-309 Oxford St, T020-7409 2619, is a sportswear superstore carrying the lastest lines from just about every big name except Fila for some reason.
Lillywhites, 24-36 Lower Regent St, T020-7930 3181. Open until 2000 Mon-Fri, 1000-1900 Sat, 1100-1700 Sun. One of the largest and most famous sports shops in Europe with 5 floors carrying all the big brands.

Niketown London, 236 Oxford St, T020-7612 0800. Mon-Wed 1000-1900, Thu 1000-2100, Fri and Sat 1000-2000, Sun 1200-1800. Landed on Oxford Circus in Jul 1999, a high-tech temple to all things Nike, the only one in the UK. In the 'launch area', a portentous inscription reads: 'To all athletes and the dreams they chase, we dedicate Niketown London'. Beyond, a multimedia 'core' claims to offer an 'in-depth look at athletes and product'. It's an introduction to the surreal presentation on 3 spacious floors of some heavily branded sportswear and accessories, all protected by 4 miked-up bouncers on the door. Whatever you may think of the Nike philosophy, the branding here is loud and aggressive.

Activities and tours

Boating
Popular on the lakes in Hyde Park, Regent's Park and Battersea Park.

Cricket
The definitive summer sport, is played from Apr-Sep. London's 2 main grounds are the **Oval**, SE11, T020-7582 7764, and **Lord's Cricket Ground**, NW8, T020-7432 1066. Test Match tickets usually need to be bought well in advance, but you should be able to get seats for county matches on the day.

Football
For Londoners, football (soccer) is still the most popular spectator sport, at least for men, that is. Tickets to see Premier League London clubs like **Arsenal**, **Chelsea**, **Tottenham Hotspurs** or West Ham can be pretty hard to come by; for information try: **Football Association**, T020-7262 4542, the **Premier League**, T020-7298 1600 or the **Football League**, T01772-325800, for games in one of the other 3 League divisions. Tickets for Premiership matches start at about £20.

Greyhound racing
Makes for a fun and different night out. Most tracks hold 2 or 3 meetings a week and the first race is usually at around 1930. Most easily accessible from central London are the tracks at:
Walthamstow, Chingford Rd, E4, T020-8531 4255 (Walthamstow Central tube), and **Wimbledon**, Plough La, SW19, T020-8946 8000 (Wimbledon Park tube). Both have restaurant and bar facilities.

Horse racing
You'll need to travel a bit further to put your money on the horses. The nearest racetracks to the capital are a shortish train ride away at Ascot, T01344 622211; **Epsom**, T01372-726311; **Sandown Park**, T01372-463072; and **Windsor**, T01753-865234. Admission prices for the general public start at about £6.

Horse riding
Hyde Park, T020-7723 2813, £30 per hr (with an escort). You can also ride in Richmond Park and on **Hampstead Heath**.

Indoor sports
Badminton, squash and swimming are available at public sport and leisure centres. The local tourist board will tell you which is the nearest, or you can call **Sportsline**, T020-7222 8000. Most leisure centres have fitness rooms and gym facilities and run martial arts, yoga, exercise and other classes.

Ice skating and dry slope skiing
For the first time, in 2000 winter open-air ice skating was possible for a couple of months in the 18th-century courtyard at **Somerset House** (see p66). Tickets cost £6 and £4 for children including skate hire. It is likely to become a regular feature, but check first on T020-7845 4600. **The Broadgate Ice Rink**, near Liverpool St tube station, T020-7505 4068, is another open-air option (open until Apr). Entry costs £5 (plus £2 skate hire) and £3 for children (plus £1 for skates).

There are also year-round indoor ice rinks at **Broadgate**, T020-7505 4068, Liverpool St tube. **Leisurebox**, T020-7229 0172, Queensway tube.
Streatham, T020-8769 7771, Streatham Station, South London.
For dry slope skiing try **Alexandra Palace Ski Centre**, T020-8888 2284; **Crystal Palace Ski School**, T020-8778 0131; **Hillingdon Ski Centre**, Uxbridge, T01895-58506; **Profiles Ski Centre**, Orpington, T01689-78239; **Woolwich Ski Slope Army Barracks**, T020-8317 1726.

Oxford and Cambridge Boat Race

You can witness this traditional contest for supremacy between England's 2 most famous universities from either bank of the Thames along the whole length of the course, but the best viewpoints are Putney Bridge, Putney Embankment and Bishops Park at the start of the race, Hammersmith and Barnes in the middle, and Dukes Meadows and Chiswick Bridge at the finish.

Rugby

Twickenham Rugby Football Ground, T020-8744 3111 (ticket information line), hosts the main national and international matches. The season last from early Sep-Apr (although a few matches may run into May).

Running

Flora London Marathon (26 miles from Greenwich and Blackheath to The Mall), in Apr each year. Serious runners wanting to enter should apply to enter a ballot. Entry forms are distributed in *Marathon News* (a free magazine available in specialist sports stores). Overseas visitors wanting to receive copies of the entry form should send a self-addressed envelope (stating the number you require), with 2 international reply coupons to: Overseas Entry Co-ordinator, 91 Walkden Rd, Walkden, Manchester, M28 7BQ, England.

Swimming

Outdoor swimming is available in the summer only in **Hyde Park**, Serpentine Lido, T020-7298 2100; **Hampstead Heath Ponds**, T020-7485 449, entry free; **Brockwell Park**, Evian Lido, T020-7274 3088; **Richmond Pool**, on the Park, T020-8940 0561.

Tennis

If you want Centre Court or Court 1 seats for **Wimbledon** you'll need to contact the All England Lawn Tennis Club, Church Rd, SW19, T020-8946 2244, at least 6 months in advance. Otherwise you can get there early and queue on the day (some people camp out overnight) to watch play on the outside courts. Determined fans can usually buy cut-price returned tickets later in the afternoon for some Centre Court action.

Transport tours

Big Bus Company, 48 Buckingham Palace Rd, T020-7233 9533, www.bigbus.co.uk. Daily sightseeing tours from hop-on, hop-off, open-top double-decker buses. Tickets include a free river cruise and a choice of walking tours. The commentary is live, or else digitally recorded in 12 languages. £15, £6 children.
Black Taxi tours of London, T020-7289 4371, www.blacktaxitours.co.uk. Sightseeing tours in licensed taxi cabs. Commentary from trained London 'cabbies'. 2-hr day and night tours. Pick-up and return to hotel. Costs £70 for up to 5 people.
Evans Evans Tours, T020-7950 1777, www.evansevans.co.uk. Half-and full-day coach tours of London with stop-offs at key sights. Prices start at £17 (£14.50 for children between 3 and 16). Sightseeing trips to major tourist destinations outside London also available, as are tours in Japanese and Spanish.
London Frog Tours, T020-7928 3132, www.frogtours.com. Starting at County Hall, these 'road and river' tours of London last 80 mins in yellow amphibious vehicles. The Frogs 'splash down' into the Thames at Lacks Dock Vauxhall and the river part of the tour lasts about 30 mins. Tours cost £12, £9 for children; family tickets are also available. Driver-guides operating general and special-interest tours for individuals and small groups in and around London are another option.
The Driver-Guides Association (DGA), T020-8874 2745, www.driver-guides.org.uk, can provide details of professional blue-badge driver-guides throughout the country.

Walking tours

Embarking on a tour is an excellent way to get to know London whether it be on your own with a map or book or as part of a group on an organized tour. More and more companies are running these tours, either pre-booked or regular, turn-up-and-go walks that leave from the same place at a fixed time every week. There are dozens of special-interest walks, from Dickens and Jack the Ripper, to Bohemians and Bluestockings, to Bishops, Brothels and the Bard. Most walks last between 1 hr 30 mins and 2 hrs and cost about £5. Also try www.london.walks.com, for further information.

The Original London Walks, T020-7624 3978, F7625 1932, www.london.walks.com, have over 40 walks to choose from. Other enjoyable walks, if the weather is good, are around London's many parks, gardens and cemeteries. One of these is the circular *Diana Princess of Wales Memorial Walk*, a 7-mile route through St James's Park, Green Park, Hyde Park and Kensington Gardens. For more information: T020-7298 2000.

Water sports

For watersports such as sailing, canoeing, rowing and Chinese dragon-boat racing (no power sports), contact
Docklands Sailing & Watersports Centre, T020-7537 2626 (Crossharbour and London Arena DLR station).

Transport

Bicycle

Cycle lanes are still not the norm in London and, compared with some European or Scandinavian cities, London is not an easy ride for cyclists. Make sure you always wear a helmet and never leave your bike unlocked. A 1000-mile cycle network is planned for the city and several organizations and direct action groups are continually pressing for improvements and to convince the Greater London Authority of the importance of making London more bicycle friendly. The best known is the *London Cycling Campaign*, T020-7928 7220 (Mon-Fri, 1400-1700 only), F020-7928 2318, www.lcc.org.uk.
Their magazine *London Cyclist*, publishes a diary of rides and related events for all London. They also publish the *Brand New Central London Map* (£4.95), a cycling map with traffic-free routes, safe cycle crossings and bike shops. Cycling.uk.com. is a cycling information station with over 200 links to other useful sites.

Boat

Daily services operate from most central London piers. Riverboats travel to and from Greenwich and the Thames Barrier in the east, and as far as Hampton Court in the west. There are over 20 piers along this stretch of the Thames and apart from Hampton Court Palace and the sights at Greenwich, the river gives access to Kew Gardens, Richmond Park and many of the central London attractions. Tickets for most trips can be bought at the pier or, in some cases, on the boat.

Bus

There's generally a bus route near you wherever you are in the city and buses are a great way of getting to know London, especially from the top deck, but traffic congestion is a serious problem in London and bus journeys often take longer than the tube. Daytime buses, like the London Underground, run until about 0030. After that, an extensive system of night buses takes over. Most areas of Greater London are within easy reach of at least 1 night bus service. All night bus route numbers start with the letter 'N'. Most of the central London night buses pass through Trafalgar Sq. The standard single Zone 1 day and night bus fare is £1.

Night buses

Night buses run hourly along more than 50 routes from about 2300 until dawn; most pass through Trafalgar Square, a good place to head for if you are unsure of which bus you need. The **Central London Bus Guide**, which includes a night bus map, is provided free at Travel Information Centres. Alternatively, call **London Transport Information**, T020-7222 1234 (lines are very busy). The following is a selection of 10 popular routes:

N5 Trafalgar Sq – Hampstead – Hendon – Edgware
N9 Aldwych – Trafalgar Sq – Hammersmith – Putney – Richmond – Kingston
N11 Liverpool St – Trafalgar Sq – Fulham – Hammersmith – Wembley
N12 Notting Hill Gate – Trafalgar Sq – Elephant – Camberwell – Peckham – Dulwich
N14 Tottenham Court Rd – Piccadilly Circus – Fulham – Putney – Roe Hampton
N31 Camden Town – Kilburn – Kensington – Earl's Court – Chelsea – Clapham Junction
N52 Victoria – Trafalgar Sq – Notting Hill – Ladbroke Grove – Willesden
N97 Trafalgar Square – Earl's Court – Hammersmith – Hounslow – Heathrow Airport
N159 Marble Arch – Trafalgar Sq – Brixton – Streatham – Croydon – New Addington
N207 Holborn – Shepherd's Bush – Ealing – Southall – Uxbridge

Car

If you are only planning to spend a short time in London, don't bother hiring a car, it's not worth it. Traffic-clogged central London is still a nightmare to drive in, despite the newly introduced congestion charges of £5 per day (congestion charging area marked out with a white 'C' on a red background on the road and on signs) Mon-Fri 0700 and 1830. Indeed, Londoners themselves tend to use public transport during the day, saving their cars for night and weekends. Apart from the heavy traffic and complicated web of one-way streets, parking is hard to find and exorbitantly expensive. The charge can be paid on the day at any one of 300 Paypoint-equipped shops, petrol stations or car parks until 2200. Failure to pay before 2400 incurs another £5 penalty fee, after which time the driver owes Transport for London £80. Call T0845-9001234 for more details, or look up www.cclondon.com. Beware of parking illegally too, as you are very likely to get a ticket or else be clamped or towed away and impounded (in which case you should call T020-7747 4747). This can set you back anywhere between £60 and £205.

Taxi

The famous London black cabs are almost as much of an institution as the old, double-decker buses. Licensed cabs can be hailed in the street when the yellow 'For Hire' sign is displayed; they all have meters which start ticking as soon as you get in, and fares increase by the min thereafter. Surcharges are added late at night and for luggage or extra passengers. Most 'cabbies' will expect a tip of 10-15%. Any comments should be made to the Public Carriage Office, T020- 7230 1631, whilst lost property should be reported to T020-7833 0996 (make a note of your taxi's licence number and the driver's badge number). **24-hour Radio Taxis**, T020-7272 0272.
As well as black cabs there are also regular taxis, which are known as minicabs. It is advisable to book these directly from the cab office, as there are many unlicensed cab drivers operating in Central London. Minicabs can be more economical, especially during busy times, as they charge a flat fee for the journey instead of using a meter, but you will need to know the going rate for a particular journey in order to avoid being ripped off. A journey from central London to somewhere in the tube's Zone 2 area will cost from around £15-20 in the evening.

Tube

The London Underground, or tube, is the fastest way of getting around town (although that's not saying much) and most Londoners use it. The 12 lines are colour coded, the map is easy to follow and the system is relatively straightforward to use. However, it is worth avoiding during rush hr (0800-0930 and 1700-1830) if at all possible. Services run from 0530 until just after midnight. Fewer trains run on Sun and public holidays. The underground is divided into 6 fare zones, with Zone 1 covering central London. Travel between 2 stations in Zone 1 costs £2 (child 60p); a journey crossing into Zone 2 will cost £2.20 (child 80p). Anyone planning to make more than 2 journeys in 1 day will save money by buying a Day Travelcard £4.30, Weekend Travelcard £6.40, or Family Travelcard £2.80 per adult and 80p per child for 1 day's travel.

Directory

Embassies

Australia, T020-7379 4334.
Canada, T020-7258 6600.
Denmark; T020-7235 1255.
France, T020-7073 1400.
Germany, T020-7824 1300.
Italy, T020-7312 2200.
Japan, T020-7465 6500.
Netherlands, T020-7590 3200.
New Zealand, T020-79308422.
South Africa, T020-74517299.
Spain, T020-7589 8989.
Sweden, T020-7917 6400.
Switzerland, T020-7616 6000.
USA, T020-7499 9000.

Hospitals

Charing Cross Hospital, Fulham Palace Rd, T020-8846 1234.
Guy's Hospital, St Thomas St, T020-7955 5000.
St Thomas's Hospital, Lambeth Palace Rd, T020-7928 9292.

Internet

There are internet cafés all over London where you can acces the internet and pick up your email.
easyEverything, probably the biggest and cheapest option (access from £1), has 5 locations in central London: 9-16 Tottenham Court Rd (Oxford St end); 7 Strand (Trafalgar Sq end); 358 Oxford St (opposite Bond St tube station); 9-13 Wilton Rd, Victoria (opposite main line station); 160-166 Kensington High St.
For other options, www.queenscene.com, has a directory of about 70 cybercafés in different areas of the capital listed by area, postcode or nearest tube station. Local **libraries** often provide cheap or free internet access.

Language schools

English in Britain website, www.englishinbritain.co.uk, lists the accredited schools and colleges in London and the rest of the UK. From the website you'll be able to search the database, contact the schools and colleges, visit their websites, and book a course.

The Southeast

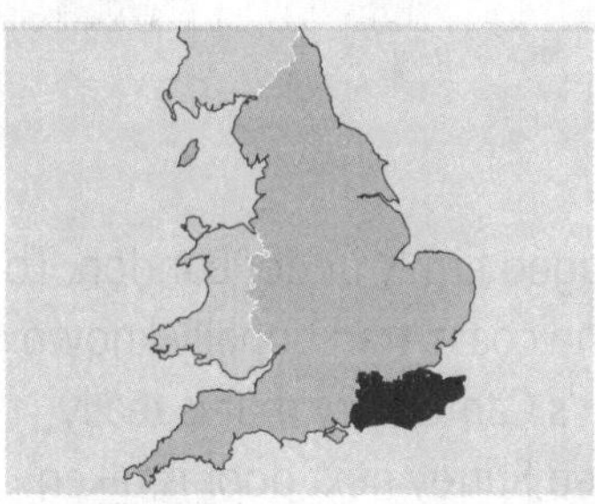

Footprint features

Introduction

The southeast of England is wedged firmly under London. To the east, Kent stretches out to the coast, traditionally known as 'the garden of England', but it's Canterbury that is really the pick of the bunch. Landlocked Surrey next door is taken up with the southwestern suburbs of the capital and beyond. Sussex is squashed beneath them both along the south coast. And much of the region depends largely on the big city for its livelihood. Millions of commuters make the return trip every day, although many of the region's towns and villages cherish fond reminders of the days when work was closer to home. From the white clapperboard High Streets of the Weald with its tile-hung Kentish farms, their hop gardens and converted oast houses, to the fishermen's huts in Hastings or Whitstable, and the grand guesthouses on the seafront at Brighton where relics of local industry still litter the landscape. Now mainly of archaeological and tourist interest, the traditional industries of the southeast could never have created the prosperity that most of the area enjoys today. This can best be appreciated with a stay at one of the many genteel farmhouse B&Bs nestling in the gorgeous countryside, while metropolitan tastes (and expense accounts) mean that in these parts you're never that far from good coffee or a top-notch restaurant kitchen.

Geologically, a young landscape relative to some other parts of the country, the soft low chalk ridges of the North and South Downs encircle a few 100 square miles of rich Wealden clay. The North Downs run from Guildford in Surrey across north Kent to fall into the sea at the white cliffs of Dover. The South Downs rise in Hampshire and run along the south coast, waving to France from Beachy Head and the Seven Sisters.

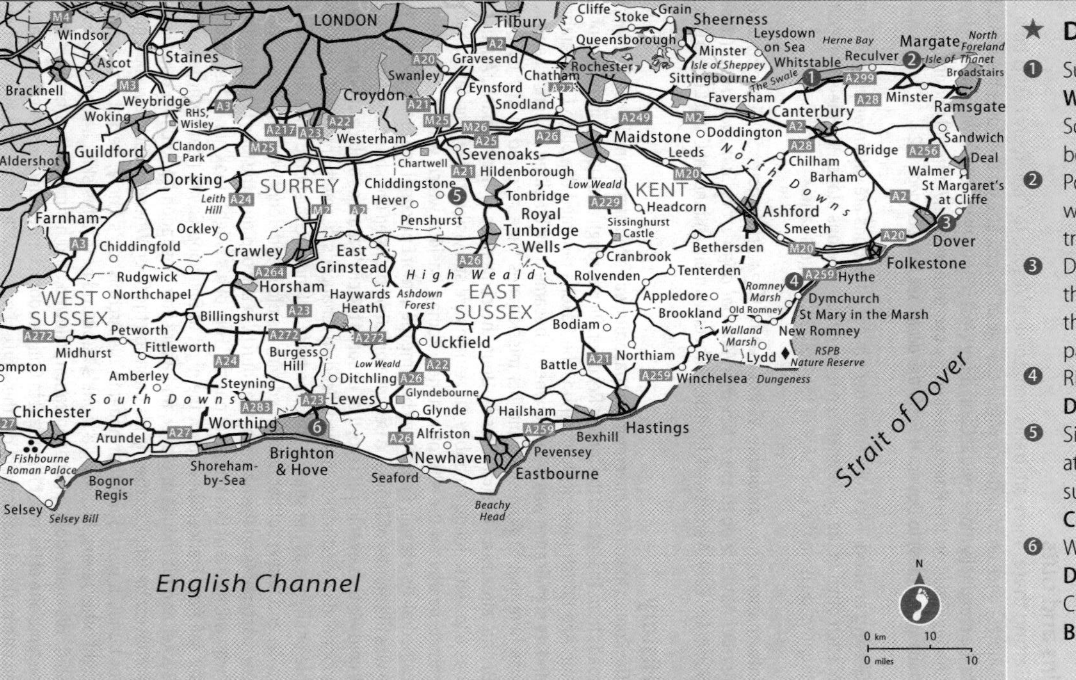

★ Don't miss...

❶ Suck down a plate of oysters in **Whitstable** and watch the sun set over Southend from Peter Cushing's favourite beach, page 156.

❷ Ponder the fate of the stuffed African wildlife and the use of the pre-colonial tribal artefacts at **Quex House**, page 159.

❸ Dive beneath **Dover Castle** to explore the entrails of the White Cliffs, from where the army was rescued from Dunkirk, page 164.

❹ Ride the miniature **Romney, Hythe and Dymchurch railway**, page 170.

❺ Sink your teeth into Elizabethan history at **Penshurst Place** before enjoying a pub supper in the Tudor village of **Chiddingstone**, page 182.

❻ Work up a thirst walking along the **South Downs Way** enjoying superb views of the Channel and then dance all night in **Brighton**, page 198.

Canterbury

→ *Colour map 3, grid B5.*

Canterbury is probably the single most popular tourist destination in the southeast. Not surprisingly it can become very congested, but the city also does an excellent job of combining its medieval roots with mass tourism, on a charming and manageable scale. Although parts of the centre of town were bombed flat in the Second World War, they have since been fairly sympathetically rebuilt and enough of the old timber-framed buildings and narrow streets remain to maintain the antique tone. The pedestrianized heart of the city, within the medieval walls, is an enjoyable place to explore, despite the crowds, and thanks to its cathedral and university Canterbury has more style and energy than anywhere else in east Kent. » *For Sleeping, Eating and other listings see pages 150-152.*

Ins and outs

Getting there There are **trains** from London Victoria to Canterbury East (1 hour 22 minutes) once an hour (twice with a change at Faversham) on the Dover mainline, or to the marginally more central Canterbury West (1 hour 25 minutes) twice an hour from Charing Cross on the Ramsgate line. By **car**, take the M2/A2 from London (about 1 hour 45 minutes) to Dover. » *For further details, see Transport page 152.*

Getting around Most of Canterbury's major attractions are within walking distance of each other in the pedestrianized town centre. The bus station for the surrounding countryside is on the east side of town off St George's Lane.

Information The **Canterbury Visitor Centre** ⓘ *34 St Margaret St, T01227-766567, Apr-Oct Mon-Sat 0930-1730, Nov-Mar Mon-Sat 0630-1700, Sun 1000-1600 (closed Sun in Jan, Feb).* A short walk from the Cathedral's main entrance at Christ Church gate.

History

The Roman town of Durovernum Cantiacorum was sited at the junction of the military roads from Thanet and the forts at Reculver, Richborough and Dover, on the site of the Iron Age British town of Durovernon. The Saxons renamed the place Cantwaraburg and its significance was secured when it became King Ethelbert of Kent's capital. It was here that St Augustine and his missionaries were received in 597 by Queen Bertha, already a Christian herself. Upon the conversion of her husband, Augustine was allowed to found an abbey (its remains are still visible today) and later another church nearby on the site of a ruined Roman basilica which was to become the cathedral. As a result, Canterbury became the senior Episcopal see in the country. But it was the murder of Thomas à Becket, sometime between Christmas and New Year on a cold winter's evening in 1170, that ensured the city's fame as a place of pilgrimage, a top holiday destination immortalized in Chaucer's 'Canterbury Tales', and final pre-eminence as the seat of the Church of England. Archbishop Becket, the son of a miller and former soldier, quarrelled with his old friend Henry II over the Royal court's encroachments on the power of the church. In a fit of pique, the King famously asked "who will rid me of this turbulent priest?" Four of his knights took him at his word and set sail from France. They spent the night at Saltwood Castle near Hythe, surprised Becket and his monks at prayer, and after some hesitation hacked him down in the northwest transept, scattering his brains on the floor. When the corpse was prepared for burial, it was found that beneath his Archbishop's finery, Becket was wearing eight other layers, including a monk's habit and next to his skin, a very grubby hair shirt. His martyrdom and canonization followed, and his miraculous healing shrine became one of the most important in Christendom. Canterbury prospered and gained an international reputation from the influx of medieval 'tourists', and even the break

The Canterbury Tales

The poet Geoffrey Chaucer is generally accepted as the father of English literature, and his late 14th-century Canterbury Tales his most famous work. "Whan that Aprill with shoures soote/ The droghte of March hath perced to the roote… Thanne longen folk to goon on pilgrimages" it begins, as 30 pilgrims set out from Southwark for Canterbury on April 17, telling tales in prose and verse as they go. They're a mixed bunch, broadly representing a cross- section of the middle classes of the day. The Knight, poshest of the crew, riding along with his son the Squire, starts the ball rolling with a chivalric romance. Then the drunken Miller takes the micky out of carpenters, and the Reeve, who has done a bit of woodwork himself, takes offence, and retaliates with a story about a dodgy miller. The Wife of Bath, one of the most popular characters, discusses the subject of who wears the trousers in married life. She's had five husbands, and speaks with some authority on the subject, arguing that all was well when she was in charge. In her tale, a woman turned into a hag is released from the spell by her hero, who's given the choice of having her 'fair by day and foul by night' or the other way around. The hero leaves it up to her and as a result she promises to be both fair and true. The Friar and Summoner then mock each other before the Clerk relates the patience of Griselda in putting up with her husband's absurd demands. The Merchant, unhappily married himself, tells a tale of old man January who suffers from the wicked wiles of his wife May. The Squire's romantic interlude involves a sadly abandoned lady, while the urbane Franklin's Tale is a fairy-tale romance about honesty in relationships, and set in Britanny. The Physician digresses on the proper education of young women. The Pardoner, very intellectual, tells the 'best short story in existence': a sermon used to extract money from gullible listeners, including the old tale of the three partygoers who find death in a heap of gold before the Shipman relates how a merchant is done out of his money and his wife by a monk. The Prioress counters with a story about a schoolboy murdered by the Jews who returns from the dead through the intercession of Our Lady to let the world know how he died. The Nun's Priest tells the charming story of Renard the fox, the cock Chauntecleer and his lovely hen Pertelote.

Part of the route they follow takes the Roman road out of Rochester to Harbledown where they first sight Canterbury, although in their day its landmark tower was yet to be built.

with Rome by Henry VIII, who had the shrine destroyed, hardly dented the city's significance. Sadly, like much of the old town centre, the birthplace of the great Elizabethan playwright Christopher Marlowe at 57 St George's St was destroyed in the so-called 'Baedecker bombings' of 1942, when the Nazis tried to undermine the nation's morale by obliterating its heritage. Luckily the cathedral itself was saved, like St Paul's in London, by a dedicated team of firewatchers.

Cathedral

ⓘ *T01227-762862, canterbury-cathedral.org. Summer Mon-Sat 0900-1900, Sun 1230-1430, 1630-1730, winter Mon-Sat 0900-1700, Sun 1230-1430, 1630-1730. £3.50, £2.50 concessions, under-5s free. Services: Sun 0800, 0930, 1100, evensong 1515 and 1830; Mon-Sat 0800 also 1100 on Wed; Thu 1815; Saints Days 1015; matins Mon-Fri 0730, Sat 0930; evensong Mon-Fri 1730, Sat 1515.*

The triple towers of the Cathedral still dominate the city. Most visitors quite rightly make a beeline for this medieval glory, the mother church of Anglicanism and most ancient Episcopal see in the kingdom, because it remains the main event and it's unlikely to disappoint. Although not the tallest, longest, oldest or even most beautiful cathedral in the country, the majesty of its old grey stones are awe-inspiring. Inside and out, the building almost seems to have grown up organically over the centuries, each generation adding, changing, removing or restoring parts, but never the whole. Most of the west end is late 14th-century. Bell Harry, as the great central tower is known, was added during the first years of the 16th century in magnificent Perpendicular Gothic, while the eastern choir had been built by the late 12th century, in the style now known as Early English. The most recent major alteration was the replacement in 1834 of the old northwestern tower with a copy of its medieval neighbour. The interior is reached through the south porch, the bas-relief above depicting the Altar of Martyrdom destroyed by Henry VIII. The tour route

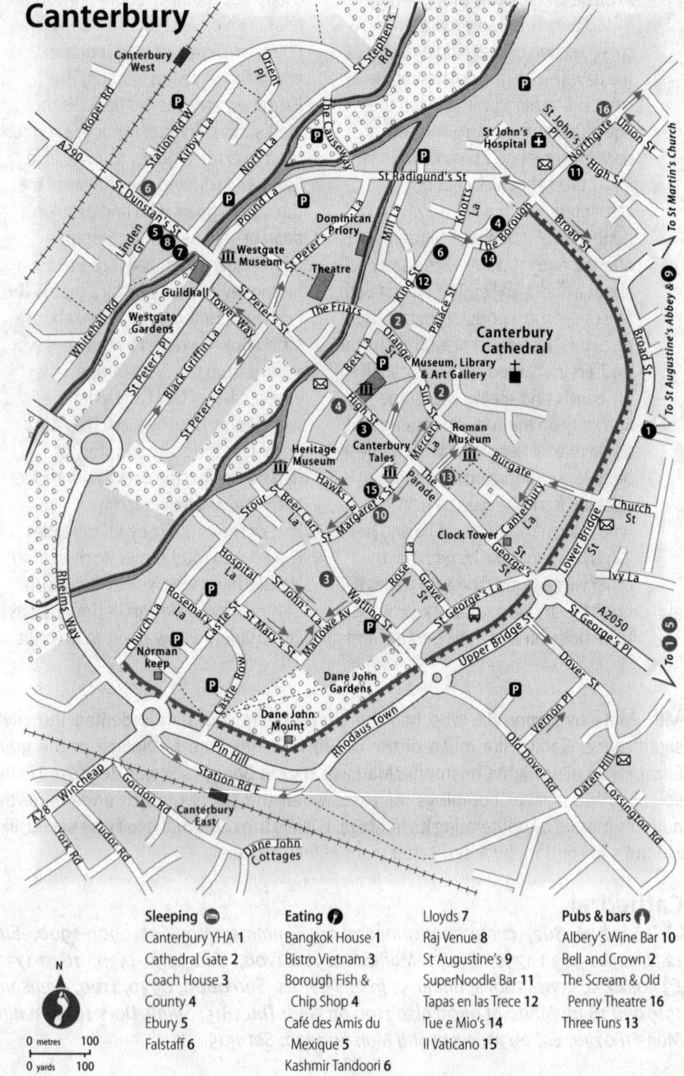

then heads down the airy nave, directly into the northwest transept, the scene of Becket's death. A modern sculpture marks the spot where he fell. His murderers would still recognize their way in here through the doorway from the cloisters. Steps then lead down into the Crypt, the earliest and most atmospheric part of the building. It's the finest Norman undercroft in the country, with remarkable stone-carving on pillars and capitals, especially on St Gabriel's chapel in the southeast corner which also features a 13th-century painted ceiling. Further along on the south aisle down here, a chapel was set aside in 1568 for French Protestants (Huguenots), where services in French are still held at 1500 on Sundays. It includes the Black Prince's Chantry, donated in 1363 by that bellicose son of Edward III's in exchange for the hand in marriage of Joan Plantagenet, the Fair Maid of Kent. Back on ground level, the tourist route enters the long Quire, with its Grinling Gibbons stalls at the west end, before heading round to the famous Royal tombs (Henry IV and the Black Prince) in the Trinity Chapel behind the High Altar. This was also the site of St Thomas à Becket's shrine, the 13th-century windows illustrated with some of the miracles he is supposed to have performed. It's well worth wandering around the precincts of the Cathedral to find the beautiful Norman staircase in King's College, an exclusive private school where the likes of Christopher Marlowe, Robert Boyle and Somerset Maugham were educated.

Central Canterbury

The visitors' entrance to the Cathedral precincts is through the ornate 16th-century Christ Church gate on the **Butter Market**. Best approached from Mercery Lane, this is the centre of tourist Canterbury and often impossibly busy with language groups and coach parties milling around the war memorial. Antiquey old Burgate heads east, with the **Roman Museum** ⓘ *T01227-785575, www.canterbury-museum.co.uk, Mon-Sat 1000-1600 also Jun-Oct Sun 1330-1700,£2.50, concessions and under-16s £1.65, family £6.50,* just off to the right down Butchery Lane. It's a subterranean museum containing a reconstruction of a Roman kitchen and dining arrangements, with several objects recovered during the excavation of the Longmarket Shopping Centre's foundations, as well as the excavated site of the Roman house that inspired the museum.

Back in the Butter Market, Sun St leads north round the Cathedral precincts into Palace St, the best shopping strip in the city (see Shopping, below). Beyond the Borough, on Northgate, and quite hard to find, are the old almshouses of **St John's Hospital** ⓘ *T01227-451621,* which have the somewhat dubious honour of housing the oldest loo in the country. The elderly residents welcome polite enquiries to see the chapel and hall. Mercery Lane heads across the High St into St Margaret's St, where you'll find the **Visitor Centre** ⓘ *St Margaret's St, T01227-479227, Nov-18 Feb 1000-1630, 19 Feb-May and Sep-Oct 1000-1700, Jul-Aug 0930-1730, £6.75, concessions £5.75, under-16s £5.25, family £25,* and also the **Canterbury Tales**, a reasonably entertaining 'visitor attraction' based on the stories told by Chaucer's pilgrims on their way from London to Canterbury. The animatronics now look badly dated but the humour of the tales comes across well.

St Margaret's St becomes Castle St (leading down to the quite impressive ruins of the city's **Norman keep** ⓘ *daily 0800-dusk, at the junction of Beer Cart Lane and Watling St,* built by William the Conqueror and sieged two centuries later by revolting peasants, its empty shell remains evocative of its history. A right turn here leads to the **Heritage Museum**, the place to learn about the history of the city, 'from Romans to Rupert...'. The story is well laid-out and informative, including a few treasures alongside the models, videos and wall displays. The highlight, though, remains the museum's premises, the 600-year-old timber-framed **Poor Priests' Hospital** ⓘ *Stour St, T01227-452747, Nov-May Mon-Sat 1030-1600, Jun-Oct also Sun 1330-1600, £2, concessions £1.30,* on the banks of the river Stour.

Lastly, the **Westgate Museum** ⓘ *T01227-452747, Mon-Sat 1100-1230, 1330-1530, £1, concessions 65p,* in the only remaining medieval entrance to the city, contains a small display of weaponry but is best visited for the views from the top.

St Augustine's Abbey and around

East down Burgate, beyond the old medieval walls, **St Augustine's Abbey** ⓘ *T01227-767345, Apr-Sep daily 1000-1800, Oct 1000-1700, Nov-Mar 1000-1600, £3, concessions £2.30, under-16s £1.50,* is the birthplace of the Roman Catholic Church in England. There's not much left of the buildings themselves now except a few old walls and foundations, but this is where St Augustine and his convert King Ethelbert are buried. The English Heritage visitor centre and audio tour try hard to bring the grassy emptiness back to life, and also detail the Abbey's use as a palace by Elizabeth I, Charles I and Charles II after Henry VIII's split from Rome.

Another short walk northeast from here brings you to **St Martin's Church**, in North Holmes Rd, the oldest church in continuous use in England, where Queen Bertha apparently worshipped before St Augustine's arrival. Now it's best visited for its position in one of the city's more pleasant districts beyond the city walls, for a look at the Norman font supposedly also comprising part of the Saxon font in which King Ethelbert was baptized, and perhaps to pay hommage at the grave of local hero Mary Tourtel, the creator of the yellow-check trousered cartoon hero Rupert the Bear in the *Daily Express*.

Sleeping

Unfortunately Canterbury is not blessed with many outstanding hotels. It makes up in quantity what it generally lacks in quality, though, especially when it comes to affordable B&Bs and guesthouses. The TIC or web is the best place to track down these, but the stretch of straightforward places on the New Dover Rd is a good place to start looking on spec. For an antique hotel just outside the city walls (and one of the more expensive) try the hard-to-beat

A-B Falstaff Hotel, 8-10 St Dunstan's St, T01227-462138, www.corushotels.com/thefalstaff. Part of its building dates from the early 15th century, but the new building within and around blends in sympathetically enough. It's part of the *Corus* chain and has all the facilities you'd expect for the price. 3 more expensive rooms with 4-poster beds.

C Ebury Hotel, 65-67 New Dover Rd, 10 mins on foot out of town, T01227-768433. 15 rooms, breakfast included. 1 4-poster, 2 family rooms.

D Coach House, 34 Watling St, T01227-784324. Six individual family rooms in a 3-storey Georgian townhouse, with a courtyard garden, breakfast included.

D County Hotel, High St, T01227-766266, F784324. A small, neat and very central Victorian townhouse.

D-E Cathedral Gate Hotel, 36 Burgate, T01227-464381, F462800. Right next to Christ Church Gate and a creaking warren of rooms of all shapes and sizes, some quite basic. The views of the cathedral – beautifully floodlit at night – from the back rooms make it quite romantic and the best value place in the centre.

F Canterbury YHA, Ellerslie, 54 New Dover Rd, T01227-462911. ¾ of a mile from Canterbury East station, fully equipped (85 beds).

Eating

£££ Lloyds, 89-90 St Dunstan's St, T01227-768222. One of the more recent openings and one of the more ambitious doing a sophisticated modern British and traditional French menu in a cunningly converted bank.

£££ St Augustine's Restaurant, 1 and 2 Longport, T01227-453063. Not quite so central, but with an enviable long-standing reputation this is the place for some thoroughly civilized and well-prepared European dishes in a restrained atmosphere.

£££ Tue e Mio's, 16 The Borough, T01227-761471. Generally agreed to be the smartest Italian in town: quite a formal but welcoming place for some traditional Italian food with Arabic and Sicilian influences.

££ Bangkok House, 13 Church St, T01227-471141. The genuinely Thai menu is served up in a long narrow stylishly-decorated room.

For an explanation of the sleeping and eating price codes used in this guide, see the inside front cover. Other relevant information is provided in the Essentials chapter, page 40.

££ Bistro Vietnam, White Horse La, T01227-760022. Highly recommended for its fish recipes from Saigon.
££ Il Vaticano, 35 St Margaret's St, T01227-765333. A very lively Italian restaurant, reasonably priced and bang in the middle of town.
££ Kashmir Tandoori, Palace St. Does as it says and specializes in tandooris from Kashmir. The Tudorbethan dining room is unusual.
££ Tapas en las Trece, 13 Palace St, T01227-762639. Does a reasonably priced Spanish menu in a typically laid-back atmosphere.
£ Borough Fish and Chip Shop, 7 The Borough, does the national dish well enough.
£ Café des Amis du Mexique, 95 St Dunstan's St, T01227-464390, combines Mediterranean and Mexican cuisine in a bright, busy atmosphere, popular with students.
£ Raj Venue, 92 St Dunstan's St, T01227-462653. A colourful Bangladeshi restaurant and take away.
£ SuperNoodle Bar, 87-88 Northgate St, T01227-457888. A good bet for some very tasty, fast and inexpensive Chinese noodles. A bright and cheerful restaurant and takeaway beyond Palace St.

Pubs, bars and clubs

As far as a decent pint is concerned, Canterbury has surprisingly few old-fashioned boozers.
Albery's Wine Bar and Bistro, 38 St Margaret's St, has long queues on Sat nights.
The Bell and Crown, 10 Palace St, T01227-462459, is one that is popular with young locals.
The Scream in the old Penny Theatre on Northgate St is a popular student hang-out.
The Three Tuns, Castle St, (top of Butchery La), with its large wooden tables and welcoming atmosphere is another good watering hole in the centre of town.

Festivals

Oct Canterbury Festival, T01227-455600. Music, dance, street theatre and performing arts, running for 2 weeks mid-month.

Shopping

Apart from all the usual big names on the High St, the place to head for more interesting finds is Palace St and its continuation beyond The Borough into Northgate St.
Canterbury Bookshop, 23a Palace St, T01227-464773, with a good selection of rare and secondhand books, especially strong on local topography.
The Canterbury Dolls' House, 36 Palace St, T01227-477036, provides superior accommodation and furnishings.
Field and Trek, 3 Palace St, T01227-470023, is a well-stocked branch of the strong national outdoor pursuits supplier.
France, 29-30 Palace St, T01227-454508, www.francecanterbury.com, does travel arrangements, maps, books, cards, games and 'everything for the francophile'.
Hollingsworth, 68 Northgate, T01227-769537 are traditional crafters of hand-sewn leather goods.
Hollywood Bread Co, 33/34 Palace St, T01227-450001, bakes the best bread in town.
National Trust Shop, 24 Burgate. Typically English souvenirs and gifts.
Stuart Heggie, 14 The Borough, T01227-470422, stocks a good range of old and vintage cameras, and also advises on repairs.
The Sugar Boy, 31 Palace St, T01227-479545, is a classic sweet shop for just about every conceivable type of boiled sweet by the bag as well as chocolate bars.

Activities and tours

Canterbury City Official Guide (tickets are available from the TIC). Walking tours lasting about 1 hr 30 mins and leaving from the centre at 1400 daily Apr-Nov, and also at 1100 daily from Jun-Aug.
Dr Thomson's Tours of Historic Canterbury, T01227-455922, 37 The Crescent. A private operator with considerable experience.
Oathill Farm Riding Centre, Pound La, Molash, near Canterbury, T01233-740573. Beginners welcome, no road-riding necessary.
Punting On the Stour from the Westgate Gardens (Jun-Sep), T07885-318301.

Transport

Bicycle
Downland Cycle Hire, Canterbury West Railway Station, T01227-479643.

Car
Drive Easy, Halletts, Station Rd West, T01227-451155; S & B Car Hire Kent Ltd, Canterbury East Railway Station, T01227-781180. Victoria Hire, 22 St Dunstans St, T01227-455001.

Taxi
Cabwise Taxi Services, 112 Sweechgate Broad Oak, T01227-712929; City Cars, Unit 26, Roper Cl, T01227-454445; Lynx Taxis Ltd, Unit 6, Dane John Works, Gordon Rd, T01227-464232.

Train
National Express, T08705-808080, from **Victoria** coach station (2hrs) every hr on the ½ hr from 0830-2030, as well as at 0700, 2200 and 2330.

Directory

Hospitals The Chaucer Hospital, Nackington Rd, T01227-455466; Kent & Canterbury Hospital, Ethelbert Rd, T01227-766877; St Martins Hospital, Littlebourne Rd, T01227-459584. **Language schools** Canterbury Language Training, 73-75 Castle St, T01227-760000; Carl Duisberg Language Centre Canterbury, 26 Oaten Hill, T01227-764123. **Police** Canterbury Police Station, Old Dover Rd, T01227-762055. **Post office** 29 High St, T0845-7223344.

North Kent Coast → *Colour map 3, grid B3/5*

Although so close to London, the southern shores of the Thames estuary are not an obvious destination for visitors. Bypassed by the M2 en route to Canterbury and Folkestone, and overshadowed by the North Downs, the riverside and coastal towns along here are surprisingly isolated. Rochester, Chatham and the Medway Towns may not be the most prepossessing places, but they all contain attractions of more than passing interest. To the east, the Isle of Sheppey is the place for strange and lonely walks along the saltings and marshes looking at weird seabirds and eerie little churches. Further along, Whitstable has fairly recently achieved considerable cachet with the capital's weekenders, not only for its famous oyster restaurants but also for its working harbour and thriving nightlife. ▸▸ *For Sleeping, Eating and other listings, see pages 160-163.*

Ins and outs

Getting there Rochester and Chatham are easily reached from London by **train**, either from Charing Cross (1 hour) or more quickly from Victoria (40 minutes) two to three times an hour on the mainline to Ramsgate. By **car**, Rochester is on the A2/M2, about 50 minutes from London, unless travelling at peak times, which can add 40 minutes to the journey. There are also infrequent **bus** services. ▸▸ *For further details, see Transport page 163.*

Getting around Rochester's one-way system makes driving around town fairly pointless, although there are plenty of car parks in the centre. Chatham's is even worse. Rochester is best explored on **foot**, while in Chatham it's always worth hopping on a **bus**.

Information Rochester Visitor Centre ⓘ *95 High St, T01634-843666, www.medway.gov.uk, Mon-Sat 1000-1700, Sun 1030-1700.*

Rochester → *Colour map 3, grid B3*

Rochester in particular has occupied its position overlooking the mouth of the River Medway since long before the Romans arrived, and boasts the second oldest cathedral in the country and one of the most impressive Norman keeps. It's also the heart of Dickens country and won't let you forget it. Either bone up on your Pickwick before visiting or track down a copy in one of the town's secondhand bookshops.

Rochester Cathedral's ⓘ *T01634-401301, daily 0800-1800, free, £2 donation requested,* Saxon foundations were laid by King Ethelbert of Kent on his conversion in 604, although the small but perfectly formed Norman cathedral of today was founded a little to the east in 1080 by Gundulf, also responsible for the Tower of London's White Tower. The rounded arches of the nave remain one of the finest examples of Norman cathedral architecture in the country. After Thomas à Becket's murder in Canterbury, the town and its abbey became an important stop-off for pilgrims en route to the shrine. One such overnighter, a Scottish baker called William, was found murdered in the Abbey. For no apparent reason, his adopted son was accused of the crime and the monks of Rochester then declared the baker a martyr, later canonized as Saint William of Perth. His shrine (long since removed) helped swell the cathedral coffers sufficiently for the restoration of the choir after a disastrous fire in 1179.

Over the road from the Cathedral's west front, the great ruined keep of the Norman **castle** ⓘ *T01634-402276, Apr-Sep daily 1000-1800, Oct-Mar 1000-1600,* overlooks the river above civic gardens incorporating fragments of the town's Roman walls. A stairway winds up the hollow shell of the old castle to the top battlements, from where the wide valley of the Medway can be seen meandering into the distance, bridged by the M2 and the new Channel Tunnel rail link.

From the castle and cathedral, the town's venerable old High St, still much as Dickens described it – "full of gables with old beams and timbers" – heads south from the old bridge. Its pedestrianized length is lined with interesting secondhand bookshops, cafés and a few ramshackle antique shops. Near the castle end, the **Guildhall Museum** ⓘ *High St, T01634-848717, daily 1000-1600, free,* is an unusually rewarding treasure trove of local Medway history and archaeological finds, including an exhibition on the grim prison hulks immortalized by Dickens, as well as an excellent array of Victoriana.

A short walk down the High St on the left, Richard Watt's **Six Poor Traveller's House** ⓘ *97 High St, T01634-845609, Mar-Oct Tue-Sat 1400-1700, free,* is a remarkable survival from 1586. Some very basic accommodation for commercial travellers was provided here free of charge, so long as you didn't mind sleeping above Rochester's original prison, in the basement (viewable on request). The galleried rooms have been preserved and a small exhibition out front gives details on the continuing work of the Richard Watt Charitable Trust and its origins.

A few steps nearer Chatham, the **Charles Dickens Centre** ⓘ *T01634-844176, Apr-Sep daily 1000-1800, Oct-Mar 1000-1600, £3.90, concessions £2.80,* is a tourist attraction on the author's life and works, with a few mildly distracting audio-visual reconstructions from his works and one of his actual desks. The star attraction is probably his gaudily painted writing chalet from Gads Hill (see below), which can be seen in the garden of the Centre even when the Centre is closed.

Almost opposite, **Restoration House** ⓘ *just off the High St down Crow La, May-Sep Thu, Fri 1000-1700, £4.50,* has recently been returned to its 16th-century condition and was supposedly the inspiration for Miss Haversham's gloomy home in *Great Expectations*. It's interesting enough to walk past.

Chatham

In its heyday Chatham had one of Britain's most important naval dockyards, this has now been skilfully converted into an entertaining visitor attraction, The **Historic Dockyard** ⓘ *T01634-823800, www.worldnavalbase.org.uk, Apr-Oct daily 1000-1800 (last entry 1600), Nov, Feb and Mar Wed, Sat, Sun 1000-1600 (last entry 1500), £7.50, concessions £7, under-16s £6, family £25, take any of several buses marked Chatham Maritime/Historic Dockyard from the train station or High St,* (or **World Naval Base** as it now likes to be known) is about a mile and a half from the

Where the Dickens?

Fans of Charles Dickens are in clover in north Kent. It's hard go far around here without being reminded of the great troubled novelist. His childhood was spent in Chatham, and his old age near Rochester, described by his first biographer as "the birthplace of his fancy" and one which still makes as much of the connection as it can. His multicoloured writing chalet, which once stood in the garden at Gad's Hill, then in the grounds of Cobham Hall, is on permanent display just off the High St in the Dickens Museum. The Cooling Marshes are the setting for the opening scenes of *Great Expectations*, in which The Bull Hotel on the High St, where Dickens himself stayed, features as the Blue Boar, while in the same novel the clock on the Corn Exchange over the road is described as 'inexpressive, moon-faced and weak'. Nearby, Restoration House was the model for Miss Havisham's Satis House and Nos 150-4 High St are where Uncle Pumblechook ran his corn shop. Rochester also figures strongly in The *Mystery of Edwin Drood* as Cloisterham, although Dickens elsewhere dubbed it less kindly Mudfog and Dullborough. While at Broadstairs on holiday, he wrote part of the *Pickwick Papers* at 31 High St, at 40 Albion St part of *Nicholas Nickelby* and completed David Copperfield at what is now called *Bleak House* .

town centre (not a very pretty sight). The dockyard itself is a must for all seadogs, especially the large Royal National Lifeboat Exhibition, with its well-presented array of life-saving boats, as well as the extraordinary **Ropery**, 'the longest room in England' at nearly quarter of a mile, and continually in use since the early 19th century. The ropemakers, who can be seen working on Wednesday to Saturday, recently made the ropes for the opening of Buckingham Palace's Garden to the public. Elsewhere around the huge site, the destroyer **HMS Cavalier** and inshore patrol submarine **Ocelot** can be looked over on guided visits. The latter feels like the ocean-going equivalent of a tank: very cramped and very dangerous. Elsewhere on the huge site, **Wooden Walls** is a fairly successful attempt to describe how the navy that defeated Napoleon at Trafalgar was built, as seen through the eyes of a young apprentice of the time. The **Harbour Master's Club** overlooking the estuary is the place to sup on home-brewed beers and ponder how much times have changed for those in peril on the sea.

One of the last river-going **paddle steamers** ⓘ *'Kingswear Castle', T01634-827648, www.pskc.freeserve.co.uk, Jul to 1st week Sep Sun, Wed, Thu, Fri 1600 back by 1645 from Rochester Pier, £5, concessions £4.50, under-16s £3, family £12,* in the world leaves from Chatham Dockyard and Rochester Pier, as well as special sailings in summer to and from Tower Bridge.

The other sight worth seeking out in Chatham is the old **Theatre Royal**, ⓘ *T01634-831028, tours Mon-Sat 1000-1500,* a 3000-seat Victorian theatre.

Around Rochester and Chatham

Just off the A2 before it becomes the M2, **Cobham Hall** ⓘ *T01474-823371, Easter and summer school holidays only (Apr, Jul, Aug), £3.50, concessions £2.75, gardens and park only £1.50,* is a beautiful old redbrick Elizabethan mansion dating from 1584. In the 17th century it was the home of 'La Belle Stuart', Frances, Duchess of Lennox, mistress to Charles II, the model for the engraver Roettier's likeness of Britannia on 50p coins and responsible for making 'navy' blue fashionable, not least with the navy itself. The ornate Darnley State Coach, an extraordinary survival from about 1715, is on display inside, but the real treats here are outside, in the architecture and the gardens landscaped by Humphrey Repton. Since 1962 the house has been an independent boarding school for girls.

In Higham, on the A289 off Junction 1 of the M2, **Gads Hill House** ⓘ *T01474-822366, first Sun of month and bank holidays 1400-1700, also during the biannual Dickens festivals, phone for details, tour £3.50, £1.50*, stands on what was once one of the most notorious stretches of road for highwaymen: 'Swift Nick Nevinson', said to have inspired the fictional Dick Turpin, robbed a man here at four in the morning, escaped across the river and established his alibi by appearing at the bowling green in York by eight that evening. On the crest of the hill, the house is where Dickens wrote *Great Expectations*, *Our Mutual Friend* and died in 1870 as he was finishing *The Mystery of Edwin Drood*. The novelist wrote of the place: "Ever since I can recollect my father seeing me so fond of it has often said to me: if you were to be very persevering and work hard you might someday come to live in it". Acquired by Dickens in 1856, it is now a private girls school, but some rooms have been preserved much as Dickens left them.

Isle of Sheppey

East of Chatham, the Isle of Sheppey is a wide, flat stretch of marshland surrounding a low ridge at the mouth of the river Medway, cut off from the mainland by a narrow stretch of water called The Swale. It is best approached from the west via the village of Lower Halstow, nestling in a yacht-filled creek where old Medway barges rot away on the mudflats and marshes. This attractive village makes a good starting point for walks along the Saxon Shore Way, which can be joined near the old church built in part with Roman bricks.

Ins and outs

Getting there By **rail**, a branch line from Sittingbourne (56 minutes from London Victoria) runs twice an hour up to Swale, Queenborough and Sheerness (20 minutes). By **road**, Sheppey's only point of entry is the dual carriageway A249 to Sheerness, which leaves the M2 at junction 5 and the M20 at junction 7. About 1 hour's drive from London. Several **buses** from Sittingbourne go to Sheerness, Minster and Leysdown-on-Sea, although the best parts of the island lack any public transport.

Getting around A **car** or **bicycle** are really the only ways of exploring the more remote and atmospheric parts of the island.

Information **Fleur de Lis Heritage Centre** ⓘ *Preston St, Faversham, T01795-534542 www.faversham.org.*

Sights

On Sheppey itself, the main towns of Sheerness and Queensborough are best bypassed en route to **Minster**, the island's highest point. Here are the remains of the abbey founded by King Egbert's mother, Sexburga in 670. Its chapel was later incorporated into the village church of Minster-in-Sheppey, blessing it with an unusual twin nave and ensuring the survival of the monastery's gatehouse during the Dissolution. The highlight of the interior is the extraordinary Gothic tomb of Sir Robert de Shurland, who died in about 1300. Next to his leg is a horse's head, according to legend because of the mortal septicaemia he suffered after kicking his horse's skull which had washed up on the

Sheppey's most famous 'resident' was former cabinet minister Jonathan Aitken, who went to two prisons here, after being convicted of perjury and perverting the course of justice.

 beach long after the trusty steed had drowned while saving him from an 'impossible' wager with Edward I. Continuing the theme, nearby is the tomb of a 15th-century knight thought to be the Duke of Clarence, brother of Edward IV, who was drowned in a butt of Malmsey wine.

The eastern end of Sheppey is covered in caravan parks and the tacky amusements of **Leysdown-on-Sea**, but from here a lonely road winds south over the marshes to the **Isle of Harty** and the now disused landing stage of the old Harty Ferry. The nature reserves around here are a twitcher's delight and good for muddy, desolate walks. The **church of St Thomas**, in Harty is a lonely little place with an interesting 14th-century wooden chest carved with the lively figures of two jousting knights. The only other trace of civilization is a convenient pub (see Sleeping and eating below).

Harty Ferry itself once crossed the Swale to **Faversham**, an old port and market town on a creek boasting 'the longest preserved medieval street in the country', Abbey St, with its rows of Tudor and Stuart townhouses. No 80 was the house of the wealthy merchant Thomas Arden, murdered by his wife and her lover, inspiring the anonymous Elizabethan drama 'Arden of Feversham'. Faversham escaped serious damage during the Second World War and has retained much of its character, including Britain's oldest independent brewery, **Shepherd Neame** ⓘ *T01795-532206, for details of brewery tours and the beer festival in Sep.* Another survivor worth seeking is the **Chart Gunpowder Mills** ⓘ *off South Rd, Easter-Oct Sat, Sun 1400-1700.*

Whitstable

Whitstable has long been associated with oysters. Those succulent molluscs have been happily breeding in the warm salty inshore waters here since Roman times. The town now depends on them for its popularity, if not for its livelihood, as it did a century ago when a dozen slithery mouthfuls were a staple meal for poor people across the land. In 1830, Whitstable also became famous as the terminus of the first passenger railway in the world, designed by George Stephenson to take steamboat passengers from London onward to Canterbury. The sea-going part of the trip can still be experienced twice each summer on the last ocean-going paddle steamer in the UK, the *PS Waverley* (for details T01227-275482), although the railway has long been defunct.

Ins and outs

Getting there Whitstable is the first properly coastal, as opposed to estuarine, town on the North Kent coast, easily reached off the A299 from the end of the M2 (junction 7) about 1 hour 30 minutes' drive from London, or by train direct from London Victoria (1 hour 15 minutes) twice an hour. ➾ *For further details, see Transport, page 163.*

Information TIC ⓘ *7 Oxford St, T01227-275482, www.whitstable.org.*

Sights

The relatively high cost of oysters today, along with the mildly decadent frisson that eating them can arouse, accounts for much of the town's current success with weekending Londoners. Also, unlike most of the towns on the coast to the east, Whitstable remains a working town, its hatchery in the harbour one of the largest in Europe. Never developed as a seaside resort, the High St casually turns its back on the sea, only a pebble's throw away. It's certainly not a quaint or even particularly attractive place, but the shingle beach (sandy at either end) affords beautiful sunsets looking across to the Isle of Sheppey and Southend beyond, the little harbour is still

Whitstable's most famous resident, Peter Cushing, had his own bench looking out to sea and even a car park named in his honour.

quite busy, and the rows of oyster huts (not all as yet converted into desirable holiday homes) were once sketched by Turner. The history of the place can be explored next door to the TIC at the **Whitstable Museum and Gallery** ⓘ *5a Oxford St, T01227-276998, winter Mon-Sat 1000-1600, summer also Sun 1300-1600, free,* through a diverting collection of local memorabilia, exhibitions on oysters and divers, as well as natural history (especially the local birdlife) and maritime history.

Isle of Thanet

Northeast of Canterbury and once cut off from the mainland by the Wantsum channel, Thanet is a wide-open stretch of flat country fringed by coastal resorts of variable quality. Margate is the most famous and now perhaps the most run down. Round the corner of the North Foreland headland, Broadstairs is a quiet family holiday haven, while handsome old Ramsgate remains a hard-working port. Inland, the Isle conceals a few surprising destinations for an unusual day out, especially the bizarre collection of pickled African flora and fauna at the Powell-Cotton Museum and Quex House.

Ins and outs

Getting there Margate, Broadstairs and Ramsgate can be reached from either London Victoria via Rochester, Chatham and Whitstable in about 1 hour 50 minutes on one of the few direct **trains**, on a good day. More regular services require a change at Faversham, adding 20 minutes to the journey time. From London Charing Cross it's necessary to change at Rochester. Ramsgate can also be reached by train from Canterbury or Dover. Margate is about 40 minutes by **car** beyond Canterbury on the A28, with Ramsgate the same off the A28 on the A253. Broadstairs snuggles between the two, all of them about 2 hours 30 minutes from London. ▸▸ *For further details, see Transport, page 163.*

Getting around There is a comprehensive network of local buses serving all three towns, which are about 15 minutes apart from each other. Bicycling is likely to be tough on the legs.

Information TIC ⓘ *12-13 The Pde, Margate, T01843-230203, www.tourism.thanet.gov.uk; on the seafront near and 17 Albert Ct, York St, Ramsgate, T01843-583333.*

Margate

No one would deny that Margate has seen better days. After all, this was one of the very first seaside resorts, established in the mid-18th century, where sea-bathing was popularized with the help of Quaker preacher Benjamin Beale's patented bathing machine. Deck chairs, donkey rides, sandcastles, rolled trousers and knotted handkerchiefs for headgear: we owe them all to Margate. Unfortunately those innocent and bracing pleasures, taken when the place used to boast of there being 'nothing between here and the North Pole', have long gone out of fashion. Today you're more likely to see crop-haired men on drugs being led by frightening dogs down windswept streets strewn with chip-cartons. There's considerable social unrest in this cultural backwater. However, with any luck that's all set to change. The home town of one of the country's most successful contemporary artists, Tracey Emin, was also once an inspiration to Britain's greatest ever painter, Joseph Mallord William Turner. TS Eliot may have written in *The Wasteland* that "on Margate sands I can connect nothing with nothing", but Turner fell in love with his landlady here, Sophia Booth, and became known to locals in his later years as plain Mr Booth. So then, thanks to some badly needed government funding, the seafront will eventually be graced with a brand new £7 million arts centre, to be called *Turner Contemporary* (not *The Booth* as some locals have already suggested). Designed by Snohetta and Spence (the architects responsible for the new Alexandra Library in

 Egypt) in the shape of a billowing sail, unfortunately it's not opening until 2007. Until that time though, if you head down to Margate Harbour, the Turner Contemporary have a **visitor centre** ⓘ *Droit House, T01843-294208, www.turnercontemporary.org*, where they will be displaying smaller exhibitions. Otherwise you will have to make do with being fleeced by the tacky amusement arcades, braving the rough pubs, and boggling at the eyesore of the crumbling 60s tower block that dominates the dilapidated sweep of old buildings around the bay. After mooching around the seafront, it's worth heading for Market Square or Trinity Square, the least spoiled parts of Margate's architectural legacy and the place to find some decent old pubs and acceptable eateries.

On the curving stretch of seafront along Marine Terrace, **Dreamland Cinema and Bingo Hall**, with its Art Deco 1935 frontage, is the most striking attraction among a host of lesser stars, which include the **Dreamland fun park** ⓘ *T01843-227011, Easter-Oct daily 1100-2200 (Oct until 1800)*, with its creaky old 19th-century rollercoaster.

In Market Square is the **Margate Museum** ⓘ *T01843-231213, Easter-Sep daily 1000-1630, Oct-Easter Mon-Fri 0930-1600, £1, concession 50p*, in the old town hall building that was also once the police station and courthouse, this is a traditional local museum that displays the town silver, a variety of military memorabilia as well as some evocative images and relics of the town's former glory.

One oddity that has long been drawing in the curious, mystified and just plain gullible is the town's famous **Shell Grotto** ⓘ *Grotto Hill, off Northdown Rd, T01843-220008, Easter-Oct daily 1000-1700, £2, under-16s £1, family £5*, quite hard to find, it's questionable whether it's really worth the effort. Clearly the work of an eccentric and astoundingly industrious English schoolmaster in the first half of the 19th century, a couple of small subterranean passages have been decorated with about 4½ million sea shells in a weird variety of patterns supposed to represent occult and gnostic symbols. Commentators as renowned as HG Wells, possibly tongue in cheek, have declared that they considered the work to be older than Stonehenge, or perhaps the work of early Phoenicians.

Broadstairs

A short hop around the coast out of reach of the penetrating northeasterlies, set higher up on the cliffs of North Foreland, Broadstairs is Margate's proper little neighbour, the kind of resort that the Victorians liked to call a 'watering-place', altogether more dignified and refined. Dickens was a great admirer, taking regular working holidays here and describing it as "one of the freest and freshest little places in the world". He wrote *Barnaby Rudge* in a house in Harbour St and other places associated with his writing and visits have been turned into quirky old museums (see Sights below). Everything looks a little tired these days as the town slopes steeply down to its little sandy beach in Viking Bay with the small port alongside. More self-contained than either Margate or Ramsgate, Broadstairs is a good base from which to explore the area. Quiet and old-fashioned – witness the survival since 1913 of the little single-screen Windsor Cinema on Harbour St (see Entertainment below) under the York Gate inscribed 1510 – it has a good selection of comfortable places to stay and several reasonable restaurants.

High on the cliffs overlooking the bay, in a prominent position way above the beach, **Bleak House** ⓘ *Fort Rd, T01843-862224, Mar-Nov daily 1000-1800, Jul and Aug 1000-2100, £3, OAPs £2.80, concessions £2.50, under-16s £2.20*, is named after the novel that Dickens planned there and where he wrote *David Copperfield*. His study with its glorious sea view has been recreated, along with his bedroom and dining room. Downstairs there's an interesting exhibition on the wreckers of the Goodwin sands during the golden age of smuggling when the town apparently did very well for itself.

The other main Dickens attraction is the **Dickens House Museum** ⓘ *Victoria Pde, T01843-864353, daily 1400-1700, £2, under-16s 50p,* down on the seafront, at the former home of Mary Strong, the inspiration for the character of Betsey Trotwood in *David Copperfield.* The little house is neatly laid out with Victoriana and memorabilia associated with the great author.

About a mile north of Viking Bay, set back some distance from the sea, is the **North Foreland Lighthouse** ⓘ *North Foreland Rd, T01843-861869, www.ekmt.fsnet.co.uk, Easter-Sep weekends (summer school holidays Tue-Sun) 1100-1700, £2, OAPs £1.50, under-16s £1, family £5.* Constructed in 1732, this stubby little beacon was the last in the country to be automated, in 1998. The views from the top stretch from Margate to Ramsgate and beyond.

Ramsgate

Ramsgate is the least tourist-orientated of the Thanet coastal resorts, still clinging on to its role as a major continental freight ferry port and private yachting centre. It's also the grandest of the three towns, the Regency terraces overlooking the harbour have solid enough character to give it some genuine 'faded charm'. Madeira Walk winds up the hill from the prom through weird rock gardens and waterfalls, emerging on Wellington Crescent, a splendid sweep of Regency architecture originally erected for retired officers of the army that fought at Waterloo. Apart from the views though, the main points of interest for visitors to the town are all down at sea level around the **Royal Harbour**, along **Royal Parade**, and the **Paragon**, each of which can be reached by a series of creaking old elevators from the top of the cliff. Also worth a look is the neo-gothic **Abbey church of St Augustine**, designed by Augustus Pugin, the architect responsible for the Houses of Parliament, and considered by him to be his best work.

In an underground building on the seafront can be found Ramsgate's pride and joy. The **Motor Museum** ⓘ *West Cliff Hall, The Paragon, T01843-581948, Easter-Oct daily 1030-1730, Nov-Easter Sun 1030-1730, £2.50, £2 OAPs, concessions £1.50, £5.50 family,* is an extensive collection of vintage cars and motorcyles, each in settings carefully designed to evoke nostalgia for the early days of motoring. In particular the selection of old British motorbikes – BSAs, Triumphs and Nortons – provides gleaming examples of mass manufacturing craftsmanship at its very best.

The place to discover the sea-going history of the area, the **Maritime Museum** ⓘ *Clock House, Pier Yard, Royal Harbour, T01843-570622, Easter-Sep daily 1000-1700, Oct-Easter Mon-Fri 0930-1630, £1.50, concessions 75p, family £4,* is a small local museum with four old-fashioned galleries displaying nautical knick-knacks alongside some unusual wrecker's booty from the Goodwin Sands.

Around the Isle of Thanet

Just outside Margate, off the A28, in Birchington, the **Powell-Cotton Museum** at **Quex House and Gardens** ⓘ *museum and house, T01843-842168, Apr-Oct Tue, Wed, Thu, Sun and bank holidays 1100-1700 (house 1400-1630), Nov, Dec and Mar Sun 1100-1600 (house closed), £4, concessions summer £3, winter £2.50, gardens only, £1,* is a peculiar and unexpected survival from another era. For almost half a century from the 1880s, Major Powell-Cotton travelled the Himalayas and sub-Saharan Africa killing and retrieving the indigenous wildlife, not for sport but for his extraordinary series of purpose-built illuminated dioramas. Disturbing and educational, three large galleries are now home to about 500 stuffed animals behind glass, surreally caught in realistic action poses from photographs using some highly skilled taxidermy. A giraffe lowers its head to drink at a pool while a leopard sits up in a tree eating an antelope. In the middle of the third gallery, which even features a stuffed elephant, stands an amazing arrangement of a lion attacking a wildebeest. Two more rooms are full of the tribal artefacts, photographs and weapons that the Major collected on his travels, amounting to one of the most complete records in the UK of African life during and after colonization. The **Regency house** next door has been preserved much as it was at the time, including some unusual Oriental furniture and a large pocket watch found suspended in Napoleon's carriage after Waterloo, possibly the one that failed to wake him up in time to win the battle. 15 acres of gardens are also open to the public, complete with a large **Victorian walled garden**, some very fine old fruit trees and a woodland walk to a folly tower with a peal of 12 bells.

Less than a mile to the south, via the low-lying village of Acol, is the **Spitfire and Hurricane Memorial** ⓘ *Manston, near Ramsgate, T01843-821940, www.spitfire-museum.com, Apr-Sep daily 1000-1700, Oct-Mar 1000-1600,* on the edge of the old RAF Manston (now London Manston airport). Mainly of interest to Battle of Britain fans, in three large rooms the building houses a cleaned-up and cutaway Spitfire fighter plane, as well as a relatively rare example of its sturdy companion the Hurricane, alongside various bits of RAF memorabilia and a souvenir shop. Across the car park is the **RAF Manston History Museum,** ⓘ *T01843-825224, Apr-Sep daily 1000-1700, £1,* a determinedly old-fashioned exhibition on the life of the aerodrome during 1940.

Sleeping

Rochester *p152*
D Gordon House Hotel, High St, T01634-831000, is also very central but in need of some refurbishment (as promised).
D Royal Victoria and Bull Hotel, 16 High St, T01634-846266, www.rvandb.co.uk. If an overnight stop is necessary this is the traditional option.

Around Rochester and Chatham *p154*
F Medway YHA, Capstone Rd, Gillingham, T01634-400788, medway@yha.org.uk. Take 114 bus from Chatham station, get off at Luton Recreation Ground.
B Newington Manor Hotel, Callaways La, Newington, out of town on the road to Sittingbourne, T01795-842053. Expensive and comfortable, this is a small old manor house with a large garden on the edge of the village, with 3 rooms in the old house (4-poster bed £98, others £78) in stable block and annexe, 12 rooms in all. Restaurant closed at weekends.

Isle of Sheppey *p155*
D-E Ferry House Inn, T01795-510214, Isle of Harty, where straightforward rooms are available and food is served all day, although it's so remote that it closes on Mon and Wed nights in the winter.
D-E Mount House, Oare, near Faversham, T01795-534735. Another Georgian house doing B&B in a pleasant little village on the Swale, single room £18.
D-E Twin Mays B&B, T01227-751346, Plum Pudding La, Dargate, in a reconstructed French barn, especially good for families.

Whitstable *p156*
Accommodation in Whitstable can be very difficult to find on Fri and Sat nights, so it's best to book well ahead, even during the week.
C Hotel Continental, 29 Beach Walk, T01227-280280, www.oysterfishery.co.uk. The most stylish place to stay in Whitstable, with its fine Art Deco frontage and renovated rooms, some with balconies looking out to sea west of the harbour. It's owned by the Whitstable Oyster Fishery Company, who also run the top-notch restaurant the *Royal Native Oyster Stores* (see 'Eating' below), so the restaurant does all manner of absolutely fresh fish very well. The same company also manages a group of self-catering converted beach huts for £125 a night, each sleeping 4, that always need to be booked months in advance. Details of more self-contained accommodation, not quite so central, can be found on T01227-280391/07702-821229.
D-E Barnsfield, out of town, 5 miles south towards Canterbury, near the village of Hernhill, T01795-536514. A pleasant B&B in a 16th-century house.
D-E Copeland House, 4 Island Wall, T01227-266207. A cosy B&B close to the beach.
D-E K Phipps, 4 Daniels Ct, Island Wall, T01227-266332. Another B&B on the beachside strip.
D-E Magellan House, 165 Island Wall, T01227-265678. Pleasant B&B near beach.
E The Windmill B&B, Millers Ct, on the outskirts of town, T01227-265963/07779-466051. Offers 4 rooms in a house attached to an old windmill.

Margate *p157*
It would be hard to recommend anywhere special for an overnight stop in Margate, although the Cliftonville area is a good bet.
F Margate YHA, 3-4 Royal Esplanade, Westbrook Bay, T01843-221616, margate@yha.org.uk, very close to Margate station, 54 beds, self-catering.

Broadstairs *p158*
C Royal Albion Hotel, Albion St, Broadstairs, T01843-868071, right on the seafront with views over Viking Bay. Sea-facing rooms including breakfast marginally more expensive.
D Hanson Hotel, 41 Belvedere Rd, Broadstairs, T01843-868936. Not in quite such a special position, but less expensive, this is a cosy little place in an old Georgian house where some of the décor seems to be stuck in the 70s but all the better for it.

Ramsgate *p159*
C Ramada Jarvis Marina Hotel, Harbour Pde, Ramsgate, T01843-588276. Modern, well-equipped and the most expensive in the area, also with sea views. No charge for children.
D The Crescent, 19 Wellington Cres, Ramsgate, T01843-591419. Continental breakfast included and in a spectacular position on top of the cliffs. Good budget options in the area are the youth hostels.
F Broadstairs YHA, Thistle Lodge, 3 Osborne Rd, T01843-604121. A clean, comfortable hostel especially popular with families.

Eating

Rochester *p152*
££ Barnacles Seafood, 86 High St, Rochester, has a small back garden and some reasonably priced fish dishes.
££ Casa-Lina Restaurant, 146 High St, T01634-844993. A good bet for pizza and pasta in a jolly atmosphere (closed Sun and Mon).
£ Eon Internet Café, 32 High St, is the place to log on with a coffee and inexpensive sandwich.

Isle of Sheppey *p155*
£££ Read's, Macknade Manor, Canterbury Rd, Faversham, T01795-5535344. A little out of town but somewhere really quite special and worth the extra spend. It's a 'restaurant with rooms' in a fine Georgian property serving up top quality fresh modern European food.
££ Dove Inn, Plum Pudding La, Dargate, T01227-751360, a *Shepherd Neame* gastro-pub some way out of Faversham off the A229. It usually needs to be booked.

Whitstable *p156*
Oysters can be had all year round, although the best homegrown varieties are only available in season (when there's an 'r' in the name of the month)
£££ Pearson's Crab and Oyster House, Sea Wall, T01227-272005, lively and very popular with locals for a drink as well as a meal.
£££ Royal Native Oyster Stores, on the beachfront, T01227-276856. The town's most upmarket (and expensive) option in the old warehouse that was once packed full of the little blighters.
££ Crab and Winkle, South Quay, The Harbour, above *St Augustine's Fish Supplies*, T01227-779377, has a pleasant balcony overlooking the harbour, and despite being a little overpriced, like the others is always busy, so needs booking.
££ El Loco, 27a Oxford St, T01227-771914, is a decent value Mexican restaurant popular with locals.
££ The Sportsman, Faversham Rd, Seasalter, 01227-273370. The uninspiring exterior gives no hint of the delights on offer inside. Sublime cooking of the strictly non-poncey variety. Kids welcome. Tue-Sat for lunch and dinner, Sun lunch. Booking advised.
££ St Augustine's Fish Supplies, below *Crab and Winkle*, T01227-771245, where fish direct from the boats can be bought during the week. Seafood aside, the town has an array of good value restaurants.
££ Wheeler's Oyster Bar, 8 High St, T01227-273311, open till 2100 Mon-Thu and Sun, 2130 Fri, 2200 Sat (closed Wed). Out front there's an old-fashioned and unpretentious counter serving a wide variety of fresh seafood and sometimes very good ginger ice cream. It's BYOB (available from *Thresher's* over the road) which makes a meal here very good value, even if dining in the cosy parlour round the back.
£ Café Rendezvous, High St. During the day the French owner puts some delicious baguettes and light meals together.
£ V.C. Jones, 25 Harbour St, T01227-272703, is one of the locally favoured chippies.

Margate *p157*

£ Peter's Fish Shop is the most popular local chain.

Broadstairs *p158*

££ Broadstairs Tandoori, 41 Albion St, T01843-865653. Indian food with a twist.

££ Marchesi's, 16-18 Albion St, T01843-862481, is a traditional Anglo-French restaurant specializing in rich sauce.

££ Osteria Pizzeria Posillipo, 14 Albion St, T01843-601133. Stands out for Italian staples.

££ Tartar Frigate, Harbour St, T01843-862013. The best fresh fish restaurant in town, although a little twee.

Ramsgate *p159*

££ Harbour Indian Cuisine, 6-8 Westcliff Arcade, T01843-580290, affords wide views over the Marina to accompany some highly accomplished sub-continental recipes.

£ Churchills, The Paragon, Ramsgate, T01843-587862. A pub with food that's popular with younger locals.

Pubs, bars and clubs

Rochester *p152*

Coopers Arms in St Margaret St behind the Cathedral.

Queen Charlotte on the High St, which sometimes has live music.

Isle of Sheppey *p155*

The Albion, Faversham, near the brewery, on the creek, has a good reputation for its food,

Shipwright's Arms, T01795-590088, Ham Rd, Hollow Shore, Oare, could win a prize for its attractive isolated position right out on the salt flats next to the boatyard.

Whitstable *p156*

There are plenty of pubs in the centre of town.

Old Neptune, Marine Terr, T01227-272262, a clapperboard place right on the beach at the east end of town, with tables outside on the wave-lapped shingle strand. One of the most characterful pubs in town.

Entertainment

Whitstable *p156*

Imperial Oyster Cinema, T01227-770829. Showing an interesting mix of mainstream and more offbeat movies several times daily. In the same beachfront building as the Royal Native Oyster Stores.

Margate *p157*

Dreamland Cinema, Marine Pde, T01843-227822, shows mainstream new releases.

Theatre Royal, Addington St, T01843-293877. A late-18th-century gem with guided tours on Fri.

Broadstairs *p158*

Pavilion Theatre, T01843-600999, is the town's home-from-home for touring shows.

Windsor Cinema, Harbour St, T01843-865726, is a tiny little 1-screen cinema showing new releases in its old purpose-built picture house.

Festivals

Rochester *p152*

Jun Dickens Festival in the first week sees Rochester jump to the great novelist's tune with even more alacrity than usual, including a Victorian pageant, music and readings from the novels all round the area.

Whitstable *p156*

Jul Whitstable Oyster Festival (details from TIC, see p156), involving a sea-going regatta of antique yawls, as well as maritime morris dances and general fairly drunken celebrations of the first small haul of the season (which actually runs Sep-May).

Broadstairs *p158*

Jun Broadstairs Dickens Festival, takes place in the middle weeks with parades, Victorian cricket matches, and other celebrations of the town's local hero.

Aug Broadstairs Folk Week, T01843-604080, is a well-respected folk music festival in the 2nd week of Aug that takes over various venues all over town.

For an explanation of the sleeping and eating price codes used in this guide, see the inside front cover. Other relevant information is provided in the Essentials chapter, page 40.

Ramsgate *p159*
May The Ramsgate Festival, T01834-580994. A usual demonstration of municipal pride.

Transport

Bus
There are infrequent daily **Greenline**, T0870-6087261, and **North Kent Express**, T01474-330330, services from **London Victoria** to both **Rochester** and **Chatham** which take around 2 hrs.

National Express, T08705-808080, coaches run 5 times a day from **London Victoria** to both **Margate** and **Ramsgate**, taking about 2 hrs 30 mins. Stagecoach East Kent, T08702-433711.

East Kent Coast

→ *Colour map 3, grid B/C5*

Kent's eastern seaboard south of Thanet is a strange and contradictory affair. The northern reaches harbour quaint old maritime towns like Deal and Walmer, still boasting their Tudor coastal defences, as well as the antique medieval streets of Sandwich, long left high and dry by the receding waters. To the south, the widest expanse of shingle in Europe juts into the Channel at Dungeness which is blessed with a weird assortment of attractions, from a nuclear power station to the UK's longest miniature railway, running between Romney, Hythe and Dymchurch. Inland, the mysterious atmosphere of Romney Marsh can best be appreciated at a handful of lonely fog-bound churches surrounded by quietly grazing sheep and unusual birdlife. Slap bang in the middle is Dover, with its impressive castle and busy ferry terminals, still many visitors' first impression of England and not always a happy one. ▸▸ *For Sleeping, Eating and other listings, see pages 165-166.*

Dover

Sitting in the mouth of the River Dour at the southern end of the North Downs, Dover and its famous white cliffs have long been an important landing-place. The Roman Dubris (one of its guiding lighthouses still stands in the grounds of the **castle**) was the starting point for Watling St, the main road up to London via Canterbury. During the Dark Ages, the Saxons fortified its position, but it's thanks to Henry II that there's something really worth seeing in the town today. In the late 12th century he ordered the construction of the great stone castle on the cliffs that has since become known as the 'key to England'. As the closest town to mainland Europe (17 miles away at Cap Griz Nez), a procession of historically significant characters have stepped its streets. Charles II landed here at the Restoration. Francois Blanchard flew across the channel from here in a balloon in 1785, followed more than a century later by Louis Bleriot in an aeroplane. In 1918 Woodrow Wilson docked in, the first US President ever to visit England. During the First World War, it was the major route to the battlefields of France, protected by the Dover Patrol, ferrying some 12 million British and American soldiers to meet their fates. In the Second World War, between 1940 and 1944, the town and harbour were shelled almost continually. Unfortunately, however, for a place with such an important place in history, modern Dover is a disappointment, hemmed in by huge roads and some seriously ugly post-war developments.

Ins and outs

Getting there **Trains** from London Charing Cross (1 hour 40 minutes) and from London Victoria (1 hour 50 minutes) pull into Dover Priory, close to the town centre. A free bus service runs from the station down to the docks. Dover is 71 miles southeast

The Southeast East Kent Coast

of London and can usually be reached in under 2 hours by **car** on either the M20 via Ashford or the M2/A2 via Canterbury. The M20 is usually quicker, except at peak times or during a French lorry strike, when the M2 is likely to be less busy. » *For further details, see Transport page 165.*

Getting around Apart from a small area in the centre, Dover is not the most attractive town to walk around, dominated by the big roads serving the docks. Negotiate the subways though, and shanks's pony (ie your legs) can probably take you wherever you might need to go.

Information TIC ⓘ *Townwall St, T01304-205108, daily 0900-1800.*

Sights

Without doubt the highlight of any visit to Dover, the remarkably well-preserved medieval **castle** ⓘ *(EH), T01304-211067, Apr-Sep daily 1000-1800, Oct 1000-1700, Nov-Mar 1000-1600, £8, concessions £6, under-16s £4, family £20,* dominates the town, a steep climb directly above the port. (In fact it is better to approach it by car from Deal and the east.) Henry II's stern square keep (1168-80s) looms proud on the hilltop, surrounded by a series of concentric walls with fortified towers. These are a familiar feature of most medieval castles but they first appeared in western Europe here, thanks to Crusaders who had got wise attacking the Moslems' fortifications. Although the castle occupies the site of an Iron Age fort, the oldest visible testament to the importance of its position is the hexagonal base of the Roman lighthouse. In the 15th century, this was heightened to become the belltower of the Saxon church next door. Inside the keep, the chapel dedicated to Thomas à Becket has some fine Romanesque carving, while the views from its battlements are superb. Most people's favourite part of a visit, though, are the secret wartime tunnels that burrow through the cliffs. Begun after the French had successfully undermined one of the northern gate towers in the siege of 1216, only to be driven back in hand-to-hand combat, the tunnels were expanded 600 years later during the Napoleonic Wars, providing barracks for up to 2000 troops ready to repel invaders below the clifftops. During the Second World War, further underground space was created from which to mastermind the retreat from Dunkirk. During the summer the castle gets busy with re-enactments of its eventful history and throughout the year there's enough to see and do to occupy most of the day.

In the centre of the town itself, there's sadly not much to linger over, except for the award-winning local history **museum** ⓘ *Market Sq, T01304-201066, www.dovermuseum.co.uk, summer daily 1000-1800, winter daily 1000-1730, £1.70, 90p concessions,* which includes the new interactive Bronze Age Boat Gallery. Archaeological finds in the area are on the ground floor, from Roman times as well as from the important Buckland Anglo-Saxon cemetery. On the first floor there are regular special exhibitions. The Bronze Age Boat Gallery is on the second floor, dedicated to the remains of the world's oldest known sea-going boat, about 3500 years old and discovered as recently as 1992.

Round the corner from the museum, in New Street, is the **Roman Painted House** – the fairly impressive remains of a **Roman 'mansio'** ⓘ *T01304-203279, Apr-Sep Tue-Sun, Jul and Aug also Mon, 1000-1700, £2, concessions 80p,* or official hotel, including its wall paintings and hypocaust.

Down nearer the seafront, **Wellington Dock** is also a good place to spend a couple of hours, reached via a subway beneath Townwall St from Castle St and Market Square. Apart from shopping at **De Bradelei Wharf** (see Shopping, below), youcan also take a **boat trip** to see the cliffs (see Activities below). Also in Wellington Dock, there's the chance to climb aboard and look around a beautifully restored **'Gentleman's Yacht'** ⓘ *T01634-376564, T07712-964276, Tue, Wed, Sat, Sun and bank holidays 1100-1700* for tours by owner, free, of 1878 called *Sorceress*. Owner Richard Grimble has painstakingly returned this fine vessel to its original condition, apparently once the scene of illicit meetings between Lillie Langtry and King Edward VII.

A mile out of town, off the A2 roundabout at Whitfield, the **Dover Transport Museum** ⓘ *Port Zone, White Cliffs Business Park, T01304-204612/822409, Easter-Oct Sun 1000-1700, also Jul, Aug Tue-Fri 1300-1700,£2, £1.50 concessions*, is exactly what it says on the label, entirely run by volunteers, who lovingly care for almost 50 vintage vehicles of all types, as well as some antique reconstructed shops and a model railway layout. Definitely another one of those curiously English labours of love undertaken by anoraky enthusiasts.

Beyond the castle to the east is the **South Foreland Lighthouse** ⓘ *St Margaret's at Cliffe (see below), T01304-852463/202756, Mar-Oct Thu-Mon 1100-1700 by 30 minute tours, £1.80, concessions 90p, family £4.50*, a National Trust property on the **White Cliffs** themselves, built in 1834 and where Marconi made his first successful experiments with wireless, from shore to ship and then to France. It's a good start/end point for walks along the cliffs.

Sleeping

Dover *p163*

B-C Churchill Hotel, Waterfront, T01304-203633, F216320. A straightforward and fairly smart *Best Western* chain hotel.

C Loddington House, East Cliff, Marine Pde, T/F01304-201947. Reasonable, if noisy, being on the main road from the ferry terminal. Breakfast included. Convenient for the ferries.

F YHA Dover, 306 London Rd, T01304-201314, F202236. About half a mile from Dover Priory station, a mile or so from the Docks, with 132 beds in 2 separate townhouses, open all year.

Eating

Dover *p163*

££ The Moonflower, 32-34 High St, T01304-212198. A Chinese restaurant with a good reputation.

££ The Park Inn, Park Pl, Ladywell, T01304-203300, www.theparkinnatdover.co.uk. Has a characterful Victorian dining room and surprisingly opulent rooms upstairs.

Shopping

Dover *p163*

De Bradelei Wharf, overlooking Wellington Dock, T01304-226616, is in a new development on the marina and stocks a wide range of designer wear for men and women at discounted prices.

Le Marché au Vin, Pérardel, Rue Marcel Doret, T0033-0321972122. Many of the shoppers in Dover could well be on their way to France, nipping across the channel on a 'duty free' booze cruise and this is a highly rated wine merchant where they know their stuff.

Activities and tours

Dover *p163*

White Cliffs Boat Trips, De Bradelei Wharf, T01304-271388, T07971-301379. £5, £3 concessions, daily. Trips last about an hr and children are often given a turn at the wheel.

White Cliffs Countryside Project, T01304-241806, organize guided walks around the area.

Transport

For Channel Tunnel information, see p179

Dover *p163*

Bus

Local Stagecoach East Kent, T08702-433711, run buses from Dover to the **North Downs**, east coast, and countryside inland.

Long distance National Express, T08705-808080, run coaches from **Victoria** Coach Station to **Dover** town centre and ferry port every hr between 0700 and 2330 taking around 2 hrs 30 mins.

Car

Practical Car & Van Rental, 17 Elms Vale T01303-279603; **Sixt Kenning Rent-a-car**, Ferry Approach Filling Station, Maison Dieu

Rd, T01304-240340; Winchelsea Car Hire, Unit 3 The Chalk Pit, Winchelsea Works,Winchelsea Rd, T01304-226633.

Ferry

P&O Stena Line, T08706-000600, www.posl.com, run about 32 ships a day to **Calais** from Dover Eastern Docks, (1 hr 15 min). Also from the Eastern Docks, Seafrance, T0870-5711711, make the trip 15 times a day, (15 mins longer but marginally cheaper). **Hoverspeed**, T08705-240241, from Hoverport Western Docks, 8 times day to **Calais** (just under an hr), or **Ostende** 2 times a day at 1100 and 1845 (2 hr).

Taxi

Dover Taxis, 53 Castle St, T01304-201915; Central Taxis, 21 Pencester Rd, T01304-204040; Star Taxis, 321 London Rd, T01304-202027.

Train

From Dover Priory the mainline runs east up the coast via **Walmer**, **Deal** and **Sandwich** to **Ramsgate**, west via **Folkestone** to **Ashford** and **London Victoria** and also northwest via **Canterbury**, **Faversham** and **Chatham** to London.

Directory

Dover *p163*

Hospitals Buckland Hospital, Coombe Valley Rd, T01304-201624. **Internet** Cafe En-Route 66, 8 Bench St, T01304-206633. **Police** Dover Police Station, Ladywell, T01304-240055. **Post office** 68 Pencester Rd, T01304-241747.

Coast north of Dover

→ *Colour map 3, grid B5.*

North of Dover, the east Kent coast facing France is a bracing and unusual backwater. If anything, the twenty or so miles up to Ramsgate have played almost as vital a role in the nation's history as Dover itself. Sandwich most famously lent its name to England's favourite lunchtime snack, thanks to an 18th-century Earl of Sandwich, a gambler who fuelled his game by devouring ham in slices of bread. But it was also an original Cinque Port, along with Hastings, Dover, Romney and Hythe, one of the five defenders of the Channel approaches in the 12th century. Close by, Richborough Castle, where the Romans first set up base in AD 43, has also been left high and dry by the receding sea. Further south, Walmer and Deal remain pleasant and unpretentious old seaside towns. Next door to Dover, a rewarding find is the little seaside village with a name that almost says it all: St Margaret's at Cliffe. ▸▸ *For Sleeping, Eating and other listings see page 168.*

Ins and outs

Getting there There are hourly **Connex trains** from Dover Priory to Walmer, Deal and Sandwich (20 minutes) on the mainline to Ramsgate. Deal is about 20 minutes northeast of Dover on the A258 by **car**. Sandwich is further, but also only about 20 minutes from Dover on the dual carriageway A256. ▸▸ *For further details, see Transport page 168.*

Information TIC ⓘ *Townwall St, Dover, T01304-205108, daily 0900-1800.* **TIC** ⓘ *Town Hall, High St, Deal, T01304-369576. Mon-Fri (May-Sep also Sat) 0900-1700.* **TIC** ⓘ *Guildhall, Sandwich, T01304-613565.*

St Margaret's at Cliffe

Three miles northeast of Dover on the minor road past the castle and the lighthouse is St Margaret's at Cliffe. This charming cliffside village tumbling down to the bay is an unexpected find, with some good pubs that have rooms (see Sleeping page 168), and is worth the detour on the way to Walmer and Deal. The **obelisk** on the corner of St Margaret's Bay commemorates the Dover Patrol, with partners on Cap Blanc Nez and in New York Harbour.

Walmer Castle

ⓘ T01304-364288, Apr-Sep daily 1000-1800, Oct 1000-1700, Nov, Dec and Mar Wed-Sun 1000-1600, Feb weekends only 1000-1600, £4.80, concessions £3.60, under-16s £2.40, family £12.

Due north up the coast Walmer and Deal go hand in hand, joined at the hip even, two ancient seaside towns, Walmer possibly the more polite of the pair with its well-kept little prom. William Penn sailed from Deal on his first trip to America in 1682. Both have Tudor castles defending the Downs, sited to catch any passing ships in a withering crossfire if they attempted to pass to landward of the treacherous Goodwin Sands. Although now less of a fort and more of a stately home, highlights of Walmer Castle include the room in which the Duke of Wellington died in 1852, kept as it was on that day, along with a pair of his famous boots, as well as memorials to other Wardens of the Cinque Ports like Pitt the Younger and Winston Churchill. The extensive gardens and park outside are delightful, part laid out to commemorate the 95th birthday of the late Queen Mother. The Broad Walk is flanked by a famously knobbly old yew hedge.

Deal

Deal Castle *ⓘ Victoria Rd, T01304-372762, Apr-Sep daily 1000-1800, Oct 1000-1700, Nov-Mar 1000-1600, £3.10, concessions £2.30, under-16s £1.60,* still looks like a proper coastal fortification, although now considerably further from the sea than when it was built by Henry VIII in the fanciful but effective shape of a Tudor rose. One of the few of a chain around the south coast to survive in its original condition, its long gloomy corridors, spooky dungeon, and interesting displays on coastal defences down the ages can easily fill a couple of enjoyable hours.

Beyond the castle, the town of Deal stretches along the seafront in a pleasing and unpompous way, with an unassuming little pier and a string of old weather-boarded and brick houses that escaped the bombs. On Victoria Parade, the 18th-century **Timeball Tower** *ⓘ T01304-201200, Jul-Aug Tue-Sun 1000-1700, £1.25, concessions 85p,* bills itself as a 'historic communications centre' containing intriguing displays on signalling, time, semaphore and telegraphy. The ball on the top drops every hour in July and August, once the only way that ships in the channel could set their watches. Second in importance to the one in Greenwich, it is one of only four in the world.

A short walk further into town, the **Maritime Museum** *ⓘ St George's Rd, T01304-381344, May-Sep daily 1400-1700, £1.50, 50p concessions,* is a small local museum dedicated to the lives of the local seamen, some of whom were expert handlers of the Deal Lugger, boats specially designed to cope with the notorious currents and tides on this stretch of coast and famously capable of outstripping any that Customs and Excise could bring into play against them.

Sandwich

About 7 miles north of Deal on the A258, Sandwich was also once an important seaport, although it's now at least 2 miles inland on the banks of the river Stour. Still recognizably a medieval town, its winding little half-timbered streets are fun to explore, full of antique shops and little tearooms. The most prominent survival from its heyday is the **Barbican**, a Tudor gate-tower to the north of the town beside the river. The drained marshland between here and the coast is taken up by pharmaceutical giant Pfizer's massive factory, pumping out Viagra no doubt. To the south the **Sandwich Bay Bird Observatory,** T01304-617341, has a visitor centre next door to the famous Royal St George golf links. **River trips** (T07957-503730) are available from the old bridge over the Stour, one of the most satisfying being the journey through the marshes to Richborough Fort (£5).

Richborough Fort

ⓘ (EH), T01304-612013, Apr-Sep daily 1000-1800, Oct daily 1000-1700, Nov and Mar Wed-Sun 1000-1600, Dec-Feb weekends only 1000-1600, £2.70, concessions £2.
Within 2 miles of Sandwich, hard to find by road but well worth the effort, is Richborough Roman Fort. Here are the impressive remains of the Roman fort of Rutupiae where the process of civilizing the British Isles began with Claudius' invasion in AD 43. Substantial sections of the walls are still standing, although ruined, with the site of a monumental triumphal arch that once marked the gateway to the new colony taking centre stage. Its original strategic position on the coast, guarding the entrance to the Wantsum channel like its counterpart Reculver in the north, is hard to appreciate today, the sea now way off in the distance. However, the outlandish features furnished by the 20th century in the wide view from this atmospheric old place are compensation enough: an abandoned power station's curvaceous cooling towers, jumbo freightliners landing at Manston airport nearby and a wind-generator. There's a 40-minute audio tour and an amphitheatre awaiting thorough excavation in the fields nearby.

West of Sandwich

From Sandwich the A256 continues north past the bleak expanse of Pegwell Bay and the mouth of the Stour, to Ramsgate (7 miles) while the A257 heads west to Canterbury (11 miles). North of the A257, small villages are hidden away down lanes crossing the marshland and orchards in the river valley. **Wickhambreaux**, 3 miles east of Canterbury north of the A257, is worth a look for the old houses that surround the church and village green as well as its pub, *The Rose*. To the south, the Church of St Nicholas at **Barfreston** is one of the most complete examples of late-Norman Romanesque in England, close to the North Downs Way long distance footpath.

Sleeping

St Margaret's at Cliffe *p166*
C-D **Coastguard Inn**, T01304-852057 or T07939-662020 (mob). Has a self-contained cottage with sea views behind the pub.
D **The Clyffe Inn**, High St, T01304-852400, F851880. Pub with rooms.

Deal *p167*
C-D **Royal Hotel**, Beach St, T01304-375555, www.theroyalhotel.com. Seafront hotel where, Admiral Nelson used to meet Lady Hamilton. Excellent breakfast room right on the beach.

Sandwich *p167*
A **Bell Hotel**, The Quay, T01304-613388, F615308. The smartest place in the area, popular with golfers.
C-D **The Sportsman**, 23 The Street, Sholden, near Sandwich, T01304-374973. A friendly pub and restaurant with 3 rooms.

Eating

St Margaret's at Cliffe *p166*
The Coastguard Inn, down near the water, T01304-853176, is a very pleasant place to sit outside and enjoy the sea views, a freehouse with good reasonably priced pub food (main courses about £7).

Deal *p167*
Dunkerley's Hotel, 19 Beach St, T01304-375016, is the smartest restaurant in Deal, on the seafront, booking advisable for meals costing about £20 a head.

Sandwich *p167*
The Admiral Owen, by the bridge, T01309-620869, is a fine place to sip a pint and watch the world go by on the water. **The Rose Inn**, Wickhambreaux, does very presentable food (about £8 for a main course), with tables outside overlooking the attractive village green.

Transport

Bus

Local There are buses from **Dover** to **Walmer**, **Deal** and **Sandwich** (1hr) are run by Stagecoach East Kent, T08702-433711 and Cardinal Coaches, T01304-212859.

Coast south of Dover

→ Colour map 3, grid B5.

Despite or perhaps because of the Channel Tunnel, Folkestone is a shadow of its former self. Even so, with its transport links and faded Edwardian splendour, it remains the most obvious place to start an exploration of one of the oddest corners of Kent. In 1287, nearby New Romney's harbour was destroyed by a ferocious storm, the Norman church's west entrance filling with pebbles and the pillars inside bearing traces of the flooding to this day. The storm also blocked the mouth of the river Rother with shingle, forcing it to find a new way out to sea at Rye. Around the same time, more than 20 small churches were being built by the wool-rich locals. Along with the sheep, the loneliness and the eerie quiet, despite the encroaching bungalows, the atmosphere around these old places make the marsh a strange and special area to explore. On the coast the marsh juts into the channel at Dungeness, a remarkably desolate shingle spit dotted with a weird array of attractions. *» For Sleeping, Eating and other listings see page 171.*

Folkestone

Sadly Folkestone these days hardly merits an overnight stay, although anyone with time to kill and an interest in Cold War technology can look over the **Russian Submarine** ⓘ *T01303-240400,* moored at South Quay, a Soviet-era hunter killer and one of only four in the world. Or take a stroll along **The Leas**, an Edwardian clifftop boardwalk reached via a water-balanced chairlift. Otherwise the town's uneasy mix of old and new makes it a faintly depressing place to linger. **TIC** ⓘ *Harbour St, T01303-258594.*

Romney and Walland Marshes

Between Hythe in the east and Rye in the west, the once sea-swamped Romney and Walland marshes, known locally as 'the marsh', is a miniature fenland. In Roman times it must have looked like the area around Hayling Island on the Hampshire coast does today. In the Middle Ages though the Rhee Wall was built between Appledore and Romney (now the B2080 and A259), allowing complete drainage of the area by 1562. Until then, sea-going ships found shelter as far inland as Smallhythe. The church at Appledore, now at least 10 miles from the sea, was built on the site of a fort established by Danish berserkers storming ashore from their longships in the Dark Ages.

Ins and outs

Information TIC ⓘ *New Romney, Magpie, Church Approach, T01797-364044.*

Sights

Appledore is a lovely little town on the **Royal Military canal.** Constructed to fend off Bonaparte, with a kink every few 100 yards for a cannon, the banks of the canal are still lined with pillboxes from 1940. Overlooking the marsh from the church, it's easy to picture the marsh under water all those years ago. Many of the local churches, with their heavy angled buttresses, look a little like upturned boats.

At **St Mary in the Marsh**, apart from the grave of E Nesbit, the author of *The Railway Children*, the church has little more than a solitary pub, the *Star Inn*, for company. Apart from New Romney, **Lydd** is the largest settlement in the area, with a faintly dilapidated air. Its church is proportionately larger than most of the others, known as 'the cathedral of the marsh', but was bombed almost flat in the Second World War. Reconstructed, it remains the focal point of this low-lying town with most major facilities.

Nearby at **Old Romney**, the church has some fine 18th-century box pews and a minstrel's gallery, as well as a beautifully carved Purbeck marble medieval font. The most unusual of all the marshes churches is at **Brookland**, with its triple-coned wood-shingle belltower in a Norwegian style, detached from the main body of the early Gothic church. Inside there's a wall painting of the murder of Thomas à Becket and a remarkable 12th-century font decorated with the signs of the zodiac and the pastoral activities with which they're associated. **Fairfield** is the most lonely of the churches, a 13th-century timber-framed building bricked over in the 18th century and restored in the 20th. It can only be reached along a raised dyke off the road in the middle of nowhere.

Apart from church visiting, fans of Second World War military hardware will appreciate the **Brenzett Aeronautical Museum**, Ivychurch Road, **Brenzett**, ⓘ *T01797-344747*, which has a couple of hangars housing a collection of Second World War memorabilia, bits of aircraft and things, many of them found dotted about the marsh.

Hythe, New Romney and Dungeness

On the eastern seaboard of the marsh, Hythe and Romney were two of the original Cinque Ports. Hythe unfortunately suffered extensive damage during the war, leaving little of note to look at now, but thankfully its magnificent **church** survived in the older part of town. In its crypt, beneath an impressive early Gothic chancel, higher than its nave, and reminiscent of Canterbury Cathedral's but on a much smaller scale, is a gruesome array of thigh bones and skulls (from an estimated 4,000 people), all very neatly stacked up. Nobody minds if you handle them. Near Hythe, the **Port Lympne Wild Animal Park**, was one of John Aspinall's exotic animal collections, with plenty of gorillas and big cats, in the grounds of Philip Sassoon's stately home.The views from the Norman ruins of **Lympne Castle** ⓘ *T01303-264647*, over the marshes are breathtaking.

New Romney is the main town of the marsh, not much to look at, although the **Museum of the Romney Hythe and Dymchurch Railway** is worth checking out. Constructed by the millionaire racing driver Captain Howey in 1927, the **Romney Hythe and Dymchurch Railway** ⓘ *T01797-362353, www.rhr.demon.co.uk, Easter-Sep daily, Mar, Oct weekends only, return £9.20 Hythe-Dungeness, with many other tickets available, phone for details,* runs for 13 miles along the coast from Hythe to Dungeness, calling at Dymchurch, St Mary's Bay, New Romney and Romney Sands. The whole thing, track, engines and carriages, is one-third full size: adorable coaches are pulled along by hard-working little replica steam and diesel engines. The journey from Hythe to Dungeness takes just over an hour and is easily the most charming way of reaching the strange and desolate tip of the shingle spit at Dungeness.

Without doubt one of the weirdest places on the south coast, **Dungeness** is not only the end of the line for the little railway, it's also home to a nuclear power station, two lighthouses, and a string of beach huts popular with recluses. One of these, **Prospect Cottage**, was famously given a delightful garden by the late artist and film-maker Derek Jarman. Although a private residence, the oddly moving layout of rocks and exotic plants is visible from the road. In another, there's an excellent source of home-smoked fresh fish at **The Smokery** ⓘ *T01797-320604*. Occasionally, the quiet is broken by a massive roar, like a low-flying jet, as the power station lets off steam. The **Dungeness A Power Station Visitor Centre** ⓘ *T01797-321815, Mar-Oct daily, Nov-Feb by appointment, booking required, free, (no under-5s)*, reassures the public that they are quite safe. The best place to appreciate the outlandish position and the peculiar light reflecting off the sea all around is from the top of the **Old Lighthouse** ⓘ *T01797-321300, May-Sep daily 1030-1700, Mar, Apr and Oct weekends only, £2.40, concessions £1.40, family £6.20*. After climbing 169 steps, you can enjoy the scale problems caused by the miniature railway steaming across the flat landscape, for all the world like the Santa Fe express heading into the desert. The fourth lighthouse on the site, built in 1901, it also contains a few displays on the local history. When the power station blocked the light, it was replaced by the award-winning modern one in 1961. Birdwatchers and nightfishers flock here to see the local colonies of rare seabirds and catch unlikely fish enjoying the warm waters of the power station's outfall ⓘ *Dungeness RSPB Nature Reserve, T01797-320588*.

Sleeping

Folkestone *p169*

C Pigeonwood House at Grove Farm, Arpinge, near Folkestone, T01303-89111. A comfortable 18th-century farmhouse, a little further afield, but nearer the Channel Tunnel.

D Chandos Guest House, 77 Cheriton Rd, Folkestone, T01303-851202. A reliable B&B.

D Kentmere Guest House, 76 Cheriton Rd, T01303-259661. Perfectly reliable.

New Romney *p170*

C Romney Bay House, Coast Rd, Littlestone, T01797-364747, F367156. Designed in the 1920s by Sir Clough Williams-Ellis, the creator of the town of Portmeirion in Wales. It's pretty much the only top-notch hotel in the area.

E Martinfield Manor, Lydd Rd, T01797-363802. Has 5 comfortable en-suite rooms overlooking the marsh.

Eating

Romney and Walland Marshes *p169*

££ Bayleaves, 33-35 The Street, Appledore, T01233-758208, (closed Mon, daytime only). Do a variety of home-made light meals, including vegetarian options, in a cheerful atmosphere, as well as first-rate cream teas.

Pubs, bars, and clubs

Romney and Walland Marshes *p169*

The Woolpack, Brookland, T01797-344321, is a delightful marsh pub with a great menu.

Red Lion, Snargate, doesn't do food, but with its garden to one side and cosy interior, it's the best place for a good pint.

Transport

Folkestone *p169*

Bus

Long distance Folkestone sits at the end of the M20, just under 2 hrs from London. National Express, T08705-808080, run coaches to Folkestone every 2 hrs between 0900 and 2330 (2 hrs 30 mins).

Ferry

Hoverspeed, T08705-240241, run regular services to **Boulogne** taking just under an hr.

Train

Folkestone is on the mainline from **London Charing Cross** via **Ashford** (1 hr 40 mins). Le Shuttle, T01303-271100, run the hourly car-on-the-train service to **France** from just north of Folkestone, journey-time about 30 mins.

For an explanation of the sleeping and eating price codes used in this guide, see the inside front cover. Other relevant information is provided in the Essentials chapter, page 40.

Rye and around

→ Colour map 3, grid C4

Rye is a sleepy market town perched on a hill overlooking Romney Marsh and the English Channel. Its maze of cobbled streets, towers and half-timber buildings make it a serious contender for prettiest town in England. This picturesque idyll belies the town's past – the centre was once encircled by water and her winding streets, secluded inns and cubby-holes made the place a safe haven for smugglers and brigands. The whole town has a fairy-tale quality. But from the 18th century, Rye cleaned up its act, becoming a magnet for artists and writers. The modern town's carefully planned tourist industry feeds on both elements of her past, with all manner of 'contraband' alongside the tributes to Henry James, former resident. Despite its understandable appeal as a day-trip venue, Rye is more than just a vacuum-packed fillet of England's past. There are some quality hotels and estimable restaurants here, many in quaint tumbledown premises, which make it worth forking out a few extra pounds to prolong your stay. Despite the crowds in high season, the legacy of a history this colourful and a setting this idyllic is hard to resist. » For Sleeping, Eating and other listings, see pages 175-178.

Ins and outs

Getting there A delightfully knackered diesel **train** links Rye to Hastings (20 minutes) and Ashford (25 minutes). From Hastings you can pick up connections to London Charing Cross (2 hours); Lewes (1 hour 30 minutes) and Brighton (1 hour 45 minutes). From Ashford you can make connections to Dover (1 hour), and Canterbury (1 hour 15 minutes). By **car**, Rye lies on the South Coast trunk route (A259), between Brighton, Lewes and Hastings and Dover. From London you can take the A21 as far as Hastings but, if you fancy a more leisurely countryside jaunt, turn off at Flimwell, just after Tunbridge Wells, and take the A268 along the sheep-strewn Rother Valley. Local *buses* link Hastings and Rye rail stations hourly. Longer distance coaches run hourly to Dover, and Brighton via Lewes with a change at Eastbourne. » For further details, see Transport, page 177.

Getting around Rye is tiny and can easily be explored on foot. To visit Winchelsea, there are hourly train services (5 minutes, £1.90), or there are various local buses (10 minutes). Camber Sands can be reached by the No11 bus (15 minutes).

Information TIC ① *Strand Quay, T01797-226696, Jun-Aug daily 0900-1730, Sep-May 1000-1600*. You can pick up a map and guide here, but if you're planning a quick trip, it might be best to opt for the Rye town walk (£1) guided tour, or an audio-tour £2/£1.

Sights

The Story of Rye ① *Strand Quay, T01797-226696, Jun-Aug 0900-1730, Sep-May 1000-1600*, at the TIC, is an audio-visual presentation, set within the Rye town model, which offers a glimpse of Rye's turbulent past. Continue up Wish Ward, and you'll come to Mermaid Street and The Mermaid Inn. The street is one that regularly features on patriotic postcards, and with its timber-framed 15th-century houses, and cobbles, it's easy to see why. The notorious Hawkhurst gang of smugglers used the Inn for riotous nights on the tiles after successful raids. These days it's a very genteel hotel and restaurant with more cocoa than contraband. A right turn at the top of Mermaid Street takes you to **Lamb House** ① *West St, T01797-227709, Apr-Oct Wed and Sat 1400-1800, £2.60, under-16s £1.30*. This lovely 18th-century house has been home to Henry James, and EF Benson, and there's a small exhibition inside containing some of the former's possessions.

At the end of West Street is the gorgeous Church Square. The **Church of St Mary the Virgin**, is a 15th-century rebuild of an earlier church, and the clock in the tower (the oldest to use a pendulum in England) features two golden cherubs who emerge on each quarter hour. You can climb the tower for a splendid view over the rooftops (£2). Leading off one corner, is **Watchbell Street**, containing yet more attractive timber-framed houses, there is a viewing-point on the little promontory over Strand Quay, affording a wide vista of the river valley.

Another corner of Church Square leads to the **Ypres Tower** (1249). Part of anti-French fortifications, the tower is now home to one half of the **Rye Castle Museum** ⓘ *T01797-226728, Mon-Fri and Sun 1000-1300 and 1400-1700, Apr-Oct Sat-Sun 1030-1300 and 1400-1700, only the Ypres section is open in winter Sat 1030-1530, £6, under-16s £1.60,* and contains smuggling memorabilia, medieval pottery, and an exhibit on the unique Romney Marsh sheep! The other half of the museum is in East St, and features locally made toys and pottery.

Heading down East Cliff, you'll come to **The Landgate**. Part of Edward III's 1329 town fortifications, the gate pays testimony to Rye's watery past: it used to be the only way in at High Tide.

Around Rye

A footpath leads off the right of Wish Street (A259), over the bridge from Strand Quay into the **salt marshes** to the town's west. Here you can see some wonderful wildlife – terns, frogs, dragonflies and some vivid wild flowers. After 1½ miles, you'll arrive at **Camber Castle** ⓘ T01797-223862, *Jul-Sep, £2, under-16s £1,* (1539-43), sited on a gravel bank between what were once the twin harbours of Rye and Winchelsea, this squat structure was built by Henry VIII to defend schismatic England from Catholic Europe. The waters may have receded but the place retains an air of atmospheric isolation.

Camber Sands, 6 miles to the south of Rye, is a sandy, windswept beach, complete with dunes, and a host of rare species of flora and fauna.

Winchelsea

Hop on a bus or train over the Brede valley and you're in this unusual little village. Originally an island in Rye Harbour, and part of the Cinque Ports system of coastal defences, the village's surviving grid pattern was installed by Edward I in 1283. These days it's a place with a few tangible reminders of a past equally illustrious and turbulent, and often less overwhelmed with visitors than its more famous neighbour. Former residences of authors including Joseph Conrad abound, and an excavation on the edge of the hill suggests that those who fell foul of the plague and French invaders are piled up in their hundreds. The village's story is told at **Winchelsea Museum**. ⓘ *Court Hall, T01797-224395, Apr-Sep 1030-1230 and 1400-1700, £1.*

Hastings

Poor old Hastings. Things started going wrong when a militant Norman now known as William the Conqueror put to shore near here in 1066 and began his successful invasion of these Isles. From that fateful moment on, history has rarely treated the place kindly. The seafront is awash with grandiose seaside retreats intended for the holidaying London bourgeoisie, but they never really came, preferring, like modern metropolitan clubbers, the racy glamour and convenience of Brighton. Adding insult to injury, Hastings is consistently overlooked by economic planners, failing to benefit much from the development of the Kent corridor to the Channel Tunnel. The town sits rather forlornly on its sandstone outcrop – home to a bedraggled fishing fleet, some of the tackiest seaside amenities in the country and some of the worst social problems in the Southeast. But kick away this crumbling façade and the place has an undeniable appeal. Okay, the New Town is an architectural eyesore, but the Old Town, with its precipitous alleyways looking over a clutter of dignified Regency pads, ramshackle Tudor houses and fishermen's cottages is a delight. The shops of George Street contain some fine antiquarian books, work by a thriving community of local artists and enough antiques and curios to satsify the most nostalgic of browsers. Moreover, the fishing fleet, based around the unique wooden huts on the beach gives the town an honest-to-goodness workaday edge lacking in most of the seaside towns on the south coast. Brighton trades on its faded glamour. Hastings was never glamorous in the first place, and that's its charm.

Information TIC ⓘ *Priory Meadow, T01424-781111, Mon-Sat 0900-1700, Sun 1000-1700*, has plenty of leaflets and a helpful accommodation service.

Sights

The **New Town**, the area west of George Street, despite containing many of the town's amenities, is not pleasant to walk around – there are tacky amusement arcades everywhere, the streets have a flyblown air about them, and the pier looks like an unhappy electricity pylon that has chosen to end it all by falling into the sea. The **Hastings Museum and Art Gallery** ⓘ *Cambridge Rd, T01424-781155, Mon-Fri 1000-1700, Sat 1000-1300 and 1400-1700, Sun 1500-1700*, contains an excellent selection of fossils and local animals, there's also an exhibit on the Hastings-born conservationist, Grey Owl.

Head for the **Old Town** for most places of interest. A good place to start is the **West Cliff Railway** ⓘ *George St, T01424-781111, Apr-Oct 1000-1730, Nov-Mar 1100-1600, 80p, concessions 40p*, a cute little funicular taking you to the grassy park atop West Hill. On a sunny day, the view over the rooftops of the Old Town and out to sea is entrancing. Also on West Hill are **Hastings Castle** and **1066 Story** ⓘ *T01424-781111, Oct-Apr 1100-1530, Apr-Sep, 1000-1700, £3.20, £2.10*. The castle was built by William I, but little remains now, while the exhibition is a good-value audio-visual synopsis for the historically challenged. **Smugglers Adventure** ⓘ *St Clements Caves, T01424-422964, Oct-Easter 1100-1630, Easter-Sep 1000-1730, £5.25, under-16s £3.40*, is a celebration of the hearty brigands who used to thrive along these shores.

From West Cliff, you can head down through the maze of vertiginous passages and alleyways, lined with timber-framed and Georgian houses, leading to George Street, where you can pick up natty antiques and prints of the area. Along the High Street, you'll find the intriguing **Flower Makers Museum** ⓘ *T01424-427793, Mon-Fri 0930-1600, Sat 1100-1600, £1*, set in the premises of a company that supplied over 100,000 rose petals for the film *Gladiator*. A little further along is the **Old Town Museum of Local History** ⓘ *T01424-781166, Apr-Sep 1000-1700, Oct-Mar 1100-1600, free*, which has a fine collection of Saxon coins and even a few interactive exhibits.

The Stade is the name given to the beach upon which the town's fishing industry is based. The area is littered with little fishing boats and tall wooden 'net-huts' unique to this part of the world. Despite ubiquitous posters blaming Eurocrats for the demise of the fisherman's lot, the industry clings on, and is in fact the largest beach-launched fishing fleet in Europe. If you're here at the right time (ie early morning), you'll catch the fleet coming in, and you can pick up some and animatedly fresh Dover sole, skate and plaice from the huts before they're whisked off to the restaurant tables of London. Also worth trying to see is the **Shipwreck Heritage Centre** ⓘ *Rock-a-Nore Rd, T01424-437452*, a fascinating audio-visual account of the many ships which have perished off Hastings. The **Fisherman's Museum** ⓘ *Rock-a-Nore, T01424-428893, Mon-Fri 0930-1600, Sat 1100-1600, free*, features *The Enterprise*, the last indigenously built sailing lugger, and exhibits on the local trade. **Underwater World Hastings** ⓘ *Rock-a-Nore, T01424-718776, summer 1000-1700, winter 1100-1600, £5.25, under-16s £3.40*, boasts a glass tunnel through shark-infested water. The **East Cliff Railway** ⓘ *Rock-a-Nore, T01424-781111, summer 1000-1700, winter 1100-1600, 80p, under-16s 40p*, is the steepest funicular in the UK, taking passengers up to the Country Park and more tremendous views over the Old Town, and along the flat stretch of coast to the west.

Around Hastings

Traditionally, the English have prided themselves on their independence and 1066 has always been a date of considerable import: the last time the country was successfully invaded. These days **Battle** is just another pretty little English town with a violent past, but there are a few remarkable remains of William the Conqueror's victory over King Harold. **1066 Battlefield and Battle Abbey** ⓘ *T01424-773792, Apr-Sep 1000-1800, 1-31 Oct 1000-1700, Nov-Mar 1000-1600, £4.30, under-16s £3.20*, is where it all took place and you can view it with the aid of videos, interactive exhibits and re-enactments of the battle by local actors. You can appreciate the owner's attempts to provide some context to what is essentially a field with a ruined church in it, but the historical marketing is laid on pretty thick. That said, it's an atmospheric place and should be on anybody's 'to do' list on a visit to the South Coast. The **Church of St Mary the Virgin** ⓘ *T01424-773649*, however, is harder to spoil, built on the site of the 1066 battle, it contains a Norman font, 14th-century wall paintings and the gilded alabaster tomb of Sir Anthony Browne, to whom Henry VIII granted the Abbey. There are a few reasonable places to eat along the high street outside the Abbey entrance.

Pevensey Castle ⓘ *T01323-762604, Apr-Sep 1000-1800, Oct 1000-1700, Nov-Mar 1000-1600 Wed-Sun, £2.50, under-16s £1.90*, is a better bet than Battle if you like your ruins not too ruined. The Outer Walls of the castle are Roman and a few traces of original brickwork remain. We have Robert De Mortain, William the Conqeror's half-brother to thank for this chunk of Roman Britain. In building his castle on the site, he left the outer walls fairly unscathed, concentrating on building a new inner Bailey and rectangular stone Keep. Derelict since the 16th century this unique fusion of the Roman and Norman styles is a captivating addition to the flat coastal plains between Eastbourne and Hastings and well worth a trip.

Sleeping

Rye *p172*

There is plenty of accommodation in Rye, from B&Bs to upmarket hotels. For B&Bs try the accommodation booking service at the TIC Rye is such a captivating place to stay, that it's worth parting with a few quid for a weekend in one of the town's finest hotels:

A The Mermaid Inn, Mermaid St, T01797-225 069, one of the oldest and prettiest hostelries.

C Rye Lodge Hotel, Hilder's Cliff, T01797-223838, in the centre of town with stunning views across the estuary, luxury suites and a decent dining room.

C White Vine House, High St, T01797-224748. Another upmarket floral gem on the High St with some luxurious rooms.

D The Little Orchard House, West St, T01797-223831. In a quiet cobbled street and does excellent breakfasts.

D The Old Vicarage, 66 Church Sq, T01797-222119. In the thick of it, opposite the church tower, a very twee, pink Georgian affair surrounded by roses.

D-E The Durrant House Hotel, 2 Market St, T01797-226639. A family-run Georgian townhouse hotel.

D-E Jeake's House, Mermaid St, T01797-222623. A stylishly restored townhouse with a book-lined bar.

D-E The Old Borough Arms, The Strand, T01797-222128. A family-run, 300-year-old former sailor's inn.

E Windmill Guesthouse, off Ferry Rd, T01797-224027. Comfortable and good value.

Self-catering

The Camber Sands Holiday Park, T01797-225555. Offers self-catering cabins along the beach.

Hastings *p173*

Hastings is awash with B&Bs, some less savoury than others, and the focus of some of the town's considerable social problems. A few of those out west, towards St Leonard's, are best avoided. As always, ask at the TIC accommodation desk. Battle is best explored on a day trip from Hastings or even London and accommodation is limited and expensive. As far as bigger hotels go, there's nothing very grand, but the following should be satisfactory.

C-D **Lansdowne Hotel**, 1-2 Robertson Terr, T01424-429605. Slightly smarter.
C-E **Chatsworth Hotel**, Carlisle Pde, T01424-720188. A vast pile.
D **Jenny Lind Hotel**, 69 High St, T01424-421392. Looks a little grotty but has acceptable double rooms and is in the heart of the old town.
E **The Apollo**, 25 Cambridge Gardens, T01424-444394. Has acceptable rooms from £20 per person.
E **Holyers**, 1 Hill St, T01424-430014. A Tudor guesthouse also in the thick of the old town.
E **Lavender & Lace**, 106 All Saints St, T01424-716290. Not quite as twee as its name suggests, and has nice rooms in a 16th-century property.
E **Tulips**, 27 Croft Rd, T01424-712511. An attractive old house up one of the old town's many steep hills.

Eating

Rye *p172*

There are restaurants to cater for all tastes and budgets in Rye. Look out for locally caught seafood, game, and the wonderfully tender Romney Lamb.
£££ **The Copper Kettle**, The Mint, T01797-222012, also offers local specialities such as rabbit and pheasant pâté, and Whitstable oysters, quite expensive with mains ranging from £12-£20.
£££ **The Landgate Bistro**, 5 Landgate, T01797-222829, has been the top gourmet destination for some time, reflected in the prices and definitely needs to be booked.
££ **The Flushing Inn**, 4 Market St, T01797-223292, provides some wonderful-looking local produce, including 'the Flushing Inn agglomeration of crustaceans and molluscs'.
££ **Union Inn**, East St, T01797-222334, is a bog-standard alehouse, with a curious penchant for outlandish food – grilled crocodile steak for example.
£ **The Bell Inn**, The Mint, T01797-222232, is a pleasant pub with a flowery beer garden. A good bet for a cheap feed, with something and chips starting at around £4.
£ **The Mermaid Inn**, Mermaid St, T01797-223065, has a bar/bistro in the pub serving drinks and bar snacks, as well as more substantial fare like Fisherman's Pie.
£ **Mermaid Street Coffee House**, West St/Mermaid St, T01797-224858, has some very naughty cakes for around £2.
£ **Rye Fish Shop**, The Mint, is your best bet for a takeaway. You can also eat-in, but the place has a uniquely English aura of conversational repression amongst cheap cutlery.
£ **Simon the Pieman**, Market St, offers some interesting sweet and savoury snacks. The fudge is delicious.

Hastings *p173*

££ **Restaurant 27**, 27 George St, T01424-42000, is a reasonable bet with a good line in local fish, more expensive with mains starting at around £12.
£ **Gannets Café/Bistro**, 45 High St, is an uninspiring but reliable diner with a huge menu in the pasta/baked spud vein.
£ **Katie's Pantry**, George St, is a tea and cakes supplier of the frilly variety.
£ **The Larder**, 49 High St, has some surprisingly good deli-style nibbles for a picnic on West Cliff or the beach.
£ **Maggies**, Rock-a-Nore Rd, T01424-430205, in one of the old fishing huts near the beach. The fish and chips are the most famous in town.
£ **Revolver Internet Café**, 26 George St. Café Latte finally reaches Hastings, in typically shrink-wrapped surroundings.

Pubs, bars and clubs

Hastings *p173*

The Anchor, 13 George St, is an implausibly ramshackle old pub where locals come to enjoy pints in booths with peculiar ceilings.
First In Last Out, 14-16 High St, is a no-frills real ale watering hole.
Ye Olde Pump House, 64 George St, is another timber-framed tavern, where you can sup up your beer (from the local Shepherd Neame brewery), with a hearty meal.

Entertainment

Rye *p172*

Understandably, as a quaint old town, there is not much in the way of nightlife in Rye. Local bands do grace the town's pubs from time to time, so keep an eye out in local papers.
Rye Art Gallery, Ockman La, off Market St, has occasional exhibitions by local painters, tending toward twee oil colours of local vistas.

Hastings *p173*
Odeon Cinema, Queens Rd, T08705-05000, is in good nick and has all the latest releases.
Stables Theatre, High St, T01424-423221, innovative theatre in intimate surroundings.
St Mary-in-the-Castle, Pelham Cres, T01424-781624. Multi-purpose arts venue, the likes of Ash and the Divine Comedy have graced the stage of the venue's 'crypt.'
White Rock Theatre, White Rock, T01424-781000. Primarily a venue specializing in horrendous tat – Freddie Mercury tribute nights and the like – this is a big venue, and has played host to the likes of Jools Holland.

Festivals

Rye *p172*
Aug Medieval Weekend, sees locals dressed up as Lords and Ladies, serving wenches, and jongleurs parade through the streets to a 2-day fair at the Town Salts, and there's a medieval street market on the High St. Fans of small-scale civic nostalgia will adore it, others may find it infuriating.
Sep Rye Festival, music, film, drama, literature, visual arts and lectures in a number of venues across the town.
Nov Rye Bonfire Weekend. Rye's 5 Nov celebrations are not on the same scale as Lewes's, but societies from all over the county parade the streets in mild anti-papal solidarity.

Hastings *p173*
Aug Hastings Old Town Carnival takes place every summer, normally in the first week of Aug, and involves, town criers, a fancy dress parade, concerts and recitals, open days at local artists' studios, and free beach concerts.

Shopping

Rye *p172*
There are scores of boutiques, clothing shops, arts and crafts shops and antiques shops in the town centre.
Gillian Tapsell Paintings, High St, sells watercolours of Rye and Winchelsea.
Iden Pottery, Conduit Hill, T01797-223413, is a good place to pick up a clay or china memento of your visit.
Needles Antiques Centre, 15 Cinque Ports St, T01797-225064, with a decent range of not too overpriced antiques and collectables.
Old Grammar School, High St, T01797-222752, situated in a lovely old building that now houses a record shop where you might just pick up some rare vinyl.

Hastings *p173*
Alexander, 25 George St, is an eye-catching jewellers.
L'Illustration, 51 George St, has some attractive-looking local prints in the 'fishing boats on the beach' mould.
Priory Meadow Shopping Centre, between Havelock Rd and Queen's Rd in the new town, has all the mainstream shops and cafes. In the Old Town the area around George St and High St has some interesting bookshops, arts and crafts and curio shops.

Activities and tours

Rye *p172*
Rye Sports Centre, The Grove, T01797-224676, is a multi-purpose sports hall.
Rye Town Salts, is the public park by the river below Fishmarket St and has a bowling green and minigolf.
Sea fishing, with local fishermen can be arranged through the TIC, T01797-226696.
Swimming at Camber Sands is excellent, if usually chilly.
Windsurfing equipment is available for hire at Camber Sands, Winchelsea Beach, and Northpoint Water, T01797-225238.

Hastings *p173*
Summerfields Leisure Centre, Bohemia Rd, T01424 781777 has all the usual facilities.
White Rock Gardens, White Rock, T01424 781111, has tennis courts, bowling greens and putting greens.

Transport

Rye *p172*
Bicycle
Rye Hire, T01797-223033. Bikes for hire from about £10 per day.

Bus
Local Buses pull up in front of Rye rail station. **Rambler Coaches**, T01424-752505 and **Coastal Coaches**, T01825-723024 provide local buses to Hastings, Camber and Winchelsea.

Long distance Stagecoach, T08702-433711, serves Brighton via Eastbourne and Hastings, and Dover.

Train
Rye station is just off Cinque Ports St, and very close to the town centre. **Connex South Central**, T08706-030405.

Hastings *p173*

Car
Hastings is on the A21 from London, and the drive takes 2/3 hrs depending on how quickly you exit the M25. The A259 is the main south coast trunk route, and continues east to Rye and Dover, and west to Lewes and Brighton. Cheap, if arduous, bus services operate from **Victoria Coach Station** in London (3 hrs), and you can also reach **Tunbridge Wells** (lhr 55 mins), **Rye** (1 hr), and Eastbourne (40 mins), for connections to **Lewes** and **Brighton** (1 hr 10 mins), **Battle** (25 mins), **Pevensey** (50 mins).

Train
Hastings is pretty well served by train. There are hourly services to **London Victoria**, (2 hr 25 mins), via **Lewes** (1 hr/£6.60) and **Eastbourne** (35 mins). Trains are half hourly for **London Charing Cross** (1 hr 30 mins) via **Tunbridge Wells** (40 mins). The line to **Ashford International** (45 mins), for trains to France, passes through **Rye** (25 mins). There are also local services to **Battle** (15 mins), **Pevensey** and **Westham** – for Pevensey Castle (25 mins).

Directory

Rye *p172*
Doctors Local doctor with an emergency surgery at Posten Gate, Cinque Ports St, T01797-224924. **Internet** Rye Library, Lion St, T01797-223355. **Police** Rye has no police station, but you can call **Sussex Police** (non-emergency), T08456-070999. **Post office** Cinque Ports St.

Hastings *p173*
Hospitals The Conquest Hospital, The Ridge, T01424-755255, has an A&E.
Internet Revolver Internet Café see Eating above; also at the Library, 13 Claremont, T01424-420501. **Post office** Cambridge Rd, T01424-464243.

North Downs and The Weald

➔ *Colour map 3, grid B/C3/4*

The North Downs stretch in an almost unbroken line all the way from Farnham in Surrey to the white cliffs of Dover. Their geology may be similar to the South Downs, but they hardly compare very favourably, lacking their sea air and being too close to all the main roads to France for comfort. That said, these rolling hills conceal a few attractions well worth seeking out and the North Downs Way is a surprisingly bracing long-distance ridgeway. Near Maidstone, lake-bound Leeds Castle draws the crowds in the summer while further east, tucked into the folds of the hills, small villages like Chilham are highly picturesque.

Southwest of the North Downs, and north of the South Downs, the Weald is a rich bowl of clay soil, unique to England and once entirely wooded. Nowadays it's affluent commuter country. The Restoration spa town of Royal Tunbridge Wells at its heart still bears traces of its 17th-century heyday, in the colonnaded Pantiles and church of King Charles the Martyr. Within easy reach are some of the most memorable old houses in southern Britain: Knole Park in Sevenoaks, Penshurst Place the ancestral home of Sir Philip Sydney and Hever Castle, millionaire newspaper proprietor William Waldorf Astor's medieval castle condo. Near Westerham, Winston Churchill's relatively modest home at Chartwell is one of the most-visited and most evocative of the National Trust's properties. To the south, Ashdown Forest is all that remains of the great Wealden wood. ▸▸ *For Sleeping, Eating and other listings see pages 186-188.*

Ins and outs

Getting there The Channel tunnel **rail** link roughly follows the line of the M20 to the south. This being commuter country, there are plenty of small stations served by stopping trains on the main Charing Cross to Folkestone line, as well as Victoria to Ashford and Folkestone. Stations with bus connections to surrounding attractions include Hollingbourne, Harrietsham, Lenham, Charing. Unfortunately, accessing the North Downs by **road** is all too easy. The A2/M2 roars along their northern side to Canterbury and Dover, while the M20 slices through them just above Eynsford, squeezes past Maidstone and hurtles along their southern slopes all the way via Ashford to Folkestone. Even so, barring the stretch around Rochester and Maidstone, the distance between these 2 big roads is just great enough to allow pockets of the Downs to remain fairly remote and secluded. A network of local **buses** operates out of Maidstone, Sittingbourne, Faversham, Canterbury and Ashford, but the Downs themselves are not very well served. » *For further details, see Transport page 188.*

Information Maidstone TIC ⓘ *The Gatehouse, Palace Gardens, Mill St, T01622-602169.*

M25 to Maidstone

Eynsford

Eynsford is a surprising find so close to the M25. A small town on the trickle of the river Darent, crossed here by both a ford and old bridge, it has not only the ruins of a Norman castle but also one of the most complete Roman floor mosaics in the country and an impressive stately home with a wonderful private chapel at **Lullingstone Roman Villa** ⓘ *T01322-863467, Apr-Sep daily 1000-1800, Oct 1000-1700, Nov-Mar 1000-1600, £2.60, concessions £1.90, under-16s £1.30*. The remarkable mosaics, of Bellerophon slaying the Chimera and of Europa being carried away by Zeus in the shape of a bull, can be found surrounded by the carefully excavated remains of a small farmer's villa. Further down the same small road, behind a large Tudor gatehouse, stands **Lullingstone Castle** ⓘ *T01322-862114, May-Aug, Sat, Sun and bank holidays 1600-1800*. The façade of the present house is a graceful early 18th-century construction, concealing the Tudor Great Hall and courtyards behind. Next door to the house, the **church** is an unusual refurbishment of a Norman church in a striking classical style, also from the early 18th century. The interior features a beautiful plaster ceiling, some fine woodwork and grand monuments to the Hart and Dyke families.

Around Maidstone

Maidstone, the county town of Kent, is really best avoided. Apart from a traffic-choked old riverbank on the Medway and a moderately diverting local museum, the town is an eyesore. Best push on past on the M20 to junction 8 to find **Leeds Castle** ⓘ *T01622-765400, Mar-Oct daily 1000-1700, Nov-Feb 1000-1500, £11, concessions £9.50, under-16s £7.50, family £32*. Proudly billing itself as the 'loveliest castle in the world', it is indeed as pretty as a picture, sitting on a pair of small islands in a large lake surrounded by wooded hills and parkland. It's also quite expensive, an undeniably successful commercial enterprise, with regular special events, ballooning, a maze, underground grotto, an aviary and series of gardens. The interior was restored in the early 20th century and features rooms from a variety of different periods. The oldest part of the castle is the Gloriette, rising straight out of the water, containing the former owner's collection of Impressionist paintings. More interesting perhaps is the unusual collection of antique dog collars in the Gatehouse, although the highlight of a visit here is likely to remain the memorable views of the lakeside. Take a picnic, but leave the dog at home.

Walks in the North Downs

- **Deal to Dover**: 8 miles one-way. Start: Deal Castle. A seaside, clifftop walk along the Saxon Shore Way past St Margaret's-at-Cliffe, round South Foreland and up to Dover Castle. OS Maps: Landranger 179, Explorer 138.
- **Wye National Nature Reserve**: 3 miles there and back. Start: Wye village. A walk along the a section of the North Downs Way, taking in Wye Crown, with its views over Romney Marsh. OS Maps: Landranger 179, Explorer 137.
- **Stour Valley**: 7 miles one-way. Start: Chilham village, 10 miles southwest of Canterbury. Part of the Stour Valley Walk, from picturesque Chilham to the village of Wye, along peaceful riverside and through woodland. OS Maps: Landranger 179, Explorer 137.
- **Ightam Mote**: 4 miles there and back. Start: Knole Park, Sevenoaks. A woodland walk from an Elizabethan palace to a medieval manor house. OS Maps: Landranger 188, Explorer 147.
- **Ide Hill and Chartwell**: 6 miles one-way. Start: Ide Hill village, 3 miles southwest of Sevenoaks. An undulating woodland walk with wide views across National Trust land to Chartwell, former home of Sir Winston Churchill. OS Maps: Landranger 188, Explorer 147.

A mile west of Leeds Castle, a much less well-known medieval treasure albeit on a much smaller scale is **Stoneacre** ⓘ *(NT), Otham, near Maidstone, T01622-862871, Apr-Oct Wed, Sat 1400-1800 (last entry 1700), £2.60, concessions £1.30,* a hall-house restored in the 1920s by the keen antiquarians, Morrisite and Fabian Aymer Vallance. Tucked away in its own wooded valley, the great oak front door gives on to the little beamed hall, beautifully restored to its former glory. A lovely little garden includes a rare gingko tree, a herb garden, and tiny back courtyard with a path leading to a summerhouse giving views over the surrounding orchards.

About 20 miles east of Otham, off the M2 between Sittingbourne and Faversham, **Doddington Place** ⓘ *T01795-886101, Wed mid-Apr to Sep 1300-1800, £3,* is a landscaped garden designed by William Nesfield in the mid-19th century with great yew hedges and tremendous views as well as formal and woodland gardens. His other work included parts of Kensington Gardens and Kew Gardens in London. Another downland garden worth seeking out is **Beech Court** ⓘ *T01233-740641, Easter-Oct daily 1000-1700, £2,* Challock, near Ashford. Eight acres of woodland surrounding a medieval house, at their very best in the last week of May when the azaleas are in bloom.

A few miles northeast, on the way to Canterbury, **Chilham** is a picture-postcard hilltop village with its very own Jacobean castle (closed to the public), antique-stuffed main square and attractive old church. Off the main tourist track, **Maps to Treasure** ⓘ *Howletts Farm, Shottenden, near Chilham, T01227-730760, Tue-Sat 1000-1800,* is an exhibition and salesroom on a working farm of over 100-year-old detailed maps of local areas all round the country.

Royal Tunbridge Wells

Shakespeare would never have heard of Tunbridge Wells, because in his day it hadn't been invented. It was only in 1606, when Dudley Lord North recovered from his 'consumptive disorder' after drinking water from a hole in the ground on the Earl of Abergavenny's estate that fashionable society began to flock down from London. As well as sampling the iron-rich or chalybeate spring, they brought with them the prosperity that is still much in evidence today. By the time Charles II visited after the Restoration, giving the place its Royal title, it had become what Brighton was to be to the Regency court 150 years later, somewhere to see and be seen. Surprisingly enough, judging from some of the local names like Mount Ephraim and Mount Sion, the town liked to project a pious puritanical image, possibly because the waters were notoriously foul. They still are, and can be sampled by the brave in their original pump room in the Pantiles. Today Tunbridge Wells is still, on the face if it, a prosperous, polite and congenial town spreading attractively up the hill. However, shattering the 'Disgusted of Tunbridge Wells' stereotype of cosy middle-class domesticity, the place also has a high homelessness rate and its chief vicar, an exorcist, was called upon during the 1990s after a bout of grave desecration in town and a matricide where the defendant was known to have been a fan of Satanic death metal.

Ins and outs

Getting there If going by **train** Tunbridge Wells is on the mainline from London Charing Cross and Waterloo East as well as London Victoria, two trains an hour (1 hour). By **car** Tunbridge Wells is just off the A21, about an hour from central London. ➧ *For further details, see Transport page 188.*

Getting around Tunbridge Wells is small and pleasant enough to explore on foot, although some of its steeper hills can be surprisingly exhausting. The countryside around is best reached on buses.

Information **TIC** ⓘ *Old Fish Market, The Pantiles, Tunbridge Wells, T01892-515675, www.heartofkent.org.uk.*

Sights

The **Pantiles** are the place to get some idea of how the town may have looked in its heyday. A dinky 18th-century colonnade stretches away from the Chalybeate Spring (pronounced Kalibiyet) and Bath house (open Easter-Sep) at one end, with its modern and much less appealing equivalent at the other. Next to the pump house is the splendid Restoration church of **King Charles the Martyr**. A small alleyway leads up from here into the High St, lined with boutiques and fashion labels, past the station and up hill to the Town Hall. **A Day at the Wells** ⓘ *T01892-546545, Apr-Oct daily 1000-1700, Nov-Mar 1000-1600, £5.50, under-16s £4.50, family £17.50,* is the inevitable see-hear-and-smell show, run by the same people as the Canterbury Tales, taking visitors through a day in the life of the 18th-century town in about half an hour. It's housed in the old Corn Exchange.

At the top of the hill, the **Tunbridge Wells Museum and Art Gallery** ⓘ *T01892-554171, www.tunbridgewells.gov.uk/museum, Mon-Sat 0930-1700, free,* in the Town Hall, is an impressive example of its kind, not only for its 'Tunbridge ware', a world-beating collection of the local talent for marquetry, but also for its antique toys, dolls and natural history displays, as well as a thorough display on the history of the town and its various claims to fame.

Just west of town, the **High Rocks** ⓘ *T01892-515532, take the A264 towards East Grinstead, just over a mile out of Tunbridge Wells is a signpost for the rocks, £2 (ticket obtainable from High Rocks Hotel by the car park),* are very strange looking sandstone rock outcrops which are worth a clamber around. This was once a Neolithic settlement and is now a Site of Special Scientific Interest, so be careful where you trample.

Around Tunbridge Wells

Sevenoaks

Sevenoaks is a reasonably attractive dormitory town on the mainline to London but the only reason to visit is the extraordinary Elizabethan pile of **Knole House** ⓘ *(NT),*

 T01732-450608, Apr-Oct Wed-Sat 1200-1600, Sun, bank holidays 1100-1700, gardens May-Sep first Wed of the month, £5.50, under-16s £2.75, a long walk uphill from the station. This is where the writer, gardener, and lover of Virginia Woolf, Vita Sackville-West grew up, at the largest private house in the country, with a room for each day of the year, and an impressive art collection. The gardens and deer park surrounding the house are as enjoyable as the house itself.

A mile to the east, and accessible across the park from Knole House, **Ightham Mote** ⓘ *(NT) T01732-811145, Apr-Oct Mon, Wed-Fri, Sun 1100-1730, £6, concessions £3,* is one of the most endearing (and popular) moated manor houses in the country. Also National Trust, its little rooms can become impossibly busy, but it's worth going with the flow to see some of the most sensitive restoration work ever undertaken. At dusk, when the coach parties have departed, the house's position in a quiet valley is quite magical.

Penshurst

Seven miles west of Tunbridge Wells, off the A26 on the B2176, Penshurst is a charming village at the confluence of the rivers Eden and Medway. Its main claim to fame is **Penshurst Place** and **Gardens** ⓘ *NT, T01892-870307, www.penshurstplace.com, Apr-Oct daily 1200-1730, gardens 1030-1800, Mar weekends only, £6.50, under-16s £4.50, concessions £6, family £18,* seat of the Sidney family since 1522. A more modest and much more charming version of Knole, the Barons Hall at the heart of the house was built in 1341, kept very much as it would have looked in the Middle Ages. Outside, the Elizabethan gardens and 11-acre walled garden are delightful, and there's also the Woodland Trail, adventure playground and walks in the surrounding parkland.

Chiddingstone

A few miles west again along the relatively unspoiled valley of the river Eden, Chiddingstone is a National Trust village, its half-timbered houses and old schoolhouse made famous as a location for Merchant Ivory's *A Room with a View*. At weekends the antique look of the village is badly compromised by the gleaming wheels stretched along its single street beside the old church. **Chiddingstone Castle** ⓘ *T01892-870347, Easter, Jun-Sep Wed-Fri 1400-1700, Sun 1130-1700, £4, concessions £2,* was rescued from dereliction by the late Denys Bower in 1955, a passionate art collector who filled his castellated Edwardian home with an exotic collection of ancient Egyptian finds, Japanese lacquerwork, Chinese Buddhist treasures and Jacobite memorabilia including Lely's portrait of Charles II's mistress Nell Gwynn posing as Venus. The Georgian room is hung with an extraordinary series of portraits of the entire Stuart dynasty who ruled Scotland and then also England for almost 400 years before being supplanted by the Hanoverians.

Hever Castle

ⓘ *T01732-865224, www.hevercastle.co.uk. Apr-Oct daily 1100-1800 (last admission 1700), Mar-Nov 1100-1600. £8.40, £7.10 concessions, under-14s £4.60, family £21.40. Gardens only £6.70, £5.70, £4.40, £17.80.* Another mile to the west, the moated little castle at Hever (since 1270) was where Anne 'of a Thousand Days' Boleyn was brought up before catching the eye of King Henry VIII and eventually losing her head on 19th May 1536. Inside the place is more country house than castle, with 16th- and 17th-century portraits and a collection of model houses showing how castles were turned into these elegant homes between 1086 and 1901. Outside is better, with excellent topiary, yew maze and water maze for the kids (open Apr-Oct only) as well as beautiful Italian gardens with ancient Roman sculpture laid out by Waldorf Astor, the millionaire newspaper proprietor, in the early 1900s. There's also a peaceful lake with piazza and waterfowl.

Chartwell

Near the idyllic little hilltop village of **Ide Hill** ① *(NT), T01732-868381, Apr-Jun, Sep, Oct Wed-Sun (Jul, Aug also Tue) 1100-1700 (last admission 1615), £6.50, concessions £3.25,* and 4 miles north off the B269, Chartwell is one of the National Trust's most popular houses, formerly the home of Winston Churchill. Not a particularly attractive house in itself, its position overlooking the Weald and preservation as the great man left it make it somewhere really special. Inside, apart from his study, dining room and bedroom, the gift room includes valuable donations from grateful well-wishers as well such as his badge of membership for the Hastings Winkle Club. The grounds are just as evocative, the rose garden's wall inscribed, "The greater part of this wall was built between the years 1925 and 1932 by Winston with his bare hands" and including Marycot, the little summerhouse he built for his youngest daughter, complete with carpet sweeper and broom.

Westerham and Biggin Hill

Close to Chartwell is Westerham, a market town with a small green, surrounded by pretty cottages, the parish church, and dominated by two statues – a large bronze of Churchill and a towering **General James Wolfe**. Wolfe fought at the Battle of Quebec capturing it from the French in 1759. His family home (Quebec House, NT) is just past the green on the Sevenoaks Road. William Pitt the younger (Britain's youngest prime minister), lived at Pitt's Cottage, on the High Street. Westerham has a hotel, plenty of antique shops (like its neighbou, Brasted), and a large range of international cuisine served up in restaurants catering from French to Thai to Indian tastes.

Three miles north of Westerham is **Biggin Hill** ① *T01689 859119, Wed-Sun, Feb-Mar 1000-1600, Apr-Sep 1000-1800, Oct 1000-1700, Nov-Dec 1000-1600, £6, concession £4.50, under-16s £3. Bus 146 from Bromley South railway station, hourly on the half hour except Sun or R2 from Orpington station at 13 and 43 past the hour except Sun*. The world-renowned Biggin Hill International Air Fair is held here every June. **Charles Darwin**, author of On the Origin of Species, lived and died at Down House, Luxted Rd, Downe, just 3 miles northeast of Biggin Hill, which has displays related to evolution and the life of the man himself.

South and east of Tunbridge Wells

Southeast of Tunbridge Wells stretches the High Weald, dubbed the 'Heart of Kent' by the Tourist Board. With its wooded and winding lanes suddenly giving onto wide south-facing views, this is one of the most rewarding parts of the southeast to explore by car. There may not be as many grand houses and castles to visit as further east, but then this is garden country. Sissinghurst is the jewel in the crown, and inevitably overcrowded, making some of the less well-known well-tended acreages more rewarding. Try Hole Park, or further south, Great Dixter. Cranbrook is the unoffical capital of the area, a very attractive white clapperboard town brooded over by a massive windmill, full of antiques and teashops and the childhood home of Elizabeth Taylor. 10 miles westwards, Tenterden church is visible from miles around. With its tree-lined avenues and one long main street, the town has a charming Frenchified atmosphere.

Sights

The local museums are the places to explore the history of the area: the **Cranbrook Museum of Local History** ① *T01580-715542, Apr-Oct Tue-Sat 1400-1630, £1.50, concessions 50p*, is located in an Elizabethan brick and timber house, full of amusing anecdotes of local derring-do as well as some antique farm implements. The **Cranbrook Windmill** ① *T01580-712256*, which can be visited at weekends, is an impressive local landmark maintained by enthusiasts who still use it to grind their flour.

Just to the north of Cranbrook can be found the famous horticultural creation of Vita Sackville-West and Harold Nicholson at their home, **Sissinghurst Castle** ⓘ *(NT), T01580-712850, Apr-Oct Tue-Fri 1300-1800, weekends 1000-1730, £6.50, concessions £3*. Now one of the most popular National Trust properties in the country, it can become impossibly busy, relying on a timed ticket system that only just manages to cope with the coach parties. Even so, it's worth braving the crowds to enjoy the staggering variety of different plantings, bursting into bloom throughout the open season, as well as the old library and tower.

The **Tenterden and District Museum** ⓘ *T01580-764310*, focuses on the considerable agricultural wealth the area once generated, with a range of scary-looking machinery and informative displays. The **Kent and East Sussex Railway** ⓘ *T01580-762943, talking timetable T01580-765155, bookings www.seetb.org.uk/kesr, May-Sep daily, Oct-Mar Sun and school holidays*, is the district's best steam railway, running the 10 miles or so from Tenterden to Bodiam Castle through some lovely countryside.

The 14th-century **Bodiam Castle** ⓘ *(NT), Robertsbridge, T01580-830436, Feb-Oct daily 1000-1700, Nov-Jan 1000-1500, £4, concessions £2*, must be the most classic example of its genre in the country. Four-square walled, with round towers rising out of the surrounding moat, it's the kind of place that sends children into whoops of delight. In fact it never really saw much action, but there's an entertaining account of its history in one tower, while the National Trust keeps it busy today with re-enactments and medieval weekends throughout the summer.

Just next door to Bodiam, at Great Dixter, **Northiam** ⓘ *T01797-252878, Apr-Oct Tue-Sun 1400-1700, gardens only also Sun, bank holidays 1100-1700, house and gardens £6, £1.50 under-16s, gardens only £4.50, £1 under-16s*, is the 15th-century manor house restored by Sir Edwin Lutyens in 1910, although the main attraction is gardening writer Christopher Lloyd's garden which blooms almost all year round with meadow flowers, beautiful borders, flower-fringed ponds and an 'exotic' garden.

To the north, **Hole Park Gardens** ⓘ *T01580-241344, Apr-Jun and Oct, Mon, Wed and 2 Suns 1400-1800, £3.50*, is a 15-acre garden in beautiful parkland providing an escape from the more crowded gardens in the area. There are extensive yew hedges, walled gardens, pools and woodlands carpeted with bluebells in spring, as well as beautiful views complete with the romantic-looking 17th-century Rolveden postmill in the distance.

In **Rolvenden** itself, halfway between Cranbrook and Tenterden, the **CM Booth Collection of Historic Vehicles** ⓘ *63 High St, T01580-241234, Mon-Sat 1000-1800, £1.50*, should please fans of both two and four-wheeled transport. It boasts a Humber Tri-car of 1904, as well as several Morgan three-wheelers from 1913-1935 alongside velocettes, and other moto-memorabilia in a surprisingly large but crowded garage tucked away behind *Falstaff Antiques* on the village's main street.

South of Rolvenden, **Great Maytham Hall** is a Georgian house redesigned by Lutyens in the 20s where Frances Hodgson Burnett lived for a while in the 19th century, and was inspired to write *The Secret Garden* and *Little Lord Fauntleroy*. It has extensive Wealden views from the back lawns, as well as the original 'secret garden' itself. To the north of the village is the **Biddenden Vineyard** ⓘ *T01580-291726, Mar-Dec Mon-Sat 1000-1700, Sun 1100-1700, Jan, Feb Mon-Sat 1000-1700*, near Biddenden. A well-established vineyard with 22 acres of vines, mostly of Germanic origin, as well as home-brewed cider.

Five miles west of Cranbrook, the pretty hilltop village of **Goudhurst** ⓘ *T01580-211702, www.finchcocks.co.uk, Easter-Sep Sun and bank holidays, Aug Wed-Thu 1400-1800 (music at 1445), £7, concessions £5*, draws the crowds in summer to see its steep little High St, duckpond and church with spectacular views. Nearby, classical music-lovers should make tracks to Finchcocks, where period recitals are given in an appropriately grand Georgian setting on one of the 100 or so historic instruments collected by the current owner.

A couple of miles to the west, **Owl House Gardens** ⓘ *Lamberhurst, T01892-891290, daily 1100-1800, £4, under-16s £1,* is a little-known woodland garden established by Lady Dufferin, Marchioness of Dufferin and Ava, who added a literal owl-theme to the statuary although named originally after the 'owlers' or smugglers who hooted to avoid the excise officers. Now the gardens are a treat in spring, when the bluebells and azaleas are in bloom, and the whole place has a pleasantly informal atmosphere missing at some of the more commercialized properties in the area.

Ashdown Forest and around

The last remnant of the forest that once covered most of southeast England, the Ashdown Forest was given by Edward III to John of Gaunt as a royal hunting ground. Also the inspiration for AA Milne's Hundred Acre Wood the 'Forest' is in fact now an isolated 6000-acre patch of relatively high scrubland covered with yellow gorse (February-Spring) and purple heather (August-September). Criss-crossed by firebreaks, the public have the right to wander here as they please and being under 40 miles from London, with East Grinstead in the north and Uckfield in the south, it's a popular place for weekend walks. One good place to start is the **Nutley Windmill** ⓘ *Jun-Sep last Sun afternoon of each month*, a 300-year-old trestle mill. From here, a circular walk includes the old smuggler's village of Duddleswell, a 19th-century army camp recognizable from the mounds left by the cookhouses and the Airman's Grave, a memorial to the bomber crew that crash-landed here in 1941. Maps of this walk and many others can be found detailed on leaflets available at the **Ashdown Forest Centre Information Barn** ⓘ *Wych Cross, Forest Row, T01342-823583, daily Apr-Sep 1400-1700, Oct-Mar Sat, Sun 1100-1700, the barn also contains displays on conservation and wildlife in the area, as well as exhibitions of local art and woodcraft.*

Sights

One of the finest and best-preserved steam railways in the country, the **Bluebell Railway** ⓘ *Bluebell Railway, Sheffield Park Station, T01825-720800, timetable information T01825-722370, www.bluebell-railway.co.uk, trains run Apr 7-Sep 30 (weekends and Aug on the hr from 1100 to 1600), Oct-Mar weekends and school holidays only, £8, under-16s £4, family £21.50,* runs through countryside between Sheffield Park and Kingscote Station which is a short hop by bus (no 473) from the War Memorial in East Grinstead. Sheffield Park station is the line's HQ, where the engine sheds and their well-oiled beasts can be seen at close quarters as well as a small museum and real ale bar serving home-cooked food. During high season, cream teas can be booked in advance to be taken on the 1500 or 1545 train to Kingscote.

Close to the station, **Sheffield Park Garden** ⓘ *(NT), T01825-790231, Mar-Oct Tue-Sun 1030-1800 or dusk (last admission 1 hr before closing), Nov-Dec Tue-Sun 1030-1600, Jan-Feb weekends only 1030-1600. £4.60, under-16s £2.30, family £11.50, combined tickets available with Bluebell Railway,* is a spectacular landscape garden set around four large lakes, laid out by Capability Brown and developed in the early part of the 20th century by Arthur Soames. Highlights include the daffodils and bluebells in the spring, rhododendrons and azaleas in early summer, while the wide variety of exotic and rare trees are at their best in autumn.

The pretty little village of **Hartfield**, where AA Milne lived, is on the northern edge of the Ashdown Forest. The Poohsticks bridge is still there and is a favourite spot for families. There's also a Winnie the Pooh shop in the village for all your Pooh memorabilia needs.

Sir Arthur Conan Doyle lived and died in Crowborough to the east of the Forest. There's a statue to him in the town.

Sleeping

Around Maidstone *p179*

A Eastwell Manor, Eastwell Park, Boughton Lees, T01233-219955/213000. A very deluxe Tudor country house hotel and health spa in 3000 acres of its own land. Also have self-contained mews cottages ideal for families.

B-C Harrow Hill Hotel, Warren St, near Lenham, T01622-858727. A reasonable no-frills place on the Pilgrim's Way, on the top of the downs near the A20.

D-E Barnfield, Charing, near Ashford, T01233-712421. A smart non-smoking B&B that represents good value for money despite being relatively expensive.

D-E Woolpack Inn, High St, Chilham, T01227-730351, F731053. The local Shepherd Neame establishment, with comfortable reasonably priced rooms above a busy pub with good food.

Royal Tunbridge Wells *p180*

C Hotel du Vin & Bistro, Crescent Rd, T01892-526455. A Georgian townhouse, this is probably the most stylish place to stay in town, with a well-respected restaurant (the Bistro bit means that a meal here can be affordable).

C Spa Hotel Mount Ephraim, T01892-520331, F510575. Overlooking the common with a stately dining room. From another era, and altogether very grand.

C Swan Hotel, The Pantiles, T01892-541450. Very convenient and recently refurbished.

D Ephraim Lodge, The Common, T01892-523053, a superior guesthouse in a quiet position near the common.

D-E Blundeston, Eden Rd, T01892-540255, a very central upmarket B&B.

Around Tunbridge Wells *p181*

B The Old Parsonage, Church La, Frant, T01892-750773. A superior and upmarket B&B.

C Jordan's, Sheet Hill, Plaxtol, T01732-810379. A tile-hung farmhouse and non-smoking B&B deep in the countryside.

D Hoath House, Chiddingston Hoath, near Edenbridge, T01342-850362. The rambling Tudor and Edwardian home of one of the oldest families in the area, the Streatfeilds.

D The Orchard House, Brasted Chart, near Westerham, T01959-563702, is a convenient but pretty basic B&B for Chartwell.

D-E The Crown Inn, Groombridge, T01892-864742, has rooms above a lovely old pub doing decent food on the village green.

D-E Egypt Farm, Hamptons, near Tonbridge, T01732-810584. The large garden, swimming pool and tennis court complement an antique-filled oast houses and barn conversion.

D-E Leicester Arms, Penshurst, T01892-870551. 7 rooms above an attractive 17th-century inn, including a couple with 4-posters, done up in a chintzy style but nonetheless good value.

D-E Windmill Farm, Chevening Rd, Chipstead, Sevenoaks, T01732-452054. At Jill and Charles Innes's fine family house guests have their own living room, in an attractive little village just outside Sevenoaks.

South and east of Tunbridge Wells *p183*

C Kennel Holt, Goudhurst Rd, Cranbrook, T01580-712032, F715495. Topiary hedges and views, tucked away with a little garden down a long drive, where Sally and Neil Chalmers do their upmost to make you feel at home in their Elizabethan manor house with its library, music collection and log fires.

D Bishopsdale Oast, Cranbrook Rd, Biddenden, T01580-291027, www.bishopsdaleoast.co.uk. Converted oast house with original beams and cosy log fire but all mod cons too. Eat alfresco in the summer (when it's warm and dry enough) in the wild flower garden.

D Maplehurst Mill, Frittenden, near Staplehurst, T01580-852203. Evening meal, £22. Needs booking well in advance to stay in a beautifully converted 18th-century watermill surrounded by a huge garden, with a heated swimming pool and delicious organic food at supper.

D-E Star and Eagle, High St, Goudhurst, T01580-211512. An old beamed coaching inn with attractive views.

Ashdown Forest and around *p185*

L Gravetye Manor, near East Grinstead, T01342-810567, www.gravetyemanor.co.uk, a pretty special country hotel, an Elizabethan house surrounded by William Robinson's 'natural garden'. Visitors to the garden are welcomed on Tue and Fri only. The hotel, on a hilltop site surrounded by deep woodland, has a long-established reputation for its restaurant and standards of service.

A Hammerwood Park, T01342-850594 Easter-Sep Sat, Wed by guided tours £5 at 1410, Victorian bedroom B&B £120 is very different but equally special, the labour of love of David Pinnegar and family, who rescued the little mansion from dereliction and ownership by Led Zeppelin in the 80s. The first house designed by Greek revivalist Benjamin Latrobe in 1792, who went on to do the Capitol and White House portico in Washington, guests are put up in a huge and draughty Victorian room with lovely views and welcomed to the family breakfast table in the morning.

Eating

Eynsford *p179*

££ **The Plough Inn**, at Eynsford, has seats outside by the river and a more ambitious menu than many.

Around Maidstone *p179*

££ **Pepperbox Inn**, Fairbourne Heath, near Ulcombe, T01622-842558, is perched up on Windmill Hill, also doing some adventurous food which can be enjoyed at tables outside with good views over the Downs.

££ **The Rose and Crown**, Perry Wood, Selling, near Faversham, T01227-752214, has cosy well-kept gardens including a 'bat and trap' pitch on the top of Crown Hill with woodland walks, great views all around from the surrounding hills. Real ales, log fires and reasonable food (not Sun, Mon).

£ **Hop Shop**, Mon-Fri 1300-1700, Sat 1000-1700 does dried flowers, foods, apple juices, at a farm just up the road in the Darent valley.

£ **The White Horse**, Chilham is an old pub in the village square, beneath Chilham Castle.

Royal Tunbridge Wells *p180*

£££ **The Hare**, Langton Rd, Langton Green, T01892-862419. A short hop out of town, this is an attractive pub with an original menu that won't disappoint foodies served in the restaurant at the back.

£££ **Thackeray's** 85 London Rd, T01892-511921. A gourmet option, serving up modern British and French food in fairly swish surroundings for a price (around £50 a head).

££ **Magic Wok**, off the High St in Little Mount Sion. A reliable and inexpensive Chinese restaurant and takeaway.

££ **Zapata Mexican Restaurant**, 1-3 Union Sq, T01892-513950, is a lively place in the modern part of the Pantiles for some fiery food from south of the border.

Around Tunbridge Wells *p181*

££ **Honours Mill**, 87 High St, Edenbridge, T01732-866757. An expensive but atmospheric small Anglo-French restaurant in the pretty little town of Edenbridge.

££ **The Spotted Dog**, Smarts Hill, Penshurst, T01892-870253, is a hilltop pub doing very good food with a garden outside giving views over the surrounding countryside.

£ **The Deli**, 1 Fuller's Hill, Westerham, T01959-569048, is a good little sandwich shop, to pick up a bite on the way to Chartwell.

South and east of Tunbridge Wells *p183*

£££ **The Lemon Tree Restaurant with Rooms**, Tenterden, T01580-762060, has received excellent reviews for its fresh recipes and comfortable rooms. Needs booking.

££ **The Peacock**, Goudhurst Rd, Iden Green, T01580-211233. A clapperboard Shepherd Neame pub near Goudhurst with good food.

£ **Cheney's the Baker's**, 63 High St, Cranbrook, good-value and popular café.

£ **Soho South**, 23 Stone St, Cranbrook T01580-714666, Wed-Sat, is the place for some delicious light meals in a bistro popular with locals.

Ashdown Forest and around *p185*

££ **Coach and Horses**, Danehill, T01825-740369 has a large garden to one side with fine views, good local walks and well-cooked food that has received very warm reviews.

££ **Griffin Inn**, Fletching, near Uckfield T01825-722890. Not just a very welcoming and cosy country pub but an accomplished restaurant out back as well.

Pubs, bars and clubs

Around Tunbridge Wells *p181*

Fox and Hounds, Toys Hill, T01732-750328, near Ide Hill. The last word in authentic country pubs.

The Queen's Arms, near Edenbridge. Only Brakspear's best on offer from the indomitable old landlady Elsie. Defiantly basic, unmade over and popular with local folkies.

Activities and tours

Around Tunbridge Wells *p181*

Bewl Water T01892-890661 Daily 0900 till sunset, for **fly-fishing** for trout T01892-890352, **mountain biking** (summer months only), **windsurfing** T01892-89100, sailing T01892-890930.

North Downs and the Weald *p178*

Walks

The **Darent Valley Path** goes past Lullingstone between Dartford and Otford. The North Downs Way is the footpath between Farnham and Folkestone, including a branch off to the north to Canterbury. In the west near Sevenoaks and Maidstone it runs along the course of the old Pilgrim's Way. The **Stour Valley Walk** runs from Sandwich via Canterbury and Ashford to Lenham.

South and east of Tunbridge Wells *p183*

Alive in the High Weald Apr-Sep Sat, Sun. Free leaflet available from Kent High Weald Project, Cranbrook T01580-715918 www.kenthighwealdproject.org. Offer guided walks, events and lectures on and around the local countryside.

Transport

North Downs and the Weald *p178*

Bus

Local 2 particularly useful routes are the No 667 run by **Poynters Coaches** T01223-812002 between **Canterbury** and **Charing** via **Chartham**, **Old Wives Lees**, **Chilham** and **Challock** 4 times a day; and for **Leeds Castle** and the **North Downs Way**, the No 10 Stagecoach East Kent, T08702-433711, service is hourly between **Maidstone** and **Folkestone** via **Bearsted**, **Harrietsham**, **Lenham**, **Charing** and **Ashford**.

Around Tunbridge Wells *p181*

Bicycle

Bewl Bike Hire T01323-870310.

Bus

Local Arriva Kent and Sussex, T01634-281100. **Chartwell Explorer**, weekends and bank holidays 26 May–2 Sep, Wed-Sun and bank holidays Jul, Aug from Sevenoaks station. T08457-696996 £3.50. **Tunbridge Wells** Heritage Hopper, T08457-696996, 5 May-16 Sep Sat, Sun and bank holidays. Departs **Tunbridge Wells** War Memorial at 1005, 1305, 1505 via **Bayham Abbey**, **Scotney Castle**, **Bewl Water**, **Bedgebury Pinetum**, **Goudhurst**, and **Finchcocks** round trips back at 1134, 1434, 1634. Also **Scotney Castle** to **Tunbridge Wells** at 1750 back at 1854. £2.50, £1.50 concessions.

Eastbourne to Brighton

The far end of the South Downs Way, between Eastbourne and Brighton, contains many of the route's most attractive features. Over the centuries, the English Channel has carved its way into the chalk hills as they meet the sea, leaving a spectacular series of cliffs. Beachy Head and The Seven Sisters remain a symbol of England as an island nation – pure white cliffs, a natural fortress against invaders. Inland too, smooth grassy hills, and toy-town settlements provide enduring examples of 'quintessential England'. The villages of Alfriston, Ditchling and Firle, with their flint and half-timber cottages and ancient churches nestling at the feet of the hills, are the stuff of wartime postcards, reminding British troops of the idyll they were fighting for. Despite being more populated than other stretches of the South Downs Way, there's still a rural feel to this part of Southern England, with some gorgeous ramshackle farmhouses and barns dotting the countryside. And there's culture amid the agriculture, the lure of a pastoral existence proving attractive to the Bloomsbury

Group of artists and thinkers who set up at Charleston Farmhouse, and the Christie family, who turned a country pile at Glyndebourne into the world's most eccentric opera venue. The area contains many a footpath away from the South Downs Way, and a wander through fields and villages followed by a few pints in one of the many excellent country pubs is a simple delight. If you want to base yourself in a town while in the area, Eastbourne and Seaford are alternatives to Lewes or Brighton. » *For Sleeping, Eating and other listings see pages 194-197.*

Ins and outs

Getting there The slow but frequent South Coast line links the area to Hastings and Ashford in the west, Chichester, Portsmouth and Southampton in the east. Direct **trains** to London Victoria run from Eastbourne via Lewes and from Brighton. The A27 **road** runs along the South Coast from Dover to Southampton and passes by Lewes, Eastbourne (where the A22 leads to London) and Brighton (where the A27 heads for Gatwick and London). **Stagecoach South Coast** buses run infrequent services along the A27 road from Hastings to Brighton via Eastbourne and Lewes. From Brighton you can pick up connections to London. » *For further details, see Transport page 196.*

Getting around Access to the South Downs Way itself is relatively easy but you will obviously have to expect to walk. If you're arriving by train, your best bet is Eastbourne, where the start of the route is about 3 miles from the station. Alternatively, you can join the path halfway between Eastbourne and Brighton by taking a train from Lewes to Southease. The tiny station is on the South Downs Way as it crosses the River Ouse. In terms of exploring the countryside and villages away from the main pathway, you'll need patience and initiative if you're not prepared to walk and don't have a car. That said, many of the major sights in the section can, with patience, be accessed by buses, which run along the A27 on the inland side of the Downs and along the A259 coastal road. Seven Sisters, Alfriston and Beachy Head all have services to Seaford and Eastbourne. Glynde, Glyndebourne, Firle, Rodmell Charleston and Ditchling, meanwhile, can all be reached by bus from Lewes.

Eastbourne

If you're taking the South Downs Way seriously, you'll end up in Eastbourne sooner or later. If you arrive with aching limbs after a trek from the west you'll not be alone in putting your feet up here. The place's reputation for retired middle-class pensioners waiting for God by the sea has earned it the moniker 'Costa Geriactrica'. If you want the fast living and tacky glamour of the English seaside, you're better off staying in Brighton. That said, Eastbourne has its advantages: it's startlingly clean, has a beautifully maintained seafront with some elegant hotels and some lovely sandy beaches when the tide is out. The town centre is pleasant if uninspiring and has a few places worth popping into. The **Lifeboat Museum** ⓘ *T01323-730717*, on King Edward Parade, is an informative homage to seaborne heroics. The **Towner Gallery** and **Local History Museum** ⓘ *Manor Gardens, T01323-411688*, includes some impressive modern and local art exhibitions. The **Eastbourne Heritage Centre** ⓘ *Carlisle Rd, T01323-411189*, is an illuminating history of the town. There as also a **TIC** ⓘ *Cornfield Rd, T01323-411400*.

Seaford

Sitting on an exposed shingle bank, where the River Ouse has carved out a valley several miles wide as it meets the sea, Seaford tends to spend the winter months being heavily battered by wind and waves. As a result it's a flyblown place, though not devoid of charm, and is conveniently situated for launching trips to the area's attractions.

Walks in the South Downs

- **Firle Beacon**: 2 miles there and back. Start: From West Firle, off the A27 east of Lewes, beacon and car park clearly signposted. A walk up onto one of the highest points of the downs, past dewponds, round barrows and cultivation terraces. OS Maps: Landranger 198, Explorer 122
- **Cuckmere Haven**, Seven Sisters and Beachy Head: 7 miles one-way. Start: Exeat Bridge, on the A259 between Seaford and East Dean. Along the wide meanderings of the Cuckmere river to the sea, then along South Downs Way. OS Maps: Landranger 199, Explorer 123
- **Devil's Dyke**: 3 miles one-way. Start: Fulking village, 6 miles northwest of Brighton, clearly signposted from car park. A steep climb up to a favourite paragliding spot with fine views above a natural amphitheatre, then a lonely walk to Pyecombe (refreshments). OS Maps: Landranger 198, Explorer 122
- **Stane Street**: 6 miles there and back. Start: Eartham village, 5 miles northeast of Chichester off A285. A dead straight walk along the tree-lined path of a Roman road up Bignor Hill and beyond. OS Map: Landranger 197, Explorer 121
- **Beacon Hill**: 4 miles there and back. Start: South Harting, 7 miles west of Midhurst, on the B2141. A fairly steep climb up to one of the highest points on the western end of the South Downs. OS Map: Landranger 197, Explorer 120.

The coast round Beachy Head and inland

If you take the coastal stretch of the South Downs Way out of Eastbourne, or travel along the A259, you feel like you're right on the edge of England. And you are: the white cliffs here put the more famous ones at Dover to shame. The views of the English Channel and Eastbourne's little bay just to the west of the town are breathtaking. From here you can reach the granddaddy of all south coast sea cliffs. It's awesome yet precipitous beauty has made **Beachy Head** at once an icon of fortitude and the nation's premier suicide spot, and at 162 m of sheer chalk leading directly to a rocky shelf and the lighthouse like a little toy below, you can see why on both counts. The **Beachy Head Countryside Centre** ⓘ *Beachy Head Rd, Eastbourne, T01323-737273*, tells the tale of the surrounding coastline and features interactive exhibits. If you fancy a scramble, it's worth heading west along Eastbourne's seafront, which eventually becomes a rocky path leading to the beach at the cliff's foot. The area around Eastbourne is as famous as the Isle of Wight for having the best weather in England (despite the temptation to mock, summer here genuinely features long sunny days) and on this little path you'll see a microclimate which allows plants to grow which otherwise only exist by the Mediterranean. From here you'll get a good view of the sheer height of the cliff, and the famous little red and white striped **lighthouse** at its foot – it's a captivating place to be at low tide. Back atop the cliff, head a couple of miles further west along the coast from Beachy Head and you'll come to **Belle Toute Lighthouse**, originally built in the 1830s. A fine example of the English triumphing over often foul natural elements, the building was recently uprooted and moved 220 yards inland as the cliff-edge threatened to recede. A little further along is **Birling Gap**, a tiny former coastguard's settlement whose terraced houses look certain not to evade the fate from which Belle Toute escaped. It's a good place to stop for a drink in the ramshackle and rather grotty hotel and, as it's a gap in the cliffs, you can clamber down onto the pebble beach.

The **Seven Sisters** ⓘ *Seven Sisters Country Park and Friston Forest, T01323-870280*, the name given to the eight (typically English that) white cliffs between Seaford and Beachy Head, are one of rural Britain's most photographed sights. A path leads from the Country Park entrance the half mile or so down to Cuckmere Haven, where the white wonders span out in all their glory. Beware, however, the place is a tourist blackspot and in summer the prevalence of day trippers means it can feel a bit like wandering around a rock festival. If you come in the evening much of the throng will have dispersed and you may even catch a sunset turning the cliffs a mellow and alluring orange. An even better view of the cliffs can be had from **Hope Gap**, a short drive (or an hour's walk) along a track leading off Seaford's eastern seafront. It's also worth a wander around the inland country park. From **Exceat Hill**, there's a wonderful view of the winding meanders of the Cuckmere and it's ox-bow lakes, leading down to Cuckmere Haven, while **Friston Forest** is a leafy reminder of what the South Downs must have been like when covered in woodland.

The inland route of the **South Downs Way** passes through sleepy **Jevington**. This tiny village, complete with ancient flint church and quaint boozer has not changed much over the years, and is a decent approximation of what the area was like in less populated, more parochial times. One of the village's flint cottages houses the estimable *Hungry Monk* restaurant (see Eating and drinking, page 195).

Alfriston and around

A tourist trap, but one it would be a shame to miss, Alfriston is an impossibly pretty little village 3 miles up the River Cuckmere from the Seven Sisters Country Park. The main street is a mish mash of half-timbered buildings in which smugglers once stashed their ill-gotten gains. The **Tye**, meanwhile, is an ancient grassy patch by the river, on which stands Alfriston's magnificent Parish Church of Saint Andrews, known modestly as the **'Cathedral of the Downs'**. The National Trust's first ever property, **Alfriston Clergy House** ⓘ *T01323-870001, Mar-Nov Sat-Mon, Wed and Thu 1000-1700, £2.80, under-16s £1.40*, stands on the edge of the Tye and is a charming 14th-century thatched affair which contains some enlightening material on life in rural Sussex. A wander along the river bank in either direction is a worthwhile journey into gorgeous countryside.

To the south of the A27, between Lewes and Eastbourne lies an enigmatic hill carving, the **Long Man of Wilmington.** Suggestions as to its origin vary wildly: some have it as an Iron Age fertility symbol, others as a Roman landmark. Thinking has recently been hijacked by sane and rational killjoys, who insist it was merely the hobby of a local farmer in the last couple of centuries... but it would be nice if the other theories were true.

Charleston Farmhouse

ⓘ *Just south of the A27, T01323-811265, 1400-1700, Jul and Aug 1100-1700, £5.50, under-16s £3.50 by guided tour only.* The country retreat of the Bloomsbury set was instigated when Vanessa Bell, Virginia Woolf's sister, moved here in 1916. It's a lovely Tudor farmhouse with well-kept gardens and striking views of the South Downs.

Glynde and Firle

These are two achingly picturesque villages at the foot of the downs. **Glynde Place**, ⓘ *T01273-858224, Jul and Aug Sun, Wed, Thu 1400-1700, Jun and Sep Sun and Wed, £5.00, under-16s £2.50*, home to the Trevor family (Viscount Hampden), is a gorgeous Elizabethan confection containing works by Canaletto, Guardi, Zuccarelli and Batoni. **Firle Place** ⓘ *T01273-858335, 23 May-27 Sep, Wed, Thu, Sun, 1400-1630, £4.50-£2,* meanwhile contains some magnificent Dutch and English artworks, and is 18th-century in appearance with medieval origins. The villages have a healthy rivalry, and cricket matches between the two are events of gladiatorial proportions.

Firle Beacon

Above the Village of Firle (and accessible from it by a road leading from the western end of the village) Firle Beacon is the highest point in this stretch of downland. From here you can get an excellent idea of the geography of the area. To the south, the Downs descend slowly to the sea at Seaford, to the east you can see them jutting into the Seven Sisters, to the west they swing inland towards Brighton, Chichester and Winchester. Look north and you'll see the whole of Sussex spanning before you. The foot of the hill is where the chalk Downs hit the Sandstone Weald, an area of rolling lowland which spans north to Surrey.

Glyndebourne

ⓘ *North of the A27 and 4 miles east of Lewes, T01273-812321.* In 1934 John Christie inherited a country pile, and decided to indulge his opera-singer wife, building her a private opera house in the grounds (crueller legends suggest that her minimal vocal aptitude meant that she could not get work anywhere else). From such beginnings the venue has developed an opera company, and clientele, of international repute, culminating in the recent completion of a wonderful new auditorium. From May until August, opera lovers don black tie and enjoy performances punctuated by a picnic in the grounds. Tickets are more coveted than gold dust, and you must be on the mailing list even to receive a £10 standing ticket. For mere mortals, the only hope is speculative blanket telephoning of the box office in hope of returned tickets, but you should try – it's an unforgettable slice of national culture. If you don't succeed, it's well worth popping along on performance days to take in the archives, a collection of exhibits charting Glyndebourne's rise from English eccentricity to international prominence.

Ditchling Beacon

Towards Brighton the coastal part of the Downs becomes depressingly built up, but the inland stretch is still a natural oasis. Once you've circumnavigated Lewes, the main pathway follows a ridge with spectacular views of the Weald as far as Pyecombe – just behind Brighton. About halfway along the ridge, you'll hit Ditchling Beacon, the highest point along the 158-km pathway; along with Firle Beacon it formed part of England's coastal defences during the Spanish Armada: fires were lit at high points along the chalk ridge warning those further along of incipient attack. From the Beacon you can take a road or pathway down to Ditchling Village – an attractive crossroads with some tumbledown cottages and a couple of nice pubs.

Lewes

If Brighton is the scruffy, hedonistic, yet ultimately sensible and successful offspring, then Lewes is its concerned but mildly nostalgic parent. Ostensibly, Lewes is your average pretty country town – built up a hill in a gap in the Ouse Valley, it is East Sussex's administrative centre, complete with Norman castle, a number of buildings of historical importance and a family-run brewery. Yet the town is also the guardian of a radical history. Simon de Montfort was an early starter, leading the rebellion which captured the King at the Battle of Lewes in 1264, Thomas Paine (of *The Rights of Man* fame) was a Lewes man and the town's uniquely raucous and extensive 5 November celebrations have their roots in a particularly virulent Puritanical strain. These days, locals spend their time supping on the brewery's syrupy outpourings, playing bowls on the Castle's ancient tilting green or at the Rotary club. The closest you'll get to radicals is an influx of middle-aged liberal intellectuals seeking respite either from the staff rooms of Sussex University and London's media offices or a misspent youth in Brighton. The town is surrounded by beautiful rolling downland.

Bonfires of the insanities

Lewes remembers the 5th November like nowhere else. The town's Protestants were always situated towards the hellfire end of the religious thermometer, and were driven into a fervour by Guy Fawkes's attempt to blow up Parliament in 1605. Over the years, the town's more boisterous citizens insisted on torching effigies of the Pope, and throwing blazing tar barrels at one another, in a violent reminder that the Fifth must never be forgot. By the 19th century, religion had less to do with it and things were just getting gratuitously nasty, people started dying and the Riot Act was read. These days the event is properly policed, devoid of any sectarian feeling, and the town's 'Bonfire Boys' organized into five societies, each with its own traditions and identity. On the 5th November, the narrow streets still play host to the world's largest torch-lit procession. After this curtain raiser, up to 50,000 onlookers follow their society of choice to fire-sites, where fireworks are thrown at society members dressed as Cardinals. Effigies of the Pope, Fawkes and 'enemies of Bonfire' (Thatcher, Blair, Clinton, Delors and most recently Osama Bin Laden have all suffered) are then unceremoniously blown sky high. It's an anarchic, politically incorrect experience. At one recent celebration, after scurrilous suggestions that Cliffe and Commercial Sq societies were about to merge, the Cliffe chief reassured his masses that he would 'never surrender' to 'the poofters from Commercial Square.' The Bonfire Boys, it seems, haven't lost the rock.

Information TIC ⓘ *School Hill, 187 High St, T01273-483448. Mon-Fri 0900-1700, Sat 1000-1700, Sun 1000-1400.* Worth popping in for a free town map and guide, and suggested walks.

Lewes Castle ⓘ *High St, T01273-486290, Mon-Sat 1000-1730, Sun and bank holidays 1100-1730, £4.20, under-16s £2.10, family £11.40,* was erected by William de Warrenne, shortly after the Battle of Hastings, and is one of only two in the country to boast two Mottes. The Keep, sections of the fortifications, and a 14th-century Barbican remain. Climb to the top of these and you'll see why William chose the spot, the panoramic views over the Ouse valley allow any invaders to be spotted a mile off. These days, invasions are confined to local amateur dramatics societies putting on summer productions in the grounds, and groups of local old codgers playing bowls in the castle Bailey. The **Barbican House Museum** has local artefacts dating from prehistoric times, and there's a scale town model of Lewes in the 1870s.

Turn right along High Street from the castle, and you'll come to **Bull House**, where famous son Tom Paine resided from 1768 and 1774 as an excise officer. Over the road is **St Michael's Church**, which has a 12th-century round flint tower, a 14th-century arcade, and a Georgian façade. Just past this on your left is **Keere Street**, Lewes's entry for the most cosily English cobbled-street-on-a-hill award. Supposedly, George IV, Prince Regent, forced his coach and horses at breakneck speed down the vertiginous route for a dare.

Southover Grange lies at the bottom of Keere Street. The House itself is a gorgeous Caen stone concoction, designed for William Newton in 1572, and was once the home of diarist John Evelyn. George IV also visited, presumably to recover from his Keere Street caper. These days the house is a popular venue for couples to wed, and the gardens are a lovely public space on a warm day. Head along Southover High Street, and you'll reach **Anne of Cleve's House Museum** ⓘ *T01273-474610, Mar-Nov Mon-Sat 1000-1700, Sun 1400-1700, £2.60, under-16s £1.30.* Dating back to the early 16th century, the house was part of the divorce settlement given to the luckless Low Countries lady. Henry VIII was disgusted to see that his advisers had found not the image of beauty depicted in Holbein's painting, but 'The Flandres Mare.' The subsequent divorce saw Anne return home red-faced and thus she never lived here. Inside is an exploration of Sussex social history and folklore including exhibits of local furniture, tapestry, sculpture and iron work, as well as a section on black magic. Just off Southover High Street is **Lewes Priory**, once a proud ecclesiastical centre of national significance, the building, like Anne, owes it's demise to King Hal, who torched it in the Henrecian Reformation. One wall of the central abbey church and a section of the latrines remain, whilst a surviving gateway at the end of Priory Crescent, several 100 yds away, gives an idea of the former scale of the building.

At the other end of High Street is **Harvey's Brewery** ⓘ *T01273-480209*, known locally as Lewes Cathedral, it supplies many a local boozer. There's a shop, and tours are available on request. One essential purchase is Harvey's floodwater, so named after a brewing cask was found happily bubbling away in the ruined building after a winter flood (2000) of biblical proportions.

Sleeping

There are hundreds of B&Bs, which are best along the western seafront area, ask at TIC

Eastbourne *p189*

L Grand Hotel, King Edward's Pde, T01323-412345. Indeed very grand, restored to its 19th century glory at huge expense, with 2 pools (outdoors and indoors) and 2 restaurants, 1 of which is The Mirabelle (see Eating).

E Lindau Lodge, T01323-640792, 71 Royal Pde, is a no-frills seaside B&B for around £20.

E YHA Eastbourne, is at East Dean Rd, T01323-721081.

Alfriston and around *p191*

C Deans Place Hotel, Alfriston, T01323-870248. An elegant establishment.

D Crossways Hotel, Wilmington, T01323-482455. Clean and friendly, although a little close to the A27 main road.

E-F YHA have hostels at Frog Firle, Alfriston, T01323-870423 and Bank Cottages, Telscombe, T01323-301357.

Seaford *p189*

D Tudor Manor Hotel, Eastbourne Rd, Seaford, T01323-896006. More elegant than the Avondale and has en-suite doubles for £35 including breakfast but is, alas, still in Seaford.

E Avondale Hotel, Avondale Rd, Seaford, T01323-890000. Has clean doubles with baths.

Lewes *p192*

Budget accommodation in Lewes is a problem, so it might be best to splash out on a couple of nights of luxury.

L Shelley's, High St, T01273-472361. The real deal, a 16th-century house with plush lounges and bar, and an excellent restaurant. The place was rumoured to be curiously full when New Labour held their Party conference in nearby Brighton last year, provoking local outrage and accusations of champagne socialism.

A The White Hart, 55 High St, T01273-476694. Does its best to look classy, but adding Holiday Inn type swimming facilities, and a rear restaurant that looks like a Travelodge to an otherwise attractive townhouse hotel, barely justifies the expense.

C Berkeley House Hotel, 2 Albion St, T01273-476057, is an attractive Georgian townhouse with an alcohol licence.

D-E Black Horse, Western Rd, T01273-473653. A cosy traditional boozer and B&B with well-maintained rooms up top.

D-E Castle Banks Cottage, 4 Castle Banks, T01273-476291. Tiny B&B.

D-E The King's Head, 9 Southover High St, T01273-474628, Pub and B&B.

D-E Pump Cottage, 6 St Nicholas La, T01273-473765. A small B&B.

E The Crown Inn, 191 High St, T01273-480760, is a curiously appealing

For an explanation of the sleeping and eating price codes used in this guide, see the inside front cover. Other relevant information is provided in the Essentials chapter, page 40.

small town hotel of the kind most towns have consigned to history.

F **YHA Hostel** at Telscombe, Bank Cottages, Telscombe, T01274-304357, £10 dorms, but by the time you've got up and trekked into Lewes it'll be dusk.

Eating

Eastbourne *p189*

£££ **Hungry Monk**, Jevington Village, T01323-482178, is housed in a couple of old flint cottages. This venerable restaurant has built up a fine local reputation over the years. You won't get much change out of £30 a head, but the gamey food and decent continental wine list make it an ideal venue for a night out.

£££ **The Mirabelle**, Grand Hotel, Royal Marine Pde, T01323-435066. Now in the hands of top German chef, Gerald Röser, offering dishes such as pike, soufflé and salad of smoked salmon, avocado and foie gras.

£££ **Oartons**, 4 Bolton Rd, T01323-731053, is as close as you'll get to decent French cuisine, but is a little overpriced nonetheless.

£ **The Townhouse**, 6 Bolton Rd, T01323-734900, draws a younger crowd than most places round these parts on account of its city-bistro appearance, modern European meals can be procured for £6 to £10.

Alfriston and around *p191*

££ **George Inn**, High St, Alfriston, T01323-870319. With its oak beams and inglenook fireplace, this place is almost too quaint, but it does decent English food at the bar and à la carte.

££ **Rose Cottage**, Alciston. You might want to descend from the Downs halfway between Alfriston and Southease for a pint and a bite here. The food is genuinely English – not an insult but a tribute to well cooked game and local lamb.

£ **Badgers**, North St, Alfriston, T01323-870749, does cakes, buns and the like in a 16th-century cottage and garden.

£ **The Sussex Ox**, Milton St, near Alfriston, T01323-870840. On the South Downs Way just to the east of Alfriston is this no-nonsense country boozer.

Ditchling Beacon *p192*

The White Horse, Ditchling, is a homely boozer at the foot of the downs, worth a bash for the giant sized portions of fresh fish and chips and a good range of real ales.

Lewes *p192*

£££ **Shelley's Hotel**, High St, T01273-472361, is Lewes's only 'posh' restaurant. There's an estimable wine list, and the food is rich and gamey.

££ **Light of Bengal**, Landsdown Pl, T01273-472493, is a good Indian eat-in or takeaway.

£ **The Friar**, Fisher St, T01273-472016. Family-run takeaway chippie that's been serving up titanic portions of battered delights to hungry locals for years.

£ **Old Needlemaker's**, T01273-471582. The café in this arts and crafts mall is your best bet for a cup of coffee and a sticky bun.

£ **Patio Pizzeria**, Market St, T01273-479539, is Lewes's best budget option, serving up excellent and simple Sardinian cuisine at wallet-friendly prices.

£ **Spaghetti Puttanesca**, near Market St, is also a bargain. You may need to book as the locals have cottoned on to a good thing, and the place is microscopic.

Pubs, bars and clubs

Eastbourne *p189*

Atlantis, T01323-410466, on the pier. The usual expensive booze and cheap thrills.

TJ's, T01323-723456, on Terminus Rd provide more of the same.

Lewes *p192*

Circa, Westgate St, T01273 471777. Lewes's attempt to join the brasserie brigade doesn't quite work, as the market isn't there to capture, but the quality of the food is reasonable.

The Lewes Arms, Castle Ditch La, off Fisher St, T01273-473152, is a classic Sussex pub, with a bar billiards table, and a top spot for a pint of the local Harvey's.

Snowdrop Inn, South St, T01273-471018. If you're in town for the evening, it's worth the trek to this eccentric little pub. With an excellent vegetarian and seafood menu, the place is popular with the town's youth and often has live music.

Entertainment

Eastbourne *p189*
Congress Theatre, on Carlisle Rd. T01323-412000. Attracts good touring companies.
The Curzon Cinema, T01323-731441, has all the latest from Hollywood.
Devonshire Park Theatre, Compton St,T01323-412000 and attract some surprisingly high-quality productions.

Lewes *p192*
Recent plans to introduce a nightclub to the High St were met with near apocalyptic reactions from the town's moral guardians...
All Saints Centre, Friar's Walk, T01273-477583. This busy local arts centre has art-house film screenings and live music.
Lewes Jazz Club, High St, T01273-473568, has live Jazz every Thu evening. £4 entry.

Festivals and events

Lewes *p192*
Jul Lewes Festival. Comprises some surprisingly good classical concerts in the town's many old churches. Call TIC for details, T01273-483448.
Nov Bonfire Night Celebrations. See box p193.

Shopping

Lewes *p192*
Not exactly Oxford St, but there are a few interesting antique and book shops:
A&Y Cumming, 84 High St, T01273-472319
Bow Windows Bookshop, 105 High St, T01273-480780.
Dieppe Market, Cliffe High St. 1 Sat each year, our French farming friends cross 'La Manche' to flog their wares to gastronomically impoverished locals. And once a month there's a local farmers' market (both on Cliffe High St), which puts Safeway's genetically enhanced anaemic produce to shame.
Emporium Antiques Centre, 24 High St, T01273-477979, is well above average.
The Old Needlemakers, Off Market St, T01273-471582. Arts and crafts shops in converted industrial environs.

Activities and tours

Eastbourne *p189*
International Lawn Tennis Centre, Devonshire Park is an unlikely venue for the stars of the women's ATP Tour, but they're here every May/Jun to warm up for Wimbledon.
Sovereign Centre, Royal Pde, T01323-738222, also has a decent swimming pool, 1 with a wave machine, as well as a sports hall.

Seaford *p189*
Downs Leisure Centre, Sutton Rd, T01323-490011 has a multi-purpose sports hall.
Seaford Head Swimming Pool is on Arundel Rd, T01323-735076.

Lewes *p192*
Convent Field, off Mountfield Rd, has some tidy grass tennis courts, and minigolf.
Lewes Leisure Centre, Mountfield Rd, T01273-486000. Indoor swimming and slide, all-purpose sports hall, and a climbing wall.
Pells Outdoor Swimming Pool, off Pelham Terr, T01273-472335. Fed by a natural spring, this was the country's first outdoor pool, and packs them in in the summer months.

Walking
The downs are a hiker's dream, and the South Downs Way passes Lewes just to the East at Southease (5 mins on the train from Lewes). From here you can walk along the ridge – with breathtaking views of the Weald to the north and the sea to the south – to Alfriston and Eastbourne, or descend at the village of Firle, for a return by bus to Lewes. Less hilly is the Ouse Valley: a leaflet available at the tourist office details 3 lovely walks to the South of town. You can also follow the river north: take the path alongside the Pells outdoor swimming pool and turn left at the footbridge. You'll soon be in open countyside, and can reach the hamlet of Hamsey, with its 13th century church, in an hr or so.

Transport

Eastbourne *p189*
For transport details for Lewes and Brighton see p197 and p198 respectively

Bicycle
Cuckmere Cycle Co Ltd, The Granary Barn, Seven Sisters Country Park, Exceat, Seaford, T01323-870310.

Bus
Long distance Eastbourne bus station is on Terminus Rd. National Express, T0870 580 8080, run 2 buses to **London Victoria** coach station per day (3 hrs). The hourly Stagecoach, T01903-237661, bus from **Dover** (4 hrs) to **Brighton** (1 hr 30 mins) also calls by. County Busline, T01273-474747, or Bus Enquiries, T01256-464501.

Taxi
Eastbourne and Country Taxis, T01323-720720; Eastbourne Station Taxis, T01323-725511.

Train
Eastbourne Station is on Ashford Rd, trains run every 30 mins to **London Victoria** (1 hr 35 mins) and 2-3 times an hr to **Brighton** via **Lewes** (45 mins) and **Hastings** (30 mins). **Seaford Station** is right in the centre and has services 3 times an hr to **Brighton** via **Lewes** (30 mins). There are also stations at **Southease** on the line from **Seaford** to **Lewes** for access to the **South Downs Way**, and at **Glynde**, on the line from **Eastbourne** to **Lewes** and **Brighton**.

Lewes *p192*
Bus
Local The Bus Station is on Eastgate St, opposite Safeway supermarket. RDH, T01273-890477, operate local services including, No 125 to **Glynde** (15 mins), **Firle** (20 mins), **Charleston** (30 mins). For **Glyndebourne**, a special bus runs from the rail station on performance days (most evenings May-Sep).
Long distance Stagecoach, T08702-433711, operate services to **Brighton** (40 mins), **Eastbourne** (1 hr), **Hastings** (1 hr 30 mins), and **Dover** (2 hr 30 mins), and inland Sussex and Kent, eg Tunbridge Wells (1 hr 30 mins). For longer routes, you're better off arriving at Brighton and making your way to Lewes by bus or train.

Car
Lewes is an easy place to get to by road, but the narrow street, of the old town are not a parker's paradise. The A27 stretches west to **Brighton**, **Portsmouth**, and **Southampton**, east to **Eastbourne**, **Hastings** and **Dover**. The quickest way from **London** is to take the A23 to Brighton, and turn off on the outskirts of the city along the A27. The A26 and A275 wind through scenic parts of inland Sussex, and can provide a more interesting route from London or Kent if you have time to spare.

Taxis
George and Graham, T01273-473692, or Becks, T01273-483838.

Train
The station is on Station Rd at the Southern foot of the hill. A local line leads west to **Brighton** (15 mins) and east to **Eastbourne** (30 mins) and **Hastings** (45 mins). There's also a branch to **Newhaven** (10 mins) for ferries to France, and **Seaford** (15 mins), which is near to the Seven Sisters Country Park (see The South Downs section). The main line has twice hourly services to **London Victoria** (1 hr 10 mins) via **Gatwick Airport** (35 mins). Connex South Central, T08706-030405.

Directory

Eastbourne *p189*
Hospitals Eastbourne District General Hospital, King's Dr, T01323-417400. **Internet** at the Public Library, Grove Rd, T01323-434206. **Police** Terminus Rd, T01323-412999. **Post office** Oklynge Rd, T01323-731277.

Lewes *p192*
Hospitals The Victoria Hospital, Offham Rd, has an emergency doctor. **Internet** Access is available at Lewes Library, on Albion St. **Police** St Johns St, T0845-6070999. **Post Office** The main post office is on High St, opposite the Castle entrance.

Brighton and Hove

→ *Colour map 3, grid C2*

From the good-time girls and gangsters of Graham Greene's Brighton Rock via the mods and rockers of the cult film Quadrophenia to its current status as clubbing capital of the country, Brighton has always had that air of dangerous cool. This is Bohemia British style. Once the Prince Regent's coastal retreat, Brighton is now home to avant-garde artists and musicians, an exuberant gay and lesbian community, thousands of students and a few blue-rinse bungalow-dwellers who must be wondering where it all went wrong. The town has an atmosphere somewhere between hippy trail and Mediterranean sleaze-pit. In summer the streets around North Laine and the Prince's bizarre oriental Pavilion are a throng of trendy stalls and cafés, the pebbly beach awash with vocal youngsters and the clubs bursting at the seams seven nights a week. Throw in an arts festival second only to Edinburgh and the best eating in England outside of London and you have a city which takes culture seriously. Surely all this enjoyment can't last forever. One day Brighton is going to have to grow up and get a job, indeed many fear this may already have happened. The place has barely been out of the press since Brighton resident DJ Fat Boy Slim married TV presenter Zoë Ball and made it the place to be. House prices have rocketed, and grotty old dives have become post-modern enormodromes with overpriced cocktails. Bohemia, it seems, has been bought. This said, Brighton remains the highlight of any trip to the south coast and if you can't find fun here, you're unlikely to find it anywhere. ▸▸ *For Sleeping, Eating and other listings see pages 203-210.*

Ins and outs

Getting there Brighton is excellently served by **rail**. There are two fast trains each hour from London Victoria (50 minutes), and two from London King's Cross, London Blackfriars and London Bridge (1 hour). There are numerous trains to Gatwick Airport (25 minutes), and Luton Airport (1 hour 45 minutes). A coastal line leads west to Chichester (40 minutes), Portsmouth (1 hour 20), Southampton (1 hour 30) and Winchester (2 hours). To the east, you can reach Lewes (15 minutes) and Hastings (1 hour). There are also less frequent through trains from Edinburgh via Manchester, Birmingham and Oxford, and from Cardiff via Bristol and Bath. Brighton is notoriously difficult and expensive to park in, so if you must come by **car** use the Park and Ride Scheme at the Withdean Stadium (clearly signposted from all main roads). From London take the A23, once you've got as far as the M25, it's about a 1 hour drive to Brighton. The A27 is the south coast trunk route and connects Brighton to Chichester, Portsmouth and Southampton to the west, and Lewes, Hastings, and Dover to the East. Getting to Brighton by bus is trouble-free, if slow, and considerably cheaper than the train. ▸▸ *For further details, see Transport page 209.*

Getting around Brighton is a relatively small city, much of which can be reached by foot. If your feet are swollen, however, there's an extensive network of local buses which ply the city's streets (1 day pass, £2.60), many continue to nearby places of interest mentioned in this chapter: Lewes, Rottingdean, Devil's Dyke and Stanmer Park. For travel at night there are night buses to most parts of town, departing from North St, until about 0300; miss these and it's a walk or queues by the taxi ranks that give Russian soup kitchens a bad name.

Information **TICs** ⓘ *10 Bartholomew Sq and Hove Town Hall, T09067-112255, Jun-Aug Mon-Fri0900-1700, Sat 1000-1700, and Sun 1000-1600, Sep-May Mon-Sat 0900-1700.*

“” Brighton remains the highlight of any trip to the south coast and if you can't find fun here, you're unlikely to find it anywhere...

History

Brighthelmstone, as it was known, was just another of the small fishing villages strung along the coast until flooding destroyed its livelihood in the 18th century. The seawater cures promoted by Dr Russell in the 1750s came to its rescue, coupled with the town's proximity to the capital, luring thousands of affluent Londoners to the coast. The town rapidly emerged as the most vibrant place outside the capital, and early in the 19th century it captured the attention of the fun-loving Prince Regent. 'Prinney' (to his friends) came looking for somewhere to keep his mistress, have wild parties and enjoy a lavish lifestyle away from his disapproving father, King George III. As a result, the seafront between Hove and Kemp Town is still remarkable for its Regency buildings and the beautiful Brunswick, Regency and Sussex squares, but it was his Pavilion that established Brighton as the most fashionable place on the south coast. Not to everyone's taste, it fell into disrepair during Queen Victoria's reign. The birth of the railways made Brighton accessible to ordinary folk and day trips to the seaside took off. Two piers were built before the turn of the 20th century, providing entertainment and a focus for the new tourists. During the late 60s and early 70s, its popularity was tinged with notoriety, thanks to violent seafront clashes between mods and rockers – scenes immortalized in the 1979 film *Quadrophenia*.

Around The Lanes and the seafront

Only Brighton could boast, as its most important piece of architecture, an Indo-Chinese royal palace inspired by an obsessive and mildly decadent half-German prince. Fresh from a thoroughly sensitive £10 million renovation programme, at the **Royal Pavilion** ⓘ *Church St, T01273-290900, Jun-Sep daily 1000-1800, Oct-May daily 1000-1700, £5.80, concessions £4, under-16s £3.40, family £15,* you can now enjoy John Nash's 1815-23 masterpiece, with its dragon-shaped chandeliers and lotus-shaped lanterns, in its full glory. Nearby, is the **Brighton Museum and Art Gallery** ⓘ *Church St, T01273-290900, Tue 1000-1900, Wed-Sat 1000-1700, Sun 1400-1700, closed Mon, free.* Two new galleries, entitled the 'Body' and 'Performance' spaces promise 'a celebration of modern humanity'. In many other cities this might involve a set of exhibits by the local Save the Whale group, but is the kind of thing Brighton normally manages to pull off, dignity intact. There are also two history galleries – one depicting life and work in Brighton – and one devoted to the seaside resort, double-entendre ridden postcards and the like.

The area between West Street and the Steine was, until the 18th century, a small fishing village named Brighthelmstone. These days **The Lanes** are a maze of passageways containing antique and jewellery emporia of varying quality, and a host of cafés, restaurants and pubs. Few original features remain, but *English's Oyster Bar* occupies a former fisherman's cottage.

The beach

Not exactly Copacabana, but a pebbly spot for a cheap ice cream, a pint in a plastic glass or, weather permitting, even a swim in the cold, green English water. In summer, come nightfall, the beach is awash with the local youth, drinking beer, lighting barbecues, patting bongos, smoking joints, fondling one another, falling in the sea, and generally making the place their own. There are also events like open-air cinema, fireworks, and live music. Perhaps the place's most captivating sight is the swallows that zig-zag around the ruined West Pier at dusk.

The tiny electric **Volks Railway**ⓘ *283 Madeira Dr, T01273-292718, 1145-1700, £1.50, family £5.20,* clicks its way along the eastern seafront. It's not exactly the bullet train but, pushing 120 years of age, it is the world's oldest electric railway.

Sharks, stingrays and all manner of piscine delights are on display at the **Sealife Centre**ⓘ *Marine Pde, T01273-604234, 1000-1700 daily, £7.95, under-16s £4.95, family £24.95,* one of the country's finest aquariums.

These days Brighton's fishing industry is confined to a handful of vessels that put to sea each evening. But at the **Fishing Museum**ⓘ *201 King's Rd Arches, T01273-723064, daily 1000-1700,* exhibits and film chart the history of Brighton's seafood trade in more prolific times. One of the city's most understated gems.

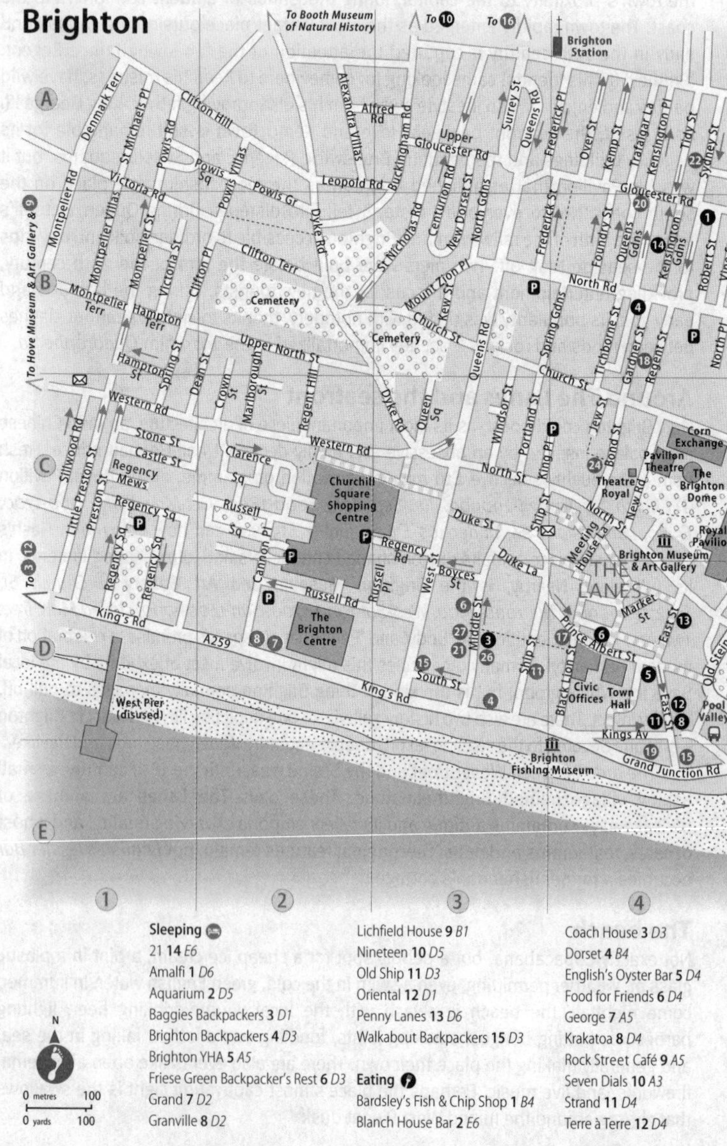

Much to the indignation of the locals, the 'Palace Pier' was renamed **Brighton Pier**ⓘ *Madeira Dr, T01273-609361, daily dawn-dusk*, to celebrate Brighton's recent entry in the great big A-Z in the sky under the section marked 'cities.' Corporate re-branding aside, it's still the unselfconsciously kitsch amalgam of fairground rides, money-swallowing machines and calorific cuisine that it always was. You can buy Brighton rock (the sickly, minty sweet with the name running through it) by the yard here, and only the staunchest cultural snob wouldn't. After all, even Fatboy Slim has been known to frequent the Hog Roast here.

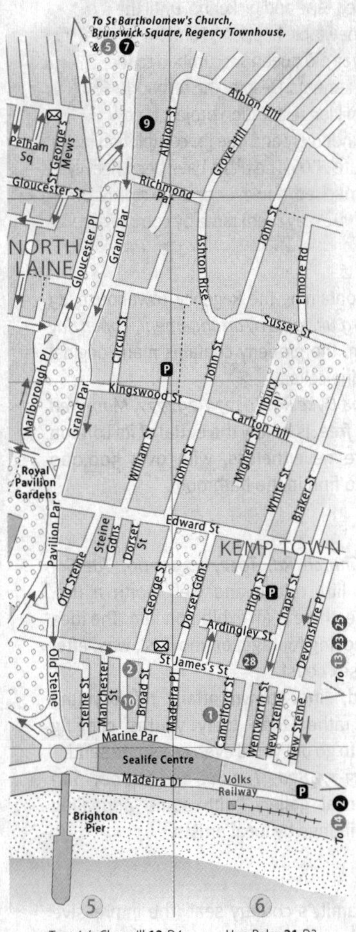

Tootsie's Chargrill **13** *D4*
Wai Kika Moo Kau **14** *B4*

Pubs & bars
Alicats **15** *E4*
Battle of Trafalgar **16** *A3*
Cricketer's **17** *D4*
Curve at Komedia **18** *B4*
Dr Brighton's **19** *E4*
Heart & Hand **20** *B4*
Hop Poles **21** *D3*
Office **22** *A4*
Pressure Point **23** *D6*
Riki Tik **24** *C4*
Sidewinder **25** *D6*
Squid & Starfish **26** *D3*
Sumo **27** *D3*
Tin Drum **28** *D6*

Around North Laine

Situated between Trafalgar St and Church St, this raggle taggle of trendy and secondhand shops, delis, cafés and pubs is the womb from which Brighton's current DJ-chic youth emerged. The denizens here are ridiculously fashion conscious, in a scruffy kind of way, and it's a great place to people-watch and pick up a few souvenirs. **St Bartholomew's Church** ⓘ *Ann St, T01273-620491*, from the exterior looks like an outsize railway shed. For trivia fans, it is the highest church without a tower in the country, is grade I listed, and has some wonderful Art Nouveau furnishings.

Around Kemp Town

Just off St James St, Brighton's eastern hills were formerly the town's gay centre. These days such pigeon-holing doesn't really apply, and it's a quiet area full of B&Bs and some quiet shops and cafés. If you have time, you should try to get out to Lewes Crescent. This vast Regency triumph bears testimony to the fact that, as London's hypochondriacs followed Prince George to the sea, the sky really was the limit when it came to real estate development. Still the preserve of the ridiculously rich, mere mortals are left dreaming of lottery wins to make a piece of it their own.

Around Montpelier and Brunswick

Brighton's **West Pier** ⓘ *King's Rd, T01273-207610*, the country's only grade I-listed pier was a magnificent piece of architecture which once featured some of the most demure restaurants and theatres in the realm. Having been in a state of woeful disrepair for some time, it fell prey to winter storms in 2002 and then to horrific arson attacks in early 2003. Remarkably the regeneration campaigns continue, watch this space.

Pier pressure

There was no greater paradigm of English seaside pleasure than Brighton's West Pier. The only Grade I listed pier in the country was once an essential feature of the Brighton seafront, but on the night of 29 December, 2002, winter storms ravaged the Edwardian Ballroom, part of which collapsed into the sea. The damage was compounded by a devastating arson attack in 2003. Built in 1866, the West Pier attracted over 2 million visitors a year in its heyday. People flocked to see plays, pantomimes and ballets performed in the 1000-seater theatre, take a day trip on a paddle steamer, or simply promenade its length. Its popularity began to wane during the course of the 20th century as the performing arts gave way to ghost trains and slot machines and it finally closed in 1975. Local residents campaigned successfully to save it from demolition but restoration work was hampered by red tape and bickering, until the inevitable happened and Brighton's frail old queen succumbed to the elements. Despite the setback, a £30 million restoration project is now underway and due for completion in late 2005. The plans have been heavily criticised, however, and the storms of 2002 may seem tame by comparison.

Brunswick Square is an elegant structure containing the Regency Townhouse, **13 Brunswick Square** ⓘ *T01273-206306, www.rth.org.uk, tours by arrangement, 1 open day per month, both £3*. Eventually to be a museum, the property contains many original features, the basement housing an untouched wine cellar.

The **Booth Museum of Natural History** ⓘ *194 Dyke Rd, T01273-292777, Mon-Wed 1000-1700, Fri-Sat 1000-1700, Sun-1400-1700, free*, is hardly the equal of its London counterpart, but a collection of some repute nevertheless, with over 500,000 specimens, many of which you wouldn't want to find in the bathroom.

Hove

The **Hove Museum and Art Gallery** ⓘ *New Church Rd, T01273-290200, Tue-Sat 1000-1700, Sun 1400-1700*, is a fascinating little place and well worth a trip. Alongside local artefacts dating to the Stone Age, there is an exhibit on film. The idea of sequencing still photographic images into moving footage, or 'movies', was, after all, conceived in this genteel haven on the Sussex coast.

The **beach** in Hove is a less cluttered, litter-strewn affair; think young professionals barbecuing swordfish steaks rather than lusty youths clinging drunkenly to one another. If you wait for the tide to go out you'll even see some sand.

The **White Gallery** ⓘ *Western Rd, T01273-774870, Tue-Sat 1000-1800, Sun 1100-1600, free*, is a contemporary commercial gallery, with some appealing jewellery and ceramics alongside prints and paintings by local artists.

Around Brighton and Hove

Stanmer Park, is the grounds of the Pelham family's country seat (the impressive abode is currently under restoration). The park is well-signposted, and you can walk into miles of unspoilt countryside, which includes panoramic views of the Sussex hinterland from Ditchling beacon, a couple miles to the north.

East of the city, **Rottingdean** seafront is a paltry affair, but walk a street or two back and you're in a charming Sussex village, complete with duckpond, flint church and cottages, and a quaint old boozer.

Prinney

A statue of the man responsible for Brighton's transformation into the most happening and fashionable place on the south coast stands largely ignored outside the North Gate of the Royal Pavilion. But then even many of those around at the time would be pushed to recognize that man in the stately statue of George IV, because it was as young Prinney, the flamboyant Prince of Wales, that the son of George III had captured their imaginations and drawn high society down from London. Prinney was introduced to Brighton by his wicked uncle the Duke of Cumberland in the 1780s, visiting several times to go to the races and take the sea cure for his swollen glands. Soon he was cavor- ting at extravagant parties here on a regular basis and had secretly married Maria Fitzherbert, an ardent Catholic, much to the concern of the establishment. He put her up in a house in Marlborough Row: North Gate House, which stood at the end of the Row, can still be seen. Ten years later, saddled with debts, he was forced by his father to part with Maria and marry the Protestant Princess Caroline of Brunswick, mother of the Princess Charlotte whose room can be seen in the pavilion. A few years on, much to the locals' delight, Prinney got back together with Maria, who settled in Steine House (now the YMCA), and the party went on. He became Prince Regent in 1811, thanks to his father's illness, and built the Royal Pavilion that stands today as an appropriate monument and backdrop to their romance. On his coronation as George IV in 1821, the slighted Princess Caroline caused a famously ugly scene by forcing her way into the celebrations. The King remained loyal to Maria though. A happy pensioner, she died in Brighton in 1841, the year the railway opened spelling the end of the town's royal heyday, the young Queen Victoria soon finding the place far too crowded and popular for her liking.

Sleeping

Around The Lanes and the seafront *p199, map p200*

There are a myriad of B&Bs (where you ought to be able to get a bed for around £20-£30 a night), in Kemp Town, and out towards Hove. They are all much the same, so it's probably best to ask the accommodation service at the TIC to make enquiries for you.

L-A **The Grand**, King's Rd, T01273-321188. Saunas, jacuzzis, swimming pools, deferent room-service, good enough for conferencing PMs and IRA bombers. Don't argue about the price, just cough up, it's the best in town.

A **Hotel du Vin & Bistro**, Ship St, T01273-718588, www.hotelduvin.com. Part of the exclusive and chi-chi hotel group, this clever conversion of Gothic-style buildings os only a stone's throw from The Lanes. Modern, well-equipped rooms with great bathrooms. Warm and enthusiastic service.

A **The Old Ship**, King's Rd, T01273-329001. The posh one that isn't the Grand, the *Old Ship* is a little overpriced for the standard, but is the epitome of Brightonian faded glamour.

C **The Granville**, King's Rd, T01273-326302. The least grand of the expensive options, but you can't knock the sea view and you're unlikely to stumble upon a fringe meeting of the Young Conservatives at their annual party conferences.

D **21 Hotel**, 21 Charlotte St, T01273-686450. Clean and moderately trendy B&B.

D **Oriental Hotel**, 9 Oriental Pl, T01273-205050. A lovely small hotel which is getting something of a reputation among weekending Londoners of the chattery, world cuisine-loving Islingtonian variety. Book early, or not at all if you want to avoid overhearing conversations about how well Josh's play is going.

D **Penny Lanes**, 11 Charlotte St, T01273 603197. Good-sized rooms with bathrooms in a quiet street near the beach, breakfast included.

E The Amalfi Hotel, 44 Marine Pde, T01273-607956. Reasonably priced and on the seafront, even if a little grotty out front.
E Aquarium Hotel, 13 Madeira Pl, T01273-605761. Clean, friendly, and close to the Pier.
F Brighton Backpackers, 75-6 Middle St, T01273-777717, stay@brightonbackpackers.com. £11/12 dorms. One of the first independent globe-trottery places in town, and consequently full of 'creative' wall-paintings by former residents, and anecdotes about smoking too much in Malawi.
F Brighton YHA, Patcham Pl, London Rd, T01273-556196. £10 dorms. All the usual hostel facilities, but a little out of the way (20-30 mins on the bus to the city centre).
F Friese Green Backpacker's Rest, 20 Middle St, T01273-747551. £10 dorms. A small, friendly hostel for people whose Bible is *The Beach*.
F Walkabout Backpackers, 79-81 West St, T01273-770232. £12 dorms. Right next to the *Walkabout Bar*, scooner-quaffing antipodeans aplenty.

Around Kemp Town *p201, map p200*

A Nineteen, 19 Broad St, T01273-675529, F675531. Small and hip hotel, one of the most stylish places in the city.

Hove *p202*

E Lichfield House, 30 Waterloo St, Hove, T01273-777740. Excellent value hostel-cum-hotel.
F Baggies Backpackers, 33 Oriental Pl, T01273-733740. £11 dorms. Better situated than the other budget options, *Baggies* is in a quiet area of Hove and near the burgers, kebabs, and noodle bars of Preston St.

Eating

Around The Lanes and the seafront *p199, map p200*

£££ English's Oyster Bar, 29-31 East St, T01273 327980. A Brighton institution: Crustaceans, molluscs, flatfish – if it swims, it's here – usually on large plates with chips garnished with green salad. A tad pricey, the place is redeemed by a pleasant outside dining area and its status in local legend.
££ Blanch House Bar, 17 Atlingworth St, T01273-603505. Technically a hotel, you can enjoy a classic French meal, and a cocktail in the retro bar, if you book. Uber-cool and rather expensive, the place is run by a former Groucho club bar manager, so you get the picture.
££ The Coach House, Middle St, T01273-719000. Mediterranean style cantina, with excellent value moules (£6/£8) and a small secluded terrace.
££ Krakatoa, 7 Pool Valley, T01273-719009. You sit on the floor Indonesian-style here, but the food is best described as oriental fusion (carnivores beware, seafood and vegetarian only). Book early as the place is attracting a national reputation.
££ The Strand, 6 Little East St, T01273-747096. Tiny, but popular restaurant offering adventurous modern-European recipes. Mains around £13. Bookings essential.
££ Terre a Terre, 7 East St, T01273-729051. Regarded by many as Brighton's finest restaurant, the vegetarian and organic menu here is mind-bogglingly innovative. Mains start at around £10, and you'd be hard put to find a finer diner in its field.
££ Tootsies Chargrill Restaurant, 16-18 Meeting House La, T01273-726777. Not for dieters or hardcore veggies, *Tootsies* serves up some of the best simple meat dishes in town to those of a hunter-gathering dietary disposition. Efficient service and a pleasant heated terrace.
£ Food for Friends, Prince Albert St, T01273-202310. An early-starter on the vegetarian scene, this self-service restaurant has been serving consistently excellent lunches, dinners and cakes over the years.
£ The Rock St Café, Rock St. Superior local caff, with mouth-watering cakes. Probably one of the most tempting places in town to while away a rainy day.

Around North Laine *p201, map p200*

££ The Dorset, 28 North Rd, T01273-605423. Half pub, half quality eaterie, this joint is bustling with beautiful but jovial punters most hours of the day. A fine example of Brighton's most prominent citizens – professional loafers – in their cig-smoking, pose-striking element.
££ Seven Dials, 1-3 Buckingham Pl, T01273-885555. New kid on the block and wowing the locals and visiting Londoners alike, this place has a fresh approach to British fusion cuisine without being too pretentious or stuffy despite to media darlings who seem to be its main source of income.

£ Bardsley's Fish and Chip Shop, 106 Gloucester Rd, T01273-681601. The best examples of the national dish are to be found away from the soggy batter and staggering Scousers of the seafront, in this little shop at the end of Kensington Gardens.
£ The George, 5 Trafalgar St, T01273-681055. When vegetarians were regarded as laughable eccentrics with dogs on strings, they could pop in here for a quality quorn burger in a dingy old boozer. These days the punters and the décor are equally modern and streamlined, and the food is some of the best (and best value) vegetarian in town. They even do vegetarian beer.
£ Wai Kika Moo Kau, 11a Kensington Gardens, T01273-671117. Wai the Stew Pid Nayme? What they mean, as honest herbivores, is that bovine mistreatment is a no-no. You can pick up a decent cheap veggie bite here, and the service is swift and friendly.

Around Montpelier and Brunswick *p201*

£££ The Gingerman, 21a Norfolk Sq, T01273-326688. Superlative French cuisine in intimate surroundings. One of the city's élite.
£££ La Fourchette, 101 Western Rd, T01273-722556. Pricey it may be (£22.50, 3 courses), but there's no doubting the skill with which the French chef prepares locally caught seafood and game.
££ China Garden, 88-91 Preston St, T01273-325065. Vast building on the seafront, and several cuts above your staple chow-mein joint – but is this enough to justify the in-house pianist? Mains start at £8.
££ India, 12 Preston St, T01273-778721. A good bet for Indian cuisine in the city centre.
££ The Nile House, Preston St, T01273-326003. The city's most outlandish eaterie offers up Sudanese and North African specialities at implausibly reasonable prices.

Hove *p202*

££ The Black Chapati, 12 Circus Pde, New England Rd, T01273-699011. Forget your Chicken Madras and Nan with the lads at chucking out time, this Indian restaurant is about as ambitiously authentic as you get in the UK. It's been there for donkey's years, and featured in virtually every discerning critic's national highlights along the way. Well worth the trip off the beaten track.
££ Harry's English Restaurant, 41 Church Rd, T01273-727410. A welcome reminder that the English can cook as long as they keep away from saturated fats and microwave dinners. Bangers and mash have never tasted this good. Mains start around £8.
££ Oki-Nami, 208 Church Rd, T01273-773777. Brilliant Sushi and the like in a very Japanese minimalist space. Mixed meal £8.50.
££ Sole Mio, 64 Western Rd, T01273-729898. Despite a glut of pizza/pasta joints in the city centre, it's well worth the trip out to Hove for the genuine article in a gorgeous, high-vaulted building. Pasta dishes from £6.

Pubs, bars and clubs

Brighton's club scene is regarded as one of the best in England outside London. Aside from the big hitters and perennial favourites listed below, there is an ever-changing local scene: good places go bad and vice versa, and there are invariably some very good nights in some very bad clubs. The best way to keep up to date is to check local listings (*The Insight* and *City News* are good bets, available free from the tourist office), or ask around in city centre pubs and bars.

Around The Lanes and the seafront *p199, map p200*

Alicats, Brills La, 80 East St, T01273-220902. After negotiating the bins and other less salubrious street smells, this underground bar is a great place to sup on a cheap brew and take in an arty film on the big screen in the corner. It's done out like a student living room, and the clientele are your housemate's 'bohemian' friends from the drama society.
The Beach, 171-181 Kings Rd Arches, T01273-722272. Despite its big, brash mainstream appearance, *The Beach* still packs in an alternative crowd most nights of the week, with a mixture of drum and bass and hard house. Curiously for a club where music is taken seriously, the bar is slap bang

For an explanation of the sleeping and eating price codes used in this guide, see the inside front cover. Other relevant information is provided in the Essentials chapter, page 40.

in the middle of things; oh well, if you can't pull you may as well just get pissed.

Casablanca Jazz Club, 2 Middle St, T01273-709710. Whilst 30-somethings appreciate a few tunes downstairs, the town's youth take advantage of student-friendly ale prices above, and get very, very drunk.

Concorde 2, Madeira Dr, T01273-207241. Never mind its association with the stars (DJ Fatboy Slim is on the sacred decks twice each month), the club is a laid-back, unpretentious venue (trainers positively encouraged), in which virtually everybody is in a chemically good mood.

The Cricketer's, Black Lion St, T01273-329472. This pub, with its wonderfully camp pink frilly décor, is a reminder of Brighton's more traditional seaside resort roots. Refreshingly, there's not a spiky hair cut or a pair of skate pants to be seen, and the gaff is heaving with hearty locals at weekends.

Dr Brighton's, 16 King's Rd, T01273-328765. One of the city's longest established gay drinking spots. The place is popular with gay men and women, and has a pre-club buzz about it most nights of the week.

Escape, 10 Marine Pde, T01273-606906. Offering an eclectic range of nights over 2 new-look floors.

Event II, Kingswest, West St, T01273-732627. The Event 'I' was an enormous, vomit-sodden shrine to all tunes tacky, all behaviour boorish and all pulling predatory. The Event II...well, take the original and double it.

Honeyclub II, 214 Kings Rd Arches, T07000-446639. Host to some seriously big-time DJs over the past few years, the *Honeyclub* is back, hopefully bigger and better.

Hop Poles, 13 Middle St, T01273-326503. Old bloke's pub in appearance, new-media lager-quaffing 20-something's bar in atmos. Mainly recommended for its cheap, varied, but surprisingly tasty all-day menu.

Jazz Place, 10 Ship St, T01273-328439. Think along the lines of stylishly clad young things strutting and smoking French fags, rather than dubiously bearded middle-aged gentlemen tapping their feet and smoking cigars, for this is the cutting edge of jazz.

The Joint, 37 West St, T01273-321692. Trends come and go, but *The Joint* seems to have weathered them all and maintained its cool.

Paradox, 78 West St, T01273-321628. The 'Dox offers big name DJs, and the famous 'Wild Fruit' gay night, about once a month.

Revenge, Old Steine, T01273-606064. The city's biggest specifically gay club, boasting cabaret nights and strippers.

Squid and Starfish, 78 Middle St, T01273-727114. Every night of the week, a stream of Brighton's young things come in here to get hopelessly plastered and yell at one another. A top spot for necking a few glasses before the club, but not the best place for a gin and tonic with granny.

Sumo, 9-12 Middle St, T01273-823344. One of the few late night bars in town, and rather self-consciously cool, best to get here early and dress like a diva.

Volks Tavern, 3 The Collonade, Madeira Dr, T01273-682828. Before Brighton's club explosion, dancing in the city often revolved around gaunt and 'ironically' dressed Jarvis Cocker types posing camply to cheesy tunes in basement venues. The *Volks*, under the arches on the Eastern seafront, is a survivor of these more innocent times.

Zap Club, King's Rd Arches, T01273-202407. Despite many years at the centre of the clubbing scene, the twin arches of the *Zap* still burst with youthful enthusiasm across musical genres ranging from cheese to hard house.

Around North Laine *p201, map p200*

Battle Of Trafalgar, 34-35 Trafalgar St, T01273-882276. Just up the hill from the station, this no-nonsense boozer is one of few left in the centre to have survived the onslaught of garishly painted walls and zebra-print sofas. Pull up a pew by the fire and sup on a pint of Harvey's (brewed down the road in Lewes), in traditional environs.

Curve Café/Bar at the *Komedia Theatre*, Gardner St, T01273-603031. Cocktails, overpriced wines, bottled beers and Fine Modern European Cuisine in pristine surroundings. Beware, however, as the watering hole of preference of Brighton's theatre folk and mediaocracy, *Curve* may be artier than thou.

The Heart and Hand, Upper Gardner St, T01273-624799. This tiny old pub used to be a pre-club haunt for the town's indie and mod glitterati. You'll still see the odd skinny guitar type in here (Bobby Gillespie of Primal Scream is rumoured to frequent), and it's a lot less pretentious than many of the centre's alehouses.

Ocean Rooms, 1 Morley St, T01273-699069. A 'super-club' which cleverly manages to cater to all tastes and maintain a certain effortless credibility. You can recline over a cocktail in the opium-den of an upstairs room, have a meal at the in-house restaurant, or bop like a banshee in the basement bar/dancefloor.

The Office, 8 Sydney St, T01273-609134. A wide range of beers, and thumping music, make this diminutive pub a good bet for a few too many mid-week pintas. The name also provides the ideal excuse to one's other half for 'working late'.

Riki Tik, 18a Bond St, T01273-683844. Ultra-modern, super-cool, pre-club warm-up zone, with budding local DJs, chill out room, and even the odd playstation. Stay away if you regard student/DJ/slacker-types as middle-class pricks.

Around Kemp Town *p201, map p200*

Pressure Point, Richmond Pl, T01273-235082. A pleasant pub with live music and club nights upstairs.

Sidewinder, 65 Upper St James St, T01273-679927. Sofas, couches, candles, this sloth-like bar raises lethargy to new heights.

Tin Drum, St James St, T01273-624777. Fine Gastro-pub, with Polish vodka-centric undertones, home to London's 30-something chattering class refugees.

Around Montpelier and Brunswick *p201*

Freemasons, 39 Western Rd, T01273-732043. This easy-going boozer is full most nights of the week and has an above-average dining room upstairs.

Hove *p202*

Cooper's Cask, 3 Farm Rd, Hove, T01273-737026. Extremely cosy alehouse with cheap, filling food options.

Nan Tuck's Tavern, 63 Western Rd, Hove, T01273-736436. Despite the unnecessary and naff ghoulish motif, this is one of the area's better pubs.

Entertainment

Brighton and Hove *p198, map p200*

Cinemas

Duke of York, Preston Circus, T01273-602503. Top draw independent arthouse cinema, a little out of the way.

Gardner Arts Centre, University of Sussex, Falmer, T01273-685861. This modern arts venue at the University offers occasional screenings, usually of small, independent films.

Odeon, Kingswest, West St, T0870-5050007. The only remaining city-centre mainstream cinema has 6 screens and all the latest releases.

UGC, Brighton Marina Village, T0541-555145. Corporate but comfortable enormodrome among the yachts and jetties.

Theatres, live music and comedy

BNI, 5 Preston St, T01273-232161. Away from the centre, and at the end of an unpromising basement staircase, this venue has a reputation for kick-starting young careers.

The Brighton Centre, King's Rd, T0870-9009100. Multi-purpose venue that stages a good few gigs. Radiohead, Oasis and the like have all graced the stage here.

The Brighton Dome, 29 New Rd, T01273-709709. 3 venues under 1 roof – between them, the **Dome Auditorium**, **Pavilion Theatre** and **Corn Exchange** offer both mainstream crowd-pullers and smaller productions.

The Event II (see above), occasionally plays host to bands of national significance.

Gardner Arts Centre, University of Sussex, Falmer, T01273-685861. This medium-sized auditorium has hosted everything from student productions, to touring companies and comedians.

Komedia, 44-47 Gardner St, T01273-647100. Now installed in a plush new home in North Laine, cabaret and comedy downstairs, theatre upstairs, both of them first-rate.

Marlborough Theatre, 4 Princes St, T01273-570028. Small but loved and respected theatre above a city centre pub.

Theatre Royal, New Rd, T01273-328488. A lovely old theatre specializing in touring companies and pre-west end productions.

Festivals and events

Brighton *p198, map p200*

May Brighton Festival, T01273-700747. England's largest arts festival takes place every year, and comprises over 800 events ranging from street performers to serious theatre. There's a good range of live music, comedy, dance, film screenings, and a fringe which is emerging as a showcase of young talent on a par with Edinburgh. If you're in Brighton in May, there'll be something to suit all but the most boorish cultural cretin, in one of the festival's many venues.

Aug Pride, Madeira Drive and Preston Park. Each year the city celebrates 'gay and trans-gendered' culture, in a British interpretation of Sydney's Mardi Gras. There's a huge parade on the seafront before participants head for a free party in Preston Park.

Shopping

Around The Lanes and the seafront *p199, map p200*

The maze of streets around Brighton Sq and Meeting House La is home to a host of antique jewellers and little boutiques. Dukes La and East St are where to head for quality chains and labels. Whilst along at the Seafront the King's Road Arches, is a swathe of seaside postcard-style tat – candyfloss, rubber rings, silly glasses, plastic bosoms, it's all here and has to be seen to be believed.

Choccywoccydoodah, 27 Middle St, T01273-381999, Mon-Fri 1000-1800, Sat-Sun 1000-1700. All manner of beautifully crafted choccies and cakes, this isn't confectionery, it's art.

Colin Page, Duke St, T01273-325954. Fine secondhand and antiquarian bookshop.

Jeremy Hoye, 22a Ship St, T01273-777207. Beautiful jewellery, crafted by the proprietor himself.

The Lanes Armoury, T01273-321357. One of the more interesting antique shops in the area, this one specializes in weapons of war.

Re-al, Dukes La, T01273-325658. Independent surf and skate establishment, dude.

Rounder Records, 19 Brighton Sq, T01273-672512. A good range of chart and indie CDs, the shop is also the best place to pick up tickets for forthcoming gigs and club nights.

Churchill Square and **Western Road**, along the Seafront. Churchill Sq is a conversion of an outdoor precinct into a covered modern complex, complete with **Virgin Megastore**, BHS, McDonald's and all the usual suspects. It has retained all the character of the 60s original, ie none. Those high street shops which they couldn't cram into the complex straddle out along Western Rd.

Around North Laine *p201, map p200*

North Laine has a markety feel about it with a colourful throng of trendy clothing (often secondhand), antiques, vintage and modern records, cafés, delis and ubiquitous ethnicraft. A few highlights are…

Ananda, 24 Bond St, T01273-725307. Plenty of the aforementioned ethnicraft, much of it in the form of attractive home furnishings.

Borderline, 41 Gardner St, Mon-Fri 1000-1730, Sat-Sun 1100-1700. Plenty of vinyl, many obscure titles.

Minky, 26 and 32 Sydney St, T01273-604490, Mon-Sat 1000-1800, Sun 1100-1700. Trendy independent labels.

Pussy, 3A Kensington Gardens, T01273-604861, Mon-Sat 1000-1730, Sun 1200-1630. Neither pertaining to felinity or female genitalia, but full of useless and very pretty things like lava lamps and miniature chrome fridges.

Rokit, Kensington Gardens, T01273-672053. Long-established purveyors of fine secondhand jeans, denim and leather jackets and amusingly-sloganed T-Shirts.

Snooper's Paradise, Kensington Gardens. Secondhand clothes, books, records, pots and pans, kitchen sinks, pretty much everything really.

Vegetarian Shoes, Gardner St, T01273-691913. Brighton's lettuce-munchers extend their creativity to footwear.

Activities and tours

Brighton and Hove *p198, map p200*

Bowlplex, Brighton Marina, Marina Way, T01273-818180. Gigantic 10-pin venue, full of junk food, crap Happy Days style décor, and bored parents trying desperately to suppress the beta-carotene rush of their hyperactive little darlings.

Brighton & Hove Albion FC, Tongdean La, T01273-776992. 2001 saw the mighty 'Seagulls' secure promotion to the second division, after a few years of indifferent form, and exile to the badlands of Gillingham, Kent.
Brighton Racecourse, Freshfield Rd, T01273-603580. Racing on the South Downs throughout the summer, often in the evenings.
Coral Greyhound Stadium, Nevill Rd, Hove, T01273-294601. It's all here, in the cockney style, flat-cap and dodgy sheepskin not included.
Hollingbury Golf Course, Ditchling Rd, T01273-500086. 18-hole public course with a view over the city, sea and Downs.
King Alfred Leisure Centre, Kingsway, Hove, T01273-290290. Modern pools and slides. Fewer plasters and tampons than the sea.
Prince Regent Swimming Complex, Church St, T01273-685692. More plasters and tampons than the King Alfred, but nearer the centre and still safer than the sea.
Sussex County Cricket Club, County Ground, Eaton Rd, Hove, T01273-827100. Sussex are to cricket what the Albion to footie, so come and give them a much-needed cheer. Recently installed floodlights mean fun one-day games in the summer.

Transport

Brighton and Hove *p198, map p200*

Bicycle
Brighton is well served by cycle paths, but you do sometimes have to plough through some chaotic traffic. You can hire a bike for a day from **Sunrise Cycle Hire**, T01273-748881 at the West Pier, or **Freedom Bikes**, 45 George St, T01273-6816980.

Bus
Local From Brighton buses call at **Lewes** (Nos 28, 28X, 729 from Churchill square or Old Steine, 30 mins); **Rottingdean** (No 22A, 30 mins from Churchill Sq); **Devil's Dyke** (No 77 from Brighton Pier, 30 mins) and **Stanmer Park** (No 25 from Churchill Sq, 25 mins), many of these buses continue from Churchill Sq into **Hove**. **Guide Friday**, T01273-746205, for open-top tours.

Long distance Intercity buses arrive at Pool Valley, near Old Steine, T01273-383744. **National Express**, T0870-5808080, for **London Victoria** (2 hrs) and long-distance. **Jetlink**, T0870-5757747, for **Gatwick** (1 hr) and **Heathrow** (2 hrs), **Luton** (3 hrs) and **Stansted** (3 hrs 30 mins) airports. Brighton and Hove buses, T01273-886200, have an extensive local network in the Brighton, Hove and Lewes areas. **Stagecoach**, T01903-237661, for **Hastings** (2 hrs), **Dover** (5 hrs), **Portsmouth** (2 hrs), **Southampton** (2 hrs), and **Lewes** (30 mins).

Car
For car hire try **Avis**, 6a Marina Village Brighton Marina, T01273-673738; **Beetle Hire**, 4 Parkmoor Terr, T01273-279926; **Europcar**, Cannon Pl, T01273-329332.

Taxi
Metered cabs congregate at various points around the centre – the main ranks are on West St (outside the Kingswest Complex), East St (opposite the Pavilion gardens), and at the Station. Otherwise try **24 Hour Cabs**, T01273 414141; **B&H Radio Cars**, T01273-204060 or **Brighton Streamline Taxi-cab Ltd**, T01273-747474.

Train
The main railway station is on Queen's Rd, a little North from the centre. There are local stations at London Rd (on the line to Lewes and Hastings), and Preston Park (served by stopping trains to London and the North). Hove Railway Station is on Goldstone Villas, a 10-min walk from central Hove, and is served by trains to Portsmouth. *Connex South Central*, T08706-030405. For **London Victoria** (1 hr), **Lewes** (15 mins), **Hastings** (1 hr 15 mins) and **Portsmouth** (1 hr 30 mins). Thameslink Trans, T08457-484950, for **London King's Cross** (1 hr 20 mins), **London Blackfriars** (1 hr 10 mins), **London Bridge** (1 hr), **Luton Airport** (1 hr 50 mins) and Gatwick Airport (30 mins). **South West** Trains, T02380-213600, for **Chichester** (50 mins) and **Winchester** (1 hr 50 mins). **Wales and West**, T08709-000766, for Cardiff, Bristol, Bath and Southampton. **Virgin Trains**, T08457-222333, for **Edinburgh**, **Manchester**, **Birmingham** and **Oxford**.

Directory

Brighton *p198, map p200*
Hospitals Royal Sussex County Hospital, Eastern Rd, T01273-696955. Has an accident and emergency department.
Internet Pursuit Internet, 22 Preston St is a good bet. There are also internet facilities at Riki Tik, 18a Bond St, T01273-683844.
Police Brighton Police are at John St, Hove at Holland Rd, T0845 60708999. **Post office** Brighton has post offices at 51 Ship St, and 142 Western Rd, Hove at 120 Church Rd. T08457-223344.

Brighton to Arundel

→ *Colour map 3, grid C2/1*

From the eerily named but extremely scenic Devil's Dyke, just behind Brighton, to Arundel in the west, the Downs move further inland. The flat coastal plain to their south is largely built-up but contains some interesting architecture at Lancing and Shoreham. To the north lie traditional villages and towns along the spring-line, like Poynings, Fulking, Bramber and Steyning and the utterly twee Amberley. There are also a number of sites of archaeological import – for example the Iron Age Settlement at Chanctonbury Ring and the Roman villa at Bignor. This stretch of downland has a more rural, wild feel to it than the rolling hills around Eastbourne and Lewes, and the area's relatively isolated nature means that access and accommodation are not as plentiful as to the east. That said, this is still southeast England, and you're never more than a few miles from a pub or a B&B. In summer, it may be best to head to these parts for a quieter and more authentic, if less spectacular, taste of the South Downs. ▸▸ *For Sleeping, Eating and other listings see pages 213-214.*

Ins and outs

Getting there The only useful **train** station aside Brighton and Arundel is Shoreham-by-Sea, where you can pick up connections to Brighton (20 minutes) and Chichester (25 minutes). You can pick up trains to London from Arundel and Brighton and there is a local service from Brighton to Chichester which stops frequently along the built-up coastal plain. Shoreham is about 5 miles from the Downs. The A22 **road** from London meets the A27 just north of Brighton and this stretches west along the coastal plain a few miles south of the Downs. Buses run along the A27 from Arundel to Brighton where you can pick up connections to London. To the North of the Downs, there are infrequent local buses connecting the towns and villages to Arundel, Chichester, Shoreham and Brighton. ▸▸ *For further details, see Transport page 214.*

Getting around You're best off accessing the Downs at Devil's Dyke, a short bus ride from Brighton, or at Arundel. Both are connected by rail to London. There are a number of minor roads which connect the villages north of the Downs to the A27 to the south, and also infrequent local buses to Arundel, Chichester, Shoreham and Brighton (see above). If you're feeling adventurous, you can also get up to the Downs from Shoreham; the station is about 5 miles from the top of the hills and Truleigh Hill Youth Hostel. If you have a car, the country lanes along the spring-line to the north of the hills are a pleasant drive but the hills themselves are best explored on foot.

Devil's Dyke

Head west beyond Hove and the city turns into a green but uninspiring sprawl of suburbs, head north just a couple of miles, and you're in some breathtaking downland scenery. This steep, sharp valley was actually carved by a stream, rather than forces from behind the fiery gates, and is a lovely spot for some fresh air at sunset.

Poynings and Fulking

Just west of the Dyke, the South Downs Way passes over Poynings and Fulking. These two pretty villages lie along the spring-line (where the chalk downs spill their excess water onto the lowlands). The church of the **Holy Trinity** at Poynings is a classic flint Sussex Church and its village a pleasant place to wander or sample some local ale. The main street at the unfortunately named Fulking, meanwhile, features an area where yokels used to dam the spring to create a sheepdip. Doing this every week in freezing cold flowing water is rumoured to have crippled much of the town's male population until the early 20th century saw more civilized agricultural practices introduced. The **Fulking Escarpment** behind the village is a Site of Special Scientific Interest, containing some fine downland flora and fauna including some rare orchids.

Bramber

Bramber is a sleepy little place about half way between Brighton and Arundel, and a good watering hole if you get tired of walking. The main sites of interest are the Parish Church of **St Nicholas**, a tiny Norman affair dating to 1073. Of the same era is the largely ruined **Bramber castle**, constructed by Norman baron William de Braose, again in 1073, to protect his fiefdom. Only the gatehouse remains in any quantity, but you can walk around the leafy ruins of the motte and bailey.

South of the Downs

To the south of the Downs, the main spots of interest are **Lancing College** ⓘ *T01273-452213, Mon-Sat 1000-1600, Sun 1200-1600, free,* and **Shoreham**. Lancing College is a fairly upmarket public school featuring a gorgeous Gothic Chapel (1868), which dominates the plain to the south. Shoreham is a straggly town on the coast, but is worth visiting for remnants of its Norman heritage. Dominated by the large Norman church of St Mary, the town is also home to the **Marlipins Museum** ⓘ *T01273-462994, High St, Tue-Sat 1030-1630*, which documents local and maritime history in an attractive Norman customs house.

North of the Downs

Steyning, to the North of the hills is an attractive place for a pit-stop. This little country town was once a port and features a number of unusually intact medieval streets, especially Church Street which has some wonderfully ramshackle old houses, and a sizeable Norman Church. A little further west along the South Downs Way, **Chanctonbury Ring** is the area's best vantage point with magnificent views over the inland countryside. Once swathed in a ring of beech trees (which fell foul of a nasty storm in the late 1980s) extensive remains of Roman and Iron Age settlements have been found.

Amberley

Amberley Village is a couple of minutes on the train from Arundel, and is perhaps even more of an English idyll. All cutesy architectural styles seem to be represented from thatch, through flint to half-timber. It's the kind of place they used to put on First World War recruitment posters to highlight to future cannon-fodder what they were fighting to preserve. Pleasingly, it doesn't suffer from the bus loads of tourists which have blighted the likes of Alfriston (see page 191) and is a lovely spot to wander for a couple of hours. The castle is now an exclusive country hotel but it's worth popping into **St Michael's church**, a Norman effort just outside the castle walls, and **Amberley Museum** ⓘ *T01798-831370*, which, given its situation in gentrified Sussex countryside, features a rather incongruous collection of industrial memorabilia.

Arundel

Travelling up the Arun valley, the casual observer could be forgiven for thinking they were arriving at Windsor, the cynical, at EuroDisney. Completely dominating this little town perched up on the Western hillside is its expansive motte and double bailey castle. There has been some kind of fortification here since well before the Norman Conquest and successive Earls of Arundel have added to it over the centuries, accounting for both its size (it is the country's biggest) and contrived appearance. Like Rye, Arundel was once a port and its history is dominated by seafaring and smuggling. The current town is a cutesy place with ubiquitous antique shops, frilly tea rooms and conservative hotels. Although you can easily see it in a day, it's worth holing up here for a bit longer as a base to explore the countryside and villages of the Arun Valley – some of the area's most beautiful. If you can, you should try and coincide your visit with a cricket match at the castle's very own cricket pitch – the spectacle of leather on willow in these surroundings being a wonderful affirmation of Englishness.

Ins and outs

Getting there Arundel is on the main line from Chichester (20 minutes) to London Victoria (1 hour 25 minutes) via Gatwick airport (45 minutes). From Chichester you can pick up connections east to Brighton and west to Portsmouth, Southampton and Winchester. Arundel lies just off the A27 Portsmouth to Brighton trunk **road** and is about an hour's drive from both, and just 20 minutes from Chichester. Coming from London, you'll need to take the A29 and turn off at Houghton, the drive can take anything from 1-3 hours. ➔ *For further details, see Transport page 214.*

Getting around Arundel is a very small town and you should be able to reach it all on foot. For Amberley village it's a single stop on the train (5 minutes) and trains run hourly.

Information TIC ⓘ *High St, T01903-882268. Apr-Sep 1000-1800, Nov-Mar 1000-1500.*

Sights

Museum and Heritage Centre ⓘ *High St, T01903-882268, 1030-1700 Mon-Sat, 1400-1700 Sun, £1,* is next to the TIC, and gives you the lowdown on the town's history.

Arundel Castle ⓘ *T01903-883136, Apr-Oct Sun-Fri 1200-1700, £9, under-16s £5.50, concessions £7, family £24.50,* was built by Roger de Montgomery, Earl of Arundel, in the 11th century, and has been the seat of the Dukes of Norfolk for over 500 years. It has been rebuilt on numerous occasions since, most thoroughly in the 19th century, and now has a fairly-tale quality, with a maze of towers and turrets perched on the hill over the Arun valley. On view inside are some personal possessions of Mary, Queen of Scots, some 16th-century tapestries and clocks, and portraits by Van Dyke and Gainsborough. If you are here during the summer months, you should try and catch a game of cricket in the castle's very own ground (T01903-882462); Sussex County Cricket club play the odd fixture here, and touring international teams play an MCC team each summer.

Outside the castle entrance on London Road is the Parish church of **St Nicholas**. Built in the perpendicular style in 1380, it is one of history's anomalies – during the Reformation, the western part of the chapel converted to the Church of England, the eastern portion, however, as part of the jurisdiction of the catholic Duke of Norfolk, was forced to stay loyal to Rome. A little further along the crest of the hill is **Arundel Cathedral** ⓘ *T01903-882297.* Despite its 15th-century style, it was actually built between 1869 and 1873 to plans drawn up by one JA Hansom, he of the Hansom cab.

A 1km walk to the North of Arundel, along Mill Road, brings you to **Swanbourne Lake and Arundel Park.** A former millpond in a quiet valley, it's now home to many species of wildlife. The park itself is 1100 acres of untampered downland, and ideal for strolling in this idyllic grassy landscape. A little further along Mill Road, is the **Waterfowl Park** ⓘ *T01903-883355, daily 0930-1730, £5.50, under-16s £3.50,* ideal for those with an eye for the birds.

Sleeping

Brighton to Arundel *p210*

B Norfolk Arms Hotel, High St, Arundel, T01903-884275. A charming 18th-century coaching inn in the shadow of the castle. The poshest in town, it's worth splashing out for a night or 2.

B The Old Railway Station, Petworth, north of Arundel on the A272, T01798-342346. Six bedrooms in converted Pullman carriages with en suite bathrooms, brass beds and breakfast on the old platform (if the weather's fine). This is 'rail' luxury...

C Burpham Country House Hotel and Resturant, Burpham, near Chichester, T01903-882160. An upmarket B&B.

C-D Woodstock House Hotel and Restaurant, Charlton, near Chichester, T01243-811666. A country-lodge style gaff.

D Bramber Castle Hotel, Bramber, T01903-812102. An olde-worlde pub with 8 doubles.

D Old Tollgate Restaurant and Hotel, The Street, Bramber, Steyning, T01903-879494. Is clean and reasonably priced.

D Springwells, 9 High St, Steyning, T01903-812446. A clean, modern B&B with outdoor heated swimming pool.

D The Swan Hotel, High St, Arundel, T01903-882314. B&B. The in-house restaurant makes the most of local seafood and game.

D Tottington Manor Hotel, Edburton, T01903-815757. Good value rooms in a 16th-century manor house.

E Arundel House, 11 High St, Arundel, T01903-882136. A 16th-century licensed restaurant with 6 characterful rooms.

E Dukes of Arundel, 65 High St, Arundel, T01903-883847. A prince amongst B&Bs with 400-year-old interior architecture.

E Poynings Manor Farm, T01273-857371. Has 3 rooms on a working farm.

E White Horse Hotel, 2 The Square, Storrington, T01903-743451, is good value with en-suite doubles for £20.

E Woodpeckers, 15 Dalloway Rd, Arundel, T01903-883948. A modern resting place in countrified surroundings near the town centre.

F Warningcamp Youth Hostel, Sefton Pl, Warningcamp, T01903-882204. Dorms £8, camping £3.90. The local budget option and is clean and friendly, if a little out of the way.

F YHA, Hostels are at Truleigh Hill, Shoreham, T01903-813419 – right on the South Downs Way, and Warningcamp, Arundel, T01903-882204, also clean and reliable.

Camping

Bridge Public House, Amberley, T01798-831619, has camping available. Next to a pub which serves simple, but excellent, food.

Eating

Brighton to Arundel *p210*

Best to confine yourself to pubs as there's very little choice, although many of the hotels above do acceptable food.

£££ Norfolk Arms, High St, Arundel, T01903-882101, does cream teas in a quaint old room; there's also a meaty, gamey English restaurant, but it has a little too much impact on the wallet for the quality.

££ Chequer Inn, High St, Steyning, T01903-814437, is a small town place with a traditional restaurant.

££ Maharajah, The St, Bramber, T01903-814746, even humble Bramber has its Indian restaurant, and it's not bad either.

££ Steyning Wine Bar and Pizzeria, 27 High St, Steyning, T01903-812820, is exactly what you'd expect from a small town wine bar and pizzeria.

££ Tudor Rose Restaurant, 49 High St, Arundel, T01903-883813, is a safe bet for English meals.

££ Xavier's, Castle Mews, Tarrant St, Arundel, T01903-883477, is a wine-bar type affair with delicious crêpes.

£ Belinda's Tea Shop, 13 Tarrant St, Arundel, T01903-882 977, has teas, coffees, light meals, and plenty of cakes.

£ Copper Kettle, 21 Tarrant St, Arundel, has lunches of the sandwich and baked spud kind.

£ Milestones, 25 High St, Steyning, T01903-812338, is a decent bet for a cheap eat.

Pubs, bars and clubs

Brighton to Arundel *p210*
The Eagle, Tarrant St, Arundel, is a quiet pub, with some excellent cold lunches à la Parma ham and melon, and Greek salad.
King's Arms, Tarrant St, Arundel, is a traditional boozer, and a good place for a swift half.
Royal Oak Inn, The Street, Poynings, T01273 857389, is an old-fashioned boozer with plenty of stodge on the menu.
The Shepherd and Dog, Fulking, T01273-857382, is an old alehouse with a decent menu and a beer garden looking up into Devil's Dyke.

Entertainment

Brighton to Arundel *p210*
The Gallery, Castle Mews, Tarrant St, Arundel, T01903-883813, has works by local artists.
Priory Playhouse Theatre, Arundel, T01903-883345, is home to the local dramatic society.

Festivals

Brighton to Arundel *p210*
Aug Arundel Festival, box office T01903-883474, is held yearly, normally in the last week of Aug. Theatrical and musical events, in a number of historic venues around town.

Shopping

Brighton to Arundel *p210*
Your only real shopping options are antiques shops and print shops, and Tarrant St is the best place for these.
Arundel Antiques, Castle Mews, Tarrant St, Arundel, T01903-883066, has a good range of books, prints, and walking sticks.
Faringdon Galley, Tarrant St, Arundel, has attractive paintings and prints of the area.

Activities and tours

Brighton to Arundel *p210*
The council has facilities for tennis and bowling on Mill Rd, Arundel.
Arundel Cricket Club, T01903-882462, is an idyllic venue in the castle grounds.
Chalk Springs Fishery, on the outskirts of Arundel, just off the A27, T01903 883742.
Lancing Manor Leisure Centre, Old Shoreham Rd, Lancing, T01273-263300 is an all-purpose sports hall.
Steyning Leisure Centre, T01903-879666, Horsham Rd, has a 25 m pool, squash courts and a multi-purpose sports hall.
Sussex County Cricket Club, T01273-827100, play a few matches here and invitation XIs take on overseas touring sides.
'Wadurs' Community Pool, Kingston Broadway, Shoreham, T01273-263100 is an indoor swimming pool.

Transport

Brighton to Arundel *p210*

Bus
Stagecoach Coastline, T01903-237661, services operate along the A27 from Brighton (2 hrs) and Chichester (1 hr).

Taxi
Cab Service 141 are at Steyning, T01903-815171. Southern Taxis are at Shoreham, T01273-464646. Castle Cars, Arundel, T01903-884444.

Train
Connex South Central, T08706-030405.

Directory

Brighton to Arundel *p210*
Hospitals Southlands Hospital, Upper Shoreham Rd, Shoreham, T01273-455622. There is also a small hospital in Arundel, T01903-882543. **Police** Shoreham police are at Ham Rd, T01273-6070999.

Chichester

→ Colour map 3, grid C1

This elegant little city has been a major centre across several eras of English history and has an extraordinarily rich architectural heritage from the Roman walls of Noviomagnus and the Villa at Fishbourne, to some fine 18th and 19th century townhouses. Dominating the skyline and incorporating virtually all aspects of the city's history is the cathedral – one of the country's finest. The modern city is a bustling if rather staid place perhaps accounted for by a rather geriatric population. Yet the architecture of the place should make it a stopping point on anybody's tour of the region and come in July and you'll be treated to regional theatre second only to Stratford-upon-Avon at the Chichester Festivities. ➤➤ *For Sleeping, Eating and other listings see pages 216-218.*

Ins and outs

Getting there Chichester is well served with regular direct **trains** to Brighton, Portsmouth and London Victoria via Gatwick airport. By **car**, the A285 or the A29 wind their way up to London, and this can take anything from 1 ½-3 hrs, depending on traffic. Portsmouth and Brighton are both about an hour away on the A27. ➤➤ *For further details, see Transport page 217.*

Getting around Chichester itself is easily covered on foot. For the outlying places mentioned in this section you'll need to head for the bus station: Bosham (15 minutes), Fishbourne (10 minutes), Goodwood (15 minutes).

Information TIC ⓘ *29a South St, T01243-775888, 0915-1700 Mon-Sat.* Plenty of leaflets, an accommodation booking service and a computerized information machine.

Sights

The **Market Cross**, is the logical place to start a walk around the city centre. Donated to the town's poor by Bishop Storey in 1501, so that they might trade 'without let or hindrance,' these days it's still the city's centrifuge and all classes meet there for a rest and a chat during a haul around the shops. Along West Street, is the city's magnificent **Cathedral** ⓘ *T01243-782595, 0730-1900. Guided tours are available Easter-Oct, Mon-Sat at 1100 and 1415, (and there is a 'roving' guide at all times), and are well worth it for a deeper appreciation of the cathedral's many treasures.* There has been a building on this spot since Roman times, and a fragment of an intricate second-century mosaic can be found to the right of the current retrochoir. Today's building began taking shape in 1076, and was ready for the consecration of Bishop Luffa in 1108. Much has been added since then – the sacristry, retrochoir and clerestory (under Bishop Seffrid II – 1180-1204), are of the Early English Gothic style; the Lady Chapel (early 14th-century), with its gorgeous Lambert Barnard ceiling, is in the Decorated style; the bell tower, cloisters and independent belfry (15th-century) were built in the Perpendicular style – but the building conveys much more of the integrity of the original than many of its English counterparts. The cathedral contains paintings, sculpture and masonry from over a millennium as a centre of worship and pilgrimage, and you should take your time over it.

Outside the Cathedral, the unique, free-standing **Bell Tower**, has a peal of eight bells, with one surviving from 1583. St Richard's walk, is a pretty walled-alleyway leading from the Cathedral down to Canon Lane, whilst **Vicar's Close** is a terrace of 15th-century houses, once occupied by the vicar's choral and their refectory. At the end of the lane, you can see the Palace Gateway, the Tudor red-brick entrance to the **Bishop's Palace**. Cut through and you'll come to the Bishop's Palace Gardens, a beautifully manicured public space, which is an ideal spot to sit down in and enjoy the view over the Cathedral and her precincts.

Pallant House, is an elegant historic house and art gallery, built in 1812, now host to an estimable collection of British art, and regular talks and events. Up on thronging North Street is the Saxon church of **St Olave's** ⓘ *9 North Pallant, T01243-774557, Tue-Sat, 1000-1700, Sun and bank holidays 1230-1700, £4, under-16s £3*, built in 1050, possibly by roving Scandinavian merchants; it contains remains of an earlier Roman foundation.

Just off Priory Rd is the **Greyfriars building**, a chancel built in the 13th century, it is now all that remains of the monastery of the Greyfriars. Genteel sacrilege now surrounds it in the form of a nicely groomed cricket pitch surrounded by the city walls.

For a good overview of the city's saga it's worth popping into **Chichester District Museum** ⓘ *29 Little London, T01234-784683, Tue-Sat 1000-1730, free*. The former cornstore contains, amongst other local delights, an array of the militaria of the Royal Sussex Regiment.

Around Chichester

Fishbourne Roman Palace ⓘ *Salt Hill Rd, Fishbourne, T01243-539266, Mar-Jul 1000-1700, Aug 1000-1800, Sep-Dec 1000-1600, Jan Sat and Sun 1000-1600, £5, under-16s £4.10*, is Britain's largest Roman residence. Built for King Tiberius Claudius Togidubnus it is a fine example of Latinate luxury dating from the first century AD. Surviving hypocausts and mosaics suggest the king was something of a bon viveur, and the gardens have been lovingly re-replanted to original plans. Alas, the decline in residential planning over the subsequent two millennia has resulted in many of the remains being housed in a building that looks like your average ring-road garden centre.

'Glorious Goodwood,' is a phrase uttered in reverence of a quasi-fictional summer upper class idyll. Normally by *Daily Mail* readers from the Rotary Clubs of Surrey. It's fair to say, **Goodwood Racecourse**, T01243-75502, is a venue of some grandeur, situated as it is in some breathtaking downland scenery. If you can bear the mild air of social aspiration and some ridiculous head attire its summer programme is a grand excuse to go and stick a few bets on the gee-gees. Distinctly less frenetic is **Goodwood House** ⓘ *T01243-755048, Apr-Oct, Sun and Mon afternoons, £7, concessions £6, teenagers and students £3.00, under-12s free*, home to the celebrated Duchess of Richmond, who organized the Franco-foxing ball on the eve of the Battle of Waterloo.

For some serious art in stately environs head for **Petworth House** ⓘ *T01798-342207, Apr-Nov, Sat-Wed, 1300-1700*. Turner, Van Dyck, Reynolds and Blake are amongst the famed artists on display in the Sussex countryside, whilst the gardens themselves a work of art, concocted according to the Lancelot theory of Capability Brown.

Chichester was once an important port, and the estuary at **Bosham** at its hub. It's a pleasant place for a stroll with a cutesy church down by the river. The estuarine mudflats are laid bare at low tide and provide an unusual landscape awash with birds.

Sleeping

Chichester *p215*

C Ship Hotel, North St, T01243-778000. A classic 18th-century townhouse hotel, perhaps a little overpriced, though.

C-D Ramada Jarvis Hotel, Westhampnett Rd, T01243-786351. Your average corporate motel with swimming, sauna and sunbeds.

D Bedford Hotel, Southgate, T01243-785766. Pleasant, if a little staid, private hotel near all the city's attractions.

D Suffolk House Hotel, 3 East Row, T01243-778899. Respectable classic Georgian affair.

D-E Encore, 11 Clydesdale Av, T01243-52827. A reliable B&B, a stone's throw from the centre.

E The Cottage, 22B Westhampnett Rd, T01243-774979. A standard B&B with clean if uninspiring rooms.

E University College Chichester, Bishop Otter Campus, College La, T01243-816070.

Lets out its student rooms for £23 per night from Jun to Aug.

Eating

Chichester *p215*
££ Chichester Inn, 40 West St, is a no-nonsense boozer with garden, wholesome stodge, bar snacks and, well, beer.
££ Little London Indian Restaurant, 38 Little London, T01243-537550, does exactly what it says on the tin to a better standard than most.
££ Pizza Express, South St, T01243-786648, if imagination deserts you, head for the superior end of generic.
£ Cathedral Refectory, Chichester Cathedral, West St, T01243-782595, in the Cathedral vaults and offers light lunch.
£ Shepherd's tearoom, 35 Little London, T01243-774761, cakes, buns and assorted sweetmeats among the frills.
£ Slurping Toad, West St, is a pub in an old church serving up plenty of beer, music and large helpings of veg and 2 meat.
£ White Horse, corner of South St and West Pallant, T01234-785804. Does panini, pasta and the like in airy accommodation.

Entertainment

Chichester *p215*
Chichester Festival Theatre, Oaklands Park, T01243-784437, since its inception in 1962, has established a national reputation for its productions; John Geilgud and Maggie Smith are amongst the stars to have performed here over the years. The venue is the nucleus of the Chichester Festivities (See Festivals) which take place every year in Jul and is complemented by the diminutive Minerva Theatre which was added to the complex in 1989.
New Park Cinema, New Park Rd, T01243-786650, is a small independent cinema which shows a mix of mainstream releases and quality film and, until seemingly interminable conflicts over the building of a multiplex cinema and bowling alley are resolved, that's your lot.

Festivals

Chichester *p215*
Jul **Chichester Festivities**, T01243-785718, takes place each year and is an impressive affair. Local and international performers make sure all organs of the body artistic are pumping – from avant-garde soireés in tiny city venues to theatre at the Festival Theatre to chamber music at Goodwood House.

Shopping

Chichester *p215*
Chichester is a small place, not exactly a shopper's paradise and your options are primarily confined to antique vendors of varying repute, but there are a few other places of note.
Butter Market, North St, contains independent producers including a very fine-looking sausage butchers.
Chichester Armoury, 43 West St, T01243-774687, hunting, shooting, fishing, and proud of all 3.
Living World, 33 West St, T01243-780360, if a trip to the cathedral sparks your redemption, you can go and read up at this well kept Christian bookshop.
Maison Blanc, South St, T01243-539292, M. Blanc may be making a pretty penny out of gastronomically deprived Brits, but you can't deny the delights of his Gallic Patisserie.

Activities and tours

Chichester *p215*
Chichester Golf, T01243-528999, has pay and play 9-hole, 18-hole, and crazy golf a few miles south of the city centre.
Chichester Harbour Water Tours, 9 Cawley Rd, T01243-786418, does some watery tours around the old harbour.
Westgate Centre, T01243-785651, has an all-purpose sports hall, swimming pool and sauna.

Transport

Chichester *p215*
Bicycle
Barreg Cycles in Fishbourne, T01243-786104. For bicycle hire.

Bus
Local The main bus station is on Southgate, opposite the rail station. Most services are run by Stagecoach, T08702-433711, but their information line will give out times for other companies.

Long distance A bus runs along the A27 from **Portsmouth** (1 hr) to **Brighton** (2 hrs) via **Chichester**.

Taxi

Central Cars, T01243-789432; Dunaways Taxis, T01243-782403.

Train

Chichester Station is just off Southgate, a few mins' walk from the Market Cross. Connex South Central, T08706-030405, and South West Trains, T02380-213600, run trains to **Brighton** (40 mins), **Portsmouth** (30 mins) and **London Victoria** (1 hr 45 mins) via **Gatwick airport** (1 hr 10 mins), **Winchester** (1 hr 10 mins) and **Reading** (1 hr 30 mins).

Directory

Chichester *p215*
Hospitals St Richard's Hospital, T01243-788122. **Internet** available at the Library on Tower St, T01243-290800. **Post office** West St.

Surrey

Colour map 3, grid B2

Surrey usually gets a bad press, written off as a polite suburban extension of southwest London, the city's stockbroker belt. Even so, once beyond the M25, the combination of affluent homeowners and strict planning regulations has promoted an attractive mix of town and country. Between Guildford and Dorking, the North Downs roll up to the highest point in the southeast at Leith Hill. Just to the north an even more popular viewpoint is Box Hill, close to the Edwardian splendours of Polsden Lacey. To the south, rolling wooded countryside and heathland dotted with little commuter villages stretches down to the border with Sussex. *For Sleeping, Eating and other listings, see page 220.*

Guildford

The county town of Guildford is not the most attractive place in Surrey but it's certainly one of the busiest. Dominated by its stark modern cathedral, there have unfortunately been other much less impressive developments in the second half of the 20th century. That said, the old High St hidden away among the multistorey car parks and office blocks remains much as it would have looked before the cathedral was built, and the banks of the Wey have recently received some much needed attention. On the whole, the town is a reasonable base from which to explore the surrounding area.

Ins and outs

Getting there Fast **trains** run from London Waterloo via Woking twice an hour taking 35 minutes. By **car**, Guildford is on the A3, about 1 hr's drive from central London. *For further details, see Transport page 220.*

Getting around Guildford is relatively car-friendly, making it less of a pleasure to walk around than some other towns. Local buses are operated by **Connex**, T0208-6897735, **Arriva**, T01483-505693, **Metrobus**, T01293-449191, **Arriva Airbus**, T08705 757747.

Sights

Guildford's cobbled High St slopes uphill lined with all the usual big names in retail. Its most famous feature is the ancient gilded clock jutting out from the old Guildhall. A pleasant retreat from the crowds, the stubby stone keep of Guildford's **Norman castle** is tucked away behind the High St in flower-filled gardens. Some distance from the town centre stands the **Cathedral**. Construction on this highly contemporary interpretation of Gothic magnificence started in 1936. The completed fabric, designed by Edward Maufe, was consecrated in 1964. Notable features, apart from its austerity and size, are the carvings outside and in by the likes of Eric Gill and Vernon Hill. Next door is the equally redbrick **University of Surrey**.

Down on the river Wey, **Dapdune Wharf** ⓘ *Wharf Rd, T01483-561389, boat trips are available from the Guildford Boat House, T01483-504494,* offers the chance to explore an old Wey barge, *Reliance*, and a good interactive exhibition on the history of the waterway.

Around Guildford

A couple of miles southeast of Guildford, near the village of Compton, **Loseley Park** ⓘ *T01483-304440, house Jun-Aug Wed-Sun 1300-1700 by guided tour, gardens only May-Sep Wed-Sun 1100-1700, house and garden £6.50,* is an Elizabethan house on a hilltop owned by the same family since 1562. Inside can be found pannelling from Henry VIII's Nonesuch Palace, while outside there's a superb walled rose garden and a herb garden. They also do very good ice cream made on the estate from their own prize-winning Jersey herd.

Three miles northeast of Guildford, off the A25, **Clandon Park** ⓘ *(NT), near West Clandon, T01483-222482, Apr-Nov Tue-Thu, Sun 1100-1700, gardens only all year Tue-Thu, Sun 1100-1700, £6, family £15,* is a very fine and stately Palladian mansion stuffed with valuable furniture, pictures and porcelain collected early in the 20th century. Capability Brown had a hand in the gardens, although these are really only at their best during the spring when the daffodils are in bloom.

In East Clandon next door, **Hatchlands** ⓘ *(NT), T01483-222482, Apr-Nov Tue-Thu, Sun 1100-1700, gardens only all year Tue-Thu, Sun 1100-1700, £5, £2.50 concessions,* was built for Admiral Boscawen, and contains some of Robert Adams' earliest known work (from 1759), a large collection of keyboard instruments as well as a few old masters.

A similar distance northeast of Guildford are the **Royal Horticultural Society's garden** ⓘ *RHS Wisley, T01483-224234, www.rhs.org.uk, all year Mon-Fri 1000-1800 or dusk, weekends 0900-1800 or dusk, £6, £2 under-16s,* 240 acres of expertly tended gardens, including a 16-acre fruit field bursting with an astonishing variety of apples, as well as herbaceous borders, ornamental walks, greenhouses, and the inevitable shop, restaurant and café. Highlights include spring in the Alpine Meadow, the specially designed model gardens, and the new Country Garden.

Just inside the M25 off the A3, **Painshill Landscape Garden** ⓘ *T01932-868113, Apr-Oct Tue-Sun 1030-1800 (last admission 1630, free guided tours weekends at 1400), Nov-Mar Tue-Thu, Sat, Sun 1100-1600 (last admission 1500), £3.80, concessions £3.30, £1.50 under-16s,* rolls out around a 14-acre lake fed by a huge waterwheel surrounded by a carefully restored landscape garden laid out from 1738-1773 by Charles Hamilton, complete with ruined abbey, Chinese bridge, Turkish tent, Gothic tower and grotto. Since 1981, the Painshill Park Trust have been returning the 160-acre plot to its former glory.

Dorking

More attractive but also more of a 'dormitory' town than Guildford, Dorking's only real attraction is **Box Hill** ⓘ *NT Warden, T01306-885502,* popular with weekenders looking for some fresh air and geography field trips exploring the peculiarities of the River Mole's course through the Downs. Just to the north of the town, it's a good 4-hour trek over stepping-stones across the river. It can also be reached off the A24. Long walks can be taken along the ridge via Pebble Combe to Reigate, or along Mickleham Down to Leatherhead.

A mile west of Box Hill, **Polesden Lacey** ⓘ *(NT), T01372-452048, Apr-Sep Wed-Sun, bank holidays 1100-1700, £7.50, grounds only all year daily 1100-1800 or dusk £4*, with its superb Edwardian rose gardens and grounds, was the lavish party home of Mrs Greville, where she entertained Edward VII and babysat the Queen Mother.

Five miles south, **Leith Hill** ⓘ *T01306-711777, Tower Nov-Mar weekends and bank holidays 1000-1500, Apr-Oct Wed, weekends 1000-1630, £1.50*, is the highest point in the southeast, from where on a very clear day, St Paul's and Canary Wharf can be seen, as well as the sea at Shoreham on the south coast. Windy Gap car park provides the nearest assault to the 19th-century viewpoint tower at the top, where the effort is rewarded with home-made cakes. The **Plough Inn** ⓘ *T01306-711793*, in nearby Coldharbour, makes a good post-climb destination, although you'll need to book the restaurant.

Sleeping

Guilford *p218*

A-B Jarvis Guildford Hotel, Upper High St, T01483-564511, F531160. A very central chain hotel in a fine old Georgian building.

C-D Hampton, 38 Poltimore Rd, T01483-572012, vgmorris@aol.com. A Tudor-style detached house in a quiet cul-de-sac with views over the town.

D Joanna's Bed & Breakfast, 30 Nightingale Rd, T01483-568873. A late 19th-century house close to the London Rd train station.

E Guildford YMCA, Y Centre, Bridge St, T01483-532555, F537161. Has a popular daytime restaurant offering home-cooked meals and award-winning service in a modern riverside location. £30 per person per night, just round the corner from the station, but needs booking well in advance.

Dorking *p219*

L Nutfield Priory, Nutfield, Redhill, T01737-824400. One of the most luxurious and expensive options in a former Gothic folly surrounded by acres of parkland, with magnificent views, a health club and everything you'd expect from a smart country house hotel, including award-winning restaurant.

D-E Herons Head Farm, Mynthurst, Leigh, T01293-862475, is a Jacobean farmhouse with jacuzzis, outdoor swimming pool and a lake.

D-E Park House Farm, Hollow La, Abinger Common, near Dorking, T01306-730101, also in beautiful countryside, close to Leith Hill.

E Bulmer Farm, Holmbury St Mary, near Dorking, T01306-730210, is an attractive old house, convenient for exploring Leith Hill, with self-contained accommodation available in an annexe.

Eating

Dorking *p219*

£££ The Dining Room, 59a High St, Reigate, T01737-226650, a treat for foodies with confident combinations of Mediterranean and British cuisine.

£££ La Barbe, 71 Bell St, Reigate, T01737-241966, do classic French food in a busy atmosphere, set dinner at about £30 per head.

£££ Mulberry Restaurant at Langshott Manor, Langshott, near Horley, T01293-786680, somewhere between the 2 in price, needs to be booked, surprisingly low-key given its smart hotel location.

££ The Parrot, Forest Green, near Dorking, T01303-621339, is a busy pub with food in an attractive position on the village green.

££ White Horse, in Shere, T01483-202518, 'the prettiest village in Surrey', is a rickety old place with decent food.

Transport

Guildford *p218*

Bus

Long distance National Express, T08705-808080, coaches leave **Victoria** at 0900, 1300, 1500, 1700, and 1900, taking about 1 hr.

The South

Footprint features

Introduction

Five counties make up the core of southern England: between them they're probably the most affluent region of the UK. For the visitor this means plenty of top-quality hotels and restaurants, well-kept villages with polite gastropubs and acres of attractive parkland.

Oxfordshire's name almost says it all, Oxford being one of the most polyglot, venerable and beguiling university towns in the world. Nearby is the Baroque splendour of Blenheim Palace, as well as the less ostentatious charms of its river valleys – the Cherwell, Windrush and Thames – winding between the Cotswold, the Chiltern and the White Horse hills. South and east, the River Thames flows on towards London past ancient Dorchester and into Berks and Bucks: through the high-tech light industry of Reading, beneath Georgian-looking Henley, literary Marlow and Conservative Cookham, to Royal Windsor, with Eton at its feet. To the north of the river stretch the rolling chalk hills of the Chilterns up to the hilltop cathedral city of St Albans.To the south, West Berkshire and Wiltshire are all about racehorses, sweeping downlands and monuments of neolithic civilization – Avebury, Stonehenge and Silbury Hill – with the extraordinary spire of Salisbury cathedral poking up out of the Middle Ages. Winchester, the county town of Hampshire next door, was the medieval capital of England, with a beautiful cathedral, school and the St Cross Hospital still to show for it. On the south coast, the New Forest was the kings' playground, and is now peaceful heathland grazed by quiet ponies.

Offshore, the Isle of Wight totters into the 21st century freighted with an ageing population, crowded prisons and some beautiful scenery – not unlike England itself.

★ Don't miss...

1. Tickle your fancy with a few totemic charms at the **Pitt Rivers Museum** in Oxford before swanning downstream in a punt, page 231.
2. Stroll up or downriver along the quiet **valley of the Windrush** from Burford, upstream for a pub lunch at the Fox Inn, Great Barrington, page 236.
3. Take to the hills on the Downs above **Marlborough** before a top cream-tea at Polly's, page 280.
4. Dredge the wellsprings of your imagination with a trip to **Stonehenge**: imagine if there were no car park... Or just go to **Avebury**, pages 285 and 281.
5. Wander through the watermeadows around the medieval monastery of **St Cross Hospital**, Winchester, page 295.
6. Jump on a ferry from the **New Forest** to **Yarmouth** on the Isle of Wight and ogle all the yachts, page 312.

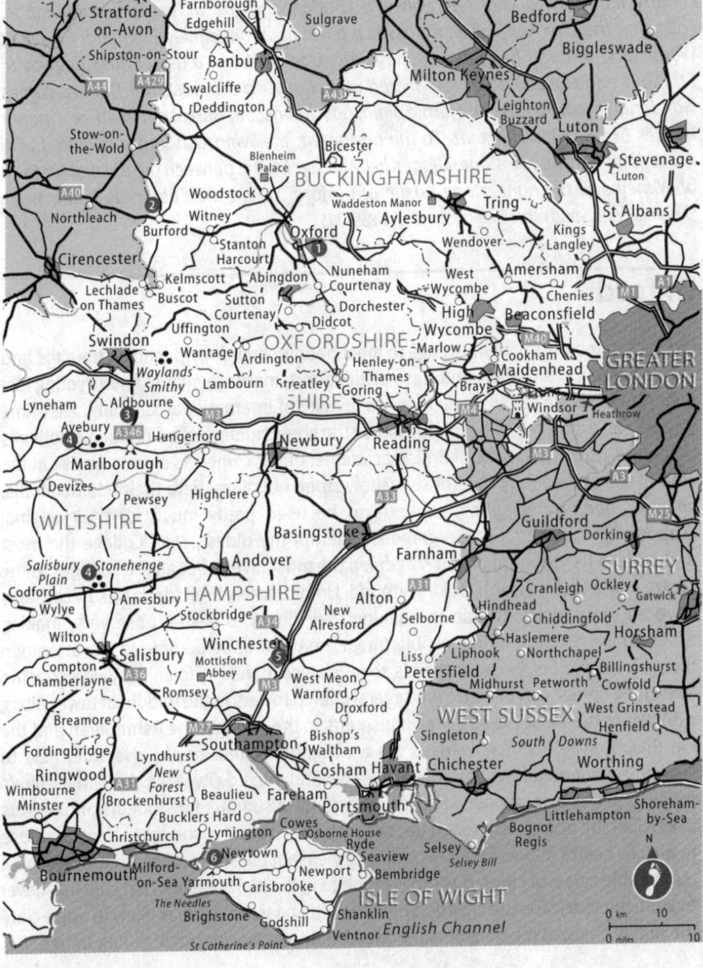

Oxfordshire

→ *Colour map 2, grid A5*

Oxfordshire is a county of slow quiet rivers and watermeadows, stone-built villages in the north near the Cotswolds, downland and old bridge towns in the south on the Thames. At its heart, where that London-bound river is joined by the Cherwell running in from the east Midlands, sits Oxford itself. Very much the capital of its county, England's oldest and most famous university town (once dubbed "the home of lost causes" by the poet Matthew Arnold), it rarely disappoints. Broader, more spread out and just as beautiful as Cambridge, its equally celebrated sister in the east, Arnold also noted that seen from a distance the city's spires, turrets and domes seem to be dreaming. Walking around the old stone colleges or through their surrounding meads and gardens, it's impossible not to be aware of the weight of centuries of scholarship, culture and learning. Thankfully, though, the streets are as alive today as they've ever been, and Oxford continues to be one of the most remarkable, least isolated and most intellectually engaging of modern European cities. To the north is the line of the canal that transformed an essentially medieval town in the late 18th century into such a vital link between London and the industrialized Midlands. Following the Cherwell Valley, it passes a few miles from stately Blenheim Palace at Woodstock, through delightful countryside up to Banbury, a useful base halfway to Stratford and close to other less-hyped attractions. To the west, the Thames comes wandering in over a wide and fertile plain, past Kelmscott, Burcot and medieval manor houses like Stanton Harcourt. To the northwest, the Windrush Valley is dotted with exceptionally attractive stone villages like Minster Lovell, between the old market town of Witney and the honeystone bustle of Burford, where the Cotswolds begin. » *For Sleeping, Eating and other listings, see pages 239-245.*

Oxford

Oxford's name means many things to most people: branding for shoes, trousers and cars, a bastion of snobbery and class distinction, a marriage market for the young idle rich. Above all though, it's still a university city of international standing. First-time visitors can hardly fail to be impressed by the sheer number of beautiful old colleges that make up this pinnacle of British academe. And it comes as some surprise at the start of the 21st century that these mellow stone buildings, with their beamed halls, chapels, quads and spires, continue to be used pretty much for their original purpose. Christ Church is the grandest, Merton the oldest, New College the most authentic in its groundplan and Magdalen the most lovely, but all the colleges in the centre of the city are worth looking around. Unfortunately their top tables necessarily have an ambivalent attitude to opening their doors to casual observers, making access unpredictable or impossible (most are open at some time in the afternoon though). No worries, because there's so much else in the city to enjoy. Views over the 'dreaming spires' can be had from several church towers in the middle of town. Along with two of the most extraordinary museums in the country, the Ashmolean and the Pitt Rivers, the Botanical Gardens are a delightful retreat on the riverside, next to flowering watermeadows and meads just beyond the old city walls. And then there's punting on the river, almost a mandatory activity in summer for students and visitors alike. If all the boats are booked up, simply taking a stroll in the green acres so close to the city centre makes for an exceedingly pleasant afternoon. One of Europe's most remarkable cities, of course Oxford is mobbed in the high season. That said, it's never too difficult to escape the crowds, while even the passing visitor is likely to appreciate the highly charged meeting of cerebral old institutions with bright young things.

Ins and outs

Getting there **Thames Trains** run twice-hourly express **train** services from London Paddington via Reading to Oxford, usually at 18 and 48 mins past the hour, taking just under an hour. Stopping services (via **Didcot Parkway** and stations along the Thames valley) take 1 hour 30 minutes. Oxford's one-way **road** system has reduced motorists to tears, and parking is almost impossible in the middle of the city without paying through the nose. Unfortunately, the pedestrianization of the city centre also means that traffic even clogs up the **Park & Ride** buses. The Botley Road Park and Ride **buses**, to the west, is the closest to the centre, but takes almost as long as the others because of the bottleneck at the railway bridge. If you must arrive on four wheels, you'll find Oxford just off the M40, about an hour from London, half an hour from the M25. Oxford is very well served by **coach** companies. ➡ *For further details, see Transport page 245.*

Getting around **Walking** or **cycling** around central Oxford is one of life's real pleasures. For some of the slightly further-flung parts of the city, **taxis** are relatively cheap and the **bus** network from Gloucester Green along the High Street and around Carfax is regular and reliable. The centre of the city of Oxford is Carfax, the crossroads at the top of the High Street coming in from the east over Magdalen Bridge. Pedestrianized Cornmarket heads north towards wide St Giles, and eventually Woodstock and Banbury. Queen Street continues the High Street west, down past the Norman Castle and prison towards the train station. St Aldate's slopes downhill south, past Christ Church college with its prominent Tom Tower, crossing the Thames at Folly Bridge and continuing out of town as the Abingdon Road.

Information The **TIC** ⓘ *15-16 Broad St, T01865-726871, www.visitoxford.org, Mon-Sat 0930-1700, Sun 1000-1530*, provide an accommodation booking service (including fee).

History

Compared to many towns and cities in England, Oxford is not that old. There's no evidence of Roman occupation, although by then there was already a major road junction just to the north near Bicester. Even the Saxons probably only used the place as a river-crossing for their cattle, hence 'Oxenford', and never settled. In the late ninth century, though, King Alfred recognized the strategic importance of the gravelly banks at the confluence of the rivers Thames and Cherwell in defending his kingdom against the Danes. The town must have prospered, because the expected attack did come in 1009. The first Norman constable Robert Doilly built a castle overlooking the river in the west (of which one tower and the keep's mound survive) and ordered the construction of one of the first stone bridges in western Europe – **Folly Bridge**, completed in 1827, incorporating the Norman bridge beneath, is now a scheduled ancient monument. It wasn't until the late 12th century, when Henry II's wars with France prevented scholars from attending the University of Paris, that Oxford's position slap bang in the middle of England, well-connected to London and the rest of the country, made it a popular meeting place for informal gatherings of masters and wannabe masters. The South Range of Worcester College's main quad gives some idea of the houses these early academics favoured. Merton's Mob Quad is the oldest of the type of accommodation that they eventually adopted, although New College remains the most complete example of the hall, chapel and staircases later adopted by all colleges. The amazing Divinity School in the Bodleian Library was the first place to be owned by the university as a whole, before colleges were set up to safeguard the investments of benefactors. These religious foundations were dealt a hammer-blow by the Reformation, but thankfully much of their architecture survived, making the city the best place in the country to explore

Gothic and later neoclassical architecture. During the Civil War, fanned in part by the St John's man, Archbishop Laud's, overhaul of the Church of England, Charles I based himself and his supporters in Christ Church. Come the Restoration, the university rose again, with illustrious alumni like Christopher Wren (architect of the Sheldonian, Tom Tower and the Clarendon building), the scientists Robert Boyle and Elias Ashmole. The 18th century was not a happy time in the university's history. Riddled with indolent Tories, this was the era that established its reputation as a feckless marriage market for aristos. The coming of the canal changed all that. The city expanded north, and today the spirit of Victorian Oxford and its industry can best be appreciated at the University Museum opposite the splendid red-brick confection of Keble College. In modern times, the Eagle Ironworks and Cowley car plant hugely increased the city's population. The suburbs in the north along the Banbury Road were for dons and their families, while Jericho was developed as affordable accommodation for artisans. East Oxford housed the workers in the car plant as it still just about does today.

West of Carfax

Most visitors using public transport approach central Oxford from the west. Walking up from the train station, the route up Hythe Bridge Street runs past the brand new **Said Business School** (quite a sight in itself, with students perched at their terminals on display behind its glass front), over the Oxford Canal, and joins George Street at the junction of Worcester Street. George Street continues gently uphill, past the Gloucester Green bus station and market square on the left. The city meets the university proper 60 yards from the bus depot at the top of George Street where it hits Cornmarket. Most of the more interesting colleges are east of here, along Broad Street and the High Street (see East of Carfax, below).

One exception is **Worcester College**. A relatively young college, founded in 1714, its very grand 18th-century neoclassical buildings and lakeside garden surround the oldest example of scholars' accommodation in the city. The medieval south range of the main quadrangle forms the adorably dinky remains of Gloucester College, a Benedictine monastery founded in 1283. Worcester Street heads north and becomes Walton Street, home to the **Ruskin Art School** (look out for degree shows by the most fashionable undergraduates at the university) and the Oxford University Press. A little further down, between Walton Street and the canal, Jericho has long been one of the most happening parts of town (see Eating and Shopping below). At the top of Walton Street, Walton Well Road heads left down to **Port Meadow**, an amazingly unspoilt medieval watermeadow, still popular with skaters in winter, and in the summer with grazing cows and undergraduates strolling over to pubs like the *Perch* and the *Trout* on the river.

A right turn eastward at the meeting of Worcester Street and Walton Street leads on to Beaumont Street. Here stands the Oxford Playhouse, opposite the Ashmolean, the oldest museum open to the public in the country. It was opened early in the 17th century by Elias Ashmole, one of Charles I's tax-men. Today it ranks as one of the most extraordinary collections under one roof outside London. The grand classical façade of the **Ashmolean Museum** ⓘ *Beaumont St, T01865-278000, www.ashmol.ox.ac.uk, Tue-Sat 1000-1700 (also Jun, Aug on Thu until 1900), Sun 1400-1700, free*, hides more than 50 rooms, some very beautiful, others not, all with stories to tell and on a very manageable scale. Past the information desk on the left, a corridor of classical sculptures stretches along the front of the building, each mounted on columns of different coloured marble. At the end are four rooms full of artefacts from ancient Egypt, including the Princesses

In the early years of the 19th century, Thomas De Quincey was up at Worcester College, where he began the experiments with drugs that would inspire his brilliant 'Confessions of an Opium Eater'.

fresco from about 1340BC, a fragment of delicate wall painting. Next door are three small treasure troves of English and European porcelain, showing up what's on offer or in use at the museum shop and café below. Straight ahead upon entry at the front door, the Department of Eastern Art occupies 12 rooms packed with Indian, Islamic, Japanese and Chinese fine and applied art. Highlights include an Islamic lamp of gilded glass and enamel from the Middle Ages and a gorgeously detailed terracotta relief from 200BC of the Indian mother goddess Yakshmi. A wide staircase to the right of the front entrance leads up to the Founder's Collection, a right turn at the top of the stairs, displaying a few of gardener John Tradescant's 'curiosities', later purchased by Elias Ashmole. These include Powhatan's Mantle, 'perhaps the most important North American Indian relic to survive anywhere' – four deerskins stitched together and decorated with shells. Sadly it's now thought unlikely that it was in fact worn by Pocahontas' dad. Other items on display, that Tradescant was either given or collected while out plant-hunting for his boss King Charles I, are Henry VIII's hawking gear, Guy Fawke's Lantern, a Chinese rhinoceros-horn cup and an African drum and trumpet. In the rooms beyond, antiquities from the Mediterranean include a Cycladic figurine carved in white marble around 2400BC and also the Alfred Jewel, a pretty gold and crystal kind of bookmark-type thing found in Somerset, inscribed in Anglo-Saxon "Alfred ordered me to be made". That's King Alfred the Great (d. 899) to you and me. In a room next door surrounded by other rare musical instruments sits one of the most precious violins in the world, *Le Messie*, made by Antonio Stradivari at Cremona in 1716. Straight ahead at the top of the stairs leads on to many people's favourite part of the museum, the Department of Western Art. Among the Italian Renaissance paintings can be found Tintoretto's *Resurrection of Christ*, Uccello's dramatic *The Hunt in the Forest* and also Pierre de Cosimo's *Forest Fire*, as well as drawings by Michelangelo and Raphael. Beyond is The Sands Gallery, opened in June 2001, for early 20th century paintings, including Picasso's *Blue Roofs*, Sickert's *Ennui*, Braque's *Le pacquet de tabac*, as well as John Piper's *June Landscape* reminiscent of his stained glass for Coventry cathedral. Works by other English artists like Stanley Spencer, Glyn Philpot's *Gabrielle and Rosemary*, and John Nash's *Gloucestershire Landscape* can also be found here. Next door, the Hindley Smith Gallery contains post-Impressionist works by, among others, Bonnard, Gauguin and also Pissarro, including his wonderful *View of the Gardens of the Tuileries in the Rain*. Round the back of the museum is the **Cast Gallery** ⓘ *Pusey La, off St John St, Tue-Fri 1000-1600, Sat 1000-1300*, with an exceptional array of casts taken from Greek and Roman sculptures in other collections around the world.

With the *Randolph Hotel* on the corner, Beaumont Street meets the wide tree-lined north-south thoroughfare of St Giles at the spikey **Martyrs Memorial**. It was put up in 1841 in memory of the Protestant bishops Cranmer, Ridley and Latimer who were burned at the stake during the counter-Reformation of 'Bloody Mary' in the mid-16th century. A cross marks the exact spot where their ashes were found outside Balliol College on the Broad (see below). Over the way is **St John's College**, consistently one of the highest academic achievers, with one of the most beautiful gardens in Oxford, fronted by a striking combination of Gothic and neoclassical architecture.

East of Carfax

The block of old streets and colleges formed by the Cornmarket, the Broad, Catte Street and the High Street is pretty much the heart of the university, embracing the University Church of St Mary the Virgin, the Radcliffe Camera, the Bodleian Library and Sheldonian Theatre, as well as Jesus, Exeter, and Brasenose colleges.

Cornmarket itself may not be the most inspiring street in the centre, but it conceals some hidden gems. The small **Painted Room** ⓘ *3 Cornmarket (opposite the HSBC bank, above the Tote Bookmakers sign), T01865-791017, free by appointment with Oxford Aunts, the current tenants*, is where Shakespeare is supposed to have stayed when in town. The bard was apparently the godfather of the son of the keeper of the *Crown Inn* that once stood on this site, John Davenant. Wooden panels on one wall slide back to reveal some remarkable Tudor wall painting, with white Canterbury bells, windflowers, roses and even a passion flower interlaced in the twisting design. Behind is the **Covered Market**, now faintly twee but nonetheless another unusual survival, and an 18th-century precursor to modern shopping malls, currently occupied by some tempting permanent stalls (see Shopping, page 243). On the way through from Cornmarket, more expansive but perhaps less significant wall paintings

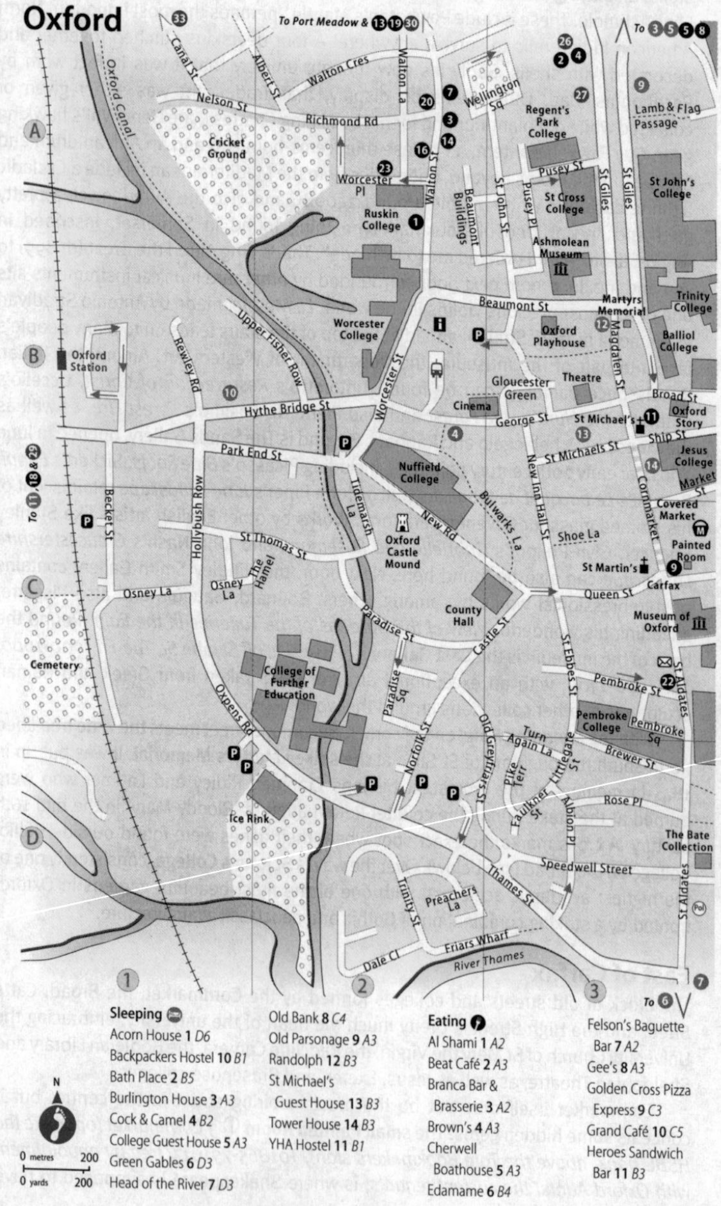

can be seen behind glass on the walls of the local *Pizza Express*, re-named the Golden Cross Restaurant in honour of the inn that once stood here behind the *Crown*. At the top of the Cornmarket, the **tower of St Michael's** ⓘ *Apr-Oct daily 1000-1700, Nov-Mar 1000-1600, £1.50, concessions £1, under-16s 80p, café for rolls and tea*, at the North Gate, on the corner of Ship Street, was built in about 1040, allowing it to be dubbed the 'oldest building in Oxford', although the rest of the church is 13th-century. The view from the top, reached via displays on the history of the church and some large bells, is definitely worth the climb.

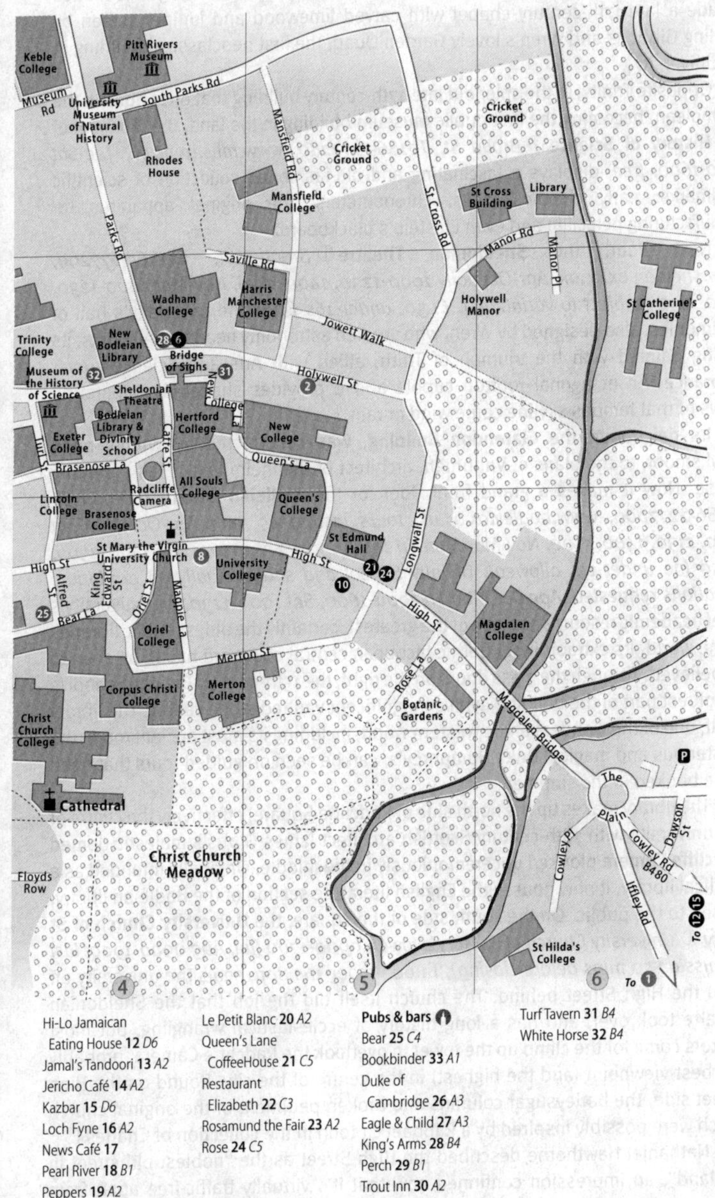

Hi-Lo Jamaican Eating House **12** *D6*
Jamal's Tandoori **13** *A2*
Jericho Café **14** *A2*
Kazbar **15** *D6*
Loch Fyne **16** *A2*
News Café **17**
Pearl River **18** *B1*
Peppers **19** *A2*
Le Petit Blanc **20** *A2*
Queen's Lane CoffeeHouse **21** *C5*
Restaurant Elizabeth **22** *C3*
Rosamund the Fair **23** *A2*
Rose **24** *C5*

Pubs & bars
Bear **25** *C4*
Bookbinder **33** *A1*
Duke of Cambridge **26** *A3*
Eagle & Child **27** *A3*
King's Arms **28** *B4*
Perch **29** *B1*
Trout Inn **30** *A2*
Turf Tavern **31** *B4*
White Horse **32** *B4*

A right turn at the end of Cornmarket heads into the Broad, perhaps the archetypical University street. On the corner, the city's inevitable see-hear-smell tourist trap, the **Oxford Story** ⓘ *6 Broad St, T01865-790055, www.oxfordstory.co.uk, Jan-Jun 1000-1630, Jul-Aug 0930-1700, Sep-Dec 1000-1630, Nov-Mar Mon-Sat 1000-1630, Sun 1100-1630, £6.75, £5 concessions*, whisks customers through the university's story in an hour as they sit at mobile desks. Opposite is **Balliol College**, not much to look at but one of the university's more radical powerhouses. Next door **Trinity** has an unassuming cottage for a porter's lodge instead of the usual grand gatehouse, but the college's beauties include a late-17th-century chapel with carved limewood and juniper screen by Grinling Gibbons and Wren's lovely Garden Quad, the first neoclassical building in the university.

Opposite Trinity, in the splendid late-17th-century building that once housed the Ashmolean, becoming the first public museum building in the land, the **Museum of the History of Science** ⓘ *Broad St, T01865-277280, www.mhs.ox.ac.uk, Tue-Sat 1200-1600, free*, displays a fascinating and old-fashioned collection of scientific landmarks: early chemical stills, chronometers, the original apparatus for manufacturing penicillin and even Einstein's blackboard.

Next door, the **Sheldonian Theatre** ⓘ *Broad St, T01865-277299, www.sheldon.ox.ac.uk, Apr-Oct daily 1000-1230, 1400-1630, Nov-Mar 1000-1230, 1400-1530 (subject to variations), £1.50, under-16s £1*, is the university's hall of ceremonies, also designed by Wren, who studied astronomy nearby at All Souls, its ceiling painted with the triumph of Truth, allied with Arts and Sciences, over Ignorance. An octagonal rooftop cupola above provides sheltered wraparound views of that famous skyline come wind or rain.

Its neighbour, the **Clarendon Building**, was constructed by Wren's pupil Hawksmoor, to the plans of Vanbrugh, architect of Blenheim Palace, as a printing house. Now it makes a grand front door for the **Bodleian Library** ⓘ *Broad St, T01865-277000, www.bodley.ox.ac.uk, tours lasting 45 mins Apr-Oct Mon-Sat 1030, 1130, 1400, 1500, Nov-Mar Mon-Fri 1400, 1500, Sat 1030, 1130, 1400, 1500. £3.50 (no under-14s allowed), Divinity School and shop, usually an exhibition, donations requested, Apr-Dec Mon-Fri 1000-1600, Sat 1000-1230*, the university's chief academic resource and one of the greatest, certainly the oldest public libraries in the world. Its extraordinary Gothic Jacobean central courtyard has to be seen to be believed. Through the glass doors on the right, the 15th-century Divinity School is the oldest part of the building, with a magnificent vaulted stone ceiling. The library itself, one of the wonders of the western world, including its most ancient room, the mysterious and magical Duke Humphrey's, can be seen on guided tours that need to be booked in the summer.

The library makes up the north side of Radcliffe Square, effectively the centre of the university with 18th-century Scottish architect James Gibbs's majestic domed **Radcliffe Camera** plonked unceremoniously in the middle. Originally intended as a medical library, it now houses the English literature section of the Bodleian library, closed to the public. On the south side of the square, the **University Church of St Mary** ⓘ *University Church of St Mary's tower, 0900-1700 (Jul, Aug 0900-1900, last admission 50 mins before closing), £1.60, under-16s 80p*, seals the university off from the High Street behind. The church itself did the job that the Sheldonian Theatre took over, and has a long history of ecclesiastical wrangling, but most visitors come for the climb up the tower to overlook the Radcliffe Camera, probably the best viewpoint (and the highest) in the centre of the city. Round on the High Street side, the barleysugar columns and broken pediment of the original church porch were possibly inspired by a Raphael cartoon in the collection of Charles I.

Nathaniel Hawthorne described the High Street as the "noblest old street in England", an impression confirmed now that it's virtually traffic-free apart from buses. It curves round to the south, with the postgraduate college **All Souls** (the 15th-century stained glass and oak roof of its chapel can be inspected on request) on the left, facing **University College**, not the oldest but certainly one of the most academic colleges. Next door, over Logic Lane, are the Victorian Examination Schools, still in use, opposite **Queen's College** which occupies flamboyant Baroque buildings. A left turn beyond up narrow Queens Lane runs past the medieval **St Edmund Hall** into New College Lane, which is lined with famous gargoyles and twists around beneath the mock **'Bridge of Sighs'** back to the Broad. **New College** is most famous for its chapel, hall and cloisters, and its beautiful gardens dominated by the old city wall and a viewing mound supposedly marking the site of a plague pit.

Back on the High Street, continuing south, the **Botanic Gardens** ⓘ *T01865-286690, Apr-Sep daily 0900-1700, Oct-Mar daily 0900-1630 (last admission 1615), Apr-Aug £2, under-12s free, donation requested at other times*, are on the right beyond Rose Lane, sheltering behind high walls and ornate Jacobean stone gates. The oldest of their kind in Britain (dating from 1621), they evolved from an apothecary's herb garden into this well-labelled horticultural wonderland, a new bog garden, tropical glasshouses and charming riverside walks. Rose Lane leads into **Christ Church meadow**, Oxford's answer to Cambridge's 'backs'.

Over the road, next to its bridge and beneath its unmistakable Perpendicular tower, stands **Magdalen** (pronounced *Maudlin*) **College**, the most spread-out and gloriously sited of all the old colleges. The medieval chapel, hall and cloisters should be seen, but the highlight is the so-called New Building of 1733, an elegant neoclassical edifice standing in its very own deer park close by the confluence of the Rivers Thames (or 'Isis' as it's called in Oxford) and Cherwell (pronounced *Char-wool*).

The Museums and parks

The wide green expanse of the **University Parks** to the north are the destination of many a leisurely punt up from Magdalen Bridge or down from the Cherwell Boathouse. The parks also border on a couple of unmissable museums. The **University Museum of Natural History** ⓘ *Parks Rd, T01865-272950, www.oum.ox.ac.uk, daily 1200-1700, free*, is housed in a striking neo-Gothic fancy of a building. Inside, the Victorian stone carvers went wild with nature, turning just about every stone surface in sight into a vegetable shape. Beneath its great glass roof, supported on graceful columns of wrought iron replete with more fecundity, the museum features many wonders from the natural world, including an observation beehive, a skeletal T-Rex, and some dodos.

Just behind, the **Pitt Rivers Museum** ⓘ *Parks Rd, T01865-270927, www.prm.ox.ac.uk, Mon-Sat 1300-1630, Sun 1400-1630, free*, displays the university's anthropological and ethnographic collections in a famously fusty Victorian way: slide open draws to discover African charms, Inuit ornaments, and peer through glass cases at shrunken heads and Native American Indian scalps. Children love it. Over the road from the museums, another Victorian marvel is the stripey red-brick and stone **Keble College**, where Holman Hunt's *Light of the World* in the chapel is the main attraction.

South of Carfax

Carfax Tower on the south side of the crossroads is all that remains of St Martin's Church, once the parish church of the city. The name Carfax derives from the Latin *quadri furcus* (four-forked), and indeed it was the church's position on such a busy crossroads that necessitated its demolition in 1896. The view south from **Carfax Tower** ⓘ *Apr-Oct 1000-1715, Nov-Mar 1000-1530, £1.20, 60p concessions*, is dominated by Wren's imposing gatehouse for Christ Church College, topped by Tom Tower.

Christ Church ⓘ *T01865-286573, www.chch.ox.ac.uk, Mon-Sat 0930-1730, Sun 1200-1530, £4; hall Mon-Fri 0930-1145, daily 1400-1730*, is the largest, most spectacular and most commercialized of the colleges. It was founded by Cardinal Wolsey, (hence 'Cardinal College' in Hardy's *Jude the Obscure*), and re-founded by Henry VIII after his break with Rome who saved some money by making its chapel the city's cathedral. The college is the university's largest and in Tom Quad you know it. Used by Royalists in the Civil War as a cattlepen, during the 18th century it became famous for the antics of its equally bovine aristocratic undergraduates or 'junior members' as they're known at 'the house'. Tom Quad, the cathedral and the picture gallery are well worth a look round. The **cathedral** ⓘ *Mon-Sat 0900-1645, Sun 1300-1630, services: Mon-Sat 0715, 0735, 1305 (Wed only), 1800; Sun 0800 (Holy Communion), 1000 (Matins and Sermon), 1115 (Sung Eucharist), 1800 (Evensong), Chapter House Apr-Sep Mon-Sat 0930-1730, Sun 1300-1730, Oct-Mar Mon-Sat 0930-1700, Sun 1300-1700*, is the country's smallest, and contains the recently restored shrine of the city's patron saint St Frideswide, as well as some beautiful pre-Reformation stained glass, including an unusual depiction of the murder of St Thomas à Becket which survived because the martyr's head was replaced with plain glass. His face is still missing. Look out too for the illustration in the south transept of Osney Abbey, long since vanished. The **picture gallery** ⓘ *Apr-Sep Mon-Sat 1030-1300, 1400-1730, Sun 1400-1730, Oct-Mar Mon-Sat 1030-1300, 1400-1630, Sun 1400-1630 (£2 additional fee)*, housed in a purpose-built modernist block sunk next to the library, is particularly famous for its collection of Old Master drawings. These include the translucent beauty of Verrochio's *Head of a Young Woman* from the late 15th century, Bellini's *Portrait of a Man* and Leonardo's *Grotesque Head*, as well as works by Raphael, Durer, Titian, Rubens and Lorrain. The paintings on display include a 14th-century triptych, Tintoretto's *Portrait of a Gentleman*, Hals' *Portrait of a Woman*, and Veronese's *Mystic Marriage of St Catherine*. One of the gallery's charms is the way that it has maintained intact the different tastes of its four major benefactors. As well as 13 future prime ministers, the Elizabethan soldier, courtier and poet Sir Philip Sydney, Robert Burton, author of *The Anatomy of Melancholy*, the poet and playwright Ben Jonson, art historian John Ruskin and archeologist William Buckland, probably the college's most famous alumnus is Charles Lutteridge Dodgson, aka Lewis Carroll, the author of *Alice in Wonderland*. The garden gate behind the cathedral that supposedly inspired the mathematician's story has become something of a shrine.

Just up the hill from Christ Church on St Aldate's, next to the Town Hall, the **Museum of Oxford** ⓘ *St Aldate's, T01865-252761, Tue-Fri 1000-1600, Sat 1000-1700, Sun 1200-1600, £2, under-17s 50p, £1.50 concessions, £5 family*, gives the full low-down on the history of the city with the help of some well laid-out artefacts and some entertaining wall texts. Off to the right down Pembroke Street, the **Modern Art Oxford** ⓘ *30 Pembroke St, T01865-722733, www.modernartoxford.org.uk, Tue-Sat 1000-1700, Sun 1200-1500, free*, is the city's top place for exhibitions of internationally respected contemporary art. A barn-like space, it's particularly suitable for large works and has a well-stocked bookshop attached.

North of Oxford

North of Oxford, the river Cherwell and the Oxford Canal twist alongside each other across wide open countryside, sneeking through a gap in the Cotswolds up to Banbury. The river may have been responsible for Oxford's strategic importance in the early Middle Ages, but it was the cutting of the canal in the late 18th century that opened the city up to the industrial heartland of the country in the Midlands, changing its character forever. Within a decade or so of its opening, though, its north-south route had been made redundant by the Grand Union canal. Now the Oxford Canal is one of the most popular pleasure boat routes, despite the proximity of the M40 that follows much of its route up to Banbury. Woodstock, a few miles west of the canal, is very famous, almost too famous for its own good, because of Blenheim Palace on its doorstep. Further north, Rousham House offers quieter pleasures to admirers of stately gardens, while to the east, the old market town of Bicester boasts a very popular purpose-built cut-price designer retail outlet. Banbury may not be much of a destination any more, but Tooley's boatyard on the canal has become the centrepiece of a brand new museum, in the gleaming Castle Quay shopping centre. The town is surrounded by less well-known places of interest, like Edgehill and Broughton Castle.

Ins and outs

Getting there Two stopping **trains** an hour, run by **Thames Trains**, head north of Oxford from London and Reading or Didcot Parkway to Banbury via Tackley, Heyford, and Kings Sutton, taking about half an hour. They carry on to Stratford-upon-Avon, while faster trains run straight through to Birmingham via Banbury and Coventry. Trains to Bicester Town (23 minutes) from Oxford and Reading also call at Islip. The main **roads** north out of Oxford are: the A44 dual carriageway via Woodstock to Chipping Norton and the Cotswolds beyond; the A34 dual carriageway up to Bicester and the M40, the fastest route to Banbury and Stratford; and also the smaller A4260 through Kidlington and Deddington to Banbury. Even the big roads can be very slow at rush hour. The X59 **Stagecoach**, T01788-535555, service shuttles Mon-Sat hourly between Banbury, Bodicote, Adderbury, Deddington, Steeple Aston, Tackley, Kidlington and Oxford (1 hour 10 minutes). Buses 25, 27, 28 and 29 run out to Bicester on a variety of different routes. From Banbury bus station, the 488 (also **Stagecoach**) runs Monday to Saturday every 2 hours to Chipping Norton via Hook Norton and Bloxham. ▸▸ *For further details, see Transport page 245.*

Information **Woodstock** ⓘ *The Oxfordshire Museum, T01993-813276, Mar-Oct Mon-Sat 0930-1730, Sun 1300-1700, Nov-Feb Mon-Sat 1000-1630, Sun 1300-1700.* **Bicester TIC** ⓘ *Unit 6a, Bicester Village, Pingle Dr, T01869-369055, daily 1000-1800.* **Cherwell Valley TIC** ⓘ *Junction 10 M40 Services, Ardley, near Bicester, T01869- 345888, Apr-Oct daily 0930-1645, Nov-Mar 1000-1545.* **Banbury TIC** ⓘ *Castle Quay Shopping Centre, T01295-265464/259855, Mon-Fri 0930-1700, Sat 0930-1700, Sun 1030-1630.*

Blenheim Palace and Woodstock

ⓘ *T01993-811091. Palace and park: mid-Mar to Oct daily 1030-1730 (last admission 1645). £11.50, under-17s £8, 5-15s £5. Park only also Nov-Mar daily 0900-1645. £7.50 with car, £2.50 pedestrians.*

Woodstock, 6 miles northwest of the A40's junction with the A34 on the ring road north of Oxford, on the A44, is an attractive stone-built market town, sadly a little spoiled by the busy road and also by the hoards of visitors that come for its star attraction, Blenheim Palace. A gift to the Duke of Marlborough for winning the Battle of Blenheim in 1704, Sir John Vanbrugh's immense Baroque building certainly deserves to be called a palace, the only one in the country in fact that isn't inhabited by royalty. Winston Churchill was born here (and is buried at Bladon nearby), but the building's chief glories now are outside rather than in. Much of the artwork in the sumptuous interior has been moved elsewhere over the years. Even so, the Long Gallery and Churchill exhibitions are worth a look, while the formal gardens and grounds have plenty to keep the masses amused: a miniature railway, butterfly house and boating lake for example. The park, hundreds of acres landscaped by

 Capability Brown around a large lake and a wonderful half-flooded bridge (also by Vanbrugh) means that there's plenty of room here to escape the crowds if you're prepared to walk a little.

Woodstock itself has long entertained royalty, most especially the Plantagenet kings. Sadly nothing remains of their medieval palace except a memorial after the Duchess of Marlborough had it removed for being an eyesore, despite protests from her husband. Apart from several top-quality eateries (see Eating and drinking below), the town boasts a predictable number of tourist-orientated boutiques. Worth seeking out, though, is the **Oxfordshire Museum** ⓘ *Fletcher's House, Park St, T01993-811456, Tue-Sat 1000-1700, Sun 1400-1700 (last admission 1645), £2.50, concessions £1, under-16s 50p, family £4.50*. This recently revamped county museum contains illuminating displays on local history, archaeology, agriculture and wildlife, right in the middle of the town.

Bicester

Nine miles northeast of Oxford on the A34, Bicester draws the crowds to its discount designer shopping outlet at **Bicester Village** ⓘ *T01869-323200*, a purpose-built home for big brand fashion labels. The town itself, once an important Roman outpost on Akeman St, became wool rich in the Middle Ages and has since settled into comfortable commuter seclusion.

Near the village of Steeple Aston, 7 miles west of Bicester, **Rousham House** ⓘ *T01869-347110, Apr-Sep Wed, Sun, bank holidays 1400-1630, gardens all year daily 1000-1630, house £3, garden £3 (no under-15s admitted)*, is a serious-looking Jacobean pile, although William Kent's early landscape garden is the main draw, virtually unaltered since it was laid out in the early 18th century.

Deddington

Also just off the A4260, heading north to Banbury, Deddington is a sleepy old market village, once an important crossroads, now packed with antique shops. Just outside the village, substantial grassy mounds covered with mature trees indicate the site of a **ruined 12th-century castle** ⓘ *(EH), open at any reasonable time, free*, a good spot for a picnic. Four miles east on the B4031 from here, the village of **Aynhoe** on the Oxford Canal is celebrated for the peach trees climbing over its stone houses and for **Aynhoe Park** ⓘ *T01869-810636, May-Sep Wed, Thu 1400-1630, £3, concessions £1*. A little disturbed by the M40 thundering past nearby, Ayhnoe Park is nonetheless a place with presence, a country house designed by Sir John Soane (also responsible for the Bank of England and the extraordinary John Soane's museum in London). The ice house has recently been restored in the 13-acre south-facing garden.

Banbury and around

Banbury itself is not the most charismatic of towns, but makes a reasonable workaday base within easy reach of both Oxford and Stratford. The 'Historic Town Trail' takes in the Victorian cross marking the spot of the one immortalized in the nursery rhyme: "Ride a cock-horse to Banbury Cross/ To see a fine lady on a white horse,/ With rings on her fingers and bells on her toes,/ She shall have music wherever she goes." before taking in various merchants' houses, churches and pubs that have also suffered the ravages of time with their dignity scarcely intact. Part of the new Castle Quay shopping centre development, the new Banbury Museum incorporates the canalside, with interactive displays on local history, the Broughton Castle coin hoard and costumes from the 17th century as well as the fully refurbished **Tooley's Boatyard**, a rare survival from the first industrial revolution, before the coming of the railways.

Three miles west of Banbury off the B4035 for Shipston-on-Stour, **Broughton Castle** ⓘ *T01295-276070, late May-mid Sep Wed, Sun (and Thu in Jul, Aug) 1400-1700, £4.50, under-15s £2, concessions £4, the park is open throughout the year*, is a beautiful moated medieval manor house, the family home of Lord and Lady Saye and Sele, still more of a home than a visitor attraction. Three miles or so further on the same road, **Swalcliffe Great Barn** ⓘ *T01295-788278, Easter-Oct Sun 1400-1700, free*, is one of the dozen best-preserved and restored medieval tithe barns in England, similar in date to Broughton Castle and built of the same ironstone. Constructed to house the produce of the farms owned by New College Oxford, the 15th-century great-beamed barn now keeps an antique agricultural implement collection dry.

Seven miles northwest of Banbury on the A422 to Stratford-upon-Avon, **Edgehill** was the site of the first major (and indecisive) battle of the Civil War. The steep hill can best be approached from Tysoe village along the ridge overlooking **Upton House** ⓘ *(NT), T01295-670266*, with its famous terraced garden descending from a Restoration house containing paintings by Stubbs, El Greco and Hogarth among others.

Six miles north of Banbury on the A423 to Coventry, is **Farnborough Hall** ⓘ *(NT), near Farnborough, T01295-690002, house and grounds, Apr-Sep Wed, Sat 1400-1800, £3.40, terrace walk, Apr-Sep Thu, Fri 1400-1800, £1*. This has been the Holbech family home since the 17th century, their garden designed in the 1750s, an early version of the grander landscapes of the later 18th century, including a charming Terrace Walk. Some of the plasterwork inside the house is exceptional too.

Seven miles northeast of Banbury off the B4525, the village of **Sulgrave** is notable for **Sulgrave Manor** ⓘ *T01295-760205, Apr-Oct Mon, Tue, Thu-Sun 1030-1730, Nov-Dec and Mar weekends only 1030-1300, 1400-1630, guided tours £4, under-16s £2, family £12*, George Washington's ancestors' sweet little pad, a stone-built manor house erected in 1539 and restored meticulously to look as it might have done in the Elizabethan era, where patriotic Statesiders are made most welcome.

West of Oxford

Although the Thames actually enters Oxford from the north, its broad valley dominates the area west of the city. Meandering through open countryside, sometimes marred by pylons and reservoirs, the river gives this part of the country its special quality. The largest town, the old market centre of Witney, in fact straddles the River Windrush, one of the most charming of the Thames' tributaries. Descending from the Cotswold hills, it passes through the beautiful honey-coloured town of Burford, famously the 'gateway to the Cotswolds'. Then it winds through peaceful villages like Asthall, past the romantic ruined manor house at Minster Lovell, before finding the Thames just beyond Stanton Harcourt. Here a complete medieval estate is still inhabited by descendants of the Harcourts. Further up the Thames, on opposite banks of the river, are two remarkable places associated with left-wing pioneers of very different types. The 16th-century manor house at Kelmscott was the delightful summer retreat of William Morris in late Victorian times, while the grey classical pile at Burcot witnessed the antics of some exotic Labour-leaning socialites and thinkers in the 1930s.

Ins and outs

Getting there The A40 **road** heads west from north Oxford via Witney (10 miles) and Burford (17 miles) to Cheltenham and Gloucester. Major roads run north-south at both Witney and Burford. **Stagecoach**, T01865-772250, run the hourly X3 **bus** between Oxford and Milton-under-Wychwood via Eynsham, Witney, Minster Lovell, and

 Burford, also the 11 and 100 between Oxford and Witney. From Witney the No 7 bus runs to Lechlade and Swindon, the No 45 to Stanton Harcourt and South Leigh, the 102 and 103 to Minster Lovell, the 19 to Bampton, and the 42 to Woodstock. » *For further details, see Transport page245.*

Information Witney TIC ⓘ *51a Market Sq, T01993-775802. Easter-Oct, Mon-Sat 0930-1730, Nov-Easter 1000-1630.* **Burford TIC** ⓘ *The Brewery, Sheep St, T01993-823558, Easter-Oct Mon-Sat 0930-1730, Sun 1000-1500, Nov-Easter Mon-Sat 1000-1630.*

Upper Thames and Windrush valleys

The Thames runs south into Oxford. But going against the stream north and west out of the city, past Port Meadow, Godstow and some old abbey ruins, and heading west just south of the A40, the river skirts **Wytham Great Wood**. These 600 acres or so of deciduous hilltop woodland have been carefully managed by the university and now provide a habitat for all manner of rare north European birds, including nightingales, warblers and also a heronry. **Eynsham**, 3 miles west of the city ring road, was an important medieval town, a fact still reflected in its market square and old town hall. A mile south, at **Swinford**, the fine 18th-century bridge over the river operates the oldest and cheapest toll in the country. A couple more miles west, north of the Thames and east of the Windrush, **Stanton Harcourt** is a peaceful little greystone village. The surprisingly grand medieval church, Norman cruciform, features one of the oldest screens in the country (13th-century) and a massive collection of monuments to the Harcourt family from the 12th century until the early 18th. Their **manor house** ⓘ *T01865-881928, open on various days (phone for details), Apr-Sep 1400-1800, £5, under-12s £3, garden £3, under-12s and concessions £2*, next door was described by Alexander Pope as "the true picture of a genuine Ancient Country Seat", high praise from the greatest satirical poet of the Enlightenment, but then he was translating Homer's *Iliad* in the top of the tower here (open by appointment), in 1718. As well as 12 acres of gardens complete with medieval fish and stew ponds, the old kitchen and private chapel both easily justify the relatively high entrance fee.

Witney and around

Bypassed by the A40, the old market town of Witney has an attractive centre and splendid church but was until recently the fastest growing town in England, with predictably hit-and-miss results. Just to its north, off the A4095, the **Cogges Manor Farm Museum** ⓘ *Church La, T01993-772602, mid-Mar to Oct Tue-Fri 1030-1730, weekends 1200-1730, £4.20, £2.10 under-16s, £2.65 concessions*, is worth the short detour. George Orwell must have been thinking of a place like this when he wrote *Animal Farm*. In fact, it's a charming reconstruction of a working farm from around 1900, with heavy workhorses, sheep, chickens, and thankfully only one pig, so there may be hope for it yet.

Three miles west of Witney, **Minster Lovell Hall and Dovecote** ⓘ *(EH), open any reasonable time, free*, is a picturesque ruined 15th-century manor house in a pleasant spot on the banks of the river Windrush, alongside an ancient dovecote.

Heading back towards the river, 6 miles south of Witney, **Bampton** is where Morris dancing is supposed to have originated, hence perhaps the unusually large number of pubs in the old town and also the unusually large number of men who enjoy them. The road south off the B4449 crosses the Thames at **Tadpole**, where there's a campsite on one of the most unspoiled stretches of the river, with a pub, *The Trout Inn*.

Six miles west of Tadpole, **Kelmscott Manor** ⓘ *T01367-252486, Apr-Sep Wed 1100-1300, 1400-1700, third Sat in Apr, May, Jun and Sep 1400-1700, first and third Sat in Jul, Aug 1400-1700 (last admissions 30 mins before closing), £7, concessions £3.50,*

Alive and kicking?

Should you arrive in an English village to find the locals waving hankies and clashing sticks to the accompaniment of a squeezebox, do not be unduly alarmed. What you are witnessing is Morris Dancing. Once the quintessence of English heritage, Morris Dancing may, however, be a dying tradition. In a recent poll only 24% of young Britons saw it as a key part of the country's heritage and it ranked just below the Rolling Stones in terms of popularity. Indeed, today's Morris Dancers are seen as practically a secret society, confined to the margins of modern life. A sad state of affairs for a 200-year-old tradition that began in the village of Bampton, in Oxfordshire. Some people, though, argue that, far from being on its last bell-clad legs, Morris Dancing is in rude health. There are now more than 1,000 teams across the UK, North America and the Antipodes. Champion Morris dancer, Simon Pipe insists that bell ringing and stick waving still has a place in modern society and states: "There's something basically all right about any country in which men, women and children can leap about in public with bells and other improbable adornments attached to their bodies."

is a very fine 16th-century house hidden behind high walls in a quiet out-of-the-way village, where the great Socialist William Morris summered from 1871 until his death in 1896. He shared it with the pre-Raphaelite poet Gabriel Dante Rossetti and the place has been restored and preserved by the Society of Antiquaries as a home for a considerable collection of Morris's works – furniture, textiles and ceramics – in his highly influential, flowery (and usually poorly imitated) neo-medievalist style. Overall, a visit here confirms what Morris believed – that a great opportunity was lost during the industrial revolution to beautify the world with mass-production rather than cheapen it.

A walk west along the Thames Path from Kelmscott passes **Buscot Weir** and the National Trust village of Buscot, with its inevitable teashop, and pleasant walks further along the river to the old Cheese Wharf. A mile or so east of Buscot village, **Buscot Park** ⓘ *(NT), T01367-240786, Apr-Sep Wed, Thu, Fri 1400-1800 (last admission 1730) and also selected weekends (including Easter) through the spring and summer – ring for details, house and grounds, £5, grounds only £4*, was once famous as the weekend retreat of the left-wing thinkers, artists and poets that gathered around Gavin Henderson, Lord Faringdon, in the 1930s. An austere late-18th-century house, it contains a particularly impressive art collection, including works by Rubens, Rembrandt and Burne-Jones's *Legend of the Briar Rose*, Sleeping Beauty to most of us, but exquisite all the same. Upstairs, there are some remarkable English paintings of the 19th and 20th centuries by the likes of Gainsborough, Reynolds and Graham Sutherland. The spectacular Italianate water garden was laid out by Harold Peto in the early 20th century. On the way to it, the east pavilion is decorated with murals depicting the heady revolutionary fervour of the dinner parties held at the house.

Lechlade and around

Three miles northwest of Buscot, Lechlade on Thames (actually in a little pocket of Gloucestershire) is the highest navigable point on the river, and consequently a Mecca for pleasure cruisers. Best seen from the old St John's Bridge, next to yet another *Trout Inn* (see below), the spire of **St Lawrence's church** rises above the trees while the river snakes lazily across the meadows. The mainly 16th-century church inspired Shelley's *Stanzas in a Summer Evening Churchyard* on his boating trip up to Lechlade in 1815. The town itself comes as a bit of a disappointment, with its slightly desperate antique shops and poky little cafés, but nonetheless has a welcoming and friendly attitude, well-accustomed as it is to a stream of strangers messing about in boats.

Lechlade is also an important road junction. The A361 heads south for 10 miles to Swindon and north for 9 miles to Burford, crossing the A417 Wantage-Cirencester road. Five miles towards Burford, beyond a perfectly preserved 18th-century watermill at **Little Faringdon**, the **Swinford Museum** ⓘ *Filkins, near Lechlade, T01367-860209, first Sun of May-Sep 1400-1700 or by appointment, free*, is one of the oldest small museums in Oxfordshire, a collection of domestic and agricultural tools housed in a 17th-century cottage.

Three miles further up the road to Burford, the **Cotswold Wildlife Park** ⓘ *T01993-823006, www.cotswoldwildlifepark.co.uk, Mar-Sep daily 1000-1700, Oct daily 1000-1600, Nov-Feb daily 1000-1530, £6.50, concessions and under-16s £4*, is set in acres of fine parkland around a Victorian manor house, a hugely popular local attraction where zebras and rhinos can be seen roaming their generous enclosures from the picnic lawns, while a miniature steam railway chugs around in the summer months. As well as caring for some endangered red pandas, the zoo also takes its gardening seriously, with a tropical house, 'hot bed', and walled garden.

Burford

Since its decline as an important medieval wool town, Burford has long billed itself as the 'Gateway to the Cotswolds' and strikingly lovely and stone-built it is too. That's no secret though, which means that during the summer months the gate pressure can be intense: the long broad High Street, sloping down to the old bridge over the little river Windrush, becomes impossibly busy. Even so, the crush in the antique shops, pubs, and tearooms can easily be avoided on the smaller side streets. One such, at the lower end of the High Street, leads to Burford's **church of St John**, the most outstanding parish church in the county. Its Norman tower has survived, later topped with a spire, easy to miss from the town if not from the river, but the medieval warren of arches, chapels, nooks and crannies inside should definitely not be missed. Apart from some intriguing monuments, including one to Henry VIII's hairdresser, featuring the first known depiction of a Red Indian in England, and a possible likeness of a fertility goddess from the second century, the font bears the scratched name of one of the mutinous Levellers imprisoned here by Oliver Cromwell for three nights in 1649. On May 17, three of them were executed, an event still commemorated in the town on the nearest Saturday to that date with some fancy dress and not-so-fancy politicizing. The town itself has retained, virtually unaltered, its medieval street plan. Originally the main road ran east-west past the 16th-century market hall, called the **Tolsey** (now housing a local history museum), and around this crossroads with the High Street there are still several houses that bear traces of the Middle Ages. From the bridge, a very pleasant walk follows the banks of the Windrush eastwards for about three miles to the village of Swinbrook, where there's another church with remarkable tombs inside and the graves of Nancy and Unity Mitford outside.

Half a mile away to the north, at **Widford**, is a tiny church in an even more idyllic setting and incorporating the remains of a Roman villa. If your legs will carry you, the pretty and relatively undiscovered village of **Asthall**, a mile further downstream, is also well worth a visit. Another riverside walk heads west along the Windrush to **Taynton**, and a couple of miles further to **Great Barrington**, where *The Fox Inn* does excellent lunches and has accommodation (see below).

Sleeping

Oxford *p224, map p228*

Hotels in Oxford are generally expensive for what you get, and hotels in the lower price brackets are almost non-existent although there are lots of B&Bs on Abingdon Rd and Banbury Rd. There are hardly enough affordable rooms for students in the city, so visitor accommodation is at a premium and you should book well in advance, for the budget options all year and all others especially in the summer. The TIC runs the usual booking service, but don't expect to be within walking distance of the sights if you leave it too late.

L **Old Parsonage Hotel**, 1 Banbury Rd, T01865-310210. Oscar Wilde's undergraduate digs, since 1989 the poshest hotel in town, run by the same people as *Gee's Restaurant*.

L **The Randolph**, Beaumont St, T0870-4008200, www.heritage-hotels.co.uk. New restaurant, champagne and oyster bar, decorated with the arms of all the colleges, businessmen and students persuading their rich parents they're not prodigal.

A **Bath Place Hotel**, 4 Bath Pl, T01865-791812, www.bathplace.co.uk. About as central as you get, a cosy 17th-century building near the city wall and *Turf Tavern*, family run and friendly.

A **Old Bank Hotel**, 92-94 High St, T01865-799599. One of the most stylish and central places to stay in the city, 42-individual room hotel (£155 a standard double, likely to have good views of the famous skyline) including *Quod Bar and Grill*, a stylish brasserie-type place with some abysmal artwork on the walls but a zinc-topped bar and sunny outdoor drinking deck in summer (£8-£12 for some accomplished pasta, pizza and main courses like slow-roast lamb shank with pumpkin and mint pesto).

B **Burlington House**, 374 Banbury Rd, T01865-513513, www.burlington-house.co.uk. Non-smoking little boutique hotel some distance up the Banbury Rd, 11 rooms, with a very good breakfast.

B **The Cock and Camel**, 24 George St, T01865-203705, F792130. Eight rooms (breakfast included) above a huge Young's pub in a lively part of town.

B **Head of the River**, Folly Bridge, St Aldate's, T01865-721600, F726158. Large Fuller's pub and hotel overlooking river to the south. Breakfast included.

B **The Tower House**, 15 Ship St, T01865-246828, www.scoot.co.uk/towerhouse. Bang in the middle of town, in a 17th-century house, tucked away off Cornmarket, 4 doubles, 3 with shared bathrooms.

C **Acorn House**, 260 Iffley Rd, T/F01865-247998. Four comfortable non-smoking double rooms, a 20-min walk into town. Both the above are similar in price and style to many of the B&Bs strung out along the main road into town from the south and east.

C **Green Gables**, 326 Abingdon Rd, T01865-725870, F723115. Has 7 double rooms, fairly clean and comfortable with breakfasts, some way out town near Donnington Bridge.

C-D **College Guest House**, 103-105 Woodstock Rd, T01865-552579, r.pal@ukonline.co.uk. £45-65 double. 10 mins walk from centre.

D **St Michael's Guesthouse**, 26 St Michael St, T01865-242101. Central, £50 for a double.

F **The Backpackers Hostel**, 9a Hythe Bridge St, T01865-721761, www.hostels.co.uk. Also close to the station, and has 10 bunkrooms for 4-10 people each. Open 24 hrs.

F **YHA Hostel**, 2a Botley Rd, T01865-727275. Just behind the railway station, fairly smart and new with 180 beds in dorms and rooms, can be reached from the westbound platform through a little alleyway. Open 24 hrs.

Camping

Oxford Camping International, on the ring-road south of Oxford, 1.5 miles from city centre. T01865-244088. Open all year, 129 sites.

North of Oxford *p232*

L **Feathers Hotel**, Market St, Woodstock, T01993-81299, F813158. The most expensive option, a very grand public house, but the food is worth every penny, booking essential, especially for the courtyard garden.

A The Bear, Park St, Woodstock, T0870-4008202, www.heritage-hotels.com. Another hotel in the same mould, more of a pub but very comfortable with all the facilities you'd expect for the price.

A Whately Hall, Banbury Cross, Banbury T0870-4008104, F271736. A smart 17th-century building in the middle of the town, although some good B&Bs near the town (see below) may be a better bet.

B King's Arms Hotel, 19 Market St, Woodstock, T01993-813636, F813737. An 18th-century townhouse that makes no concessions to its antiquity in its décor or with its stylish Mediterranean-style restaurant. Not quaint at all.

C The Castle Inn, Edgehill, near Banbury T01295-670255, F670521. Offers the unusual opportunity to stay in a folly tower on the top of Edgehill, above a reasonable pub with a big garden, on the site that Charles I mustered his army before the battle.

C Mill House, Shenington, near Banbury, T01295-670642. Distinctly superior, a large south-facing house with a snooker table.

D Wemyss Farm, Sulgrave, Banbury, T01295-760323. A working farm with one double room.

West of Oxford *p235*

L Bay Tree Hotel Sheep St, Burford, T01993-822791, www.cotswold-inns-hotels.co.uk. Wysteria-clad on the outside, chintzy within, country townhouse hotel, very comfortable with a reputable restaurant.

L Burford House Hotel, 99 High St, T01993-823151, www.burfordhouse.co.uk. Non-smoking family-run hotel with plenty of friendly touches and pleasant easy-going atmosphere.

A The Lamb, Sheep St, Burford, T01993-823155. Log fires, flagstone floors and formerly the home of Sir Lawrence Tanfield, Lord Chief Baron of the Exchequer in the reign of Queen Elizabeth I around 1580. Real ales and a fairly expensive restaurant doing top-notch food (about £30 a head), as well as well-filled sandwiches at the bar. Most famously 'good pub' in Burford.

B Jonathan at the Angel, Witney St, Burford, T01993-822714, is a very highly rated non-smoking old pub-restaurant (about £12 a main course) with 3 attractive double rooms. Recommended.

C The Ferryman Inn, Bablock Hythe, Northmoor, a couple of miles from Stanton Harcourt, has a foot ferry across the river, T01865-880028. A famous waterside freehouse with pub grub, right on the water and very cheery.

C The Fox Inn, Great Barrington, near Burford, T01451-844385. Pulls a very good pint in a charming riverside pub with a garden, and also manages some very decent English country cooking 7 days a week. 3 rooms with bathroom en suite. Recommended.

C The Old Vicarage, Minster Lovell, T01993-775630. A beautiful old house beside the Windrush, £350 per week in the summer for the self-catering garden house, sleeping 6.

C Rectory Farm, Northmoor, Near Witney, T01865-300207. A very fine early 17th-century stone farmhouse that once belonged to St John's College, Oxford.

Eating

Oxford *p224, map p228*

£££ The Cherwell Boathouse, Bardwell Rd, T01865-552746, is the place to have a fine 'modern European' feast (about £30 a head for lunch) in a clapperboard hut, then hire a punt perhaps, or a more expensive and leisurely supper on the waterside.

£££ Le Petit Blanc Oxford, 71-72 Walton St, T01865-510999. Brasserie style dishes at Raymond Blanc's chain, such as a main course of fillet of sea bream, fricassée of squid, rouille and bouillabaisse jus in Terence Conran-designed surroundings, although many think it's not particulary good value for money.

££ Al Shami, 25 Walton Cres, T01865-310066, around £15 a head will buy you some superior Lebanese cuisine, with a particularly good array of mezes.

££ Branca Bar Kitchen, 111 Walton St, T01865-556111, has trumped it, a newish Italian peasant favourite, marginally cheaper, with an Eyestorm Damien Hirst spot painting on the wall, the kitchen upstairs on the balcony, above the snazzy low-lit dining room.

££ **Brown's**, 1-5 Woodstock Rd, T01865-311415, the flagship restaurant, which started well but has gone a little downhill.

££ **Edamame**, 15 Holywell St, T01865-246916. Lunches Tue-Sun, sushi on Thu night, a Japanese tapas bar at lunchtimes, very good value dinners, no bookings taken, popular with students who queue up some nights.

££ **Gee's**, 61 Banbury Rd, T01865-553540, do good value set lunches (£10) in an old flowershop with a conservatory style atmosphere and an eclectic, confidently presented menu.

££ **Golden Cross Pizza Express**, T01865-790442, in the old Golden Cross Inn off the Cornmarket, heavily restored in 1988 (see p229). A good fall-back, and has no bookings.

££ **Hi-Lo Jamaican Eating House**, 70 Cowley Rd, T01865-725984, a Caribbean institution, for fresh red snappers perhaps in a laid-back occasionally riotous West Indian atmosphere (about £25 a head).

££ **Jamal's Tandoori**, 108 Walton St, T01865-310102, is an excellent and locally popular Indian where you can take in your own alcohol.

££ **Kazbar**, 25-27 Cowley Rd, T01865-202920, is a Spanish and North African restaurant owned by the same people as the *Grand Café* on the High St.

££ **Restaurant Elizabeth**, 82 St Aldate's T01865-242230. About £18 a head for some highly rated French country cooking.

££ **Rosamund the Fair**, Cardigan St, T01865-553370, is a charming restaurant boat based in Castlemill Boatyard.

£ **Felson's Baguette Bar**, 32 Little Clarendon St, T01865-316631, is a highly rated sandwich stop.

£ **Pearl River**, Botley Rd. Down by the station, on the other side of town, beyond the railway bridge is this takeaway Chinese understandably popular with students and local backpackers.

£ **Peppers**, 84 Walton St, their pure beef burgers a hit with students (yoghurt and mint with your vegeburger?), the bar stacked with flyers for clubnights. Some say the best takeaway burger in Oxford is to be found here.

Cafés

The Beat Café, Little Clarendon St, T01865-553543, do a mean Mexican tortilla for £4, fresh soup for £3.50, and have a downstairs bar.

Grand Café, 84 High St, T01865-204463. Claims to be the oldest coffee house in England, completely refurbished of course. Charming service but high prices for some superb cafetière coffees, American-style sandwiches and light meals.

Heroes Sandwich Bar and Takeaway, 8 Ship St, T01865-723459, open until 2100 Mon-Fri, has a good array of innovative fillings.

Jericho Café, 112 Walton St, a popular haunt for egg and chips.

News Café, 1 Ship St, T01865-242317, is a pleasant place to rest your feet away from the crush on the Cornmarket during the day, with light meals for about £8 and lots of newspapers to read.

Queen's Lane Coffee House, 40 High St, T01865-240082. Considerably more authentic these days and very popular with students, for some sensibly priced espresso (£1), cakes and a legendary BLT.

The Rose, 51 High St, T01865-244429, is a bright, refurbished little café with an imaginative menu (buckwheat pancakes with smoked salmon, capers and crème fraiche anyone?), main courses about £6 and promising to do meals on summer evenings.

North of Oxford *p232*

The Bell, High St, Adderbury, 3 miles south of Banbury off the A4260, T01295-810338, is a charming folksy pub in a little village, doing fresh food in the restaurant and a good range of bar snacks.

The King's Head, Chapel Hill, Wootton, near Woodstock, T01993-811340, is a gourmet's haven serving up an imaginative menu either in the traditional pub or non-smoking restaurant, in a village that has consistently won the 'best-kept' award.

The Red Lion, Steeple Aston, near Rousham House, T01869-340225, is the place for smart, fresh but reasonably expensive (about £30 a head) food in intimate surroundings on Tue and Sat evenings, complemented by a very good wine list and worth booking well in advance.

Stag's Head, Swalcliffe, which does food with a high reputation.
The Star Inn, Manor Rd, Sulgrave, near Banbury, T01295-760389. Ideal for anyone visiting Sulgrave Manor.
The Swan Inn, Lower St, Islip, Near Kidlington, T01865-372590. Excellent home-made meals (except on Sun) near the spot where Edward the Confessor was born. The village station makes it a convenient walking base too.
Thai Orchid, 56 North Bar St, Banbury, T01295-270833 is highly rated for its authentic menu, costing about £20 per person.

West of Oxford *p235*

Mermaid Inn, High St, Burford, T01993-822193, is in a very old building, with decent enough pub grub.
The Priory Tearoom, High St, Burford, do good breakfasts.
The Royal Oak, Ramsden, near Witney, T01993-868213. A freehouse that does very good food, (monkfish, game pies, vegetarian specials) and a few outside tables opposite the war memorial in a quiet village on Akeman St, the Roman road that connected Bicester and Cirencester.
The Swan Inn, Swinbrook, T01993-822165, near the Windrush. An even older place that hasn't changed much in 50 years, where the food's all home-made and the ales are well-kept.
The Trout Inn, St John's Bridge, Lechlade on Thames, T01367-252313, www.the-trout-inn.sagenet.co.uk. Does good food, is a busy waterside oasis and also the base for *Cotswold Boat Hire* (see below).

Pubs, bars and clubs

Oxford *p224, map p228*

The other option for food as well as booze is one of the pubs, of which Oxonians are understandably proud, even if they can become too smoky or beery to make eating a pleasure.
The Bear, 8 Alfred St, T01865-728264, is a cosy wood-panelled old pub popular with the local Christ Church students, and also with rugby union clubs from around the world judging from the array of old ties in the back bar (lunch served 1200-1500). Not for tall people (ie anyone over 5ft 5).
Duke of Cambridge, 5-6 Little Clarendon St, T01865-558173, is a popular and lively new 'young person's pub' with bar snacks.
Eagle and Child, St Giles, known as the *Bird and Baby*, is another cosy place to drink, once the favourite haunt of JRR Tolkien and CS Lewis.
King's Arms, T01865-242369, on the corner of Holywell St and Broad St, for some good Young's beer but quite expensive grub. Popular with students.
The Perch, in Binsey (open lunch and evenings only), with its tree-shaded riverside garden. A little out of town but makes for a pleasant walk across Port Meadow.
The Trout Inn, Lower Wolvercote, T01865-302071, (diners usually need to book), beside an old bridge and weir.
Turf Tavern, beyond Bath Pl off Holywell La, does a truly staggering array of real ales (and an award-wining Scrumpy) under low ceilings, with reasonably priced pub grub served up all day (cash only), outside to heaving crowds beneath the old city wall of New College and inside in the snug low-ceilinged bars.
The White Horse, 52 Broad St, T01865-728318, is a donnish, cosy little place and another of TV detective Inspector Morse's favourite haunts.

West of Oxford *p235*

The Bell, Ducklington, Near Witney, T01993-702514. A thatched pub that has extraordinary flowers outside, live folk music and real ales inside.
The Plough Inn, Kelmscott. A gorgeous little village pub in the process of being done up, hopefully with sympathy (and with moorings on the river).
White Hart Inn, Wytham, near Oxford, T01865-244372. Near the River Thames, nestling in the shade of the A34. Heated barn for winter surrounded by flowerbeds, on a quiet backroad.

Clubs

Surprisingly short on good nightspots, Oxford's clubs come and go.
Bar Ris, 3-5 Hythe Bridge St, have popular cheesy dance nights.

Cellar Bar, Frewin Ct, T01865-244761, is studenty, for techno, drum'n'bass, and house nights Wed-Sat until 0200.
The Love Bar, 3 King Edward St, T01865-200011, is one of the latest uber-cool offerings, complete with unisex loos and a glass ceiling between the ground floor and the dancefloor in the basement below. Pumps out the tunes till 0200.
Park End Club, 37-39 Park End St, near the train station, T01865-250181, open Thu-Sat 2130-0200. With 3 floors of house, R'n'B and party sounds, this is the people's choice, the biggest and brashest in Oxford, smart casuals (no trainers), £7.50 after 1000.
PoNaNa Bar, 13-15 Magdalen St, T01865-249171. Popular club for students and locals alike.
Thirst Bar, 7/8 Park End St, T01865-242044, until 0100, is very loud, lively, late and free.

Entertainment

Oxford *p224, map p228*
Oxford doesn't lack excitement, but much of it is student-generated. The invaluable broadsheet posted in most college lodges and some bars and restaurants, daily during termtime, weekly at other times, is *Daily Information*, T01865-554444.

Cinemas

Odeon ABC, Magdalen St and **Odeon ABC**, George St, T0870-5050007, are the mainstream screens in the centre of town. **The Phoenix**, Walton St, T01865-512526, is the arthouse. The **Ultimate Picture Palace**, T01865-245288, the mainstream and independent cinema.

Live music

Live music for all types can be found in pubs and halls all over the city during term (check the *Daily Information*).
Backroom at the Bully, 162 Cowley Rd, T01865-244516. Crams the punters in for more of the same at the *Bullingdon Arms*.
Freuds, 119 Walton St, T01865-311171, usually have live music, jazz and blues mainly, in their old Palladian church on Fri or Sat (charging after 2200).
Zodiac, Cowley Rd, T01865-420042. A student hang-out and a popular stage for indie bands during the week. Indie club on Sat nights and cheesy listening on a Thu.

Theatre and comedy venues

Apollo, George St, T0870-6073500. Large-scale touring productions, musicals, operas and pantomimes.
Burton Taylor Theatre, Gloucester St, T01865-798600. For smaller-scale productions.
Jongleurs, 3-5 Hythe Bridge St, T01865-722437, T0870-7870707, is a regular comedy club chain, Thu-Sat.
Old Fire Station, George St, T01865-297170, for short-run fringe theatre, student and small-scale touring productions.
Oxford Playhouse, Beaumont St, T01865-305305, www.oxfordplayhouse.com. The main theatre for drama and middle-scale touring productions by the likes of the National Theatre and Almeida Theatre Company.
Pegasus Theatre, Magdalen Rd, T01865-722851, smaller fringe theatre.

North of Oxford *p232*
The Mill Theatre, Spiceball Park, Banbury, T01295-279002. Hosts small-scale fringe touring productions, some of a very high standard. Banbury also has a single-screen **Odeon** cinema.

Shopping

Oxford *p224, map p228*
Little Clarendon St is the place for gift shops, and funky home furnishings, while **The Grog Shop**, 13 Kingston Rd (continuation of Walton St), T01865-557088, is an independent off-licence who do good value mini-barrels of ale (36-pint polypins) for about £50.
Morris Photographic Centre, 102 High St, T01865-244434, for cameras and film.
The Oxford Organiser in Turl St, for all your smart stationery requirements.
Unicorn, in Ship St, has an extraordinary collection of vintage clothing for hire (mainly) or sale, popular with partying students getting up in drag or Sixties gear.
University of Oxford Shop, 106 High St, does all those monogrammed sweatshirts and souvenirs to show the folks back home.

Books

Blackwell's, 48-51 Broad St, T01865-792792. The University booksellers, with an excellent secondhand section as well as all the latest new and academic titles.
Border's, next to Debenhams on Magdalen St (the continuation of Cornmarket north).
Thornton's of Oxford, 11 Broad St, T01865-242939. A large independent bookseller (new and secondhand).
Waterfield's, 52 High St, T01865-721809. An interesting secondhand and antiquarian bookseller.
Waterstone's, Broad St, T01865-790212.

Markets

For picnic materials, the **Covered Market** is home to: **Ben's Cookies**, T01865-247407, for award-winning chocolate biscuits in all shapes and sizes. **Cake Shop** for cakes, bsicuits and sweet decorations as well as doughs. **Cold Pantry** for picnic meats. **Je-mi-ni** florists. **Palms Delicatessen** for picnic favourites. **Oxford Cobbler** for your worn-out shoeleather. There's also a market on Wed afternoons in Gloucester Green, for cheapish new clothes, fruit and veg and the odd speciality stall.

Activities and tours

Oxford *p224, map p228*

The biggest sports centre in the city, with pool, fitness rooms, squash and tennis courts is the **Peers Sports Centre**, in Littlemore near Cowley (buses 1,5, 5a and 16 from the city centre). **Oxford Ice Rink**, Oxpens Rd, T01865-467000, has sessions on Mon, Tue, Thu 1745-1945, 2000-2230, Fri 1800-2230, Sat 1400-1600, 1800-2230, Sun 1400-1600, 2100-2230. £2.80-£4.50 per session. **Yogagarden.co.uk**, some way out in Summertown, is the place to wind down after all that fun, with a very healthy café.

Boating

Punts can be hired at: **Cherwell Boathouse**, T01865-515978, the most rural. **Head of the River**, Folly Bridge, T01865-721600, the one on the Thames. **Magdalen Bridge Punt Hire**, T01865-761586, the busiest. Boat trips on the Thames are run by **College Cruisers**, Combe Rd Wharf, Combe Rd, T01865-554343, www.collegecruisers.com, hire out cruising boats on the river by the week. **Salter Brothers**, Folly Bridge, T01865-243421 www.salterbros.co.uk

Walking

Official guided tours leave from the TIC, where there are also some good self-guiding leaflets available on walks along the river or canal and around the town. The Oxford Canal walk runs all the way up to Coventry, on level ground, through picturesque countryside. The **Thames Path** can also be joined here (see p248). **The Oxford Guild of Guides** also offer walking tours, T01865-250551.

North of Oxford *p232*

More details from Banbury TIC who also have a good selection of free leaflets describing enjoyable circular walks in the area. There are golf courses near Kidlington, Bicester, and several west of Banbury.

Fishing

Cheyney Manor, Barford St Michael, T01869-338207, with 4 fly-fishing lakes.
College Farm Fishing, Aynho, T01869-810258. For coarse fishing.
Farmoor Reservoir, Cumnor Rd, Farmoor, Near Oxford, T01865-863033. Well-stocked with brown and rainbow trout, for fly fishing.

Horse riding

DHE Polo School, Heathfield Village, Bletchingdon, T01869-351660.
Oaklands Riding School, Shipston Rd, Upper Tysoe, T01295-688045.

West of Oxford *p235*

Boating

Cotswold Boat Hire, T01793-700241, same-day enquiries T07946-655730 (mob). 6-seater rowing boats £6 per hr, £30 full day. Electric boats £12 per hr, £30 for 3 hrs, £55 full day, all from St John's Bridge on the river next to *The Trout Inn*.
Riverside (Lechlade) Ltd, Park End Wharf, Lechlade, T01367-252229, www.riverside-lechlade.co.uk. For rowing boat hire.

Transport

Oxford *p224, map p228*

Bicycle
Oxford is great for cyclists. You can hire a bike for a day/week/or month from Bike Zone, at the back of the Covered Market on Market St, T01865-728877 for £10 a day, £60 a week.

Bus
Long distance The intercity and local bus terminus is at Gloucester Green, very close to the city centre. **National Express**, T08705-808080, for **London Victoria** and long distance. Also **City Link Oxford Express**, T01865-785400, **Oxford Tube**, T01865-772250 (24 hr London-Oxford Express, every 12 mins.
Local Most local buses are run by Stagecoach Oxford, T01865-772250. **Jetlink** for airport buses T08705-757747, **Guide Friday**, T01865-790522, for open-top tours.

Car
Car hire Thrifty, Osney Mead, T01865-250252; **Oxford Hatchback Hire**, Longcot, Shotover Kilns, Old Rd, Headington, T01865-763615; **Midlands Vehicle Rental Ltd**, Salle Suit, Wolvercote Mill, Wolvercote, T01865-311180.
Car parks Central car parks (many of which have hefty overnight charges) include Gloucester Green, Westgate, Worcester St, Abbey Pl and Oxpens Rd. Park and Ride is run by **Oxford Bus Co**, T01865-785400. Day return bus fare £1.50.

Taxi
Relatively cheap in Oxford, and not usually a problem finding one on the street. Otherwise **City Taxis** T01865-201201; **Eurocabs** T01865-43043; or 24-hr minicabs from **001 Taxis** T01865-24000.

Train
The main railway station is in the west of the city, where the Botley Rd meets Hythe Bridge street, a 15-min walk into the centre. Trains are run by **Thames Trains** T0118-9083678 (recorded train info T08457-300700) www.thamestrains.co.uk, and **Virgin Trains** T0870-7891234 (recorded train info T08457-222333), www.virgin.com/trains and First Great Western T01793-499400 (booking T0845-7000125) www.firstgreatwestern.co.uk. On from **London Paddington**, to **Birmingham** via **Banbury**, and **Leamington Spa**, to **Bicester**, **Buckingham** and **Milton Keynes**, and to **Hereford** and **Worcester** via the **Cotswolds**.

North of Oxford *p232*

Car
Budget, Unit 6, Thorpe Way Industrial Estate, Banbury, T01280-704433.

Taxi
Castle Cars, Banbury Railway Station, T01295-270011; **Cherwell Cars**, 53 George St, Banbury, T01295-255555.

West of Oxford *p235*

Bicycle
Riverside Cycles, Lechlade T01367-253599 from boathouse, £10 per day.

Taxi
A to B Taxis, Kerrieview, Burford Rd Minster Lovell, T01993-706060; **Fairways Airport & Tour Cars**, Burford, T01993-823152; **Keylocks**, Burford, T01993-823234.

Directory

Oxford *p224, map p228*

Hospitals John Radcliffe Hospital, Woodstock Rd, T01865-311188, is the nearest casualty department.
Internet Mices.com, 118 High St, T01865-726363, open daily 0900-1100 (Sun from 1000), £1 for 30 mins; **Internet Exchange**, 8-12 George St, T01865-241601.
Language schools EF Language Travel Ltd, 3rd floor, Cherwell House, London Pl, T01865-200720; **Oxford Brookes Unversity**, Gipsy La, Headington, T01865-483692.
Libraries The Central Library is at Westgate, T01865-815509. See Sights above for other University libraries.

West of Oxford *p235*

Medical facilities The nearest doctor is at The Surgery, Sheep St, Burford, T01993-822176; **John Radcliffe Hospital**, Oxford, T01865-741166 for nearest casualty department. **Police** Witney T01993-703913.

River Thames

→ Colour map 2, grid A/B5

The water that flows through central London has streamed softly for some 150 miles through the southern English countryside. Below Oxford, about 70 miles from its source in Gloucestershire, the country's most venerable waterway winds through the pages of history. Abingdon claims to be the oldest town in the land and Wallingford still looks pretty quaint. Before Dorchester, the river is also known as the Isis, but here it's joined by the river Thame, at a place that has been continuously settled for more than 3000 years. At polite little Goring, the river carves its way gently through the Chiltern hills, crossing the prehistoric Ridgeway that runs east-west between Avebury and Tring south of the Vale of the White Horse, named after the 3000-year-old tribal totem carved into the chalk hills. Roughly halfway between Oxford and London, the city of Reading has boomed and become one of the most prosperous places in the south. Just downstream, Henley-on-Thames retains its Georgian atmosphere, attracting thousands dressed up in old-fashioned style in the summer to watch its famous rowing regatta. More appealing in some ways, Marlow has provided a riverside home for a succession of celebrated writers. Next door, Cookham nurtured the eccentric genius of the painter Stanley Spencer. It's overlooked by the palatial hilltop estate of Cliveden, notorious for its 'scandalous' contribution to British political life in the last century. Going with the flow, Windsor can boast the oldest inhabited royal castle in the world and, over the bridge at Eton, probably the most famous school in the world. The Thames Valley isn't exclusively the playground of the privileged few though. It's still a good place to mess about in boats, the Thames Path National Trail along its banks, is one of the most rewarding, and the affluence of the London-Bristol 'M4 corridor' ensures that gourmets and bon viveurs are not usually disappointed either. ⏩ For Sleeping, Eating and other listings, see pages 253-255.

Vale of the White Horse to Goring Gap

The ancient riverside town of Abingdon is the adminstrative centre of the Vale of the White Horse. It has lost much of its antique appeal over the last 30 years, but its town hall, bridge and old churches still make it memorable. It's not surprising that most visitors prefer to escape the traffic chaos and head west into the Vale instead. This broad watery valley, named after the old hill figure at Uffington, is overlooked by the Ridgeway, the prehistoric east-west line of communication across the country. The views afforded from here over Oxfordshire and the upper Thames Valley are some of the finest in the south. As the river flows on to Dorchester, an old abbey and substantial evidence of pre-Roman settlement testify to the area's Celtic and early Christian significance. A few miles further downstream, Wallingford is a river town with a history as ancient as Oxford. Now it seems to be stuck charmingly in the 1950s. From here, along stretches of the river that inspired Kenneth Grahame's *Wind in the Willows*, the river winds on to Goring and Streatley, twee little towns facing each other across a gap in the Chiltern hills.

Ins and outs

Getting there Didcot Parkway **train** station is on the mainline from London and Reading to Oxford, Bicester, and Birmingham. Trains to Bicester and/or Oxford also usually stop at Goring and Streatley, Cholsey, Radley and Appleford. Connecting **bus** services X3 from Oxford and 32 from Didcot Parkway run to Abingdon. Wantage can also be reached by bus from Didcot Parkway. By **road** take the M40 Junction 7 to

Abingdon, Junction 6 to Wallingford. Vale of White Horse most easily reached via Junction 13 on the M4, following A34 dual carriageway up to Didcot. ▸▸ *For further details, see Transport page 255.*

Getting around Although Abingdon and several other Thameside towns can be reached by **train**, really the only way to explore the Vale of the White Horse is by **car** or **bike** or on **foot** along the Ridgeway. One useful **bus** is the 47a, which links up the villages strung along the line of springs in the valley, and the **Ridgeway Explorer Bus** which runs April to October on Sunday only T01865-810224. The local bus networks are run by **Stagecoach**, T01865-77250, **Oxford Bus Company**, T01865-785400, **Thames Travel**, T01491-837988 and **Whites** (Oxfordshire County Council transport line T01865-815683).

Information Abingdon TIC ⓘ *25 Bridge St, T01235-522711, Apr-Oct, Mon-Sat 1000-1700, Sun 1330-1615; Nov-Mar, Mon-Fri 1000-1600, Sat 0930-1430.* Helpful with details of local transport and accommodation. **Wallingford TIC** ⓘ *Town Hall, Market Pl, T01491-826972, Mon-Sat 0930-1700.* **Faringdon TIC** ⓘ *7a Market Pl, T01367-242191, Apr-Oct, Mon-Fri 1000-1700, Sat 1000-1300, Nov-Mar, Mon-Sat 1000-1300.* **Wantage TIC** ⓘ *Vale and Downland Museum, 19 Church St, Wantage, T01235-760176.*

Abingdon and around

South of Oxford, the River Thames slips beneath the ring road alongside the A34 and flows on to Abingdon. On a wide bend the river passes the house and parkland of **Nuneham Courtenay**, where All Saints' Old Church is an unusual Palladian temple overlooking the Thames. It was erected in the middle of the 18th century by Lord Harcourt when he cleared away the old village – an action that inspired Oliver Goldsmith's poem 'The Deserted Village' – to make room for his new estate after quitting Stanton Harcourt in the north. The 17th- and 18th-century Italian fittings of the interior can be seen on application for the key. The 18th-century Gothic novelist Horace Walpole thought Nuneham Courtenay the "most beautiful landscape in the world", now enjoyed by the conferencees at the house and pleasure cruisers on the river.

Abingdon, once Berkshire's county town, was subsumed into Oxfordshire in 1974 and since then has almost trebled in size, now ringed with high-tech industrial complexes that cause traffic chaos every rush hour. It's also famously the 'oldest inhabited town in England'. Best seen from the river or from the bridge (medieval but reconstructed in 1927) little now remains of the **Benedictine abbey** ⓘ *Apr-Oct Tue-Sun 1400-1600, 60p*, founded in the seventh century that once dominated the site. Its scale can still be appreciated though, near the 15th-century Gateway and Long Gallery. A little upstream from here, **Abingdon Lock** and **Andersley Island** are celebrated for their population of greedy mute swans.

Two sights in the town are particularly well worth a look though. Hard to miss is the 'Wrenaissance' magnificence of the **County Hall**, one of the grandest in the country, now the Town Hall and home to the **Abingdon Museum** ⓘ *T01235-523703, Apr-Oct 1100-1700, Nov-Mar 1100-1600, free, (roof viewpoint open Apr-Sep Sat only, £1, under-16s 50p*. The museum tells the history of the town 'from the Stone Age to the MG' (the cars were built here for 50 years and regular vintage rallies occur in the summer, for details T01235-555552), although the highlight has to be the view from the roof. East St Helen Street heads down to the river from here, where no 26A is a late-15th-century **merchant's hall house** ⓘ *T01865-242918, open by appointment*, complete with remarkable wall paintings, an oak ceiling and traceried windows. At the end of the street, where the River Ock flows into the Thames, some charming 15th-century almshouses make up the close of big, broad **St Helen's Church**. The pumphouse for the church organ is a unique survival in England, while inside the church the remarkable 14th-century painted roof in the Lady Chapel depicts the tree of Jesse beneath a series of Kings and Prophets.

Pleasant riverside walks downriver from Abingdon along the **Thames Path** reach **Sutton Courtenay** (2 miles), an attractive village with a late 12th-century manor house, church and the grave of one Eric Arthur Blair – better known as George Orwell – in the churchyard. On the north bank, a 4-mile walk fetches up in **Clifton Hampden**, where there are a couple of long-standing old pubs. A mile further south of Sutton Courtenay, although a little too close to the A34 for comfort, **Milton Manor** ⓘ *T01235-862321, daily for first 2 weeks of May and Aug 1400-1700, also bank holiday weekends, tours at 1400, 1500, 1600, £4, under-16s £2, grounds only £2.50, under-16s £1*, is a pretty little brick-built doll's house supposed to have been designed by Inigo Jones in the 17th century, still well lived in. Pony rides are given from the stables in the summer.

A mile or so to the east, the town of **Didcot** is dominated by the great concave cooling towers of its power station, and its main (perhaps only) attraction is one of the largest steam railway museums in the south. Highlights of the **Didcot Railway Centre** ⓘ *T01235-817200, www.didcotrailwaycentre.org.uk, Apr-Sep daily 1000-*

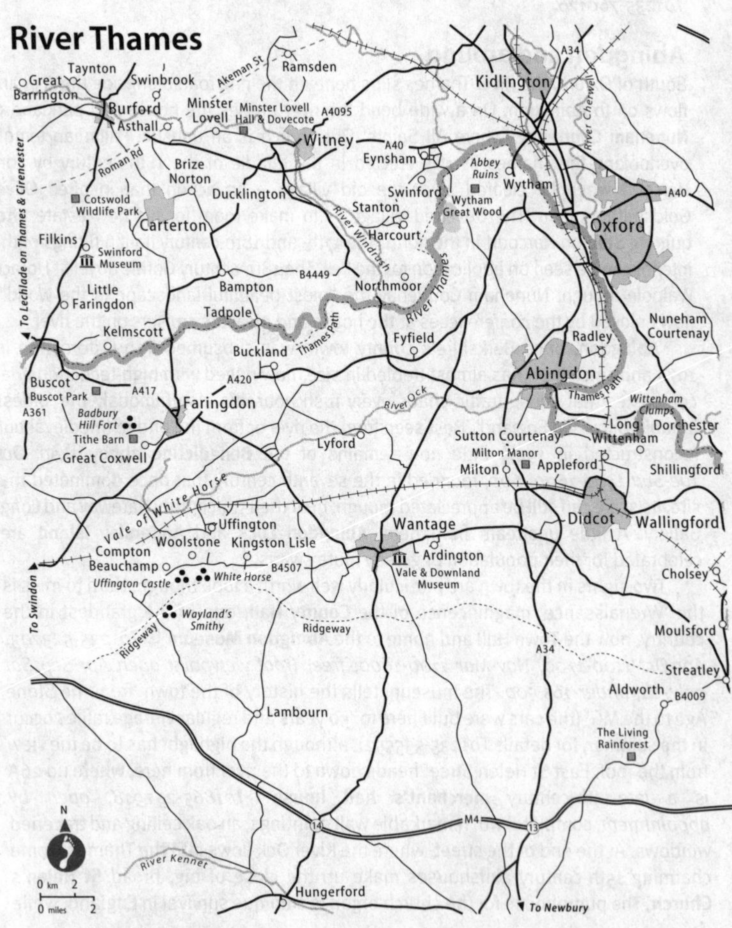

1700, Oct-Mar weekends only 1000-1700, Nov-Feb 1000-1600, £4-£8 depending on events, steamdays with rides, first and last Sun of month, all Sun Jul-Aug, also Wed, Sat in Aug, include the Travelling Post Office mail exchange, where the rapid changeover of mail bags can usually be seen in operation at 1500 on steamdays (when enthusiasts stoke up the boilers and get the stock rolling). The engine shed is the main event at other times, surrounded by a wealth of railway memorabilia, from Frome signal box to the Coaling Stage. The Centre is right next door to Didcot Parkway Train Station on the main line between London and Bristol, once Brunel's broad gauge Great Western railway.

Vale of the White Horse

Named after the 3000-year-old chalk hill figure above Uffington, the watery Vale of the White Horse now has Abingdon as its administrative headquarters. The broad flat floodplains of the River Thames and its little brother the Ock spread west from the town, overlooked by soft undulating downlands topped by the **Ridgeway**, a national trail and prehistoric east-west line of communication. Small brick-built villages like Woolstone and Kingston Lisle are strung along the spring-line of the downs, delightful

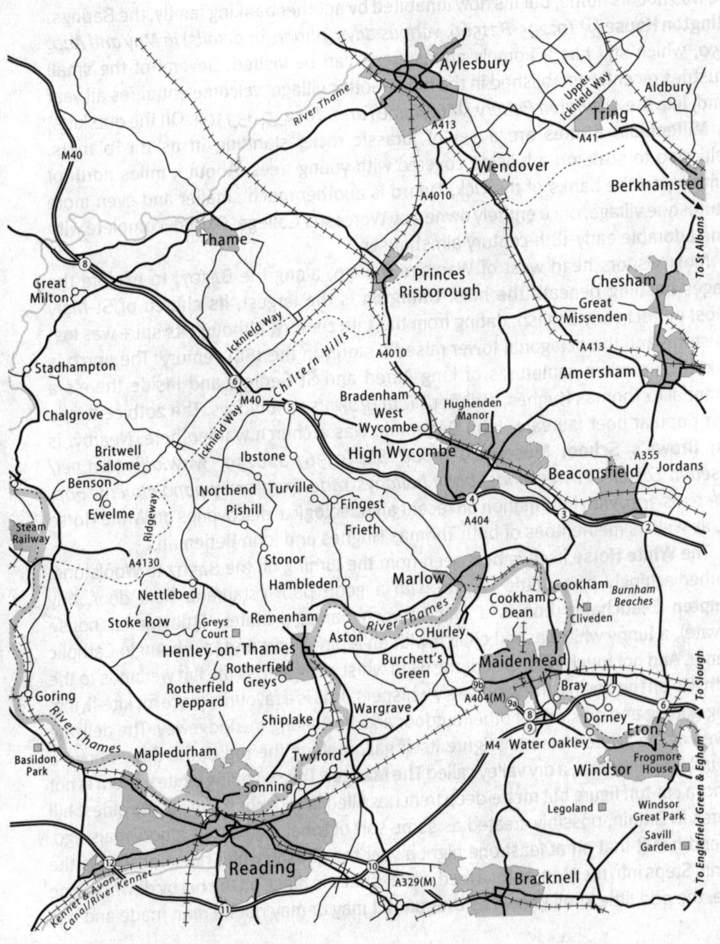

 places to drop down into for refreshment after tramping the grassy heights. The Ridgeway itself runs for 85 miles from Avebury in Wiltshire to Tring in the Chilterns, but this is its most historic (and most popular) stretch.

The birthplace of Alfred the Great in 848, **Wantage** is the old market town at the heart of the region. Narrowly bypassed in the 19th century by the Great Western Railway between Didcot and Swindon, it missed out on the Industrial Revolution and became severely depressed, earning the nickname 'Black Wantage'. Colonel Loyd Lindsay, the inheritor of a banking fortune, came to its rescue, reviving the ironworks and linking the town to the railway with the first steam tram (now defunct) in the country. The **Vale and Downland Museum** ⓘ *Church St, T01235-771447, www.wantage.com/museum, Mon-Sat 1000-1630, Sun 1430-1700, £1.50, under-16s £1, family £4*, tells the full story, an accomplished local history museum, with a few interactive displays, including a push-button illuminated landscape of the Vale, a Victorian kitchen, a video narrated by David Attenborough, as well as contemporary PR from local concerns like *Crown Technologies*, the designers of the Coke bottles, and Damon Hill's Williams team Formula-one racing car.

The good works of Lord Wantage, as Col Lindsay later became, can be appreciated at the village of **Ardington**, a couple of miles east, where the Lockinge Trust still maintains the village on his estate. The beautiful early-Georgian 'big house' here was not his home, but it's now inhabited by another banking family, the Barings. **Ardington House** ⓘ *T01235-821566, various days (phone for details) in May and Aug, £3.50*, which still has a homely atmosphere, can be visited. Several of the small industries recently established in the mock-Gothic village welcome enquiries all year round, like the *Ardington Pottery* ⓘ *15 Home Farm, T01235-833302*. On the outskirts, the **Millennium Stones** are a set of Jurassic rocks standing in as the planets, positioned to scale on a hillside covered with young trees. About 5 miles north of Wantage, on the banks of the Ock, **Lyford** is another much smaller and even more picturesque village, once entirely owned by Worcester College, Oxford, complete with some adorable early-18th-century almshouses.

Most visitors head west of Wantage though, along the B4507, to explore the villages nestling beneath the hills. **Uffington** is the largest, its church of St Mary almost perfect early English, dating from the 13th century, although its spire was lost in a storm and the octagonal tower raised a storey in the 18th century. The porch is flanked by modern sculptures of King Alfred and St George, and inside there's a memorial to Thomas Hughes, author of *Tom Brown's Schooldays*. The 20th century's most popular poet laureate, John Betjeman, was a church warden here. Nearby, is **Tom Brown's School Museum** ⓘ *Broad St, T01367-820259, www.uffington.net/museum, Easter-Oct weekends, bank holidays 1400-1700 or by appointment, 60p, under-16s 30p*, with information on recent archaeological discoveries on White Horse hill, as well as mementoes of both Thomas Hughes and John Betjeman.

The **White Horse** itself is best seen from the turning off the B4507 to Woolstone, another achingly pretty little village, with a good pub/restaurant. Next door, tiny **Compton Beauchamp** boasts a fancy French name, a stately little manor house (private), a funny whitewashed church with an Alpine turret and lavish Anglo-Catholic interior. And not much else, except the wind whispering across the flat wetlands to the north. Up on the downs, the wind rarely whispers. This is a favourite place for kite-flying, hang-gliding and all kinds of other outdoor activities along the Ridgeway. The delicate curves of the White Horse hill figure itself gallop along the top of the ridge above a natural amphitheatre, a dry valley called **The Manger**. The sweeping white pattern is not in fact a cut-turf figure but metre-deep trenches filled in with chalk, one of the oldest hill figures in Britain, possibly created as some sort of tribal logo about 3,000 years ago. Legend has it that on at least one night a year the ghostly white horse descends the Giants Steps into the Manger for a feed, always back in place on the hill by dawn. To one side, the odd little knoll known as **Dragon Hill** may or may not be man-made and has caused as much speculation about its origin and purpose as the horse. Was this where St George slew the dragon, hence the bald chalk patch on top where its poisonous blood was spilled? Or was it raised up as a sacrificial site? Probably neither, but the almost abstract design of the horse looks good from the summit. Above the horse, an Iron-Age hill fort, **Uffington Castle**, commands wide-reaching views over the Upper Thames Valley towards the Cotswolds in the distance. A mile to the west, **Wayland's Smithy** is one of the finest and most mysterious neolithic chambered long barrows in the country, much older than the horse, dating from around 2500BC. Archaeologists think it may once have been covered in white chalk as one of a series of shining monuments along the ridge marking a processional route for neolithic funerals. Set in a grove of peaceful trees, it too has spawned many legends, including that of the mythical blacksmith Wayland's apprentice, Flibbertygibbet. He dawdled on an errand, got hit on the heel by a boulder thrown by his impatient boss, and can apparently still be heard nearby at Snivelling Corner.

About five miles north of Uffington, **Great Coxwell Tithe Barn** ⓘ *(NT), near Faringdon, open daily at any reasonable time, 50p*, is an impressive 13th-century stone-built barn, with a stone roof, one of the best-preserved in the country and favourably compared to a cathedral by the Medievalist William Morris. **Buscot Park** (see Oxfordshire section above, page 224) is just over Badbury hill fort (carpeted with bluebells in the spring) from here. Heading back east on the A420, beyond Faringdon, the 'threshold of the Cotswolds' and a market town in a pretty position on a limestone ridge, **Buckland House** stands in the Upper Thames Valley next to the well-kept little village of the same name. It's a very grand 18th-century mansion clearly visible from the road, facing an uncertain future after being on the market for a few years (yours for about £4 million), with grounds featuring several lakes and the finest ice-house in the county.

Dorchester and Wallingford

Back beside the Thames below Abingdon, Dorchester was once the vital fortified meeting point of three tribes of ancient Britons at the confluence of the rivers Thames and Thame. Then it became a small Roman town on the river. Now it's more of a large and rather dignified village. As well as the extensive Iron Age and Roman earthworks nearby, the main attraction is **Dorchester Abbey** ⓘ *T01865-340703, May-Sep, also Easter, weekends in Apr, early Oct Tue-Sat 1100-1700, Sun and bank holidays 1400-1700, free*, originally founded as a cathedral in the seventh century by St Birinus. With another Decorated Jesse window, similar to the one in Abingdon, and the medieval tomb of Sir John Holcombe – drawing his sword in an unusually dramatic manner – and some of the oldest stained glass in England, the Abbey was eventually superseded by Winchester in the 15th century. A museum tells the story in the Old Monastery Guest House, a 14th-century building itself.

Just before reaching Dorchester, the river curves round the **Wittenham Clumps**, an ancient and atmospheric group of tree-topped hillocks. Round Hill and Castle Hill both afford tremendous views over the river valley and there's an attractive and undemanding riverside walk down into Dorchester from here. Part of the area is a **nature reserve** ⓘ *T01865-407792*. In Long Wittenham, the **Pendon Museum of Landscape and Transport in Miniature** ⓘ *T01865-407365, www.pendonmuseum.com, all year weekends 1400-1700, also on Wed in Jul, Aug, £4, under-16s £3.50, concessions £3*, reproduces the Vale of the White Horse in the 1930s in miniature detail (cottages 4 ins high) on a 70-ft model landscape, next door to the Madder Valley Model Railway. Engineered in the 1930s, both are craftworks of astonishing patience and detail.

The Wittenham Clumps

Two small hills near the Thames at Dorchester are prominent local landmarks riddled with legend and superstition. Both are one of the places across the country where King Arthur is supposed to have rallied his troops. Castle Hill, also known as Sinodun Hill, was certainly once a fort and also contains a hollow known as the 'Money Pit'. A villager digging here once found a metal casket but was disturbed by a raven's shriek. Taking this to mean that the treasure was not for him, he filled in the hole and no one has found it since. The spinney of trees on the top of the hill is known as the 'cuckoo pen': an ancient country belief held that if a cuckoo could be successfully kept in the clump and prevented from escaping, then summer would never end.

Wallingford is another ancient riverside town, like Oxford also founded by Alfred the Great, and still looks and feels much like Abingdon may have done about 40 years ago. Across the medieval bridge, with its 17 arches, rises the openwork spire of **St Peter's Church**, designed on its prime site beside the river by Sir Robert Taylor in 1777. Sir William Blackstone, the lawyer who had a hand in the US constitution, is buried in the churchyard. Across the road, a grassy mound marks another of the Norman Robert d'Oily's castles, slighted by Cromwell's forces in the Civil War. The open-plan ground floor for the Town Hall, constructed in 1670, stands in the middle of the market square (fruit, veg and cheap consumer durables on Fridays, farmers market on Wednesdays), near the **Wallingford Museum** in Flint House – an old-fashioned 'time-warp walk' through Saxon and medieval Wallingford, with a reconstructed Victorian shop, pub and living room. Agatha Christie, who is buried in the back corner of Cholsey Churchyard, lived in Wallingford from 1935 until her death in 1976, and parts of town would still seem quite at home featuring in one of her murder mysteries. If you want to pay homage at her grave, it may not be quite the Orient Express, but the **Cholsey and Wallingford Steam Railway**, T01491-835067, steams up on weekends Apr-Aug, down the short 2½ mile long stretch of branch line to Cholsey. Transport buffs of the two-wheeled variety might be interested in the **Benson Veteran Cycle Museum** ⓘ *61 Brook St, Benson T01491-838414, mornings Apr-Aug by appointment only, free*, a collection of about 600 vintage cycles – pushbikes, bicycles, penny farthings – from 1818 to the 1930s.

Goring and Streatley

About six miles downriver from Wallingford, beyond Moulsford – one of the stretches of river that inspired Kenneth Grahame's *Wind in the Willows* – prehistoric man forded the Thames at Goring as he tramped along the Ridgeway. Today the almost over-tended little riverside town is still a popular springboard for hikers setting off for the hills. The bell in the church is one of England's oldest, dating from 1290, while **Lardon Chase** (NT), on the hillside overlooking the river, is a popular spot for picnics in the woods.

Three miles west of Streatley, the little village across the river bridge from Goring, on the B4009, **Aldworth's** Church of St Mary is worth travelling to find, described by Simon Jenkins as "a dormitory of knights and ladies of the time leading up to the Hundred Years War". Five generations of the de la Beche family lie enshrined in early-14th-century monuments, known as the Aldworth Giants. Queen Elizabeth I made a special trip to see the effigies, known as John Long, John Strong, John Never Afraid and John Ever Afraid (who has since disappeared). The poet Laurence Binyon, who wrote *For the Fallen*, the moving poem of remembrance for the First World War dead recited every November 11, is buried in the churchyard near a thousand-year-old yew tree. In the church, there's also a selection of leaflets suggesting good **walks** (from 5-8 miles) over the surrounding downs.

Three miles further along on the same road, the **Living Rainforest** ⓘ *T01635-202444, www.livingrainforest.org, daily 1000-1715 (last admission 1630), £4.50, concessions £3.50, under-14s, £2.50, family £12*, is an unusual visitor attraction and educational resource on the Wyld Court estate. Small monkeys, large spiders, hungry piranha fish, and rare butterflies can be seen surrounded by lush exotic vegetation and water features in some large and humid glasshouses. It's great for kids.

A couple of miles south along the river from Goring in Lower Basildon, **Basildon Park** ⓘ *(NT), T0118-9843040, Apr-Oct Wed-Sun 1300-1730, £4.40, under-16s £2.20, family £11, park and gardens only £2, under-16s £1, family £5*, is a large Palladian mansion constructed out of profits made in India in the 18th century, set in acres of rolling parkland above the river. Its first owner, Sir Francis Sykes, spent some time locked up in the Black Hole of Calcutta. After falling into disrepair, the place was bought last century by Lord and Lady Iliffe, who restored it lovingly to its original condition, adding a few 20th-century comforts upstairs. Highlights include the Shell Room and Lady Iliffe's bedroom, with Graham Sutherland's painted study for his Crucifixion tapestry in Coventry cathedral.

Sleeping

Abingdon and around *p247*

A **The Upper Reaches Hotel**, Thames St, Abingdon, T0870-4008101, www.heritage-hotels.co.uk. In a converted mill, with smart chintzy rooms but you're paying for the 'heritage' location right on the river.

C **22 East St Helen St B&B**, Abingdon, T01235-550979, F533278. Bang in the middle of town, in an old house full of character close to the river, with an eminently capable family atmosphere, 1 double room, 1 single and 1 twin.

D **Helensbourne**, 34 East St Helen St, Abingdon, T01235-530200, F201573. B&B also right in the centre of town, and competitively priced, 1 double and 1 family room.

D **Hollies Guest House**, 8 New Rd, Radley, Near Abingdon, T01235-529552, F529552. Very friendly, well connected by bus to Abingdon 3½ miles away, also on the mainline to Oxford, 2 double rooms.

Vale of the White Horse *p246*

C **Coach and Horses**, Uffington, is an unprepossessing place that is considerably more friendly than it looks from the outside and sells excellent ales and is a good place to view the Horse from.

C **The Craven**, Fernham Rd, Uffington, T01367-820449, has a family atmosphere in a thatched cottage freshly done up.

C **Lamb Inn**, Buckland, T01367-870484, is a pub grub restaurant with rooms above (about £50 a night) in a secluded estate village.

C **Old Bull's Head**, in Ardington, a pub with rooms in the old estate village.

C **White Horse Inn**, Woolstone, T01367-820726 does superior food and cosy accommodation.

F **The YHA Ridgeway Centre**, Court Hill, Wantage, T01235-760253, F768865. Converted barns close to the long distance path, above Letcombe Regis Ridgeway Centre, one of a series of barns rescued by Dick Squires, founder of the Vale and Downland Museum. Open Dec-Mar Fri, Sats only, Sep-Nov not Sun, Mon.

Camping

Eco-friendly camping (without facilities, leave the pitch as you found it) is acceptable in many places along the Ridgeway.

Dorchester and Wallingford *p251*

L **Beetle and Wedge Hotel**, Ferry La, Moulsford, T01491-651381, F651376. Small riverside lawns, 2 restaurants with good reputations, on the stretch of river where the *Wind in the Willows* was set, where the old ferry crossed to South Stoke.

B **Crazy Bear Hotel**, Bear La, Stadhampton (north of Dorchester), T01865-890714,

F400481. Highly idiosyncratic place with wacky furnishings.

B The George Hotel, Dorchester, T01865-340404, F341620. Marginally more expensive, and more spruce, less character but pleasant enough.

B The White Hart Hotel, Dorchester, T01865-430074, www.oxford-restaurants-hotels.co.uk. Standard doubles £80.

C Fords Farm, Ewelme, Wallingford, T01491-839272. Sheep farm B&B in a pretty little village right opposite the Chaucer church, with its heraldic shields.

D North Farm B&B, Shillingford Hill, Wallingford, T01865-858406. A welcoming working farm.

Goring and Streatley p252

F YHA Streatley-on-Thames, Reading Rd, Streatley, T01491-872278, F873056 although it's not open all year. Call for opening times.

Eating

Abingdon and around *p247*

£££ Le Manoir aux Quat'Saisons, Church Rd, Great Milton, T01844-278881, is a 2-Michelin starred restaurant with very plush (and equally expensive) rooms above. Book many months ahead.

££ The Plough Inn, Abingdon Rd, Clifton Hampden, T01865-407811, is an old pub with a good reputation for its food, entirely non-smoking and also with rooms (**B**), within walking distance of Abingdon along the river.

£ Peking House, Bridge St, is a reliable enough Chinese takeaway.

Dorchester and Wallingford *p251*

££ The Goose, Britwell Salome, T01491-612304, is a successful gastropub established by Prince Charles's former chef, dinner about £26 for 3 modern British courses.

££ Queen's Head, Crowmarsh, near Wallingford, an offbeat hybrid of a Thai Orchid restaurant in an old Fuller's pub.

££ The Red Lion, Chalgrove, T01865-890625, is an attractive old pub with food that comes highly rated.

Goring and Streatley p252

££ The Bell Inn, Aldworth, T01635-578272, a virtually unspoilt 14th-century inn, with geese in the back yard, patriotic family-owned and doing very popular lunches and ales.

££ The John Barleycorn pub in Goring, serves one of the best pints of Brakspear's Special you'll get outside Henley – worth sampling over a game of bar billiards.

££ The Leatherne Bottle, Goring-on-Thames, T01491-872667, does rooms, and an exotic fairly expensive, very popular menu in cramped surroundings. It's often very busy, so booking is advisable.

Bars, pubs and clubs

Abingdon and around *p247*

Barley Mow, Clifton Hampden, T01865-407847, popular beamed and thatched old local. Within walking distance of Abingdon along the river.

The Harcourt Arms, Nuneham Courtenay is another good pub near the river.

Old Anchor, St Helen's Wharf, where the river Ock meet the Thames, is a characterful old pub also doing decent food.

White Hart, Fyfield, T01865-390585, does excellent real ales, a medieval pub with reasonably priced modern pub grub.

Entertainment

Dorchester and Wallingford *p251*

Corn Exchange Cinema and Theatre, Wallingford (contact TIC for details of what's on or try T01491-825000). Is an old Palladian building in the market square.

Festivals and events

Dorchester and Wallingford *p251*

May Wallingford Regatta takes place on the Thames.

Jul Wallingford Raft Race, for charity.

Activities and tours

Abingdon and around *p247*

Boating

Abingdon Boat Centre, The Bridge, Nag's Head Island, T01235-521125. Does boat hire.

Redline, Wilsham Rd, T01235-521562. For boat hire in Abingdon.

Salter Bros, T01865-243421, run river trips from May-Sep, to Oxford from Nags Head island in Abingdon.

Thames Hire Cruiser Association, Secretary Mr P Allen, T0208-9791997. Contact for longer boat trips.

Dorchester and Wallingford *p251*

Boating

Benson Waterfront, near Wallingford, T01491-838304.

Upper Thames Passenger Boat Association, T0870-2415016, for wine and dine, a disco dance, commentaries and steamboats on the river.

Transport

Abingdon and around *p247*

Cycle hire Braggs, 2 High St, Abingdon, T01235-520034. **Pedal Power**, 92 The Vineyard, Oxford Rd, T01235-525123.

Taxi Top Cabs, 70 Hamble Dr, Abingdon, T01235-537333.

Dorchester and Wallingford *p251*

Taxis Rural Car Services, Castle House, Castle St, Wallingford, T0800-0743494.

Directory

Dorchester and Wallingford *p251*

Hospitals **Wallingford Hospital**, T01491-835533; surgery T01491-835577.

Police T01235-776000.

Reading to Maidenhead

→ *Colour map 2, grid A6*

Reading, the largest town on the river between London and Oxford, is hardly a beauty. But then that's not the point. Berkshire's administrative headquarters, the transport hub of the south and one of its most thriving business centres, tries instead to pull in the punters with its special events and clublife. Henley-on-Thames, on the other hand, just downstream, seems to be stuck in a dream of England past, one that becomes a fantastic spectacle every July at its historic regatta. Marlow is less pompous and has long been culturally more interesting, while Cookham is a popular riverside spot with weekending Londoners. Just down the river at Bray are some of the finest restaurants outside the capital in the country. ▸▸ *For Sleeping, Eating and other listings, see pages 259-261.*

Ins and outs

Getting there Reading is a major national transport interchange, on the mainline to Bristol and the west country down to Penzance (and also Birmingham and the north) from London Paddington. Well-served by **rail**: frequent **Thames Trains** (stopping at Twyford and Maidenhead for Henley and Marlow) take about 45 minutes; express trains, run by **First Great Western**, about 25 minutes. From London Waterloo, **South West Trains** run a stopping service to Reading via the western suburbs of London, with interconnecting services to Windsor, taking about 1 hour and 20 minutes. For Henley, one stopping train an hour (more at peak times) runs on the branch line from Twyford (10 minutes), via Wargrave and Shiplake. Reading is on the **M4**, 30 minutes from central London. Henley is a few minutes closer, easily reached using the A404(M) Maidenhead bypass at Junction 8/9 on the M4. **National Express**, T08705-808080, run **coaches** to Reading-Calcot, Savacentre, M4 Junction 12 from London Victoria, once an hour between 0745 and 2330, taking 1 hour 15 minutes (£8 one-way). ▸▸ *For further details, see Transport page 261.*

Getting around Reading's small town centre is relatively pedestrian-friendly and there are reliable bus services to most parts of town and outlying areas. Buses between Reading and Henley are run by **Arriva**.

 Information Reading Visitor Centre ⓘ *Church Ho, Change St, T0118-9566226. Mon-Fri 0930-1700, Sat 0930-1600.* **TIC Henley** ⓘ *The Barn (beside the Town Hall), Kings Rd, T01491-578034, daily 0900-1700.* **TIC Marlow** ⓘ *31 High St, T01628-483597, Mon-Fri 0900-1700, Sat 0930-1700 (until 1600 Nov-Mar).*

Reading

Reading, at the confluence of the rivers Kennet and Thames, is Berkshire's capital city and the largest town on the congested 'M4 corridor' between London and Bristol: the buckle of England's affluent southern belt. Surrounded by thousands of acres of light industry, hi-tech office complexes and business parks, most of its ancient riverside character has long been buried beneath the consequences of this 21st-century prosperity. Today, with its massive brand new shopping and entertainment mall, The Oracle, its rock and world music festivals, a thriving university and intriguing museum, Reading has more than enough going for itself. Even so, it has trouble providing affordable homes for its bus drivers (some of whom commute into work weekly from as far away as Lincolnshire apparently), and somehow it's little wonder that it attracts only a few passing visitors. Then again, it doesn't really need them.

The centre of town, pedestrianized Broad Street and parallel Friar Street, is cut off from the river Thames by the railway. Five minutes' walk from the station, on the Market Place, the **Museum of Reading** ⓘ *Town Hall, T0118-9399800, www.readingmuseum.org.uk, Tue-Sat 1000-1600 (Thu until 1900), Sun 1100-1600, free*, is well worth a look for its archaeological finds. Here are most of the Roman artefacts dug up at Silchester, (see page 279), including a British brooch uncannily similar in design to the White Horse, and the little 'Silchester Eagle' that inspired Rosamund Sutcliffe to write her best-selling historical novel for children, *The Eagle of the Ninth*. The painstaking copy of the Bayeux Tapestry, embroidered in 1835 by over 35 industrious hands, is housed in its own purpose-built gallery, allowing this medieval comic strip celebration of the battle of Hastings to be seen in full light, unlike the original in France. The **John Madejski Art Gallery**, in the same complex as the museum and named after the billionaire owner of the local football club, mounts changing exhibitions of the city's extensive art collection in a refurbished Victorian space, next door to galleries featuring Epstein's *Rebecca* and a display of local biscuit-makers *Huntley and Palmers'* decorated biscuit tins, including one that was given to Captain Scott for his ill-fated expedition to the South Pole.

Apart from taking a stroll beside the river Thames (best undertaken along the Thames Path west of Caversham Bridge) there's not much else in the way of sightseeing in Reading. A 10-minute walk east of the station, through a 13th-century gatehouse, the extensive **Abbey** ruins are where the embalmed left hand of St James was found in a casket in the 19th century (now in Marlow's church of St Peter). They stand next to **Reading Gaol**, still very much in use, a Victorian prison famous for accommodating Oscar Wilde as he wrote *De Profundis* in 1897, on being betrayed by his lover Alfred Lord Douglas – his *Ballad of Reading Gaol* was written in Paris after his release. A dreary 15-minute walk along the Kennet and Avon canal past the ruins and the prison leads to **Blakes Lock Museum** ⓘ *T0118-9399800*, of canal life, currently being refurbished. The **Kennet and Avon**, linking Reading to Bath 57 miles away, is one of the most beautiful canals in the country, opened fully in 1810, but unfortunately this terminus is hardly one of the most inspiring.

A little further afield, at the University, the **Museum of English Rural Life** ⓘ *Chancellors Way, Shinfield Rd, T0118-9318663, Tue-Sat 1000-1300, 1400-1630, £1*, and the **Ure Museum of Greek Antiquities** are two little-known academic curiosities, displaying outmoded agricultural implements and artefacts from ancient Greece respectively.

Around Reading

Two miles west of Reading, on the north bank of the river Thames is **Mapledurham** with its imposing red-brick **Elizabethan mansion** ⓘ *T0118-9723350, www.mapledurham.co.uk, Apr-Sep weekends, bank holidays 1400-1730 (last admission 1700), house £4.50, mill £3.50, house and mill £7, can be reached by 45-min river cruise from Caversham Bridge in Reading, leaving at 1400 on open days, £4.50 return, at 1700*, still lived in by descendants of the Blounts, whose famously beautiful daughters inspired the hunchback satirist Alexander Pope in the 18th century. The secluded estate village, right beside the river, has been immaculately preserved and includes the last working watermill on the Thames. Some may recognize it as the timewarp location for the film adaptation of Jack Higgins' *The Eagle has Landed* as well as various screen versions of *The Wind in the Willows*.

Henley-on-Thames and around→ *Colour map 2, grid A6*

Henley-on-Thames, 8 miles downriver from Reading, is a very well-to-do riverside town, not much changed at its heart since the early 19th century. Most famous for its summer regatta, held since 1839, when it becomes very busy indeed, it's also a popular launch pad for walks in the Chiltern hills and along the Thames Path. East of the station, the town itself perches neatly on the north bank of the river, Hart Street running up from the bridge to the Market Place and grand Town Hall. Most of the boating action in July takes place downstream of the bridge on the south bank, much of it enclosed for members only. All year this proper little town place boasts a healthy array of independent retailers and good quality restaurants.

West of the station, the revamped **River and Rowing Museum** ⓘ *Mill Meadows, T01491-415600, www.rrm.co.uk, May-Aug daily 1000-1730, Sep-Apr daily 1000-1700, £4.95, under-16s £3.75, family £13.95*, tells the story of the town's obsession with paddling with oars on the river as fast or as elegantly as possible, from old tubs and beautiful launches to super-sleek Olympic eights. Apart from the permanent displays of boats ancient and modern, the temporary exhibitions are often well worth a look, on subjects as diverse as the town's 18th-century gentility and the reasons for the Thames' flooding.

Three miles west of the town, near the village of Rotherfield Greys, **Greys Court** ⓘ *(NT), T01491-628529, T01494-755564, house open Apr-Sep Wed-Fri, bank holidays 1400-1800, garden open Apr-Sep Tue-Sat, bank holidays 1400-1800, £4.60, under-16s £2.30, family £11.50, gardens only £3.20, family ticket £8*, is a beautiful (and quite popular) little 14th-century house perched on a hill next to an old church in quiet rolling countryside. The house has many a tale to tell, of murderous Jacobean countesses and court intrigue, as well as a Tudor donkey wheel and path maze. One tower survives from 1347 while rooms around the old courtyard are decorated with some exceptional 18th-century plasterwork.

Downriver from the town, the **Thames Path** along the southern bank passes through a string of well-kept and pretty little villages. One mile along is the tiny village of **Remenham**, with its sad church lychgate commemorating the death of Violet Constance Noble who died suddenly of scarlet fever in 1884 aged 14. Two miles further, **Aston** is an old ferry village with a good pub popular with fisherfolk. Going with the flow for 3 more miles, at a complex of locks, **Hurley** is an altogether grander place, with a venerable 12th-century church housing the remarkable **Lovelace** monument and a well-stocked Old Farm Shop in its old barn. Unusually, the villagers saw fit in 1976 to buy the Lordship of their Manor.

A couple of miles out of Henley on the Marlow road along the north bank of the river, a left turn heads for quaint little **Hambleden**, where bookseller W H Smith (later Lord Hambleden) is buried. Lord Cardigan, who ordered the charge of the Light Brigade, was born in this charming spot, from where the road leads on up to a clutch of attractive villages nestling in the Chilterns.

Marlow

About 8 miles downriver from Henley, Marlow is another old river town, exceptional for its clutch of unusual former residents and beautiful situation. Mary Shelley wrote *Frankenstein* here, in Albion House on West Street, where she lived with Byron's illegitimate daughter Allegra, the girl's mother, and her new husband Percy Bysshe Shelley. He visited all the local places of interest within a day's walk and was considered by most of the local gentry to be mad. The novelist and poet Thomas Love Peacock also lived in the town, and over a century later, Jerome K Jerome's comic classic *Three men in a Boat* was inspired by his experiences living on the waterside here. TS Eliot too had a house in Marlow, next door to Sir William Borlase's school. The impressive old Georgian house on the High Street called Remnantz, close to the town centre, was the birthplace of the Royal Military Academy now at Sandhurst. Today, despite being a London commuter dormitory, the town remains a dignified but unassuming little place, immediately more friendly than Henley and a pleasure to go poking around.

The Roman Catholic church of **St Peter's** ⓘ *St Peter St, T01628 483696*, was designed by Augustus Pugin (also responsible for the Houses of Parliament – his son did the school next door) and preserves an unusual medieval relic, believed to be the left hand of Saint James, brought to England by the Empress Matilda. The thing was dug up in its casket in the ruins of Reading Abbey and can be viewed on request. On the river, next to the splendid wobbly old suspension bridge put up in 1836, stands the tall spire of **All Saints' Church**. A curiosity inside is a painting of 'the spotted negro boy', an eight-year-old Caribbean albino exhibited as a freak in 1812.

Cookham

Cookham, 3 miles east of Marlow, is a small, smart riverside village, pretty in a self-conscious kind of way, most famous for accommodating the tortured religious artist Sir Stanley Spencer. By public subscription a memorial **gallery** ⓘ *T01628-471885, Easter-Oct daily 1030-1730, Nov-Easter weekends, bank holidays 1100-1700*, dedicated to his extraordinary paintings was opened in 1962 in the old Methodist chapel in the middle of town. Occasional temporary exhibitions by other artists are also shown here. Nearby, the town centre is marked by the **Tarry Stone**, once used as a racing mark for games on the village green on the Feast of the Assumption and believed by some locals to be a meteorite. **Cookham Lock** is one of the most beautiful on the river, although the first to be mechanized in the 1950s. **Boulter's Lock** nearer Maidenhead still tends to draw the summer crowds, which makes Cookham's all the more attractive.

Between Cookham Lock and Maidenhead, along one of its most beautiful stretches, the river runs quietly beneath the majestic beech woods surrounding **Cliveden** ⓘ *(NT), T01628-605069, information T01494-7555562, garden mid-Mar to Dec daily 1100-1800, Nov and Dec 1100-1600, £6, under-16s £3, family £12.50, house and Octagon Temple Apr-Oct Thu, Sun 1500-1730 (entry by timed ticket, £1 extra on cost of garden admission)*, perched high up on the north bank with spectacular views. An Italianate villa designed in the middle of the 19th century by Sir Charles Barry for the Duke of Sutherland it was bought by the American newspaper millionaire William Waldorf Astor in 1893. A house purpose-built for lavish entertainment has stood on this extraordinary site since 1666 when the Duke of Buckingham chose it for "pleasure, frolic and extravagant diversion". The south-facing brick terrace he had built still survives, now complemented by the Astors' extravagant formal gardens and their recently renovated secret garden, as well as the Octagon Temple with its amazing mosaics. In the last century, Cliveden achieved notoriety for entertaining Nancy Astor's political 'set' of Hitler appeasers and later the protagonists of the Profumo scandal in the 60s. Appropriately enough, it's now a super-luxury hotel, although still in the care of the National Trust.

Bray and Maidenhead

Downstream from Cookham, the riverside village of Bray on the outskirts of Maidenhead boasts a couple of the best restaurants in the country (see below). Maidenhead itself is a busy commuter town, famous for Boulter's Lock, a popular Edwardian pleasure ground, and its river bridges. **Brunel's rail bridge** uses a pair of the widest brick arches in the world, the northern one known as the 'sounding arch' because of its strange echo on the river. The bridge was immortalized by Turner in his *Rain, Steam and Speed*. The old stone **road bridge** was built in the 1770s by Sir Robert Taylor, who later endowed the Taylorian Institute of Modern Languages at Oxford University.

Sleeping

Around Reading *p257*

A The French Horn, Sonning-on-Thames, downstream of Reading, T0118-9692204, F9442210. Small smart riverside hotel, complete with restaurant praised to the skies by no less experienced a diner than director Michael Winner, as well as some luxury riverside cottages for hire.

A The Great House at Sonning, Thames St, Sonning, T0118-9692277, F9441296, www.greathouseat sonning.co.uk. The other smart hotel on the river here, in a beautiful spot, likes to use the word 'luncheon' and its 'country house' furnishings now also look a bit dated.

A White Hart Hotel, Nettlebed, T01491-641245. Individually designed rooms in an immaculate modern pub conversion, like something out of *Elle* magazine, with the superior clean-cut *Nettlebed Restaurant* and *White Hart* pub below, the new venture of Chris Barber, formerly chef to Prince Charles.

Henley-on-Thames and around *p257*

C Appletree Cottage, Backsideans, Wargrave, on the A321 between Reading and Henley, T0118-9404306. A small and secluded cottage tucked away behind the High St of an attractive town 3 miles upriver towards Reading from Henley.

C Avalon 36 Queen St, Henley, T01491-577829. A very central B&B in a Victorian house in Henley.

C Stag and Huntsman, Little Hambleden, north of Henley, T01491-571227. Victorian flint and brick pub with highly rated food and accommodation in a charming old village.

D Flowerpot Hotel, Ferry La, Aston, Near Henley, T01491-574721. A large old Victorian pub which has a prepossessing fishing theme, real wood fires, very reasonably priced grub and big garden. There are big riverside campsites at Hurley and Swiss Farm in Henley (contact TIC for details).

Marlow *p258*

L The Compleat Angler, Marlow Bridge, T0870-4008100, www.heritage-hotels.co.uk. Riverside rooms in a beautifully situated hotel from £208 per night. See also p260.

L Danesfield House, Henley Rd, near Marlow, T01628-891010, www.danesfieldhouse.co.uk. Very grand late-19th-century country house hotel overlooking the Thames Valley, with health spa, swimming pool, and conference facilities.

C Acorn Lodge, 79 Marlow Bottom, Marlow, T01628-472197, small and welcoming B&B run by the Acorn Natural Therapy Centre.

Bray and Maidenhead *p259*

L Cliveden Taplow, T01628-668561, F661837, www.clivedenhouse.co.uk. One of the most luxurious hotels in the country, offering the chance to stay in Nancy Astor's bedroom (about £30,000 for the run of the whole place for 24 hrs, £1200 for the riverside cottage per night including champagne, £900 for most expensive rooms per night, £400 standard) with its oak-panelled hall, library with tremendous views. Restaurants include the French Dining Room with panelling imported by Waldorf from Madame de Pompadour's chateau outside Paris. Set menu £60 for 3 courses in Waldo's, £20 for 2 courses on Terrace, chef from the *Waterside Inn* at Bray.

Eating

Reading *p256*

The Crooked Billet, Stoke Row, Near Reading, T01491-681048. Very good food (especially fish) in a serious wine-lovers' country pub.

Henley-on-Thames and around *p257*

Loch Fyne Restaurant, 20 Market Pl, T01491-845780, is a particularly good branch of the fish-friendly chain, with cool tiles in the oyster bar out front and a barn-like restaurant beyond a cosy bar area.

Marlow *p258*

££ **Compleat Angler** is the top-end option, its 3-course set lunch costing £23.50. Wonderful wraparound views of the river and weir, see also p259.

££ **Da Ciro**, T01628-482180, a decent Italian established in 1980.

££ **Wok Wok**, T01628-488544, for some efficient Chinese.

Cookham *p258*

££ **Alfonso's**, 19 Station Pde, T01628-525775, is an innovative Italian.

££ **Bel and the Dragon**, High St, T01628-521263, is overpriced but does do very good modern European food.

££ **Jolly Farmer**, Cookham Dean, T01628-482905, is a typical 18th-century country pub, not too woefully refurbished.

££ **Malik's**, High St, T01628-520085, is the best Indian restaurant in Cookham, in the old *Royal Exchange* pub, run by renegade Bangladeshi staff from the *Cookham Tandoori* down the road.

Bray and Maidenhead *p259*

£££ **The Fat Duck**, High St, Bray, T01628-580333, is sensational with exotic and unusual combinations that stretch the imagination being conjured up by celebrity chef Blumenthal.

£££ **The Waterside Inn**, Ferry Rd, Bray, T01628-620691, has 3 Michelin stars, – a gourmand's treat by Albert Roux for about £100 a head.

££ **The Belgian Arms**, Holyport, T01628-634468, a friendly old pub overlooking the village green, with no-nonsense pub grub and real ales, not too far from Bray.

££ **The Fish at Bray**, Old Mill La, Bray, T01628-781111, an old pub with a very good fish menu, decent wine list and real ales.

Pubs, bars and clubs

Reading *p256*

Dew Drop Inn, hidden away up the tiny road to Burchetts Green opposite Hurley off the A4130, with good walks in the woods and views over the valley.

Eldon Arms, Eldon St, near the university, is a good old friendly place serving up a decent pint and some reasonable live music.

The Greyhound, Gallowstree Rd, Rotherfield, Peppard, T0118-9722227 £10 main courses, very good value, attractive garden and fishpond.

Sweeney and Todd, 10 Castle St, Reading, T0118-9586466, is a highly individual and inexpensive home-made pie shop and pub with very good real ales.

Clubs

After Dark, 112 London St, T0118-9576847. Grungy indie club with some reasonable live bands every now and then.

The Matrix, 75 London St, Reading, T0118-9590687. On Thu this is a happy combination of 'old, new and future funkin' disco' and very cheap (£1 a drink) booze. Also a platform for UK Garage and hard house artistes.

Henley-on-Thames and around *p257*

The Anchor on Friday St and the Three Tuns in the Market Pl are 2 good pubs of the many in Henley.

Marlow *p258*

The Clayton Arms, Oxford Rd, T01628-478620, is a pigeon-fanciers' and anglers' pub in an old chair-bodgers stopover.

For an explanation of the sleeping and eating price codes used in this guide, see the inside front cover. Other relevant information is provided in the Essentials chapter, page 40.

Entertainment

Reading *p256*

Hexagon, Queen's Walk, Reading, T0118-9606060. A democratic selection of everything from 'An Evening with Keith Harris and Orville' to English Touring Opera productions.

Henley-on-Thames and around *p257*

Kenton Theatre, New St, Henley, T01491-575698. Amateur theatricals and professional touring productions.

Regal Cinema, Bell St, Henley, T01491-414160, www.regalcinema-henley.co.uk. Single screen upper-crust mainstream releases.

Nettlebed Folk Club, T01628-636620, www.nettlebed.freeserve.co.uk. Mon, Wed 2000. Bluegrass and other American acoustic sounds, folk on Mon.

Festivals

Reading to Maidenhead *p255*

Jun Marlow Regatta, third Sat, a 1-day event.

Jul Henley Royal Regatta, T01491-572153, takes place in the first week of Jul (finishes on the first Sun).

Jul Swan-upping in the 3rd week along the river from Cookham to Windsor.

Jul WOMAD, the country's largest festival of world music, takes place in Reading, T01225-744494, www.womad.org.

Aug The Reading Festival is organized by Mean Fiddler group, T020-88961549, a thumping great feast of Aug bank holiday indie rock, dance and always a few suprises.

Sep Cookham Regatta on the 1st Sat.

Shopping

Reading *p256*

Reading has all the major chains and big department stores, including **John Lewis**, House of Fraser and **Debenhams** at 2 malls including the **Oracle**, as well as a few interesting one-offs.

County Delicacies, 35/37 St Marys Butts, T0118-9574653, if you're after some superior picnic provisions – why not take them to the festivals?

The Sound Machine, 24 Harris Arcade, T0118-9575075 and 112 Broad St Mall, Reading T0118-9599040. For rock, pop and indie on CD and vinyl.

Vickers Game Butchers, 20 West St, T0118-9572904, who do some great pies.

Henley-on-Thames and around *p257*

Baileys, 21 Duke St, T01491-573214, a top-class old-fashioned butchers also with a fine array of pies.

Du Vin, 2 Friday St, T01491-637888, a superior wine merchant.

The Ferret, 4 Friday St, T01491-574104, with its intriguing bric-a-brac and affordable 'antiques and things'.

Activities and tours

Boating

Bray Boats, Maidenhead, T01628-637880.

Hobbs of Henley, Station Rd, Henley, T01491-572035. 1-hr trips (£4.25, under-16s £3) on Henley Reach and self-drive motor boat hire. Apr-Sep 0930-1730.

IPG Marine, Marlow, T01895-235347, both run passenger services on the river, and also motor boats for hire at Higginson Park, Marlow.

J Hooper Boat Hire, Riverside 54, Ancastle Green, T01491-576867, downstream from the bridge.

Transport

Reading *p256*

Car

Rabbit Vehicle Hire, Wolsey Rd, Caversham, Reading, T0118-9461661. **Thrifty**, 15 Trafford Rd, Reading, T0118-9511123.

Taxi

1st Yellow Cars Ltd, Reading, T0118-9660666. **Talbot Taxis**, T01491-574222.

Directory

Reading to Maidenhead *p255*

Hospitals Townlands Hospital in Henley (minor injuries), T01491-572544. **Royal Berkshire Hospital**, London Rd, Reading, T0118-9875111. **Police** Kings Rd, Henley T01491-410600.

Windsor and Eton

→ *Colour map 3, grid B1*

Everyone who loves anything royal loves Windsor. English Kings and Queens have lived in the impressive castle that glowers over the town since the 15th century and it remains the monarch's preferred residence. During the First World War it gave a good name to the current royal family (the Saxe-Coburg-Gothas), after a precedent established by Edward III in the 14th century. Easily accessed from London, tourists descend on the place in thousands during the summer and are generally not disappointed. Apart from the castle itself, the town centre is an attractive place to explore and the crowds can easily be escaped in the Great Park or along the river. Over the old bridge, visitors clog up Eton's quirky little High Street on their way to see the world-famous school, one of the oldest in the country. ▸▸ *For Sleeping, Eating and other listings, see pages 265-266.*

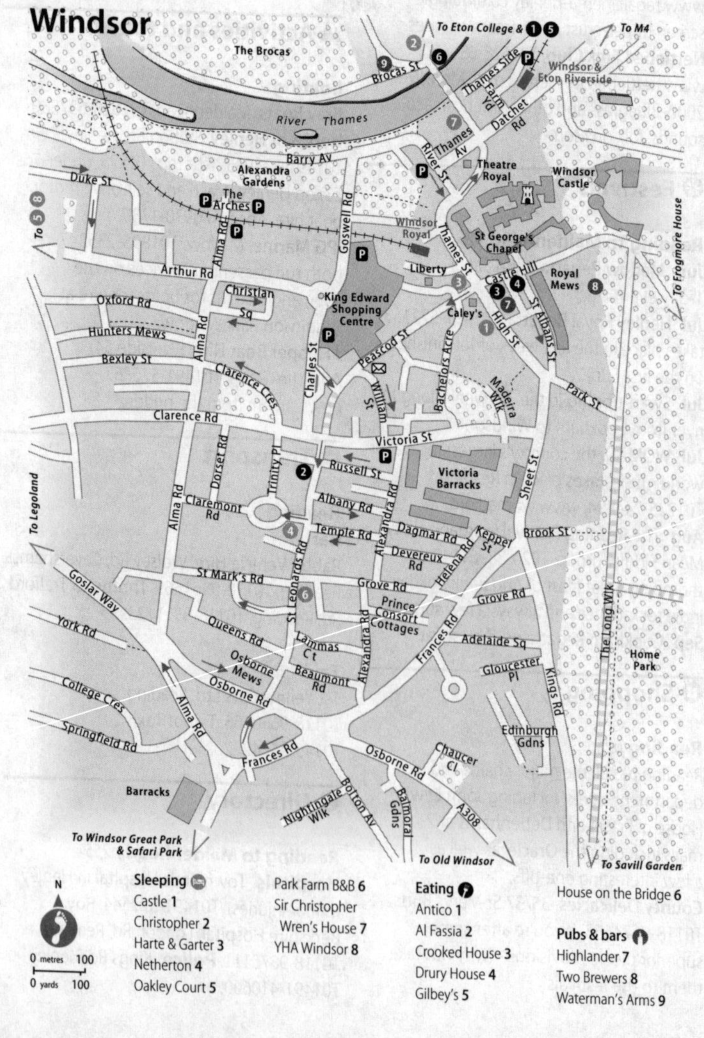

Ins and outs

Getting there South West Trains operate a twice-hourly service from London Waterloo to Windsor and Eton Riverside, taking about 50 minutes. From London Paddington, **Thames Trains**, T0800-3583567, run regular connecting services from Slough (on the mainline from London to Reading) taking 6 minutes. **National Rail Enquiries** T08457-484950. Windsor is just south of the M4, 26 miles from London at Junction 6, a journey from central London that can take 30 minutes to 1 hour, depending on the traffic. **Green Line**, T0870-6087261, operate bus services to Windsor from London. » *For further details, see Transport page 266.*

Getting around The Long Walk stretches dead straight for several miles from the castle gates into the Great Park, but Windsor town centre and the castle are easily small enough to walk around. Eton College is a 15-minute walk from the castle over the river.

Information Royal Windsor TIC ⓘ *24 High St, T01753-743900 (accommodation booking T01753-743907), www.windsor.gov.uk, Mon-Fri, Sun 1000-1600, Sat 1000-1700. Also small free exhibition upstairs on 'Town and Crown'.*

History

Windsor has been associated with the monarchy since William the Conqueror chose to hunt in the local forest, but it wasn't until the reign of Edward III, who was born in the castle and decided to live in the Round Tower, that it became firmly established as their favourite residence. He also sometimes referred to himself as Edward of Windsor, hence the current monarch's surname. In 1348 he also established the order of the Garter in St George's Chapel. When the Emperor Sigismund was made a Companion of the Order in 1416 he brought with him the heart of St George, which was kept in the castle until the reign of Henry VIII. That merry monarch had more than enough other castles to enjoy, his daughter Elizabeth I was very fond of Windsor, though, and used to walk on the castle's famous terrace for an hour before lunch every day, unless it was too windy. According to Daniel Defoe she particularly "loved to walk in a mild calm rain with an umbrella". Apart from the town blacksmith, Windsor declared for Parliament during the Civil War. Even so, on the restoration of the monarchy, Charles II used to spend his summers here and appointed Wren as the castle's Surveyor-General. George III also very much enjoyed the terrace, showing off his large family on processional walks. Under George IV (who raised Edward's Round Tower by 30 ft in 1827) and William IV, the castle became notorious for extravagance, only stamped out when Queen Victoria's husband Prince Albert discovered his staff enjoying a ball dressed up as the 'Queen' and her 'Consort'.

Eton is an older settlement than Windsor and was once almost as large. On its narrow High Street, in the olde-worlde *Cockpit Restaurant* the sunken pit where Charles II liked to watch fighting birds kill each other can still be seen. Eton College was founded by the 20-year-old Henry VI in 1441, closely connected a few years later to King's College, Cambridge. The Lower School, facing the chapel across School Yard, is the original schoolroom, one of the oldest in the country. Upper School was completed in 1694, and the founder's statue erected in 1719. Despite the famous top hat and tails uniform, first worn in mourning for George III, during the 19th century conditions for the boys here were not much better than a workhouse.

Windsor Castle

ⓘ *T01753-869898, www.the-royal-collection.org.uk, (24-hr information line T01753-831118). Mar-Oct daily 0945-1715 (last admission 1600), Nov-Feb daily 0945-1615 (last admission 1500). Semi-State Rooms also open Oct-Mar only. State Rooms usually closed for 1 week mid-to late-Jun and occasionally at other times. £11*

(£5.50 when State Rooms closed), over-60s £9 (£4.50), under-17s £5.50 (£2.70), under-5s free, family £27.50 (£13.70). Guided tours of the restored areas not on the main public route including the medieval Undercroft and Great Kitchen. One tour each morning and afternoon on Tue and Wed Oct-Mar only.

Windsor Castle is hard to miss. Walk uphill anywhere in the town and you'll find yourself beneath its walls. It was built as part of a circle of Norman control around London. Unlike the other castles – Rochester, Tonbridge, Reigate, Berkhampstead, Ongar, Hertford and Guildford, all roughly equidistant from the Tower of London – it has survived intact and been much extended over the centuries. Today, the Royal control extends to banning dogs, radios, mobile phones, bicycles or alcohol from the castle precincts. Founded on a strategic sight affording far-reaching views by William the Conqueror within a day's march of the Tower of London, it ensured the dominance of the invading monarch over the western approaches to the city. The Queen still lives here most of the year. The public are admitted throughout the year (except on state occasions, phone first), to the **State Apartments**, including Charles II's apartments and the Waterloo Chamber, decorated with paintings from the Royal Collection by Van Dyck, Holbein, Rubens and Rembrandt and some very fine furniture; the castles' precincts and Henry VIII's gorgeous Gothic **St George's Chapel**, where 10 sovereigns are buried (and where Edward and Sophie tied the knot). The highlight of the State Apartments is **St George's Hall**, fully restored after the fire in 1992, where the Queen holds banquets and receptions.

From April to June, the **Changing of the Guard** occurs here at 1100 Monday-Saturday. From July to March, the ceremony takes place on alternate days. The best vantage points are the Lower Ward of the Castle or outside on Windsor High Street. During summer, the Semi-State rooms are also open, featuring some of the Castle's most splendid interiors. One very popular curiosity is Queen Mary's Dolls' House, the most famous of its kind in the world, a complete palace built to a scale of 1 in 12 by at least 1,000 master craftsmen in the 1920s. All the little palace's fixtures and fittings are in full working order, including the bathrooms, lifts and electricity supply.

Other sights

South of the Castle stretches the wide expanse of the **Great Park**, most easily reached from town via the fine Georgian street Park Street. Look out for the large and noisy flock of incongruous green parrots at the top of the Long Walk, which runs dead straight south for 3 miles towards a distant statue of George III on horseback. There are very fine views of the castle and Thames Valley from this giant statue, which by car is closest to the Bishop's Gate entrance to the Great Park.

Not inhabited and very rarely open, **Frogmore House** ⓘ *Home Park, T01753-869898, www.royalresidences.com, 3 days in mid-to-late May 1000-1900 (last admission 1800), £3 gardens and mausoleum, under-17s free, Aug bank holiday, 1000-1700 (last admission 1600) £5.20, £3.20*, was Queen Victoria's favourite retreat in Windsor. The house itself is a fairly restrained white Georgian building, but the beautiful landscaped gardens are well worth a glimpse if possible.

In the far eastern corner of the park, the **Savill Garden** ⓘ *Wick La, Englefield Green, Egham, T01753-847518, www.savillgarden.co.uk, daily Mar-Oct 1000-1800, Nov-Feb 1000-1600, Apr-May £5, Jun-Oct £4, Nov-Mar £3 (concessions 50p less)*, is a woodland garden popular with recent monarchs, created in the 30s, and unusual for being open all year.

Back in the town, **Castle Hill** runs down from the visitors' entrance past Henry VIII's gate into Peascod Street, the main shopping drag. The High Street comes up from the south, past the grand Guildhall designed by Wren. The TIC is just opposite, next to the department store *Caleys*. Continuing north, Thames Street runs along the foot of the castle walls down to the river bridge. On the corner of River Street is the birthplace of Robert Keayne 1595-1656, a founder of Harvard University and also of the oldest military organization in America the Honourable and Ancient Artillery Company of Massachusetts in 1638.

Over the bridge, Eton High Street begins, running north for a few hundred yards before fetching up outside **Eton College** ⓘ *T01753-671177, Mar-Oct daily term-time 1400-1630, school holidays 1030-1630, £4.50, ordinary £3.50, guided tours 1415, 1515, includes the Museum of Eton Life*. The guided tours illuminate the history of this the most exclusive boys school in the country, its high fees once described by 'old boy' George Orwell as "a tax the middle classes must pay to join the system".

Around Windsor

Just south of Junction 7 off the M4, **Dorney Court** ⓘ *T01628-604638, May bank holiday Sun and Mon 1330-1630, Aug Mon-Fri, Sun 1330-1630 (last admission 1600), £5, concessions £3*, is a very well-preserved Tudor manor house, replete with early Tudor fireplaces, panelling and fittings, still inhabited by the Palmer family that bought it in 1624. The first pineapple in England was grown in the garden and the 18th-century Kit Kat club used to meet in the house.

Well-signposted from Windsor and the M4, expensive but generally hugely enjoyable, **Legoland** ⓘ *Winkfield Rd, T08705-040404, www.legoland.co.uk, daily mid-Mar to Oct 1000-1800 (until 1900 in late Jul and Aug, until 1700 various days Mar-Jun, Sep-Oct, phone for details), £19, under-15s £16, OAPs £13*, is a fairly large theme park adored by under 12s, with lots of mini rides – castles, rollercoasters, speedboats and waterslides – as well as models using more than 20 million of the plastic bricks with knobs on.

Sleeping

L The Castle Hotel, High St, Windsor, T0870-4008300, F01753-621540. Heritage hotel, as central as it gets, front rooms with views of the castle and changing of the guard.

L Oakley Court Hotel, Windsor Rd, Water Oakley, T01753-609988. Famous film location and now top-end moat house hotel with lawns sloping down to the river.

L Sir Christopher Wren's House Hotel, Thames St, Windsor, T01753-861354, F442490. Individually designed rooms in Sir Christopher's old house which he designed himself down by the river bridge, as well as a top-notch restaurant.

A Christopher Hotel, 110 High St, Eton T01753-852359, www.christopher-hotel.co.uk. Best Western hotel in an old coaching inn with *Renata's* restaurant.

A Harte and Garter Hotel, High St, Windsor, T01753-863426, F830527. Beneath the castle walls although a little shabby for the price.

B Netherton Hotel, 98-98 St Leonard's Rd, Windsor, T01753-855508, F621267. Family-run hotel within walking distance of the Castle.

C Park Farm B&B, St Leonard's Rd, Windsor, T01753-866823, F850869. Smart and fairly central guesthouse.

F YHA Windsor, Edgeworth House, Mill La, Windsor, T01753-861710, F832100. In a big old house on the outskirts of town.

Eating

Fine dining has really yet to arrive in Windsor, marginalized perhaps by the establishments upstream at Bray.

£££ Al Fassia, 27 St Leonard's Rd, Windsor, T01753-855370 (about £30 a head) has a good reputation for its North African food served up in a friendly and intimate atmosphere.

£££ Antico, 42 High St, Eton, T01753-863977, is a long-established Italian very popular with the locals.

£££ Gilbey's Bar and Restaurant, 82 High St, Eton, T01753-854921, is also usually busy, a wine bar with a fairly expensive menu.

For an explanation of the sleeping and eating price codes used in this guide, see the inside front cover. Other relevant information is provided in the Essentials chapter, page 40.

£££ The House on the Bridge, Windsor Bridge, Eton, T01753-860941, does accomplished French cooking for about £40 a head, £30 set menus.

Cafés

Tearooms abound in Windsor town. Two archetypal examples of the genre are:
Crooked House, Queen Charlotte St (apparently the shortest street in Britain), is a funny little non-smoking tearoom doing real clotted Cornish cream teas next to the impressive Guildhall.
Drury House, 'Windsor's oldest teashop', at 4 Church St, right opposite King Henry VIII gate.
Pret a Manger, on the main drag of Peascod St, this is allegedly where the Queen likes to order her sandwiches from.
Waitrose in the *The King Edward Court Shopping Centre*, for picnic materials.
Windsor Farm Shop, Datchet Rd, Old Windsor, T01753-623800, offer food and drink from the Royal Farms and Royal Dairy.

Eton High St is something of a Mecca for collectors, with a string of quirky independents and collectors shops, like: **Asquiths Teddy Bear Shop**, 32 High St, T01753-831200, leather goods specialists; **Clarke and Co**, 103 High St, T01753-862824; **Rose and Co Apothecary**, 61 High St, T01753-622160.

Pubs, bars and clubs

Highlander on Church La, is worth seeking out for its Caley 80 ale and reasonably priced grub.
The Two Brewers, 34 Park St, Windsor, T01753-855426 a cosy old place at the entrance to the Long Walk in the Great Park, doing a fairly ambitious menu decently enough.
Waterman's Arms Brocas St, Eton is a traditional local close to the river.

Entertainment

Theatre Royal, T01753-853888. The local repertory theatre for touring and amateur productions.
Windsor Arts Centre, St Leonard's Rd, T01753-859336, www.windsorarts centre.org. Small independent repertory cinema, theatre, gallery, dance and music venue with an innovative and often exciting programme of events.

Shopping

Caleys of Windsor, High St, Windsor, T01753-863241, is the town's department store, a branch of **John Lewis**, next to the **Castle Hotel**.
Liberty, Station Pde in the old station includes the only branch of the store outside London as well as plenty of other posh names.

Activities and tours

For walking along the Thames Path, contact National Trails Office T01865-810224.
French Brothers Ltd, Clewer Boathouse, Clewer Court Rd, Windsor T01753-851900 Easter-Oct 1100-1700, boat trips.
Orchard Poyle Carriage Hire, T01784-435983, T07836-766027 (mob). 30 min £19, 1 hr £38. Victorian Hackney carriage pulled by 2 bay horses.

Transport

Bicycle

Windsor Cycle Hire, Alexander Gardens, Windsor, T01753-830220.

Car

D.J.B Self Drive Hire, Homelands, North St, Winkfield, T01344-890608; **Baldocks**, 43-44 The Arches, Alma Rd, Windsor, T01753-868870.

Taxi

Windsor Radio Cars, 59b St. Leonards Rd, T01753-677677.

Directory

Hospitals King Edward VII Hospital, St Leonard's Rd, Windsor, T01753-860441.

Chilterns and St Albans

➔ *Colour map 3, grid B/A1*

The Chiltern hills stretch from near Henley-on-Thames in the south to just beyond Tring in the north, almost as far as the Midlands. These rolling chalky hills are often overlooked by visitors heading for Oxfordshire or stopping at Windsor, even though they offer some superb open and wooded walking country, as well as a handful of the prettiest villages in the south. That said, it's also the greenback belt – the expensive and closely guarded northwestern homeland of the high-salaried London commuter – and hence hardly goes out of its way to advertise its charms. The M40 motorway slices through the middle of the region, choked every morning and evening, although thanks to some sensitive landscaping, it leaves much of the surrounding countryside undisturbed. The model village at Beaconsfield enshrines the kind of dream village many of the cars would like to come from and that can still be found nestling nearby. To the north, with its hilltop cathedral, St Albans is the most historically interesting town within 20 miles of London, where even a fleeting visit provides an insight into the developing course of English settlements since the Iron Age. ➧ *For Sleeping, Eating and other listings, see pages 275-277.*

Chiltern Hundreds

From proper old Beaconsfield with its model of Little England in the east, to the Goring gap on the river in the west, the southern end of the Chiltern hills is the most well-to-do and the most accessible region of these chalky woodlands. Their low ridges are capped with magnificent beech trees planted to provide wood for City carriages and Windsor chairs. Their dry valleys shelter well-ordered commuter villages with cosy pubs, providing fine walking country within easy reach of London. They're also blessed with a surprising profusion of flora and fauna, including rare orchids and red kites. Just south of the M40 but a world away from the rush of the big road, the pretty villages of Turville, Fingest and Ibstone are each good starting or finishing points for exploratory rambles. To the north, High Wycombe isn't much to write home about, although just next door West Wycombe is a peculiar survival: a village bought by the Royal Society of Arts in the 1920s, now in the hands of the National Trust. Its single old street is complemented by the strange follies at West Wycombe Park and the caves where its owner Sir Francis Dashwood held his Hellfire Club revels in the 18th century.

Ins and outs

Getting there High Wycombe and Beaconsfield are served by **Chiltern Railways,** T08705-165165, from London Marylebone, on the line to Birmingham via Bicester, Banbury and Leamington Spa. Journey times to Beaconsfield about 30 minutes, to High Wycombe about 35 minutes. There's also another line from London via Aylesbury which goes to Great Missenden and Princes Risborough. The southern Chilterns can be reached most easily on the M40, which slices through the hills between junctions 5 and 6, about 30 minutes' drive from central London. ➧ *For further details, see Transport page 276.*

Getting around A **car** is unfortunately the only really practical way of exploring the Chilterns. Local **buses** to the more attractive villages and walking areas are few and far between.

 Information High Wycombe TIC ⓘ *Paul's Row, T01494-421892, Mon-Sat, 0930-1700.* **Thame TIC** ⓘ *Market House, North St, T01844-212834, www.thame.net Mon-Fri 0930-1700, Sat and Sun, 1000-1600.*

Beaconsfield

The star attraction in Beaconsfield is well-signposted off the M40. A five-minute walk from the station, the 'model village' called **Bekonscot** ⓘ *Warwick Rd, Beaconsfield, T01494-672919, www.bekonscot.org.uk, Feb-Oct daily 1000-1700, £4.50, under-15s £2.75, concessions £3.50, family £12.50*, was started in 1929 by Roland Callingham as a hobby and now claims to be the oldest of its type in the world. About 1½ acres of little paths and waterways are dotted with 2-ft tall model houses served by the most extensive gauge 1 model railway in the country. Billing itself as "a little piece of history that is forever England", it certainly preserves a typically 1930s vision of little England: cricket on the green, windmills and even a fishing fleet. Children are thrilled by the small scale of everything and spotting what's going on around the place.

Bekonscot nestles in the heart of Beaconsfield New Town, although half a mile up the hill **Beaconsfield Old Town** looks more like it could have been the inspiration for the model village. Like Amersham, just to the north, this ancient crossroads on the Oxford to London road just about maintains some 18th-century dignity under the onslaught of traffic. GK Chesterton lived here for most of his life, in a house with a theatre for a dining room, opposite what is now the National Film and Television School. The great orator and interpolator of 'the sublime', Edmund Burke, is buried in the church, close to a strange lodge house for the old Hall Barn estate clad entirely in carved black Renaissance oak.

Milton's Cottage

ⓘ *Deanway, Chalfont St Giles, T01494-872313, Mar-Oct Tue-Sun 1000-1300, 1400-1800, £2.50, under-15s £1.*

Three miles northeast of Beaconsfield, beyond Jordans (where William Penn, his two wives and five of his children are buried next to the atmospheric old Quaker Meeting House) in Chalfont St Giles, Milton's Cottage is one of the few memorials to England's greatest epic poet. Fleeing the plague in London, Milton stayed in this 'pretty box' for 11 months finishing *Paradise Lost*. A fine collection of his works can be seen, the sweet garden enjoyed, and the curator is happy to share his enthusiasm for the great blind poet and his works.

Burnham Beeches

Two miles south of Beaconsfield, Burnham Beeches is an ancient and beautifully maintained stretch of rolling woodland. The fantastic shapes of the old trees are the result of 400 years of pollarding, when the beeches provided a sustainable supply of wood for the City of London's carriage wheels – iron rims were banned in the square mile because they cut up the streets. The woods are still owned by the Corporation of London and are understandably very popular in the autumn when the fallen leaves are a joy to go kicking through.

High Wycombe and around

Six miles west of Beaconsfield, High Wycombe (pronounced *Wick'em*) is the largest town in the area, a sprawling and fairly unappealing place on the river Wye. That said, the **Wycombe Swan Theatre** ⓘ *T01494-512000*, has an enviable reputation for modern dance. Just to the north of the town, in a surprisingly peaceful valley, **Hughenden Manor** ⓘ *(NT), Valley Rd, High Wycombe, T01494-755573, house Mar weekends 1300-1700, Apr-Oct Wed-Sun 1300-1700, £4.30, under-16s £2.15, family £10.50, garden only £1.50*, is an 18th-century manor occupied by Queen Victoria's favourite PM, Benjamin Disraeli, with nine rooms still furnished much as he might have left them in the late 19th century. His wife's garden is a riot of colour every summer, and the surrounding park and woodlands a tranquil retreat.

West Wycombe and around

A couple of miles west of High Wycombe, **West Wycombe** could hardly be more different from the High one. A single street of 16th-18th-century houses has been preserved by the National Trust, along with reminders of some of the area's traditional livelihoods, like the chair bodgers that once knocked up a wooden chair a minute. Far from being too nicely pickled or over-restored, West Wycombe remains quite dilapidated, struggling to cope with the traffic along the A40. Overlooking the village behind long walls is **West Wycombe House** ⓘ *(NT), T01494-513569, grounds only Apr-May Mon-Thu, Sun 1400-1800, house and grounds Jun-Aug Mon-Thu, Sat 1400-1800 (last admission to time with tours 1715), house and grounds £5, £2.50, family £12.60, grounds only £2.60*, the home of the Dashwood family since the 18th century. Most extraordinary is the Rococo landscape garden surrounding the striking Italianate house. Various classical temples and follies are artfully dotted about the lakes and artificial vistas. The interior of the house is famous for its Palmyrene ceilings.

Overlooking West Wycombe House to the north are the **church, mausoleum and caves** ⓘ *caves, T01494-533739, Mar-Oct daily 1100-1730, Nov-Feb weekends 1100-1730, £3.50, concessions £2.50*, built in the 1750s by the first Sir Francis Dashwood on the site of an old quarry. The surprisingly extensive caves have been turned into a visitor attraction, complete with ridiculous mannequins in 18th-century costume representing Dashwood's famous friends: the likes of Benjamin Franklin, Lord Sandwich and radical MP John Wilkes, some of them members of the scandalous Hellfire Club. In some ways the church, standing in an Iron Age hill fort, with its interior copied from the Sun Temple at Palmyra in Syria and offering superb views from its tower, as well as the hexagonal roofless mausoleum next door, combine to make more of an impression than the tacky caves beneath.

A minor road left off the A40 just west of West Wycombe leads under the M40 and into one of the most picturesque parts of the Chilterns. In the village of **Fingest**, the old church of St Bartholomew looks very venerable with its Norman double-capped tower beneath hanging beech woods. Next door, Turville is even more cute, (and was used as the location for the TV comedy series the *Vicar of Dibley*), while the Fingest to Ibstone road runs high along a ridge past a renovated windmill (private) and down a deep dell past a lonely Saxon church.

From Northend, 2 miles west of Turville, a beautiful walk leads north up into the hills to the **Chiltern Sculpture Trail** ⓘ *T01865-723684, daily all year*, where 22 contemporary sculptures by the likes of Laura Ford and Andrew Sabin are carefully sited in a small young wood on the Chiltern escarpment. Especially well worth seeking out is Anya Gallaccio's *Forest floor*, 1996, a kind of outdoor room, a simple square of carpet with young trees growing through it. Catch it while it quietly rots. Over the road, overlooking Oxfordshire, is the **Aston Rowant Nature Reserve** ⓘ *run by English Nature, T01844-351833*, a wild preserve for rare orchids, juniper and yew scrub, beech, ash, and wild cherry.

Another 2 miles south of Northend, rarely open but worth a look on a summer Sunday afternoon, is one of the oldest continuously occupied Roman Catholic aristocratic seats in the country. The 18th-century red-brick façade of Lord and Lady Camoys' home at **Stonor** ⓘ *T01491-638587, www.stonor.com, Apr-Sep Sun, bank holidays (also Jul, Aug on Wed) 1400-1730 (last admission 1700), house and garden £4.50, gardens only £2.50*, conceals a 13th-century interior and chapel, magnificently sited in a Chiltern valley, surrounded by a deer park and terraced gardens. A shrine to recusancy.

Hundreds of Aylesbury and around

Although Aylesbury itself is hardly a tourist destination, the Chiltern towns along the Icknield Way and the Ridgeway to its southeast are quite popular with walking weekenders from London. For good reason: Wendover is the most charming little place, with its gently sloping old high street and clock tower. Neighbouring Tring, tucked beneath the splendid viewpoint at Ivinghoe Beacon, also boasts an extraordinary and exotic outpost of the Natural History Museum in the form of the Walter Rothschild Zoological Museum, a glass-cased Victorian array of stuffed animals and even insects. The Rothschilds' other contribution to the region was even more striking, Waddesdon Manor, a grand 19th-century replica of a Renaissance French chateau, now home to one of the most impressive collections of pre-Revolutionary French decorative art in the world.

Ins and outs

Getting there By **train,** Amersham is at the top of the Metropolitan tube line, slow journey time just over 1 hour and 30 minutes from Baker St in central London. Aylesbury, Wendover and Amersham are all on the mainline from Marylebone run by **Chiltern Railways,** T08705-165165, with about two trains an hour taking just over an hour to Aylesbury. Tring can be reached from London Euston, twice an hr on services run by **Silverlink Trains,** T08457-818919, taking about 40 minutes. Usually accessed via the notoriously congested dual-carriageway A41 from Junction 20 on the M25 (off Junction 5 of the M1), Aylesbury is surprisingly hard to reach considering its position at such an important road junction. The journey from central London is likely to take at least an hour and 20 minutes. At busy times, and certainly from west London, it can be quicker to use the M40, getting off at Junction 2 for Amersham and then taking the A413 via Wendover.

Getting around As with the Chilterns further south, a **car** is easily the most convenient way of exploring the area. Many of the local **buses,** such as they are, are run by **Arriva,** T0870-7288188 and **Red Rose Travel,** T01296-399500.

Information **Aylesbury TIC** ⓘ *8 Bourbon St, T01296-330559.* **Wendover TIC** ⓘ *The Clock Tower, High St, T01296-696759, www.chilternweb.co.uk/wendover.*

Chenies

Quite a surprise just 3 miles northwest of Junction 18 on the M25, Chenies must be one of the most unspoilt estate villages in the Chilterns. As well as a decent pub and hotel (see below), an attractive church and village green, it comes complete with an imposing red-brick **Tudor manor house** ⓘ *T01494-762888, Apr-Oct Wed, Thu, bank holidays 1400-1700, house and garden £5, under-15s £2.50, gardens only £3, under-15s £1.50,* built by the first Earl of Bedford, Lord Privy Seal to Henry VIII. The gardens created by the present owner are a treat, including a medieval well and early 16th-century banqueting house, while ancient tapestries, furniture and paintings decorate the interior of the main house.

Amersham

Three miles further west on the same road, Amersham is an attractive and dignified old town with an impressive town hall bang in the middle of its 18th-century High Street. The railway station is in the new town, called Amersham on the Hill, separated from the old pubs and antique atmosphere of the original town by a Tesco's superstore off the bypass roundabout.

Around Wendover

The A413 bypass continues northwest towards Aylesbury, passing Great Missenden where children's author Roald Dahl lived for much of his writing life in Gypsy Cottage, and reaches Wendover after about 9 miles. Wendover nestles prettily in a gap in the hills on the edge of the Chilterns. Short walks out of town lead up onto the Ridgeway and there's a very helpful tourist information outfit housed in the clock tower at the bottom of the old High Street.

Tring

Tring, 5 miles northeast of Wendover, is another ancient market town, where the Ridgeway hands over to the Icknield Way as it heads into the East Midlands. Most unusual here though is the **Walter Rothschild Zoological Museum** ⓘ *Akeman St, Tring, T020-79426171, Mon-Sat 1000-1700, Sun 1400-1700, free*. Now an outpost of the Natural History Museum in London, the land and money to build the place was given to Walter on his 21st birthday in 1889 by his father, who considered his son's interest to be no more than an absorbing hobby. Little did he realize that this hobby would eventually amass one of the largest single collections of stuffed wildlife in the world. The museum today preserves its Victorian design and layout, the glass cases and wrought ironwork considerable craftworks in themselves. Highlights of the collection's mildly ghoulish fascination (very popular with children), spread out over six different galleries, are the grinning polar bear, dead giant tortoises, cheeky-looking fox, a disturbing array of stuffed dogs, and the tiny pair of dressed fleas in the fish gallery. One room has been set out as a Victorian office to give some idea of the salubrious conditions in which the original curators worked, but there's sadly not much information on exactly how such an extraordinary variety of animals, reptiles, insects and fish from across the globe ended up pickled in this small Buckinghamshire town.

Aldbury

A mile's walk eastwards uphill from Tring station (itself a mile to the east of the town) brings you into Aldbury, a pretty village on the edge of the National Trust's extensive **Ashridge Estate** ⓘ *T01442-851227*, where there are fine woodland and high downland walks with wide views over the Vale of Aylesbury. The best view of all, and also the most popular, is from **Ivinghoe Beacon**, at the very northern end of the Chilterns, about 4 miles north of Tring.

Aylesbury

Aylesbury is the administrative centre of Buckinghamshire, almost completely overwhelmed with major road roundabouts. In Church Street, the **Bucks County Museum** ⓘ *Church St, Aylesbury, T01296-331441, www.buckscc.gov.uk/museum, Mon-Sat 1000-1700, Sun 1400-1700*, is worth a look if you happen to be passing through, especially with children and time on your hands. Part of this innovative local history museum includes the Roald Dahl Children's Gallery, which features the Fantastic Mr Fox's tunnel and also the Giant Peach.

Waddesdon Manor

ⓘ *(NT), near Aylesbury, T01296-653203, www.waddesdon.org.uk, grounds Mar-Dec Wed-Sun 1000-1700, house Apr-Oct Wed-Sun 1100-1600 (by timed ticket, T01296-653226 for advance booking plus £3), grounds £3, under-15s £1.50, family £7.50 (Nov, Dec free), house £7, under-15s £6 (needs grounds ticket too).*

A huge mock-Renaissance French chateau has been plonked on a hilltop in the middle of the Buckinghamshire countryside. Waddesdon Manor, 5 miles northwest of Aylesbury, was built in the 1870s by Baron Ferdinand de Rothschild as an extravagant expression of his family's success in bankrolling the Napoleonic Wars. The gardens feature some beautiful statuary and the house itself is stuffed with a world-beating collection of 18th-century French treasures calmly overlooked by a few Englishmen beautifully portrayed by Thomas Gainsborough. The house and garden have been painstakingly restored since 1996, enshrining a fantastic example of Victorian opulence and exhibitionism.

St Albans

Hertfordshire is oddly hidden away, usually dismissed by Londoners as an expensive suburb, but much of it is rural enough, away from all the main roads thundering north. With the possible exception of Windsor in the west, St Albans is the most tourist-orientated and certainly the most tourist-friendly town within easy reach of London. A modern commuter town as well, it provides the opportunity to appreciate at a glance the development of a small English city over the last 2000 years. Buried beneath municipal football pitches in Verulamium Park, the Roman fortified town is overlooked by the great Norman abbey church, its tower built using Roman bricks. From the park itself the whole monastic complex seems to float above the trees beside the lake. A continuously prosperous northern satellite of London, at the very least St Albans makes for a very pleasant day trip from the capital.

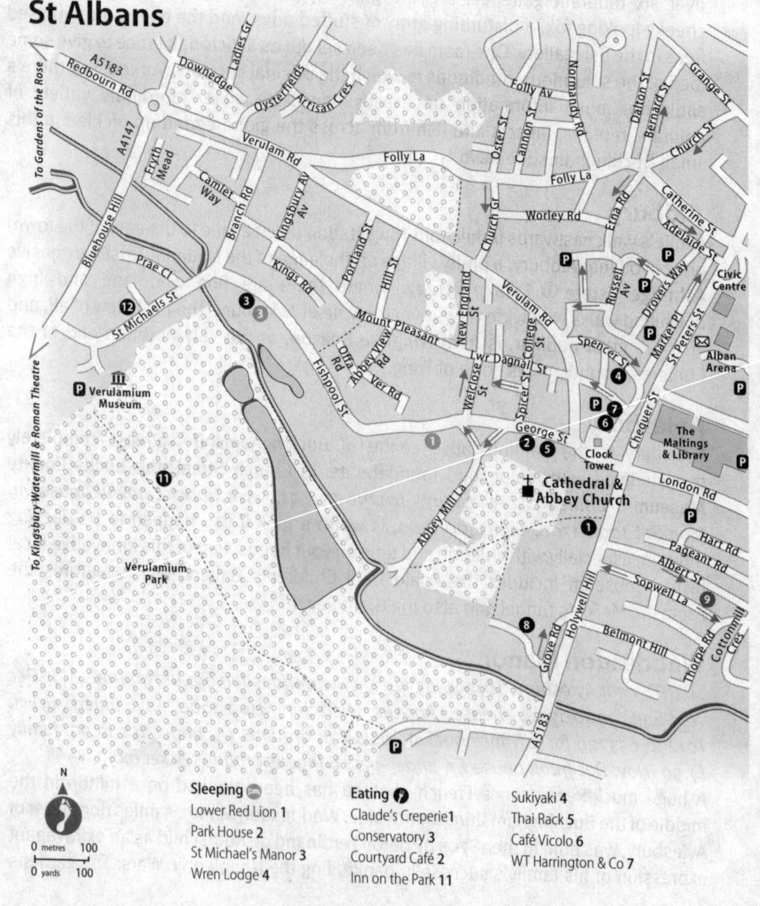

Ins and outs

Getting there St Albans is on the King's Cross **Thameslink** line from Luton via London to Brighton, about four **trains** an hour, journey time usually about 20 minutes. By **road**, St Albans is 20 miles from London, just off the M25 at Junction 21a, near M1 junction 6. Journey time from central London is usually about 45 mins. **Green Line** buses run services from west London to St Albans, also connected by **bus** to Luton. ▸▸ *For further details, see Transport page 276.*

Getting around St Albans' small town centre is perfectly manageable on **foot** and also surprisingly easy to park a **car** in or near.

Information St Albans TIC ⓘ *Town Hall, T01727-864511, www.stalbans.gov.uk, Easter-Oct Mon-Sat 0930-1730, Jul-mid-Sep also Sun 1030-1600, Nov-Easter Mon-Sat 1000-1600.*

History

Named after England's first Christian martyr, a Roman soldier called Albanus who was beheaded in 303 for protecting the priest that had converted him, St Albans started life in the Iron Age when it was known as Verlamion, 'the settlement above the marsh', and the tribal capital of the Catuvellauni. It was captured by Julius Caesar in 54BC and Beech Bottom Dyke, a few miles to the northeast of the modern city, is the place to see all that remains of their town. They collaborated peacefully with the Roman invaders, ensuring the prosperity and prestige of what then became Verulamium but infuriating Boudicca, Queen of the Iceni, who razed the town to the ground in AD 61 on her way from Colchester to London. During the Dark Ages, in 793, King Offa of Mercia founded a Benedictine abbey on the hilltop site of St Albanus' execution, already a Romano-Christian shrine. By the Middle Ages the abbey became the wealthiest and most prestigious in England, educating Nicholas Breakspeare, the only Englishman ever to become Pope, as Adrian IV in 1154. After the monastery's dissolution by Henry VIII, the market town still prospered, benefiting from the coaching trade and has since become a prosperous base for London commuters.

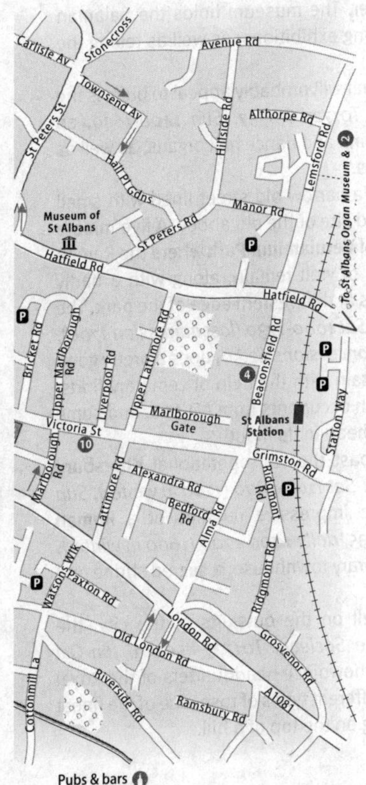

Pubs & bars
Duke of Marlborough **8**
Goat Inn **9**
Horn **10**
Rose & Crown **12**

Cathedral

ⓘ *The Cathedral and Abbey Church of St Alban, Sumpter Yard, T01727-860780. Daily 0900-1745 (guided tours T01727-890200). Services Mon-Fri 0700, 0730, 1700, Sat 0830, 0900, 1600, Sun 0800, 0930, 1100, 1215, 1830.*

 Although by no means the most beautiful cathedral in the country, St Albans is one of the most dramatically situated (along with Lincoln) and also has the longest nave. The central crossing remains much as it was when built by the first Norman abbot, Paul of Caen, and completed in 1116. The nave achieved its claim to fame by 1235 and the east end of the church was also remodelled from that date until the early 14th century. Sir George Gilbert Scott began restoration in 1856 but the west front was badly mucked around a little later by Lord Grimthorpe, a fanatical ecclesiastical and architectural controversialist. Highlights of the interior include the 13th-century wall paintings, including one of the Crucifixion by Walter of Colchester, and St Albans chapel with a monument to the brother of Henry V, Humphrey, Duke of Gloucester decorated with the only surviving pre-Reformation statues of English kings.

Other sights

The centre of the town is the **Clock Tower** ⓘ *Market Pl, open Easter-Oct weekends 1030-1700*, put up by the townsfolk in the early years of the 15th century as a statement of their independence from the all-powerful abbey, overlooking the city and the only surviving medieval belfry in the country. Its bell, cast in 1355, is known as Gabriel. The views from the top are well worth the very small admission fee.

The market place runs north from the tower as St Peter's St to the **Museum of St Albans** ⓘ *Hatfield Rd, T01727-819340, Mon-Sat 1000-1700, Sun 1400-1700, free*, on the right just before the church of St Peter. The museum holds the Salaman collection of trade tools, and mounts interesting exhibitions, as well as telling the story of the city after the Romans had gone.

Some way out of town, another museum that will probably appeal to buffs is the **St Albans Organ Museum** ⓘ *326 Camp Rd, T01727-851557, Sun 1400-1630*, an extensive collection of Wurlitzer and other cinema and dance hall organs, as well as mechanical pianos and Victorian musical boxes.

South of the Clock Tower, **French Row** is a narrow old street lined with small shops leading down towards the cathedral and site of the old abbey. A five-minute walk down Abbeymill Lane reaches the edge of **Verulamium Park** where the Roman town once stood. Quite substantial sections of wall remain, along with a badly vandalized hypocaust, but the star attraction is at the western edge of the park. The **Verulamium Museum** ⓘ *T01727-751810, Mon-Sat 1000-1730 (last admission 1700), Sun 1400-1730 (last admission 1700), £3.50, concessions £2.50*, does a pretty good job of illuminating everyday life in Roman Britain with the help of cemetery finds, including Roman pottery, coffins complete with occupants from AD 200, and some impressive mosaics of a lion holding a stag's head in its mouth.

A 5-minute walk west of the museum, past the still operational **Kingsbury Watermill** ⓘ *St Michael's, T01727-853502, Tue-Sat 1100-1800 (1700 in winter), Sun 1200-1800 (1700 in winter), £1.20*, are the impressive remains of a **Roman amphitheatre** ⓘ *Bluehouse Hill, T01727-835035, daily 1000-1700 (1600 in winter), free*, as well as the foundations of a contemporary townhouse, a sacred shrine and a Roman shop.

Still heading west, just beyond Chilswell on the outskirts of the city, the **Gardens of the Rose** ⓘ *(Royal National Rose Society), T01727-850461, Jun-Oct Mon-Sat 0900-1700, Sun 1000-1800*, is the showpiece headquarters of the Royal National Rose Society. Here are over 30,000 different types of rose, one of the finest collections in the world, in an inspiring setting on the top of a hill.

Sleeping

Chiltern Hundreds *p267*

B Chequers Inn Hotel, Kiln La, Wooburn Common, T01628-529575, www.chequers-inn.com. 17th-century tavern done up in a typically country commuter belt style with a popular restaurant.

C George and Dragon, High St, West Wycombe, T01494-464414, www.george-and-dragon.co.uk. An ancient coaching inn, a couple of old rooms with 4-poster beds.

C Little Parmoor Farm B&B, Frieth, T01494-88160. R&F Emmett, brick and flint farm up on the downs.

D Swan Inn, High St, West Wycombe, T01494-527031. Has bags of character, does just passable food but in an environment seemingly unchanged since the 50s or early 60s. Extraordinary.

F Bradenham YHA Bradenham, High Wycombe, T01895-673188, T01494-562929. Within walking distance of Saunderton train station, a small hostel in an old schoolhouse in the National Trust village of Bradenham, a good launchpad for walks into the Chilterns.

F Jordans Youth Hostel, Welders La, Jordans, near Beaconsfield, T01494-873135, F875907. Open Apr-Dec, small wooden lodge in 2 acres of grounds with 22 beds in dormitories and family rooms.

Hundreds of Aylesbury and around *p270*

L Hartwell House, Oxford Rd, Near Aylesbury, T01296-747444, www.hartwell-house.com. Easily the best luxury option in the area, an immaculately restored stately home in acres of landscaped parkland, where King Louis XVIII of France waited for Bonaparte to be defeated, with health spa, swimming pool and lots of antiques.

A Bedford Arms Hotel, Chenies, Rickmansworth, T01923-283301, www.bedfordarms-hotel-chenies.com. Award-winning restaurant in an old country pub done up to be more country house hotel. Sat bar lunches particularly good value.

C The Red Lion Hotel, High St, Wendover, T01296-622266. Fairly basic accommodation in an old coaching inn-cum-pub in the middle of town.

D Dunsmore Edge, London Rd, Wendover, T01296-623080. Upmarket B&B close to the Ridgeway surrounded by farmland.

D Severn House, 127 High St, Old Amersham, T/F01494 725352. Comfortable B&B in period home right on Old Amersham's characterful High St.

St Albans *p272, map p272*

L St Michael's Manor, Fishpool St, T01727-864444, www.stmichaels manor.com. A very peaceful place for a full pampering with a beautiful garden and top-notch restaurant.

C Lower Red Lion, 34 Fishpool St, T01727-855669, is one of the city's many real ale pubs (also does rooms) in a 17th-century coaching inn.

C Park House, 30 The Park, T01727-832054. 3 double rooms in a comfortable, fairly central B&B.

C Wren Lodge, 24 Beaconsfield Rd, T01727-855540. A comfortable ETB recommended B&B with 4 double rooms.

Eating

Chiltern Hundreds *p267*

££ Bull and Butcher, Turville, good value food, including Brunswick Stew apparently made with squirrel. Jolly and welcoming landlord a fount of local knowledge.

££ The Crown Inn, Pishill, a 15th-century brick-built food pub with real fires.

££ Yew Tree, Frieth, T01494-882330. Very 70s menu, country pub and restaurant £13 main courses.

St Albans *p272, map p272*

£££ The Conservatory, St Michael's Manor, Fishpool St, T01727-864444. The closest St Albans comes to a gourmet modern British restaurant, in a pleasant greenhouse affair with lawns and lake, about £40 a head for dinner.

££ Claude's Creperie, 15 Holywell Hill, T01727-846424, as it says on the label, and for some reliable Italian staples,

££ Sukiyaki, 6 Spencer St, St Albans, Herts T01727-865009 is an excellent Japanese restaurant doing good value set lunches for around £10.

££ Thai Rack, 13 George St, T01727-850055, is very popular for its Royal Thai cuisine in a theatrical setting.
£ Café Vicolo, 3 French Row, T01727-860609.
£ The Courtyard Café, 9 George St, T01727-844233, has a sweet little secret garden.
£ Inn on the Park, open daily, near the Verulamium Museum. In the park itself, good coffee and snacks (no alcohol) can be had indoors or out.
£ WT Harrington and Co, 3 Market Pl, T01727-853039, is the place to pick up a fine handmade sandwich or pie in the centre of town.

Pubs, bars and clubs

St Albans *p272, map p272*
Duke of Marlborough, 110 Holywell Hill, T01727-858982, for its beers and position near Verulamium Park.
The Goat Inn, 37 Sopwell La, T01727-833934, an ancient real ale provider.
The Horn, Victoria St, T01727-853143 does Sun lunchtime jazz.
Rose and Crown, 10 St Michael St, T01727-851903, close to the Abbey, another old pub specializing in American sandwiches.

Entertainment

St Albans *p272, map p272*
Abbey Theatre T01727-857861, for small to mid-scale touring productions.
The Alban Arena, T01727-844488, www.alban-arena.co.uk, for the big-name acts.
Maltings Arts Theatre, T01727-844222, for smaller performances.

Shopping

St Albans *p272, map p272*
Main market every Wed and Sat, art market on Sun during the summer. **Farmers Market** in the market square on the 2nd Sun of every month 1000-1500.

Antique, crafts and specialist shops on High St, George St and Holywell Hill, such as **Clarks Camera Centre**, 14 Holywell Hill, T01727-852991, for repairs, films and wide-range of secondhand and new cameras.
James of St Albans, 11 George St, T01727-856996. Antiques, teddy bears and gifts.
Lawrence and Goodman, 12 George St, T01727-852112, for handmade furniture.
Paton Books, 34 Holywell Hill, T01727-853984, www.patonbooks.co.uk. Large secondhand stock.

Festivals

St Albans *p272, map p272*
Jul St Albans Festival biannually from 2004, T01727-844222. A classical music and theatre festival.
Jul St Albans International Organ Festival, biannually, from 2003, T01727-844765, www.organfestival.com.
Aug St Albans Carnival during the Bank Holiday, with processions, bands, and a lot of drinking.
Sep/Oct CAMRA Beer Festival in last week of Sep or early Oct, www.hertsale.org.uk.

Activities and tours

St Albans *p272, map p272*
Chiltern Chuggers Dayboat Hire, Bulbourne, Near Tring, T01442-827673, on the Grand Union Canal. For messing about in boats.
The Flitch Way through Hatfield Forest, T01799-510490, is idea for bicycle rides.
Westminster Lodge Leisure Centre, St Albans, T01727-846031, close to Verulamium park, free car park, waterslides (aquazoom), huge swimming pool.

Tours
Free guided tours, T01727-833001, leave the Clock Tower on Sun at 1115 and 1500, and from Verulamium Museum at 1415 and during summer also on Wed from the Clock Tower at 1500.
St Albans Travel Service, 4a Spencer St, T01727-866533.

Transport

St Albans *p272, map p272*
Bus
Sovereign Bus, T01727-854732, runs the regular direct Intalink services to **Luton** (45 mins) and **Cambridge** (2 hrs 20 mins) at

0939 changing at **Luton**. National Express, T08705-808080, runs the hourly direct service to **London Victoria** (1 hr 10 mins). The regular service to **Stansted airport** (1 hr 40 mins) changing at University of Herts is run by **University Buses**, T01707-255764, and **Cambridge Coach Services**, T08705-757747. There are no direct services to Oxford or Ipswich.

Car
St Albans Car and Van Hire, 138 St Albans Rd, Sandridge, T01727-838151. Thrifty, 39 London Rd, T01727-811815.

Taxi
Alban Cab Co, T01727-837777. City Cabs, T01727-868687.

Train
City Station, Station Way, (off the Hatfield Rd) for **London King's Cross**, **Brighton**, **Gatwick airport**, **Luton**, **Bedford** and connections to the **East Midlands**. Abbey Station, St Stephens Hill, for **Watford** and connections to the **West Midlands**, **North West** and **Scotland**. (Buses from St Peter's St).

Directory

St Albans *p272, map p272*
Hospital St Albans City Hospital minor injuries only T01727-866122. Hemel Hempstead General, T01442 213141. A&E. **Library** Central Library, The Maltings, T01438-737333. **Police** Victoria St, T01727-796000. **Post office** 14 St. Peter's St, T0845-7223344.

West Berkshire and Wiltshire

→ *Colour map 2, grid A5/6*

West of Reading, Newbury is the next major stop along the congested but prosperous 'M4 corridor', with quite a few of its big neighbour's problems in miniature. Consequently not high on most visitors' list of places to visit, it sits on the river Kennet surrounded by countryside made famous in Watership Down. *Rabbits do abound, but more picturesque in many ways are the downland gallops and rides set aside for the racehorses still trained up around here. Further west along the valley of the Kennet, Marlborough is a much more attractive destination, with beautiful downs of its own to the north and the extraordinary prehistoric remains at Avebury just to the west. Wiltshire was apparently the homeland of the earliest human inhabitants of the British Isles and they made an impression on the landscape that has survived to this day. On Salisbury Plain, Stonehenge is the pièce de résistance of course, although just one of a wealth of longbarrows, stone circles, tumuli and other earthworks dotted about the region. Seven miles to the south, the use of stone in the Middle Ages achieved one of its most dramatic expressions in the spire of Salisbury Cathedral, pointing skyward above a lively and beautiful market city surrounded by watermeadows and quiet little river valleys.* ▸▸ *For Sleeping, Eating and other listings, see pages 287-290.*

Newbury and the Berkshire Downs

Newbury itself may not be much to write home about, but some of the sights within its reach are well worth a trip in themselves. Highclere Castle is one of the most gloriously situated Victorian stately homes in the country. Nearby, the Sandham Memorial Chapel is a deeply moving and idiosyncratic commemoration of the carnage of the First World War. On the downs to the north, Ashdown House is a peculiar little Dutch confection standing in proud isolation surrounded by wonderful walking country.

Walks in the North Wessex Downs

- **The Ridgeway**: 2 miles there and back. Start: Whitehorse Hill Car Park. Along the Ridgeway from the White Horse to Wayland's Smithy. OS Maps: Explorer 170 Landranger 174.
- **Lambourn Downs**: 4 miles there and back. Start: Seven Barrows Car Park, 2 miles north of Lambourn village off the B4001. A quick walk up onto the top of the downs, along neolithic burials mounds and then a hike to views north from Blowingstone Hill. OS Maps: Explorer 170 Landranger 174.
- **Tan Hill**: 4 miles there and back. Start: Alton Priors. Past a 19th-century White Horse and up the hill for views over the Vale of Pewsey. OS Maps: Explorer 157 Landranger 173.
- **Fyfield Downs and Barbury Castle**: 10 miles there and back. Start: Avebury. Northeast up on to the Downs past the Grey Wethers along the Ridgeway to the hill fort at Barbury. OS Maps: Explorer 157 Landranger 173.
- **Kennet Valley**: 10 miles there and back. Start: Marlborough. A riverside valley walk from Marlborough to Ramsbury via Axford (after 3 miles, refreshments). OS Maps: Explorer 158 Landranger 174.

Ins and outs

Getting there **Trains** to Newbury are run by **First Great Western** and **Thames Trains**, leaving London Paddington hourly and taking just over an hour. By **car**, Newbury is 5 miles south of junction 13 on the M4, about 40 minutes from the M25. The countryside to north and south is easily accessed from the large A34 that bypasses the town. **National Express**, T08705-808080, **coaches** stop at Calcot, Newbury and Hungerford on some of their route journeys from London Victoria. Most local **buses** are provided by **Reading Transport Ltd**, T0118-9594000.

Information **Newbury TIC** ⓘ *The Wharf, T01635-30267, www.westberks.gov.uk. Oct-Mar Mon-Sat 1000-1600, Apr-Sep Mon-Fri 1000-1700, Sat 1000-1630.*

Sights

This area is the horse-racing centre for the south of England: rolling downland covered in threads of white fencing marking out the gallops and every other field home to some retired thoroughbred put out to grass. Second only in racing parlance to Newmarket in East Anglia, Newbury itself is a medium-sized market town on the river Kennet. Sadly it's not a top tourist destination, having suffered the same fate in recent years as Abingdon to the north. Passing visitors may be interested though in the **West Berkshire Museum** ⓘ *The Wharf, Newbury, T01635-30511, www.westberks.gov.uk, Oct-Mar Mon, Tue, Thu, Fri, Sat 1000-1600, Apr-Sep Mon, Tue, Thu, Fri 1000-1700, Sat 1000-1630, free*. The 17th-century **Cloth Hall** and the 18th-century **Granary** overlooking the Kennet and Avon Canal is a decent enough local history museum with galleries devoted to the Civil War battles of 1643 and 1644 as well as the history of Greenham Common and its famous feminist peaceniks who protested against the Cruise missiles once stationed here.

North of Newbury towards the Vale of the White Horse, the Berkshire Downs are the heart of horsey country. **Ashdown House** ⓘ *(NT), T01488-72584, Apr-Oct Wed, Sat by guided tours at 1415, 1515, 1615, gardens Apr-Oct Wed, Sat 1400-1700, £2.10*, near Lambourn, is an unusual 17th-century hunting lodge in a Dutch style associated with the Winter Queen, Elizabeth of Bohemia, sister of King Charles I. There are extraordinary

Cereal thrillers

In the late 1980s and early 90s, Britain was gripped by Crop Circle fever. Across the south of England, and mostly in Wiltshire, farmers woke to find a series of giant pictograms carved into their fields of cereal crops. What was going on? Many theories were posited as to the origin of these strange designs, ranging from nightly visitations by extra-terrestrial draughtsmen to the more mundane idea of an elaborate hoax. Crop circles are not a new phenomenon, however. Illustrations showing crop circles date from as long ago as 1647, and crop circles were appearing, in much simpler form, in the early 1970s. But it is only since 1990 that they have taken on their now familiar complex geometric patterns. The Centre for Crop Circle Studies was established in 1990 to give some serious thought to the matter and have revealed some interesting facts. For instance, many of the circles appeared close to sacred sites such as Avebury, Stonehenge, Silbury Hill and Old Sarum, the original site of Salisbury, lending credence to the notion that they could have been formed by ley lines, the powerful current that flows through the earth. The CCCS also discovered that crop yields increased significantly following the appearance of circles, that electronic equipment malfunctioned inside the circles and that people even showed physical side effects such as nausea and dizziness. Crop circles were thrust back into the limelight with the release of the Walt Disney movie, *Signs*, starring Mel Gibson.

views from the roof over the now rather shabby formal gardens and empty surrounding downland, as well as a great staircase lined with paintings from hall to attic. Good walks in the woodlands and up to King Alfred's castle on a hill nearby.

Ten miles east of Newbury off the A4 is **Silchester**, a complete Roman town discovered in the late 19th century, excavated and then reburied. The finds are mostly in the Museum of Reading (see page 256) but the site still has a short stretch of very well-preserved town wall, a recently restored amphitheatre and a little church. Silchester is unusual not only for being laid back to rest after its discovery, but also for its failure to develop after the Saxon invasions, possibly because it was such an important road junction and close to the tribal homelands of the powerful Atrebates. In the uncertain times following the departure of the legions, the new settlers generally avoided the old roads for fear of attack. Three miles to the south is **The Vyne** ⓘ *(NT), Sherborne St John, near Basingstoke, T01256-883858, house and grounds, Apr-Oct Mon-Wed, Sat, Sun 1100-1700, grounds only also Feb, Mar Sat, Sun 1100-1700, £6.50 (grounds only £3)*, a Tudor palace remodelled in the 17th century with the addition of the first classical portico in the country. Originally the house was owned by Henry VIII's Lord Chamberlain, and still boasts some exceptional panelling, hoards of antiques and lovely grounds, now in the care of the National Trust.

Five miles south of Newbury, in a spectacular position overlooking the rolling Berkshire countryside, the Earl of Carnavon's palatial home at **Highclere Castle** ⓘ *T01635-253210, www.highclerecastle.co.uk, Jul and Aug Mon-Fri 1100-1600, Sat 1100-1430, castle and grounds £6.70, concessions £3-£5, grounds only £3, concessions £1.50*, was designed by Charles Barry (also responsible for the Houses of Parliament) as an appropriate setting for Victorian high-society parties. The fifth Earl accompanied Howard Carter on his expedition to unearth the tomb of Tutankhamun, and an exhibition in the basement contains some of his finds. The current Earl (sixth) was been the Queen's Horseracing Manager and has set up an tion on the subject. The views from the gardens and romantic walks around the are worth the price of admission in themselves.

Close to Highclere, on the other side of the A34, a red-brick **chapel** ⓘ *(NT), ndham Memorial Chapel, Harts La, Burghclere, T01635-278394, Apr-Oct Wed-Sun 100-1700, Mar and Nov Sat, Sun 1100-1600, £2.80*, was purpose-built in the 1920s for Cookham artist **Stanley Spencer** to decorate with his astonishing and moving murals commemorating the dead of the First World War. The paintings, inspired by his own experience of the war and entirely filling the interior, are a stirring testament to the artist's own faith and his sharp eye for the everyday details of soldiers' lives. The lack of artifical light in the chapel means that it's best visited on a fine day.

Marlborough and around

About 17 miles west of Newbury, higher up the valley of the River Kennet, Marlborough is a considerably more rewarding destination. During summer, its wide Georgian high street throngs with visitors exploring the surrounding downland and making for Avebury, possibly the centre of the most developed neolithic culture in England. Unlike Stonehenge, you can get close to the stones here and in many lights their brooding presence around their ancient earthwork can be quite magical. To the south, Pewsey lies at the foot of a peaceful valley threaded by the Kennet and Avon Canal. To the west, Devizes is another solid Georgian market town, home to the acclaimed Wiltshire Heritage Museum.

Ins and outs

Getting there **Trains** from London Paddington serve Pewsey (1 hour) on the line to the Southwest and Exeter. By **car**, Marlborough is about 9 miles south of junction 15 on the M4, reachable in under 2 hours from London. Pewsey is a 15-minute drive south, Devizes about 30 minutes west of here. Local **buses** are run by the **Wiltshire Bus Line**, T08457-090899.

Information **Marlborough TIC** ⓘ *George La car park, T01672-513989, Apr-Oct Mon-Sat 1000-1700, Nov-Mar Mon-Sat 1000-1630.* **Avebury TIC** ⓘ *United Reform Chapel, T01672-539425, Tue-Sun 1000-1700, Wed-Sun.* **Devizes TIC** ⓘ *Cromwell House, Market Pl, T01380-729408, Apr-Oct Mon-Sat 0930-1700, Nov-Mar Mon-Sat 0930-1630.*

Sights

Marlborough itself is a quiet and attractive place, once an important market town and staging post on the old London to Bath and Bristol coach road, now more of a tourist-pleasing stopover for visitors to Avebury and Stonehenge. Its colonnaded high street is one of the widest in Europe, topped by a Victorian town hall and church with a Norman arch in the west front. Many of the solid stone-built Georgian buildings along its length were erected after the town was almost completely destroyed by a disastrous fire in 1653, prompting thatch to be banned by order of Parliament. One of the finest, **No 132 High Street** ⓘ *T01672-511491*, was built in 1656 for a wealthy silk merchant and is in the process of being restored to open to the public, featuring the Great Panelled Chamber with original floor-to-ceiling oak panelling. At the west end of town, **Marlborough College** is a famous public school, founded in 1843 for the sons of the clergy. The grounds contain a mound said to be Merlin's tomb, known as Merle Barrow. Some consider this to be the origin of the town's name, although it's more likely to derive from the local chalk 'marl'.

East of Marlborough, the ancient expanse of **Savernake Forest** stretches out between the river Kennet and the Kennet and Avon Canal. Famous for its butterflies, the forest has been in the stewardship of the same family since 1066, relatives of Henry VIII's wife Jane Seymour, criss-crossed by bridleways and a mile-long, dead-straight avenue through the beech trees.

North of Marlborough, the A346 heads up to Swindon 10 miles away, leading up out of the valley into the distinctive chalky landscape of the **Marlborough Downs**. Seven miles to the northeast, the downland village of **Aldbourne** is a picturesque spot, its old houses clustering higgledy-piggledy around a sloping green overlooked by a venerable old church. A similar distance to the northwest, the ancient **Ridgeway** recovers from the trauma of being crossed by the M4, keeping to the heights as it passes the Iron Age hill fort at Barbury Castle and runs down into Avebury.

Avebury and around

Anyone remotely interested in British prehistory eventually makes a pilgrimage to the UNESCO World Heritage Site of Avebury. In some ways more impressive and certainly more atmospheric than Stonehenge, the broken monoliths here make up for what they lack in architectural accomplishment with sheer quantity and the extent of their original plan, which appears to include a large number of other monuments close by. **Fyfield Down** and **Lockeridge**, 3 miles west of Marlborough, are also neolithic sites of great significance, dry valleys littered with sarsens, including a particularly fine group called the **Grey Wethers** and a capped dolmen called the **Devil's Den**. They both make a good introduction to the wealth of neolithic remains in and around Avebury itself. Much of the village is surrounded by the stone circle, ditch and bank, and was built in part using old sarsen stones. The ditch and stone circle were probably in place about 4,500 years ago, the latter now consisting of about 27 standing stones out of an estimated original total of 250. Their story is thoroughly explored, questioned and intriguingly not fully explained at the **Alexander Keiller Museum** ⓘ *T01672-539250, Apr-Oct 1000-1800, Nov-Mar 1000-1600, £4, concessions £2, family £10*. Named in honour of the champion golfer and archaeologist who found and relocated many of the stones in the 1930s, the museum is adjacent to the **Barn Gallery** (NT), a 17th-century thatched barn housing an interactive exhibition entitled 'Avebury 6000 Years of Mystery', included in the museum entrance fee. Nearby, complete with a beautiful walled garden, **Avebury Manor** ⓘ *(NT), T01672-539250, Apr-Oct Tue, Wed, Sun, bank holidays 1400-1730, £3.70, under 16s £1.90, garden only £2.80/£1.40*, is also worth a look in wet weather for its Queen Anne interior and Edwardian renovations.

A mile south of the village, via the West Kennet Avenue of standing stones alongside the B4003, **Silbury Hill** is an even more spectacular and strange survivor from prehistory, the largest Bronze Age man-made mound in Europe. Clambering up the grassy slopes is forbidden but its looming 130-ft bulk has an impressive presence at dusk despite the A4 rushing past its foot. About half a mile beyond, south of the A4 from here, **West Kennet Long Barrow** is an unusually large chambered tomb dating from around 3700BC. The West Kennet Avenue in fact heads east from Avebury to The Sanctuary, possibly an even older stone circle, now consisting of two concentric rings of stone and six that were wooden, their position now marked by concrete posts.

Pewsey and Devizes

Seven miles south of Marlborough, Pewsey is a quaint little town at the head of the Vale of Pewsey, one of the most lovely stretches of the Kennet and Avon Canal. Another White Horse overlooks the town from Pewsey Hill. At the other end of the valley to the west, beyond a string of little villages with beguiling names like Honey Street and Etchilhampton, sits Devizes, the major market town in north Wiltshire. Devizes's market place is the largest in England, and is still surrounded by grand old

 Georgian houses and two Norman churches. An hour's walk west from the centre of Devizes, the Cain Hill flight of 29 locks on the Kennet and Avon Canal is an inspiring feat of Victorian engineering. In Long Street, the accomplished county **museum** ⓘ *Wiltshire Heritage Museum, Gallery and Library, 41 Long St, T01380-727369, Mon-Sat 1000-1700, £3, concession £2, free on Mon,* contains galleries of artefacts on Natural History, Stone Age, Bronze Age, Iron Age, Roman, Saxon, Medieval and recent history. It's especially rich in its prehistoric finds. The art gallery, with its John Piper stained-glass window, puts on temporary exhibitions by local artists.

Salisbury

Salisbury wins out in the league of beautiful cities of the south mainly because it has been lucky enough to keep out the way of big new road-building programmes. Which comes as some surprise given that nine major old roads meet here near the confluence of four rivers on the banks of the River Avon. The Market Square is the centre of things, alive and busy every Tuesday and Saturday, while the Close and its Cathedral remain very peaceful and serene behind their old walls a few hundred yards away. The Cathedral, with its magnificent spire, is still the main event, although Salisbury is large enough to boast some thriving nightlife, characterful pubs and one of the best rep theatres in the south.

Ins and outs

Getting there Southwest Trains run hourly services to Salisbury from London Waterloo, taking 1 hour and 30 minutes. Relatively off the beaten track, Salisbury is about 7 miles south off the main A303 between London and Exeter, and about 14 miles north of the main A31 between London and Bournemouth. A major **road** junction itself, it's nonetheless very easy to reach by car, taking on average about 1 hour and 30 minutes from the M25 London Orbital. **National Express,** T08705-808080, run three direct services from London Victoria daily (3 hours). ⏩ *For further details, see Transport page 290.*

Getting around Salisbury City Centre is small and charming enough to make walking around it a pleasure. Destinations out of town can be reached on **Wilts and Dorset Buses,** T01722-336855.

Information Salisbury TIC ⓘ *Fish Row, Salisbury, T01722-334956, May-Sep Mon-Sat 0930-1700 (Jun-Aug until 1800), Sun 1030-1630 (Jul and Aug until 1700), Oct-Apr Mon-Sat 0930-1700, free accommodation booking service.*

History

The Romans set up camp overlooking one of their most important crossroads on a small hill now known as Old Sarum. Sorbiodunum, as they called it, was conquered by the Saxons and called Searesburgh, which the Normans later called Searesbyrig, hence Salisbury. Old Sarum is still quite an extraordinary place to visit, partly because the settlement was abandoned completely in 1219 when the cathedral was relocated onto the plain below. Legend has it that Bishop Poore had an arrow fired from Old Sarum down into the valley and founded the new cathedral where it fell. Since then, Salisbury's history has been quiet and largely uneventful, something that its heritage industry today can be grateful for.

Sights

Although most visitors are inevitably drawn towards the Cathedral's towering spire, the city centre is also worth exploring. Unlike the twisting Saxon layout of Canterbury, the regular grid of old medieval streets around Market Square can reasonably claim to be one of the earliest examples of new town planning in Europe. Clearly Salisbury's Norman founders had learned a thing or two from the Romans. Dominated by the **Guildhall**, the square still lives up to its name on Tuesdays and Saturdays, at other times doing service as a fairly grand car park.

North of Market Square, Castle Street runs alongside the Avon. To the east, Blue Boar Row leads into Winchester Street, one of the city's more intriguing shopping strips for antiques and other one-offs. Just to the west, **St Thomas's Church**, consecrated to Canterbury's Thomas à Becket, was founded in the 13th century, at the same time as the Cathedral, but rebuilt in the 15th. Inside, the chancel arch is decorated with a superb Doom painting, and there are medieval murals depicting the Annunciation, Visitation and Nativity as well as some fine pre-Reformation stained glass.

From St Thomas's Square, the High Street leads south to the **Close**, although St John Street provides the most satisfying approach to the Cathedral. Pretty much undisturbed by the passing of time, the Close seems to be in a world of its own, its gates locked at night, protecting the seclusion of residents such as former Conservative

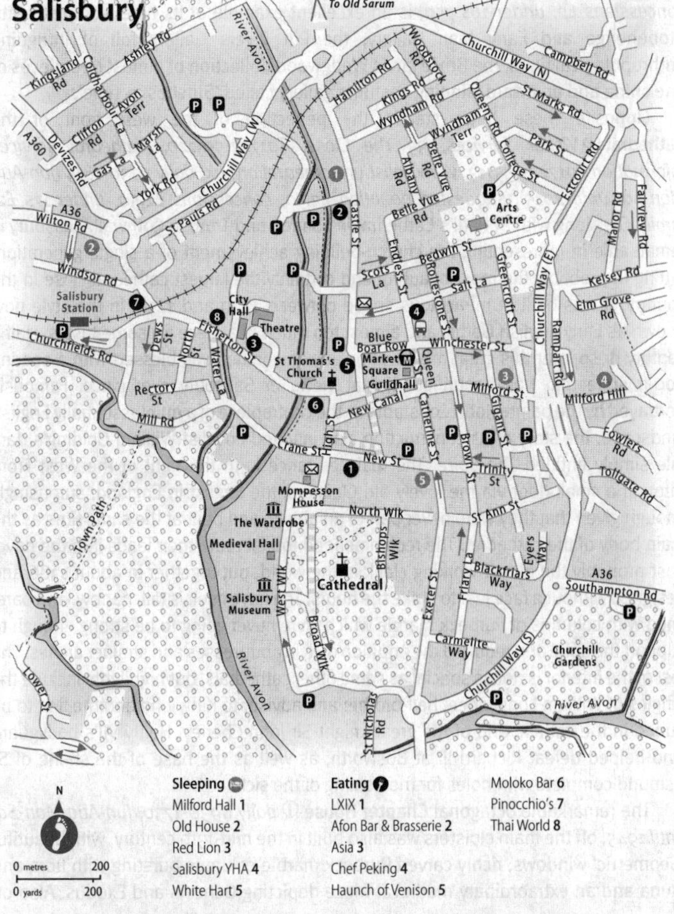

 prime minister Edward Heath. The High Street entrance leads into Choristers Green, where stands **Mompesson House** ⓘ *(NT), The Close, T01722-335659, Apr-Oct Mon-Wed, Sat, Sun 1200-1730 (last admission 1700), £3.90, under-16s £1.95, garden only 80p*, a stately Queen Anne building with a remarkable interior featuring some very fine plasterwork and oak staircase, as well as an 18th-century collection of drinking glasses, antique furniture and a walled garden. It featured as Mrs Jennings' home in Ang Lee's film adaptation of Jane Austen's *Sense and Sensibility*.

The **West Walk**, backing onto the watermeadows of Queen Elizabeth Gardens, is home to three engaging attractions that can satiate the most anoraky thirst for local history. The first is the most specialized and often the least overwhelmed: **'Redcoats in the Wardrobe'** ⓘ *58 The Close, T01722-414536, www.thewardrobe.org.uk, Apr-Oct daily 1000-1700, Feb, Mar, Nov, Dec Tue-Sun 1000-1700, £2.50, concessions £1.90, under-16s 50p*, is the Royal Gloucestershire, Berkshire and Wiltshire Regiment's museum with beautiful gardens leading down to the river and watermeadows.

A few doors down, 'The Secrets of Salisbury' in the **Medieval Hall** ⓘ *10 Shady Bower, T01722-412472, Apr-Sep 1100-1700, £1.50, under-18s £1*, the old 13th-century dining hall of the Deanery, one of the oldest domestic buildings in the close, offers a 40-minute presentation shown continuously from 1100.

Next door, the **Salisbury Museum** ⓘ *The King's House, 65 The Close, T01722-332151, Mon-Sat 1000-1700 (also Jul and Aug Sun 1400-1700), £3, concessions £2, under-16s 75p*, is an excellent example of its type, complete with Stonehenge and Early Man Gallery, the Pitt Rivers Gallery full of intriguing anthropological finds, the Brixie Jarvis Wedgwood Collection of almost 600 pieces of fine china and an award-winning costume gallery called 'Stitches in Time'.

Opposite these three stands the perfection of the west front of the **Cathedral** ⓘ *Visitor Services, 33 The Close, T01722-555120, Cathedral services information T01722-555113, www.salisburycathedral.org.uk, daily 0730-1815 (Jun-Aug Mon-Sat until 2015), suggested donation £3.50, concessions £2.50, under-17s £2, family £8*. Along with St Paul's Cathedral in London and Truro in Cornwall, Salisbury is remarkable in representing the church-building achievement of a single generation. Sitting in probably the most beautiful and certainly the largest cathedral close in the country, it was built at miraculous speed between 1220 and 1258, in the style now known as Early English Gothic and almost too much of a piece for some tastes. Half a century or so later this great medieval palace of worship was blessed with a soaring 400-ft spire that has beautified distant views of Salisbury ever since. Famously portrayed by the painter John Constable as the centrepiece of a quintessentially English landscape, the story of its construction also inspired novelist William Golding's dark tale simply entitled *The Spire*. The main entrance is to the right of the West Front through a small door via the lovely old Cloisters, the largest in England, surprisingly enough given that they were never part of an abbey, and built at the same time as the main body of the cathedral. The recommended tourist route then leads into the nave, past probably the oldest working clock in the world, put together in about 1386 and designed without a face just to strike the hours. The nave itself is tall, narrow, and bare, lined with columns of Purbeck marble which were never going to be strong enough to support the spire and required the addition of flying buttresses and strainer arches. The rest of the interior is not as special as some other cathedrals, but highlights include the effigies of William Longespee, half-brother and advisor to King John and the first to be buried in the church, and of the great knight Sir John Cheney, Henry VII's bodyguard who helped defeat Richard III at Bosworth, as well as the base of the shrine of St Osmund complete with holes for the healing of the sick.

The remarkable octagonal **Chapter House** ⓘ *daily 0930-1730, Jun-Aug Mon-Sat until 1945*, off the main cloisters was also built in the mid-13th century, with beautiful 'Geometric' windows, richly carved Purbeck marble columns bursting with flora and fauna and an extraordinary medieval frieze depicting Genesis and Exodus. Also on show is one of the four surviving original copies of the Magna Carta, the foundation stone of the rule of law in the country during the despotic reign of King John.

Almost a mile north of the city centre, **Old Sarum** ⓘ *(EH), Castle Rd, T01722-335398, Apr-Jun, Sep daily 1000-1800, Jul and Aug 0900-1800, Oct 1000-1700, Nov-Mar 1000-1600, £2, £1.50 concessions, £1 under-16s*, is a beautifully situated hill fort. Constructed in the Iron Age, it was continuously inhabited until the Middle Ages when the church moved its cathedral into the valley below. Good views from the walks around the walls and the foundations of the original Norman cathedral can still be seen, where William the Conqueror made all the landowners in the country swear allegiance to him.

North of Salisbury

Stonehenge

ⓘ *T01980-624715, www.stonehengemasterplan.org. Jun-Aug daily 0900-1900, Mar 16-May and Sep-Oct 15 daily 0930-1800, Oct 16-Oct 23 daily 0930-1700, Oct 24-Mar 15 daily 0930-1600 (closed 25, 26 Dec, Jan 1), £4.20 including free audio tour, £3.20 concessions, £2.20 children, personalized out-of-hours tours, T01980-626267.*
Almost halfway to Exeter from London on the A303, and 7 miles north of Salisbury, stands Britain's most famous and most visited prehistoric monument, Stonehenge. First impressions may be disappointing: big roads rush very close by; the whole place is often mobbed with visitors; walking among the stones is forbidden; and if you've only seen photographs, the standing stone doorways may seem unimpressively small. That said, the informative and entertaining audio guide quickly provokes a sense of wonder at humankind's achievement here during the Bronze Age. The main features of the monument are a circular ditch and bank (a henge), the ancient Heel Stone just outside it (the only naturally shaped stone on site), and in the middle the ruins of a circle of sarsens capped with lintels, a circle of bluestones, a horseshoe of trilithons and the fallen Altar Stone. Speculation continues as to the true purpose of the thing, broadly agreed to have been erected over the period 3000BC to 1500BC. It's sobering to think that it was probably in use for at least 3,000 years, the hub of one of the earliest cultures on the planet. Whether a temple to the sun, an astronomical clock, or gruesome site of ritual sacrifice, its importance can be judged from the fact that many of its stones were somehow transported all the way from the mountains of Wales. Others, including the distinctive 30-ton sarsens and their capping stones, were dragged off the Marlborough Downs some 20 miles to the north. At present, the car park, ticket queues and gift shop keep visitors firmly in the present until they pass through a tunnel under the road to emerge the other side of the fence. Big plans for the future include burying the roads, creating a visitor centre further from the stones in a 4,000-acre Prehistoric Millennium Park, and hence restoring the monument to its magnificent isolation. Sadly it's hard to see how they're ever going to be able let people wander among the stones ever again though.

North of Stonehenge stretches **Salisbury Plain**, much of it an army training ground and off-limits. Walks from the monument itself are pretty limited therefore, although a good overview of its position surrounded by a litter of related earthworks and burial mounds can be found at the crest of **King's Barrow Down**, best reached up a tiny road north just east of the fork in the A303 that pens in Stonehenge with the A344. Just beyond, a minor road south heads down into the Avon valley and the **Woodfords**, a string of attractive manorial riverside villages crossed by the long-distance Monarch's Way footpath. In Middle Woodford, **Heale Gardens** ⓘ *T01722-782504, Tue-Sun 1000-1700, £3.50, concessions £1.70*, surround a mellow old house (private) with a gorgeous profusion of roses, hedgework and herbaceous borders.

Druids: Bronze Age to New Age

When Julius Caesar invaded Britain in the first century BC he already knew from his experiences conquering Gaul that the Druids would give him trouble. Recent research suggests that these warrior priests presided over a settled and sophisticated agrarian Celtic community, probably undertaking most of the roles occupied by the professional classes today. They were doctors, lawyers and chartered surveyors all rolled into one. Indeed the Romans only finally crushed their resistance more than a century later at a bloody battle on Anglesey Island in Wales. Archaeologists have suggested that the siting of burial mounds and stone circles over former domiciles indicates that the Druids practised a religion that believed in an underworld peopled by their tribal ancestors. These monuments were taken to be the gateway to the land of the dead. Sadly the historical evidence is at odds with the popular image of the priesthood epitomised by Getafix in the Asterix cartoons. Rather than wandering affably around in search of mistletoe with their golden sickles, they're more likely to have been found ritually garotting young men – the probable fate of Lindow Man, now preserved in the British Museum – and instilling their followers with a casual lack of concern for personal safety, something that bothered the Roman legionaries. Modern Druids espouse a more limited faith – in the sanctity of the seasons and respect for mother nature, in the animistic spirits of wood and stream and in flowing facial hair.

It is these gentle although not entirely unprofessional souls that have earned the right to celebrate their faith at Stonehenge on the summer solstice each year and thankfully not their reincarnated Bronze Age brethren.

South and west of Salisbury

Down the Avon valley on the A338, just north of the New Forest and Fordingbridge, at **Breamore**, there's a beautiful Elizabethan **manor house** ⓘ *T01725-512233 or 512468, Aug daily, May-Jul and Sep Tue-Thu, Sat, Sun, Apr Tue, Wed, Sun 1400-1730*, still lived in by descendants of its early 18th-century purchaser Sir Edward Hulse, physician to Queen Anne and the first two Georges. The interior contains paintings from the 17th- and 18th-century Dutch schools, a unique set of Mexican ethnological paintings and a rare Jacobean carpet. The **Countryside Museum** next door illustrates the lives led in the surrounding 17th-century village and boasts a very unusual Bavarian four-train turret clock from 1575. The village church, detached from the main cluster of buildings, is one of the finest examples of pre-Conquest Saxon architecture in the south.

West of Salisbury, the rivers Wylye, Nadder, and Ebble flow down into the Avon, and each is lined with attractive villages that make good bases for riverside walks. The Ebble is the least developed, overlooked by the Iron Age hill fort of **Clearbury Ring** with great views of the surrounding downs and Salisbury from a thickly overgrown old earthwork on the top of the hill. A mile or so west of Salisbury up the Nadder valley, **Wilton House** ⓘ *T01722-746729, www.wiltonhouse.com, Apr-Oct daily 1030-1730 (last admission 1630), £7.25, concessions £6.25, under-15s £4.50, grounds only £3.75, under-15s £2.75*, is quite a commercialized stately home, owned by the Earl of Pembroke, but very special inside, with a visitor centre in the Old Riding School, featuring a Victorian laundry and Tudor kitchen. Its most famous room is the Double Cube Room, by Inigo Jones, hung with paintings by Van Dyck and Joshua Reynolds. There's an adventure playground and 21 acres of romantic gardens and the strange Italianate church in town is also worth a look.

A little further west on the A30, past the lovely parkland and church of picturesque Compton Chamberlayne, **Philipps House** ⓘ *(NT), T01985-843600, house, Apr-Oct Mon 1300-1700, Sat 1000-1300. £3, park, daily 0800-dusk, free*, is a fine Palladian mansion containing Regency furniture in a lovely setting in Dinton Park with renovated and restored parkland walks stretching down to a lake.

Other villages in the Nadder valley worth exploring are **Teffont Magna**, positively the last word in cute thatched villages, near the *Howard's Hotel* (see below) and tiny **Fyfield Bavant**, with a 13th-century church like a little cowshed with a belfry.

A peculiar sight south of the A30 are the **Fovant Badges**, a series of large hill carvings in the strange shapes of regimental badges created by the troops stationed here during the First World War, including the YMCA, the Royal Corps of Signals' figure of Hermes and the London Rifle Brigade. Close by, at Compton Chamberlayne, with more acres of attractive parkland, picturesque thatched village and manor, there's also a map of Australia carved into the hill by the many Aussies stationed here.

Sleeping

Newbury and the Berkshire Downs *p277*

A **Newbury Manor Hotel**, London Rd, Newbury, T01635-528838, F523406. Most swish hotel in Newbury (5 mins outside) with the river running through its grounds.

A **The Royal Oak Hotel**, The Square, Yattendon, Near Newbury, T01635-201325, F201926. Comfortable rooms in an old village inn with very good restaurant (see below) but a rather institutionalized air these days.

C **Fishers Farm**, Ermin St, Shefford Woodlands, Near Hungerford, T01488-648466. Working farm with indoor swimming pool, handy for walks on the Downs.

D **Peak House Farm**, Cole Henley, Whitchurch, T01256-892052, peakhousefarm@tesco.net. Another working farm B&B that represents good value for money.

Camping

F **Bishops Green Farm**, Bishops Green, Near Newbury, T01635-268365, with all the usual facilities.

Marlborough and around *p280*

B **Castle and Ball Hotel**, High St, Marlborough, T01672-515201, with rated 'Taste of the West' restaurant.

B **Ivy House**, Marlborough, T01672-515333, is another decent option on the High St.

C **Castle Hotel**, New Park St, Devizes, T01380-729300, www.castledevizes.com. Welcoming and cheerful family-run establishment where nothing seems too much bother.

C **Red Lion**, High St, Avebury, T01672-539266. 4 rooms, needs booking well in advance, in the middle of the village (and the circle).

Salisbury *p282, map p283*

A **Milford Hall**, 206 Castle St, T01722-417411, F419444. Close to the centre, family-run in an extended Georgian mansion.

A **Red Lion**, 4 Milford St, T01722-323334, www.the-redlion.co.uk. Founded in the 13th century, courtyard hotel in the middle of the city with a reliable restaurant.

A **White Hart**, St John St, T0870-4008125, www.heritage-hotels.com. Very comfortable refurbishment of an old townhouse, with real fires, clean rooms and friendly service.

C **Old House**, 161 Wilton Rd, T01722-333433. Beamed rooms and friendly family home with charming garden, within walking distance of the city centre.

F **Salisbury YHA**, Milford Hill, Salisbury, T01722-327572, F330446. Has 70 beds in one single, one double, 7 4-bedded and dormitory rooms, within walking distance of the Cathedral.

South and west of Salisbury *p286*

A Howard's House Hotel, Teffont Evias, near Salisbury, T01722-716392, www.howardshousehotel.com. Small and very comfortable country hotel in an idyllic setting with a sweet little garden and boasting a high-quality restaurant that draws in diners from Salisbury and further afield (£30 a head without wine). Recommended.

C The Bell Inn, High St, Wylye, T01985-248338. In the shadows of the A303 and A36 but a lovely old pub with comfortable rooms and good local ingredients in its accomplished restaurant.

D Pembroke Arms, Fovant, T01722-714201. Creeper-clad coaching inn on the A30 with a hearty local atmosphere and displays on the First World War camp on the downs that created the Fovant Badges.

Eating

Newbury and the Berkshire Downs *p277*

£££ Dew Pond, Old Burghclere, T01635-278408. Ambitious menu in olde-worlde cottage setting.

£££ Royal Oak, The Square, Yattendon, T01635-201325. Smart dining in a country pub just north of the M4 with a lovely garden.

£££ The Vineyard at Stockcross, Newbury, T01635-528770. Opulent minimalist surroundings and Californian cuisine offered at a restaurant owned by winemaker and industrialist Sir Peter Michael.

£ Crown and Horns, East Ilsley, T01635-281205, an unpretenious and very friendly local with reliable if unexciting fare.

£ Hare and Hounds, T01488-71386, at Lambourn Woodlands, with its more ambitious menu and contemporary approach to pub décor.

£ Pot Kiln, Frilsham, near Yattendon, with its own West Berkshire brewery round the back, an open fire and basic pub grub.

Marlborough and around *p280*

£££ Harrow Inn, Little Bedwyn, T01672-870871. Cosy gourmet restaurant in a converted pub, about £50 a head for some accomplished 'modern European' food.

££ 2XS, 7 Kingsbury St, Marlborough, T01672-514776. Another Marlborough restaurant with a good reputation.

££ Bell Inn, Ramsbury, T01672-520230. Another village local with reputable food.

££ Coles, Kingsbury St, Marlborough, T01672-515004. Do a modern European menu confidently enough, main courses about £12, large starters available at lunchtimes.

££ George and Dragon, High St, Rowde (just north west of Devizes), T01380-723053. Very fresh fish from Cornwall deep inland (about £30 a head) in a bog-standard boozer.

££ Red Lion, Axford, T01672-520271. Pub on the river with highly rated food and a favourite with the locals.

££ Royal Oak, Wootton Rivers, T01672-810322, half-timbered and thatched, fairly expensive food (£12 main courses) but very welcoming atmosphere, jolly in summer when the canal is busy with passing punters.

£ The Bear, Market Pl, Devizes, pub with good food.

£ Circle Restaurant, High St, Avebury, T01672-539514. Vegetarian and organic restaurant catering expertly to the new agers visiting the stones, with wholesome lunches for under £10.

£ The Polly Tearooms, High St, Marlborough T01672-512146. The most famous tearooms in Marlborough, always buzzing with tea-drinkers wondering whether to have one more tempting piece of patisserie.

£ Taste of Bengal, 58 New Park St, Devizes, T01380-725649. Main courses about £8, excellent innovative Indian cuisine.

£ Truffles Bakery, 7 Little Brittox, Devizes, T01380-720049, can provide delicious ingredients for a picnic.

£ Tudor Tearooms, 115 High St, Marlborough, T01672-52853. Less expensive than the *Polly* with less sophisticated home-made cakes for £3.50, sometimes less crowded too.

£ Wellington Arms, T01672-512954, on the High St in Marlborough is good for pub food.

Salisbury *p282, map p283*

££ Asia, 90 Fisherton St, T01722-327628. A reliable but quite pricey Indian restaurant.

££ The Haunch of Venison, 1/5 Minster St, T01722-322024. A famous old pub with a very decent menu of pub grub in the restaurant upstairs.

££ LXIX, 67-69 New St, T01722-34000. The most stylish restaurant in the city, if not the whole of Wiltshire (and it knows it), booking essential for modern British cuisine in sleek designer surroundings.
££ Pinocchio's, near the station, T01722-413069. A busy and cosy old-style Italian.
£ Afon Bar and Brasserie, Millstream Approach, off Castle St, T01722-552366. A vaguely Australian-style, reasonable value menu in a pleasant enough spot beside a confined stretch of the Avon stream where boats and punts can be hired.
£ Chef Peking, Fisherton St, T01722-326063. A very tasty and popular Chinese with a lively atmosphere.
£ Thai World, off Fisherton St, T01722-333870, is a good Thai alternative.

Pubs, bars and clubs

South and west of Salisbury *p286*
The Cartwheel, Whitsbury, T01725-518362. A proper country pub with a pool table, garden, good value pub grub and well-kept beers.
The Crown Inn, Alvediston, is a charming thatched 15th-century pub.
Radnor Arms, Nunton, T01722-329722. Do an interesting modern European menu backed up with some real ales.
Three Horsehoes, Bishopstone (left at *White Hart* pub on main road), is a very old thatched pub, no food but completely unchanged since the 1950s. Pool table and jukebox, although the beer isn't up to much.

Entertainment

Newbury and the Berkshire Downs *p277*
The Hennessy Cognac Gold Cup takes place at Newbury Racecourse, T01635-400155, www.newbury-racecourse.co.uk, at the very end of Nov every year.
Watermill Theatre, Bagnor, near Newbury, T01635-460444. Wide and often interesting range of in-house, small-scale touring and amateur productions in a converted old watermill.

Marlborough and around *p280*
Palace Cinema, Devizes, T01380-722971, restored Art Deco cinema showing mainstream releases.

Salisbury *p282, map p283*
A useful leaflet giving details of many concerts throughout the year in the City Hall and Cathedral as well as churches and schools around the city is also available: T01722-330179, www.musicinsalisbury.org.
Salisbury Arts Centre, Bedwin St, T01722-321744, www.salisburyarts.co.uk. Performing and visual arts in a converted church beside parkland.
Salisbury Playhouse, Malthouse La, T01722-320117, www.salisburyplay house.com. Well-established haven for touring productions, some warming up for the West End.

Festivals

Salisbury *p282, map p283*
May/Jun Salisbury Festival, usually last week of May and first of Jun, T01722-332977/323888, box office T01722-320333, www.salisburyfestival.co.uk. A formidable multi-arts festival with fireworks, outdoor classical concerts, theatre and street shows.

Shopping

Marlborough and around *p280*
Marlborough is something of an antiques centre, with a couple of shops on Kingsbury St, just above the Town Hall, but most clustered around The Parade near the Mill Stream.
Anthony Spranger, 6 Kingsbury St, Marlborough, T01672-514105. A decent collection of secondhand books.
Katharine House Gallery, The Parade, T01672-514040, for unusual antiques and 20th-century British Art.
Mackintosh of Marlborough, 42a High St, Marlborough, T01672-514069. High-quality picnic materials.
Nick Wheatley at Katharine House Yard, Kennet Pl, T01672-512111, with a large stock of Arts and Crafts movement furniture.
White Horse Bookshop, 136 High St, Marlborough, T01672-512071. Good for new books.

Salisbury *p282, map p283*
Pritchetts, 5 Fish Row, T01722-324346. Top quality butcher doing mean pork pies and superb sausages.

Reeve the Bakers, 2 Butcher Row, T01722-320367. Another place to pick up some delectable picnic materials.

Activities and tours

Marlborough and around *p280*

Marlborough Downs Riding Centre, Rockley, Marlborough, T01672-511411. About 3 miles northwest of Marlborough for rides around Barbury Castle and along the Ridgeway.

Marlborough Leisure Centre, Barton Dene, Marlborough, T01672-513161. Municipal pool.

Salisbury *p282, map p283*

Cameron Balloon Flights Southern, T01672-562277, flights from the Leisure Centre.

Old Sarum Flying Club, Old Sarum Airfield, T01722-322525, www.old-sarum-flying.demon.co.uk.

Salisbury Racecourse, Netherhampton, T01722-326461 www.salisburyracecourse.co.uk. Horse racing May-Oct at one of the country's oldest and most picturesque courses.

Thruxton Motorsport Centre, Thruxton Circuit, Andover, T01264 882222, info@thruxtonracing.co.uk.

Transport

Salisbury *p282, map p283*

Car hire Europcar, Fisherton Yard, Fisherton St, T01722-335625; **Thrifty**, Brunel Rd, Churchfields Ind Est, T01722-411919. **Cycle Hire** Hayball Cycle Centre, Black Horse Chequer, 26-30 Winchester St, Salisbury T01722-411378. **Taxi** City Cabs Salisbury Ltd, T01722-334477.

Directory

Salisbury *p282, map p283*

Hospitals Salisbury District Hospital, Odstock Rd, T01722-336262.

Hampshire

→ *Colour map , grid B5*

Hampshire is a county with three faces: chalk downlands above the winding valleys of the swift little Itchen, Test and Meon streams; the open heathland and woods of the New Forest in the south; and in the east, the hanging beaches around Selborne in a small hilly area known with charming overstatement as 'Little Switzerland'. In the middle sits Winchester, a bit mauled by the M3 motorway, but still boasting one of the most noble cathedrals and most beautiful old schools in the country. On its outskirts, beside the river Itchen, the abbey and almshouses at St Cross are probably the best-preserved medieval sight in England. West of Winchester, Romsey is the setting for another great Norman church, while the Test Valley runs north-south, still brimming with trout and attracting some alarmingly well-equipped anglers. East of Winchester, Alresford is an attractive old town, just north of the Meon Valley, with its string of pretty villages. Selborne, just north of Petersfield, has become permanently associated with the great naturalist Gilbert White. South of Winchester, the New Forest is a popular playground for cyclists, walkers and pony-trekkers, as well as being the last extensive stretch of lowland heath to survive in the whole country. East of the Forest, across the Southampton Water, Southampton and Portsmouth are the most important maritime cities in the south, the former still heaving with merchant shipping, and the latter limping along as the historic birthplace of the Royal Navy. ▸▸ *For Sleeping, Eating and other listings, see pages 304-309.*

Winchester

Quondam capital of the country under King Alfred the Great, Winchester lost out to London some time in the late Middle Ages. Its Royal glory days may be over but it remains a very prosperous city with a distinctive ecclesiastical and scholarly air. The great cathedral's interior is one of the most inspiring in the land and William of

Wykeham's public school for boys provided the model for most others. In fact the cathedral with its close, the college and its grounds taken together make up one of the most beautiful medieval complexes in the country, capped by the almost undisturbed peace of St Cross Hospital, still standing quietly close to lovely watermeadows a mile or so to the south, where Keats was inspired to write his Ode to Autun. That said, the city centre itself is only slowly recovering from some seriously ill-advised urban planning; and the destruction of Twyford Down by the M3 caused widespread protest as areas of outstanding natural beauty and sites of special scientific interest surrounding the city were brutally destroyed.

Ins and outs

Getting there Twice hourly direct **trains** from London Waterloo take about 1 hour, by **South West Trains,** T023-80213650. Winchester is off the **M3** at junctions 9-11, about a 1 hour drive from London. **National Express,** T08705-808080, have nine **coach** services a day to Winchester from London Victoria (2 hours). ▸▸ *For further details, see Transport page 308.*

Getting around Winchester, the cathedral close, town and college, is easily small enough to **walk** around, although the walk from **train** station to the city's outskirts at St Cross would take at least an hour. The network of local **buses** are run by **Wilts and Dorset Buses,** T01722-336855 (to the southwest, Salisbury, Romsey etc) and **Solent Blue Line,** T023-80618233 (to Southampton, Eastleigh). The council also subsidizes some local buses T01962-846924.

Information Winchester TIC ⓘ *Guildhall, The Broadway, T01962-840500, www.winchester.gov.uk. Jun-mid Sep Mon-Sat 1000-1800, Sun 1100-1400, mid Sep-May Mon-Sat 1000-1700.* Accommodation booking service (£3 per booking, online booking £5). **Andover TIC** ⓘ *Town Mill Ho, Bridge St, Andover T01264-324320, www.exploretestvalley.com.* **Romsey Heritage and Visitor Centre** ⓘ *13 Church St, Romsey, T01794-512200, Mon-Sat 1000-1600.*

History

The earliest settlement, home of a Celtic people during the fifth century BC, discovered in the Winchester area was on St Catherine's Hill, just south of the modern city, recognizable today by its distinctive 'clump' of trees on the summit. Around 150BC a tribe of Belgae set up a trading centre near this spot and two centuries later, the Romans turned it into a major regional administrative centre which they called 'Venta Belgarum'. Long after they'd left, shortly after the Dark Ages, when the town is thought by some to have played a part in Arthurian romance as Caer Gwent, Egbert was crowned King of England here in 829. More famously, 42 years later, the Anglo-Saxon King Alfred the Great followed in his footsteps, founding a new Minster, establishing the capital here and masterminding resistance to the Vikings. Construction of the cathedral that stands today began just after the Norman Conquest. William the Conqueror was crowned both here and in London. Two hundred years later, Bishop William of Wykeham founded Winchester College. In 1538, Henry VIII's split with Rome mauled the city's monasteries, and by the time his successor 'Bloody' Mary Tudor married the Catholic Philip of Spain, the Cathedral had been stripped of its famous shrine to St Swithun, venerable adviser to the Saxon kings. Less than a century later, Winchester backed the losers in the Civil War, the west window of the Cathedral was smashed and Oliver Cromwell's cannon pounded the castle and city into submission. His vantage point to the south is still known as Oliver's Battery. At the Restoration, Charles II took a shine to the place, and planned to build a palace here. It was never built though, and after the Glorious Revolution of 1688 the city's Royal star faded. Since the 18th century, Winchester has settled into provincial obscurity, and is now a prosperous and polite London satellite.

Westgate and Great Hall

From the railway station in the northwest of the town, a 5-minute walk brings you to the old medieval **Westgate** ⓘ *T01962-848269, Apr-Oct Mon-Sat 1000-1700, Sun 1200-1700, Feb and Mar Tue-Sat 1000-1600, Sun 1200-1600, 30p, concessions 20p*, at the top of the High Street. Inside there's a brass rubbing centre, and some debtor's graffiti testifying to its use as a prison for more than a century. Better perhaps to hurry on next door to the **Great Hall** ⓘ *T01962-846476, Apr-Oct 1000-1700, Nov-Mar 1000-1600, free*, the last remnant of Winchester Castle, impressive nonetheless, where the city's famous Round Table has hung on the wall for more than 500 years. Long associated with King Arthur, he is depicted at its centre in the Tudor costume of the time when it was repainted. Big enough to seat all 24 of his knights, it probably actually originates from sometime in

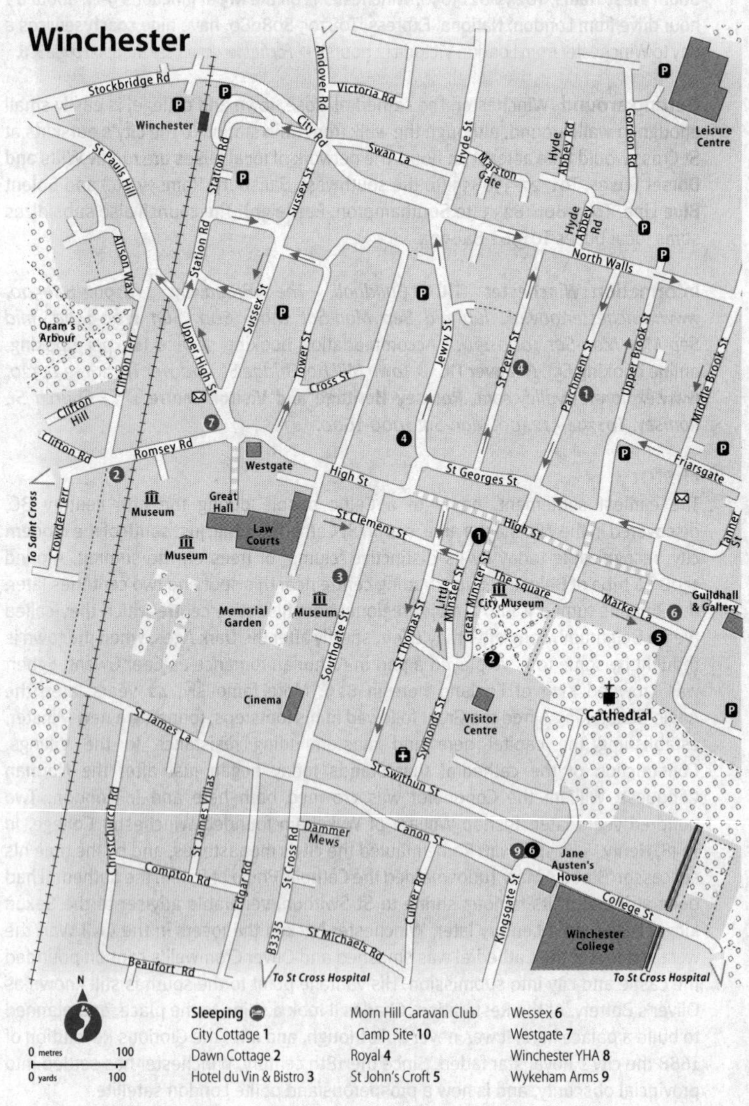

the 13th century. Henry VIII took the Emperor Charles V to see it in 1522. Queen Eleanor's pretty little medieval garden has been reconstructed outside.

Peninsular Barracks

ⓘ *Royal Green Jackets Museum, T01962-828549, Mon-Sat 1000-1300, 1400-1700, Sun 1200-1600, £2, concessions £1.*

A little further down the High Street, Southgate Street heads off to the right for St Cross Hospital (see below) past the Peninsular Barracks. No less than five military museums are now housed here: The **Light Infantry Museum** ⓘ *T01962-828550, Mon-Sat 1000-1600, Sun 1200-1600, free*, the most modern of them with displays on the collapse of the Berlin Wall and the Gulf War; the **Gurkha Museum** ⓘ *T01962-828536, Mon-Sat 1000-1700, Sun 1200-1600, £1.50, concessions 75p*, with exhibits from their homeland in Nepal; the **King's Royal Hussars Museum** ⓘ *T01962-828541, Tue-Fri 1000-1245, 1330-1600, week- ends 1200-1600, free*, featuring the history of three cavalry regiments and the Charge of the Light Brigade; the **Royal Hampshire Regiment Museum** ⓘ *Serle's House, Southgate Street, T01962-863658, Mon-Fri 1000- 1230, 1400-1600, Apr-Oct also weekends 1200-1600, free*, with displays on the history of the local militia; and last but by no means least, the **Royal Green Jackets Museum** ⓘ *T01962-828549, Mon-Sat 1000-1300, 1400-1700, Sun 1200-1600, £2, concessions £1*, featuring the Rifle Brigade and a diorama of the Battle of Waterloo. All in all, a feast for military types young and old (more probably).

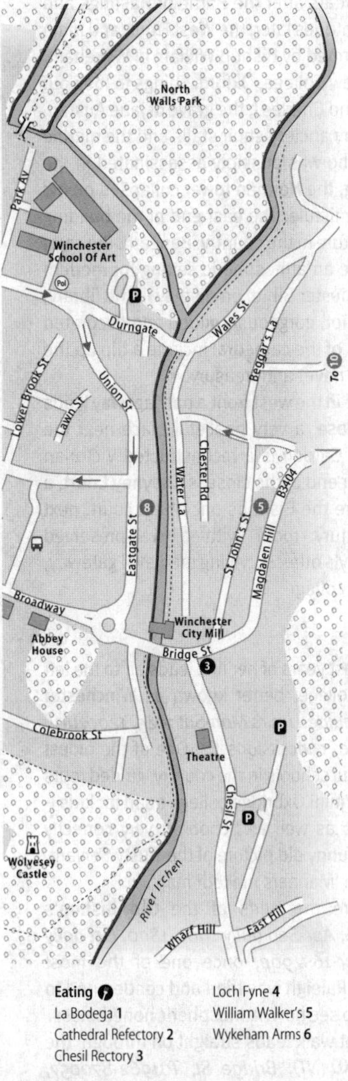

City Museum

Continuing down the High Street, the **Buttercross** is the local youth hang-out, kids sitting vacantly around the heavily restored 15th-century market cross. A passage through the old shops on the right leads into the Square, site of the City Museum and a good approach to the west front of the cathedral. The recently re-vamped local **museum** ⓘ *T01962- 848269, www.winchester.gov.uk/heritage, Apr-Oct Mon-Sat 1000-1700, Sun 1200-1700, Nov-Mar Tue-Sat 1000- 1600, Sun 1200-1600, free*, tells the story of the city's former national importance entertainingly enough and also includes some of the latest archaeological finds from the site of King Alfred's grave.

Eating

La Bodega 1
Cathedral Refectory 2
Chesil Rectory 3
Loch Fyne 4
William Walker's 5
Wykeham Arms 6

Winchester Cathedral

ⓘ *T01962-857200, www.winchester-cathedral.org.uk, daily 0830-1700. Services Mon-Sat 0740, 0800, (Thu and Saints days 1200), 1730, Sun 0800, 1000, 1115, 1530. Donations suggested, £3.50, concessions £2.50, family £7. Visitor Centre, T01962-857258, open daily 0930-1700. Free.*

Even a passing visitor to the city should not fail to look inside Winchester Cathedral. On low ground beside the river Itchen – so low in fact that it began to sink into the marshy ground and was only saved by a brave diver called William Walker pumping concrete into its rotten wooden foundations in the 1920s – the stubby tower may make first impressions disappointing. Approaching the west front from the Square though, the building's scale and grandeur gradually make themselves felt. Inside, the longest medieval nave in Europe never fails to stir the spirit, soaring up to a magnificent vaulted ceiling supported by a splendid march of perpendicular columns. Work was begun on the building 13 years after the Battle of Hastings and completed 14 years later in 1093. Almost two centuries later, the West Front (and main entrance) was remodelled and the nave transformed by Bishop William of Wykeham, founder of St Mary's College (see below) and New College, Oxford. Things to look out for inside include fine statues of Kings James I and Charles I, the grave of Jane Austen, the 12th-century black marble font, extraordinary ancient choir stalls and the marble tomb of William Rufus. Shortly after Rufus – who was possibly assassinated in the New Forest – was buried in the central crossing, the Norman tower collapsed on his grave, many thought as a consequence of his misrule. The east end of the building boasts some of the earliest pure Gothic architecture in the country. Beneath, the crypt – which is still prone to flooding – has become an atmospheric setting for modern sculptor Anthony Gormley's *Sound II*. The Winchester Bible, on display in the library, is a beautiful illuminated 12th-century manuscript, gorgeously gilded and decorated with lapis lazuli from Afghanistan. Guided tours of the cathedral include a trip up the tower, or round the library, triforium (above the nave) and treasury.

To the right of the cathedral's main entrance in the west front a passageway leads beneath flying buttresses into the **Deanery Close**, a very peaceful place near the remains of the old monastery. Dean Garnier's Garden is a reconstructed Victorian garden beneath the cathedral walls. At the other end of the close is **Cheyney Court**, a much-photographed half-timbered house where the Bishops once held court, next door to **Pilgrim's Hall**, an early 14th-century room with a well-preserved hammer-beam roof. Through the old wall, the city's other surviving medieval gateway, the Kingsgate separates the cathedral from the college.

Around College Street

College Street, where Jane Austen lived out the last years of her life, leads off to the left and the impressive main gate of St Mary's College, better known as **Winchester College** ⓘ *T01962-621209, www.wincoll.ac.uk, guided tours Mon-Sat 1045, 1200, also 1415, 1530 (not Tue, Thu), Sun 1415, 1530, £2.50, concessions £2*. One of the oldest (founded 1382), most exclusive and most beautiful schools in the country, guided tours include the dinky little Chamber Court – a sort of mini Oxbridge college quad for kids – the chapel, quiet cloisters and old dining hall, as well as School, a very correctly proportioned building attributed to Wren, and a funny old picture of the Trusty Servant, a hybrid creature embodying the school's motto: 'Manners maketh man'.

On the other side of College Street are the ruins of the **Old Bishop's** Palace ⓘ *Wolvesey Castle (EH), T01962-854766, Apr-Sep daily 1000-1800, Oct daily 1000-1700, £1.80, concesssions £1.40, under-16s 90p*, once one of the most important medieval buildings in Europe, where Raleigh was tried and condemned to death, although there's not a huge amount left to see now. Atmospheric nonetheless.

At the end of College Street, a very pleasant walk leads straight on through 'the weirs' of the Itchen to a working **watermill** ⓘ *(NT), Bridge St, T01962-870057,* *www.winchestercitymill.co.uk, Apr-Sep Wed-Sun (daily Jul and Aug) 1100-1645, £2,* almost back in the middle of town with an impressive rushing water race and island garden. It's also a youth hostel (see below). A right turn at the end of College Street heads towards the **watermeadows**, a delightful tract of reedbeds and tiny waterways burgeoning with wildlife. A good mile's walk between these meadows and the school's playing fields along the riverbank finally reaches the other unmissable highlight of a visit to Winchester, **St Cross Hospital** ⓘ *T01962-851375, Apr-Sep Mon-Sat 0930-1700, Oct-Mar Mon-Sat 1030-1530, £2, £1.50 concessions, guided tours bookable in advance in writing.* Founded in 1136, these beautiful old almshouses (the oldest in England) and their wonderful Norman abbey on the riverbank survived the dissolution of the monasteries thanks to being for lay brothers rather than the clergy. Today it must be one of the most perfectly unspoiled medieval places in the country. The current occupants still hand out the Wayfarer's Dole – a bit of bread and beer – to visitors or pilgrims during visiting hours and show people around their adorable church with its chunky round Norman pillars, wealth of zigzag stonework and adjoining Tudor courtyards.

West of Winchester

Romsey and the Test Valley

Romsey, 10 miles southwest of Winchester on the A3090, is a pretty little market town most famous for its great Norman nunnery. **Romsey Abbey** ⓘ *T01794-513125, daily 0830-1800*, was founded by King Alfred's son Edward in 907, demolished by the Danes and rebuilt by the Normans in 1130. Like St Cross Hospital in Winchester, it was lucky to survive the Dissolution, being bought by the citizens of the town for £100. In the reign of William Rufus, the third Abbess Ethelflaeda disguised the Saxon princess Aedgyth as a nun to shield her from the King's desire for a dynastic alliance of the Norman and Saxon crowns. According to local legend, the Abbess was also in the habit of reciting her psalms naked by moonlight in the river Test. Today the church is crowded around by the town but remains one of the grandest set-pieces of Norman architecture in the country.

In the market place of Romsey stands a statue of Lord Palmerston, the mid-19th-century Prime Minister who changed from Tory to Whig and on his deathbed said "Die, my dear Doctor, that's the last thing I shall do!" He lived at **Broadlands** ⓘ *T01794-505010, www.broadlands.net, Jun-Aug daily 1200-1730, £5.95, under-16s £3.95, concessions £4.95*, the grand 18th-century stately home with landscaped grounds sloping down to the river. Later it became the home of Lord Louis Mountbatten, last Viceroy and first Governor General of India, and the stable-block houses an exhibition on his life's achievements and naval exploits.

Five miles north of Romsey on the A3057 is **Mottisfont Abbey** ⓘ *(NT), T01794-340757, grounds, mid-Mar to Sep Mon-Wed, Sat, Sun 1100-1600 (rose garden until 2030 in Jun), house, 1300-1700, picture gallery Mon, Tue, Sun 1300-1700, £6*, the remains of another 12th-century priory on the river Test with an 18th-century house built round it, featuring Rex Whistler's trompe-l'oeil drawing room, a 19th-and 20th-century art collection and peaceful gardens famous for their old-fashioned rose collection.

Six miles further north, the same road following the course of the river Test arrives in **Stockbridge** (9 miles west of Winchester). A picturesque one-street town lined with antique shops and twee tearooms, this is the trout fly-fisherman's favourite Hampshire residence and a popular staging post on the long-distance walk the **Test Way**, 71 miles from Eling Wharf to Inkpen Beacon.

Danebury Vineyard ⓘ *T01264-781851, www.danebury.com, Mon-Fri 0900-1630*, 3 miles northwest of the town is a 6-acre vineyard in the grounds of Danebury House, with tastings and food in a grand south-facing setting. Close by is **Danebury Hill fort**, one of the south's more spectacular Iron Age hill forts. The history of the fort can be explored in **Andover**, 7 miles north of Stockbridge, at **The Museum of the Iron Age** ⓘ *6 Church Close, Andover, T01264-366283, Tue-Sat 1000-1700, Sun 1400-1700, £1.50, concessions 75p*. Just beyond Danebury, in Middle Wallop, the **Museum of Army Flying** ⓘ *T01980-674421, daily 1000-1630, £4.80, under-16s £3.20*, is a pretty impressive example of its type, with a unique collection of military gliders and more than 35 other flying machines, from biplanes to choppers. It also includes a popular interactive science education gallery for kids called Explorer's World, featuring a camera obscura with views over the surrounding countryside that adults might well enjoy too.

East of Winchester

With the Itchen valley north and south of Winchester pretty much destroyed by the M3, it's refreshing to escape east on the B2177 to the uncommercialized old town of Bishops Waltham. On the way, five miles south east of Winchester, is **Marwell Zoological Park** ⓘ *Colden Common, near Winchester, T07962-943163, www.marwell.org.uk, Apr-Oct daily 1000-1800, Nov-Mar daily 1000-1600 (last admission 1 hr before closing), £9, concessions £8*. Admission may be expensive but then there are a surprising number of rare and endangered species being well looked after here. As well as roomy enclosures for the likes of lemurs, penguins and gazelles on the 100-acre site, there are also plenty of sideshow activities for kids.

Bishops Waltham, about 9 miles southeast of Winchester, was once wholely owned by the Bishops of Winchester. The attractive Georgian town on the river Hamble now clusters around the evocative remains of their **palace** ⓘ *(EH), T01489-892460, Apr-Sep daily 1000-1800, Oct 1000-1700, £2, concessions £1.50, under-16s £1*, built by Bishop Henry of Blois in the Middle Ages, with moated grounds, ruined great hall and chapel. How Oxbridge Colleges might have looked if abandoned after the Dissolution.

Slightly further east, the A32 winds up from Fareham and Gosport through the **Meon Valley**, passing through a string of well-to-do and very well-kept towns and villages like Droxford, Warnford and West Meon. Nearby, **Old Winchester Hill**, just to the east, is another Iron Age hill fort worth a climb, with excellent views towards the sea and over the surrounding downs.

New Alresford, 7 miles east of Winchester on the A31, is an attractive old market town (christened 'new' in the 13th century) with a good variety of interesting shops and pubs, as well as the terminus of the **Mid-Hants Watercress Line** ⓘ *The Watercress Line, The Railway Station, Alresford, T01962-733810 www.watercressline.co.uk*. Like the Bluebell in Sussex, the Watercress Line is also popular with families not wholely obsessed with steam because its 10-mile journey from Alresford to Alton via Ropley, Medstead and Four Marks (the highest station in southern England) runs through delightful countryside. The steamtrains link up with the national rail network at Alton.

Not far from Alresford, the formal and informal hillside gardens with great views around a fine Georgian house at **Hinton Ampner** ⓘ *(NT), Bramdean, Alfresford, T01962-771305, grounds, Apr-Sep Tue, Wed, Sat, Sun 1330-1730, house Apr-Sep Tue, Wed (Sat, Sun in Aug only) 1330-1730, £5*, are a joy to behold in season.

Selborne, 5 miles southwest of Alton, is a quaint little village nestling beneath the Hangar. This steep wood was made famous by the writer **Gilbert White** whose *Natural History of Selborne* published in 1789 set the standard for many early ecologists. His **house** ⓘ *The Wakes, Selborne, Alton, T01420-511275, daily 1100-1700, £4.50, concessions £4, under-16s £1*, and an original manuscript, have been preserved, and his garden restored to its 18th-century state. On the upper floors of the house, the Oates

Museum honours the memory of Captain Oates, who sacrificed his life for his fellows on Scott's ill-fated expedition to the Antarctic by leaving the tent during a blizzard saying "I am just going outside and may be some time."

New Forest → *Colour map 2, grid B4/5*

Neither new, nor really a forest, the New Forest remains without doubt one of the most individual stretches of countryside in the south of England. Ever since William the Conqueror made it his personal hunting ground almost a thousand years ago, the forest has been a playground for Londoners. Much of the area could now more aptly be described as open heathland, one of the most ecologically important sites in lowland Britain, although the wooded parts do contain a notable variety of trees. The Norman king's son and successor, William Rufus, was shot by an arrow in mysterious circumstances while out hunting – and the Rufus Stone, an unremarkable 18th-century boulder near Fordingbridge, marks the spot. Deer do still abound, but their stocky little four-legged cousins, the New Forest ponies, are much more high profile around here. Amiable enough when not with foal, these peaceable free-range grazers give the area its special character. The historic towns and villages dotted about heave with visitors during summer, but it's always possible to get away from them all by taking a walk in the woods.

Ins and outs

Getting there **Trains** to Ashurst from Waterloo every 2 hours take about 1 hour and 20 minutes. **Southwest Trains, Connex South Central** and **Virgin Cross Country** trains to Brockenhurst leave Waterloo about three times an hour, taking 1 hour and 30 minutes. Change at Brockenhurst for Lymington. Beaulieu Road is a station in the middle of nowhere between Lyndhurst and Beaulieu, a good starting point for walks. The New Forest stretches away to the coast south of the M3/M27/A31 between Southampton and Ringwood, most of it accessible in about 2 hours from London. A fairly comprehensive network of local **buses** is run by **Wilts and Dorset**, T01202-673555. ▸▸ *For further details, see Transport page 308.*

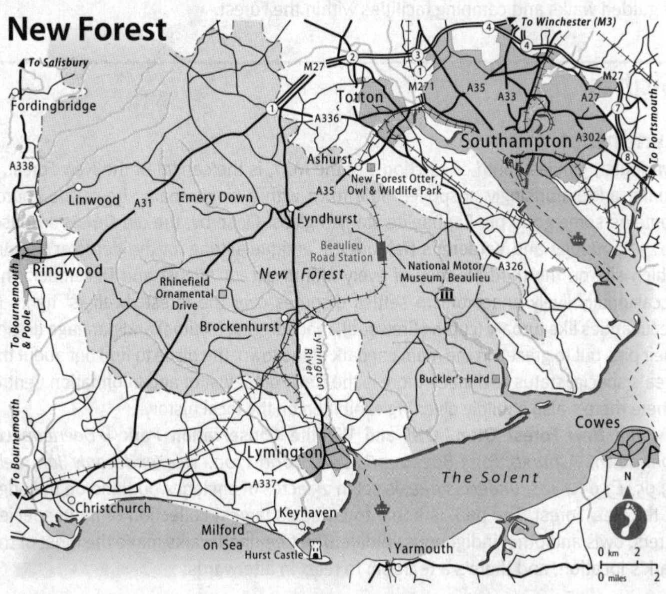

Walks in the New Forest

- **Bolderwood Green**: 4 mile circle. Start: Bolderwood Grounds carpark, on the minor road from Emery Down to Linwood. A woodland walk that includes a labelled arboretum, deer sanctuary and ancient Douglas firs. OS Maps: Outdoor Leisure 22.
- **Portuguese Fireplace**: 5 mile circle. Start: Millyford Bridge, on the road from Emery Down to Linwood. An easy walk south from a memorial to Portuguese allies through the woods to the Knightwood Oak. OS Maps: Outdoor Leisure 22.
- **Brock Hill**: 3 mile circle. Start: Rhinefield Ornamental Drive. A walk up an avenue of the oldest and tallest pine trees in the forest, past its first enclosure at Vinney Ridge, to a clump of ancient oaks and beeches. OS Maps: Outdoor Leisure 22.
- **Beaulieu**: 4 miles there and back. Start: Beaulieu village. A walk down the Beaulieu river to Buckler's Hard and back along the Solent Way. OS Maps: Outdoor Leisure 22.
- **Queens Bower**: 1 mile there and back. Start: Ober Corner, west of Brockenhurst. An open and marshland stroll to the confluence of the Lymington and Ober rivers near an old hunting lodge. OS Maps: Outdoor Leisure 22.

Getting around The New Forest is best explored on foot, pony or by bike. Local **buses** require some patience but connect the main towns and villages during the main part of the day, except on Sun.

Information New Forest TIC ⓘ *Lyndhurst, T023-80282269, www.thenewforest.co.uk, Apr-Oct daily 0900-1700, Nov-Mar daily 1000-1600*. Efficient, friendly and well-stocked information centre with accommodation booking service. **Lymington TIC** ⓘ *New St, T01590-689000, Apr-Oct, Mon-Sat 1000-1700, Nov-Feb Mon-Sat 1000-1600*. **The Forestry Commission** ⓘ *T023-80283141*, provides details of guided walks and camping facilities within the Forest.

Sights

Lyndhurst

Lyndhurst, 5 miles south of Junction 1 of the M27, is the capital of the New Forest, a quaint and surprisingly unspoiled little town with a single main street. The church contains some good pre-Raphaelite stained glass. Close by, the old **Queen's House**, T023-80282052 and **Verderer's Hall** are the antique setting for the Verderer's Court, which sits on the third Monday of every month except August and December. This occasionally lively anachronism settles disputes over the forest dwellers' rights to peculiarities like turbary (cutting firewood), marl (digging for lime) and pannage (letting their pigs out to graze). In the main car park of the town, the place to find out about the area's special status and much more is the New Forest Visitor and Information Centre, where there's also a mildly diverting exhibition on the local history.

The **New Forest Otter, Owl and Wildlife Conservation Park** ⓘ *Deerleap La, Longdown, Ashurst, T023-80292408, daily 1000-1700, weekends only Jan, Feb, £5.95, £3.95 4-14s, under-4s free*, is set in 25 acres of ancient woodland on the edge of the New Forest. The park is home to Europe's largest collection of multi-specied otters, owls and other indigenous wildlife. The tree-lined walks make the most of the park's location, and there's a tearoom to relax in afterwards.

Beaulieu and around

From Lyndhurst, three roads fan out across the forest. The most attractive (and often a slow-moving traffic jam in high season) is the B3056 to **Beaulieu**, past Beaulieu Road station. Beaulieu is indeed a 'beautiful place', its ancient **Abbey**, brooding at the head of the river estuary across the water from the peaceful old estate village. Most of the cars are quite likely to be heading for Lord Montagu's **National Motor Museum** ⓘ *T01590-612345, www.beaulieu.co.uk, May-Sep daily 1000-1800, Oct-Apr 1000-1700, £11.95, concessions £9.95, under-16s £6.95, family £33.95*, in the grounds of his family's old house, once the gatehouse of the Abbey. The Museum was started to indulge Montagu's own interests, and now there are over 250 vehicles to see, including the recordbreaker Bluebird. Almost as much a theme park as museum, you can also take a stroll down a 1930s street and race through time in a space-age pod. In the house itself are Victorian costumed guides and there's an exhibition on monastic life at the Domus of Beaulieu Abbey, dating from 1204. Or try a ride on the monorail. The high price of admission is usually justified, especially during one of the regular motoring club events at weekends.

From Beaulieu a narrow road winds for 3 miles down the estuary to **Buckler's Hard** ⓘ *T01590-616203, www.bucklershard.co.uk, Apr-Sep daily 1030-1700, Oct-Mar daily 1100-1630, £3, concessions £2, children £1.50*, built from scratch in the 18th century by Montagus as a speculative sugar harbour and then used as a Naval dockyard for the construction of several of Nelson's ships of the line. The single grassy street slopes down to the riverside, often very crowded in summer but well worth an overnight stay to enjoy the tranquility of the place once all the trippers have gone home. Now it's also a popular yachting centre with a couple of museums on the living quarters and activity in the shipyard during its heyday.

Lymington and around

From Buckler's Hard the long-distance footpath the **Solent Way** heads along one of the few undeveloped stretches of forest coastline, passing the impressive ruins of one of the largest medieval tithe barns in England at St Leonard's Grange, to Lymington, 7 miles west. A yachting centre to rival Cowes further up the Solent, Lymington is the leaping off point for Yarmouth on the Isle of Wight and scarcely preserves its dignity under the onslaught of braying boaties and their flashy fibreglass toys. The little harbour area throngs with holidaymakers looking over the tackle and cramming into dinky alleyways lined with gift shops, tearooms and nautical nick-nacks. Sloping uphill, the town's Georgian High Street is also worth a look. The **St Barbe Museum and Art Gallery** ⓘ *New St, Lymington, T01590-676969, www.stbarbe-museum.org.uk, Mon-Sat 1000-1600, Jul and Aug also Sun 1400-1700, £3, concessions £2, family £6*, puts on temporary exhibitions of contemporary artists, and is also a small permanent local history museum.

Keyhaven, 4 miles west of Lymington, is a small village at the foot of a long shingle spit sheltering a tidal nature reserve. At the tip of the spit, **Hurst Castle** ⓘ *(EH), T01590-642500 (ferry information T01425-610784), Apr-Oct daily 1000-1730 or dusk, £2.70, concessions £1.50, child £1.50*, is another of Henry VIII's coastal fortifications, extended massively by the Victorians. Charles I was held prisoner here before being transferred to Carisbrooke. You can take a boat through the salt marsh nature reserve from Keyhaven to the grim-looking place, the nearest point to the Isle of Wight, and enjoy the amazing views and warren of atmospheric rooms. Alternatively, you can walk out to the castle along the calf-stretching shingle beach.

On the coast west of Keyhaven, **Milford-on-Sea** is one of the area's prettier seaside towns, with a village green and good swimming beach. **Christchurch**, 8 miles further west, sits at the mouth of the river Avon on the outskirts of Bournemouth. It's managed to resist being swamped by that Victorian holidaymakers' Mecca though, and its central marketplace is still recognizably medieval. The large **Priory Church** (the longest parish church in the country) dates from that time and is decorated inside with some of the most extraordinary stone carving in the south. The church's north transept is described by church-reviewer Simon Jenkins as "one of the most spectacular works of Norman design in England". High praise for such an under-visited church, now sadly hemmed in by the banal retirement homes stretching along the coast.

From Christchurch, the B3347 winds for 7 miles up the Avon valley to **Ringwood**, a forest town whose character has almost been obliterated by the A31 and A348 coming up from Bournemouth. Six miles north on the A338 **Fordingbridge** is a much more attractive old town on the banks of the river. West of Fordingbridge can be found one of the largest **Roman Villas** ⓘ *T01725-518541, Apr-Sep 1030-1800, £1.75, 95p concessions*, ever excavated in the country, relatively recently discovered, spanning several of the first few centuries AD. There's an informative display on Roman life here, followed by a well-signposted look around the site itself, highlights being the exposed underfloor heating of the two bath houses from AD 150 and the mosaic still intact on the dining room floor.

Portsmouth

Portsmouth usually hits the news for all the wrong reasons, like when a mob here attacked a paediatrician they had mistaken for a paedophile. Since the millennium regeneration of the harbourfront, though, the city's future has been looking up. That said, it still bears the scars of the ill-conceived regeneration of its extensive Second World War bomb damage during the 60s and first impressions are likely to be uninspiring. The Historic Dockyard remains most visitors' favourite destination, and quite a sight it is too, still just about a working naval base and also a series of very popular old ships in dry dock, including HMS Victory and the Tudor warship Mary Rose. From the dockyard's main entrance, The Hard stretches along the harbourfront, recently the subject of a much-needed facelift. A millennium walk now leads past the new Gun Quay leisure and shopping development to Old Portsmouth and the 'hot walls'. These old stone defences still manage to conjure up the city's importance in its seafaring heyday, a good introduction to a small cluster of old buildings and pubs that either survived the bombs or have been carefully restored.

Ins and outs

Getting there By **road**, Portsmouth is at the end of the A3, just over 1 hour from London, although at peak times the M3 and M27 can be marginally quicker. **South West Trains** leave frequently throughout the day for Portsmouth Harbour from London Waterloo. ▸▸ *For further details, see Transport page 308.*

Getting around South Downs Explorer Bus linking Portsmouth, Gosport, Fareham with Petersfield and the Meon Valley. **Solent Blue Line Buses,** T023-80618233.

Information Portsmouth TIC ⓘ *Clarence Esplanade, Southsea, T023-92826722, daily 0930-1745, also on The Hard, daily 0930-1745, www.visitportsmouth.co.uk,* includes an accommodation service.

History

On an unusual island site, Portsmouth was a small natural harbour in the Middle Ages and has been continuously fortified ever since. It first became the royal dockyard under Henry VII. Some Tudor fortifications remain, such as Henry VIII's Southsea castle, but it was Charles II who turned the city into the country's foremost naval base. As well as being home to various eminent Victorians, the likes of Dickens, Brunel and

Conan Doyle, the city also boasts connections with just about every Englishman who has ever sailed the seven seas, especially Nelson of course. Along with Southampton, it was also the main port of embarkation for D-Day in June 1944.

Sights

Most visitors to Portsmouth with time to kill make a beeline for **Portsmouth Historic Dockyard** ⓘ *1-7 College Rd, HM Naval Base, Portsmouth, T023-92861512, www.historicdockyard.co.uk, daily 1000-1630, £17.50 all attractions, £15.50, £12.50 under-16s, £12.50 (3 attractions), under-16s £9.30, concessions £11, single attraction £6.50, concessions £5.80, under-16s £4.80*, a 10-minute walk west of the station. **HM Naval Base**, once the world's largest industrial complex, is still home to a significant part of the fleet, including three aircraft carriers and a variety of destroyers, frigates and minesweepers. In the reign of Charles II the world's largest dry docks were built here, now harbouring HMS Victory, Nelson's flagship at the Battle of Trafalgar, and the *Mary Rose*, a Tudor warship salvaged in remarkable condition from the Solent silt. In 1802, the world's first steam-powered factory, the Blockmills, was built here, turning out pulley blocks for sailing ships and designed by the father of Isambard Kingdom Brunel. Apart from its historical associations, the dockyard now draws in the punters to its five visitor attractions. The most authentic of them are HMS Victory and HMS Warrior. The Victory, the oldest and most symbolic attraction in the yard, is enormously popular and frequently has to operate a timed-entry system. The measures are not that surprising, given that she remains one of the best preserved and most rewarding ships in the yard to visit: see the very planks upon which the one-eyed Admiral fell in 1805, the cockpit where he begged Hardy to kiss him (or muttered 'kismet' as some have suggested), and marvel at the cramped conditions in which men had to fight. The nearest attraction to the main entrance, HMS Warrior, is also a treat, the first iron-clad steam-powered battleship, which thanks to successfully avoiding any action remains in pristine condition, as good as when she first steamed into the Channel in 1860. The latest and predictably most gimmicky attraction is Action Stations, 'showcasing the modern Royal Navy' with a multimedia exhibition that tries to let you in on the glamour of life in the navy using a huge screen showing a film called *Command Approved*, a simulator ride and some pretty effective Naval PR. All in all it's a marked improvement on the press gang as a method of recruitment. Opposite HMS *Victory*, the **Royal Naval Museum** features *Trafalgar*!, a multimedia portrait of the decisive sea battle, as well as displays on the history of the sailing navy and the life of Nelson. The salvaged remains of the **Mary Rose**, not particularly impressive in themselves, can be found a short walk away. This Tudor warship was built in 1511 and capsized within sight of port in 1545. The televised and tricky salvage operation has ensured the vessel's continuing celebrity even though its original performance hardly seems to justify it. That said, the exhibition does a good job of illuminating life at sea in the very early days of the great age of sail. Finally, Warships by Water offers water-borne 40-minute tours ofo the modern dockyard in summer for £3.50.

Portsmouth Harbour was transformed for the millennium, with the creation of a new harbourside walkway. The new **Gun Quays** development (T023-92836700) features all the usual suspects of noisy mass-market retailing, with cinemas, discount fashion outlets, a bowling alley and chainstores aplenty, but it has also reinvigorated a tired and run-down stretch of the harbour between the naval base and Old Portsmouth. More controversial (because of its impact on the old harbour's skyline) has been the 500 m **Spinaker Tower**, due to open in 2003 and destined to be a very prominent landmark and observation tower dominating the waterfront. Beyond, the 'hot walls' stretch around Old Portsmouth, a 20-minute walk south from the Historic Dockyard.

Around Portsmouth

Over the waters of Portsmouth Harbour lies Gosport, not much of a destination except for submarine buffs heading for the **Royal Navy Submarine Museum** ⓘ *Haslar Jetty Rd, Gosport, T023-92529217, www.rnsubmus.co.uk, Apr-Oct daily 1000-1730, Nov-Mar daily 1000-1630, £4, concessions and under-16s £2.75, family £11*, which offers guided tours of HMS *Alliance* and displays the navy's first submarine *Holland I*. Further up Gosport's Millennium promenade, **Explosion!** at the **Museum of Naval Firepower** ⓘ *Priddy's Hard, T023-92505600, Apr-Oct daily 1000-1730, Nov-Mar 1000-1630, £5 child/concessions £3*, is likely to be a surefire hit with kids for its celebration of big bangs at sea set in the Grand Magazine.

At the top of the harbour, on a prime defensive site for the last 2000 years, **Portchester Castle** ⓘ *(EH), near Fareham, T023-92378291, Apr-Sep daily 1000-1800, Oct daily 1000-1700, Nov-Mar daily 1000-1600, £3.50, concessions £2.60, under-16s £1.80*, has the most complete Roman walls in Europe still standing, as well as a squat Norman keep, the remains of Richard II's palace and the prison where thousands of French prisoners were 'sardined' during the Napoleonic wars. Great views over the Solent.

Nearby, the Victorian fort on Portsdown Hill is home to the **Royal Armouries museum** ⓘ *Fort Nelson, Down End Rd, Fareham, T01329-233734, www.armouries.org.uk, Apr-Oct daily 1000-1700, Nov-Mar Thu-Sun 1030-1600, free*, with underground magazines, tunnels and pieces of the Iraqi supergun and displays on artillery in action.

Southampton

Like Portsmouth, Southampton's position on a peninsula jutting into the deep-water estuary of the rivers Itchen and Test has ensured its maritime importance since the Middle Ages. The Mayflower sailed from here, as did the Queen Mary and the Titanic. Nowadays it's a thriving commercial port thanks to its unusual 'double tides', allowing supertankers to nose their way deep inland. No surprise then that it was virtually flattened by the Luftwaffe and fairly unattractively redeveloped after the war. A few older parts of town have survived to give the town centre some character, especially the Old Bargate at the top of the High Street, but apart from a quick look around the city's museums or art galleries, and a stroll along the harbour front around Town Quay, there's not a huge amount to keep visitors long as they pass through to the New Forest, the Isle of Wight or France and beyond.

Ins and outs

Getting there Direct **train** services link Southampton with many parts of the UK. **South West Trains** operates a 15 minute interval daytime fast service between London Waterloo and Southampton Central. **South West Trains, Wales and West, South Central Trains** and **Virgin Trains** operate regular services along the south coast. Southampton is even better connected by **road,** to London via the M27 and M3 (about an hour away), and to Birmingham via the M40 and A34 (about 2 hours and 30 minutes). Junction 3 on the M27 accesses the city centre quickest via the M271. » *For further details, see Transport page 309.*

Getting around The centre of Southampton is clustered around the **railway** station and stretches down to the harbour (a 20-minute walk) along Above Bar Street. **Stagecoach,** T01256-464501, run frequent **bus** services throughout the city and surrounding area, including Eastleigh, Hedge End, Fareham, Portsmouth and Southsea, Chandlers Ford, Romsey, Totton, and the New Forest. Other buses around town and beyond are run by **Solent Blue Line,** T023-80618233, **Wilts and Dorset,** T015900-672382, and **First Southampton,** T023-8022 4854. **Blue Funnel Cruises** T023-80223278 operate tours of Southampton Water.

The Shipping Forecast

Broadcast four times a day on BBC Radio 4 Long Wave, shortly before 0500, 1200, 1800 and midnight, the shipping forecast has become almost as sacred an English institution as Trooping the Colour and cream teas. Heard for the first time in 1924, it uses a strange set of seemingly totemic names and mysterious coded shorthand to warn mariners of the weather conditions over the next 24 hours. The names pinpoint 30 sea areas. Some, such as Dover, Plymouth, Irish Sea and Hebrides, are self-explanatory and provide handy summaries of what it's likely to be like beside the seaside. The sound of others – Dogger, Bailey, Rockall, Sole, and Forties – brings the smack of the cold and briny open sea into cosy homes across the land. After the gale warnings and general synopsis, the forecast begins in the northeast with Viking, North and South Utsire, near Norway, and moves clockwise around the British Isles, through Tyne, Humber, Thames, Dover, Wight, Portland, Plymouth, and Lundy, and back up to the Faeroes, Fair Isle and southeast Iceland in the north again. Each sea area is followed by a three-part forecast describing the wind direction and strength on the Beaufort Scale, the weather expected, and the visibility: 'Cromarty, southwesterly backing southerly 4, increasing 5 or 6, occasionally 7. Rain spreading northeastwards. Moderate, becoming poor.' Controversy has recently surrounded the proposed replacement of the lullaby tune, Sailing By, that has introduced the midnight forecasts since 1965. Originally commissioned by the BBC to accompany an epic hot-air balloon ride over the Alps, its twee and lilting harmony would apparently be sorely missed by grizzled seafarers and snug landlubbers alike.

Information Southampton TIC ⓘ *Civic Centre Rd, T023-80833333, www.southampton.gov.uk/cityinfo, Mon-Sat 0830-1730*. Accommodation booking service (no fee, 10% deposit).

Sights

Most visitors head south on arrival at the train station, towards Town Quay and the boats for Hythe and the Isle of Wight. However, there are two art galleries worth looking into on the way. The **Southampton City Art Gallery** ⓘ *Guildhall, Commerical Rd, T023-80832277, Tue-Sat 1000-1700, Sun 1300-1600, free,* for its permanent collection of mid-20th-century artists and others, as well as temporary exhibitions. And, beyond the Civic Centre with its prominent clock tower and the East Park, the **Millais Gallery** ⓘ *T023-80319916, www.millais.solent.ac.uk, Mon-Wed, Fri 1000-1700, Thu 1000-1900, Sat 1200-1600*, which is an innovative space for contemporary art with regularly changing exhibitions.

The route south past the TIC leads past the **Tudor House Museum and Garden** ⓘ *Bugle St, T023-80635904, Tue-Fri 1000-1700, Sat 1000-1600, Sun 1400-1700, free.* The house was built for Sir John Dawtry and his family in 1495, and has been reconstructed to illustrate life in Tudor, Georgian and Victorian times. There's also a Tudor Knot Garden with fountains, bee skeps and appropriate 16th-century herbs.

A short distance away is **Medieval Merchants House** ⓘ *French St, T023-80221503, Apr-Nov, daily 1000-1800, £2.30 including audio tour*, which illustrates the history of the house decorated as it would have been in the 14th century, as shop, office, and home to a wealthy merchant of the time.

On Town Quay itself, the **Southampton Maritime Museum** ⓘ *Town Quay, T023-80635904, Tue-Fri 1000-1700, Sat 1000-1600, Sun 1400-1700, free*, has displays on the history of the port and a model of how it might have looked in the 1930s on the ground floor, while upstairs there's the Cunard town display, a 22-ft model of the *Queen Mary* and the story of the *Titanic*.

Sleeping

Winchester *p290, map p292*

L Wessex Hotel, Paternoster Row, T0870-4008126, www.wessexhotel.co.uk. Long-time the smart option (if a touch impersonal) in an excellent position on the close, many rooms with cathedral views, only scrapes into this price bracket (superior rooms £170 per night).

A Hotel du Vin and Bistro, 14 Southgate St, T01962-841414, www. hotelduvin.com. Stylish and comfortable hotel with pleasantly informal service and top-notch brasserie. Great views of the Cathedral's west front and over Winchester from the top rooms.

A Royal Hotel, St Peter St, T01962-840840, www.the-royal.com. Renovated old hotel of great character with beautiful garden and famous conservatory dining room.

B Westgate Hotel, 2 Romsey Rd, T01962-820222. Fairly recently refurbished family-run hotel close to the top of the High St with good bar and fresh, interesting ingredients on the menu in the restaurant.

B Wykeham Arms, 75 Kingsgate St, T01962-853834, F854411. Comfortable rooms in one of the best pubs in the city, right by the College and Cathedral Close.

C Dawn Cottage, Romsey Rd, T01962-869956. Professional non-smoking B&B a mile from the centre with views over town.

C St John's Croft, St John's St, T01962-859976. Period house B&B on St Giles Hill with high ceilings, 10-min walk from the cathedral.

D City Cottage, 51 Parchment St, T01962-863971. Sweet little B&B in small old terraced street tucked behind the main shopping drag.

D Mrs Fetherston-Dilke, 85 Christchurch Rd, T01962-868661. Large Victorian family house some way out of city centre but close to St Cross.

F Winchester YHA, 1 Water La, T01962-853723, F855524. Worth booking well in advance for pole position in National Trust City Mill on the Itchen, at the foot of the High St and Broadway. 31 beds in 1-, 4-, 9- and 18-bedded rooms.

Camping

F Morn Hill Cararvan Club Site, Morn Hill, 3 miles east of the city centre, off the A31, T01962-869877. Open Apr-Oct.

West of Winchester *p295*

A Lainston House Hotel, Sparsholt, Near Winchester, T01962-863588, www. exclusivehotels.co.uk. Charming William and Mary manor house at the top of a long drive in acres of attractive grounds with very good afternoon teas, at a price. Top end of this price bracket.

B The Greyhound Inn, 31 High St, Stockbridge, T01264-810833. Smart restaurant with 4 comfortable rooms, typically Stockbridge.

C Carbery Guest House Salisbury Hill, Stockbridge, T01264-810771, F811022. Quiet Georgian house a mile or so from Stockbridge, with a heated outdoor swimming pool and landscaped gardens overlooking the Test.

C The Grosvenor Hotel High St, Stockbridge, T01264-810606, F810747. Home of the famous Houghton Fishing Club, hence very busy in May, but a reasonably good 'country house' bet in the middle of town and this bracket (£75 per room with breakfast).

C Malt Cottage, Upper Clatford, Near Andover, T01264-323469, F334100. Very comfortable B&B in the Test Valley, surrounded by immaculate gardens.

East of Winchester *p296*

C Dean Farm, Kilmeston, Near Alresford, T01962-771286. An 18th-century farmhouse B&B on the edge of the Hampshire Downs.

D Priory Inn, Winchester Rd, Bishops Waltham, T01489-891313. Friendly pub with rooms.

New Forest *p297*

L Chewton Glen, New Milton, T01425-275341, www.chewtonglen.com. Frequently voted top hotel in the south, at £370 per night you expect a lot. The old house and grounds are elegant but the facilities are no less than one would expect and the pervading feel is slightly corporate.

L Master Builder's House Hotel, Buckler's Hard, Beaulieu, T01590-616253, www.themasterbuilders.co.uk. Done up in that slightly characterless but ever-so tasteful style beloved by smart hotels in the country. Its location on the banks of the Beaulieu river, at the end of the single grassy street that is Buckler's Hard, makes the *Master Builder's House Hotel* somewhere quite special.

A Stanwell House Hotel, High St, Lymington, T01590-677123, www.stanwell househotel.co.uk. Right on the town's main drag, funky restaurant and bar with garden out back and non-chintzy rooms.

A Westover Hall Hotel, Park La, Milford-on-Sea, T01590-643044. Charming informal atmosphere in a Victorian millionaire's seaside villa, with individual rooms of great character, many with sea views as well as a beautiful restaurant, bar and garden. Recommended.

B Gordleton Mill, Silver St, Near Lymington, T01590-682219, F683073. Attractive pub and restaurant hotel with twee water gardens and rated restaurant.

C Alderholt Mill, Sandelheath Rd, Fordingbridge, T01425-653130, www.alderholtmill.co.uk. A working watermill doing B&B with a lovely back garden. Very good value. Recommended.

C Compasses Inn, Damerham, near Fordingbridge, T01725-518231. Pleasant rooms in an attractive pub doing reasonable grub on the western fringe of the forest.

D Carrington Farmhouse, 22 Keyhaven Rd, Milford-on-Sea, T01590-642966. A 16th-century cottage B&B close to Keyhaven ferry.

F Burley YHA, Cott La, Burley, near Ringwood, T/F01425-403233. Former family house with 36 beds in 1-, 4-, 6- and 10-bedded rooms, next to the *White Buck Inn*. Quite hard to reach without a car.

Portsmouth *p300*

A Portsmouth Marriott Hotel, Southampton Rd, Portsmouth, T023-92383151, F92388701. 24-hr room service with conference facilities available accommodating up to 400 delegates. A corporate favourite but also one of the most comfortable options for holidaymakers.

B Old House Hotel, The Square, Wickham, T01329-833049, F833672. Acclaimed restaurant in a pleasant old-style hotel with walled garden and period features.

C The Sally Port, 57-58 High St, Old Portsmouth, T023-92823045. A 16th-century pub with comfortable rooms, opposite the Cathedral, 2-min walk along the 'hot walls'. Recommended.

D Hotel Ibis, Winston Churchill Av, Portsmouth, T023-92640000, F92641000. Budget chain option.

D Langdale Guest House, 13 St Edwards Rd, Southsea, T023-92822146, F9235-3303. Friendly, family guesthouse.

D Sailmaker's Loft, 5 Bath Sq, Old Portsmouth, T023-92823045. 3 double rooms, 2 with views over the water, in the old town.

D Woodville Hotel, 6 Florence Rd, Southsea T023-92823409, F92346089. Family-run hotel, 2 mins from the sea and centrally located close to all of Southsea's entertainments.

F Portsmouth and Southsea Backpackers, 4 Florence Rd, Southsea, T023-92823045, www.portsmouthbackpackers.co.uk. £10 per night, 2 double rooms £22 per night.

F YHA Portsmouth, Old Wymering La, Cosham, T023-92375661, F92214177. Tudor manor house in the north of the city, some way from the seafront.

Southampton *p302*

Southampton is not the most thrilling place to stay although its range of business hotels and chain diners caters well enough for the transient population. The options below stand out in their price range:

L De Vere Grand Harbour, West Quay Rd, T023-80633033, F023-80633066. The most expensive hotel in Southampton, smart corporate feel, with rated haute cuisine in *Allerton's* restaurant (£50 a head without wine).

B Novotel, 1 West Quay Rd, T023-80330550, F80222158. Clean and efficient mid-range chain option, with swimming pool, restaurant and bar.

C The Star, 26 High St, T023-80339939. Top end of this bracket, bang in the middle of town in an old building that survived the bombs.

D Linden Guest House, The Polygon, T023-80225653. Passable budget option close to the train station.

Eating

Winchester *p290, map p292*

£££ The Bistro in the *Hotel du Vin* (see p304) has become easily one of the best dining options in the city, and needn't break the bank with its liberal attitude to combining choices from the simple Frenchified menu (anything from £15 to £40 a head).

£££ Chesil Rectory, Chesil St, T01962-851555. Smart modern food (£37 set 3 courses), Michelin-starred, in one of the oldest buildings in the city.

££ Cathedral Refectory, Inner Close, T01962-857258. Reasonably priced fresh local ingredients (about £8 main courses) confidently put together in the shadow of the cathedral with tables outside.

££ La Bodega, 9 Great Minster St, T01962-864004. Tapas bar downstairs, proper Italian upstairs (main course of home-made pasta £7, kilo of ribeye £15).

££ Loch Fyne, 18 Jewry St, T01962-872930. One of the very fresh fish chain from Scotland in a renovated 16th-century building (£12 mains, £7 starters).

££ The Old Manor House, 21 Palmerston St, Romsey, T01794-517353. Very good Italian food in a typically English setting.

££ William Walker's in the *Wessex Hotel* (see above) has good value 'carvery' deals and views of the cathedral's south transept.

££ Wykeham Arms, 75 Kingsgate St, T01962-853834. Very popular top-quality old pub with wholesome traditional food and welcoming scholarly atmosphere. Reliable cooking for about £15 a head. Recommended.

New Forest *p297*

£££ Bistro on the Bridge, 3 Bridge St, Christchurch, T01202-482522. Simple fresh ingredients well-presented at this offshoot of Bournemouth's famous *Bistro on the Beach* (dinner about £20 a head).

£££ Westover Hall Hotel, Park La, Milford-on-Sea, T01590-643044. Has a beautiful little dining room, overlooking Christchurch Bay with views of the Needles in the distance, doing an excellent dinner menu for non-guests at £25 a head, which should be booked.

££ East End Arms, Lymington Rd, East End, T01590-626223. New Forest gastropub run by the same people as the *Master Builder's House Hotel*.

££ Egan's Restaurant, 24 Gosport St, Lymington, T01590-676165. Cheerfully decorated fresh fish restaurant just off the High St in Lymington (mains £12-£15). Good value £10 3-course lunch.

££ Marryat Restaurant, Chewton Glen, New Milton, T01425-275341. 1 Michelin- starred cooking overlooking the exclusive hotel grounds, good for a special occasion.

££ Nurse's Cottage, Station Rd, Sway, T01590-683402. Local produce like freshly caught fish, farm eggs, English cheeses and an impressively extensive wine list. No smoking throughout. B&B for £60 a night as well.

Portsmouth *p300*

££ Spice Island, Bath Sq, Old Portsmouth, next door to *Still and West*, does food all day and also has tables outside overlooking the harbour.

££ Still and West, Bath Sq, Old Portsmouth, T023-92821567. Right on the seafront with a good range of seafood dishes and a few real ales.

££ Sur La Mer, 69 Palmerston Rd, Southsea, T023-92876678. Reliable little French restaurant with a variety of good deals on its set menus and fish dishes.

££ Tang's, 125 Elm Grove, Southsea, T023-92822722. Superior Chinese in salubrious surroundings (about £20 a head).

For an explanation of the sleeping and eating price codes used in this guide, see the inside front cover. Other relevant information is provided in the Essentials chapter, page 40.

Pubs, bars and clubs

East of Winchester *p296*

Brushmakers Arms, Upham, Near Bishops Waltham, T01489-860231. Real ale free house with outside seating and reliable food.

The Globe on the Lake, The Soke, Alresford, T01962-732294. Ambitious menu on the shores of Old Alresford pond with large waterside garden and real ales.

Harrow Inn, Steep, Petersfield, T01730-262685. Traditional old country pub, beers through the hatch and big fireplace in attractive village in 'little Switzerland'.

Sun Inn, Bentworth, Near Alton, T01420-562338. Cosy log-fired pub hidden down a country lane with very good real ales and a few tables outside.

White Horse Inn, South Hill, Droxford, T01489-877490. An old coaching inn in the Meon valley with fine homemade pies, real ales and colourful flower-filled courtyard.

White Horse Inn (The pub with no name), Priors Dean, Near Petersfield, T01420-588387. Perched up on the downs, good food and own-brew beers in a popular destination pub celebrated by the poet Edward Thomas.

New Forest *p297*

The Chequers Inn, Lower Woodside, Lymington, T01590-673415, www.chequersinn.com. Country pub with barbecue, very popular with the hearty boating community.

Gun Inn, Keyhaven, T01590-642391. Basic inexpensive food and good beer in a cheery old local boozer near the ferry to Hurst Castle and Isle of Wight.

New Forest Inn, Emery Down, T023-80282329. Large back garden (and B&B) in a picturesque village at the heart of the forest with standard pub food.

Red Lion, Ropehill, Boldre, T01590-673177. Flower-bedecked boozer on the edge of the forest with beamed rooms and bar food.

Royal Oak, North Gorley, T01425-652244. A thatched country pub in picturesque surroundings on the western edge of the Forest, where you can sit and watch the ducks on the pond while supping your pint from the local Ringwood Brewery. Good value pub grub too.

Entertainment

Winchester *p290, map p292*

The Screen at Winchester, Southgate St, T01962-877007/recorded information T01962-856009, www.screencinemas.co.uk. 2 cinema screens with luxurious auditoria showing middle-to-high-brow new releases. Very good value.

Theatre Royal, Jury St, T01962-840440, www.theatre-royal-winchester.co.uk. Touring middle-scale dramas of a high standard.

Festivals

Winchester *p290, map p292*

Jul Winchester Hat Fair, 5a Jewry St, T01962-849841, www.hatfair.co.uk. Usually in early Jul, is the longest running festival of street theatre in Britain. Over 40 companies from all over the world take part in the festival.

Shopping

New Forest *p297*

Branksome China Works, Shaftesbury St, Fordingbridge, T01425-652010, www.branksomechina.co.uk. Hand-glazed and crafted fine porcelain crockery with tours of the factory.

Lymington Antiques Centre, 76 High St, T01590-670934. A hotbed of local antique collecting activity.

Activities and tours

Burley Wagonette Rides, Burley, T07000-924667/07712-074486. 20 mins to 1 hr 30 mins £2.50-£7.50 Easter-Oct daily 1100-1600.

Boating

Puffin Cruises from Lymington Town Quay to Yarmouth, Isle of Wight, T0850-947618. Sea fishing trips from Keyhaven, 8-6 hr deep sea trips, 3 hr mackerel trips Ray Pitt T01425-612896.

Leisure centres

Calshot Activities Centre, Calshot Spit, Fawley, New Forest, T023-80892077, www.hants.gov.uk/calshot. One of the largest in Britain: 3 ski slopes, climbing wall, indoor

velodrome, watersports, in an extraordinary position next to Calshot Castle on the spit.
New Forest Waterpark, Ringwood Rd, North Gorley, T01425-656868. Water-skiing, jet-skiing, inflatable banana boats. Jun-Sep daily 1000-2100, Apr and Oct weekends only, May Wed-Sun. Water-skiing from £15; aquarides £6; jet-skiing £30. Advisable to book.
River Park Leisure Centre, Gordon Rd, Winchester, T01962-869525. Daily 0630-2300 with swimming pool, 'twister' flume ride, sauna, steam rooms, fitness suites.

Riding

Burley Villa School of Riding, Near New Milton, T01425-610278, www.burleyvilla.co.uk, for riding Western style.
New Forest Riding Centre, The Old Barn, Dale Farm, Manor Rd, Applemore, T023-80843180. Tue-Sun 0900-1500 30 mins horse rides, 1 hr rides (£15), swimming on horseback and residential holidays.
New Park Manor Stables, New Park, Lyndhurst Rd, Brockenhurst, T01590-623919. Another reputable residential riding school and stables, marginally less expensive than most.

Walking

Long distance walks Pilgrim's Trail: 28 miles from Winchester to Portsmouth. St Swithun's Way: 43 miles from Winchester to Farnham. South Downs Way: 100 miles from Winchester to Eastbourne. Clarendon Way: 26 miles from Winchester to Salisbury, www.hants.gov.uk/leisure/paths. Solent Way: Milford-on-Sea to Emsworth (60 miles), a long-distance coastal footpath.
Guided Walk of Old Southampton, free tour every day at 1030 and 1430 Jun-Sep, Sun at 1030 all year, bank holidays at 1030, T023-80221106.
New Forest Badger Watch, T01425-403412, www.badgerwatch.co.uk. Evening trips (Mar-Oct) to watch badgers above and below ground through glass hides £10, under-15s £5.

Transport

Winchester *p290, map p292*

Car

Enterprise Rent-a-Car, Winchester Train Station,T01962-844022; **Hendy Hire**, Easton La, T01962-891891.

Taxi

A1 Alpha Cars, 15 West Hayes,Sarum Rd, T01962-820416. **Winchester Airport Link**, 171 Stanmore La, T01962-843057.

New Forest *p297*

Cycle

AA Bike Hire, Lyndhurst, Fernglen, T023-80283349, www. aabikehire newforest.co.uk. **Adventure Cycles**, 97 Station Rd, New Milton, T01425-615960. Beaulieu, T01590-611029. **Burley Bike Hire**, Burley, T01425-403584. **Cyclexperience**, Island Shop, 2-4 Brookley Rd, Brockenhurst, T01590-624204, www.cycleX.co.uk. **Perkins**, 7 Provost St, Fordingbridge, T01425-653475 Inexpensive tourers for £5 a day.

Taxi

Marchwood Motorways Taxi service T0800-5250521.

Portsmouth *p300*

Bus

National Express, T08705-808080, run the local services from Portsmouth, **The Hard Interchange** direct every 2 hrs to **London Victoria** (2 hrs 30 mins), direct twice hourly to **Brighton**, **Pool Valley** (3 hrs 40 mins), direct at 1040 to **Bournemouth Travel Interchange** (1 hr 40 mins) and also 8 times per day direct to **Southampton Harbour Parade** (50 mins).

Boat

Ferries from Portsmouth for France and Spain with P&O, T0870-2424999, to **Cherbourg**, **Le Havre** and **Bilbao** or Britanny Ferries, T08705 360360, to **Caen** and **St Malo**. For the **Isle of Wight** Wightlink, T0870-5827744, runs services over 3 routes to and from the island. Portsmouth to **Ryde** (High Speed Passenger Service) £12 standard return, taking 15 mins, every ½ hr. Portsmouth to **Fishbourne** (Car and Passenger Service) £67 standard return car and driver, £9.80 each additional passenger, taking 40 mins, every ½ hr. £39 night service for car and driver valid for a month so long as you travel both ways between 2300 and 0400.

Train

South West Trains, T08456-000650, run the frequent direct service from Portsmouth Harbour to **London Waterloo** (1 hr 45 mins).

Wessex Trains, T08709-002320, runs the regular direct service to **Southampton Central** (45 mins) and the frequent service to **Bournemouth** (1 hr 30 mins), changing at **Southampton**. South Central Trains, T08708-306000, run the hourly direct service to **Brighton** (1 hr 30 mins).

Southampton *p302*

Air

Southampton Airport has its own dedicated railway station, Southampton Airport Parkway. Fast trains run 3 times an hr from **London Waterloo** directly to the airport station. From Southampton Airport, business and leisure passengers can reach 22 direct destinations, together with over 200 long haul worldwide destinations via 6 key hubs including Amsterdam, Brussels, Paris, Frankfurt, Manchester and Dublin.

Boat

Red Funnel, T023-80334010, run passenger/vehicle services to **East Cowes** from Southampton (55 mins, £67 standard return, plus £9.40 per passenger) every 50 mins. Red Jet Hi-Speed service to and from **West Cowes** (£13.50, 22 mins) every 30 mins.

Bus

National Express, T08705-808080, run the direct service to **Bournemouth** (50 mins) 7 times per day and 9 times to **Portsmouth Hard Interchange** (50 mins). There is also an hourly direct service to **London Victoria** (2 hrs 35 mins) and a direct service to **Salisbury** (40 mins) at 1000, 1330 and 2125.

Train

South Central Trains, T08708-306000, run the regular direct service from Southampton Central to **Bournemouth** (40 mins). Wessex Trains, T08709-002320, run a regular direct service to **Salisbury** (35 mins) and 3 direct morning services to **Portsmouth Harbour** (50 mins). South West Trains, T08456-000650, run the direct service to **London Waterloo** (1 hr 25 mins) every 15 minutes.

Directory

Winchester *p290, map p292*

Hospitals Royal Hampshire County Hospital, Romsey Rd, T01962-863535.
Internet The Byte, 10 Parchment St, T01962-863235.

Isle of Wight

Colour map 2, grid C5

Like many of its fairly half-baked attractions, the Isle of Wight charges an entrance fee. If you're taking the car, it's likely to cost you more than a trip to France. That said, this 23-mile wide, 13-mile deep 'sunshine isle' does have a quirky charm. It's often observed that it represents the south of England in miniature. Geologically speaking that's certainly accurate, the heavy clay in the north giving away to a pair of downland chalk ridges, one of them breaking up in quite spectacular style in the sea to the west at the Needles. And there's more than a touch of little England about the place as a whole, with its old Norman castle, high-security prisons and social problems besetting the capital Newport in the middle, busy harbours in the north and tidy manor house villages snuggled up in the rolling hills inland. The east coast, best served by public transport, is where the majority of trippers fetch up, in the retirement and seaside entertainment resorts of Sandown, Shanklin and Ventnor. The south has the most beautiful coastline, while the north can boast one of the epicentres of world yachting at Cowes. Cycling, walking, bucket-and-spade and boating holidays are what the Isle of Wight does best. Nothing fancy, not that cheap, even a bit tired perhaps, but all jolly good clean fun. *For Sleeping, Eating and other listings, see pages 317-319.*

Ins and outs

Getting there Car ferries leave the mainland for the Isle of Wight from Southampton (at the end of the M3, 77 miles from London, at least 1½ hour's drive), Portsmouth (about 10 miles from the M3, down the M27 eastwards and M275), and Lymington (about 22 miles beyond Southampton via the M27 westwards and the A337 across the New Forest, at least a 2 hour drive). Mainline rail services to Southampton run from London Waterloo about twice hourly taking 1 hour and 30 minutes, to Portsmouth more often, also from London Waterloo, taking about 1 hour 45 minutes. Like Southampton, Lymington is on the mainline to Weymouth. **Wightlink**, T0870-5827744, runs **ferry** services over three routes to and from the island. Portsmouth to Rydge (high speed passenger service) £12 standard return, taking 15 minutes, every 30 minutes. Portsmouth to Fishbourne (car and passenger service) £67 standard return car and driver, £9.80 each additional passenger, taking 40 minutes, every 30 minutes. £39 night service for car and driver valid for a month so long as you travel both ways between 2300 and 0400. Lymington to Yarmouth (car and passenger service) £67 standard return car and driver, £9.80 each additional passenger, taking 30 minutes, every 30 minutes. **Red Funnel**, T023-80334010, run passenger/vehicle services to East Cowes from Southampton (55 minutes, £67 standard return, plus £9.40 per passenger) every 50 minutes. **Red Jet Hi-Speed** service to and from West Cowes and Southampton (£13.50, 22 mins) every 30 minutes. **Hovertravel**, T01983-811000, run passenger services between Ryde Esplanade and Southsea in under 10 minutes (£11.30 return). They have a frequent service running seven days a week. For day tripping foot passengers, the cheapest and most charming option late May to September is the tiny **Keyhaven to Yarmouth Ferry**, T01590-642500, which takes about 40 minutes leaving Keyhaven at 0915, 1030, 1230, 1630 and returning from Yarmouth at 1000, 1130, 1330, 1530, 1715. £7 day return.

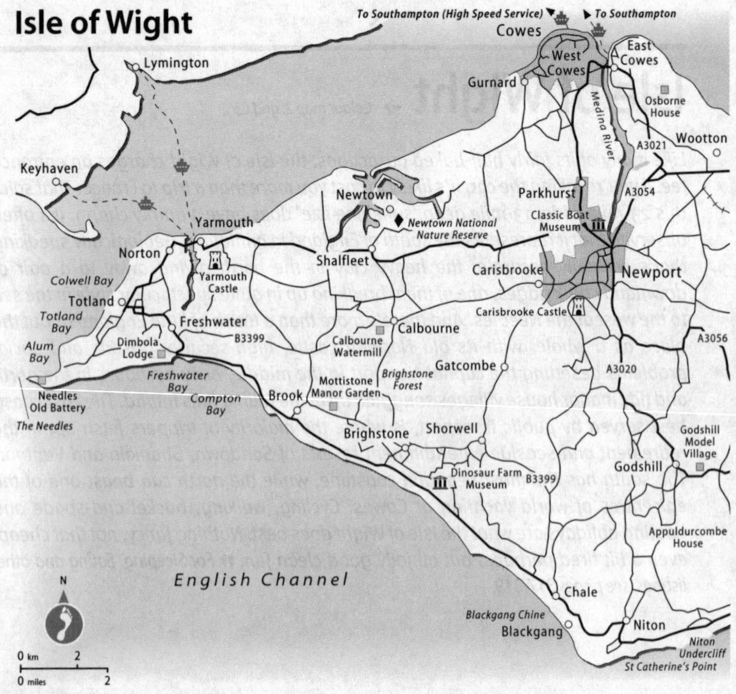

Getting around The east coast resorts of Ryde, Sandown, Shanklin and Ventnor are fairly well served by public transport, by the **Island Line**, Isle of Wight Steam Railway, T01983-884343, and by buses run by **Southern Vectis**, T01983-522456. Buses also serve the west end of the island (including Southern Vectis' useful Island Explorer) but much less regularly. A car or bicycle are easily the best ways of reaching some of the island's more impressive beauty spots. Bicycling especially is a joy out of season on the smaller roads that criss-cross the southwest of the island around Godshill, Wroxall and Brading, or from Yarmouth to the south coast. During the summer traffic usually finds its way into the remotest corners of the island.

Information Isle of Wight Tourism ⓘ *Westridge Centre, Brading Rd, Ryde, T01983-813800, accommodation booking service, T01983-813813, www.islandbreaks.co.uk.*

Northwest Wight

The old harbour town of Yarmouth is the most attractive port of entry on the island. The pubs, restaurants and hotels gathered around its small town square can become impossibly busy in the summer, but out of season they can make a very enjoyable day trip from the New Forest. A few miles east the marshland around the pretty little estuarine village of Newtown throngs with visiting birdlife. Almost bang in the middle of the island, Carisbrooke Castle on its little hill looks suitably noble and battered given its long history as a Royal prison and Norman powerhouse. Next door, the island's capital on the river Medina at Newport is a sorry sight although it does have a beautiful Guildhall, housing an informative local history museum. Directly due north, at the mouth of the Medina, Cowes has become synonymous with international yachting and all that that very expensive sport entails.

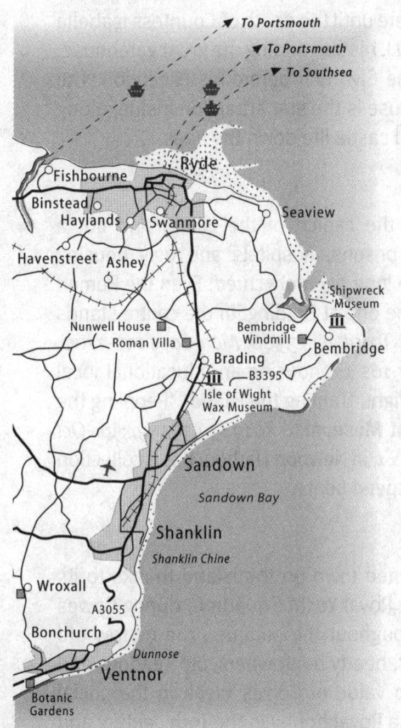

Ins and outs

Getting there Bus services 1/1A: Cowes, Newport, Ryde, Tesco, Bembridge. 7/7A: Ryde, Sandown, Shanklin, Ventnor, West Wight, Ryde, Binstead, Wootton, Newport, West Wight and Ryde, Newport, Brighstone, Brook, Totland. 33/34: Ryde, Havenstreet, Newport, Gurnard, Cowes and Ryde, Haylands, Swanmore, Ryde. All hourly during the main part of the day. ▸▸ *For further details, see Transport page 319.*

Getting around Two buses serve the area. 42: Yarmouth, Alum Bay, Needles Battery and 43: Newport, Yarmouth.

Information Yarmouth TIC ⓘ *The Quay, T01983-760015, Mon-Sat 0930-1630 Sun 1000-1600.* **Cowes TIC** ⓘ *Fountain Quay, T01983-291914, Tue-Sat 0930-1630.* **Newport TIC** ⓘ *The Guildhall, High St, T01983-823366, Mon-Sat 0900-1730 Sun 1000-1600.*

Yarmouth

Yarmouth is one of the most attractive towns on the island, its old harbour and town square yet to be overwhelmed by tourist tat, although it gets very crowded in the summer. Overlooking the harbour, **Yarmouth Castle** ⓘ *(EH), T01983-760678, Apr-Sep daily 1000-1800, Oct daily 1000-1700, £2.50, concessions £1.90, under-16's £1.30*, was Henry VIII's final coastal fortification, completed in the mid-16th century to protect the town from the French, now an impressive building housing changing exhibitions of local painting and photos of old Yarmouth, with battlements affording fine views over the Solent, good for picnics.

Newtown

About 5 miles east of Yarmouth, north of the main road to Newport, the tranquil little village of Newtown often wins the 'best-kept' award on the island, its cottage gardens a feast for the eyes in spring and summer. The strangely isolated little 17th-century brick and stone **town hall** ⓘ *(NT), T01983-531785, Apr-Oct Mon, Wed, Sun 1400-1700, Jul and Aug Mon-Thu, Sun 1400-1700, £1.60, under-16s £1.30*, is evidence that this was an important town in the Middle Ages, and one that became an infamous 'rotten borough', hugely over-represented in Parliament and done away with by the Reform Acts of the 1820s. Birdwatching and excellent coastal and marsh walks can be enjoyed in the **Newtown National Nature Reserve**.

Carisbrooke Castle

ⓘ *(EH), T01983-522107. Apr-Sep daily 1000-1800; Oct daily 1000-1700; Nov-Mar daily 1000-1600, £5, concessions £3.80, under-16s £2.50, family £11.50.*

The island's most important castle, at Carisbrooke, 5 miles further east on the A3054, commands tremendous panoramic views from its wallwalk and remains surprisingly complete, its great stone walls and gatehouse standing proud at the top of a small hill. It started life as a Saxon camp, parts of which can still be seen below the Norman keep. The Redvers family ran the island from here until the death of Countess Isabella in 1293, when the castle was bought by Edward I, his son adding the great gatehouse. King Charles I was imprisoned here during the Civil War before his execution. The working donkey wheel deep well in the wethouse is the star attraction inside, along with engaging museum displays on island and castle life down the ages.

Newport

Carisbrooke is on the outskirts of Newport, the capital of the island and not a particularly appealing sight. Surrounded by prisons, hospitals and ugly housing developments, the town's ancient origins have long been obscured. Even the Roman villa discovered here is best passed over for the one at Brading. In the centre stands John Nash's fine early 19th-century **Guildhall** ⓘ *T01983-823366, Mon-Sat 1000-1700, Sun 1100-1530, £1.80, concessions and under-16s £1*, housing an educational local history museum with displays on prehistoric Wight, 'Taming the Island', 'Peopling the Island' and a heritage gallery. The **Classic Boat Museum** ⓘ *T01983-533493, Apr-Oct daily 1030-1630, £3, concessions £2, under-16s £1*, in Newport Harbour has a collection of vintage boats, including early dinghies and speed boats.

Cowes

Back on the coast, Cowes is the most renowned town on the island thanks to its global yachting associations. The home of the Royal Yacht Squadron, during Cowes Week (early Aug), and at boating events throughout the summer, the narrow old streets of Cowes are awash with yellow wellies, hearty boatowners, old seadogs and very focused professional yachties. The snob value of Cowes Week in the social calendar was confirmed when sailing became a Royal hobby in the 19th century and shows no sign of diminishing, although the whole event has become significantly less amateurish. At any other time, the old town of West Cowes is an attractive and genteel place to poke around, connected to the more workaday East Cowes by the floating chain bridge (£1.30 per car).

Northeast Wight

Queen Victoria's favourite summer retreat at Osborne House now draws in hordes of curious visitors. The opulence of its interior is unlikely to disappoint. Further west, Ryde is the other main ferry port, a Victorian town that has never quite achieved its grand aspirations. The more unassuming and quietly well-to-do seaside village of Seaview just along the coast is more of a magnet. Bembridge is another major yachting centre at the mouth of the River Yar. At Brading the downs rise up to the south and the island's holiday spirit gets into gear.

Ins and outs

Getting there and around Ryde is the main **ferry** port on the eastern side of the island. The **Island Line** electric **railway** links Ryde with Smallbrook Junction, Brading, Sandown, Lake and Shanklin. The **Isle of Wight Steam Railway** runs from Smallbrook (£9 Island Liner ticket allows unlimited all-day travel on both). **Island Explorer** runs bus services 7/7a (see page 311); service 8 Tesco, Oakfield, Ryde, Seaview/Nettlestone; services 33/34, and an hourly service round the island in both directions. **Southern Vectis,** T01983-532373, services 1/1A, (see page 311); services 4/5 Ryde, Binstead, Wootton, East Cowes, Newport, Osborne, East Cowes. ⏩ *For further details, see Transport page 319.*

Information **TIC Ryde** ⓘ *Western Esplanade, T01983-562905, Mon-Sat 0900-1630 Sun 1000-1600.*

Osbourne House

ⓘ *(EH), East Cowes, T01983-200022, Apr-Sep daily 1000-1800 (last admission 1600, house closes at 1700). £8, concessions £6, child £4, family £20, grounds only £4.50/£3.40/£2.30.*

A mile or so east of East Cowes, Osborne House is the single most visited place on the island, especially since featuring in the film *Mrs Brown*. Queen Victoria's little holiday home, where she grieved well nigh inconsolably for her beloved Albert, is a pretty extraordinary Italianate palace looking down on wide-terraced gardens and acres of rolling parkland. Designed by Thomas Cubitt (responsible for the look of Pimlico in London) around an old Georgian house in 1846, the inside is finished in an opulent style, full of marble, gilt, statuary and portraits of 19th-century European royalty. Also on show are the Queen's Dining Room, with place settings showing the 'order of precedence' and the Durbar Wing, where her youngest daughter Beatrice lived, including a magnificent room designed by Bhai Ram Singh in the 1890s to show off India, the jewel in Victoria's crown. An exhibition explains the lavish furnishings' contemporary relevance to the subcontinent today.

Ryde and Seaview

Ryde is the main ferry terminal on the east of the island but not somewhere many people would otherwise choose to visit. It has a certain amount of 'faded charm' but even in that department can't really beat the competition further south and west. Getting into the holiday spirit, though, old London tube trains take ferry passengers inland along the pier, depositing them at the bottom of Union Street. East of the Hoverport, the Esplanade might like to become the next Brighton, complete with its miniature oriental pavilion, but it clearly has some way to go. Anyone with a car or bike is likely to do much better heading east for a couple of miles to Seaview, still a quiet little seaside village with a selection of good hotels, sandy beaches, warm breezes and views across the Solent of the twinkling orange lights of Portsmouth.

Bembridge

Next stop round the coast is Bembridge, popular with yachters, houseboat-dwellers and the retired. The **Shipwreck Museum** ⓘ *Sherbourne St, T01983-872223, Apr-Oct daily 1000-1700, £2.75, concessions £1.75, under-16s £1.35*, has lots of old photographs, a few videos, model ships, nautical bric-a-brac and tales to tell of HMS *Bounty*. Half a mile south of Bembridge on the B3395 is the last surviving **windmill** ⓘ *(NT), T01983-873945, Apr-Jun, Sep, Oct Mon-Fri, Sun 1000-1700, Jul and Aug daily 1000-1700, £1.70*, on the island, built in the early 18th century with its wooden workings still intact.

Brading

From Bembridge a quite spectacular road heads over Culver Downs. Here is the well-sited but bog-standard pub, the *Culverhaven Inn*, as well as various gun emplacements, and good views overlooking Sandown and Shanklin. After 3 miles or so the road arrives in Brading, which provides a foretaste of the full-on appeal to the tourist purse made further along the coast. As well as the **Isle of Wight Wax Museum** ⓘ *T01983-407286, daily 1000-1700, £5, under-14s £3.40*, with its inevitable Chamber of Horrors, there's **Morton Manor** ⓘ *near Sandown, T01983-406168, Apr-Oct Mon-Fri, Sun 1000-1730, £4*, a 13th-century manor house surrounded by an ancient 6-acre garden – a sight for sore eyes in spring – as well as a maze and vineyard. The remarkably good value **Lilliput Antique Doll and Toy Museum** ⓘ *T01983-407231, www.lilliputmuseum.com, daily 1000-1700, £1.95, under-16s £1*, is typical of the island in many ways: the museum's really impressive collection of old playthings is presented in a charming and amateurish way. Equally, the privately run **Roman Villa** ⓘ *T01983-406223, Apr-Oct daily 0930-1700, £2.75, under-16s £1.35*, with its well-preserved hypocaust, intriguing and beautiful floor mosaics in a Roman room with a view crying out for a new roof, is much more accessible and enjoyable than many an overtended English Heritage site. A mile northwards, a stiff walk past Morton Manor over Brading Down and through the Devil's Punch Bowl, stands **Nunwell House** ⓘ *T01983-407240, Jul and Aug Mon-Wed 1000-1700, Sun 1300-1700, £4*, a place with beautiful views and set in a garden designed by Vernon Russell-Smith. It's a fine-looking establishment where King Charles I spent his last night of freedom as a guest of the Oglander family, one of the oldest on the island, who still look after the place today.

Southeast Wight

The island's reputation for seaside holiday heaven (or hell) emanates from the resorts of Sandown and Shanklin, amusement arcade wonderlands with a tacky style all their own – love 'em or loathe 'em. Round the corner, Bonchurch is quietly superior to their boisterous charms, tucked into the peculiar geological landslip bursting with exotic vegetation known as the Undercliff. Next door, Ventnor is a solidly picturesque seaside town tumbling down to a little sandy bay. A short hop inland, Godshill draws in the crowds to wonder at its picture-postcard setting, model village and remarkable church.

Ins and outs

Getting there and around **Route Rouge** services 2/3/3A/3B, Cowes-Newport-Shanklin-Sandown-Ryde; Cowes, Newport, Godshill, Ventnor; and Cowes, Newport, Robin Hill, Sandown. **Island Explorer Services** services 7/7A, (see page 311). Service 47, Sandown-Shanklin (Old Village-Town-Esplanade).

Information Sandown TIC ⓘ *8 High St, T01983-403886, Mon-Sat 0930-1730.* **Shanklin TIC** ⓘ *67 High St, T01983-862942, Mon-Sat 0930-1630 Sun 1000-1600.* **Ventnor TIC** ⓘ *T01983-853625, Apr-Oct only.*

Sights

Two miles south of Brading, the wide sweep of Sandown Bay is almost entirely taken up with the twin resorts of Sandown and Shanklin. These two fulfill most people's ready image of the 'holiday island', with their esplanades, sandy beaches, crumbling hotels and relentless tacky amusements. Sandown is marginally more geriatric, while Shanklin boasts the thatched, illuminated (May-Sep) and awesomely twee **Shanklin Chine** ⓘ *T01983-866432, www.shanklinchine.co.uk, Apr-Oct daily 1000-dusk*, a ravine running down the cliff full of rare plants and used as a training ground for Commandos during the war. Henry 'Hiawatha' Longfellow visited it in 1868, leaving some verses on the drinking fountain near the top of the chine.

Bonchurch and Ventnor

Round the corner beyond Dunnose, 3 miles along the pretty Undercliff, the closest the Isle of Wight comes to a corniche road, Bonchurch and Ventnor are a much more solidly attractive south-facing mix of seaside amusements, good restaurants and reasonable accommodation. All of which contributes effectively to a happy holiday mood, nestling below St Boniface Down. The aesthetic poet Algernon Swinburne lived in a house called East Dene in Bonchurch as a boy and played with Dickens' sons when the novelist stopped over in 1849, but he found the air distasteful and left for breezy Broadstairs in Kent.

The **Ventnor Botanic Garden** ⓘ *T01983-855397, Apr-Oct 1000-1700, free*, features several acres of exotic plants from the Antipodes, South Africa and Mexico as well as a herb garden and banana trees. Also in the Garden, the **Museum of Smuggling History** ⓘ *T01983-853677, Apr-Sep daily 1000-1730*, has three basement rooms dedicated to all things contraband, with life-size models and over 300 exhibits illustrating the smugglers' trade. Good for a rainy day.

Three miles north of the Botanic Gardens along the B3327, a narrow track leads off to the left and a striking ruined stately home set in Capability Brown-landscaped gardens. **Appledurcombe House** ⓘ *Wroxall, T01983-852484, www.appuldurcombe.co.uk, May-Sep daily 1000-1700, Oct-Apr daily 1000-1600, £2, under-16s £1.50, concessions £2.25*, was once the grandest on the island but fell prey to some strange adulterous shenanigans amongst its owners, an amusing story told on information boards in the empty shell. Now its austere Palladian architecture stands lonely and elegant in its gardens, crying out to be sketched. The grounds are a beautiful spot for a picnic and there's a falconry centre next door.

Godshill

As if the Chine were not enough, Godshill, 5 miles west of Shanklin on the A3020, must rank as one of the most ridiculously quaint little villages in England. Its unusual double-naved church claims to be among the top 10 'most visited' in the country, perhaps to see the wonderful Lily Crucifix mural from 1440 – painted over during the Reformation and uncovered in the 19th century – but also no doubt to ask forgiveness for the huge cream teas taken in the village. Almost inevitably, in the gardens of the old vicarage, there's a **model village** ⓘ *T01983-840270, Mar-Sep 1000-1700 (Jul and Aug until 1800), £2.75, under-16s £1.25, concessions £2.50*, a good example of its type, with tiny people enjoying a very hearty variety of outdoor activities dotted about between 1/10-scale stone houses with miniaturized gardens and a 1/20-scale model railway. The other attraction, the Shell Museum, a collection of fossils, shells and minerals, is almost overwhelmed by its gift shop.

South and west Wight

The least over-developed and most scenic part of the island, the southern coast path around St Catherine's Point, St Catherine's Hill and the downs above Brighstone provide the best walking country. Along with a few less busy old villages like Shorwell and Calbourne, the southwest is also home to several good quality visitor attractions like the gardens at Mottistone Manor, the Dinosaur Farm Musem, the working watermill at Calbourne and Dimbola Lodge, the former home of pioneer portrait photographer Julia Cameron. To the west, the island peters out beyond Freshwater in dramatic style with the sea-swept chalk stacks of the Needles.

Ins and outs

Getting there and around Island Explorer services 7/7A (see page 311) and 42 Yarmouth, Alum Bay, Needles Battery.

St Catherine's Point

Six miles west along the coastal A3055 from Ventnor, St Catherine's Point is the most southerly headland on the island, a lovely cliffside spot with a little lighthouse overlooked by St Catherine's Hill, the highest point on the island (by 1 m over St Boniface Down to the east). On the summit, a medieval **lighthouse** known as the Pepperpot, officially St Catherine's Oratory, stands next to the **Saltcellar**, an abortive 19th-century attempt at a lighthouse (because of the frequent fog), used as a gun emplacement during the Second World War. On the road at the foot of the hill, close to the rather desperate **Blackgang Chine Amusement Park** (partly because it's gradually falling into the sea), there's a strange little **temple to Shakespeare**, a shrine quoting verses from the *Two Gentlemen of Verona* put up by Thomas Letts of diary fame.

The A3055 runs northwest along the coast, a military road constructed to repel French invaders, after six miles passing the **Dinosaur Farm Museum** ⓘ *T01983-740401, www.wightonline.co.uk/dinosaurfarm, £2, concessions £1.50, under-16s £1.* Established following the discovery of a well-preserved brachiosaurus in 1992, it's where fossils found on hunts can be identified and rare specimens can be seen in the process of conservation by experts.

Shorwell and Brighstone

At Chale, the B3399 heads north inland to the picturesque village of Shorwell, an excellent base for walks on the central downland. **Limerstone Down**, 2 miles west of the village, provides particularly wide-reaching views of almost the entire sea-girt little island. At the foot of the hill is another sweet village, Brighstone, with an interesting Village Museum in a row of cute thatched cottages with a National Trust shop. The Trust's most impressive property on the island is 2 miles west of Brighstone, at **Mottistone Manor** ⓘ *(NT), T01983-741302, garden open Apr-Oct Tue, Wed 1100-1730, Sun and bank holidays 1400-1730, £2.80, concessions £1.30*, the place to take in sea views, teas and some colourful herbaceous borders in a 16th-century manor house garden.

Three miles inland north of Mottistone through **Brighstone Forest** (past the NT car park where the Tennyson Trail through beautiful hillside beech woods and along the ridge of the downs can be followed west to the Needles about eight miles away), at **Calbourne**, there's a working **watermill** ⓘ *T01983-531227, Apr-Oct daily 1000-1700 (Jul and Aug until 1900), £4, concessions £3, under-16s £2*, with grinding demonstrations at 1500 daily, surrounded by quirky museums, punting on the mill pond, and bouncy galleon for kids. Good café selling homeground cakes and bread.

Freshwater Bay and The Needles

Back on the south coast, at Freshwater Bay, five miles west of Mottistone, the large seaside house called **Dimbola Lodge** ⓘ *Terrace La, Freshwater Bay T01983-756814, www.dimbola.co.uk, Tue-Sun 1000-1700, £3, under-16s free*, where the pioneer photographer Julia Cameron lived and worked has been preserved, with a permanent exhibition of her Victorian portraits 'Famous Men and Fair Women' and also changing shows on contemporary photographers, an excellent vegetarian restaurant with sea views as well as workshops and other events.

The walk from Brighstone continues west along Compton Down affording magnificent sea views southwards. To the south below is **Compton Bay**, famous for its very clean beaches. The chalk ridge continues along **Tennyson Down** and **High Down**, ending up at The Needles in the west. It's worth arriving in time to check out the **Old Battery** ⓘ *(NT), West Highdown, Totland, T01983-754772, Apr-Jun, Sep, Oct Mon-Thu, Sun 1030-1700, Jul and Aug daily 1030-1700, £3.50, family £7.50*, built into the cliffs here, alongside a strange rocket testing site. The fort was built in 1862 to protect against the threat of French invasion, with a 200-ft tunnel leading to spectacular views of the Hampshire and Dorset coast. Its gun barrels are still in place, and the searchlight position accessible up winding spiral staircase. The 1940s tearoom is a treat.

Sleeping

Northwest Wight *p311*

A **The George Hotel**, Yarmouth, T01983-760331. One of the best hotels on the island, run by the same people as the *Master Builder's House Hotel* in Buckler's Hard, New Forest, see p305. Very good airy brasserie with outdoor seating next door to a rather stuffy smart restaurant.

C **Fountain Arms** High St, Cowes T01983-292397. A central pub with comfortable rooms, if not that quiet.

C **Duke of York**, Mill Hill Rd, Cowes T01983-295171. A very lively and friendly old pub just up from the floating bridge. Expect the whole town to be booked solid in the summer.

D **Jireh House**, St James Sq, Yarmouth T01983-760513, and

D **Wavell's**, Yarmouth, T01983-760738, above their own deli, with a clean, comfortable guest annexe.

Northeast Wight *p313*

A **Biskra Beach Hotel**, 17 St Thomas's St, Ryde, T01983-567913, www.biskrahotel.com. The other contender in the style stakes, right on the beach with a top-notch Italian restaurant.

A **Priory Bay Hotel**, Priory Dr, Seaview, T01983-613146, www.priorybay.co.uk. Probably the classiest hotel on the island, on the site of an old priory with converted barns, gardens and a highly rated restaurant.

B **Northbank Hotel**, Seaview, T01983-612227. Pleasant 18-room family-run Victorian hotel right on the beach in the middle of the village boasting an Aga-cooked menu.

B **Seaview Hotel**, High St, Seaview, T01983-612711, www.seaviewhotel.co.uk. Popular award-winning restaurant and comfortable hotel in the centre of the village, both acclaimed by the national press, something of a haven for the more affluent Seaviewers.

B **Springvale Hotel**, Seaview, T01983-612533. Beautifully positioned Edwardian house overlooking the Solent makes an eccentric alternative to staying in the village.

C **Crab and Lobster Inn**, 32 Foreland Fields Rd, Bembridge, T01983-872244. Busy pub with rooms in a fine position on the most eastern tip of the island. Local seafood is a speciality, but parking in summer can be next to impossible.

For an explanation of the sleeping and eating price codes used in this guide, see the inside front cover. Other relevant information is provided in the Essentials chapter, page 40.

C **Little Upton Farm**, Gatehouse Rd, Ashey, T01983-563236. Working farm on the outskirts of Ryde, close to the Steam railway stop at Ashey.

C **Newham Farm**, Binstead, Rude, T01983-882423, www.newhamfarm.co.uk. 17th century working farm built on the site of an abbey. Easy-going, friendly atmosphere, impeccable service and magnificent breakfasts. A real find. Highly recommended.

Southeast Wight *p314*

A **Royal Hotel**, Belgrave Rd, Ventnor, T01983-852186, www.royalhoteliow.co.uk. The grandest hotel in Ventnor, recently refurbished in a restrained and airy way, with heated outdoor pool and sea views.

A **Windcliffe Manor**, Sandrock Rd, Undercliffe T01983-730215. The other smart option near Ventnor.

B **Shanklin Manor House Hotel**, Manor Rd, Old Village, Shanklin, T01983-862777. Welcoming and friendly old house with pool indoor, outdoor and in the games room, close to thatched old Shanklin.

C **Kerne Farm**, Alverstone, Sandown, T01983-403721. Crangly old farmhouse B&B with self-catering cottages, conservatory and large garden.

D **Hillside Hotel**, Mitchell Av, Ventnor, T01983-852271. Small family-run thatch-roofed hotel overlooking Ventnor from the foot of Boniface Down. Good value vegetarian menu.

D **Spyglass Inn**, Esplanade, Ventnor, T01983-855338, F855220. Small rooms with sea views above a very convivial pub (see below).

F **Sandown YHA**, The Firs, Fitzroy St, T01983-402651, F403565. A 47-bed hostel in a converted townhouse 300 yds from the Esplanade.

South and west Wight *p316*

A **Swainston Manor Hotel**, Calbourne, T01983-521121. Grand old country house in a beautiful garden with old-fashioned, slightly run-down furnishings.

B **Sandpipers**, Coastguard La, Freshwater Bay, T01983-758500 with *Fat Cat on the Bay* restaurant.

C **North Court**, Shorwell, T01983-740415. Jacobean mansion, snooker table in the library, set in 14 acres of carefully tended gardens, croquet and lawn tennis. No smoking.

C **Rockstone Cottage**, Colwell Chine Rd, T01983-753723. B&B with attractive garden, Near Totland.

D **Westcourt Farm**, Shorwell, T01983-740233. Charming old Elizabethan manor house with beautiful views and cosy rooms. No smoking.

F **Totland Bay YHA**, Hurst Hill, Totland Bay, T01983-752165, F756443. The best budget option near the Needles.

Eating

Northwest Wight *p311*

££ **Café Mozart**, 48 High St, T01983-293681, do some Frenchified light meals, main courses about £10.

££ **The New Inn**, Mill Rd, Shalfleet, T01983-531314, is a pub with riverside garden doing food to a high standard (£10 mains) and a reputation for excellent fish dishes.

££ **Salty's**, Quay St, Yarmouth, T01983-761550, is a harbourside restaurant patronized by the locals who come for the fish and busy downstairs bar, one of the most highly rated places on the island.

££ **Valentino's**, 93 High St, Carisbrooke, T01983-522458, is a mid-range Italian restaurant popular with the locals.

£ **Murray's**, 106 High St, T01983-296233, has a long-standing reputation for its fresh fish and seafood.

£ **Primefood**, 62 High St, Cowes, T01983-291111, is a superior deli, a good place to pick up provisions for your boat or put together a picnic.

£ **Yorkies Fish and Chips**, 55 High St, Cowes, T01983-291713, is a famous old-fashioned chippy.

Northeast Wight *p313*

££ **Ivar Cottage**, Hillway, Bembridge, T01983-874758. Sweet little cottage garden on the B3395 4 miles west of Bembridge, where absolutely fresh crab and lobster can be enjoyed or taken away for a picnic.

££ The Net, Sherbourne St, Bembridge, T01983-875800, is a newish style restaurant that's a winner with the sailing fraternity with a brasserie menu (about £4) and regularly changing fusion food dinner menu (£12 main courses).
££ The Old Fort, Esplanade, Seaview, T01983-612363, a strange combination of diner and bar, a social hub right on the seafront doing competent cuisine.

Southeast Wight *p314*
££ Bonchurch Inn, The Shute, Bonchurch, T01983-852611. Italian food and English staples in a curio-crammed olde-worlde pub in a very pretty village.
££ Spyglass Inn, Esplanade, Ventnor, T01983-855338. South-facing and right beside the sea, very popular with families (also does rooms) and doing reasonably good food that can be enjoyed outside braving the gulls and spume at high tide.

South and west Wight *p316*
££ Bay View Restaurant, Totland, T01983-756969. Great position on the beach, with stunning sunset views, unfortunately only complemented by adequate and expensive cuisine and a noisy bar area.
££ The Red Lion, Church Pl, Freshwater, T01983-754925. Quiet but very popular pub doing an above-average menu prepared from fresh ingredients, in one of the more attractive corners of Freshwater, up by the old church. Recommended.
£ The Buddle Inn, St Catherine's Rd, Niton Undercliff, T01983-730243. Attractive old pub with a large garden and model of Carisbrooke Castle out front, near the south coast path, doing reliable and reasonably priced pub grub (cod and chips £5.25).
£ Gatcombe Tearooms, Little Gatcombe Farm, Newbarn La, Gatcombe, T01983-721580. Sidney the peacock patrols outside this modern farmhouse where good home-made teas can be taken just beneath the downs in the middle of the island (also a B&B).
£ The Oasis, Castlehaven Caravan Site, Niton, T01983-730461, winter T01983-855556. Do basic snacks in a funny little hut near St Catherine's Lighthouse, good for coast pathers.

Activities and tours

Northwest Wight *p311*
Boating
Southerne Belle For trips on the River Medina, the Belle cruises into Newport Harbour from Cowes during summer, T07703-217888 for times and prices.

Riding
Romany Riding Stables, T01983-525467, on a minor road to the north off the A3054, 3 miles west of Newport, signposted Little Whitehouse. Offers very good value riding lessons and hacking, £10 for beginners, in a welcoming if rather scruffy yard.
Brickfields, Newnham Rd, Binstead, near Ryde, T01983-566801, www.brickfields.net. Daily all year 1000-1700. Apr-Oct £4.95, concessions £4.50, under-16s £3.75, family £15. Sep-Mar £4.50, concessions £3.50, under-16s £2.50. Also have pigs, rare breeds, a tractor museum and special events.

Transport

Northwest Wight *p311*
Bicycle
Isle Cycle Hire, T01983-760219, Yarmouth, **Wight Mountain**, T01983-533445, Newport, **Offshore Sports**, T01983-290514, Cowes.

Car
Ford Rental, River Way, Newport, T01983-523441; **Solent Self Drive Ltd**, 32 High St, Cowes, T01983-282050.

Northeast Wight *p313*
Bicycle
Battersby Cycles, Ryde, T01983-562039; **Bikestore**, Ryde, T01983-812989; **Bikemech**, Freshwater, T01983-756787; **GP Rentals**, Benbridge, T0800-9173494; **Isle of Bikes**, Brading, T01983-406306. **Island Cycle Hire**, Sandown, T07712-363134; **Offshore Sports**, Shanklin, T01983-866269.southeast

Car
Bartletts Service Station, 5 Langbridge, Newchurch, Sandown, T01983-865338; **Hillstone Self Drive Car Hire**, Osborne Rd,

Shanklin, T01983-864263. **Volkswagen Rental**, George St, Ryde, T01983-562322.

Directory

Hospitals Isle of Wight Healthcare NHS Trust, Parkhurst Rd, Newport, T01983-524081. The Orchard Hospital,189, Fairlee Rd, Newport,PO30 2EP, T01983-520022. **Library** East Cowes Library,York Centre,York Avenue, East Cowes, T01983 293019.

The Southwest

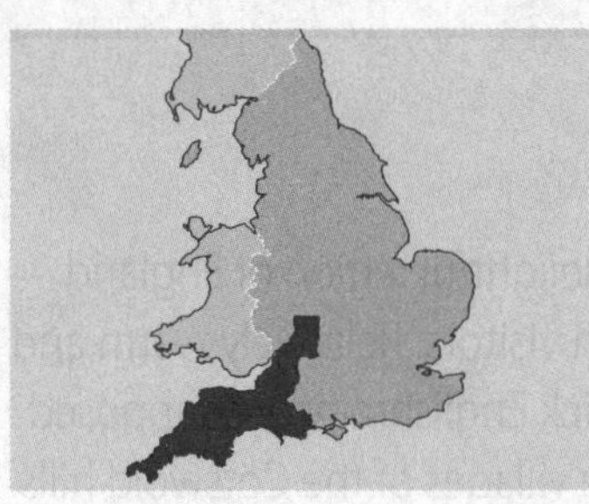

Footprint features

Introduction

The Southwest is a consistently delightful region of England and one of the most popular with visitors. Relatively warm and wet, here's the place that homesick Englishmen are supposed to see in dreams: the honeystone villages of the Cotswold hills in Gloucestershire; the golden flagon of cider from Somerset's apple orchards; the winding green lanes and clotted cream of Dorset; the foaming breakers on Devon's rocky coast; and the mystical light bathing lonely Cornwall. Surprisingly enough it does still exist, but you'll need to escape the endless traffic, overpriced food and shabby accommodation to really live the dream. A refreshing place to wake up might be its unofficial capital, Bristol, an earthier and more businesslike kind of Brighton. Next door, Bath isn't slumbering either, as it makes the most of its Roman spa town heritage and elegant 18th-century architecture. Gloucestershire is one of the most aristocratic of counties, its rolling Cotswolds hardly a guarded secret though, with a glorious cathedral in Gloucester and another 18th-century spa town at Cheltenham. To the south, Dorset boasts the beach-life of Victorian-built Bournemouth and the stonemason's rugged Isle of Purbeck on its coast, ancient manor houses, abbeys, hill forts, and Thomas Hardy inland. Further west, in Devon, the natural wildernesses of Dartmoor and Exmoor are sandwiched between a high wooded coastline to the north and the reddish rocks of the Jurassic Coast in the south. Even further west, Cornwall entices visitors with some brilliant beaches, headlands and harbour towns before England finally peters out with the subtropical granite rocks that are the Isles of Scilly. Cornwall is also home to the magnificent climate-controlled biospheres in a disused clay pit called the Eden Project, a millennium project that sums up something about the Southwest as a whole: it's all about the sea, stone and whatever can be done with what's in between.

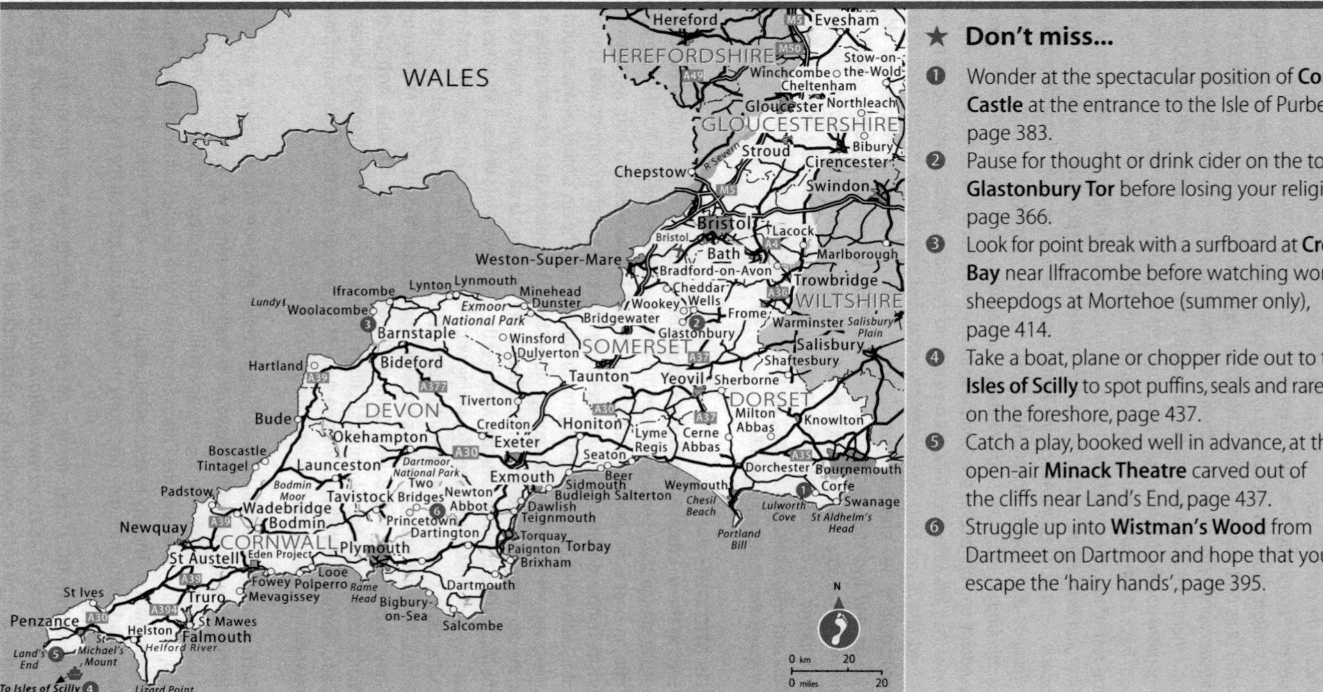

★ Don't miss...

1. Wonder at the spectacular position of **Corfe Castle** at the entrance to the Isle of Purbeck, page 383.
2. Pause for thought or drink cider on the top of **Glastonbury Tor** before losing your religion, page 366.
3. Look for point break with a surfboard at **Croyde Bay** near Ilfracombe before watching working sheepdogs at Mortehoe (summer only), page 414.
4. Take a boat, plane or chopper ride out to the **Isles of Scilly** to spot puffins, seals and rare flora on the foreshore, page 437.
5. Catch a play, booked well in advance, at the open-air **Minack Theatre** carved out of the cliffs near Land's End, page 437.
6. Struggle up into **Wistman's Wood** from Dartmeet on Dartmoor and hope that you'll escape the 'hairy hands', page 395.

Bristol
→ *Colour map 2, grid A2*

Though the city of Bristol may not quite be the San Francisco of England, it is certainly an idea worth conjuring with. Stuck out on the west coast of the country, it has all the fresh air and sunlight (when it's not raining) of a city built on hills, a large expanse of shimmering water at its centre and a beautiful, swooping suspension bridge as its main icon. It is the artistic capital of the region. And though its inhabitants are yet to wear flowers in their hair (and there's no particularly visible gay scene), there is nonetheless a palpable spirit of optimism and freshness about a place that can only be described as positively bristling with fresh ideas and spanking new developments. But it was not until the early 1990s that the rest of the country began to associate Bristol with anything more than crumbling Georgian terraces and headbanging cider drinkers. At that point, a triumvirate of triphop bands – Tricky, Massive Attack and Portishead – determinedly mining a deep vein of alienation and despair, nonetheless linked the city in the popular imagination with a certain kind of urban cool. By the time of the millennium, the prosperity of a booming local economy and of herds of predominantly middle-class students was really beginning to make itself felt. Most obviously, the area around the floating harbour was opened up and turned into a vast Euro-style visitor attraction, featuring a funky modern bridge, and incorporating two previously established arts centres, open-plan eateries, an IMAX cinema and two state-of-the-art multimedia '@Bristol' exhibits. Heading uphill, the hitherto rather staid Park Street now boasts a riot of trendy clothes shops and coffee bars and, further on, a section of sedate Whiteladies Road has become a continuous line of bars and restaurants, earning itself the new, semi-ironic name of 'the strip'. ▸▸ *For Sleeping, eating and other listings, see pages 329-333*

Ins and outs

Getting there **Bristol International Airport**, T0870-1212747, is just south of the city. A regular shuttle bus operates between the airport and the city centre. There is at least 1 **train** an hour from London Paddington to Bristol Temple Meads (1 hour 45 minutes). Bristol Temple Meads is only 15 minutes away from Bath and also connects with services into South Wales and the West Country. Bristol Parkway, the city's other railway station – unless you need to catch a train going north – should be avoided, as it is several miles out of the city centre. By **road**, London to Bristol is 122 miles, or about 2 hours, straight down the M4. The M4 then heads further west over the River Severn into Wales. It also links up, just west of Bristol, with the M5, taking you either north up to Birmingham and the Midlands, or south down deeper into the West Country. There are plenty of car parks in Bristol. **National Express**, T08705-808080, from London Victoria to the Marlborough Street **bus** station and **Bakers Dolphin**, T01934-413000, from Marble Arch to the Marlborough Street Bus Station and Clifton Triangle. Local services, including buses to Bath, Glastonbury, Wells and Weston-super-Mare, also run from the Marlborough Street bus station. ▸▸ *For further details, see Transport, page 333.*

Getting around Bristol is becoming increasingly pedestrian-friendly, which is a definite bonus for the visitor. However, to walk between, say, Clifton and the Old City is quite a hike, even if one is going downhill. There are plenty of buses, however. The 8, 9, 180 and 500 all link the Clifton Triangle with the Centre Promenade and Temple Meads Station. The city is also cycle-friendly and has an extensive network of cycle lanes and paths, including one along the Avon which goes all the way to Bath.

Information TIC ⓘ *next to the @ Bristol exhibits in the harbourside area, T0117-9260767/9462222, www.visitbristol.co.uk, open daily.* It's well worth getting hold of a copy of the excellent A3 map produced by the city council, available free from the TIC and from many different shops. In addition, *Venue* magazine, Bristol's answer to London's *Time Out*, will keep you up to date with what's on in the city, as well as being a lively read in itself.

Sights

Bristol divides itself into a number of different pockets, each with its own distinctive atmosphere. Of these, four are of particular interest to the visitor: the **harbourside**; the **Old City** and the pedestrian area around the **Old Vic Theatre**; a two-mile stretch of road linking the Anglican cathedral, just above the harbour, up Park Street, past the university and museum at the top of the hill and on to the Clifton Triangle of shops and restaurants, finally veering right up into Whiteladies Road; and **Clifton Village**, elegant if slightly precious, with its desirable Georgian properties, chi-chi boutiques and beauty parlours, set below the famous Clifton Suspension Bridge. In addition, **Montpelier**, the bohemian quarter of town, boasts at least one great restaurant and one great pub.

Harbourside

Standing beside the statue of Neptune in the middle of the Centre Promenade, Bristol lies all around you. Looking south towards the ornamental fountains, the harbourside area is directly in front of you. A good way of taking it all in is on a **ferry ride** around the harbour from Bordeaux Quay. There are four companies plying for your trade, all at much the same price (£3.50/£2.00 for a 40-minute tour or £1.20/80p for a one-way trip). Glimpse the SS *Great Britain* and the Clifton Suspension Bridge, or stop off at the **Bristol Industrial Museum** ⓘ *T0117-9251470, Apr-Oct Sat-Wed 1000-1700, Nov-Mar weekends only, free,* to learn a little about the history of this port, including its murky role in the slave trade of the 18th century. The history of the slave trade is also covered at the worthwhile **British Empire and Commonwealth Museum** ⓘ *1000-1700 daily, £4.95, concessions £4.35, child £2.45,* next to Bristol Temple Meads railway station.

The **SS Great Britain** ⓘ *T0117-926 0680, Apr-Oct 1000-1730, Nov-Mar 1000-1630, £6.25, child £3.75,* the world's first luxury ocean liner and, alongside the Clifton Suspension Bridge, one of Brunel's great Bristolian triumphs is now almost completely restored to its original glory in the dock where she was first built in 1843. Its passengers included 15,000 emigrants to Australia, as well as the first England cricket team going on tour down-under. In 1886, however, she was caught in a storm off Cape Horn and abandoned in the Falkland Islands. Your visit to the dock, accessible also by foot or the little harbour railway (£1 return) beside the Industrial Museum, includes a ticket to a maritime heritage centre and a replica of the *Matthew*, John Cabot's tiny three-masted caravel, which, in 1997, re-enacted Cabot's voyage across the Atlantic. Next door to the *SS Great Britain* is the **Spike Island Artspace** ⓘ *T0117-929 2266, daily 1200-1700, free,* a co-operative of artists' studios which also stages exhibitions at most times during the year.

On the westerly side of the harbour is the **Watershed**, a media centre that is also a two-screen arts cinema (though it is about to undergo a major refit). On the right surrounding the tourist information centre, is **Millennium Square**, a wide expanse of stone piazza that doesn't quite seem to know what it's there for, other than to provide lots amusement for kids cooling off in the fountains during the summer. The emphasis here is on size, including the two, very popular **At Bristol** attractions ⓘ *T0845-3451235, £8.95/£7 for each of these 3 attractions, with special deals for multiple tickets*, vast, glass-fronted structures of hidden promise, which can each take up several hours of your time. These are **Explore**, an interactive science museum, with additional planetarium and simulator ride, and **Wildwalk**, a three-dimensional meditation on mankind's relationship to nature – featuring a walk-through rainforest. Wildwalk is also home to the **IMAX cinema**, showing an increasingly varied selection of films on its big screen. There are also big restaurants – *Pitcher and Piano*, *Firehouse Rotisserie*, *Bar Room Bar* – and a big stainless steel ball (the planetarium of the Explore exhibit). At the back of the piazza is rather a small statue of Hollywood star Cary Grant, who was born and grew up in the city as plain Archibald Leach, now Bristol's golden boy.

Now cross over Pero's Bridge, named after a slave boy belonging to John Pinney (see Georgian House below) and a very trendy nod to slave guilt, with its strange postmodern horns. Straight ahead of you is the interesting **Bristol Architecture Centre** ⓘ *T0117-9221540, 1100-1700 Tue-Fri, 1200-1700 at weekends, free.* To the right, the **Arnolfini Arts Centre** ⓘ *T0117-9299191,* housed in a converted warehouse is

currently undergoing a massive refurbishment, but you can still go inside to visit the shop and see smaller exhibitions. Directly outside you will see a bronze statue of a man looking intently towards the west. This is **John Cabot**, one of Bristol's favourite adopted sons (formerly Giovanni Caboto of Genoa and Venice), who, hitching a ride with Bristolians, sailed from here to Newfoundland in 1497, five years after Christopher Columbus had stepped ashore in the Bahamas. Cabot is also remembered at **Cabot Tower**, a Victorian minaret offering fine views from its site on **Brandon Hill**, just off Park Street. (Brandon Hill is a superb place for a picnic lunch if you're near Park Street.)

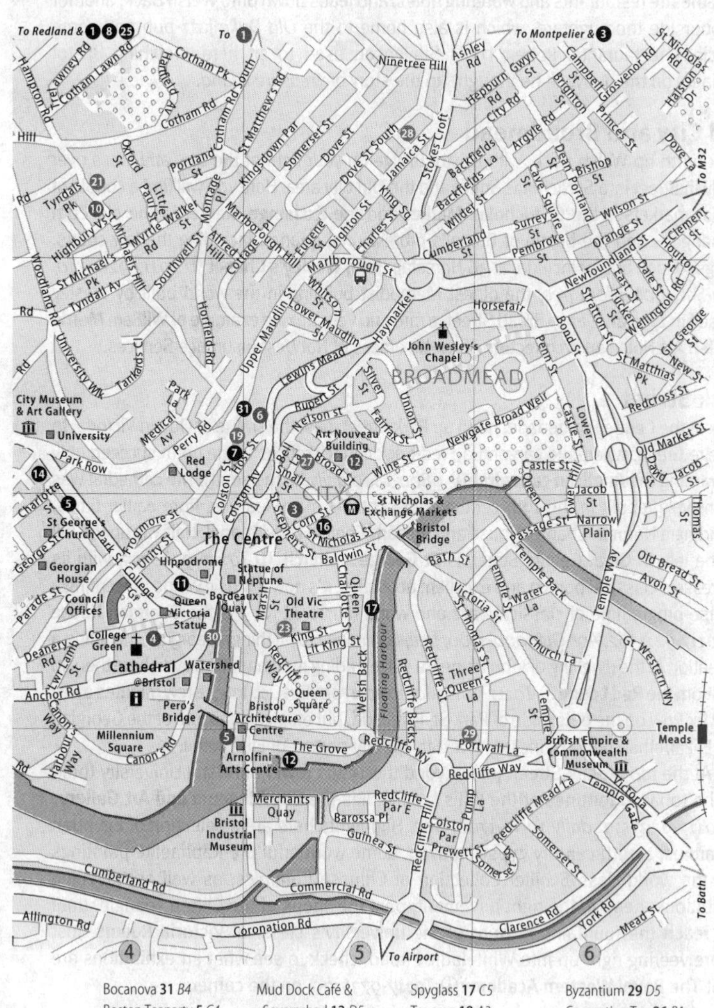

Bocanova **31** *B4*
Boston Teaparty **5** *C4*
Brown's **6** *B3*
Budokan **7** *A3, B4*
Carmen Miranda **8** *A4*
Deason's **9** A3
Fish Works **10** *A3*
Harveys **11** *C4*
Mud Dock Café & Severnshed **12** *D5*
Quartier Vert **13** *A3*
Rajdoot **14** *B4*
Red Snapper **25** *A4*
Saha **15** *B2*
San Carlo **16** *C5*
Sands **32** *B3*
Spyglass **17** *C5*
Touareg **18** *A3*

Pubs & bars

Arc **27** *B5*
Bag o'Nails **33** *C3*
Bell **28** *A5*
Brewery Tap **19** *B4*
Byzantium **29** *D5*
Coronation Tap **26** *B1*
E Shed & The River **30** *C4*
Eldon House **20** *B3*
Highbury Vaults **21** *A4*
Lion **22** *C3*
Renatos **23** *C5*

Old Vic and Welsh Back

Behind the Arnolfini, are the lawns of Queen Square, centred around the fine equestrian statue of William III. To the left, the north side of the square links up with King Street, site of the **Old Vic** ⓘ *T0117-9877877, tours most Fri and Sat mornings, except Jul and Aug.* Behind the theatre's original Georgian façade is a spacious 1970s foyer, which itself contains the original 18th-century galleried auditorium, one of the very few of that period still in existence and a real treat for theatregoers. If you can't make it to a show, you may want to join a tour of the theatre. King Street itself has a number of pre- or post-theatre restaurants and watering holes, and leads down onto Welsh Back, another harbourside thoroughfare, which is also home to the *Old Duke* jazz pub and some top-class restaurants. Robert Louis Stevenson used to sit here, watching Bristol mariners on the quay, as he thought up the story of *Treasure Island*.

The Old Vic theatre school in Clifton, opened in 1947 by Sir Laurence Olivier, was nursery to such talents as Jeremy Irons and Miranda Richardson.

Old City and Broadmead

Walk north up Welsh Back, with Bristol Bridge on your right at the top, and cross over Baldwin Street into St Nicholas Street and the Old City area. Here you will find a couple of indoor markets – the **St Nicholas Market** and the **Exchange Market** in the old Corn Exchange – and the bustle of Bristol's professional quarter, including the law courts. Things to look out for include, at 36 Horsefair, **John Wesley's Chapel** ⓘ *T0117-9264740, Mon-Sat 1000-1800, free,* the oldest Methodist building in the world built by Wesley himself in 1793 and, at 37 Broad Street, a rare and very striking example of **William Morris English Art Nouveau architecture**, now the offices of NatWest Insurance Services.

Park Street

Back at the Centre Promenade, head up Park Street, past the statue of Queen Victoria, to College Green, where the gargantuan red-brick council offices to the north succeed only in dwarfing the **Anglican cathedral** ⓘ *0800-1800 daily,* to the south. The cathedral was extensively rebuilt in the 19th century, but contains many features from earlier times, including a Norman Chapter House and an early English Lady Chapel. Halfway up the hill on the left, in Great George Street, is **St George's Church** ⓘ *T0117- 9230359,* with its impressive classical portico and excellent acoustics, it's now a music venue presenting a diverse programme of classical, jazz and world music. At No 7 is the **Georgian House** ⓘ *T0117-9211362, Apr-Oct 1000-1700, free,* a homage to all things Georgian, including a recreation of the dwelling of John Pinney, a slave trading merchant who lived here then. In addition, the **Red Lodge** ⓘ *T0117-9211360, 1000-1700 Apr-Oct, free,* a few minutes away on Park Row on the other side of Park St, is an odd, but engaging mixture of the Georgian and Elizabethan periods, including a 16th-century portrait of Elizabeth I.

At the top of Park Street, just beyond the 1920s tower of Bristol University (built on the tobacco fortunes of the Wills family), lies the **City Museum and Art Gallery**. ⓘ *T0117-9223571, daily 1000-1700, free.* Highlights here are a selection of Egyptian mummies, a 19th-century gypsy caravan, some wonderful pre-Raphaelite paintings and the world-class Schiller Collection of Chinese Ceramics; as well as travelling exhibitions. Keep to the right pavement, past the shops of the Clifton Triangle, until you reach the fountains in front of the university's classical **Victoria Rooms**. Just before veering right up into Whiteladies Road, check to see what art exhibitions are on at **The Royal Western Academy** ⓘ *T0117-9735129,* on the corner.

Clifton

Alternatively, turn left along Queen's Road, past the monstrous students' union building, across Victoria Square where the great Victorian cricketer Dr WG Grace lived at number 16, and then on under an archway into **Clifton Village**. Walk along Royal York Crescent to experience the grandeur of the Georgian architectural vision, the rows of other perfectly proportioned terraces beneath and the green fields that lie beyond the city limits. Pop into the Coronation Tap, in Sion Place, for a half or three of poky West Country cider.

Turn right at the west end of the crescent up Sion Hill to discover the **Clifton Suspension Bridge**, the engineering masterpiece of Isambard Kingdom Brunel. If you have come by train from London, you are already the beneficiary of this man's genius, as he was largely responsible for building the railway. (Bristol Temple Meads station is also his design.) The bridge – approximately 700 ft across and 250 ft above the River Avon – is lit up by strings of fairy lights at night. An informative visitor centre ⓘ *daily 1000-1700, £1.90, child 1.70*, presently 200 m away in Sion Place, is about to move to a site much nearer the bridge. On the hill above the bridge, where views continue to be spectacular, there is a **camera obscura**, an observatory and an entrance to an ancient tunnel burrowed into the hillside, leading to the **Giant's Cave**, site of a Roman Catholic chapel in the 15th century.

Brunel died in 1859 aged 53, 5 years before the completion of his bridge, the result, it is said, of a combination of overwork and 40 cigars a day.

Just north of Clifton Village, if you like zoos, **Bristol Zoo** ⓘ *Guthrie Rd, T0117-9706176, daily 0900-1730 summer/1630 winter, £8.90, concessions £7.90, children £5.20*, is well-presented – incessantly proclaiming its environmental credentials – with links to Bristol's award-winning BBC wildlife department and the At Bristol Wildwalk exhibit (see above). From the zoo, walk past **Clifton College**, where as a schoolboy Monty Python's John Cleese had his first taste of the absurdities of the English class system, to the modernist Clifton **Roman Catholic Cathedral** ⓘ *Clifton Park, T0117-9738411, open at most times during the day, free*, where the retro groove of 1970s architecture and interior design is the unlikely mother of an impressive sacred space.

Sleeping

A **Avon Gorge Hotel**, Sion Hill, Clifton, T0117-9738955. Great situation in Clifton Village just below the Suspension Bridge, a bit rough around the edges for the price, but good for an afternoon drink on the terrace overlooking the bridge.

A **Bristol Marriott Royal Hotel**, College Green, T0117-9255100. A bit staid, but imperiously located on College Green, just above the harbourside – with Queen Victoria overlooking the front door.

L **Hotel du Vin and Bistro**, The Sugar House, Narrow Lewins Mead, T0117-9255577. This super-stylish warehouse conversion brilliantly mixes the sensibilities of New York loft living and old-fashioned French chic. A hotel of real imagination and individuality in the centre of the city. Suites/loft suites from £170-295.

C **Number 31**, 31 Royal York Cres, Clifton, T0117-9735330. Live like a Regent, in Bristol's finest Georgian terrace, with stunning views and a secluded garden.

C **Thistle Hotel**, Broad St, Old City, T0870-3339130. Smart, inexpensive and bang in the middle of the Old City, with good gym/indoor pool.

C **Seeleys Hotel**, 17-27 St Paul's Rd, Clifton, T0117-9738544;

C **Washington Hotel**, 11-15 St Paul's Rd, Clifton, T0117-9734740; and

C **Westbourne Hotel**, 40-44 St Paul's Rd, Clifton, T0117-9743552, are a row of similar, reasonably priced and pleasant hotels in a good situation between Clifton Village and Whiteladies Rd. The *Washington* has the cheapest rooms.

D **Oakfield Hotel**, 52-54 Oakfield Rd, Clifton, T0117-9735556. Near the Roman Catholic Cathedral in the heart of Clifton.

D **St Michael's Guest House**, 145 St Michael's Hill, T0117-9077820. If you fancy starting the day with a big, fry-up breakfast in the company of recalcitrant students and the best jukebox in town, this is the place for you.

D **Sunderland Guest House**, 4 Sunderland Pl, Clifton, T0117-9737249. A tidy, little guesthouse, tucked away in a secluded side street off Whiteladies Rd. Vegetarian breakfast only.

D **Tyndall's Park Hotel**, 4 Tyndall's Park Rd, Clifton, T0117-9735407. A Victorian house with a slightly old-fashioned atmosphere near to Bristol University and just off Whiteladies Rd. Special weekend rates.

F Bristol Backpackers, 17 St Stephen's St, Old City, T0117-9257900. Dorm beds £13 a night, cheaper if you book in advance. Comfortable lounge and a bar in this central location.

F Bristol YHA, 14 Narrow Quay, Harbourside, T0117-9221659. Clean, modern and superbly sited on the harbour. From £12.50 for a dorm bed, also twin and family rooms.

Eating

£££ Bell's Diner, 1 York Rd, T0117-9240357. Effortless bohemian chic in this Montpelier favourite which prides itself on the best ingredients and a French-English style. Smokers are banished to the waiting area.

£££ Fish Works, 128 Whiteladies Rd, T0117-9744433. One of the new breed of sleek, classy fish brasseries – all stainless steel and chunky wood – that also doubles as a fishmonger, an offshoot of the one in Bath. Main course about £15.

£££ Deason's, 43 Whiteladies Rd, T0117-9736230. This first-time venture by young chef Jason Deason meets with high praise. Classy food in contemporary setting. No-smoking dining room. Starters about £7, main courses about £15.

£££ Quartier Vert, 85 Whiteladies Rd, T0117-9734482. Humming tapas bar in the middle of 'the strip' with à la carte Mediterranean dining at the back. Starters about £6, main courses about £17.

££ Ahmed's Curry Café, Chandos Rd, Redland, T0117-9466466. A bit of Bradford comes to Bristol in this basic, reasonably priced, formica-top, candlelit eating den serving curry in a haandi.

££ Azuma, 4 Byron Pl, Clifton Triangle, T0117-9276864. Sushi chef Yuji recently moved to this central location after 15 years at his old, Redland restaurant. Simple, authentic, personal, slightly quirky and delicious – without being particularly pricey for Japanese food.

££ Bocanova, 90 Colston St, T0117-9291538. Lively and expert Brazilian with BYOB on Tue.

££ Brown's, 38 Queens Rd, Clifton, T0117-9304777. The winning Brown's formula rides again, in Bristol University's old refectory. Open plan dining, great cocktails, attractive waitresses and a terrace and steps from which to survey life from on high.

££ Fuchsia, Nelson Ho, Nelson St, T0117-945 0505. Combining a sleek Chinese restaurant with a sassy club.

££ Rajpoot, 83 Park St, T0117-9268033. A beautiful statue of the goddess Parvati presides over this beautifully decorated, slightly old-fashioned Indian – a notch above your average curry house.

££ Red Snapper, 1 Chandos Rd, Redland, T0117-9737999. A seasonal fish restaurant with fresh red and yellow décor. Still the best fish place in Bristol.

££ San Carlo, 44 Corn St, T0117-9226586. Bristol's answer to London's *La Caprice*. Glitzy Italian bistro, also serving shellfish and oysters.

££ Spyglass, Welshback, T0117-9277050. Alfresco Mediterranean barbecue on a canopied boat (with heaters). Little sister to the posher *Glass Boat* restaurant next door. Main courses, sardines to steaks. Only open in the summer.

£ Budokan, Colston St and Whiteladies Rd, T0117-9141488. 2 Asian fuelling stations in traditional Japanese canteen setting, serving Thai, Japanese and Indonesian food.

£ Sands, 95 Queen's Rd, Clifton, T0117-9739734. An atmospheric Lebanese restaurant serving reasonably priced good food in a cavern-like interior, or outdoors on the terrace (with heaters). They also have sheesh pipes to smoke or share. Apple is the most popular flavour.

Cafés

Blue Juice, 39 Cotham Hill. Fruit/veg juices and herbal shots just behind Whiteladies Rd.

The Boston Teaparty, 75 Park St, T0117-9298601. Comfy, old sofas upstairs and mellow terrace-garden at the back in this popular unlicensed café. Open all week.

Carmen Miranda, Chandos Rd, Redland. Relaxed verging on the chaotic. Licensed café, serving lunch and teas, a box or 2 of second-hand books, some vegetables and a few plants for sale, with a basement chill-out zone for the evenings.

Saha, 12-13 Waterloo St, Clifton Village, T0117-3179696. Leave Clifton for Marrakesh, in this cool, unlicensed Moroccan café that also doubles as a gallery. Closes 1800.
Mud Dock Café, 40 The Grove, T0117-9349734. Popular harbourside spot for Sat/Sun brunch, with a bicycle shop underneath. Licensed, with DJs, for evening dining. About £8 for a main course.

Pubs, bars and clubs

Arc Bar, Broad St, T0117-9226456. An arty live performance space.
Bag o'Nails, St George's Rd, Hotwells, T0117-9406776. Very fine ales in a small wood-panelled pub, that can get impossibly busy.
The Bell, 18 Hillgrove St, T0117-9096612. One of the city's original music pubs.
The Brewery Tap, T0117-9213668. The modern wooden interior and chequer tile floor creates the perfect, unpretentious setting to savour the Smiles beers brewed on site. Contains a no-smoking room and will also arrange tours of the brewery.
Byzantium, Portwall La, Redcliffe, T0117-9221883. Swish, stylish pleasuredome with deep sofas and Eastern notes. Also a decent place for a quality bite to eat.
Coronation Tap, Sion Pl, T0117-9739617. This pub usually has four or five brews of West Country cider to choose from, advisedly sold in halfs. Clifton-based students and serious cider heads.
E Shed, Canon's Rd, T0117-9074287. Waterside place described by its designer as possessing "high-class New York hooker-chic". Its neighbour, *The River*, T0117-9300498 is also worth a peek.
Eldon House, 6 Lower Clifton Hill, T0117-9264964. Friendly, individualistic, no-nonsense boozer with a snug, back parlour. Live music.
Ether, 2 Trenchard St, T0117-9226464. "The bar that fell to earth". Enjoy a super-trendy and absinthe-fuelled evening amongst the stark sci-fi setting and 'collagen injected' swivel chairs. Specials include 'The Etherist' cocktail.
The Farm, Hopetown Rd, St Werburghs, T0117-9442384. Further afield but a bit more real, move from pub garden to DJs inside.
Highbury Vaults, St Michael's Hill, T0117-9733203. Popular student pub near the university, dark and cosy inside with a terrace at the back for alfresco drinking. Declared itself a 'football free zone' during the last World Cup.
The Lion, Church La, Clifton Wood, T0117-9268492. Bristol at its laid-back best. Serving good food – including a wild boar roast on Sun – this is the kind of pub people move house to be near. DJs at the weekend.
Nocturne, 1 Unity St, T0117-9292555. A cutting-edge drinking, formerly owned by Massive Attack, decorated with Brit-art. Non-members should look smart.
The Palace Hotel, 1-2 West St, Old Market, T0117-9557095. Revamped grand old Victorian hotel bar celebrating the city's revved up music scene.
The Park, 38 Triangle West, Clifton, T0117-940 6101. Bristolians endure the tight squeeze to enjoy the tunes and vodka at this hip bar.
Renato's, 33 King St, T0117-929 7712. A fairly standard Italian trattoria by day, site of frenzied thespian revelry by night for after-show drinkers from the Old Vic.
Severnshed, The Grove, T0117-9251212. Large and airy waterside Victorian warehouse designed by Brunel (girders and all) with good organic food.
The Star and Garter, 33 Brook Rd, Montpelier. At the other end of the chic scale from Nocturne, this is a characterful old West Indian boozer, playing reggae sounds all night and morning long, with a pool table in the front room and, er, a large, black coffin in the back.
The White Lion Inn, Avon Gorge Hotel, Sion Hill, T0117-973 8955. Fabulous sun terrace, with unrivalled views of the Clifton Suspension Bridge and barbecue in the summer.

Clubs

Club nights in Bristol change regularly, so check *Venue* or the free *Synergy* magazine for the latest listings. Many of the places listed under Bars above are worth dancing at too, especially round Frogmore Steet: eg Ether.
Cosies, in St Paul's, 34 Portland Sq, T0117-9424110. Gets seriously chilled. Then find out what's playing at: **Blue Mountain**, Stokes Croft; **Creation**, in Baldwin St; **The Fez Club**, 26-28 St Nicholas St, T0117-9259200 or the **The Old Firestation** in Silver St.

Elbow Room on Park St, T0117-9300242, dance upstairs or shoot pool downstairs.
Pam-Pam, 3 Beacon Ho, Queens Av, Clifton, T0117-973 1249. Bouncers keep out the hoi-polloi from this glam club. Dress to impress.

Shopping

Bristol's shopping opportunities are by no means limited to the Broadmead area, where you will find all the usual high street outlets. Try Park Row and the Christmas Steps for an eclectic range of shops, including specialists in crystals, tarot, piercing, stamps, jokes, glassware and violins. As a souvenir, buy either a piece of deep, dark Bristol Blue glass or something to do with Wallace & Gromit – Nick Park's *Aardman Animations* are still Bristol-based.
The Bristol Guild, at the top of Park St, T0117-9265548. Contains 11 departments of household goods, all of a high standard.
Clifton Village is the place for the more mature shopper for jewellery, beauty products, 'mistress' boutiques and art galleries.

The nodding dance music aficionado is also well served, try:
Bangbang Records on Park Row; **Eat The Beat**, St Nicholas St and **Rooted Records** at 9 Gloucester Rd .

Entertainment

Cinema

The main cinemas include:
Odeon, Broadmead, T0870-5050007;
Orpheus, Northumbria Dr, near the university halls of residence, T0117-9621644 and
Showcase on the outskirts of town towards Bath, T0117-9723800.
Watershed, T0117-9253845. Arthouse flicks.

Theatre

Old Vic, King St, T0117-9877877. A great theatre and well worth visiting.
Hippodrome, on the other side of the Central Promenade, T0870-6078500, has a much bigger auditorium and tends to stage blockbuster musicals – and occasionally opera.
The largest of the fringe theatres are:
QEH on Jacob's Wells Rd, T0117-9250551;
The Redgrave, in Percival Rd, Clifton, T0117-3157600.
The Tobacco Factory, Raleigh Rd, Southville (outside the centre), T0117-9020344. Shows excellent theatre regularly. It also boasts views of the massive 19th-century tobacco depositories that dominate the skyline and has a very cool bar-restaurant and events centre.

Live music

There's a busy music scene in the city. The larger venues are:
Bristol Academy, Frogmore St, T0117-9279227;
Colston Hall, Colston St, T0117-9223686;
St George's Church, see p328, and
Victoria Rooms, see p328.
There are also plenty of other smaller places.
Bristol Bierkeller, The Pithay, All Saints St, T0117-926 8514;
The Fiddlers, Willway St, T0117-9873403;
The Thekla, a boat moored at Phoenix Wharf in the harbour, are some of the best. Again, check *Venue* or *Synergy* for the listings.

Festivals

Jul Bristol Community Festival. Ashton Court Estate, T0117-9042275. Held over the course of 1 weekend.
Jul St Paul's Carnival. St Paul's, T0117-944 4176. A celebration of West Indian culture, is held at about the same time as the above.
Aug Bristol Balloon Fiesta and Nightglow. T0117- 9535844. Watching coloured balloons floating gently overhead is one of Bristol's happiest sights.
Sep Bristol International Kite Festival. Ashton Court, T0117-9772002.

Activities and tours

For an unusual and fascinating tour of mercantile medieval Bristol, ask at the main tourist office, T0117-9260767/9462222, about the possibility of a **tour of Redcliffe caves**, a network of about 8 miles of caves and cellars stretching under the city centre, where merchants hoarded their valuables and slaves piled Bristol's wealth into vast caverns. Usually available at 2 days notice from a local guide. Wellies and torches essential.
Bristol Balloons, T0117-9637858, or
Bailey Balloons, T01275-375300, for personal balloon trips.

Transport

Air
Bristol International Airport, T0870-1212747, offers direct flights to 27 UK and European destinations, including low cost flights with EasyJet and Ryanair.

Bicycle
Black Boy Hill Cycles, 180 Whiteladies Rd, T0117-9731420. For repairs go to the Bristol Bicycle Workshop, 84 Colston St, T0117-9268961.

Bus
Long distance National Express, T08705-808080, run services at least hourly to **London Victoria** (2 hrs 30 mins) and to many other towns throughout England, eg **Exeter** (2 hrs), **Birmingham** (2 hrs).

Car
National, Bristol International Airport, Lulsgate, T01275-474821 and 248 Muller Rd, Horfield, T0117-9525414; **Sixt Kenning**, 59 Hartcliffe Way, T0117-9662296; **Thrifty**, 127 Queen Anne Rd, Barton Hill, T0117-9711133.

Taxi
Apex, 433 Gloucester Rd, T0117-9232626; Bristol Taxi Co, 204a Cheltenham Rd, T0117-9428080; **Dads Cabs**, 138 Grosvenor Rd, T0117-9350044.

Train
First Great Western serve Bristol Temple Meads station from **London Paddington** (1 hr 45 mins). Other stations on this line are **Reading** (1 hr 15 mins), **Swindon** (45 mins), **Chippenham** (30 mins) and **Bath Spa** (15 mins). Services continue on to **Taunton** (30 mins), **Exeter** (1 hr), **Plymouth** (2 hrs) and **Penzance** (4 hrs). Virgin Trains serve **Cheltenham** (40 mins) and **Gloucester** (50 mins).

Directory

Hospitals Bristol Royal Infirmary, Maudlin St, T0117-9230000. **Internet** The Netgates Café, 51 Broad St, T0117-9074040; Oncoffee.net, 11 Christmas Steps, T0117-9251100. **Police** Avon and Somerset Constabulary, PO Box 37, Valley Rd Portishead, T01275-818181. **Post office** Prince St, T0845-7223344.

Gloucestershire

→ *Colour map 4, grid C3*

Gloucestershire, like Norfolk, was fabulously wealthy in the Middle Ages. Unlike Norfolk, the county has also largely escaped the ravages of 20th century agribusiness. Wool-rich then, untouched by the Black Death and with plentiful and superbly crafted stone all around, its main port was Bristol, reached from the docks surprisingly far inland at Gloucester. Along with the Stroud Valley cloth mills, the first industrial revolution in the 17th century only adds to the charms of the county today. They're no secret though. The limestone Cotswolds are overwhelmed with admirers every summer and many of their genteel honey-coloured villages pander to a nostalgic vision of England past. That said, their immaculate state of preservation and the apparently organic way they seem to have grown up from the soil makes them truly irresistible. This is also superb walking country and the tourist hordes can easily be escaped on foot or bike along quiet river valleys. Gloucester is the county town, with one of the most wonderfully well-preserved cathedrals in the country. Its very different neighbour is the elegant Regency spa town of Cheltenham. Both sit on the western edge of the Cotswolds overlooking the Severn Valley. In the south of the county, hearty Cirencester is the regional capital, an ancient Roman town surrounded by river valleys. To its west, workaday Stroud nestles amid glorious scenery peppered with neolithic remains giving wide views into Wales. ▸▸ *For Sleeping, eating and other listings, see pages 342-346.*

Ins and outs

Getting there and around There are **railway** stations at Gloucester, Cheltenham, Kemble, Stroud, Stonehouse, Moreton-in-Marsh and Lydney. Many areas of Gloucestershire's countryside are accessible by **bus**, rural bus services make The Cotswolds, the Forest of Dean and the Severn Vale all accessible by public transport. Buses run from the main towns such as Cirencester, Cheltenham, Gloucester and Stroud, or from the rural railhead stations at Kemble, Lydney and Moreton-in-Marsh. There are weekday and Sun services. The Message Link Information Line, T01452- 425543, is a telephone service for bus and rail timetable information (available Mon-Fri 0745-2000, Sat 0800-1700, Sun 0900-1400, and bank holidays 0800- 1700).

Information Gloucestershire Tourism Information ⓘ *T01452-425673*.

North Cotswolds

Beyond Burford, north of the A40, the heartland of the Cotswolds is so popular that the roads in summer often become choked with coaches and cars. The scenery is almost as stunning in winter though. If anything the warm yellowy-grey limestone-built villages, becoming more and more honey-coloured in the north, look even prettier in clear winter sunshine. The trio of Bourton-on-the-Water, Stow-on-the-Wold and Moreton-in-Marsh are the top destinations, but many of the smaller villages also suffer from serious congestion. And it's not hard to see why: the combination of rolling little hills, sparkling streams and tidy old villages is hard to resist. They're also sprinkled with a variety of rewarding and carefully maintained attractions, especially gardens and great houses. The Indian dream of Sezincote is one of the most extraordinary, although even more eccentric is the collection of antique crafts and handiwork on display at delightful Snowshill Manor. To the northeast is Chipping Campden, one of the most distinctive and fiercely protected of Cotswold towns. To the west, the countryside becomes impossibly picturesque, especially around Stanway and Broadway.

Ins and outs

Getting there Moreton-in-Marsh is on London Paddington-Worcester **train** line. **National Rail Enquiries**, T08457-484950. From London the M40/A44 is the most direct route, although the A44 is a notoriously slow **road**. Even so, Moreton-in-Marsh can usually be reached in 2 hours. See also Ins and outs for Gloucestershire above. ▸▸ *For further details, see Transport, page 345.*

Walking is one of the best ways to see the surrounding countryside and there are many footpaths to choose from. The Cotswold Way, is 100 miles from Chipping Camden to Bath via the outskirts of Cheltenham. The Gloucestershire Way, travels 100 miles from Tewkesbury to Chepstow via Winchcombe and the Forest of Dean. The Warden's Way and Windrush Way are circular routes that link Winchcombe and Bourton-on-the-Water, 26 miles in all. The North Cotswold Diamond is a 60-mile circular route around Stow-on-the-Wold taking in Chipping Camden, Moreton-in-Marsh and Northleach. The Cheltenham Circular Footpath circles the town of Cheltenham.

Cotswold Walking Holidays ⓘ *10 Royal Pde, Bayshill Rd, Cheltenham, T01242-254353, www.cotswoldwalks.com*, is a local company specializing in self-guided and guided walks. **Compass Holidays** ⓘ *T01242-250642*, organize luggage transfers and accommodation along the Cotswold Way.

Information Cotswold TIC ⓘ *Hollis House, Market Sq, Stow-on-the-Wold T01451-www.chippingcampden.co.uk, Apr-Oct daily 1000-1730, Oct-Mar daily 1000-1700, £1* *accommodation booking fee.* **Winchcombe TIC** ⓘ *Town Hall, High St, T01242-602925, www.visitcotswoldsandsevernvale.gov.uk. Apr-Oct daily 1000-1700, Nov-Mar Sat, Sun 1000-1600.*

Bourton-on-the-Water

Bourton-on-the-Water is one of the most typical and also the most touristy of Cotswolds villages and worth a look for all that. It has been making the most of its charms since it made its name by reducing itself to a ninth of its size in 1937, using the same stone and water as the village, similar small scale trees and shrubs, and a model of the model at the **Model Village** ⓘ *T01451-820467, www.theoldnewinn.co.uk, £2.75, under-16s £2, concessions £2.25.* A series of other attractions celebrating miniaturism could now also claim a place in the model: **The Cotswold Motoring Museum** ⓘ *The Old Mill, T01451-821255, Feb-Nov daily 1000-1800, £2.50, under-16s £1.75,* is popular with kids, being the home of Brum from the TV series, as well as a variety of other (full scale) vintage vehicles. Another kids' favourite, with 400 sq ft of displays, is the **Model Railway** ⓘ *Box Bush, High St, T01451-820686, www.bourtonmodelrailway.co.uk, Apr-Sep daily 1100-1730, Oct-Mar Sat, Sun 1100-1730, £1.90, under-16s £1.50, concessions.* Small birds, as well as larger ones like penguins, pelicans and flamingos, can be seen at the **Birdland Park**. ⓘ *T01451-820480, Apr-Oct daily 1000-1800, Nov-Mar daily 1000-1600, £4.60.* A more unusual visitor attraction is the **Perfumery Exhibition** ⓘ *Victoria St, T01451-820698, www.cotswold-perfurmery.co.uk, daily 1000-1700, £2, concessions £1.75,* which manufactures scents on site and includes a 'smelly-vision' cinema.

Stow-on-the-Wold and around

Some of Bourton's tourist hordes spill over in high season into the **Slaughters**, Upper and Lower, a pair of impossibly twee little stone villages. Three more miles up the A429, **Stow-on-the-Wold** is the capital of the Cotswolds, where most roads meet before heading off across the hills. Its market place and sidestreet sheep-runs become crammed in summer with crowds browsing the antique shops. Even so, along with **Moreton-in-Marsh**, 5 miles north, Stow has a more businesslike and workaday air than many Cotswold settlements, and both are surrounded by some of the region's most enticing destinations for a day out. Moreton's famous **Tuesday market** is still a sight to behold and the town benefits from being on the main London-Worcester railway.

Six miles east of Moreton, near the utterly idyllic village of Great Tew, the **Rollright Stones** are an eerie collection of standing stones. The King's Men and the Whispering Knights, as the two main groups are known, are shrouded in legends of their supernatural powers. They sit in a shrubby enclosure some distance from the solitary King Stone. This is apparently a petrified invading monarch who had been told by a wise old woman that he would rule the land if he could take seven strides and see Long Compton. Foiled by the lie of the land, he was turned to stone, some distance from his men and the knights plotting his downfall whatever the outcome.

Just west of Moreton, **Batsford Arboretum** ⓘ *T01386-701441, Mar-Nov daily 1030-1730, £4, under-16s free,* is a 50-acre plot covered with rare and exotic shrubs and trees. Close by, beneath Bourton-on-the-Hill, **Sezincote** ⓘ *Sezincote House, May-Jul, Sep Thu, Fri 1430-1800, gardens Jan-Nov Thu, Fri 1400-1800, house and garden £5, gardens only £3.50, under-16s £1,* is an even rarer wonder. The inspiration for the Brighton Pavilion, this extraordinary onion-domed affair was designed by SP Cockerell surrounded by an Oriental water garden.

Snowshill and Stanway

Stranger still is the collection of things gathered together at **Snowshill Manor** ⓘ *(NT), T01386-852410, Mar-Nov, Wed-Sun 1200-1700, garden 1130-1730, £6.40, under-16s £3.20.* From the early 1920s the eccentric architect and craftsman Charles Wade amassed an array of ordinary domestic antiques, musical instruments, suits of armour, Japanese masks, tapestries, reliquaries and furniture among other things, the emphasis being on anything and everything individually hand crafted. He himself lived in Spartan conditions in the cottage next door as the results of his insatiable antique hunting crowded out the manor house itself. He also created a beautiful terraced and very intimate garden, which winds and descends from one 'room' to another, partial enclosures revealing his mysterious handmade miniatures. Wade gave the property to the National Trust on his death in 1956. Both house and gardens are surprising. Every corner hides a new fantasy on the theme of lost local labouring skills and forgotten handicrafts. Wade's equally astonishing costume collection, with which he used to surprise guests like Graham Greene, Virginia Woolf, JB Priestley and John Betjeman, can be seen by appointment at Berrington Hall, near Leominster in Herefordshire, T01568-613720, see page 587.

A couple of miles away from Snowshill as the crow flies, **Stanton** and **Stanway** are a pair of delightful honey-coloured villages. At the latter, **Stanway House** ⓘ *near Winchcombe, T01386-584469, Jul, Aug Tue, Thu 1400-1700, £3.50, under-16s £1,* where Lord Neidpath has lovingly and imaginatively restored the garden, stands out. The pyramid folly overlooks a 185-yd long waterfall as it cascades gently down from the canal. Fountains and dreamy gardens to wander through. Lord Neidpath is most accommodating if you wish to arrange a visit on out of season days. Close by, **Hailes Abbey** ⓘ *(NT/EH), T01242-602398, Apr-Sep daily 1000-1800, Oct daily 1000-1700, £2.80, concessions £2.10, under-16s £1.40,* was a Cistercian monastery founded in 1246 by King Henry III's brother Richard, Earl of Cornwall, who was buried here in 1272, and dissolved in 1539. A series of the leaping arches of its cloister are all that survive in a quiet Cotswold valley, complemented by a small museum on its history.

Broadway and Chipping Campden

Broadway is yet another contender for most beautiful village in the Cotswolds. A few miles north, Chipping Campden is not as commercialized as many parts of the Cotswolds, fiercely protective of the architectural legacy of the woollen boom and its sedate atmosphere. The gently curving and really quite grand High Street is a delight, surrounded by various styles of well-preserved terraced housing. The magnificent 15th-century church, built with the profits of a lucrative wool industry, has a stirring skybound tower, while the Market Hall, built in 1627, is the centrepiece of the town. Chipping Campden was also famous for the artisan centre set up by Arts and Crafts designer CR Ashbee with relocated East End workers in 1902. The experiment failed in 1908 because in those days the town was too remote for the results of their labour to be effectively distributed. Chipping Campden is also the start of the 102-mile long-distance footpath to Bath – the **Cotswold Way** ⓘ *www.cotswold-way.co.uk. The walk can be completed in a week or less depending on your fitness. There is plenty of accommodation along the way, but it gets booked up soon, especially during the summer months so make sure you plan well ahead if you want to do this walk.*

Two miles north of Chipping Campden, **Hidcote Manor Garden** ⓘ *T01386-438333, daily except Thu and Fri, 1030-1630, £6,* is one of Britain's most extraordinary gardens. Created by Major Lawrence Johnson on what seemed to be hostile terraine, windy and cold, a maze of imaginative settings have been nurtured. High hedges and garden rooms of spectacular colour and combinations. A must-see, but often very crowded in summer. Often less busy but in many ways as rewarding is **Kiftsgate Court** ⓘ *T01386-438777, Apr, May, Aug, Sep Wed, Thu, Sun 1400-1800, Jun, Jul Wed, Thu, Sat, Sun 1200-1800, £4, concessions £1,* on the edge of Glyde Hill nearby, a superb hill garden famous for the largest rosebush in Britain twisting up a copper beech tree.

Winchcombe

Heading southwest again on the beautiful B4632 towards Cheltenham from Broadway, Winchcombe was the ancient capital of the Anglo-Saxon kingdom of Mercia, with very old squat stone buildings and a prosperous air. Close by is 15th-century **Sudeley Castle** ⓘ *T01242-602308, Apr-Oct daily 1100-1700, £6.70, concessions £5.70, under-16s £3.70, family £17.50,* which despite being a hot tourist destination deserves its accolades. It boasts fantastic shrub roses in the Queen's garden, sculptured yews and pools in the grounds. The venerable and rambling home of the Dent-Brocklehursts has a long history and inside a slightly less absorbing display of Victoriana and old master paintings. Close to Charlton Abbots, **Belas Knap** ⓘ *EH, open any reasonable time,* is the county's most impressive neolithic longbarrow, a superbly positioned chambered tomb for at least 30 people which has been opened up so that visitors can see inside. The B4632 continues southwest through beautiful **Cleeve Hill** with its fabulous viewpoints, and past the racecourse of the Regency spa town of Cheltenham, a very different kettle of fish from crumbly old Winchcombe.

Cheltenham and Gloucester

Two very different towns of similar size within 6 miles of each other either side of the M5 Bristol-Birmingham motorway. To the east Cheltenham is a very polite and conservative Regency spa town set in a bowl of the western Cotswolds. Famous for its hunting and horse-racing events, which draw huge horsey crowds, it also bills itself as a year-round festival town building on the strengths of its world-famous music and literature bunfights. It also has a surprisingly young population thanks to the variety of different colleges and schools based here. Gloucester could hardly be more different: an ancient county town, its magnificently preserved cathedral is the main draw, visible from afar, as well as its tiny Beatrix Potter museum. Its Victorian docks have been effectively redeveloped into a visitor attraction, featuring the National Waterways Museum and an absorbing military museum. Otherwise Gloucester is not a particularly pretty sight, but the whole workaday city provides a refreshing counterbalance to ever-so slightly ever-so Cheltenham.

Ins and outs

Getting there There are frequent **trains** from London Paddington (2 hours) to both towns. **First Great Western** have some direct services, otherwise change at Swindon, other operators include **Virgin** and **Central Trains**. Bristol and the West Country have direct rail services to Gloucester, as does Wales and the Midlands. **National Rail Enquiries,** T08457-484950.

By road, from London take the M4 for approx 110 miles, then join the northbound M5 until junction 12 followed by the A38 which enters Gloucester from the south, alternatively you can exit the M5 at the new junction 11a to the west of the city. Approximate driving time: 2 hours 20 minutes; distance: 140 miles. The M40/A40 is the main route to Cheltenham, about 2 hours from London. By bus from Victoria coach station the journey is between 3 hours and 3¾ hours. Buses generally leave hourly throughout the day. **Traveline,** T0870-6082608. ▸▸ *For further details, see Transport, page 345.*

Getting around Cheltenham and Gloucester are small enough to **walk** around. In Cheltenham especially it's easily the best way to enjoy the town. **Buses** to the Cotswolds and outlying villages are run by **Stagecoach,** T01452-527516. There are now six bus routes from Gloucester to Cheltenham. For a fast journey, try the X94 along the Golden Valley bypass. To avoid Gloucester City Centre, the 90 goes direct from the estates. From Hucclecote and Brockworth, service 10 runs every 20 minutes into Cheltenham. Service 94 provides a service all day and late bus N94 runs until 0200 on Friday and Saturday. The 97 and 98 provide a service for Innsworth and Churchdown. Dayrider tickets are available from the driver offering a day's travel by **Stagecoach** buses. Some areas have a lower priced Dayrider for travel after the rush hour.

Information **Cheltenham TIC** ⓘ *77 Promenade, T01242-522878, www.visitcheltenham.gov.uk. Mon-Wed, Fri, Sat 0930-1715, Thu 1000-1715*. Produces a good mini-guide to the town and is generally very helpful. **Gloucester TIC** ⓘ *28 Southgate St, T01452-421188, www.gloucester.gov.uk/tourism. Mon-Sat 1000-1700 (also Jul, Aug Sun 1100-1500)*. Free accommodation booking service.

Cheltenham

Cheltenham is a really very pretty town and it knows it. The elegant Tunbridge Wells of the west, the medicinal properties of its waters were 'discovered' in the early 18th century, encouraging George III to spend more than a month in town sampling them for his health. Competing spas were developed in the early 19th century at Pittville (where the Pump Room remains, still dispensing waters to the brave) and Montpellier, which is now the town's exclusive shopping strip. Cheltenham Ladies College was founded in 1841 for the education of young society girls and became one of the most exclusive girls schools in the country. Cheltenham, with its stucco and limestone, shady tree-filled squares and crescents, delicate ironwork verandas and balconies, on a small scale still presents one of the most complete Regency townscapes in Britain, on a par with Bath and Edinburgh. The wide and partly pedestrianized Promenade is the main drag, with the TIC and bus station tucked behind in front of Royal Crescent, a fine little half-moon of a terrace built in

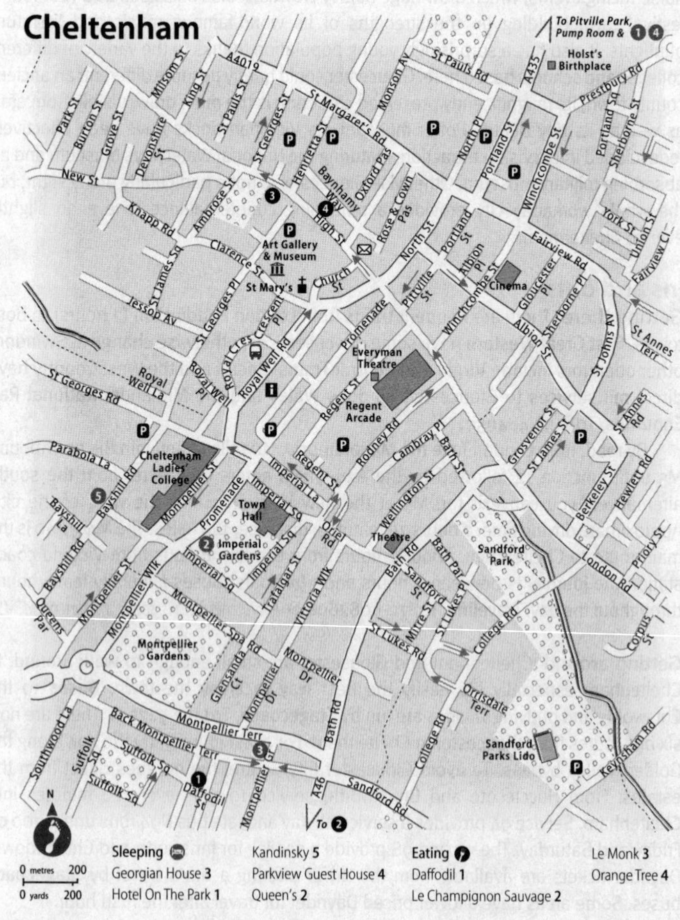

1805. A few steps north, on Clarence St, a world-beating collection of furniture, ceramics and jewellery from the Arts and Crafts movement as well as displays on the town's 18th-century development and social life can be seen at the **Cheltenham Art Gallery and Museum** ⓘ *T01242-237431, www.cheltenhammuseum.org.uk, Mon-Sat 1000- 1720, Sun 1400-1620, free.* Next to the museum's late-Victorian building stands Cheltenham's oldest survivor, the **church of St Mary's** with its severe stone spire. Five minutes' walk north up North St, the **birthplace** of the composer **Gustav Holst** ⓘ *4 Clarence Rd, Pittville, T01242-524846, www.holstmuseum.org.uk, Tue-Sat 1000-1600, £2.50, under-16s £1.25,* preserves his memory and his piano, as well as giving a glimpse inside a Regency terraced townhouse, with its cosy Victorian drawing room, nursery and working kitchen.

Continuing north along West Drive, past two dignified Georgian squares, Clarence and Wellington, a 20-minute walk brings you to **Pittville Park**, a bit spoiled by all the traffic on Evesham Road. The **Pump Room** ⓘ *T01242-523852, Mon, Wed-Sun 1100-1600,* has been refurbished on the ground floor to what it may have looked like when built in the 1820s, the centrepiece of Joseph Pitt's ambitious and ultimately failed development of Cheltenham's spa capacity. The waters can still be tasted though.

Heading south on the Promenade leads into the boutique shopping area Montpellier, full of rare books and antiques, designer dress shops and jewellers. Beyond Imperial Square and the grand Edwardian Town Hall, where spa water is still dispensed in the foyer from a Royal Doulton urn, the Queen's Hotel's impressive colonnaded portico stands at the end of the Promenade, between the Imperial and Montpellier gardens. The famous 30 armless **Cheltenham ladies** then process down Montpellier Walk, a striking series of caryatids imitating the Acropolis and supporting the roof of Montpellier Arcade, an early shopping mall. At the end of the street, the Rotunda, now a bank, was the second of Cheltenham's spa developments.

Gloucester

Cheltenham's workaday brother, the capital of Gloucestershire, may not be much to look at, either at its centre or on its outskirts, but the distant views of the **cathedral** ⓘ *T01452-528095, www.gloucestercathedral.uk.com, Mon-Fri 0730-1800, Sat 0730-1700, Sun 0730-1600, services, Sun 1015, 1500, Mon-Fri 1730, Sat 1630,* (which has found new fans after featuring in the Harry Potter film *The Philosopher's Stone*) are compensation enough. Close up, beneath its glorious Painswick-stone tower, the church turns out to be very well preserved. Standing proud on College Green, this is English Perpendicular architecture at its very best. Built over the course of a century with funds raised from pilgrims to the shrine of Edward II, the astonishing embellishment of the original Norman church began in the 1330s. Highlights of the interior are the huge Norman columns of the nave, and the way that the 14th-century vaulting leaps around them, as well as the East window of the same date, the largest in Britain. Beyond the south transept the wooden effigy of William the Conqueror's eldest son Robert dates from around 1260. Robert died in 1134 imprisoned in Cardiff Castle by his younger brother King Henry I. On the other side of the fabulous vaulted choir is the tomb of Edward II, horribly murdered in Berkeley Castle in 1327. The exquisite Lady Chapel is the most recent major structural alteration to the fabric of the cathedral, late 15th-century and artfully designed not to obscure the East window. The cathedral's other unmissable sight is the late 14th-century cloisters with their extraordinary fan vaulted tracery.

Close by, **The House of the Tailor of Gloucester** ⓘ *9 College Ct, T01452-422856, 1000-1600 Mon-Sat,* is popular with Beatrix Potter fans, a tiny little museum and shop in the original house sketched by the author for her favourite story. A not particularly inspiring 10-minute walk west down College St past Robert Smirke's Shire Hall of 1816 brings you to England's deepest inland port and terminus of the canal to Sharpness, the **Gloucester Docks**. Here, in a converted Victorian warehouse, is the **National Waterways Museum** ⓘ *T01452-318054, daily 1000-1700, £5, £4 concessions,* which should satisfy the most curious of canal fans with its array of interactive displays and working models illustrating the history of the first industrial revolution's transport network. The museum also runs regular boat trips on the **Gloucester and Sharpness Canal**. At the other end of the docks, the **Soldiers of Gloucestershire Museum** ⓘ *daily 1000-1700, £4.25, under-16s £2.25, concessions £3.25,* tells the absorbing story of the county's soldiers' lives (and deaths) over the last 300 years. Over the water, on the other side of the main basin, the **Antiques Centre** ⓘ *T01452-422900, Mon-Sat 1000- 1700, Sun 1300-1700,* provides room for a host of different stallholders in another converted warehouse, with 70 different shops.

Back in the centre of town, the **Gloucester City Museum and Art Gallery** ⓘ *T01452-396131, Tue-Sat 1000-1700, £2,* has a lively and well-presented collection of dinosaur models, archaeology, furniture and Gloucestershire arts and crafts. A couple of miles north of the city centre, at **Wallsworth Hall** ⓘ *Twigworth, T01452-731422, Tue-Sun 1000-1700, £3.35, under-16s and concessions £2.75,* a Georgian mansion contains a display on art inspired by nature with interesting special exhibitions.

South Cotswolds

Much less tourist-tramped and slightly less picturesque than the northern Cotswolds, the area south of the A40 between Northleach and Cirencester is prosperous commuter country. Northleach once rivalled Chipping Campden in wool wealth and remains fairly unspoiled. Cirencester was a very important Roman town and is still a confident regional centre blessed with another beautiful church, marketplace and a clutch of 17th- and 18th-century houses. To its west, Stroud was once a thriving centre for the first industrial revolution. A few impressive cloth mills still stand, but its major draw is the spectacular rolling scenery all around which affords wonderful views at every turn.

Ins and outs

Getting there Kemble and Stroud are on the main London to Bristol and South Wales lines via Gloucester, change at Swindon. Regular trains take just over 2 hrs. By road from London the M4/A419 via Swindon is the quickest route to Cirencester taking about 2 hrs. An alternative would be the M40/A40/A429, sometimes much less congested.

Information **Cirencester TIC** ⓘ *Corn Hall, Market Pl, T01285-654180.* **Malmesbury TIC**, *The Town Hall, Cross Hayes, T01666-823748. Easter-Sep Mon-Thu 0900-1630, Fri 0900-1620, Sat 1000-1600, Oct-Easter Mon-Thu 0900-1630, Fri 0900-1620.* **Northleach TIC** ⓘ *Cotswold Heritage Centre, Fosse Way, T01451- 860715/820211. Easter-Oct Mon-Sep 1030-1700, Sun 1200-1700.* **Stroud TIC** ⓘ *Kendrick St, T01453-760960.*

Northleach

Beyond Burford in Oxfordshire, the 'gateway to the Cotswolds' (see page 238), the A40 heads into Gloucestershire up the Windrush valley. After 9 miles it bypasses **Northleach**, in the Middle Ages the most prosperous of the Cotswold wool towns. Now it's much less commercialized than many and its magnificent church survives as a reminder of its glory days. The **church of St Peter and St Paul** is more impressive on the outside than in, with its great porch, tower and battlements, but the brasses paid for by rich wool merchants are exceptional. The town's other unmissable attraction is the **World of Mechanical Music** ⓘ *The Oak House, High St, T01451-860181, www.mechanicalmusic.co.uk, daily 1000-1800, £5, concessions £4, under-16s £2.50,* a hymn to self-playing musical instruments, from tiny singing birds in snuff boxes to grand pianolas, with its rare clocks, musical boxes, automata and mechanical music machines, visitors are often lucky enough to be shown round by the collection's enthusiastic owner Keith Harding.

Three miles south of Northleach, in a wooded valley near Yanworth is the **Chedworth Roman Villa** ⓘ *(NT), T01242-890256, Mar, Oct Tue-Sun 1100-1600, Apr-Oct Tue-Sun 1000-1700, £3.90, child £2, family £9.80,* one of the best in the country, the surprisingly extensive remains of a rich Roman's house, complete with floor mosaics, two bathhouses and a hypocaust. There's also a small museum of finds from the site, which as a whole is a kind of museum of Victorian archaeology in itself.

Bibury and Barnsley

Bibury, about 5 miles southeast of Chedworth, is another of the Cotswolds' picture-postcard villages, a peaceful string of stone-built cottages nestling beside the little river Coln. Arlington Row, a terrace of cottages purpose-built for weavers in the 17th century, must be some of the most photographed in the county. There's also a mill museum, several teashops and some good pubs.

Heading towards Cirencester from Bibury on the pretty B4425 fetches up after 3 miles in Barnsley. Less to see as far as the village is concerned, although the pub has a formidable reputation for its food, the big draw is **Barnsley House.** ⓘ *T01285-740561, daily 1000-1730 Apr-Oct, £3.* Pioneering TV gardener Rosemary Verey's well-publicized garden and darling box-hedged potager has changed little since her death in 1999. Everything in this Reptonesque wonderland is on a delightful scale, each area with a different mood.

Cirencester and around

Cirencester is the most important town in the southern Cotswolds, an ancient meeting of the roads and still a thriving, good-looking market town with a hearty complement of agriculture students. The Romans called it Corinium, second only to Colchester and London in importance, and retired their legionaries here, since when it's never really looked back. The grassy remains of their amphitheatre can still be seen west of the town. The **Corinium Museum** ⓘ *Park St, T01285-655611, Mon-Sat 1000-1700, Sun 1400-1700, £2.50, concessions £2, students £1, under-16s 80p,* offers a quite exceptional insight into their way of life, easily comprehensible to kids, as well as displaying the famous Hunting Dogs and Four Seasons mosaics, along with other less spectacular finds from the area. Otherwise, 'Siren' as the locals call it, is good for browsing around in the old marketplace and its mini-cathedral of a church testifies to the wealth it once enjoyed from wool in the 15th century.

Northwest of Cirencester, the delightful valley of the Dunt is lined with adorable villages called Duntisbourne something. At **Duntisbourne Rous** the tiny Norman church is in a charming situation and has a remarkable ancient lychgate. Excellent walks lead through rolling well-hedged countryside towards **Sapperton**, where the tunnel for the canal is the one of the longest in the country. The tunnel runs beneath the Cotswolds for almost 3 miles, emerging close to the **source of the River Thames** near Kemble. There's not much to see except for a headstone at this mystical spot in a lonely field – Old Father Thames keeps shifting his ground. Close by at **Rodmarton Manor** ⓘ *May 5-end Aug, Wed, Sat and bank holidays and all Mons in Jun and Jul, £3.00,* there's another stunning garden, this one designed by Ernest Barnsley and Claud Biddulph in the 19th century. This Arts and Crafts design has topiary punctuating the natural circumference of the garden rooms. Roses bushes and herbaceous borders lead towards the woodland walks.

Further down the A433 past Tetbury, **Westonbirt Arboretum** ⓘ *5 miles southwest of Tetbury on A433, T01666-880220, daily 1000-1700, Jan-Mar £5, Apr-May and Sep-Dec £6, Jun-Sep £7.50, children £1,* covers 600 acres of landscaped grounds, where 17 miles of paths run through a collection of over 18,000 trees begun in 1829 by Robert Holford, who made his fortune piping clean drinking water into London. Westonbirt is magnificent at any time of year but is at its dizzying best in autumn when the leafy sunlit glades become a thousand luminous hues, from lustrous gold to flaming scarlet and blazing orange. Try to avoid weekends, however, when half the country seems to be visiting.

Stroud

Sapperton's canal heads on west towards Stroud, once an important woollen mill town, now something a hotbed of 'green' thinking. Not much to look at itself, the town is surrounded by spectacular scenery: villages clinging to escarpments, wooded hills and rolling fields. The **Elliott Nature Reserve** just outside Slad affords some of the finest views in Gloucestershire. More spectacular views can be had from the roofed longbarrow called **Hetty Pegler's tump** in winter, while **Ulebury Iron Age Hill Fort** on the Cotswold Way also presents far-reaching vistas towards Wales. Near the **Nimpsfield** an unroofed longbarrow looks over the Severn Estuary into Wales, as does the Coaley Peak Picnic Site, part of a swathe of land over 400 ft.

Painswick Rococo Garden ⓘ *T01452-813204, daily 1100-1700 Jan-Nov, £3.60, concessions £3.30, child £1.80*, is a delightful journey into the past following the uncovering and restoration of a garden from a 1748 painting by Thomas Robins. Gothic houses with sculptures frescos and alcoves and pools are dotted throughout the winding paths. The informal Rococo style is brilliantly eye catching and imaginative.

Sleeping

North Cotswolds *p334*

L Buckland Manor Hotel, Buckland, near Broadway, T01386-852626, www.bucklandmanor.com. A 13th-century manor house surrounded by a 10-acre garden with only 14 bedrooms, a putting green, swimming pool, tennis and croquet lawns.

L Cotswold House Hotel, Chipping Campden, near Moreton-in-Marsh, T01386- 840330, www.cotswoldhouse.com. This Edwardian manor house has been recently refurbished in a mixture of contemporary and antique styles. Special rates on weekdays.

L-A The Royalist Hotel, Digbeth St, Stow-on-the-Wold, T01451-830670, www.theroyalisthotel.co.uk. Supposedly the oldest inn in the country. Owned by the Knights of St John in AD 947 and used then as an almshouse. Beams, fireplaces, nooks and crannies abound.

A Dormy House, Willersey Hill, Broadway, near Cheltenham, T01386-852711, www.dormyhouse.co.uk. This 17th-century farmhouse is set high on Willersey Hill looking over the Cotswolds. Welcoming, with fresh flowers and oversized club chairs. *Tapestries* restaurant is of a very high standard using only the freshest available ingredients (about £40 a head).

A Lords of the Manor Hotel, Upper Slaughter, near Cheltenham and Stow-on-the-Wold, T01451-820243, F820696. This former rectory was built in 1650 and is set in one of the prettiest villages in the Cotswolds. Meticulously manicured gardens. Riding, tennis, and croquet on offer.

A Lower Slaughter Manor, Lower Slaughter, T01451-820456, F822150. This manor house was built in 1651 on the site of a 1068 Domesday manor. A lavish fine dining award-winning restaurant (approx £50 a head) and 16 well-appointed rooms with home-made biscuits and English toffee in each.

A The Malt House, Broad Campden, near Chipping Campden, T01386-840295, F841334. Welcoming and comfortable former 18th-century malt house now a family-run hotel with an eye on detail. Roaring fires and hosts that oversee meals made from their own garden vegetables.

A The Noel Arms Hotel, High St, Chipping Campden, T01386-840317, www.cotswold-inns-hotels.co.uk. 2 bars and food made fresh to order. Well-run with all modern conveniences.

A Old Bakery, Blockley, near Chipping Campden, T01386-700408. Better than most country-house hotels, a stay here is a sheer delight, not to say a privilege. Superb cooking from the kitchen to complement the deliciously-decorated rooms. Highly recommended.

A The Painswick Hotel, Kemps La, Painswick, near Gloucester, T01452-812160, www.painswickhotel.com. Luxurious soft fabrics and embroidery, fine furnishings and artwork throughout. All 19 rooms have stunning views and there's a good restaurant.

B-C King's Head, The Green, Bledington, near Stow-on-the-Wold, T01608-658365, F658902. A 16th-century inn in an idyllic setting. Burbling brooks and quacking ducks surround this stone inn with its exposed beams, benches and fireplaces. The bedrooms are comfortable in the annexe off the courtyard.

B-C Westward, Westward Sudeley Lodge, Winchcombe, T01242-604372, www.westward-sudley.co.uk. Looking over Sudeley Castle, this Georgian manor house has grand formal gardens and perfect lawns, superb work in the kitchen.

C The Crown Inn & Hotel, High St, Blockley, Moreton-in-Marsh, T01386-700245, www.crown-inn-blockley.co.uk. A family-run old coaching inn. Put your feet up in front of a roaring fire and enjoy a pint before a meal in the rated seafood restaurant.

C Guiting Guest House, Post Office La, Guiting Power, T01451-850470, www.guitingguesthouse.com. Full English breakfast. Formerly an Elizabethan pub, this has been tastefully transformed into a home using local stone and timber.

C Rectory Farm, Rectory Farm, Salford, near Chipping Norton, T01608-643209. This 18th-century farmhouse is set in an uninhabited 450-acre valley. Well-stocked trout fishing lakes on their property.

D Wyck Hill Lodge Wyck Hill, near Stow-on-the-Wold, T01451-830141. Former 19th-century lodge transformed into a tranquil home with flowers from the garden dotted throughout, giving a fresh and well-looked-after atmosphere.

F YHA, Stow-on-the-Wold, T01451-830497.

Cheltenham *p337, map p338*

A The Greenway, Shurdington, Cheltenham, T01242-862352, www.the-greenway.co.uk. £190 including dinner and full English breakfast. Built in 1584, this 21-bedroom Elizabethan manor house has formal grounds and a croquet pitch. The coach house is more modern but spacious and quiet.

A Hotel On The Park, Evesham Rd, Cheltenham, T01242-518898, www.hotelonthepark.co.uk. A stylish Regency townhouse, 6 mins' walk from the centre of Cheltenham. The 12 rooms are beautifully decorated with fine linens and antiques. The *Bacchanalian* restaurant also has a good reputation.

A The Queen's Hotel, The Promenade, Cheltenham, T08700-4008107, www.heritage-hotels.com. A 4-star historic hotel done up in faintly characterless style but in a superb position bang in the middle of things.

B Hotel Kandinsky, Bayshill Rd, Cheltenham, T01242-527788, www.hotelkandinsky.com. 5 mins' walk from the town centre, a Regency townhouse with a cheerful atmosphere and clean, comfortable rooms. There's a retro nightclub in the basement called U-bahn.

C Georgian House, 77 Montpellier Terr, Cheltenham, T01242-515577, F545929. Across the park from fashionable Montpellier, with individually designed bedrooms in a house that lives up to its name.

C Moorend Park Hotel, 11 Moorend Park Road, Cheltenham, T01242-224441, F572413. Family-run refurbished Victorian mansion about 15 mins' walk from the town centre with ample private parking.

D Orion Guest House, 220 London Rd, Cheltenham, T01242-233309. Small, family-run guesthouse with an environmentally friendly attitude, about a mile from the town centre.

D Parkview Guest House, 4 Pittville Cres, Cheltenham, T01242-575567. A fine Regency house 5 mins' walk from the centre of Cheltenham in Pittville Park close to the Regency Pump Room thus providing a peaceful place to stay.

South Cotswolds *p340*

L Calcot Manor, near Tetbury, T01666-890391, F890394. 16th-century manor house with extensions in the heart of the Cotswolds. Converted 16th-century barn and courtyard. Top restaurant.

L Lucknam Park, Colerne, near Chippenham, T01225-742777, www.lucknampark.co.uk. Famous spa and country house hotel, approached through a mile-long avenue of beech trees, with haute cuisine in its restaurant and a family atmosphere.

A Bibury Court Hotel, Bibury, T01285-740337, www.biburycourt.co.uk. A lovely place, a Tudor mansion with a venerable history, the river running through its fine back garden (a good place to take afternoon teas), a gate into the churchyard from the orchards and river walks into Bibury and up to Coln St Aldwyns. The rooms are comfortable and the restaurant has a good reputation.

A Hatton Court, Upton Hill, Upton St, Leonard's, near Painswick, T01452-617412,

F612945. Overlooking the Severn Valley, this 17th-century manor house has peerless views. Have drinks or tea on the terrace overlooking the woodlands below.

A Swan Hotel at Bibury, Bibury, T01285-740695, www.swanhotel.co.uk. Built in the 17th century, this hotel overlooks the river. Expect terry white robes and cotton bath sheets. Restaurant with awards and good wine list.

B The New Inn at Coln, Coln-St-Aldwyns, T01285-750651, www.newinn.co.uk. This old coaching inn has 14 rooms and a restaurant that serves old English recipes from ancient cookbooks. Family-run with courteous staff and beamed ceilings in rooms.

C Winstone Glebe, Winstone Glebe, Winstone, near Cirencester, T01285-821451, www.winstoneglebe.com. A former Georgian rectory set in 5 acres of garden and fertile grazing land. The proprietor is also a professional chef.

C 1 Cove House, 1 Cove House, Ashton Keynes, south of Cirencester, actually in Wiltshire, T01285-861226. Expect a hearty greeting at this 16th-century manor house, with 5 beautiful bedrooms, all en suite and lovely gardens and lawns.

C Hampton Fields, Hampton Fields, Meysey Hampton, east of Cirencester, T01285-850070. A renovated 19th-century barn with a sunken garden, orchard and fields with horses grazing. Gorgeous views abound.

C The Rose and Crown, Nympsfield, Stonehouse, T01453-860240. Clean, comfortable rooms in this refurbished pub near Uley.

C The Village Pub, Barnsley, near Cirencester, T01285-740421. Comfortable rooms in a handsome boozer not much like your average local. Down-to-earth top-quality food.

Owlpen Manor, Owlpen, near Uley, T01453-860816, www.owlpenmanor.co.uk. Self-catering cottages (sleeping from 2-10, £30-70 per person per night, £125-140 per person per week). This splendid building dates from the 13th-century. With its long and romantic history, it is gutsy and rarefied. As to be expected, the cottages are appointed with the fabrics and furniture of an English country house and are well-stocked with amenities.

Eating

North Cotswolds *p334*

£££ Lygon Arms Hotel, High St, Broadway, T01386-852255. *Oliver's* restaurant for brasserie style lunches and the splendid oak-panelled *Great Hall* restaurant for dinner (set menu £39.50 for 3 courses) at this renowned member of the Savoy group.

££ Baker's Arms, Broad Campden, T01386-840515. Good value bar food in a pretty village pub.

££ Eagle and Child, Digbeth St, Stow-on-the-Wold, T01451-830670. Outshines *The Royalist* next door, also claims to be England's oldest inn.

££ Eight Bells Inn, Church St, Chipping Campden, T01386-840371. Fresh pub food in an old stonemasons' lodgings with good real ales.

££ The Craven Arms, Brockhampton, T01242-820410. Real ale destination pub with a large garden, good bar snacks and full meals in the restaurant which needs to be booked at weekends.

££ Churchhill Arms, Paxford, near Chipping Campden, T01386-594000. Superb cooking pulls in the crowds for lunch and dinner to this village pub.

Cheltenham *p337, map p338*

£££ Le Champignon Sauvage, Suffolk Rd, T01242-573449. Ambitious French cuisine is on offer at this Michelin-starred and now the city's most famous restaurant (book 3 weeks in advance for a Sat night).

££ Choirs, 5 Well Walk, T01242-235578. Do a good job of French country cooking at reasonable prices (dinner about £18 for 3 courses, less at lunchtime).

££ Daffodil, 18 Suffolk Pde, T01242-7000055. One of the city's more lively venues, in an airy converted Art Deco cinema with straightforward English and fusion food (£10 2-course lunches, about £20 a head for dinner) done well.

£ Belgian Monk, 47 Clarence St, T01242-511717. Good-value £5 lunches of moules and frites with usual strong lagers.

£ Orange Tree, 317 High St, T01242-234232. A very useful vegetarian restaurant and café.

Gloucester *p337*
££ **Golden Dragon**, 95 Northgate St, T01452-523819. A decent enough Chinese.
££ **Pattaya Thai**, 7 College St, T01452-520739. A popular Thai restaurant.
£ **King's Café**, 42 Southgate St, T01452-502147. Vegetarian café option.

South Cotswolds *p340*
££ **The Bear Inn**, George St, Bisley, near Stroud, T01452-770265. Excellent home-made food in this cosy village pub. Check out the Roman well in the village which still refuses to allow street lighting. Book well ahead. Recommended.
££ **Daneway Inn**, Sapperton, T01285-760297. A delightful old pub near the western end of the Sapperton tunnel.
££ **Trouble House Inn**, Tetbury, T01666-502206. £18 per head in a superb pub restaurant.
££ **Woolpack Inn**, Slad, T01452-813429. Where Laurie Lee drank his cider with Rosie, a very good freehouse famous for its pies.

Festivals

North Cotswolds *p334*
Sep Chipping Campden Cheese Festival on the last weekend of Sep, T01452-425673, www.thecheeseweb.com. Over 750 different varieties of the humble fermented curd can be sampled at venues around town.

Cheltenham *p337, map p338*
Mar Cheltenham National Hunt Festival with the Cheltenham Gold Cup is the nation's most prestigious steeplechase. There are also important meetings in **Nov.**
Jul The Festival of Music. As big festival, started in 1945 like the Edinburgh Festival, mainly classical.
The Festival of Literature in **Oct**, also an oldie, one of the longest-running in the world. Also **Jazz** in **May**, **Science** in **Jun**, and **Folk** in **Feb**, all using a variety of venues around the town, including the Pump Room, Town Hall, Everyman Theatre and various restaurants, pubs and bars.
Festivals line: T01242-237377, www.cheltenham festival.co.uk.

Activities and tours

Walking
The Wysis Way is a 55-mile long-distance footpath (linking the Rivers Wye, Severn and Thames) that runs from Monmouth via Gloucester to the source of the Thames near Kemble, joining up Offa's Dyke Path with the Thames Path. Further details from Cotswold TIC, T01451-831082.

Transport

North Cotswolds *p334*
Bicycle
Cotswold Country Cycles, Longlands Cottage Mickleton, Chipping Campden, T01386-438706. **Country Lanes Cycle Centre**, Station Rd, Moreton-In-Marsh, T01608-650065.

Car
Cotswold Private Hire, 3 Wolds End Cl, Chipping Campden, T01386-840500. Also taxi.

Taxi
David Prout, Herons Gate, Rissington Rd, Bourton-on-the-Water, T01451-821478. Cotswold Private Hire, see above.

Cheltenham and Gloucester *p337*
Bicycle
Compass Holidays, Queens Rd, Cheltenham, T01242-250642; **Forest Adventure**, Coleford, T01594-834661.

Bus
National Express, T08705-808080, run regular direct services from Gloucester to **London Victoria** (3 hrs 30 mins), 3 direct services daily to **Birmingham Digbeth** (1 hr 45 mins) and 4 to **Bristol** (55 mins). There is also a service to **Bristol airport** (1 hr 55 mins) 4 times per day, changing at Bristol and services to **Bath** (2 hrs 5 mins) at 1405 and 1435, also changing at Bristol. There is no direct service to Cardiff.

Car
Avis Rent a Car, Unit 7, Chancel Cl Trading Est, Gloucester, T01452-380356; **Bristol Street Motors**, Hayden Rd,Tewkesbury Rd, Cheltenham, T01242-229922; **Cotswold Car Hire**, Unit 1, Mead Rd, Cheltenham, T01242-

230900; **Jackies Self Drive Hire**, The Old Airfield Moreton Valence, Gloucester, T01452-720666; **Sixt Kenning Rent-a-Car**, 271 Bristol Rd, Gloucester, T01452-310511; **Thrifty Car Rental**, 153a, Bristol Rd, Gloucester, T01452- 383866.

Taxi

ABC Private Hire, 61 Hartland Rd, Gloucester, T01452-424369; **John's Private Hire**, Unit 7a, Woodcock Trading Estate, 277 Barton St, Gloucester, T01452-385050; **Station Taxis**, Gloucester, T01452-423070; **Central Taxis**, Royal Well Rd, Cheltenham, T01242-228877; **A2B Private Hire**, 12 St James St, Cheltenham, T01242-580580.

Train

Wessex Trains, T08709-002320, www.wessextrains.co.uk, run the regular services direct from Gloucester to **Bristol Temple Meads** (45 mins) and to **Bath Spa** (1 hr 15 mins) changing at Bristol Temple Meads. There is also a regular service to **London Paddington** (2 hrs 20 mins) changing at **Bristol Parkway**. Virgin Trains, T08707-891234, www.virgintrains.co.uk, run the regular direct service to **Cardiff Central** (1 hr) and **Birmingham New St** (1 hr).

Directory

North Cotswolds *p334*
Medical facilities Moreton-in-Marsh District Hospital, T01608-650456.

Cheltenham and Gloucester *p337*
Medical facilities Cheltenham and Gloucester Nuffield Hospital, Hatherley La, Cheltenham, T01242-246500.

Bath and around

➔ *Colour map 2, grid A3*

Quite a serious contender for top prize in the beautiful cities of Britain pageant, Bath attracts crowds in thousands during the summer. If arriving by rail, first impressions may be a little disappointing, although it only takes a five-minute walk north to begin to appreciate what all the fuss is about. Better perhaps to approach the city from north or south by bike, when it suddenly reveals itself spread out below in all its honey-stoned glory nestling in a wooded loop of the Avon Valley, cradled by seven hills. Eighteenth-century fashionable society's mania for the place is what makes it a sight to behold, the highlights of their architectural legacy being the neoclassical Palladian splendours of the Circus, the Royal Crescent and Pulteney Bridge with its famous weir. Most visitors, though, still come to see the thing that's got everyone going for at least the last 2,000 years – the only hot springs in the British Isles. After seeping through the Mendip limestone for some 10,000 years, warmed in the bowels of the earth, like few others the waters that gave the city its name have been worshipped, channelled, contained, drained and splashed about in. Waterfights are out now, but the Roman Baths remain the main event, one of the country's most popular and intriguing archaeological sites. The city also does a fine line in other museums, of costume, of East Asian art, of 18th-century property development and interior design and of fine art, and it also just about manages to avoid being a museum itself. Although famously soporific, the city boasts a wealth of distinctive hotels, shops, restaurants and small businesses, and remains resolutely independent of its much bigger brother Bristol, 10 miles downriver.

Luxury hotels and beauty spas hide away by the dozen in the gorgeous countryside around Bath and Bristol, but most visitors will want to make a stop in Bradford-on-Avon, a lovely old woollen mill town a few miles upstream of Bath. Further upriver, Lacock is a feudal village preserved in aspic, while to the south Iford Manor is a surprising Italianate dream of a garden near the quaint old market town of Frome. The area's biggest visitor attraction by far is the Safari Park at Longleat, which conceals some disturbing surprises, and nearby the landscaped gardens at Stourhead are possibly the most beautiful in the country. ➤➤ *For Sleeping, eating and other listings, see pages 356-361*

Ins and outs

Getting there **First Great Western trains** serve Bath Spa from London Paddington every 30 minutes, direct services taking about 1 hourr 30 minutes. Trains running on the **Alpha Line** and **Wales & West** services between Southampton and South Wales stop at Bradford-on-Avon, as well as direct services to London Waterloo, and connecting services (via Bath) from London Paddington. Estimated time from London by **car** is about 2 hours. Total distance: 116 miles. From London take the M4 west (about 100 miles) exit at junction 18, head south on A46, and follow signs to town centre. From London, Victoria **coach** station, to Bath Spa, **bus** station, Manvers Street, the coach takes between 2 hours 30 minutes – 3 hours 50 mins. Bradford-on-Avon is 8 miles east of Bath on the A363. Buses from Bath (X5, X6 on the Bath-Salisbury route). **Wiltshire Bus Enquiries,** T08457-090899, **Wilts and Dorset Buses,** T01722-336855, **Badgerline,** T01225-464446. ▸▸ *For further details, see Transport, page 361.*

Getting around In the absence of Bath chairs, Bath is best walked around at a leisurely pace, although its hills can prove surprisingly wearing on the legs. Local buses are infrequent and unnecessary to take in the town centre. It's worth taking one of the double-decker tour buses for insight into the city's history and convenience. Taxi ranks are found outside the train station and the Abbey. Bicycles can be hired in Bradford from the Lock Inn, T01225-868068.

Information **Bath TIC** ⓘ *Abbey Chambers, T01225-477101, www.visitbath.co.uk. May-Sep Mon-Sat 0930-1800, Sun 1000-1600, Oct-Apr Mon-Sat 0930-1700, Sun 1000-1600. Accommodation booking, T0906-7112000 (premium rate 50p), 10% deposit on first night's accommodation and £5 booking fee.* **Bradford-on-Avon TIC** ⓘ *34 Silver St, T01225-865797, Easter-Dec daily 1000-1700, Jan-Easter daily 1000-1600.*

History

Celtic legend has it that Bath was founded by the father of Shakespeare's King Lear, Bladud, son of the King Lud who had founded London. Exiled on account of his skin condition, he became a swineherd. Luckily for him, his pigs stumbled on the only hot springs in Britain. Bladud noticed that their skin condition benefited from a wallow in the warm mud and dived in himself. Miraculously cured, he ordered the construction of a city and temple to the Celtic goddess Sul. When the Romans arrived in the first century AD, they must also have been delighted at their luck to discover this warming reminder of Rome in chilly Britannia. They called the place Aquae Sulis, constructing a temple to their goddess of wisdom, Minerva, and also one of the finest bathhouses in western Europe, almost certainly visited by all their top brass and possibly even by the emperors Trajan and Hadrian. When they left, the Anglo-Saxons seem to have avoided the place, possibly for superstitious reasons, dubbing it Het Bath. It wasn't until the seventh century that they resettled the area, after defeating the Celts at the Battle of Dyrham, when King Osric established a monastery here close to the springs. In 973 Eadgar was crowned King of all England in the abbey. After the Norman Conquest, the abbey's power and prestige grew and grew, the present church being constructed on the site of the Saxon church in the early 16th century. The collapse of the wool trade and dissolution of the monasteries soon after ushered in another period of decline for the city, despite James II's wife being cured of her infertility after taking a dip here in the 1680s, and the baths became associated with all manner of vice. Foul-mouthed and alcoholic, Queen Anne visited them in 1703 and inadvertently initiated a reversal in the city's fortunes. Enter drop-out aristocrat Beau Nash, who had come down to indulge his gambling habit, but then raised money for new roads and staged concerts of such class that society was soon squabbling over when they should make the two- and-a-half-day coach trip down from London. In 1738 he organized the visit of Frederick, Prince of Wales under George II (an obelisk with a motto reluctantly penned by Alexander Pope commemorates the occasion in Queen Square) and the city's status as the favourite playground of the beau monde was confirmed. Thanks to the efforts of stone magnate, postmaster and property developer Sir Ralph Allen, grand new Palladian buildings, many of them designed by John Wood and even more, later on, by his son, sprang up rapidly all over town and on the surrounding hills. By the time Jane Austen arrived in 1801, Bath was already gracefully going out of fashion but had become an essential stop on the tourist map of Britain, which it remains to this day. Victorians and Edwardians continued to descend on the baths to 'take the cure', which were only closed in the late 1970s, ironically enough because of a health scare. The city's latest initiative is an ambitious revival of its role as a resort spa with the multi-million pound redevelopment of the old Cross Bath into a luxury health and beauty centre.

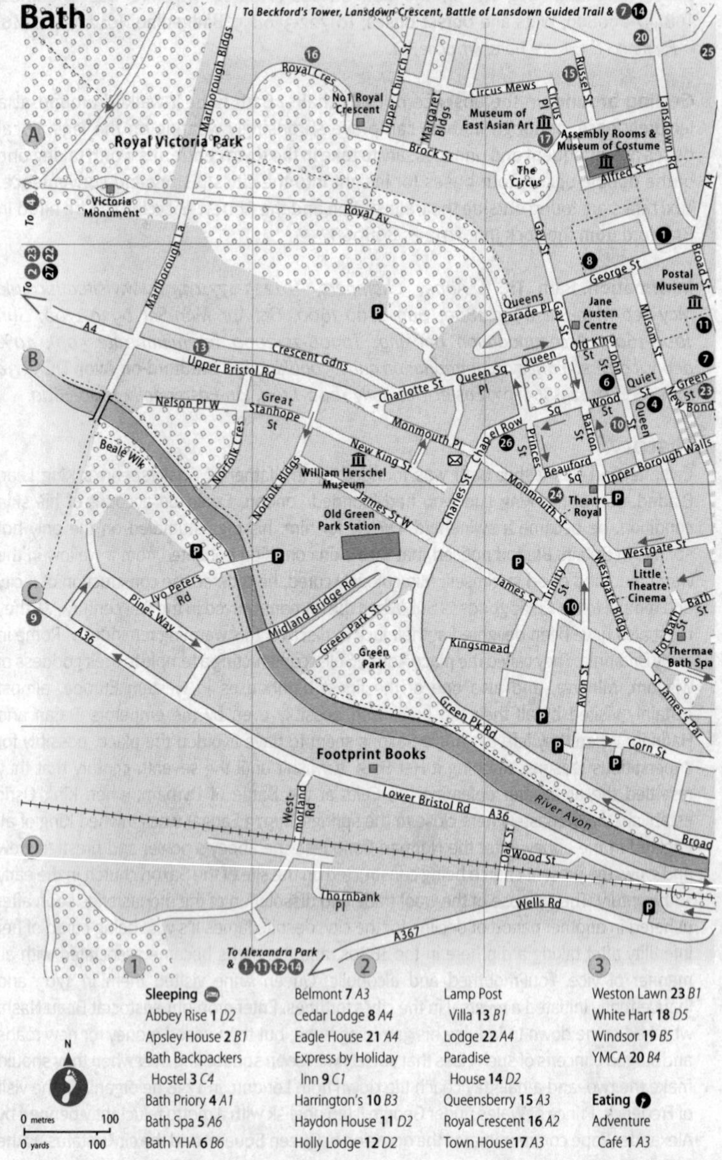

Sights

Roman Baths

ⓘ *T01225-477785, www.romanbaths.co.uk Daily except 25 and 26 Dec. Nov-Feb 0930-1730, Mar-Jun, Sep-Oct 0900-1800; Jul-Aug 0900-2200. Last entry 1 hr before closing. After 1800 daily torchlit evenings in Aug with last admission 2100, until 2200). £8.50, concessions £7.50, unemployed/under-16s £4.80, family £22. (Combined ticket with Museum of Costume for £11). Free guided tours on the hour every hour. Free audio handset tours.*

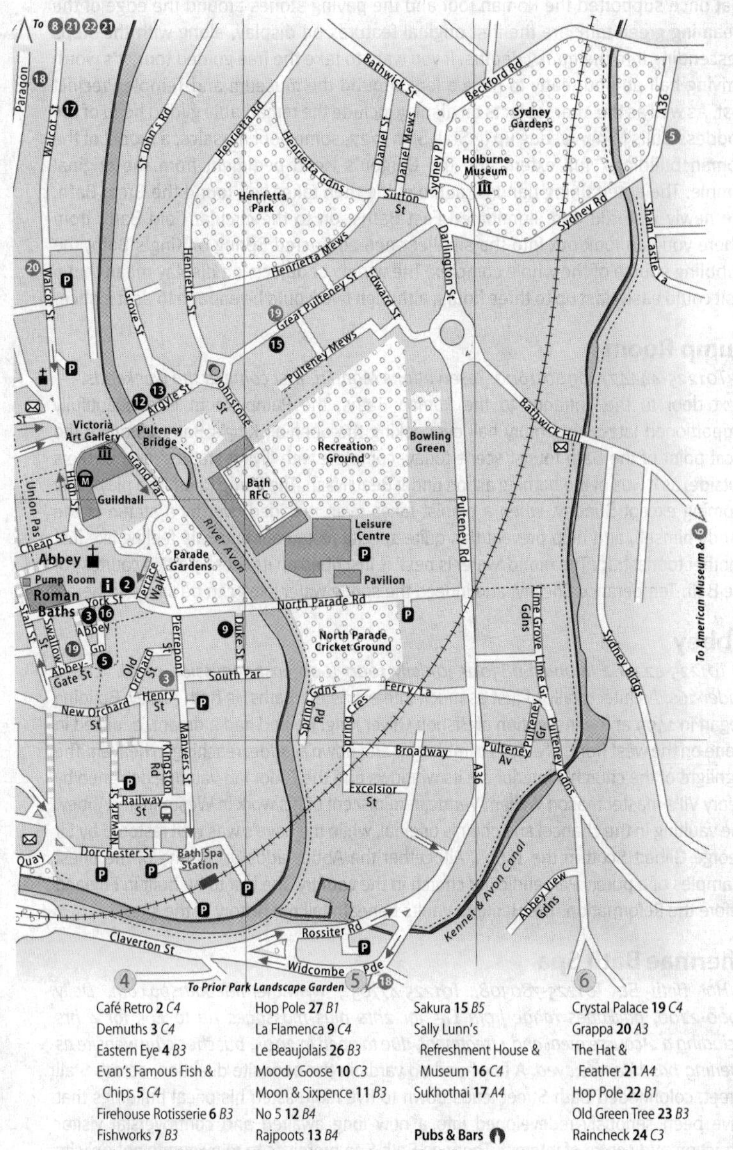

To this day the centre of Bath remains its hot springs and Roman Baths, now one of the most popular fee-paying visitor attractions in the country. Expect to have to queue (although it's generally quieter before 1000, and after 1800 in August) although they're well worth the wait. All in all, they provide one of the best insights in northwestern Europe into the Romans' achievement and their remarkably comfortable and sophisticated way of life. The Roman remains only began to be excavated in the late 19th century and first impressions today are still of the fine 18th-century neoclassical buildings erected on the site at the height of the hot springs fashionable heyday. After looking down into the open-air Great Bath from the Victorian gallery terrace, visitors descend to the water level. The bases of the columns that once supported the Roman roof and the paving stones around the edge of the steaming green tank are the first original features on display, along with the steps descending into the murky depths. If you want to take the free guided tour, it's worth arriving half an hour early to have a look around the museum and Temple Precinct first. As well as the altar, objects on display include the remarkable gilded head of the goddess Sulis Minerva, dug up in Stall St in 1727, some floor mosaics, a model of the Roman buildings' full extent and the Gorgon's Head pediment from the original temple. The entertaining handset audio guide then takes you round the Great Bath, the newly restored and illuminated East Baths, on to the circular Cold Bath, from where you can look out into the smaller open-air Sacred Spring or King's Bath, the bubbling source of the whole complex. The variety of objects on display mean that a visit could easily last up to three hours, although two would be enough to do it justice.

Pump Room

ⓘ *T01225-444477, 0900-1600, reservations Mon-Fri, first come at the weekends.* Next door to the entrance to the Roman Baths, the Pump Room is a beautifully proportioned late-18th-century hall overlooking the open-air King's Bath, as much the focal point of the Bath tourist scene today, complete with 'living statues' and buskers outside, as it was of the bathing action under Beau Nash. The Pump Room Trio play every morning except Sunday, when a pianist takes over, presided over by a statue of the dandy himself, and help prevent this quite special restaurant and café feeling like just another tourist trap. The motto 'water is best' is inscribed on its Greek portico courtesy of the Bath Temperance Society, and indeed the spring water itself can be sampled here.

Abbey

ⓘ *T01225-422462 (Mon-Fri 0830-1530)daily 1000-1600 (last admission 1530). £2, £1 under-16s.* Architecturally of just as much interest as the Baths, is Bath Abbey. Building began in 1499 at the instigation of Bishop Oliver King. He had had a dream, depicted in stone on the west front, of angels climbing up and down a ladder reaching to heaven. The highlight of the church's interior are its windows and the Tudor fan-vaulting designed by Henry VII's master mason William Vertue, reminiscent of his work in Westminster Abbey. The vaulting in the chancel and choir is original, while the nave's was well restored by Sir George Gilbert Scott in the 1860s. Altogether the Abbey adds up to one of the finest examples of a purely Perpendicular church in the country, the last to be built in England before the Reformation. The Heritage Vaults beneath tell the history of the site.

Thermae Bath Spa

ⓘ *Hot Bath St, T01225-780308, T01225-477051, www.thermaebathspa.com. Daily 0900-2200, packages range from £45 for 2hrs plus massages up to £65 for 4 hrs including a 2-course meal and 1 treatment, due to open in 2004, but check the website as opening has been delayed.* A few hundred yards in the opposite direction, across Stall Street, colonnaded Bath Street leads down to five more listed historical buildings that have been seriously redeveloped into a new long awaited and controversial visitor attraction and centre of interest. Thermae Bath Spa promises to reinvigorate not only its clients but also spa culture across the land. The 18th-century **Hot Bath** and sweet little **Cross Bath** are the centrepiece of the development, with a new building designed by Nicholas Grimshaw behind the Hot Bath, which will house the centre's medical facilities, as well as a Turkish bath, beauty treatment salons, restaurant and bar. The Cross Bath itself lies close to the original Sacred Cross spring, and has been remodelled to feature a small open-air thermal pool.

William Herschel Museum

ⓘ *19 New King St, T01225-311342, www.bath-preservation-trust.org.uk, Feb-Nov Mon-Fri 1400-1700 except Wed, Sat and Sun 1100-1700, £3.50, under-16s £2, family £7.50.* A five-minute walk west of the Cross Bath, the William Herschel Museum preserves the home of a prominent figure in 18th-century Bath society. William Herschel was an organist, composer and amateur astronomer. In 1781, from the garden of his home here, using a telescope of his own design, he discovered the planet Uranus. The museum is a great find for keen astronomers.

Theatre Royal and Queen Square

Heading north from the Cross Bath leads uphill via Westgate and Barton streets towards the parts of town that have justifiably made its architectural legacy world-famous. Before you come to Queen Square, the first of three 18th-century set pieces that are really the unmissable sights in the city, on the left at the foot of Barton Street is the Theatre Royal (see page 360), its elegant façade constructed in 1805.

Heading north, Queen Square was the first of architect John Wood the Elder's projects, built between 1728 and 1734, beautifully proportioned, right down to the windows (now with their original panes restored), and its north side making up a complete palace frontage.

Jane Austen Centre

ⓘ *40 Gay St, T01225-443000, www.janeausten.co.uk, Mon-Sat 1000-1700, Sun 1000-1730, £4.45, concessions £3.65, under-16s £2.45, family £11.95.* A stiff climb up Gay Street passes the Jane Austen Centre. No recreated rooms here, but the museum aims to show how the city influenced her works, especially *Northanger Abbey* and *Persuasion*, both set in the city, and 'find out why Jane Austen's TV adaptations are so popular'. The costumed guide outside poses for photographs with a world-weary expression on her face.

The Circus

ⓘ *Mon-Fri 1000-1700.* At the top of Gay Street, the second architectural set piece was planned by John Wood the Elder, but carried out by his son and completed in 1767. The Circus was the first of its type in the country and represents Georgian architecture at its most ladylike, with its little balconies (originally painted not black, but dark red and green), and delicate columns beneath arcane decorative symbols and stone acorns, apparently in honour of Bladud's pigs' favourite food. Thomas Gainsborough moved into No 17, when just starting out on his highly successful career as society's favourite portrait painter. And in its time the Circus also accommodated the missionary David Livingstone, General Clive of India, and the arctic explorer Parry. Based on the dimensions of Stonehenge, its three graceful crescents surround five majestic plane trees planted in 1804. The garden at No 4 has been restored to something like its Georgian appearance.

The Royal Crescent

ⓘ *Number 1, T01225-428126, Feb-Nov Tue-Sun 1030-1700 (last admission 1630) and first 2 weekends of Dec, £4, concessions £3.50, family £10.* A hundred yards down Brock Street, past the chi-chi shopping strip of Margaret's Buildings, the ground opens up in front of the third and most spectacular of the Wood developments. The Royal Crescent sweeps round to the right, facing south over **Royal Victoria Park** and

Fashion victim

As the Bath Tourist Office never ceases to remind the thousands of visitors who come to the city each year, Jane Austen, the unrivalled mistress of English prose, lived in Bath from 1801 to 1806 with her parents. But what they don't tell you is that she was never very fond of the place and left it 'with what happy feelings of escape'. By then it was already going out of fashion, and it's the moribund nature of society in the town that features strongly in both Northanger Abbey and Persuasion, published in 1818. (Many of the places mentioned in these novels are still recognizable: the Pump Rooms, Assembly Rooms, Queen Square and Laura Place among others. Her father is buried in Walcott church.

In recent years, however, Bath has regained some its lost cachet. Soho House, a favourite with London luvvies, opened its country branch at Babington House, several miles to the south, and house prices in the area continue to soar as more and more of the metropolitan set decant to the southwest, preferring the M4 commute to paying risible London house prices. The southwestern spa town may not exactly be the height of fashion, but at least it appears to be shaking off its image as the graveyard of ambition.

the river valley with views right over to Beechen Cliff beyond. Completed by John Wood the Younger once the Circus was finished, over a period of seven years, its positioning, its rhythm, scale and scope, still give just as lively an impression of fashionable 18th-century life as any Jane Austen adaptation. And if it's period detail you're after, at No 1 the interior of the very grand end house was painstakingly returned to its Georgian condition in the late 1960s. Surprisingly modern in atmosphere, despite the lack of electric light fittings, the dining room on the ground floor, as well as the drawing room and lady's bedroom on the first, would delight the most finicky art director. The kitchen in the basement, however, is less convincing.

Museum of East Asian Art

ⓘ *12 Bennett St, T01225-464640, Mon-Sat 1000-1700, Sun 1200-1700, £3.50, concessions £2.50.* Back in the Circus, Bennett Street leads northeast past the Museum of East Asian Art, which devotes three floors to treasures from East and Southeast Asia, dating from 5000 BC to the present day, with an extensive collection of Chinese jade and ceramics, as well as gourds, sculpture, including ivory and bamboo carvings.

Assembly Rooms

ⓘ *Bennett St, T01225-477789, www.museumofcostume.co.uk, daily 1000-1700 (last admission 1630), £5, concessions £4, under-16s £3.50, family £14.* The Assembly Rooms, once the social hub the city, are now owned by the National Trust. The Ball Room, Octagon, Tea Room and Card Room are the public rooms designed by John Wood the Younger in 1769 that have recently been restored, including the nine great chandeliers. The **Museum of Costume** in the basement is an exhibition of fashion wear from the 16th century to the present day, featuring over 150 dressed-up life-size dolls.

Building of Bath Museum

ⓘ *Feb-Nov Tue-Sun and all bank holidays 1030-1700 (last admission 1630). £4, concessions £3, under-8-18, £1.50, family £10.* Round the corner off Guinea Lane, on the Paragon, the place to gain an understanding of exactly how the city was developed is in an 18th-century Gothic chapel commissioned by the Methodist evangelist Selina, Countess of Huntingdon. (Her face in a portrait reminded Edith Sitwell of 'a fillet of boiled plaice'.) The Building of Bath Museum gives the full low-down on the construction of 18th-century Bath, how it came to look the way it does, as well as how it was decorated and inhabited, with models, architects' drawings and paintings in the Building gallery, engravings, house plans, gilding and cabinet-work in the Interiors gallery.

Postal Museum

ⓘ *8 Broad St, T01225-460333, www.bathpostalmuseum.org Mon-Sat 1100-1700, £2.90, senior citizens £2.20, students and under-16s £1.50.* Heading back toward the city centre above the banks of the Avon, the Postal Museum celebrates the honour of being the place where the first postage stamp in the world was used on 2 May 1840, and illustrates '4000 years of communication from 'clay mail' to 'e-mail'. It's also in honour of Ralph Allen, Bath's first postmaster, quarryman and general bigwig, who invented a system whereby letters weren't forced to go via London to the rest of the country.

Pulteney Bridge

Walcot Street continues south into the High Street, back into the boundaries of the medieval city. To the left, down Bridge Street, stands the last unmissable piece of 18th-century architecture in the city. Pulteney Bridge was designed by Robert Adam in the early 1770s and is unique in the country for still being lined with its original booths for shopkeepers. Along with the famous horseshoe weir on the Avon, it provides one of the most popular images of Bath. The bridge is best seen from North Parade, but a walk across it is mandatory in order to appreciate the splendour of Great Pulteney Street. The widest in Europe when it was built, wide enough for a horse and carriage to turn without having to back up, it provided the inspiration for the dimensions of the Champs Elysées. Up to the right are the old pleasure gardens of Henrietta Park.

Holburne Museum

ⓘ *T01225-466669, www.bath.ac.uk/holburne Mid-Feb-Nov Tue-Sat 1000-1700, Sun 1430- 1730, £3.50, concessions £3, under-16s £1.50.* In a commanding position at the end of Great Pulteney Street, the Holburne Museum in a former 18th-century hotel is the appropriately elegant setting for the fine art collection of 19th-century collector Sir William Holburne. It features a number of Old Masters, as well as silver, porcelain, furniture and portrait miniatures (including one of Beau Nash), alongside a strong showing from great English landscape and portrait painters like Turner and Gainsborough.

No 4 Sydney Place

Behind the museum stretch the leafy Sydney Pleasure Gardens, crossed by Brunel's railway and with their ornate bridges over the Kennet and Avon Canal. Jane Austen lived at no 4 Sydney Place for three years and there are views of the Sham Castle built by Sir Ralph Allen to provide a romantic view from his house on North Parade in 1760.

Victoria Art Gallery

ⓘ *Bridge St, T01225-477233, www.victoriagal.org.uk, Tue-Fri 1000-1730, Sat 1000-1700, Sun 1400-1700.* Back on Bridge Street, near the High Street, the Victoria Art Gallery is a fairly straightforward municipal art gallery with a good permanent exhibition of European art from about 1500 onwards and regular temporary shows by local artists and touring collections of interest. A few doors down on the High Street, the **Guildhall** contains perhaps the finest Georgian public rooms in the city, in Robert Adam style with superb chandeliers and a selection of royal portraits.

Around Bath

With more time, a few places just beyond the city are well worth seeking out. To the north, a couple of miles up Lansdown Road, **Beckford's Tower** ⓘ *Lansdown Rd, T01225-460705, Easter-Oct Sat, Sun, bank holidays 1030-1700, £2.50, concessions £2, family £6,* stands in the Lansdown Burial Ground, the last surviving monument to the huge wealthy and eccentric early champion of the neo-Gothic architectural style eventually beloved by the Victorians. William Beckford had this Italianate tower built in 1827, as a kind of mausoleum. There are great views over the countryside from the little belvedere at the top (Bristol and the Severn are visible on a clear day) but unfortunately not over Bath itself. The belvedere has been lovingly restored to its original condition and in the rooms downstairs, a small museum pays tribute to Beckford and includes a model of his fantastic house at Fonthill (no longer standing). (If you want decent views of the city, head for **Landsdown Crescent**, another sweeping crescent, designed by John Palmer in the early 1790s, on the way back into the city.)

A couple of miles east, up Bathwick Hill, is the **American Museum** ⓘ *Claverton Manor, T01225-460503, Apr-Sep Tue-Fri Gardens 1300-1800, Museum 1400-1700, Sat, Sun Gardens 1200-1800, Museum 1400-1700, also 23 Nov-15 Dec Tue-Sun 1300-1630, £6, concessions £5.50, under-16s £3.50, (less for Grounds, Folk Art and New Galleries only), from the bus station to the university (bus no 18) 5-10 min walk.* North Americans may find this place faintly patroniszing – a bit like coming across an English Museum in California full of bowler hats and brollies – but it's one of the oldest museums dedicated to Americana in the country. Assembled into a series of period-furnished rooms from colonial times up to the Civil War, it includes displays of Shaker furniture, some remarkable quilts, Native American artefacts, and much else. In the grounds, the copy of Washington's garden in Virginia is apparently pretty authentic.

To the southeast, some of the finest views of the city from afar can be had at **Prior Park Landscape Garden** ⓘ *Ralph Allen Dr, T01225-833422, Feb-Nov Mon, Wed-Sun 1100-1730 (or dusk if earlier), Dec and Jan Fri-Sun, £4, under-16s £2 (£1 off with valid bus or train ticket),head south across the river into Widcombe, at the White Hart pub, either head straight up Ralph Allen Dr or, if on foot, take a detour through the old village, up Widcombe Hill and along Church St, before joining Ralph Allen Dr,* designed by Alexander Pope and Capability Brown for Sir Ralph Allen, one of the city's most industrious supporters. Prior Park mansion has long been a Roman Catholic school, but the beautiful grounds, now in the care of the National Trust, include a Palladian bridge and three lakes.

For possibly the best view of Bath make your way south of the river and walk up Wells Way, across the roundabout, towards Bear Flat. Once in Bear Flat take a left up Shakespeare Avenue and you will arrive at **Alexandra Park**. The views are wonderful, and when the sun shines on the city it looks like a toy town. You can descend through the houses enjoying a bit of Bath's Victorian architecture and day-to-day life.

One of the great pleasures of Bath is to stroll along the towpath of the **Kennet and Avon Canal**, which runs all the way from Bristol to Reading. You can join the canal at the basin by the *Hilton* hotel (just off the A36, Rossiter Road) or a bit further on, by the bridge on Bathwick Hill, and follow your nose east as far as you like. A good stopping-off point is *The George Inn* at Bathampton (see page 359). More energetic souls can continue all the way to Avoncliff (about an hour by bike), where the *Cross Guns* pub does decent grub and has a beer garden overlooking the river. You could also hire a bike and go all the way to Bradford-on-Avon or alternatively go west following the old railway track to Bristol (see page 361 for bike hire).

Bradford-on-Avon and around

Upstream of Bath, just inside Wiltshire, Bradford-on-Avon is a kind of a mini-Bath, built from the same stone, without the 18th-century splendour but in a similar setting. The birthplace of the British rubber industry and for centuries a rich woollen mill centre, the old town snuggles up to the Avon, its old stone bridge still supporting a little 17th-century shrine which was later used as a lock-up. A short walk from the bridge via the Shambles, a shopping strip, via **Dutch Barton**, the area made prosperous by Huguenot weavers, the architectural highlight of the town is the Saxon Church of **St Laurence**. It was only discovered in 1856, having been a school, warehouse and private house, and is believed to have been rebuilt in the 11th century after being founded by St Aldhelm in the late 700s. Now it stands surrounded by later housing, an empty and atmospheric old place. A half-mile walk away along a footpath across the river is another, the **Tithe Barn** ⓘ *daily 1030-1600, free.* This medieval great barn once belonged to Great Barton Farm, an outlyer of Shaftesbury Abbey, a Benedictine nunnery of considerable wealth. It was built in the mid-14th century and used primarily for farm produce although parish tithes would also have been stored here. Also very atmospheric, with its cathedral-like cross window in the west wall and old oak-beamed roof, it's surrounded by old farm buildings that have been turned into tearooms, antiques and gift shops. Back in the middle of town, there's a history **museum** ⓘ *Bridge St, T01225-863280, Easter-Oct Wed-Sat 1030-1230, 1400-1600, Sun 1400-1600, Nov-Easter Wed-Fri, Sun 1400-1600, Sat 1030-1230, 1400-1600, free,* featuring a reconstruction of a 19th-century pharmacy. Other things worth seeking out are the concerts at the **Wiltshire Music Centre** ⓘ *Ashley Rd, T01225-860100,* walks and boat trips along the **Kennet and Avon Canal**, and the beautiful views over the town from the little medieval chapel of **St Mary Troy**, at the top of Conigre Hill.

Another 8 miles upriver from Bradford lies the National Trust village of **Lacock**. Mobbed in summer, the pretty little stone-built feudal village has been immaculately preserved, apparently almost unchanged since the 13th century. **Lacock Abbey** ⓘ *Abbey, museum, cloisters and garden (NT), T01249-730227 (abbey), T01249- 730459 (museum), Mar-Oct daily 1100-1730 (abbey Apr-Oct Wed-Mon 1300-1730), £6.50, under-16s £3.60, family £17.60,* was converted into a manor house at the dissolution and its 19th-century resident, William Fox Talbot, discovered the principle of photographic negatives. Appropriately enough, his home featured in the film of *Harry Potter and the Philosopher's Stone*. A museum of photography commemorates his discovery. The Church of St Cyriac, Perpendicular with a beautiful late-15th-century Lady Chapel, is also worth a look.

Just west of Lacock and 9 miles northeast of Bath, **Corsham Court** ⓘ *T01249-701610, Apr-Oct Tue-Sun 1400-1730, Oct-Mar Sat, Sun 1400-1630,* is a grand Elizabethan house, the home of the Methuen family, with an extraordinary array of Old Master paintings and landscaped grounds.

South of Bath

Heading 6 miles south of Bath, a mile south of the pretty little village of Wellow, **Stoney Littleton longbarrow** is one of the best-preserved prehistoric monuments in Somerset. One hundred feet long, the stone support of the door to its entry chamber looks as if it has been deliberately chosen for its ammonite.

European garden design at its tidy best can be found at the romantic Italianate terrace garden designed by Harold Peto between 1899 and 1933 at his home, **Iford Manor** ⓘ *Peto Garden, Iford Manor, 8 miles south of Bath, off the A36, T01225-863146, www.ifordmanor.co.uk, May-Sep Tue-Thu, Sat, Sun 1400-1700, Apr and Oct Sun 1400-1700, £3, concessions and 10-16s £2.50, under-10s welcome weekdays only.* As well as wonderful flowers, it is full of all kinds of surprising ornamental classical sculptures, the best displayed in his Romanesque cloisters, and there are beautiful views over the Frome valley too.

Frome, 10 miles south of Bath, is an endearing market town, with a dinky little shopping street (Cheap St) with its open drain running down the middle, reminiscent of York on a very small scale, and a foretaste of places like Wells, with its Old Market Cross at the bottom of the street and Catherine Hill worth a wander up for the views.

Cider country

As well as perfecting ritual human sacrifice, the Druids are said to have introduced apples to Britain. Both the Romans and the Normans improved age-old recipes for distilling their juice and, by the 17th century cider was second only to beer as the drink of choice among farm labourers. Somerset is the cider county, although few of its traditional orchards remain. Recently though there has been a resurgence of interest in small-scale, unprocessed, farm-produced 'scrumpy': dry, flat, cloudy and usually very alcoholic. Most ciders are now made from a selection of proven cider apples: Kingston Black (Bittersharp), Yarlington Mill and Dabinett (Bittersweets), Sweet Coppin (Sweet) and Brown's Apple (Sharp) are the main varieties.

Three miles south of Frome stands the first stately home to open its doors to the public on a regular basis: **Longleat House and Safari Park** ⓘ *T01985-844400, www.longleat.co.uk, house open Easter-Sep daily 1000-1730, Oct-Dec by guided tours 1100-1500. £9, concessions and under-14s £6. Safari Park mid to Mar-Oct Mon-Fri 1000-1600, Sat, Sun, bank holidays (and school holidays) 1000-1700. £9, concessions and under-14s £6. Longleat Passport to all attractions £15, concessions and under-14s £11.* Longleat is a strange place. The grand Elizabethan house is approached along a 2-mile drive through beautiful ornamental woodland, overlooking the star attraction that first made the estate a household name, the safari park. Deer, giraffe and rhino can be seen grazing in the distance, matchbox-sized cars crawling around among them, getting close to the famous lions, as well as hippos, seals and zebra. Otherwise there's plenty else for all ages to enjoy at this highly commercialized entertainment complex (Adventure Castle, Blue Peter world, miniature railway etc), including the gaudy interior of the old house itself, featuring the current Lord Bath's erotic murals. The worst taste though is reserved for the display of Nazi memorabilia in the Life & Times of Lord Henry Bath exhibition. Visitors stumble unawares here on disturbing 'mementoes' like a napkin from the Belsen commandant's supper table, below horrific photos of the camp's burial pits, as well as lots of Adolf Hitler's boring but technically accomplished artwork. It's quite enough to make the pleasures of 'the world's longest hedge maze' and other attractions round about quickly pall, even in bright sunshine.

Stourhead ⓘ *(NT), Stourton, near Warminster, T01747-841152, garden open daily 0900- 1900 (or dusk if earlier), house open Apr-Oct Fri-Tue 1100-1700, King Alfred's Tower (NT), Apr-Oct daily 1200-1700, house and garden £8.90, under-16s £4.30, family £21.20, garden or house only £5.10, under-16s £2.90,* is one of the most beautiful English landscape gardens, 6 miles south of Longleat. Designed by the amateur landscape gardener and banker Henry Hoare between 1741 and 1780, it embraces a large lake with woodland walks revealing surprising views of neoclassical monuments and follies all the way round, right up to the original Bristol city market cross. The house itself has a remarkable library and contains a variety of Old Master paintings and interesting sculpture. A 2-mile walk across the estate leads to King Alfred's tower, a brick folly with fabulous views over the surrounding countryside.

Sleeping

Bath *p346, map p348*

Accommodation prices vary widely according to the season. Central options are either budget or top-end, and both should be booked well in advance during the summer tourist season.

L Bath Priory Hotel, Weston Rd, a little way out, beyond the Royal Victoria Park, T01225-331922, F448276. A comfortable place, with spa facilities, garden and charming drawing room (great for afternoon teas) and Michelin-starred cooking in the dining room.

L Bath Spa Hotel, Sydney Rd, T0870-4008222, F444006. Plush, comfortable spa hotel set in 7 acres of gardens. Rooms at the front have good views. Facilities include 2 restaurants, CD player in every rooms, car valeting service and an excellent health and leisure spa.

L Royal Crescent Hotel, 16 Royal Cres, T01225-823333, F339401. The smartest hotel in the city, at the smartest address bang in the middle of its grandest architectural feature, with quiet back gardens and Roman-style spa facilities, oozing discreet Georgian elegance.

A Harrington's Hotel, 8 Queen St, T01225-461728, www.haringtonshotel.co.uk. Charming and very central, very comfortable townhouse hotel with quiet rooms.

A Queensberry Hotel, Russell St, T01225-447928, www.bathqueensberry.com. Stunning series of townhouses that are only marginally less grand than the Royal Crescent, very well-respected *Olive Tree* restaurant, and courtyard garden for summer drinks behind.

A Windsor Hotel, 69 Great Pulteney St, T01225-422100, F422550. A refurbished 200-year-old building in a superb position, with its own guides and sedan chairmen.

B Apsley House Hotel, 141 Newbridge Hill, T01225-336966, www.apsely-house.co.uk. Once the Duke of Wellington's house, now a welcoming family home on the main road some 20 mins from the centre, with parking.

B Eagle House, Church St, Bathford, T01225-859946. Grand-looking but informal family-run Georgian hotel.

B Haydon House, 9 Bloomfield Pk, T01225-444919, F427351. Highly rated Edwardian 5-bedroom guesthouse on the edge of the city, with a couple of golden retrievers, Laura Ashley interior and antiquey living room. Easy parking.

B Holly Lodge, 8 Upper Oldfield Pk, T01225-424042, www.hollylodge.co.uk. Some distance from the centre but with views over the town from Oldfield Park, a cosy place crammed with antiques and statues and a small garden.

B Lodge Hotel, Bathford Hill, a couple of miles outside the centre, in the pretty village of Bathford, T01225-858575, F858172. A friendly country home, with swimming pool and even a narrowboat on the canal for guests use.

B Paradise House, Holloway, T01225-317723, www.paradise-house.co.uk. Large and grand 11-room guesthouse with spectacular garden giving good views over the city, 5 mins' walk from the station.

C Cedar Lodge, 13 Lambridge, Bath, T01225-423468. Tasteful 18th-century house 15 mins' walk from the centre with delightful garden.

C Express by Holiday Inn, Lower Bristol Rd, T0870-4442792, www.hiexpress.co.uk. Big (126 rooms), new bed factory only a 15-min walk from the bus and train stations and offering comfortable, no-frills accommodation. Car parking, price includes continental breakfast. Front upper rooms have good views of the Royal Crescent.

C Grey Lodge, Summer La, Combe Down, Bath, T01225-832069. Smart B&B with great views, but some way out of town.

C The Town House, 7 Bennett St, T01225-422505. Two-room good-value guesthouse just off the Circus, very central cosy and comfortable.

C Weston Lawn, Lucklands Rd, Weston, T01225-421362, www.westonlawn.co.uk. Friendly, traditional 3-room B&B in elegant family home 20 mins' walk from city centre. Fresh flowers in the very comfortable rooms and breakfast with home-baked bread in the conservatory overlooking a delightful garden. Babysitting available.

D Abbey Rise, 97 Wells Rd, T01225-316177. 3-room Victorian guesthouse with good views over the city from the south, also on a main road but convenient for the train station.

D Belmont, 7 Belmont, Lansdown Rd, T01225-423082. Seven-room spacious guesthouse 10 mins' walk uphill from the Royal Crescent.

D Lamp Post Villa, 3 Crescent Gardens, Upper Bristol Rd, T01225-331221. Popular little 4-bedroom B&B at the bottom of Victoria Park, on the main road but quiet nonetheless.

E YMCA, International House, Broad St, T01225-460471, www.bath.org/ymca. Very central basic accommodation in dorms (£12), singles and doubles (£32), including breakfast. Best budget option in town. Recommended.

F Bath Backpackers Hostel, 13 Pierrepont St, T01225-446787, www.hostels.co.uk. No frills, 50 beds close to the station. No breakfasts.

F Bath YHA, Bathwick Rd, T01225-465674, F482947. Italianate mansion with 124 beds uphill from the station (take Badgerline No 18).

F White Hart, Claverton St, Widcombe, T01225-313985, www.whitehartbath.co.uk. Recently refurbished pub south of the river, within 5 mins of station, providing some of the best value beds in town, from backpacker dorms at £12.50 per person to en suite and family rooms. Self-catering kitchen, licensed café/bar, enclosed garden at back. Recommended, booking advisable.

Around Bath *p354*

L Babington House, Kilmersdon, near Radstock, T01373-812266, www.babington house.co.uk. Excellent swimming pool and spa facilities at this country house offshoot of the trendy London members club, Soho House. £250 a double.

L Woolley Grange, Bradford-on-Avon, T01225-864705. Family-friendly hotel.

B Priory Steps, Newtown, Bradford-on-Avon, T01225-862230. Family-run Wolsey Lodge in a row of old cottages on the edge of town with good views and cosy dining room.

D The Hermitage, Bath Rd, Box, Corsham, Wilts, T01225-744187. Small country house with fine heated outdoor swimming pool.

D Sturford Mead Farm, Corseley, near Warminster, T01373-832213. Welcoming farmhouse B&B close to Longleat.

Eating

Bath *p346, map p348*

Bath boasts a bewildering variety of places to eat and drink, generally of quite a high standard despite the obvious temptation to make a fast buck. If you know what you want, you're almost sure to find it done well here somewhere.

£££ Moody Goose, 7a Kingsmead Sq, T01225-466688. Top-notch modern British seafood and game with distinct French and Italian influences for about £35 a head in an inviting subterranean restaurant and cosy vaulted dining room. Two Michelin stars for chef Stephen Shore.

£££ Olive Tree at the *Queensberry Hotel* (see above). The other serious foodie option in the city.

£££ Fishworks, 6 Green St, T01225-448707. Ardent piscivores can confidently head here. It's quite expensive but very wholesome and absolutely fresh, all served up in TV cookery show-type surroundings.

£££ Sakura, 69 Great Pulteney St, T01225-422100. The city's top, fairly expensive Japanese restaurant.

£££ Sukhothai, 90 Walcot St, T01225-462463. A cheery and not-too-expensive Thai restaurant.

££ Le Beaujolais, 5 Chapel Row, just of Queen Sq, T01225-423417. A French bistro-style restaurant, with plenty of ambience but rather small portions. Good value lunch menu.

££ Demuths, 2 North Parade, off Abbey Green, T01225-446059. A long-standing, straightforward but versatile veggie restaurant (about £8 for a main course).

££ Eastern Eye, 8 Quiet St, T01225 422323. Grand décor, very central and not too expensive for top-notch variations of the new national dish, a good curry.

££ Firehouse Rotisserie, 2 John St, T01225-482070. Delicious brick oven-fired pizzas at this stylish restaurant. Generous portions and attentive service. The salmon and crab fishcakes are also recommended.

££The George Inn, Mill La, Bathampton, (30-min stroll from the centre of Bath), T01225-425079. Venerable old pub by the side of the canal, perfect for an outdoor drink on a summer's evening, or for Sunday lunch.
££Hole in the Wall, 16 George St, T01225-425242. Another enduringly popular vaulted brasserie, serving Michelin award-winning modern British cuisine. Good-value set menus during the week.
££La Flamenca, 12a North Parade, T01225-462626. Go underground for tapas and vino tinto at Bath's authentic Spanish-run tapas bar and restaurant. Eat at the barrel-turned-tables in the cellar bar or in the next door restaurant with live flamenco shows at weekends.
££Moon and Sixpence, 6a Broad St, T01225-460962. Intimate candlelit bistro, tucked away up a little passageway, in the middle of town. Eclectic dishes, including corn-fed chicken with spicy Thai risotto. The best tables are downstairs. There is a small, friendly bar area and tables in the peaceful courtyard outside.
££No 5, 5 Argyle St, almost on Pulteney Bridge, T01225-444499. Also a laid-back local favourite, good value despite being in pole position for tourists, doing very competent French cuisine.
££Paragon Wine Bar & Bistro, 1a Paragon, T01225-466212. Firm favourite with Bath locals. Offering informal dining with a contemporary menu. A warm and cosy environment, with a lovely fire in the winter.
££Rajpoots, Argyle St, T01225-466833. Fine Indian cuisine. Diners eat in booths beneath lanterns.
££Richmond Arms, 7 Richmond Pl, Lansdown, a little way from the centre, T01225-316725. Looks like a humble neighbourhood pub from the outside but inside it's a cosy bistro/wine bar with an enviable reputation amongst the town's culinary cognoscenti. The beer garden is perfect for a pre-prandial pint on a summer's evening.
££Sally Lunn's Refreshment House and Museum, 4 North Parade Passage, T01225-461634. The most famous medieval house in the city, still purveying the buns perfected by French Huguenot refugee Sally Lunn in the 1680s. Candlelit suppers and cream teas. The museum in the basement contains the original kitchen and a cellar full of stalactites and stalagmites.
££-£Tilleys Bistro, 3 North Parade Passage, T01225-484200, www.tilleysbistro.co.uk. Innovative French cuisine catering for all budgets. 2 extensive menus, 1 of which is vegetarian. Highly recommended
£Evan's Famous Fish and Chips, Abbey Gate St. If you're looking for the old-style national dish this place will oblige. See also Cafés below.

Cafés

Adventure Café, 5 Prince's Buildings, George St, T01225-462038. Extremely popular with locals and tourists alike who come in their droves to worship at the temple of great coffee. Also good smoothies, cakes and a range of sandwiches and panini. Outside seating catches the sun as well as the traffic fumes.
Doolallys, 51 Walcott St, T01225-444122. Bijou, boho café-cum-bar in the city's artisan quarter, with a laid-back feel and live music in the evenings.
Café Retro, 18 York St, T01225-339347. Just behind the abbey, this café/bistro is very popular with local 20- and 30-somethings. Downstairs is a good place to hang out for a leisurely brunch (service is not the quickest) while upstairs in the evenings the menu is Anglo-French and a little more formal at around £20-25 a head for dinner.

Around Bath *p354*
Bridge Tea Rooms, 24 Bridge St, Bradford-on-Avon, T01225-865537.
Beehive Pub, 253 Trowbridge Rd, Bradford-on-Avon, T01225-863620. A walk east along the canal towpath with good home-made food.
Maples Delicatessen, 4 The Shambles, Bradford-on-Avon, T01225-862203. For excellent picnic materials.
Sagebury Cheese Delicatessen, 21 Cheap St, Frome, T01373-462543.

Pubs and bars

Bath *p346, map p348*
The Bell, 103 Walcot St, stands out for its live music and real ale.
Grappa, 3 Belvedere, Landsdown Rd, T01225- 448890. Minimalist bar/pub but a large bar, beams, open fire and soft lighting makes it inviting and relaxed. Good lagers, wines and cocktails. Busy at weekends.

Ha Ha Bar and Canteen, The Tramshed, Walcot St, T01225-421200. Shiny new bar that's all exposed brickwork, wood floors and leather couches. Good place to chill or enjoy some solid bistro-style fare.

The Hat & Feather, 14 London St, T01225-425672. This pub offers a glimpse of the seamy side of Bath. DJs play upstairs and downstairs and though downstairs is predominantly a pub, some weekends you'd swear it was a club.

Hop Pole, 7 Albion Buildings, Upper Bristol Rd, T01225-425410. A 5-min walk west of Queen Sq, just below Victoria Park, this locals' pub is worth the stroll. It has a fine selection of ales and an excellent menu. Lovely garden filled with tables, plants, lanterns and a few pagoda-type constructions in which to sit. Good for Sunday lunch but book.

The Old Green Tree, 12 Green St. A popular locals' pub with very good real ales, wood-pannelled rooms (including a no-smoking one) and cheery chatter.

Raincheck, 34 Monmouth St, T01225- 444770. Convivial atmosphere, table service and perhaps the best cocktails in town.

The Star, 23 Vineyards, on the Paragon, snug and wood-panelled.

Clubs

Moles, 14 George St, T01225-404445. Moles is a popular, but tiny, live music venue on two floors. It offers everything from live world music to techno DJ sets, as well as themed nights including the 'Big Cheese' for the tacky but fun-loving and 'Purr' for indie kids, punks and weirdos.

Entertainment

Bath *p346, map p348*

Cinema

Little Theatre, St Michael's Pl, T01225-466822, www.picturehouses.co.uk. Popular cinema offering arthouse films. Check website for what's on.

Comedy

The Porter, 15 George St, T01225-424104. Popular Sun night sets. See also the listings in *Venue* magazine.

Theatre

Theatre Royal, T01225-448844, www.theatreroyal.org.uk. West End previews, touring opera, dramas and comedies in the Georgian main house, and more experimental work in the smaller Ustinov studio. £3 tours on the first Wed and Sat of each month, 1100 and 1200.

Festivals

Bath *p346, map p348*

Mar Literature Festival in early-Mar.

May/Jun Bath Festival (box office, T01225-463362, www.bathmusic fest.org.uk) in late-May and early Jun, is a very prestigious music festival, spanning world, jazz and classical genres.

Nov Mozart Festival in Nov.

Shopping

Bath *p346, map p348*

Bath is something of a shopper's paradise, with a wide variety of interesting one-offs, and more than enough antique shops, most of them expensive. **Milsom St** is the main drag with all the usual high street names, and also pedestrianized Union St, which has beautiful wooded views to the south.

North of the centre, **Walcot St** is a good browsing ground and is referred to as the 'artisan' centre of the city with shops selling everything from secondhand clothes to quality furnishings.

Also to the north of the centre, **Margaret's Buildings** is a very refined little strip of boutiques, for antiques and classy womenswear. Try: **Alexandra May**, 23 Brock St, T01225- 465094, for vintage costume jewellery; and **Bankes Books**, at No 5, T01225-444580, **Bath Old Books**, No 9, T01225-422244, and **Patterson Liddle**, No 10, T01225-426722, for rare books. Another antiquey spot is **Savile Row** behind the Assembly Rooms.

The Bath Deli, 7 Savile Row, T01225-315666. Good for picnic materials.

The Fine Cheese Company, 29-31 Walcot St, T01225-483407. Top-quality picnic materials aplenty with more than 150 handmade curds, as well as bread and wine.

Green Park Market, T01225-789613. A skilful conversion of the old Green Park station into a

covered market, with food stalls, art and crafts from Wed-Sat, antiques on Thu, and the original Farmers Market every Sat.
Harvest, 37 Walcot St, T01225-465519, for organic wholefoods.
Itchy Feet, 4 Bartlett St, T01225-337987. An independent retailer of travel gear.
Paragon Antiques Market, 3 Bladud Buildings, T01225-463715. Takes place every Wed from 0630-1500 for antiques, bric-a-brac and 'bygones'.
Paxton and Whitfield, 1 John St, T01225-466403. A venerable old cheesemonger.
Shannon, 68 Walcot St, T01225-424222, for its contemporary Scandinavian furniture.
Shoon, 14 Old Bond St, T01225-480095. Worth seeking out for its well-chosen clothes, shoes and outdoor gear.

Activities and tours

Bath *p346, map p348*

Boat tours

Cleopatra Boat Trips, T01225-480541, from the riverside next to the Rugby Football Ground. The only tour boat that cruises downstream of the weir. £5.95, concessions £4.95, under-16s £3.95, hourly departures daily.
Bath Boating Station, Forester Rd, T01225-466407. Skiff and punt hire for river expeditions upstream from Pultney Bridge to Bathampton.

Walking tours

The Mayor's Corps of Honorary Guides, T01225-477411. Entertaining and free 2-hr walking tours leave from outside the Pump Room throughout the year Mon-Fri, Sun at 1030 and 1400, Sat 1030 only, and also May-Sep Tue, Fri and Sat at 1900.
Bizarre Bath, T01225-335124. A comedy walk that leaves the *Huntsman Inn* every evening at 2000 Apr-Sep.
Ghost Walks, from Garrick's Head T01225-463618 at 2000.

Transport

Bath *p346, map p348*

Bicycle

Avon Valley Cyclery, Bath Spa Railway Station, Dorchester St, T01225-442442; **John's Bikes**, 82 Walcot St, T01225-334633.

Bus

First Bus, runs the frequent direct X39 service to **Bristol** (40 mins). **National Express**, T08705-808080, runs the direct service at 1225 to **Cardiff** (2 hrs 35 mins), 10 direct services per day to **London Victoria** (3 hrs 20 mins) and a regular service to **Bristol airport** (2 hrs), changing at Bristol bus station. **Traveline**, T0870-6082608.

Car

Parking in central Bath is a bit of a problem. On-street parking is available via the purchase of Pay & Display tickets from machines located by the roadside. Areas are clearly signed for 1 and 2 hrs maximum stays. In the 1 hr zones the cost is £1 per half hr, and in the 2 hr zones £1 per hour. In Zone 1 (Pulteney St area) pay and display costs are 10p per 10 mins up to a maximum of 2 hrs duration. If spending a day in Bath, the best option are the Park and Ride car parks in Landsdown (from north), Bath University or Odd Down (from south) or Newbridge (from west).

Avis, Unit 4b Bath Riverside Business Park, T01225-446680; **A1 Self Drive Hire**, 376 Wellsway, T01225-830630; **Ford Rental**, Kingsmead Motor Co Ltd, 5-10, James St West, T01225-402234; **Hertz**, Bath Spa Rail Station, Dorchester St, T01225-442911.

Taxi

Abbey Radio Taxis, South Parade, T01225-444444; **Bath Taxis**, Cheltenham St, T01225-447777; **Widcombe Cars**, 21 Greenacres, T01225-422610

Train

First Great Western, T08457-000125, runs the frequent direct service from Bath Spa to **Bristol Temple Meads** (15 mins) and twice hourly direct to **London Paddington** (1 hr 30 mins). **Wessex Trains**, T08709-002320, run the direct hourly service to **Cardiff Central** (1 hr 5 mins). **National Rail Enquiries**, T08457-484950.

Directory

Bath *p346, map p348*

Internet Click Internet Café, 13 Manvers St, near the station, T01225-481008.
Hospitals Royal United Hospital, Combe Park, T01225-428331.

Somerset → *Colour map 2, grid B1/2*

Somerset is often portrayed as a place of insular, cider-guzzling farming communities and new-age freaks, but this is one of the most ancient and sacred parts of the country, evidenced by the miniature cathedral-city at Wells and confirmed at nearby Glastonbury. Here all the myths come together – not just of Arthur, Wessex, and Joseph of Arimathea, but also of every type of alternative philosophy. To the west, the county town of Taunton sits beneath the Quantocks, a charming little range of sandstone hills, where acres of wild oaks and heather give glimpses of the sea. Further west still, Exmoor, round 267 square miles of windswept, rainlashed sandstone upland, is one of the most romantic of England's national parks. » *For Sleeping, eating and other listings, see pages 372-375.*

Wells and the Mendips

Perhaps because of its close proximity to Glastonbury, Wells – the smallest cathedral city in England – feels eminently sensible and well-behaved, curled up at the foot of the Mendip hills. Whilst its crazy cousin – just 6 miles down the road – is all bohemian unruliness and mystical excess, the small scale and dignified character of Wells count as evidence of the design of an altogether more rational divine hand. Its awe-inspiring medieval cathedral, which many consider to be the loveliest in the country, might today as easily serve a vast urban sprawl. But Wells remains a reminder of a time when English provincial towns retained altogether more comfortable and more manageable proportions. Next door to the cathedral, swans ring a bell to be fed in the moat of the Bishop's Palace – home also to the Bishop of Bath and Wells – whose lawns play host to regular games of croquet in the summer. A lively market sets up its stalls on Wednesdays and Saturdays in the affable Market Place next door. And, as a playful touch, the waters from the natural wells that give the place its name run down the High Street in swift, little channels, the gift to the city in the 15th century of a certain Bishop Beckynton. Though possibly not grand enough to count as a destination in its own right, Wells certainly makes a highly satisfactory stopover, the evening floodlighting of its historic buildings adding extra atmosphere to an overnight stay. To the north and west, the Mendips provide some fine walking country, as well as the limestone 'wonders' of Wookey Hole and the Ebbor and Cheddar Gorges. Weston-Super- Mare is the now fairly jaded resort that has grown up where the Mendips fall into the Bristol Channel.

Ins and outs

Getting there From London by **car**, turn off at Shepton Mallet onto the A371. Buses go almost every hr from Bristol and Bath. If you are making a round, day trip to Wells and Glastonbury, ask for an Explorer ticket, which enables you to hop on and off whenever and wherever you want. There is virtually no free parking, but the city contains a number of public car parks where you can leave your car for 24 hrs for about £3-4.

Getting around Wells is small enough to negotiate on foot. If, however, you feel like exploring the city and its vicinity on two wheels, try **Bike City**, in Broad St, T01749-671711.

Information Wells TIC ⓘ *Town Hall, Market Pl, T01749-672552, wells.tic@ukonline.co.uk. Mar to Nov, daily.* Provides a useful accommodation and information guide for 50p. **Weston-Super-Mare TIC** ⓘ *Beach Lawns, T01934- 888800. Apr-Sep 0930-1730, Oct-Mar Mon-Fri 0930-1700, Sat 0930-1600. www.somersetcoast.com.*

Wells

Having had your fill of browsing in the Market Place, walk through the stone gateway at the top left of the square to find the **cathedral** ⓘ *daily, voluntary donations of £4.50-1.50 welcome, evensong 1700 Mon-Sat and 1500 on Sun*, rising up before a magnificent expanse of greensward. You will need to take a few steps back to take in the full extent of the 13th century west front, which contains the largest gallery of medieval sculpture in the world – a veritable panoply of bishops, kings, saints and apostles with the figure of Christ, at its apex, a modern piece installed in 1985. Once inside, your eye is immediately drawn to the unique 'scissor arches' at the east end, a superbly elegant design of deceptively modern appearance, which was, in fact, a 14th-century solution to the problem of redistributing the weight of a building threatening to sink into its foundations. Look out for the ancient astronomical clock in the north transept, whose jousting knights revolve in ceaseless tournament, before climbing the worn stone steps up to the octagonal Chapter House, where ecclesiastical business was traditionally conducted. Undoubtedly the best way to experience the great beauty of the cathedral is to sit through choral **evensong**. If your visit is at lunchtime, however, the cloisters – with its 15th-century library – also includes a shop and restaurant (main courses about £5, with an impressive array of cakes made by the ladies of the diocese). On the north side, the quiet precincts of the cathedral include the **Vicar's Close**, said to be the oldest continuously inhabited street in Europe, which – with its miniature Gothic architecture, cobbles and extraordinary chimneys – is almost a work of art in its own right. The **Wells Museum** ⓘ *T01749-673477, daily Easter-Oct, Wed-Mon Nov-Easter, £2.50*, the pinkish building looking onto the green, contains a display of local history and archaeology, including the macabre remains and belongings of the legendary witch of the Wookey Hole caves. On the south side, negotiate the drawbridge and portcullis of the **Bishop's Palace** ⓘ *1030-1700 Tue-Fri and 1200-1700 Sun, Apr-Oct and most days in Aug, £3.50* – some of whose rooms are open to the public – and stroll around the grounds, which contain some unusual trees and, at the back, a pool produced by the 40 gallons of water supplied per second by the natural springs seen bubbling up at its base.

The Mendips and Weston-Super-Mare

The large caves called **Wookey Hole** ⓘ *2 miles west of Wells, T01749-672243, www.wookey.co.uk, Apr-Oct daily 1000-1700, Nov-Mar 1030-1630, £8.80, under-16s £5.50,* hollowed out of the Mendips by the river Axe over thousands of years, have been turned into a full-blown tourist attraction. Admission includes a 40-minute tour of the illuminated cave system, with observations of the stalactites, stalagmites ('mites go up and tites go down') and rock formations with silly names, including the 'Witch of Wookey', as well as a Victorian papermill, still in production, old-fashioned penny arcade, mirror maze and the Caves Museum, which explains their geological and local history. Allow a couple of hours to do the whole lot.

Heading west towards the Mendip hilltop village of **Priddy**, which is indeed pretty, the road passes **Ebbor Gorge**, a beautiful nature reserve that provides on a smaller scale evidence of how the much more famous **Cheddar Gorge** ⓘ *Cheddar Caves and Gorge T01934-742343, www.cheddarcaves.co.uk, Apr-Oct daily 1000-1700, Nov-Mar 1000-1630, £8.90, under-16s £5.90,* a few miles further on might have looked before its commercialization. Cheddar may have given its name to the world's most famous cheese (thanks to Victorian local man Joseph Harding and his wife who invented its scientific manufacture), but visitors today are more likely to come for its caves. Wookey's main rival charges for parking, although it has the added attraction of the gorge (its lower and more spectacular end spoilt by the traffic) and boasts two slightly smaller caves, Gough's and Cox's, as well as a Crystal Quest, Jacob's Ladder (a long flight of steps leading up to a viewpoint), and an open-top tour bus. The Cheddar Man exhibition displays the remains of someone buried here about 9000 years ago, whose DNA was matched in 1997 with that of local teacher Adrian Target.

Weston-Super-Mare, 9 miles west of Cheddar, is Bristol's seaside and retirement resort. Bungalow heaven, the seafront now looks run-down, although it still does donkey rides, miniature railway rides along Beach Lawns and the Grand Pier, and boat trips out to tiny **Steepholm Island** in the middle of the Bristol Channel from Knightstone Harbour (details from TIC).

Glastonbury

→ *Colour map 2, grid B2*

There is nowhere more imbued with the mythical – even mystical – idea of England than Glastonbury. The romantic ruins of the town's ancient abbey, a sacred well, a thorn tree from the holy land and the tor – a kind of miniature magic mountain – have variously become part of the warp and woof of two of this country's greatest stories. Glastonbury has been identified both as the Isle of Avalon, the site of King Arthur's final resting place and, also, as the birthplace of English Christianity, where Joseph of Arimathea – who made the arrangements for Jesus' burial – is said to have brought the holy grail, the vessel used by Christ at the Last Supper. The town has inspired writers and poets throughout the ages, from Lord Tennyson to the singer Van Morrison.

Somewhat more prosaically, the first thing the visitor to Glastonbury is likely to be struck by is the cornucopia of shops selling all the paraphernalia of the modern spiritual bazaar – crystals, incense, buddhas, beads and the like. The town is home to so many healers and seekers of different shapes and sizes that, without the solid centre that the abbey must once have provided, the whole thing can occasionally feel like rather a dispiriting, amorphous mess. The other way to look at it, perhaps, is that this proliferation of unconventional minds is an expression of the intrinsic pulling power of Glastonbury, still capable of magnetizing seekers of all persuasions. It does remain a special place and some genuinely interesting people do live here. Anyway, who's to say that that dreadlocked hippy, playing the bongos rather badly, isn't actually on – or rather onto – something?

Ins and outs

Getting there If you're driving from London, take the M3 and then the A303 – breaking your journey at Stonehenge – before turning off at Wincanton on the A371 to Shepton Mallet, by which time either Glastonbury, or 'The Ancient Isle of Avalon', is well-signposted. The town is also about 10 miles from the M5, turning off at junction 23 onto the A39. There are regular, hourly buses from Bristol and Bath – via Wells – to Glastonbury. Traveline, T0870-6082608. There is also a daily National Express, T08705-808080, service between Glastonbury and Dorchester, leaving Dorchester at 0955 and returning from Glastonbury at 1655. There is very limited street car parking in the town, with public car parks in St John's Sq behind the High St, in Silver St and next to the abbey grounds.

The nearest railway station is 10 miles away at Castle Cary (from London Paddington, 2 hours direct or 2½ hours if you change at Bath, £35 return). However, there is only one bus a week (Tue at 1000) that goes direct from Castle Cary to Glastonbury. Otherwise, a spasmodic Mon-Sat service goes – very slowly – as far as Street, from where there are regular buses to Glastonbury. A taxi from Castle Cary might cost you anything up to £30. It is probably easier to go by train to Bath or Bristol Temple Meads and catch the hourly bus which stops outside the railway station to Glastonbury.

Getting around The town centre – once you have penetrated the unprepossessing modern development on the outskirts – essentially consists of two streets, the High St and Magdalene St. These are joined together at right angles at the Market Pl, the focus of much of the town's life – including impromptu, beery singing – and site of a striking mid-19th-century cross. The abbey is 60 yds away to your left along Magdalene St, while

All the fun of the fayre

The summer music festival is an intrinsic part of British life, and the most famous of all, Glastonbury, is as much a part of the cultural calendar as Last Night of the Proms or the panto season. From humble origins when it was known as Glastonbury Fayre, 'Glasto' has grown into a musical behemoth and, according to many, largely lost its radical kudos, as well as having gained a nasty reputation for crime. It was very different back in September 1970 (on the day after Jimi Hendrix died), when local farmer, Michael Eavis, allowed the first festival to take place on his land, charging the princely sum of £1 (which included free milk from his cows) and 1500 turned up to hear Marc Bolan and Al Stewart amongst others. Now well over 100,000 are charged over £100 a head for the privilege of attending. But at least the purists don't moan about changes to the on-site sanitation and greater security measures first put in place in 2002 seem to have given rise to a happier vibe, if making it harder to jump the fence.

the other two sites of particular interest – the Chalice Well and Glastonbury Tor – are quite some walk away, perhaps 20-30 minutes. There is, however, a Tor Bus which operates a round trip from St Dunstan's car park beside the abbey, via the well and the Rural Life Museum, to the foot of the tor. (About every 30 mins, 0930-1700, £1/50p). To reach the top of the tor involves a steep 10-15-minute climb, which would be very demanding to anyone using a stick or a wheelchair.

Information Glastonbury TIC ⓘ *at the bottom end of the High St, in The Tribunal, a lovely old medieval building which used to be where the town's abbot would decide local legal matters, T01458-832954, glastonbury.tic@ukonline.co.uk, www.glastonbury tic.co.uk. Apr-Sep Sun-Thu 1000-1700, Oct-Mar 1000-1730, Fri and Sat 1000-1630.* A very useful accommodation guide, with a map and other information is available for 50p, and *The Oracle*, a monthly news-sheet with listings and small adverts, is free.

Sights

Glastonbury Abbey ⓘ *T01458-832267, daily 0930-1800, or dusk if earlier, 0900 Jun-Aug, and 1000 Dec-Feb, £3.50, child 1.50.* Begin your tour of Glastonbury at the abbey, a stone's throw away from the Market Place and the main bus stop. Like so much of England's Christian heritage, the reason this once-great building is now all but a ruined shell is that it was demolished during the Protestant Reformation of the 16th century on the orders of Henry VIII and subsequently used as a stone quarry. It is, surely, an indication of the unique significance of Glastonbury that Henry, astonishingly, repented of this one particular act of desecration on his deathbed. This was where the Christian gospel was believed to have first taken root on English soil.

The only complete building to survive Henry's onslaught is the abbot's kitchen, a pyramidal structure dating from about 1340. Still vaguely intact is the beautiful Lady Chapel, of Norman style, which is believed to have been built over the site of a much earlier church – some say Joseph's own. The ghostly ruins of the nave contain the grave of King Arthur and his queen Guinevere – now marked by a simple wooden sign – which was discovered in 1191. The relics were then placed in a marble tomb before the high altar: the debate still rages on as to whether or not this was an elaborate fake, a piece of monkish mummery invented to capitalize on this royal cult. There is also a museum attached to the abbey, included in the entry fee.

Continuing south along Magdalene Street, tucked away on your right is the medieval **St Margaret's Chapel**, which originally served a small hospice and is now the base of a group of Christians called the Quest Community. ⓘ *Prayers at 1200 Mon-Sat, free.* At the end of the street, if you turn right up Street Road – into what was once Glastonbury's red light district – you will come to **Wearyall Hill**, where another thorn tree marks the spot where Joseph is first said to have planted his rod. Carrying on, however, and turning left up Bere Lane, you will eventually come to the **Rural Life Museum** ⓘ *T01458-831197, Tue-Sun (Sat only from Nov-Mar) 1000-1800, £2.50, concessions £2, child £1,* set in and around a splendid 14th-century barn, displaying all manner of farm and domestic practices – from threshing machines to cheeses – of the 19th and early 20th centuries.

At the top of Bere Lane, turn right into Chilkwell Street where, a 100 yards further on, you will find the **Chalice Well** ⓘ *T01458-831154, www.chalicewell.org.uk, daily Apr-Oct 1000-1800, Nov, Feb and Mar 1100-1700, Dec and Jan 1200-1800, £2.30, concessions £1.60, child £1.20, disabled parking and guide dogs only,* a natural spring which for centuries has been renowned for its spiritual and healing properties. The water is full of red iron, which may have added fuel to the belief that this was where the holy grail was buried. The gardens surrounding the spring are immaculate and support an atmosphere of great peacefulness. In recent years, Prince Charles has come here to take the waters after breaking his arm in a polo accident.

The **Lake Village Museum** ⓘ *daily 1000-1700 summer, 1000-1600 winter, £2, concessions £1.50, child £1,* is a display of local archaeology going back to Iron Age times, on the first floor of the Tribunal building. The ancient **Church of St John** ⓘ *admission free only on Tue mornings, at other times, contact the church warden via the TIC,* – largely rebuilt in the 15th century – half way up the High Street is also worth visiting. Its stained-glass windows include a depiction of Joseph of Arimathea and the churchyard contains yet another holy thorn tree, from which a cutting is sent every year to decorate the Queen's Christmas breakfast table.

Glastonbury Tor ⓘ *24 hrs daily, free.* From St John's, the tor can be reached either by a path on its westerly flank – beginning at the corner of Chilkwell Street and Wellhouse Lane – or by a shorter path to the east – beginning in Stone Down Lane, a 10-minute walk up Wellhouse Lane from Chilkwell Street. Rising some 164 yards above sea level, this natural feature of the landscape is – depending on who you talk to – a meeting point of ley lines (mysterious channels of energy that run through the earth), a temple dedicated to the great Goddess, or a secret entrance to the underworld. The distinctive patterns of its terraced slopes, generally understood to be the result of a medieval field system called strip lynching, have also been interpreted as the remains of an esoteric labyrinth. Whatever is truly the case, the summit of the tor is an indisputably exhilarating place to sit – take a picnic with you – due in no small part to the wonderful sense of place and space and the 360 degree view of the Somerset countryside, extending as far as the Bristol Channel. From the tor, one can appreciate how Glastonbury really was once an ancient isle, rising out of marshy land that was often flooded in the winter. Like St Michael's Mount in Cornwall and the Mont St Michel in Normandy, the tor is dedicated to St Michael, the great destroyer of demons. It is impossible to say when it was first regarded as a holy place. The tower on the tor is all that remains of a medieval church – built to replace an earlier building destroyed by earthquake – and archaeologists have unearthed material from the sixth century and what seem to be 10th-century monastic cells. The tor is also where Richard Whiting, the last abbot of Glastonbury, was taken to be hanged and beheaded by Henry's men on 15th November 1539.

Somerset Levels, Taunton and the Quantocks

South and west of Glastonbury stretch the drained flatlands of the Somerset Levels, famous for their cider farms and with distant views of the Quantocks. The geology of these lovely sandstone hills introduces the characteristic look of Exmoor (see page 368) and much of north Cornwall. As well as being fine walking country, the Quantocks have a literary reputation disproportionate to their size thanks to the Romantic poets Wordsworth and more especially Coleridge, and writers like Evelyn Waugh. Nether Stowey nestles on their northern flank, within reach of the sea, and the site of Coleridge's Cottage, one of the earliest of literary shrines, now preserved by the National Trust. At their feet in the south sits Taunton, the county town of Somerset. Not much to write home about itself but close by are the famous gardens of Hestercombe.

Ins and outs

Getting there **First Great Western** run the service to Exeter from London Paddington (2 hours) via Reading (1½ hour) passes through Taunton, and there are also **Virgin Trains** from Bristol (30 minutes) and the West Midlands. **National Rail Enquiries,** T08457-484950. Taunton can usually be reached in less than 2½ hours from London on the M4 and M5 (junction 25), and in about 30 minutes from Glastonbury, about 18 miles away along the A361, sometimes in slightly less time by using the A39 and M5. A fairly comprehensive and reliable network of local buses are run by **First National,** T01823-272033. **Traveline,** T0870-6082608.

Getting around Walking and cycling are the best way to get around the Quantocks. TIC offices below can provide a set of leaflets on local walks. **Ian's Cycle Centre,** Taunton, T01823-365917.

Information **Taunton TIC** ⓘ *in the Library on Paul St, T01823-336344. Jun-Sep Mon-Thu 0930-1730, Fri 0930-1900, Sat 0930-1700.* Accommodation booking service (in person only). **Fyne Court Information Centre** ⓘ *T01823-451587.*

Somerset Levels

The ancient history of the Somerset Levels can be explored 5 miles west of Glastonbury at **Westhay**, where the council's **Peat Moors Centre** ⓘ *Shapwick Rd, T01458-860697, Apr-Oct 1000-1630, £2.50, concessions and under-16s £1.95, family £8,* demonstrates how neolithic man lived in these marshes, with entertaining mock-up huts and a reconstruction of the extraordinary pre-fab wooden track they used to get about on.

Eight miles southwest of Glastonbury, **Muchelney Abbey** ⓘ *(EH), T01458-250664, Apr-Sep daily 1000-1800, Oct daily 1000-1700, £2.50, £1.90 concessions,* is a little-visited treasure: the remains of a monastery founded in the seventh century and re-founded in 950. The Abbot's lodging still looks much as it would have done when handed over to Henry VIII in 1539. **Muchelney Pottery** ⓘ *T01458-250324,* is worth a visit for the work of John Leach and there's also an old **Priest's House** (NT) in the village.

At **Montacute** ⓘ *(NT), Montacute, T01935-823289, Apr-Oct Mon, Wed-Sun 1100-1700, £6.50, under-16s £3,* 12 miles south of Glastonbury, stands one of the finest late Tudor mansions in the country containing a series of Elizabethan and Jacobean portraits, surrounded by a formal garden with yew hedges, a lake and gazebo. The place became famous after featuring in the film adaptation of Jane Austen's *Sense and Sensibility*.

Eight miles west, the finest church on the Somerset Levels can be found at **Isle Abbots**, with a tower complete with 'hunkypunks' or ornamental gargoyles.

Taunton

Another 7 miles to the west lies Taunton, in the valley of the river Tone, between the Quantocks and the Blackdown hills. A congested local centre, it has a well-respected **Flower Show** (The Chelsea of the West) on the first weekend of August and also the **county history museum** ⓘ *Castle Green, T01823-320201, www.somerset.gov.uk/museums, Apr-Oct Tue-Sat, bank holidays 1000-1700, Nov-Mar Tue-Sat 1000-1500, free,* in its old castle, with displays on the landscape, flora and fauna of the region and also the Somerset Light Infantry. Once famous for its cattle market, the **Taunton Antiques Market** ⓘ *Silver St, T01283-289327, every Mon 0900-1600*, is probably of more interest to visitors, with over 100 dealers in antiques and collectables.

A couple of miles north of Taunton, **Hestercombe Gardens** ⓘ *Cheddon Fitzpaine, near Taunton T01823-413923, www.hestercombegardens.com, daily 1000-1800 (or dusk if earlier), £4.50, child £1,* are the masterpiece of the collaboration between garden designer Gertrude Jekyll and architect Edward Lutyens. His Orangery is a highlight, and her 4-acre plantings in the Edwardian garden are another. A Victorian shrubbery and 40 acres of Georgian pleasuregrounds, with lakes, follies and woodland walks, are in the process of being restored.

Quantocks

Hestercombe sits on the sheltered southeastern tip of the Quantocks, which roll for 12 miles or so northwest towards the sea. The name apparently derives from the celtic word for 'rim'. They are a delightful place to explore. Their official visitor centre and the headquarters of the Somerset Wildlife Trust is a couple of miles north at **Fyne Court** ⓘ *Fyne Court, T01823-451587, daily 0900-1800 (or sunset if earlier),* in the old pleasure gardens of the home of pioneer electrician Andrew Crosse, now demolished. Maps, walking trails and general information on the area are provided here, as well as a teahouse and ruined folly being turned into a haven for bats.

After 6 miles along the same road, the Quantocks suddenly dip down into **Nether Stowey**. **Coleridge's Cottage** ⓘ *T01278-732662, Apr-Sep Tue, Wed, Thu, Sun 1400-1700, £3, under-16s £1.50,* is a sweet little place with three rooms on show, as well as a good bookshop on the Romantics and an exhibition room including manuscripts. Although much altered, having been a pub for a while, the house gives you a good idea of how the great man lived during his most creative period (aged 23), when he was writing the *Rime of the Ancient Mariner* and *Kubla Khan*, disturbed by a man on business from Porlock.

The road over to Crowcombe from Nether Stowey heads through wild oak woodland up onto the top of the heather-clad, bracken-infested hills, laced with footpaths, and dotted with white puffballs in season (Sep, Oct). **Crowcombe** has an excellent pub. A few miles further down the west side of the hills, the main A358 passes **Combe Florey**, where Evelyn Waugh and then his son Auberon lived in the manor house. The **West Somerset Railway** ⓘ *T01643-704996, www.west-somerset- railway.co.uk* runs steam engines in summer up this side of the hills, from **Bishop's Lydeard** 20 miles to **Minehead**, popular with hikers, birdwatchers and families.

Exmoor → *Colour map 1, grid A5/6*

Around 267 square miles of windswept, rainlashed sandstone upland, Exmoor is one of the most romantic of England's national parks. Wordsworth, Coleridge, Hazlitt and co. didn't do quite such a thorough job on it as the Lake District though, despite all three staying nearby in their twenties and Shelley honeymooning on the coast. RD Blackmore sealed its Victorian reputation for boddice-ripping adventure with his novel *Lorna Doone*. Wooded valleys, tidy farmland and winding roads in its eastern and northern parts give way to bare tracts of bleak moorland in the west. If the sun happens to shine, the rolling acres of heather, bracken and bog can seem quite tame. But don't be fooled. When the sea mists descend and the wind gets up, it can become thoroughly inhospitable.

Most of the park is privately owned, but it's criss-crossed by more than 700 miles of public paths and bridleways. Simonsbath sits in the centre of the moor, about 440 yards above sea level. A few miles away the river Exe rises five miles from the sea, but flows south instead all the way to Exeter. Serious and lonely little Exford is the first town it passes on its way, followed by the softer and more picturesque village of Winsford, from where it carves out a path south between the moor and the Brendon Hills. Dulverton, bridging the river Barle quaintly enough in the moor's southeastern corner, is the headquarters of the National Park service and the main point of entry from the south. Most visitors still approach from the north, however, because the magically wooded Exmoor coast ranks as one of the most delightful and idiosyncratic land and seascapes in the country. From the old town of Dunster to the Victorian resort at Lynton, the A39 climbs along the northern edge of the moor taking in snug little Porlock with its tiny harbour at Porlock Weir, and also Lynmouth, the north Devon coast's 'Little Switzerland on Sea'.

Ins and outs

Getting there No trains penetrate Exmoor itself, but the **West Somerset Railway,** T01643-704996 (24-hr talking timetable T01643-707650), runs a summer steam service (and some weekends in winter) from Bishops Lydeard (4 miles west of Taunton) via Williton, Watchet, Cleeve Abbey, Blue Anchor and Dunster to Minehead on the moor's northeastern corner. The A39 from Bridgewater (about 2 hours 30 minutes from London down the M4/5) is a slow road in the holiday season. Bridgewater to Lynton, some 35 miles as the crow flies, 44 miles by road, can sometimes take anything up to 2 hours to cover. The southern edge of Exmoor is much more easily reached along the A361 from Tiverton, junction 27 on the M5 (almost 3 hours from London). Tiverton to Dulverton usually takes about 45 minutes. There are buses between Barnstaple and Lynton. Local travel information, T01823-251151.

Getting around **Car, bike** or **horse** are the only alternatives to footwork on Exmoor, although there is a network of local **buses**, contact **Devon Busline,** T01392- 382800. **First Southern National,** T01823-272033 (0830-1730), run the no 300 bus service shuttle along the A39 daily in summer, at weekends in winter, between Ilfracombe and Taunton via Porlock and Minehead. Distances can be deceptive, so it's worth being equipped with a good map, plenty of wet-weather gear and ideally a compass.

Information National Park Authority Information Centres, www.exmoor-nationalpark.gov.uk. **Dulverton** ⓘ *Fore St, T01398-323841, Apr-Oct daily 1000-1700, Nov-Mar daily 1030-1530.* **Dunster** ⓘ *The Steep, T01643-821835, Apr-Oct daily 1000-1700, Nov-Mar Sat, Sun 1100-1500.* **Lynmouth** ⓘ *the Esplanade, T01598-752509, Apr-Oct daily 1000-1700, Nov-Mar Sat, Sun 1100-1500.* **Combe Martin** ⓘ *Cross St, T01271-338819, Apr-Oct daily 1000-1700.* **County Gate** ⓘ *A39 at Countysbury, T01598-741321, Apr-Oct daily 1000-1700.* **Porlock Visitor Centre** ⓘ *West End, High St, T01643-863150, www.porlock.co.uk.*

Exmoor National Park

All the moorland of interest falls within the boundaries of the National Park, but the essence of Exmoor is the almost treeless expanse of Exmoor Forest around Simonsbath. To the east the landscape becomes enclosed, farmed and also wooded. The park is crossed by four main **rivers** which all have their sources near an area of Exmoor Forest known as The Chains. The Exe rises north of Simonsbath and flows southeast towards Exford and Winsford, then heads south on its long journey, passing a few miles from Dulverton. The Barle rises west of Simonsbath and flows through down to Withypool and southwest to Dulverton. The West Lyn river flows north from Pinkery Pond, the East Lyn north through Malmsmead, Brendon and Watersmeet, both meeting the sea at Lynmouth. Little **Exmoor ponies** wander around many parts of the National Park, especially off the B3223 north of Simonsbath, around Withypool in the valley of the Barle and on Winsford Hill. If you're lucky you might also spot some of the largest herd of red deer in England, buzzards, bats and badgers, and even perhaps an otter.

Apart from the main A39 north coast road, the only roads of any size to cross the middle of Exmoor are the A396 from Dunster to Tiverton via Bampton, and the B3224 from Wheddon Cross through Exford and Simonsbath to Blackmoor Gate. This road is joined by and becomes the B3223 from Dulverton to Lynton via Simonsbath, passing close by Withypool and Winsford Hill. **Dulverton** is the main centre on Exmoor for organizing activities like walking and fishing on the moor, very busy with holidaymakers in summer. A minor road off to the left leads down to the **Tarr Steps**, an ancient and quite impressive clapper bridge over the Barle, about 170 ft long, washed away in the floods of 1952 and since restored.

Winsford, off the B3223 to the right, is another huntin', shootin', and fishin' centre and also a minor-road junction. Picturesquely placed at the coming together of several streams, including the river Exe, with thatched cottages and old stone bridges, it makes a good base for walks, especially up to the heights of **Winsford Hill**.

The other major settlement in this generally more gentle, farmed and well-wooded part of Exmoor is **Exford**, upstream of Winsford on the Exe. Not quite as pretty, it boasts a petrol station and various teashops, pubs and hotels of middling quality. To its northeast, **Dunkery Beacon** (519 m), the highest point on Exmoor and reachable by road from Cloutsham, provides spectacular views over the **Holnicote Estate** (see below), a large swathe of farmland, woodland and moorland stretching from Wheddon Cross to the sea between Minehead and Porlock.

Simonsbath, named after a pool on the Barle river, is the most isolated settlement on the moor, surrounded by the former Royal Forest of Exmoor. Sold off in 1818, the forest consisted of almost 10,000 acres of open moorland, bought by the industrialist John Knight who attempted to farm the land, with limited success. To the southeast of the village, **Birch Cleave** is an unusually high stretch of beech woodland.

Exmoor Coast: Dunster to Lynton

Just under a mile from the coast, on the northeastern edge of Exmoor, Dunster is a little medieval village in the adorable valley of the River Avill. Frequently overrun with tourists, it's not hard to see why. With its steam train and marshy beach, its higgledy-piggledy roofscape and funny little 17th-century octagonal yarn market, all overlooked by a picturesque castle and curious folly tower looming out of the trees above on each side, it

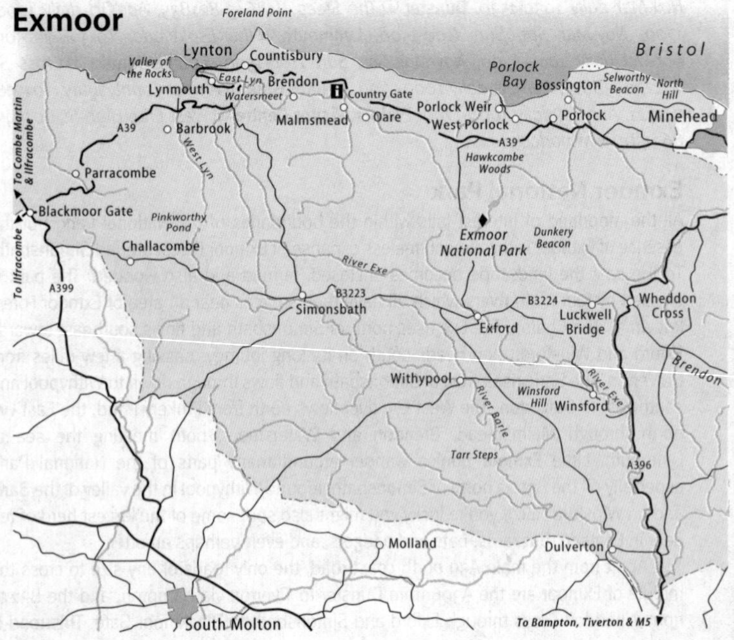

adds up to a picture-postcard treat. Once an important port, rich in Exmoor wool, it now manages quite nicely thanks to its olde-worlde charm. Apart from its antique shops and tearooms, the main visitor attraction is **Dunster Castle** ⓘ *(NT), T01643-821314/823004, Apr-Oct Mon-Wed, Sat, Sun 1100-1700 (-1600 in Oct), garden and park, Apr-Sep daily 1000-1700, Oct-Mar daily 1100-1600, £6.40, under-16s £3.20, family £16,* built in the Middle Ages but completely remodelled in the 19th century, in a deliberately scenic manner. Inhabited by the Luttrell family for 600 years, it now belongs to the National Trust. Highlights of the interior include late-17th century plaster ceilings and a great carved wooden staircase. Outside, sloping parkland and a terraced garden look over the roofs of the village. The 18th-century folly tower on Conygar Hill is a remarkable eyecatcher. The little packhorse Gallox bridge is also worth a look and the views from Grabbist hill over the village are memorable too.

Two miles west of Dunster on the A39, **Minehead** is this coast's main seaside resort, with all the usual entertainments and also once famous for its massive Butlin's holiday camp. A minor road winds west out of town up North Hill, overlooking the minehead Bluff and on to the quite spectacular viewpoint at **Selworthy Beacon**, with views of Porlock. In the National Trust village of **Selworthy**, on the **Holnicote Estate** ⓘ *T01643-862745, Mar-Sep daily 1000-1700 and shop,* there's a National Trust information centre. The coast path here heads down to the breached shingle beach at **Bossington** (NT).

Porlock is the next tourist hotspot on the coast road, famous for its hill, which also contributes to its magnificent position in a natural amphitheatre looking out over Porlock Bay. Its thatched cottages and stone streets heave with visitors in summer. Cars choose to climb out of the place westwards either on the very steep A39 or on the lovely twisting toll roads (£2 cars, £5 caravans). The coast road leads down to charming little **Porlock Weir**, the old harbour, from where the **South West Coast Path** wanders along just inland past the lonely and peaceful woodland church at **Culbone**, supposedly the smallest in the country. Inland from Porlock, off the A39 on the left, **Hawkcombe Woods** are a superb stretch of old oak woodland.

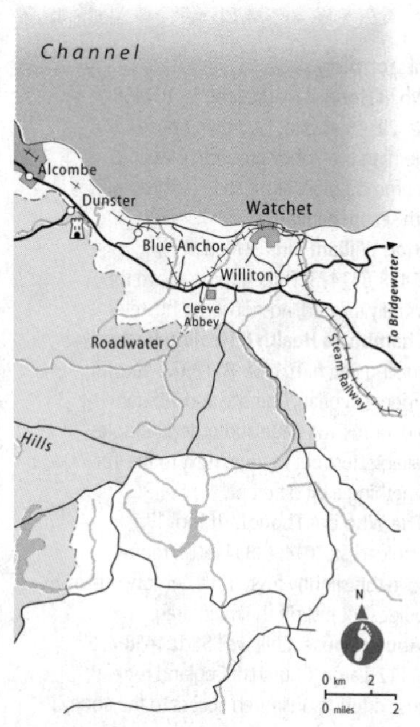

At County Gate the A39 enters Devon, close to **Malmsmead**, where there's another little 17th-century pack- horse bridge, and from where Doone Country stretches up the valley onto Exmoor. The setting for Blackmore's novel *Lorna Doone* is virtually unrecognizable, but includes the church at Oare where all the films have the heroine shot on her wedding day. The coast path here runs up to **Foreland Point**, the highest cliffs in England.

Watersmeet Tea Gardens ⓘ *(NT), Watersmeet Rd, Lynmouth, T01598-753348, Apr-Oct daily 1030-1730 (-1630 in Oct),* have been up and running since 1901 in an old fishing lodge and are set in quite a dramatic wooded combe, surrounded by beautiful woodland walks, at the confluence of the East Lyn and Hoar Oak Water.

At Countisbury the A39 begins the steep descent into **Lynmouth**, a delightful little harbourside village nestling in a wooded valley that within living memory was the scene of destruction on a biblical scale. On the main street is a mark of the mud level set on 15 August 1952, when 20,000 cu ft of water swept through the village, killing 34 people and destroying 62 buildings. Over 9 in of rain had fallen on Exmoor in the previous 24 hous. Like every self-respecting catastrophe, this one also has its conspiracy theorists, something to do with secret cloud-seeding tests on the hills above. Reminders of that terrible day are everywhere: the distinctive lookout and beacon on the dockside, originally built as a water tower in the 1820s, and modelled on Rhine towers, has an inscription that reads simply: "destroyed 1952, rebuilt 1962". The tide of visitors ebbing and flowing through the village is the chief concern today, although nothing can detract from the superb location. The village's main tourist attraction is the **Glenn Lynn Gorge** ⓘ *T01598-753207, Easter-Oct daily 1000-1700, £3, concessions £1.50,* "opened 1854, devastated 1952, re-opened 1962" where visitors are encouraged to "Experience the awesome power of nature in this place of mystery, tragedy and extreme beauty". The ravine contains an informative 'Power of Water' exhibition, water pumps and jets, and the largest privately owned hydro-electric scheme in England. Water is also put to good use by the water-powered **Lynton and Lynmouth Cliff Railway** ⓘ *T01598-753486, Mid-Feb to mid Nov daily 1000-1900 (or dusk if earlier), £2.20 return, £1.20 single,* a feat of Victorian engineering that takes passengers up 500 ft to the clifftop resort of Lynton.

Lynton sits at the top of the gorge. It was developed by George Newnes, millionaire publisher of a popular cheap newspaper for the working classes called *Tit-Bits*. He paid for the cliff railway, the rail link to Barnstaple and the town hall, but sadly died penniless in 1910. The legacy of the building boom that followed his proposal to build a pier for steamers still remains, some of it providing the lowest cost accommodation in the area.

A mile round the coast to the west of Lynton and Lynmouth, the **Valley of the Rocks** is a popular but desolate spot, a dry valley where wild goats roam and the rocks were squashed into weird shapes during the Ice Age. Apparently this was the destination of Coleridge, Wordsworth and his sister Dorothy in 1797 on a walk over from Ash Farm near Culbone, where the Wordsworth's were staying, a walk that inspired the *Rime of the Ancient Mariner*.

Sleeping

Wells and the Mendips *p362*

L **Ston Easton Park**, Ston Easton, near Midsomer Norton, T01761-241631. Palladian country house set in Repton parkland, with comfortable bedrooms.

B **Swan Hotel**, 11 Sadler St, T01749-836300. One of several traditional coaching inns on this street. Log fires, 4-poster beds and English food, with a door leading straight onto the cathedral green.

C **The Crown**, Market Pl, T01749-673457. A large 15th-century inn at the heart of Wells, with lively bar, a French bistro and spacious courtyard. Four-poster beds available. B&B from £32.50 per person.

D **Canon Grange**, Cathedral Green, T01749-671800. B&B in a 15th-century house looking onto the west front of the cathedral.

D **The Old Poor House**, 7A St Andrew St, T01749-675052. A secluded 14th-century cottage away from all traffic.

Glastonbury *p364*

B **No. 3 Hotel**, 3 Magdalene St, T01458-832129. An elegant Georgian house adjoining the abbey grounds. Classy accommodation, all en suite bathrooms, with secure parking.

C **King William Inn**, 19 Market Pl, T01458-831473. Three rooms above this centrally located, no-nonsense hostelry.

C **Shambhala Health & Healing Retreat**, Coursing Batch, T01458-831797. Peaceful garden, Egyptian, Chinese and Tibetan-style rooms, massage and other therapies available, just out of town next to the Tor. Something a bit different.

C **The Who'd A Thought It Inn**, 17 Northload St, T01458-834460. 5 rooms above this slightly fussy 18th-century pub in a quiet spot just off the main drag.

D **Abbey House**, Chilkwell St, T01458-831112. Large, Church of England retreat house offering unlimited access to the abbey grounds. Mainly for groups, but does take individual bookings. Full board £35.

D The Bolthole, 32 Chilkwell St, T01458-832800. B&B just opposite the Chalice Well and near the Tor with its own parking. Shared bathroom only.

D Hawthornes Hotel, 8-12 Northload St, T01458-831255. The best value hotel in Glastonbury, just off the High St. Not a trace of the New Age in its tasteful, contemporary décor, with a civilized restaurant, bar and lounge.

D Tordown, 5 Ashwell La, T01458-832287. Healing and 'higher self' sessions available at this B&B. Shared bathroom .

E Little St Michael's, Chilkwell St, T01458-831154. A delightful house that is part of the Chalice Well gardens with rooms from £20 a night for anyone paying an additional £18 to become a 'companion to the well'. Vegetarian.

F Glastonbury Backpackers, 4 Market Pl, T01458-833353. Dorm beds at £10 a night and rooms at £25/30 a night in this converted 16th-century coaching inn right in the centre of things. Communal kitchen and living room upstairs, with bar and café downstairs.

Somerset Levels, Taunton and the Quantocks *p366*

A The Castle at Taunton, Castle Bow, Taunton, T01823-272671, www.the-castle-hotel.com. High standards in this hotel with restaurant which has launched the careers of TV chefs such as Gary Rhodes.

C Frog Street Farm, Beercrocombe, near Taunton, T01823-480430. An old farmhouse tucked into the Somerset countryside, with exposed beams and good cooking. £30 per person, optional £18 supper.

D Carew Arms, Crowcombe, near Taunton, T01984-618631, 3 rooms, fairly basic and not en suite, £44 including breakfast, £40 per night for more than 1 night, above a cheerful old pub with a roaring fire and locally grown food well prepared in the kitchen. Open all year.

E Quantock Hills YHA, Sevenacres, Holford, near Nether Stowey. A country house with 28 beds (4 6-bedded and 2 4-bedded) in a fine position on the northern Quantocks.

Exmoor *p368*

C Little Quarme, Wheddon Cross, T01643-841249, www.littlequarme.co.uk, farmhouse accommodation near Luckwell Bridge.

D Twitchen Farm, Challacombe, near Simonsbath, T01598-763568, courtyard farmhouse with wonderful views and home cooking.

D Larcombe Foot, Winsford, T01643-851306, comfortable farmhouse with fine south-facing views near pretty Winsford.

D Little Brendon Hill Farm, Wheddon Cross, T01643-841556, www.exmoorheaven.co.uk, non-smoking professionally run farmhouse accommodation with en-suite rooms.

F Exford YHA, Exe Mead, Exford, T01643-831288, F831650, with 51 beds in 2 2-bedded, the rest 4-6 bedded rooms, in a Victorian house close to the river Exe.

Camping

Westermill Farm, near Exford, T01643-831238. **Camping barns**, T01200-420102, at Woodadvent, near Roadwater, and at Northcombe.

Dunster to Lynton *p370*

A Porlock Vale House, Porlock Weir, T01643-862338, www.porlockvale.co.uk. Price includes dinner. Former hunting lodge set in wooded countryside with views over the Bristol Channel. Specialise in equestrian holidays.

A Tors Hotel, Lynmouth, T01598-753236, www.torslynmouth.co.uk. A classy option, in a spectacular position on the hillside overlooking the village, but with far less character than the *Rising Sun*.

B Rising Sun Hotel, Harbourside, Lynmouth, T01598-753223. The best upmarket option and probably the place where Shelley actually stayed, it's a thatched pub and top- notch restaurant with quirky little rooms up the tiny staircase.

C Andrews on the Weir, Porlock Weir, T01643-863300. Also a highly rated restaurant, serving up local produce innovatively and well, with rooms overlooking the little harbour, £19 3-course set dinner and boasting one of the best cheeseboards in the West Country.

C Bales Mead, West Porlock, T01643-862565. A well-known B&B in an Edwardian country house with a few extra frills.

C Glenville House, Tors Rd, T01598-752202. Another good value place right on the river.

C Orchard House Hotel, Watersmeet Rd, Lynmouth, T01598-753247. At the lower end of this bracket, this is very good value guesthouse accommodation.

C **Riverside Cottage**, Lynmouth, T01598-752390. Overlooking the sea (rooms with balconies) and right on the main street, also has a little café.

C **Shelley's Hotel**, Lynmouth, T01598-753219, www.shelleyshotel.co.uk. Very comfortable, and has rooms that have some amazing views.

F **Lynton YHA**, Lynbridge, Lynton, T01598-753237, F753305. With 36 beds in 2 2, 2 4- and 4 6-bedded rooms.

F **Minehead YHA**, Alcombe Combe, Minehead, T01643-702595, F703016. Comfortable country house up a private road between Dunster and Minehead.

Eating

Wells and the Mendips *p362*

££ **The Good Earth**, Broad St, T01749- 678600. An organic and vegetarian restaurant in a country cottage setting, doubling as a health food shop and potager. Open from 0900-1700.

Glastonbury *p364*

££ **Elaichi Tandoori Restaurant**, 62 High St, T01458-833966. If all the wholefood is getting you down, a retreat to this bog-standard Indian may be just what you need.

££ **Hawthornes Hotel**, 8-12 Northload St, T01458-831255. Smart, attractive lentil-free zone in this unpretentious hotel brasserie, specializing in fish, with a garden courtyard.

£ **Blue Note Café**, 4 High St, T01458-832907. Vegetarian eating with outside tables in a tranquil little courtyard tucked away off the High St. Main course about £6.

£ **Café Galatea**, 5a The High St, T01458-834284. Vegetarian food in this lively café, with internet access, which also serves as a gallery for local arts and crafts. Closed Tue. Main course, lunch/evening about £5/7.

£ **Knights Fish Restaurant**, 5 Northload St, T01458-831882. Sit down for your fish supper in one of England's oldest chippie's, established in 1909.

£ **Spiral Gate Organic Café**, 24 High St, T01458-834633. Friendly atmosphere in a relaxed setting. Live music and juice bar. Open fires in winter, courtyard seating in summer.

Somerset Levels, Taunton and the Quantocks *p366*

£££ **The Castle at Taunton**, see Sleeping above.

££ **Brazz**, Castle Bow, Taunton, T01823-252000. One of the best bets in Taunton, a fairly smart brasserie in the middle of town.

Exmoor *p368*

The London Inn, Molland, near South Molton, T01796-550269. A thatched 15th-century inn, pretty much unchanged for some years with a garden and interesting village church next door.

Dunster to Lynton *p370*

££ **The Bistro**, 7 Watersmeet Rd, T01598-753302. A cheaper alternative for fresh seafood in the evenings (£12 main course, £4 starter).

££ **Crown Hotel**, Lynton, T01598-752253, does very well-prepared country pub food – sausage and mash and the like.

££ **Exmoor Sandpiper**, Countisbury, T01598-741358. Locally caught seafood on offer at this hilltop coaching inn as well as home-made stews and soups.

££ **The Restaurant in the High St**, 3 High St, Dunster, T01643-821304. Award-winning local fare, especially game and seafood, in a typically Dunster-ish ambience.

££ **Thai-Lyn Restaurant** at the Waterloo House Hotel, Lydiate La, Lynton, T01598-753391, does inventive things with local produce and Thai spices.

£ **Sir George Newnes**, 14 Lee Rd, Lynton, T01598-753478. A traditional English tearoom famous for its genuine ginger cream teas, opposite generous George's Town Hall.

£ **Watersmeet Tea Rooms** also do justice to the institution (see p 371).

Pubs, bars and clubs

Wells and the Mendips *p362*

City Arms, Chamberlain St, T01749- 673916. A good range of beers in what used to be Wells' jail in Tudor times. Look out through the bars on the windows, or sit in freedom in the cobbled courtyard off the street.

Glastonbury *p364*

King Arthur, 31 Benedict St, T01458-831442. Cavernous pub, which often has live music.

Market House Inn, 12-14 Magdalene St, T01458-832220. The biggest pub in Glastonbury just opposite the Town Hall, which has just undergone a major refit.

Somerset Levels, Taunton and the Quantocks *p366*

Somerset Distillery and Cider Farm, Pass Vale Farm, Burrow Hill, Kingsbury Episcopi, T01490-240782 www.ciderbrandy.co.uk.

Brown and Forrest, The Smokery, Bowdens Farm, Hambridge, Somerset, T01458-250875. Top-quality smoked eels and other classics.

Festivals and events

Wells and the Mendips *p362*

Horticulturists might be interested in the **Wells in Bloom** festival, which takes place in **Jul**. There are also regular antiques and crafts fairs, as well as classical concerts, throughout the year – check with the TIC for details.

Glastonbury *p364*

Jun Glastonbury musical festival. For information on the famous annual festival – which actually takes place on a farm at the neighbouring village of Pilton – look up www.glastonburyfestivals.co.uk. For 2004 the festival dates are: **25-27 Jun**.

There is often something either weird or wonderful going on in Glastonbury, from live music in one of the cafés on the High St to a visiting speaker in the Town Hall.

The Assembly Rooms at the bottom of the High St is the most lively venue and publishes a What's On guide which you can pick up there for free. Recent years have also seen conferences on the **crop circle** phenomenon and the **Great Goddess** in **Aug**, and a **fun fair** beside the Tor in **Sep**.

The Church of England bought back and reconsecrated the abbey ruins in 1907, since when an annual Anglican **pilgrimage** – followed immediately by a Roman Catholic pilgrimage – has taken place here in **Jul**.

Shopping

Glastonbury *p364*

The courtyard of the **Glastonbury Experience**, opposite the Tribunal, is just the spot for a nice cup of herbal tea, surrounded by a number of other idiosyncratic retailers. One of the nation's leading marijuana campaigners, by the name of **Free Rob Cannabis**, has a shop in the Market Pl, containing the obligatory shrine to the dope-smoking Indian god, Shiva. Benedict St, a stone's throw away, contains 2 more interesting specialists: **Waistcoat Shop**, selling only waistcoats, the **Music Shop**, stocking everything from flutes to lutes. There are markets at St John's Sq, behind the north side of the High St, every Tue and on the 4th Sat of the month (farmer's market).

Activities and tours

Exmoor *p368*

Canoeing

On the Barle: **Taunton Canoe Club**, T01823-274651, from Dulverton.

Cycling

The **West Country Way** runs along the National Park's southwestern edge, between Barnstaple and Tiverton via Bampton.

Pony trekking

Outovercott Riding Stables, off the A39 between Barbrook and Parracombe, near Lynton, T01598-753341.

Horsedrawn Tours in cart pulled by Shire horses from **West Ilkerton Farm**, Barbrook, near Lynton, T01598-752310, www.westilkerton.co.uk. Must be booked in advance.

Walking

Barle Valley Safaris, from the Old Blacksmith's Gallery, Dulverton, T01398-323699 or T01643-851386.

Exmoor Safaris, from the *White Horse Inn* in Exford T01643-831229/831112. 2 hr 30 mins tours in an 8-seat Landrover with knowledgable local guide.

South West Coast Path Association, T01752-896237, www.swcp.org.uk. Publishes a guide to the entire route.

Directory

Glastonbury *p364*

Alternative health Archangel Michael's Soul Therapy Centre, 01458 832482, George St. **Hospitals** Butleigh Cottage Hospital, Kingweston Rd, Butleigh, T01458 850237. **Library** Glastonbury Library, 1 Orchard Ct, The Archers Way,T01458-832148.

Dorset → *Colour map 2, grid B3*

Dorset is little England at its most rural, cosy, and green. Apart from Bournemouth, which was always traditionally in Hampshire, it has no large conurbations. Its scenery embraces acres of rolling farmland, landscaped parks, and lots of small manor houses and castles, rather than a few big stately homes, all set beside villages with impossibly quaint names like Purse Caundle, Toller Porcorum or Hammoon, near Fiddleford. Like Wiltshire, it also seems to have been a hotbed of Iron Age activity. Every other hillock has been carved into a crumpled hill fort. And of course this is Thomas Hardy country. Its centre is Dorchester, the busy county town, where he became a fatalistic old curmudgeon and great poet, but the county is scattered with scenes memorably described in his novels. Hilltop Shaftesbury and warm-stoned Sherborne with its astonishing Abbey are the two medieval market towns in the north. In the middle, the unpromisingly named 18th-century town of Blandford Forum proves to be anything but, a tasty backwater with a church and quirky costume collection. Bournemouth needs little introduction, a coastal boomtown on the site of the Victorians' favourite watering place, its hillside villas change hands for rocketing prices almost as quickly as polite Poole's next door. Across Poole Harbour, the Isle of Purbeck is the stonemason and quarryman's heartland, a strange and until relatively recently all but forgotten corner of the south coast. Now it's been designated a World Natural Heritage Site. No doubt the steam railway that goes puffing past one of the most popular ruined castles of them all at Corfe, and has long provided a regular service for locals across Purbeck to rum old Swanage on the coast, will soon be linked into the national rail network. On the freshly branded 'Jurassic Coast' then, the most popular spots are still the rock arches at Durdle Door and the beach at Lulworth Cove, but it's the wonder of Chesil Beach and the resort of Lyme Regis and its surrounding cliffs that have really earned the attentions of UNESCO. ▸▸ *For Sleeping, eating and other listings, see pages 387-391.*

Shaftesbury and Sherborne

The old town of Shaftesbury overlooks the rich clay farmland of the Blackmore Vale from a sandstone spur jutting out of the rolling wooded hills and fields of Cranborne Chase. The scenery of these two prosperous areas competes for prizes in the best-tended category in the south of England. Cranborne Chase hides the exotic delights of the Larmer Tree gardens and the romantic ruins of Old Wardour Castle, as well as the little Baroque delight of Chettle House. Shaftesbury lacks the confidence of mellow-stoned Sherborne on the other side of the Blackmore Vale, probably because Sherborne can still boast a spectacular old Abbey. In between the two, the countryside is peppered with quaint manor houses, like those at Fiddleford and Purse Caundle, both open to the public.

Ins and outs

Getting there About 1 slow train an hr leaves London Waterloo for Gillingham (near Shaftsbury), and Sherborne, taking around 2½ hours. **National Rail Enquiries,** T08457-484950. Shaftesbury is about 2 hours from London down the M3 and A303. Sherborne 30 minutes further down the road. **National Express,** T08705-808080, serve Shaftesbury and Sherbourne by coach direct from London Victoria (3½ hours -4 hours) but there is usually only one service a day. **Traveline,** T0870-6082608.

Getting around A fairly good network of local **buses** is run by the **Wilts and Dorset Bus Company,** T01202-673555, but a **car** or **bicycle** are easily the most convenient ways of exploring the Blackmore Vale.

Information **Shaftesbury TIC** ⓘ *T01747-853514, www.ruraldorset.com. Apr-Oct daily 1000-1700, Nov-Mar Mon-Sat 1000-1700, Jan-Mar Mon-Wed 1000-1300, Thu-Sat 1000-1700.* £3 accommodation booking fee. **Sherborne TIC** ⓘ *T01935-815341, www.sherbornetown.co.uk, www.westdorset.com. Apr-Oct Mon-Sat 0900-1700, Nov-Mar Mon-Sat 1000-1500.* Free accommodation booking service.

Shaftesbury and around

Shaftesbury is an old town, dramatically positioned on a sandstone bluff overlooking the vale of Blackmore, 18 miles west of Salisbury down the A30. Famous for the view down Gold Hill, a steep old cobbled street lined with partly thatched cottages, the place has been continuously occupied since 880, growing up around a wealthy nunnery and Royal abbey at the top of the hill. It owes its olde-worlde charm today to the more-or-less consistent use of local building materials ever since. In 1820 it was a pocket borough controlled by the Grosvenor family. They sold up in 1919, by which time Shaftesbury had become famous as a manufacturing centre for underwear buttons, but like most of the rest of Dorset, industry never really took hold here. It remains a quiet, old-fashioned market town, a little depressed since losing much of its passing trade along the A30 with the opening of the A303 bypass in the 1960s. Gold Hill (its name a corruption of Guild Hall Hill), off the High St behind the Church of St Peter's, runs steeply down alongside the impressive remains of **Shaftesbury Abbey's precinct walls**, just along the ridge. A peak inside one of the quaint little houses on Gold Hill can be had at the volunteer-run **Shaftesbury Museum**ⓘ *Sun and Moon Cottage, Gold Hill, T01747-852157, Apr-Oct daily 1030-1630*, which displays the Byzant, central to the history of the town's water supply, and some locally made firedogs, ladles and a trivet. The walk along the top of the hill is certainly memorable, to the site of the **old Abbey** ⓘ *Abbey Museum and Garden, T01747- 852910, Apr-Oct 1000-1700, £1.50, concessions £1, under-16s 60p*. Although not much remains of it now, the museum here does a very good job of explaining its former importance – founded by Alfred the Great, it became the wealthiest Benedictine nunnery in the land – and the lives of the community that lived here.

Northeast of Shaftesbury, a couple of miles southwest of Tisbury, stands the empty shell of Lord Lovel's six-sided 14th-century castle, next to a lake in beautiful gardens. Designed to impress, the **Old Wardour Castle** ⓘ *(EH), T01747-870487, Apr-Sep daily 1000-1800, Oct daily 1000-1700, Nov-Mar Wed-Sun 1000-1300, 1400-1600, £2.50, concessions £1.90, under-16s £1.30*, was damaged in the Civil War, and now contains a display on the life of the castle in its heyday.

South of Old Wardour, over Winklebury Hill fort and near the superb views from the top of the downland ridge at Win Green in the middle, stretch the green acres of the old Royal hunting grounds of **Cranborne Chase**. At the mystical-sounding **Larmer Tree Gardens** ⓘ *T01725 516228, www.rushmore-estate.co.uk, mid Apr-Oct Mon-Fri, Sun 1100-1800 (last admission 1700), also usually closed in July and early Aug for ticket-only music festivals, £3.50, concessions £3, under-16s £1.50*, the exotic park created by General Pitt Rivers in 1880 has been carefully restored along with its eccentric collection of garden buildings: including a Roman Temple, Open Air theatre and various Oriental and Colonial pavilions. Quite magical. Nearby is another rare thing, a small English Baroque country house, **Chettle House** ⓘ *Chettle, near Blandford Forum,T01258-830209, Easter-July Sun, bank holidays, Aug Mon-Fri, Sun 1100-1700, £2.50*. Designed by Queen Anne's architect Thomas Archer, with rounded corners and beautiful gardens, it has survived almost unmodified.

Sturminster Newton, 8 miles southwest of Shaftesbury, is a typical Dorset town, known locally as 'Stur'. Hardy called it Stourcastle, and moved here with his newly wed Emma in 1876 for a couple of the happiest years of their lives. Sturminster is connected to Newton by a six-arched medieval bridge over the river Stour. A mile to the east, a small part of a medieval manor house, with extraordinary roof structures and upper living room, has been preserved at **Fiddleford** ⓘ*Fiddleford Manor (EH), Sturminster Newton, Apr-Sep daily 1000-1800, Oct-Mar 1000-1600, free.* 6 miles west at **Purse Caundle** ⓘ*Purse Caundle Manorhouse, T01963-250400, May-Sep Thu by appointment £2.50,* this sweet little Tudor manor house is just that bit more modern.

Sherborne

The jewel in Dorset's crown, Sherborne is set in a thickly wooded valley amid beautiful countryside immortally associated with the name of Digby. With its raised pavements and warm red Ham-stone houses, it has a very well-to-do air, despite being mistaken for Yeovil by German bombers in the Second World War. Digby Hill and Cheap St are the two main shopping streets, but the pièce de résistance is its rusty-red old stone abbey. **Sherborne Abbey** was a cathedral until 1075 and displays a continuous procession of confident church-building up to the 15th century and the Reformation. Its Perpendicular fan vaulting is the astonishing highlight of the interior, as well as a variety of monuments (such as a full-length statue of the late-17th-century local squire John Digby) and the air of ancient peace. Sherborne town surrounds but does not hustle its abbey, fended off by some impeccably polite medieval almshouses. An interesting antiques and **fleamarket** ⓘ*T01963-250108,* takes place on the fourth Saturday of each month in the Digby Church Hall up Digby Road opposite the Abbey. Built by Sir Walter Raleigh in 1594, **Sherborne Castle** ⓘ*T01935- 813182 Easter-Sep Thu, Sat, Sun, bank holidays 1230-1700,* is the Digby family seat but it's not really a castle at all, more of a big old house beside a lake. The real thing is half a mile east of town, the 12th-century **castle ruins** ⓘ*Sherborne Old Castle, T01935-812730 Apr-Sep daily 1000-1800, Oct daily 1000-1300, 1400-1700, Nov-Mar Wed-Sun 1000-1300, 1400-1600, £1.80, concessions £1.40, under-16s 90p,* also inhabited by Raleigh, which once took Cromwell over a fortnight to capture during the Civil War.

Dorset Downs

The centre of Dorset is Hardy country through and through. Dorchester, the county town, in the south, is separated from the dignified backwater of Blandford Forum and the mini-cathedral town of Wimborne Minster by the last few vestiges of the novelist's beloved heaths. This is a landscape dominated by Iron Age hill forts: Maiden Castle, just outside Dorchester, is the largest in Europe. Others, like the Badbury Rings, Hambledon Hill and Knowlton, each have their distinctive qualities. Dorchester itself is a prosperous but not entirely prepossessing market town, milking the tourist dollar for all it's worth. Nearby, the carved hill figure wielding a club above his proud phallus draws the crowds to the little village of Cerne Abbas, while Milton Abbas is a very dinky set of thatched 18th-century cottages next door to another amazing Abbey.

Ins and outs

Getting there Dorchester South is on the **Southwest Trains** mainline to Weymouth from London Waterloo (2½ hours) but not many trains stop there. **Wessex Trains** from Bath and Bristol (2 hours) to Weymouth call at Dorchester West. Hardy Country is most easily reached using the M3 and A31 via Ringwood. Wimborne Minster is about 1½ hrs from London. From Wimborne, Blandford is another 20 minutes up the A350 and Dorchester another ½ hour or so along the A31 and A35. Dorchester Wimborne and Blandford Forum can be reached by **National Express,** T08705-808080, bus in 1 hour from Bournemouth. **Traveline,** T0870-6082608.

Information Blandford Forum TIC ⓘ*1 Greyhound Yard, T01258-454770, www.ruraldorset.com Apr-Oct Mon-Sat 1000-1700, Nov-Mar Mon-Sat 1000-1300.*

Blandford Forum

The dignified town of Blandford Forum sits to the south of Cranborne Chase. To the southwest stretch the remains of the Dorset Downs, embracing Thomas Hardy's celebrated Egdon heath on the edge of the Isle of Purbeck. Blandford is a later Georgian version of Marlborough, very much of a piece in its 18th-century architecture, epitomized by the superb Baroque **Church of St Peter and St Paul.** Like the town hall, it was designed by the local Bastard brothers, John and William, after the fire that razed Blandford in 1731. The story of the great fire is told at **Blandford Museum** ⓘ *Bere's Yard, Market Pl, T01258-450388 Apr-Sep Mon-Sat 1100-1600 £1.50,* an endearing small town museum with displays on local agriculture and wildlife as well. Another, more eccentric museum can be found up the road from the Church, a remarkable collection of old-fashioned costumes collected by local woman the late Mrs Betty Penny, **The Cavalcade of Costume** ⓘ *Lime Tree House, The Plock, T01258-453006. Apr-Sep 1100-1630 Oct-Mar 1100-1530, £3, £2.50 concessions, under-16s £1.50.* Her dressing-up box for her amateur theatricals caused quite a stir when she decided to take it on tour as a catwalk show. Now back to rest in Blandford, special themed exhibitions and parts of the collection are displayed on mannequins and in the laceroom. A tearoom is attached

Techies may well be more interested by the **Royal Corps of Signals Museum** ⓘ *Blandford Camp, T01258-482248, Mon-Fri 1000-1700, Sat, Sun 1000-1600, £4.50, concessions £3.50, under-16s £2.50, family £11,* an enlightening exercise in Army PR, billing itself as a museum of Interactive Science & Technology Communications, the displays and exhibitions include the Enigma codebreaking machine, how a radio works and the invention of Morse code. Three miles northwest of Blandford Camp, **Hambledon Hill** boasts two Iron Age hill forts, superb views and a wonderful tract of wild oak woodland.

Wimborne Minster

Wimborne Minster lies 9 miles southeast of Blandford on the outskirts of Bournemouth. A venerable old town, the eponymous church is still the main draw, a miniature cathedral that's a strange mixture of styles from Norman to Perpendicular on the outside, full of extraordinary tombs, effigies and wondrous peace on the inside. The town itself struggles to keep out of Bournemouth's way, but nostalgic adults and kids will enjoy the **Wimborne Model Town** ⓘ *T01202-881924, www.wimborne-modeltown.com Apr-Sep daily 1000-1700, £3, concessions £2.50, under-16s £2,* a replica one-tenth scale version of the town as it sort-of looked in the 1950s.

The most attractive route to Wimborne from Blandford, the B3082, passes beneath the **Badbury Rings**, yet another Iron Age hill fort but this one's in the care of the National Trust: no dogs are allowed and the plantlife thrives. The Rings lie on the **Kingston Lacy estate** ⓘ *(NT), T01202-883402 Apr-Oct Wed-Sun, bank holidays 1200-1730 (last admissions 1630), £6.50, under-16s £3, family £17 gardens only £3, under-16s £1.50,* once the seat of the Bankes family (after they'd moved from the ruin of Corfe Castle), and still a grand 17th-century house modified by the Victorian architect Sir Charles Barry containing William Bankes' splendid art collection. Point-to-point horse races are held here in late Feb, Mar and early Apr.

Seven miles north of Wimborne, at **Knowlton,** a ruined Norman church stands in the middle of neolithic earthworks, an evocative symbol of paganism meeting Christianity. For wide-sweeping views, the sea can be seen from **Chalbury**'s church, with its quaint 18th-century interior, 3 miles to the southeast, even though at least 10 miles inland. Three miles further up the rolling B3078 from Knowlton, at **Cranborne,** the beautiful Elizabethan manor house (private) ⓘ *Cranborne Manor, T01725-517248 Easter-Sep Wed 0900-1700, £3.50,* is surrounded by exceptionally pretty gardens, a series of 'outdoor rooms' divided by old yew hedges, originally laid out by John Tradescant and significantly enlarged in the 20th century.

West of Blandford Forum

On the edge of Hardy's heath, now much prettified, **Milton Abbas** is a ridiculously cute thatched estate village created from scratch in the 18th century, when the Earl of Dorchester decided to improve the view from his house, **Milton Abbey** ⓘ *T01258-860489, daily 1000-1730, £2 in July and Aug.* Now a private school for boys, the medieval abbey church was transformed to spectacular effect by Augustus Pugin's glass for the south window in the 19th century. Worth a look for that alone, it's also set in sweeping parkland next to the grand house that the architect William Chambers described as "terribly ugly".

Dorchester and around

Milton Abbas is almost halfway from Blandford on the road to the headquarters of Hardy Country at Dorchester. The novelist's Casterbridge and Dorset's county town is an old market town with attitude, wooing tourists with a shameless variety of attractions, the strangest of all being run by *World Heritage Ltd*, some more successful than others. On its outskirts it has also provided the site of Prince Charles's surreal experiment in town-planning at **Poundsbury.** The Prince no doubt regrets that the town's single main street will be almost unrecognizable to readers of *The Mayor of Casterbridge* but Hardy fans can find plenty of solace elsewhere: **Max Gate** ⓘ *(NT), T01305-262538, www.thomas-hardy.connectfree.co.uk, Apr-Sep Mon, Wed, Sun 1400-1700 £2.40, under-16s £1.30,* was the house that he designed himself and lived in from 1885 until his death in 1928. The dining and drawing rooms can be seen, with some of his furniture. Better still, the **Dorset County Museum** ⓘ *T01305-262735, May-Oct daily 1000-1700, Nov-Apr Mon-Sat 1000-1700, £3.50, under-16s £1.70, family £8.70,* recreates his study, tells the story of Maiden Castle and the local geology, flora and fauna in its wonderful old Victorian exhibition hall. The setting for Victorian and Georgian justice can be seen nearby at **The Old Crown Court and Cells** ⓘ *High West St, T01305-252241, www.westdorset.com court room Mon-Fri 1000-1200, 1400-1600 free cells Aug Tue, Thu, Fri 1415-1615, Wed 1015-1215,* where the Tolpuddle Martyrs (see below) were tried and transported.

Over the road, Dorchester's other attractions are harder to explain: the latest is the **Terracotta Warriors Museum** ⓘ *High East St, T01305-266040 daily 1000-1730, £4.75, under-16s £2.95,* with eight full-size Chinese-made replicas of the figures unearthed in 1976 in Xian. They've joined the recreation of **Tutankhamun's tomb and treasures** ⓘ *High West St, T01305-269571,* the most popular, and for kids **The Dinosaur Museum** ⓘ *Icen Way, T01305-269741,* and the **Teddy Bear House** ⓘ *Antelope Walk, T01305-263200 or T01305-269741, details for all 3 can be found at www.world-heritage.org.uk,* with its human-sized soft toys full of diced sponge.

Views over the town can be had from the extensive **military museum** ⓘ *T01305-264066, www.keepmilitarymuseum.org Mon-Sat 0930-1700 (also Sun 1000-1600 in Jul, Aug,* in the mighty mock-medieval Victorian castle gate: medals, machine guns and interactive displays.

Escaping from Dorchester itself, a variety of less carefully stage-managed attractions may prove more rewarding. A mile to the south, **Maiden Castle** is the mother of all hill forts, the largest in Europe and astonishing proof of our early ancestors' ability to shape the landscape to their own ends. Apparently it would have been home to about 200 families, quite possibly fiercely resistant to the Roman invasion of AD 43 but incapable in their isolation of joining up with other tribes to be effective in the struggle. The evidence of their colonization is the site of a Roman temple within the earth ramparts.

Seven miles north of Dorchester on the road to Sherborne, the delightful little village of **Cerne Abbas** is regularly overwhelmed in summer with visitors, the site of the country's most famous hill figure, the priapic Cerne Abbas giant. Sadly this extraordinary chalk figure, fully aroused and wielding his club, is more likely to be Roman than Celtic. It's now in the careful hands of the National Trust, who discourage couples from copulating on the chalky phallus by moonlight in the time-honoured

❝❞ The Cerne Abbas giant is now in the careful hands of the National Trust, who discourage couples from copulating on the chalky phallus by moonlight in the time-honoured tradition...

tradition. The Trust also look after Thomas **Hardy's birthplace** ⓘ *3 miles northeast of Dorchester, T01305-262366 Apr-Oct Mon-Thu, Sun 1100-1700 £2.80,* a small cottage in Higher Bockhampton, little altered since being built by his great grandfather. Four miles east, on the edge of the Isle of Purbeck and the remains of Hardy's wild Egdon Heath at Affpuddle, the Elizabethan manor house at **Athelhampton** ⓘ *T01305-848363, www.athelhampton.co.uk Mar-Oct Mon-Fri, Sun 1030-1700 Nov-Feb Sun 1100-dusk,* is still a family home with spectacular Victorian gardens.

Bournemouth and around

Bournemouth, the grand dame of the South Coast, is enjoying a second honeymoon. Miles of long golden sands and safe waters continue to lure holidaymakers from far away to its sturdy cliffside seaside attractions as they have done since it first drew the steam-railway crowds in 1870. Recently recast as a more upmarket sunshine resort, Bournemouth's clean-cut and rather staid image – compared to its bohemian rival Brighton – has suddenly caught on. Since horticultural fashions have become all the televised rage, Bournemouth's generous array of immaculate Victorian gardens makes it a year-round choice for big firms and pre-retirement types. It's a city with all the mod cons within commuting distance from London, proudly expanding its position between the south coast's ring roads and the ferry ports, making it the leafy and upwardly-mobile place to be. Villa-lined valleys slope towards the sea boasting house prices that would make even Londoners think again. Youth culture has also arrived with the new prosperity and looks all set to give Brighton a run for its money.

Ins and outs

Getting there Bournemouth station greets the passenger with its impressive original iron and glass arch. Regular trains run by **South West Trains,** T0845-6000650, on the mainline to Weymouth from London Waterloo taking around 2 hrs, also calling at Southampton. **National Rail Enquiries,** T08457-484950.

Bournemouth is very well connected to London via the M3 then M27, from London takes under 2 hours. Poole maybe half an hour more. **National Express,** T08705-808080, run coaches 16 times a day between Bournemouth, Poole and London. With connecting services to Wareham, Corfe Castle, and Swanage or Wareham, Dorchester and Weymouth. **First,** T01305-766393, runs services between London and Weymouth, Dorchester, Blandford Forum, and Wimborne. **Traveline,** T0870-6082608. ▸▸ *For further details, see Transport, page 391.*

Getting around Bournemouth is a relatively small city, much of which can be reached by foot, bus or taxi. The **Guide Friday** buses operate here for a guided tour of the city, T01789-294466. Or explore the whole seafront by train and Cliff Lift T01202-451781. Its hills can make a cycle tough on the legs. Local bus routes run by **Yellow Buses,** Bournemouth T01202-636060 and **Wiltshire & Dorset Buses,** T01202-673555.

 Information Bournemouth TIC ⓘ *Westover Rd, T0906-8020234, www.bournemouth.co.uk. Mon-Sat 0930-1730 (0930-1900 and also Sun, mid Jul-Aug).* **Poole TIC** ⓘ *4 High St, T01202- 253253, www.pooletourism.com.*

History

Bournemouth was named by a Dorset squire, Lewis Tregonwell, who founded a summer home on the site of what is now the *Royal Exeter Hotel* in 1811. In 1837 Sir George Tapps-Gervis, a local landowner, established a resort next to the Tregonwell estate, and Westover Villas, Westover Gardens and the *Bath Hotel* were all built. A jetty was built in 1856 which became the iron pier in 1880 and in 1866 the Arcade was built on the site of a rustic bridge crossing the Bourne stream. With the arrival of the railway, Bournemouth didn't look back, becoming the most successful seaside resort of the Victorian era on the south coast. The legacy of their solid and comfortable housing stock, and the fact that unlike elsewhere on this coast, much of it survived Second World War bombing, has contributed to the old place's renaissance.

Sights The centre of Bournemouth is a curious mix of concrete and heavy-handed modern architecture, side by side with swathes of abundant lush greenery and tailored Victorian arcades. The beachfront starts at the grand old **pier**, which houses an active theatre and traditional seaside sideshows (a carousel, a gaming arcade, and a palm reader among others). Its view is unfortunately blighted by a spanking new Waterside development boasting a vast 3-D IMAX cinema, but the fun and excitement of the seaside remains undiminished. The walk from the sea is cut up by the toughest of one-way systems, but the hordes can clamber up through the pleasantly cooling **Lower Gardens** to a mosaic-paved 'Square' and central Camera Obscura café which kick off the pleasant central pedestrian precinct. In Lower Gardens, wraparound views are also available from the **Bournemouth Eye** ⓘ *T01202-314539, Apr-Sep 0730-2300, Oct-Mar 0900-dusk, £10, concessions £7.50, child £6,* offering 'the thrill of ballooning for a fraction of the cost of a hot-air flight...' The tethered balloon lifts up to 28 passengers 500 ft above sea level, giving panoramic views across town from Poole to the Isle of Wight. The original Victoriana shop fronts curve upwards in a distinctive hillside sweep and fans off into little arcades, each creating pockets of teenage excitement and domestic bustle down below. Back on the ground level, the bigger department stores offer vast car parks and indoor watering holes. The open-air restaurants and old stores are nearly all madeover trendy bars and chic chain stores, calculated to serve the aspirational Big-Brother voter after hours, yet still catering for quieter daytime cappuccino and cream tea-drinkers. They might be happier at the **Russell-Cotes Art Gallery & Museum** ⓘ *East Cliff, T01202-451800 Tue-Sun 1000-1700 free,* an awarding-winning museum, newly restored with Heritage Lottery funding, displaying a wealth of famous Victoriana, as well as Japanese artefacts and contemporary art exhibitions. The seafront itself teems with all the usual attractions. The **Oceanarium** ⓘ *Bournemouth Seafront, T01202-311993, www.oceanarium.co.uk, daily 1000-1800, £6.25, concessions £4.95, child 3-15 £3.95, family of 4 £18 or family of 5 £21,* boasts over 10,000 sea creatures and also a charming 'turtle beach café'. Watch sharks, turtles and rays being fed daily. **Bournemouth Pier** ⓘ *0900-2100, toll 40p for adults, 20p for children,* is an old-fashioned iron pier, with theatre and mini funfare at the end. It's the place to book local trips on eg Grand Firework Cruise, Scenic Tour to Sand Banks, Poole Harbour or 'Old Harry' Rocks and Swanage. Prices and times vary. The best **beaches**, although always crowded in summer, are Sandbanks, Branksome Chine, Flaghead and Alun Chines. Beach huts can be hired T07980-616208. £10/12 per day or £60 for the week (high season). *Durley Craft Hire* offer rowing boats, canoes and floats at half hourly rates starting from £4. Deck chairs, windbreaks, parasols and sunbeds for hire for daily rates starting at £1.50. ⓘ *The West Cliffe lift opens Mon, Wed, Thu, Sat and Sun 0930-2145 Tue 0930-1815 and Fri 0930-2300 (weather permitting).*

Poole

A polite harbour extension of Bournemouth, Poole lives up to its name thanks to Sandbanks and the Isle of Purbeck creating tranquil Poole Harbour, with lovely **Brownsea Island** ⓘ *(NT), T01202-707744,* in the middle, the last refuge of the red squirrel. In the town itself, the **Poole Aquarium and Serpentarium** ⓘ *Hennings Wharf, The Quay, T01202-686712, daily 1000-1730 (Jul, Aug 0900-2100), £6.50, concessions £5,* is a cut above the average fishtank exhibition, including a variety of scary reptiles. The **Study Gallery** ⓘ *Poole College, North Rd, Parkstone, T01202-205200,* is home to Bournemouth and Poole College's important mid-20th century art collection, with works by Henry Moore, Barbara Hepworth and Bridget Riley. Poole is also the official start of the **South West Coast Path** ⓘ *T01752-896237, info@swcp.org.uk,* the longest and arguably most attractive National Trail in the UK.

Isle of Purbeck

Not strictly an island, the Isle of Purbeck is a delightful stretch of chalky upland that drops into the sea in the east beside the funny old seaside town of Swanage. This is quarry country, the coast bearing witness to centuries of stone extraction and recently blessed with the grand designation of World Natural Heritage Site, the first of its kind in the country. Branded the Jurassic Coast, the ancient rock formations between Durlston Head and Weymouth have been pulling in the crowds for some time, to the limestone sea arch at Durdle Door and crescent bay of Lulworth Cove especially although the whole coastline is well worth exploring. As well as being great walking country, the Isle of Purbeck also hides good wet weather curiosities like Lawrence of Arabia's retreat at Clouds Hill, stately Lulworth Castle's renovated shell and the Bovington Tank Museum.

Ins and outs

Getting there Wareham is on the main line to Weymouth from London via Bournemouth and Poole. A regular and very good value steam train service runs from Norden, 3 miles south of Wareham, via Corfe Castle to Swanage. The town is about 20 mins west of Poole on the A351. Swanage would take at least another 30 mins to reach, possibly more in high season when Purbeck's roads can become congested.

Information Swanage TIC ⓘ *Shore Rd, T0870-4420680, www.swanage.gov.uk. Easter-Oct daily 1000-1700, Nov-Easter Mon-Fri 0900-1700.* **Wareham TIC** ⓘ *South St, T01929-552740, www.purbeck-dc.gov.uk. Easter-Oct daily 0930-1700, Nov-Easter Mon-Sat 1000-1500. Accommodation booking service free.*

Wareham to Swanage

The main town at the entrance to the Isle of Purbeck, Wareham is a solid, well-to-do market town with a prosperous air on the banks of the rivers Piddle and Frome. Boats can be hired from its old bridge, and beautiful walks across the floodplain of the Frome head towards its mouth in Poole Harbour. In the distance rise the Purbeck Hills, with the dramatic ruins of **Corfe Castle** ⓘ *(NT), T01929-481294, Apr-Oct daily 1000-1800, Nov-Feb daily 1000-1600, Mar daily 1000-1700, £4.40, under-16s £2.25, family £11,* sitting on a small mound in their central gap. A Norman and early English castle which once commanded the entire island, it was destroyed in the Civil War. Now one of the most popular and extraordinarily situated ruins in the country, it's often overrun with visitors in season playing hide and seek and scrambling up and down its grassy flanks.

Just north of Corfe Castle on the Wareham Road, Norden is the jumping off point for the superb **Swanage Steam Railway** ⓘ *T01929-425800, Mid-Mar to Oct daily,*

 Nov-Dec at weekends, £6 return, from Norden Park and Ride, via Corfe Castle, Harmonds Cross, and Herston, to Swanage. Steam trains run down to Swanage with wonderful views of Nine Barrows Down on the left, good for great breezy ridge walks (four miles) back to Corfe Castle across the neolithic burial mounds.

Swanage and Durlston Head

Swanage is one of England's most endearing seaside towns, just out of the way enough not to be competely ruined by the hordes. It does all the usual seaside things in a mini way, with regular visits from the steam paddleship *Waverley* in the summer. The town hall boasts a Baroque façade originally from the Mercer's Hall in Cheapside, and various other bits of old London were collected and brought down here by the indefatigable George Burt in the 19th century. The most rewarding of his eccentric collection can be found after the stiff walk up out of town to the south, on Durlston Head, a great big globe of Portland Stone. **Durlston Head** is the most easterly point of the World Heritage Site now branded the Jurassic Coast as far as Exmouth. The first natural World Heritage Site in Britain, it celebrates the variety of rocks Triassic (200-250 million years old), Jurassic (140-200 million years old) and Cretaceous (65-140 million years old) and the unique forms, fossils, flora and fauna they have created and supported. The most spectacular of its geological features are the sea arches and rock stacks at Durdle Door and the extraordinary shingle bank of Chesil Beach (see page 386). Less obvious features include ripple marks on the rocks around Osmington that suggest Dorset once enjoyed a Bahaman climate and the fossil forest just east of Lulworth Cove.

St Aldhelm's Head to Lulworth Cove

From Durlston Head, a superb 5-mile stretch of the **South West Coast Path** runs along to St Aldhelm's Head. A couple of miles along, at Dancing Ledge, there's a swimming pool blasted out of the spectacular rocks by quarrymen. All along here, the quarries have left their mark, the stone being loaded at great risk into boats beside vertical walls of rock. Swimming in the sea along here is still only for the brave. **Seacombe** has a good rocky beach, and so does **Winspit**, just before steps lead up onto the wild and lonely St Aldhelm's or St Alban's Head itself. An atmospheric Norman chapel, a coastguard's lookout and cottages brave the south-westerlies in this desolate spot, although quiet valleys filled with gorse and blackberry bushes run inland to the little village of **Worth Matravers**.

Continuing along the coast path, beyond the eerie quiet of **Chapman's Pool**, a seaweed filled bay, you arrive after 4 miles in **Kimmeridge**, a popular spot with surfers. The Clavel Tower on the headland was built in 1820. The path on from here is at the discretion of the MOD, who use this beautiful 6-mile shoreline for target practice. The walks are usually open at weekends and during school holidays, but it's worth contacting the Lulworth Range Information Officer, T01929-404819, to check. He should also be able to provide information as to the accessibility of **Tyneham**, the village requisitioned by the army at the start of the Second World War and never given back. Its story and that of the surrounding area has been vividly told by Patrick Wright in his book *The Village that Died for England*. As well as the tumbledown old cottages, schoolroom and manor houses, there are impressive walks out onto the headland and beach at **Worbarrow Tout** from here. Overlooking the ranges on the tiny road between East Creech and Lulworth, the **Franklin Viewpoint** commands a tremendous coastal panorama.

Lulworth Cove itself, 3 miles west of Tyneham, is a picturesque semicircle of sandy beach beneath the cliffs that can become impossibly crowded in summer. Almost as popular is **Durdle Door**, with its famous sea arch and beaches beneath Chaldon Down with views of Weymouth and the Isle of Portland. A little inland, **East Lulworth** village was moved in the 1780s by the Catholic Weld family, to clear the view from Lulworth Castle. Originally built as a very grand Jacobean hunting lodge, **Lulworth Castle** ⓘ *Lulworth Castle, T01929-400352, Apr-Oct Mon-Fri, Sun 1030-1800, Nov-Mar Mon-Fri, Sun 1030-1600 (or dusk if earlier), £5.50, concessions £5, under-16s £3.50, family £15,* was converted spectacularly into a country house in the 18th century and equally spectacularly went up in flames in the 1920s. The shell has been restored by English Heritage at great expense. The **Great Chapel of St Mary's** close by was built in 1786, apparently the first free-standing Roman Catholic chapel to be built after the Reformation, allowed by George III "on the condition that it looked more like a mausoleum than a chapel". Various events like jousting and falconry take place throughout the summer.

Inland from Lulworth Cove

Three miles further inland, the **Bovington Tank Museum** ⓘ *T01929-405096 daily 1000-1700 (last admission 1630), £7.50, £6.50 concessions, £5 under-16s, family £21, shop T01929-405141,* has about 150 armoured vehicles on show, all undercover. Bovington Camp's most famous soldier was TE Lawrence 'of Arabia', under the pseudonym TE Shaw. He lived nearby in a cottage at **Clouds Hill** ⓘ *T01929-405616. Apr-Oct Thu-Sun, bank holidays 1200-1700 (or dusk if earlier), £2.80.* The man indirectly responsible for the British Mandate in Palestine, by organizing the Arab resistance to Turkish occupation, lived here in retreat from 1925 until his death in a motorbike accident in 1935, 600 yds down the road, at the age of 46. His simply furnished home has been kept much as it was, without electric light.

Three miles north, in February 1834, at **Tolpuddle**, six farm labourers were arrested for establishing the first trade union, tried in Dorchester and transported to Australia. Thomas Standfield's cottage, where they took their illegal oath, still stands next to the Methodist chapel. **Tolpuddle Martyrs Museum** ⓘ *T01305-848237, Apr-Oct Tue-Sat 1000-1730, Sun 1100-1730, Nov-Mar Tue-Sat 1000-1600, Sun 1100-1600, free.*

Weymouth to Lyme Regis

The Jurassic Coast continues west of Weymouth, a jolly seaside resort in summer, pretty sad in winter, past Portland Bill on to Chesil Beach, a remarkable shingle strand braving the breakers beneath superb downland scenery. It's well worth heading inland around these parts to enjoy the countryside: tucked away down tiny lanes are hidden gems like Mapperton Gardens, or Eggardon hill fort, among villages lost in time like Compton Valence and Punchknowle.

Ins and outs

Getting there The terminus for **trains** via Bournemouth and Poole (50 minutes) from London Waterloo (2 hours 40 minutes), Weymouth also has direct services to Bath (2 hours), Bristol (2 hours 20 minutes) and Wales. Weymouth is about 30 minutes beyond Dorchester down the A354. A car or bike is really the only way to explore the coast.

Information Lyme Regis TIC ⓘ *T01297-442138.*

Weymouth

Weymouth has an attractive old Georgian seafront and not much else to recommend it. It's a family holiday place that looks good from a distance. The sandy beach gets very busy in summer, the blue and white deck chairs giving lovely views out to the Purbeck coast and Weymouth's best feature: **Portland Bill**. Another mock island, the Isle of Portland is a strange outcrop of rock that has long provided the stone for many of Britain's grandest buildings, St Paul's Cathedral for example. Some of its old quarries have been turned into visitor centres. The best visitor centre, however, is at the **Lighthouse Visitor**

Centre ⓘ *T01305-861233, Apr-Sep Mon-Fri, Sun 1100-1700 (last tour 1630),* on its most southerly point. It's worth the trek out here for the fine views of **Chesil Beach**, a long straight 7-mile strip of pebbles sheltering a lagoon rich in wildlife called The Fleet. The beach is not safe for swimming but good for walks.

The best views of Chesil's complete extent can be had from the top of the **Hardy Monument** ⓘ *Black Down, T01202-882493, Apr-Sep Sat, Sun 1100-1700 £1.* Not a memorial to the novelist, but to Nelson's flag-captain on HMS *Victory* at Trafalgar, Sir Thomas Masterman Hardy.

Abbotsbury is a thatched village near the coast that's almost too cute for its own good, with its swannery and subtropical gardens ⓘ *Abbotsbury Subtropical Gardens, T01305-871387, www.abbotsbury-tourism.co.uk. Mar-Oct daily 1000-1800 Nov-Feb daily 1000-1600.* Another good view can be had by climbing up to **St Catherine's Chapel** perched on the top of the hill, with a turret once used as a lighthouse.

The **coast road** from Abbotsbury to Bridport is glorious, rolling through wild gorse and heather with the sea shining bright down below. The coastal settlements themselves are a little disappointing, although Bridport's seaside village at **West Bay** has a couple of good restaurants and a little harbour. Best to press on to Lyme Regis or head inland to visit **Eggardon Hill**, a spectacular Iron Age hill fort, or **Mapperton Gardens** ⓘ *T01308-862645, Mar-Oct daily 1400-1800 (from 1300 Wed, Thu, Sat),* near Beaminster for their ornamental lakes and terraces in a spellbinding valley beneath a crumbling old manor house, little church and tearoom barn. Nearby, **Loscombe Woodland Garden** ⓘ *Apr-Sep Mon, Tue, Sat, Sun 1100-dusk,* is also worth seeking out to escape the crowds in high season.

Lyme Regis

Lyme Regis may not quite live up to being twinned with St George's, Bermuda, but it's undeniably very pretty. Approached through rolling woodland on the coast road, this little fishing village was the setting for John Fowles' *French Lieutenant's Woman* and has a sandy dog-free beach at low tide. Its Marine Parade was the first public prom created in England, in 1771, its lower part being a cart road. The rebellious Duke of Monmouth landed here in 1685 and Jane Austen was fond of the place a century later. More interestingly, Mary Anning 'the Fossil Woman' discovered the Icthyosaurus in the fossil encrusted cliffs, lower Jurassic topped by younger rocks, cliffs created by continual landslips. She invented the word 'dinosaur' and has even been immortalized in the tongue-twister 'she sells sea shells on the sea shore'. The origins of Lyme Regis stretch back to the eighth century when monks distilled salt from the seawater here. Today, people enjoy strolling along the prom and up the town's impossibly quaint little streets and looking out over the **Cob**, the medieval

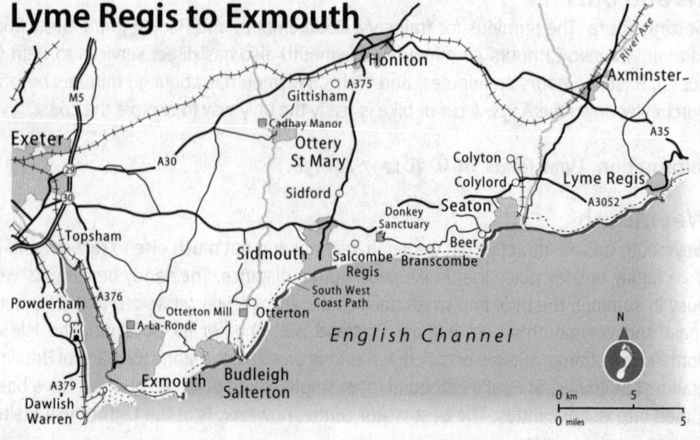

harbour wall. At its tip, the **Marine Aquarium** ⓘ *T01297-443678, Easter-Oct daily 1000-1700 £1.40*, is a sweet little display of sealife, as well as wreckage, fishing gear and old photographs. There are great views out to Portland along Chesil Beach and it's possible to take a trip out to see the Jurassic Coast by boat. Try *Phone a Boat*, T07765-501539. For anyone with kids, it's well worth checking with the TIC when the Lifeboat station will be showing off its extraordinary sea-tractor.

Sleeping

Shaftesbury and Sherborne *p377, p378*

L **Stock Hill Country House**, Gillingham, near Shaftesbury, T01747-823626, stockhillhouse.co.uk. Gracious 1830 Victorian-built house with garden, tennis and croquet. Convenient for days out castle, garden and museum viewing.

A **Plumber Manor**, Sturminster Newton, T01258-472507/472507, F473370. Homely family-run hotel B&B with a good traditional restaurant in a delightful Jacobean manor house with garden crossed by the Devilish stream. Rooms in the main house and in the converted stables.

C **Benett Arms**, Semley, near Shaftesbury, T01747-830221, www.benettarms.co.uk. Does English favourites in a friendly 3-storey pub on the green, with local ingredients: Wiltshire ham and good ploughman's lunches. With 5 rooms with en suite bathrooms too.

C **Cromwell House**, Long St, Sherborne, T01935-813352. Three bedrooms in a Georgian townhouse B&B bang in the middle of town.

C **The Lamb**, Hindon, T01747-820573. Rooms above a jolly country pub doing reasonable pub grub in the attractive village of Hindon, Frenchified by its boulevard of limes.

D **Paynes Place Barn**, New Rd, Shaftesbury, T01747-855016. Converted Victorian stone barn B&B with great views over the Blackmore Vale.

D **Quiet Corner Farm**, Oak Vale La, Henstridge, T01963-363045. An 18th-century farmhouse with a glorious garden and Shetland ponies, halfway between Shaftesbury and Sherborne.

Dorset Downs *p378*

L **Summer Lodge**, Evershot, near Dorchester, T01935-83424, F83005. A charming 1789- built lodge with swimming pool. Expertly prepared local seafood, beef, pheasant, rabbit and game are on the menu.

A **Beechleas Hotel & Restaurant**, 17 Poole Rd, Wimborne Minster, near Bournemouth, T01202-841684, www.beachleas.com. A Georgian townhouse hotel a few mins' walk from Wimborne Minster with 9 rooms.

B **Yalbury Cottage**, Lower Bockhampton, near Dorchester, T01305- 262382, www.smoothhound.co.uk/hotels/yalsbury. 2 350-yr-old cottages with pine- furnished rooms overlooking fields or the garden. The restaurant also specializes in local produce and makes its own bread and ice cream.

B **Fox Inn**, Corscombe, Dorchester, T01935-891330. Rose-covered thatch from 1620 and 3 bedrooms, very good food.

Bournemouth and Poole *p382, p383*

There are countless hotels and B&Bs in both Bournemouth and Poole, many some way from the centre out towards Boscombe. Clearly holiday lets are a popular thing to do, eg **Clifton Apartments**, T01202-302562, which overlook the sea from Boscombe.

L **The Bath Hotel**, Bath Rd, Bournemouth, T01202-555555. A definite top of the range choice in Bournemouth.

A **The Mansion House Hotel**, Thames St, Poole, T01202-685666, www.themansion house.co.uk. Set in this old historic town this 32-room hotel boasts the top restaurant in Poole. All rooms are modernized and have Edwardian antique furnishings.

A **The Norfolk Royale Hotel**, Richmond Hill, Bournemouth, T01202-551521. Offers faded Edwardian grandeur in the middle of town.

B **Langtry Manor**, Derby Rd, Bournemouth, T01202-553887, F290115. This Edwardian manor house was built by the Prince of Wales (King Edward VII) as a hideaway for his paramour, Lillie Langtry. All rooms have individual themes and are spacious. A beautiful dining hall with stained-glass windows and a gallery.

C The Antelope Inn, Old High St, Poole, T01202-672029. This old coaching inn boasts a carvery, cask-conditioned bitters and a fireplace dating from 1465, a lively place, once serving as a molasses store, a 19th-century Judges Court and a base for commando operations in the Second World War; 21 rooms, 1 with 4-poster.
B Menzies East Cliff Court, T01332-513330. Set in an endless row of hotels overlooking the sea, this peppermint green one stands out with its newly refurbished cool summer stucco front, stylish rooms, 4-star rating, private pool and waft of cocktails from the terrace.
C The Studland Drive, Studland Dr, T01202-765445. A corner hotel on West Cliffe, high on the promontory, with an enticing Thai 'Pacific bar and Restaurant' included.

Isle of Purbeck *p383*

A Priory Hotel, Church Green, Wareham, T01929-551666, F554519. Set on the banks of the river Frome, this 16th-century priory is peaceful and quiet. The owners have converted the former boathouse into 2 luxury suites. Rooms in the priory look onto the Purbeck Hills. The restaurant has moorings for diners arriving by boat (about £50 a head).
D Bradle Farmhouse, Bradle, near Church Knowle, T01929-480712, www.bradlefarmhouse.co.uk. Some comfortable rooms with en suite bathrooms in a delightful location near Corfe Castle.
D Scott Arms, Kingston, T01929-480270. A pub with tremendous views over Corfe Castle in the distance from its garden, decent food and 2 double rooms, breakfast included.

Weymouth to Lyme Regis *p385*

A Manor Hotel, West Bexington, near Bridport, T01308-897785, F897035. With flagstone floors, intricately carved panelling, a low ceiling cellar bar, stone walls and oak, this 16th-century stone building is an olde worlde kind of place. Rooms with sea views.
B Bay View Hotel, Marine Parade, Lyme Regis, T01297-442059. Right on the seafront, with a hip 50s feel to it, and a very fresh fish restaurant doing 2 courses for £19.50.
B Thatch Lodge Hotel, The Street, Charmouth, near Lyme Regis, T01297-560407, F560407. Thatch Lodge was built in 1320 as a resting place for monks. The rooms are all unique and the cooking is based on fresh local produce. The cottage has 200-year-old vines and hand-picked grapes.
D Melcombe Villa Guesthouse, Weymouth, T01305-783026. A good central option, close to the beach.
D Old Monmouth Hotel, Bridge St, Lyme Regis, T01297-442456, www.lyme-regis-hotel.co.uk. Good value option just over the road from the TIC.

Eating

Shaftesbury and Sherborne *p377, p378*

££ John Peel, 52 High St, Shaftesbury, T01747-853178, is a good value restaurant (no more than £15 a head), with vegetarian options and generous portions. BYOB.
££ Rose and Crown, Trent, near Sherborne, T01935-850776. A good local pub with a large garden, and slightly fancy menu, but open fires and flagstone floors beneath the thatch.
££ The Ship Inn, Bleke St, Shaftesbury, T01747-853219. An 'olde-worlde pubbe' in scenic Shaftesbury, with a refurbished 17th-century interior and boules pitch outside.
££ White Horse, Hinton St Mary, Sturminster Newton, T01258-472723. Home-made traditional English food on the menu for lunch and supper and a flower-filled garden with a lovely prospect. Book for the weekends.
££ Ye Olde Two Brewers, 24 St James St, Shaftesbury, T01747-854211. Great views and a wide variety of locally produced food on offer in a roomy pub off Gold Hill.

Dorset Downs *p378*

££ The Acorn Inn, Evershot, near Dorchester, T01935-83228. Comfortable village pub with good food.
££ The Crown, Fontwell Magna, near Shaftsbury, T01747-812222. Good selection of well-crafted meat, fish and vegetarian dishes.
££ The Crown, Ibberton, near Blandford, T01258-817448. Nestling in the Blackmoor Vale below Bulbarrow Hill, an old little pub with a large fireplace.
££ Hambro Arms, Milton Abbas, T01258-880233. Pool table and big log fires in the middle of thatched model village, also doing fresh local produce.

££ **Frampton Arms**, Moreton, T01305-852253. Conveniently close to the station, in the village where TE Lawrence is buried, with wide menu of home-made food.

Bournemouth *p382*

££ **Alcatraz Brasserie**, 127 Old Christchurch Rd, T01202-553650. Modern Italian dining in a cool elegant dining room with open-air patio overlooking the start of the gardens.

££ **Coriander**, 22 Richmond Hill, T01202-552202. A Mexican eaterie with a friendly local buzz, that beats the constant diet of seaside fish bars or big pick-up joints.

££ **West Beach**, Pier Approach, T01202-587785. A fish and seafood restaurant that's a real summer find. Right on the beach it overlooks the pier and nestles under the cliff. The main restaurant offers mussels and fresh catch of the day in some Cote d'Azur style. There's even a separate deck right out over the beach, shading the beau monde from the scalding sun under its blue uniform umbrellas. Either side of the long windows are little outlets for the bikini-clad masses to purchase their dishes at takeaway prices, and the burgers and ices prove the popular favourite.

£ **Delice des Champs**, 13 Gervis Pl, T01202-319094. Everything French.

£ **Harry Ramsden's**, Undercliffe Drive, East Beach, T01202-295818. Open 0900-1000 Established in 1928, "The World's Most Famous Fish & Chips" – an institution. Serving large helpings of fresh fish to take out or sit upstairs and enjoy a more sheltered view over the bathing beaches.

£ **Trawlers Bistro Café**, 42c Sea Rd, Boscombe Spa, just beyond Bournemouth, T01202-309238. Offers an all-in bargain tea or coffee and scone for £1.50 (or bigger bites) after a long hike from Bournemouth to Boscombe, it's next door to an archetypical bucket and spade 'Rock Shop' which dares to offer 'turf2surf' clothing from New Zealand!

Poole *p383*

££ **Hardy's Restaurant**, 14 High St, T01202-660864. A family-owned bistro offering baked snapper in a friendly more authentic atmosphere.

££ **John B's**, 20 High St, Old Town, T01202-672440. Does French double-fronted dining offering snails and all the usual gourmand treats in a formal manner.

££ **Topogigio**, 22 High St, T01202-670181. A popular pizzeria with a sunny white interior.

£ **Oriel Café & Restaurant**, The Quay, T01202-679833. Summery white and cream suitable for families and high tea.

£ **Shell Bay**, Poole. A great spot overlooking the sea with resplendent dining rooms and patios serving delicious local seafood.

Isle of Purbeck *p383*

£££ **Nomad**, 12a North St, Wareham, T01929-555275. Wed-Sat do superb suppers.

££ **Fox Inn**, West St, Corfe Castle, T01929-480449. Has log fires, views of the castle and daily specials on the menu.

£ **Square and Compasses**, Worth Matravers, T01929-439229. An unreconstructed old boozer with beer-through-the-hatch, basic snacks and regular live music of sorts, pretty much the heart of the headland. The landlord will probably find room for your tent if you ask nicely.

Weymouth to Lyme Regis *p385*

£££ **Riverside Restaurant**, West Bay, T01308-422011. Laid-back freshly prepared seafood restaurant right on the water. Booking advisable.

££ **The Bridport Arms Hotel**, West Bay, T01308-422994. A thatched hotel beside the beach, with daily fish specials.

££ **Perry's**, 4 Trinity Rd, The Old Harbour, Weymouth, T01305-785799. Simple fresh fish dishes in a cosy spot on the harbourfront.

££ **Spyway Inn**, Askerswell, near Bridport T01308- 485250. Close to the impressive hill fort at Eggardon, good home-cooked food and superb views from the garden.

££ **Three Horseshoes**, Powerstock, T01308-485328. Excellent local produce and seafood with spacious gardens and panelled dining room in a working village.

Pubs, bars and clubs

Bournemouth *p382*

Casa, 4-15 Bourne Av, T01202-780154. A vast wooden and highly modern bar and sofa home. Where the male of the species checks out the female of the species over a meze or J-2-0 cocktail jug during 'happy hour'. During all day dining, the students and designer wearer can munch and chatter before the DJ kicks in for the dating crowd at night.

Consortium, The Square. Another music bar directly opposite *Casa*, offering the same vibe. Free till 2230, £5 afterwards. Tue £1.
Daisy O'Briens, 77 Old Christchurch Rd, T01202-290002. A long way from Tipperary, but this old one-off Irish pub in the heart of the high-street shopping district offers a break from the chainstore stranglehold.
Goat and Tricycle 22-29 West Hill, T01202-314220. Does billiards, an old-fashioned place with reasonable pub grub.

Clubs

Bournemouth's club scene is hotting up. Wave FM on 105.2 seems to plug the local scene and most bars offer DJs in the evening and cater to students during term time.
The Brasshouse, 8-9 Westover Rd, T01202-589681. A vast cavernous pub in the day, with request DJs and grooves every night.

Poole *p383*

King Charles Pub, Thame St, Poole, T01202-674950. A traditional old tavern with low ceilings and hearty hot pot suppers.
Oyster Quay, Port Saint James, the Quay, Poole, T01202-668669. There's high summer fun with weekend DJs at this waterfront bar and grill, sporting live tropical fish behind the bar and biweekly firework displays.
Poole Arms, The Quay, Poole, T01202-672309. A burnished green tiled-fronted pub offering a friendly pint on the old harbour.

Entertainment

Theatres, live music and comedy

The **Box Office** T01202-456456 caters for Pavilion and Pier Box Offices and the IMAX or visit www.bic.co.uk for online ticketing.
Bournemouth Symphony Orchestra, 2 Seldown La, Poole T01202-670611, www.bsolive.com, an established touring orchestra, offers classical firework summer proms at local houses.
Forest Arts Centre, Old Milton Rd, New Milton, Hampshire, T01425-612393. Thriving arts centre, an arty alternative.
The Pavilion is the original home of the Bournemouth Symphony Orchestra opened in 1929 and includes a 1,600 seat theatre, ballroom, restaurant and terraces over-looking the Lower Gardens. This thriving theatre offers tours, ballroom dancing, afternoon tea dances, country line dancing, lunchtime organ concerts, balls, military tattoo, and touring concerts and events – see box office for details.
The Pier Theatre, is literally at the end of Bournemouth pier, full of holiday fun, offering respectable touring classics from Ayckbourne to Coward with the extra twinkle of a familiar TV celebrity cast in a leading role.

Festivals

Shaftesbury and Sherborne *p377, p378*

May Sherborne Town and Abbey Festival. Regular concerts on Sat nights in the Abbey.
Aug/Sep Great Dorset Steam Fair, Tarrant Hinton, near Blandford at the end of Aug, early Sep, T01202-456456, www.steam-fair co.uk. All the tackle and steam at the fair on a 500-acre site, widely renowned as the leading event of its kind in the world. Attracting the steam buff from miles around.

Bournemouth and Poole *p382, p383*

Bournemouth Carnival **29 Jul-4 Aug**.
Boscombe Carnival **22 Jul – 28 Jul**. Red Arrows – annual visit.

Shopping

Bournemouth and Poole *p382, p383*

Beales is the local department store www.Beales.co.uk After all the usual chains from Marks & Sparks to Debenhams, the local favourite remains this old staple.
BIC Purbeck Hall and Lounge, Tregonwell, T01202-456501. Something is usually staged for the bric-a-brac hunter as well as xhibitions from antiques fairs in the Pavilion Ballroom to the Ideal Home Exhibition.
Outdoors, 3 Gervis Pl, T01202-318210. "We've got it covered" is their slogan. An exhuberant travel shop for the intrepid backpacker replenishing their supplies, or the casual walker in need of advice.
Quiksilver, 79 Old Christchurch Rd, T01202-295412, do cheerful and trendy beachwear and accessories, part of the south coast 'Just Add Water' chain for designer surf-n-sun wear.
Westover Gallery, 4 Westover Rd, T01202-297682. Present local artists and glassware in one of the prettiest Victorian covered arcades.

Woodside, 3 Westover Rd, T01202-290509. This airy boutique offers designer labels for well-heeled ladies-who-lunch.

Activities and tours

Bournemouth and Poole *p382, p383*
AFC Bournemouth, T01202-456456. For information on all forthcoming football matches from the local team.
Island Ferries, T01929-462383. "For the perfect day out on the famous yellow boats of Poole".
Leisure Pool and The Zone Fitness Suite, T01202-456580. Over 700 sq m of water, separate toddlers pool, 'Sharkspin' giant 52 m waterslide, wave-making maching, sauna, steam and solarium. Free parking for patrons, free for under 3 year olds.
Poole Harbour Boardsailing, 284 Sandbanks Rd, Lilliput, Poole, T01202-700503.
Poole Sea Angling Centre, rear of 5 High St, Poole, T01202-676597.
Self-Drive Boat Hire, Poole Harbour, T01202-710448.

Transport

Bournemouth and Poole *p382, p383*

Bicycle
Rent a Bike, 88 Charminster Rd, T01202-315855; **Action Bike**, Dolphin Centre, Poole, T01202-680123.

Car
Avis, 33-39 Southcote Rd, T01202-296942; **Europcar**, Station Approach, Ashley Rd, T01202-293357.

Taxi
Central Taxis, 13 The Triangle, Bournemouth, T01202-394455; **Bournemouth Taxi Ranks**, Central Station, Bournemouth, T01202-556166; **Star Cars**, Christchurch Rd, Boscombe, T01202-391919.

Directory

Bournemouth and Poole *p382, p383*
Hospital Bournemouth Nuffield Hospital, 67-71 Lansdowne Rd, Bournemouth, T01202-291866.

Devon

Devon, England's biggest and most beautiful county is huntin', fishin', shootin' and farmin' country. So it rains, the roads may be impossibly busy in the middle of the day, and nothing much happens after midnight. Instead, visitors can enjoy the best cream tea of their lives, mile upon mile of well-tended organic farmland (pretty much back to normal after the worst outbreak of foot and mouth in the south) and the choice of two delightful coastlines. The russet-red south Devon coast became fashionable in the early 19th century, especially around the polite Regency resort of Sidmouth, while Exeter remains the adminstrative heart of the county. Slightly bewildered perhaps, the atmosphere of this ancient cathedral city can best be summed up as the living embodiment of the generation gap. On the coast to the south, the seaside resorts of Torbay have no such doubts – the English Riviera really does consider itself a cut above, whatever your age, even though the weather generally fails to deliver. The prosperous land south of the river Dart, known as South Hams, contains the epicentre of free-thinking in the Southwest at Totnes as well as the Royal Naval College at Dartmouth and the boating middle-classes' favourite seaside rendezvous at Salcombe. The Navy crops up again in a big way at Plymouth, the biggest city in the county and one with an undeniable sense of its place in the history of the world. In its heyday it sent its prisoners north, to Dartmoor, still one of the most strange and eerie stretches of moorland in England. The north Devon coast is the most romantic wooded shoreline in the British Isles and birthplace of British surfing. It finally peters out in the west with the rocks and wilds of Hartland.

Exeter and south Devon coast

➔ *Colour map 1, grid B5/6*

Exeter, at the mouth of the River Exe, is a city with a very visible generation gap. The regional capital of the Southwest, it has only fairly recently begun to cotton on to the various different ways in which today's 20- or 30-somethings like to divest themselves of their cash. There is an old-fashioned decency about the place, a pride in its central role in county affairs and in its civic status, which – though not without a certain charm – can sometimes make it seem a bit stodgy. There is more to life, after all, than a medieval cathedral (however beautiful) and a worthy provincial museum. Now attracting a youngish crowd that increasingly regards the city as a lively base from which to explore the various outdoor attractions of Devon and Cornwall, Exeter's teashops are just waking up to the fact that the shop next door is now just as likely to be selling skateboards and Pacific-style surfwear, than it is sensible shoes and tweed caps. At the forefront of this revolution, the Quay development down on the river is in the process of carving out the kind of space familiar to many European cities: a stretch of water to perambulate by, a slight whiff of culture, and a selection of bars, cafés, restaurants and nightclubs for the discerning punter.

East of Exeter, the World Heritage Coast runs from Exmouth to the Dorset border. There's a wonderful beach walk from lovely Branscombe, just past the little fishing village of Beer, to the Regency resort of Sidmouth. Very different from Lyme, Sidmouth just about preserves the memory of more formal pleasures taken in past times, coming fully alive once a year with an internationl folk festival. Inland, the mini- cathedral at Ottery St Mary is also worth a look, while the market town of Honiton is one of the antique dealing centres of the Southwest. Exmouth itself, round the corner from the polite retirement homes at Budleigh Salterton, is a straightforward low-rent seaside town for family holiday fun. ➤ *For Sleeping, eating and other listings, see pages 397- 400.*

Ins and outs

Getting there Exeter International Airport is 6 miles out of the city. A regular shuttle bus, T01392-367433, serves the centre. Exeter is well served by rail. From London trains depart about once an hour from both Paddington (2 hours 20 minutes) and Waterloo (3 hrs 20 minutes). The Waterloo trains, though a lot slower, have the advantage of depositing you at Exeter Central, right in the middle of the city, while the Paddington trains go to Exeter St Davids, a 15-minute walk, or a short taxi (about £3.50) or bus ride (take the H or N) into town. Axminster is the closest mainline station to Seaton, with a regular bus service 885 to the coast. Honiton is the closest mainline station to Sidmouth, connected by bus service 340. **National Rail Enquiries**, T08457-484950. From London, the safe bet is to stick to the M4 and M5 motorways getting off at junction 30 (about 3 hours). The M3/A303/A30 route is more direct and more interesting, but it is by no means dual-carriageway all the way, so you can find yourself stuck behind a lorry or a caravan, especially at peak holiday times. There are plenty of car parks in the city centre, where 24 hours parking will cost you from £4-8. **National Express**, T08705-808080, operate coaches to Exeter from most parts of the country (9 coaches a day from London). Exmouth and Budleigh Salterton are both easily reached by bus from Exeter. **Traveline**, T0870-6082608. ➤ *For further details, see Transport, page 400.*

Getting around The centre of Exeter is compact enough to negotiate on **foot**. Regular buses, run by **First** in Dorset, Edward St, Weymouth, T01305-783645, and **Stagecoach Devon**, Belgrave Rd, Exeter, T01392-427711, connect Lyme Regis with Seaton, Sidmouth, Budleigh Salterton and Exmouth. **Axe Valley Mini Travel**, 26 Harbour Rd, Seaton, T01297-625959, run a coastal service from Seaton via Beer and Branscombe to Sidmouth.

Information Exeter TIC ⓘ *Paris St, opposite the coach and bus station, T01392-265700, www.exeter.gov.uk. Mon-Sat 0900 1700 and Sun in summer only.* Pick up a copy of *The List*, Exeter's free listings magazine to find out what's on. **Seaton TIC** ⓘ *The Underfleet, T01297-21660.* **Sidmouth TIC** ⓘ *Ham La, T01395-516441.* **Budleigh Salterton TIC** ⓘ *Fore St, T01395-445275. Exmouth, Manor Gardens, Alexandra Terr, T01395-222299.* **Exe Cruises,** 1215, 1445, from Ferry Steps, T01395-279693.

Exeter

History

Historically, traces of an early settlement at this shallow, fordable bend in the river go back a couple of hundred years BC. It was not until the Romans built a legionary fortress here in AD 55, though, that the city began to take its place on the map. The Romans departed in 410, leaving a robust set of city walls which, repaired by King Alfred in the ninth century to keep out the marauding Danes, remain in parts to this day. The next set of invaders, the Normans, gave the city its greatest foreign legacy: the two towers of the cathedral, whose main body was rebuilt in medieval times. Exeter also retains some fine examples of medieval architecture, despite the attentions of Hitler's Luftwaffe which, in a bombing raid on 4 May 1942, destroyed great swathes of the old centre, most of it – regrettably – replaced by unprepossessing, uninspired examples of 1960s architecture.

Sights

A good place to begin a tour of the city is outside the *Royal Clarence Hotel* looking out onto the Cathedral Green. On your left are *Mol's Coffee Shop* – now selling maps – allegedly an old Tudor haunt of Sir Francis Drake and St Martin's Church, and an interesting little red sandstone church dedicated in 1065; whilst ahead of you is the sedentary figure of Richard Hooker, the great Anglican theologian of the 16th century, who – on a summer's day – is surrounded by people recumbent in less formal postures on the grass. The **cathedral** itself is named after St Peter, who stands naked with a fishing net in his hands at the apex of the building, a recent, 1980s addition to the other statues of the 14th/15th century image screen. Once inside the impressive, vaulted nave, look out for the minstrels' gallery on the north side, with its 14 musical angels, and the 15th-century astronomical clock in the north transept. Wander past the gigantic oak Bishop's Throne, dated 1312, near the altar and explore the series of intimate chapels that surround the north end of the chancel. The Exeter Rondels, the tapestry cushions that line both sides of the nave, form a fascinating record in pictures and text of Exeter's history from Roman times right up to 1983, having taken 65 local ladies 4 years and 14 million stitches to complete.

Retrace your steps past the *Royal Clarence Hotel* up St Martin's Lane, a narrow alleyway leading onto the High Street. A few yards to the left is the **Guildhall** ⓘ *T01392-265500 limited opening times free,* quite possibly the oldest municipal building in the country. Straight ahead of you, down Queen Street, is the **Royal Albert Memorial Museum** ⓘ *T01392-665858, Mon-Sat 1000-1700 free,* whose ground floor hotchpotch of natural and local history is surmounted by an interesting 'world cultures' exhibit on the first floor. Tucked away to the right and parallel to Queen Street is the cobbled Gandy Street, home to some quirky boutiques and cafés. Further to the right up the High Street, a left turn up Castle Street will take you to the gardens of **Rougemont House**, containing some of the original walls of William I's castle and a memorial to the last four witches to be hanged in Devon in 1685. In Romangate Passage, next to *Boots*, you have the opportunity to descend into the **Underground Passages** ⓘ *T01392-665887, Mon-Sat 1000-1700 summertime, 1200-1700 at other times of year, £3.75, child £2.75,* a network of 14th-century tunnels used to bring fresh water into the city.

Heading back along the High Street, continue over the brow of the hill into Fore Street down towards the Quay. Right, along a street called The Mint, is the 11th-century **St Nicholas Priory** ⓘ *T01392-665858, Easter-Oct 1400-1630, 50p,* containing an exhibition about the history of the Devon and Dorset Regiment. **Tuckers Hall** ⓘ *T01392-412348, 1030-1230 Tue, Thu and Fri in summer, Tue only at other times free,* further down Fore Street, is the guildhall of the weavers, fullers and shearmen of Exeter, with a barrel roof and attractive panelling. Take a quick look, in front of you, at the city's **medieval bridge**, now marooned on dry land in the middle of a traffic gyratory system, before turning left and down onto the Quay. There, amongst the bars and cafés, you will find a handsome 17th-century **Customs House** ⓘ *T01392-265213, daily 1000-1700 Apr-Oct, weekends only 1100-1600 Nov-Mar, free,* with a Visitor Centre, containing a display about the history of the Quay and an audio-visual story of Exeter, both a little bit past their sell-by date. The Quay is also the place to hire a bicycle or canoe to head out into the waterways and countryside of the Exe estuary, see Activities, page 399.

Finally, the **Exeter University campus** ⓘ *T01392-263999, weekdays 0900-1800 and Sat mornings, free,* on a site about a mile outside the centre, contains a sculpture walk – including works by Barbara Hepworth and Henry Moore – and a fine botanical garden.

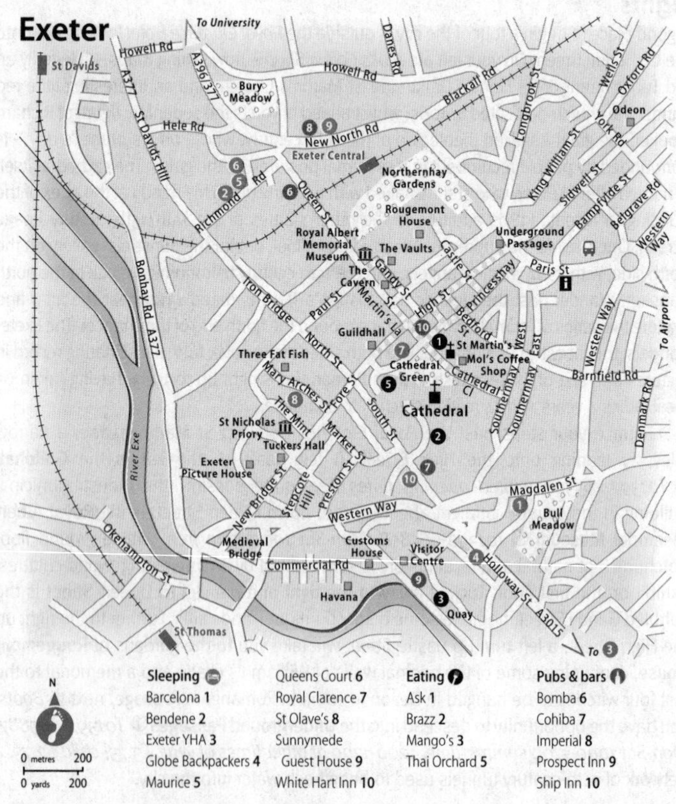

Walks in Devon

- **Wistman's Wood, Dartmoor**: 4 mile circle. Start: Two Bridges. Twisted dwarf oaks and mossy boulders in a mysterious wood 2 miles north of Two Bridges. OS Maps: Outdoor Leisure 28
- **Buckland Beacon, Dartmoor**: 2 miles there and back. Start: Buckland-in-the-Moor. A short walk up to one of the moor's finest viewpoints. OS Maps: Outdoor Leisure 28
- **Exmoor**: 4 mile circle. Start: Simonsbath. Riverside walks south-east of the village down the Barle to the hillfort at Cow Castle. OS Maps: Outdoor Leisure 9
- **North Devon coast**: 3 mile circle. Start: Woody Bay, 3 miles west of Lynmouth. Clifftop and woodland walks past the inspiration for the Coleridge's 'Rhyme of the Ancient Mariner'. OS Maps: Outdoor Leisure 9
- **South Devon coast**: 6 miles there and back. Start: Beer, 10 miles west of Lyme Regis. Along the South West Coast path to Branscombe and back. OS Maps: Explorer 116/115

South Devon coast

Seaton

Six miles west of Lyme Regis, past the landslip nature reserve, at the mouth of the river Axe, Seaton is a slightly disappointing little place, although it does have a small harbour, prom and seaside amusements, and grassy green chalky cliffs sloping down to its sloping pebble beach and beach huts. It's popular with pensioners, who enjoy the nostalgic trips on the open-air double-decker trams that run from here to Colyford and Coltyon (details from TIC), whistling their way up the pretty floodplain of the Axe valley.

Beer

The coast becomes more picturesque a little further on, at the tiny little fishing village of Beer. Very twee, with the *Anchor Inn* on the seafront, ragstone walls and a few small boats, its small pebbly beach is also sheltered by limestone cliffs. On sunny days it can become almost Mediterranean. The village was once home to the most notorious smuggler in the Southwest, Jack Rattenbury, who would certainly have been familiar with the warren of **caverns** ⓘ *T01297-20986/680282, www.beerquarrycaves. fsnet.co.uk, Apr-Oct daily 1000- 1600 by guided tour, £4.75, concessions and under-16s £3.50, family £15,* carved into the hill at its main low-key tourist attraction today, Beer's 2000-year-old stone **quarry.** The chilly quarry provided material for buildings like Exeter and Winchester Cathedrals and also a secret Catholic chapel.

Branscombe

Branscombe is another picture-postcard thatched village 2 miles west, with a wonderful wide pebbly **beach** protected by the National Trust (parking fee £3) and good walks all around. The Trust also runs the **Old Bakery tearoom** in the village, next to the **Manor mill** and still-working **Forge** ⓘ *(NT), T01297-680333. Bakery Easter-Oct daily 1100-1700, Nov-Easter Sat, Sun 1100-1700. Mill Apr-Oct Sun (also Wed in Jul and Aug) 1400-1700, £1. Forge T01297-680481, daily.* The **Millennium Rose garden** just above the church is spectacular, laid out on the slopes of a combe heading down to the sea. From here a 7-mile beach walk to Sidmouth passes lost coves only accessible from the sea, and places where potatoes were once grown on the undercliff. At **Salcombe Regis,** a footpath leads a mile down to another lonely beach, from the old church with its rare cherry tree, half a mile from the sea. Just beyond Weston, one of the country's largest donkey sanctuaries is at **Slade House Farm** ⓘ *T01395-578222, daily 0900-dusk, free,* home to over 500 of the "devil's walking parody of all four-footed things" as GK Chesterton called them, their days of working the beaches done.

Sidmouth

Sidmouth, approached from the west through another deep wooded dell with fine beech trees, is a sight to behold, sitting snug between its russet-red cliffs basking in the southern sun looking out to sea. A speculative development of a certain Emmanuel Lousada at the close of the 18th century, the town became one of the most fashionable and exclusive seaside resorts on the south coast. Here, even more than the Torbay resorts round the corner, was somewhere that really did rival the Riviera. A fair bit of the architecture from those glory days survives, some of it along the Esplanade, but more especially in the *cottages ornés* that decorate the slopes up Glen Road and Bickwell Valley, beyond the Victoria and Royal Glen Hotels, where Princess Victoria stayed with her parents in 1819. Lousada overlooked his creation from Peak House, which still stands above the fine Connaught Gardens on the seafront. The whole town has become famous for its flower displays and clings on to its dignity even in high summer, remaining fairly unspoilt (ie not a huge amount for the kids to do). The **Sid Vale Heritage Centre** ⓘ *Hope Cottage, Church St, T01395- 516139, Easter-Oct Mon 1400-1630, Tue-Sat 1000-1230, 1400-1630,* is full of photos of the town in its heyday, displays on its illustrious residents, and staff lead guided tours of the town on Tuesdays and Thursdays at 1015. Otherwise, you can enjoy descending to **Jacob's Ladder** (sandy at low tide) on the Western Beach from Connaught Gardens, strolling along the Esplanade and admiring the Georgian architecture of York Terrace behind, browsing in the shops up Fore St or climbing the steep footpath up **Salcombe Hill Cliff** east of the town.

Inland from Sidmouth

Eight miles inland from Sidmouth, through **Sidbury** with its seventh-century crypt in the church (July-Sep, Thu 1400-1700), **Honiton** is a prosperous market town, dominated by its 104-ft church tower and a large number of antique shops and auction houses. A good place to browse, the **Thelma Hubert Gallery** ⓘ *Elmfield House, Dowell St, T01404-45006, Feb-Dec Tue-Sat 1000-1600, free,* is also worth a look, a public art space for changing exhibitions of work by local artists as well as international names thanks to its links with the Hayward Gallery in London.

Ottery St Mary, 7 miles west towards Exeter, has one of the most remarkable parish churches in the West Country, partially constructed in 1260 and remodelled on Exeter Cathedral around 1340. It too has an astronomical clock, in the south transept, believed to date from the late 14th century and an equally ancient weathervane on the tower. In the vicarage next door, Samuel Taylor Coleridge was born in 1772, 13th child of the vicar of St Mary's. A mile to the northwest, **Cadhay Manor** ⓘ *T01404-812432, Jul and Aug Tue, Wed, Thu 1400-1700, £4.50, under-16s £2,* is a peaceful medieval house with Elizabethan and Georgian alterations, the interior shown on guided tours.

Exmouth and around

From Otterton Mill, a 2-mile footpath leads downriver to the Otter's mouth at **Budleigh Salterton**. No prom here to speak of, but instead a curving pebbly beach under the russet-red cliffs, with their pebbled seams, and an atmosphere that provides a foretaste of genteel South Hams round the corner. A little thatched house contains the **Fairlynch Arts Centre and Museum** ⓘ *27 Fore St, T01395-442666, Easter-Oct daily 1400-1630 (mid-Jul to Aug 1100-1300 also)*, with displays on costume, social history and geology.

Next door, **Exmouth's** broad sweep of sandy beach fronts a faintly neglected esplanade, nonetheless popular for family-holiday fun, with fish and chips aplenty and donkey rides on the beach in summer. Boat trips run across the mouth of the river Exe to **Powderham Castle** and the even larger beach at **Dawlish Warren**.

★ Five of the best beaches in Devon and Cornwall

- **Lusty Glaze**, Cornwall, is very safe and clean for swimmers, page 423.
- **Daymer Bay**, Cornwall, for very good windsurfing, page 421.
- **Strangles**, Cornwall, for rock formations, seclusion and naturists, page 419.
- **Bigbury-on-Sea**, Devon, for sand, swimming and snorkelling, page 403.
- **St Martin's Flats**, Isles of Scilly, for wildlife and seclusion, page 442.

... and five of the best-placed lighthouses

- **Trevose Head**, near Padstow, page 422.
- **Pendeen**, near Penzance, page 432.
- **Hartland Point**, north Devon, page 416.
- **Lizard**, Lizard Head, page 429.
- **St Agnes**, Isles of Scilly, page 442.

Just outside Exmouth off the Exeter road is the world-famous folly house, **A La Ronde** ⓘ *A La Ronde (NT), Summer La, Exmouth, T01395-265514, late Mar-Oct Mon-Thu, Sun 1100-1730, £3.80, under-16s £1.90,* built with 16 sides to the designs of the Parminter spinsters, Jane and Mary, apparently inspired by the church of San Vitale in Ravenna. Completed in 1798, it still displays the fruits of their 18th-century Grand Tour of Europe and their curious taste in interior design: a shell-decorated gallery (only viewable via CCTV), and a feather frieze. Only once owned by a man, the house can be compared with the Parminters' other pet project, up the road, called 'Point of View', a chapel and almshouses purpose-built for single women only.

Sleeping

Exeter *p393, map p394*

A **Royal Clarence Hotel**, Cathedral Yard, T01392-319955. The first English inn to use the French term 'hotel', its regal site at the very heart of the city injects a sense of history and occasion.

A **St Olave's**, Mary Arches St, T01392-217736. Intimate, characterful hotel in an elegant Georgian merchant's house with its own walled garden.

B **Hotel Barcelona**, Magdalen St, T01392-281000. Exeter's biggest surprise. A funky, Gaudi-inspired designer fantasy, in what used to be the West of England Eye Infirmary.

B **White Hart Inn**, 66 South St, T01392-279897. The genuine article. A real 14th-century coaching inn, all beams, flagged floors and dark panelled rooms.

C **Bendene Hotel**, 15-16 Richmond Rd, T01392-213526. A 5-min walk, over the iron bridge, to the cathedral. Good value, with pool.

C **Queens Court Hotel**, 6/8 Bystock Terr, T01392-272709. Recently refurbished family-run hotel, in central location, with French-style restaurant.

D **Hotel Maurice**, 5 Bystock Terr, T01392-213079. Non-smoking, family-run hotel in a quiet Georgian square.

D **Sunnymede Guest House**, 24 New North Rd, T01392-273844. Small, non-smoking guesthouse in a Grade II listed building a short walk from the centre.

F **Exeter YHA**, Mount Wear House, 47 Countess Wear Rd, Countess Wear, T01392-873329. Exeter's youth hostel is 4 miles out of the city on the way to the pretty estuary town of Topsham. Dorm beds for £11.25, rooms from £29.

F **Globe Backpackers**, 71 Holloway St, T01392-215521. Centrally located hostel, with communal TV lounge, dining area and kitchen. Dorm beds for £11.

South Devon coast *p395*

A **Combe House Hotel**, at Gittisham, near Honiton, T01404-540400. An Elizabethan manor house hotel with an exceptional restaurant and lovely quiet grounds.

A **Hotel Riviera**, The Esplanade, Sidmouth, T01395-515201, www.hotelriviera.co.uk. The grandest of the town's Regency hotels.

B **Masons Arms**, Main St, Branscombe, T01297-680300. A large pub and hotel with reasonable food in the middle of the village, thatched roof and even thatched umbrellas outside.

C **Mariner's Hotel**, The Esplanade, Seaton, T01297-20560. Good seafront option.

C **Royal York and Faulkner Hotel**, Sidmouth, T0800-220714. Considerably less expensive than the *Hotel Riviera*, but also in a good position on the Esplanade.

D **Bay View**, Trevelyan Rd, Seaton, T01297-20400. Overlooks the harbour and has reasonable rooms.

D **Glendevon Hotel**, Cotmaton Rd, Sidmouth, T01395-514028, www.glendevon-hotel.co.uk. Another good option, tucked up Glen Rd.

D **Lower Pinn Farm B&B**, Peak Hill, Sidmouth, T01395-513733, www.lowerpinnfarm.co.uk. In an excellent position on the coast road beyond Peak Hill to the west. Friendly and comfortable farmhouse accommodation.

D **Ryton Guest House**, 52-54 Winslade Rd, Sidmouth, T01395-513981. A comfortable B&B in the middle of town.

F **Beer YHA**, Bovey Combe, Beer, T01297-20296. At the top of the town, above the Pecorama gardens, 40 beds in an airy country house.

Eating

Exeter *p393, map p394*

£££ Michael Caine's, Royal Clarence Hotel, Cathedral Yard, T01392-310031. Part of the growing empire of the eponymous award-winning chef and the poshest venue in town.

£££ Thai Orchard, The Three Gables, Cathedral Yard, T01392-214215. Welcoming Thai eaterie with a good reputation, looking onto the cathedral. 5 set menus from £20.50-£26 per person, or à la carte main dishes about £8. Also cheaper set lunch menu .

££ Brazz, 10-12 Palace Gate, T01392- 252525. A tropical fish tank dominates the modern interior of this stylish brasserie-bar-café. Cheaper express menu at lunchtime.

££ Café Paradiso, Hotel Barcelona, Magdalen St, T01392-281010. A stunning contemporary space – a kind of organic, circus tent – serving a genuine Mediterranean menu. Pizzas from the wood-burning oven about £6.

£ Ask, 5 Cathedral Cl, T01392-427127. Its setting within the elegant, panelled rooms of an ancient, ecclesiastical building right next door to the cathedral gives this dependable pizza joint a real touch of class.

£ Mango's, King's Wharf, The Quay, T01392-438538 (closes at 1700). Colourful, friendly café serving sandwiches, salads, tortilla wraps, cakes, teas and breakfasts at reasonable prices.

South Devon coast *p395*

£££ The Galley, 41 Fore St, Topsham, T01392-876078. Very good fish restaurant looking out to sea downriver, quite expensive though (about £40 a head).

££ Fountain Inn, Street, just up from Branscombe, T01297-680359. Seafood and own-brew beers in a cosy and ramshackle little place, also with benches on logs outside.

£ Kingfisher, Dolphin St, Colyton, T01297-552476. A friendly local in a once-prosperous wool town, a good stop on the Seaton Tramway.

£ The Dolphin, Beer, does huge portions of fish and chips and has a little garden.

£ The Bridge Inn, Bridge Hill, Topsham, south of Exeter, T01392-873862. Excellent sandwiches, tables by the creek and rambling old rooms inside, very friendly landlord and superb real ales.

Pubs, bars and clubs

Exeter *p393, map 394*

Bar Bomba, 44 Queen St, T01392-412233. Bar Bomba has brought cocktails and lounge living to Queen St – 60 different ones from £3.95 in this Latin American Cuban Caribbean subterranean space, with a restaurant on ground level.

For an explanation of the sleeping and eating price codes used in this guide, see the inside front cover. Other relevant information is provided in the Essentials chapter, page 40.

Cohiba, South St, T01392-678455. Subdued mellow lighting make this upholstered tapas bar one for the evenings.

Double Locks, Canal Banks, T01392-256947. Hire a canoe or a cycle and head down to this very popular riverside pub, serving good food, a mile and a half away from the Quay, with the option of cruising further down the canal to the *Turf Hotel*.

The Imperial, New North Rd, T01392-434050. Grand, old mansion near the university. Very cheap drinks at the *Monday Club* and an orangery designed by Isambard Kingdom Brunel.

The Prospect Inn, The Quay, T01392-273152. Lots of different levels, nooks, crannies and fireplaces – and a fairly bogus nautical theme. The best place for a pint down on the Quay.

The Ship Inn, St Martin's La, T01392-272040. Reputedly a watering-hole of Francis Drake and Walter Raleigh, this busy, low-ceilinged pub just off Cathedral Yard still retains a certain olde-worlde charm.

Clubs and live music

The club scene is getting steadily more sophisticated, though the contrast between streetlife on Friday and Saturday nights (adolescent, alcoholic mayhem) and the rest of the week (quite quiet, really) is still marked.

The Cavern, 83 Queen St, T01392-495370. At the forefront of live music in Exeter, with a particular emphasis on punk, indie and hard rock. Also drum'n'bass Djs.

Havana, The Quay, T01392-498181. Live music, comedy and salsa in this club, which also features a mysterious blue room – a dining area serving French-style food at £5 a plate. Cuban/ Mexican flavour to the main club area.

Kino, Hotel Barcelona, T01392-281000. Non-members must arrive before 1000 to pass through the magic door into this intimate little club with subtle retro groove.

Three Fat Fish, Mary Arches St, T01392-209037. New venue for local and national live bands – and some comedy – in the evening, food and art during the day.

Timepiece, Little Castle St, T01392-493096. Specializes in a mixture of world music – reggae, arabic, salsa, African and latin, with a comedy night on Sun.

The Vaults, 8 Gandy St, T01392-203939. Predominantly gay clientele in this underground bar with regular cabaret, karaoke and theme nights.

There are also several restaurants and cafés that put on, live music performances, such as **Michael Caine's Café**, in St Martin's La, T01392-310130, and **Pizza Express**, on Cathedral Yd, T01392-495788.

Entertainment

Exeter *p393, map p394*

Cinema

The Exeter Picture House, Bartholomew St, off Fore St, T01392-430909. Has a lively bar.

The Odeon, Sidwell St, at the north end of the High St, T01392-217175.

Theatres and other arts venues

The city's premier drama venue, the **Northcott Theatre**, is on the university campus, T01392-493493, though it stages an annual outdoor show in the Rougemont Gardens. There's also **The Phoenix** art centre, Bradninch Pl, just off Gandy St, T01392-667080.

Festivals

Exeter *p393, map p394*

Jul/Aug The Exeter Fringe Festival annually from end of Jul, beginning of Aug, T01392-667080.

Aug Bishopstock Blues Festival is the biggest blues festival in the country. For more details, T01392-875220, www.bishopstock.co.uk.

South Devon coast *p395*

Aug Folk Festival, T01629-760123. Starting on the Friday before the first Mon of every Aug for a week, Sidmouth hosts this internationally famous event drawing in aficionados from all over the world, with the main events selling out.

Activities and tours

Exeter *p393, map p394*

Canoe Control, T01392-677167 or Haven Banks Outdoor Education Centre, T01392-434668 for canoeing in the Exe Estuary and other watersports. Exeter also

extends the hand of friendship to its visitors by offering a free guide service.
The Red Coats, T01392-265203, are a collection of local history enthusiasts, who share their expertise in a wide variety of daily tours conducted throughout the year, including, for instance, a catacomb experience concentrating on death and burial in the city. See the noticeboard by the cathedral for the latest details.

Transport

Exeter *p393, map p394*

Air
Exeter International Airport runs flights to **Dublin, Belfast, Guernsey**, the **Channel Islands, Toronto**, a wide variety of Mediterranean destinations, but no flights within England or Scotland.

Biycle
Saddles and Paddles, on the Quayside, T01392-424241. For hiring out bikes.

Bus
Long distance Stagecoach, run the 56 service hourly to Exeter Airport (30 mins). National Express, T08705-808080, run directly 4 times daily to **Plymouth** (1hr 5 mins), 4 times to **Bristol** (1 hr 50 mins), 8 times to **London Paddington** (4 hrs 30 mins) and directly to **Bournemouth** (3 hrs 35 mins) at 1135. Traveline, T0870-6082608, www.traveline.org.uk.

Car
Avis, 29 Marsh Green Rd, East Marsh Barton Trading Estate, T01392-259713; **Thrifty**, 2 Elm Units, Grace Rd South Marsh Barton Trading Estate, T01392-204460.

Taxi
A1 Cars, 54 Queen St, T01392-218888; Castle Cars, 81 Victoria St, T01392-436363.

Train
Virgin Trains, T08707-891234, run the services twice hourly direct to **Plymouth** (1 hr 5 mins) and regularly direct to **Bristol Temple Meads** (1 hr 15 mins). First Great Western, T08457-000125, run the hourly direct service to **London Paddington** (2 hrs 20 mins to 3 hrs). There is no direct service to Bournemouth or Exeter Airport. Exeter St Davids also connects with trains north to **Birmingham**, south into **Cornwall** and operates the Dawlish Donkey steam service to **Paignton** in the summer.

Directory

Exeter *p393, map p394*

Internet Hyperactive, 1b Central Station Buildings, Queen St, T01392-201544.
Hospitals Royal Devon and Exeter Hospital, Gladstone Rd, T01392-411611.

Torbay and South Hams

→ *Colour map 1, grid B5*

The river Exe finally finds the sea at Dawlish Warren sands, opposite Exmouth and about 10 miles south of Exeter. The sheltered east-facing coastline that then runs south from here has long been dubbed the 'English Riviera'. Although finding any similarities to the Cote d'Azur can test the imagination, its situation, temperate climate and cabbage palms probably come as close as England gets. Torquay, the capital of the region, is certainly stacked up on Hope's Nose, a headland faintly reminiscent of St Tropez, if you like, overlooking the sweep of Tor Bay to the south. It even boasts a tiny corniche road twisting down to Babbacombe Bay in the north. Down beside the seaside, Paignton is its more family-orientated neighbour, with the busiest sandy beaches, while the fishing town of Brixham nestles further south on Berry Head. This distinctive threesome adds up to the south Devon coast at its most marketed, most visited and often most congested.

West and south of Torbay, South Hams has become one of the most expensive and desirable places to live in Devon. Totnes is the capital, centre for all thinkers-with-a-difference, at the head of the wonderfully winding Dart estuary, but it's the rhomboid of pretty farmland between Dartmouth, Start Point, Salcombe and Ivybridge that has given the area its reputation for haute-cuisine and fine living. Dartmouth, across the foot ferry from Kingswear, is a naval yachting port of impeccable pedigree with a laid-back atmosphere. Salcombe is the tidiest and most picturesque of all south Devon holiday resorts. Marginally less well-known and frequented coastal treats include Bantham and Bigbury-on-Sea. » *For Sleeping, eating and other listings, see page 404.*

Ins and outs

Getting there The main express line from London Paddington to Plymouth via Exeter usually calls at Newton Abbot. Otherwise, regular services from Exeter St Davids run to Exeter St Thomas, Dawlish, Teignmouth, Newton Abbot, Torre, Torquay, Paignton and Totnes. **National Rail Enquiries,** T08457-484950. From the M5 at Exeter take the A380 for Torquay, Paignton and Brixham, the A379 for Dawlish. **Stagecoach Devon,** T01392-427711, run the No 85 bus from Exeter every 30 mins to Dawlish Warren, Teignmouth, Shaldon and Torquay. Bus No 12 links Torquay with Paignton and Brixham. There are regular bus services from Newton Abbot to Totnes. **Tally Ho!,** T01548-853081, run service 164 7 times a day between Totnes and Kingsbridge.

Getting around Regular local **bus** services make it easy to hop around Torbay, although these too can get caught up in holiday traffic. A bicycle would be the best bet, although the rolling roads can be punishing on Shanks's pony. The Dawlish Donkey is a hop-on, hop-off steam train that runs from Exeter to Paignton in Aug during the week, T0871-8714119, departing Exeter at 0935 and 1440, arriving at Paignton (calling at Dawlish Warren, Dawlish and Torquay) at 1050 and 1545. Unfortunately a car is the most efficient way of exploring South Hams, and if there weren't as many of those, then a bike would be much more fun. The tiny lanes between Dartmouth, Kingsbridge and Salcombe are often quite dangerous for cyclists in summer.

Information **Teignmouth TIC** ⓘ *The Den, T01626-215666.* **Dawlish TIC** ⓘ *The Lawn, T01626-215665.* **Torquay, Vaughan Parade** ⓘ *T01803-297428, www.theenglishriviera.co.uk.* **Paignton TIC** ⓘ *The Esplanade, T01803-55383.* **Brixham TIC** ⓘ *The Old Market House, The Quay, T01803-852861.* **Totnes TIC** ⓘ *The Town Mill, Coronation Rd, T01803-863168. Open all year.*

Around Torbay

A ferry ride away across the mouth of the Exe from Exmouth, or a couple of miles south of Exeter by road, **Powderham Castle** ⓘ *T01626-890243, www.powderham.co.uk, Apr-Oct Mon-Fri, Sun 1000-1730, £6.45, under-16s £2.95, concessions £5.95, family £15.85,* is the rambling ancestral home of the Earl of Devon. In the late 18th century, long before the scandal surrounding Oscar Wilde, it was here that William Beckford met the aesthetic 13-year-old William Courtenay, with disastrous effects on both their social lives. William Courtenay's refined taste is preserved in the domed music room of the castle, which today is also a full-on visitor attraction, complete with pet's corner, miniature railway, and medieval jousting. There are beautiful views of the Exe from the Belvedere in the woods.

Another very different stately home can be found 8 miles southwest at **Ugbrooke** ⓘ *Ugbrooke House, T01626-852179, www.historichouses.co.uk, mid-July to early Sep Tue, Wed, Thu, Sun, bank holidays 1300-1730, £5, under-16s £2.* The seat of the powerful Catholic family of Cliffords, it looks like a little toy fort, remodelled by Robert

Adam in the 18th century, with a sumptuous chapel attached. The homely interior contains some remarkable portraits (including one of the rebellious Duke of Monmouth), tapestries and furniture and the lakeside grounds were laid out by – you guessed it – Capability Brown, now a little spoiled by the dual carriageways close by.

On the coast 6 miles directly east, Dawlish is a dignified retirement resort, famous for the steam train the **Dawlish Donkey** that puffs along the prom in the summer. Passengers are likely to be on their way to **Teignmouth** (pronounced *Tinmouth*), which Keats found very much to his liking in 1818. Today it's still quite a charming seaside town, with a pier, working harbour and the cliffside tranquility of Holcombe next door.

Torquay

Torquay is the epitome of suburbia-on-sea, immortally lampooned by John Cleese's bitter, bigoted, and frustrated hotelier in one of TV's best sitcoms *Fawlty Towers*, but still providing holidays to remember for thousands each year. Cleese no doubt drew inspiration from the town's most famous resident, Agatha Christie, who died in 1976 and lived at Ashfield House. Before her time, the great Irish playwright Sean O'Casey settled on these mild shores and even before that, William of Orange landed here in 1688 to begin the bloodless Glorious Revolution. Today the resort boasts lots of language schools, and all the usual seaside amusements, with that added frisson of class. On a warm summer evening, the twinkling lights and cafés around the harbour are just about Riviera enough. Apart from the exceptionally clean beaches, the town's other attractions include **Torre Abbey** ⓘ *T01803-293593, www.torreabbey.co.uk, Apr- Oct daily 0930-1800 (last admission 1730), Nov-Mar Mon-Fri by appointment, £3, under-16s £2,* with its 20 historic rooms, stunning paintings and Victorian tearooms and monastic remains, small Agatha Christie room with some of her personal belongings including her typewriter, and nightgown. Not too far from here is **Kent's Cavern** ⓘ *T01803-215136, www.kents-cavern.co.uk, Apr-Oct daily 1000-1630, £5.70, under-15s £3.60, family £17,* a cliff railway leads down to Babbacombe beach, open by guided tour, with geological and archaelogical explanations, in candlight and every other type of light, taking about 45 mins at a constant 11 degrees centigrade. Real Agatha Christie fans won't want to miss the **Torquay Museum** ⓘ *T01803-293975, www.devonmuseums.net/torquay, Mon-Sat 1000-1700 Apr-Oct also Sun 1330-1700, £3, £2 concessions,* with much more information (although less genuine artefacts than at Torre Abbey), in the Agatha Christie gallery, as well as a few BBC costumes, and from Kent's Cavern the oldest remains (31,000 years old to be precise) of modern humans in Britain. There's also an entertaining Devon farmhouse gallery.

Paignton and Brixham

Just down the road from Torquay, Paignton is the jolly one, with candy floss, toffee apples and crazy golf, and also very clean beaches. Brixham, beyond the caravan parks at Goodrington, is still a working fishing port, though a very polite one, with seafood restaurants galore and a busy yachting marina. This is where Napoleon was expected to arrive after his defeat at Waterloo, off Berry Head. Four miles to the south, **Coleton Fishacre** ⓘ *(NT), T01803-752466, Mar Sat, Sun 1100-1700, Apr-Oct Wed-Sun 1030-1730. £5, under-16s £2.50, family £12.50,* was designed in 1925 for the D'Oyly Cartes, the impressarios responsible for Gilbert and Sullivan. The house is a good example of the Arts and Crafts style, but is most famous for its luxuriant 25-acre exotic gardens thriving in their mild south-facing situation. They include a formal pool garden, and wild flower walks winding down to the sea. Delicate plants flourish in the microclimate here.

South Hams

Totnes and around

Totnes, 5 miles west of Paignton, is the centre of New Age and alternative thinking in the Southwest. 'Strange Listings' of events and courses can be picked up at the museum on the High St. A pretty town, overlooked by its redbrick church and old castle sitting on the top of the hill, its steep High St has a formidable history. Next to a shop called *Forever England* (and next door too to the *House of Gifts*) is the **Brutus Stone**, commemorating the landing of King Brute, descendant of Aeneas, here in 1170BC according to Geoffrey of Monmouth. A right turn just beyond leads onto the Ramparts Walk, and good views round the Castle. The *Riverside Café* near the ferry port on Steamer Quay is always busy during the summer with people enjoying the river trip down to Dartmouth, and riverside walks opposite the famous Baltic Boatyards run downriver into open countryside. On the other side of the river, a little 75p ferry leaves from the *Steampacket Inn*, taking you up to the steam railway, one of the most popular in England: **the South Devon Railway** ⓘ *T0845-3451420, mid-Mar to Oct*, from Totnes to Buckfastleigh, on the edge of Dartmoor, calling at Staverton on its way along the banks of the Dart.

A mile from Staverton, **Dartington Hall** has beautiful terraced gardens dotted with sculpture, and has been a centre for the arts since 1925 when it was bought by the Elmhirsts. They also set up the scandal-rocked liberal public school where people like Bertrand Russell, Barbara Hepworth, Ben Nicholson, Jacob Epstein and the Freuds sent their kids. **High Cross House**, an inspiring piece of Bauhaus architecture, designed in 1936 by William Lescaze, now mounts exhibitions from the Elmhirst's art collection.

Dartmouth

Nine miles by riverboat, 16 by road from Totnes, Dartmouth is a photogenic yachting centre, with quaint eateries and B&Bs in abundance, and it's also the home of the prestigious **Royal Naval College**. Designed by Aston Webb, also responsible for Admiralty Arch on Trafalgar Square and the front of Buckingham Palace, the College looks down on the little harbour from a commanding position on the hill above. The **Butterwalk** is a Caroline half-timbered building that now houses the local history museum. Higher Street is also very picturesque, leading up to Ridge Hill and **Newcomen Lodge**, where the town's most famous son, Thomas Newcomen, developed an atmospheric steam engine in 1712.

Salcombe and around

Salcombe, 17 miles south of Totnes on the A381, is a very desirable and well-established little resort, on a picturesque estuary, with cafés overlooking the water, and even a Park and Ride. Three miles west inland, **Buckland** is a sweet little thatched village tucked away down narrow lanes, near Bantham on the sea. From here an estuary walk skirts the Avon for 9 miles, a way of crossing the river when the ferry is out of action (mid-Apr to Oct). **Bantham** itself is a string of whitewashed and dark green thatched cottages leading up the main street, to the estimable *Sloop Inn*.

West to Plymouth

On the main A379 to Plymouth, **Modbury** is a typically charming South Hams town, in a steep little valley near **Flete House**. This grand Victorian oak-panelled country house bears comparison to Castle Drogo on Dartmoor for its early-20th-century take on medievalism. At **Bigbury-on-Sea**, a sandy beach looks out towards the *Burgh Island Hotel*. Designed in 1929 in pure Art Deco style, facing the mainland, it was visited in its time by Noel Coward and Agatha Christie, and was also the location for John Boorman's first film *Catch Us If You Can* as well as a recent BBC adaptation of Christie's *Evil Under the Sun* (see below).

Sleeping

Torbay *p400*

L **The Imperial Hotel**, Torquay, T01803-294301. Top of the range in Torquay and worth the expense for the superior ambience.

B **Gabriel Court Hotel**, a couple of miles from Paignton, T01803-782206. Perfect seclusion with an Elizabethan garden near Stoke Gabriel on the river Dart, 4 miles or so from Totnes and Brixham.

B **Nonsuch House**, Church Hill, Kingswear, T01803-752829. Overlooks the mouth of the Dart, with balconies and en suite bathrooms.

C **Mulberry House**, 1 Scarborough Rd, Torquay, T01803-213639. Rooms above an excellent dinner restaurant.

D **Belmont** 66 Belgrave Rd, Torquay, T01803-295028. Good value.

D **The Garlieston Hotel**, Bridge Rd, Torquay, T01803-294050. Friendly, family-run guesthouse with 5 en suite rooms, 10 mins walk from the sea behind Torre Abbey.

D **Leicester House** 2 Winterbourne Rd, Teignmouth, T01626-773043. A reliable B&B in a tall Victorian house overlooking the sea.

South Hams *p400*

L **Burgh Island Hotel**, Bigbury-on-Sea, T01548-810514. Restored in the 1980s by fashionistas, it's now a somewhat expensive trip down memory lane at £260 per night including dinner (1930s black tie requested). It's worth stopping for a cocktail in the bar.

B **The Sloop Inn**, Bantham, T01548-560489. Does excellent bar meals and also has rooms that need to be booked well in advance during high season.

C **The Dolphin Inn**, Kingston, near Bigbury, T01548-810314. Has 3 small rooms above a flowery pub in a pretty flowery village.

C **Gara Rock Hotel**, T01548-842342. Isolated on the southern tip of South Hams, not far from upmarket Salcombe.

C **Tally Ho!**, Littlehempston, near Totnes, T01803-862316. Antiques and low beams, very good Brixham fisherman's pie and 4 en suite bedrooms, open all year.

F **YHA Salcombe**, Sharpitor, Salcombe, T01548-842856 On the National Trust Overbecks property with lovely gardens and coastal views, 51 beds, popular with families and always very busy in summer.

Eating

Torbay *p400*

££ **The Crown and Sceptre**, 2 Petitor Rd, St Marychurch, Torquay, T01803-328290. A good real ale pub that does fresh pub grub high up above Petitor beach.

££ **Nobody Inn**, Doddiscombsleigh, T01647-252394. A popular pub in the middle of nowhere with famous food and wines.

££ **Remy's**, 3 Croft Rd, just up the hill off Belgrave Rd, Torquay, T01803-292359. 3 courses of good French food for £18.75.

South Hams *p400*

£££ **The Carved Angel**, 2 South Embankment, Dartmouth, T01803-832465. Has one of the most rated menus in South Hams served up overlooking the estuary (about £40 a head).

£££ **Clare's**, 55 Fore St, Salcombe, T01548-842646. Absolutely fresh fish in cheerful surroundings for about £30 a head.

£££ **The Galley**, 5 Fore St, Salcombe, T01548-842828. More very fresh local fish in a very straightforward seafront café (about £30 a head).

£££ **Oyster Shack**, Millburn Orchard Farm, Stake Hill, near Bigbury-on-Sea, T01548-810876. Views towards Burgh Island and again, very good seafood (about £25 a head).

££ **Church House**, Rattery, South Brent, T01364-642220. Claims to be the oldest pub in the country, apparently connected to the church by a tunnel. Has real ales.

££ **Church House Inn**, Harberton, near Totnes, T01803-863707. Another very ancient old pub, oak-panelled and serving up fresh local food.

££ **The George Inn**, Main St, Blackawton, T01803-712342. A friendly village pub with exceptionally good beer.

££ **Maltsters Arms**, Tuckenhay, near Totnes, T01803-732350. Another waterside pub on a tributary of the River Dart, also with Brixham fish on the menu.

££ **Mill Brook**, Southpool, near Kingsbridge, T01548-531581. Right on the waterside with reliable food.

Plymouth and Dartmoor

➔ *Colour map 1, grid B4*

Devon's biggest city, in a strategic setting overlooking Plymouth Sound, is even more dramatically bound up with the navy, the sea and seafaring than Portsmouth, its great naval rival on England's south coast. Epic arrivals and departures from the Sound characterize its long history, and like mercantile Liverpool, it was the launchpad of the British Empire. It too was heavily bombed during the Second World War but its subsequent redevelopment has been marginally happier than the others'. The city centre is divided by a long wide strip of lawn running south up to the Hoe which, with its superb views and memorable sense of place, is top of most visitors' list of places to visit. A 10-minute walk to the east, beneath the massive Royal Citadel, the Barbican is the oldest part of the city and site of most of its tourist attractions, including the Mayflower steps and the excellent National Marine Aquarium on Coxside.

The last wilderness in the country, a mineral-rich moorland 1500 ft above sea level, the largest expanse of granite upland in the country, the biggest open space in the south of England, Dartmoor is about 200 bleak and lonely square miles between Plymouth and Exeter, the source of the Dart, the Tavy, the Taw, the Plym and the Teign rivers. It's a chilling landscape is surrounded by sweet little villages nestling in green valleys, very different though from Exmoor, its little neighbour to the north. Dartmoor's most famous characteristic – along with Her Majesty's prison, the ghosts, bogs and 'letterboxes' – are its distinctive Tors, stumpy granite towers left behind during the last Ice Age. ▸▸ *For Sleeping, eating and other listings, see pages 410-412.*

Ins and outs

Getting there **Plymouth Airport** is about 4 miles north of the city centre on the Tavistock road. T0345-222111. Regular direct **trains** from London Paddington take 3-3½ hours. There are also direct services to South Wales, the Midlands, the North and Scotland. Plymouth train station is about half a mile north of the city centre, at the top of Armada Way, a mile from the Hoe and Barbican. Plymouth, Exeter and Newton Abbot are the closest mainline rail stations to Dartmoor. Okehampton can be reached by train on a branch line from Exeter on Sun. **Wessex Trains** to Crediton on the Tarka Line from Exeter to Barnstaple. **National Rail Enquiries,** T08457-484950. Plymouth is about 3½ hours-4 hours (240 miles) from London down the M5 to Exeter and then the A38. Leave London west on the M4 and continue for around 110 miles, join the M5 at junction 20 and take that southwest for around 80 miles, join the A38 after Exeter continue south for around 37 miles. Head into town on the A374. This route is usually at least ½ hour quicker than the M3/A303 route which saves you around 15 miles in distance. **National Express,** T08705-808080, run a Rapide luxury coach service taking about 4½ hours. Other services take 4 hours 40 minutes – 6 hours 25 minutes. Most go via Heathrow Airport. **Traveline,** T0870-6082608. ▸▸ *For further details, see Transport, page 412.*

Getting around The Hoe and city centre are fairly compact and can be explored on foot. Local **buses** are run by **Plymouth Citybus,** T01752-662271/222221, and **First Western National,** T01752-402060. No 25 bus service runs a circular route from Plymouth railway station, along Royal Parade, through The Barbican, over The Hoe and past Plymouth Pavilions. There are many 'Pay and Display' car parks in the city centre but, owing to limited parking available in the Barbican area, it's a good idea to leave your vehicle in the multi-storey car park at Coxside and walk across the lock gates. Park & Ride facilities are available at Coypool (near Marsh Mills roundabout) and at Milehouse (follow the signs to Plymouth Argyle). For walkers, a surprising amount of Dartmoor is accessible by bus. **Traveline,** T0870-6082608, or Devon County Council publish annually an excellent *Discovery Guide to Dartmoor by Bus and Train*, available from most National Park and Tourist Information Centres. **DevonBus**, *T01392-382800*.

Information Plymouth TIC ⓘ *Island House, The Barbican, T01752-304849, www.plymouth.gov.uk. Mon-Sat 0900-1700, Apr-Oct also Sun1000-1600*. The main Dartmoor National Park headquarters is at **High Moorland Visitor Centre** ⓘ *Old Duchy Hotel, Princetown, Yelverton, T01822-890414, www.dartmoor-npa.gov.uk. Apr-Oct daily 1000-1700, Nov-Mar 1000-1600*. Other information centres can be found at: **Newbridge** ⓘ *T01364-631303, Easter-end Oct 1000-1700, and winter weekends 1000-1600*, **Postbridge** ⓘ *T01822-880272, Easter-end Oct 1000-1700*, **Haytor** ⓘ *T01364-661520, Easter-end Oct 1000-1700*. A good range of leaflets on walks in the entire surrounding area is available at these offices and the following TICs. **South Dartmoor TIC** ⓘ *Leonards Rd, Ivybridge, T01752-897035*. **Okehampton TIC** ⓘ *Museum Courtyard 3, West St, T01837-53020*. **Tavistock TIC** ⓘ *Town Hall, Bedford Sq, T01822-612938*. All are open all year round but have reduced opening times in winter.There are **Community Information Points** in the smaller towns around the moor: **Moretonhampstead CIP** ⓘ *11 The Square, T01647-440043*. **Ashburton** CIP ⓘ *Town Hall, T01364-652142*. **Buckfastleigh CIP** ⓘ *The Valiant Soldier, 80 Fore St, T01364-644522. Easter-Oct*. **Dartmoor Military Firing Range** ⓘ *T0800-4584868, www.dartmoor-ranges.co.uk*, for firing times. **Forestry Commission** ⓘ *Bullers Hill, Kennford, Exeter, T01392-832262*.

Plymouth

History

Originally a small village called Sutton, Plymouth grew up around Sutton harbour, which the Barbican's old buildings overlook to this day. The first record of a ship weighing anchor here was in 1211, almost a century before Edward I's fleet set off for France to begin the 100 Years' War. Henry VI granted the town of Plymouth a charter in 1440 and the Barbican was built in 1572. Five years later Sir Francis Drake set off in the *Golden Hind*, circling the globe before his return in 1579. Nine years on he was vice admiral of the fleet that took on the Spanish Armada, famously only after he had finished his game of bowls. In 1620 the 120 so-called Pilgrim Fathers headed west in the *Mayflower* and established the Massachusetts Bay Colony. Some of them overnighted before in Island House, 9 The Barbican, now the TIC, still recognizably a Jacobean house. Plymouth held out for Parliament during the Civil War that followed, surviving a three-year siege by the Royalists, resulting in the construction of the intimidating Royal Citadel on the Hoe by Charles II when he was restored to the throne. In 1768, James Cook set sail to find Australia in the *Endeavour* from here and less than a century later Plymouth was to become a major embarkation point for emigrations and deportations. Between the wars, Sutton Harbour became a major fishery and in 1921 Ernest Shackleton departed on his final voyage to the Antarctic from here. More recently, in the 1980s, the Falklands Task Force followed in his wake.

Sights

The Hoe, a stirring place to contemplate the death of Empire, is where Drake insisted on finishing his game of bowls as the Armada sailed up the channel. His statue stands here still, hand jauntily on hip, surrounded by a host of other naval greats and less-than greats, an obelisk commemorating the death of Queen Victoria's grandson at Pretoria stands out, beyond the Regency café. But not as surely as the former Eddystone lighthouse, **Smeaton's Light**, with its revamped interactive exhibition on the history of the Hoe inside. Next door is the **Plymouth Dome** ⓘ *T01752-600608*, daily 0900-1700, which tells the city's history in a gimmicky, interactive way. More enticing probably is the fairground that occupies the Hoe each summer. In the centre of the city, **St Andrew's Church** was badly bombed, but its restored windows by John Piper repay a visit. Dominating the Hoe and the city as a whole, the **Royal Citadel** ⓘ *guided tours May-Sep Tue 1430, £3 bookable through the TIC*, is home to 292 Commando Regiment Royal Artillery. They also give superb views and the old chapel is worth seeing, to which all are welcome for morning service every Sunday at 1115.

Otherwise, the main attractions are clustered around the **Barbican**, from where the Pilgrim Fathers set sail in 1620, commemorated by a dinky little Greek arch, erected in 1934. Here skippers tout for trade like market criers for boat trips round the Sound. The latest visitor attraction to arrive on the Barbican is the **Plymouth Mayflower** ⓘ *T01752-306330, Apr-Oct 1000-1800 (last admission 1730), Nov-Mar 1000-1700 (last admission 1630), £3.50, child £1.50, joint ticket with Aquarium £10, child £5*, an illustrated account of the city's history on three floors, with excellent views over the old harbour from the top. A short film, model ships (of the *Mayflower* and *Golden Hind*), a treasure chest, Jacobean pottery and interactive graphic panels are among the things on display.

On Coxside, across a swing bridge (access possible daily 0730-2000) and lock gate from the Barbican, in a large glass-front building, is the city's lottery-funded asset, one of the best and certainly the biggest, aquariums in the country. The **National Marine Aquarium** ⓘ *T01752-600301, information line T01752-220084, www.national-aquarium.co.uk, 1000-1800 (last entry 1700), £8, under-16s £4.50, concessions £6.50, family £22, joint tickets including admission to the Plymouth Mayflower Exhibition are*

Plymouth

also available (see above), boasts Europe's deepest fish tank, holding two and a half million litres of water, and home to an enormous number of fish, including sharks and seahorses. Various other water-based habitats are also displayed, from the Dartmoor stream to offshore reefs, and at feeding time the excitement is palpable. » *For Sleeping, eating and other listings, see pages 410-412.*

Dartmoor

Okehampton

Okehampton, a solid-looking place, is the main town on the north of the moor, 24 miles west of Exeter on the A30. **All Saints** parish church stands in the middle of the High St, and the ruins of a Norman castle can be found on its western outskirts, but the town has never been prosperous enough to build a market place. Next door to the TIC, an understanding of the way life was once led on the moor can be gained at the **Museum of Dartmoor Life** ⓘ *West St, T01837-52295. Easter-Oct Mon-Sat (also Sun Jun-Sep), 1000-1700, Nov-Easter by appointment Mon-Fri.* It has the usual information panels, artefacts and sound recordings and also a working waterwheel, in a Georgian mill, next to the *Victorian Pantry Tea Rooms*, T01837-53988.

Northeast Dartmoor

Okehampton is also an army town, with a large base on the edge of the Okehampton Common, servicing the **Ministry of Defence firing ranges** that occupy most of northeastern Dartmoor. These desolate restricted areas provide some of the very best yomping country. They are always accessible in the summer and in fact very rarely closed for live firing (contact the free information line above to check). **Yes Tor**, the highest point in the National Park, is one of the most popular destinations for a serious ramble. Not far away is the **source of the Dart** and several other rivers, **Cranmere Pool**, a notorious bog in one of the most remote and inaccessible stretches of the moor. This was also where the first 'letterbox' was placed by James Perrott of Chagford in 1854.

The rolling half-wooded hills east of here, strung with stone walls and beech hedges, could hardly be a greater contrast to the open moor. Buffalo roam, within their enclosures of course, near **Cheriton Bishop**, and just to the south, an Edwardian cornershop baron, Julius Drew, founder of Home and Colonial Stores, discovered his ancestral roots. **Castle Drogo** ⓘ *(NT), Drewsteington, T01647-433306, Apr-Oct Mon-Thu, Sat, Sun 1100-1730, garden open daily all year 1030-dusk, £5.90, under-16s £2.90, gardens and grounds only £3, under-16s £1.50,* was the result, disappointingly small because unfinished when building work stopped in 1930, but remarkable for being an early-20th-century mock-medieval castle of solid granite with an extremely comfortable fully electrified country house inside. Lutyens was also responsible for the interior, adding amazing Italian glass chandeliers (carefully adapted to carry electric bulbs instead of candles) in the elegant green-panelled drawing room and a very complicated shower system in the bathroom. Outside there are great views over the surrounding woodland, a beautiful rose garden and a large circular croquet lawn (which can be used on application to reception) surrounded for privacy by a thick green hedge and some bright red benches.

Moretonhampstead, 3 miles southeast, is an attractive stone-built village, the 'Gateway to the High Moor' and indeed easily the most scenic approach to the National Park from the east and Exeter on the B3212. Along with the slightly more-out-of-the-way **Chagford**, its neighbour 3 miles to the northwest, these two large unspoiled villages are the last outposts of refined civilization before the moor begins. Moretonhampstead has more pubs, some interesting 17th-century arcaded granite almshouses and a church in a glorious position, its 15th-century tower visible for miles around. Chagford is slightly smarter, tucked away down leafy lanes. It has a popular open-air swimming pool and walks up to the pine wooded Fenworthy Reservoir on the edge of the High Moor.

The Moor

One of the most popular National Parks, and one of the earliest to be given that status, in 1951, walking is the way most people choose to enjoy Dartmoor. Free-range rambling on foot, preferably well-equipped with a good map and hiking boots, covers almost half its area (see page 412). The blanket bog, upland oakwood, caves and mines are natural habitats of tremendous ecological significance, home to a huge variety of flora and fauna, many almost invisible, including endangered species like the southern damselfly, marsh fritillary butterfly and blue ground beetle. The landscape is also amazingly rich in archaeological remains.

From Moretonhampstead the B3212 continues its lonely way southwest on to the moor itself. A tin rush occurred in the middle of the 12th century along this road, which is famously haunted by the 'hairy hands'. They suddenly grab motorbike handlebars and car steering wheels, so it's best not to exceed the 40 mph speed limit. Two miles past the **Miniature Pony Centre**, a haven for the diminutive Dartmoor breed, a small road on the left leads to **Grimspound**, one of the finest remains of a Bronze Age settlement in the country. The places where 24 huts would have stood can be seen, in a 4-acre enclosure surrounded by a low stone wall. The site can usefully be compared with the gravemounds near Chagford at Shoveldown and especially the other Bronze Age settlement at Merrivale (see below), which also has some impressive standing stones.

The B3212 rolls on over the bare land to **Postbridge** (3 miles), passing the isolated *Warren House Inn*, the third highest pub in England with a fire in the grate that has been burning for almost 130 years. On the distant moors opposite, four walled enclosures in the shapes of a suit of playing cards were apparently dropped by a certain Jan Reynolds riding with the Devil. Postbridge is a tiny one-horse town, distinguished by its impressive 13th-century granite clapper bridge. A left turn here leads to the hamlet of **Bellever**, a good jumping-off point for walks along the East Dart river.

Three miles further on, the tree-clad settlement of **Two Bridges** is the crossroads at the heart of the High Moor on the West Dart. Not much to look at, although the

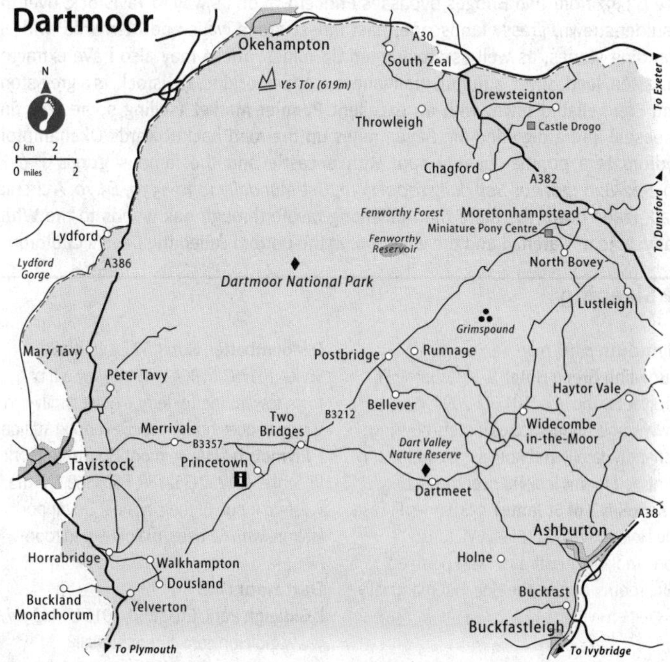

 smart *Two Bridges Hotel* provides congenial refreshments. A left turn onto the B3357 runs the 4 miles into **Dartmeet**, a delightful but very popular spot where the East and West Dart rivers come together, surrounded by the extensive **Dart Valley Nature Reserve**. A choice of small roads beyond leads either to Buckland in the Moor, where the 10 commandments are inscribed on a rock high above the sinful cluster of thatched cottages beside the river, or to Widecombe-in-the-Moor.

Widecombe-in-the-Moor has been immortalized in Devon's anthem *Tom Pearce*, who has a grey mare (of ghostly origin) that's required to reach Widecombe Fair with "Bill Brewer, Jan Stewer, Peter Gurney, Peter Davey, Dan'l Whiddon, Harry Hawke, old Uncle Tom Cobleigh and all!" It's no surprise then that this is the most popular village in Dartmoor. A green and very picturesque oasis, its beautiful Perpendicular church tower is a reassuring landmark seen across the eastern moor. The Devil had a hand in this too, apparently, pulling it down one stormy night in 1638, killing four people and injuring others. A poem in the church by the local schoolmaster at the time records the event. Outside, **Church House** (NT) is a quaint 16th-century building that has been a brewhouse, almshouse and is now the Village Hall.

Back on the B3212 at Two Bridges, the road continues for a mile and a half into **Princetown**, the grey, hard-bitten and gloomy capital of the moor, where the main National Park Information Centre is based, before carrying on to **Yelverton**. The atmosphere in Princetown emanates entirely from the **prison** and its situation, constructed in 1809 by French prisoners of war, out of solid granite, and used as an overflow for the prison hulks in Plymouth Sound during the war with America. It became a convict prison in the mid-19th century, and still houses about 700 low-risk criminals. There's a small **museum** ⓘ *T01822-890305, Apr-Oct Tue-Sat 0930-1630, Nov-Mar 0930-1230, 1330-1630 (last admission 30 mins before closing), £2, under-18s £1,* on its history, in the old stables, with chain-gang leg-irons and a mock-up cell, which hardly does much to lift the spirits.

Tavistock to Lydford

The B3357 from Two Bridges bypasses Princetown on its way to Tavistock, over the boulder-strewn, grassy landscape, past mossy stone walls and **Merrivale**, with its standing stones, as well as abandoned tin mines. These may also have extracted tungsten, lead, silver, sulphur, manganese, copper, or zinc. Tavistock, is a grey-stone and crennellated town, with an excellent **Pannier Market** (selling some very fine cheeses) and a dignified air. Seven miles up the road back towards Okehampton, Lydford is a popular beauty spot with a castle and the famous **gorge** ⓘ *(NT), T01822-820320, Apr-Sep daily 1000-1730, Oct-Mar daily 1030-1530, £3.70*. A circular walk leads down the more than mile-long ravine through oak woods to the **White Lady**, a 30 m waterfall and the whirlpool at the bottom called the Devil's Cauldron.

Sleeping

Plymouth *p406, map p407*

C **Bowling Green Hotel**, 9-10 Osborne Pl, Lockyer St, The Hoe, T01752-209090, www.smoothhound.co.uk/hotels/bowling. A friendly, family-run hotel with comfortably furnished rooms looking over the Hoe.

D **Berkeley's of St James**, 4 St James Pl East, The Hoe, T01752-221654. A Victorian non-smoking guesthouse with plush en suite rooms, also on the Hoe, but marginally less expensive.

D **Mountbatten Hotel**, 52 Exmouth Rd, Stoke, T01752-563843. A little way out of town toward the Tor ferry, a quiet family-run Victorian guesthouse near Devonport station.

F **Plymouth YHA**, Belmont House, Belmont Pl, Stoke, T01752-562189, F605360. On the western fringe of the city, near Devonport station, with 62 beds, mainly 4-bed rooms.

Dartmoor *p408*

L **Gidleigh Park**, Chagford, T01647-432367, www.gidleigh.com. Internationally renowned mock-Tudor country house boutique hotel, with 15 luxurious rooms and celebrity West Country chef Michael Caines' menu in the restaurant (about £60 a head, needs booking in advance).

A Holne Chase Hotel, Two Bridges Rd, Ashburton, T01364-631471. Country house hotel with 16 rooms in a former hunting lodge, 5 or 6 miles outside Ashburton. Accomplished restaurant about £45 a head.

A The Horn of Plenty, Gulworthy, Tavistock, T01822-832528. Great views over the Tamar valley and inventive food.

B Lydgate House, Postbridge, T01822-880209, www.lydgatehouse.co.uk. In a superb location beside the East Dart River, a small award-winning non-smoking country house hotel with 7 rooms (bathroom en suite).

C Castle Inn, Lydford, near Oakhampton, T01822-820242. Close to the White Lady waterfall and the Devil's Cauldron, local cheeses and home-made soups on the menu.

C Cherry Brook Hotel, Two Bridges, T01822-880260, www.cherrybrook-hotel.co.uk. Right in the middle of the moor, between Two Bridges and Postbridge, also with 7 cosy bedrooms (bathroom en suite).

C Church House Inn, Holne, near Ashburton, T01364-631208. Organic food on the menu and views over the moor from a good pub in the middle of a small village. Comfortable rooms.

Quarter of a mile outside Widecombe-in-the-Moor are a couple of good B&B options, book well ahead for high season:

D Brookside, Lustleigh, T01647-277310. Nice B&B option.

D East Wray, Lustleigh, T01647-277338. Good B&B.

D Higher Venton Farm, Widecombe, T01364-621235, with 2 double rooms, 1 twin, in a thatched longhouse, as well as 2 double rooms next door.

D Little Meadow B&B, T01364-621236, Widecombe, an attractive clapperboard house.

F Bellever YHA, near Postbridge, T01822-880227, F880302. Right in the middle of the moor, with 38 beds.

F Okehampton YHA, Klondyke Rd, Okehampton, T01837-53916, F53965. With 102 beds in a converted railway goods shed.

F Steps Bridge YHA, near Dunsford, near Exeter, T01629-592707 (for bookings more than a week in advance), T01647-252435, F252984. With 24 beds in a variety of rooms in a chalet in the Teign Valley on the edge of East Dartmoor.

Camping

F Cockingford Farm, T01364-621258, allows you to camp for £2.50 a night.

F YHA Camping Barns (to be booked on T01200-420102) at Runnage (2, on a working farm near Bellever Forest and the River Dart), at Houndtor (near Manator, and Widecombe, in a former farmhouse with 2 upstairs sleeping galleries), at the Fox and Hounds (near Lydford, with a pub next door), at Lopwell (on the banks of the Tavy not far from Plymouth), and at Watercombe (with bunk beds, close to Cornwood on the southern tip of the moor).

Eating

Plymouth *p406, map p407*

£££ Chez Nous, 13 Frankfort Gate, T01752-266793, does highly rated French food in slightly run-down surroundings near the Theatre Royal, for about £40 a head.

££ Thai Palace, 3 Eliot St, The Hoe, T01752-255770. An efficient, tasty Thai restaurant.

£ Café Emmaus, a little café below the Hoe.

Dartmoor *p408*

£ Mountain Inn, Old Church La, Lutton, near Cornwood, Ivybridge, T01752-837247. Fish and chips and good beer.

£ Rugglestone Inn, Widecombe-in-the-Moor, T01364-621327. Open fires and stone floors as well as home-cooked food and lots of dogs.

Pubs, bars and clubs

Dartmoor *p408*

The Cleave, Lustleigh, T01647-277223. Thatched pub on the edge of Dartmoor.

Drew Arms, Drewstaignton. A fine old pub where they still pass beers through the hatch.

Peter Tavy Inn, T01822-810348, near Tavistock,convenient for walks onto the moor.

The Rock, Haytor Vale, T01364-661305. Is a locals' local with good beers and a garden.

Warren House Inn, Postbridge, T01822-880208. Has had a fire burning continually for 129 years, with pool table. It's the third highest in England, 1425 ft above sea level, close to the King's Oven prehistoric entrance grave.

Activities and tours

Dartmoor *p408*

Climbing

Shilstone Rock Stud, near Widecombe-in-the-Moor, T01362-621281.

Cycling

The Granite Way on an old railway line runs from Okehampton to Lydford, part of the Devon Coast to Coast Cycleway.

Tavistock Cycles, Paddons Row, Brook St, Tavistock, T01822-617630. Cycle hire.

Okehampton Cycle Hire, Bostock Garden Centre, Okehampton, T01837-53248.

Letterboxing

Letterbox 100 Club, 1 Dryfield, Exminster, Exeter, T01392-832768. Membership available after collecting 100 stamps.

Walking

Rambler's Association (Devon), Mrs EM Linfoot, 14 Blaydon Cottages, Blackborough, Cullompton, www.ramblers.org.uk.

Riding

British Horse Society, Dartmoor Representative: Mrs Radford, T01364- 631287.

Survival in the Wild Weekend, near Exeter, T01799-526526. £119 per person per weekend.

Swimming

Open-air swimming pool, Chagford, T01647-432929. May-Sep daily 1400-1900.

Transport

Plymouth *p406, map p407*

Air

Direct flights to Plymouth airport, T0345-222111, from **London Gatwick**, **Bristol**, **Cork**, **Newquay**, **Paris**.

Boat

Britanny Ferries, T08705-360360, to and from **Santander** and **Roscoff** embark and arrive at Millbay Docks, a mile and a half west of the city centre and the Barbican, overlooked by the West Hoe. (Regular bus service via the city centre to the train station.) Children under 4 years of age travel free. **Cremyll Pedestrian Ferry**, T01752-822105, operates from Admiral's Hard (off Durnford St, Stonehouse) to **Mount Edgcumbe Park** in Cornwall. A ferry timetable may be purchased at the Cremyll Tollgate. **Plymouth Boat Cruises**, T01752-822797, operate boat trips from Plymouth Barbican, also linking with the Tamar Valley Line trains. The **Torpoint Ferry**,T01752-812233, is a regular and frequent car and pedestrian ferry service operating between Torpoint and **Devonport**.

Car

Thrifty, 20-28, Cattedown Rd, Cattedown, T01752-210021; **Sixt Kenning**, 11 Regent St, T01752-221860.

Taxi

Tower Cabs, 138 North Rd East, T01752-252525; **Central Taxis**, Wolseley Rd, T01752-363636.

Train

Plymouth Railway Station is on the main London-Penzance railway line. **First Great Western** provide a frequent service throughout the day and an overnight sleeper to **London Paddington** while **Virgin Trains** operate through cross-country services to major cities in the **Midlands**, the **North of England** and **Scotland**. Wessex Trains operate the Tamar Valley Line to destinations such as **Gunnislake**, **Callington**, **Cotehele House**, **Morwellham Quay**. These services operate from Devonport, Dockyard, Keyham and St Budeaux stations as well as Plymouth station. On Sun in the summer, special trains along the Tamar Valley Line link with a planned network of buses at Gunnislake to give access to **Dartmoor** and beyond. For details of the Tamar Valley Line in general T01752-233094.

Directory

Plymouth *p406, map p407*

Communications **Internet**: Fab Electronics, 50 Armada St, Greenbank, T0870-0756256. **Medical facilities** Glenbourne Hospital, Morlaix Rd, Derriford, T01752-763103.

North Devon coast

→ *Colour map 1, grid A3/5*

Apart from the tourist hotspots at the seaside resort of Ilfracombe and pickled cliffside fishing village of Clovelly, the North Devon coast just about continues to remain unspoiled although hardly undiscovered. It's a wonderland of sweeping sands, crumbling cliffs, tiny roads and wild rocky headlands. Ilfracombe gives a good taste of what's in store with its crazy coastal scenery, while Woolacombe and Croyde are the original English surfers' beaches. Barnstaple is the staid and slightly bewildered market town at the heart of the region, wondering how to keep up with arty Bideford and its little neighbour Appledore. From both Bideford and Ilfracombe boats run out to Lundy Island, famous for its occasional glimpses of puffins but also a day trip for a walk. Boats also go to Lundy from Clovelly, but most visitors are content to struggle up and down its impossibly photogenic main street, awestruck by how quaint a singularly sited fishing village in private hands can be. Beyond Clovelly, the Hartland peninsula is one of the best places in Britain to get lost in. Head any way towards the setting sun and you'll end up on a dramatic nub of granite butting the Atlantic. ▸▸ *For Sleeping, eating and other listings, see pages 416-417.*

Ins and outs

Getting there The Tarka Line, run by **Wessex Trains**, T08456-000880, reservations on T0870-9000773, covers 39 exceptionally scenic miles between Exeter and Barnstaple, every couple of hrs or so, taking just over an hr, and passing through Crediton and small villages like Umberleigh, Eggesford, Morchard Road, Copplestone and Newton St Cyres en route. National Rail Enquiries, T08457-484950. By road, the quickest way of reaching Barnstaple, Bideford and the north coast between Lynton and Ilfracombe is via junction 27 on the M5 to Tiverton and then the A361. The A39 is a beautiful but congested route from Bridgewater (junction 24 on the M5). Barnstaple is about 4 hrs from London by car by the former route, about 5 by the latter. ▸▸ *For further details, see Transport, page 417.*

Getting around Barnstaple is the hub of the bus network in the area, with regular services to Ilfracombe and Bideford, fewer out to Hartland. Many of the buses are run by First in Devon, T01271-376524. Good bus maps and guides can be obtained from Devon Bus, T01392-382800. Cycling is a very good option round the coast and in Hartland.

Information **Barnstaple TIC** ⓘ *36 Boutport St T01271-375000.* **Bideford TIC** ⓘ *The Quay, Kingsley Rd, T01237-477676. Ilfracombe TIC, The Seafront, T01271-883319.* **Lynton TIC** ⓘ *The Town Hall, Lee Rd, T01598-752225.* **Woolacombe TIC** ⓘ *The Esplanade, T01271-870553.*

Lynton to Barnstaple

From the Valley of the Rocks, a mile west of Lynton, the **South West Coast Path** winds past the leafy combes and secret coves of Woody Bay towards the beauty spot of **Heddon's Mouth**, full of large round pebbles, some way below the peaceful wooded seclusion of the **Hunter's Inn**. Four miles further west, the overgrown village of **Combe Martin** nestles in a valley with a view of the sea, a popular family seaside spot where silver was once mined. The kids might well enjoy a day at **Watermouth Castle** ⓘ *T01271-863879, www.watermouth.com, Easter-Oct phone for times, £7, under-16s £6,* a little toy fort of a house with an adventure theme park attached just up the hill near the pretty village of Berrynarbor. Nearby on the coast, **Watermouth Cove,** where Enid Blyton set some of her *Famous Five* stories, is a charming sheltered little cove with a safe beach.

Ilfracombe and around

A couple of miles to the west, Ilfracombe, the largest, busiest and most chaotically situated resort on the north Devon coast, spreads itself out over a confusion of low cliffs, beaches and bays looking out to sea. A Victorian and Edwardian resort of considerable note, today, with its bluffs, hidden beaches and big seabirds, it looks like the perfect setting for a B-movie. Carefully tended allotment gardens stretch up quiet wooded slopes on the approach, before the town suddenly gets into its stride on the bustling narrow High Street, surrounded on all sides by the crumbling Victorian boomtown architecture that gives the place its faded English charm. A walk up bald **Capstone Hill** on the seafront beyond the pepperpot cones of the Landmark Arts Centre and TIC will clear the head and give uninterrupted views of the town's peculiar layout behind its old Promenade, little harbour and the sea. The holiday spirit is strong here in summer, and also more innocent than the seaside resorts in south Devon. Old-timers looking to escape the crush for more tranquility head for the old Quay and boat trips round the bay or out to Lundy island (see below) on *MS Oldenburg* (tickets from TIC or the office on Ilfracombe pier T01271-863636), families make for the rockpools on the **Tunnel Beaches**, gaining access thanks to Welsh miners who burrowed through the cliffs from the Bath House in the late 19th century. The whole town goes mad for old times during the **Victorian Celebrations** in the middle of June, dressing up in crinolines and bonnets. **Ilfracombe Museum** ⓘ *T01271-863541, Apr-Oct daily 1000-1730, Nov-Mar Mon-Fri 1000-1230, £1.50, concessions £1, under-16s 50p,* close to the Landmark Arts Centre, is a collector's paradise, an extraordinary array of odds and ends from days gone by in an old laundry house. As well as a Lundy Island display, here be clocks, hats, bells, bats, shells, chandlery as well as a pickled two-faced kitten, a two-headed gosling and a four-legged chicken in the natural history section.

The very fine **Torrs Walk** zigzags through impressive coastal scenery (NT) west of Ilfracombe to the much smaller resort at **Lee**, famous for its fuschias and also the sweet secluded Lee Bay, reached via the Lee Abbey Toll road (50p cars).

Nearby, 1½ hours' worth of working Collie dogs going head-to-head with woolly sheep while falconry action rages overhead can be enjoyed near the village of **Mortehoe** at the **Woolacombe Working Sheepdog and Falconry** ⓘ *Borough Farm, Jul Thu, Aug Wed, Thu at 1800, £2.50, under-16s £1.* Displays are given by the sheepdogs that have been immortalized in the bestselling amateur video *Year of the Working Sheepdog* as they brave the local cliffs in an Atlantic gale.

Woolacombe

Round the promontory of Bull Point and Rockham Bay, Woolacombe's sandy beach stretches for almost 3 miles south. Half close your eyes and the breakers heading onto the sweep of the bay could almost be pounding on Laguna Beach. Very popular with surfers as well – the first full-time surf hut in England was established here in the 60s – who head for the Putsborough end of the beach, it never seems that crowded even though surrounded by holiday homes and camping parks spread around the *Bay Hotel*. Woolacombe Beach Huts can be hired, each with a table, four chairs and a windbreak, bookable in advance, T01271-870234. Round the promontory of Baggy Point to the south, little **Croyde Bay** is the place the surfers go when Woolacombe won't deliver.

Barnstaple

Nine miles east of Croyde, past the 4-mile wide expanse of Saunton Sands, Barnstaple is the region's market town, a pleasant enough place spoiled by too much traffic, at the head of the Taw Estuary. With an ancient history stretching back to the foundation of Wessex, in the ninth century it was the most westerly port in Alfred's kingdom and continued to prosper after being fortified by the Normans and later traded with the Americas. The impressive remains of its role as a marketplace can be seen in the centre of town at the **Pannier Market** and along Butcher's Row, although the shops and markets themselves are a bit tired. Queen Anne's Walk, an 18th-century colonnade housing a heritage centre complete with laughable costumed mannequins, is along the riverside on The Strand, near the old Castle Quay. There's not much else to keep visitors here long, most using the town as a convenient base for exploring the area inland and along the coast.

Lundy Island

Ins and outs

Getting there Departures on *MS Oldenburg* March to December various days, T01271-863636, from Bideford usually between 0800 and 1000, from Ilfracombe usually 1000 or 1030, arriving back at either between 1800 and 2100. Sailing time just under 2 hours. £25 day return, £12.50 under-16s, £4 under-4s, family £60. Period return £40, under-16s £21. Also the *Jessica Hettie* sails April to October, Wednesday, Thursday from Clovelly £22.50 return, T01237- 431042 www.clovelly-charters.ukf.net.

Information Lundy Shore Office ⓘ *The Quay, Bideford, T01237-470422. Lundy Island T01237-470074, www.lundyisland.co.uk.* Short stays available on the island March to June, September to December through **Landmark Trust** ⓘ *Shottesbrooke, Maidenhead, Berkshire, T01628-825925, www.landmarktrust.co.uk.*

Sights

A flattened granite outcrop 3 miles long and half a mile wide, 10 miles north of the Devon coast, windswept Lundy Island sits in the middle of the Bristol Channel like a giant petrified whale. Boats run out to it regularly in summer from Ilfracombe, Bideford and Clovelly. Inhabited by about 30 people, as well as lots of seabirds, rabbits, Soay sheep and a herd of Sika deer, it's owned by the National Trust and run by the Landmark Trust, who maintain and let the small amount of delightful but quite pricey self-catering and B&B accommodation. The island's own ship, *MS Oldenburg*, carrying its capacity of 267 passengers in the summer, makes regular day trips most months of the year. On arrival at the jetty on the very southern tip of the island, a fairly steep climb up past the lighthouse arrives at the main settlement, gathered around the *Marisco Tavern* (see below). Day trippers usually have about 5 or 6 hours to spend on the island: admiring the strange rocks on the coastline, looking hard for puffins (only a good idea in June when these colourful burrowing birds breed on the west coast) and just enjoying the fresh air. The island has a long history of piracy and later, comfortable respectability, which it pretty much still maintains thanks to the restrictions on access. No dogs allowed either.

Bideford to Hartland

Seven miles southwest of Barnstaple is its great maritime rival, Bideford. Marginally more picturesque, and smaller, it was described by local novelist Charles 'Water Babies' Kingsley as the "the little white town". It once owed its prosperity to its 27-arch medieval bridge over the River Torridge. Walter Raleigh first landed tobacco here. Trips to Lundy (see above) can be taken aboard *MS Oldenburg*, while next door to Victoria Park is the **Burton Art Gallery** ⓘ *Kingsley Rd, T01237-471455, www.burtonartgallery.co.uk, Apr-Oct Tue-Sat 1000-1700, Sun 1400-1700, Nov-Mar Tue-Sat 1000-1600, Sun 1400-1600,* an interesting space for temporary exhibitions, with the local history museum on the first floor.

Further upriver, the little fishing village of **Appledore** is a surprising delight: a kind of mini St Ives in north Devon, with an arty but unpretentious atmosphere, its pretty little harbour feeding small boats into the mouth of the Torridge where it meets the Taw. On the opposite bank, near Instow, **Tapeley Park Gardens** ⓘ *T01271-860528/342371, Easter-Oct Mon-Fri, Sun 1000-1700, £4, under-16s £2.50, concessions £3.50,* are an Italian garden created by the architect Sir John Belcher in the 19th century, with a walled vegetable garden, curious shell grotto, ornamental terraces lined with lavender and fuschia, a variety of other gardens and a lake surrounded by ancient evergreens. Beautiful views over the estuary on the walk to a newly designed labyrinth and monument too.

Clovelly, 12 miles west of Bideford on the A39, must be one of the most photographed villages in Britain. A privately owned and immaculately preserved fishing village that tumbles down a steep gorge on a wooded hill to a tiny harbour, it's a rivulet of cobbles, dinky cottages, and tearooms trickling between gently crumbling russet cliffs. Really only for the very sweet-toothed, it nonetheless has to be seen to be believed. And thousands do want to do just that, despite the entry fee (£4) charged at the the **Clovelly Visitor Centre** ⓘ *T01237-431781, www.clovelly.co.uk, daily 0930-1730*, at the top of the hill. After the crowds have toiled up and down the single main street, 'up-along' and 'down-along' as it's called, and headed home, the *Red Lion Hotel* right on the tiny quayside really comes into its own, as do the peaceful walks along the cliffs and the Hobby Road. Despite being a museum, Clovelly is still alive, with a lifeboat station (T01237-431781), fishing and boating trips to Lundy, donkeys dragging provisions or carrying children up and down, residents and visitors enjoying the two hotels in the evenings. The Long Walk leads up to **Clovelly Court**, the home of the Rous family who own the place, with a fine Victorian kitchen garden. ⓘ *Apr-Sep 1000-1600*. From here too, **Angel's Wings** provides a romantic clifftop walk through tangled old woods with glimpses of the sea below to Gallantry Bower, a sheltered and spectacular viewpoint.

About 7 miles south of Clovelly, near the village of West Putford, the **Gnome Reserve** ⓘ *T0870-8459012, late Mar-Oct daily 1000-1800, £2.45, under-16s £1.90,* is an epiphany to little people made of clay. More than 1,000 of the blessed garden ornaments are dotted around 2 acres of beech woodland. Visitors get a gnome hat to get into the spirit, and there's also a labelled wild flower garden.

West of Clovelly, some of England's most beautiful and rugged coastal and inland scenery stretches out towards **Hartland Point**. The town of Hartland itself seems to be pretty much stuck in another era, a peaceful enclave of whitewashed houses with lead roofs. A mile to the west, in a beautiful sheltered valley about a mile from the rugged Atlantic coast, **Hartland Abbey** ⓘ *T01237-441264/441234, www.hartlandabbey.com, Apr-Sep Wed, Thu, Sun, bank holidays (also Tue in Jul and Aug) 1400-1730, gardens only Apr-Oct Mon-Fri, Sun 1400-1730,* is an unexpected oasis of ordered calm. The mock-medieval house stands on the site of an Augustinian priory founded in the mid-12th century and the last to be dissolved, given by Henry VIII to his wine keeper. A lovely mile-long wooded walk leads down to the sea.

Sleeping

Lynton to Barnstaple *p413*

A Saunton Sands Hotel, near Braunton, T01271-890212. Lively hotel with smallish rooms but 4-star facilities, including a heated outdoor pool, health club, babysitting and a private path to the beach, with magnificent views over the sands from its terrace.

C Broomhill Art Hotel, Muddiford, near Barnstaple, T01271-850262, www.broomhillart.co.uk. Small country house hotel with a heated swimming pool, in a wooded valley with a sculpture park. Dog friendly.

C Greyven House, 4 St James Pl, Ilfracombe, T01271-862505. Cosy place close to the harbour and TIC.

C Headlands Hotel, Beach Rd, Woolacombe, T01271-870320, www.headlands-woolacombe.com. Beautiful situation overlooking the beach and coast.
C Huxtable Farm, West Buckland, near Barnstaple, T01598-760254, www.huxtablefarm.co.uk. 16th-century working farmhouse 5 miles east of Barnstaple, with local produce on the table.
C Lyncott House, 56 St Brannock's Rd, Ilfracombe, T01271-862425. Comfortable non-smoking Victorian guesthouse close to Bicclescombe gardens.
C Seapoint House, The Esplanade, Woolacombe, T01271-870439. Apartments within a stone's throw of the sea.
D Bradiford Cottage, Halls Mill La, Bradiford, near Barnstaple, T01271-345039, www.humesfarm.co.uk. Little old cottage in a quiet out-of-the-way village, just outside Barnstaple towards Braunton.

Bideford to Hartland *p415*
C Golden Park, Hartland, near Bideford, T01237-441254. 17th-century farmhouse with sea views and walled garden, 3 bedrooms with en suite bathrooms.
C Hartland Quay Hotel, Hartland, T01237-441218. Sweet family-run hotel in a spectacular position overlooking the spume-ridden waves.
C Red Lion, Clovelly, T01237-431781, www.clovelly.co.uk. Comfortable accommodation right by the harbour, with good food.
D Camberley Guest House, Beach Rd, Woolacombe, T01271-870231, www.camberleybandb.co.uk.
F Ocean Backpackers, 29 St James Pl, Ilfracombe, T01271-867835. One double room (£30) with 38 beds, £10 a night, and a cheap restaurant and a late bar.
F Camping Barn at Mullacott Farm, Ilfracombe, bookings T01200-420102.

Eating

Lynton to Barnstaple *p413*
££ Hunters Inn, Heddon's Mouth, near Parracombe, T01598-763230. A good place for a pub lunch in a secluded wooded spot with peacocks roaming in the gardens.
££ Pyne Arms, East Down, near Barnstaple, T01271-850207. Flower-filled tubs in the garden and good food on the table in a low-ceilinged pub.
£ Rolle Quay, Rolle's Quay, Barnstaple, T01271-345182.
£ Corner House, 108 Boutport St, Barnstaple, T01271-343528. Popular working-men's local with decent bar snacks and unspoilt interior.

Lundy Island *p415*
££ Marisco Tavern, Lundy, T01237-431831. The only pub on the island, and luckily it's a good one, with a garden and traditional filling pub grub, ideal after a bracing day hunting puffins. Booking office for Lundy Island: T01237-470074.

Activities and tours

Lynton to Barnstaple *p413*
Horseriding
Woolacombe Riding Stables, Eastacott Farm, T01271-870260, www. Woolacombe-ridingstables.co.uk.

Surfing
Surf South West, Croyde Bay, T01271-890400, www.surfsouth west.com. Apr-Oct daily 1030-1230, 1330-1530. Half day £20, full day £40, mid-week special (5 lessons) £85. **Surfseekers Surf School**, Woolacombe Bay, T07977-924588.

Transport

Bideford to Hartland *p415*
Bicycle
Bideford Bicycle Hire, Torrington St, East the Water, Bideford, T01237-424123. **Torridge Cycle Hire**, The Station, Torrington, T01805-622633, Mar-Oct 0915-1700. £9 full day.

For an explanation of the sleeping and eating price codes used in this guide, see the inside front cover. Other relevant information is provided in the Essentials chapter, page 40.

Cornwall

England's far southwestern corner, Cornwall is as Celtic as Britanny. A sainted, holy place, it was Christian long before the rest of England, buzzing with missionaries from Ireland and Wales, and today still possesses a proudly independent spirit, a significant and surprisingly serious separatist movement mustering under its black and white banner and nurturing the Cornish language. But it also has the lowest income per capita in the country, and in parts remains severely depressed, something which the yearly influx of holidaymakers, most heading west determinedly for the sea, only goes some way towards alleviating. Quite apart from the instability of the tourist trade generally, the popularity of certain areas of the peninsula with visitors, especially in July and August, threatens to rob them of any magic. The north Cornish coast has the busiest beachlife and harbours: the Arthurian mysteries of Tintagel, the gourmet's haven at Padstow on the Camel estuary, and Newquay, the full-on surf capital of the UK. In the middle of the county squats the bare granite wastes of Bodmin Moor, sliced in half by the A30, but surrounded by amazingly luxuriant gardens. Now easily the most famous of them is the Eden Project, an extraordinary 21st-century redevelopment of a disused clay pit into a spectacular greenhouse. The south coast nearby is worth exploring for its more traditional gardens and tiny little harbour villages. Further west, Falmouth and the Lizard repay a visit for their mild climate and coastal scenery. Arty St Ives sets the tone for the Penwith Peninsula, which peters out at Land's End with a notorious visitor attraction hailing the 'Relentless Sea'. Some 30 miles beyond, the Isles of Scilly are a delightful little subtropical archipelago where our Bronze Age ancestors went to bury their dead in the path of the setting sun.

North Cornish coast

→ *Colour map 1, grid A3-B2/3*

The continuation of the superb North Devon coast to the south and west into Cornwall is one of the most spectacular stretches of the South West Coast Path. Sure it's had its fair share of ill-advised developments, bungalows and fixed caravan parks, but the cliffs and beaches between Bude and Newquay keep hikers and surfboarders happy throughout the long season. Bude is the typical north Cornish seaside resort, flanked by wonderful surfing beaches at Sandy Mouth and Widemouth, both better for beginners on the board than overcrowded Newquay to the south. Boscastle is the most picturesque fishing village on the coast, owned by the National Trust like much of the treasured coastline along here, and very busy in summer. Crowds and coaches also make for Tintagel, legendary birthplace of King Arthur, but out of season the dramatic situation of this ruined coastal castle should satisfy the most demanding romantic. On the Camel Estuary, the only large river to meet the sea in north Cornwall, the medieval harbour town of Padstow has been given a new lease of life by TV chef Rick Stein, whose restaurants draw people down from London. And the arrival of low-cost airfares to Newquay looks set to boost that resort's already booming reputation for being up for it – surf culture and Ibizan nightlife that is. ▸▸ *For Sleeping, eating and other listings, see pages 423-424.*

Ins and outs

Getting there Ryanair fly daily to Newquay from Stansted, T0871-2460000, www.ryanair.com. Newquay Airport, T01637-860600, is about 15 minutes from town with regular buses run by **Summercourt Travel**, T01726-861108. Barnstaple is the closest train station, on the Tamar Valley line from Exeter. Padstow can easily be reached by bus from Bodmin Parkway (4 hours from London Paddington), on the main line to Penzance, and a branch line runs out to Newquay (5-6 hours). **National Rail Enquiries**, T08457-484950. By road, Hartland Point and the north Cornish coast remain one of the most remote and inaccessible destinations in the southwest. The only express routes by road involve either the A361 via Barnstaple from the Tiverton exit on the M5, or the A30 and A3079 via Holsworthy, joining the A39 at Bude. Either way will take a good 5 hours from London. Padstow is about 15 miles from the main M5/A30 route, 4 hours from London on a very good day, Newquay a little further on the same route. **National Express**, T08705-808080, run daily services to Bude from London Victoria, via Exeter (7 hours) and to Newquay (7 hours) direct once a day.

Getting around **First Western** run a good network of buses around the North Coast to places like Tintagel and Bude from Truro, Bodmin, Okehampton, Plymouth, and Exeter, but covering any distances, will require patience.

Information **Tintagel Visitors' Centre** ⓘ *T01840-779084. Apr-Oct 1000-1700, Nov-Mar 1030-1600 daily.* **Padstow TIC** ⓘ *The Red Brick Building, North Quay, Padstow, T01841-533449, www.padstow.uk.com, Apr-Oct 0930-1700, Nov-Mar Mon-Fri 0930-1700.* Accommodation booking service £3. **Newquay TIC** ⓘ *Marcus Hill, T01637-854020, www.newquay.co.uk. Accommodation booking service £3.50. There's also a state-of- the-surf information line, T09068-360360 (60p a min).*

Bude and Boscastle

Morwenstow, the most northerly village in England's most southerly county, lies a mile from the impressive coastal scenery of the **Sharpnose Points**, Higher and Lower. The village itself is immortally associated with one of the Anglican church's most eccentric vicars, the Rev RS Hawker, who tirelessly buried the local shipwrecked dead around his Norman church here (against the custom of burying them on the beach) between 1834 and 1875. A friend of Tennyson, he would retire to Hawker's Hut, a bothy he made for himself on the cliff from ship's timbers, to smoke opium and have visions, after visiting his flock with his pet pig. He also decorated his vicarage with chimneys in the shape of his favourite church towers and erected the figurehead of the wrecked *Caledonia* in the graveyard.

South of Morwenstow, as far as Tintagel, Cornwall's Atlantic coast provides one of the country's finest walks along a particularly inspiring stretch of the **South West Coastal Path**. **Sandy Mouth** beach (NT) gets the ball rolling, a 3-mile long surfer's delight but easily big enough for everyone to enjoy. At its southern end sits Bude, quite a sweet Regency seaside resort, developed but not ruined, with donkey rides on the prom and peace and quiet only a short walk away. Except that here the Atlantic rages higher and harder than anywhere else in Cornwall, apparently audible up to 10 miles away. The town straddles a little estuary, flanked by superb cliffs, looking out over miles of sand at low tide.

Even more popular with surfers is Widemouth Bay, 3 miles to the south. Pronounced *Widdymuth* but true enough to its name anyway, it gives a good mile of steady breakers. Widemouth is fairly heavily commercialized though, so those looking for a less rowdy spot press on for 5 miles or so round Dizzard Point to **Crackington Haven** (NT). With a teashop, a few pubs and a little sandy beach (also with reliable surf) tucked behind the Cambeak headland, the place has also long been a favourite with crusties, campers and alternative types. Even more seclusion can be found just south at the **Strangles**, a lovely beach with no facilities and quite tricky to reach down a 500-ft drop from the clifftop but worth the effort to find weird rock formations and sea arches.

About five miles south, **Boscastle** is a National Trust village that was once a delightful little harbour town and the main point of embarkation for Delabole slate. A bit overwhelmed by tourism these days, nothing can detract from its extraordinary position wedged into the valley of the Valency like a miniature Norwegian fjord. It's worth walking out beyond the pretty thatched riverfront and stone harbour onto the sea slates for the impressive views of the coastline north and south. If the tide is right, near here the blow-hole called the **Devil's Bellows** may be rumbling and throwing up spray. A mile or so up the valley, Thomas Hardy worked as a young architect on the tower of the church at **St Juliot's** and turned his experience into material for his novel *A Pair of Blue Eyes*, calling the village Endelstow. Hardy also married the leader of the church choir, Emma Gifford.

Tintagel and around

ⓘ *Tintagel Castle (EH), T01840-770328. Late Mar to mid-Jul and Oct daily 1000-1800, mid-Jul to Aug daily 1000-1900, Nov-Mar daily 1000-1600. £3, concessions £2.30, under-16s £1.50. Special evening events at 1800 on Wed in Jul and Aug. Introductory talks daily during the summer.* The 4-mile **clifftop walk** from Boscastle to Tintagel has often been described as one of the finest in England. No surprise that it's popular then, especially as its passes through **Rocky Valley** just north of Tintagel, but in part the sentiment must have something to do with the destination and the peculiar place that Tintagel occupies in the English imagination. Arthur is the name of the game here. The village's single street takes the commercialization of the legendary King to the heights of tack. But then again it can't escape the fact that no one comes here to see the village. The spectacular ruins of the 14th-century cliffside castle and thin neck of land leading out to the 'island' rock are the main event and would be worth a trip even if they weren't believed to be the birthplace of King Arthur. A crumbling battlemented wall runs up the sheer 300-ft headland and on the other side of the chasm, the mystical spot itself, **Arthur's Castle** perched on a rock battered by the sea. This is where his father Uther Pendragon is supposed to have seduced Queen Igraine, with help of the magic of Merlin, whose **Cave** roars in the waves down below. It's also where the tragic lovers Tristan and Isolde are buried, according to the poet Swinburne, just one of the literary greats to have been inspired by Malory's *Morte d'Arthur* and Geoffrey of Monmouth's imaginative 12th-century *History of Britain*, if not by Tintagel itself. In high summer, the popularity of the place and bright sunshine can undermine the mystery, but at any other time the atmosphere seems absolutely appropriate to England's Dark Age warrior king and his gallant knights. The Norman court that inspired so many of the details of the romance can most easily be summoned up in the church of **St Materiana** perched on the clifftop a short distance away, with its altars, candles, round arches and tiny windows.

Other sights in the village of Tintagel itself include **King Arthur's Great Halls**, an extraordinary building constructed out of solid granite in 1933 by Masonic-style enthusiasts, with some exceptional stained-glass windows, and the **Old Post Office** ⓘ *(NT), T01840-770024, late Mar-Oct daily 1100-1730 (-1600 in Oct, Nov), £2.30, family £5.70,* a wonderfully weathered stone cottage dating from the 14th century, with one of its rooms restored to its role as a Victorian post office.

A mile or so south of Tintagel, the beautiful sandy beach at **Trebarwith Strand** is reached over wonderful stream-gouged rocks and delightful paddling pools, overlooked by a few beach shops, teashops and holiday homes. Lovely walks head up into the woods round about. After 5 miles the coast path south arrives in the little fishing village of **Port Isaac**, renowned for its crab and lobster catch but worth avoiding in high season when visitors clog the narrow streets. Nearby **Port Quin** is similar, but less commercialized. The sad little Gothic tower on **Doyden Point** close by commemorates the loss of the Portquin boat with all hands.

Also very busy in summer, but this time with surfers and their sport, is the seaside resort of **Polzeath** just round the spectacular lonely headland of Pentire Point. From their fine position at the foot of the Pentire peninsula, the holiday homes of Polzeath look down on the wide curve of the bay where cars pull up on the beach in their hundreds much of the year, wet-suited boarders running for the breakers to escape the

Walks in Cornwall

- **Bedruthan Steps**: 2 miles there and back. Start: Trenance, car park on the B3276. A spectacular section of the South West Coast Path above massive slate cliffs and caves. OS Maps: Explorer 106, Landranger 200.
- **South Cornish Coast**: 2 mile circle. Start: Pencarrow, 4 miles west of Polperro. A walk out onto the dramatic triangular headland, with wide views along the coast east and west. OS Maps: Explorer 107, Landranger 201.
- **North Cornish Coast**: 6 miles one way. Start: Coombe village, 4 miles north of Bude. Nature trails wind through wooded valleys to the coast, and north past Morwenstow to Henna cliff. OS Maps: Explorer 126, Landranger 190.
- **Lizard**: 4 miles one way. Start: Kynance Cove, off the A3083 between Helston and Lizard. A bracing walk along the cliff tops to Mullion Cove. Loe pool is another 5 miles further on. OS Maps: Explorer 103, Landranger 203.
- **St Anthony-in-Roseland**: 7 mile circle. Start: Froe Creek, near Gerrans off the A3078. A walk around the temperate coastline of Roseland via Towan Beach. OS Maps: Explorer 105, Landranger 200.

crowds and join their own. A charming coast path leads round to **Trebetherick**, where the pet poet of Middle England John Betjeman is buried in the graveyard of the old church of St Enodoc, half-buried itself in the sand. **Daymer Bay** here is another good spot for surfing. A mile further, strung along the Camel estuary looking across to Padstow (see page 422), connected by foot ferry, the village of **Rock** has become known as 'Fulham-on-Sea' thanks to the influx of second-homers from London.

Bodmin Moor

Inland, east of Tintagel, the wide tract of bleak granite upland that comprises Bodmin Moor is surrounded by surprisingly beautiful gardens. At **Pencarrow House** ⓘ *Washaway, T01208-841369, Apr-Oct Sun-Thu, £6,* there are 50 acres of woodland around this little stately home with a world-renowned parkland of specimen conifers. Formal gardens designed by Sir William Molesworth boast many varieties of rhododendrons and camellias. From the house one views geometric gardens with a fine turf maze, Victorian rockery from Bodmin Moor, palm trees and peacocks fanning their tails. Pencarrow, in its unpretentious grandness, makes for a leisurely and gracious day out. Much better known, **Lanhydrock gardens** ⓘ *Lanhydrock (NT), near Bodmin, T01208-73320, £7 house and garden, £3.90 garden and grounds only, Duchy of Cornwall Nursery, T01208-872668,* feature formal parterres surrounded by yew and box and unusual circular herbaceous borders, designed in 1857, as well as some exceptional magnolias. This is also the grandest house in Cornwall, so a house and gardens visit could make for a lovely afternoon combined with a stop at the **Duchy of Cornwall Nursery** which is only a couple of miles away for shrubs, trees and perennials. Nearby, towards Lostwithiel in the valley of the River Fowey, **Restormel Castle** ⓘ *(EH), T01208-872687, Apr-Sep daily 1000-1800, Oct daily 1000-1700, £2, under-16s £1,* is a remarkable Norman castle, much of its extraordinary circular keep still standing and in very good condition. Once the home of Edward, the Black Prince, its commanding position on a round wooded hillock gives fine views across the countryside around. On Bodmin Moor itself, **Dozmary Pool** is considered to be the most likely spot to find Excalibur and the Lady of the Lake, if you fancy looking. Otherwise, there are moorland walks to be had all around. A little to the south, the church in the little town of **St Neot** is worth travelling to for its magnificent stained glass, telling the story of Adam and Eve.

Cornwall for the Cornish...

'After you've rinsed the glus-dyns out of your mouth with dowr, you might feel like taking a tollgar down to the treth through fields full of woolly davas' . Apologies to Mebyon Kernow – the Cornish separatist party – for the attempt at Cornglish, but then they're likely anyway to have more important matters in hand than cleaning their teeth for a taxi ride to the beach through the sheep fields. The Cornish language, closely related to Breton, belongs to the family of Celtic tongues of which Irish Gaelic remains the most robust member. Like Scottish Gallic, it flourished until the 17th century, when a combination of official repression and local snobbery contributed to its decline. Unlike the Gallic, by the late 19th century it had died out completely as a native tongue, although the scholastic efforts around that time of one Henry Jenner ensured its survival. What is now called Standard Cornish was developed in the last century under the guidance of Morton Nance. More information on learning the language and contributing to its revival can be found at www.clas.demon.co.uk.

Meanwhile, Cornish separatists are gaining growing support for their vision of a self-governing county, a backlash against perceived ignorance of the area's economic plight in Westminster. The possibility of a devolved assembly for the region is in fact being discussed, in English.

Padstow and around

Back on the crowded coast, across the Camel Estuary from Rock, Padstow is a busy fishing and holiday harbour town, made famous and apparently almost single-handedly kept in business by TV-chef Rick Stein. People still travel for miles to eat in one of his several fish restaurants here. Others are happy just to wander around the old streets sloping down to the harbourside or pick up some absolutely fresh shellfish when the boats come in. The **National Lobster Hatchery** ⓘ *T01841-533877, May-Aug daily 1000-1800, Sep-Apr 1000-1600, £1.50, under-16s £1,* on the quayside opens its doors to visitors interested in the farming and life-cycle of the delicious things with tasty pincers. Named after St Petrock, who came over from Ireland in a coracle, Padstow provided sanctuary for criminals before the Reformation and was once packed with shrines to saviour saints. **St Petrock's,** the town church on the hill, is the only one to survive, its 15th-century tower resting on a 13th-century base. Just outside Padstow, **Prideaux Place** ⓘ *near Padstow, T01841-532411, Easter-late Apr, late May-Oct Mon-Thu, Sun 1330-1700, £5, under-16s £2,* is a small Elizabethan house in a superb position overlooking the estuary. Modified in the 18th century, with attractive gardens, it's been in the hands of the same family for the last 400 years and has become a popular film location. It's also where Humphrey Prideaux, Dean of Norwich in 1702, wrote a Life of Mahomet. At **Trevone Bay,** near St Cadoc's Point, the shoreline is full of intriguing rock pools with a rare population of sea slugs.

Newquay and around

South along the coast road from Padstow, the 3-mile stretch of sand at Watergate Bay is a good place to learn to surf and introduces the capital of surf culture in the UK at Newquay. Although it does have a tiny harbour, Newquay has been pretty much taken over by the sport and its enthusiasts and has the biggest and busiest beaches in Cornwall. Once a fairly quiet family holiday resort, it now imitates Ibiza-style nightlife, can easily be reached on a cheap flight with Ryanair, and milks youth culture for all its worth. **Watergate and Fistral Bays** are the most popular beaches for the sport, at either end of the scale in difficulty, Fistral particularly unpredictable in the challenges it throws up. Special surfing areas operate here from mid-May to September, 1000-1800. The **Extreme Academy** on Watergate Bay has won a reputation for reliable instruction in way-out ways to enjoy the beaches, from kite-surfing to mountainboarding to land-yachting. Most of the locals only return or come out of their houses in winter, while a huge number of B&Bs and guesthouses compete ever more fiercely for the passing trade throughout the year. Best of the beaches is **Lusty Glaze**, a naturally sheltered privately run cove, with exceptionally high water quality and headquarters of the National Lifeguard Training Centre.

Five miles inland, the proud Victorian town of **St Columb Major** could hardly be more different. Much less affected by the tourist industry, the grand buildings of this hilltop town have remained largely unspoiled, clustered around a 15th-century church overlooking the wonderfully green Vale of Mawgan. One oddity near here is the **Japanese Garden and Bonsai Nursery** ⓘ *T01637-860116, www.thebonsainursery.com, Apr-Oct daily 1000-1700, Nov-Mar 1000-1630, £3.50,* in St Mawgan Village, based on an actual Zen garden, it's an acre and a half of Japanese maples, azaleas, abundant grasses, bamboo and a 'teahouse', with a Bonzai nursery next door.

A couple of miles to the west of St Columb Major, **Castle-an-Dinas** is a great Iron Age hill fort, while the **Nine Maidens**, also worth a visit, are an ancient stone avenue beneath a wind farm on the Breock Downs to the northwest. **Trerice** ⓘ *(NT), Kestle Mill, Newquay, T01637-875404, £4.50 house and gardens,* is a very popular gem of an Elizabethan house and garden with a fruit orchard. Its gold and purple colour scheme bursts into full bloom in the summer.

Sleeping

Bude and Boscastle *p419*

C **Manor Farm**, Crackington Haven, Bude, T01840-230304. Lluxury in an 11th-century manor house a mile inland from the sea. Prearranged dinners where guests meet in the drawing room for drinks and proceed together for their meal (£25 per person). Dress smart.

C **St Gennys House**, St Gennys, Bude, T01840-230384. Tucked in a spring-fed woodland, a long driveway leads to this former 16th-century vicarage with Georgian additions. Views straight onto the sea and sandy beaches. Secluded, comfortable and idyllic.

C **Trerosewill Farm**, Paradise, at the top of Boscastle, T01840-250545. Working farm with good sea views.

C **Trevigue**, Crackington Haven, near Bude, T01840-230418, F230418. The Crocker family farm has small plots of worked land produce, eggs from heaven, and their own bacon and sausages. The stone house is a stone's throw from the sea. Period features surrounded by a cobbled courtyard and lush verdant foliage.

Tintagel and around *p420*

B **The Mill House Inn** Trebarwith Strand, Nr Tintagel, T01840-770200. Stone building with 9 rooms that are understated but luxurious. The old mill is surrounded by fully mature pines. The restaurant is good and the bar a bit trendy.

C **Slipway Hotel**, Port Isaac, T01208-880264, www.portisaac.com. Young, friendly seaview hotel on the harbour front with rated seafood and a bit of a buzz about it.

D **The Old Mill**, Tintagel, T01840-770234. Fresh breakfast and a helpful hostess in this old stone mill. Surrounded by idyllic countryside and good value.

E **Cornish Tipi Holidays**, Tregildrens Quarry Tipi Site, Trelill, Nr Port Isaac, T01208-880781, www.cornish-tipi-holidays.co.uk. Family of 4 for £340 a week in a surprisingly comfortable wigwam from late Jul-early Sep.

Bodmin Moor *p421*

B **Anchorage House**, Nettles Corner, Tregehan, T01726-81407. This Georgian house has been meticulously cared for. The American owner can tell you about anywhere in the area. Dinners are occasional and cost £25 per person.

C **Cabilla Manor**, near Mount, Bodmin, T01208-821224, F821267. An 18th-century manor with tennis court and manicured lawns. Stroll in the gardens and over the edge into Bodmin Moor or even catch a concert in the small opera house in the barn.

C Porteath Barn, St Minver, near Wadebridge, T01208-863605, F863954. Restored stone barn with exposed beams and granite walls. The feel is not unlike a Provençal French mas. Fresh flowers and antiques in a chic and cool setting.

D Bokiddick Farm, Bokiddick, near Lanivet, T01208-831481, F831481. An 18th-century farmhouse on a 200-acre working dairy farm, the breakfasts here are fresh and delicious. Plenty of space to read and take long unobstructed walks in nature.

Padstow and around *p422*

A The Seafood Restaurant, Riverside, T01841-532700. Top of the range, Rick Stein's restaurant with rooms, overlooks the estuary and harbour from a converted granary.

D Khandalla Sarah's La, T01841-532961. A popular B&B with views over the Camel Estuary.

Newquay *p422*

No one in their right mind would come to Newquay without a surf board and a strong desire to drink copious amounts of alcohol. Consequently, much of the accommodation is of the hostel variety, or surf lodges as they're called here.

D-E Aqua Shack Surf Lodge, 30-32 Island Cres, just behind the bus station, T01637-879611, www.aquashacksurflodge.com. Dorm accommodation with restaurant, café-bar and rooftop BBQ and drinks terrace. Surfboard storage and lessons also arranged. Broadband internet access.

D-E Base Surf Lodge, Tower Rd, T01637-874852, www.basesurflodge.co.uk. The town's newest surf lodge and has double and twin rooms as well as dorms.

D-E Home Surf Lodge, 18 Tower Rd, T01637-873387. Close to surf central, Fistral Beach, and the town centre, this has the benefits of a monster TV and a bar open till 0400 most nights. Dorm-style rooms with sea views. Price includes cooked breakfast served till 1000. Free tea and coffee.

Eating

Padstow *p422*

££ Margot's, 11 Duke St, T01841- 533441. Another superior option.

££ The Old Custom House, South Quay, T01841-532359, F533372. Also right on the harbour, and with an estimable fish restaurant.

££ Rick Stein's Café, 10 Middle St, T01841-532359. The youthful, economy version of Mr Stein's fêted seafood restaurant (see above).

For other eating options in the area, see sleeping above.

Pubs, bars and clubs

Newquay *p422*

Recommended local club action includes: **Springbok**, 27-29 Cliff Rd, T01637-875800. **Tall Trees**, Tolcarne Rd, T01637-850313. Ibiza foam parties on Fridays. Both until 0200.

Activities and tours

Fishing

Blue Fox Fishing Charters, with Phil Britts, Padstow, T01841-533293. £200 a day for 6, £75 late run.

Surfing

British Surfing Association, T01736-360250, for a list of surf schools in the area. **Extreme Academy**, Watergate Bay, Newquay, T01637-860840. Run courses in a variety of unusual and high-risk watersports.

Walking

Kernow Trek, T01637-881752, www.walkingincornwall.co.uk. Organize reputable walking holidays.

Transport

Taxi

Bluebird Taxis, 8 Station Parade, Newquay, T01637-852222; **Padstow Private Hire Taxi Service**, T01208-813383. **Padstow Cycle Hire Ltd**, South Quay, Padstow, T01841-533533.

Directory

Hospitals Newquay Hospital, St Thomas Rd, T01637- 893600.

South Cornish coast

→ *Colour map 1, grid B2-4*

The big noise in South Cornwall since the end of the 20th century has been the Eden Project, near St Austell. This astonishing conversion of a disused clay pit still causes controversy in the local area, but visitors to its two enormous 'biomes' are generally not disappointed (once they manage to get in) by the stunning array of international plantlife inside and the Project's upbeat, colourful and urgent ecological message. Sailing perilously close to becoming a victim of its own success, it's not the only attraction that this part of the county has to offer, although gorgeous gardens are something of a theme. Just across the water from Plymouth, Rame Head is the isolated and scenic coastal setting for Mount Edgcumbe's formal gardens and country park, near the lonely mariner's chapel of St Michael. To the north, the Tamar Valley is a wooded riverside wonderland. Back on the coast, Fowey is a still fairly unspoiled harbour fishing town, a fate that others like Looe, Mevagissey and Polperro have not managed to avoid. Beyond St Austell, the coast to St Mawes hides tiny harbours like charming Portloe. Falmouth's naval legacy and lively contemporary art scene are worth lingering around for, while outside the towns and villages, the natural beauty of the area is as stunning as it is varied. The Lizard peninsula stretches 12 miles south from Helston and the secluded charms of the Helford Estuary to the spectacular crags and crashing waves of Britain's most southerly point. Delightful subtropical gardens, secluded fishing villages, rocky coves and miles of unspoilt coastal paths draw in considerable crowds around the summer. The mild climate also keeps The Lizard warm in winter, and off-season primroses may be found here before Christmas and even daffodils in January. ►► *For Sleeping, eating and other listings, see pages 429-431.*

Ins and outs

Getting there From Plymouth (see also page 412) the lovely Tamar Valley line runs up to Gunnislake. Regular buses link Bodmin Parkway, a beautiful station on the main London to Penzance line, with Padstow. Falmouth is on a branch line 20 minutes from Truro, trains run every 1 hour 30 minutes or so. Change at Truro for mainline services to Penzance in the west or Exeter (2 hours) and London (7-8 hours) in the east. **National Rail Enquiries,** T08457-484950. From Plymouth the A38 runs up to Liskeard, from where the A390 forks off to St Austell. Plymouth to the Eden Project should take about 45 minutes. National Express, T08705-808080, run regular coaches from London Victoria to St Austell (7 hours). The A39 takes you 20 minutes southwest to Falmouth from Truro traffic depending (double road journey times in high season) and the A393 will bring you over from the north coast via Redruth in about the same time. Helston is about 30 mins southwest on A394. The A3083 takes you 40 minutes south, down the spine of the peninsula to the Lizard Point, with smaller roads to Mullion on the west and St Keverne and Coverack in the east. **National Express** run numerous buses from Falmouth to destinations including twice daily to London, (7½ hours), Bristol (6 hours), and twice daily to Penzance (1 hour). Change at Truro for Newquay and St. Ives. **The Truronian** run four buses from Truro to Lizard Village daily (not Sunday) via Falmouth and Helston taking 1 hour 30 minutes (£2.75). Connecting service to Coverack and St Keverne. **Traveline,** on T0870-6082608. The nautically inclined can take a boat to Falmouth in the summer from Truro (bus to Malpas at low tide). The trip takes 1 hour and costs £2.50.

Getting around **Cars** overload the area in summer so go on **foot** or **bicycle** wherever you can. **Truronian Buses,** T01872-273453. Calstock Ferry and Motor Launch Co, Calstock, T01822-833331. Buses to the Eden Project go from Newquay and St Austell.

 Information St Austell TIC ⓘ *Southbourne Rd, T01726-879500.* **Tamar Valley Tourism Association** ⓘ *6 Fore St, Calstock, T01822-835874, www.tamarvalleytourism.co.uk.* **Falmouth TIC** ⓘ *T01326-312300, www.falmouth-sw-cornwall.co.uk.* **Helston TIC** ⓘ *Meneage St, T01326-565 431, info@helstontic.demon.co.uk. 1000-1630. See also www.lizard-peninsula.co.uk.*

Rame

The most easterly part of Cornwall, **Rame Head** is still distinctively Cornish. Much of it is taken up with the grounds of **Mount Edgcumbe House and Country Park** ⓘ *Cremyll, Torpoint, T01752-822236, Apr-Sep Wed-Sun, bank holidays 1100-1630, £4.50, concessions £3.50, under-16s £2.25, family £10,* now owned by Plymouth City Council. The Cremyll Ferry from Admiral's Hard, in the Stonehouse district of Plymouth, provides the best approach to the house itself, the first country house in England to be built for its prospect. Badly bombed in the Second World War, the interior is now less full of treasures than it might have been, but the gardens still command great views of Plymouth Sound. The formal gardens, near the Cremyll Ferry landing, are also special, laid out in the 18th century and divided into French, Italian, English, and more recently American and New Zealand styles. The Earl's Garden, behind the house, was laid out at the same time, and features magnificent cedars, classical garden houses and a shell seat. Two miles away is the small village of **Rame**, with its candelit old church, while right out on the headland, 20 minutes' walk from the village, is the lonely St Michael's mariners chapel, with coastguards cottages and radio mast for company and superb views south, east and west.

From Plymouth, Rame can be reached by boat to Cawsand (a mile from Mount Edgcumbe) from the Mayflower Steps during summer.

Tamar Valley

North of Plymouth, Cornwall's border with Devon runs up the picturesque Tamar Valley, passing close to Tavistock, on the edge of Dartmoor, and up beyond Launceston. Trains run the 14 miles from Plymouth to Gunnislake via Bere Ferrers, Bere Alston and Calstock on the scenic **Tamar Valley Line** throughout the year, crossing the Tavy and Tamar on a series of great viaducts. **Boat cruises** (*Tamar Cruising*, T01752-822105 and *Plymouth Boat Cruises* T01752-822797) also head upriver to **Calstock**, the unoffical capital of the region, described by John Betjeman as the "least known and most uninterruptedly Cornish town". Just downstream is the estate of **Cotehele** ⓘ *(NT), T01579-351346, Apr-Oct Mon-Thu, Sat, Sun 1100-1700 (-1630 in Oct), garden open all year daily 1030-dusk (last admission 30 mins before closing), £6.60, family £16.50, garden and mill only £3.80/£9.50,* the ancient seat of the Edgcumbe family. A wonderful medieval house built between 1485 and 1627, without electric light, it's surrounded by beautiful woodland, as well as being close to a restored watermill, and the old Quay on the river houses an outstation of the National Maritime Museum, and the industrial heritage of the Danescombe Valley. A walk through the woods leads to a 15th-century chapel on a bluff overlooking the river, built by Sir Richard Edgcumbe in gratitude for his dramatic escape from Richard III's men, putting his pursuers off the scent by throwing his hat and a big rock into the river.

Looe to Fowey

Back on the coast, Looe is a typically touristy south Cornish seaside town, still with a few boats working out of its harbour. A walk west round Hannafore Point, though, arrives at a naturalist's dream: a series of gullies and tidepools with an abundant variety of sea flora. Since 1964, the seaside woods around Looe have been set aside for a colony of **woolly monkeys** ⓘ *Monkey Sanctuary, Murrayton, Looe, T01503-262532, Easter-Sep Mon-Thu, Sun 1100-1630,* endangered in their natural habitat, the Brazilian rainforest. See them swing through high beech trees, apparently enjoying life in south Cornwall.

Round the corner and Talland Bay, the quaint appeal of the old fishing village of **Polperro** draws thousands to its single valley street of tacky souvenir shops. That said, the old harbour is undeniably picturesque, immortalized by the artist Oskar Kokoshka and despite being a shadow of its former role as a storm-battered fishing boat haven, the village does well as a happy holiday spot in the summer.

Next stop along the coast, **Fowey** is a dear little harbour town, closely associated with the novelist Daphne du Maurier. A deep-water working port, it is also popular with tourists, who drop into the **Du Maurier Literary Centre** in narrow Fore Street running parallel with the waterfront. **St Fimbarrus Church** is also worth a look, as are the town's secret gardens, such as the **Old Boys Grammar School**, alive with roses in summer. Alternatively, climb the granite steps of Bull Hill, or find the small sheltered beach at Cove. The **Hallwalk** is a memorable 2-mile circular walk with wonderful views across the river to Fowey and down the estuary mouth to Polruan. Catch the ferry across to **Bodinnick**, where there's a wide choice of places to eat. The walk continues to **St Catherine's Point** and the ruins of **St Catherine's Castle**, built by Henry VIII, guarding the entrance to the harbour. Across the river the boat building centre of **Polruan**, with its narrow streets clinging to the hillside leading down to the old waterfront and quay, is less touristy than Fowey and well worth the foot ferry trip.

Eden Project

ⓘ *Bodelva, T01726-811911, www.edenproject.com. Apr-Oct daily 0930-1800 (last admission 1630), Nov-Feb daily 1000-1630 (last admission 1500), £10, concessions £5, under-16s £4, OAPs £7.50, family £25. Buses from St Austell and Newquay rail stations, T01872-273453.*

North of St Austell is the main event in south Cornwall, sometimes with queues 10 miles away from the site, and signs saying 'Eden Full'. The Eden Project is not a wet weather attraction apparently, but no one's listening. Then again, it has gathered very positive world-wide publicity. Architecturally stunning, educationally stimulating, and culturally on the money, the Eden Project is an extraordinary enterprise: a 'Living Theatre of Plants and People' as it likes to bill itself, its highlights are the great high-tech greenhouses in an abandoned chinaclay pit: the **Humid Tropics Biome** for rainforest plantlife is the largest and most spectacular. Slightly smaller, the **Warm Temperate Biome** contains thousands of plants from South Africa and California. The **Roofless Biome** is outdoors (note the Roofless bit), planted with hemp, sunflowers and tea. Allow three hours to see the whole thing.

St Austell to St Mawes

Another, very different, old-fashioned garden in the area is also worth seeking out. **Tregehan** ⓘ *T01726-814389, £3.50,* at Par, near St Austell has an imposing 1846 glasshouse (making useful comparison with the Eden Project's biomes) and formal walled garden, these 20 delightful acres have belonged to the Carlyon family since 1565. With lovely terraces and colourful border scheme. Focusing on genera from temperate regions and a green gene bank for source plants. The camellias are award winning. Stroll down a path of yews to a doggie graveyard and statues of beloved and lost dogs. Fully mature oaks shelter them in the parkland.

The coast from St Austell to St Mawes has remained remarkably unspoiled, partly because it's more difficult to reach by road. At **Mevagissey**, a crowed little fishing village in summer, roads of any size peter out, leaving the rest of the coast relatively quiet. Inland, **Caerhays Castle Garden** ⓘ *Porthluney Cove, T01872-501310, £4.50 garden, £4.50 house, £8 combined,* was created by JC Williams' sponsored plant gathering expeditions to China in the 19th century. The bounty of his efforts are visible today with rare shrubs and flowers delighting the eye in a wooded garden. Noteworthy are the camellias again, magnolias and rhododendrons. On rolling hills the castle estate offers tea with walks winding down to the sea. More well-known perhaps are the

 Lost Gardens of Heligan ⓘ *Pentewan, T01726-845100, £6,* with over 80 acres making it apparently the largest restored garden in Europe. Miles of footpaths have been uncovered and reinstated with thousands of newly planted trees providing shelter. There are walled gardens with exotic plants, a melon house, Italian garden and Japanese garden, and acres of subtropical jungle to monkey around in too.

A series of tiny villages are sprinkled along the rocky coast. **Portloe** is one of the most attractive, with its minuscule landing slip, cliffwalks and jolly tearooms. Further west, dinky little **St Mawes** looks across to Falmouth across Carrick Roads. **Lamorran House Gardens** ⓘ *T01326-270800, £3.50, under-16s free,* is a beautiful 4-acre tropical garden with a Mediterranean grace and gorgeous views to St Antony's Headland and the sea. As with other gardens in Cornwall the mild climate allows the most delicate plants to thrive: azaleas, desert agaves and yuccas are just a few examples. Walk amidst statuary and columns and palms set in a landscape inspired by an Englishman's garden abroad.

Falmouth

Though one of Cornwall's largest towns, Falmouth is perhaps the least dominated by tourists. There is a large art student community and the world's second deepest natural harbour has so far dissuaded the Navy from embarking. Seeded on the slopes of three buxom hillocks, Falmouth grew from the inconsequential hamlets of Smithwick and Arwenack to a bustling town at the centre of the Old World's postal system. There are three reasonably clean **beaches** within easy reach – Gyllyngvase, Swanpool and Maenporth. The new **Maritime Museum** ⓘ *T01326-313388, www.nmmc.co.uk, Easter-Oct daily 1000-1700, Oct-Mar Mon-Sat 1000-1500, £2.20,* has an impressive collection of boats old and new as well as contemporary projects such as fine landscape photographs of Cornish seascapes. **Pendennis Castle** ⓘ *T01326-316594, 1000-1800 (1600 in winter), £4.20, concessions £3.20, child £2.10,* is Cornwall's oldest and offers splendid views though never had quite the range that Henry VIII was looking for: it was still possible to sail up the river out of range of both Pendennis and St Mawes opposite. **Falmouth Art Gallery** ⓘ *T01326-313863, weekdays 1000-1700, Sat 1000-1300,* also has an interesting collection.

Neighbouring **Penryn** is a quiet little town that also happens to be among the oldest in the country. It was the site of Glasney College – a centre of learning and pilgrimage until the Reformation – and there is little doubt that the town would have claimed Truro's cathedral had Henry VIII and successive generations of builders left it standing. Not that there was much need for scavenging as Penryn remains at the centre of some of the best granite quarries in the world.

Helston

While the town has a noble history, gentrification started early and a magnificent bowling green dating from 1764 now stands on the site of the castle built by Edward The Confessor's brother. At the entrance to the green stands an impressive Victorian Gothic arch, commemorating the hero of a battle against the closure of a local mine, but unless you've timed your visit to coincide with the celebration of **Furry Dance** on St Michael's Day, you'll find it is the monuments to late 20th century tourism that dominate the rest of the town. A **Folk Museum** ⓘ *T01326-564027, 1000-1700 all year plus 5-7 school holidays, £2, 12-16 years 50p,* is housed in the old Market House and details the long history of the Furry Dance, essentially a customized celebration of the Spring Rite, complete with top hats, morning coats and ball dresses.

Lizard Peninsula

The **Helford Estuary** would quell arguments even on the most demanding of family holidays. Nature lovers are particularly spoiled with the **National Seal Sanctuary** ⓘ *T01326-221361, 0900-1700 daily (call for times in winter, £7.50, child £5.50,* numerous walks along the estuary's wooded creeks and two fine gardens. With its 150-year-old laurel maze, **Glendurgan** ⓘ *(NT), T01326-250906, Tue-Sat, Feb-Oct 1030-1730, £4, family £10,* at the eastern end of the river is one of the great subtropical gardens of the Southwest. Exotic trees and shrubs flourish amidst open glades carpeted with wild flowers in season. **Trebah Gardens** ⓘ *T01326-250448, www.trebah-garden.co.uk, daily 1030-1700,* has colourful displays of azaleas and rhododendrons in spring and hydrangeas later in the year. **Trevarno Estate Gardens and National Museum of Gardening** ⓘ *T01326-574274, 1000-1700 daily,* brings the green fingered tally to three.

In the west, follow the coastal path south through rocky **Porthkerris** to warm-hearted **St Keverne** a mile inland. **Coverack**, once a notorious smuggling haunt, retains its charm as a fishing village as does **Cadgwith** with its thatched cottages spilling down into the sea. For a day at the beach, head to the expanse of **Kennack Sands** or the stunning low-tide perfection of **Kynance Cove** on the east coast. The **Lizard** village itself is expanding rapidly preferring quantity to quality but the coves at **Housel Bay** and **Mullion** retain their charm.

Radioheads should follow their antennae to **Marconi's Museum** at Lizard Point or if it's size you're after, **Goonhilly Earth Station** ⓘ *T0800-679593, www.goonhilly.bt.com,* is the largest satellite station in the world, with a purpose-built multimedia Visitors Centre. Naval and helicopter enthusiasts can call **RNAS Culdrose** ⓘ *T01326-565085,* to arrange a guided tour.

Sleeping

Rame *p426*

B **The Old Rectory**, St John-in-Cornwall, near Torpoint, T01752-822275, F823322. Oh so peaceful with kippers and organic eggs for breakfast. Snooker in the afternoon and long views from the bedrooms.

Tamar Valley *p426*

C **Botelet**, Herodsfoot, Liskeard, T01503-220225. If you like animals this is the place for you. Charolais bulls, ducks and a goat. Pretty drive and country setting. Reflexology and aromatherapy treatments available. Good breakfasts and fresh fish, home-made biscuits and tea. Dinners Sun, Wed, Thu and Fri nights.

C **Cotehele Holiday Cottages**, run by the National Trust in the wooded Tamar Valley, T01579-351346.

Looe to Fowey *p426*

A **The Cormorant Hotel**, Golant, near Fowey, T01726-833426, F833026. (£150 double occupancy including breakfast and 5-course dinner.) On a high cliff with a spellbinding view of the River Fowey, this is truly an enchanted part of Britain. This hotel is well managed with many amenities. Glorious views from most rooms. A heated pool and numerous walks into the countryside. A dedicated young chef brings enthusiasm to the preparation of fresh local fare.

St Austell to St Mawes *p427*

L **The Lugger**, Portloe, Truro, T01872-501322, F501691. Perched atop the tiny harbour, this hotel is a treasure. Let the staff know if lobster is your thing and the local fishermen will bring it in. People travel for this restaurant. Meticulously clean and fresh. A small and romantic hotel.

B **Crugsillick Manor**, Ruan High Lanes, near St Mawes, T01872-501214, barstow_crugsillick@csi.com. This Queen Anne manor house is a perfect stopover for the pillage and plunder tour of Cornwall. A winding smugglers' path takes you down to the sea from the house. The splendid plaster ceiling was moulded by Napoleonic prisoners which the former owner Admiral Sir Arthur Kemp brought back from seafaring adventures. He apparently still haunts the place. Also 3 self-catering cottages with an additional cottage on the Lizard Peninsula with views.

B **Nanscawen House**, Prideaux Rd, Luxulyan Valley, Par, T01726-814488, keithmartin@compuserve.com. Set in the heart of a woodland this 16th-century manor house has an abundance of charm. Lovely light in the rooms and panoramic views.

B **Sharksfin Hotel**, The Quay, Mevagissey, T01726-843241. The Sharksfin is set right on the harbour of this pretty but crowded little fishing village. With a dozen rooms, all are comfortable with sea views. The restaurant is renowned for fresh seafood, all bought straight from the local fishermen. Lobster, mussels, shellfish, plaice, sea bass are standards on the daily menu. £59.50 per person includes B&B and supper. £20 allowance for those who prefer to order à la carte instead of from the daily menu.
C **Creed House and Gardens**, Creed, Grampound, Truro, T01872-530372. This listed house with outstanding gardens is notable for its gracious hospitality.
D **Piggy's Pantry**, The Willows, Gorran Haven, T01726-843545. Cheerful bungalow within walking distance of the sea.
D **Woodlands Guest House**, Trewollock, Gorran Haven, near Mevagissey, T01726-843821. South facing bungalow with sea views, close to the South West Coast Path.

Falmouth *p428*
A **Budock Vean Hotel**, Falmouth, T01326-252100. Spectacular gardens, near very fresh crabs at the *Ferryboat Inn*.

Helston *p428*
B **Nansloe Manor**, near Helston, T01326-574691. A Grade II listed building, parts of which date back to the 1600s. Set in 4 acres, the property is further surrounded by National Trust and privately owned woodland and farmland.
E **The Grange Fruit Farm**, Gweek, T01326-221718. Among the best.

Lizard Peninsula *p428*
C **The Housel Bay Hotel**, at the southernmost tip, T01326-290417. A number of high Victorian hotels dot the area, this is the best, with its piano bar, eclectic photograph collection and warm welcome. Although there are countless B&Bs in the area, they do get booked quickly, try:
D **Meaver Farm**, Mullion Cove, T01326-240128;
E **Trevinock**, St Keverne, T01326-280498.
Self-catering for longer visits is highly recommended with cottages around Helford:
B-C **National Trust** at one end of the scale, T01225-791133;
D **Helford River Cottages**, T01326-231666;
D-F **Criggan Mill Timber Lodges**, Mullion, T01326-240496, www.criggan mill.co.uk.

Camping
Widely available try:
Little Trevothan, Coverack, T01326-280260;
Kennack Sands, T01326-290631.

Eating

Looe to Fowey *p426*
Food for Thought, Fowey, T01726-832221. A small cottage on the harbourside. There are choices for those of you who don't fancy seafood but this is what people have been coming back for, for over 25 years. Fixed 3 course menu £19.95 Mon-Fri. Sat à la carte. 90 bottles on wine list, £10-£50.

St Austell to St Mawes *p427*
£££ The Rosevine Hotel, Rosevine, Portscatho, T01872-580206. Enjoy a seafood platter in the lovely garden that leads down to the cliff's edge.

Falmouth *p428*
££ **The Penmere Manor Hotel**, T01326-211411. Splash out with finest local fish and meat (£20.50 for 3 courses).
££ **The Sticky Prawn**, T01326-373734, on the quayside in Flushing has reasonably priced fish and meat sourced locally.
££ **Three Mackerel** at Swanpool offers fine food in a lovely location.
££ **Trengilly Wartha Inn**, T01326-340332, in a lovely setting at Constantine, west of Falmouth, near the Helford River. Bar food at lunchtime, the Full Monty at dinner (book ahead and stay for the night).

Helston *p428*
Pasties, ice creams and junk food come at you from all sides in Helston. But for more natural produce try the **Farmer's Market** happens fortnightly on Mon in Helston.

For an explanation of the sleeping and eating price codes used in this guide, see the inside front cover. Other relevant information is provided in the Essentials chapter, page 40.

£ Blue Anchor, T01326-562821, a 15th-century inn brewing powerful 'Spingo' ales with water from a nearby well.
£ Cadgwith Cove Inn, T01326-290513. Delightful but crowded pub serving up crab sandwiches (£5.00), jacket potatoes (£4.50) and ploughman's (£5.50) for lunch and more substantial fish dishes in the evening (£10-15 for a main), afternoon teas also available.

Lizard Peninsula *p428*
££ Halzephron Inn, Gunwalloe, T01326-240406. Wonderful westerly views and a good wine list.
££ The Lion's Den Pub and Bistro, Manaccan, T01326-231331.
££ The White Hart, St Keverne, T01326-280325. Offers locally reared and gathered fare with more elbow room (£5 for a quick lunch or £20.75 for 3 courses).
Also well worth a visit.
The Quayside Fish Centre, Porthleven, T01326-562008. Has the works in terms of freshly-caught fish daily.

Entertainment

Falmouth *p428*
Many of the pubs organize theme nights and karaoke as well as the odd concert. Look out for details of local entertainments in the local press and the weekly 'the guide' available free across the area.
Falmouth Arts Centre, Church St, T01326-212300. Changing contemporary art exhibitions, especially of students from the *Falmouth College of Arts*, T01326-211077.
The Lady Street nightclub caters to sailors on shore leave at the nearby naval base.
The Pirate, Grove Pl. This is where bands play most nights and a 0100 licence keeps things busy.
The Star and Garter's Monday jazz nights in The Old High St, Falmouth, are also worth attending.

Festivals

Looe to Fowey *p426*
May Daphne Du Maurier Festival. Fowey and the surrounding area hold this renowned festival every year, and very popular it is too. There is also usually free entertainment on Town Quay.

Falmouth *p428*
Jul-Sep The Tall Ships Race in Jul and a regatta in **Aug** while studios open their doors in Aug- Sep to reveal kitsch coastal watercolours mingling with some more interesting contemporary work from the town's eclectic residents and students from the art college.

Helston *p428*
May The Furry Dance. 8 May sees Helston's spring perambulations here. Dancing, buildings swathed in garlands of flowers, buskers, stalls and fairground rides take over the town with much carousing and drinking.

Activities and tours

Falmouth and Lizard *p428*
Watersports
Boats are available on the river whatever your experience: from dinghies (£10.50 for 2 hrs) to diesel pilots (£19.50 per hr). Hire is available at St Anthony and Helford village, T01326- 231357. **Diving** at all levels can be arranged at T01326-221446, www.lizardiver.co.uk. For other watersports including land yachts, katamarans and windsurfing go to **Windsport**, Mylor Harbour, Falmouth, T01326-376191/373363, daily 0900-2000 (summer) 1000-1600 (winter).

Riding
Nanfan Farm, Church Rd, Cury, Helston, T01326-240591. Daily 0900-1800 (summer), 0900-1500 (winter), £8.00 per hr.

Walking
The South West Coastal Path is a magnificent treat for walkers of all levels. Pick up the invaluable National Trust leaflets at NT car parks and TICs.

Transport

Bicycle
Bike Services, 13 Meneage Rd, Helston, T01326-564564. Bissoe Tramways Cyclez Hire, Carnon Downs, T01872-870341; Pentewan Valley Cycle Hire, 1 West End Pentewan, St Austell, T01726-844242.

Penwith Peninsula

→ Colour map 1, grid C1

Miles of incomparable coastline offer swathes of golden sand, crystal waters and clifftops strewn with wild flowers, though in less benign mood nature's pounding surf, fierce squalls and treacherous reefs require all the vigilance the area's ubiquitous lighthouses and coastguards can muster. Just as extreme are the contrasts between the impossibly crowded town centres, fit for only the very bravest in high season, and the romantic splendour and unspoilt grandeur of the countryside in between. The delights of exploring a small, well-chosen area on foot keep smitten fans returning year after year. Packing it all in on a whistle stop tour could well ensure a rapid U-turn for the road bound. Where given the opportunity, the taste guardians of the National Trust have achieved the practically impossible, and maintain a delicate balance between the insatiable demands of holidaymakers and the wonderful natural surroundings that draw them. The delights of St Michael's Mount or the coastal path west from St Ives? Or the 'Relentless Sea' experience at Land's End? Pay yer money, take yer choice. ▸▸ *For Sleeping, eating and other listings, see pages 436-437.*

Ins and outs

Getting there **First Great Western** have five trains a day from London Paddington to Penzance (6 hours), with direct service to St Ives every other hour (5 hours 30 minutess) and a regular local connecting service taking 20 mins. **National Rail Enquiries,** T08457-484950. Penzance is the last major stop on the A30 30 minutes from Redruth, with Land's End another tortuous 9 miles. Turn off 5 miles before Penzance for St Ives and the north coast. The southern coast road takes in Mousehole, Lamorna and Porthcurno on the way to the tip, continuing on through St Just to St Ives. **National Express,** T08705-808080, have 7 buses a day to London from Penzance (9 hours) or St Ives (8 hours 30 minutes). Local service takes 25 minutes to St Ives every other hour. Newlyn, Mousehole, Land's End, and Zennor are all well served locally but allow plenty of margin at peak times. **Traveline,** 0870-6082608.

Information **Penzance TIC** ⓘ T01736-362207, close by the train and bus stations has a broad brush approach with as many leaflets for Penzance residents wanting to go elsewhere as information for incoming visitors. 0900-1700 Mon-Fri, 0900-1600 Sat and 1000-1300 Sun. **St Ives TIC** ⓘ T01736-796297, is more conventional, focusing on the town's own numerous attractions. 0900-1700 Mon-Fri, 0900-1600 Sat and 1000-1300 Sun.

Penzance

Sheltered in the western end of fertile Mount's Bay, this bustling town gets first prize for sticking its head in the sand and getting on with the unglamorous business of being a transport hub. Its shopping streets can hardly be distinguished from any other conventional English town, the seafront does its job as prosaically as possible and the elegant dome perched on the top of the town passes itself off as a Lloyds bank. To be fair though, the 16th and 17th centuries saw the town's embryonic attempts at growth burnt to the ground twice; first by the Spanish and then by the English so perhaps it's no surprise that it prefers to remain inward looking. Hard-working Newlyn is one of the busiest fishing ports in the Southwest though the plaintive 'Save our Fish' sign above the market paints a bleak picture for the future. The new marina will no doubt draw a different catch as a drink with the sun setting behind you lighting up the clouds as you look east to The Lizard will keep the shore densely packed even when all the fish are long gone.

Now owned by The Landmark Trust, The **Egyptian House** ⓘ *Chapel St, T01628-825925, apartments bookable by the week long in advance (see page 436)*, was built in 1836 by John Lavin, a Penzance mineralogist, to house a geological museum. The former home of a wealthy miller and merchant, **Penlee House** ⓘ *Morrab Rd, T01736-363625, Oct-Apr Mon-Sat 1030-1630, last admission 1600, May-Sep Mon-Sat 1000-1700, last admission 1630, £2, under-18s free,* offers a modern gallery concentrating on the Newlyn School of Artists (1880-1930) as well as a fine Natural History and Antiquarian museum covering 6000 years of Cornish history. The **Newlyn Gallery** ⓘ *New Rd, T01736-363715, free,* displays contemporary work. The **Pilchard Works** ⓘ *T01736-332112, 17 Apr-28 Oct Mon-Fri 1000-1800 plus Sat mornings in Jul and Aug, £2.95, child £2.20,* offer an interesting insight into a 90-year-old working factory. Finally, enterprising **Harry Safari** ⓘ *T01736-711427, (£15 per hour),* offers history on horseback on the moors above Penzance to beginners and more experienced riders.

St Michael's Mount

ⓘ *T01736-710265, 25 Mar-Oct Mon-Fri 1030-1730, last admission 1645. Most weekends during the season also include admission to the garden, call to check times. £4.60, child £2.30. Boats run regularly at high tide. £1 each way, children 50p.*

The archangel is said to have appeared in shining form at the top of this spectacular rock, rising sharply from the sea at the eastern end of Mount's Bay, thereby ensuring that monks, pilgrims, soldiers and aristocrats would conspire to create one of the most picturesque and charming of monuments in the country. A causeway takes you across the sands at low tide, where you may then stroll along the delightful quay before climbing **The Pilgrim's Steps** (not for the infirm or stillettoed) amidst towering pine trees, and cascading subtropical gardens to the castle and chapel of St Michael perched above.

Originally a monastery affiliated with the Benedictines of Mont St Michel in France, it was used as a stronghold and during the Reformation – it was here that the Armada was first sighted – before being converted after the Civil War by the fortunate Col St Aubyn into a family seat of unique distinction. The labyrinth of rooms reflect the Mount's rich history with styles ranging from stark Medieval to playful Rococo. Helpful and welcoming guides are a mine of information while views from the upper levels – whatever the weather – give a powerful yet comforting sensation of being at sea.

Land's End

Nature has been generous to a fault at Land's End, man unfortunately less so. While tourists used to come and enjoy the simple pleasures of taking photos and totting up the miles they'd travelled to get here, the barren splendour of the promontory is now dominated by a monument to the unfulfilling greed of the 1980s. Perhaps the best thing is the promotional fanfare of billboards that bids you farewell, alerting you to other 'highlights' nearby. It serves as a salient reminder – though one is hardly needed – that you need something quick to remove the taste of your visit, while warning you of the dangers that lie ahead from 'themed' smugglers, miners and shipwrecks. Hopefully the **Relentless Sea** ⓘ *T01736-871501, 0930-1700 every day, £12.50, child £4.95,* will, in time, sweep the peninsula clear with a one-way 'Return to the Last Labyrinth' for the whole ill-advised eyesore. A short walk will take you on to the coastal path and sweeping **Whitesands Beach** in Sennen Cove. Don't look back.

St Ives

The light that drew the eponymous St Ia to embark from her native Ireland on a magic leaf to this beautiful bay 1,500 years ago has inspired artists, writers, surfers and sun worshippers to follow in her footsteps ever since. The town's beaches, cobbled streets and shimmering sea are bathed in a serene brightness that soothes the soul even when the summer season pulls its biggest crowds. The inspirational Tate, built on the site of an old gasworks, makes as much of a show of the beach and sea through its wide windows and thoughtful design as it does to the illustrious artists the town has inspired. Ben Nicholson, Barbara Hepworth and Bernard Leach are the much celebrated early-20th-century trio while the legacy lives on in the work of Terry Frost and Willy Barnes-Graham not to mention architect Richard Gilbert, who built the now-revered slate fronted council houses next to the Tate, a subtle variation on the town's symphony in grey. These two remarkable generations have left their graceful marks on the town and such momentum is unlikely to stop there. The more discerning visitor may find the numerous smaller galleries and craft shops too commercial but stroll up the steep streets that lead back from the sea front or up to St Nicholas' Chapel and leave the crowds behind, the hidden corners and expansive views flattering you into thinking the many rewarding discoveries on hand your own. A number of good fish restaurants, cafés and colourful pubs cater for the sore-footed and sunburnt but booking in advance for food and accommodation is a must at busier times of the year.

St Ives

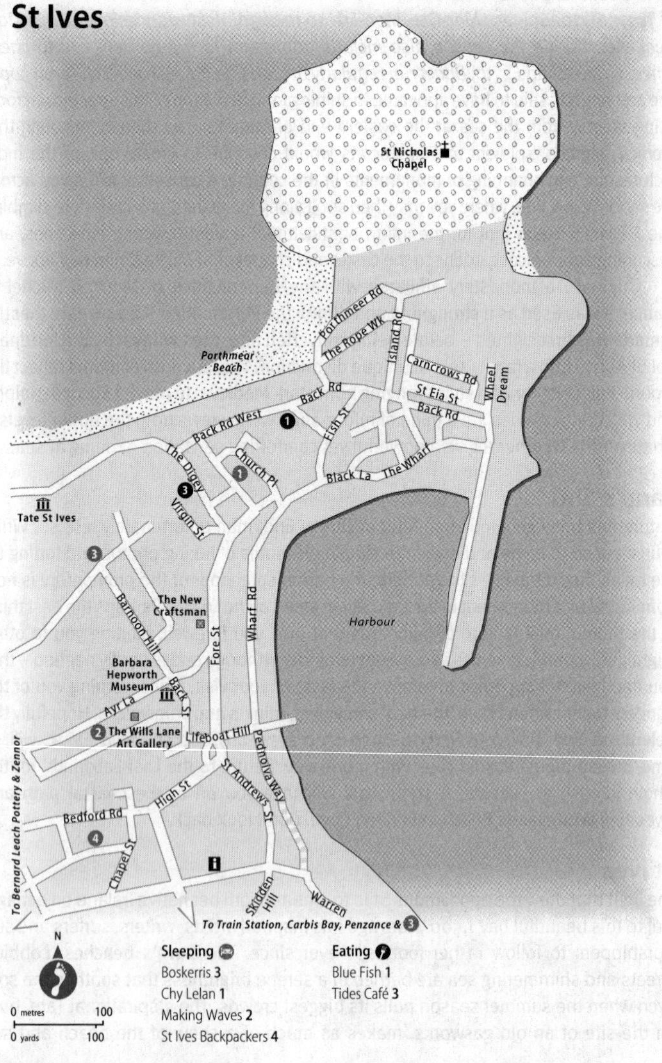

Barbara Hepworth (1903-1975)

Barbara Hepworth was a key figure in the abstract movement in British art, famous for her 'sculptures with holes'. Her use of this technique grew more complex as she stretched the hole into oval and spiral shapes and, like her friend Moore, created sculptural forms derived from nature, especially inspired by the sea-washed rocks near her home in Cornwall. Born in Wakefield, Yorkshire, Hepworth studied at Leeds School of Art, then from 1921 at the Royal College of Art, before living in Italy for a spell. She met and married the painter Ben Nicholson in 1931 and together they explored the possibilities of abstraction, visiting the studios of Arp, Brancusi, Braque, Picasso and Gabo among others. In 1939, Hepworth moved to St Ives, Cornwall, where she became an influential member of the artistic community, being a founder member of the Penwith Society in 1949. Sadly, in 1975 she died in a fire in her studio in St Ives, where the fine Barbara Hepworth Museum was opened in her memory.

The empty building of the **Tate** ⓘ *T01736-796226, 1030-1730 Tue-Sat, daily in Jul and Aug, £3.95 or £6.50 includes the Barbara Hepworth Museum,* would be worth a visit in its own right but as it masterfully complements the small but extremely inspiring collection of local talent and the well-considered temporary exhibitions, to visit it is to see modern art in a constant state of self-creation, inspiration, artist and viewer all contributing to the whole. An impressive array of work from one of the greatest sculptors of the last century is beautifully arranged at the **Barbara Hepworth Museum** ⓘ *T01736-796398, 1000-1700 weekdays, Sat in summer,* in the house, workshop and garden where she lived from 1949 until 1975. Her bare forms resonate immense power with their calculated simplicity, and are a perfect tonic for overstimulated visitors suffocated by the crowds. The ceramics of **Bernard Leach,** inspired by a long stint in Japan, share the same preoccupation with abstraction yet the day to day practicality of his bowls and cups combines function and form with great grace and distinction. Visitors to his pottery on the Zennor road will see why he occupies such a pre-eminent and influential position as a ceramicist and will be struck by how contemporary his work appears nearly 100 years later. Other galleries worth seeing in St Ives include the **Wills Lane Art Gallery** and the **New Craftsman.**

Around the Peninsula

The 25-mile stretch of coastline from Penzance to St Ives has some of the most spectacular scenery of the whole **South West Coastal Path** and is well worth exploring. In season, the clifftops are strewn with wild flowers and the mild climate ensures a colourful and botanically diverse display pretty much all year round. The route has it all: sensational coves, towering cliffs, good surf and long clean beaches. Beyond the small but crowded village of Mousehole (pronounced *Mowsle*), the traffic thins out a little but go by foot and you'll find some space for yourself at any time of the year.

Lamorna Cove and **Loggan Rock** a few miles further on are beauty spots well worth the name while the beach at **Creen** is charming. If you are in need of intrigue, try the **Museum of Submarine Telegraphy** ⓘ *Porthcurno, T01736-810966, 24 Mar-31 Oct Sun-Fri, daily Jul and Aug.* It was once the largest international cable station and used as a secret communication centre in the Second World War from which contact was kept with Allied forces. Both sides of Land's End are extremely impressive and walking there ensures not getting caught up in the 'Experience'. Sennen Cove will clear your head if you do. **St Just-in-Penwith** is a good base from which to explore the extreme west and the surrounding country is starkly desolate, dotted with prehistoric monuments such as **Lanyon Quoit**, The **Mên-an-Tol** and **Chysauster Iron Age Village**. If you feel like a short stretch of walking, **Zennor to St Ives** is particularly beautiful and can be done in an afternoon or a morning, stoking up a good appetite for lunch and a snooze on the Porthmeor Beach or a well-earned dinner.

Sleeping

Penzance *p432*
See www.go-cornwall.com for a huge selection of holiday lets. Self catering is available at the Egyptian House from The Landmark Trust, T01628-825925.
B **The Abbey Hotel**, Penzance, T01736-366906. Penzance's finest and worth it if you really do want to stay in town.
C **The Summer House**, T01736-363744, www.summerhouse-cornwall.com. A former artist's home, bright and stylish with good food.
D **Chymorvah**, Marazion, T01736-710497. Overlooking St Michael's Mount, family run and out of the hustle.

St Ives *p433, map p434*
C **The Boskerris**, in Carbis Bay, T01736- 795295, www.boskerrishotel.co.uk. Caters to the comfortable with views out to Godrevy Island.
D **Chy Lelan**, T01736-797560. A charming 17th-century cottage guesthouse.
D **The Porthmeor**, T01736-796712, www.porthmeor.com. Peers out over The Tate from the middle of town.
E **Making Waves**, T01736-793895. For the organically minded, welcoming with its simplicity.
F **St Ives Backpackers**, T01736-799444. Basic and informal.

Around the peninsula *p435*
C **The Gurnard's Head**, T01736-796298. In a wonderful location high on a cliff top between St Ives and Land's End.
D **Kerris Farm**, T01736-731309. A working dairy farm B&B about 4 miles west of Penzance beyond Mousehole.
D **Tregurnow Farmhouse**, T01736-810255. A handsome and welcoming farmhouse above Lamorna Cove.
E **Rose Farm**, near Mousehole, T01736-731808. More friendly farm accommodation.
F **The Old Chapel Backpackers Hostel**, Zennor, T01736-798307. Cheap and peaceful with a good pub to hand.

Eating

Penzance *p432*
£££ **Chapel Street Bistro**, Chapel St, T01736-332555. More informal than The Abbey (see below), with a boho atmosphere, but nothing relaxed about the quality of grub on offer.
££ **The Abbey**, in Abbey St, T01736-330680, www.theabbeyonline.com, will sweep you off your feet at the higher end of the scale (mains £10 and above).
££ **The Bake House**, in Chapel St. Pleasant and popular restaurant at the top end of the price range.
££ **The Hungry Horse**, Newlyn, T01736-363446. Has the best of the local fish.
££ **The Old Coastguard Hotel**, T01736-731222. Superior pub food.
£ **Coco's** has tapas and sandwiches for £5 and upwards.
£ **The Mount Haven**, Marazion, T01736-710249. Spectacular views over St Michael's Mountand ample car parking.
£ **The Sail Loft**, at the foot of the Mount itself, T01736-710748. Teas and light lunches in National Trust comfort.

Around the peninsula *p435*
£££ **The Cornish Range**, Mousehole, T01736-731488. Intimate and delightful with rooms upstairs although quite expensive.
££ **The Gurnard's Head**, T01736-796298. A welcome sight in the wilds of Zennor with good fish and stunning views.

St Ives *p433, map p434*
££ **Blue Fish**, T01736-794204, above The Craft Market. The highlights of St Ives. Has a lovely terrace with rooftop views of the sea, delicious fish (£12.50 main course) and desserts to finish you off.
££ **The Old Chapel**, T01736-798307. The place for a healthy sustaining lunch and to cleanse your palate.
££ **The Porthminster Beach Café**, T01736-795352. Will do you well at the same price.

££ **The Restaurant in The Tate**. Suitably cool yet unpretentious and has unbeatable views.
£ **Tides Café**. Cheaper with a bohemian feel.

Entertainment

Around the Peninsula *p435*
Acorn Theatre, T01736-365520, in an old Wesleyan Chapel has a lively and varied programme including dance, comedy, music (especially in the summer) and drama. Evening performances from 1900. Tickets £2.00-£10.00.
Minack Theatre, T01736-81018, south of Porthcurno. Outdoor amphitheatre perched on the cliffside with the best view of any theatre in the world. Bring something to sit on, as seats are hard, and a bottle of the best you can afford and enjoy good performances of anything from Shakespeare to Alice in Wonderland. Late May-Sep. Book well in advance.

Festivals

Around the Peninsula *p435*
In Penzance the Golowan Festival **21st-30th Jun** fills the town's streets with processions and music to celebrate the Feast of St John and the arrival of midsummer. It culminates in Mazey Day on 29th. **Aug 6th** is Morvah Pasty Day. **Aug 26th** is Newlyn Fish Festival. St Ives Arts Festival from **9-14th Sep**.

Transport

Penzance *p432*
Car hire Europcar, Station Yard, Penzance, T01736-360356.

Isles of Scilly

→ *Colour map 1, grid C1*

The most southern and westerly outpost of England, the Isles of Scilly are a granite archipelago about 30 miles west-south-west of Land's End. Of around 150 of the low lumps of rock, only five are inhabited, although many more also support vigorous and varied wildlife and flora. The comparatively balmy climate, crystal clear blue water and white sand beaches make this England's best go at a subtropical paradise and a surprisingly good one it is too. Although a very popular family holiday destination in high summer, remarkably the Scilly Isles have not entirely succumbed to the blandishments of year-round mass tourism. After the October half-term school holiday, the Scilly Isles pretty much close down until the next March and get on with growing flowers, fishing and getting online. The administrative hub of the islands' life is Hugh Town, on St Mary's, the largest of the five although only just over two square miles, but each of the other four main islands have distinctive and independent identities: Tresco is the pretty, glamorous, and exclusive one, with its famous gardens and timeshare cottages; St Martin's sheltered, quieter and hard-working, a naturalist's heaven with amazing beaches; Bryher the most rugged and storm-battered; and self-contained little St Agnes, the furthest south. Boat trips to the uninhabited islands reveal their peculiarities: Samson's deserted village, the Western Rocks for seals (pups in September) and raucous seabird life, Annet for puffins from mid-April to late July, and Bishop's Rock, the most westerly lighthouse in the UK. ▸▸ *For Sleeping, eating and other listings, see pages 442-444.*

Ins and outs

Getting there **Skybus** from Bristol (£240 return), Exeter (£190 return), Newquay (£102 return, £75 day return), Land's End (£95 return, £60 day return). No flights on Sun. Short break returns available. Out by sea, back by air also cheaper. Flight time: 15 minutes from Land's End. **Isles of Scilly Travel**, T0845-7105555, www.ios-travel.co.uk. By helicopter, **British International Helicopter Travel Centre**, T01736-36871, www.scillyhelicopter.co.uk. From Penzance to St Mary's or Tresco (£100 return, £72 day return). Flight time 20 minutes. First Class from London with

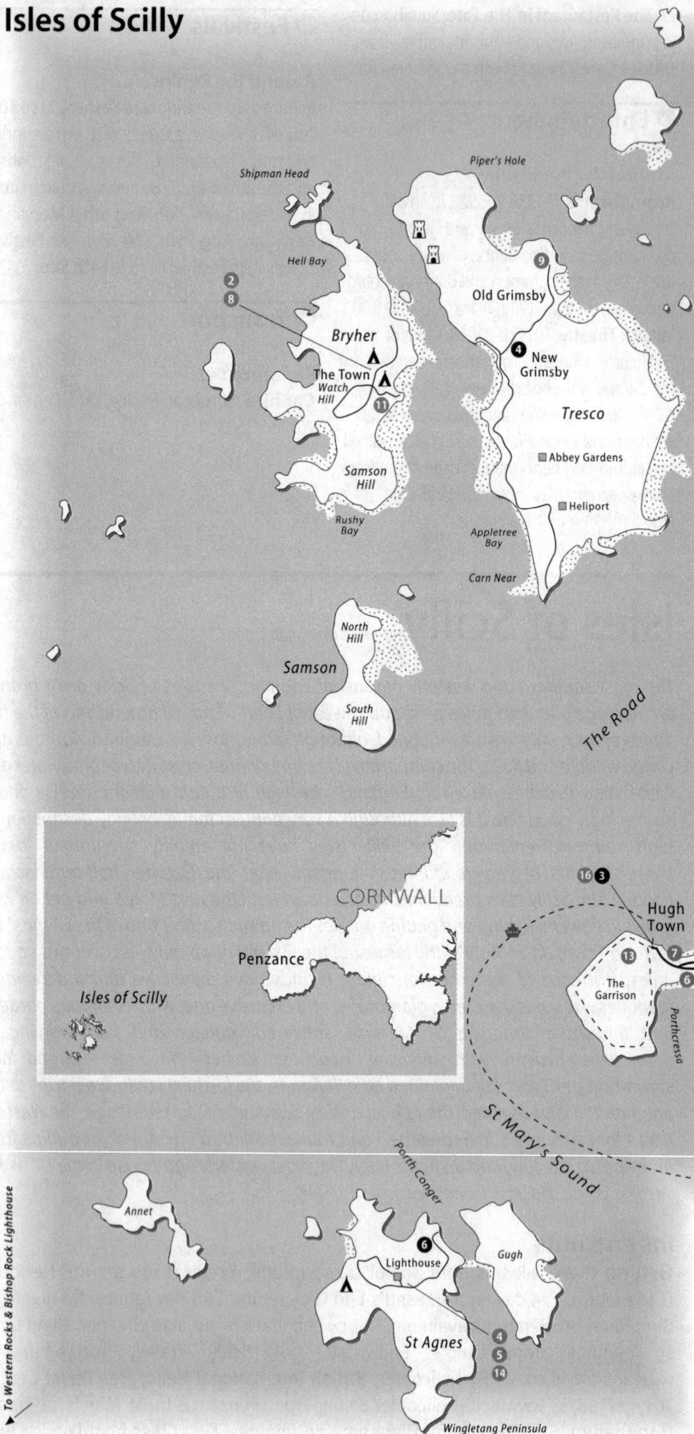

Shipman Head
Piper's Hole
Hell Bay
Old Grimsby
Bryher
New Grimsby
The Town
Watch Hill
Tresco
Abbey Gardens
Samson Hill
Heliport
Rushy Bay
Appletree Bay
Carn Near
North Hill
Samson
South Hill
The Road
CORNWALL
Penzance
Isles of Scilly
Hugh Town
The Garrison
Porthcressa
St Mary's Sound
Porth Conger
Annet
Gugh
Lighthouse
St Agnes
Wingletang Peninsula
To Western Rocks & Bishop Rock Lighthouse

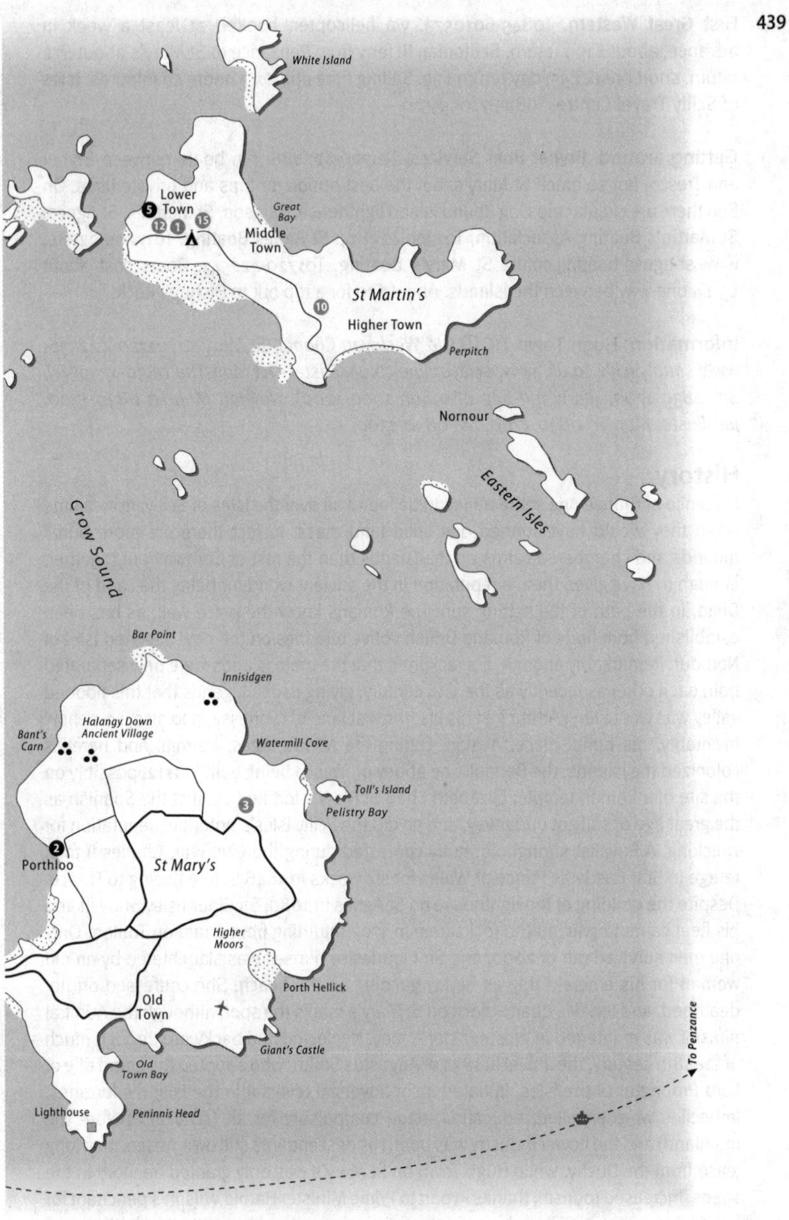

White Island
Lower Town
Great Bay
Middle Town
St Martin's
Higher Town
Perpitch
Nornour
Eastern Isles
Crow Sound
Bar Point
Innisidgen
Halangy Down Ancient Village
Bant's Carn
Watermill Cove
Toll's Island
Pelistry Bay
Porthloo
St Mary's
Higher Moors
Porth Hellick
Old Town
Giant's Castle
Old Town Bay
Lighthouse
Peninnis Head
To Penzance

Sleeping
Ashvale 1
Bank Cottage 2
Carnwethers Country House 3
Coastguards 4
Covean Cottage 5
Crebinick House 6
Evergreen Cottage 7
Hell Bay 8
Island 9
Parsonage 14
Polreath 10
Soleil D'Or 11
St Martin's on the Isle 12
Star Castle 13
Travean 15
Tregarthens 16

Eating
Harbour View & Fraggle Rock 1
Juliet's Garden 2
Mermaid Inn 3
New Inn 4
Seven Stones 5
Turk's Head 6

N
0 metres 500
0 yards 500

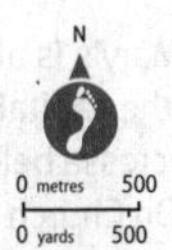

 First Great Western, T0845-6010573, via helicopter, booked at least a week in advance, about £190 return. **Scillonian III** ferry from Penzance to St Mary's about £72 return, short break £55, day return £35. Sailing time approx 2 hours 40 minutes. **Isles of Scilly Travel Centre**, T0845-7105555.

Getting around Bryher Boat Services, T01720-422886, run boats between Bryher and Tresco, not so much St Mary's, but the best option for trips and private hires. On Sun there are circular trips, eg Round Island lighthouse, Samson, St Martin's, St Agnes. **St Martin's Boating Association**, T01720-422814. **St Agnes Boating**, T01720-422704, www.st-agnes-boating.co.uk. **St Mary's Boating**, T01720-422541. Boats cost about £3-£4 one-way between the islands. About £10 for a trip out to Bishops Rock.

Information Hugh Town TIC ⓘ *Old Wesleyan Chapel, St Mary's, T01720-422536, www.simplyscilly.co.uk, www.scillyonline.co.uk. Easter-Oct Mon-Thu 0830-1730, Fri, Sat 0830-1700, (early Jun-Sep also Sun 1000-1200), Nov-Jan Mon-Fri 0830-1700, Jan-Easter Mon-Fri 0830-1700, Sat 0830-1300.*

History

Evidence of Bronze Age settlement can be found all over the Isles of Scilly, from a time when they would have formed one solid land mass. In fact there are more burial mounds and chambered cairns on the islands than the rest of Cornwall put together, enough to have given them a reputation in the ancient world for being the Land of the Dead, in the path of the setting sun. The Romans knew the place well, as has been established from finds of Romano-British votive offerings on the now deserted islet of Nornour. Remarkably enough, it's reckoned that the main islands were only separated from each other as recently as the 11th century, giving rise to legends that this flooded valley was where King Arthur lost his life, the lost land of Lyonesse, and also, somehow inevitably, his burial place, Avalon. During the Middle Ages, hermits and heretics colonized the islands, the Benedictine abbey on Tresco being built in 1112, possibly on the site of a Roman temple. Elizabeth I had St Mary's fortified against the Spanish as the great age of sail got underway, and so did the Scilly Isles's notorious reputation for wrecking. A Royalist stronghold, hotly contested during the Civil War, Charles II took refuge in Star Castle as Prince of Wales for six weeks in 1646 before fleeing to France. Despite the building of the lighthouse on St Agnes in 1680, Sir Cloudesley Shovell and his fleet came to grief on the rocks here in 1707 returning from a raid on Toulon. Only one man survived out of 2000, and Sir Cloudesley himself was slaughtered by an old woman for his emerald ring as he lay gasping on the beach. She confessed on her deathbed, and today a quartz block on St Mary's marks the spot, although the Admiral himself was re-interred in Westminster Abbey. Neglected and backward through much of the 18th century, the arrival in 1834 of Augustus Smith, who adopted the grand title of Lord Proprietor of the Isles, initiated a controversial reversal in the island's fortunes. Imbeciles were expelled, education made compulsory for all (40 years before the mainland) and the flower industry was born. His descendants still own Tresco, on a long lease from the Duchy, while Hugh Town on St Mary's was only granted freehold in the 1940s. Increased tourism, thanks in part to Prime Minister Harold Wilson's penchant for holidaying with his dog here in the 60s, has steadily replaced fishing and flower-growing as the islanders' main source of income.

St Mary's

The largest of the islands, a little over two square miles in area, St Mary's is also the most 'normal' of them, although still far from ordinary. Hugh Town, the capital of the archipelago, sits on a sandy isthmus between Town Beach and Porthcressa below the Garrison headland, grey-roofed and whitewashed and unprettified. On Church St, the antiquated local history **museum** ⓘ *T01720-422337, www.iosmuseum.org, Easter-*

Oct daily 1000-1200, 1330-1630 (also Whitsun-Sep 1930-2100), Nov-Easter Wed 1400-1600, video evenings on Scilly past and present are given on Wed from Jun-Sep at 2015, tells the story of Scilly with much shipwrecked gear, including a cannon from the wreck of Sir Cloudesley Shovell's HMS *Association* and Roman brooches from Nornour in the Eastern Isles.

The **Garrison Walk** around the headland to the southwest takes about an hour and gives tremendous views of the other islands and an historical insight into the islands' strategic significance at the entrance to the Bristol and English Channels. On the top of the low hill, approached through an impressive stone gateway, near the 18th-century **Rocket House**, which holds an exhibition on the Garrison's history, the granite bulk of **Star Castle** (now a hotel) was built for Elizabeth I in 1593, a pointed defence against the Spanish after the defeat of the Armada. Continuously fortified until the 20th century, the Garrison Walls and Civil War fortifications remain largely intact.

Heading the other way out of Hugh Town to the southeast leads up to the **Old Town** and **Peninnis Head**, with its lighthouse and strange weathered granite rocks, the Pulpit, Laughing Man and Tooth Rock. Overlooking **Old Town Bay**, the Old Church is a sacred old stone funeral chapel, candlelit only and surrounded by an evocative graveyard. One man was buried vertically here so he could go on looking out to sea. Beyond the airfield, civilization recedes as you approach **Porth Hellick**, site of Sir Cloudesley's grave and countless rock pools at low tide, past the **Giant's Castle rocks** and up to the passage graves and barrows on the Higher Moors. Further round the coast, beyond Pelistry Bay, a small sandy beach opposite Toll's Island, and Watermill Cove, are two well-preserved chambered tombs, at **Innisdgen**. Pointing north, **Bar Point** is one of St Mary's most remote and peaceful beaches.

Continuing anti-clockwise round the island, **Halangy Down Ancient Village** is a pre-Celtic settlement overlooked by **Bant's Carn**, the most impressive of Scilly's chambered tombs, dating from 2000BC. The coast path continues back to Hugh Town giving views across **The Road** the stretch of water between St Mary's and Samson, Bryher and Tresco.

Tresco

Considerably smaller than St Mary's, 20 minutes across The Road by boat, Tresco is the most prettified and most famous of the Isles, thanks to its extraordinary subtropical Abbey Gardens laid out by Augustus Smith on south-facing terraces around his well-wooded Victorian manor house. The whole private island has a strange and slightly unreal atmosphere, being entirely dedicated to plant propagation and mild, polite holidaymaking. Like Portmeirion in Wales, with palm trees in place of eccentric Italian architecture, all the accommodation (including a good selection of self-catering cottages) on the island needs to be booked through the estate office. That said, the northern part of the island is as wild, rugged and lonely as anywhere in the Southwest, its heather and gorse dotted with barrows and chambered cairns.

At low tide, boats are forced to use the landing quay at Carn Near on the very southern tip, near Appletree Bay, a delightful beach of white sand so fine that it was once much in demand for blotting ink. Beyond the Heliport is the main entrance to **Tresco Abbey Garden**. Windbreaks, terracing and careful horticulture allow an exotic and wonderfully varied range of plants, trees and shrubs to flourish here, natives of Mexico, South Africa and Australasia in particular abound. Not too formally arranged, kind of Californian in style, the 12-acre gardens are full of surprises, not least the large collection of ships' figureheads rescued from wrecks in a stone cabin called Valhalla near the entrance. The current lady of the manor has decorated a shell temple and Father Neptune sits imperiously at the top of the Lighthouse walk leading up the hill. There's also a wholesome café. A stunning coast road with views of Bryher over Appletree Bay runs along the west coast of the island to **New Grimsby**, Tresco's main harbour and settlement. On the coast to the north, Cromwell's and King Charles's ruined castles guard the channel between the two islands. At the harbour the road turns east over the back of Tresco, past the New Inn, the island's one and only pub, to the delightful *Island Hotel*, in a superb position perched on the northeastern nub of civilization. Low-lying, it looks out over a sandy beach and a scattering of rocky desert islands. Beyond the hotel, a lonely track climbs into wilder countryside and back round to the castles. Halfway round, **Piper's Hole** is an impressive sea cave with an underground freshwater pool on the coast that can be reached on foot in less than an hour and explored with a torch.

Bryher and Samson

Just west of Tresco, separated by a tidal channel, Bryher is very different, the least domesticated of the inhabited islands, facing the full force of the Atlantic from the west. At its northern end, around Hell Bay, mountainous seas in gale force winds frequently overwhelm the spur of rock known as **Shipman Head**. The island's one settlement, called simply **The Town**, straggles along the eastern, Tresco side of **Watch Hill**, which true to its name gives glorious wraparound views across the entire archipelago. As well as its wild and broken west coast, Bryher has beautiful beaches on its southern shores, at Rushy Bay below Samson Hill, from where there are also extraordinary views in all directions and yet more lumpy tumuli in the rough grass. **Samson** itself, immediately due south, is the largest of the uninhabited islands. Its last 10 impoverished occupants underwent enforced evacuation by Augustus Smith in the mid-19th century, the remains of their village and industry still visible today on South Hill. Both North and South Hills, separated by a low sandy isthmus, are also topped with chambered cairns.

St Martin's

Many visitors' favourite island, but still unlikely to be at all crowded, St Martin's lies north of St Mary's beyond Crow Sound, in the comparative shelter afforded by Tresco, Bryher and Samson to its west. A ridge of granite, the northern coast is rugged, with the exception of **Great Bay**'s sandy beach, one of the widest and most remote in Scilly. Beyond Great Bay, a tidal causeway links the northwest of the island with lonely and mysterious **White Island**. The southern side has more superb beaches, especially **Par**, **Perpitch** and **Lower Town**, and is lined with flower farms along the mile-long road between Lower Town and Higher Town, where the boats come in. As well as its lovely beach, Lower Town also boasts a hotel to rival Tresco's and the island's one and only pub, the *Seven Stones*.

St Agnes

The smallest, most southerly and most independent of the inhabited islands, separated from the others by the deep water channel of St Mary's Sound, St Agnes is like a child's drawing of an island. A little white lighthouse, one of the oldest in the country, stands proudly in the middle, surrounded by a wonderful array of places to explore: sandy beaches, coves, tidal islands, high-hedged little flower farms, an ancient stone maze, a mysterious well, and strange rock formations among other things. Boats land at Porth Conger, in the north of the island, near the only pub, *The Turk's Head*. A single track road then climbs up to the hill to the lighthouse (disused), passing a small turning on the left leading to the tidal sand bar connecting St Agnes to Gugh, with its megalithic remains and weather-beaten castles of rock. **Beady Pool** on the remote Wingletang Peninsula gets its name from small Spanish glass balls still very occasionally found here over 200 years after the ship carrying them went down just offshore.

Sleeping

Please note that most accommodation on Scilly needs to be booked well in advance, especially in high season.

St Mary's *p440*

A **Tregarthens**, close to the quay, T01720-422540. The island's oldest hotel (150 years in 1999), which has recently undergone a much-needed refurbishment.
B **Carnwethers Country House**, Pelistry Bay, T01720-422415. Out of the thick of things, a mile and a half from Hugh Town on the other side of the island.
B **Star Castle Hotel**, The Garrison, St Mary's, T01720-422317, F422343. Quite expensive and chintzy but probably the smartest St Mary's has to offer, with superb sea views from some of the rooms and others in the old stone castle itself.
C **Crebinick House**, Church St, Hugh Town, T01720-422968. Another good B&B option.
C **Evergreen Cottage**, Parade, in Hugh Town, T01720-422711. A comfortable 300-year-old cottage.

Tresco *p441*

A **Island Hotel**, Tresco, T01720-422883, www.tresco.co.uk. Closed Nov 4th-first week Mar. Top of the range and the smartest hotel on the Scilly Isles, it's in a gorgeous position with a very accomplished restaurant and unfussy rooms that are very comfortable. Most have sea views and many their own sun terraces. The swimming pool is warm if you don't dare brave the waves.
See also Eating below.

St Martin's *p442*

A **St Martin's on the Isle**, T01720-422090, www.stmartinshotel.co.uk. Gives the *Island Hotel* (above) a run for its money in the comfort stakes, converted out of a terrace of fishing cottages in Lower Town.
C **Ashvale**, Ley-Greaves, Lower Town, T01720-422544. Closed Dec only. An old farmer's cottage on the top of the hill with superb sea views, where guests have their own shared living room. Very good value at the lower end of this bracket.

B&Bs in Higher Town worth looking into include:
C **Polreath**, T01720-422046, 4 bedrooms in a little cottage near the quay, it's the most famous B&B on the island and also runs the tearooms.
C **Travean**, T01720-423211;
F **Campsite**, T01720-422888, between Middle Town and Lower Town.

Bryher *p442*

A **Hell Bay Hotel**, T01720-422947, F423004. Owned by the Dorien-Smiths, not quite on the Bay but all the more restful for that.
C **Bank Cottage**, T01720-422612, although no children under 10;
C **Harbour View and Fraggle Rock**, T01720- 422222. The island's pub, which also has accommodation.
D **Soleil D'Or**, T01720-422003. B&B.
Campsite run by Kathy Stedeford of the Bryher Boat Service, T01720-422886. Apr-Oct only. Spectacularly positioned.

St Agnes *p442*

C **Turk's Head Pub**, T01720-422434. Famous Island pasties, crab sandwiches and very good real ale. Also B&B with views across St Mary's Sound and towards Gugh.
B&Bs include:
C **Coastguards**, Wendy Hick, T01720-422373;
C **Covean Cottage**, T01720-422620, also with *Garden Café* with home-made cakes and cream teas; and
C **The Parsonage**, Pam Beresford-Smith, T01720-42230; all of whom also do self-catering.
Try also **The Lighthouse** in the gatehouse, Carol Hicks, T01720-422514.
Camping on superb ground at Troy Town Farm, T01720-422360.

Eating

St Mary's *p440*

£££ **Juliet's Garden**, Seaways Flower Farm, Porthloo, T01720-422228. Mar-Oct daily 1000 and in the evenings Tue-Sun high season. A 20-min walk from Hugh Town, with superb views from its rockery garden, a good place to enjoy a very fine crab salad and the best restaurant on St Mary's by miles.

££ Mermaid Inn, overlooking the harbour in Hugh Town. Strewn with smugglers' loot and wreckage and evening meals feature freshly caught fish.

Tresco *p441*
££ The New Inn, New Grimsby, T01720-422883. The island's pub: the restaurant section a bit characterless but the bar area usually lively. Open all year. Cottage rental on T01720-422566. Open all year.

St Martin's *p433*
££ Seven Stones pub in Lower Town, T01720-423560. The island's pleasant pub. Open 1000-1630 and 1830-1100, less regularly in the winter. Sun lunches a speciality and can be booked.

Festivals

Gig racing is the big spectator sport in the Scilly Isles, when locals compete to row their old pilot boats from Nut Point to St Mary's as quickly as possible, a reminder of the days when first on won the contract, sometimes to take ships as far as Liverpool. **May** The World Pilot Gig Championships take place in the first May Day Bank Holiday. Throughout the season, Wed nights the women race, Fri the men.

Activities and tours

Watersports

Mark Groves, 'Nowhere', Old Town, St Mary's, T01720-422732, T07747-615732 (mob). Snorkelling with grey atlantic seals (£34), all equipment provided. Also does diving safaris, 3-hr instruction £40. 0900 or 1400 and sea safaris in an RIB.
St Martin's Diving Services, Highertown, St Martin's, T01720-422848. Dive school and canoeing instruction.
Pettifox, T01720-422511. Trips on a 36ft gaff cutter, a registered tall ship, with Scillonian skipper Alfie Hicks.

Tours

Open Top Vintage Bus Tour, T01720-422901. Tour round St Mary's with enlightening commentary. Leaves daily from the park in Hugh Town.

Transport

Bicycle

Buccabu Bike Hire, Porthcressa, St Mary's, T01720-422289. Mon-Sat with erratic opening hrs. Bike hire on Tresco T01720-422849.

Taxi

Island Taxis, T01720- 422635; St Mary's Taxis, T01720-422555; Luke's Taxis, T01720-423424; all on St Mary's.

Directory

Banks There are 2 banks on Scilly, both on Hugh St, St Mary's. **Lloyds TSB**, T01720-422418 and **Barclays** T01720-422678. Both are generally open Mon-Fri, 0900-1600. Lloyds has a cash machine. The Co-op store in Hugh St offers a 'cashback' facility, accepting Switch and Delta. **Post office** There are offices on all the islands offering National Girobank and National Savings facilities. **St Mary's**, T01720-422454; **St Agnes**, T01720-422364; **Bryher**, T01720-422010/422858; **Tresco**, T01720-423363; **St Martin's**, T01720-422801. Mon-Fri (0815-1630) and Sat (0815-1215). **Medical facilities** Doctor T01720-422628; **dentist**, T01720-422694. The only chemist on the islands is R Douglas at The Bank, Hugh Town, St Mary's, T01720-422403.

East Anglia

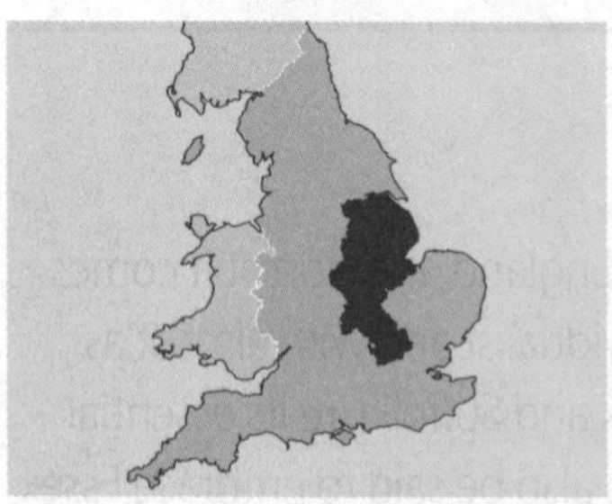

Footprint features

Introduction

East Anglia is a peculiar corner of England, the closest it comes to Holland, both offbeat and individualist and with almost as settled and civilized an air. Norfolk and Suffolk are its essential counties, although the region can also be said to embrace Essex in the south and Cambridgeshire in the west. Geologically the youngest part of the country, its eastern seaboard practically shares the sea bed. Relatively isolated from the rest of the country, it's the endless flat horizons of Norfolk's north coast, Suffolk's eerie seashore and the level watery marshland of the Broads that draw the most discerning visitors.

Cambridge is a hotbed of cutting-edge technologicaland intellectual activity; Norwich is the home of the flourishing University of East Anglia (UEA) and the world-class Sainsbury Centre of Visual Arts; Suffolk has received a shot in the armfrom emigrant Londoners, the towns on its unearthly coastline – Southwold, Dunwich, Aldeburgh, Orford – all awash with metropolitan gossip; and Essex, well it's one of the most mixed-up, in-yer-face counties within spitting distance of London: think The Prodigy, Squarepusher and loud pointy-chested girls as well as the watercolour prettiness of Constable Country. This is the county that embraces both militarized Colchester and the olde-worlde charm of Saffron Walden. The latter sits at the heart of an area endearingly named Uttlesford, including sleepy market towns like Thaxted and Great Dunmow. On the coast to the south, Southendsoaks up weekending Eastenders, while to the east Clacton and Frinton compete in both their class and the cleanliness of their beaches.

★ Don't miss...

1. Come over all nostalgic about English rural life at the Alfred Munnings museum in **Dedham**, heart of Constable Country, page 452.
2. Discover more about the Anglo-Saxons at **Sutton Hoo** near Woodbridge and see how they liked to bury their dead, page 463.
3. Spot rare wading seabirds like avocets at **Minsmere** RSPB reserve on the strange Suffolk Coast, page 466.
4. Wonder at the art in the **Sainsbury Centre**, Norwich, after looking around one of the finest medieval cities in the country, page 482.
5. Find the horizon at **Holkham Beach** after looking around the palatial neo-classical pile of Holkham Hall, page 487.
6. Go punting along 'the backs' of the colleges in **Cambridge** and thank God you're not Rupert Brooke, page 493.

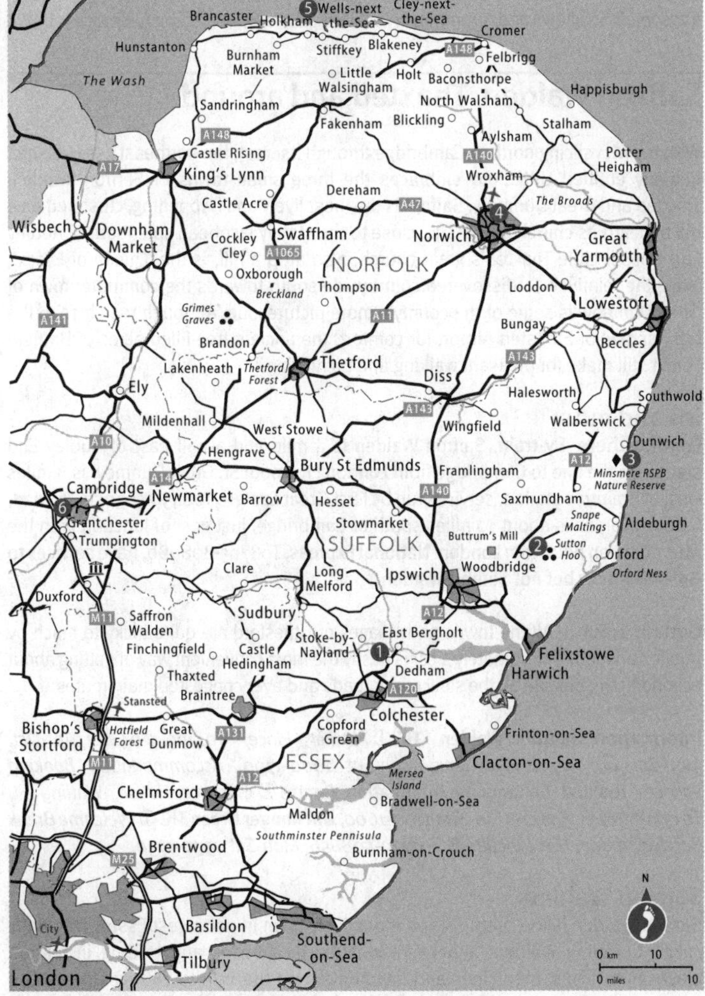

Essex

→ *Colour map 3, grid A3*

Essex is the English county that has famously become the butt of many bad jokes, full of 'wannabe' girls and boys ridiculed for their easy virtue, flash consumerism and one-time worship of Margaret Thatcher. In fact, although it may not be very fashionable, Essex conceals some relatively undiscovered countryside within reach of London and many of its villages are just as pretty as those of its more salubrious neighbour, Suffolk. To the east of the county, Uttlesford embraces the three prosperous market towns of Saffron Walden, Thaxted and Great Dunmow. In the west, Colchester is a strange mixed-up kind of place on the site of one of the oldest towns in England and close to the countryside on the river Stour that the painter John Constable committed to canvas in the 19th century. Along the coast, Southend-on-Sea has long been many Eastenders' favourite seaside resort, competing with Clacton-on-Sea further north. Nearby, Frinton-on-Sea is famous for being irredeemably middle class, perhaps in reaction to its neighbours. Beyond is the tidal marshland of Hamford Water inspiration for Arthur Ransome's Swallows and Amazons. » *For Sleeping, Eating and other listings, see pages 455-457.*

Saffron Walden, Thaxted and around

With the M11 slicing north to Cambridge through its west, the northeast Essex district quaintly entitled Uttlesford embraces the three small towns of Saffron Walden, Thaxted and Great Dunmow. Saffron is the most lively and happening, clustered on a hill beneath its church and castle, close to the stately Jacobean splendour of Audley End House. Little Thaxted's great church, also atop a hill, is the 'Queen of Essex', while the relatively undiscovered countryside south towards the commuter town of Great Dunmow is some of the county's more picturesque. Although too close to the busy sprawl of Stansted Airport for comfort, the ancient tree-filled acres of Hatfield Forest still make for pleasant walking and picnicking.

Ins and outs

Getting there By **train**, Saffron Walden is a mile and a half east of Audley End station on the line to Cambridge from London Liverpool St. Great Dunmow is 8 miles west of Braintree station, services run by **First Great Eastern** T08459-505050. By **road**, Saffron Walden is about 10 miles south of Cambridge, just east of Junction 9 on the M11, about an hour from London. **National Express**, T08705-808080, have services to Great Dunmow but not Saffron Walden.

Getting around All the towns and villages of Uttlesford are quite tricky to reach by public transport. Unfortunately a car is easily the most convenient way of getting about beyond them, despite all the slow minor roads and over-congested main routes.

Information Saffron Walden TIC ⓘ *Market Place, T01799-510444. Apr-Oct, Mon-Sat 0930-1730, Nov-Mar, Mon-Sat 1000-1700. Accommodation Booking service.* **Thaxted Community Information Centre** ⓘ *Clarance House, Watling St, T01371-831641. Apr-Oct Thu-Sun 1100-1600.* **Birchanger Green TIC** ⓘ *Welcome Break Service Station, M11 Junction 8, T01279-508656. Mon-Sat 0930-1730.*

Saffron Walden

Saffron Walden is the prettiest and most lively town in northwest Essex. Originally called Chipping Walden, it became wealthy by growing and trading in saffron crocuses for dyes, medicines and flavouring from the 15th to 18th centuries. The dinky little **Market Square** remains the centre of town, its neoclassical old **Corn Exchange** (now a small library open Sunday only) overlooking market stalls on Tuesday and Saturday and a congested car park the rest of the week. A few steps north of the square, the graceful spire of **St Mary's** (the largest church in Essex) is a useful landmark and Church Street a good place to begin an exploration of the town's warren of gabled, half-timbered streets. The patterned plasterwork on the 15th-century **Sun Inn** (now an antique bookshop) is a fine example of the 17th-century art of pargeting. Others can be seen along the High Street and Castle Street, beyond the church, and adjacent to **Bridge End Gardens** ⓘ *Viewable by appointment with the TIC*. These attractive Victorian formal gardens contain a restored yew hedge maze, pavilions and a kitchen garden. Also on Castle Street, with similar origins to the gardens, is the **Fry Art Gallery** ⓘ *Castle St, T01799-513779, www.fryartgallery.org, Easter-Oct Tue, Sat, Sun, bank holidays 1400-1700, free, donations suggested*, with its interesting permanent collection of work by eminent local artists, especially the mid-20th century painters and engravers from Great Bardfield, like John Aldridge, Edward Bawden and Eric Ravilious, as well as Marianne Straub and Tom Deakins. At the top end of the street is the **Saffron Walden Museum** ⓘ *Museum St T01799-510333, Mar-Oct Mon-Sat 1000-1700, Sun and bank holidays 1400-1700, Nov-Feb Mon-Sat 1000-1630, Sun and bank holidays 1400-1630, £1, concessions 50p, under-16s free*, with the ruins of the town's Norman castle in its grounds. The museum's highlights include a Viking necklace, antique porcelain and the history of saffron as well as plenty to entertain the kids. A 5 minute walk east, on the Common, is the most extensive ancient **turf maze** in Europe – not much to look at but surprisingly tricky to complete.

Audley End House

ⓘ *T01799-522399. Apr-Sep Wed-Sun, bank holidays, Grounds 1100-1800, House 1200-1700 (last entries 1 hr before closing), Oct Wed-Fri 1100-1600, Sat and Sun 1100-1000. £6.95, concessions £5.95, children £3, grounds only £4, concessions £3. Miniature railway, T01799-541354, www.audley-end-railway.co.uk. Mainly weekends and Aug.*

Half a mile or so west of Saffron Walden, Audley End House is a remarkable Jacobean palace set in lovely landscaped grounds and all the more remarkable because a substantial part of the original house was demolished in the early 18th century. It was built in the early 17th century for the Earl of Suffolk, Lord Treasurer to the indigent James I. Charles II later bought it as a convenient base from which to enjoy the Sport of Kings – going to the races at Newmarket. As well as the restored Victorian parterre and the ha-ha giving onto rolling green hills dotted with eyecatcher monuments, highlights of the interior are a magnificent carved oak screen in the great hall, an early 18th-century Gothic private chapel, and a string of rooms sumptuously decorated in the 1820s (hung with paintings by Canaletto and Holbein among others). Best of all though is the delicate, painted beauty of the Robert Adam-designed apartments on the ground floor. Friendly well-informed guides are at hand to elucidate each of the rooms' finer points. Also at Audley End, great for the kids, is Lord Braybrooke's **miniature railway** chugging through the woods alongside and over the river Cam for a mile and a half.

James I supposedly remarked that the house was too big for a King but about right for a Lord Treasurer.

South of Audley End, **Mole Hall Wildlife Park** ⓘ *Widdington, near Newport, T01799-541359, T540400, www.molehall.co.uk*, offers a family-fun day out featuring otters, butterflies and other exotic fauna around a moated old manor house.

Thaxted and around

Thaxted is another picturesque town but much quieter than Saffron, with its fine crumbly medieval Guildhall at the top of the High Street, a cobbled walkway below its flying-buttressed **church** on the hilltop where Holst was organist. Inside, a chapel commemorates John Ball, one of the leaders of the Peasant's Revolt in 1381, and there's lots of medieval stone carving and a beautiful 15th-century stained-glass window of Adam and Eve. The other prominent landmark is the early 19th-century brick-built **windmill** ⓘ *T01371-830285*. Another 5 miles to the east, **Finchingfield** is a pretty little village with a duck pond surrounded by teashops and old pubs, also overlooked by a much smaller church at the top of its hill.

Another six miles east of Thaxted, **Castle Hedingham** ⓘ *T01787-460261, Apr-Oct daily 1000-1700*, is quite an impressive Norman keep that has survived since 1140, strongly associated with the De Veres and the Earls of Oxford. The interior will be familiar from many an Errol Flynn movie, featuring a banqueting hall, minstrels gallery and yet another room where Elizabeth I is supposed to have slept. A couple of miles to the east, **Little Maplestead**'s round church is one of only four in England.

Great Dunmow

Uttlesford's third town is Great Dunmow, with much less immediate appeal than Thaxted or Saffron, it is more of a commuter dormitory town though blessed with an attractive rolling green and pond. Just to its northeast, **Little Easton** is a very pretty village with lakeside gardens and an atmospheric church containing marble monuments to the local Maynard family. HG Wells lived here and you can visit his **house** ⓘ *Jun-Sep Thu*. Also worth a look, perhaps for a picnic, are the strangely atmospheric **Gardens of Easton Lodge** ⓘ *T01371-876979*, a hotch-potch work-in-progress by the Creasey family restoring and adding to Harold Peto's original layout of 1902. There's a great swing hanging from a mighty cedar of Lebanon.

Hatfield Forest

ⓘ *Hatfield Forest (NT) T01279 870678. Café open Easter-Oct daily 1000-1630, Nov-Easter weekends and school holidays 1000-1530.*

Six miles west of Great Dunmow, off the road to Bishop's Stortford, Hatfield Forest is a medieval royal hunting forest still home to fallow deer, where the woods have been carefully coppiced and pollarded for centuries. Pleasant walks around the grasslands are slightly marred by the air traffic overhead. The long-distance footpath the **Flitch Way** passes through the forest. A little 18th-century lakeside picnic house decorated with shells is now also a café and education centre.

Colchester, Constable Country and around

Colchester is and always was an army town. It confidently lays claim to being 'the oldest town in Britain', thanks to a mention by Pliny in AD 77. First known as Camulodunum, meaning 'fortress of the war god Camulos', in pre-Roman days, it is now the base for battalions of the Parachute Regiment, aka the 'Paras', the shock troops of the British Army. No change there then. Possibly also named after Old King Cole, the merry old soul, Colchester is a strange mix of ancient heritage and urban deprivation. Northeast of Colchester, the undeniable charms of Constable Country are milked for all they're worth round Dedham. Several other villages close by, including the painter's birthplace at East Bergholt, are usually appreciably less mobbed than the famous Flatford Mill.

Ins and outs

Getting there Hourly **trains** from London Liverpool Street to Colchester Town Station (1 hour 8 minutes) from **First Great Eastern**, T08459-505050. By **road**, leave London from the east on the A12. Continue northeast on the A12 through Chelmsford, exit A12 at Beacon End on the outskirts of Colchester (1½ hours, 60 miles). **National**

Battle of the Essexes

Essex Man (Tabloidicus Hooliganus) has become part of English folklore. Recognizable by his bleached hair and copy of the Sun newspaper in the back pocket, he and his sun bed-fricaseed female equivalent can usually be seen breaking the speed limit on the A127 in a souped-up Ford Escort with customary sunstrip bearing the legend 'Darren and Tracy'. Poor Essex. It must surely be the most maligned of England's counties, provoking fear and derision in equal measure. John Peel, the nation's favourite DJ, even makes a massive detour to and from his home in Suffolk in order to avoid having to drive through the place. But it's not all negative. Essex has made a major contribution to the world of music, from art rockers Blur (who hail from Colchester) to Canvey Island's finest, pub rockers Dr Feelgood. The country that the rest of England loves to ridicule doesn't really give a monkey's anyway. As the late, great Ian Dury sang in his paen to Essex: "I'm not a bleedin' thicky, I'm Billericay Dickie and I'm doing very well".

Express, T08705-808080, have services from London Victoria coach station to Colchester bus station, via Stansted Airport (3½ hours). Direct services are less frequent (2½ hours). » *For further details, see Transport page 457.*

Getting around Colchester Town Centre is about a mile square based around the ancient town layout with the River Colne flowing along the north and down the east side. To the northeast Colchester links with Ipswich on the A12 and the A14 route to Birmingham and via the M1/M6 to the Midlands and the North of England. It is 45 minutes from Stansted Airport and 30 minutes from the East Coast ports of Harwich and Felixstowe. Tendring Peninsula is minutes away from Colchester by car, bus or train. Or can easily be cycled via the Wivenhoe Riverside Path. **Arriva Colchester,** 38 Magdalen St, T01206-764029 is the local bus service.

Information Colchester TIC ⓘ *1 Queen Street, T01206-282920 and Flatford La, Flatford, East Bergholt T01206-299460.*

History

Shakespeare's Cymbeline, chief of the Trinovantes, founded a settlement at Lexden, 2 miles west of present-day Colchester, where the rudimentary earthworks of his Camulodunum can still be seen. In AD 43, the Roman Emperor Claudius captured Camulodunum, forcing 11 British kings to submit to his rule, and ordering a temple to be constructed here in his honour, which indicates the importance of this outpost. The town was attacked 17 years later by the revolting Iceni tribe led by Boudicca. She torched the temple, savaged the town and most of its inhabitants, before rampaging south and west through St Albans and on to London. After she and her tribe had in turn been massacred by the legions of Suetonius Paulinus, the town was heavily fortified with a 20-foot wall and large triumphal gateway, the remains of which still stand to this day. In 1079 the Normans constructed one of their larger castles over what was left of Claudius's temple. Five centuries later the town's wealth and importance was increased by the arrival of emigrant Dutch weavers who settled in an attractive part of town now called the Dutch quarter, north of the High Street. In 1648, during the Civil War, Colchester stubbornly sided with the King and suffered badly during a three-month siege. Today the town remains an important base for the army.

Colchester

Okay, so Colchester may not look very Roman today. Even so, with a fair bit of imagination, the original rectangular shape and scale of Camulodunum can still just about be made out. The modern High Street follows the dead straight east-west line of the Roman town laid down over the hill in the first century AD. At its western end, the **Balkerne Gate** was the Romans' entrance from the west, and its remains can still be seen. It looks like a bit of old subway, a short clammy tunnel with a curved brick roof giving onto the A134 rushing past just beneath, but it can claim to be the only surviving Roman gateway in Britain. That fact, along with its age and its setting – in the shadow of the striking bulk of the brick-built Victorian watertower, a hilltop landmark affectionately known as Jumbo, and next to the *Hole in the Wall* pub (aptly named) and Mercury Theatre – make the gate quite a strange and unusual sight.

A beeline east of the gate along Camulodunum's main street passes through the mock-Tudor timber frame of the town's **Post Office** and on to the modern High Street. Half way down the High Street, behind the imposing **Town Hall** with its prominent clocktower, is the **Dutch quarter**, a warren of attractive old streets between West and East Stockwell Streets. On the opposite side of the road, south of the High Street, **Tymperleys Clock Museum** ⓘ *Trinity St, T01206-282939. Apr-Oct, Tue-Sat 1000-1300, 1400-1700, free*, houses a collection of antique tickers in a 15th-century timber-framed building. Nearby, **St John's Abbey Gate** ⓘ *open at any reasonable time*, is all that remains of the vast Benedictine abbey of St John.

The substantial remains of the **Norman castle** ⓘ *T01206-282939, Mon-Sat 1000-1700, Sun 1100-1700 (last admission 30 mins before closing), £4, under-16s and concessions £2.70, guided tours (£1.50) explore the foundations of Claudius's temple and take in the views from the roof*, built on the site of Claudius's temple, using bricks from the Roman town, stand at the top of East Hill, a few hundred yards above the old east gate (long vanished). Set back from the High Street in a pretty park, it was the largest keep ever built by the Normans, between 1076 and 1175, and adapted in the 18th century by the local MP 'for his own personal use', with the addition of large windows, domed tower and tiled roof. The **museum** inside is particularly strong on Roman finds, and medieval life in the town.

Near Colchester Town station is **St Botolph's Priory** ⓘ *T01206-282931, open any reasonable time, free*, where the nave of the first Augustinian priory in England can be seen, including an original arcade at its west end.

Constable Country: the Stour Valley

Northeast of Colchester, the river Stour (usually pronounced 'store') divides Essex from Suffolk and more famously inspired John Constable, one of Britain's greatest landscape painters. Remarkably enough many of the scenes that he made famous, brooded over by his magnificent skies, are still perfectly recognizable today. Dedham is the centre of 'Constable Country', although his birthplace **East Bergholt** and the charming village of **Stoke-by-Nayland** are in some ways more rewarding places to seek out the picturesque rural idyll of his paintings. The mills of Stratford St Mary also inspired the painter, although today the village is a bit spoiled by the A12. All are in the **Dedham Vale**, a protected AONB ('Area of Outstanding Natural Beauty').

Dedham village itself is worth a look though, with its row of grand and carefully preserved Georgian houses lining its main street alongside the 17th-century church. Attractive wooden tiller rowing boats can be hired on the river from here, at **Dedham Boathouse** ⓘ *T01206-323153, Apr-Sep only, £10 an hr*, on the bridge just outside the village, for a row downstream to Flatford Mill. A 20-minute walk south down a charming narrow alley beside the **Dedham Art and Craft Centre** ⓘ *T01206-322666, daily 1000-1700*, across municipal playing fields and past an extraordinary pink timber-framed Elizabethan courtyard house (*garden open*), brings you to **Castle House** ⓘ *T01206-322127, Easter-Sep, Wed, Sun, bank holidays 1400-1700, also Thu,*

Sat 1400-1700 in Aug), £3, concessions £2, under-16s 50p. This grand rectory was the home of the quintessentially English portrait painter Sir Alfred Munnings from 1919 until 1959. Most of his portraits involve horses, taking the races and country life as their subject, and the whole place has a quiet, elegiac atmosphere, a shrine to rural ways of life that are all but extinct.

Flatford Mill, the most celebrated of Constable's subjects, featured in several pictures, is reached by road through East Bergholt where the church bells are kept in a spooky old wooden cage in the churchyard, apparently because the devil stole the bell tower. Down by the river, the complex of attractions includes a John Constable Exhibition in thatched **Bridge Cottage** ⓘ *T01206-298260, May-Oct daily 1000-1730, Mar-Apr Wed-Sun, bank holidays 1100-1730, Nov-Feb Wed-Sun 1100-1530, not Wed-Fri in Jan and Feb, free*. There's also the **Museum of Rural Bygones** in the old Granary, and the **Flatford Visitor Information Centre** ⓘ *T01206-299460, Mar Sat, Sun 1000-1700, Apr-Sep daily 1000-1700, Oct Mon-Fri 1000-1600*. The latter provides details on Dedham Vale and walks in the surrounding countryside. The **Stour** Trust ⓘ *T01206 393680, Wed during summer holidays, and every Sun Easter-Oct 1100-1700, every 30 mins, £2.50*, run silent electric launch river trips.

South of Colchester

Two miles south of the town centre, well-signposted, **Bourne Mill** ⓘ *(NT), Bourne La, Colchester, T01206-572422, Jun-Aug Tue and Sun 1400-1700, £2*, was built as a fishing lodge in 1521, and still has watermill machinery intact inside and out. Also a couple of miles south, on the B1022 towards Maldon, is **Colchester Zoo** ⓘ *Stanway, T01206-331292, www.colchester-zoo.co.uk, daily 0930-1730 (or dusk, whichever is earlier), £9, under-14s £5.75*, one of the better zoos in England and the home of over 200 species, including rhino, elephants, cheetahs, and the only white tiger in the UK. The well-designed complex could easily occupy a whole day and kids are usually enthralled.

Four miles further south of Colchester on the same road, tucked away down a maze of narrow lanes near Birch, **Layer Marney Tower** ⓘ *T01206-330784, Apr-Oct Mon-Fri, Sat 1200-1700, £3.50, under-16s £2, family £10*, is the tallest Tudor gatehouse in the country and quite a surprising find in this relatively out-of-the-way area. Designed in the late 1500s to outdo Hampton Court, its palace was never built. There are fine views from the top. Next door, the **church of St Mary** was also built to be fit for a palace.

Five miles southwest of Colchester, off the A12, **Copford Church** boasts some of the most splendid Norman paintings in the country. A restored 12th-century church, the *Raising of Jairus's Daughter* is in its original condition above the pulpit. Another 2 miles down the A12, **Feeringbury Manor** ⓘ *near Coggeshall, Feering, T01376-561949, Mon-Fri, Apr-Jul 0800-1300*, is an old moated house with a beautiful garden.

Essex Coast: Southend to Harwich

There's not a huge amount to recommend the Essex coast apart from its convenience for Londoners. That fact has been quite enough though to ensure that it's still very lively in summer, and it also conceals a few more secluded spots beloved by birdwatchers and oyster-eaters. Southend is the largest seaside resort, a full-on strip of seaside amusements overlooking the longest pier in the world. Further up the coast, succulent Colchester oysters can found at Burnham-on-Crouch and Mersea Island, while the nature reserve at Northey Island in the Blackwater estuary is one of the best for birdwatching within easy reach of the capital. Clacton-on-Sea and Frinton-on-Sea on the Tendring peninsula east of Colchester are where Essex really gets into its stride along the coast and amusingly different in the steps they take to entertain summer visitors. Harwich is the major international ferry point on the North Sea, with a quaint old town still relatively intact.

Ins and outs

Getting there Southend can be reached by **train** from London Fenchurch Street in less than an hour. Trains for Burnham-on-Crouch leave from Liverpool Street and also take about an hour. Clacton-on-Sea and Frinton-on-Sea are on a branch line from Colchester. By **road**, Southend is about 1 hour's drive from central London down the A13. Other parts of the coast are easily reached along the A12. Maldon is about 1½ hours from London, Harwich more like 2 hours. **National Express,** T08705-808080, run regular coaches to Southend, Colchester and Harwich from London.

Information **Southend TIC** ⓘ *19 High St, T01702-215120, www.southend.gov.uk, Mon-Sat 0930-1700, Jul-Aug also Sun 1000-1600.* **Clacton TIC** ⓘ *23 Pier Avenue, T01255-423400 www.essex-sunshine-coast.org.uk, Mid-May to mid-Sep daily 1000-1730, rest of year, Mon-Sat1000-1700.* **Harwich TIC** ⓘ *Safeway, Iconfield Park T01255-506139.*

Southend

Southend, the closest seaside resort to the capital, has long been London's East End-on-Sea. Considerably more cheerful than some of its competitors on the opposite bank of the Thames estuary, the 7-mile long beach is surprisingly clean and fronts a south-facing esplanade that still retains some of its Regency splendour if none of its dignity, dominated as it is by loud pubs, fast-food joints and noisy amusement arcades. Younger kids always want to head straight for **Adventure Island** ⓘ *Marine Pde and Western Esplanade, T01702-468023, daily Easter-mid-Sep 1100-1800 (until 2000 Jul-mid-Sep)*, on the Western Esplanade, where entry is free and a variety of rides for all ages are paid for one at a time. The rainy day option is the revamped sealife centre, now called **Sea Life Adventure** ⓘ *Eastern Esplanade, T01702-601834, daily 1000-1900, £4.95, under-14 £3.60*, with an underwater tunnel, ray bay, piranha tank and one of the largest tiny tots play areas in the country. The resort's most famous feature, its over a mile-long **pier** ⓘ *Western Esplanade, T01702-215622, Apr-Sep Mon-Fri 0815-2100, Sat and Sun 0815-2200, Oct, Nov, Feb, Mar Mon-Fri 0815-1800, Sat, Sun 0815-2000, Dec and Jan Mon-Fri 0815-1600, Sat, Sun 0815-1800, The Pavilion (on the Pier Head) T01702-469405*, is definitely worth the train ride or walk along it right out into the estuary, even if the Pavilion and viewpoints at the end are not the most inspiring destination. .

Southminster peninsula

Seven miles north of Southend as the crow flies (considerably longer by road), **Burnham-on-Crouch** is a popular yachting centre, and makes a good day trip by train from London. Famous for its oysters, its on the south side of the Southminster peninsula. On the north side, **Bradwell-on-Sea** has a nuclear power station that's just been decommissioned. Standing in a remote and eerie spot nearby, the church of St Peter-on-the-Wall is a seventh-century place of worship, built using stones from the local Roman fort of Othona. At the foot of the peninsula is the little port of **Maldon** on the river Blackwater, with its triangular-towered church and Washington window: the town was home to the captain of the *Mayflower*. A tidal causeway leads out to **Northey Island** ⓘ *(NT), Northey Cottage, Maldon, T01621-853142, open by appointment with the warden with 24 hours notice, £1.50*. The island was the site of the Battle of Maldon in 991, celebrated in a remarkable Anglo-Saxon poem recounting the defeat of local hero Brythnoth and his men by the Vikings. Today it's a top birdwatching site.

Mersea Island

On the north side of the Blackwater estuary, about 10 miles east of Maldon, Mersea Island is reached over a low causeway liable to flooding at peak tides, and is also famous for its oysters. The *Company Shed* is a good place to eat them (see Eating and drinking below), looking south across the estuary to the sound of tinkling halyards in the boatyard.

Clacton and Frinton

East of Colchester, the main seaside resorts are Clacton-on-Sea and Frinton-on-Sea. Both are favourites with Londoners during the summer, comical in their appeal to different classes. Clacton was recently ranked 'top for totty' by the Alternative Beach Guide, not entirely to its tourist board's amusement. The pier claims to be the largest in the country, and features a Seaquarium and Reptile Safari. Otherwise it's a very straightforward and well-maintained summer family holiday centre. Much more genteel, just up the coast, Frinton has an attractive grassy promenade, absolutely no amusement arcades and an orderly rank of neat little multicoloured beach huts stretching along the sandy beach.

Halfway to Colchester on the A133, in Elmstead Market, unpromising ground conditions were capitalized upon by top horticulturalist Beth Chatto over 40 years ago to create **gardens** ⓘ *Elmstead Market, T01206-822007, Mar-Oct Mon-Sat 0900-1700, Nov-Feb Mon-Fri 0900-1600, £2.50*, with outstanding herbaceous borders, as well as dry Mediterranean and bog gardens. There's also a very highly rated nursery full of exotic plants if you want to try something similar at home.

Just to the north of Frinton, **Hamford Water** is a wide stretch of shallow water, mudflats and reedbeds covered by the tides. Popular with dinghy sailors, its maze of little creeks and islands was popularized by Arthur Ransome in *Swallows and Amazons*. Horsey Island sits in the middle, accessible at low tide only.

Stour Estuary

Further north, **Wrabness Nature Reserve** provides another wetland habitat worth exploring, near the old estuary villages of Mistley and Manningtree on the river Stour. Mistley Towers were designed by Robert Adam, now standing oddly on the ground bereft of their church in an enclosure beside the main road. At the mouth of the Stour, **Harwich** is an international ferry port with boats to Holland and Germany. A mile east of the main terminals, the Old Town is well worth a look around, sensitively restored since the war. Easily reached from the Main Road railway station, the Electric Palace Cinema on King's Quay Street was purpose-built in 1911 and still shows films. Other sights worth a look are the 17th-century Treadwheel Crane, the maritime museum in the Low Lighthouse and TV museum in the High Lighthouse.

Sleeping

Saffron Walden, Thaxted and around *p448*

A The Starr, Market Pl, Great Dunmow, T01371-874321, www.the-starr.co.uk. Salubrious, expensive old restaurant with rooms where TV-chef Jamie Oliver cut his teeth. The 8 rooms are comfortably and traditionally furnished.

A Whitehall Hotel, Church End, Broxted, T01279-850603, www.whitehallhotel.co.uk. Part of the Heritage group, with characterful beamed rooms and good restaurant, 3 miles from Thaxted.

C Archway Guest House, 13 Church St, Saffron Walden, T01799-501500, F503006. Opposite the church, non-smoking family-run place full of old toys and rock memorabilia.

C Crossways Guest House, 32 Town St, Thaxted, T01371-830348. 3 rooms in an old house right opposite the crumbly Guildhall.

C The Plough Inn, Sampford Rd, Radwinter, 5 miles east of Saffron Walden, T01799-599222. Great local with fairly basic rooms (from £25 per person) and very good home-made pub food, real ales and some unusual wines.

F YHA Castle Hedingham, 7 Falcon Square, Castle Hedingham, T01787-460799. 50 beds available in the heart of the attractive old village clustered beneath the Norman castle.

F YHA Saffron Walden 1 Myddyton Pl, Saffron Walden, T01799-523117, F520840. Forty beds in a 600-year-old oak-beamed maltings, complete with a courtyard garden.

Colchester, Constable Country and around *p450*

B Red Lion Hotel, High St, T01206-577986, F578207. A timber-framed building but the *George Hotel* (see below) has more character.

B-C George Hotel, High St, Colchester, T01206-578494, F761732. If an overnight stop in Colchester is necessary this is an honest-to-goodness revamped coaching inn on the High St with a lively bar.

C Elm House, 14 Upper Holt St, Earls Colne, near Colchester, T01206-240456. Another reasonable bet for B&B.

C Gladwins Farm, Harper's Hill, Nayland, near Colchester, T01206-262261. B&B which welcomes dogs and children, with smoking allowed in some rooms.

C The Old Vicarage, Higham, T01206-337248. Out of town, this is a charming B&B in an attractive old village near Stoke-by-Nayland.

Essex Coast: Southend to Harwich *p453*

C Cap and Feathers, 8 South St, Tillingham, near Southminster, T01621-779212. Attractive and cosy clapperboard pub with its own smokehouse, a no-smoking room, and some very good real ales. 3 double rooms upstairs.

C Olde White Harte, The Quay, Burnham-on-Crouch, T01621-782106. Very busy in Burnham Week when the world's yachties turn up to drink beside their boats, but otherwise a pleasant spot right on the water.

C White Hart B&B, Manningtree, T01206-392768, has comfortable rooms in an old period house in the middle of the village.

Eating

Saffron Walden, Thaxted and around *p448*

£££ The Pink Geranium, Station Rd, Melbourn, near Royston, Cambs, T01763-260215. Once Prince Charles' favourite restaurant, doing upmarket (about £35 a head) accomplished French-influence food in a starched and cottagey setting.

££ The Axe and Compasses, Arkesden, T01799-550272. Offers good food in an old thatched pub.

££ The Kings Arms, Market Hill, Saffron Walden, T01799-522768. Does real ale and food with an ambitious evening menu.

££ The Restaurant, 2 Church St, Saffron Walden, T01799-526444. Offers organic basement dining in the evenings – possibly the best food in Saffron.

£ Jo's Coffee House, 5 Hill St, Saffron Walden, T01799-513553. Straightforward lunches beside the Jubilee gardens.

Colchester, Constable Country and around *p450*

£££ Baumann's Brasserie, Coggeshall, 4-6 Stoneham St, T01376-561453. Expensive and ambitious (£40 a head at least) but distinctly a cut above most of the competition.

£££ Le Talbooth, Dedham, T01206-323150. The haute cuisine option, £30 a head for formal dining in a low, beamed room next to the river but within earshot of the A12.

£££ Lemon Tree, 48 St John's St, Colchester, T01206-767337, is a relatively innovative modern British restaurant with added atmosphere thanks to some Roman walls.

££ The Angel Inn T01206-337324, Stoke-by-Nayland is a very popular food pub in a 16th-century building on Nayland's main street.

££ Toto's Pizza and Pasta, 517 Museum St, T01206-76200, is a basic, cheap and cheerful Italian with the added value of an outside courtyard with views of the castle.

££ The White Hart, Poole St, Great Yeldham T01787-237250 does good-value pub meals.

££ White Hart Inn, T01206-263382, Stoke-by-Nayland, has rooms and a good-value restaurant madeover by Michel Roux.

Essex Coast: Southend to Harwich *p453*

£££ Blue Strawberry, Hatfield Peverel, T01245-381333. About £35 a head for a sophisticated menu in a cosy cottage setting.

£££ Pipe of Port, 84 High St, Southend, T01702-614606. Straightforward bistro food but probably the best on offer.

££ Company Shed, West Mersea, open shop hrs (not Mon) 0900-1700, Sun 1000-1700, bring your own bread and wine, last orders for eating taken at 1600.

Bars, pubs and clubs

Saffron Walden, Thaxted and around *p448*

The Compasses, Littley Green, Great Waltham, near Great Dunmow,

T01245-362308. Regularly voted CAMRA pub of the year, a Victorian drinking palace serving Essex huffers – well-filled buns.
White Hart, The Street, Great Saling, near Braintree, T01371-850341. Worth seeking out for their food as well as their beer.

Colchester p450
Hole in the Wall, Balkerne Passage, T01206-576392, popular pub with the local students.
Twisters, 45 North Hill, T01206-500204, Colchester, highly recommended for their stylish interiors and friendly staff.
V-Bar, 105 High St, Colchester, T01206-561611, friendly staff.

Transport

Colchester, Constable Country and around *p450*
Rail
A direct service to **Ipswich** (20 mins) is run every 15 mins by **Anglia Railways**, T08700-409090. There is also a direct service to **London Liverpool Street** (50 mins), which runs every 15 min. There is no direct service to Cambridge or Stansted airport. **National Rail Enquiries**, T08457-484950.

Bus
Long distance National Express, T08705-808080, runs a direct service to **Ipswich** (30 mins). There are direct services to **London Victoria** (2 hrs 20 mins), **Cambridge** (2 hrs 15 mins) and **Stansted airport** (1 hr 10 mins). **Traveline**, T0870-6082608.

Bicycle
Colchester Cycle Stores, 50 St Johns St, Colchester. T01206-563890; **Action Bikes**, 24 Crouch St, Colchester, T01206-541744.

Car
Avis Rent a Car, 213 Shrub End Rd, Colchester, T01206-541133; **Hertz rent-a-car**, Clacton Rd Frating, Colchester, T01206-252251; **CC Hire**, 67 Layer Rd, Colchester, T01206-761011; **SIXT KENNING**, 11 Commerce Way, Colchester, T01206-797990.

Taxi
A1 Taxis, T01206-544744; **Five Sevens Taxis**, T01206-577777; **Mersea Cars**, T01206-729691; **Panther Taxis**, T01206-525525; **Town Cars Ltd**, T01206-515515.

Suffolk

→ *Colour map 3, grid A4/5*

Suffolk is an odd county. Famously known for being 'sleepy', the arrival in recent years of large numbers of commuters fleeing London house prices has livened up the area considerably. And yet the good people of Suffolk cling fiercely to their rural roots, carefully preserving their wonderful old medieval wool towns and well-ordered little villages. Bury St Edmunds is the capital of northwest Suffolk, a charming old place with a quietly prosperous air, a cathedral still in the process of completion, a beautiful Georgian theatre and fine central square dominated by the medieval abbey gatehouse. To the north, the almost deserted forests and heaths of Breckland stretch into Norfolk. To the south, one of the area's most popular tourist destinations is provided by the wool-enriched splendours of Lavenham, Long Melford and also Clare. To the southwest, Ipswich deserves a mention, not least for being the county's largest conurbation and its industrial powerhouse, squatting on the Orwell estuary. Which brings us to the coast, really the county's pride and joy and an unmissable treat. From Woodbridge, high up the estuary of the river Deben, all the way to the delapidated seaside entertainments at Lowestoft, the A12 runs just inland of some of England's most peculiar and memorable coastal towns, villages and scenery. Orford, with its Norman castle, smokehouses and eerie shingle Ness, is the first stop. Next up is Aldeburgh, famous for its classical music festival and increasingly for the émigré London novelists that stalk its long pebbly beach in the footsteps of composer Benjamin Britten. Then Southwold, even more classy, coupled with its arty little neighbour Walberswick. ▸▸ *For Sleeping, Eating and other listings, see pages 467-471.*

Bury St Edmunds

Famous for its brewery, sugar beet and medieval abbey, Bury St Edmunds has the happy atmosphere of a town completely at ease with itself. 'Bury' to the locals, it's long been the pride of Suffolk, billing itself as the 'Shrine of a King, Cradle of the Law', reminders of the pilgrim's wealth that the medieval monastery accrued and the hospitality it offered to the barons forcing bad King John's hand to make a gesture towards democracy. Today the town is the focus of the local farming community, pretty much slap bang in the middle of East Anglia.

Ins and outs

Getting there London Liverpool Street to Bury Street Edmunds (1 hour 45 minutes) with **Anglia Railways.** About 80 miles from London by **road** (1½ hours). Take the M11 North, at junction 9 take the A11 then the A14 to Bury St Edmunds. **National Express,** T08705-808080, run services (3 hours 25 minutes) from London Victoria to Bury St Edmunds bus and coach station, St Andrews St North, four minutes walk from the town centre, via Cambridge (30 minutes' stop). Fewer direct services (2 hours 10 minutes). ▸▸ *For further details, see Transport page 470.*

Getting around Bury St Edmunds is a small town with a part-pedestrianized centre; its layout is still based around the original medieval market town and pleasant enough to walk around. Bury St Edmunds Station, Station Hill, T01284-484950, is ¼ mile north of the town centre, with bus connections. There is a taxi rank outside. St Andrews St South/Cattle market is the main short stay car park 4 minutes' walk from main shopping centre.

Information **Bury St Edmunds TIC** ⓘ *Angel Hill, T01284-764667. Easter-Oct Mon-Sat 0930-1730, Sun 1000-1500, Nov-Easter Mon-Fri 1000-1600, Sat 1000-1300.* **Lavenham TIC** ⓘ *Lady St, T01787-248207. Easter-Oct 1000-1645.* **Sudbury TIC** ⓘ *Town Hall, Market Hill, T01787-881320. Easter-Sep 1000-1645, Oct-Easter 1000-1445.*

History

The town is named after the Anglo-Saxon king of East Anglia, who was martyred to the Danes in 869. After the Norman conquest, Abbot Baldwin laid out a grid-iron street plan, the first of its kind in the country and still very much in evidence today. Less remains of one of the most powerful monasteries in medieval Europe, where the Barons forced King John to accept the need for Magna Carta, the famous 'bill of rights' that can be seen in Salisbury cathedral's chapter house.

Sights

For visitors, the centre of Bury St Edmunds is **Angel Hill**, an attractive square overlooked by the imposing old abbey gatehouse. This great gateway was constructed in the early 14th century, and now leads into the fairly ordinary municipal gardens that were once the site of the old monastery. West of the gate, the compact size of Bury's town centre means that most of its sights can be seen in less than an hour's stroll around.

Abbeygate Street heads uphill a short distance to the **Buttermarket** and a trio of fine early 19th-century buildings. The neoclassical Corn Exchange stands at the top of Abbeygate, inscribed with the pious motto 'The Earth is the Lord's and the Fulness thereof'. Turning right, into Cornhill, another dignified square with a South African War Memorial in the middle, the third of the town centre's grand trio of buildings is now the **Bury St Edmund's Art Gallery** ⓘ *T01284-762081, www.burystedmundsartgallery.org, Tue-Sat 1030-1700. £1, concessions 50p*, the Market Cross, which stages a series of interesting exhibitions by contemporary artists and has a shop selling innovative craftworks and jewellery. On the opposite side of the square is the **Moyse's Hall Museum** ⓘ *T01284-706183, Mon-Fri 1030-1630, Sat and Sun 1100-1600*, a renovated local history museum featuring the Suffolk Regiment gallery in an 800-year-old building, possibly once a Jewish merchant's house.

Back at the top of Abbeygate Street, turning left instead of right, Guildhall Street heads south lined with attractive 17th-and 18th-century houses flanking the Guildhall itself with its 15th-century porch. Just beyond, another left turn leads back downhill along Churchgate Street, originally lined up with the Norman church's high altar. At the foot of the street stands the particularly fine Norman tower, all that remains of the church. Next to it is **St Edmundsbury Cathedral** ⓘ *T01284-748726*, its Gothic tower due for completion at the end of 2004, to look like Bell Harry at Canterbury, and since the completion of Liverpool, the last unfinished cathedral in the country. Its nave was constructed in 1503, as part of the abbey of St Edmund, but ran out of funds. It was added to in the 1950s and again today. To one side there's a pleasant refectory with seats outside beside the old abbey walls, next to the Abbey Gardens, doing basic snacks like jacket potatoes for lunch (closed Sun).

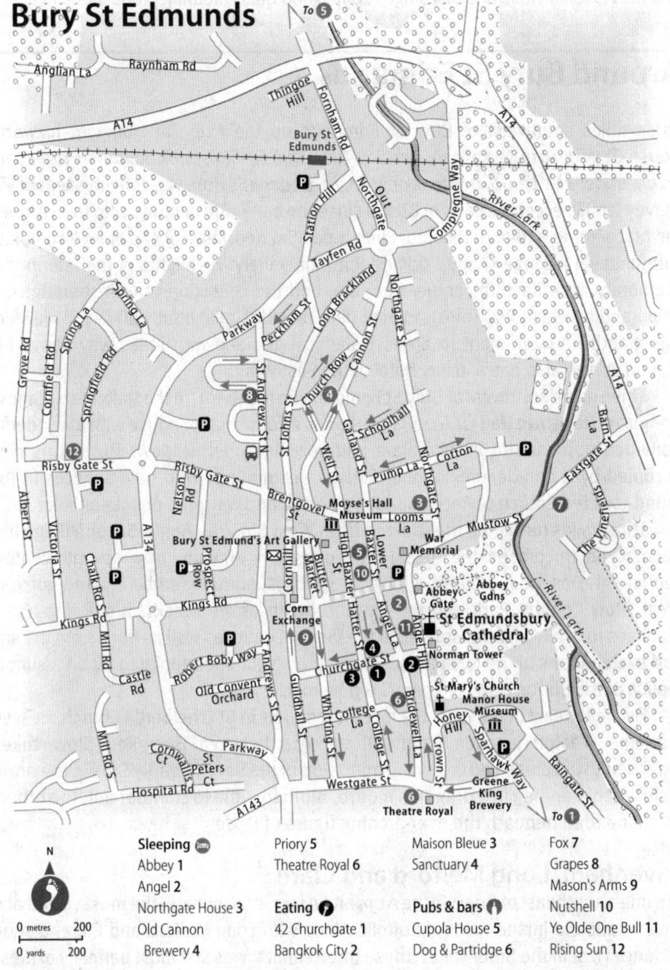

A right turn at the bottom of Churchgate Street leads into Crown Street, past **St Mary's Church** ⓘ *T01284-754680*, which has a spectacular nave and rare hammer-beam roof, as well as being the last resting place of 'Bloody' Mary Tudor. A left turn beyond the church down Honey Hill leads to the **Manor House** Museum, ⓘ *T01284-757072, Wed-Sun 1100-1600*, a Georgian house overlooking the Abbey Gardens behind the town's two most important churches, with a strange collection of antique costumes and all kinds of clocks.

Carrying straight on along Crown Street ends up at the **Greene King Brewery** ⓘ *Westgate St, T01284-714297, Mon-Fri 1300-1600, Sat and Sun 1100-1600. £2, under-16s £1, tours (2 hrs 30 mins, £5) of the brewery Mon-Fri at 1000, 1400, 1900, and on Sat 1100, 1400*, where beer has been brewed continuously since 1799 and where the company runs a small and accomplished promotion of its product. The *Brewery Tap* pub provides the freshest possible Old Speckled Hen, Abbot Ale and Ruddles County.

Beyond the Brewery, at the end of Westgate, the **Theatre Royal** ⓘ *T01284-769505, www. theatreroyal.org, May-Sep Tue, Thu 1100-1300, 1400-1600, free, guided tours Tue, Thu 1130, 1430, Sat 1130, £2 for members*, is a rare example and one of the best-preserved Georgian playhouses in the country (built in 1819), now owned by Greene King and the National Trust, and still stages some good quality touring productions.

Around Bury St Edmunds

Three miles southwest of Bury St Edmunds on the A143, at Horinger, **Ickworth** House ⓘ *(NT), T01284-735270, Apr-Sep Tue, Wed, Fri-Sun, bank holidays 1300-1630. £5.95, under-16s £2.60, gardens only £2.70, under-16s 80p*, was long the seat of the Hervey family, eccentric Earls of Bristol since the early 18th century, who transformed the place at the end of that century into a palatial neoclassical showpiece complete with unusual lozenge-shaped domed Rotunda gallery. Highlights of the interior are the library, with its 18th-century furniture, and the collection of Gainsboroughs, a Titian and a Velasquez. The 1800-acre park provides delightful walks with views of this grandiose monument to an ecclesiastical grandee with ideas way above his station. It now also has a luxury hotel in the East Wing.

Three miles northwest of Bury St Edmunds up the A1101, in the thatched village of Hengrave, **Hengrave Hall** ⓘ *T01284-701561*, is a Tudor manor house with a wonderful pollarded approach to its elaborate and very fine oriel window. The hall is now occupied by a non-denominational Christian community who hold services in the round-towered Church of Reconciliation close by and welcome people on retreat. .

Three miles further up the same road, at West Stow, an **Anglo-Saxon Village** has been reconstructed on the actual site, unusually enough, of a seventh-century settlement. Deserted, unless on fancy dress days, surrounded by firs and gorse in **West Stow Country Park** and the lowland heath of the Brecks, it still just about manages to evoke an atmosphere. In the Visitor Centre, as well as finds from the site and explanations of the local archaeology, there's an opportunity to try on a simple replica of the Sutton Hoo (see page 463) helmet.

Five miles east of Bury, are the medieval murals in **St Ethelbert's Church**, Hesset, near the Woolpit junction south off the A14 between Bury and Stowmarket. Particularly well preserved is a mural from 1460 of the Seven Deadly Sins in the north aisle, each standing in a dragon's mouth, Sloth too idle to clamber out, the others all suspended beneath the over-arching figure of Pride.

Lavenham, Long Melford and Clare

Ten miles southeast of Bury via the A134 and A1141 is Lavenham, the most visited and picturesque old inland town of Suffolk. Along with Long Melford and Clare, a short distance west in the Stour valley, these three small towns still most perfectly express the wool-rich elegance of the 16th and 17th centuries. Lavenham is the most tourist-orientated, even going so far as to boast a £3 headphone tour of the town available from the local pharmacy as punters wonder at the galleries of local contemporay art, the Al Paca studio, antiques shops, and Martin Hogg's china shop emblazoned with the declaration that 'this shop is deceptively large'. The old *Swan Hotel*, the Crooked House gallery, and *Greyhound* pub are strung along the main street, the A1141, along with an impressive array of half-timbered, plastered and pargeted houses. But the **Market Place** on top of the hill is the real highlight of the town, along with its mini-cathedral of a church, a 20-minute walk south. The **Guildhall** ⓘ *(NT), T01787-247646, Mar, Nov Sat, Sun 1100-1600, Apr, Oct Wed-Sun, bank holidays 1100-1700, May-Sep daily 1100-1700, £3*, is a 16th-century timber-framed building on the Market Place with a small local history museum, walled garden and displays on the wool trade including a working loom. Also in the Market Place is the **Little Hall**, a medieval hall house and nearby in Water Street, the Priory, converted into a home by a wealthy merchant at around the same time.

Lavenham church was built in the 15th century to rival Long Melford's, by the De Veres of Hedingham Castle and the clothiers called Spring. Restrained and serene, the length of the nave, the height of the tower and beautiful chancel arch make it an extraordinary parish church.

Four miles west of Lavenham, nestling in the valley of the river Stour, **Long Melford** lives up to its name as it stretches along its single main street just above the river, a Mecca for antique dealers. The medieval church of the Holy Trinity here is reckoned by many to be the most splendid in Suffolk. The outside of the tower was redone in the early 20th century but inside there's a magnificent procession of stained glass, including a window supposed to have inspired John Tenniel's illustrations for *Alice in Wonderland* and a rare Lily Crucifix.

Nearby, across the green, similar in date to the Tudor almshouses that cluster around the church, **Melford Hall** ⓘ *(NT), T01787-880286, Apr Sat, and Sun 1400-1700, May-Sep Wed-Sun, bank holidays 1400-1700, £4.50, under-16 £2.25*, has been lived in by the Hyde Parkers since the late 18th century, a fine red brick house where Elizabeth I was once entertained in lavish style by Sir William Cordell. Now two magnificent copper beeches set off its front lawns, with an adorable octagonal Elizabethan gazebo set into its wysteria-covered garden wall. Inside there's an impressive library and staircase, and unusual pictures done by Beatrix Potter, once a regular visitor to the house.

Six miles west of Long Melford, **Clare** is another old wool-rich town in the Stour valley, smaller and less touristy than Melford or Lavenham, set in good walking country with an attractive old high street and sweet country park surrounding the grassy remains of the town's **Norman castle**. The church of **St Peter and St Paul** is another perpendicular masterpiece, flooded with light and medieval faces looking down from the ceiling which avoided the iconoclast Dowsing's attempt to shoot them down.

Pakenham Water Mill ⓘ *T01787-247179, Easter-Sep, is a working mill run by the Suffolk Preservation Society, home-ground flour available.*

Suffolk Coast: Ipswich to Southwold

Without doubt one of the most mysterious and enchanting stretches of coast in the south of England, fairly recently declared an Area of Outstanding Natural Beauty, Suffolk's shoreline has also recently become distinctly fashionable. The character of the area is slowly changing as Londoners snap up holiday homes in their droves. And it's not hard to see why: the North Sea pounds along its pebbly beaches, seemingly intent on breaking inland to the ancient acres of forest at Rendlesham and Tunstall; at Orford Ness the waves have even moved tons of shingle down the coast forcing the river Alde to take a ten-mile detour south. Aldeburgh and Southwold are the seaside towns at the heart of the area, both still quite magical places to wile away a few days. Between them lie the wildflower strewn heaths of Dunwich and one of the RSPB's best reserves at Minsmere.

Ins and outs

Getting there and around Anglia Railways, T08700-409090, www.anglia railways.co.uk, runs the local **rail** service, with journeys direct from London Liverpool Street (1 hour 15 minutes) to Ipswich several times per hour. Travel to Norwich (40 minutes) is twice hourly direct and to Cambridge direct (1 hour 15 minutes) is every 2 hours. The local Anglia stopping service runs from Ipswich to Woodbridge, Wickham Market, Saxmunham, Halesworth, Beccles and Lowestoft (1 hour 30 minutes). There is no direct service to Stansted airport. **National Express,** T08705-808080, runs a **bus** direct service from Ipswich to London Victoria (2-3 hours). Travel to Norwich (3 hours) involves changing at least once and can be arranged through **Traveline,** T08706-082608. The only direct service to Cambridge (1 hour 40 minutes) leaves at 0950. There is no direct service to Stansted airport. **Eastern Counties Buses,** T01473-253734, serve most towns and villages in Essex, Suffolk, Norfolk.

Information Aldeburgh TIC ⓘ *152 High St, T01728-453637, Easter-Oct daily 0900-1715.* **Beccles TIC** ⓘ *The Quay, Fen La, T01502-713196, Easter-Oct daily 0900-1300, 1400-1700.* **Felixstowe TIC** ⓘ *Leisure Centre, Seafront, T01394-276770, Easter-Oct daily 0900-1730, Oct-Easter daily 0900-1700 (Sun 1000-1300).* **Ipswich TIC** ⓘ *St Stephen's Church, St Stephen's La, T01473-258070, Mon-Sat 0900-1700.* **Lowestoft TIC** ⓘ *The East Point Pavilion, Royal Plain, T01502-533600, daily all year 0900-1700.* **Southwold TIC** ⓘ *69 High St, T01502-724729, Easter-Oct daily 1000-1730.* **Woodbridge TIC** ⓘ *Station Buildings, T01394-382240, Easter-Oct Mon-Fri 0900-1730, Sat 0930-1700, Sun 0930-1700, Oct-Easter Mon-Fri 0900-1730, Sat 1000-1700, Sun 1000-1300.*

Ipswich

The county town of Suffolk has suffered badly at the hands of the post-war developers, denying it much in the way of tourist trade and it has struggled to shrug off a reputation for being an ugly backwater. Even so, its official strapline – "You'd be surprised!" – is not entirely unjustified. The waterfront docks have recently been quite attractively revamped and the town has a friendly and unpretentious atmosphere. Some half-timbered buildings that survived the bombs even give the city centre some charm. A short walk from the centre, Christchurch Park contains a fine Tudor mansion boasting paintings by Constable and Gainsborough. On the High Street, the **Ancient House** is the best of the town centre old buildings, a pargeted and timbered Tudor confection, now a branch of Lakeland. Also on the High Street, **Ipswich Museum** ⓘ *High St, T01473-433550, Tue-Sat 1000-1700, free,* is a Suffolk history and wildlife museum with a woolly mammoth and reconstructed Anglo-Saxon burial, not quite as impressive as the real thing nearby at Sutton Hoo (see page 463).

The helpful TIC in St Stephen's Church is tucked away off the High Street near the Buttermarket shopping centre.

Tolly Cobbold Brewery ⓘ *Cliff Rd, T01473-261112, www.tollycobbold.co.uk,* is one of the oldest breweries in the country, with fine Victorian buildings on the banks of the river Orwell. The *Brewery Tap* pub is on site, and there are tours of the process on Monday and Friday afternoons at 1430 in July and August, complete with unusual views of the river and largest collection of commemorative bottled beers in the country.

Christchurch Mansion is a good-looking Tudor house built on the site of an Augustinian Priory, once owned by Queen Elizabeth I's favourite Robert Devereaux, Earl of Essex; it holds the largest collection of Constable paintings outside London. There's a decent café and also the **Wolsey Art Gallery** ⓘ *T01473-433554, Mon-Sat 1000-1700, Sun 1430-1630, free,* for exhibitions by local artists.

Walks on the Suffolk Coast

- **Orford**: 3 mile circle. Start: Orford harbour. A walk along the the River Alde overlooking Havergate Island and its birdlife, up the Ore and back to Orford. OS Maps: Explorer 212 Landranger 169/156
- **Covehithe**: 2 miles there and back. Start: Covehithe village, 4 miles north of Southwold. A 10-minute walk along the low clifftop to the beach and then north along the beach to a lagoon and nature reserve. OS Maps: Explorer 231, Landranger 156
- **Shingle Street**: 4 miles there and back. Start: Shingle Street. A walk along the eerie shingle beach landscape from the mouth of the Ore to Bawdsey (refreshments). OS Maps: Explorer 197, Landranger 169
- **Tunstall Fores**t: 2 mile circle. Start: 2 miles east of Tunstall on the B1078. A woodland walk through the ancient Forest of Aldewood, home to red squirrels, old conifers and oaks. OS Maps: Explorer 212, Landranger 156
- **Dunwich Heath**: 3 mile circle. Start: Dunwich village. A walk up onto the wildflower National Trust heathland overlooking the sea. OS Map Explorer 231 Landranger 156

Woodbridge and around

Woodbridge itself is a small and attractive market town on the River Deben, as well as being something of a transport hub. The **Tide Mill** ⓘ *T01473-626618, May-Sep daily 1100-1700, Apr and Oct Sat, Sun 1100-1700, £1.50*, its wheel dependent on the turning of the tides, dates from the 18th century and was restored in the early 1970s. On Market Hill, the **Woodbridge Museum** ⓘ *Easter-Oct Thu-Sat and bank holidays 1000-1600, Sun 1430-1630, £1*, is a sweet local museum with an intriguing display on the local 19th-century translator and poet Edward Fitzgerald. A short distance out of town, on the B1079, **Buttrum's Mill** ⓘ *T01473-583352, Apr-Sep Sun and bank holidays 1400-1730 (also Sat, May-Aug)*, was built in 1836, one of the finest tower windmills in the country and was used until 1928. Its huge sails are made up of almost 200 Venetian Blind-style shutters, turned into the wind by the little six-bladed 'fantail'.

However, the best reason for a visit to Woodbridge is to see the extraordinary Anglo-Saxon burial site nearby at **Sutton Hoo** ⓘ *Sutton Hoo (NT), 2 miles east of Woodbridge on the B1083, T01394-389700, mid-Mar-May and Oct Wed-Sun and bank holidays 1000-1700, Jun-Sep daily 1000-1700, Nov-Feb Sat, Sun and bank holidays 1000-1600. £4, under-16s £2*. The new National Trust visitor centre features a full-scale reconstruction of the famous Anglo-Saxon ship burial c AD 625 with grave treasures on loan from the British Museum, next door to the site of the discovery in 1939. There's a sincere attempt to illuminate the Dark Ages and a little room of finds, although the reconstruction of a grave is a bit spurious. **Sutton Forest**, devastated by the 1987 'hurricane' is nevertheless still a good place for a walk, and it's interesting to see how much recovery has already taken place here.

Aldeburgh and around

Aldeburgh itself is a tidy, tranquil little town stretched along the coast with only one main street. Not entirely successfully developed for tourism in the late 19th century, its fortunes later declined with its fishing fleet (remnants of which survive, hauled up onto the shingle beach by winches). Things took a turn for the better thanks to classical music with the success of the **Aldeburgh Festival**, founded by Benjamin Britten in 1948 (now relocated to Snape Maltings nearby). Increasingly, houses in the town and on the seafront are being converted into holiday homes for the rich, and the town's prosperity has become more and more reliant on the tourist industry. The **marina** provides entertainment for yachty types but the place still has a genteel and faintly literary air.

Apart from strolling along the long pebbly beach (safe for swimming), enjoying top-notch fish and chips, or watching the sun rise out of the North Sea at dawn, there's not a whole lot to see or do in Aldeburgh itself, although it serves as an ideal base for explorations of the coast. The new lifeboat station is worth a look, as is **The Moot Hall** ⓘ *Apr-May Sat, Sun 1430-1700, Jun, Sep and Oct daily 1430-1700, Jul and Aug daily 1030-1230, 1430-1700, 80p*, the timber-framed Tudor building that was

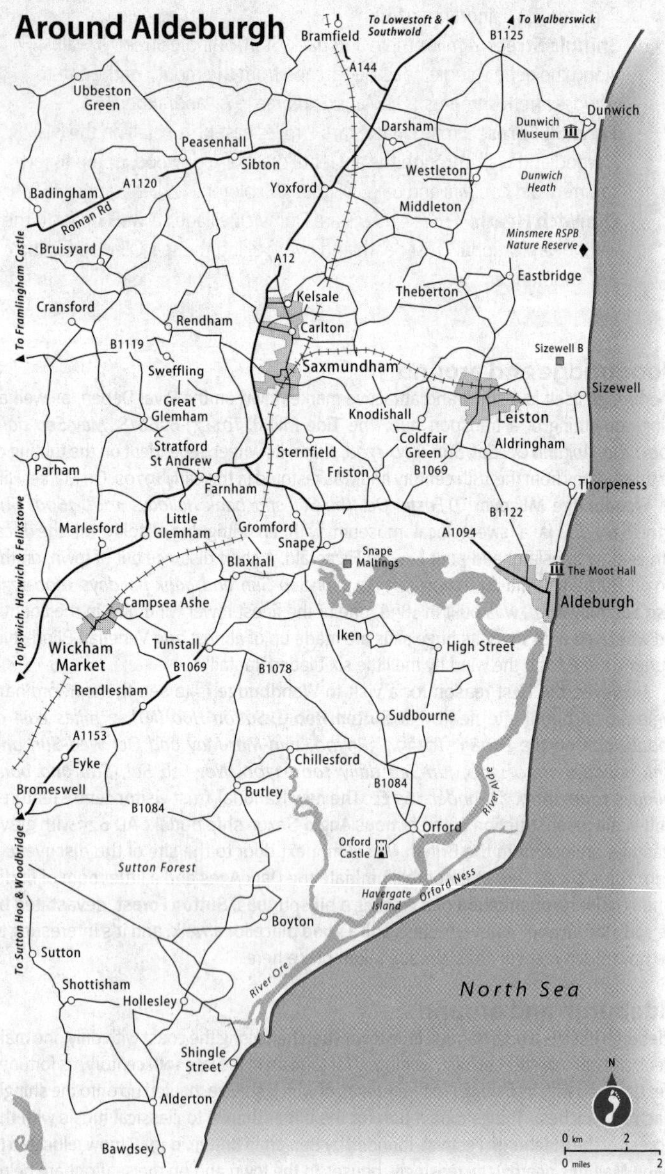

In memoriam WG Sebald

On December 12, 2001, the German writer WG Sebald was killed in a car crash in Norwich at the age of 57. An unspeakable loss to his family, friends and colleagues, East Anglia also lost one of its most exceptional literary talents. With the The Rings of Saturn (Die Ringe des Saturn: Eine Englische Wallfahrt, 1995), Sebald describes a partly fictional walk along the Suffolk coast from Lowestoft to Aldeburgh and beyond, that becomes a dreamlike evocation of the area's past, its associations, history and atmosphere. With intense precision his prose details a morbid fascination with death and decay. The poignant irony of the fact that he too has joined the ranks of his favourite subject matter will never be lost on his still growing number of fans.

once the town hall and stood in the middle of town and is now a museum only a stone's throw from the breakers. It contains some interesting old maps of the area in the council chamber, where Peter Grimes was tried in Britten's opera, and objects downstairs from the Snape Ship Burial, older by some years than Sutton Hoo, as well as other seafaring relics.

Five miles inland from the town, **Snape Maltings** concert halls stand on the beautiful reed-filled marshes on the River Alde. The main **Aldeburgh Music** Festival ⓘ *T01728-453543, www.aldeburgh.co.uk*, is in June, but there are also the Proms in August, and an Early Music festival usually in October, as well as regular concerts throughout the year. The interesting maltings buildings are also busy commercial enterprises, including house and garden shops and a brand new pub, as well as Hepworth sculptures and the Britton-Pears School of Music.

Orford and along the River Ore

Five miles south of Aldeburgh as the crow flies, although 12 by road, Orford is an attractive little red-brick Georgian town, nestling on the banks of the river Alde behind the strange shingle spit of Orford Ness and dominated by the 12th-century keep of **Orford Castle** ⓘ *EH, T01394-450472, Apr-Sep daily 1000-1800, Oct daily 1000-1700, Nov-Mar Wed-Sun 1000-1600, £4, under-16s £2, concessions £3, family £10*. There are fabulous views over the marshes, river and town to the sea from the top of the castle. The town itself can become very crowded during summer, with Orford Quay a busy little boatyard. From here there are beautiful walks along the River Ore to the sound of tinkling halyards, a chance to spot wild geese, swans, and hares, although if you want to see the sea you'll have to cross to **Orford Ness** ⓘ *NT, T01394-450900, Mar-Jun and Oct Sat only, Jul-Sep Tue-Sat ferries from 1000-1400, last return from the Ness at 1700, £5.70, children £2.85*, on the National Trust ferry. The largest vegetated shingle spit in Europe, it's littered with bizarre structures erected by the Ministry of Defence while it was a secret weapons research establishment from 1913 until the 1970s. Given to the National Trust in 1993, the windswept desolation now provides a unique habitat for numerous rare flowers, mosses and lichens.

Another less happy story of the MOD's hand in the history of this coast is rumoured 7 miles further south down the coast, at **Shingle Street**, near the village of Hollesley and at the mouth of the River Ore. Here the coastguard's cottages are just about the only two-storey buildings in a line of individualistic bungalows lining another unique shingle strand opposite the end of Orford Ness and a Site of Special Scientific Interest. The eerie atmosphere of its pebbly beach is compounded by the existence of a secret file on the 'Evacuation of the population of Shingle Street' during the Second World War. Apparently underwater pipes full of petrol were tested here to repel invaders, setting the sea on fire and horribly burning the sappers, giving rise to gruesome tales of charred corpses being washed up on the beach. Nowadays, however, it's a popular spot for dog walking and nightfishing.

North of Aldeburgh

Two miles north of Aldeburgh, **Thorpeness** is a holiday village purpose-built in the 1920s in an eccentric attempt to recreate the medieval atmosphere of 'merrie England'. Nowadays that translates into a golf course, large boating lake (£12.50 for 2 people for 2 hrs), and lots of half-timbered and clapperboard houses. Escape the crowds by walking along the attractive coastline, an unmistakable presence just north being the **Sizewell B** ⓘ *T01728-653890, www.british-energy.com*, nuclear power station. The vibrating floor in the turbine hall has to be felt to be believed, which it can be on the 1100 and 1300 tours that are often fully booked.

Four miles further north, **Minsmere** is one of the Royal Society for the Protection of Bird's best **nature reserves** ⓘ *Westleton, T01728-648281*, famous for its avocets, which can be seen in the spring (they head southwest in the summer) and other rare waders from hides overlooking the lagoons. Closed on Tuesdays, but the public footpath along the dyke protecting the reserve from the sea is open all the time. There's also a lovely walk down to the dyke from the *Eel Foot Inn* in Eastbridge (see below).

A couple of miles further north is **Dunwich**, the Suffolk coast's famous lost town. In the Middle Ages it was one of the country's busiest seaports and boasted 14 churches, a 70-vessel fishing fleet and a population half as large as the City of London's. The story of its gradual collapse into the hungry sea is enthusiastically told at the **Dunwich Museum** ⓘ *St James St, T01728-648796, Apr-Sep daily, 1130-1630, Mar Sat and Sun 1430-1630, Oct daily 1200-1600, free*. It includes a scale model of the town in its heyday as well as references to the many writers and artists – Henry James, Jerome K Jerome, Algernon Swinburne, WG Sebald and William Turner – who were inspired by its peculiar fate. All that can be seen today in the tiny village are the ruins of Greyfriars, a sweet little beach café and some crumbling cliffs. **Dunwich Heath**, a mile south of the village, is a wonderful heather-clad stretch of National Trust coastline (T01728-648505) also with a tearoom and visitor centre.

Inland from Aldeburgh

Twelve miles inland west of Aldeburgh, Framlingham is a delightful market town, much enhanced by **Framlingham Castle** ⓘ *T01728-724189, Apr-Sep daily 1000-1800, Oct daily 1000-1700, Nov-Mar daily 1000-1600. £3.90, under-16s £2, concessions £2.90, family £9.80*, once the seat of the Dukes of Norfolk (the 3rd Duke was the uncle of Anne Boleyn and Catherine Howard), with remarkable and beautifully preserved tombs from the mid-16th century in the church of St Michael and superb views over the town from the remarkably complete 12th-century walls and their 13 towers, still looking much as they would have done when built. There's no central keep, but a 17th-century poor house survives inside, now home to an interesting display on moated buildings called the Lanman Museum.

Nine miles north of Framlingham, **Wingfield Old College** ⓘ *Gardens and Galleries, Church Rd, Wingfield, T01379-384505, www.wingfield-arts.co.uk, Apr-Sep Wed 1400-1700, Sat, Sun and bank holidays 1400-1800, £3.90, £3 concessions*, is an unusual combination of an old school founded in 1362 alongside a handsome palladian mansion, with topiary gardens and a visual arts centre in the restored Great Barn.

Southwold and around

Twelve miles north up the coast from Aldeburgh, Southwold is an older, more sedate and picturesque seaside town, its Georgian townscape set back from the sea, perched up on the cliffs and grouped around several spacious greens laid out as firebreaks after a devastating conflagration in the 17th century. The home town of

George Orwell, who despaired of its precious gentility, Southwold remains a very dignified resort. Down beside the beach and the row of brightly painted beach huts, the 623-ft **pier** ⓘ *T01502-722105, www.southwoldpier.demon.co.uk*, recently reopened to great acclaim, the "first pier to be constructed in Britain for over 45 years!": its telescopes, tearoom and family amusements are just about the town's only concession to seaside tack.

Back in town, a charming 20-minute walk over the common and across the old iron footbridge brings you to **Walberswick**, even quieter and more rarified, the sort of place favoured by Sunday afternoon watercolourists. This is a very popular spot for crabbing and also a small yacht haven. Its one pub, *The Bell*, can become impossibly busy on sunny summer afternoons, while in winter the little creekside village has a cosy and somnolent air.

Sleeping

Bury St Edmunds *p458, map p459*

A **Angel Hotel**, Angel Hill, T01284-753926, F714001. Old ivy-clad coaching inn opposite the Abbey gate, done up in a comfortable way, the most central address in Bury, where Dickens wrote some of *The Pickwick Papers*.

A **Priory Hotel**, Tollgate, T01284-766181, www.prioryhotel.co.uk. Comfortable hotel on the outskirts.

B **Northgate House**, 8 Northgate St, T01284-760469, F724008. Smart B&B in the restored Georgian splendour of novelist Norah Loft's old house.

C **Abbey Hotel**, 35 Southgate St, T01284-762020, www.abbey hotel.co.uk.Reasonable option with spacious accommodation in outbuildings although fairly cramped rooms upstairs.

C **Old Cannon Brewery**, Cannon St, T01284-768769, F701137. Modern Japanese micro-brewery opened in 1999 in an old Victorian building 5 mins to the east of the centre.

E **Theatre Royal** Westgate St, T01284-755127. Twin and single-bedded self-catering accommodation next door to the old theatre.

Around Bury St Edmunds *p460*

A **Swan Hotel**, Lavenham, T0870-4008116. The most upmarket option. Heavily beamed and pannelled but also slightly characterless, there are mementoes of Second World War airmen in the bar. Recently refurbished.

B **Angel Hotel**, Market Pl, Lavenham, T01787-247388, www.lavenham.co.uk/angel. Angel Hotel is the more laid-back option, with its rooms above a loud, cheerful pub on the market place. Tables outside in the square, reasonable food.

C **Brighthouse Farm**, Melford Rd, Lawshall, T01284-830385. Roberta Truin offers a warm welcome at her 18th-century farmhouse B&B with 3-acre garden.

D **Church Farm**, Bradfield Combust, T01284-386333. Good value B&B in an 18th-century house on a working fruit farm.

D **Gannocks House**, Old Rectory La, Shimpling, T01284-830499. Good views of the countryside from pleasant B&B on the outskirts of a small village.

Suffolk Coast: Ipswich to Southwold *p461*

A **Hintlesham Hall**, Hintlesham, near Ipswich, T01473-652334, www.hintleshamhall.com. Easily the best top-end option in the area, a grand Elizabethan country house with charming beamed rooms in a newly refurbished annexe and a restaurant with a good reputation.

C **Great White Horse Hotel**, Tavern St, T01473-256558, F253396. Comfortable airy old refurbished hotel in the middle of town near the shops.

C **Melton Hall**, Melton, near Woodbridge, T01394-388138. Lovely B&B in a Georgian house in its own fine grounds.

C **Old Rectory**, Campsea Ashe, Woodbridge, T01728-746524. Wolsey Lodge with rated restaurant in a Georgian rectory.

D **Clifden Hotel**, 21 London Rd, T01473-252689, F252685. Reasonably priced, friendly hotel a 10-min walk from the centre.

Camping

Forest Camping, Sutton Forest, Tangham Campsite, near Butley on the B1084 from Woodbridge, T01394-450707.

Aldeburgh and around *p463, map p464*

A Swan Hotel, Market Pl, Southwold, T01502-722186. The local brewers Adnams pretty much have the local hotel accommodation sewn up, and this is their flagship. Quite stuffy but great for a traditional tea.

A Wentworth Hotel, at the northern end of the prom in Aldeburgh, T01728-452312, www.wentworth-aldeburgh.com. Has been top of the range for traditional teas and ocean view chintzy rooms since 1920.

A White Lion Hotel, Market Cross Pl, Seafront, T01728-452720, www.whitelion.co.uk. Not quite as grand, but has a pleasant oak-pannelled restaurant and comfortable rooms, some overlooking the Moot Hall and the beach, at a price.

B The Brudenell, The Parade, Aldeburgh, T01728-452071, www.brudenellhotel.co.uk. The town's 3rd high-class hotel is on the southern tip of the town, with a fine terrace for cocktails overlooking the sea and modern, comfortable rooms.

B Crown and Castle, Orford, T01394-450205 www.crownandcastlehotel.co.uk. The top place to stay in Orford, a renovated pub with rooms and the award-winning *Trinity* restaurant (with a Michelin 'Bib' gourmand) below and good deals on weekend breaks for 2.

B Crown Hotel, 90 High St, Southwold, T01502-722275. The less expensive or formal Adnams option with a very good brasserie restaurant and bar.

C Acton Lodge, 18 South Green, Southwold, T01502-723217. Antiques abound in a solid Victorian B&B overlooking one of the town's attractive greens.

C Bell Inn, Ferry Rd, Walberswick, T01502-723109. Cosy old pub with estuary views.

C Butley Priory Gatehouse, T01394-450 482, run by Frances Cavendish is a charming B&B in the remains of a medieval priory.

C Ocean House, 25 Crag Path, Aldeburgh, T01728-452094. Good B&B option right on the beach with pleasant non-smoking family atmosphere. Deservedly immensely popular, so booking well ahead essential, preferably for the seaview room on the first floor.

C King's Head, Front St, Orford, T01394-450243. A good B&B option in the town.

C Ship Inn, St James St, Dunwich, T01728-648219. Does comfortable, snug little rooms.

D Eel's Foot Inn, Eastbridge, T01728-830154. B&B, see Eating & drinking below.

D Jolly Sailor, Quay St, Orford, T01394 450243. Cheaper and cheerful B&B.

D Margaret's, 50 Victoria Rd, Aldeburgh, T01728-453239. A good-value place in a Victorian house 10 mins' walk from the beach.

D Prospect Place, 33 Station Rd, Southwold, T01502-722757. A Victorian house in the middle of town, 3 mins from the beach.

Self-catering

B Martello Tower right at the southern tip of the town, the round Napoleonic fort guarding the approach to Orford Ness with 2 twin rooms, can be booked (well in advance) through the Landmark Trust, T01628-825925.

C Crabbe Cottage, Crabbe St, Aldeburgh T01359-270444. Self-catering in a quiet street close to the beach, not for dogs or children but cosy and recently refurbished.

Eating

Bury St Edmunds *p458, map p459*

£££ 42 Churchgate, 42 Churchgate T01284-764179. £25 a head, 3 course £22 lunch and dinner, in a quaint provincial setting with a good variety of vegetarian options.

£££ Maison Bleue, 30 Churchgate St, T01284-760623 (closed Mon and Sun). About £30 a head for some very well-prepared fish dishes in a rustic setting, easily one of the best restaurants in town.

££ Bangkok City, 19 Angel Hill, T01284-7048700. Decent Thai cuisine, about £10-15.

££ The Sanctuary, Langton Pl, T01284 755875 does reasonably priced café meals on a roomy corner site.

Around Bury St Edmunds *p460*

£££ The Great House, Market Pl, Lavenham, T01787-247431, www.greathouse.co.uk. Does cosy rooms and very good French food in an attractive old house with dining outside in the inner courtyard (about £30 a head).

££ The Beehive, Horringer, near Ickworth, T01284-753260, is a pretty pub on the fringe of Ickworth park with a good menu of ambitious pub grub.

££ The Star Inn, Lidgate, T01638-500275, is a pub-cum-restaurant that does an innovative Spanish menu that draws people in from quite far afield.

Suffolk Coast: Ipswich to Southwold *p461*

££ The Captain's Table, 3 Quay St, Woodbridge, T01394-383145, is a pleasant little local seafood restaurant with tables outside, about £15 a head.

££ Il Punto, The Brasserie on the Quay, Neptune Quay, T01473-289748, is run by the same people as *The Great House* in Lavenham. Offers an excellent French menu at very reasonable prices (about £20 a head), on a boat moored in the newly developed Wet Docks.

££ King's Head, Gorman's La, Laxfield, T01986-798395. Thatched pub doing very good real ales and a hearty homemade menu for lunch and supper. (Laxfield was the birthplace of iconoclast William Dowsing.)

££ Spice Bar Restaurant and Café, 17 The Thoroughfare, Woodbridge, T01394-382557, a Malaysian restaurant with a good reputation.

Aldeburgh and around *p463, map p464*

Aldeburgh is well supplied with good restaurants along its High St, thanks in part to the fastidious tastes of weekending Londoners.

££ 152, 152 High St, Aldeburgh, T01728-454152. A rated Mediterranean menu served up in a mellow environment that's been around some time. Mains about £12, starters £6.

££ The Butley Orford Oysterage, Market Hill, Orford, T01394-450277 (lunch only in low season Mon-Thu, Sun) serves very fresh seafood in simple surroundings, excellent value and often very busy.

££ De Cressey's of Walberswick, Manor House, Main St, Walberswick, T01502-723243, is a small country restaurant using local produce, open all day but closed 1700-1900 when the fuller evening menu makes its appearance.

££ The Lighthouse, 77 High St, Aldeburgh, T01728-453377. Another old-timer, a breezy café during the day, serving an accomplished modern British prix fixe menu (3 courses about £17) in the evenings. Booking advisable.

£ The Anchor Inn, Walberswick, T01502-722112, uses fresh local ingredients in a traditional pub as well as freshly cut sandwiches and rolls.

£ The Coastguards Tearooms, Dunwich Heath, T01728-648505, is a National Trust tearoom with views of the sea and fresh home-made cakes.

£ The Lord Nelson, East St, Southwold, T01502-722079, is a cosy pub close to the cliffside seafront, with fresh traditional food.

£ The Parish Lantern, Village Green, Walberswick, T01502-723173. A tearoom in a listed building in the middle of the village.

£ Regatta, 171 High St, Aldeburgh, T01728-452011. Another with a seafaring theme, slightly less expensive with very good value 'early bird' deals (£10 for 3 courses) and tasty seafood.

£ Scandelicious, 165 High St, T01728-452880. A café that offers a smorgasbord of Swedish and Scandy specialities at reasonable prices.

£ Sizewell T Rooms, Sizewell Beach, T01728-831108, are housed in a curious old beach hut serving up burgers, strong tea and the like in the shadow of the nuclear power station.

£ The White Horse in Rendham, T01728-663497 for excellent Scottish dishes like Haggis and Loch Ffyne kippers.

Pubs, bars and clubs

Bury St Edmunds *p458, map p459*

Nutshell, The Traverse, T01284-764867, stands out for being the smallest pub in England, with a bar that can only accommodate about 8 people, at the top of Abbeygate St.

Other pubs worth seeking out for the quality of their ales and/or pleasant atmosphere include the **Mason's Arms**, Whiting St; the **Dog and Partridge**, Bridewell La; **Rising Sun**, Risbygate St; **The Fox**, Eastgate St; **The Grapes**, St Andrews St North, well-known for its live music, and **Ye Olde ne Bull**, nicknamed 'the Womble', Angel Hill in the middle of town, most popular with the local youth.

Suffolk Coast: Ipswich to Southwold *p461*

Fat Cat Pub, Spring Rd, does some top real ales and has a nice little beer garden.

Butt and Oyster, Pin Mill, near Chelmondiston on the B1456 from Ipswich, T01473-780764, is a very popular and famous riverside pub with reasonable food, unfortunately often almost too busy for its own good in the summer.

Aldeburgh and around *p463, map p464*
The Eel's Foot Inn, Eastbridge, T01728-830154, does decent enough pub grub with a quiet, pretty garden overlooking Minsmere bird reserve. Also does B&B.
The Ship at Blaxhall, T01728-688316, for locally brewed real ales and home-cooked food, specializing in seafood from the local area as well as B&B.
The Victoria, in Earls Soham. A country pub worth seeking out. An outlet for the tiny Earl Soham Brewery.
The White Hart, High St, especially popular with the locals.
Ye Olde Crosse Keys, Crabbe St, right on the seafront with tables outside. The best pub for genial conversations with strangers.

Entertainment

Bury St Edmunds *p458, map p459*
Bury St Edmunds Art Gallery, the Market Cross, T01284-762081 www.burystedmundsartgallery.org, Tue-Sat 1030-1700, £1, concessions 50p.
Theatre Royal, Westgate St, T01284-769505 www.theatreroyal.org. Guided tours May-Sep, exceptional Georgian theatre hosting some good quality touring productions.

Shopping

Bury St Edmunds *p458, map p459*
Barwell Foods, 39 Abbeygate St, T01284-754084, for quality picnic materials.
Bury Bookshop, 28 Hatter St, T01284-703107.

Aldeburgh and around *p463, map p464*
Richardson's Smokehouse in Orford, down a little alley off the High St with piles of logs and smoke billowing out of a shack, smokes just about everything edible: eels, pigeon, hams with burnt treacle glaze, cheddar and stilton. The fishcakes are made with wild Alaskan smoked salmon.

Activities and tours

Aldeburgh and around *p463, map p464*
Aldeburgh Yacht Club, Slaughden Rd, Aldeburgh, T01728-452562. Sailing events at weekends throughout the summer.
Kite surfing, www.kitesurfing.org, is possible on the beach at Dunwich, but check with coastguard first, T01493-451338.
Lady Florence, a converted 50ft Admiralty supply vessel, leaves from Orford Quay, for 3-course American brunch cruises, watching the birdlife, up and down beside Orford Ness. T7831-698298, 0900-1130, about £20.

Transport

Bury St Edmunds *p458, map p459*

Bicycle
Micks Cycle Centre, 68-69 St Johns St, T01284-753946.

Bus
Infrequent **First Eastern** buses, T01284-766569, run out to the surrounding countryside.

Car
Ford Rental, Springfield Rd, T01284-775900; **Europcar** in *The Bird In The Hand Motel* Beck Rd, Mildenhall, T01638-714747; **British Car Rentals**, Passenger Terminal, Mildenhall, T01638-515002; **Enterprise Rent-a-Car (UK) Ltd**, Linnett Service Station Maynewater La, T01284-750575; **Arriva Vehicle Rental**, The St Barton Mills, T01638-717452. **Thrifty**, Ames Rover, Dettingen Way, T01284 700222.

Taxi
The main taxi rank in Bury St Edmunds is on Cornhill, and there is another at the Railway Station. Local minicab firms include: **Premier Cars**, T01284-704004; **BuryTaxis**, T01284-752260; **A-2-Z Taxis**, T01638-510820; **United Cars**, T01284-762288 and **Tudor** Cars, T01284-760707.

Train
There are at least 5 train services daily between Bury St Edmunds and **Ipswich** and **Cambridge** (both 45 mins). **Anglia** Railways have an Anglia Plus One Day Pass. Unlimited travel within the Anglia Plus area

for £9 and up to 4 accompanied children can travel for just £2 each with this fare. You can use One Day Passes at any time at weekends and bank holidays or after 0845 Mon-Fri. You can also take your bicycle on board for a £1 supplement.

Aldeburgh and around *p463, map p464*

Bicycle

Alton Cycle Hire, Alton Reservoir, Holbrook Rd, Stutton, Ipswich, T01473-328873.

Byways Bicycles, Priory La, Darsham, near Saxmundham, T01728-668764, www.bywaysbicycles.co.uk. Bikes for hire by day or week, closed Tue.

Car

Fleetway Car and Van Hire, 110 Bramford Rd, Ipswich, T01473-231888. **National**, 538 Woodbridge Rd, Ipswich, T01473-724665. **Thrifty**, 549a Wherstead Rd, Ipswich, T01473-68595.

Taxi

A to B Private Hire, 31 Kingfisher Cres, Reydon, Southwold, T01502-722111. **M&R Cars**, Woodbridge Railway Station, T01394-386661. **Orwell Cars**, 42 Ganges Rd, Shotley Gate, Ipswich, T01473-788302. **B Dobson**, 29 Linden Cl, Aldeburgh, T01728-454116.

Norfolk

→ *Colour map 5, grid C4/5*

Norfolk is the county that typifies East Anglia for most people: big skies, wide views over the flat land and hazy horizons. Now people have discovered the delights of this expansive rural backwater beside the North Sea, with its strange ways and square watery light. Norwich, the capital of the county, was the third richest city in England during the Middle Ages and today rivals York as the best-preserved medieval townscape beneath cathedral and castle in the land. Great Yarmouth is Norfolk's top seaside resort, less happy but still one of the most spirited on England's east coast, and behind it lie the Broads, where pleasure-boating was born in the mid-19th century and is still going strong. These waterways winding through marshland and open lakes are busy all summer with motorcruisers and sailing boats as well as hiding more peaceful and secluded spots alive with rare water birds and also, much to the concern of the farmers, the coypu. Another unusual and much less well-known landscape can be found in Breckland, where acres of pine forest and scrub cover the sandy hills and heaths. The jewel in Norfolk's holiday box of tricks is undoubtedly its north coast. From Blakeney to Brancaster, the seemingly limitless sandy beaches, salt marshes, tidal inlets and quiet fishing villages have won the hearts of London's second-homers who work in film and a particular ruminative breed of regular epicurean re-visitors. ▸▸ *For Sleeping, Eating and other listings, see pages 488-493.*

Lowestoft, Great Yarmouth and around

Although strictly speaking in Suffolk, Lowestoft almost joins up with Great Yarmouth in the north to form an urban coastal strip east of the Norfolk Broads. Both are ancient seafaring towns, although their fishing fleets are now a tiny fraction of the size that once made them rich. Sadly Lowestoft has the delapidated air of a town that's down on its luck, but it still pulls in a considerable number of punters and young families in the summer months to enjoy its sandy beaches and seafront amusements. Great Yarmouth seems to have fared better than its southern neighbour during the post-war decline, thanks to the North Sea oil industry and also its more interesting situation on a peninsula of land formed by the river Yare as it sidles into the sea. Even busier during the summer, it claims to be Norfolk's most popular seaside resort and perhaps fancies itself as the Vegas of East Anglia.

Ins and outs

Getting there Lowestoft is about 40 minutes from Norwich, and almost 1 hour 30 minutes from Ipswich by slow stopping **trains** calling at Woodbridge, Wickham Market, Saxmundham, Halesworth and Beccles. Great Yarmouth is connected to Norwich (30 minutes away) by regular stopping trains. Lowestoft is the penultimate port of call for the A12, usually about a 2 hour 30 minute **drive** from London. Great Yarmouth is 9 miles further north, although reached more quickly from London along the dual-carriageway A47 via Norwich. **National Express,** T08705-808080, run coaches from London to both and there's a regular service from Norwich. ▸▸ *For further details, see Transport page 492.*

Getting around Both Lowestoft and Great Yarmouth are easily navigated on foot and reliable bus services connect the towns. Exploring the Broads inland is best done by boat (see page 474) or bike and the countryside inland by car or bike.

Information Lowestoft TIC ⓘ *East Point Pavilion, Royal Plain T01502-533600, www.visit-lowestoft .co.uk, daily 1000-1700.* **Great Yarmouth TIC** ⓘ *Marine Parade, T01493-842195, www.great-yarmouth.co.uk, also at the Town Hall T01493-846345.* **Broads Authority Information Centre** ⓘ *The Quay, Fen La, Beccles, Suffolk T01502-713196, www. broadsauthority.gov.uk, Apr-Oct daily 0900-1700.* **Bungay TIC** ⓘ *T01986-896156. Wells TIC* ⓘ *Staithe St, T01328 710885, Mid-Mar to Oct Mon-Sat 1000-1700, Sun 1000-1600.*

Lowestoft

Sadly there's not much to keep visitors that long in Lowestoft unless it's busy beaches, fish and chips and family amusements you're looking for. That said, the old **harbour** is worth exploring and the esplanade still conjures up memories of the town's glory days despite heavy bombing during the war. The older part of town lies north of the harbour and Lake Lothing, the mouth of the river Waveney after it has expanded into Oulton Broad. Whapload Road runs past the massive Bird's Eye fish finger factory near the **Ness**, the most easterly point in the British Isles, and also past the **Lowestoft Maritime Museum** ⓘ *T01502-561963, May-Oct daily 1000-1700 (last admission 1630), 50p.* This sweet little museum in the Sparrow's Nest in a park below the lighthouse is packed with models of boats and a mock-up of a trawler's cabin. The last deep-sea beam trawlers to fish out of Lowestoft were decommissioned in August 2002, bringing the town's 600-year fishing history to a close. Back by the harbour, the **East Point Pavilion**, a strange mock-Edwardian glass construction, is the centre of the boardwalk action, overlooking a big and busy sandy beach.

Great Yarmouth

Nine miles north of Lowestoft, Great Yarmouth was one of the wealthiest towns in East Anglia during the Middle Ages thanks to its control of the seaport for the inland waterway system leading to Norwich. Substantial sections of its old town walls, built between 1261 and 1400, have been carefully preserved and restored, although like its southern neighbour, much of the rest of the town was flattened by bombing in 1942. It sits on a long sandy promontory south of the harbourside train station that proved vital to the town's prosperity during the Victorian herring boom. This situation is what gives the place its dubious charm, a combination of quiet old riverside quays and full-on seaside resort. Nowadays the town does just well enough for itself thanks to the North Sea oil industry and tourism, drawing in crowds of fun-seekers during the summer. They usually make straight for **Marine Parade** and the beach. Along its seafront in high season, Great Yarmouth makes a tremendously tacky neon-lit spectacle of itself: horse-drawn carriages ply the prom, fairground rides pump up the volume and its two piers, Britannia and Wellington, buzz with arcade amusements and slot-machine activity. Even in winter, this scene doesn't quite let up entirely.

The calmer 'inland' face of the town is South Quay, with its famous **'rows'**, little alleyways running like a ladder down from the impressive **Church of St Nicholas** with its wide west front and nave, the largest of any parish church in England. Gutted by fire during the war, it was restored in Victorian style in 1962. Three 17th-century houses in **Row 111** ⓘ *Apr-Oct daily, by guided tour only at 1000, 1200, 1400 and 1600, £3, concessions £2, children £1.50*, along with the Old Merchant's House, have been restored by English Heritage, with plasterwork ceilings and oak pannelling. South of the Market Place, where stands the cute little **Fisherman's Hospital**, built as almhouses for old seadogs in 1702, surrounded now by the town's main shopping area, the redundant **quayside** has recently been redeveloped as a heritage attraction, including a new **Nelson Museum** ⓘ *26 South Quay, T01493-850698, Apr-Sep Mon-Fri 1000-1700, Sat, Sun 1400-1700, £2, concessions £1.50*, featuring the Ben Burgess Nelson Memorabilia Collection of paintings and things connected to the one-armed and one-eyed naval hero. At no 4 South Quay, the **Elizabethan** House ⓘ *T01493-855746, Apr-Oct Mon-Fri 1000-1700, Sat, Sun 1315-1700. £2.60, concessions £2, family £6*, has been restored to give some idea of life in Tudor times as well as the Conspiracy Room, where the downfall of Charles I was supposedly plotted, and some Victorian kitchens. Tucked behind South Quay is **The Tolhouse Museum** ⓘ *Tolhouse St, T01493-858900, Apr-Oct Mon-Fri 1000-1700, Sat, Sun 1315-1700, £2.50*, one of the oldest civic buildings in the country with medieval cells beneath and displays on crime and punishment down the ages.

Like Margate, the town has an ambitious high-profile government-funded project underway that it is hoped will boost its fortunes: a brand new £4.3 million **museum** ⓘ *T01493-745526*, on the herring industry and Yarmouth local history opened in the Tower Curing Works on Blackfriars Road in 2004. Great Yarmouth's **North-west Tower** is a Medieval tower on the North Quay beside the Bure, built in 1344 as part of the town walls. Now it's used as a Broads Information Centre and wherry exhibition. North of the centre of town, back by the sea, the RSPB reserve at **North Denes Beach** provides room for a breeding colony of rare little terns, visible simply nesting on the sand from May to August.

Around Beccles and Bungay

Seven and 14 miles inland from Lowestoft up the river Waveney respectively, Beccles and Bungay are two quaint old market riverside towns that compete with each other for the passing tourist trade to the southern Broads. Beccles boasts a busy **quayside** on the river and the remains of one of the largest 19th-century printing houses, complete with a Lion Press from 1866, one of only three surviving in the world, alongside other machines and binders dating from 1834, at the **William Clowes Museum of Print** ⓘ *Corner of Caxton St and Newgate, T01502-712884, Whit Mon (May/Jun)-Sep, Mon-Fri 1400-1630, free.* Also just in Suffolk, Bungay was rebuilt in Georgian style after a disastrous fire in 1688, sitting in a loop of the river commanded by the ruins of Baron Roger Bigod's 13th-century castle. South of Bungay, a medieval moated manor house makes a pleasingly antique setting for some top-notch real ales, at **St Peter's Brewery and St Peter's Hall** ⓘ *St Peter South Elmham, near Bungay, T01986-782322, www.stpetersbrewery.co.uk.*

Between these towns, to the north, a couple of miles up the A146 towards Norwich, are a few places well worth seeking out. **Hales Hall Barn** is a wonder:180 ft long, a thatched brick-built barn constructed in 1480 with defensive loopholes in its walls and stepped gables, standing beside a lawn in front of the old Tudor hall. It's the largest and most spectacular thatched barn in Norfolk, approached across Hales Green, a large wildflower-strewn piece of common, and is also the site of **Reads' nursery** ⓘ *T01508-548395*, a long-standing plantsman's paradise. Sitting quietly in a meadow nearby, **St Margaret Hales** is an adorable thatched pre-Gothic church with a flint tower and sparse interior maintained by Redenham Church fund. Nearby, the plantsmen make tracks for **Raveningham Gardens** ⓘ *T01508-548222, www.raveningham.com, Apr-Sep, Wed, Sun, bank holidays 1400-1730, £3*, with its proper ha-ha and beautifully renovated walled garden.

Four miles inland between Lowestoft and Great Yarmouth, **Somerleyton** Hall ⓘ *T01502-730224, www.somerleyton.co.uk, Easter-Oct Thu, Sun, bank holidays (also Tue, Wed in July and Aug) 1200-1730. £5.80, child £2.90*, is a very grand Victorian industrialist's residence. There's not that much to see inside, visitors being restricted to the ground floor only, passing through the dining room and library, although the carved entrance hall with two large stuffed polar bears and an impressive hat collection is worth a look. Outside it's the maze, immense walled garden with extraordinary old greenhouses, loggia, and superb mature trees that are the real draw.

The Broads

Norfolk's most popular tourist destination, very busy in summer, and also one of Europe's most important wetland habitats, the Broads are made up of about 127 miles-worth of shallow but navigable waterways twisting through reedbeds and marshland, the flat landscape dotted with ruined windmills, occasionally opening out into wider lakes – the 'broads' themselves. The whole area is the main place that the British love to mess about in boats. Five rivers provide the water as they make their way east across the county to the sea at Great Yarmouth: the Waveney is the most southerly, creating the county's border with Suffolk as it flows in via Bungay and Beccles; the Yare comes in from Norwich; the Bure from Aylsham, joined by the Ant and Thurne near Ranworth. Clearly this strange and usually peaceful landscape can only really be appreciated and explored by boat. The sheer number of motor cruisers that ply the channels in high season once came close to ruining the peace they seek but steps have been taken in recent years to limit their use. The most picturesque craft still in use on these waters are the Norfolk wherries, their tall masts and sails gliding quietly through the flat landscape.

Ins and outs

Getting there The main **road** access points to the Broads are at Norwich, Loddon, and Lowestoft (for the southern section) and at Great Yarmouth, Wroxham, Horning, Stalham and Potter Heigham (for the northern section). Broadland villages that give some idea of the area's charm and can be reached by car include Rockland St Mary in the south, and Ranworth, Horsey and Woodbastwick in the north. Local **bus** services (few and far between) are run by **First Eastern Counties**, T08456-020121. The Broads can be reached by fairly regular **rail** services within an hour from Norwich, with stations at Reedham, Wroxham and Acle and also to Berney Arms which has no road.

Getting around Most obviously by **boat**, although the Broads can also be very enjoyably explored on foot and by bike. One of the best boatyards on the Broads is **Martham Boats**, in Martham on the outer-reaches of the northern broads, T01493-740249, www. marthamboats.com. They have a variety of traditional wooden sailing and also wooden motor boats which they build themselves, also available for day hire. **Hoseason's**, Lowestoft, T01502-516900, www.hoseasons.co.uk. The big commercial operators in the area. **Moore and Co**, Staitheway Rd, Wroxham, T01603-783311, www.boatingholidays.co.uk are another very popular option.

Information Hoveton TIC ⓘ *Station Rd, T01603-782281.* **Ranworth TIC** ⓘ *The Staithe, T01603-270453.* **Loddon TIC** ⓘ *The Old Town Hall, 1 Bridge St, T01508-521028.* **Broads Authority Information Line** ⓘ *T01603-610734,*

Natural born cullers

It was a relatively short affair and it ended acrimoniously. The coypu, a huge South America rodent the size of a sheep was introduced to Norfolk in 1929 and bred for its pelt, known to the fur trade as nutria, and fashionable at the time. By the outbreak of war there were some 3000 being farmed for fur but a great flood in the 1940s enabled them to escape from their enclosures. They soon spread along a tributary of the Yare and then to the Broads. In no time at all they had settled happily into the East Anglian countryside. Numbers were initially limited by the demand for pelts but when nutria went out of fashion the population spiralled out of control to an estimated 200,000 by the late 1950s. The coypu were now seen by the government as a serious threat to riverbanks and crops, particularly sugar beet and carrots. The Coypu Clearance Campaign for East Anglia was quickly followed by the ominous-sounding "Operation Broadland" as tens of thousands of the prolific little breeders were culled. The Ministry of Agriculture pumped millions into its coypu control centre and by 1990 announced it was ending its field checks. The war was won.

www.broads-authority.gov.uk. **Broads Authority Information Centres** ⓘ *Beccles, Great Yarmouth, Hoveton, Loddon, Ludham, Potter Heigham and Ranworth.*

Orientation The area divides neatly into northern and southern navigations: the former, based on the Bure, Ant and Thurne being the more popular and the most scenic (all the rivers are more attractive in their upper reaches) and with more of the broads themselves. These reed-fringed lagoons were created by peat-cuttings started in the 13th century which have slowly flooded over the years. They vary in size from small pools to the largest expanse at Hickling Broad. There are about 50 of them altogether, mostly in the northern area. Thirteen are open for free-range boating, as well as the navigable channels on Martham and Sutton Broads, and Womack Water. Two more, Black Horse Broad and Horsey Mere, are open during the holiday season. All have been damaged by agribusiness and pleasureboating. Cockshoot and Barton Broads are in the process of being restored to their 1930s condition, involving the reduction of the phosphate concentration in the rivers. On Barton Broad, where Nelson learnt to sail, the cost of mud-pumping and purification will be over £2 million. Wind-powered mills in varying states of delapidation can be seen all over the Broads, although only one (Clayrack Mill at How Hill) is still used to drain marshland, while several others (Herringfleet, Thurne Dyke, Berney Arms, Horsey and Stracey Arms) have been restored, some by the Norfolk Windmills Trust.

Southern Broads

Breydon Water is the large 2000-acre tidal lake next to Great Yarmouth, with glistening mudflats at low tide, fed by the rivers Yare and Waveney. Four miles up the Yare, **Berney Arms** boasts its own request-stop on the railway, no road, and the tallest drainage **windmill** ⓘ *(EH), T01493-700605 or T01223-582700, Apr-Oct daily 0900-1300, 1400-1700, £2, concessions £1.50, children £1,* in the UK with magnificent views over Breydon Water and the surrounding marshland from the top. It stopped pumping water as recently as 1951.

Berney Marshes RSPB nature reserve includes the Halvergate Marshes and much of Breydon Water, teeming with waders and wildfowl, a pleasant walk from the village of **Reedham** where a chain ferry for cars crosses the river and there's a swinging railway bridge. A couple of miles upstream, the Hardley Cross obelisk marks the boundary between the navigational jurisdiction of Great Yarmouth and Norwich, near the mouth of the twisting river Chet, flowing in the three miles or so from **Loddon**. This little 18th-century market town is a good alternative to Yarmouth or Lowestoft for boat hire. Its Holy Trinity Church dates from 1490, with a fine hammer-beam roof, and also a panel on the rood screen depicting William of Norwich, a 12th century boy martyr, and a very old almsbox.

The largest stretch of open water in the Yare valley is nearby at **Rockland Broad**, where day boats can be hired and there's a decent pub in Rockland St Mary. **Surlingham Broad**, at Brundall, has a Swallows-and-Amazons style maze of little channels connecting its two lakes. Seven miles or so further upstream stands Norwich, the centre of which can be reached along the river Wensum.

Following the river Waveney upstream from Breydon Water passes **Burgh Castle** (open any reasonable time) where the impressive remains of a walled third-century Roman fort overlook the river. Five miles further the river is bridged at **St Olave's**, a small single-street 17th-century village named after the patron saint of Norway. The ruins of its 13th-century Augustinian priory stand too close to the busy A143 for comfort. The river runs on into **Oulton Broad** and Lowestoft passing close to Somerleyton Hall (see page 474) and bends round beneath Burgh St Peter, with its thatched church. Seven miles further on is the dignified old town of Beccles (see page 473), from where the river's most beautiful reaches run past **Geldeston Lock** where there's an atmospheric old pub (see below).

Northern Broads

The Bure enters Great Yarmouth from the north after an unattractive and congested three-mile stretch of the river below Stokesby. Five miles further upstream, the Bure comes into its own as it's joined by the Thurne, which has run south for three miles from **Potter Heigham**. A boat hire centre second only to Wroxham, Potter Heigham has an entertainingly difficult medieval bridge to navigate, where larger boats are required to take on a pilot to shoot the central arch at full speed. Southwest of the town, near Ludham, is **Toad Hole Cottage** ⓘ *Electric Eel, How Hill, T01692-678763, Apr-Oct daily 1000-1800, free*, an old eel catcher's cottage that conjures the atmosphere of Victorian country living and also runs quiet **boat trips** ⓘ *Apr-Oct 1000-1700 Apr, May, Oct weekends only 1100-1500, £4, concessions £3, family £8*, through fen and reedswamp on the river Ant aboard the *Electric Eel*.

Further up the Thurne, the sea feels very close. **Hickling Broad**, the largest of the Broads, is owned by the Norfolk Wildlife Trust, and comes closest to most people's idea of a typical broadland scene. Boats can be hired from the *Pleasure Boat Inn*, from where nature trails also head round the lake on boardwalks and dry land. A narrow channel leads into **Horsey Mere** ⓘ *(NT), T01493-393904, Apr-Sep daily 1100-1700 (last admission 1630), £2, children £1*, another secluded lake, owned by the National Trust and overlooked by their **Horsey Windpump**, restored following lightning damage in 1943.

Expect to see the relatively rare swallowtail butterflies here in summer.

Back on the Bure at the mouth of the Thurne stands a well-preserved white **windmill** (T01603-222705 for the key), from where a beautiful two-mile walk leads up to the picturesque ruins of **St Benet's Abbey**. These are the remains of the only religious house in Norfolk founded before the Norman conquest, by King Canute, enclosed with a wall and battlements in 1327. It was also reputed to be the only religious house in England not actually dissolved by Henry VIII, and the Bishops of Norwich have remained Abbots to the present day. The Bishop arrives by wherry and preaches at the annual service on the first Sunday in August. In the 18th century a windmill was built in the ruins, its battered stump remains, and a cross of oak from the Royal Estate at Sandringham was erected on the site of the High Altar in 1987.

The best way to reach the Abbey is by hiring a boat at **Horning**, beyond the mouth of the river Ant. The route passes the entrance to **Ranworth Broad**, where the delightful broad-side village of **Ranworth** (which can also be reached by car) is blessed with a **church** ⓘ *T01603-270511*, dating from 1370, containing an outstanding medieval painted screen. There's also an antiphoner book of 285 sheepskin pages with versicles and responses for the seven services for every day of the year illuminated with exquisite lettering. There are superb views over broadland from the top of its tower. **Ranworth Conservation Centre** is a floating information centre run by the Norfolk Wildlife Trust at the end of a boardwalk through woodland and fen habitats, dealing with the creation of the broads, their wildlife and conservation.

Five miles northwest of Ranworth, further up the Bure, **Wroxham** is the capital of the Broads sitting next to its 112-acre lake. The town is almost completely overrun with boaties, tourists and geese during summer, and the broad itself crammed with sailing dinghies. It's a reasonably good value place to hire a boat for the day though and also pick up picnic provisions. The **Bure Valley Railway** ⓘ *Norwich Rd, Aylsham, T01263-733858, May-Sep*, a narrow-gauge railway, built in 1990, runs the 9-mile, 45-minute trip from Wroxham to Aylsham via Coltishall, Buxton and Brampton. Nearby, **Hoveton Great Broad Nature Trail** was laid out in 1968, the first nature trail to be established in the region. Affording excellent views of Hoveton Great Broad, its adjoining fens and alder woodland, it can only be reached by boat. Moorings are available on the north bank of the Bure opposite Salhouse Broad.

North Walsham and **Stalham** are at the furthest northern tip of the Broads. In Sutton, the **Sutton Windmill and Broads Museum** ⓘ *T01692-581195, www.broadsmuseum.co.uk, Apr-Sep daily 1000-1730*, claims to be the tallest windmill in Britain and has excellent views of the surrounding Broads from the top. In use until 1940, it now also houses a museum of local life that includes a complete pharmacy from the 1880s, and a tobacco room. At Stalham Staithe, the Museum of the Broads, has several buildings housing a variety of boat-related exhibits and displays on traditional Broadland industries.

Swaffham and Breckland

Between Newmarket and Norwich, north of Bury St Edmunds, the thinly populated expanse of sand hills and heath called the Brecks comes as a distinct surprise in the chalk and wetland landscape of East Anglia. Never much use to farmers, in the last century whole tracts of the area were planted with eerie acres of conifers by the Forestry Commission to form Thetford Forest. The Ministry of Defence moved in too, appropriating training areas and establishing massive RAF and US airbases at Lakenheath and Mildenhall. The combined effect could almost be described as Soviet. Even so, large areas have been set aside for ramblers along forest trails, and attractive stretches of the ancient Peddar's Way traverse the east of the region on its path up to the North Sea at Hunstanton. Unusually for the east of England, water is at a premium here: the only settlements of any size being clustered on the Little Ouse and Wissey rivers. Thetford, the birthplace of Thomas Paine, and Swaffham, with its Georgian dignity still intact, are the major market towns. Evidence of very early human industry can be explored near both at the Neolithic flint mines called Grimes Graves, and at Cockley Cley, where there's a funny little reconstruction of an Iceni village, popular with the kids. More recent architecture is beautifully represented at the medieval moated manor of Oxburgh Hall.

Ins and outs

Getting there Brandon and Thetford are on the Ely/Cambridge **train** line to Norwich (50 and 30 mins). **National Rail Enquiries,** T08457-484950. Thetford is bypassed by the A11 **road** that runs up past Newmarket, about 2 hours (on a good day) from London. Swaffham is about 17 miles away up the A1065. Local **bus** services are run by **First Eastern Counties,** T08456-020121. ▸▸ *For further details, see Transport page 492.*

Getting around Unfortunately a **car** is really the only practical way to access Breckland's more remote walking areas, although a cycle hired in Thetford would be a good alternative.

Information Swaffham TIC ⓘ *Market Pl, T01760-722255, www.aroundswaffham.co.uk. Apr-Oct Mon-Sat 1000-1630.* **Attleborough TIC** ⓘ *Victoria Gallery, Cyprus House, Queen Sq, T01953-452404. Mon-Sat 0900-1730.* **Watton and Wayland** ⓘ *The Clock Tower, High St, Watton, T01953-882058, www.wayland.org.uk, May-Sep Mon, Tue, Thu 0930-1200, Wed, Fri, Sat 0930-1430.*

Thetford and around

The largest centre of population in the area, Thetford is a quiet market town, peacefully situated on the banks of the rivers Little Ouse and Thet but disfigured by recent housing developments. Not much remains of its ancient roots apart from an Iron Age castle mound and the 14th-century gatehouse of Thetford Cluniac Priory, near the train station. The other thing worth looking at if you happen to be passing through is the **Ancient House Museum** ⓘ *21 White Hart St, T01842-752599, Mon-Sat 1000-1230, 1300-1700 Jun-Aug also Sun 1400-1700, £1, 80p concessions*, in a 15th-century timber-framed merchant's house. A local history museum with a small display on Thomas Paine who was born in the town and long disowned by the place for publishing his revolutionary *Rights of Man* in 1791.

Acre upon acre of pine wood stretches north and west of the town towards Brandon, the **Thetford Forest** planted in the 1920s by the Forestry Commission. Seven miles to the northwest, well-signposted, in a clearing in the trees near the middle of the forest, the strangely dimpled hillocks betray the presence of the best-preserved Neolithic flint mines in the country. Called **Grimes Graves** ⓘ *(EH), T01842-810656, Apr-Sep daily 1000-1800, Oct daily 1000-1700, Nov-Mar Wed-Sun 1000-1600 (last admissions half hr before closing), £2.30, concessions £1.70*, after the pagan god Grim, their 4000-year-old purpose was only understood in 1870. Visitors can descend 30 ft underground by ladder down an excavated shaft to see how some of the material for the weapons and tools (reconstructed in the visitor centre) were extracted from the chalk. Flint-knapping demonstrations are occasionally given in the summer.

Seven miles to the northeast of Thetford, the local council has established the **'Great Eastern Pingo Trail'** around the little village of Thompson. The route passes through some typical Breckland scenery where walkers are encouraged to spot pingos, the shallow depressions left in the ground by ice bubbles 20,000 years ago. The village itself is also a good leaping-off point for the **Peddar's Way**. This ancient pre-Roman track runs almost dead straight 30 miles from near Thetford to the north coast.

Swaffham

Swaffham, 14 miles north of Thetford, stands on the northern edge of the Breckland wilds. It has a spacious and unusual triangular **Market Place**, surrounded by elegant Georgian houses. Every Saturday a busy open-air market and public auction is held here beneath the Market Cross presented to the town by the Earl of Orford in 1783. Just off the Market Place is the Church of Peter and Paul, with a fine double hammer-beam roof.

Two miles southwest of Swaffham, in the village of **Cockley Cley**, there's a fanciful little reconstruction of an **Iceni Village** ⓘ *T01760-724588, Apr-Oct daily 1100-1730, £4, £3 concessions*, from the days of Queen Boudicca. In fact it's more of a family villa than a village, but its attraction is boosted by the presence of an odd assortment of other features: the remains of a Saxon church found in a 17th-century farm cottage, a nature trail, lake and the somehow inevitable World War memorabilia exhibition.

Five miles further on the same road, **Oxburgh Hall** ⓘ *(NT), T01366-328258, Apr-Oct Mon-Wed, Sat, Sun, house 1300-1700, bank holidays 1100-1700, gardens, daily in Aug 1100-1730, £5.50, under-16s £2.80, family £14.50, gardens only £2.80*, is a delightful medieval moated manor house. The Bedingfield family added the grand Tudor gatehouse in 1482 and their descendants still live here, amid rooms ranging from the gritty Middle Ages to cosy Victoriana, enhanced by an embroidery collection worked up by none other than Mary Queen of Scots herself.

Four miles north of Swaffham off the A1065, the **Peddar's Way** passes through the old village of **Castle Acre**, well worth a visit for its impressive remains of its **Norman manor house-cum-castle** ⓘ *(EH), open at any reasonable time*, and also the ruins of the **Castle Acre Priory** ⓘ *(EH), Castle Acre, T01760-755394, www.english-heritage.org.uk, Apr-Sep 1000-1800, Oct 1000-1700, Nov-Mar Wed-Sun 1000-1600, £3.70, concessions £2.80*. The splendour of this religious establishment in the 12th century can be appreciated from the elaborately decorated arch of its west front, which still stands and comes as quite a surprise in this remote spot. The 15th-century gatehouse, porch and prior's lodging are still habitable. There's also a modern herb garden on site demonstrating some of the medicinal plants the nuns might have used.

Norwich

Norwich, never loud or brash, is quietly confident of itself. Stranded in the middle of the flatlands of East Anglia, it is, as its inhabitants are fond of saying, a "fine city", a typically understated boast that is nonetheless born out by the way in which the place manages to combine so many different layers of English history within the bustle of a busy provincial capital, set off by some bold forays into cutting-edge modernism. As recent excavations have shown, this bend in the River Wensum was used as a place of settlement in Bronze Age times and was subsequently occupied by successive waves of invading forces, from the Vikings and the Romans to – most significantly – the Normans, whose spectacular castle and cathedral still stand at the heart of the city. It is, though, entirely possible to tire of medieval churches – of which Norwich has a surfeit – the natural antidote to which is the **Sainsbury Centre of Visual Arts**, a latter-day temple to the new religion of modern art and a truly world-class museum. Norwich's churches are famously only outnumbered by the city's pubs, where a large student population ensures that the nightlife, while not desperately fashionable, is far from dull. Norwich also provides an ideal base for those interested in exploring Norfolk's many stunning beaches or the more discreet charm of the county's numerous villages and market towns.

Ins and outs

Getting there **Stansted International Airport**, 85 miles away by road, is linked to Norwich by a **Jetlink** coach service, T08705-757747, www.gobycoach.com. Norwich also has its own **airport**, T01603-411923; www.norwichinternational.co.uk, a few miles to the north of the city, operating daily 40-minute flights to Amsterdam and other worldwide connecting flights via Manchester, Paris and Amsterdam. **Anglia Railways**, T08700-409090, operate a half-hourly service direct from London Liverpool Street (1 hour 50 minutes) as well as services from other local towns and villages. For trains to or from the Midlands, the North or Scotland, change at Peterborough. **Central Trains,** T08700-006060, operate local services. The **drive** to Norwich from London, just over 100 miles, is likely to take you about 3 hours. Take the M11 as far as Cambridge and turn off onto the A11. The city contains a number of multi-storey and pay-and-display car parks, as well as some short-term parking spaces in the centre of town. **National**

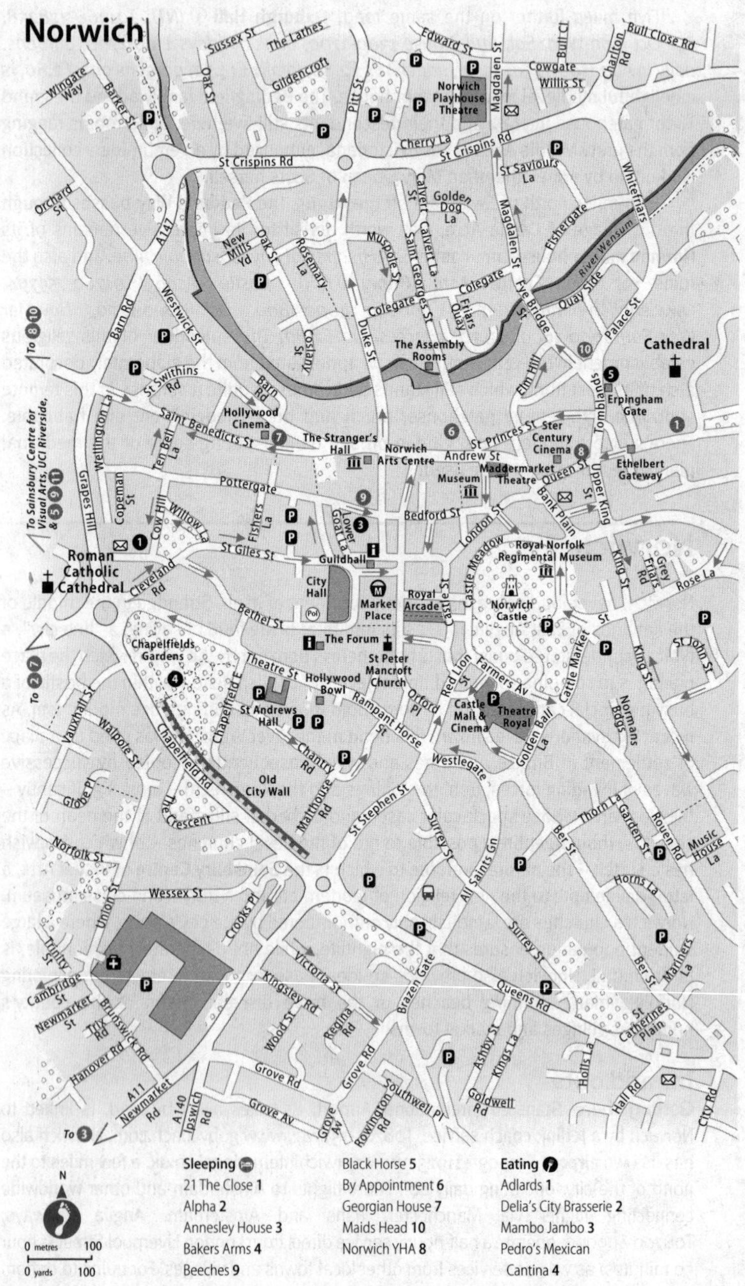

Express, T08705-808080, operates daily services to Norwich from most cities in England. London to Norwich, 3 hours. ▸▸ *For further details, see Transport page 492.*

Getting around Norwich city centre is compact enough to make most places accessible by foot. The 25 bus links the centre with the train station and the 21 or 22 take you to B&B land to the west of the city. For the Sainsbury Centre, a few miles away on the University of East Anglia campus, take the 25, 26 or 27 from the city centre.

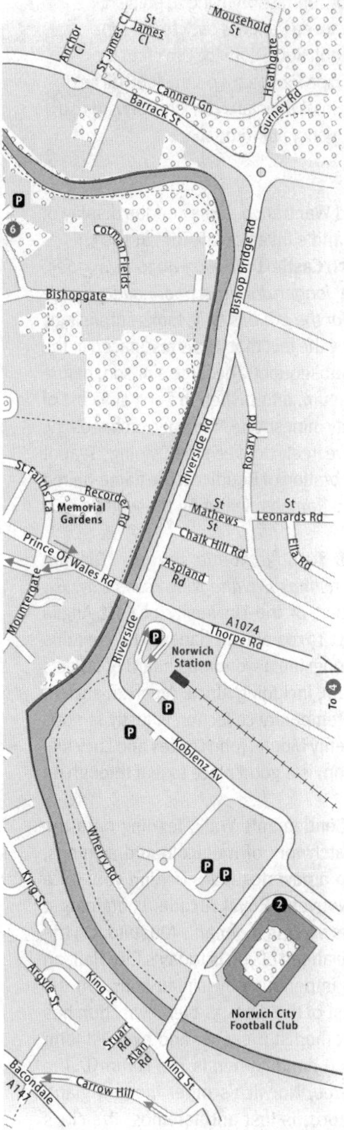

Information The main tourist office *T01603-666071, Apr-Oct 1000-1800 Mon-Sat, 1030-1630 Sun, Nov-Mar 1000-1730 Mon-Sat*, is on the ground floor of The Forum, the vast, hi-tech library and visitor centre on the southwest corner of the marketplace.

Sights

Begin your tour where the city began, inappropriately enough at a place called Tombland, the original heart of Norwich. The **Erpingham Gate**, given to the city by the eponymous gent who led the English archers at Agincourt in 1420 and whose statue stands above the archway, acts as an entrance to the cathedral grounds. The **cathedral** ⓘ *T01603-218321, vis&profficer@cathedral.org.uk, Mid-May to mid-Sep daily 0730-1900, mid-Sep to mid-May daily 0730-1800, visitors' centre open all year Mon-Sat 1000-1600, shop open all year Mon-Sat 0915-1700, services daily, free*, itself was begun in 1096 and finally completed in 1278, though the roof and spire (315 ft) date from the later medieval period, following a fire in 1463. Look under the bishop's throne, behind the high altar, for the remains of a more ancient Norfolk throne, symbolizing the continuity of local worship. A series of 255 painted bosses set high in the nave vaulting depict the entire Bible story, while other treasures include the exquisite carving around the prior's doorway leading onto the cloisters and the medieval paintings in St Luke's Chapel.

Leaving the second-hand bookshops of Tombland behind, walk up the hill into Upper King Street and then left into Castle Meadow for the castle. If you have time, visit the **Royal Norfolk Regimental Museum** ⓘ *Market Av,*

Tatlers **5**
Garden House **11**
Lounge **7**
Orgasmic **8**

Pubs & bars
Adam & Eve **6**
Belgian Monk **9**
Fat Cat **10**

Food-ball crazy

English football grounds are not the obvious places to find haute cuisine, but Carrow Road, home of Norwich City, is different. Nicknamed the canaries for their bright yellow shirts, Norwich have a very famous Chairman in Delia Smith, doyen of TV celebrity chefs and saviour of many a Middle England dinner party. Delia, a lifelong Norwich City supporter, has taken to her now role like a duck to plum sauce and has even given up her TV work to concentrate on trying to guide her beloved Canaries back to the top flight. But if Norwich can't find the recipe for success on the football field, at least their fans can look forward to a superior half-time snack.

T01603-493625, where you will find a First World War trench and a curious display of Buddhist souvenirs from Sir Francis Younghusband's invasion of Tibet in 1903.

Perched high up on its grassy mound, **Norwich Castle** ⓘ *T01603-493636/493625, Mon-Sat 1030-1700, Sun 1400-1700 and slightly longer during school holidays, café and shop, £4.70 for the whole castle, child £2.25 for the exhibits only*, looks surprisingly modern for a Norman building, explained in part by the fact that it was resurfaced in the 19th century. Originally built as a royal palace, it subsequently became a prison, before its present incarnation as Norfolk's principal museum, refurbished in 2001 at a cost of £11.8 million. For that money, you get a high-quality minestrone of history, archaeology, natural history and fine art, both old and new. Move freely between the Twinings Teapot Gallery, the Norwich School of Painters and a celebration of Boudicca, the flame-haired local harridan who led the resistance against the Romans, featuring the world's only virtual-reality chariot ride.

The **Sainsbury Centre for Visual Arts** ⓘ *T01603-456060/593199, Tue-Sun 1100-1700, (1100-2000 on Wed) closed Mon, Christmas Eve and New Year's Day, £2, concessions £1, including special exhibitions*, part of the University of East Anglia (motto: "Do different"), is in Norman Foster's vast 1970s aircraft hangar and contains top-notch modern art, provocatively displayed alongside a wondrous hoard of objects gleaned from all parts of the space-time continuum, including Africa, America, ancient Egypt, the Pacific and medieval Europe. The contemporary collection is justly famous for works by Francis Bacon, Alberto Giacometti, Henry Moore, John Davies and Lucy Rie. The coffee bar, beside the main entrance and shop, is a good place to leaf through an arty purchase.

Back at the castle, stroll west down into Gentleman's Walk, leading onto the main market place, filled by an eyecatching patchwork of multicoloured awnings, where you can buy anything from jellied eels to a new dog lead. Behind you, for a more refined shopping experience, is the Art Nouveau **Royal Arcade**, containing a shop dedicated to one of Norwich's most famous exports, Colman's Mustard. On the right is the flint-clad 15th-century **Guildhall**, while ahead of you is today's **City Hall**, an Art Deco Egyptian-style massif, guarded by two imperious Abyssinian lions. On the left of the square is **St Peter Mancroft**, the largest of the city's 31 medieval churches and a particular favourite of the 18th-century Methodist preacher and hymnist John Wesley. Soaring evermore heavenward, in the left-hand corner, is **The Forum** ⓘ *The Forum, T01603-610524, daily 0700-midnight, free*, Norwich's other modern giant, designed by Michael Hopkins and opened in 2001, is first and foremost the city's main public library, including an important archive dedicated to the American servicemen stationed in the area during the Second World War. The glass-fronted central atrium also has coffee bars and pizza restaurants, the tourist information centre and **Origins** ⓘ *T01603-727920.£4.95, child £3.50*, a multimedia interactive journey through 2000 years of Norwich and Norfolk.

Passing the entrance to the city hall on your left, head up into Upper and Lower Goat Lane, leading into Pottergate and, further on, to St Benedict's Street to find a concentration of independent clothes shops and characterful bars and restaurants. The **Stranger's Hall** ⓘ *T01603-629127*, at the bottom of St Benedict's, is a medieval merchant's house now given over to an interesting museum of English domestic life from Tudor to Victorian times. Head straight on into Princes Street and make a left and right into **Elm Hill**, an atmospheric, cobbled street of timber-framed 16th-century merchants' houses, now home to crafts and antiques shops – a favourite haunt of Lovejoy, BBC's fictional antique-dealing rogue. If it's that time of day, this is also a good place to find a restorative cup of tea and a scone.

North coast: Cromer to King's Lynn

Beyond Cromer, the crumbling clifftop seaside resort in Norfolk's northeast corner, a really superb coast road wends west towards King's Lynn. It travels through a strange but no longer undiscovered seashore, half land and half sea, made up of shifting sands, shallow tidal inlets and wide stretches of salt marshes alive with waders, seabirds and geese. On the way, it takes in precious, little, one-time ports like Cley-next-the-Sea and Blakeney and the dilapidated dignity of Wells-next-the-Sea, its beach now more than a mile away. Holkham beach nearby must be one of the most beautiful in England, where the Household Cavalry sends its thoroughbreds for rest cures and partially owned by the very grand estate of the Earls of Leicester at Holkham Hall. A little inland, Felbrigg is another extraordinary country house, much more homely, while the Queen's modest retreat at Sandringham also draws in punters during the summer.

Ins and outs

Getting there Cromer and Sheringham are on a branch line run by **Anglia Railways,** T08700-409090, from Norwich called The Bittern Line. The A149 is the main coast road, about 3 hours from London at either end. Local **buses** are run by **First Eastern Counties,** T08456-020121, who operate the Coastliner, T0845-3006116, which runs almost all the way along the A149.

Getting around Although the Coastliner bus and rail to Cromer make this coast perfectly accessible without a car, many of the more surprising and secluded sights inland can only really be reached with your own transport.

Information **Wells-next-the-Sea TIC** ⓘ *Staithe St, T01328-710885. Mid-Mar to Oct Mon-Sat 1000-1700, Sun 1000-1600.* **Walsingham TIC** ⓘ *Common Pl, T01328-820510, www.northnorfolk.co.uk, Easter-Oct daily 1000-1630. Very cheery.*

North of the Broads

North of Great Yarmouth, the coastline curves round in one continuous beach all the way to Cromer and Sheringham. It has little to recommend itself to holidaymakers though, being not much good for swimming (dangerous in many places) and lashed by biting winds. Even so, the coast road has a certain breezy charm, dipping in and out of the sea view, especially beyond the tiny village of **Happisburgh** (pronounced *Hazebrugh* by the locals). It's worth stopping here for a look into the church, and climbing the tower if it's open to look out to sea and over the Broads. The village also has a lighthouse, caravan park and a good solid country pub, the *Hill House*, see page 489.

Walks on the Norfolk coast

- **Blakeney Point**: 6 miles there and back. Start: Cley Beach car park, a mile north of Cley-next-the-Sea. A challenging and strange walk along the Norfolk Coast most spectacular shingle spit. OS Maps: Explorer 24, Landranger 133/132
- **Holkham**: 2 miles there and back. Start: North entrance to Holkham Hall, A149. A walk through pine woods to marram grass dunes and an awesome sweep of shimmering sand. OS Maps: Explorer 24, Landranger 132
- **Scolt Head Island**: 2 miles there and back. Start: Brancaster Staithe, 4 miles west of Burnham Market. Boat trip out to a national nature reserve and walks through sandy marshes. OS Maps: Explorer 23, Landranger 132
- **Beacon Hill**: 3 miles there and back. Start: Beeston Regis, 3 miles west of Cromer. A gentle walk up to Norfolk's highest point around the aptly named Pretty Corner. OS Maps: Explorer 25, Landranger 133

Cromer

The first town of any size, more than 30 miles from Great Yarmouth, is faded, sunbleached Cromer. Standing on an impressive cliff, overlooking its long pleasure pier braving the steady ranks of breakers, the place was once quite grand. Dominated by a church with the tallest tower in the county, large Edwardian buildings line the clifftop promenade, but the prevailing atmosphere is forlorn and unloved. The reek of greasy fish and chips stubbornly defies the sea breezes, though this is a top spot for local crab. **Bob Day's Cromer Crabs** at the end of Brunswick Terrace, and the **Lifeboat Café** near where all the crab-boats pull up on the slipway, are both reasonable bets for fresh crustacea. The **Cromer Museum** ⓘ *T01263-513543, Mon-Sat 1000-1700, Sun 1400-1700*, in a former fisherman's cottage next to the church has been converted into a sweet little local history museum. Meanwhile the show gamely goes on at the **Cromer Pier and Pavilion Theatre** ⓘ *T01263-512495, www.thecromerpier.com, performances late Jun-Sep.*

Inland from Cromer

A mile or so inland to the south, **Felbrigg Hall** ⓘ *(NT), T01263-837444, Apr-Oct Sat-Wed 1100-1700 (house open from 1300), £6, children £3*, is the well-preserved seat of a Norfolk country gentleman that has been left as it was when given to the National Trust in 1969. Four generations of the Windham family's furniture, books and pictures fill the comfortable rooms almost as if it were still lived in, but its chief glory is architectural. The hall itself is best seen from the south west, to appreciate the startling change in style that took place over the course of the 17th century. The south front looks like a delightful little Jacobean house, built in 1620, while the west wing, added in the 1680s, represents one of the earliest examples of the handsome Italianate architectural style that came to dominate vernacular English buildings for over a century, and is now known as 'Georgian'. The walled garden has recently been restored, with a thousand doves in the cote, and there's a pretty little church some distance away across the park.

Seven miles further inland, off the A140, stands probably the finest unmodified example of Jacobean architecture in the country, at **Blickling Hall** ⓘ *Blickling (NT), T01263-738030, house, Apr-Oct Wed-Sun, bank holidays 1300-1630 (Oct -1530), garden, Apr-Oct Wed-Sun, bank holidays (also Tue in Aug) 1015-1715 (Oct -1530), Nov and Dec Thu-Sun 1100-1600, Jan-Mar Sat, Sun 1100-1600, £6.70, gardens only £3.80*, 15 miles north of Norwich. Built between 1610 and 1630, and probably designed by the same architect as Felbrigg, it's altogether a much more stately affair, little changed externally but revealing centuries of passing fashions and tastes inside. Highlights include the long gallery with its fabulous plasterwork ceiling, the Peter the Great Room designed to display a huge tapestry woven in 1764 of the mounted Tsar, given to Lord Buckinghamshire by Catherine the Great, and the surrounding parkland complete with a mile-long lake. The place is said to be haunted by the ghost of Anne Boleyn, who may have lived on this site as a child almost a century before the present house was built.

Five miles west of Blickling, a cluster of Norfolk villages are worth seeking out for their remarkable churches and unexpectedly cosy setting in this industrially farmed landscape. **Heydon** is a privately owned village that seems hardly to have changed in a couple of hundred years. The most recent construction was the well in commemoration of Queen Victoria's Jubilee in 1887. It clusters at gates leading to a jewel of an Elizabethan house, restored in the 1970s and set in a beautiful old park. A couple of miles away through thick hedges along tiny lanes, the village of **Salle** (pronounced *Saul*) boasts Norfolk's 'rural cathedral'. Apart from its sheer scale, evidence of the wealth that the cloth industry once brought to these parts, the church's interior contains remarkable carvings, including an angelic host supporting the chancel roof. Nearby, the church at **Cawston** has a mighty 15th-century tower, visible from miles around, and inside one of the best old hammer-beam roofs in the county. A mile or so to the west, near Reepham, the church at **Booton** is another matter entirely: it's the eccentric fantasy of a devout Victorian parson, displaying exuberant Gothic Revivalism dreamed up by Whitwell Elwin, an ascetic who was descended, like others around here, from the native American princess Pocahontas. He won the devotion of several rich young women who paid for the place and are commemorated in the windows of the nave as angels wandering through the fields.

Heading back towards the coast, **Baconsthorpe Castle** ⓘ *(EH), daily 1000-1600, free*, was built by local despot Sir John Heydon in the 15th century during the Wars of the Roses. Peaceful and substantial ruins beside a moat are all that remain, a good spot for a picnic. Beyond the old market town of Holt, **Letheringsett Watermill** ⓘ *T01263-713153, Whitsun-Oct Mon-Fri 1000-1700, Sat 0900-1300 (demonstrations 1400-1630), Nov-Whitsun Mon-Fri 0900-1600, Sat 0900-1300 (demonstrations 1330-1530), £2/£3 with demonstration*, is the county's last working watermill, restored in 1982, with enthusiastic and knowledgeable volunteer millers. Three miles west of Holt, the **North Norfolk Steam Railway** ⓘ *T01263-820800 for train times, www.nnrailway.co.uk*, runs 7 scenic miles from here to the coastal resort of **Sheringham** along 'the poppy line'. It shares its headquarters with the regular rail service's station at Sheringham, a sea-level imitation of Cromer, although the seafront has been badly disfigured by modern defences against coastal erosion.

The north Norfolk coast road

Cley-next-the-Sea and Blakeney

The A149 coast road from Sheringham to Hunstanton, another 30 miles or so, ranks as one of the most delightful coastal routes in England. The North Sea is never more than a couple of miles away to the north, occasionally visible across gleaming mudflats or glistening salt marsh, sometimes hidden completely behind woods and sand hills, as the road rolls through a string of places called 'next-the-sea' that have long been left high and dry. Cley-next-the-Sea (pronounced *Cly*) is the first, an adorable little town and another that was once an important medieval port. Its church with its great south porch now looks over a meadow instead of a harbour, and contains some extraordinary windows and medieval carvings in its nave. Potteries, cafés and restaurants line its old High Street and this is also the jumping off point for the long (5 miles) and lovely walk out to **Blakeney Point Nature Reserve**. An easier option is to catch one of the grey seal-spotting boats that leave from Blakeney and Morston quaysides a few miles down the road, see page 492.

One mile on from Cley, its medieval rival Blakeney also has an interesting **church**, belittling the harbour below, with an extra tower that was once believed to be a lighthouse. Apparently unlikely given that the main tower is taller, suggestions are now invited inside as to its true purpose. Another of the town's sights is the 14th-century cellar of a merchant's house called the **Blakeney Guildhall**. The village itself has the calm and unhurried air of a place dependent on the tides and several good overnight stops. Not surprisingly very popular (especially with birdwatchers) is the section of the **Norfolk Coast Path** leading through the salt marshes from here to Wells-next-the-Sea.

Stiffkey

Two miles beyond Morston, the path passes to seaward of Stiffkey (pronounced *Stewkey*), once famous for its mighty cockle women who lugged back huge bundles of the 'Stewkey blues' revealed on the mudflats at low tide. The village also once revelled in being the scene of a sobering Victorian morality tale about a philandering vicar who left the village in disgrace to become a lion tamer and was eaten. No such dramas today, but instead an almost ruined Elizabethan village hall, 15th-century brasses in the church and a very good pub called the *Red Lion*. Two miles deeper inland, at **Binham Priory** ⓘ *EH, T01328-830434, open any reasonable time*, are the extensive remains of a Benedictine priory, its great Norman nave still in use as the parish church, with a 13th-century west front that gets architectural historians going because it may have contained the earliest window tracery in the country.

Wells-next-the-Sea

Four miles down the road is the old town of Wells-next-the-Sea, not next the sea at all now, but nonetheless a fairly dignified, slightly down-at-heel seaside resort with a dinky little harbour, a cluster of rock shops and a sandy beach that's a mile's walk or narrow-gauge **steam train** ⓘ *runs mid-Jul to mid-Sep, then weekends only to end of Sep, daily 1030-2310, every 40 mins to the Pinewoods campsite*, ride from the quay. The town itself is not a bad place to poke around for a while, browsing in its small shops on Staithe Street or picking up some chips on the quayside.

Little Walsingham

Probably still the most important pilgrimage shrines in the country, the most comparable thing to Lourdes on offer, is 4 miles south of the town at Little Walsingham. Since the 11th century, Kings, Queens and commoners have made their way to Little Walsingham which these days caters for a wide variety of different denominations. The main two shrines are in the **High Anglican parish church** and in the **Roman Catholic Slipper Chapel**, with major pilgrimages to the former on the bank holiday Monday at the end of May, to the latter by Roman Catholic Mothers in late July, and an ecumenical pilgrimage to both in mid-August. All year the village is busy with believers. Unfortunately the vicar of Walsingham who established the Anglican shrine in the 1920s was 220 yards out in his estimation of the location of the original shrine which was set up in 1061 by the local lady of the manor, who had supposedly seen the Virgin Mary.

Pilgrims from the sea can enjoy the last leg of their journey from Wells on the Wells and Walsingham Light Railway. T01328-71-0631 for talking timetable.

Holkham

Two miles west of Wells stands one of the most stately homes in England, the imposing neo-Palladian bulk of **Holkham Hall** ⓘ *T01328-710227, www.holkham.co.uk, late-May to Sep Mon-Thu, Sun 1300-1700, £5, under-16s £2.50*. This ponderous yellow brick-built palace, solidly Roman in inspiration, took over 30 years to complete, designed by William Kent who started work in 1734 for Thomas Coke. It's still inhabited today by his descendant the Earl of Leicester and both inside and out remains remarkably little altered since the 1770s, housing a great collection of old masters by the likes of Claude, Poussin and Rubens, powerfully evocative of the tastes of the time. There's also a Bygones Museum, famous pottery shop and a History of Farming exhibition in honour of the family's great mid-19th-century agriculturalist and pioneer of seed improvement, Coke of Norfolk.

A mile's walk towards the sea from one of Holkham Hall's many gates leads through pine woods and sand dunes to **Holkham Beach**, a serious contender for the title of most spectacular beach in England and up there with the best in the world. At low tide, mile upon mile of shining sand stretches towards the horizon, the sea seeming to have vanished from view. It returns faster than a man can run, rolling in to lap or break on the wide expanse of tussocky dunes.

Burnham Market to Hunstanton

Four miles west of Holkham, a group of four villages called Burnham-something surround Burnham Market, a very smart Georgian town with plenty of antique shops and some good restaurants. **Burnham-Overy-Staithe** is the most picturesque of the villages, especially around its old creak. Further west, **Brancaster** is another charming place in a similar mould, but with better access to the sea and sandy beaches. After 6 more miles the road arrives at the seaside resort of **Hunstanton**, a marginally upmarket version of Cromer at the west end of the north Norfolk coast and milder in climate thanks to the fact that it faces west. Donkey rides, deck chairs, beach huts and rolled trousers are still just about in fashion here, alongside the usual amusement arcades and seaside tack overlooking the beach beneath the cliffs. Just south of the town, more than 100 different varieties of lavender are grown at the **National Lavender Centre** ⓘ *Caley Mill, Heacham T01485-570384, www.norfolk-lavender.co.uk, daily 1000-1700 (field tours mid-June until harvest)*, some of their essences distilled and a 50-acre field of the purple scented stuff viewable by minibus. There's a fragrant plant centre and impressive herb garden too.

Sandringham and around

ⓘ *T01553-772675, www.sandringhamestate.co.uk, Apr-Jul, Aug-Oct daily 1100-1645. £6, concessions £4.50, children £3.50.*

Eight miles south is Sandringham, the Queen's country house. Edward VII had the place built in 1870 when he was Prince of Wales as a very grand shooting lodge. It still comes across more like a very comfortable late-Victorian home than a royal palace. As well as tours of the house and gardens, there's a museum housing some Royal possessions, ranging from a 1900 Daimler to a half-scale Aston Martin used by Princes Harry and William.

Five miles east, 10 miles west of Fakenham, **Houghton Hall** ⓘ *T01485-528569, Mid-Apr to Sep Thu, Sun, bank holidays 1300-1730, £6, under-16s £3*, is a much more grand and beautiful affair, an 18th-century Palladian mansion designed by James Gibbs for Sir Robert Walpole, the first prime minister of Britain from 1721-42. He was the father of Horace, the Gothic novelist and Strawberry Hill arbiter of 18th-century taste, who apparently hated the place but is nonethelesss buried in the church which was stripped of its village to make way for the park, the inhabitants being relocated in smart estate cottages a short distance away. The estate was later inherited by the first Marquess of Cholmondeley whose descendants still live here.

Three miles south of Sandringham, **Castle Rising** ⓘ *T01553-631330, Apr-Sep daily 1000-1800, Oct daily 1000-1700, Nov-Mar Wed-Sun 1000-1600, £3.25, concessions £2.50*, is a remarkably well-preserved 12th-century domestic keep standing in the middle of mighty earthworks. It was once the palace and home of Isabella, dowager Queen of England.

King's Lynn

The castle stands near the outskirts of King's Lynn, once one of the most important seaports in the country. It suffered throughout the 20th century, during the Second World War and later at the hands of the developers, but is still an important local centre. The two towers of its church raise their heads above the mess, and beneath them can be found a remarkable Norman west front, and pockets of the town as much of it would have looked in its heyday.

Sleeping

Lowestoft, Great Yarmouth and around *p471*

B Hotel Elizabeth, 1 Marine Pde, Great Yarmouth, T01493-855551, F853338. Next door to the Winter Gardens with sea views. A reasonable top-end option.

B Imperial, North Drive, Great Yarmouth, T01493-842000 www.imperialhotel.co.uk. The best smartish option in town, overlooking the prom at its northern end, with a reputable restaurant.

B Ivy House Farm, Ivy La, Oulton Broad, Lowestoft T01502-501333, is an unusual farm-conversion into a hotel, with large quiet rooms and attractive gardens.

D Fairholme Hotel 23/24 Princes Rd, T01493-843447.

D Silverstone House, 29 Wellesley Rd, Great Yarmouth, T01493-844862. A clean and fairly comfortable B&B option, as is the

F Great Yarmouth YHA, 2 Sandown Rd, Great Yarmouth, T01493-843991, F856600. Has 40 beds close to the seafront at the north end of Marine Pde.

The Broads *p474*

The best place to sleep on the Broads is on a boat. Otherwise these are some of the other options.

A The Norfolk Mead Hotel, Coltishall, T01603-737531, www.norfolkmead.co.uk. A Georgian manor house that has become a discreet and sophisticated country house hotel, with individually furnished rooms and attractive grounds sloping down to the river Bure.

C Fisherman's Return, Winterton-on-Sea, near Martham, T01493-393305. Close to a sandy beach in an out-of-the-way spot with good value bar-food and 3 bedrooms.

C Le Grys Barn, Wacton Common, near Long Stratton, T01508-531576, F01508-532124. A newly converted barn decorated in a way that reflects its owner's African travels.

D Hall Green Farm, Norton Rd, Loddon, T01508-522039, www.geocities.com/hallgreenfarm. A 10-min walk outside the village of Loddon, a Georgian farmhouse with 2 double rooms, both with en suite bathrooms.

D Lower Farm B&B, Horsford, T01603-891291, www.norfolkbroads.com/lowerfarm. Attractive old 17th-century farmhouse with 2 double rooms with en suite bathrooms.

D The Old Chapel, Horsey, T01493-393498. An interesting converted church B&B.

Swaffham and Breckland *p477*

A Strattons, 4 Ash Close, Swaffham, T01760-723845, www.strattons-hotel.co.uk. Off the Market Square, a delightful old Queen Anne house with 8 fairly spacious rooms above a rated restaurant.

B Riverside Hotel, Mill St, Mildenhall, T01638-717274. A fairly small but comfortable hotel on the river and main road.

C College Farm, Thompson, near Thetford, T01953-483318. Old priest's house with a long history.

C Crown Hotel, Crown St, Mundford, T01842-878233. Reasonable food at one of the area's rare pubs and also has a few very comfortable little rooms.

C Litcham Hall, Litcham, near King's Lynn, T01328-701389. A very fine 18th-century country house B&B.

F Old Red Lion, Castle Acre, T01760-755557, www.oldredlion.here2stay.org.uk. Informal hospitality (sleeps 23),double rooms and 2 dormitories. Exclusively wholefood catering. Kitchen available and log stoves. No smoking. Venue for hire, groups, courses. Retreats.

Norwich *p479, map p480*
Accommodation is hard to come by bang in the middle of town and the majority of visitors to Norwich find themselves booking into a B&B – for around £25-30 per person – in the area just west of the city centre down the Dereham and Earlham Rd.

A **The Beeches**, T01603-621167. 3 converted Victorian houses grouped around the Roman Catholic Cathedral, offer 3-star accommodation within acres of well-kept gardens within walking distance of the city centre.

B **By Appointment**, 25-29 St George's St, T01603-630730. For something a little theatrical, this is a 15th-century merchant's house in the middle of the city centre, which includes a well-respected restaurant.

B **The Georgian House Hotel**, 32 Unthank Rd, T01603-615655. Also opposite the Roman Catholic Cathedral, this is a family-run hotel within easy reach of the centre.

B **Maids Head Hotel**, in central Tombland, T01603-209955. Offers rooms at a wide range of prices.

C **Black Horse**, Earlham Rd, T01603-624682 , pleasant pub accommodation.

E **21 The Close**, T01603-662562. A friendly 1-room B&B at a desirable address right next to the cathedral.

E **The Baker's Arms**, St Leonards Rd near the railway station. Rooms above the pub.

F **Norwich YHA**, 112 Turner Rd, a 20-min walk west of the city centre, T01603-627647. A dorm bed is £10.25 (£7 for under-18s).

The north Norfolk coast road *p485*
L **Morston Hall**, Holt, T01263-741041, www.morstonhall.com. Small manor house with attractive rooms, a well-tended garden and really top-quality restaurant.

A **Blakeney Hotel**, Blakeney, near Holt, T01263-740797, www.blakeney-hotel.co.uk. Straightforward and comfortable modern 3-star hotel overlooking the marshes with friendly and efficient staff.

B **Hoste Arms**, The Green, Burnham Market, T01328-738257. In the middle of Burnham Market, this place thinks a lot of its kitchen and charges accordingly. Fresh local ingredients on the extensive modern British menu. The service tends towards the supercilious but the rooms are spacious and quiet.

B **The White Horse Hotel and Restaurant**, 4 High St, Blakeney, near Holt, T01263-740574, F741303. Ten cosy rooms, some overlooking the harbour, in an old coaching inn, with a highly rated restaurant below in the old stables. Recommended.

C **Buckinghamshire Arms**, Blickling, T01263-732133. Comfortable rooms in Blickling Hall's old stable block. Decent bar food too.

C **Cley Mill**, Cley-next-the-Sea, T01263-740209. A remarkable converted windmill with wonderful marshland views and very good food.

C **The King's Arms**, Westgate St, Blakeney, T01263-740341. Snug low-ceilinged old pub in 3 fishermen's cottages with cosy good-value little rooms and tempting fare on offer.

C **The Old Laundry**, Heydon Hall, T01263-587343. Right next to the Elizabethan house of Heydon Hall, where rooms can also be hired for special occasions, at a price. Recommended.

C **Old Town Hall House**, Cley-next-the-Sea, T01263-740284. Has large rooms in the middle of the village with good breakfasts.

C **Saracen's Head**, Wolterton, near Erpingham, T01263-768909. Hard to find but worth the effort, for its superb food (booking advisable), real ales and cosy rooms with en suite bathrooms. Recommended.

C **Whalebone House of Cley** High St, Cley-next-the-Sea, T01263-740336. Available by advance booking for stays of 2 nights or more. Homespun philosophy, contemporary vegan, vegetarian and organic, small and exclusive.

D **Cambridge Guest House B&B**, East Cliff, Cromer, T01263-512085. Right on the seafront, with sea views.

D **The Hill House**, Happisburgh, T01692-650004. Largish rooms above a characterful freehouse pub (once one of Arthur Conan Doyle's favourite haunts), in a quiet coastal village with great views over the Broads and out to sea. Recommended.

F **Sheringham YHA**, 1 Cremer's Drift, T01263-823215. A short walk from the train station.

Eating

Lowestoft, Great Yarmouth and around *p471*

£££ Seafood Restaurant, 85 North Quay, Great Yarmouth, T01493-856009. About £35 a head but the only really good seafood restaurant in the town.

££ St Peter's Brewery and St Peter's Hall, St Peter South Elmham, near Bungay, T01986-782322, www.stpetersbrewery.co.uk. Do good local-recipe lunch and dinners on Fri and Sat and lunches on Sun 1100-1800.

Norwich *p479, map p480*

££ 39 Steps, 17 St Benedicts St, T01603-619040. Live jazz every night and dining on 3 floors. A la carte menu and a special deal offering a glass of wine and main course for £8.

££ Adlards, 79 Upper St Giles St, T01603-633522. A British restaurant with a strong French influence, in an elegant, contemporary dining room. Norwich's only Michelin star, yet not outrageously expensive.

££ Delia's City Brasserie, Norwich City Football Club, T01603-218705, where you can combine an afternoon watching the beautiful game and an evening of the recipes of television chef Delia Smith, a director and majority shareholder of Norwich's first division football team, aka 'the Canaries'. The restaurant, inside one of the football ground's stands, is only open on Saturday nights.

££ Tatlers, 21 Tombland, T01603-633511. Probably Norwich's best-known restaurant, serving modern English cooking made with local produce in a chic yet homely setting.

£ Mambo Jambo, 14 Lower Goat La, T01603-66802, offers good-value southern cooking – Creole, Cajun, Mexican – with an upbeat ambience.

£ Pedro's Mexican Cantina, Chapelfields Gardens, T01603-614725. Large plates of nachos and enchiladas with a salsa backing track ensure a loyal student following at this fun old favourite.

£ Sainsbury Centre, T01603-456060/593199. Join history of art students in the centre's licensed café at the west end. A good value lunch (1200-1400, about £3). A proper, table-service restaurant, next to the café, and where it is better to book in advance, is also an option.

The north Norfolk coast road *p485*

Apart from many of the places listed above, a variety of restaurants and pubs in the region are also very good at serving up fresh local produce in imaginative ways amid homely surroundings.

£££ The Crown Hotel, Buttlands, Wells-next-the-Sea, T01553-771483. Does modern British cooking of a very high standard and fairly high price (about £40 a head) in an old converted cottage.

£££ Yetman's, 37 Norwich Rd, Holt, T01263-713320. Smart restaurant (about £50 a head) serving top-quality local produce backed up by an excellent wine list.

££ Fishes, Market Pl, Burnham Market, T01328-738588. Know how to prepare their namesake with panache.

££ Jolly Sailors, Brancaster Staithe, T01485-210314. Accomplished restaurant serving local seafood and very good ales in a quiet (although popular) creek-side village. Booking advisable.

££ Lifeboat Inn, Ship La, Thornham, T01485-512236. Does very good things with local produce at reasonable rates in a rambling 16th-century inn.

££ The Red Lion, Stiffkey, T01328-830552. Very good fresh local seafood in a hearty and unpretentious atmosphere.

££ Three Horseshoes, Bridge St, Warham All Saints T01328-710547. Imaginative recipes for local produce at this atmospheric pub.

£ Cliff Top Café, Cliff Rd, Overstrand, T01263-579319. Steve and Les's delightfully eccentric café overlooking the sea and offering wholesome inexpensive food and afternoon cream teas. Open Jun-Sep 0800-1600.

Pubs, bars and clubs

The Broads *p474*

Fur and Feather, Woodbastwick (between Ranworth and Wroxham), T01603-720003. Large pub that serves as the main outlet for the local award-winning Woodfordes brewery and also does reasonable food.

Horsey Nelson, Horsey, T01493-393378. A straightforward and cosy country pub, also close to the beach.

Locks Inn, Geldeston, T01508-518414. Beside the river but hidden away down a farmyard track, does decent pub grub, although it's the location and candlelit interior of the old place that makes it.

Swaffham and Breckland *p477*
The Swan, Hoxney. A good Elizabethan-looking pub with huge open fires, beams and brickwork, real ales, bright and welcoming with reasonable food.

Norwich *p479, map p480*
The Adam and Eve, Bishopsgate, is Norwich's oldest pub in the shadow of the cathedral walls. Sit outside with your pint and admire the ivy.
The Belgian Monk, 7 Pottergate, T01603-767222, allows you to complement your research into an unholy array of 18 Belgian beers and 12 fruit Jenevers with mussels and chips and other examples of robust gastronomie.
The Fat Cat, 49 West End St, off Dereham Rd, is beloved of real ale drinkers, stocking a genuinely impressive range of barrelled beers and a good stock of the Belgian bottled variety too.
The Garden House, Pembroke Rd, off Earlham Rd. Like the above, another pub in the so-called 'Golden Triangle' of student living. Very popular, with a pool table, pinball table, huge garden and occasional Djs.
Lounge, 13 St Benedicts, is from the school of cool, minimalist styling and ambient beats, offering a cocktail hour and a light bar menu.
Orgasmic, Queen St, you shouldn't let the trendy crowd put you off. This brand new bar caters for all ages and serves a good pizza too.

Clubs
The Prince of Wales Rd, leading away from the city centre towards the railway station, is lined with noisy pubs and nightclubs.
Concept is a smaller, basement club with garage and swing nights.
Liquid, all bubble projections and lava lamps is the biggest and most well known.
The Loft is a predominantly gay club playing 60s and 70s soul sounds, with a live band on Friday nights.
Time contains a vast dance floor and enormous video screen. Just over the river, in the new Riverside development.

Entertainment

Norwich *p479, map p480*
Cinema
Norwich has 3 multiplex cinemas: **Hollywood Cinema** in Anglia Sq, T01603-621903; **Ster Century** in the Castle Mall shopping centre, T01603-221900 and **UCI Riverside** in the new Riverside development, T0870-0102030.
Cinema City, St Andrews St, T01603-622047. Is the art house cinema.

Theatre
The city also has 3 theatres, the **Norwich Playhouse** in St George's St, T01603-598598, the **Theatre Royal** in Theatre St, T01603-630000, and the more alternative **Maddermarket Theatre**, in St John's Alley, T01603-620917.

Music
Classical concerts are held in **St Andrew's and Blackfriars' Halls**, T01603-628477 and also in **The Assembly Rooms**, Theatre St, T01603-626402. There might also be something happening at the friendly **Norwich Arts Centre**, in St Benedicts St, T01603-660352 – Nirvana played here on their first UK tour to an audience of 87 people.

Festivals

Norwich *p479, map p480*
The city is also host to a variety of festivals throughout the year.
Jan-Mar **The Visiting Writers' Festival** is held from the end Jan-mid-Mar at the University of East Anglia, where the creative writing course under Malcolm Bradbury and Andrew Motion has produced such luminaries as Ian McEwan, Timothy Mo, Graham Swift and Kazuo Ishiguro.
Oct An **animation film festival** is often held throughout the month
Oct **Norwich Beer Festival** in the last week of the month.
Nov **East Coast Jazz Festival** in the 1st 2 weeks of Nov.

Shopping

Norwich *p479, map p480*
As well as all the usual big name brands in the Castle Mall shopping centre, the area around the cathedral harbours a few little surprises such as the
Colman's Mustard Shop, 15 Royal Arcade, T01603-627889. All things bright yellow and mustard-themed from the famous Norwich mustard manufacturers, including a museum.

The north Norfolk coast road *p485*
The Cley Smokehouse famously good for picnic materials like fresh-dressed crabs, home-made pâté, wild salmon, wild smoked salmon, anchovies and crayfish tails, on the High St, next door to
Made in Cley, T01263-740134 , an interesting home-made potters shop.
Picnic Fare Delicatessen, Cley, is a highly rated East Anglian foodshop.

Activities and tours

Lowestoft, Great Yarmouth and around *p471*
Caister Riding Stables, Caister Rd, Great Yarmouth, T01493-720444.
Lowestoft Harbour Boat Tours, T01502-569087.
Yarmouth Stadium, 1930 every Mon, Wed and Sat for greyhound racing atthroughout the year, T01493-720343.

Norwich *p479, map p480*
Blue Badge Guide, walking tours lasting approximately 1 hr 30 mins depart from the tourist centre. Apr-Oct. City Ghost and Horror Walk. May-Oct. T01603 607262, www.norwich-ghost-walks.co.uk.
City Boats Boat trips are available departing daytime and evening from Elm Hill Quay and Norwich Station Quay, T01603-701701.
The sports centre, T01603-592398. Swimming, athletics, fitness centre, squash, basketball, fencing, hockey, trampolining, climbing etc, is at the UEA Sportspark down the Earlham Rd. Daily 0730-1000.
Hollywood Bowl, T01603-631311 in the new Riverside development – 26 bowling lanes, with bar and food area.

The North Norfolk Coast Road *p485*
Bishop's Boats, Blakeney Quay, T01263-740753, also do seal-spotting trips.
Blakeney Harbour Sailing Instruction Charter, Tide's Reach, Morston, T01263-740377, www.charlieward-trad-boats.co.uk. Laid-back instruction in sturdy Norfolk Oyster dayboats. The same company also operates day trips on the luxury sailing barge *Juno*.
Temple's Ferry Service, T01263-740791, £5, under-16s £3.50. Leaves from Morston Quay for 1- or 2-hr trips to see the seals and land on Blakeney Point (NT), ticket office in *Anchor* pub.

Transport

Lowestoft, Great Yarmouth and around *p471*
Car
Central Motors, 50 St Georges Rd, Great Yarmouth, T01493-851515. **Thrifty**, Newcombe Rd, Lowestoft, T01502-580333.

Taxi
Five-One Taxis, Unit 8, Harbour Rd, Lowestoft, T01502-500700. **PR Miller**, 103 Station Rd, North Belton, Great Yarmouth, T01493-781680.

Swaffham and Breckland *p477*
Car
B M R Vehicle Hire, Brickfields Way, Thetford, T01842-761265. **Willhire Vehicle Rental**, Mundford Rd, Thetford, T01842-761578.

Norwich *p479, map p480*
Bicycle
Streetlife, 54 West End St, T01603-626660. **Broadland Cycle Hire**, The Rhond, Hoverton, T01603-783096.

Bus
National Express, T08705-808080, www.nationalexpress.co.uk, run direct services from Norwich Bus Station to and from **London Victoria** (3 hrs) and every 2 hrs to **Stansted airport** (1 hr 45 mins). Services to **Cambridge** (2 hrs 30 mins), changing at **Newmarket**, are run by **Stagecoach** at 0915 and 1115. To **Ipswich** (3 hrs) can be arranged through Traveline, T0870-6082608.

Car
Avis, Norwich Airport, T01603-416719. **Thrifty**, 1 Paddock St, T01603-666300.

Taxi

City Hall Taxis, 41 Hurricane Way, T01603-789333. **Five Star Taxis**, 43a Prince of Wales Rd, T01603-455555.

Train

Anglia Railways, T08700-409090, www.angliarailways.co.uk, runs the main service to and from Norwich. Trains are twice hourly to **London Liverpool Street** (1 hr 45 mins), twice hourly direct to **Cambridge** (1 hr 15 mins) and twice hourly direct to **Ipswich** (40 mins). Central Trains, T0121-6541200, www.centraltrains.co.uk, run the regular service to **Stansted airport** (1 hr 50 mins), changing at **Ely**.

Directory

Norwich *p479, map p480*

Hospitals **Norfolk & Norwich University Hospital NHS Trust**, Colney La, Colney, T01603-286286. **Internet** Flying Classrooms Internet Café, 14 Bank St, T01603-619091. **Norwich Market Internet** Café, 40-41 Provision Market, T01603-760808. **Police** Norfolk Police Norwich Division, Bethel St, T01603-768769. **Post Office** Post Office Services, 84/85 Castle Meadow Walk, Castle Mall, T0845-7223344.

Cambridgeshire

→ *Colour map 5, grid C2/3 and colour map 3, grid A2/3*

Apart from the university town at its heart, Cambridgeshire is not a particularly prepossessing place to visit. Its fertile soil and the demands of agribusiness have created a dull and lifeless landscape across large areas, although the few pieces of high or wooded ground are consequently all the more interesting. Cambridge itself draws in millions of visitors each year to admire its colleges world-class museums and string of well-run festivals. A relatively small and undeniably very pretty town, it's mobbed most of the year with students and tourists who give it a lively buzz on the streets. In summer, a punt along the river here is still a must for a full appreciation of the place. The river winds out to Grantchester, the village immortalized by the poet Rupert Brooke but only one of a series of endearing Cambridge satellites like Trumpington. To the south of the city, off the M11, is the Imperial War Museum's vast museum of militarized flight at Duxford, just before the unexpected prominence of the mystical Gog Magog Hills. To the north, Ely Cathedral sails majestically above the well-drained farmland all around, the Queen of the Fens. ▸▸ *For Sleeping, Eating and other listings, see pages 502-506.*

Cambridge and around

More than anything else, Cambridge is its university. Unlike Oxford, its traditional rival, the city would otherwise be little more than a fairly unremarkable market town south of the Wash. For the last 700 years or so, academia has made its mark in this little place more impressively than just about anywhere else in the world. If it's old colleges you want to see, with their medieval and Renaissance chapels, libraries, halls, gardens and courts, Cambridge is the place to come. Partly because of the tourist pressure, the whole town has a slightly unreal, self-conscious atmosphere, an impression compounded by the type of twee flannels-and-blazers pastoral idyll once promoted by the cult surrounding local poet Rupert Brooke. Women were admitted to the University in 1947 though, the first in a series of reforms that has turned it into one of the most dynamic centres for research in the country, building on its strengths in mathematics and the sciences. The city itself, only granted that status in the 1950s, now has a growing population of about 108,000, drawn in to work for the high-tech industries discreetly placed along the ring road.

Ins and outs

Getting there Cambridge **railway** station is on Station Rd, a 20-min walk from the centre. The main operators are **WAGN** (West Anglia Great Northern Railway), T0870-8508822. Direct trains from Cambridge to: London King's Cross via Royston, Hitchin, Stevenage, Finsbury Park (every 30 mins peak times, journey time 45 mins-1 hr), and to London Liverpool.St via Audley End, Bishop's Stortford, Harlow Town. There are frequent direct trains from Cambridge to London. From London take M11 north (which passes close to Stansted airport and Saffron Walden), at Junction 13 take the A1303 east and follow signs to city centre (1 hr 15 mins, 63 miles from central London). Cambridge is well served by express coach services, all of which terminate

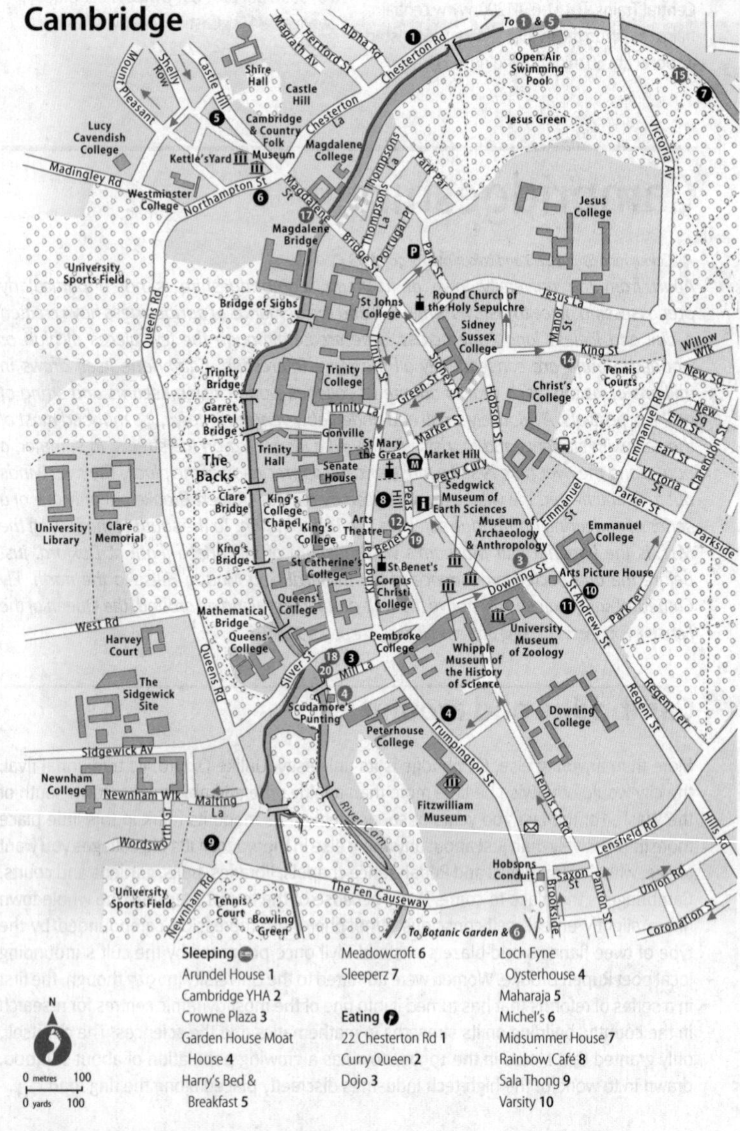

at the Drummer St coach stands, adjacent to the bus station. The main operators are **Jetlink, Stagecoach** and **National Express,** T08705-808080. The travel office at the bus station has full details of all services and sells tickets for scheduled coach services and coach excursions to places of interest. **Traveline,** T0870-6082608, or **GoByCoach** helpline, T0121-4238477. ▸▸ *For further details, see Transport page 505.*

Getting around Cambridge town centre is only about a mile or so in diameter bordered to the north and west by the river Cam and the river Granta and its green banks which include the Midsummer Common and Jesus Green. The town centre is easily navigated by foot or by bicycle.

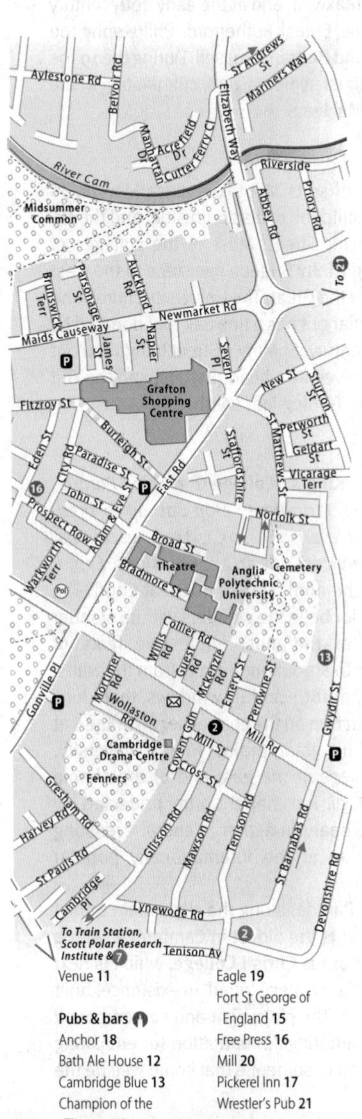

Venue 11

Pubs & bars
Anchor **18**
Bath Ale House **12**
Cambridge Blue **13**
Champion of the Thames **14**
Eagle **19**
Fort St George of England **15**
Free Press **16**
Mill **20**
Pickerel Inn **17**
Wrestler's Pub **21**

Information Cambridge TIC ⓘ *Wheeler St, T01223-322640, www.tourismcambridge.com. Mon-Fri 1000-1800 (until 1730 Nov-Mar), Sat 1000-1700, Easter-Sep Sun and bank holidays 1100-1600,* seem to charge for most things and has a rather indifferent/world-weary attitude.

History As its name suggests, Cambridge owes its existence to its location at a solid bridgeable point on the river Cam. A settlement called Camboritum grew up here, at the junction of Akeman Street (between London and King's Lynn) and the Via Devana (between Lincoln and Colchester). The Romans established a fort on the outer bend of the river, on the spot later chosen by the Normans for their castle, just over Magdalene Bridge (Castle Mound marks the place today). Medieval myth-making aside (one legend has it that the University was founded by none other than King Arthur), the received wisdom is that the University as such first took shape thanks to scholars fleeing riots in Oxford in 1209. They soon made themselves unpopular with the locals, resulting in the burning of the University records in St Mary's church and the subsequent execution of 18 townsmen. Church and Royalty favoured the scholars and they prospered. The first major phase of the University's expansion occurred after the Black Death in 1349, when, as in the country as a whole, almost half the town's population was wiped out. Colleges sprang up along the course of the old High Street, now King's Parade and Trinity Street, while the University's European status and reputation was confirmed with the arrival of Erasmus in the early 16th century. Despite dissolving the monasteries, Henry VIII chose to demonstrate his munificence with the foundation of Trinity but stole much of the other colleges' silver. As a result, they were forced to open their doors to the rich and compromise their scholastic ideals. In the 17th century, Cambridge was at the centre of the Puritan revival, shaping the ideology that inspired the Civil War and also exporting it to the colonies of America. Oliver Cromwell briefly attended Sidney Sussex as a commoner. Surprisingly perhaps, after the Restoration and then the Glorious Revolution of 1688, the University became staunchly Royalist and Tory: like Oxford, during the 18th century it earned a reputation for debauching the sons of the gentry. Victorian Cambridge saw the salvation of the University's credibility with stunning developments in science, nurturing greats like Charles Darwin, electrical pioneer James Clerk-Maxwell, and in the early 20th century electron-discover JJ Thompson and atom-splitter Ernest Rutherford. Philosophy too was a strength, thanks to Ludwig Wittgenstein and Bertrand Russell. During the 1930s the University bred an alarming number of Stalinist sympathizers, culminating in the celebrated traitors Burgess, Blunt, Philby and Maclean.

Sights

Market Hill, a square where a general market of sorts still takes place Monday to Saturday, is the centre of Cambridge, with the Guildhall on its south side, and the TIC round the corner in the Old Library on Wheeler Street. Most of the colleges of particular interest to a visitor are lined up along Trinity Street a few steps to the west down St Mary's Street past the church of St Mary the Great. The University church and parish church of Cambridge is not that spectacular but has a fine oak roof donated by Henry VII, reconstructed at the end of the 15th century. St Mary's Street brings you out on Trinity Street opposite Senate House, the University's headquarters, and the Old Schools behind. Turning right here heads north. Turning left, south.

South of Market Hill

Top of most visitors' places to visit is **King's College** ⓘ *King's Parade, T01223-331250, www.kings.cam.ac.uk, during term-time: Mon-Sat 0930-1530, choral evensong 1730, Sun 1315-1415, choral evensong 1030, 1530, vacations, Mon-Sat 0930-1630, Sun 1000-1700 (no services), £3.50, concessions £2.50, under-12s free*, for the spectacular chapel on the north side of its Great Court. The simple elegance of the chapel's plan and exterior belie the wonders within: slender fan-vaulting soars overhead – surely one of the most impressive feats of ceiling-making in the western world – seeming to sprout organically from the walls, the whole space illuminated by a brilliant array of 16th-century windows, thankfully spared by the 17th-century iconoclasts. Construction on the chapel began in 1446 at the instigation of Henry VI, the centrepiece of his grand project for the University, and was completed by Henry VIII. The altarpiece at the east end of the simple rectangular plan is Rubens' *Adoration of the Magi*. The chapel's other pride and joy is its world-famous boys' choir, which can be heard in action at choral evensong most afternoons during term-time, as well as at the internationally popular Christmas carol service.

Continuing south a few yards down King's Parade, along the city's main tourist drag, the little church tucked up **St Bene't** Street is the oldest in Cambridge, with a Saxon tower and arch, originally the chapel of **Corpus Christi College**, which is next up on the left. The Old Court of Corpus is the earliest college 'quad' in existence, built shortly after the foundation of the college in 1352. The playwright and contemporary of Shakespeare **Christopher Marlowe** began Cambridge's reputation for educating future spies here in the 16th century and a portrait of someone that could well be the man himself hangs in the college hall.

Opposite Corpus is **St Catherine's College**, known as 'Cats', with an attractive 18th-century brick courtyard. Behind, down Silver Street or King's Lane, is **Queens' College**, founded as Queen's by the wife of Henry VI in 1448, rechristened and endowed by the wife of Edward VI (hence the relocated apostrophe). One of the smallest and prettiest colleges in the city to look at, it provided lodgings in the Pump Court tower for the great Humanist Erasmus who saved the University's academic reputation throughout Europe in 1511 by bringing the teaching of Greek to England. The combination of Queens' red-brick Tudor buildings – Gatehouse, Cloister Court and President's Lodge – is charming. Crossing the Cam, but best seen from Silver Street, is the **Mathematical Bridge**, a much-restored 18th-century design.

Heading down to the river, Mill Lane is the most popular place in the city to hire a punt, near the Garden House Hotel.

Back on Trumpington Street, the continuation of King's Parade, on the left is **Pembroke College**, with a fine classical chapel designed by Wren – his first major church project no less. The college has a long list of famous alumni, including Pitt the Younger – Prime Minister at the age of 23 – the poets Edmund Spenser and Ted Hughes, and comedian Peter Cook.

Opposite Pembroke is **Peterhouse**, the smallest and oldest college in the University, founded by the Bishop of Ely in 1281. The college hall remains much as it was when built, while its well-kept garden and pretty octagonal courtyard are also worth a peek. The Fitzwilliam Museum is next door.

The Museums

Thanks to the University, for a market town Cambridge is blessed with an unusually large and well-endowed collection of museums, at least 10 in total. Next door to Peterhouse stands their flagship, the grand neoclassical façade of the **Fitzwilliam Museum** ⓘ *Trumpington St, T01223-332900 www.fitzmuseum.cam.ac.uk, Tue-Sat 1000-1700, Sun 1415-1700, free*, without doubt one of the best reasons to visit the city in the first place. Founded in 1816, it houses a host of antiquities from Ancient Egypt, Greece and Rome, as well as applied arts from sculpture and furniture to clocks and rugs, alongside precious manuscripts and an outstanding collection of Old Master paintings, drawings and prints. Be sure to look up as you pass beneath its grand portico to enjoy its extraordinary gem-like Victorian coffered ceiling. Undergoing a comprehensive redevelopment of its main galleries at the time of writing, highlights of the collection on display in the magnificent Founder's Building include paintings by Titian, Vernonese, Rubens, Canaletto, Hogarth, Reynolds, Stubbs, Modigliani, Renoir, Cezanne and Picasso; Breughel's *Flowers in Stoneware Vase*, Monet's *Poplars*, and Vecchio's *Venus and Cupid*.

Back past Peterhouse and a right turn up Pembroke Street brings you into the heart of the University's scientific and museum quarter. First on the left is the **Whipple Museum of the History of Science** ⓘ *Free School La, T01223-330906, www.hps.cam.ac.uk, Mon-Fri 1330-1630*, housed in an Elizabethan hall. Highlights include the Grand Orrery, an astronomical model made by George III's instrument maker, George Adams, as well as displays of scientific instruments from the Middle Ages to the present day.

Close by in Downing Street, is the **University Museum of Zoology** ⓘ *New Museums Site, Downing St, T01223-336650, www.zoo.cam.ac.uk, Mon-Fri 1000-1300, 1400-1645, free*, reopened after refurbishment in 2001, displaying a wide array of recent and fossilized skeletal animals, including a huge whale, and an almost comprehensive display of stuffed British birds.

Over the road is the **Museum of Archaeology and Anthropology** ⓘ *T01223-333516, www.cumaa.archanth.cam.ac.uk, Oct-May Tue-Sat 1400-1630, Jun-Sep Tue-Fri 1030- 1630, Sat 1400-1630, free*. It holds important archaeological collections from palaeolithic Europe, Asia and Africa, pre-Columbian

Ten-to-three?

The image of Cambridge that has proved most enduring remains that surrounding the short, beautiful life of the poet Rupert Brooke before the First World War. His famous lines from The Old Vicarage, Grantchester, "Stands the church clock at ten-to-three/ And is there honey still for tea?" have come to epitomize the university and its gilded youth's immortal charms. The persistence of this sentimental picture of the place was guaranteed by his death aged 27 on board a troopship bound for Gallipoli in April 1915. He was buried in an olive grove on the Greek island of Skyros, giving the stamp of truth to his other equally famous lines: "If I should die, think only this of me:/ That there's some corner of a foreign field/ That is forever England".

South America and early Mediterranean civilizations and anthropological collections from the South Seas and Northwest America, including the inevitable Totem pole, as well as lots of interesting photographs.

Next door is the **Sedgwick Museum of Earth Sciences** ⓘ *T01223-333456, www.sedgwick.esc.cam.ac.uk, Mon-Fri 0900-1300, 1400-1700, Sat 1000-1300, free*, the oldest museum in the University, where you are greeted by a full-size (18ft) model of an iguanodon. Highlights include the colourful mineral collection, and also some 250 million-year-old fossilized lightning, looking like a miniature volcano (about two or 3 inches across) from prehistoric beaches on the isle of Arran. It is the third biggest geology museum in Britain, with no restrictions on photography and new displays on interplanetary travel.

A right turn south at the end of Downing Street, onto St Andrews Street, and a half-mile walk arrives at the **Scott Polar Research Institute** ⓘ *Lensfield Rd, T01223-336540, www.spri.cam.ac.uk, Mon-Fri 1430-1600, free*, founded in 1920 in memory of Captain Scott's ill-fated expedition to the South Pole. The small museum, dividing into Arctic and Antarctic galleries, includes maps, journals, photographs and equipment related to polar exploration past and present.

A few hundred yards further on down Hills Road and right onto Bateman Street is the University **Botanic Garden** ⓘ *Cory Lodge, Bateman St, T01223-336265, www.botanic.cam.ac.uk, daily Apr-Sep 1000-1800, Nov-Mar 1000-1600 (glasshouses daily 1000-1545), Mar-Oct and weekends all year £2, £1.50 concessions, other times free*, a plant-lovers paradise in a formal garden that can't quite escape the sound of traffic from the A1307 close by.

The Backs

As the location of Peterhouse suggests, the University was founded between the High Street (now Trinity Street, King's Parade and Trumpington Street) and what was once called Milne Street (now only surviving as Trinity Lane and Queen's Lane) which ran alongside the river. Until the 18th century, 'the backs' of colleges like King's, Clare, Trinity and St John's overlooked busy coal and corn wharves. Now the view could hardly be more different. The Backs are one of the city's most celebrated assets, beautiful green lawns, playing fields and meadows, ablaze with flowers in the spring, strung together with charming old stone bridges crossing the Cam into college gardens. Their leafy extent can easily be viewed by cars or bikes crawling along the congested Queen's Road, but can only be fully appreciated by walkers and especially by punters. **Punting** could almost have been invented for the purpose of idling away a few hours here floating past some of the most beautiful old buildings in England. That's no secret though, which can mean that the footpaths are sometimes less crowded than the water. Private footpaths across the Backs head straight over the bridges into the colleges, open whenever the colleges are. Punts can be hired from Silver Street, Granta Place, Garret Hostel Lane or Magdalene Bridge (see Activities page 504). Granta Place on Mill Lane is the most popular, because here you have the choice of either heading upriver towards Grantchester, or downriver through the Backs. What the Grantchester way lacks in architectural wonder it makes up for in delightful pastoral stretches – cows ruminating on Coe Fen and entirely non-urban.

North of Market Hill

Back in the centre of town in the market square, a right turn on **Trinity** Street leads past the street's eponymous college, the University's largest (with over 600 undergraduates) and most grand. In fact it's a union of two old colleges, Michaelhouse and King's Hall, amalgamated by Henry VIII. At about two acres, its Great Court is also the most spacious of all Oxbridge quads, made famous in the film *Chariots of Fire* for the Great Court Run. A traditional wacky race in which undergraduates in full evening dress after a heavy supper try to complete a circuit of the court in the time it takes for the clock to strike midnight. It's only been successfully achieved once, by Lord Burghley in the early 1920s, an ancestor of Queen Elizabeth I's chancellor. During her reign, the oldest part of the Court was built using stones from the old Grey Friars monastery which stood where Sidney Sussex now stands. The college's other highlight is its magnificent Wren library, along the west side of Nevile's Court. Two decades or so before it was built, Isaac Newton was up at Trinity, in 1661. (He published *Principia Mathematica* in 1687 after being made Professor of Mathematics and allegedly hit on the head by an apple.)

Trinity Lane twists down the south side of the college towards the Backs, and the front door of **Clare College**, tucked behind the Old Schools. With its austere and beautiful 'Carolean' buildings dating from the 1640s, part of the Classical Revival, and one of the University's most beautiful gardens, it's well worth a look around, as is the very fine **Clare Bridge**, with its stone balls balanced on its parapet. As a jolly jape, undergraduates apparently replaced one of them with a polystyrene replica, nonchalantly toppling it off onto a terrified punt-load of tourists beneath.

Beyond Trinity is **St John's College**, the second largest in the University, founded by Bishop Fisher, who was martyred in the same year as Sir Thomas More under Henry VIII. Along with its fine Tudor gateway, the college has some of the most extraordinary buildings in the city, including its hammer-beamed hall, beautiful Tudor Second Court, and Combination Room, with a spectacular pannelled gallery and ornate plaster ceiling. The College also has some of the most beautiful and imaculately-kept gardens. The neo-Venetian **Bridge of Sighs** makes a picturesque river crossing from the college.

St John Street, as Trinity Street has become, ends at the junction of Bridge Street and Sydney Street, where stands the **Round Church of the Holy Sepulchre** ⓘ *Bridge St, T01223-311602, Mon-Sat 1000-1700, Sun 1300-1700*. As its name suggests, this unusual round church was based on the one in Jerusalem, and now houses a Christian visitor centre offering guided college tours, services on Wednesdays and a video on Cambridge history. It's one of only four round churches in England, founded by the Knights Templar.

A left turn onto Bridge Street leads down to the river and **Magdalene Bridge** and **Quayside**, a pleasant pedestrianized riverside spot for a drink outdoors. A boardwalk runs to the right along the river from here to Jesus Green, passing the old monastic buildings of Magdalene College. The river here is always busy with punts and chauffeur-punt touts in high season. Over the river on the left-hand side, the **Cambridge and County Folk Museum** ⓘ *Castle St, T01223-355159, www.folk museum.org.uk, Mon-Sat 1030-1700, Sun 1400-1700 (closed Mon, Oct-Mar), £2.50, concessions £1.50,*

Celebrated Trinity alumni include Lord Byron, who famously kept a bear in his rooms, Wittgenstein, Nabokov, the spies Philby, Burgess and Blunt, and Prince Charles.

is housed in an old pub with eight different displays on various facets of local history, including domestic crafts, fens and folklore, and also the University and the City. A few yards up the road is another slightly more sophisticated local operation, **Kettle's Yard** ⓘ *Castle St, T01223-352124, www.kettlesyard.co.uk, house Apr-Sep Tue-Sun 1330-1630, Oct-Mar Tue-Sun 1400-1600, gallery Tue-Sun 1130-1700, free.* Founded in 1957, the house contains artworks by the likes of Ben Nicholson, Barbara Hepworth, Brancusi and the St Ives School, and also holds chamber music concerts. The gallery puts on changing exhibitions of contemporary art.

A right turn onto Sydney Street from Bridge Street heads south again, towards **Sidney Sussex,** Oliver Cromwell's college, with a dissenting chapel orientated north-south. Just before it Jesus Lane leads off to the left. **Jesus College** was founded in 1496 by another Bishop of Ely on the site of the St Radegund's nunnery. Its Cloister Court was created by improving the nunnery's cloisters and its chapel is equally ancient, with some fine stained glass by the Arts and Crafts movement. Opposite the college stands the outstanding but neglected Victorian church of **All Saints'**. Beyond to the north are the green acres of **Jesus Green** and **Midsummer Common**, attractive places to take a picnic or go for a walk beside the river.

Around Cambridge

A couple of miles southwest of the city centre, best reached by a leisurely stroll or punt along the Cam, is **Grantchester,** the epicentre of the Rupert Brooke cult that contributed so much to Cambridge's image between the wars. The Old Vicarage, where the poet stayed while at the university, is now the home of disgraced ex-Tory party chairman Jeffrey Archer. The church clock doesn't still stand at 10 to three although there could well be honey for tea, or a refreshing pint in one of the three pubs in the village. **Trumpington**, a mile away, is an even more cute, well-kept little village, less mobbed by day trippers.

Six miles south of Trumpington, near Junction 10 of the M11, the **Imperial War Museum** ⓘ *Duxford, T01223-835000, www.iwm.org.uk, Mid-Mar to Oct 1000-1800, Nov to mid-Mar 1000-1600, £8.50, concessions £6.50, children free*, has one of the finest collections of antique and modern military aircraft in the world, with about 150 of the things in five vast hangars with an American Air Museum SR71 Blackbird spy-plane, the B24 bomber, Spitfires, Lancaster bombers, a flight simulator and also a land warfare museum full of frightening tanks and things in their natural habitat.

A mile southeast of Trumpington the **Gog Magog hills** are named after the legendary giants slain by the ancient British King Brute. Hardly giants themselves, the 300-ft hills still provide good views over the surrounding flatlands, as does **Wandlebury** Iron Age hill fort next door.

Five miles further on down the A1307, **Linton Zoo** ⓘ *Hadstock Rd, Linton, T01223-891308, www. lintonzoo.co.uk, daily 1000-1800 (or dusk if earlier), £5.50, £5 concessions, 2-13 years olds £4.50*, is famous for its big cats, a well-managed zoo with giant tortoises and other exotic species in about 16 acres.

Ely and the Fens

The Fens stretch out north of Cambridge and west of Breckland – a completely flat, oddly depressing area of rich farmland divided up by drainage ditches and dykes. One of the earliest entirely man-made and hence industrialized landscapes in Europe, the area was once a mysterious and inaccessible tract of marshland dotted with gravelly little islands. These provided safe havens in the east from Neolithic times right up to the 17th century and the accomplishment of the first serious drainage scheme. Down the ages they attracted a variety of colourful characters, from monks, monarchs and hermits to outlaws, traitors and poets. The most striking survivor from those times is Ely, best approached through fenland mists, when its extraordinary cathedral and octagonal lantern loom ahead, floating on a rise in the ground in the distance. The Isle of Ely, named after all the delicious eels that once squirmed round its shores, still boasts very little other than its beautiful cathedral, marooned in modern East Anglia as surely as it was once in marshland.

Ins and outs

Getting there A surprisingly important **rail** junction for a place of its size, Ely can be reached direct from Liverpool, Norwich, London and Cambridge. Ely is about 20 mins north of Cambridge up the A10. **Buses** run to Ely from King's Lynn and Cambridge. » *For further details, see Transport page 505.*

Getting around Although there is a local bus networks, a car or bike are easily the best ways of exploring the fens.

Information Ely TIC ⓘ *29 St Mary's St, T01353-662062, www.eastcambs.gov.uk, Apr-Sep daily 1000-1730, Nov-Mar Mon-Sat 1000-1700, Sun 1115-1600.*

History

Ely was effectively founded by a seventh-century Northumbrian Queen on the run. Etheldreda was fleeing her husband Egfrid, whom she had denied any sexual favours for 12 years in order to maintain a vow of chastity. She was so pious that she founded a monastery here (in 673) and blamed the throat infection that finally killed her on her necklace. Known locally as St Audrey, in her honour the townsfolk took to wearing lace in Tudor times instead of jewellery, some of it so cheap and showy that it gave us the word 'tawdry'. Between times, Ely also became famous as the site of the last stand against the Normans of the outlaw Hereward the Wake. William the Conqueror tried unsuccessfully to oust him and his gang of Danes several times by building pontoon causeways across the marshes from the village of Aldreth. Belsar's Hill, near the village of Willingham, was the site of one of the Conqueror's wooden siege forts. Hereward was finally betrayed by the monks, who provided William with local information and were heavily fined for their trouble. Since those days, because of its peculiar position, it has retained a remarkable number of medieval and Tudor buildings, many now attractive restaurants and teashops.

Sights

One of the most beautiful **cathedrals** ⓘ *Chapter House, The College, T01353-667735, Apr-Oct daily 0700-1900, Nov-Mar Mon-Sat 0730-1800, Sun 0730-1700, £4, £3.50*, in the country, Ely's was re-built by the Normans. In the 14th century it was embellished with the inspiring octagonal tower that can be seen for many miles around on a clear day. This beautiful Gothic structure was designed and built by one of the greatest of medieval architects, local monk Alan de Walsingham. In Febuary 1322, as the brothers were retiring to bed, the old Norman tower collapsed. Alan rushed out to survey the ruins, and swore with God's help to 'set his hand to work'. The Lady Chapel has the broadest medieval vaulted ceiling in the country. In the Treforium, the **Stained Glass Museum** ⓘ *T01353-660347, www.stainedglassmuseum.org, Apr-Oct Mon-Sat 1030-1700, Sun 1200-1800, Nov-Mar Mon-Sat 1030-1700, Sun 1200-1630, £3.50, under-16s £2.50, family £7*, contains over a hundred examples of coloured glass and courses on making it.

Relocated to the Old Gaol in 1997, the local history **museum** ⓘ *Market St, T01353-666655, Apr-Sep daily 1030-1730, Nov-Mar 1030-1630, £2, concesssions £1.25*, does a good job of filling the background, with the usual fossils, prehistoric weapons, Roman and Anglo-Saxon finds, as well as an exhibition on the treatment of the Cambridgeshire Regiment as POWs by the Japanese during the Second World War.

At **Wicken**, the oldest **nature reserve** ⓘ *T01353-720274, www.wicken.org.uk, daily dawn to dusk, £3.80, under-16s £1.20*, in the country and the last surviving piece of the wilderness that once covered most of East Anglia, can be found. **Stretham Old Engine** ⓘ *T01353-649210, Apr-Aug second Sun each month, bank holidays, 1330-1700, £2, concessions £1*, has an impressive land-drainage beam steam engine put in place in 1831 to pump out the fen. The **William Thorpe Visitor Centre** ⓘ *Tue-Sat 1000-1700, Apr-Oct Sun, bank holidays 1400-1700*, is in the Stoker's cottage next to the Old Engine, with displays on the history and people of the Fens.

Sleeping

Cambridge and around *p493, map p494*
Accommodation in central Cambridge is expensive. There are plenty of B&Bs on the outskirts, some of the best along Milton Rd, and also in Chesterton Rd. Given that the nightlife is hardly jumping, though, it might be as good to go for better value rooms in one of the villages just outside town, many with regular and reliable bus services to and from the city.

L **Garden House Moat House Hotel**, Granta Pl, Mill La, T01223-259988, www.moathousehotel.com. The smartest hotel in the city, with a lovely terrace bar and brasserie backing onto the punt-crammed Cam, as well as spacious, comfortable rooms with river views.

A **Crowne Plaza**, Downing St, T01223-464466, www.crowneplaza.com. Thoroughly modern and upholstered city centre option, popular with corporate clients as well as tourists.

A **Meadowcroft Hotel**, 16 Trumpington Rd, T01223-346120, www.meadowcroft.co.uk. A small, slightly chi-chi hotel with fine gardens and tasteful individually designed bedrooms.

B **Arundel House Hotel**, 53 Chesterton Rd, T01223-367701, www.arundelhouse hotels.co.uk. Terraced Victorian hotel overlooking the river Cam with reasonable menu in the restaurant.

B **The Grange Manor House**, Lolworth, T01954-781298, www.hotels.uk.com/thegrange. Has 7 gardens and a swimming pool set around a large non-smoking Victorian manor house off the A14.

C **Suffolk House**, 69 Milton Rd, T01223-352016, F566816. Family-run impeccably clean non-smoking guesthouse in a quiet area about 20 mins walk from the centre.

D **Harry's Bed and Breakfast**, 39 Milton Rd, T01223-503866. Small B&B in an Edwardian house about 20 mins from the city centre.

D **Sleeperz Hotel**, Station Rd, T01223-304050, www.sleeperz.com. Clean and comfortable budget option in a converted granary close to the station.

D **Springfield House**, 16 Horn La, Linton, T01223-891383, www.smoothhound.co.uk/hotels/springf2. B&B in a Victorian schoolhouse with a bus service into Cambridge.

F **Cambridge YHA**, 97 Tenison Rd, T01223-354601, F312780. Close to the station, a Victorian townhouse about 15 mins' walk from the centre with 100 beds in 2-8 bedded rooms. Booking well in advance advisable.

Ely and the Fens *p500*

B **Cathedral House**, 17 St Mary's St, Ely, T01353-662124, www.cathedralhouse.co.uk. Large rooms, a walled garden and also very close to the cathedral.

B **The Lamb Hotel**, 2 Lynn Rd, Ely, T01353-663574. Part of the Old English Hotels chain, perfectly comfortable in a slightly bland sort of way and very close to the cathedral.

C **The Grove**, Sutton Gault, T01353-777196, a large farmhouse with gardens running down to a river.

C **Old Egremont House**, 31 Egremont St, Ely, T01353-663118, is another highly rated small B&B with cathedral views.

C **Palace Green Cottage**, T01353-662185, www. palacegreen.co.uk. Smaller and more cosy, closer by and nearer the bottom-end of this price-backet.

C **Spinney Abbey** Wicken, T01353-720971, a large Georgian farmhouse on the edge of the national nature reserve.

C **Sycamore House**, 91 Cambridge Rd, Ely, T01353-662139, www.sycamorehouse.gb.com. Very comfortable, but a 10-min walk from town.

Eating

Cambridge and around *p493, map p494*

There are many mediocre restaurants in Cambridge doling out comfort food to careless students and tourists. Finding good-quality cooking is quite a challenge

£££ **22 Chesterton Rd**, 22 Chesterton Rd, T01223-351880. Also fairly expensive (set 4-course dinners for about £25), it's another classy joint that also needs to be booked. Quite staid but with a surprisingly innovative menu served up in an Edwardian dining room.

£££ **Loch Fyne Oysterhouse**, 37 Trumpington St, T01223-362433. In the middle of town, this is a fine example of the reliable national seafood chain doing very fresh fish in cheerful and easy-going surroundings (about £30 a head).

£££ **Midsummer House**, Midsummer Common, T01223-369299. Universally acknowledged to be the best (and most expensive – about £50 a head for dinner, considerably less for lunch) but it deserves all the praise. Innovative and delicious gourmet cuisine is served up with unfailing attention to detail in a delightful conservatory and garden, with a balcony area overlooking the Cam. Booking essential.

£££ **Venue**, 66 Regent St, T01223-367333. Another central option, also about £30 a head for supper, a sleek modern British restaurant not quite as swish as it likes to think it is but decent enough nonetheless. Booking advisable.

££ **Dojo**, 1-2 Millers Yard, Mill La, T01223-363471. An Asian fusion restaurant and noodle bar that has received warm reviews.

££ **Maharaja**, 9-13 Castle St, T01223-358399. Quite expensive but reasonably central.

££ **Sala Thong**, 35 Newnham Rd, T01223-323178. A small and straightforward place doing excellent Thai cuisine.

££ **Varsity**, 35 St Andrew's St, T01223-356060. A 'continental' restaurant with a vaguely Greek theme, that has been around for years and remains popular for its cheap and cheerful approach.

£ **Curry Queen**, 106 Mill Rd, T01223-351027, is one of the city's more reliable curry houses that often gets the student vote.

£ **Michel's**, 21 Northampton St, T01223-353110. A modern Italian restaurant just over Magdalene Bridge, doing fairly good-value £9 3-course lunches.

£ **The Rainbow Café**, 9a King's Parade, T01223-3211551. A vegetarian basement place tucked away right on the main tourist drag.

The other less expensive dining options can be found in one of the city's many pubs, of which the locals are justifiably proud. 4 of the best for decent grub are the

£ **Pickerel Inn**, 30 Magdalene St, T01223-355068, and down by the river

£ **The Mill**, Mill La, T01223-357026 (lunchtimes only), and next door

£ **The Anchor**, Silver St, T01223-353554 (no food Fri and Sat evenings) and the

£ **Bath Ale House**, Bene't St, T01223-350969.

Ely and the Fens *p500*

£££ **Old Fire Engine House**, 25 St Mary's, T01353-662582, is a welcoming place that has indeed been around for years and some think it shows, but it remains the smartest option in town (about £38 a head).

£ **The Almonry**, The College, High St, Ely T01353-666360 is a large tea room, with tables outside giving views of the cathedral.

Pubs, bars and clubs

Cambridge and around *p493, map p494*

The Cambridge Blue, Gwydir St, T01223-361382, is an eccentric drinking hole with conservatory and good bar snacks.

Champion of the Thames, King St, T01223-352043, is the place for an atmospheric and traditional pint (no food) in a snug.

The Eagle, Bene't St, T01223-505020, is the Cambridge equivalent of Oxford's *Bird and Baby*, see page 242, a rambling pine-pannelled old place with famous 'RAF ceiling' scribbled on during the Second

For an explanation of the sleeping and eating price codes used in this guide, see the inside front cover. Other relevant information is provided in the Essentials chapter, page 40.

World War by locally based British and American airmen.
Fort St George of England, next to Midsummer House, is good in summer, with outside seating on the river beside the boathouses.
Free Press, Prospect Row, T01223-368337, is a sporty non-smoking Greene King pub in an old terraced house with attractive little garden.
The Wrestler's Pub, 337 Newmarket Rd, T01223-566553, does highly praised Thai food in a basic and busy boozer.

Ely and the Fens *p500*
The Maltings Arts Centre, T01353-669757, has a decent wine bar and brasserie on the Great Ouse's waterfront to go with its cinema and theatre.
The Prince Albert, 62 Silver St, Ely T01353-663494 is a very jolly flower-festooned town pub with a good garden and reasonable grub. The best in the city.

Entertainment

Cambridge and around *p493, map p494*
Student amusement abounds during term-time: bands, drinking sessions and post-exam hysteria in May/Jun Try also www.cambridge events.com.

Film, theatre and music
Arts Theatre, St Edward's Passage, T01223-503333. Local rep playhouse with a high reputation as well as the reputable *Roof Garden Restaurant*, T01223-578930.
Arts Picture House, St Andrews St, T01223-504444, www.picturehouse-cinemas.co.uk. 3-screen general release art house films.
Cambridge Drama Centre, Covent Garden, T01223-511511. Fringe drama and small-scale touring productions.
Corn Exchange, Wheeler St, T01223-357851 is the city's front-rank venue for larger touring productions, including opera, dance and live music.
The Junction, Clifton Rd, T01223-511511, www.junction.co.uk. Club nights, comedy and live music.
Kettle's Yard (see North of Market Hill above), for intimate classical and folk concerts.

Festivals

Cambridge and around *p493, map p494*
Mid-Mar Cambridge Science Week. With lectures and other science-related events.
May Cambridge Beer Festival on Jesus Green, usually penultimate week in May, www.camra.co.uk.
Jun May Week, in the middle of Jun has student japes and general hilarity to celebrate the end of exams.
Jun Strawberry Fair A Full-on hippy trippy festival on Midsummer Common, held on a Sun in early-mid Jun.
Jul Cambridge Film Festival T01223-504444 for further details.
Jul Cambridge Folk Festival, near the end of the month, T01223-457245, www.cam-folkfest.co.uk. Booking essential for one of the world's first and most prestigious 4-day folk music festivals.
Jul-Aug Cambridge Shakespeare Festival, in the college gardens, T01223-357851.

Shopping

Cambridge and around *p493, map p494*
Andy's Records, 29-33 Fitzroy St, T01223-361038 Good selection of vinyl, tape and CDs.
Heffer's Bookshops, 20 Trinity St, Cambridge, T01223-568568 www.heffers.co.uk. Established in Cambridge in 1876, stocks over 300,000 book titles and multimedia products on all subjects, as well as: art, graphics and craft materials, maps, stationery (including personal organizers), and an extensive range of pens, videos and music CDs.

Activities and tours

Cambridge and around *p493, map p494*
Cambridge Parkside Pools and Kelsey Kerridge Sports Centre, T01223-446100, www.parkside pools.co.uk. The main city council swimming and sports centre.
Scudamore's Punting Company, Granta Pl, Mill La, T01223-359750, www.scudamores.com. Mar-Oct 0900-dusk, Nov-Feb Sat, Sun only 1000-dusk. £12 an hr. In high season, expect to queue if you want a punt any time after 1300. Choose either an

upriver boat, for Coe Fen and the 3-hr round-trip to Grantchester or a downriver boat for the Backs and the 2-hr, 2-mile round-trip to Jesus Green Lock. The upriver boats and the stretches of river they ply are generally less busy and more rural than the downriver ones.

Walking tours (£7.35 per person) leave the TIC at 1030 (July-Sep, Mon-Sat), 1130 (Apr-Oct daily, Nov-Mar Sat only), 1330 (daily all year), 1430 (daily July-Aug), 1830.

Costumed drama tours: £4.50 Tue in July and Aug.

Ely and the Fens *p500*

Fenland River Cruises, T01353-777567. Apr-Sep 1200-1700 £3.50, under-16s £2.50 ½ hr boatrides along Ely's waterfront in an old river launch from Ship La.

Transport

Cambridge and around *p493, map p494*

Bicycle

Cycle King, 195 Mill Rd, T01223-212222; **Geoff's Bike Hire**, 65 Devonshire Rd, T01223-365629; **Ben Hayward & Son**, 69 Trumpington St, T01223-352294; **N.K. Bike Hire**, Cherry Hinton Rd, T01223-505485 and **University Cycles**, 9 Victoria Av, T01223-355517.

Bus

Long distance Stagecoach runs the service to **Norwich** (2 hrs 30 mins) every 2 hrs, changing at **Newmarket**. The direct service to **Ipswich** (1 hr 55 mins) is run by **National Express**, T08705-808080, and departs from Drummer Road coach stop at 1650. They also run the direct hourly service to **London Victoria** (2 hrs 20 mins), the regular direct service to **Stansted airport** (50 mins) and the direct service to **Luton** (1 hr 10 mins) every 2 hrs. **Traveline**, T08706-082608.

Local Cambridge is well served by **local buses**. There is a free City Centre Shuttle bus service which operates every 15 mins from 0900 till 1700 (buses marked: City Centre Shuttle) on this route: Emmanuel St, Fair St (Grafton Centre), Newmarket Rd, Jesus La, Bridge St, St Johns St, King's Parade, Silver St, Pembroke St, Downing St, St Andrews St. The main operator is **Stagecoach** in Cambridge who provide most city services. Services towards Bedford are run by *Stagecoach* in Bedford, and towards Huntingdon and St Ives by Huntingdon & District. Other local companies include **Go Whippet**, T01480-463792, and **Myalls**. **Dayrider** tickets are available in Cambridge (£2.60, includes unlimited travel on Park & Ride services and other *Stagecoach* and *Cambus* routes across the city). For travel all over the region (apart from routes into London), there is the **Explorer** ticket: £5.99, £4.25 for children and senior citizens and £7.99 for 2 adults (max) and up to 3 kids. Buy from the driver on your first *Stagecoach* bus.

Car

Avis, 245 Mill Rd, T01223-212551; **Budget Rent-a-Car**, 303 Newmarket Rd, T01223-323838; **Cambridge Car Hire**, Coldhams La Garage, T01223-515151; **Europcar**, 22 Cambridge Rd, Impington, T01223-233644; **Hertz**, 264 Barnwell Rd, T01223-416634; **National Car Rental**, 264 Newmarket Rd, T01223-365438.

Taxi

Ranks on Drummer St, Emmanuel St, St Andrews St and at the Train Station. Local minicab firms: **A1 Taxis**, T01223-525555; **Camtax**, T01223-313131; **Diamond Taxis**, T01223-523523; **Panther Taxis**, T01223-715715; and **Regency Taxis**, T01223-311388.

Train

The twice hourly direct service to **Norwich** (1 hr 15 mins) is run by **Anglia Railways**, T08700-409090, as is the direct line to **Ipswich** (1 hr 20), which departs at 1009. The direct service to **London King's Cross** (50 mins) is run every 15 mins by **WAGN**, T08708-508822. **Central Trains**, T0121-6541200, run the direct hourly service to **Stansted airport** (30 mins), also **Peterborough** (1 hr), **Leicester** (1hr 50 mins) and **Birmingham** (3 hrs). There is no direct service to Luton.

Directory

Cambridge and around *p493, map p494*
Language Schools Language Studies International, 41 Tenison Rd, T01223-361783; Aspect International Language Academies, 75 Barton Rd, T01223-357702. **Internet** CB1, 32 Mill Rd, T01223-576306; CB2, 5-7 Norfolk St, T01223-508503; La Pronto Internet Café, 2 Emmanuel St, T01223-312700; The Internet Exchange, 2 St Mary's Passage, T01223-327600. **Medical facilities** Addenbrooke's NHS Trust, Hills Rd, T01223-245151. Brookfields Hospital, Mill Rd, T01223-723000. **Police** Parkside Police Station, Parkside, T01223-358966. **Post office** 9-11 St Andrews St, T0845-7223344.

East Midlands

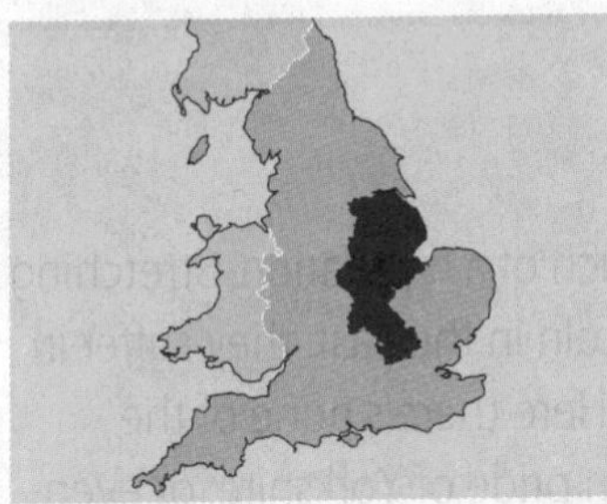

Footprint features

Introduction

The East Midlands don't have much of a reputation. Stretching from Leicester in the west to Lincoln in the east, they suffer in comparison to their neighbours. Here there's none of the kudos of Cambridge, the northern pride of Yorkshire, or even the sheer balls of the West Midlands with their Brummies and Herefordshire bulls. Instead, unassuming and overlooked, the East Midlands reward visitors with a few world-class sights, some vibrant forward-looking towns and an old-fashioned attitude in the countryside.

Leicester is the comfortable multicultural heart of the region, next door to the smallest, most stubborn little county in the country, Rutland. To the north, Nottingham has been reborn as the dance music capital of the UK while Derby, the first factory town, can boast a World Heritage Site on the River Derwent. Close by, Ashbourne is the proper little southern gateway to the scenic delights of the Peak District. Further north and east, Lincoln struggles gamely on beneath the finest Gothic cathedral in the land, close to the lost villages of the Wolds around lovely Louth and a coast dominated by the grey pound. Stamford, at the southern end of the county, is an immaculately preserved stone-built Georgian town on the A1. To the south of the region, Bedfordshire and Northamptonshire are all about Bunyan and boots, squires, spires and watery mires.

★ Don't miss...

1. See all that remains of the castle where Mary Queen of Scots got her head chopped off at **Fotheringhay** and enjoy a pint in the local pub, page 514.
2. Explore the stratosphere at the **National Space Centre** outside Leicester and come down to earth for a curry on the Golden Mile, page 518.
3. Check out the latest in UK Garage at any number of **Nottingham** club nights, page 533.
4. Walk through the Exchequer Gate in **Lincoln** and experience a sight that's been stopping people in their tracks for centuries: the west front of the cathedral, page 537.
5. Amble around **Louth** in the Lincolnshire Wolds, marvelling at its refusal to move with these commercial times, page 540.

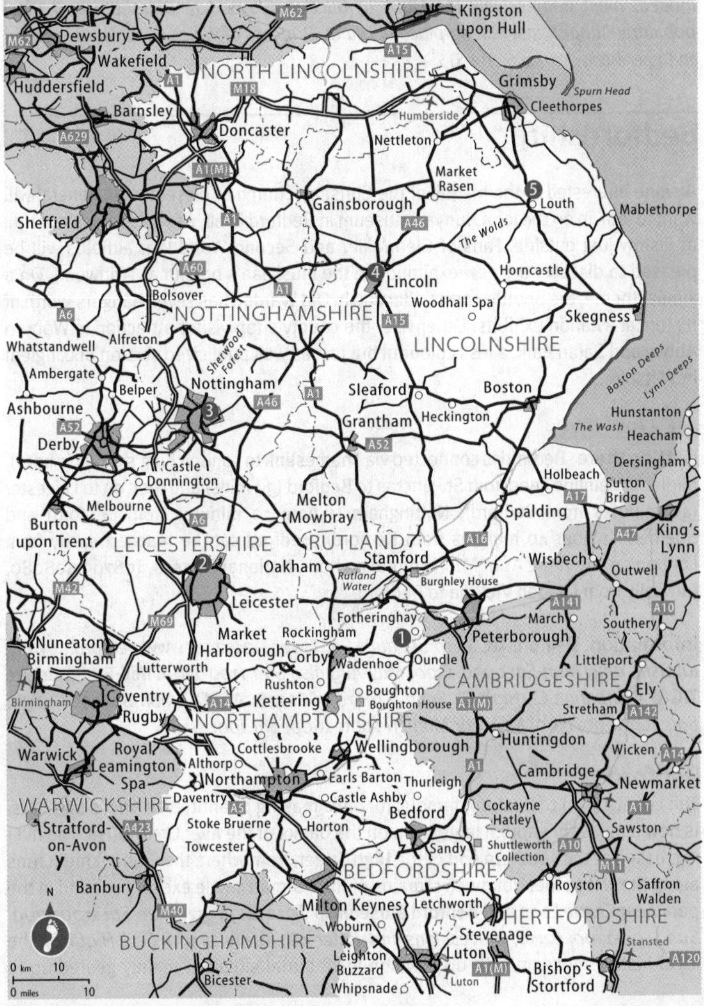

Bedfordshire and Northamptonshire

→ Colour map 3, grid A1/2

Both these Midland counties are usually overlooked by visitors, not without some reason, although Northamptonshire embraces some beautiful countryside dotted with old stone-built villages, grand stately homes and innumerable church spires. Bedfordshire's defining character derives from the broad floodplain of the River Ouse, its clay soil traditionally used for bricks. The greensand ridge in the middle of the county is its most attractive feature though, with the much-publicized safari park and stately home at Woburn Abbey at its western end, and quaint Victorian estate villages like Old Warden at its eastern. Folded combes and windswept downs fan out from Barton. Bedford itself is chiefly famous for bricks, hats, and being the place of imprisonment of John Bunyan. Northamptonshire boasts some very grand houses indeed, most impressively the Duke of Buccleuch's pad at Boughton and most popularly Althorp, last resting place of Diana, Princess of Wales. ▸▸ *For Sleeping, Eating and other listings, see pages 514-515.*

Bedfordshire

Anyone interested in the history of the Christian church or dissenters in general will want to look in on the John Bunyan museum in Bedford itself, as well as the Moot Hall at Elstow just outside. Fans of Glen Miller and Second World War airfields will be pleased to discover the new exhibition in the musician's honour at Twinwood. On a similar theme, the Shuttleworth Collection in Old Warden has seven hangars-worth of historical aviation exhibits. Otherwise, the county's top visitor attraction is Woburn Abbey and Safari Park, a less colourful but just as well publicized version of Longleat in Wiltshire.

Ins and outs

Getting there Bedford is connected via **Thameslink** to London King's Cross (1 hour). Midland Mainline goes from St Pancras to Bedford (30 mins) and then on to Leicester (40 minutes from Bedford), Nottingham (1 hour 10 minutes from Bedford) and Sheffield (1 hour 40 minutes from Bedford). Bedford can be reached easily from London on either the A1 or M1 in around an hour. **National Express**, T08705-808080, run daily from London Victoria to Bedford.

Information **Bedford TIC** ⓘ *10 St Paul's Sq, T01234-215226, www.bedford.gov.uk/tourism, daily Mon-Sat 0930-1700, May-Aug also Sun 1100-1500.* **Mid-Bedfordshire TIC** ⓘ *5 Shannon Ct, High St, Sandy, T01767-682728. Apr-Oct Mon-Sat 1000-1630, Sat, Sun 1000-1500, Nov-Mar Mon-Fri 1000-1600, Sat 1000-1500.*

Bedford

The county town of Bedford, famous for once making quantities of bricks and hats, is now a pleasant enough large town on the banks of the river Great Ouse. The river is crossed at the southern end of the High Street, from where the Embankment runs along the waterside. Not much remains of the Norman castle except a mound in the park near Castle Lane and **Bedford Museum** ⓘ *T01234-353323, Tue-Sat 1100-1700, Sun 1400-1700, £2.10, concessions and under-18s free (also with Cecil Higgins)*, the local history museum with displays on local burial sites but mainly geared up to deal with schools. Next door is the highlight of a visit to the town, the **Cecil Higgins Art Gallery** ⓘ *Castle La, T01234-211222, www.cecilhigginsartgallery.org, Tue-Sat 1100-1645, Sun 1100-1645*, a reconstructed Victorian mansion and modern art gallery with an exceptional collection of watercolours, as well as sculpture, furniture, glass, ceramics and metalwork by internationally famous artists. The watercolour collection includes works by the likes of Turner, Constable, Blake, Landseer, Sickert, Lowry, Hepworth, Nicholson, and Henry Moore among others. The gallery also contains a room dedicated to the eccentric Victorian architect and designer William Burges, a leading exponent of the Gothic Revival. Interesting temporary exhibitions from the collection are also mounted.

Behind the museum, in Mill Street, the bronze doors of the **Bunyan Meeting Free Church** were donated by the Duke of Bedford in 1876, with 10 panels depicting scenes from *The Pilgrim's Progress*. Written by the preacher and Parliamentarian John Bunyan while he was imprisoned in Bedford jail for 12 years under Charles II's religious laws, it still ranks as one of the most influential pieces of Christian literature of all time. Bunyan bought a barn and orchard on his release from prison, which in 1707 was replaced by a Meeting House, and in 1850 by the church that stands here today. Next door, the **John Bunyan Museum** ⓘ *The Church Office, Bunyan Meeting Free Church, Mill St, T01234-213722. Mar-Oct Tue-Sat 1100-1600*, was opened in 1998, displaying exhibits and artefacts associated with his life and an illustrated display on *The Pilgrim's Progress*.

Around Bedfordshire

The late-15th-century **Moot Hall** ⓘ *T01234-266889, Apr-Sep*, at Elstow, was where John Bunyan saw the light while mucking about on the green opposite (he was born here in 1628). Moot Hall is now a museum of 17th-century English life and tradition.

Fans of Second World War big band music will want to take a trip to the new **Glen Miller Museum** at Twinwoods Airfield, ⓘ *T01234-350413, www.twinwoodevents.com, Sat, Sun 1030-1600*. There's another new museum at Thurleigh, the **306 Bombardment Group Museum** ⓘ *T01234-708715, Mar-Oct Sat, Sun 1000-1600, £3*. On the 9 October 1942 a formation of B17 Flying Fortress left Thurleigh on the first of what was to be 341 daylight bombing missions over occupied Europe. Thurleigh airfield became the first base in England to be handed over completely to the Americans, giving them full sovereignty and control of these few acres. The museum is housed in the original airfield's control tower.

Set in a 3000-acre deer park, **Woburn Abbey** ⓘ *T01525-290666, daily Apr-Sep 1100-1600, Sat and Sun Jan-Mar, Oct 1100-1600, £8.50, concessions £7.50, under-16s £4.Take exit 13 off the M1 motorway, or leave the A5 at Hockliffe for the A4012. The Abbey is well signed from here, Safari Park £13, children £9.50*. It is the home of the Marquess and Marchioness of Tavistock and their family and houses one of the most important private art collections in the world, including paintings by Van Dyck, Gainsborough, Reynolds, and Canaletto as well as 18th-century French and English furniture, silver, gold and porcelain. Visitors can also enjoy the renowned antiques centre, coffee shop, gift shops, pottery and beautiful grounds including a safari park.

Opened in 1931 as the first open zoo in Europe, **Whipsnade** ⓘ *T01582-872171, www.whipsnade.co.uk, Mar-Sep 1000-1800, Oct-Feb 1000-1600, £12.50, £9.50 for under-16s, in Dunstable, just west of Luton. The zoo is signposted from the M1 (junctions 9 and 12) and all major roads*, is the country base of London Zoo, with over 200 different species in about 600 acres of Chiltern downland. Larger animals, such as elephants, have been gradually moved here from the city.

The **Shuttleworth Collection** ⓘ *T01767-627288, www.shuttleworth.org.uk Apr-Oct daily 1000-1700, Nov-Mar daily 1000-1600, £7.50, under-16s free*, off the A1, near Sandy, about 12 miles east of Bedford, is an impressive museum of antique

Walks in the East Midlands

- **Snipe Dales**: near Horncastle, Lincolnshire: 2 mile circle. Start: Winceby. A walk through a small but perfectly formed nature reserve at the southern end of the Wolds. OS Maps: Explorer 273, Landranger 122.
- **Gibraltar Point**. Start: 3 miles south of Skegness, Lincolnshire. Freshwater and saltwater marshes favoured by a wide variety of birdlife, including waders in the Autumn. OS Maps: Explorer 274, Landranger 122.
- **Belvoir Castle**, Leicestershire: 3 miles there and back. Start: Knipton village, 10 miles northeast of Melton Mowbray. On to the Terrace Hills west of the castle through woods and fields. OS Maps: Explorer 247, Landranger 130.
- **Salcey Forest**: 2 mile circle. Start: Hartwell, 5 miles south of Northampton. An ancient woodland next to the M1, but quiet, with a large clearing in the middle. OS Maps: Explorer 207, Landranger 152.
- **Eyebrook Reservoir**: 3 mile circle. Start: Stoke Dry, 2 miles south of Uppingham, Rutland. Peaceful well-planted woodland walks around a reservoir close to Rockingham Castle. OS Maps: Explorer 233, Landranger 141.

aircraft, biplanes and triplanes, as well as the Swiss Gardens, and a bird of prey centre in Old Warden Park. **Cockayne Hatley,** 10 miles east of Bedford on the border with Cambridgeshire, has one of the most remarkable parish church interiors in the country in its church of St John. Furnished with loot from the Napoleonic Wars by Henry Cockayne Cust including the choir from the Abbey of Oignies, the poet WE Henley, friend of both Robert Louis Stevenson and JM Barrie, and his daughter, who is said to have been the model for Wendy in 'Peter Pan', are buried in the churchyard.

Northampton and around

The county of 'squires, spires and mires' attracts fewer visitors than it deserves, perhaps because it's generally perceived to be in the middle of nowhere. The M1 slices through the southeastern part on its way north. Northampton itself sits right beside the motorway, ruined by recent developments but concealing some extraordinary churches and an unusual collection of footwear. Shoemaking once made this part of the country famous, although its wealth has always come from manufacturing industry and agriculture, both currently down on their luck. Large estates cover most of its northern part, the most spectacular and pompous being Boughton House, the most popular, for mawkish reasons, being Althorp. Otherwise the pleasures of the county are to be found in exploring its small villages, especially along the valley of the River Nene, with its fine gardens and churches.

Ins and outs

Getting there Northampton is on the main London-Birmingham line, with regular services running into London Euston (1 hour). Northampton is just off the M1, easily reached in 1 hour 30 minutes from London. **National Express,** T08705-808080, run coaches to Northampton four times a day, taking about 2 hours from London Victoria.

Getting around Town buses are run by **First Northampton,** T0870-6082608, and the network of local buses to outlying villages by **Stagecoach,** T01604-676060. Northampton itself can easily be walked around, but exploring beyond the town really requires a car.

Information **Northampton TIC** ⓘ *Northampton Museum and Art Gallery, Guildhall Rd, T01604-622677, www.northampton.gov.uk/tourism, Mon-Sat 1000-1700, Sun 1400-1700.* **Oundle TIC** ⓘ *14 West St, T01832-274333, Mon-Sat 0900-1700.*

Northampton

Northampton was once synonymous with shoemaking. As recently as the 1930s, almost half the town's population were cobblers of one sort or another. Today it's a fairly unprepossessing modern market town with little to suggest its ancient roots except a handful of fine churches. Charles II destroyed the Norman castle on his restoration but the **Church of the Holy Sepulchre** survives, one of the four round churches still standing in England. Like the castle, it was built by the Norman knight Simon de Senlis, inspired by his crusading experiences and looking more like the one in Jerusalem than the others. Its heavy rounded columns in a ring are original, topped with late-14th-century arches.

A few steps southeast from the church down Sheep Street is the wide expanse of **Market Square**, the centre of modern Northampton and still used for a market of sorts most days of the week. Just to the south again, **All Saints church** is a wonderful late-17th-century building, a vivid essay in Baroque enlivening the town centre. Its echoing interior is covered with a dome, a kind of mini-St Pauls. The poet John Clare used to worship here.

Further south, towards the train station, St Giles Square contains the Victorian neo-Gothic **Guildhall** and opposite, the local **Northampton Museum and Art Gallery** ⓘ *Guildhall Rd, T01604-238548, Mon-Sat 1000-1700, Sun 1600-1700, free,* contains an extensive boot and shoe collection. The Followers of Fashion Gallery displays Manolo Blaniks down the ages, as it were, while the Life and Sole Gallery charts the history of the shoe. The most popular exhibits are the DMs worn in 'Tommy', and a shoe made for an elephant.

Around Northampton

Five miles northwest of Northampton is the county's most popular visitor attraction, for the saddest of reasons. **Althorp** ⓘ *T01604-770107 (advance booking on T0870-1679000) www.althorp .com, July-Sep daily 1000-1700 (last admission 1600), £11.50, concessions £9.50, under-16s £5.50, off A428 to Rugby,* has been the stately seat of the Spencer family for the last few hundred years but is now much more famous for being the childhood home and last resting place of Diana, Princess of Wales. Her grave lies on an island in the middle of a lake overlooked by a classical temple restored in her memory. As well as an exhibition of some of her personal effects, the house also contains an internationally renowned collection of paintings by Gainsborough, Reynolds, Van Dyck and others.

More elegant gardens can be seen six miles north at **Cottesbrooke Hall**. ⓘ *T01604-505808. House Easter-Sep Thu, (Sat and Sun in Sep) 1400-1700, grounds Easter-Sep Tue-Fri 1200-1730, house £5, gardens only £3.* Very refined, they were designed around an almost unaltered Queen Anne mansion, supposely the model for Jane Austen's *Mansfield Park* and laid out by a variety of eminent designers in the last century. They include a philosophers' walk, Dutch garden, water gardens and a formal garden.

Near the village of Rushton, 9 miles to the northeast, 5 miles northwest of Kettering, a **Triangular Lodge** ⓘ *(EH), T01536-710761, Apr-Sep daily 1000-1800, Oct daily 1000-1700, £1.95, concessions £1.50, under-16s £1,* was built by Sir Thomas Tresham in 1597 for his rabbit-breeder. A devout Catholic, Sir Thomas designed a tricksome fantasy of a place in honour of the Holy Trinity. The three-sided building stands in the park of Rushton Hall and is embellished with all kinds of arcane religious symbolism. It's now the highlight of a 'Tresham Trail' round the area.

Four miles northeast of Kettering stands the palatial Northamptonshire home of the Duke of Buccleuch, **Boughton House** ⓘ *T01536-515731, www.boughtonhouse.org, house open Aug daily 1400-1630, grounds open May-Sep daily 1300-1700, £6, concessions £5, grounds only £1.50, concessions £1,* which has been compared to Versailles. The grounds include acres of parkland, lakes and long tree-lined avenues. The house itself took on its current imposing French appearance in the late 17th century and contains an array of Old Masters and fine furniture.

East of Boughton toward Thrapston the landscape opens up into the valley of the River Nene. **Oundle** is a quiet little town dominated by an exclusive private school. A few miles downstream, the riverside village of **Wadenhoe** is often cited as the most picturesque in the county. Just to the north, **Fotheringhay** has a remarkable church, the first thing that strikes visitors, whether arriving by road or river. The tower was designed for a much larger church that no longer exists. The castle that once stood on the mound nearby was thoroughly dismantled by James I for the role it had played in the death of his mother, Mary Queen of Scots, in 1587. Her traumatic execution involved several blows of the axe, the interference of the Queen's dog and a loose wig.

East of Northampton, two spectacular gardens are worth seeking out. On the edge of Yardley Chase, at the **Menagerie**ⓘ *Horton, T01604- 870957, May-Sep Thu 1000-1600 or by appointment, £3,* a Rococo folly was lovingly restored in the 1970s and since then an intriguing garden has been designed around the place, including grottos, ponds, and caves. Close by are the much more stately splendours of the Marquess of Northampton's home at **Castle Ashby** ⓘ *T01604-696187, www.castleashby.co.uk, daily 1000-dusk, £2.50.* The grounds include an Italian garden, an orangery and lakeside walks.

Just to the north across the valley of the Nene, All Saints church, Earls Barton has a famous Saxon tower. The **Earls Barton Museum of Village Life**ⓘ *T01604-811735, Sat 1000-1600, otherwise by appointment*, has a permanent exhibition of a shoe worker's cottage at the turn of the century, a lace case and corner shop. There is also an exhibition of Earls Barton footwear manufacture, a collection of early photographs and other local memorabilia.

Seven miles south of Northampton, **Stoke Bruerne** is England's most famous canal village, approached by a flight of seven locks from the River Tove. The canal forms the main road, and there's a museum of barge life. Just up the way is the **Blisworth Tunnel**. Boats can be hired from *Blisworth Tunnel Boats*, Mill Wharf, Gayton Rd, Blisworth, T01604-858868, to explore the 3000-yd long Blisworth Tunnel. It has no towpath so all boats once had to be 'legged' through the watery darkness.

Sleeping

Bedford *p510*

A **Swan Hotel**, The Embankment, Bedford, T01234-346565. This elegant hotel is in the heart of Bedford, built in 1794 for the Duke of Bedford. The staircase now in use here originally came from Houghton House in Ampthill, reputedly the inspiration for 'House Beautiful' in *The Pilgrim's Progress*.

B **De Pary's Hotel**, 41-45 De Pary's Av, Bedford, T01234-352121. Elegant Victorian hotel, secluded gardens with play area.

B **The Embankment Hotel**, The Embankment, Bedford, T01234-261332. Impressive black and white building overlooking the River Great Ouse.

D **Bedford Park House**, 59 De Pary's Av, Bedford, T01234-215100. Lovely Victorian House in tree-lined avenue, close to town centre.

E **Saxby**, 38 Chaucer Rd, Bedford, T01234-301718. 3-storey family house, close to railway station.

For an explanation of the sleeping and eating price codes used in this guide, see the inside front cover. Other relevant information is provided in the Essentials chapter, page 40.

E Tithe Farm, Renhold, T01234-771364. Farmhouse (16th-century) with secure parking, 5 miles from Bedford.

Northampton and around *p512*

B Lime Trees Hotel, 8 Langham Pl, Barrack Rd, Northampton, T01604-632188, www.limetreeshotel.co.uk Half a mile north of the centre, the only 3-star hotel in the town, with about 20 rooms.

C Coach House Hotel, 8-10 East Park Pde, Kettering Rd, Northampton, T01604-250981, www.coach-house- hotel.com. 10 mins east of the centre, with 11 double rooms.

C Wold Farm, Old, near Northampton (8 miles north), T01604-781258. Charming 18th-century house with glorious gardens, a billiard table, and good breakfasts.

D The Elms, Kislingbury, near Northampton (4 miles west), T01604-830326. Comfortable rooms on a working farm. Very good value.

D The King's Head, Church St, Wadenhoe, near Oundle, T01832-720024. In a conservation village, the *King's Head* on the River Nene is a popular focal point for the area, with a variety of different bars, good food and a couple of bedrooms.

D Wendy Cox, Stoke Bruerne, T01604-863865. Does cosy cottage B&B.

Eating

Bedford *p510*

££ Villa Rosa Ram Yard, High St, Bedford T01234-269259. Busy restaurant, offering the traditional along with innovative cuisine.

££ Breadlines, 4 Mill St, Bedford T01234-341006. Excellent quality and value, serving all-day English breakfast, plus sandwiches, rolls, French sticks, salad and jacket potatoes.

££ Pizzeria Santaniello, 9-11 Newnham St, Bedford T01234-353742. Original family-run pizza and pasta restaurant. Traditional family fare and atmosphere.

££ Three Horseshoes, 42 Top End, Renhold, T01234-870218. Welcoming pub with open fires on the road from Bedford to St Neots.

££ Carpenter's Arms, Slapton, near Leighton Buzzard, T01525-220563. Rambling old 16th-century village pub with an above- average menu, well-kept real ales and a long stone's throw from the Grand Union Canal.

Northampton and around *p512*

££ The Falcon Inn, Fotheringay, T01832-226254. Quality food served up in this polite village local. Nearby, **££ The Shuckburgh Arms**, Stoke Doyle, near Oundle, T01832-272339, is a cosy stone-built pub a couple of miles west of Oundle with a log fire.

££ Bruerne's Lock, 5 The Canalside, Stoke Bruerne, T01604-863654. Serves up an ambitious menu in a picturesque setting by the canal.

Leicestershire and Rutland

→ *Colour map 4, grid B5/6*

Leicestershire is a quiet, comfortable and undramatic sort of county. Undemonstrative in landscape or manner, it's considerably enlivened by the multicultural and reinvigorated city at its heart. Leicester itself rewards a visit not with its architecture or streetscape, but with its upbeat attitude and a clutch of innovative sights. Most prominent of these is the National Space Centre, a lottery-funded Millennium project that looks set to last. With its 'Golden Mile' of curry houses and thriving arts scene, Leicester has little reason to be nostalgic for the days when it was dominated by light and heavy industry. The countryside around the city harbours a few surprises, especially the rolling hills or wolds beyond and en route to Melton Mowbray, home of the British pork pie. Definitely not in Leicestershire, but similar in its landscape, is England's smallest county, Rutland. Today this embattled outpost of fox-hunters and old stone villages is most famous for Rutland Water, the largest man-made expanse of water in the UK. ▸▸ *For Sleeping, Eating and other listings, see pages 521-523*

Leicester

Until the launch, in 2001, of the National Space Centre, voyagers to these regions have generally plotted a wide, circumnavigatory course around Leicester. The popularity, though, of this imaginative and inspiring attraction is drawing large numbers of visitors into the city's orbit and establishing a new place for the city on the tourist map. Somewhat akin to the rings of the planet Saturn, Leicester is surrounded by both a notoriously tricky traffic system and a thick miasma of southern snobbery, which tends all too readily to dismiss it as a run-down manufacturing town of little cultural significance. In fact, Leicester has from Roman times been recognized as the very centre of England – the furthest point from any coast or border – and has regularly played a pivotal historical role. The city contains a number of interesting

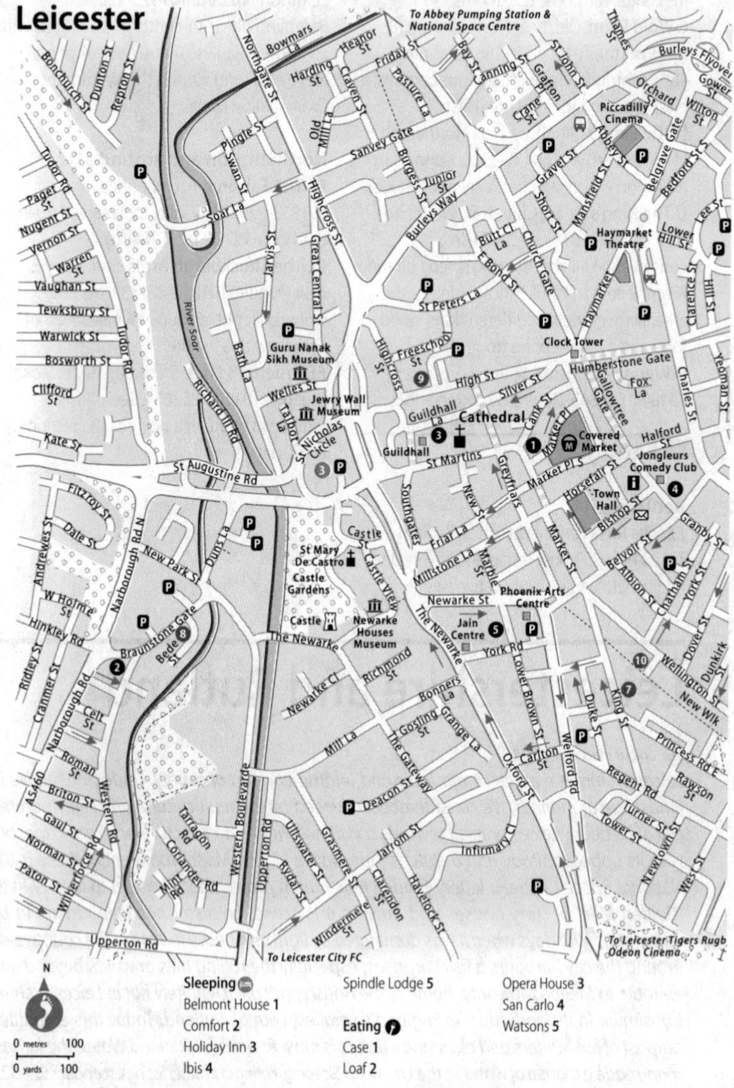

buildings and monuments, and – indicative of a return from a period of industrial decline – a recent rash of sharp little restaurants and bars. With its Asian community making up almost a third of its 290,000 population, Leicester is also one of the very best examples of England's modern, integrated multicultural society. In particular, the shopkeepers and restaurateurs of the city's Belgrave Road, or 'Golden Mile', have created a vibrant streak of Indian life that is now as much a part of the city as its famous 700-year-old covered market.

Ins and outs

Getting there East Midlands Airport, T01332-852852, and **Birmingham International Airport**, T0121-7675511, are, respectively, 30 and 45 minutes away by car. There are several trains every hour on the **Midland Mailine** service from London St Pancras (1 hour and 10 minutes by the fast service). **Road** Leicester is 100 miles, or about 2 hours, from London by car, straight up the M1. The M1 is also linked, at junction 21, with the M69 west to Coventry, which is itself linked to the M6 for destinations in the West Midlands and the Northwest. For the city centre, turn off the M1 at junction 21 onto the A5460 Narborough Rd, before turning right onto St Augustine Road, immediately crossing the river to the car park at St Nicholas Circle, where 24 hours parking costs £6. **National Express**, T08705-808080, offers services throughout the country from St Margaret's Bus Station, just north of the city centre. ▸▸ *See Transport, page 523, for more details.*

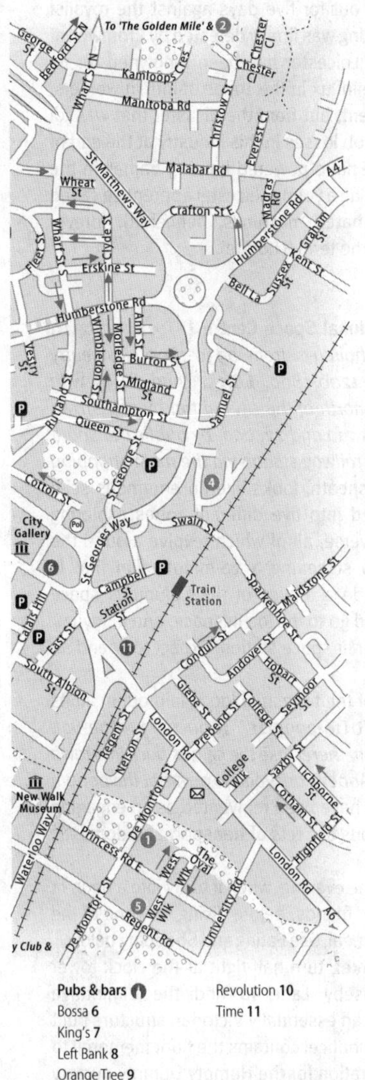

Pubs & bars
Bossa **6**
King's **7**
Left Bank **8**
Orange Tree **9**
Revolution **10**
Time **11**

Getting around The centre of Leicester is encompassed, unprepossessingly, by the busy A594 ring road. Inside this circle, the city is small enough to negotiate on foot. However, a trip out to the Belgrave Rd area or the National Space Centre will definitely require the use of a bus for at least one stretch of the journey.

Information Leicester TIC ⓘ *7-9 Every St, T0906-2941113, Mon-Sat 0900-1730, opens 1000 Thu, closes 1700 Sat.* Its detailed website, www.discoverleicester.com, is well-worth checking out before your visit.

History

The name Leicester comes from 'Legro Ceaster', meaning the Roman "camp on the River Legro", now called the River Soar. The settlement, first established in AD48, stood near the crossroads of two great Roman thoroughfares, Watling Street and the Fosse Way. Another Roman road, the Via Devana, is preserved as a pedestrian street called New Walk, whilst the remains of the second century Roman baths can be seen at the Jewry Wall Museum. Leicester was an important town under both the Danish and Norman invaders and a pleasant park now surrounds the mound or motte of the 11th-century castle.

The city's relationship with its kings has been fraught. In 1264, the sixth Earl of Leicester, Simon de Montfort – whose statue adorns the 19th-century clock tower at the city centre and after whom one of the city's two universities is named – led a revolt against Henry III and briefly set up the first English parliament in the city. The 11th Earl, John of Gaunt, was the father of Henry of Lancaster, who defeated Richard II to become Henry IV. In 1485, the Wars of the Roses came to an end when Richard III rode out of Leicester to his death at the Battle of Bosworth Field – his monument may be found in the chancel of the cathedral. In 1645, during the next civil war, Leicester's brave and vastly outnumbered citizens held out for five days against the royalist troops of Charles I, only two weeks before the king was finally defeated by Cromwell at the Battle of Naseby. In more recent times, Leicester has been renowned for its hosiery trade, one of the chief reasons for the influx in the 1970s of Indian workers, many of whom came not from the subcontinent, but from the disaster that was Idi Amin's Uganda. Computerization led to huge job losses in this industry at the end of the 20th century, just as the invention of the hand-powered knitting frames in the 19th century had led to job losses then, provoking a young Leicester apprentice called Ned Ludlam to smash a couple of these hated machines, henceforth forever lumbering technophobes the world over with the term 'Luddite'.

Sights

From a distance, the rocket tower of the **National Space Centre** ⓘ *T0116-2582111, www.spacecentre.co.uk, Tue-Sun and bank holidays from 0930-1800, last entry 1630, and on Mon during school holidays 1200-1800. £8.95, child £6.95 with concessions for families and groups, 2 miles north of the city centre, by car, brown signs give directions from the M1 via junctions 21a and 22, and, by public transport, the 54 bus departs regularly from outside the railway station via the main shopping area of town*, enveloped in a hi-tech, silver sheath, looks like an enormous sci-fi maggot. Once inside, the museum is divided into five different zones exploring different aspects of space travel and the universe, all of which revolve around the Space Theatre, a huge, wraparound cinema screening a 20-minute film that is included in the ticket price. Highlights include a replica of the Columbus space station, showing how astronauts eat, sleep and go to the loo in space, and a Soyuz T space capsule used to ferry astronauts to the Mir space station. Expect to spend an absorbing 3 or 4 hours.

Coming back down to earth, the history of the terrestrial loo is laid out in all its glory at the **Abbey Pumping Station** ⓘ *T0116-2995111, 1000-1700 Mon-Sat, Sun,1300-1700, closed 1600 Oct- Mar, free, from there, take the 54 bus back into town or walk down the River Soar and then left onto Abbey Park Road to arrive at the bottom of Belgrave Road*. The Victorian sewage works have been reinvented as an engaging and slightly eccentric museum recording various aspects of transport and domestic life from the first half of the last century.

The **'Golden Mile'** is actually best seen in the evening, when it turns into a neon-lit promenade, a place to window shop and meet friends, before diving into one of the many different eateries for a bite or a full-blown meal. See Eating and Shopping below.

Returning by 22 or 37 bus to the Haymarket, turn half-right at the clock tower along the High Street and left down Loseby Lane to find the diminutive **Cathedral** ⓘ *T0116-2625294, open daily, free*, an essentially Victorian structure built over the remains of a much older church. The chancel contains the floor memorial to Richard III – with his hunched back, the inspiration for the Humpty Dumpty nursery rhyme – and the engravings on the modern glass doors illustrate the Escape from Egypt. The **Guildhall**ⓘ *To116-2532569, Mon-Sat, 1000-1700, Sun 1300-1700, closes 1600 Oct-Mar, free*, right beside the cathedral, is a beautifully preserved 14th-century half- timbered structure, the venue for many of the most significant events in Leicester's history and still in use for some civic functions to this day. Continue back along the High Street and over the A594 to find the **Jewry Wall Museum** ⓘ *To116-2473021, Mon-Sat 1000-1700, Sun 1400-1730, free*, site of the moderately exciting remains of the Roman baths and display of local archaeology, that includes two genuinely impressive Roman mosaics.

From here, head a few steps north to the **Guru Nanak Sikh Museum** ⓘ *To116-2628606, Thu only, 1300-1600, or by appointment, free*, a working Sikh Gurdwara open daily for worship and free food, with a museum of Sikh history upstairs. A short walk south takes you to the castle gardens, containing the mound of the Norman castle and the **Newarke Houses Museum** ⓘ *To116-2473222, Mon-Sat 1000-1700, Sun 1300-1700, closes 1600 Oct-Mar, free*, home to an eclectic collection of such things as clocks, toys and Indian embroidery, including the portrait and various possessions of Daniel Lambert, an enormously fat 19th-century gentleman, who tipped the scales at 52 stone 11 lbs. Just behind the museum, the church of **St Mary de Castro** ⓘ *To116-2628727, Sat and bank holidays 1400-1700 or by special arrangement*, with its exceptional Norman chancel, was the site of the 14th-century poet Geoffrey Chaucer's second marriage.

Returning once more over the A594, look in at the **Jain Centre** ⓘ *To116-2543091, daily from 1400-1700, free*, in the converted congregational chapel on Oxford Street, the only Jain temple in the western world, which contains some fine imported Indian carvings. Walk past the gargantuan Leicester City Council offices onto King Street and amble down leafy New Walk to the **New Walk Museum** ⓘ *To116-2554100, Mon-Sat 1000-1700, Sun 1300-1700, closes 1600 Oct-Mar, free*, of natural history, history and art, which happens to include a celebrated collection of German expressionist paintings. 10 minutes away, in Granby Street, the **City Gallery** runs exhibitions by local and visiting contemporary artists and craftsmen. ⓘ *To116-2540595, closed Mon, free.*

Around Leicester

Melton Mowbray, 15 miles northeast of Leicester, is an unassuming Midlands market town, justly famous for its mighty pork pies, beloved of the horsey set and cheese-eaters. One of the many places (and also one of the most likely) that Stilton cheese is supposed to have originated is at Wymondham, 6 miles west of the town. The Melton Mowbray TIC shares a building with the **Carnegie Museum** ⓘ *Windsor House, Windsor St, To1664- 480992, Mon-Fri 0930-1630, Sat 1000-1600*, that tells the story. **St Mary's Church**, with its extraordinary array of celestory windows (48 of them in all), is also worth a look. If you want to hunt down a pork pie, **Ye Olde Pork Pie Shoppe** and **The Sausage Shop** ⓘ *8-10 Nottingham Street, To1664-482068*, should be more than happy to help.

North of Melton, the A607 heads up towards **Grantham**. Any turn left westwards leads up into delightful undiscovered villages in the wolds, a surprising area of rolling hills overlooking the Vale of Belvoir (pronounced *Beaver*) and giving beautiful views over Leicestershire. **Belvoir Castle** ⓘ *To1476-870262, www.belvoircastle.com, May-Sep daily 1100-1700, Oct Sun 1100-1700, £7.25, concessions £6.75, under-16s £4.75*, the home of the Duke of Rutland, is an imposing exercise in Regency romantic medievalism, full of remarkable paintings and once the scene of very grand house parties.

Fifteen miles southeast of Leicester, **Market Harborough** is another even less assuming Midlands market town. The attractive old part of town, including a grammar school founded in the reign of James I, clusters beneath the impressive broach spire of St Dionysius. Nine miles east of the town, **Rockingham Castle** ⓘ *T01536-770240, www.rockinghamcastle.com Easter-Sep Sun, bank holidays 1300-1700 (also Tue, Thu in Jul, Aug), £7, concessions £6, under-16s £4.50, family £18.50,* is an impressive Tudor house built within the walls of a Norman castle. Charles Dickens was inspired to model Chesney Wold in *Bleak House* on the place and today the interiors and wild gardens (including a 400-year-old elephant hedge) and their superb views are still worth a look.

Rutland

Defiantly not in Leicestershire at all, Rutland is an independent county, England's tiniest, that has been forced to reassert its identity. Oakham is the county town, the epicentre of resistance to the county boundary changes introduced in the 1970s and the fight to retain its Mercian roots. Uppingham is the only other town of any size. Rutlanders have won back their right to self-government, and the county still retains an old-fashioned, decidedly genteel atmosphere. About 17 miles long and 17 wide, old stone buildings, ancient villages and countless sheep dot its verdant landscape, but this is no longer the land that time forgot. At its centre, Rutland Water, is a vast reservoir that draws in watersport enthusiasts, fishermen and ramblers from miles around.

Ins and outs

Getting there Oakham **train** station is a 10 minute walk west of the town centre, with trains running to Birmingham and Norwich, regular connections with the main North-South lines via Peterborough and Leicester. Rutland is about 100 miles north of London, easily reached in 2 hours on the A1.

Getting around Rutland is best explored by **car** or **bike**, although Oakham is easily negotiated on foot and there's a reasonable network of local buses. Contact **Busline** on T0116-2511411.

Information Rutland TIC ⓘ *Oakham, T01572-724329.* **Rutland Water TIC** ⓘ *T01572-653026.*

Sights

Oakham is the miniature capital of Rutland, a prosperous town famous for being mad about horses and fox-hunting. First impressions may be a little grim, but the Market Place is attractive enough, next to **Oakham Castle** ⓘ *T01572-758440, Apr-Oct Mon-Sat 1000-1300, 1330-1700 (Nov-Mar -1600), Sun 1300-1700 (Nov-Mar -1600), free.* Although not much of a castle, being more of a defensive moated townhouse, its Norman Great Hall still stands and repays a visit to look at its medieval sculptures and strange collection of horeshoes. Probably the most unusual array of Royal memorabilia in the country, it was built up thanks to the forfeit paid by the reigning monarch passing through the town since the 15th century.

A 5-minute walk down Catmose Street arrives at **Rutland County Museum** ⓘ *Catmose St, T01572-758440, www.rutland.gov.uk, Mon-Sat 1000-1700, Sun 1400- 1700.* Housed in the old stables of the Rutland Fencibles, a volunteer cavalry force raised by a local landowner in 1794, the museum gives a good picture of the history of this strange little corner of the country and also holds the 13th-century Brooke Reliquary, a rare enamelled casket.

Around Oakham, horseshoes put in another appearance at the working forge at **Tinwell**, T01780-756341, while the nearby village of **Ketton** is famous for its stone quarry. Geoff Hamilton and Gardener's World have made the gardens at **Barnsdale** famous nationwide – 8 acres divided up into 37 different types of garden. ⓘ *The Avenue, Exton, near Oakham, T01572-813200, www.barnsdalegardens.co.uk, Mar-Oct daily 0900-1700 (-1900 Jun, Jul, Aug). Last entry 2 hrs before closing, £5.* Further east, near Stamford, **Tickencote Church** is worth a detour to see its extraordinary carved Norman chancel arch.

Rutland Water looks like an outsize waterhazard on a golf course, a very large (5-mile-long) reservoir created in the mid 1970s by flooding the valley of the Gwash. The main settlements on its 24-mile perimeter are Empingham, Whitwell and Barnsdale. Near Empingham there's a visitor centre, and the **Butterfly Farm and Aquatic Centre** ⓘ *Sykes La, T01780-460515, Easter-Aug daily 1030-1700, Oct 1030-1630.* **Rutland Water Nature Reserve** ⓘ *Egleton, T01572-770651, www.ospery.org.uk*, run by *Anglian Water*, offers the chance to see ospreys fishing from April through August.On the southern shore, the church at **Normanton** ⓘ *T01572-653026*, was rescued from the rising waters and now includes a museum on the construction of the reservoir.

Sleeping

Leicester *p516, map p516*

A Holiday Inn, 129 St Nicholas Circle, T0116-2531161. Next door to the remains of the Roman baths, this modern hotel is built on the site of a Roman temple to the Persian god Mithras. Conveniently located for the motorway and the city centre, facilities include an excellent gym and indoor pool.

C Belmont House Hotel, de Montfort St, T0116-2544773. This country house hotel is just 5 mins' walk from the city centre along the tree-lined New Walk, an old Roman road.

C Spindle Lodge Hotel, 2 West Walk, T0116-2338801. Victorian townhouse still with many of its original features, in a quiet location close to the city centre.

D Comfort Hotel, 23-25 Loughborough Rd, T0116-2682626. At the north end of the 'Golden Mile', this well-appointed hotel features the amazingly kitsch *Kabalou* restaurant, serving Indian food in an interior of mock Gothic-Indian- Egyptian-Greek design.

D Ibis Hotel, St George's Way, T0116-2487200. Right next door to the railway station, this functional, barn of a building offers Leicester's best-value accommodation.

Rutland *p520*

L Hambleton Hall Hotel, Hambleton, T01572-756991. Top of the range – a Victorian house on a peninsula in the middle of the reservoir with an expensive gourmet restaurant and wonderful views.

B Barnsdale Lodge Hotel, The Avenue, Rutland Water, T01572-724678. Partly a converted farmhouse hotel with views over the reservoir, well-placed for visiting attractions around about.

C Lake Isle, 16 High Street East, Uppingham, T01572-822951. Ambitious restaurant in another small hotel in a similar vein.

C Lord Nelson's House, 11 Market Pl, T01572-723199. A small hotel with the highly rated *Nick's* restaurant downstairs, this is the best bet in Oakham itself. Booking essential.

Eating

Leicester *p516, map p516*

£££ The Opera House, 10-12 Guildhall La, T0116-223666. Leicester's classiest eaterie, housed in 2 17th-century cottages, has won several awards for its modern English cooking since its opening in 1999. About £17 for a main course.

££ The Case, 4 & 6 Hotel St, St Martins, T0116-2517675. Champagne bar on ground floor and European-style restaurant upstairs, with occasional jazz accompaniment. Starters/main courses about £6/12, with a slightly cheaper lunch menu.

££ Loaf, 58-62 Braunstone Gate, T0116-2999424. Stylish bar and restaurant, serving a well-presented mix of Mediterranean and Asian dishes

For an explanation of the sleeping and eating price codes used in this guide, see the inside front cover. Other relevant information is provided in the Essentials chapter, page 40.

just the other side of the Soar, on Leicester's unlikely Rive Gauche. Starters/main courses about £6/10.

££ **San Carlo**, 38-40 Granby St, T0116-2519332. The nearest thing to *La Caprice* in Leicester. White tiles, blue neon, chrome and high quality Italian food. Antipasti/main courses about £7/12.

££ **Watsons**, 5-9 Upper Brown St, T0116-2227770. Glass walls, wooden veneer floors and bright, modern paintings. A more contemporary, less stuffy experience than its competitor the *Opera House*. Starters/main course about £6/12.

Golden Mile

££ **Chaat House**, 108 Belgrave Rd, T0116-2660513, (closed Tue). A little different, an intimate den serving many different versions of the eponymous North Indian snack.

££ **Sharmilee**, 71 Belgrave Rd, T0116-2668471, (closed Mon), for takeaways and eat-in.

££ **Bobbies**, 154 Belgrave Rd, T0116-2662448, (closed Mon). Sweets and vegetarian savoury takeaways, and thalis and dosas in the restaurant.

££ **The Curry Fever**, 139 Belgrave Rd, T0116-2662941, (closed Mon). The menu here contains few surprises, but is very highly regarded.

Rutland *p520*

£ **Flores House Deli**, Oakham is a good place to pick up a picnic.

£ **Olive Branch**, Main St, Clipsham, T01780-410355, is an upbeat and charming village pub with much better than average food, in a village with a remarkable topiary yew hedge.

Pubs and bars

Leicester *p516, map p516*

Bossa, 110 Granby St, T0116-2334544. You might be in a small town in Italy, stepping inside this civilized little bar with its rack of weird spirits, coffee machine and glass case of ciabata sandwiches.

The King's, 36 King St, T0116-2551477. Leicester's most relaxed boozer. Soothing green benches, big wooden tables and newspapers, a selection of ales and decent food for a very mixed, laid-back clientele.

Left Bank, 26 Braunstone Gate, T0116-2552422. One of the first trendy bars to spring up in this popular little nightlife enclave west of the river. Also serves excellent fresh food.

The Orange Tree, 99 High St, T0116-2235256. Mellow wooden floors and wooden tables, an easy-going crowd, a wide range of cocktails and happy hours throughout the week.

Revolution, New Walk, T0116-2559633. Big, retro-style vodka bar, with high ceilings and groovy 70s decor, on this very pleasant, leafy pedestrian thoroughfare.

Time, 48a London Rd, T0116-2619301. A vast, warehouse-style establishment next to the railway station, with a concrete floor and chrome barspace that gets busy at weekends.

Entertainment

Leicester *p516, map p516*

Cinema

Odeon, just south of the city centre, Freemans Park, T0870-5050007;
Piccadilly Cinema, Abbey St, T0116-2519699;
Phoenix Arts Centre, Newarke St, T0116-2554854, which also runs a programme of theatre, dance and other performance .

Theatre

Haymarket Theatre, Belgrave Gate, T0116-2539797. Often used as a test bed for shows heading for London's West End.

Jongleurs, Granby St, T0870-7870707. The place to catch some stand-up comedy.

Festivals

Leicester *p516, map p516*

Feb Leicester **Comedy Festival** is held over 10 days in the middle of Feb, featuring established stars alongside brand new talent. T0116-2257770.

May Early music lovers descend on Leicester in late May and early Jun for the **Early Music Festival** held in museums, churches, the cathedral and Castle Park. T0116-2709984.

Jun It's usually followed in mid-Jun by the Leicester International Music Festival, specializing in chamber music but also featuring jazz and world music. T0116-2473043.
Aug The city's big **carnival**, at the beginning of Aug, is a celebration of the Caribbean community in the city. T0116-2257770.
Nov Leicester stages the biggest **Diwali** celebrations outside India. Marking the start of the Hindu New Year, this festival of light is held at the beginning of Nov, when the 'Golden Mile' is illuminated in spectacular style, the road is closed to traffic and a stage put up at the flyover end for music and dancing, with a firework display as a grand finale. T0116-2998888.

Shopping

Leicester *p516, map p516*
Daminis, 87 Belgrave Rd, T0116-2664357. A cut above the other sari shops for chic east-west fashions.
TF Cash & Carry, 93 Belgrave Rd, T0116-2660946, is an underground Aladdin's Cave, stocking everything from Hindi DVDs and Indian cooking pots, to a life-sized framed photographs of the Indian master Sai Baba.
The Sangam Pan House, just off the south end of the strip in Roberts Road, is one of the more luxurious shops specializing in the mysterious Indian art of pan, the traditional areca nut pick-me-up wrapped in a green betel leaf.
Sona, 112-114 Belgrave Rd, T0116-2661142. For gold jewellery from the subcontinent.

Activities and tours

Leicester *p516, map p516*
Leicester City Football Club at Filbert St, T0116-2915000.
Leicester County Cricket Club has its ground a mile further south at Grace Rd, T0116-2832128.
The Leicester Tigers, one of the top rugby union sides in the country, play at Welford Rd T0116-2541607.

Rutland *p520*
Rutland Sailing Club and School, Gibbet La, Edith Weston, T01780-720292.
Rutland Water Cruises on the *Rutland Belle* from Whitwell, leaving at 1300, 1400, 1500, calling at Normanton Church on the south shore. Daily May-Sep.
Rutland Water Cycling, Whitwell Car Park, on Rutland Water, T01780-460705, (also on the south shore at Normanton, T01780-720888).
Rutland Watersports, Whitwell Car Park, T01780-460154, www.rutlandwater.net.
Rutland Water Trout Fishery, Normanton Car Park, T01780-686441.

Transport

Leicester *p516, map p516*

Bus

Long distance National Express, T08705-808080, run regularly direct to **Nottingham Broad Marsh** (45 mins) and direct every 2 hrs to **London Victoria**. They also run direct services 6 times per day to **Birmingham Digbeth** (1 hr to 1 hr 30 mins) and 7 times per day to **Derby** (1 hr).

Car

Avis, 1 Samuel St, T0116-2626523; Thrifty, Garden St, T0116-2620444.

Taxi

A1 Airport Taxis, 146 Belgrave Gate, T0116-2513188; Swift Taxis, 77a Church Gate, T0116-2531138.

Train

Midland Mainline, T08457-125678, run the regular direct services to **Nottingham** (35 mins), **Derby** (30 mins) and **London St Pancras** (1 hr 20 mins). Central Trains, T0121-6541200, run the regular direct service to **Birmingham** (1 hr).

Directory

Leicester *p516, map p516*
Hospitals Leicester Royal Infirmary, Infirmary Sq, T0116-2541414.

Nottinghamshire and Derby

➔ *Colour map 4, grid A5/6*

The M1 runs up its western flank and Lincolnshire squeezes its eastern side. Nottinghamshire is a through-county where the North meets the South and few visitors are likely to want to stop for very long with much more enticing places all around. The city of Nottingham itself is easily the main draw, an up-and-coming focus for nightlife and entertainment in the East Midlands, with a venerable history to match. Dropping into the city for a night's clubbing is bound to be memorable. Unfortunately there really is precious little to recommend a special journey elsewhere in the county. Sherwood Forest is pushed hard by the Tourist Board, but is just a few hundred acres of waymarked paths through woods the like of which can be found in more magical shapes and sizes all over the country. One place worth seeking out, though, is Newstead Abbey, the childhood home of Lord Byron and still strangely evocative of his peculiar strain of romanticism, admirably maintained by the County Council. ›› *For Sleeping, Eating and other listings, see pages 531-535.*

Nottingham

Like Newcastle, Nottingham is visibly in a state of fashionable flux. Massive new building projects are underway right across the city centre as this once-drab Midlands manufacturing centre reinvents itself as a modern European cityscape. Paul Smith designerwear, Nottingham Forest Football Club and a thriving dance music scene have become the booming exports of a place that was once synonymous with hosiery and lace. Only bits of the old industrial city survive, much of it thankfully submerged beneath gloomy but marginally more liveable in housing projects and road junctions of the 60s. These bits are still likely to be of most interest to the visitor though: the area around the Lace Market and St Mary's church, neighbouring Hockley, and Nottingham castle, about two day's worth of exploration.

Ins and outs

Getting there **East Midlands airport**, T01332-852852, and Birmingham International airport, T0121-7675511, are, respectively, 20 and 30 minutes away by car. There are several **trains** every hour from London St Pancras (1 hour and 20 minutes by the fast service). Nottingham is 122 miles, or about 2 hours, from London by car, straight up the M1, 1 hour 30 minutes from Leeds further up the M1. At Junction 24, the A42 becomes the M42 on its way to Birmingham, about 30 minutes away. **Bus National Express,** T08705-808080, offers services throughout the country from Broadmarsh Bus Station, just south of the city centre. ›› *See Transport, page 534, for more details.*

Getting around The centre of Nottingham, within a busy ring **road**, is easily small enough to negotiate on **foot**. **Victoria Centre Bus Station**, nos 737, 747 and 757 for Newstead Abbey, or the 'Sherwood Forester' service.

Information **Nottingham City Information Centre** ⓘ *Council Ho, Smithy Row, off Market Sq, T0115-915 5330, www.visitnottingham.com, Mon-Fri 0930-1730, Sat 0900-1700 (and Sun 1000-1600 in Aug). Accommodation service £2.50.* **Nottinghamshire County Information Centre** ⓘ *County Hall, West Bridgford, T0115-977 3558 (open same hrs).*

History

Unlike many Midland towns, Nottingham dates back to the Dark Ages. The Saxons settled in the area, only to be ousted by the Danes. When Edward the Elder took the town back in the 10th century, he built a bridge over the River Trent nearby and by the time the Normans arrived, Nottingham was the strategic key to the centre of the country. All that remains of the formidable stronghold they constructed is the gatehouse, much restored. The rest of the castle was demolished by the Parliamentarians after the Civil War. Shortly afterwards, the Duke of Newcastle built an Italianate mansion on the site, which was put to the torch itself during rioting over the Reform Acts in the 1830s. By that time, Nottingham was already a heaving industrial centre, riddled with slums, turning out hosiery and lace in huge quantities thanks to Hargreaves' Spinning Jenny and other technical breakthroughs. The Luddites smashed up the looms here with exceptional ferocity. The city suffered considerable bomb damage during the Second World War, but it was only in the late 60s that Nottingham's traditional industries, including shoemaking, began to die on their feet. What looked like terminal decline has fairly recently been arrested with some bold enterprise initiatives, an injection of European cash, and by the never-say-die spirit of Notties themselves.

Sights

Market Square is the centre of Nottingham, about 600 yds almost directly north of the train station over the canal. The areas of the city of most interest to visitors fall either side of this north-south line passing through the Broadmarsh shopping centre. Beneath the shopping centre, though, **The Caves of Nottingham** ⓘ *Broadmarsh Centre, T0115-9520555, Mon-Sat 1000-1700 (last admission 1615), Sun 1000-1700 (last admission 1600), £4, concessions £3,* are quite an unusual visitor attraction, large caves laid out to show how they have been used down the ages, up to their use as an air-raid shelter during the war. The self-guided audio tour is entertaining enough too.

Before Market Square, to the east, clustered around the church of St Mary's, the **Lace Market** area covers the site of Saxon Nottingham. **St Mary's Church**, High Pavement, is home to the Nottingham Bach Choir, who rehearse on Tuesday evenings, and is worth a look in itself, especially the door in the south porch which frames a bronze Art Nouveau relief of Christ with the Virgin.

Just before the church is the **Lace Market Heritage Point** at the Shire Hall, where you can take a half-mile audio tour round the area, voiced by Joanna Lumley, called *The Lace Market Unveiled*. The tour capitalizes on some of the few old buildings left standing by the urban planners in the 60s: red brick warehouses now converted into fashionable bars and shops. In the old **Shire Hall**, ⓘ *Galleries of Justice Experience, Shire Hall, High Pavement, Lace Market, T0115-9520555, www.galleriesofjustice.org.uk, Apr-Oct Tue-Sun 1000-1700, Nov-Mar Tue-Sun 1000-1600,* dating from the mid-18th century, the Galleries of Justice is an interactive see-hear-and-smell show on the theme of crime and punishment, lent some authenticity by the original Victorian courtrooms and the old cells, where you're encouraged to "feel the atmosphere of 300 years of suffering seeping through the walls, bars and chains..." Not for delicate sensibilities then, but most kids seem to love it.

Opposite the *Pitcher and Piano* (see Pubs and bars, below) in the old Lace Hall, the **Lace Market Centre** ⓘ *3/5 High Pavement, Lace Market, T0115-9881849,* are two shops dedicated to local lace and silk, where you can see lace being handmade most days except Mondays. North of St Mary's, St Mary's Gate and Stoney Street lead up into **Hockley**, another area of reclaimed and renovated old buildings that make for rewarding browsing. Heading 100 yds west out of Hockley brings you back to Market Square, dominated by the Baroque **Council House** on pedestrianized Smithy Row.

Nottingham

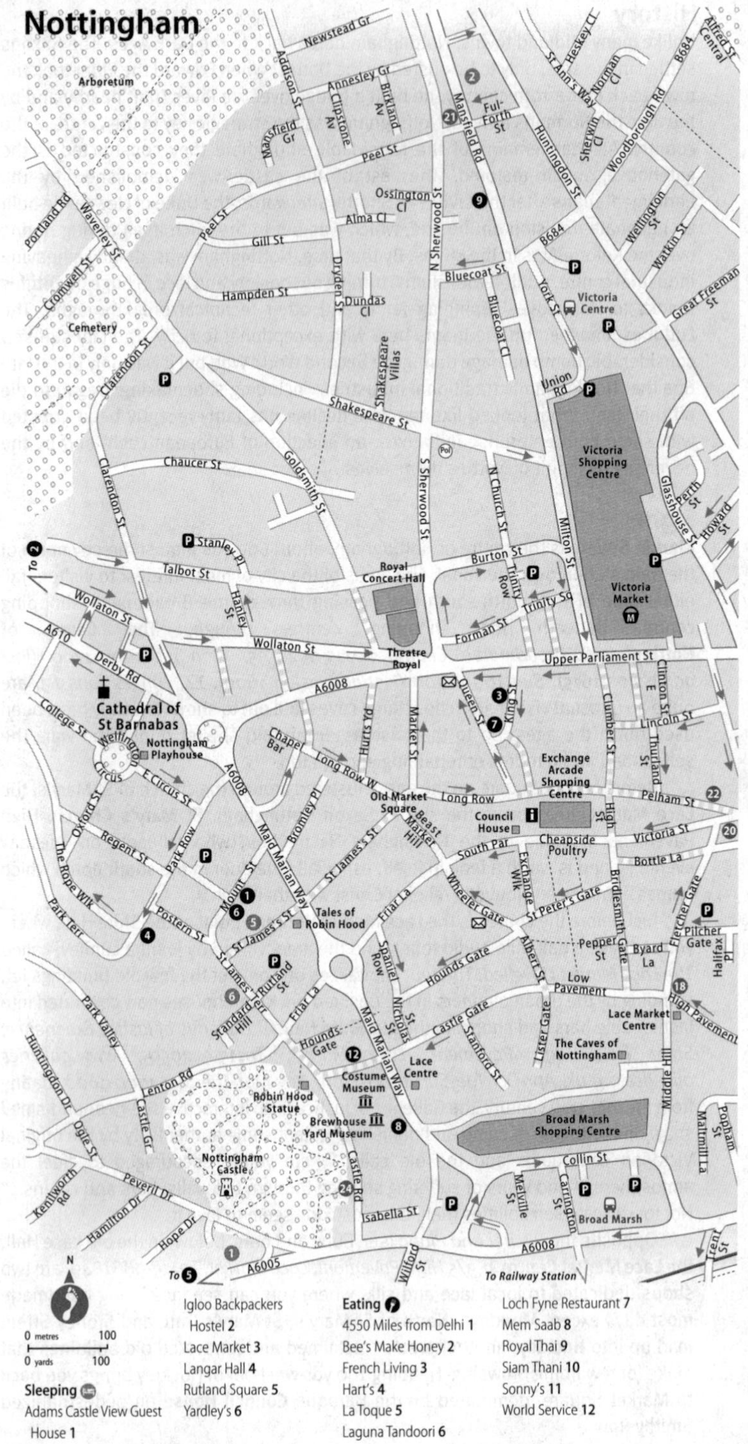
Arboretum
Cemetery
Newstead Gr
Addison St
Annesley Gr
Clipstone Av
Birkland Av
Mansfield Gr
Mansfield Rd
Ful-Forth St
Huntingdon St
St Ann's Way
Heskey Cl
Norman Cl
Sherwin Cl
Woodborough Rd
B684
Alfred St Central
Peel St
Ossington Cl
Alma Cl
Gill St
Dryden St
N Sherwood St
Wellington St
Watkin St
Portland Rd
Waverley St
Cromwell St
Hampden St
Dundas Cl
Bluecoat St
Bluecoat Cl
York St
Victoria Centre
Great Freeman St
Clarendon St
Shakespeare Villas
Shakespeare St
Union Rd
Victoria Shopping Centre
Chaucer St
Goldsmith St
S Sherwood St
N Church St
Milton St
Glasshouse St
Perth St
Howard St
Stanley Pl
Talbot St
Royal Concert Hall
Burton St
Trinity Row
Trinity Sq
Victoria Market
Wollaton St
Hanley St
Forman St
A610
Derby Rd
Theatre Royal
Upper Parliament St
A6008
Queen St
King St
Clinton St E
Cathedral of St Barnabas
College St
Wellington Circus
Nottingham Playhouse
Chapel Bar
Hurts Yd
Market St
Lincoln St
Thurland St
Clumber St
E Circus St
Long Row W
Exchange Arcade Shopping Centre
Oxford St
Old Market Square
Long Row
Pelham St
Regent St
Park Row
Maid Marian Way
Bromley Pl
St James's St
Beast Market Hill
Council House
High St
Victoria St
The Rope Wlk
South Par
Cheapside
Poultry
Bottle La
Mount St
Exchange Wlk
Park Terr
Postern St
Tales of Robin Hood
Friar La
Wheeler Gate
St Peter's Gate
Bridlesmith Gate
Fletcher Gate
Pilcher Gate
Halifax Pl
St James' Terr
Rutland St
Spaniel Row
Hounds Gate
Albert St
Pepper St
Byard La
Park Valley
Standard Hill
Low Pavement
High Pavement
Lace Market Centre
St Nicholas St
Castle Gate
Stanford St
Lister Gate
Huntingdon Dr
The Caves of Nottingham
Lace Centre
Costume Museum
Lenton Rd
Robin Hood Statue
Middle Hill
Brewhouse Yard Museum
Broad Marsh Shopping Centre
Castle Gr
Ogle St
Popham St
Maltmill La
Nottingham Castle
Collin St
Castle Rd
Melville St
Carrington St
Peveril Dr
Kenilworth Rd
Hamilton Dr
Isabella St
Broad Marsh
Hope Dr
A6008
Wilford St
A6005
Trent St
To 2
To 5
To Railway Station
N
0 metres 100
0 yards 100
Sleeping
Adams Castle View Guest House 1
Igloo Backpackers Hostel 2
Lace Market 3
Langar Hall 4
Rutland Square 5
Yardley's 6
Eating
4550 Miles from Delhi 1
Bee's Make Honey 2
French Living 3
Hart's 4
La Toque 5
Laguna Tandoori 6
Loch Fyne Restaurant 7
Mem Saab 8
Royal Thai 9
Siam Thani 10
Sonny's 11
World Service 12

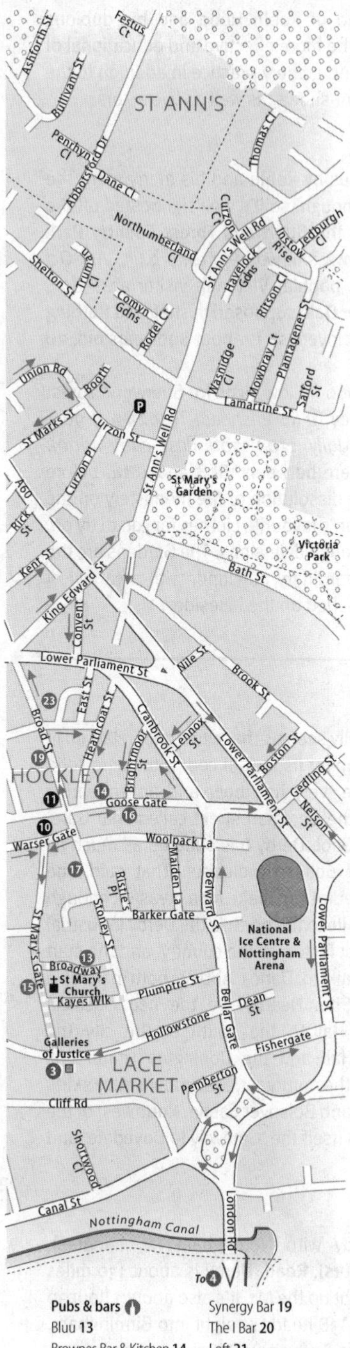

Pubs & bars
Bluu 13
Brownes Bar & Kitchen 14
Lizzard Lounge 15
Market Bar 16
Old Angel 17
Pitcher and Piano 18
Synergy Bar 19
The I Bar 20
Loft 21
Social 22
Wax Bar 23
Ye Olde Trip to Jerusalem 24

Anyone interested in the history of the city should head west from the Broadmarsh centre towards Nottingham Castle, home to an impressive municipal art gallery. On the way, the old buildings by the castle gate contain the **Costume Museum** ⓘ *Castle Gate, T0115-9153500, www.nottinghamcity.gov.uk, Wed-Sun 1000-1600, free.* Six period room settings from 1790-1950s are inhabited by period costume-wearing dummies in faintly realistic action poses, as well as a textile exhibition and a history of lace room. Look out too for the cushion-cover possibly embroidered by Elizabeth I, the Map tapestries of the city embroidered in 1632, and from a similar date, the oldest pair of boys' stockings in the UK, in fine knitted silk. **Nottingham Castle** ⓘ *off Maid Marian Way, T0115-9153700, daily 1000-1700 (last admission 1630), free Mon-Fri, £2, £1 concessions on Sat, Sun and bank holidays,* is well worth a look for its very fine collection of medieval alabaster carvings, a skill in which the city once excelled, as well as an intriguing array of Victorian paintings in a wonderful old gallery. There's also a Nottingham history room, 'The Story of Nottingham', illustrating the city's past with the help of the latest interactive technology.

A stone's throw away, the **Brewhouse Yard Museum of Nottingham Life** ⓘ *Castle Boulevard, T0115-9153600, daily 1000-1630 (last admission 1600) Mon-Fri free, Sat, Sun, bank holidays £1.50, concessions 80p,* covers the social history of the city rather than its manufacturing pride, with mock-ups of shopfronts and a period living room and kitchen.

A small cave under the castle can be seen on guided tours at 1400, 1500 (£2) leaving from the top of the castle. Northwest of the castle up Maid Marian Way, the Roman Catholic Cathedral of **St Barnabas**, Derby Road, is another impressive piece of ecclesiastical design by Pugin. Just by the junction of Maid Marian Way with Friar Lane, the **Tales of Robin Hood** ⓘ *T0115-9483284, www.robinhood.uk.com, Apr-Sep 1000-1800, Oct-Nov 1000-1730, £6.50, £4.50 under-16s, £5.25 concessions,* is the inevitable dark ride exploiting the legend of Robin Hood and his dubious association with the city. That said, it's one of the more effective and educational of the genre, with falconry in the castle grounds and archery practice in addition to the usual mannequins, sound effects and tacky light shows, as well as live actors.

Sherwood Forest

There's not much left of the forest made famous by Robin and his merry men. The tourist board make as much of it as they can though, so it's well signposted off the M1. **Robyn Hode's Sherwode Exhibition** is at the **Sherwood Forest Country Park Visitor Centre** ⓘ *T01623-823202/824490, www.sherwood-forest.org.uk, Apr-Oct daily 1030-1700, Nov-Mar daily 1030-1630*, a popular Victorian visitor attraction, admired by Washington Irving in 1835. The **Major Oak**, supposed trysting and trothing spot of Robin and Marian, its hollow trunk their lovenest, is about 800 years old, 20 minutes' walk from the Visitor Centre.

Twelve miles north of Nottingham on the A60 (follow signs for Sherwood Forest from Junction 27 of the M1) is **Newstead Abbey** ⓘ *Ravenshead, T01623-455 900, www.newsteadabbey.org.uk, house Apr-Sep daily 1200-1700 (last entry 1600). Grounds daily 0900-dusk.* Lord Byron lived here between 1808 and 1814, before selling his ancestral home (since 1540 and the dissolution of the monastery on the site) in 1818. Medieval cloisters, Great Hall, Byron's favourite clothes for you to try on, and a mock-up of his quarters are all decent enough diversions. The Gardens are the main event, though – over 300 acres of extraordinary parkland, with a variety of different gardens from around the world established on the lakeside.

Derby and around

Fifteen miles west of Nottingham, Derby is usually seen as that city's poor relation. In fact it's a very different kind of place, making up for its lack of cool with some solid industrial heritage, mild-mannered local pride, very fine beer and an endearing cathedral. Not much to look at, except along the Georgian street called Friar Gate, home to the Pickford Museum and Old Derby Gaol, Derby has suffered as much as most other Midland towns at the hands of 60s redevelopers. That said, the pedestrianized area west and south of the cathedral can make for a pleasant enough wander around of an afternoon. A quarter of a mile to the north is the Derby Industrial Museum, housed in the first factory in the country, and the start of a mile-long riverside walk to Darley Abbey, both part of a UNESCO World Heritage Site. Nearby are the neo classical splendours of Kedleston Hall.To the south of the city the extraordinary formal gardens at Melbourne Hall and the Donington Grand Prix Collection racetrack and racing car museum. To the northeast, the Amber Valley skirts abandoned mining country up to Hardwick Hall and Bolsover Castle. Northwest of the city, dignified old Ashbourne proudly proclaims itself the 'Gateway to Dovedale' and hence the Peak District as a whole.

For the Peak District part of Derbyshire, see the North-west Chapter, page 625.

Ins and outs

Getting there Regular **trains** connect Derby with Nottingham (25 minutes), Leicester (35 minutes) and on to London (2 hours). **Road** Derby is about 130 miles from London, reachable in 2 hours by car, straight up the M1. It's also about 1 hour 30 minutes from Leeds further up the M1. The big A38 heads straight into Birmingham, no more than 30 minutes away. **National Express**, T08705-808080, run six coaches a day to Derby from London Victoria, taking 3½ hours).

Getting around Derby is a surprisingly large city.The centre is Market Place, about a mile and a half west of the **train** station (catch a **bus**, the walk's no fun) and a stone's throw from the grotty bus station in Morledge. But most of the sights worth seeing are within easy walking distance of each other.

Information **Derby TIC** ⓘ *Assembly Rooms, Market Pl, T01332-255802, Mar-Oct Mon-Sat 0930-1700, Nov-Feb Mon-Sat 1000-1600.* **Ashbourne TIC** ⓘ *13 Market Pl, T01335-343666, Mar-Oct Mon-Sat 0930-1700 (also Sun in Jul and Aug), Nov-Feb Mon-Sat 1000-1600.* **Amber Valley TIC** ⓘ *Town Hall, Market Pl, Ripley, T01773-841488, www.ambervalley.gov.uk.*

History

One of the five major towns of the Danelaw (alongside Lincoln, Nottingham, Leicester and Stamford), Derby became an important local centre in the Middle Ages. It was only in the 18th century, though, that the city's fortunes really began take off, with the success of the Lombes' silk mill, arguably the first factory in the country (now the Industrial Museum). Chinaware (Royal Crown Derby) and the Midland Railway enhanced its industrial base, and in the early years of the 20th century Rolls Royce moved their works to the city. Recently the Derwent Valley from Cromford to Derby was declared a World Heritage Site by UNESCO thanks to its starring role in the dawn of the Industrial Revolution and the machine age.

Derby

By car, Derby shows itself to its best advantage when approached from Ashbourne and the west down the red-brick Georgian street called Friar Gate, the opposite side of the city from the station. On Friar Gate itself, the **Derby Gaol** ⓘ *50 Friar Gate, T01332-299321,* reveals what lay in store for the offenders during the city's industrial heyday. A few doors down, the **Georgian townhouse** ⓘ *Pickford's House Museum, 41 Friar Gate, T01332-255363, Mon 1100-1700, Tue-Sat 1000-1700, Sun 1400-1700, free,* home of the architect Joseph Pickford has been restored to its c.1800 appearance. Some rooms have been furnished as they might have been when the Pickford family lived in the house. Others contain displays of costume and textiles and also the Frank Bradley collection of toy theatres.

At the end of Friar Gate, where it meets The Wardwick, a left turn down Curzon Street arrives at the Strand and the **Derby Museum and Art Gallery**. ⓘ *T01332-716659, Mon 1100-1700, Tue-Sat 1000-1700, Sun 1400-1700, free.* This holds a fine collection of Joseph Wright of Derby's paintings, as well as a refurbished interactive ceramics gallery, and displays on the local archaeology, history, wildlife and geology.

A few steps down St James Street from here leads into Market Place, from where it's a short walk up Iron Gate to the cathedral. With its airy 18th-century neo classical nave, designed by Gibb and restored by Comper, and a medieval tower over the entrance porch, **Derby Cathedral** ⓘ *T01332-341201, www.derbycathedral.org, daily 0830-1800,* is delightful but only just deserves the name. In fact until fairly recently it was a parish church. Inside, highlights include the monument to the formidable Bess of Hardwick (1607) and Robert Bakewell's elegant early 18th-century ironwork.

A three-minute walk from the cathedral down Sowter Road arrives at the **Derby Industrial Museum** ⓘ *Silk Mill La, off Full St, T01332-255308, Mon 1100-1700, Tue-Sat 1000-1700, Sun 1400-1700, free.* This UNESCO World Heritage Site on the banks of the Derwent is an 18th-century Silk Mill. It now houses a museum solely dedicated to Derby's role in the birth of manufacturing industry, including Rolls Royce aero engines – Frank Whittle's prototype jet engine for example – displays on lead mining, silk weaving (this is illustrated by a loom that worked at the Ashbourne narrow fabrics factory until the early 1970s) and wrought iron work. The silk mill itself remains the main event, built between 1717 and 1721 for the Lombe brothers, it was unfortunately hard-hit in the 19th century by overseas competition but only ceased production in 1908.

A mile away by footpath along the river, the **Darley Abbey and Park** is also part of the World Heritage Site, the remains (much altered and redeveloped) of a late-18th-century factory village developed by Thomas Evans.

About a mile south of Market Place, on the road to Melbourne, the **Royal Crown Derby Visitor Centre** ⓘ *194 Osmaston Rd, T01332-712800, Mon- Sat 0900-1700, Sun 1000-1600, factory tours bookable in advance at 1000, 1100, 1330 and 1430*, provides hands-on introductions to ceramic paintings as well as factory tours.

Derwent and Amber Valleys

North and upstream of Derby the Derwent and Amber Valleys embrace the towns of Belper, Ripley, Heanor and Alfreton. The area's manufacturing heritage can be explored at the magnificent **Belper North Mill** ⓘ *Derwent Valley Visitor Centre, Belper North Mill, Bridgefoot, Belper, T01773-880474, www.belpernorthmill.org, Mar-Oct Wed- Sun 1300-1700, Nov-Feb Thu-Sun 1300-1700, £2, £1.50*, once a state-of- the-art water-powered and fire-proof cotton mill. The huge iron-framed building was completed in the early 1800s by the son of Jedediah Strutt, whose 1786 building had been destroyed in a fire. Models and a few original spinning machines can be seen.

The **National Heritage Corridor** ⓘ *T01773-841485, www.nationalheritagecorridor.org.uk*, is a celebration of one of the country's hardest worked rivers: the Derwent. Particularly attractive woodland stretches can be found at **Whatstandwell** (yachtswoman Ellen MacArthur's home town) and **Ambergate**. The river runs on throuth Belper and down into Derby.

Seven miles north of Alfreton, just east of Junctions 28 and 29 on the M1, **Hardwick Old Hall** ⓘ *(EH), T01246-850431, Apr-Sep Mon, Wed, Thu, Sat, Sun 1000-1800, Oct Mon, Wed, Thu, Sat, Sun 1000- 1700, £3.10, childen £1.60, concessions £2.40*, is the ruin of Bess of Hardwick's Elizabethan family home. Spectacular views from the roof. Next door to the Hardwick Old Hall is the palatial Elizabethan residence that Bess built for herself in the 1590s. Highlights of its interior are the wealth of 16th-century furniture, tapestries and needlework. Outside, the glorious gardens stretching over to the Old Hall give superb views over the M1 and surrounding countryside. ⓘ *Hardwick New Hall (NT), T01246-850430. Apr-Oct Wed, Thu, Sat, Sun 1230-1700, £6.60, children £3.30, family £16.50.*

Also visible from the M1, and particularly spectacular when floodlit at night, **Bolsover Castle** ⓘ *(EH), T01246-822844, Apr-Sep daily 1000-1800, Oct daily 1000-1700, Nov-Mar Wed-Sun 1000-1600, £6.20, concessions £4.60, children £3.10, off junctions 29 or 30 on the M1, in Bolsover 6 miles east of Chesterfield*, was built in the 17th century as a romantic lovenest on the site of a medieval castle. It was constructed by Sir Charles Cavendish as a retreat from the world, where he could indulge his fondness for all things chivalric and medieval. The Venus Fountain in the grounds, featuring cherubs relieving themselves into the water below, is typical of the playful tone Sir Charles wanted his guests to appreciate.

Ashbourne and Dovedale

Eleven miles northwest of Derby up the A52, Ashbourne is a quaint red-brick town, proudly proclaiming itself the 'Gateway to Dovedale'. Its preserved medieval street pattern and Georgian rebuilding give the place its peculiar charm. St John Street is the most interesting architecturally, with its gallows cross still standing. Ashbourne was dubbed 'Oakbourne' by George Eliot in her novel *Adam Bede*. She also described St Oswald's Church with its beautiful spire as the "finest mere parish church in the kingdom". The interior is full of surprises, including carvings, and fine stained glass, and the Cockayne chapel commemorating two centuries-worth of local bigwigs. With its cobbled market place and old pubs, Ashbourne does make a good base from which to set off into the Peak District.

South of Derby

To the south of Derby, a couple of very grand houses are worth seeking out. **Kedleston Hall** ⓘ *(NT), T01332-842191, Apr-Oct Mon-Wed, Sat, Sun 1200-1630, £5.50, under-16s £3.20, family £13.20*, is a beautiful neo classical mansion built in the mid-18th century for the Curzons, its interiors designed by Robert Adam. Also an Eastern Museum displaying the loot acquired by Lord Curzon as Viceroy of India at the turn of the last century. More elegant Adam buildings dotted around the sweeping parkland.

Not far to the east, the village of **Melbourne** is also worth a detour: the church is a remarkably complete (especially on the inside) Norman church that looks like a small cathedral. It has three towers, the central one a 17th-century belltower with 12 bells. Inside are superb carvings, a sheela-na-gig or pagan fertility symbol, and Australian flags. The latter can be explained at **Melbourne Hall** ⓘ *T01332-862502, House Aug Tue-Sun 1400-1700, gardens Apr-Sep Wed, Sat, Sun 1330-1730, House or Garden £3, concessions £2, both £5 concessions £3*, with its formal, well-tended and little-altered French gardens designed in the late 17th-century in the style of Le Notre by Henry Wise and George London (who also worked at Hampton Court, Longleat, Petworth and Chatsworth). This was once the home of Victorian PM William Lamb Lord Melbourne, troubled husband of Byron's lover Caroline Lamb.

At **Donington** ⓘ *Donington Park Grand Prix Collection, Castle Donington, T01332-812829, www.donningtoncollection.com*, you'll find one of the country's most extensive collections of Formula 1 cars at an historic racetrack just off the M1. It features more than 130 of the snarling machines, dating from the early 20th century to the present day.

Sleeping

Nottingham *p524, map p526*

A Lace Market Hotel, 29 High Pavement, T0115-8523232, www.lacemarkethotel.co.uk. Boutique hotel with snazzy contemporary design and restaurant called *Merchants* to match.

A Langar Hall, Langar, T01949-860559, F861045 Regency house with bags of character in a beautiful village setting and acres of parkland, some way southeast of the city.

C Rutland Square Hotel, St James St, T0115-9411114, www.zoffanyhotels.co.uk Clean and comfortable chain hotel close to the castle.

C Yardley's, 11 St James Terr, T0115-9411997. Small hotel close to the castle with reasonable food in a recently refurbished restaurant and quiet, comfortable rooms.

D Adams Castle View Guest House, 85 Castle Boulevard, T0115-9500022. Victorian house with comfortable rooms, close to the city centre.

F Igloo Backpackers Hostel, 110 Mansfield Rd, T0115-9475250, www.igloohostel.co.uk. 36 beds in 4 rooms, £11 per person not including breakfast. See also National Water Sports Centre, in Sport below for camping and bunkhouse options.

Derby and around *p528*

A Callow Hall, Mappleton Rd, Ashbourne, T01335-300900, www.callowhall.co.uk. The smart option, an independent hotel about a mile west of the town in a large Victorian house. Good English food in the restaurant.

C Beresford Arms Hotel, Station Rd, Ashbourne, T01335-300035, www.beresford-arms.co.uk.Quite a large hotel in a Victorian house in the middle of town.

D The Plough Inn, Station St, Ashbourne, T01335-343437. B&B above a pleasant freehouse.

D Beechenhill Farm, Ilam, T01335-310274. 2 double rooms and a self-catering cottage with superb views and colourful garden.

D **Throwley Hall Farm**, Ilam, T01538-308202, www.throwleyhallfarm.co.uk. Good B&B.

Eating

Nottingham *p524, map p526*

£££ **Hart's**, Standard St, Park Row, T0115-9110666. Generally considered to be the city's finest dining experience, a sophisticated ambience, professional service and superior modern European cuisine can be enjoyed here for about £35 a head with wine.

£££ **La Toque**, 61 Wollaton Rd, T0115-9222268. About £40 a head for superior and elaborate French cuisine in a small bistro setting some way out on the road to Beeston. Booking advisable, essential on Sat.

£££ **Sonny's**, 3 Carlton St, T0115-9473041. Brasserie with a good reputation behind the Lace Market, about £30 a head, reliable seafood and meat dishes.

£££ **World Service**, Newdigate House, Castle Gate, T0115-8475587. Fusion food with garden and sumptuous surroundings in a Georgian house, also for about £35 a head. Booking essential.

££ **4550 Miles from Delhi**, 41 Mount St, T0115-9475111. New designer North Indian restaurant in the middle of town.

££ **Bee's Make Honey**, 12 Alfreton Rd, T0115-9780109. Good seafood in a popular restaurant within walking distance of the Playhouse. BYOB.

££ **French Living**, 27 King St, T0115-9585885. Very good value (especially the *plat du jour* at lunchtime) rustic French fare in the middle of town. Snails, game and pud for about £20, 5 mins' walk from Market Sq.

££ **Laguna Tandoori**, 43 Mount St, T0115-9411632. A reliable north Indian restaurant that's been around for 26 years. A meal here costs about £17 a head.

££ **Mem Saab**, 12 Maid Marian Way, T0115-9570009. Another good Indian restaurant in the middle of town with a few south Indian recipes on the menu.

££ **Royal Thai**, 189 Mansfield Rd, T0115-9483001. Reliable Thai restaurant about 20 mins' walk from the middle of town uphill. About £16 a head.

££ **Siam Thani**, 16 Carlton St, Hockley, T0115-9582222. Modern Thai restaurant with good food for about £20 a head.

Derby and around *p528*

£££ **Darley's on the River**, Darley Abbey Mill, Derby, T01332-364987, www.darleys.com. Probably the smartest restaurant in Derby, with an ambitious but accomplished Frenchified menu at about £30 a head for lunch and supper. A 20-min walk along the river. Derby is famous for its pride in and devotion to real ale and several good pubs pull pints of the stuff at its best.

££ **The Brunswick**, 1 Railway Terr, Derby, T01332-290677. One of the city's most popular real ale pubs, with an exceptional variety in barrels and on the pumps, very close to the railway station.

££ **The Flower Pot**, 25 King St, Derby, T01332-204955. Just round the corner of the cathedral, with a small beer garden, lots of books and some very fine ales.

££ **The Smithfield**, Meadow Rd, Derby, T01332-370429. On the banks of the Derwent, next to the old cattle market, another pub with about 10 different real ales on offer.

££ **Ye Olde Dolphin**, 6 Queen St, Derby, T01332-267711. A beamed 16th-century pub within walking distance of the cathedral, serving reasonable pub grub.

£ **Ye Olde Vaults**, 21 Market Pl, Ashbourne, T01335-346127. Another rambling, popular old pub right at the bottom of the market square with good value square meals.

Pubs and bars

Nottingham *p524, map p526*

Bluu, 5 Broadway, T0115-9505359. Modern British cuisine in a separate restaurant (booking advisable), at this happening bar run by the same people as the club in London's superhip Hoxton Sq, with a downstairs lounge bar licensed until 0200 on Fri, Sat.

For an explanation of the sleeping and eating price codes used in this guide, see the inside front cover. Other relevant information is provided in the Essentials chapter, page 40.

Brownes Bar and Kitchen, 17-19 Goose Gate, Hockley, T0115-9580188. Another very large, very cool bar with interesting tapas type food in the evenings.
The I Bar, 36 Carlton St, Hockley, T0115-9555150. Smart designer bar with a couple of large bars, lots of designer cocktails and very popular with the pre-club warm-up crowd.
Lizzard Lounge, 41-43 St Mary's Gate, Lace Market, T0115-9523264. Still a very 'trendy' spot, a 3-floor bar with Thai restaurant attached and relatively laid-back, assorted crowd. It's late license means it gets busy mid-evening and entry is charged at weekends.
The Loft, 217 Mansfield Rd, T0115-9240213. Back-to-basics decor that pulls in the city's ambitious musos who appreciate its designer touches: innovative lighting and muted colour scheme. Burgers and chips, Thai and Indian platters and specials of the day.
Market Bar, 16-22 Goose Gate, T0115-9599777. Very popular with the more happening section of the city's student population, the Market Bar is also one of its most girl-friendly joints.
Old Angel, 7 Stoney St, Lace Market, T0115-9502303. Straightforward grub in a decent pub with music to the fore downstairs and a small late-licensed live music (local bands) or DJ venue upstairs (entrance charge).
Pitcher and Piano, High Pavement, Lace Market T0115 9586081. A chain-bar but quite out of the ordinary, established in the late 90s in a converted Unitarian church. Fine setting for some utterly secular drinking and a 'world menu' served until 2130.
The Social, 23 Pelham St, T0115-9505078. Relative newcomer to the latenight music scene, this offshoot of London's Portland St outfit is a harder-drinking DJ-driven club-bar with a late licence and bags of attitude.
Synergy Bar, Broad St, Hockley, T0115-9241555. Ignore the name and enjoy one of the city's more sophisticated operations, with decidedly superior cocktails (served to your table in the lounge upstairs at weekends).
Wax Bar, 27 Broad St, Hockley, T0115-9590007. Small music bar (also serving baguettes and omelettes), open until midnight most nights and until 0100 on Fri, Sat.
Ye Olde Trip to Jerusalem, Castle Rd, T0115-9473171. Reputedly the oldest pub in Britain, where the Crusaders gathered before setting off to bash up the infidels. Today it's a quiet, interesting place, gouged out of the rock beneath the castle.

Clubs

As well as many of the bars listed above, where flyers abound, possible options include:
Arriba Club, 28 St Jame's St, T0115-9227832, for mainstream dance sounds every night of the week until 0200.
Bar None, Stoney St, Lace Market, has resident DJs playing funk until 0200.
Media, the Elite Building, Queen St, T0115-9101101. On the button DJs until 0200 on Fri and Sat.

Entertainment

Nottingham *p524, map p526*

Cinema

Broadway Cinema, 14-18 Broad St, T0115-9526611, www.broadway.org.uk. Mainstream arthouse releases.
Screen Room 'The World's Smallest Cinema', 25b Broad St, Hockley, T0115-9241133, www.screen room.co.uk. On corner of Old Lenton St, opposite Lord Robert's pub. Arthouse mainstream releases in rep with classics.
Warner Village Cinema 12-screens in The Cornerhouse, a large leisure and entertainment complex opposite the Theatre Royal and Royal Concert Hall.

Music

Nottingham Arena, National Ice Centre, Lower Parliament St T0870-1210123. Venue for big names on tour.
The Old Vic, Fletchergate, T0115-9509833. The place to hear Nottingham's up and coming indie bands.

Theatre

Nottingham Playhouse T0115-9153591. Contemporary drama and dance.
Sandfield Theatre, T0115-9526611, for experimental work.
Theatre Royal, T0115-5895555, for West End musicals, ballet and classical concerts.

Festivals

Nottingham *p524, map p526*
Now Festival, Nu Art from the Creative Edge, late Oct-early Nov. Box Office, Broadway, 14-18 Broad St, T0115-9526611. T0115-915 3581, www.nowthatswhaticallart.org.uk

Shopping

Nottingham *p524, map p526*
Apparently there are something like 1200 shops in Nottingham, including 6 department stores and 4 covered shopping malls. The largest of the latter is the Victoria Centre, home to **House of Fraser** and **Miss Selfridge**, along with the Broadmarsh Centre close to the station, where you'll find the likes of **Allders**, **Argos** and **Allsports**. Hockley, the area north of Carlton St, is where many of the city's specialist and independent retailers have set up shop, while King's Walk, a few steps west of the Victoria Centre is another place for boutiques and jewellers. South of the County Hall in Market Sq you'll find **Marks & Spencer** and the **Body Shop** amongst others.

Activities and tours

Nottingham *p524, map p526*

Art galleries

The 1851 Gallery, Waverley Building, Nottingham Trent University, Dryden St, T0115-8486131. The old art school, has exhibitions of contemporary art and performances.
Angel Row Gallery, Central Library Building, 3 Angel Row, T0115- 9152869. Innovative public space with interesting temporary exhibitions by contemporary artists.
The Bonington Gallery, Bonington Building, Nottingham Trent University, Dryden St, T0115-8486131, www.future-factory.org.
Djanogly Art Gallery, Lakeside Arts Centre, University of Nottingham, T0115-9513192, www.lakesidearts.org.uk Nottingham Unversity's art gallery, with changing exhibitions of contemporary art as well as displays from the university's collection.

Sports

Nottingham Forest Football Club, The City Ground, T0115-9824444, www.nottinghamforest.co.uk. Past their glory days in the Premiership but still in the First Division.
Nottingham Tennis Centre, University Boulevard, T0115-9150000.
National Ice Centre, Lower Parliament St, T0115-8533000, www.nottingham-arena.co.uk Home to the Nottingham Panthers Ice Hockey team, with 2 large rinks for skating on.
Nottinghamshire County Cricket Club, Trent Bridge, T0115-9823000, www.nottsccc.co.uk. 1 of the 6 Test Match venues, with Notts CCC playing Apr-Sep.
National Water Sports Centre, Holme Pierrepont, Adbolton La, Holme Pierrepont, T0115-9821212, www.nationalsportscentres.co.uk. 3 miles east of the city centre, in 250 acres of parkland.
Buggyland, T0115-982 4721. Waterskiing, canoeing, kayaking, white water rafting, windsurfing and powerboating.

Transport

Nottingham *p524, map p526*

Car

Chegwidden Brothers, 28 Abbey Road West, T0845-6032901; **Jaeban UK Ltd**, 50 Lower Parliament St, T0800-212636; **Pacer Vehicle Rental**, 601 Woodborough Rd, T0115-9693166.

Bicycle

Bunneys Bikes, 97 Carrington St, T0115-9472713.

Bus

Trent Buses, T01773- 712265, run the regular direct service to **Derby** (35 mins) from Victoria bus station. **National Express**, T08705-808080, run a direct service from Broad Marsh bus station 5 times per day direct to **Birmingham Digbeth** (1 hr 15 mins to 2 hrs 15 mins) and 7 times to **London Victoria** (3 hrs 25 mins). There is also a regular direct service to **Leicester** (45 mins) and a direct service to **Manchester** central coach station (3 hrs 10 mins) at 1115 and 1535.

Taxi

Phonacar, 22a Lower Parliament St, T0115-9112211; **Streamline Taxis**, 63 Derby

Rd, T0115-9242499; Yellow Cars, 8 Pavillion Building, Pavillion Rd, T0115-9818181.

Train

Central Trains, T0121-6541200, run the regular direct services to **Birmingham New Street** (1 hr 20 mins), **Derby** (25 mins) and the direct hourly service to **Manchester Oxford Road** (2 hrs). Midland Mainline, T08457-125678, run the frequent direct service to **Leicester** (35 mins) and the direct hourly service to **London St Pancras** (1 hr 45 mins).

Directory

Nottingham *p524, map p526*
Hospital Nottingham City Hospital, Hucknall Rd, T0115-9691169. **Internet** Chill Out, 33 Heathcoat St, T0115-9476323.
Police Nottingham Police HQ, Sherwood Lodge Arnold, T0115-9670999. Lincolnshire
Post office Nottingham Branch Office, Queen St, T0845- 7223344.

Lincolnshire

→ *Colour map 5, grid B1-2*

Lincolnshire is a large and not very densely populated county which advertises itself as the 'drier side of Britain'. There's some truth in that strapline, as regards both the prevailing weather and sense of humour. Biting winds whipping in from the North Sea can make even the sunniest days a trial in the east of the county. Lincoln itself sits on an escarpment in the west, its cathedral one of the most stunning examples of Gothic architecture in the land. Otherwise, like much of its county, this ancient city's atmosphere is reserved, old-fashioned even, some might say quietly desperate. To the east, the Lincolnshire Wolds are a surprising belt of chalky downland concealing a variety of little villages and dropping down to a gem of a market town at Louth. Along with Lincoln, Louth deserves to be much better known, for its neat Georgian town centre and fabulous church spire, but is quite content to slumber on in obscurity. Bypassed by the main roads north-south, Lincolnshire doesn't attract hordes of visitors, although some do stop off on the Norwich-York trail. ▸▸ *For Sleeping, Eating and other listings, see pages 543-546.*

Lincoln

Lincoln deserves to be seen, rising up out of the surrounding flatlands, its medieval cathedral and castle sitting high above the masses huddled down below. Even today the most polite parts of town remain 'up hill', comfortably close to those imposing Gothic and Norman edifices, while the majority of recognizable retail brands and their target populace sprawl around 'down hill'. Anyone arriving by public transport faces a stiff 20-minute climb up the well-named Steep Hill to reach the main event, which is undoubtedly the cathedral. It rewards the effort with its superb west front and thoroughly awe-inspiring interior. A stone's throw away on the top of the same hill, the castle is now much less impressive than it must have been once but does command wide, sweeping views. Between the two nestles a rambling array of half-timbered and stonebuilt 16th- and 17th-century houses, along with a few stately Georgian houses.

Ins and outs

Getting there Much better connected by **train**, with at least one **GNER** train an hour departing London King's Cross (2-3 hours depending on connection) with a change at Peterborough or Newark. Lincoln is 20 miles east of the A1, which is the most direct approach from the North or London, some 200 miles away and taking 3½ hours to reach. **National Express** run an 1600 coach to Lincoln from London Victoria, and a morning (0755) return one, each taking just over 4 hours. ▸▸ *See Transport, page 545, for more details.*

Getting around From the train station over the hill to Bailgate is a 30-min walk. Most of the centre of Lincoln is pedestrianized. Local bus services, run by County Council, T0870-6082608.

Information Lincoln TIC ⓘ *9 Castle Hill, T01522-873213, also at Cornhill, T01522-873256.* £4 accommodation booking fee. Also arrange walking tours of the up hill area of town for £2.50.

History

The Romans occupied the British settlement on the site of modern Lincoln in about AD 47. For some time this was the northernmost frontier of their empire, and later it became an important garrison town called Lindum Colonia. One of its gates, the Newport Arch in Bailgate, the centre of the Roman town, still survives (much restored) today, the only Roman archway in use by traffic in the country. Come the Normans, Lincoln was already the fourth most prosperous city of the kingdom after London, York and Norwich, with its own mint for making coins. Only two years after conquest, William ordered the construction of the castle, much of which still stands, on the site of the Roman fortifications. The cathedral was constructed in the shape still recognizable today during the early 13th century under a Bishop who was head of a diocese which stretched from the Humber to the Thames. Wool brought great riches, and Lincoln Green became the serge favoured by Robin Hood and other outlaws. With the decline of the wool trade, the city's star waned and for much of the 18th and early 19th centuries it was little more than the social centre of an impoverished agricultural hinterland. The population of Lincoln doubled between 1801 and 1851, less than in many Midland towns, but the railway arrived in 1846. By the mid-20th century Lincoln had become famous for its heavy engineering, building cars, lorries and tanks. Its economy now rests largely on tourism, agriculture and local administration.

Sights

Best approached by car from the north along Ermine Street, the Roman road that is now the A15, Lincoln Hill and its cathedral towers can be seen a good 15 miles off and you will probably want to head straight up hill to this medieval wonder. If arriving by train or bus, this involves slogging up the High Street first. Close to the station, at the bottom of the street, the church of **St Mary-le- Wigford** has a crumbling Saxon tower. Heading north, the wide ugly street passes over **High Bridge**, crossing the tiny River Witham, home to a formidable flotilla of lovely swans. One of the last bridges in the country still bearing its 16th-century house, it's now the venerable *Stokes of Lincoln*, a very good value coffee shop and restaurant established since the building's restoration in 1902. Steps down the side of the building allow a glimpse of the original bridge of 1160, and a walk leads west from here to the redeveloped **Brayford Waterfront** and marina with its new restaurants and boat hire.

Pressing on up the High Street, the **Stonebow** is the very fine 15th-century town gate, still in use as the Guildhall and the centre of the 'down hill' part of Lincoln. A right turn here leads down Saltergate to the **Greyfriars Exhibition Centre** ⓘ *T01522-530401, Tue-Sat 1000-1300, 1400-1600, free*, on Broadgate. A variety of themed exhibitions culled from the county's archaeological and historical archives are mounted here in a 13th-century building, the oldest Franciscan church in the country.A left turn northwards up Broadgate arrives after a couple of hundred yards outside the **Usher Gallery** ⓘ *Lindum Rd, T01522- 527980, Tue-Sat 1000-1730, Sun 1430-1700, £2, concessions and under-16s 50p*, the home of the county's impressive art collection, which includes several paintings by local Victorian stars William Logsdail and Frank Bramley amongst other, and of the city and surroundings by the likes of Turner, Lowry and Piper. Pride of place goes to Peter de Wint's remarkable watercolours.

Back at the Stonebow, the High Street continues uphill, narrowing through the Strait where it becomes Steep Hill and the going gets tougher. On the left **Jews Court** is a medieval merchant's house now home to the Lincolnshire History and Archaeology Society, with an intriguing bookshop specializing in the county's topography and a smart restaurant in the **Jews House** next door, a building which dates from the late 12th century. From here it's a couple of hundred yards up past interesting small shops, pubs and restaurants to Castle Hill. A right turn heads through the 14th-century **Exchequer Gate** to the cathedral, a left turn leads to the castle.

The Cathedral and around

Walking through the Exchequer Gate to be confronted by the massive West Front of **Lincoln Cathedral** ① *T01522-544544, www.lincolncathedral.com, Apr-Oct daily 0800-2000, Nov-Mar daily 0800-1800, £3.50, concessions £3,* is Lincoln's most impressive coup de théâtre. An earthquake in 1185 destroyed much of the church begun in 1072 but its rounded Romanesque arches remain here, incorporated into the mighty west front dramatically redeveloped in the 13th-century Early English style. The recently restored frieze, inspired by the cathedral at Modena, depicts scenes from the Old Testament on the south side and the New Testament on the north. The magnificent open nave and choirs behind demand at least an hour to explore thoroughly, soaking up the spirit of 900 years of worship. First stop on the tourist trail is the sturdy late-Norman **font**, made from black Tournai marble in the 12th century, on the south side of the broad nave with its carved columns of local limestone and Purbeck marble. On reaching the crossing, or Great Transept, beneath the central tower and its five-ton bell, 'Great Tom', the **Dean's Eye** is on the left and the **Bishop's Eye** on the right. These two beautiful stained-glass rose windows are another glorious effort, the former Early English (about 1230) and the latter Decorated (about a century younger). Straight ahead is the most ancient part of the Gothic cathedral, **St Hugh's Choir**, with its canopied choir stalls. Beyond this is the cathedral's pièce de résistance and its most holy place, the **Angel Choir**. An exquisitely carved angelic host looks down on the shrine of St Hugh, the Bishop responsible for the Early English reconstruction of the cathedral. Everyone looks for the **Lincoln Imp** here, a Puckish figure on the north side that was adopted as the city's logo in the late 19th century. To the north of the choirs, the peaceful cloisters lead into the 10-sided **Chapter House**, scene of one of the first English parliaments, called by Edward I in 1301. Above the cloister, the library is also well worth a look, remodelled by Wren in 1647.

Just to the south, by English Heritage, the **Medieval Bishop's Palace** ① *Minster Yard, T01522-527468, Apr-Sep daily 1000-1800, Oct daily 1000-1700, Nov-Mar Wed-Sun 1000-1600, £3.20, concessions £2.40, under-16s £1.60*, is a little-known treasure in the shadow of the cathedral. The romantic medieval ruins, include an impressive vaulted undercroft and kitchen, set in gardens with views over the city. Various special events are held here including summer productions by the Lincoln Shakespeare Company.

Across Castle Hill, past the TIC, **Lincoln Castle** ① *T01522-511068, Mon-Sat 0930-1730, Sun 1100-1730 (Nov-Mar daily until 1600), £2.50, under-16s £1, concessions £1.50, family £6.50*, unusually constructed like Lewes Castle with two mottes, is also worth exploring, especially for its views over town and a look at the disturbing Victorian prison chapel, with pews that are literally 'boxed', designed to prevent prisoners fraternizing. Also on display is one of the surviving copies of Magna Carta.

Behind the Castle, **The Lawn** ① *Union Rd, T01522-873629, Easter-Sep Mon-Thu 1000-1700, Fri 1000-1630, Sat, Sun 1000-1700, Oct-Easter Mon-Fri 1000-1630, Sat, Sun 1000-1630, free*, is an imposing former mental hospital converted into a visitor centre and conference venue. Attractions include the Sir Joseph Banks Conservatory with tropical plants, butterflies and fish, the Lincoln Archaeology Centre; and large gardens with an adventure playground and picnic tables. Pub, restaurant, coffee shop, gift shop and other specialist shops including a fudge shop, with a range of special events throughout the year.

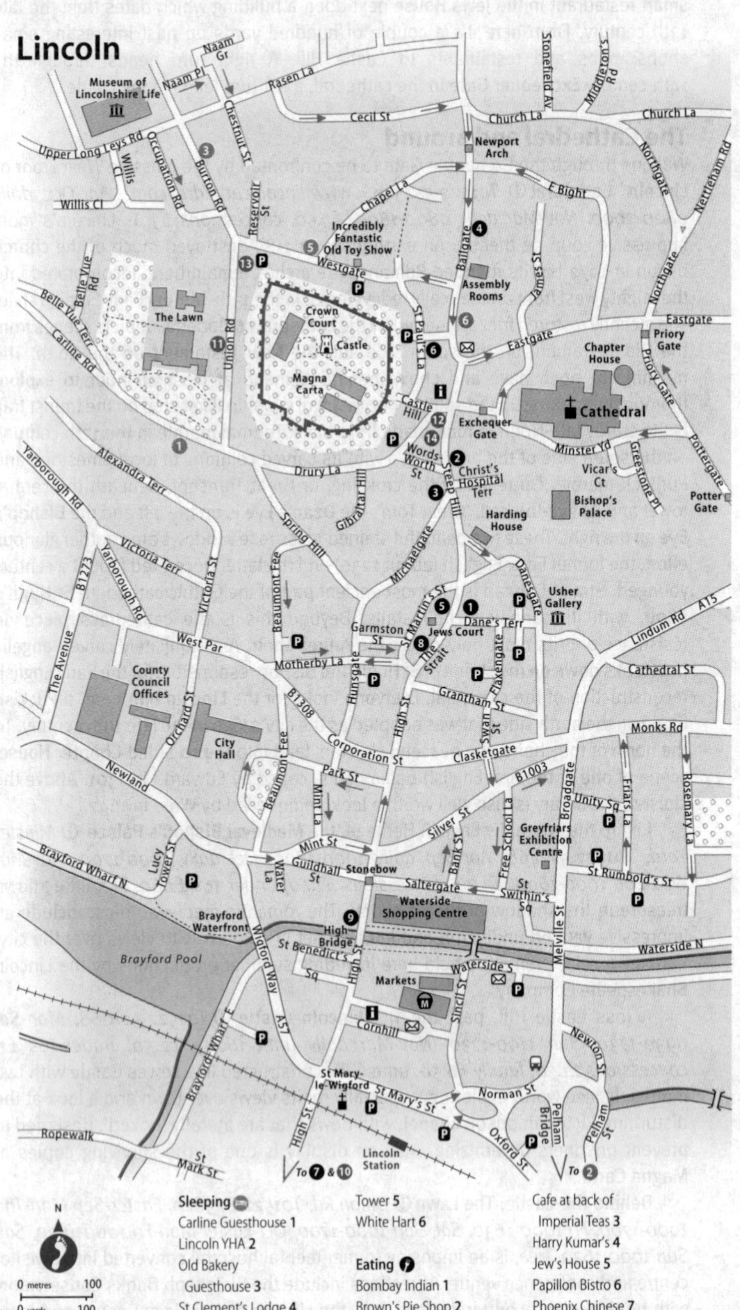

Sleeping
Carline Guesthouse 1
Lincoln YHA 2
Old Bakery Guesthouse 3
St Clement's Lodge 4
Tower 5
White Hart 6

Eating
Bombay Indian 1
Brown's Pie Shop 2
Cafe at back of Imperial Teas 3
Harry Kumar's 4
Jew's House 5
Papillon Bistro 6
Phoenix Chinese 7

East of the Westgate, the **Bailgate** is a particularly attractive old street, lined with independent shops and leading up to the **Newport Arch** out of the city. This much restored Roman gateway features a smaller entrance to one side, an 'Eye of the Needle' of the type mentioned in the Bible with reference to camels and rich men.

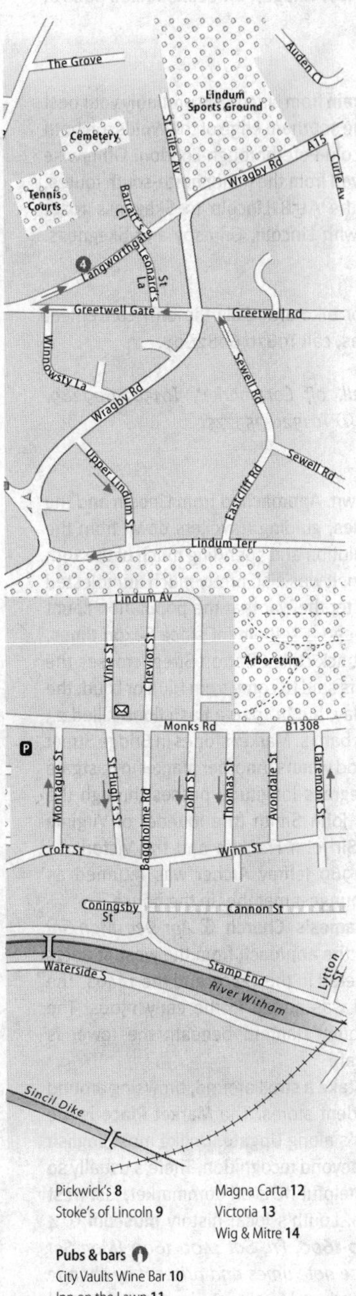

West of the Bailgate, on Burton Road, the **Museum of Lincolnshire Life** ⓘ *T01522-528448, May-Sep daily 1000-1730, Nov-Apr Mon-Sat 1000-1730, Sun 1400-1730, £2, under-16s 60p, family £4.50*, is the county's social history museum housed in the old barracks of the Royal Lincolnshire Regiment, with a recently refurbished museum on the subject. A wide variety of displays include the interiors of Victorian shops and workshops, chemists, co-operative store, and a wheelwrights. Also tractors, steam engines and the oldest First World War tank to survive are displayed, with occasional steam days. A great place for a rainy afternoon, suitable for all ages. Gift shop, tearoom, toilets.

Gainsborough

Gainsborough, 20 miles northwest of Lincoln, is a fairly unprepossessing market town, but it does boast one unmissable sight, the **Gainsborough Old Hall** ⓘ *Parnell St, T01427-612669, www.lincolnshire.gov.uk, Mon-Sat 1000-1700, Sun 1400-1700*. Built by the wool-rich merchant Sir Thomas Burgh in about 1460, this medieval manor house is now completely hemmed in by the town, but it once stood at the centre of a large rural estate. The exterior is remarkably little altered since the 15th century, highlights of the interior being the magnificent Hall, with its splendid oak-beamed roof, and the massive kitchen. The audio tour, and regular period costume events, help to bring the place alive.

The Wolds and around

Despite its reputation for being flat, boring farming country, Lincolnshire does have some pretty countryside. Marketed as 'Poacher Country', and designated an Area of Outstanding Natural Beauty, the Lincolnshire Wolds stretch from the Humber Bridge to Spilsby, a low rolling ridge of chalk upland between Lincoln and the east coast. Louth is the unofficial capital of the area, a picture of a place that resolutely resists the blandishments of 21st-century commercialism. Cycling and walking are a good way to enjoy this stretch of the country, seeking out remarkable old churches, lost villages, unreconstructed pubs or even former second world war airbases.

Ins and outs

Getting there Market Rasen, 20 minutes by **train** from Lincoln, is probably your best bet for Louth. Sleaford is useful for accessing the southern edge of the Wolds, on both the Nottingham-Skegness line as well as Lincoln-Peterborough-London. Otherwise the area is not well served by trains. Well removed from the major north-south routes, the Wolds can most easily be reached off the A158 Lincoln to Skegness **road**. **Stagecoach** run services that connect Louth with Lincoln, Grimsby and Skegness. **Traveline,** T0870-6082608.

Getting around Apart from **walking**, a **car** or **bike** are really the only convenient ways of exploring the Wolds. **TransLinc Services,** call T0870 6082608.

Information Louth TIC ⓘ *New Market Hall, off Cornmarket, T01507-609289, www.poachercountry.co.uk.* **Woodhall Spa TIC** ⓘ *T01526-353775.*

Louth

Louth is a delightful little red-brick Georgian town. Approached from Lincoln and the west, the spire of St James's is visible for miles, guiding travellers down from the Wolds. Almost bypassed by the Industrial Revolution and spending much of the 19th century in the grip of the agricultural depression, it was also pretty much unmolested by the Second World War. In fact it was only after the war that the population count rose again to its 1820s level. The place has been a settlement since Saxon times, sitting at the foot of the Wolds where the old track called Barton Street crosses the River Lud flowing into Middle Marsh. The name is said to come from Hlud or Loud, the river that is, which may seem calm enough today, but in 1920 a flash flood killed 23 people and destroyed all the buildings along its banks. Marker stones in Bridge Street and James Street still show the height of the flood waters. Another marker in Eastgate shows where the Greenwich Meridian of 0 degrees longitude passes through the town. Famous sons of Louth include Captain John Smith (the founder of Virginia rescued by Pocahontas), the Arctic explorer Sir John Franklin and the Victorian's favourite Poet Laureate, Lord Tennyson. In 1969 Jeffrey Archer was returned as Conservative MP for the town, becoming the youngest member in the house.

Louth's most prominent landmark, **St James's Church** ⓘ *Apr-Dec Mon-Sat 1030-1600, Sun afternoons in Aug*, dominates the approach from the west. It dates from the 12th century but was substantially altered in the 1240s and the 1440s. The 295-ft spire (the tallest of any parish church) was added in the early 1500s. The interior is more modest, although the 'starburst' lantern beneath the tower is spectacular. It hovers over a serviceable little café

The best way to enjoy the town is simply to take a stroll around, browsing around the unusually large number of small independent stores. The **Market Place** is the centre of town, about 100 yds east of St James's along Upgate. Unlike most English towns, the centre has yet to be pedestrianized beyond recognition. There's usually so little traffic that it hardly seems necessary. The helpful TIC is off Cornmarket, just west of the Market Place. A few steps to the north, Louth's local history **museum** ⓘ *4 Broadbank, T01507-601211, Apr-Oct Wed 1000-1600, Fri, Sat 1400-1600 (Mon-Sat 1000-1600 in Aug), £1, concessions 50p (please note times and prices may change after refurbishment in 2004),* is a little gem, and undergoing major extension and refurbishment designed to capitalize on the presentation of the *Louth Panorama*, a replica of an extraordinary early 19th-century painting by William Brown capturing a bird's eye perspective of a day in the life of the town during the 1840s.

The Wolds

West of Louth, nearer Lincoln, small villages like Tealby, Donington-on-Bain and especially Nettleton are worth seeking out for walks in the hills around. Dry valleys, glacial tills (large 'erratic boulders' that may have been carried from as far away as Norway by the last Ice Age), and fossils are some of the things to look out for. Many of the most attractive parts of the Wolds can most easily be explored along the **Viking**

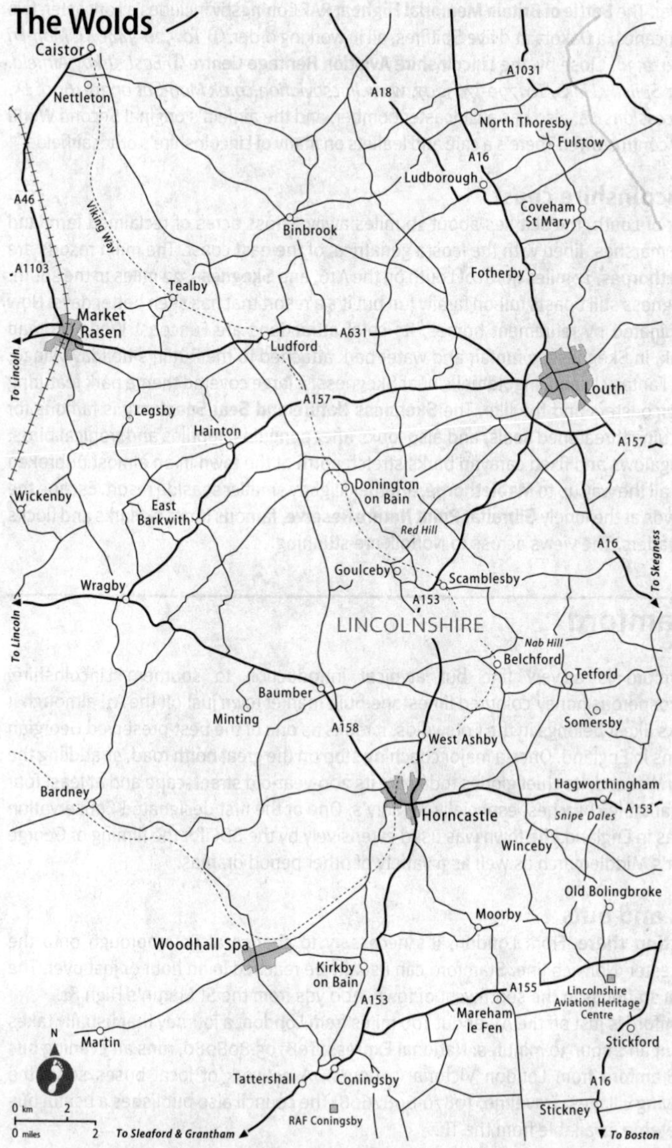

 Way, a long-distance footpath that runs for 116 miles from the Humber Bridge to Oakham, in Rutland. From Donington, with its mill, weir and ruined manor, and Nettleton, with its relatively dramatic scenery, and also Belchford, are particularly good starting points. Belchford lies near the **Bluestone Heath Road**, a prehistoric ridgeway, with fine views from **Nab Hill** nearby. Near Donington, **Red Hill** also gives superb views over Lincolnshire. Further south, Somersby was the childhood home of Tennyson: his father was the vicar at Bag Enderby and the terraces of Harrington Hall (private) are supposed to have inspired his lines "Come into the garden, Maud". The area around Somersby also makes for rewarding exploratory rambles, with its shaded lanes and crumbling churches.

At the southern extremity of the Wolds, fans of military aviation history are in clover. The **Battle of Britain Memorial Flight** at RAF Coningsby includes a Lancaster, two Hurricanes, a Dakota and five Spitfires, all in working order. ⓘ *T01526-344041. Mon-Fri 1000-1530*. Close by, the **Lincolnshire Aviation Heritage Centre** ⓘ *East Kirkby Airfield, near Spilsby Links, T01790- 763207, www.lincsaviation.co.uk Mon-Sat 0930-1600. £5, concessions £4*, also has a Lancaster bomber, and the airfield's original Second World War control tower. There's a café and leaflets on many of Lincolnshire's other airfields.

Lincolnshire coast

East of Louth, the sea lies about 10 miles away across acres of reclaimed farmland and marshes, lined with the 'costa geriatrica' of the east coast. The main resorts are **Cleethorpes**, 17 miles north of Louth on the A16, and **Skegness**, 22 miles to the south. Skegness still boasts full-on family fun but it's a resort that has seen better days. Now dominated by retirement homes, its chief attractions are Funcoast World, Roman Bank, in Skegness; a funfair and water park attached to the Butlin's holiday village; and Fantasy Island, Ingoldmells near Skegness, a large covered theme park featuring rollercoasters and the like. The **Skegness Natureland Seal Sanctuary** is famous for rescuing threatened seals, and also looks after penguins, reptiles and tropical birds. Bungalows and fixed caravan parks stretch north of the town in an almost unbroken line all the way up to **Mablethorpe**, another slightly smaller seaside resort. Escape the crowds at the lonely **Gibraltar Point Nature Reserve**, famous for its skylarks and flocks of waders. The views across to Norfolk are stunning.

Stamford

Stamford is a very fine but atypical introduction to southern Lincolnshire. A prosperous honey-coloured limestone-built market town just off the A1, although it looks like it belongs in the Cotswolds, it ranks as one of the best-preserved Georgian towns in England. Once a major coaching stop on the great north road, straddling the river Welland, its chief glories today are its 200-year-old streetscape and at least four remarkable churches, especially St Mary's. One of the first designated Conservation Areas in England, the town was used extensively by the BBC for the filming of George Eliot's Middlemarch as well as a variety of other period dramas.

Ins and outs

Getting there From London, it's necessary to change at Peterborough onto the Leicester- Norwich line. Stamford can usually be reached in an hour or just over. The **train** station is in the southwest of town, 200 yds from the St Martin's High St.
Stamford is just off the A1, about 100 miles from London, a journey that usually takes about an 1 hour 30 minutes. **National Express**, T08705-808080, runs an evening **bus** to Stamford from London Victoria (3 hours). A network of local buses serve the outlying villages. **Traveline**, T0870-6082608. The council also publishes a useful bus timetable, available from the TIC.

Stamford is best approached from the south, up St Martin's High Street, a street still recognizable as the one painted by JMW Turner in the 19th century. On the right, before the old stone bridge over the Welland, **St Martin's church** contains some fine late-medieval stained glass and the tomb of Queen Elizabeth's Treasurer, Cecil. Daniel Lambert (see below), the 53-stone man who died in 1809, takes up his fair share of space in the graveyard. Up the hill and over the bridge stands St Mary's, its magnificent early Gothic tower and broach spire one of the town's most prominent landmarks. Inside, all is perpendicular: look out for the embossed roof of the north chapel, and wonder at the High Church Arts and Crafts woodwork.

A right turn at the top of the hill by St Mary's leads past the TIC in the Arts Centre into **St George's Square**, an atmospheric quiet old square that was used as the scene of the hustings in *Middlemarch*. **St George's church**, at its eastern end, contains heraldic stained glass depicting the arms and mottoes of the 200 original Knights of the Garter, a collection granted in a bequest of Sir William de Bruges in 1449.

From here Maiden Lane heads another hundred yards north to the parquet-paved pedestrianized High Street, emerging opposite the grand neo classical portico of the Public Library. Behind is **Stamford Museum** ⓘ *Broad St, T01780-766317, Mon-Sat 1000-1700 (also Sun 1400-1700 Apr-Sep),* the former home of Daniel Lambert, so hugely overweight they needed to knock the house down to get him out when he died. The small museum, accessed from Broad Street, contains a life-size replica of the man, displays on the history of the town and a collection of Stamford Ware, locally thrown pottery.

A left turn on Broad Street from the museum leads past **Browne's Hospital**, an impressive late-15th-century almshouse, part of which is now a pub. Continuing westwards downhill, **All Saints church** is also worth a look for its early Gothic architecture and the collection of brasses commemorating the wool-rich Browne family.

Outside Stamford

One of the finest houses of the early Elizabethan period, grander than Longleat, **Burghley House** ⓘ *T01780-752451, www.burghley.co.uk, Apr-Oct daily 1100-1700 (last admission 1630), House by guided tour only, except weekends and bank holidays £7.10, concessions £6.50, under-16s £3.50 (1 free with each adult),* can be seen a mile to the east of Stamford, thoroughly well signposted. Designed by Cecil, Elizabeth's Lord High Treasurer from 1565 to 1587, the place is still inhabited by his descendants. It includes 18 state rooms, one of the most important private collections of 17th-century Italian painting in the UK, as well as priceless Japanese ceramics. Antonio Verrio's *Heaven Room* is an extraordinary trompe l'oeil masterpiece, decorated with scenes from ancient mythology, another highlight being the Hell Staircase. The Gardens are also extraordinary.

Sleeping

Lincoln *p535, map p538*

A The White Hart, Bailgate, T0870-4008117. Pretty much top of the range in Lincoln, a perfectly acceptable offering from the Macdonald chain of hotels in the thick of things on the Bailgate. The feature rooms are worth the extra spend, but service is rumoured to be a bit slack.

C Carline Guesthouse, 1-3 Carline Rd, T01522-530422. Well-respected B&B just at the bottom of the hill, clean, comfortable and quiet.

C The Tower Hotel, 38 Westgate, T01522-529999, F560596. Close to the castle walls, with quiet, comfortable but plain rooms.

D Old Bakery Guesthouse, 26-28 Burton Rd, T01522-576057. Has comfortable bedrooms close to the castle.

D St Clement's Lodge, 21 Langworth Gate, T01522-521532. Close to the cathedral, a B&B with a pleasant family atmosphere.

F Lincoln YHA, 77 South Park, T01522-522076. On the outskirts of town to the south of the train station.

Louth *p540*

A **Kenwick Park**, near Louth, T01507-608806, www.kenwick-park.co.uk. Part of the Classic British Hotels chain, and the high-end option in the area, with a golf course and oddly corporate atmosphere for such a charming setting.

B **The Beaumont**, 66 Victoria Rd, T01507-605005, F607768. A better bet, on the edge of Louth itself, a hotel 'with an Italian twist', comfortable rooms and friendly staff.

D **Mason's Arms**, Cornmarket, Louth, T01507-609525. A couple of reasonable double rooms bang in the middle of town, and a jolly pub doing decent enough food downstairs.

Stamford *p542*

A **George Hotel**, 71 St. Martins High St, T01780-750750, www.georgehotelofstamford.com. In a very grand old building, a former coaching inn, with a monastic garden and widely acclaimed restaurant and brasserie serving English and Italian food in comfortable, elegant surroundings. The good service and friendly atmosphere make this a popular choice.

B **Garden House Hotel**, St Martin's High St, T01780-763359, www. gardenhousehotel.com. An 18th-century townhouse, true to its name with an attractive garden and about 100 yds up from St Martin's church, with 20 rooms with en suite bath.

C **Stamford Lodge Guesthouse**, 24 Scotgate, T01780-482932, www. stamfordlodge.co.uk. A fairly small, quiet but also very central guesthouse with 7 double rooms en suite.

The Willoughby Arms, Station Rd, Little Bytham, near Stamford, T01780-410276, www.willoughbyarms.co.uk Has its own microbrewery and a variety of guest ales as well as small but comfortable rooms.

The Wolds *p539, map p541*

A **Petwood Hotel**, Stixwould Rd, Woodhall Spa, T01526-352411, www.petwood.co.uk. A fairly smart hotel (3-star) in what was once the Officer's Mess of the Dambusters squadron.

D **The Grange**, Torrington La, East Barkwith, near Market Rasen, T01673-858670. A Georgian farmhouse B&B, very warm and welcoming with large rooms and a lawn tennis court.

F **YHA Woody's Top**, Ruckland, near Louth, T0870-7706098. Extended and modernized former farm buildings with 20 beds in 2,4, or 6-bedded rooms, 6 miles south of Louth.

Eating

Lincoln *p535, map p538*

£££ Harry Kumar's, 80 Bailgate, T01522-537000. Reasonably priced food all day in a relaxed, bistro kind of atmosphere.

£££ Jew's House Restaurant, 15 The Strait, T01522-524851. A smart modern European restaurant in a 12th-century building: white tablecloths, high-backed chairs, competent cuisine.

£££ Papillon Bistro, St Paul's La , off Westgate, T01522-511284. A friendly informal bistro serving a wide-ranging French menu (on blackboards) including lots of fish and vegetarian options, super wine list. Nearly always busy.

££ Bombay Indian Restaurant, 6 The Strait, T01522-523264. Classic dishes in this recently redecorated restaurant, speedy service, usually quiet until 2200. Very tasty food.

££ Brown's Pie Shop, 33 Steep Hill, T01522-527330. An informal restaurant with rugged wooden furniture serving a wide range of dishes as well as its famous pies. Large portions, cheap wine and friendly service. Good value Sunday lunches.

££ Garmstons, 262 High St. Appealing café with wide range of wholesome food and tempting cakes. Sandwiches made to order, jacket potatoes, soup, salads and daily specials. Order and pay at counter before finding a table. Popular with locals.

££ Phoenix Chinese Restaurant, Newark Rd end of High St, T01522- 527682. Large popular Chinese restaurant in downhill Lincoln. Large menu, set meals are good value, buzzing atmosphere.

££ Pickwick's, 14 The Strait, T01522-545991. A splendidly old-fashioned sort of restaurant, unashamedly serving up platefuls of liver and bacon at remakarbly low prices.

£ Stoke's of Lincoln, High Gate, T01522-512534. A 2-course lunch for £3.50 and a commendable array of teas and coffees to boot in a wonderful old place at the bottom of the hill.

£ Imperial Teas Café, Steep Hill, T01522-560008. Small café aimed particularly at vegetarian and vegan customers. Quality tea and coffee.

Stamford *p542*

There's no shortage of reasonable places to eat in Stamford. Most of the pubs in town do food, while the top end of the market is catered for by the *George Hotel*.

££ Bombay Cottage Indian Tandoori, 52 Scotgate, T01780-480138, is a popular locals' choice.

££ Loch Fyne Seafood Restaurant, All Saints Pl, T01780-761370.

££ Pizza Express, 1 High St, T01780-767902.

££ The Warehouse Restaurant, 9a North St, T01780-762868, specializes in Spanish and Mexican food.

The Wolds *p539, map p541*

£ The King's Head, Tealby, T01673-838347. A thatched pub in a pretty setting beside the river in this attractive Wolds village, with reasonable food.

£ Tealby Tearooms, T01673-838261. Do a brisk trade in home-made lunches, toast and tea.

Pubs, bars and clubs

Lincoln *p535, map p538*

City Vaults Wine Bar, High St, T01522-521035. Lots of wines by the glass as well as the usual beers. Friendly, useful stopping off point on the way into town from the south.

The Inn on the Lawn, Union Rd. Quite smart with French windows overlooking Castle. Useful if The Victoria is full.

The Magna Carta, Castle Sq. Friendly atmosphere, good location, popular with all ages. Can be very busy at weekends but usually quiet at other times. Well-placed for uphill restaurants.

The Victoria, Union Rd. Real ale pub with wide range of guest beers and ciders. Very small and popular.

Wig and Mitre, 30/32 Steep Hill. A famous and comfortable old pub with a well-rated menu.

Entertainment

Lincoln *p535, map p538*

Theatre

Theatre Royal, Clasketgate, T01522-525555, Hosts a wide variety of shows, from pantomime to opera. Small and friendly, with reasonable ticket prices. Lincoln's only permanent theatre .

Lincoln Shakespeare Company, T01522-528294, performs in various venues, including the Bishop's Palace, the Cathedral and The Lawn, with 3 plays a year. Worth seeking out.

Louth *p540*

Cinema

Kinema in the Woods, Woodhall Spa, T01526-352166. A strange old-fashioned little place, where the films are still back-projected.

Playhouse Cinema, Louth, T01507- 603333. Offers 3 screen mainstream new releases.

Shopping

Lincoln *p535, map p538*

Brown's Pie Shop, 33 Steep Hill, 5217330.

Elite Meats, 89 Bailgate, T01522-523500. Butchers selling wide range of game, free range meat and unusual items like ostrich.

Goodie's, 5 The Strait, T01522-523307. Traditional sweet shop.

Reader's Rest, 13-14, Steep Hill, T01522-543217. A large secondhand bookshop, great for browsing in, open Sun.

Whisky Shop, 87 Bailgate, T01522-537834. All kinds of whisky and spirits.

Transport

Lincoln *p535, map p538*

Bus

Long distance National Express, T08705-808080, run a direct service to **London** King's Cross (4 hrs 45 mins) at 0735. Contact **Traveline**, T0870-6082608, for other direct services from Lincoln.

Car

Avis, Ermine Filling Station, Riseholme Rd, T01522-511200; **Thrifty**, Chieftain Way,Tritton Rd, T01522-568777.

Train

Central Trains, T0121-6541200, run the regular direct service to **Nottingham** (1 hr) and the regular services to **York** (1 hr 40 mins) changing at **Doncaster** (50 mins) and to **London** King's Cross (2 hrs 30 mins) changing at Newark. **Arriva Trains Northern**, T08706-023322, run the regular service to **Manchester** Piccadilly or Manchester Oxford Road (2 hrs 40 mins) changing at Sheffield (1 hr 20 mins).

Taxi

County Cars, 381b High St, T01522-567878; Handsome Cabs, 10 Clasketgate, T01522-545352.

Louth *p540*

Bicycle

DB Cycles, Ayscarth Farm, Legbourne Rd, Louth, T01507-603109.

Car

Practical Car and Van Rental, 186 Eastgate, Louth, T01507-604626; **Thurlby Motors (Rental)**, Tattershall Way Fairfield Ind Est, Louth, T01507-607070.

Taxi

Danny's & Co Ltd, 18a Queen St, Louth, T01507-609629; **Marsh Villages Taxi Services**, Golden Limes, Ludney, Louth, T01507-358663.

West Midlands

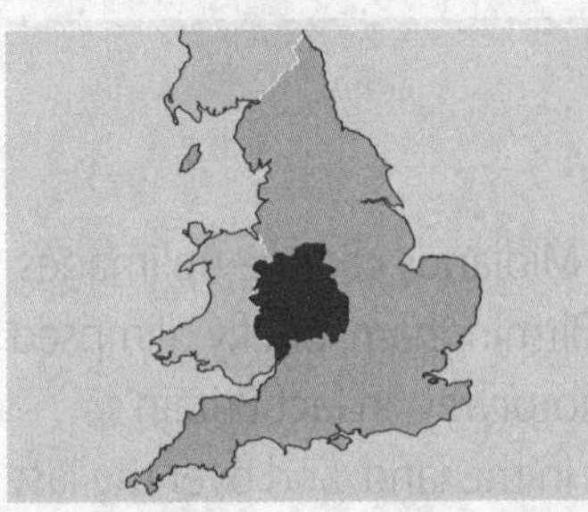

Footprint features

Introduction

For many British people the West Midlands conjure up images of an anonymous sprawl around Birmingham, briefly glimpsed to little advantage from the M6 motorway. In fact Britain's second city is one of the greenest in the land, and over the last couple of decades has transformed itself from industrial wasteland into a consumerist heaven. It also boasts the widest ethnic diversity of any city outside London, everyone enjoying a whole new type of cuisine known simply as the 'Balti'. On its outskirts, the New Art Gallery Walsall is the most exciting space for contemporary art to open since Tate Modern. Next door, Coventry was badly bombed during the Second World War, but is still a proper working city, with two Cathedrals, the modern commemorative one a masterpiece.

Its youth culture found a voice in some style during the 1970s and 80s with the two tone sound. It's a far cry from Kenilworth and Warwick close by, both dominated by their castles while Leamington Spa is the poor relation of Bath and Cheltenham. Just south, at Stratford-upon-Avon, the Bard is all around and theatrical performances of Shakespeare's plays reach new heights . To the west, Worcestershire nestles on the banks of the river Severn, embracing the picture-postcard Malvern Hills. Herefordshire welcomes in the river Wye from Wales, passing through delightful countryside from the home of old books at Hay-on-Wye, to dainty little Ross-on-Wye and the spooky Forest of Dean on its way to the Severn Estuary and the Bristol Channel. To the north, Shrewsbury is Shropshire's county town, the first in a string of attractive towns – Church Stretton, Ludlow, Bishops Castle – along the high border with Wales. From Shrewsbury, the Severn Valley skirts charming Much Wenlock before heading on to Worcester and Gloucester.

★ Don't miss...

1. Check out a gem of a fine art collection at the **Barber Institute** in Birmingham before heading into the Gas Street Basin for a cocktail, page 555.
2. Hire a canoe from Brockweir in the **Wye Valley** for a riverside view of Tintern Abbey or climb up into the Devil's Pulpit, page 587.
3. Stride across the **Malverns** trying to hum Elgar's Enigma variations as you go, page 580.
4. Taste some of the finest cuisine this side of the Welsh border in **Ludlow** after looking around its old castle, page 601.
5. Learn to paraglide from the **Long Mynd** near Church Stretton or walk up onto the hills for spectacular views, page 600.
6. Ask yourself in **Stratford-upon-Avon** whether Shakespeare knew he was going to be a household name in four hundred years' time, and then see what all the fuss has been about, page 561.

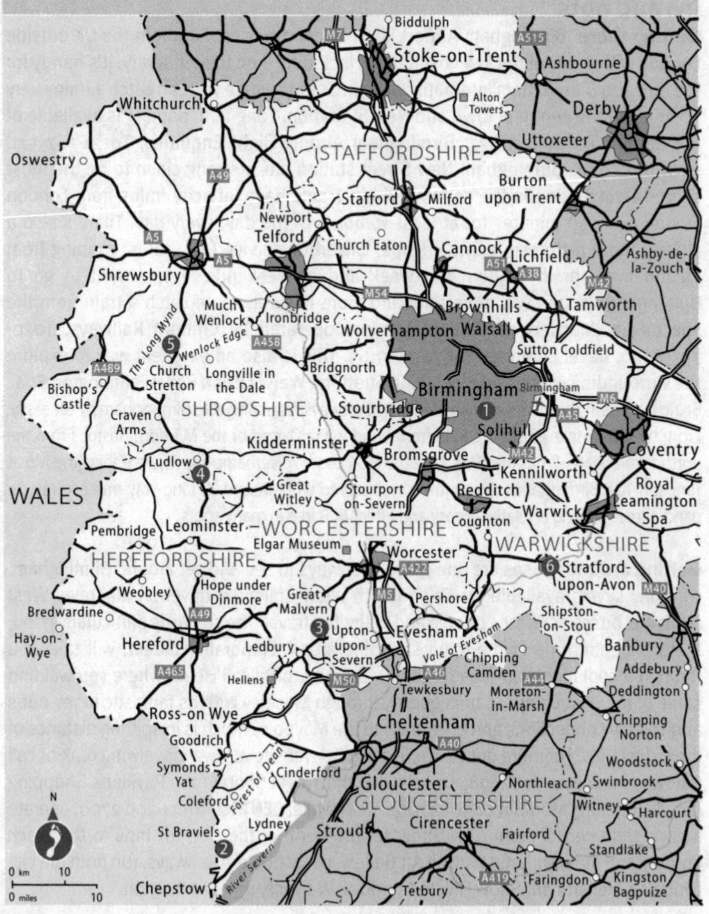

Birmingham

→ *Colour map 4, grid B3/4*

Perhaps because for too many years Birmingham has been the butt of many a comedian's joke about smoking chimneys and heavy metal music, people are surprised to learn that it is Britain's second city. It's easy to be snobbish about Birmingham – it's easy to be a Birmophobe or sniffy about where it gets the money to maintain such splendid facilities as Birmingham City Museum and Art Gallery and the Barber Institute, and many people are. But ironically, heavy metal in the form of iron, steel and particularly gold and silver has played a very important part in the town's development and still does. Birmingham, or Brummagem as it is colloquially known, is a world-famous jewellery quarter and as for the smoking chimneys, it's worth remembering that Birmingham has more trees than people, over a million. It's also probably Britain's most racially integrated city, with Chinese, Sikh, Moslem, Hindu, Irish, Jewish and Afro-Caribbean communities. Twenty four million visitors came to Birmingham in the year 2000 and since the 1970s when the mighty Spaghetti Junction made Brum synonymous with pollution, the city has really cleaned up its act, in more ways than one. » *For Sleeping, Eating and other listings, see pages 556-561.*

Ins and outs

Getting there **Birmingham Airport** is the second busiest airport in the UK outside London with many of the low-cost airlines including it on their itinerary. It's handy for the NEC and Birmingham International Train Station where you can catch a train every 30 mins for the centre of town and New St Station. Long-term parking is available at the airport, T0800-0137477. **Birmingham Airport Flight Enquiries,** T0121-7675511, www.bhx.co.uk. **Birmingham New Street** station has a strong claim to be the most central **train** station in the country. **Virgin Trains** have Intercity trains from London Euston every 30 minutes for at least 16 hours of the day, every day. There's also a slower, more picturesque and cheaper **Silverlink** service (2¼ hours) running from Euston every hr throughout the week and at weekends. If you want to go to Birmingham by an even more rural and more leisurely route catch a train from the spectacular Marylebone Station, London, operated by **Chiltern Railways,** T020-73333190, travel enquiries T08705-165165. This is also an excellent way to explore the surrounding countryside including Stratford, Warwick and Royal Leamington Spa.

Being famous as the meeting point of three motorways, you can get to Birmingham by car easily. From the south take either the M40 from London via Oxford or the M5 from Bristol. From the north take the M6. From the West take the M54 past Wolverhampton where it joins the M6 at Junction 10a. Birmingham city centre is well served with around 20 long-stay multi-storey car parks. Street parking is relatively easy and after 1800 free in many spots.

Getting around **Buses** are one of the best ways to see and get around Birmingham, with day savers available for £2.50 which allow unlimited travel on all **Travel West Midlands** buses or £4 for 4 people and unlimited travel. The 50 bus is particularly good: it starts behind one of the main shopping areas, Corporation Street, will take you through a cool nightclub area (Digbeth), then on to Balsall Heath where you will find some of the best curries in the country, through Moseley with its fantastic hippy pubs and Tolkein connections and eventually to the Maypole, which is in spitting distance of the Lickey Hills. For more details there's a good website at www.travelwm.co.uk or call traveline on T0870-6082608. There's also the **Travel Shop** in the Pavilions Shopping Arcade (opening Mon-Sat 0830 –1700). Meanwhile, **CENTRO,** T0121-200 2700, operate a good train service from New Street for the north of the City, for trips to the Black Country and the wonderful Walsall Art Gallery, while Chiltern Railways, run from the city centre's other station, Snow Hill, to Stratford, Warwick, and Leamington.

Information There are four large tourist offices, all managed by **Marketing Birmingham** ⓘ *Level 2 Millennium Point, Curzon St, Birmingham, B4 7XG, T0121 202 5115, 0930-1730 Mon-Sat*. There is also the **Ticket Shop and Tourism Centre** in the City Arcade ⓘ *T0121-643 2514, Mon-Sat 9.30-5.30*, the **International Conference Centre Office** ⓘ *Centenary Sq, off Broad St, T0121-780 4321, Mon-Sat 0930-1730, 24 hour automated phone for accommodation information*, and the **Colmore Row Travel Centre** ⓘ *130 Colmore Row, T0121-693 6300, 0930-1730, Mon-Sat*.

History

Birmingham is laced with canals – 32 miles compared to Venice's 28 miles – and the city is justifiably proud of its claim to be the cradle of the Industrial Revolution. The world's first steam engines were built in Birmingham by Boulton and Watt and the city is littered with fascinating sites of industrial heritage, most of them accessible by leisurely canal trips which start in the Brindley Place canalside development, easily accessible from New Street Station. Known as the 'workshop of the world', Birmingham nurtured cutting-edge manufacturing from jewellery to chocolate for over three centuries. More recently Birmingham became Britain's Motown, with the Leyland Longbridge plant originating the Mini, the ultimate icon of Britcool. That was before the second industrial revolution, when Mrs Thatcher smashed the unions and Birmingham became known for the ferocity of its strikes and a symbol of all that was wrong with British industry. Recently written up in Jonathan Coe's brilliant novel 'The Rotters Club', this was a period where Brum flourished more as a cultural centre spawning bands like Slade, The Electric Light Orchestra and the immortal Black Sabbath, fronted by the unforgettable Ozzy Osbourne, probably now the most famous Brummie in the world – certainly the only Brummie to have bitten the head off a bat *and* been personally invited to the White House by a US President (although Birmingham did play host to Clinton during a G8 summit). Now Birmingham has evolved – some would say beyond all recognition – from its old industrial past into a new industries future where huge conferences and tourism lie at the heart of the city's success.

Sights

Victoria Square and the Museum and Art Gallery

For a fresh-out-of New Street introduction to the city and all it has to offer walk up recently pedestrianized New Street to Victoria Square, where there is a tourist office and one of the largest fountains in Europe featuring a rampant naked lady and about 3000 gallons of water. Nicknamed **'The Floozie in the Jacuzzi'**, all Brummies know where this is and the square affords great views of **The Council House** ⓘ *guided tours on T0121-303 2759*, a fine building which features a proud mural of Britannia rewarding the manufacturers of Birmingham. On the other side of the square stands **The Town Hall**, a magnificent replica of the Temple of Castor and Pollux in Rome. It's currently being refurbished, but as the former home of the City of Birmingham Symphony Orchestra it's a building rich in musical heritage, having played host to musos as diverse as Elgar and The Beatles.

Round the corner from The Council House is **Birmingham Museum and Art Gallery**. With one of the world's finest collections of Pre-Raphaelite art, the roomy but gloomy galleries allow you to relive DG Rossetti's obsession with the opium-addled Miss Siddall, the foremost Pre-Raphaelite model. Other Pre-Raphaelite highlights include Edward Burne-Jones' mighty *Star of Bethlehem*, one of the largest paintings you will see anywhere and his tapestry collaborations with Arts and Crafts head honcho William Morris.

True to the city's manufacturing heritage, there's also a terrific **Applied Arts Collection** featuring a treasure trove of enough ornamental gold and silver to fuel a dozen heist movies. Other unexpected delights include Jacob Epstein's brilliant sculpture *Lucifer* presiding magisterially over the Museum Shop and the Edwardian

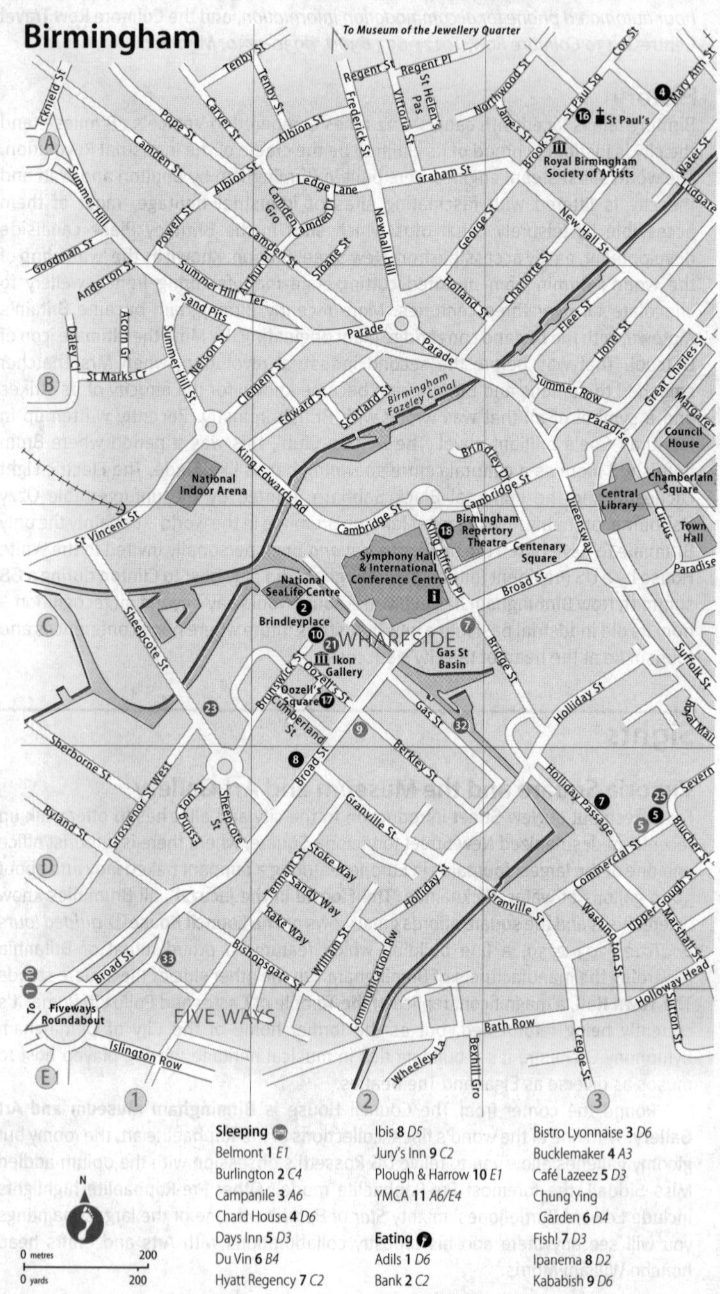

Tearoom. The newly opened **Waterhall Gallery** ⓘ *Chamberlain Sq, T0121-303 2834, www.bmag.co.uk, Mon-Thu, 1000-1700, Fri 1030-1700, Sat 1000-1700, Sun 1230-1700, free, contributions welcomed*, contains the modern art collection.

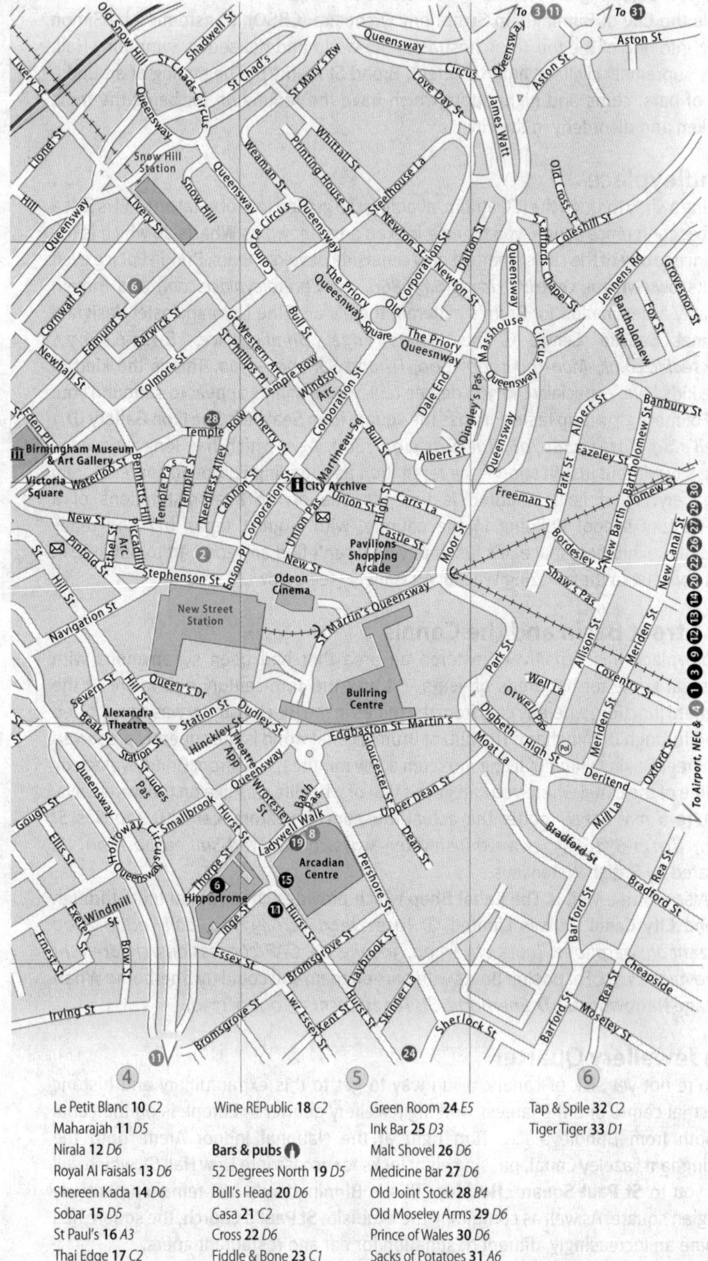

Le Petit Blanc **10** *C2*
Maharajah **11** *D5*
Nirala **12** *D6*
Royal Al Faisals **13** *D6*
Shereen Kada **14** *D6*
Sobar **15** *D5*
St Paul's **16** *A3*
Thai Edge **17** *C2*
Wine REPublic **18** *C2*

Bars & pubs
52 Degrees North **19** *D5*
Bull's Head **20** *D6*
Casa **21** *C2*
Cross **22** *D6*
Fiddle & Bone **23** *C1*
Green Room **24** *E5*
Ink Bar **25** *D3*
Malt Shovel **26** *D6*
Medicine Bar **27** *D6*
Old Joint Stock **28** *B4*
Old Moseley Arms **29** *D6*
Prince of Wales **30** *D6*
Sacks of Potatoes **31** *A6*
Tap & Spile **32** *C2*
Tiger Tiger **33** *D1*

Centenary Square and Broad Street

Passing through Chamberlain Square with the **Central Library** on the right (a monstrosity likened by some to a bus shelter) and crossing the inappropriately named Paradise Circus you come to **Centenary Square** with the **International Conference Centre** (T0121-200 2000, www.necgroup.co.uk) and **Symphony Hall** (see page 559) adjoining the top end of **Broad Street**.

While the City of Birmingham Symphony Orchestra (CBSO), transformed by Simon Rattle into one of the top 10 orchestras in the world and housed in Symphony Hall, offers supremely civilized entertainment, Broad St marks the beginning of around a mile of bars, clubs and night spots which have the reputation for being the most drunken and disorderly in the city.

Brindleyplace

Passing swiftly through the ICC atrium, avoiding the guided tour of what after all is just a very big conference centre, you emerge into an area known as **Wharfside** which is the entrance to one of the city's smartest new canalside developments. Brindleyplace even has its own **visitor centre** ⓘ *T0121-6436866, www.brindleyplace.com*, and though primarily a destination for Brum's glitterati, there's also the Norman Foster-designed **National SeaLife Centre** ⓘ *The Waters Edge, Brindleyplace, T0121-6436777, www.sealife.co.uk, Mon-Thu 1000-1600, Fri and Sat 1000-1500*. This is the kind of place kids love, especially the 360 degree tank where sharks appear to surround you.

For more grown-up tastes, across the square from SeaLife is **The Ikon Gallery** ⓘ *1 Oozell's Sq, T0121-2480708, Tue-Sun 1100-1800, free*, which has long enjoyed – some say without justification – the reputation as a leading European contemporary art gallery. What isn't disputed is that it's one of the best restorations of a 19th-century school building in the country, with a great tapas bar and really wonderful exhibition space. It's just a pity they can't find any good art to put in it, in stark contrast to the amazing Walsall Art Gallery (see below).

Gas Street Basin and the Canals

Brindleyplace has sensitively restored an area that had been synonymous with industrial grime for hundreds of years – it was the 19th-century equivalent of the spaghetti junction, whereby coal from the mines in the Black Country was transported to and through Birmingham. The hub of Brum's canal world is the superbly preserved Gas Street Basin, a kind of living museum a few minutes' walk from Brindleyplace by the side of the canal where you can get a taste of what life was like on the waterways. If you're a real barge-spotter the actual **museum** or **visitors' centre** ⓘ *42a Gas St Basin, T0121-6326845, www.britishwater ways.co.uk, Wed-Sun 1000-1800*, is operated by British Waterways.

Also worth a visit is **The Canal Shop** which provides cheap canal tours through **Second City Canal Cruises Limited**, ⓘ *T0121-2369811/6437700, daily 0800-2000 and 24hr answerphone. Tours 1 hr £3.00, 30 mins £2, OAP/concessions/children 1hr £2, 30 mins £1.50*. For posher boats with bars on them you could try **Sherborne Wharf Heritage Narrowboats**, ⓘ *Sherborne St, T0121-4555153, 0900-1730*.

The Jewellery Quarter

If you're not yet sick of canals, a fun way to get to this extraordinary and historic industrial centre and the largest working jewellery quarter in Europe is on the canal towpath from Brindleyplace. Turn right at the National Indoor Arena onto the Birmingham Fazeley Canal, passing eight locks for access into New Hall St, which will take you to **St Paul Square, Hockley**. This is Birmingham's last remaining entirely Georgian square. As well as containing the exquisite **St Paul's Church**, the square has become an increasingly affluent destination for bar and restaurant-goers.

A perfect way to digest your lunch is to visit the **Royal Birmingham Society of Artists** ⓘ *4 Brook St, St Paul's Sq, T0121-2364353, www.rbsa.org.uk, Mon, Tue, Wed, Fri 1030-1730, Thu 1030-1900, Sat 1030-1700, free*. One of the lesser-known galleries in the city, the RBSA has strong Pre-Raphaelite connections (Sir Edward Burne-Jones was a former president) and there's some spectacular locally designed jewellery for sale too.

To find out whether diamonds really are a girl's best friend – or is it gold, silver, emeralds, rubies or sapphires – you can visit over 500 shops concentrated round **Vittoria Street, Frederick Street** and **Vyse Street** where you'll also find **The Museum of the Jewellery Quarter** ⓘ *75-79, Vyse St, T0121-554 3598, www.bmag.org.uk, Mon-Fri 1000-1600 and Sat 1100-1700, closed Sun, free*, which includes a demonstration of jewellery-making techniques.

Hurst Street and around

One of Birmingham's key sites of regeneration, the city elders took a fairly ropey collection of old pubs and the Hippodrome theatre and turned it into one of the trendiest, safest and smartest areas the city has to offer. A fantastic pot-pourri of the **Chinese Quarter**, the gay district and a brand spanking new development called The Arcadian, this is definitely worth a visit if you're spending one night in Brum.

The Barber Institute of Fine Arts

Though few can believe it, Birmingham really is incredibly green and just 15 minutes south of the city centre, you hit **Edgbaston**, supposedly Brum's poshest and leafiest suburb. Take the 61, 62 or 63 Bus from Navigation St. down the Bristol Road (the continuation of Broad St after Five Ways) and get off next to *The Gun Barrels* pub. Halfway up Edgbaston Park Road is **The Barber Institute of Fine Arts** ⓘ *Edgbaston Park Rd, T0121-4147333, www.barber.org.uk, Mon-Sat 1000-1700, 1400-1700 Sun, free*, housing a truly superlative collection of Old Masters with some stunning impressionists and modern pieces. The award-winning Art Deco building comes complete with a concert hall, modest café and a full programme of concerts and History of Art lectures.

Moseley and The Tolkein Trail

Though there's currently a battle royal underway between Oxford and Birmingham to claim JRR Tolkein as a native son, Brum has by far the better claim, as he was educated at King Edward's School and spent much of his childhood around Moseley and King's Heath. Moseley Village is an excellent place to start the Tolkein trail, perhaps in the smoke room of **The Prince of Wales** where the youthful JRR had secret assignations with his bride to be. From there, it's just a quick stagger down the road to Alcester Rd where you can see a plaintive blue plaque commemorating the youthful Tolkein's residence. If you're requiring more refreshment as well as another stop on the Tolkein pilgrimage, the new Weatherspoon's pub **The Elizabeth of York** in Moseley plays host to a sculpture commemorating *The Lord of the Ring*s designed and built by the author's great-nephew Tim Tolkein. But the real Tolkein afficionados will want to make the mysterious journey down The Wake Green Road to **Sarehole Mill** and the rather sinister-sounding **Moseley Bog** which was undoubtedly the inspiration for Bilbo, Frodo and other assorted hobbits' beloved Shire. Tolkein loved this area and even in later life when he was living in posh North Oxford donated money to have Sarehole Mill restored.It's another of those perfectly restored living museums with a vistors' centre. Moseley Bog, on the other hand is still in a wild state, carefully preserved as a virtually tourist-free zone.

Walsall and The Lickey Hills

So called because the grime and pollution turned every man, woman and child's face a darker shade of grey, **The Black Country** which lies to the north of Birmingham has been avoided by tourists for at least two centuries. But now there's an excellent reason for making a beeline for Walsall, which lies at its heart. **The New Art Gallery Walsall** is a stunning, award-winning £21million building, housing a really superb collection, amassed by Jacob Epstein's widow and the daughter of an American industrial magnate. ⓘ *T01922-654400, Gallery Sq, Walsall, www.artatwalsall.org.uk Tue-Sat 1000-1700, Sun 1200-1700. Free.* Once you're in Walsall you might as well visit **The Walsall Arboretum**ⓘ *T01922 653148, Lichfield St, daily, free*, a 19th-century pleasure garden with its famed **Illuminations** (21 September to 3 November) and boating lake. For more information on walks in the area, phone Walsall Countryside Services on T0121-360 9464.

The Lickey Hills to the west of Birmingham City Centre and easily accessible on a 63 bus, only 15 minutes from town, are also a splendid country location where you can stretch your legs and see some wonderful flora and fauna.

Sleeping

Five Ways is awash with cheap and not-so-cheap hotels and B&Bs. The Birmingham Convention Bureau offers a free hotel booking service on T0121-7804321

L-A The Hyatt Regency, 2 Bridge St, T0121-6431234. The flashest hotel right next to the ICC, so it's popular with conference delegates, but try not to let that put you off. It's also got a sauna, steam room, gym and swimming pool.

A The Burlington Hotel, 6 Burlington Arcade, 126 New St, T0121-6439191. A consummately posh experience with fine dining in the Berlioz bar and restaurant: perhaps Brum's top hotel.

A Hotel Du Vin, Church St, T0121-2360559. A fantastic conversion of the old eye hospital, this place is one of the city's finest hotels. The wine cellar is unmatched by anywhere else in the region and the brasserie is wonderful. It's not as pretentious as the *The Burlington* and it looks superb both on the outside and inside.

A Plough and Harrow, 135 Hagley Rd, T0121-4544111. The poshest pub you're ever likely to spend the night in, without things like swimming pools or saunas, but a beautiful, peaceful garden instead.

B-C Days Inn, 160 Wharfside St, The Mailbox, T0121-6439344. A perfectly serviceable if somewhat utilitarian place, ideally situated for expensive shopping sprees in The Mailbox or a night out on Broad St.

C Ibis, Ladywell Walk, T0121-6226010. Like other Ibis hotels it's short on décor but long on convenience, especially if you want to gorge yourself on Chinese food; it's in the heart of Brum's Chinatown.

C The Campanile, Chester St, Aston, T0121-3593330. Uncomfortably close to the Aston Expressway, this is nevertheless a very conveniently located hotel with views of the canal.

C Jury's Inn, Broad St, T0121-6069000. A huge tower-block-like structure, right round the corner from the thriving melee of Broad St.

D Belmont Hotel, 419 Hagley Rd, T0121-4291663. A perfectly presentable bed and breakfast.

D-E Chard House, 289 Mackadown La, T0121-7852145. A friendly, clean guesthouse, with a family atmosphere but also very quiet for those who need a bit of peace to recover from the hustle and bustle of Brum's nightlife.

E YMCA, 200 Bumbury Rd, Northfield, T0121-4756218. There's a gym, squash courts and sauna which you have to pay for separately.

F YMCA, 300 Reservoir Rd, Erdington, T0121-3731937. Despite being in a fairly unsalubrious area this YMCA is clean and simple. It's also the closest you're likely to get to central Brum for this price.

Eating

£££ Bank, 4 Brindleyplace, T0121-633 7001. 'Liberated French cuisine', according to the menu, with a great view of the canals and an altogether upmarket dining experience.
£££ Le Petit Blanc, 9 Brindleyplace, T0121-6337333. Raymond Blanc's Brummie Brasserie has raised the stakes for French cuisine in the city.
££ Bistro Lyonnaise, 13 St Mary's Row, T0121-4499618. A bizarre but welcome addition to the city's offering of French cuisine, its dinky interior belies a great French cook and some gorgeous dishes.
££ The Bucklemaker, 30 Mary Ann St, St Paul's Sq, T0121-2002515. A bizarre mixture of tapas and traditional English cuisine in a truly atmospheric converted silversmith's cellar.
££ Café Lazeez, 116 Wharfside St, The Mailbox, T0121-6437979. Although another chain, it has a truly original twist on Indian food – quite an achievement in Balti city, though don't expect it to be as cheap.
££ Fish!, Wharfside St, The Mailbox, T0121-6321212. If you don't yet know this superior chain, then this is a great introduction. An elegant, airy, slimline interior, the staff are good and the food better.
££ Ipanema, 60 Broad St, T0121-6435577. Novel Brazilian restaurant and bar, with crazy dancing, another welcome change from the tack-fest that is Broad St.
££ Leftbank, 79 Broad St, T0121-6434464. A posh English cuisine restaurant on Broad St – wonders will never cease.
££ Sobar, The Arcadian Centre, T0121-6935084. Though it's near the old-school Chinese quarter, this ultra-modern noodle-bar is a great addition to the area. Plenty of room outside and a private members bar upstairs.
££ Chung Ying Garden, 17 Thorpe St, T0121-6666622. Arguably Brum's best Chinese restaurant in the heart of the Chinese district, with a family atmosphere and authentic feel.
££ St Paul's, St Paul's Sq, T0121-6051001. It's chic, bijou and rivals *Bank* as Brum's smartest restaurant with a menu of the ubiquitous 'modern English cuisine'. It does taste good though, if you can bear the somewhat 'considerably richer than yow' clientele.
££ Thai Edge, 7 Oozell's Sq, Brindleyplace, T0121-6433993. A really excellent Thai restaurant with stunning décor and reasonably priced.
££ Wine REPublic, Centenary Sq, T0121-6446464. The Rep Theatre's in-house bar, the wine selection's not bad and the food's unsurprising but alright, especially if you're planning a night at the theatre.

Curry houses

The large Pakistani and Kashmiri communities in Birmingham invented this dish in the mid 70s and there are still many of the café-style restaurants with glass-topped tables that appeal to Balti purists dotted around this slightly down-at-heel but still perfectly safe area. The easiest way to get to the Balti Triangle is to go down the Moseley Rd (A435) or The Stratford Rd (A34). Both will take you to Sparkbrook and Balsall Heath where the best Balti houses are to be found, many of them on Ladypool Rd dubbed 'the corridor of curry'.
££ Adils, 148 Stoney La, T0121-4490335. Allegedly this is where it all started – it's one of the oldest balti houses and possibly the best. Beware of the green chilli bhaji starter – not for the faint-hearted.
££ Kababish, 29 Woodbridge Rd, T0121-449 5556. If you're looking for a more upmarket balti experience than can be found in Sparkbrook, this is the place for you.
££ Maharajah, 23/25 Hurst St, T0121-6222641. Another contrast to the Balti Triangle, this is upmarket Indian as you've never tasted it before and is apparently patronized by the Indian cricket team when they're playing down the road at Edgbaston.
£ Nirala, 530 Moseley Rd, T0121-4407600. Don't be put off by the flock wallpaper and smoky windows – if you're a connoisseur of balti, this is quite unbeatable for flavour.
£ Royal Al Faisals, 136-140 Stoney La, T0121-4495695. Another early arrival on the balti scene, it made its name by pioneering the 'family' naan which in one instance (the 747) could almost accommodate an entire family. Now it's famed for its Balti Buffet where you can eat as much as you like for £6.95.

£ **Shereen Kada**, 543 Moseley Rd, T0121-4404641. If you're into sugar overloads then this is the place for you, as its reputation as an Indian sweet centre is unparalleled. The baltis are pretty good too, and prepared in front of you.

Pubs, bars and clubs

52 Degrees North, The Arcadian Centre, T0121-6225250. There's that permanent hubbub around this place that you'd expect of a trend-setting bar which is the undisputed market-leader round these parts. Louche décor, glam types and pricey drinks all come as standard.
The Bull's Head, St Mary's Row, Moseley, T0121-7020931. An offshoot of the *Medicine Bar* in Digbeth and in keeping with the laid-back atmosphere established there, lots of banging tunes and cool punters.
Casa, Brindleyplace, T0121-6333049. It may be part of a chain, but compared to other bars in Brindleyplace it's cooler and looks better.
The Cross, Alcester Rd, T0121-4494445. Moseley's movers and shakers flock to what is a stylish addition to the Moseley pub scene, with a great space out front for that boulevardier feeling.
Fiddle and Bone, 4 Sheepcote St, T0121-2002233. A good canal pub with lots of live music.
The Green Room, Hurst St, T0121-6054343. It's opposite the Hippodrome Theatre (hence the name), is very camp and a good starting off point (though not too full-on) for sampling Brum's gay scene.
Ink Bar, 117 Wharfside St, T0121-6321321. Probably the trendiest bar the Mailbox has to offer, with an interior like a sci-fi set and a 'salon privé' for special events.
Medicine Bar, The Custard Factory, Gibb St, T0121-6936333. Along with *52 Degrees North* this place has a claim to be the trendiest bar in town, but it's definitely more grunge than glam.
The Old Joint Stock, 4 Temple Rd West, T0121-2001892. You can tell from the spectacular interior that this place used to be something very grand – in fact it was the Birmingham Stock Exchange. Worth a visit, if only to see the domed ceiling.
The Old Moseley Arms, 53 Tindall St, T0121-440 1954. Despite being a down-home traditional boozer with excellent beer, this place is becoming a trendy young thing hang-out.
The Malt Shovel, 20 Brighton Rd, T0121-4422561. The former local of the band UB40 – they still pop in from time to time.
The Prince of Wales, 118 Alcester Rd, Moseley, T0121-4494198. Trendy bars come and go, but the *PoW* has remained unchanged for decades and is one of the least pretentious pubs you're likely to find anywhere. Highly recommended.
The Sacks of Potatoes, 10 Gosta Green, Aston Triangle, T0121-5035811. Though the surrounding area's a bit grim, this is definitely one of the highlights with a peerless pint and friendly landlord.
The Tap and Spile, Gas St, T0121-6325602. A real old-fashioned boozer with an older crowd, but a superlative pint.
Tiger Tiger, Broad St, T0121-6439722. It's a restaurant, a boozer and a nightclub that manages to lift itself above the norm by attracting a more discriminating crowd.

Clubs

The Birmingham Academy, Dale End, T0121-2623000.This place used to be home to Brum's early rappers and toasters when it was the *Hummingbird*. Now it's more indie as well as being one of the best live music venues in the city, with more character than the massive National Indoor Arena or National Exhibition Centre.
Code, Heath Mill La, Digbeth, T0121-6932633. The closest Brum gets to a super-club with all the young raveaholics that you'd expect. God's Kitchen on Fridays is the night to go for.
DV8, 16 Kent St, T0121-6666366. The talk of the town, as it's the newest and trendiest gay club in a quarter packed with camp.
Liberty's, 184 Hagley Rd, Edgbaston, T0121-4544444. With ultra-glam and gang-star Moneypenny's a regular weekly feature on a Saturday night, there's an air of dangerous cool and sophistication about this place.
Moseley Dance Centre, 572-574 Alcester Rd, Moseley, T0121-4490779. A delightful throwback to the days of the school disco but without the annoying music. They do have regular 70s nights, though.

Nightingale, Essex House, Kent St, T0121-6221718. Stiff competition, for *DV8*, it's the oldest gay club and consequently has a more varied crowd.
Snobs, 30 Paradise Circle, Queensway, T0121-6435551. Having thrown off its mantle as a haven for the white socks brigade, this place has unaccountably mutated into the indie and goth Mecca for a new generation.

Entertainment

Cinema

IMAX Theatre, Millennium Point, Curzon St Bookings, T0121-2022222. Attached to the new Science Museum – 'the Thinktank', this enormous screen is more novelty than genuine contribution to the cinema scene in Brum.
Mac (Midlands Arts Centre), Cannon Hill Park, T0121-4403838. An intelligently programmed *and* cheap independent cinema.
Odeon, New St, T0121-6436103.
UGC, Arcadian Centre, Hurst St, Ladywell Walk, T08701-555177; also at FiveWays Leisure Park, Broad St, T0121-6430631, T0870-9070723.
Warner Village Cinemas, StarCity, 100 Watson Rd, Nechells T0870-2406020.

Music

Since the replacement of Ronnie Scott's Birmingham outpost with a lap-dancing venue, you'd be forgiven for thinking that Brums aren't too bothered about the delights of live music. And you'd be right, kind of.
The Barber Institute, Edgbaston Park Rd, T0121-4147333. It's not only got a fantastic gallery, but there's also a concert hall which specializes in chamber music and small ensembles.
Birmingham Academy, Dale End, T0121-2623000. A whole lot cooler than either the *NIA* or *NEC*, the Academy is smaller but with bags of musical heritage, it manages to attract some excellent acts.
The Jam House, 3 St Paul's Sq, T0121-2003030, The mantle of cool tunes has passed over to this place, which has rhythm and blues acts mainly throughout the week with the don himself – Jools Holland – who co-owns the joint making the odd appearance.
NEC, M42, Junction 6, T0121-7673888. For those who prefer their rock large, loud and epic, here's one of the original stadia for which the term stadium rock was invented. Not surprisingly, it's a personality-free zone.
NIA, King Edward Rd, T0121-6446011. It's owned by the same people who own the NEC, so it's got the same sort of character (ie none), but you can catch the B list acts there.
Symphony Hall, Broad St, T0121-2002000. Does what it says on the tin – one of the best, most acoustically perfect, purpose-built venues in the country, the regular home of the CBSO and almost worth a visit even without live music. But the real thing is an incomparable experience.

Theatre

Alexandra Theatre, Station St, T0870-6077544. West End hits as well as local fare.
Birmingham Repertory Theatre, Centenary Sq, Broad St, T0121- 2364455, www.birmingham-rep.co.uk A good programme of ancient and modern, this place offers the best, most thought-provoking theatre outside Stratford.
The Hippodrome, Hurst St, T0870-7305555. The beneficiary of a million pound refurbishment, hosts the Birmingham Royal Ballet and the Welsh National Opera when they're on tour. It's also got the facilities to stage the really big West End hits when they come to town.
Mac (Midlands Arts Centre), Cannon Hill Park, T0121-4403838. An eclectic mix of slightly more avant-garde theatre pieces with a world-renowned children's puppet theatre.

Festivals

Jul Birmingham Jazz Festival (2nd week in Jul). Guaranteed to be more fun than the TV festival (see below), with dozens of live venues round Birmingham. Gas St Basin used to be full of jazz dives and even though poor Ronnie Scott's club has departed, there's jazz to suit all tastes at this superb week-long jamboree.
Sep Artsfest (1st weekend of Sep). Though this has a slightly worthy feel (on account of

being arranged and paid for by Birmingham City Council), it is chock full of free events which include live performances by some of the city's Bhangra combos, Asian dub or house. There's also performance art and all the best other art the region has to offer.

Oct Ramadan and Diwali. The city has a vocal and active Asian community and they celebrate their festivals in style, often with fireworks, big park parties and delicious food.

Shopping

Birmingham is having its bicentennial facelift on the famous Bull Ring, where once live bulls were baited for the entertainment of baying hordes. One trusts that once the bandages come off, we'll have a considerably more civilized centre than what has gone before, including the Bull Ring Shopping Centre, a hideous concrete 70s monstrosity. Meanwhile most of the shopping is concentrated around **New Street**, **Corporation Street**, **The Minories** (off Bull St), **High St** and **Martineau Square** (off Union Passage). All of the major chains are represented around here.

Markets

Markets of Birmingham beside St Martin's in the Bull Ring, are justly famed for the diversity of goods at bargain prices. Here you can find clothes, fabrics, china, kitchenware as well as exotic produce, serving the region's multicultural citizens (4 mangos for £1).

Indoor Markets, Edgbaston St, T0121-6076000, which also sell fish and meat and are open at the same times as the outdoor market every day except Sun.

Outdoor Market, Edgbaston St, T0121-3030300, Tue, Fri, Sat, 0900-1730.

Miscellaneous

Brecknells, 23 Union St, T0121-6431986, is another great speciality shop – it's a wonderful old-school milliner (hat shop) and is just round the corner from *Powell and Son*. Every type of fancy ladies hat you can imagine – from Jackie Kennedy pillbox to the Philip Treacy leopard skin floppy number worn by Boy George – is on offer and the staff are charming.

Powell & Son (Gunmakers) Ltd, 35-37 Carr's La, T0121-6430689. This extraordinary speciality shop has been purveying sporting guns to the gentry and other folk since 1802. Visiting Powell's antique but perfectly preserved shop is, not surprisingly, like going back in time and with a wonderful fishing tackle department as well as country clothing, it's the ultimate place to visit before a sporting weekend. There's also an antique restored shotgun – price, a cool £45k.

Music

Jibbering Records, Alcester Rd, Moseley T0121-449 4551, is for the younger connoisseur of the finest rap, dub, world, phat, funky and generally kicking tunes. It's a great place to have a coffee and also get the latest on where the cool clubs are. A friendly shortcut for danceaholics who want to know about the latest hot destination.

Reddington's Rare Records, Lower Ground Floor, Smithfield House, Digbeth T0121-622 7050, is as good as any Nick Hornby creation from *Hi gh Fidelity* and if you're a fan of vinyl this place has a truly rare groove selection to suit the most esoteric tastes.

Activities and tours

Cricket

Warwickshire Country Cricket Club, The County Ground, Edgbaston T0121-4464422. One of the best grounds in the world, Edgbaston has seen its fair share of test triumphs and tragedies.

Football

All 3 of the big Brum teams are in the Premiership at the time of writing. The city has always been football crazy, and the teams that inspire most insanity are **Aston Villa**, Villa Park, T0121-3272299, (with its Jorvik style ride, celebrating the claret and blues, you'd be forgiven for thinking that Villa is more of a theme park than a football team – and you'd be right); **Birmingham City FC**, St Andrew's Rd, T0121-7720101, Brum's true lions, they recently beat Villa meeting them for the first time in 16 years, a local derby that passed off without violent incident; **West Bromwich Albion**, The Hawthorns, Halford La, T0121-5258888. The baggies by nickname and Frank Skinner's favourite team.

Greyhound racing

Hall Green Dog Track, Hall Green, T0121 777 1181. Admission £4. Racing on Tue and Fri at 1935 and Sat at 1930.

Karting

Brum Kart Track, near Aston, T0121-327 7617. £20 per half hour. Sat and Sun, bring ID and you must be over 12 and/ or accompanied by a parent. It's pricey but a lot of fun.

Swimming

Moseley Baths, Alcester Rd, T0121-464 0150. Mon, Thu and Fri 0700-2000. One of the oldest public baths in the city, this is an amazing building with Brum's proud coat of arms emblazoning the entrance – FORWARD!

Cocksmoor Leisure Centre, King's Heath T0121-4641196. Admission £2.40, for opening times call information line.

Directory

Bureaux de changes AmEx, Bank House, 8 Cherry St, T0121-6445533. Thomas Cook, 130, New St (inside HSBC), T0121-6435057. **Hospitals** Birmingham Children's Hospital, Steelhouse Lane, T0121-3339999. Birmingham Heartland's Hospital, Bordesley Green East, T0121-4242000. City Hospital, Dudley Rd, T0121-5543801. Has A&E. NHS Medical Centre at Boots, 66 High St, T0121-6266000. University Hospital, Raddlebarn Rd, Selly Oak, T0121-6271627. **Internet** Trulyeverything.co.uk, Pavilions Shopping Centre, T0121-6326156. £1 for 30 mins. Mon-Wed, Fri and Sat 0900-1800, Thu 0900-1900, Sun 1100-1700. **Police** City Centre, T0121-6265000. Digbeth Police Station, 113 Digbeth, T0121-6266000. Also houses lost property office. **Post office** 1 Pinfold St, and 19 Union Passage, T08457-223344.

Warwickshire

→ *Colour map 4, grid B/C4-5*

A mixed-up county in the south-eastern shadow of Britain's second city, Warwickshire more than holds its own in the face of metropolitan Birmingham. The most famous of its attractions, and one of the most visited in the country, remains Stratford-upon-Avon, birthplace of the bard and epicentre of Shakespeare Country. Surprisingly enough, the town itself manages to sustain the atmosphere of an ordinary Midland market town amid all the tourist trappings. Nearby, Royal Leamington Spa repays a visit for its antique tone and thriving student scene keeping it awake at night. The university and county town of Warwick is next door, its much-publicised castle easily the star attraction. Warwick Castle, run by Madame Tussaud's, makes a terrifically entertaining and tourist-friendly meal of its fairytale architecture and bumpy history. Its less-hyped neighbour, Kenilworth, has even more extraordinary tales to tell about its crumbling ruins. Just to the north, the city of Coventry makes a much less obvious tourist destination. With its two extraordinary cathedrals and civic pride in the school of hard knocks it maybe says more about contemporary life in the Midlands than all the rest put together. » *For Sleeping, Eating and other listings, see pages 570-576.*

Stratford-upon-Avon

As the world centre of an ever-expanding Shakespeare industry, and Britain's second most visited tourist destination after London, you would naturally expect there to be a preponderance of bard-related attractions in and around Stratford, but the place has nevertheless still managed to hold onto its authentic small market town atmosphere. The Royal Shakespeare Company is one of the artistic triumphs of the United Kingdom and no visit to Stratford is really complete without seeing some of Shakespeare's drama – the play really is the thing in comparison with the Birthplace Trust Shakespeare trail. But if you haven't got enough time, and you still want to do the 'Willgrimage', you might drop in on Shakespeare's birthplace which has a tolerable exhibition, or see where Shakespeare was buried in Holy Trinity Church. As for the locals, they live in peace with the bard's sometimes troublesome legacy.

Ins and outs

Getting there As far as **trains** are concerned, there's an embarrassment of riches including Britain's fastest steamtrain service The **Shakespeare Express,** T0121-7074696, which runs 2 return journeys a day from Birmingham's Snow Hill station. For those not so enamoured of the age of steam, **Chiltern Railways** go from London and Birmingham twice an hr and even offer brilliant discounts for unlimited travel in the region over 1 and 3 days. Since the 1980s the mighty M40 **motorway** has provided a speedy route for those coming from the north or south. Simply take exit 15 onto the A46, where Stratford is clearly signposted. If you prefer a more picturesque route coming up from the south, there's the A3400 from Oxford which will take you straight into Stratford town centre via some delightful Cotswolds towns like Shipston on Stour. From the southwest and the M5, take exit 9 at Tewekesbury and take the A46 to Evesham, then follow the signposts to Stratford. There's also a great deal of parking space in Stratford.

Information There are 2 tourist offices for Stratford. The first is the **official TIC** ⓘ *near the Royal Shakespeare Theatre at the corner of Bridgefoot and Broadway, Apr-Oct Mon-Sat 0900-1800, Sun 1100-1700, Nov-Mar Mon-Sat 0900-1700, Sun 1100-1600, T01789-293127, www.shakespeare-country.co.uk.* Handily, it's also right next to the bus station which is on Bridgeway. You can book accommodation from here or by calling the main number. The other tourist office is provided by **Guide Friday** ⓘ *14 Rother St, adjoining the old Market Sq, T01789-299866,* and while it's well equipped, beware of its tendency to recommend its own tours of the town, Warwick Castle and the Cotswolds.

Sights

From the tourist office and Art Gallery see above, it's very easy to get to Stratford's main raison d'être: **The Royal Shakespeare Theatre,** towering over the landscape like an Art Deco power station. In fact it's quite a complex set of buildings, carefully designed to serve the great god Thespus with a varied platter. Also nestling within the arms of this great beast is a more delicate flower, **The Swan Theatre,** which specializes in performing works by Shakespeare's contemporaries, like the bloodthirsty John Webster who loved his grand guignol. They also perform standard and not-so-standard pieces such as Chekhov and *Cosi Fan Tutte.*

As befits such a dramatic place, the theatre has a chequered history including fire, passion and suicide. The present building was designed by Elizabeth Scott and was opened in 1932, but the original theatre on this site dates back to 1879 when a local brewer Edward Flower donated the land for the building. For a fascinating view behind the scenes take a **theatre tour** ⓘ *24 hrs ticket availability T01789-403404, box office bookings T01789-403403. For the theatre tour pre-booking is essential, T01789-403405, theatretours@rsc.org.uk.* Over 400 staff make scenery and costumes, maintain the theatre and administer its business. A £100 million project is proposed to develop the theatres replacing the present house with a state-of-the-art playhouse and to build yet another theatre on the car park of **The Other Place,** a warehouse theatre space which has been closed since the summer of 2002, but formerly staged a diet of experimental pieces by new writers and radical interpretations of more traditional texts performed by adventurous members of the Royal Shakespeare Company. Its fate now hangs in the balance, awaiting the arrival of the new artistic director Michael Boyd.

Purists will warn you off what rightfully should be your next port of call: **Shakespeare's Birthplace** ⓘ *1 Nov-24 Mar, Mon-Sat 1000-1600, Sun 1030-1600, 25 Mar-31 May and 1 Sep-31 Oct Mon-Sat 1000-1700, Sun 1030-1700, 1 Jun-31 Aug Mon-Sat 0900-1700, Sun 0930-1700, £6.50, child £2.50, family £15*, the jewel in the crown of the Shakespeare Properties. Even if there are a few gaps in our knowledge of the truth of Will's life (just who was the Dark Lady?), the Birthplace Trust are determined to do Will proud. There is clearly quite a formidable team of Shakespeare scholars

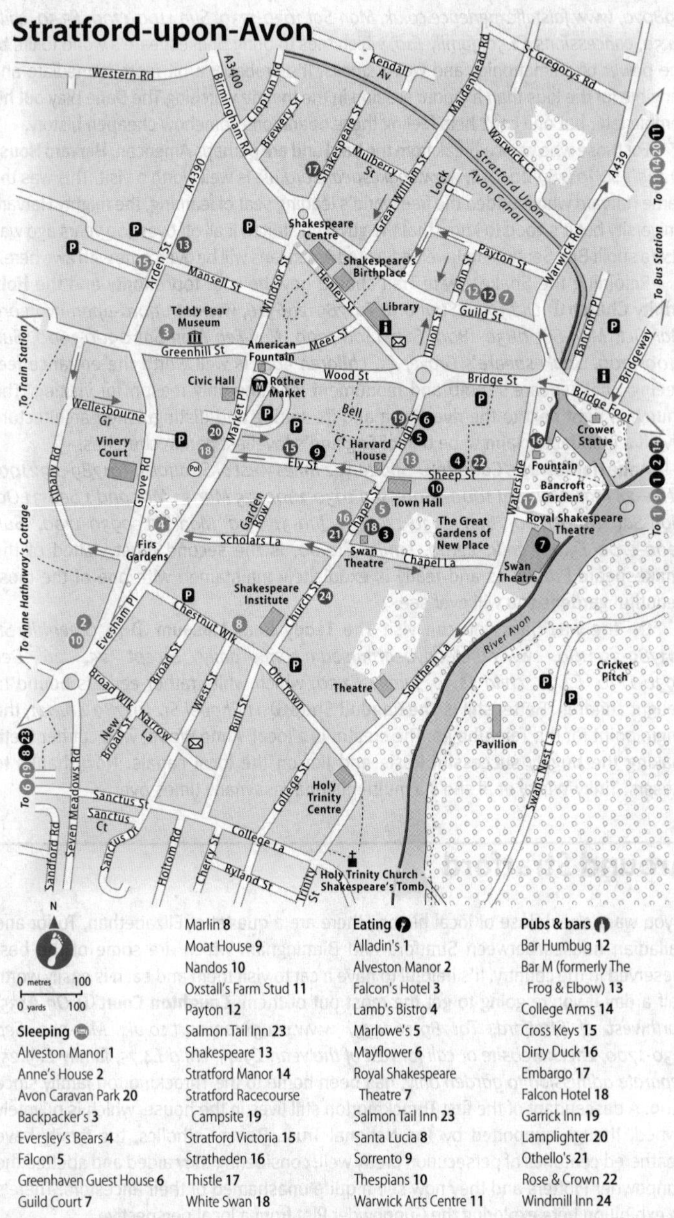

 working with the Birthplace Trust and if you really want to do what they offer justice, you need to vist **The Shakespeare Centre and Library Birthplace** ⓘ *Birthplace Trust, The Shakespeare Centre, Henley St, T01789-204016, library, Mon-Fri 1000-1700, Sat 0930-1230 except at bank holidays,* which may not be the most picturesque of the properties, but is easily the most informative. With academics coming from round the world to look at this unique collection of first editions, history and scholarship, the centre can genuinely claim to be a site of world heritage.

In complete contrast, there's **The Falstaff Experience** ⓘ *40 Sheep St, T01789-298070, www.falstaffexperience.co.uk, Mon-Sat 1030-1730, Sun 1100-1700, £3.50, child £1.50, concessions £2.50, family £10,* which tries to bring Shakespeare's world to life by the power of animatronics and weird smells. It's probably a bit more immediate and tangible for the kids than a 5-hour session in the theatre watching The Dane play out his terrible fate, but one can't help feeling these operations somehow cheapen history.

For those who want a break from the bard and are perhaps American, **Harvard House** ⓘ *High St, T01789-204016, www.shakespeare.org.uk,* is well worth a visit. This was the same Harvard who founded the free world's leading seat of learning, the mighty Harvard University but it's good to know that the guy who started it all off over 300 years ago was also a spoilt Brit. Sentimental, well-educated Americans will be overcome with awe here.

Rejoining the Shakespeare Trail should now be your top priority and the **Holy Trinity Church** ⓘ *Old Town Stratford, T01789-266316, www.stratford-upon-avon.org Mar-Oct, Mon-Sat 0830-1800, Sun 1400-1700, Nov-Feb Mon-Sat 0900-1600, Sun 1400-1700, Shakespeare's Grave, £1, children 50p,* is well worth the entrance fee. Seeing Shakespeare's tomb and monument isn't the only reason for visiting. The church is right next to the river Avon and its setting and distinguished architecture give it a justifiable claim to be one of England's loveliest parish churches.

Anne Hathaway's Cottage ⓘ *Shottery, 2 miles west of Stratford, T01789- 292100, 1 Nov-24 Mar, Mon-Sat 1000-1600, Sun 1030-1600, 25 Mar-31 May and 1 Sep-31 Oct Mon-Sat 1000-1700, Sun 1030-1700, 1 Jun-31 Aug Mon-Sat 0930-1700, Sun 1000-1700 £5.00, child £2.00, family £12.00,* is the second most visited of the Shakespeare Properties and really is exquisitely maintained with one of the most beautiful gardens you will ever see.

On the way back you can visit **The Teddy Bear Museum** ⓘ *19 Greenhill St, T01789-293160, www.theteddybearmuseum.com, daily except 25, 26 Dec 0930-1730, £2.50, child £1.50, family £7.50,* which while rather eerie is bound to delight children. Better still is **The Ragdoll Shop** ⓘ *11 Chapel St, T01789-404111,* the origin point for the Teletubbies. The creator is a local, Anne Wood, who cut her teeth making the hugely successful Rosie and Jim on the local canals. Now thanks to Messrs. Tinky-Winky et al she's a multi-millionairess many times over.

Around Stratford

If you want a real dose of local history, there are a quartet of Elizabethan, Tudor and Palladian houses between Stratford and Birmingham which are some of the best preserved in the country. It's helpful to have a car to visit them and each is easily worth half a day if you're going to get the most out of them. **Coughton Court** ⓘ *On A435, northwest of Stratford, T01789-762435, www.coughtoncourt.co.uk, Mar-end Sep 1130-1700, check website or call for rest of the year, £9.45, child £4.75, family £29.25, separate admission to garden only,* has been home to the Throckmorton family since 1409. A descendant of the first Throckmorton still lives in the house, which is privately owned, though supported by The National Trust. Being Catholics, the family have weathered centuries of persecution pretty well, considering they aided and abetted the Gunpowder Plotters and they now seem quite unashamed of their ancestors. There's an exhibition here exploring the Gunpowder Plot from a local perspective.

And if you're in the area there's one more house you must go to which is an amazing example of neo-Palladian architecture. **Ragley Hall** ⓘ *8 miles west of Stratford, T01789-762090, park and house £6, child £4.50, family £22, phone for opening times*, is the family seat of the Marquess and Marchioness of Hertford and was built in 1680 and has probably the finest collection of painting and antiques in the county.

As for **The Forest of Arden**, supposedly the inspiration for Shakespeare's forests from the one in *Midsummer Night's Dream* to Falstaff's stamping ground, it's all around; there are dozens of lovely country walks to enjoy while quoting your favourite passages.

Royal Leamington Spa

The most magnificent example of Royal Leamington Spa's heyday is the **Royal Pump Rooms**, first opened in 1811, and to this day the elegant heart of this miniature Regency town. Certainly the poor relation of Bath and Cheltenham, Leamington was nevertheless granted a royal charter by Victoria in 1838. Anxious to shake off the somewhat sad and decaying but genteel retirement atmosphere perfectly illustrated in John Betjeman's poem 'Death in Leamington', the place does have something to offer. With its nearby large student population from Warwick University, the town now has a reputation for unruly partying on its main streets, and out of term-time and during the week, Leamington is a charming treasure trove of distinguished architecture, pleasant walks and upmarket eateries.

Around Leamington

There are a profusion of delightful south Warwickshire villages to visit nearby, many of which have great walks and opportunities for wining and dining as well as the odd spectacular view, the best of which can probably be found in **Ufton**, on the A425 Daventry Rd between Leamington Spa and Southam, about 4 miles from Leamington, where there's also a **Nature Reserve.** The village pub is called *The White Hart* (signed from the main road). It has a good reputation for food and a beer garden with a good view over rolling countryside. Other excellent villages rejoice in names like **Bishop's Itchington** which has a great pub, appropriately called *The Great Western*. It's nothing, however, in comparison to the *Fleur De Lys* in **Lowsonford** a gem of a village, right next to the **Stratford Canal.**

Warwick and Kenilworth

Warwick and its environs is really a tale of two castles. One is a romantic ruin and the other is a ruined opportunity. Between them, Kenilworth and Warwick Castles dominate this part of the world and have done for centuries. From medieval pageants to pitched battles, the castles are a fantastic double act. As always, it's the powerful elite who really grab our interest in the history of this little and fairly quiet town, the county capital of Warwickshire. Throughout history, royals couldn't keep away from the place, so it's not surprising that the local population have developed a habit of turning a blind eye to the more outlandish excesses of visitors. Since Warwick Castle still employs many local people – just as it used to when it needed an army of servants to satisfy the whims of its pampered weekenders – the locals have learnt the value of discretion, unlike some royal butlers. This all leads to a very pleasant atmosphere – intensely peaceful, although some might find it a mite too stately for their tastes. Never mind, if you want nightclubs, go to Leamington. If you want superb slices of history, vividly portrayed and well preserved, however, stick to Warwick and Kenilworth.

 Getting there Train Warwick station is 10 minutes' **walk** from the town centre and castle. Regular **trains** run from Birmingham on the Chiltern Line which can be picked up in London from Marylebone Station or Paddington for other services. Use Leamington Spa for connections to Banbury, Coventry and Oxford. The best way to approach Warwick from the north is either via the M1, taking the M69 and A46, or M6 taking the M42 to M40 junction 15, then A429 to Warwick. From London also use the M40 to junction 15 then A429 to Warwick.

Information Warwick Castle has its own impressive visitors' centre and PR operation (see below). Warwick's **main Tourist Office** ⓘ *Jury St, T01926-492212, www.warwick-uk.com*, within easy striking distance of the castle and most other attractions.

Warwick Castle

ⓘ *T0870-442 2000 (24 hr), T01926-406600, www.warwick-castle.co.uk (also for information on all events held at the castle). Daily except Christmas Apr-Sep 1000-1800, Oct-Mar 1000-1700. £11.25, child £6.95, concessions £7.35, student £7.80, family £34 (all prices less in winter).*

Admittedly Warwick Castle seems to be a classic tourist trap. It's full of live archers, waxwork tableaux and living exhibits which are all the trademarks of the 'heritage industry' – in this case Tussaud's, its most successful beneficiary and the owners since 1978. Actually Tussaud's have done a rather good job and spent over £20 milion restoring the castle from a fairly parlous state.

Warwick Castle is now a major site of historic interest with close to a million visitors a year. It's not only an incredible structure – a proper medieval fort – but it has also been an icon of taste and style for the upper classes of the past four centuries. Canaletto immortalized several famous prospects and even JMW Turner couldn't resist its perfect lines and fairy-tale romanticism. The real money shots, however, are to be found above the castle – where you can see the outlines of the original earthworks which Aethelwade built to defend herself over 1000 years ago.

Tussaud's come into their own, though, once you enter the castle through the magnificent **Gatehouse** and **Barbican**. The main precinct enclosed by the east and south walls is in tip-top condition with an immaculate lawn sometimes used for torchlit feasts. Immediately, you are surrounded by the walls and battlements of an honest-to-goodness fairy-tale castle.

Assuming you're going to leave a stroll around the **towers and ramparts** for later, a good place to start your tour is at **The Kingmaker Experience**, commemorating the almost total power one Earl of Warwick, Richard Neville, enjoyed over the kingdom.

Just around the corner from Kingmaker, there's the **Chapel, Great Hall and State Rooms**, where you'll find the Warwicks' fairly large collection of antiques, gorgeous furniture and slightly boring portraits. There are things in these rooms that betray a certain lack of taste and borderline vulgarity, especially the **Blue Boudoir** which is powder blue and very camp. There is, however, a superb school of Holbein portrait of Henry VIII looking very macho. But the magic of waxworks really comes into its own in the adjacent rooms to the chapel and state rooms which are occupied by **The Royal Weekend Party** a faithful reconstruction of a house party held in 1898 at which two future kings were present as guests. But the holy of holies in this sequence is undoubtedly **The Kenilworth Bedroom,** a room set aside permanently for the Prince of Wales because he was such a frequent visitor.

But the Earls also handed out their fair share of punishment and there's the **Armoury and Dungeon** cheerfully called **Death or Glory** as testament to a history of barbarism and bullying, with the odd myth thrown in. And if you like that lot then you'll love **The Dungeon and Torture Chamber**.

As you'd expect the grounds are immaculate and absolutely litter free; showing off some spectacular features like the **Victorian Rose Garden** and the **Pageant Field**

“” If you want superb slices of history, vividly portrayed and well preserved, stick to Warwick and Kenilworth...

as well as the **Peacock Garden** designed by 19th-century landscapist Robert Warnock. There's also a truly fabulous **Conservatory** designed in 1786 to house the famous **Warwick Vase** an enormous piece of Roman pottery gifted to an 18th-century Earl in recognition of his diplomatic skills.

Kenilworth Castle

ⓘ (EH), T01926-852078, www.english-heritage.org.uk Apr 1st-Oct 31st daily 1000-1800 (1700 in Oct); Nov 1st-Mar 31st daily, 1000-1600. Closed 24-26 Dec and Jan 1st. £4.50, child £2.30, concessions £3.40, family £11.30. By car: at M6 junction (M42 Junction 7) take A452 south into Kenilworth. From Coventry and Warwick, Kenilworth is off the A46 on the A452 and the castle is signposted from the town centre. By train: Coventry Station is 8 miles. By bus: Stagecoach company – Leamington Spa from bridge outside Coventry Railway Station: X 18 stops near Castle, X16 stops nearby Clock in town.

In many ways, Kenilworth Castle has more history to offer than Warwick as its bloody story has witnessed savagery, skulduggery and at one point it even played its part in regicide. But unlike Warwick Castle it's an honest-to-goodness ruin, a fact not lost on its most famous chronicler, Sir Walter Scott, whose novel of 1821 describing the spectacular culmination of an alleged love-affair between Elizabeth I and Robert Dudley, Earl of Leicester, really put Kenilworth on the tourist map and helped to draw crowds wanting to experience the romance of an ancient ruin first-hand. Dickens used to pay frequent visits and more recently, the Castle has helped inspire modern fabulists obsessed by the medieval and spooky – JRR Tolkein and JK Rowling to name but two.

The current structure was begun in around 1120 by Geoffrey De Clinton, a counter-jumping Chamberlain to Henry I. De Clinton's formidable grasp of warcraft can be seen in the mighty Norman stone keep called **Caesar's Tower**, built in the style of a Roman fort – very high and very square, with walls that are over 20 ft thick. De Clinton also thoughtfully encircled his stronghold with water – the largest artificial lake in the kingdom at that time. It was this feature, along with **The Curtain Walls** surrounding the castle which King John later built, that helped the structure withstand a nine-month siege and every type of military onslaught when in 1266, Henry III tried to put a stop to the current castle-keeper Simon De Montfort's campaign to curb the power of the monarchy in the wake of the Magna Carta (1215).

De Montfort had started the process of turning the castle into a palace and centre of scholarship and when Henry III took it over and gave it to his son Edmund Earl of Lancaster later to become Earl of Leicester; it was one of the five licensed jousting and royal tournament centres in the kingdom. In celebration of the defeat of the Barons, a splendid gathering of over 100 knights, known as 'the round table' took place at Kenilworth in 1279 and all kinds of noble revelry, including jousting was staged in **The Tiltyard**, a purpose-built gaming and tournament field which can still be visited.

The castle passed ultimately to John of Gaunt, a medieval 'Godfather' figure who as son of Edward III became de facto king on the accession of Richard II who was only twelve at the time. His influence can be seen everywhere, but particularly in the remains of **The Great Hall** to the left of the **Keep**.

But the beautification of Kenilworth reached its apotheosis under Robert Dudley, Earl of Leicester who wanted to impress his royal patron (and possibly mistress) with the most incredible reception and party which lasted nineteen days in 1575. He even built a special tower **The Leicester Building** for the Queen and her retinue as well as a new triumphal entrance to the castle, **Leicester's Gatehouse**. **Leicester's Barn** currently houses the **restaurant** and **gift shop**, which contains some great things if you've got the cash, including replica tapestries and medieval swords for around £200. The barn is also the starting point for most guided tours of Kenilworth.

Other sights around Warwick

Like Coughton Court near Stratford-upon-Avon, **Baddesley Clinton** ⓘ *6 miles northwest of Warwick off A4141, T01564-783294. Phone to check opening times*, made its name as a haven for Catholics and it contains three priest holes secreted about its beautiful structure, which is an outstanding example of a moated manor house dating back to the 15th century.

But for real fans of exquisite interiors, there's peerless **Packwood House** ⓘ *Maintained by same people as Baddesley Clinton, 10 miles northwest of Warwick, T01564-783294, phone to check opening times,* a building first lived in in the 16th century. Famed designer Graham Baron Ash got his hands on it in the interwar period in the 20th century and he turned it into one of the smartest country houses in Britain, but cleverly preserved its connection with the past by decorating it with 16th-century period textiles and furniture. The gardens are also a marvel and are known for their herbaceous borders and yew trees.

Coventry

The paradox of Coventry is that it's one of the oldest towns in the country but has one of the newest centres. There were Anglo-Saxon settlers arriving before AD900, but thanks to Herr Hitler and his first most devastating bombing raid in November 1940, only fragments of Old Coventry remain. So there's a decidedly 70s urban concrete nightmare feel to some of it, and this, combined with Coventry's reputation in recent years as a bit of a rough place, has made it distinctly unappetizing for the average tourist. Of course, the reason Coventry was targeted by the Nazi bombing raids in the first place was because it was an important industrial centre, especially for the automotive industries, who are still big employers in the area, so you wouldn't necessarily expect it to be all medieval mews and grassy banks. And it's this big difference between Coventry and its near neighbours Stratford and Warwick that you should bear in mind when visiting – it's a proper working city. That's not to say that it hasn't got its fair share of magical history – the Lady Godiva story alone would be enough to guarantee it a place in the pantheon of British folklore, quite apart from the fact that the story benefits from being largely true. And right in the middle of the Cathedral precinct, next door to one another, are the perfect symbols of Coventry's past and present: the old and new Cathedrals. The modern one is a masterpiece.

Ins and outs

Getting there Trains are every 30 minutes from London Euston on Virgin Intercity, or every 30 minutes most of the day from Birmingham (also Virgin). **Road** From London M1, Junction 17, take the M45 which become the A45 at Thurlaston for the south side of the city. Or take the M1 to Junction 19, then the M6 to Junction 2 and then the A4600 for the northeast of the city. From the north take the M1 to Junction 21 and the M69 to Junction 2 and then the A4600, or the M6 the Junction 3 and then the A444. **National Express** from Victoria every 2-3 hours, £17 return, journey time about 2 hours 10 minutes.

Getting around Most places that you would want to see in the centre of Coventry are accessible on foot, but you will probably need to catch either the 17 or 27 from the station

Two Tone Town

Racially diverse youth culture has always been in evidence in this big-city melting pot. And it was this ethnic stew which led in the late 70s and early 80s to the emergence of a genuinely important youth movement which had its own distinctive sound: Two Tone. Even its name reflects the euphoric moment when black and white kids got together to make great tunes in the same bands, the best of which was The Specials who were originally called 'The Coventry Specials'. Their seminal Ghost Town was about Coventry, its sad concrete wastelands featuring extensively in a rare early example of the pop video which was released to accompany the song. Sadly the Tic Toc Club where it all started is no longer standing, but if you really want to hear the ghosts of Jerry Dammers et al, you can still get close to the original site.

Nowadays, Coventry's biggest connection with youth culture and especially music is genius pop entrepreneur Pete Waterman, the man who gave us Kylie, a whole host of other mega success stories and, er, Jason Donovan.

which will take you to Broadgate, the main shopping facility, a stone's throw from the Cathedral, Priory Visitors' Centre and the Museum and Art Gallery. **Allens Taxis,** T0247-6555555. **Centro Hotline** (buses and trains) local to Coventry T0247-6559559.

Information The tourist office is right next to the Cathedral in the precinct on Bayley Lane ⓘ *T0247-6227264/7266, www.coventry.org Summer Mon-Fri 0930-1700 Sat-Sun 1000- 1630, winter Mon-Fri 0930-1630 Sat-Sun 1000-1630.*

Alighting from the train the number 17 bus takes you straight into town to the Cathedral. Get off at the pseudo Tudor striking black and white *Flying Standard* pub and walk up Priory Row. **Holy Trinity Church** is on your right, notable for containing three styles of English Gothic and some very lovely stained glass. It's spire and tower collapsed in 1666 killing a passer-by, but was rebuilt even higher (237 ft). To its left is the sunken green of the **Priory Visitor's Centre** ⓘ *Priory Walk, T0247-6832383, free.* Exhibits include a glass painting of a woman's face, perhaps Lady Godiva as she has flowing wavy hair.

On to **The Cathedral** ⓘ *Visitors' Centre, 7 Priory Row, T0247-6227957, www.coventrycathedral.org, Visitors' Centre Easter-Oct Mon-Sat 1000-1600, Nov-Easter 1100-1500, adult, £2, child £1, Cathedral Easter-Oct daily 0930-1800, Nov-Easter 0930-1730*, truly wonderful, awe-inspiring and filled with many beautiful things. After the bombing of the old cathedral of St Michael's on 14th November 1940, Sir Basil Spence was charged with creating a suitable memorial to an ancient city which had suffered terribly in the Second World War. What he delivered between 1956 and 1962 was one of the most striking high-modernist buildings this side of Le Corbusier.

Some of the wonders on display include Epstein's sculpture outside the Cathedral of St Michael vanquishing the devil; *Christ Crucified*, a sculpture made from the metal of a wrecked motor car by Helen Jennings; John Piper's stained glass Baptistry window; and also the engraved glass screen, *Saints and Angels*, by John Hutton, which is a particular highlight. The tiny Gethsemone Chapel displays a mosaic of the *Angel of Agony* (by Steven Sykes) seen through a beautifully designed crown of thorns (by Basil Spence). Graham Sutherland's tapestry above the altar, *Christ in Glory*, isn't to everyone's taste, but it's still an impressive sight dominating the east end of the nave.

In the remains of the **old Cathedral**, which has the eerie beauty of a living ruin, is Epstein's *Ecce Homo* and the statue *Reconciliation*, two figures embracing in sadness, an identical one is in the Peace Garden in Hiroshima. The statue was made by Josefina De Vasconcelos when she was 90 and was given to the Cathedral in 1995 by Richard Branson.

Leaving the Cathedral from the East end and turning right you come to the **Herbert Museum and Art Gallery** ⓘ *Jordan Well, T0247-6832381, Mon-Sat 1000-1730, Sun 1200-1700, free*, a miscellaneous collection of Coventry related memorabilia. Upstairs there are a clutch of wonderful sculptures, a Henry Moore and Barbara Hepworth, for instance. There's an entertaining exhibition illustrating the history of the Sky Blues, Coventry's famous football team. And there's a whole room devoted to the famous story of **Lady Godiva**, who founded a famous Abbey in Coventry. But she's probably more famous as the wife of a local nobleman, Leofric, who was known for his cruel taxes. She appealed on behalf of the people of Coventry and he agreed to relent only if she rode naked through the city, which obligingly she did. It is said that only one citizen shamed himself by looking at her, a young man called Thomas and for ever after, the name *Peeping Tom* has been synonymous with sleazy voyeurism.

You can also get a feel for ancient Coventry at **Spon Street**, a partially reconstructed replica of an honest-to-goodness medieval street. The area lay outside the city walls along the banks of the river Sherborne which is now mostly underground. It was here that the noxiously stinky trades such as the tanning of hides and various other processes connected with wool were carried out.

Coventry Toy Museum ⓘ *Much Park St, T0247-622 7560* is in the 13th-century Gatehouse of Whitefriar's Monastery and has toys and games dating from the 18th century. Whitefriar's was a medieval Carmelite monastery, and is soon to be opened to the public.

Museum of British Road Transport ⓘ *Hales St, T0247-6832425, 1000-1700, free*, has the largest collection of British-made vehicles in the world, illustrating the development of transport from the bicycle to the jet engine. There's also a Blitz Experience illustrating Coventry's darkest hour.

Sleeping

Stratford-upon-Avon *p561, map p563*

L Alveston Manor, Clopton Bridge, on the way out of the town on the Oxford Rd, T0870-4008181. The best hotel in Stratford, it enjoys a spectacular view of the river and is within walking distance of the theatre. Pleasant Art Deco(ish) structure.

A The Moat House Hotel, Bridgefoot, T01789-279988. Originally built as a Hilton, you'd expect high standards, except when it comes to the building. Despite being 1960s, it manages to retain some character though and is next to the leisure centre.

A The Shakespeare, Chapel St, T0870-4008182. Central, good lounge area, historic building, a cosy atmosphere that nevertheless promises luxurious accommodation a stone's throw from all the attractions.

B The Stratford Victoria, Arden St, T01789-271000. A handsome Victorian townhouse. This is very superior accomodation at a more affordable price.

C The Falcon Hotel, Chapel St, T01789-279953. A very comfortable, pleasant and informal hotel with a great bar and lounge.

C Stratford Manor, Warwick Rd, T01789-731173. Has a great indoor swimming pool and all mod cons. A very tidy modern building.

C The Thistle Hotel, Waterside, T01789-294949. Theatre stopovers £110, including the pre-theatre dinner, performance and full English breakfast. Per person this is not a bad deal, especially considering the respectable quality of this ubiquitous chain.

C The White Swan, Rother St, T01789-297022. A cosy inn-type hotel, with oak beams and open fires. Highly recommended.

D **The Payton**, 6 John St, T01789-266442. Perfectly respectable guesthouse.
D **Stratheden**, 5 Chapel St, T01789-297119. Another of Stratford's many B&Bs which offers consistently good service and hospitality.
E **Eversley's Bears**, 37 Grove Rd, T01789-292334. Another budget rooming house.
E **Greenhaven Guest House**, 217 Evesham Rd, T01789-294874. Dog-lovers and smoking-haters are more than welcome here.
E **The Marlin Hotel**, 3 Chestnut Walk, T01789- 293752. A really good value establishment that takes dogs and lets you smoke.
E **Nandos**, 18-19 Evesham Pl, T01789-204907. There's a smoking lounge, dogs are welcome and there is ample parking for this very cheap B&B.
E-F **Backpacker's Hotel**, 33 Greehill St, T01789-263838. It's in the middle of town, does weekly rates and gets hideously booked up in season so be sure to book early.

Self-catering

Guild Court, 3 Guild St, T08080-555000. £350 for up to 6 people per week. £60-90 per night. Very superior 1- and 2-bedroom apartments that overlook Shakespeare's birthplace. Rather fussily decorated but this really is the lap of luxury for those who don't like the impersonality of hotels. **Anne's House**, 6 Evesham Pl, T01789-550197. £240-575, 4 adults and 2 children. Three-bedroom townhouse centrally situated, a nice period structure. **Oxstall's Farm Stud**, Warwick Rd South, T01789- 205277. £225-325 for 4 or 5 people. A bungalow on Stud Farm where they really breed beautiful gee-gees, there's even disabled access.

Caravans and camping

Avon Caravan Park, Warwick Rd, T01789-293438. A beautiful location on the banks of the river with touring pitches and also static caravans. Toilets and showers on site.
Stratford Racecourse, T01789-267949. Caravan pitches and tents Easter to Sep for all those gypsies out there and those who fancy a flutter.

Leamington Spa *p565*

Leamington has an elegant sufficiency of hotels, B&Bs and inns, though what the tourist people like to call 'Shakespeare Country' has a much wider range.
South Warwickshire Tourism, T01789-293127 and T01926-742767, provide a free booking service if you get stuck.
A-B **The Manor House Hotel**, Avenue Rd, T01926-423251. A substantial Victorian pile, it's probably the best hotel in town and benefits from its sheltered location. You can imagine the Victorian glitterati parading their stuff round these elegant rooms and halls.
C **The Angel Hotel**, Regent St, T01926-881296. Older and more laid-back than some of the stuffier joints in town, as it allows dogs and benefits from extensive parking facilities.
C **The Avenue Heritage Hotel**, 15-17 Spencer St, T01926-425601. An outstanding contribution to the unspoilt pub-inn genre just round the corner from The Pump Rooms.
D **Avenue Lodge**, 61 Avenue Rd, T01926-338555. This is a lovely Victorian House run by a friendly soul called Mr. Pandy Nijjar.
D-E **The Charnwood Guesthouse**, 47 Avenue Rd, T01926-831074.

Warwick *p565*

A-B **The Rose and Crown**, 30 Market Pl, Warwick, T01926-411117. A very smart newly opened hotel. Lots of bright colours, a cool bar and a somewhat trendy clientele.
C **Charter House**, 87-91 West St, Warwick, T01926-496965. Benefits from a great deal of privacy and a lovely garden. There's even a grand piano for the 'serious musician' and a strict no-smoking policy.
D **The Seven Stars**, Friar's St, Warwick, T01926-492658. Jolly inn-style establishment, enjoys the patronage of locals and is highly recommended.
E **Austin House Guest House**, 96 Emscote Rd, Warwick, T01926-493583. Perfectly acceptable guesthouse in the guesthouse ghetto of Warwick.

Coventry *p568*

If you need to stay the night here, it's worth looking outside the centre of the city.
L **The Hilton**, Walsgrave Triangle, T0247-660300. Luxurious inner city accomodation, but it'll cost you dearly.

A The Coombe Abbey Hotel, Brinklow Rd, Binley, T0247-6450450. The site of the old Abbey where Elizabeth daughter of James I was imprisoned during the Gunpowder Plot. Superb grounds and facilities, a little way out of Coventry with award-winnind dining.

A MacDonald Ansty Hall Hotel, Main Rd, Ansty, T0247-6612222. Ten minutes from the city centre, this is a 17th-century building which serves delicious food using produce from the hotel's own walled garden.

B The Allesley Hotel, Birmingham Rd, Allesley, T0247-6403272. A sprawling modern hotel in an old village centre, with traditional menus and a disco on a Saturday night.

B Brandon Hall Hotel, Brandon, T0870-400 8105. Former shooting lodge in extensive grounds.

B-C The Marriott, London Rd, Ryton on the A46 on the edge of Coventry, T0247-6301585. As you'd expect from this chain, a tolerable degree of comfort and its very near the largest organic gardens in Europe. Good deals at the weekend.

D Ansty Arms, Brinklow Rd, Ansty, T0247-6611817. A farmhouse converted into one of those rather handy Travel Lodges, look out for Alan Partridge at the local double-glazing conference.

Eating

Stratford-upon-Avon *p561, map p563*

Stratford restaurants are an amiable mix of beautiful country pubs some of which have had the 'gastro' makeover, and smart, if a little old-school, silver service-type establishments. And of course, this being the Midlands, there are plenty of curry houses.

£££ Alladin's, Tiddington Main St, Tiddington Rd. Friendly curry house reasonably priced, recommended by locals.

£££ Falcon's Hotel, Chapel St, T01789-279953. Traditional English food, very reasonably priced in an extremely comfortable ambience.

£££ Lamb's Bistro, Sheep St, T01789-2922554. Fine dining, one of Stratford's best, but extremely busy, so book ahead.

£££ Marlowe's Restaurant, 18 High St, T01789-204999. A stunning late 16th-century building, this is one of the best restaurants in Stratford, though it is rather formal and prides itself on silver service waitering.

£££ Royal Shakespeare Theatre, T01789-403414. The complex has 2 restaurants – a bistro-style affair which is always overflowing with punters, and a classier, and of course more expensive, restaurant serving a variety of modern English and French cuisine. Both have spectacular views of the river.

£££ Salmon Tail Inn, Evesham Rd, T01789-551913. Traditional English pub between the town centre and the racecourse with excellent restaurant.

£££ Santa Lucia, 37 Shottery, T01789-414629. More family-orientated restaurant, boasting live music most weekends and some fairly over the top murals, but it's a fun place nevertheless.

£££ Sorrento, 8 Ely St, T01789-297999. Italian trattoria, simply but elegantly decorated with a pleasant easy-going atmosphere.

££ Mayflower, 22 High St, T01789-297161. One of Stratford's best Chinese restaurants it also does a roaring takeaway trade.

££ Thespians, 26 Sheep St, T01789-267187. An army of smiling, extremely courteous staff in this place which, despite its name specializes in north Indian cuisine, including Baltis. Caters for pre- and after-theatre dining.

Warwick *p565*

££ Cellar Restaurant, 5/6 The Knibbs Smith St, Warwick, T01926-400809. This is one of the best restaurants in Warwick with an eerie atmosphere, located as it is in the cellar.

££ Fanshawe's Restaurant, 22 Market Pl, Warwick, T01926-410590. Not nearly as posh as the *Cellar*, it's a much more modest affair with an informal feel to it and more affordable, less fancy fare.

££ Findons Restaurant, 7 Old Sq, Warwick, T01926-411755. This place has a claim to being the best restaurant in Warwick. They do take themselves a bit seriously, though. Specialities include Seared Scottish King Scallops and Roast Leg of English Lamb.

£ Giovanni's Restaurant, 15 Smith St, Warwick, T01926 494904. A friendly and unsurprising Italian restaurant, though try to avoid the large parties of office workers out for an upmarket works do.

£ Hermans, 11 Old Sq, Warwick, T07974-951257. This is a small friendly coffee shop with a distinctly cosmopolitan flavour, though the prices are very reasonable. Sandwiches, snacks, cakes, all day breakfast £2.60.

Leamington Spa *p565*

Leamington has responded well to a local appetite for fine wining and dining with a handful of outstanding restaurants and bars.

£££ Amor's, 15 Dormer Place, T01926-778744. The real deal when it comes to authentic French food in Leamington, if you really want to push the boat out, this place also knows how to treat a discriminating diner.

£££ Casa Valle, 42 Regent St, T01926-741128. A fine Italian restaurant, not as old school as *Piccolinos*, *Casa Valle* isn't cheap at £25 a head, but there's something to be said for peerless pasta and strawberry tiramisu to die for.

£££ Dorjes, 9 Regent Pl, T01926-311056. Rivals *Solo* (below) for the best food, but where it really scores is the unparalleled wine cellar.

£££ Solo, 23 Dormer Pl, T01926-422422. Arguably the best restaurant in Leamington. The food is really inventive with great soups, almost a meal in themselves and the service is unfussy with plenty of informed comment on your wine and food choices.

£ The Basement Restaurant, 1 Spencer St, T01926-887288. A budget option with quite a lot going for it, not least the live jazz that this smoky 80s dive hosts on a regular basis.

£ Paprika Club, Regent St. An original take on the traditional curry house with cool decor and really excellent cuisine simply prepared.

Coventry *p568*

£££ The Cosy Cottage Restaurant, 1-3, Ryley St, T0247-6551234. Despite its decidedly dowdy name, it has a head chef who was previously at the Savoy, so expect good traditional food. It's in a renovated 16th-century building behind the Belgrade Theatre and has a pre-theatre menu from 1730-1900.

£££ Kakooti, Spon St, T0247-6221392. Featuring organic Italian wines and world cuisine, this is well situated on one of the most picturesque streets in Coventry. There's the occasional live sax night, but don't let that put you off. It also caters for allergies.

£££ Millsy's Café and Bar and the **Gallery Restaurant**, 20 Earlsden St, Earlsden, T0247-6713222. Two superb dining experiences in one location. The *Gallery* was listed in The Guardian as one of the UK's top 40 eating places. Some very inventive cuisine.

££ Allesley Hotel (details see 572). Traditional menu and Saturday Carvery, it's a little bit like a superior Berni Inn.

££ The Athenia Greek Restaurant, 49 Corporation St, T0247-6634949. This has got the lot; a live bazooki band, plus lots of plate-throwing and a disco, it's not the place for a quiet night out, but the food's reasonable, if you can hear yourself think.

££ Browns, Earl St, T0247-6221100. It's immensely popular with the townsfolk, no wonder because the food's freshly prepared, it has a strong veggie menu, a pleasant ambience and a terrace overlooking the Cathedral.

££ Cheylsmore Balti, Daventry Rd, T0247-6506147. A reasonable balti house, though don't expect Brummie standards. It is open late on Fri and Sat.

££ The Dragon Phoenix, Hertford Pl, The Butts, T0247-6258688. A Chinese buffet restaurant open 7 days a week – it's very popular so make sure you book ahead.

££ Ristorante Etna, Hertford St, T0247-6223183. A lovely old-school Italian trattoria, much patronized by the locals, with Sicilian cuisine as well as the usual Italian fare.

££ Thai Dusil, London Rd, T0247-6227788. The only Thai in Coventry with a good menu.

Pubs, bars and clubs

Stratford-upon-Avon *p561, map p563*

Bar Humbug, Guild St, T01789-292109. This ever-expanding chain is actually quite good news for the trendier type of punter. Beer garden and acceptable restaurant.

Bar M (formerly *The Frog and Elbow*), Arden St, T01789-297641. This is about the only place for a late night drink in Stratford, it also features live music every now and again, but there's quite a draconian door policy.

The Cross Keys, Ely St, T01789-293909. A great night out for younger types, this is one of the premier youth pubs in the area and is the assignation point for lots of foreign language students on the pull.

Dirty Duck, Waterside, T01789-297312. The ultimate luvvies pub in Stratford, frequented by members of the RSC and the multitude of hangers-on the theatre world has always attracted. Beware of the somewhat arrogant publicans; the smell of greasepaint seems to have gone to their heads.

Embargo, 1 Shakespeare St, T01789-293400. Not quite as exotic as its name, but a superb warm-up spot for a night on the town.

Falcon Hotel, Church St, T01789-279953. The pub attached to a very pleasant hotel, not quite as packed with the young 'uns as some of the other pubs on this list.

Garrick Inn, High St, T01789-292186. This is the place to come if you like your pubs seriously beautiful and like a movie set from Olde Englande. The beer's not bad, either.

The Lamplighter, Rother St, T01789-293071. Another hang-out of the young and trendy, this is a good place to go before a gig at The Civic Hall which used to have live music, but doesn't seem to have that much these days. It's got very friendly bar staff and a lovely open fire, as well as that old favourite Sky TV.

Othello's, Chapel St, T01789-294562. It's attached to quite a posh restaurant, and subsequently the clientele's a bit more upmarket and mature than your average Stratford teen hang-out.

The Rose and Crown, Sheep St, T01789-297884. Some would say the ultimate under-age drinking pub in Stratford, but it's pretty lively and there's lots of vibrant cheeky young things if you're after a sociable night out.

The Windmill Inn, Church St, T01789-297687. Another youth hang-out but extremely friendly with a network of cosy, really picturesque rooms that are begging to be occupied for at least an entire day of supping the local ale, Flowers.

The College Arms, Lower Quinton, T01789-720342. An historic 16th-century inn on the edge of the Cotswolds, originally owned by Henry VIII.

Coventry *p568*

The town has always loved partying, so you'd expect to find lots of drinking holes, plus of course some nightclubs of a rather dubious stripe.

The Old Windmill, Spon St, T0247-6252183. Another great reason for visiting this historic street, this is the oldest and possibly the nicest pub in the city. Better known as Ma Brown's it sells great real ale and some interesting English wines like elderberry, sloe and mead. It is also a popular pre-club drinking place. Beautiful beams, real fires and a warren of pannelled rooms.

The Golden Cross, Hay La, T0247-6222311. This place claims to have been a student pub since 1583. It's really a classic city centre boozer built on the site of a medieval mint, but the upstairs bar is open till 0100 Wed-Sat for dance events and live music.

The Varsity, Little Park St, T0247-6630862. Also popular with students.

Black Eagle Bar, in the Leofric Hotel, Upper Precinct, T0247-6221371. Once Coventry's smartest, most chic hang-out, it's enjoying a reasonably successful revival on the back of the cocktail boom. It also has live music from time to time.

Clubs

Coventry West Indian Club, Spon St, T0247-6225967. It's a community centre, but it still has some wicked dancing opportunities especially if you like reggae.

The Irish Centre 2000, Watch Cl, Spon St, T0247-6229132. This is a place for over 21s, playing a selection of retro music from the 60s to the 80s.

Over The Rainbow, Short St, T0247-6551738. Coventry's only gay club, playing the usual selection of gay anthems as well as loads of cabaret, drag and boy bands.

Entertainment

Stratford-upon-Avon *p561, map p563*

Music

The Bandstand on the Recreation Ground has bands on some Sunday afternoons during the summer.

The Civic Hall, 14 Rother St, box office T01789-414513, www.civichall.co.uk. The venue for variety shows, classical music, big band, pantomime and dance nights. Licensed bar.

Festivals

Stratford-upon-Avon *p561, map p563*

Apr Shakespeare's Birthday Celebrations. Morris dancing, street entertainers, the ceremony of the unfurling of the flags, the floral procession of dignitaries from all over the world between the Birthplace and Holy Trinity Church, dancing by local children and much more.

Jun Stratford Regatta (3rd Sat in Jun), on the River Avon.

Jul Stratford-upon-Avon International Flute Festival, T01789- 261561, stratflute@aol.com, 30 chamber music concerts.

Oct Stratford-upon-Avon English Music Festival, T01926-496277, www.warwickarts.org.uk.

Oct Stratford Mop Fair. The central streets of Stratford are closed to traffic for this annual traditional street fair with fairground rides and stalls, and the roasting of a whole ox, the first piece of which is auctioned for charity by the Mayor. It is one of the biggest mop fairs in the country.

Oct Runaway Mop. A smaller version of the Stratford Mop Fair.

Shopping

Stratford-upon-Avon *p561, map p563*

Antiques

Barns Antiques Centre 5 miles from Stratford, T01789-721399. The largest antique centre in south Warwickshire, it's crammed full of collectables, bygones and antiques in a huge barn.

Clothes

As the town's various luvvies wouldn't be seen dead in anything but the finest togs, there's a surprisingly decent collection of clothes shops. You'll find **Jaeger** at 13 Bridge St, **Monsoon** at 2 Red Lion Court and **Oxford Campus Stores** at 31 Henley St. There's a **Ragazzi** at 7 Shrieve's Walk just down from the **Prima Donna Boutique** also on Shrieve St, off Rother St. If you're in need of 'fashion therapy', try **Gemini** at 15 Wood St, or **Gemini Shoes**, 3 Cook's Alley, where the proprietor offers healing hands for the fashion traumatized.

Markets

Selling of a more basic kind happens at the famous Traditional Chartered Markets (all over town, but particularly Market Square), which still take place every week throughout the year. Stratford has been a market place for centuries, receiving its charters over 800 years ago. **The Farmer's Market** takes place once a week, where you can buy superb fresh produce from some of the best farming land in the country.

Activities and tours

Stratford-upon-Avon *p561, map p563*

Air

Heart of England Hot Air Balloons, Cross Lans Fram, Haselor, Warwick, T01789-488219.

Heli Air LImited, Wellesbourne Airfield, Wellesbourne, T01789-470476.

Angling

Daily tickets can be obtained for coarse fishing from the Water Bailiffs opposite the Theatre. Water Authority Licences may be obtained from:

Dave Jones, 17 Evesham Rd, T01789-293950;

Alcester Sports & Tackle, 3a High St, Alcester, T01789- 762200;

Stratford Angling Association, T01789-205700/299637.

Boating

Avon Cruises (Passenger Boats), Swan's Nest, Boat House, T01789-267073.

Stratford-on-Avon Boat Club, The Boat House, T01789-297265.

Golf

Ingon Manor Golf and Country Club, Ingon La, T01789-731857.

Stratford Golf Club, Tiddington Rd, T01789-205749.

Stratford Oaks, Bearley Rd, Snitterfield, T01789-731980.

Gliding

Bidford Gliding Centre, Honeybourne Rd, Bidford-on-Avon, T01789- 772606.

Stratford-upon-Avon Gliding Club, Snitterfield Airfield, Snitterfield Rd, Bearley, T01789- 731095.

Horse racing

Stratford-upon-Avon Racecourse, Luddington Rd, T01789-267949.

Horse riding

Woodland Stables, School La, Bearley, T01789-731774.

Pathlow Riding Centre, Featherbed La, Pathlow, T01789-299984.
W.J. Pettigrew, Ettington Park Stables, T01789-450653.
The Sport Horse Training Centre, The Wolds, The Green, Snitterfield, T01789-730222.
Pebworth Vale, Moat Farm, Pebworth, T01789-720900.

Tennis
Stratford Lawn Tennis Club, Swan's Nest La, T01789-295801.

Transport

Stratford-upon-Avon *p561, map p563*
Bus
Long distance National Express, T08705-808080, run 3 direct services per day from **London Victoria** (3 hrs) at 0830, 1330 and 1830, **Birmingham** (1 hr). **Guide Friday** run an open top double decker tour of the town and of the surrounding areas. Details are available from **Guide Friday**, Stratford Civic Hall, 14 Rother St, T01789-294466.

Car
Marbella Car Hire, 1 Central Chambers, Henley St, T01789-268002. **Hertz Rent-a-car**, Rail Station, Station Rd, T01789-298827.

Cycle
Spencer-Clarke's Cycles, Guild St, T01789-450788.

Taxi
Ranks are situated in Wood St, Rother St and Briedge St, Bridgefoot and the Railway station. **Shakespeare Taxis**, 17 Greenhill St, T01789-266100; **Stratford Taxis**, 27a Windsor St, T0800-243061.

Train
Stratford Railway Station is off the Alcester Rd. For timetable details call **Warwickshire Council's Traveline**, T01926-414140. There are 3 direct **Virgin Trains** services from **London Paddington** daily (2 hrs 30 mins) as well as many other slower services from Paddington, **Euston** or **Marylebone** stations. Hourly trains to and from Birmingham New Street (1 hr).

Leamington Spa *p565*
Bus
Leamington is well served by bus and coach with frequent **National Express**, T08705-808080, services from the north and south.

Car
Leamington is within easy striking distance of the extensive motorway network in the area. From north and south via the M40 take junctions 14 and 15, or the M1. Travelling from the west-south-west, take the M5 and leave it at Bromsgrove picking up the M42.

Taxi
A2B Taxis, Station Approach, T01926-470048; **Avon Knight Cars**, 15 High St, T01926-420041; **Dialacab**, 13 Maple Rd, T01926-882965.

Train
Chiltern Railways, T08705-165165, run 2 trains an hr from **London Marylebone** (hourly on Sun) (1hr 40 mins). There are also trains from **Paddington**. Coming from the north the same service will depart from either **Birmingham Snow Hill** or **Moor St** (30 mins) and is also twice hourly. From the East and West Midlands and from East Anglia, Manchester and Wales, **Central Train Services**, T0870-0006060, run frequent services at subsidized prices.

Directory

Stratford-upon-Avon *p561, map p563*
Hospitals Stratford Hospital, Arden St, T01789-292209. Minor injuries unit 0900-1700 daily. **Warwick Hospital**, Lakin Rd, Warwick, T01926-495321. 24 hr A&E. **Arden Medical Centre**, Albany Rd, T01789-414942. **Internet** The Cyber Junction, 28 Greenhill St, T01789-263400. **Post office**: Henley St, T0845-7740740. **Library** Public library on Henley St, T01789-292209. See page 564 for details of Shakespeare Centre Library. **Police** Rother St, T01789-414111.

Coventry *p568*
Hospitals Coventry and Warwick Hospital, Stonystanton Rd, T0247-6224055. **Police** Little Park Police Station, Little Park Rd, T0247-6539010.

Herefordshire and Worcestershire

→ Colour map 4, grid C2-3

Along with its northern neighbour Shropshire, Herefordshire still just about remains one of the least 'spoiled' counties in England. Famous for its ruddy cattle, it hardly deserves its bovine reputation. Hops, hedgerows and rural scenes are what the county does best. Anyone in search of villages, landscapes and locals who have yet to embrace the tourist dollar and London escapees could do worse than start looking here. This well-wooded border country was never industrialized and agriculture has continued here on a smaller scale than elsewhere. The beautiful river Wye runs through the south of the county, with Ross-on-Wye the official gateway to the Wye Valley. Halfway up, the old market town of Ledbury and then the capital Hereford, both reward visitors thanks to their unhurried way of life and outstanding local produce. To the west, just over the border in Wales, the town of Hay-on-Wye has become synonymous with the book trade. Tourist activity in the north of the county tends to stick to the Black and White village trail around the delightful town of Leominster. Worcestershire to the east is most famous for its elegant and watery Malvern Hills, inspiration for no less a great cause than the Enigma Variations. **▸▸ *For Sleeping, Eating and other listings, see pages 590-597.***

Worcester, the Malverns and the Vale of Evesham

Worcester is a perfect gem of a city nestling on the banks of the Severn river to the south of the Malvern Hills, some of the best countryside the West Midlands has to offer. The city is full of great history, quirky shops and beautiful medieval streets. Sir Edward Elgar, its most famous son, is commemorated admirably both in the Cathedral (a magnificent structure) and in the nearby countryside where he grew up and which was often the inspiration for his music. And once you start exploring the town, you realize that Worcester has a lot going for it, especially if you like superb bars, pubs, restaurants and some really stylish shopping opportunities. To the southeast, the town of Evesham is swaddled in delightful and highly productive countryside best-known for its market-gardening and spring blossom.

Ins and outs

Getting there There are regular **trains** from London Paddington to Shrub Hill Station Worcester, the journey takes around 2 hours 15 minutes. There are also twice hourly trains at peak times from Birmingham New Street to Foregate, which is more convenient for the centre.

The M5 is an excellent nearby thoroughfare and by exiting at Junction 7, you'll get to Worcester very quickly. This serves travellers from Birmingham in the north and as far southwest as Exeter. Coming from London the M4 joins the M5 just outside Bristol or if you prefer a more historical route passing through Oxford, you can take the M40 to Birmingham and then the M42 will connect you with the M5. **National Express** coaches, T08705-808080, stop on the edge of the city with links to scheduled city bus services. **Cambridge Coach Services** go direct to Crown Gate Bus Station. Enquiries T0870-6082608.

The City stands on the banks of the River Severn and the Worcester & Birmingham Canal so there are plenty of opportunities to get a **boat** either from Bristol and Cardiff, or a canal barge from Birmingham.

Getting around Making your way round Worcester centre can be fraught with frustration because of one major 2-lane road that divides most of the town from the wonderful Cathedral Precinct. Once you're away from this road, however, much of the centre is pedestrianized.

Information TIC ⓘ *in The Guildhall on the High St, T01905-726311, www.cityofworcester.gov.uk, daily 0930-1730.*

Worcester

On a purely visual level, Worcester does have an extraordinary range of spectacular street architecture from imposing Georgian Churches converted into smart bars to perfect examples of early Tudor buildings which have been pubs for over 300 years. There's an old saying that Worcester has a different pub for every day of the year and it's true that Friar Street – the superlatively preserved mainly Elizabethan and Tudor pedestrianized walkway – is a cornucopia of great restaurants, pubs and even smarter shops than those on the High Street.

The Guildhall is as good a place as any to start your trip round Worcester and even though it's a walk from Foregate Station where most of the trains from London and Birmingham arrive, you'll get a taste of how smart Worcester is. Designed by a local, Thomas White, the building looks like an 18th-century palace from the outside with its amazing wrought iron gate and Italianate façade. The real glories, however, are reserved for the inside and the **Pump Room** which is like a beautiful highly decorated ball room, but now full of the worthy burghers of Worcester wolfing down roast dinners – the place is also a self-serve restaurant and tea room. ⓘ *Phone and address as tourist office.*

The Worcester History Centre and Archives is full of the inevitable genealogy buffs but also has some fascinating stuff on the history of Worcester. Although it's really only for hardcore lovers of history, at the time of writing half of the **Worcester Museum and Art Gallery** ⓘ *Foregate St, T01905-25371, www.worcestercitymuseums.org.uk, Mon-Fri 0930-1730, Sat 0930-1700 closed Sun, free*, collection was languishing in a basement under the building beyond Foregate Station, so the **History Centre** ⓘ *Trinity St, T01905-765922, www.worcestershire.gov.uk/records, free opening Mon 0930-1900, Tue-Thu 0930-1730, Fri 0930-1900, Sat 0930-1600*, **The Museum of Local Life** on Friar Street (see below) and **The Commandery** (see below) are the best places to go to find out about historic Worcester.

Turning right from *The Pheasant Inn*, a 3-storey Tudor building dating from 1540, you will be facing down Friar St, in the direction of the main reasons for being there, namely the great historic sights, bijou shops and restaurants that typify this touristic paradise. **Greyfriars** ⓘ *Friar St, T01905-23571, 1 Apr-31 Oct, tours should be arranged in writing with Mr V Hemingway at Greyfriars, £3, child £1.50, family £7.50*, from which the street takes its name, is probably the oldest building on the street. Its imposing, somewhat forbidding, gabled rear-end runs down the side of Friar St, but it's only accessible from a picturesque walkway running off on the left of Friar St a little way down from *The Pheasant*. Built as a townhouse in 1480 next to a very early medieval monastery, this site dates from the beginnings of the Cathedral in the 10th century. There's also a really magnificent garden.

From here it's a short walk to **The Museum of Local Life** ⓘ *Friar St, T01905-722349, Mon-Sat 1030-1700, closed Thu and Sun, free*, which is housed in yet another Tudor delight. Even though they claim to specialize in Victorian Worcester with a few really good tableaux such as 'Bathtime for little Alphonse' and a great 19th-century schoolroom, they've also got a fascinating exhibit on the archaeological dig on a local suburb called White Ladies Aston, tracing it back to the Iron Age. Round the back there's a Victorian machine yard, featuring a hop press, some 19th-century advertising hoardings and a picture of the world-famous Worcester Sauce being unloaded in a most novel way.

Once you do make it into the grounds of what has been called 'the most beautiful cathedral in Britain' you begin to realize what all the fuss is about. It's not as majestic as Salisbury, as weird as Exeter or as imposing as Durham. But if you want a church where you can really feel the mystery of history and the kind of awe that people must have felt a thousand years ago when they saw the majesty of this holy place, then **Worcester Cathedral** ⓘ *Chapter Office, 10a College Green, T01905-28854/21004, www.cofe-worcester.org.uk*, is for you. Not that the Cathedral was above burying the odd unholy man, like King John whose body lies in a tomb near the main altar. In a codicil to his will he asked to be buried in Worcester Cathedral and being 'the faithful city', they obliged with a handsome tomb closer to the most sanctified part of the building than anyone else. Apart, that is, from **Prince Arthur's Chantry** which was built to house the remains of Henry VIII's elder brother. There's also a **Norman Crypt** – the oldest in the country – some really lovely Victorian stained glass which rivals Notre Dame and Canterbury, and an intriguing Georgian outbuilding called **The Guesten House** which may only be available for corporate events, but apparently does occasionally entertain tourists with talks which may also have to be pre-arranged with the Tourist Officer.

The Cathedral Precinct consists also of **The King's School** and the world-renouned **Choir School**. Every year the Cathedral Choirs of Worcester, Hereford and Gloucester get down and strut their funky stuff in competition with each other. **The Three Choirs Festival** (see page 595) takes place in Worcester once every three years.

Leaving the Cathedral square by **The Edgar Gate** which looks as if it could be the inspiration for Worcester's Coat of Arms you enter a little network of streets but have to cross the dreadful Sidbury road to get to **The Commandery** ⓘ *Sidbury, T01905-361821, www.worcestercitymuseums.org.uk, Mon-Sat 1000-1700, Sun 1330-1700, £4, child £2.50*, which started life around the time of St Wulfstan, founder of the current Cathedral in the 11th century. The place was originally a hospital where the sick were tended to by monks, but it really came into its own when a local wealthy clothier called Wylde put what was now his family home at the disposal of **Charles II** and his Royalist Army prior to the Battle of Worcester in 1651. It manages to score with a really thorough presentation on the history of this turbulent time, complete with a tableaux of the sentencing of Charles I to death by beheading.

Just across the road from the Commandery **The Royal Worcester Visitor** Centre ⓘ *Royal Porcelain Works, Severn St, T01905-23221, www.royal-worcester.co.uk Mon-Sat 0900-1730, Sun 1100-1700*, is the perfect contrast to the blood, guts and diseases of the Commandery. With guided tours of the factory, a great little museum which shows you how the elite have coped with changing trends in place-settings over the last 300 years and a fabulous shop showcasing the work of the oldest continuous porcelain manufacturer in the country, this is one of the top places to visit in the city.

Around Worcester

There is a wonderful new attraction a little way out of Worcester, the **Elgar Birthplace and Museum** ⓘ *Crown East La, Lower Broadheath, Worcester, T01905-333224, www.elgar.org, museum open daily, 1100-1700 last admission 1615, exclusive evening visits by prior booking. Longer hours 1000-1730, in Aug for Three Choirs Festival. Closed Christmas-end Jan. Just about accessible by public transport, but you need to call the County Busline for details T0345-125436*. Here you'll find all manner of Elgar treasures with regular concerts of his work and rare manuscripts to help you unlock the secret of the man who wrote 'Land of Hope and Glory', as well as a brilliant cello concerto. You'll also be in striking distance of the beautiful Malvern Hills (see below) where Elgar probably came up with that famous piece of patriotism.

 There's one other place near Worcester that's really worth a visit if you're a fan of stately ruins and excellent sculpture – as well as the odd monster. **Witley Court and the Jerwood Foundation** ⓘ *Great Witley, Worcestershire, T01299-896636, Apr-Oct, 1000-1800, Oct-Mar 1000-1700*, is maintained by English Heritage and is a really stunning and spooky ruin surrounded by some important work by 18th-century monumentalist sculptor Nesfield.

The Malvern Hills

For some England has no more beautiful countryside to offer than the Malvern Hills, an ancient and mysterious eruption of 650-million-year-old granite and crystalline rock. Pushing their way upwards dramatically from the surrounding flat landscape, the hills lie a few miles southwest of Worcester and divide the counties of Herefordshire and Worcestershire. The aptly named 'Land of Hope and Glory' may well have been inspired by the composer Elgar's frequent visits to this extraordinary and serene geographical anomaly, and he certainly first conceived the original tune upon which the *Enigma Variations* were based while walking here. William Langland, a 14th-century Christian radical mystic, was also so moved by the incomparable countryside that he was struck by a vision which became the basis for the epic poem *Piers Plowman*.

Information TIC ⓘ *21 Church St, Great Malvern, T01684-892289, www.malvernhills.gov.uk, daily 1000-1700.*

Malvern

The logical place to start, whether you're a walking fan or a water fan attracted to the famous English rivers Severn, Avon and Teme, is really the town of **Malvern**, which actually consists of seven different 'Malverns' spread around the slopes of the hills, from **West Malvern** via **Great Malvern** to **Little Malvern** in the south. Great Malvern is really the centre, with fantastic views to the west over the town as well as being the best starting point for the obligatory walk on the hills. It's also the oldest part of Malvern and because of its remoteness was chosen by the Norman Benedictine Monks for the location of the Great Priory Church (see below), built in 1085. Malvern continued as a relatively sleepy location until the 19th century when ailing city types and sophisticates were drawn by the famous Malvern 'water-cure', now transformed into a thriving bottled spring water business. Consequently, this Victorian blooming led to the architectural flavour of much of the town, best exemplified by Bellevue Terrace, a sort of faux Georgian front which runs at right angles to Church St, the main drag of Great Malvern.

The magnificent 11th-century **Priory Church** ⓘ *Parish Office, T01684-561020, www.greatmalvernpriory.org.uk*, has a rich heritage going back over 900 years. The building itself is a combination of Norman and Perpendicular Gothic and has some extraordinary stained glass depicting a rare example of the *arma Christi* – the wounds of Christ – which miraculously survived the English Reformation. The **gatehouse** originally housed visitors to the Abbey, dates back to around 1400 and is an extraordinarily ornate structure which now is the location of **Malvern Town Museum** ⓘ *Abbey Gateway, T01684-567811, Easter-Oct 1030-1700.*There's a fascinating exhibit on the water-cure doctors and their hydropathic establishments, and the bottling of water since 1622.

The TIC will supply you with a plethora of walking guides to the Hills, but the best way to get to them is via the **North Hill** and **Worcesterhire Beacon,** at the north end of the range. The reward for reaching the top is a truly amazing view – one of the best in England and from which it is said you can see six counties. Luckily there's somewhere you can fortify yourself before attempting this climb: **St Ann's Well** ⓘ *Café, T01684-560285, reached from right next to the TIC via a leafy path and 99 steps*, a lovely little building dating back to 1815, which became very popular for those taking the water-cure as there's a fresh-water spring on site. An elaborately carved font is one of the main attractions and you can still 'take the waters' there, (although a highly conscientious note from the council suggests that you boil it first). For those not wishing to take a risk, there's a more recently built octagonal extension to St Ann's Well which houses a superb café with a wide range of health drinks and some wonderful cake.

Other unmissable treats of the region include **Upton-upon-Severn** which used to be an important port on the Severn and still houses a splendid marina as well as The **Upton Heritage Centre** ⓘ *T01684-592679, Easter-Oct 1300-1630 daily*, in an extraordinary building known as *The Pepperpot*. The **TIC** ⓘ *4 High St, T01684-594200*, as usual is the best place to find out about local accomodation and events, the most famous of which is the Upton Jazz Festival which usually takes place during the last weekend of June.

The Vale of Evesham

Evesham owes its beginnings to a humble swineherd called Eoves who in AD 709 had a vision of the Virgin Mary while searching for an escaped pig in an area called 'The Lomme'. Unable to believe his eyes, he persuaded his boss, Ecgwin, Bishop of Worcester, to come and have a look. The bishop was so impressed by the quality of the vision and the general holiness of the location that he decided to build a great Abbey there, which at the height of its power was one of the top three most important religious sites in the country.

Easily reached from Birmingham on the A435 or from Oxford in the south on the A44, the area around Evesham produces most of the country's fruits and probably the best asparagus in the world (which is cheap, available in virtually every pub, restaurant and hotel and served, in the local style, with brown bread and plenty of delicious butter). The optimum time for experiencing what the local tourist Tsars have dubbed **'The Blossom Trail'**, is from late March to early May. The plum orchards explode with colour first, rapidly followed 10-14 days later by the apple blossoms.

Evesham itself is a bustling market town with its roots going back to well before the Middle Ages. The River Avon has always played a central part in the history of the town and in the 19th century became the chief reason for the town becoming so popular with Victorian day trippers who saw messing about on the water as a healthy, wholesome outdoor pursuit akin to cycling and walking. To this day there's a plethora of boating activities to be explored and one of the best is the trip boat *Handsam Too* which can be boarded in Abbey Park, right next to the Almonry and **Tourist Information Centre** ⓘ *T01386-446944, www.evesham.uk.com, Mon-Sat 1000- 1700, Sun 1400-1700, closed for 2 weeks at Christmas and New Year*. The **Almonry** is a wonderful and extremely well-preserved 14th-century building which also used to be the home of the chief Entertainments Officer of the Abbey. It now contains a museum spread out over a warren of period rooms which reflect the town's history. There's a particularly interesting exhibit on local lad Simon De Montfort, arguably the founder of Parliamentary Democracy.

Evesham Abbey was largely dismantled at the orders of Henry VIII in 1540, but the tourist people have thoughtfully provided markers as to the original structure's boundaries and still standing are the twin churches of All Saints and St Lawrence and Abbot Lichfield's fine 16th-century bell tower. These buildings within the Abbey precincts form an impressive backdrop to the **Abbey Park** with its grassy banks, shady trees and flower beds sweeping down to the River Avon (where some of the best boat trips and angling are to be had for miles around). The Battle of Evesham, the last skirmish of the Baron's War against an autocratic monarchy, was fought here in 1265. De Montfort led the charge for the Barons but was defeated by Edward, Henry III's son. His body was hacked to pieces and sent to the far flung corners of the Kingdom. However, the monks of the Abbey were able to save a fragment of De Montfort's remains and buried him with due ceremony before the High Altar of the Abbey, a spot now commemorated by a simple Stone Memorial.

Hereford and around

Hereford has a slightly stodgy reputation which is really unfair. In fact, it's a dignified, solidly built place on the banks of the Wye in the process of reinventing itself as a 'City of Living Crafts' thanks to the growing reputation of its technical college. Craft shops and cottage industries are doing well here, part of an increasingly diversified rural economy. Approached from the east across the broad floodplain of the Lug, unmissable sights in the city include the diminutive cathedral and its most prized possession: the Mappa Mundi. This extraordinary survival from the Middle Ages, a parchment atlas of the world, is on display in a purpose-built annexe that also provides room for the largest chained library in the world. The Cathedral also plays host to The Three Choirs Festival every three years, the oldest event of its type in Europe. The countryside around Hereford repays a visit with its sleepy and smart little villages. The meanderings of the Wye run past rolling hills until they meet the Welsh border at Hay-on-Wye, secondhand book centre of the free world. To the north, the 'Black and White' village trail leads up through half-timbered settlements clustered around ancient churches towards charming old Leominster with its impressive Priory church, flourishing bric-a-brac shops and market produce.

Ins and outs

Getting there There are a few direct **trains** a day from London Paddington to Ledbury, Hereford and Leominster taking around 2 hours 40 minutes-3 hours, but generally you will have to change either at Newport in Wales or Worcester. It's also at least a 2 hour journey to the area from Birmingham via Worcester. Hereford is 20 miles west of Junction 2 of the M50 , bypassing Ledbury on the A417 and the A438, about 3 hours' **drive** from London. **National Express,**T08705-808080, run two coaches a day to Hereford from London Victoria, taking about 4 hours.

Getting around Local **bus** services (patience needed to reach the outlying villages) are run by **First,** T01905-763888, and **Lug Valley Primrose Travel,** T01568-612759, out of Leominster. **Stagecoach,** T01633-485118, head into South Wales. All the towns in the area are easily walked around.

Information Hereford TIC ⓘ *1 King St, T01432-268430, www.visitorlinks.com, daily 0900-1700, Sun 1000-1600*. **Ledbury TIC** ⓘ *3 The Homend, T01531-636147*. **Leominster TIC** ⓘ *1 Corn Sq, T01568-616460*. **Hay-on-Wye TIC** ⓘ *Craft Centre, Oxford Rd, T01497-820144, www. hay-on-wye.co.uk, Easter-Oct daily 1000-1700, Nov-Apr 1100-1600*.

Hereford

Hereford is a solid, red-brick, Victorian-looking town on the banks of the river Wye, very much the heart of its county. The centre of the town today is **St Peter's Square**, a triangular road junction dominated by the imposing neoclassical Shire Hall. A few strides west lead into High Town past the Old House. Dating from 1621, the **Old House** is now a faintly forlorn-looking survival at one end of High Town, the broad pedestrianized open space in the middle of town lined with all the big brand names in retail. The ancient Jacobean half-timbered building contains a **museum** ⓘ *Old House Museum, High Town, T01432-260694, Apr-Sep Tue-Sun, bank holidays, Oct-Nov Tue-Sat*, reconstructing a few period rooms. Look out especially for the bargeboard carving of a cow being tugged at from both ends by two farmers, a lawyer milking their argument in the middle.

South of St Peter's Square, **Castle Green** is an early Georgian prom overlooking Castle Pool, still very pretty and a delightful place to picnic near the river. The park was laid out on the site of the city's Norman castle, hence the name. From here Castle St provides the most attractive approach to Hereford's idiosyncratic **Cathedral** ⓘ *T01432-374200, www.herefordcathedral.co.uk, 0800-2100 daily, Jul, Aug Mon-Sat. Services Sun 0800, 1000, 1130, 1530, Mon-Sat 0730, 0800, Choral evensong (except Wed) 1730*. Dedicated to St Ethelbert, it's an endearingly small-scale affair, much of its well-weathered knobbly old pink stone covered in green lichens, situated in an atmospheric little close just north of the river. The building demonstrates just about the entire gamut of English cathedral architecture: the great round pillars of the Nave with their carved capitals stepping the unexpectedly short distance down to the carved 14th-century choir; beyond the High Altar, the Lady Chapel is one of the finest examples of the 13th-century Early English style in the country and has been undergoing urgent restoration; the tower and eastern transept are good examples of 14th-century Decorated. Other highlights of the interior include the early 16th-century Chantry of Bishop Audley and the Early English crypt, the most recent (13th century) of its kind in the country.

Next to the Cathedral, in a modern purpose-built cloister-style library building funded by Sir Paul Getty, the church's ancient **chained library** ⓘ *Mappa Mundi and Chained Library, Apr-Sep Mon-Sat 1000-1615, Sun 1100-1515, Oct-Nov Mon-Sat 1100-1515, £4.50, concessions £3.50, family £10*, (the largest of its type in the world) has been restored and reconstructed. It makes an appropriate setting for the extraordinary **Mappa Mundi**, a medieval world atlas that puts the Holy Land firmly at the centre of things. The Mediterranean Sea divided the known world into three parts: Asia, Europe and Africa. Britain is drawn much larger than it should be and is marked up with a variety of cathedral towns. Elsewhere there be dragons and depictions of various scenes from the Old Testament.

From the Cathedral Close, narrow Gwynne St (named after Nell, the local actress who won the heart of Charles II) leads down to the **Left Bank Village** and the **Old Wye Bridge**. A pleasant stroll can be taken over the pedestrianized stone bridge to the

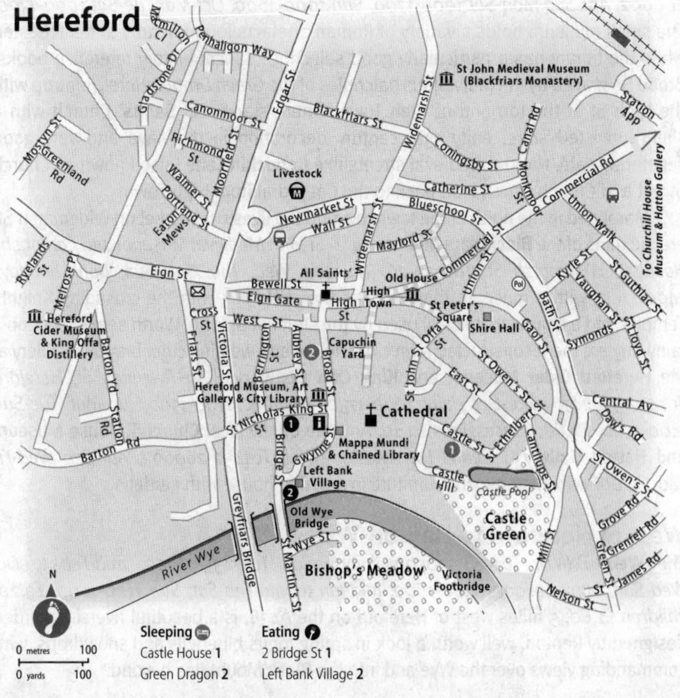

Walks in Herefordshire and Forest of Dean

- **Offa's Dyke and Devil's Pulpit**: 3 miles one way. Start: Wintour's Leap Car Park, off the B4228, 5 miles south of St Briavels. Following the winding course of the Wye along Offa's Dyke Path past a succession of spectacular viewpoints. OS Maps: Outdoor Leisure 14
- **Littledean**: 3 miles there and back. Start: Littledean Hall, 1 mile south east of Cinderford. A stiff climb up to magnificent views of the river Severn's widest meander and then on through the woods along the ridge to the Dean Forest Visitor Centre. OS Maps: Outdoor Leisure 14
- **Goodrich Castle**: 2 mile circle. Start: Goodrich, 4 miles south of Ross-on-Wye. Riverside and woodland paths around one of the most impressively situated castles in the country. OS Maps: Outdoor Leisure 14
- **Hay-on-Wye**: 8 miles there and back. Start: Hay-on-Wye. A walk up into the Welsh foothills of the Black Mountains, south of the town and up on to Hay Bluff (2220ft) above Gospel Pass. OS Maps: Outdoor Leisure 13
- **Merbach Hill**: 2 miles one way. Start: Bredwardine, 7 miles east of Hay-on-Wye. Riverside walks along the Wye Valley Way and then a fairly steep climb up Merbach Hill for fine views of the Wye Valley and Welsh hills. OS Maps: Outdoor Leisure 13

Bishop's Meadow and across the Victoria Footbridge back into Castle Green. A right turn on Bridge St heads back towards the middle of town and Broad St, home to the **Hereford Museum and Art Gallery** and also the **City Library** ⓘ *Broad St, T01432-260692, Apr-Sep Mon-Sat 1000-1700, Sun 1000-1600, Oct-Mar Tue-Sat 1000-1700*. The small museum holds a variety of Roman artefacts found nearby at Kentchester, while the library has a particularly good selection of local history reference books. Broad St, graced by the marvellous balconies of the *Green Dragon Hotel*, joins up with the High St at the top end of High Town, where stands **All Saints' Church** with a slightly twisted spire, early 13th century decoration in the nave and very good vegetarian café. Narrow medieval streets like **Capuchin Lane** (also known as Church Street and Church Lane), lead back to the Cathedral from High Town.

Marooned in the north of the town, beyond the livestock market on Widemarsh St, are the ruins of the **Blackfriars Monastery** ⓘ *St John Medieval Museum and Coningsby Hospital, Widemarsh St, T01432-267821, Tue, Wed, Thu, Sat, Sun, bank holidays 1400-1700*, with a museum that explains the site's link with the crusading Knights Templar and a chapel that is still used by the Order of St John. Worth seeking out on a rainy day are the reconstructed farm cider house and working cider brandy distillery at the **Hereford Cider Museum and King Offa Distillery** ⓘ *21 Ryleands St, Hereford T01432-354207, Apr-Oct daily 1000-1730, Nov-Dec 1100-1500, Jan-Mar Tue-Sun 1100-1500. £2.60, concessions £2.10*. And the quirky local **Churchill House Museum and Hatton Gallery** ⓘ *Venns La, Aylestone Hill, T01432-260693, Apr-Sep Wed-Fri 1400-1700*, with costume and furniture in a period house with gardens.

West of Hereford to Hay-on-Wye

The Weir ⓘ *(NT), T01981-590509, information T01743-708100, mid-Feb to Oct Wed-Sun, bank holidays 1100-1800, mid-Jan to mid-Feb Sat, Sun 1100-1600, £3.20, children £1.60*, 5 miles west of Hereford on the A438, is a beautiful riverside garden designed by Repton, well worth a look in spring for its bluebells and snowdrops, with commanding views over the Wye and into the Black Mountains beyond.

Three miles south of Bredwardine, off the B4352, **Moccas Court** ⓘ *T01981-500381, Apr-Sep Thu 1400-1800, £2, under-16s 50p,* with its 2000-year-old oak tree and Capability Brown parkland, is also highly recommended viewing, especially for its Robert Adam interiors.

Arthur's Stone ⓘ *(EH), open at any reasonable time, free,* seven miles east of Hay-on-Wye off the B4348 near Dorstone, not far from Moccas Court, is quite an impressive prehistoric burial chamber, its mound of earth stripped away to reveal the huge stones at its core. From Dorstone, the B4348 runs down the beautiful **Golden Valley** alongside the river Dore. Nestling in the green acres here, the remains of the Cisterician monastery at **Abbey Dore** ⓘ *T01981-240419, Abbey open dawn to dusk, free, gardens open Mar-Sep Tue, Thur, Sat, Sun £3,* are a remarkable survival, thanks in part to the attentions of the Scudamore family in the 17th century, who perhaps felt remorseful about their ill-gotten gains after the Dissolution.

In the village of **Wormelow**, 7 miles southwest of Hereford, a tiny **museum** ⓘ *Cartref, Wormelow, T01981-540477. Apr-Oct daily 1100-1300, 1400-1600, phone to check,* of old photographs and mementoes commemorates Violette Szabo, the SOE agent who was parachuted several times into occupied France. Eventually she was captured and executed shortly before the end of the war. The museum is in the house that she used to rest up at between missions.

About 5 miles from both Wormelow and Abbey Dore, **Kilpeck Church** is an extraordinary Norman survival, richly carved and reputed to be the finest example of its type in the country. The church's red sandstone has withstood the weather over the centuries, and the vivacity and sheer variety of the different carvings – a pig, wrestlers, rude women and dogs – is astonishing.

Back on the A438, just beyond Whitney, a little old toll bridge (50p) takes the B4350 over the Wye and past **Clifford Castle**, 3 miles north of Hay- on-Wye. This very overgrown and ruined medieval fortification is properly picturesque, unprettified and almost unvisited. An atmospheric and forlorn place beside the river.

Hay-on-Wye

Something of a phenomenon, over the last four decades Hay-on-Wye has been transformed into an international centre for second-hand books. Now it makes for a seriously enjoyable destination for anyone searching for illumination and fed up with mass-market retailing and dumbed-down attractions. Just over the border in Wales, surrounded by wooded hills and sheep-cropped fields, its wonderful position on the banks of the Wye would justify a visit in itself. Bookworms, though, will find themselves in seventh heaven. Steep narrow little streets are lined with shops laden with books ancient and modern. A clambering browse up to the small hilltop **castle** is bound to turn up a few irresistible surprises, although prices can be high too. The castle is now inhabited by the self-proclaimed King of Hay himself, local man Richard Booth. He was largely responsible for the town's renaissance, establishing his bookshop here in 1961 and never looking back. An ardent supporter of all things regional, local and decentralized, he has been helped in his crusade by the success of the annual **Literary Festival** in early June, founded here in 1988 by Norman Florence and his son Peter.

Crossing the Wye, still quite narrow here, from Hereford, a right run onto Broad St leads into the town's main square below the town clock. From here almost all the bookshops are within easy walking distance, most of them on the way up to Castle St and the TIC at the top of the town.

East of Hereford

Ledbury is a dignified market town nestling beneath the Malvern Hills, halfway between Hereford and Gloucester. Famous for its half-timbered Jacobean market hall at the top of the High St, the place could make a good alternative base to Worcester for exploring the Malverns. Nearby is an immaculate Gothic Romantic folly built in 1812 by the Hervey Bathurst family, **Eastnor Castle** ⓘ *T01531-633160, www.eastnorcastle.com, 1100-1700 check for seasonal variations, £6, child £3.50 (there's also an adventure playground), just outside Ledbury on the A449*, designed by Robert Smirke. The family still live there in considerable splendour surrounded by a deer park, arboretum, lake and a truly unmissable interior stuffed with medieval tapestries and other delights such as the Pugin Room.

Hellens ⓘ *Much Marcle, T01531-660504, Easter-Sep Wed, Sat, Sun and bank holidays by tour at 1400, 1500, 1600, £4, under-16s £2, family £10*, 3 miles south of Ledbury, is a strange old manor house first built in 1245 and almost continuously occupied by the same family down to the present day. A variety of unusual historical mementoes connected with the likes of Charles I, James II and Anne Boleyn are displayed amid ancient rooms with a vaguely contrived air of antiquity. The recently restored gardens are an education in Elizabethan and 17th-century garden planning.

North of Hereford

The **Black and White village trail** is the star attraction north of Hereford. **Weobley** is the quintessential example, with the *Red Lion* hotel, nestling in a village of black timber-frame and white brick. *The Olde Salutation* Inn ensconced behind topiary hedges could hardly be more typical of the area. The *Studio* gallery tearoom with its 'watercolour of the week' also cocks its hat at passing trade. **Eardisland** is another village typical of the area, while the *New Inn* at **Pembridge** is the local gathering place of the county's Sloane Rangers.

Hay-on-Wye

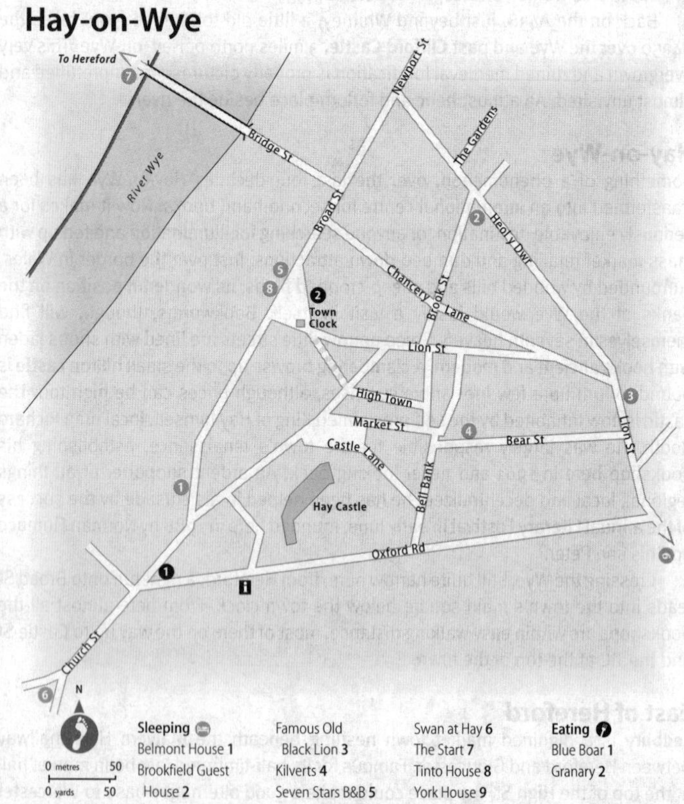

The town of **Leominster** can repay a visit thanks to its market square and quiet air of unhurried calm. School Lane is an alleyway of interesting independent shops, with the Old Merchant's House tearoom. East of Leominster, rolling green hills stretch along the A44 to Bromyard.

Hampton Court Gardens ⓘ *Hope Under Dinmore, near Leominster, T01568-797777, Apr-Oct Tue-Sun 1100-1700, £5, under-16s £3, concessions £4,* one of the most important early fortified manor houses in England, has been transformed by garden designer Simon Dorrell. A little tower in the Maze reached by a secret tunnel is just one of its many surprises.

Just north of Leominster, **Berrington Hall** ⓘ *T01568-615721 Apr-Oct Mon-Wed, Sun, Sat 1300-1700 (-1630 Oct, Nov), £4.40, grounds only £3. The costume collection can be seen by pre-arranged appointment only, contact the Costume Curator T01568-613720,* is the home of an astonishing costume collection, which Colonel Wade used to surprise guests like Graham Greene, Virginia Woolf, JB Priestley and John Betjeman at Snowshill Manor, his home in the Cotswolds. Berrington Hall itself is an austere neoclassical pile overlooking Capability Brown-landscaped gardens and the Brecon Beacons, with a surprsingly delicate and elegant interior.

Wigmore Castle ⓘ *(EH), open any reasonable time, free,* 8 miles west of Ludlow on the A4110, is a ruined medieval fortress that has subsided into itself over the centuries, leaving its curtain walls and towers surrounding a mess of crumbling masonry that kids love to scramble over.

The Wye Valley and Forest of Dean

Below Ross-on-Wye, and the famous viewpoint at Symonds Yat, the river Wye is worked almost as hard by canoeists and fishermen as it once was by barges taking the Forest of Dean's iron ore down to Bristol. The Wye Valley is treasured today – but still officially unprotected – for the ecological value of its broadleaf woodlands which step down the steep sides of its gorge, its early industrial archaeological remains, and its picturesque viewpoints. Sandwiched between the valleys of the Severn and the Wye, the Forest of Dean has long been a strange and isolated backwater. This is the kind of place that breeds expert bareback horseriders, as well as tortured playwrights like Dennis Potter, and also unfortunately the mass murderer Fred West. A wooded, hilly little landscape that is said to have inspired Tolkein's vision of Middle Earth in *The Lord of the Rings*, it's the mini-Appalachians of the West Midlands. Many of its valleys and secret 'scowles' (disused iron ore quarries) are hidden from access by car, below ridges of greenery that give sudden views of distant blue hills. These 36 square miles can be spooky then, but they still provide some of the best strolling, cycling and pony hacking country this side of the Welsh border.

Ins and outs

Getting there The nearest **train** station to Ross-on Wye is at Gloucester, about 30 minutes **bus** ride away. The Forest of Dean can also be accessed from Lydney on the north bank of the Severn river. **National Rail Enquiries,** T08457-484950. Ross-on-Wye is at the end of the M50, an arm of the M5 Birmingham-Exeter motorway. From London, though, it's most easily reached via the M4 and Severn Road Bridge (toll £4.40) to Chepstow (in Wales), then up the beautiful but often congested A466 to Monmouth and then the A40. Journey time approx 3 hours. This is also the quickest route to the Forest of Dean from London. **Stagecoach,** T01452-523928, Red and White service 34 from Gloucester to Monmouth.

 Getting around Stagecoach, T01452-523928, and **H&H**, T01989-566444, run most of the network of **buses** in the area, but otherwise a **car** or **bike** are the best options for exploring the area. The **Wye Valley Wanderer** is a useful Sunday bus service linking Worcester, Malvern, Hereford, Ross-on-Wye and Symonds Yat. It runs May to September on Sundays and also on bank holidays.

Information **Ross-on-Wye TIC** ⓘ*T01989-562768, www.visitorlinks.com, Easter-Sep Mon-Sat 0930- 1715, Oct-Easter Mon-Sat 0930-1630, mid-Jul to mid-Sep also Sun 1000-1600.* **Coleford TIC** ⓘ *T01594-812388, www.forestofdean.gov.uk, Nov-Mar Mon-Fri 1000-1600, Sat 1000-1400, Apr-Oct Mon-Sat 1000-1700, also Sun 1000-1400.*

History

The Wye Valley can make a reasonable claim to being the birthplace of British tourism. In the mid 18th-century it drew the first tourist in search of the purely picturesque, William Gilpin in 1770. He was looking at landscape for its own sake, and not for its moral qualities – as the likes of William Kent had before him. Poets and writers – Pope, Coleridge and Burke – followed in his footsteps, and most famously William Wordsworth, whose poem on Tintern Abbey remains one of the best-loved in the language. The valley has few ancient remains, apart from sections of Offa's Dyke, the Saxons' line of defence against the Celts. The Romans are known to have established a town called Ariconium on the site of modern-day Weston-under-Penyard, the centre of their iron-smelting industry.

Forest of Dean

The Forest of Dean covers about 35 square miles, much of it maintained by the Forestry Commission. Surprisingly for one of the first 'national forests' in the country, the Forest of Dean is not designated officially with any legal protection. On its edge, **Cinderford** is the most easterly town, its mining life long gone but it's still struggling gamely on. A couple of miles south, in between Upper and Lower Soudley, the **Dean Heritage Centre** fills an old mill with four well-presented displays (recently refurbished courtesy of the Heritage Lottery Fund) on the history and working life of the area. ⓘ *T01594-822170, Apr-Oct daily 1000-1700, Nov-Feb 1000-1600. £4, £3.50 concessions.* Nearby, the **Blaize Bailey** viewpoint gives stunning views eastwards over the Severn's wide horseshoe bend while **Littledean Hall** ⓘ *T01594-824213, Apr-Oct daily 1100- 1700, £3.50*, boasts a *Guinness Book of Records* entry as the oldest inhabited house in the country thanks to its being built around a supposed Anglo-Saxon mead hall. Four miles further east from Cinderford, on the A48 to Gloucester, **Westbury Court Gardens** ⓘ *(NT), T01452-760461, Mar-Jun, Sep and Oct Wed-Sun 1000-1700, Jul and Aug daily 1000-1700, £3*, are a very fine late 17th-century ordered Dutch water garden, restored in the early 1970s and planted with period trees quietly reflected in beautiful canals.

Just north of Cinderford, half a mile beyond the village of Drybrook on the road to Puddlebrook, at Hawthorns Cross, the **Forest of Dean Mechanical Organ Museum** ⓘ *'Springfields', Hawthorns Cross, Gloucs, T01594-542278, Apr and May, Jul and Aug, Tue and Thu 1400-1700 or by appointment, £2.50, £2 concessions*, is an enchanting private collection of old music machines. A De Cap Café Organ, Gasparini fairground organ and extraordinary Imhof and Muckle orchestrion are among the prize exhibits, all in working order, as well as musical boxes, gramophones and a Chiappa street piano.

From Cinderford the B4226 makes its 5-mile wooded way west towards Coleford, the capital of the Forest. Almost half way along, the **Speech House** is the heart of the area. Now a hotel, it was built as the meeting place of the Court of the Verderers, which dates back to the reign of King Canute and had the power to order trespassers skinned alive and their hide nailed to the Speech House door. Nowadays all the woods around are free-range and most of the Forest's points of interest within easy reach along well-signposted paths. To the south, the **New Fancy Viewpoint** is one of the best of its type. A couple of miles further on the road towards Blakeney, at **Blackpool Bridge**, a small stretch of Roman road has been uncovered and preserved. The bridge can also be reached via the lovely Soudley valley from the Dean Heritage Centre.

More Roman remains can be discovered at **Lydney Park** ⓘ *T01594-842027, gardens Apr and May Sun, Wed, bank holidays 1100-1800, £3 (£2 Wed), Roman Temple Apr to mid-Sep*, where JRR Tolkein helped to unearth a Roman Temple surrounded by wonderful Spring gardens with lakes and statuary.

Seven miles west of Lydney up the B4231 and B4228, **St Briavels** ranks as one of the most delightful of the Forest's traditional villages, with its imposing old castle (now a spectacular youth hostel), views over the river, decent pub and a common beneath with an amazing patchwork of fields and ancient commoner's rights. Heading north the B4228 back towards Coleford passes the **Clearwell Caves** ⓘ *near Coleford, T01594-832535, www.clearwellcaves.com, Mar-Oct, Dec daily 1000-1700*, a popular visitor attraction featuring go-as-you-please iron-ore mines, a few 'freeminers'. Nine caverns or 'churns' at a constant temperature of 10°C are lit up, dank, with safety walls. Ochres are still mined here.

To the south of St Briavels, **Brockweir**, just upstream from Tintern Abbey across the river in Wales, is another beautiful village with a good pub and canoes for hire on the river.

Ross-on-Wye and around

The place where appreciation of the Wye's scenic qualities first became a fashionable activity, Ross-on-Wye stands on a bluff overlooking a wide horseshoe bend in the river. A pretty neatly proportioned little place, it's still dominated by the spire of **St Mary's Church** which stands next to the Prospect. The spire was heightened and the Prospect laid out by John Kyrle 'The Man of Ross' in the early 18th century, capitalizing on the town's picturesque position. Kyrle's name is still remembered in the town for his philanthropy, and his hedgehog crest adopted as the town's unofficial logo. Nowadays a visit is unlikely to take up more than half a day, looking around the antique shops, admiring the view from the Prospect and look over the Church. The **Farmer's Market** on the first Friday of the month, 1000-1400, boasts a particularly impressive range of local produce and the general market on Thurs and Sat is also worth a look. The mid 17th-century **market house** ⓘ *The Market House Heritage Centre, Market Pl, T01432-260675, Apr-Oct Mon-Sat 1000-1700, Sun 1030-1600, Nov-Mar Mon-Sat 1030-1600*, has been quite entertainingly converted into a local history **museum** and heritage centre.

Below Ross, the Wye winds through increasingly sheer drops to the water. The next point of interest, **Goodrich Castle** ⓘ *(EH), T01600-890538, Apr-Sep daily 1000-1800, Oct daily 1000-1700, Nov-Mar Wed-Sun 1000-1300, 1400-1600, £3.70,concessions £2.80, children £1.90*, is best seen from the river in a canoe from Ross. Five miles downstream of the town, sitting on a red sandstone outcrop, Goodrich Castle has dominated this stretch of river since the Stone Age. Within its massive medieval outer walls nestles a perfect little Norman keep, possibly built by Godric (hence the name) in the 12th century. The formidable Gate Tower contains sluices designed for molten lead and boiling oil. Besieged for four months by the Parliamentarians in the Civil War, the castle was rendered useless on their victory but remains the most impressive in Herefordshire. Charming footpaths lead down to the river.

A couple more miles downstream, one of the most popular viewpoints on the Wye is at **Symonds Yat**, an old hill fort on the east side of the river. Very busy in high season, complete with toposcope, some of the crowds can be escaped by climbing up to **Yat Rock**, a limestone outcrop 160 yards above the water, a steep walk up from the *Forest View Hotel*. In summer the **Birds of Prey Centre** ⓘ *T0870-9901992* in Newent put on spectacular displays from the rock. Further downstream, **Doward Wood** is a particularly lovely wood managed by the Woodland Trust, not driveable into, with **King Arthur's Cave** tucked away inside, a natural cave of passing interest, as well as another hill fort. The **Devil's Pulpit** is another superb viewpoint on the Offa's Dyke national trail along the border, near St Briavels and overlooking the remains of Tintern Abbey.

Sleeping

Worcester *p577*

B **Fownes Hotel**, City Walls Rd, Worcester, T01905-613151. This converted glove factory is a little bit outside the city centre but is extremely tasteful, has an à la carte restaurant and is a really comfortable base from which to enjoy Worcester in style.

B **The Giffard Hotel**, High St, Worcester, T01905-726262. Though it claims to have wonderful views of the Cathedral, it is not a particularly nice view itself, resembling something out of Thunderbirds. Nevertheless one of Worcester's smartest hotels and you can't fault the level of comfort.

B **The Star Hotel**, Foregate St, Worcester, T01905-24308. An extremely comfortable billet right next to the hustle and bustle of Foregate and the station, very convenient if you've arrived by train and suitable levels of luxury.

C **The Diglis House Hotel**, Severn St, Worcester, T01905- 353518. The nicest thing about this hotel is its location nestling right on the river bank in a beautifully preserved old part of Worcester. For lovers of history and convenient locations.

D **Burgage House**, 4 College Precincts, Worcester, T01905-25396. Slap bang next to the Cathedral, this handsome Georgian guesthouse is very good value with tolerable levels of comfort and a great garden for strolling in, taking in views of the Cathedral.

E **Mrs V A Rogers**, Little Lightwood Farm, Lightwood La, Cotheridge, T01905-333236. It's a fair way out of Worcester, but you'll be hard put to to find anywhere cheaper or friendlier. Take the A44 out of Worcester in the direction of Broadwas, after about 4 miles you'll find a turning to the right into Lightwood La (direction Lower Broadheath). The farm is about half a mile up the road.

Malvern *p580*

C **Bredon House Hotel**, 34 Worcester Rd, Great Malvern, T01684-566990. A fairly small but impeccably respectable establishment enjoying spectacular views from the vantage point of the main Worcester Rd and also very near to the middle of Great Malvern.

C **Brook Farm**, Hanley Swan, T01684-310796, www.brookfarm.org.uk. A lovely converted farmhouse with ample accommodation and fantastic walking country all around. It's a little way out of Malvern – take the A449 to Powick and then head south on the B4424 towards Upton. This road turns into the B4211 and then turn right on to the B4209 which will take you into the delightful village of Hanley Swan.

C **Wyche Keep**, 22 Wyche Rd, Malvern, T01684-567018. Experience Elgar Country in style at this superb Malvern countryside location. A delightful house with incredible views across the county. Take the A449 south out of Great Malvern, about a mile down the road turn right into Wyche Rd (B4218).

D **The Firs**, 243 West Malvern Rd, near Malvern, T01684-564016. Small, quiet and cheap this benefits from being actually on the hills and is ideal for the serious walker.

E **Como House**, Como Rd, Great Malvern, T01684-561486, kevin@como-house.freeserve.co.uk. A lovely 1850s Malvern stone house this is a good value, comfortable hotel within easy walking distance of Malvern town centre. They're also most obliging about lifts to the station and good vantage points for walks.

Vale of Evesham *p581*

A-B **Wood Norton Hall**, Wood Norton, Evesham, T01386-420007. Definitely the poshest hotel in the region, this place is owned by the BBC and used for all those brainstorming sessions that turned the BBC into what it is today. A beautiful grade II listed Victorian building nestling in 170 acres of glorious parkland undoubtedly the best place to experience The Vale in bloom.

C **Best Western**, Waterside, Evesham, T01386-40322. Not quite as posh as Wood Norton, it's still a handsome Georgian building right next to the river and packed full of amenities. About 5 mins from Evesham station so is pretty handily situated both for the town and The Vale.

D **The Stables**, High St, Old Badsey, Evesham, T01386-830380. Handily attached to a pub, this lovely old inn is definitely a superior B&B with the advantage of a really classic drinking house next door.

Hereford *p582, map p583*

A **Castle House**, Castle St, Hereford, T01432-356321. The most up-to-date in the city, in the most picturesque part of town and with beautifully appointed rooms.

B **Green Dragon Hotel**, Broad St, Hereford, T01432-272506, F352139. Genuinely ancient, fully refurbished Heritage hotel in the middle of the city, close to the cathedral, somehow more impressive outside than in but unbeatably convenient.

C **The Green Man**, Fownhope, about 5 miles southeast of Hereford on the B4224, T01432-860243, www.smoothhound.co.uk/hotels/greenman. Pretty gardens not far from the River Wye and plenty of historical associations stretching back centuries at this welcoming family-run hotel. Also has leisure facilities close by, such as tennis, swimming and gym.

C **Grove House**, Bromsberrow Heath, near Ledbury, T01531-650584. A very superior B&B, the core of the house dates from the 14th century, with a large garden and large pond, and there are also recently refurbished rooms in the old dairy and summerhouse.

C **The Stagg**, Titley, T01544-230221, has a couple of bedrooms above a destination food pub in delightful border village about 12 miles west of Leominster. Near the Black Mountains and Golden Valley,

D **Mrs Ev Lloyd**, T01873-890263 and C **Diana Palmer**, T01873-890675, with her rare breeds farm, are both close to Abbey Dore.
F **The Pandy Inn**, on the main road in the bordertown of Pandy, about 20 miles southwest of Hereford on the A465, T01873-890208. Does B&B with bunkhouse accommodation. Useful for the Golden Valley and Black Mountains.

Hay-on-Wye *p585, map p586*
NB Book early if you plan to stay during the Hay Festival.
B-C **The Swan at Hay**, Church St, T01497-821188, F821424. Probably the smartest option, with deluxe rooms at £47 per person in a Georgian mansion in the middle of town, very clean and well-maintained with a garden too. The C **Famous Old Black Lion**, Lion St, T01497-820841, www.oldblacklion.co.uk. Comfortable rooms and highly rated food (see Eating, page 594).
C **Seven Stars B&B**, 11 Broad St, T01497-820886. Bang in the middle of things, with an indoor heated pool, and a sauna too.
C **Tinto House**, Broad St, T01497-820590, www.tintohouse.co.uk. A Georgian townhouse, built around 1780, right opposite the Clock Tower.
C **The Start**, T01497-821391. An 18th-century house a short walk from the centre of town, down by the river, with a large garden.
C **York House**, Cusop, near Hay-on-Wye, T01497-820705. An elegant, late Victorian residence on the edge of Hay-on-Wye, also with large, southerly facing garden and aiming for a country house atmosphere.
C **Kilverts Hotel**, The Bullring, T01497-821042, F01497-821580. Privately owned and has a relaxed and informal atmosphere.
C **Brookfield Guest House**, Brook St, T01497-820518, www.brookfieldguesthouse.btinternet.co.uk. A beamed 16th-century house with inglenook fireplace close to the town centre.
D **Belmont House**, Belmont Rd, T01497-820718. An antiquey B&B with large bedrooms, at the bottom of Castle St.

Camping
F **Radnors End**, Hay-on-Wye, a short walk over the river, T01497-820780, £3.50 per night.

The Wye Valley and Forest of Dean
p587, map p588
B **Royal Hotel**, Palace Pound, Ross-on-Wye, T01989-565105, www.oldenglishinns.co.uk. A fully refurbished Greene King hotel about 2 mins' walk from Market Sq. Dickens stayed here when planning his American tour.
C **Glewstone Court Hotel**, Glewstone, near Ross, T01989-770367, www.glewstonecourt.com. Good value this: a country house hotel with 8 rooms, the front rooms have beautiful views over the surrounding countryside, as well as a decent restaurant and bar.
B **Speech House Hotel**, Coleford, Forest of Dean, T01594-822607, F823658. Chintz and pleated valances in one of the most historic houses in the forest, a 17th-century hunting lodge where the Verderer's Court was held.
C **The George**, St Briavels, next to the castle, T01594-530228, www.thegeorgeinn.com. 2 doubles and a twin, is a convivial freehouse with a garden and passable pub grub.
B **Wyndham Arms Hotel**, Clearwell, T01594-833666, www.thewyndhamhotel.co.uk. A venerable old beamed and family-run establishment on the edge of the forest. Comfortable rooms (price includes breakfast) and oodles of traditional charm. Also serves straightforward and delicious home-cooked food.
F **YHA St Briavels Castle**, T01594- 530272, F530849. 1 4-bedded, 3 6-bedded, 2 8-bedded and 3 dorms in this moated Norman castle, once King John's hunting lodge.

Camping
Doward Park Camp Site, Great Doward, Symonds Yat West, near Ross, T01600-890438. Easter-Oct. £5-£8 per pitch per night. A small family-run campsite surrounded by woods.

Eating

Worcester *p577*
In Worcester, well-heeled citizens take their fine dining seriously and you can have a substantial gastronomic odyssey.

£££ Glasshouse, Church St, T01905-611120. Tucked away behind Church St, this place has superb interior decor, with plenty of stained glass. And the food's pretty good, too.

£££ The Little Sauce Factory, 55 London Rd, T01905-350159. Benefiting from having a master chef on the premises, this eclectic mixture of international cuisine does know what it's about, even if the interior feels a little cramped.

£££ Il Pescatore, 34 Sidbury, T01905-21444. A cut above the above, this is a proper Italian restaurant with outstanding fish and meat dishes.

££ Azure, 33-35 Broad St, T01905-25832. If you want Med eclectic, this place claims to be influenced by cuisine from Provence, Andalucía, Cyprus and Morocco, as well as a few other places in the sunnier climes. It's pretty laid back and has some great brunch treats.

££ Four Seasons, 61 Lowesmoor, T01905-27026. As good a Chinese as you'll find in this town, with friendly helpful waiters.

££ King Charles II, 29 New St, T01905-22449. Not an amazingly innovative menu, but it's worth it to be in this seriously historic setting, the place where Charles lodged before taking on the marauding troops of Cromwell at the battle of Worcester of 1651.

££ Little Venice, 1 St Nicholas St, T01905-726126. A simple, modern trattoria that resembles Pizza Express, but it's a good family place and pretty reasonable value for money.

££ Pasha Indian Cuisine, 56 St John's, T01905-426327. An innovative approach to the food of the subcontinent.

££ Souvlaki Taverna, 50 Friar St, T01905-22972. Don't expect too much plate-throwing, it's an altogether more sedate Greek dining experience, but the menu is very authentic and you'll have a really great evening here.

££ The Vauxhall Inn, Abbey Rd, Evesham, T01386-446333. A great big place that proudly boasts over 20 different varieties of pie and of course lots of great big thick chunky pieces of steak. Also pretty conveniently situated right next to the Almonry Heritage Centre.

£ Drucker's Vienna Patisserie, 27 Chapel Walk, Worcester, T01905-616870. Though it specializes in creamy and cakey things you will also find some delicious savoury items here, too and although you shouldn't expect a full meal, it's a good place to fortify yourself at affordable prices.

£ Olive Tree Pizza and Coffee Shop, 80 Barnards Green Rd, Great Malvern, T01684-577446. A slightly fey pizza house, but a nice atmosphere and with the average pizza costing around £6 you can't go wrong.

£ Royal Balti Restaurant, 50 The Tything, Worcester, T01905-25694. The competition for your custom between this curry house and the *Bombay Palace* which is just down the road is definitely to your benefit, but the *Royal Balti* probably has it by a nose, though it's a bit more expensive at around £10 a head.

Hereford *p582, map p583*

There's not yet a huge variety of choice in the town.

££ The Left Bank Village is the latest development, with good views of the river and the old Wye bridge, but it's also a rather characterless all-in restaurant bar complex. Reasonable food though.

£ 2 Bridge St, T01432-279714. A charming old-fashioned little coffeeshop on the corner of Bridge St.

£ Café in All Saints' Church, High St, T01432-370415. A good stop for a vegetarian lunch inside the Church.

Around Hereford*p582*

££ The Bell, T01531-640285, at Bosbury, 4 miles north of Ledbury off the B4214. Has bar skittles, and is another ancient black and white pub in an interesting little village where the tower got separated from its church.

££ Carpenter's Arms, Walterstone, T01873-890353. A cosy cottage pub close to the Welsh border and the Black Mountains with reasonable pub grub.

££ Crown and Anchor, Lugwardine, a couple of miles east of Hereford on the road to Ledbury, T01432-851303. Another beamed pub but with an accomplished menu.

££ **Five Bridges Pub**, T01531-630040, near Much Cowarne, 8 miles northwest of Hereford south of the A465.

££ **Grape Vaults**, Broad St, Leominster, is a snug, cosy and creaky little town pub with a highly rated menu and old-fashioned Edwardian decor. About the 8 miles from Hereford but north of the A465.

££ **New Inn**, Pembridge, T01544-388427, does well-prepared local produce, with a fine array of ales, and it's the pub of choice of the young horsey set in the area.

££ **Salutation Inn**, Weobley, T01544-318443, is a superb village local in an ancient black and white building with a smartish restaurant attached.

££ **The Stagg**, Titley, T01544-230221, is another destination food pub with a couple of bedrooms and food that has attracted the attentions of the Michelin inspectors.

££ **Three Crowns**, in Ullingswick, T01432-820279, a destination food pub specializing in organic and local produce in an ancient purpose-built hostelry.

£ **The Pandy**, Dorstone, T01981-550273, is a dinky old free house (apparently the oldest in Herefordshire) with a reasonable menu of bar meals in the wonderful Golden Valley east of Hay.

£ **The Cider House**, Dunkertons Luntley, Pembridge, T01544-388161, serves organic Hereford beef, vegetables and herbs as well as home-baked cakes and pastries and ices.

Hay-on-Wye *p585, map p586*

££ **Famous Old Black Lion** Lion St, T01497-820841, is top of the range for eating.

£ **The Granary Café and Restaurant**, T01497-820790, at the top of the approach from Hereford is a wholesome vegetarian as well as cottage pie type place, in a reasonably priced casual, scruffy bookish canteen with waitress service.

£ **Blue Boar** also does good pub food.

The Wye Valley and Forest of Dean *p587, map p588*

££ **Boat Inn**, Long La, T01600-712615. A proper pub popular with walkers and canoeists, accessed via a footbridge over the river Wye. Reasonable grub (all day on Sat) and a precipitous garden overlooking the water.

££ **Hostelry**, T01600-890241, in Goodrich. Has won plaudits for its food.

££ **The Lough Pool**, T01989-730236, Sellack. Also draws people in from some distance away to enjoy its ambitious and reasonably priced menu.

Ross-on-Wye *p590*

£££ **The Pheasant**, 52 Edde Cross, T01989-565751. Has a good reputation doing modern British food at about £25 a head.

££ **China Boy Jo's**, 27 Gloucester Rd, T01989-563533. A superior Chinese restaurant: expect to pay about £20 a head, but it's worth it.

££ **Canio's**, Cantalupe Rd, T01989-567155. A popular local Italian close to the public library, about £15 a head.

££ **Cloisters**, High St, T01989-567717. The locals' favourite bistro-type restaurant, with an emphasis on fish.

Pubs, bars and clubs

Worcester *p577*

The Courtyard, St Nicholas St, T01905-23050. A far cry from the poncey *Conservatory Bar* on Friar St, this place is riotous at weekends with some good music events in an extremely historic setting. Very popular with the trendy and rather outré youth of Worcester, it's well worth a visit if you like your evenings hot and sweaty.

Don Pedro's, The Cellar Bar/90 Worcester Rd, Malvern, T01684-577666. Slightly more upmarket clientele with a great wine list and decidedly superior bar snacks.

Farmers Arms, Birts St, Birtsmorton, Malvern, T01684-833308. A bit more sleepy than some of the other Malvern pubs, it nevertheless is worth a visit for its cosy ambience and family atmosphere.

Farriers Arms, 9 Fish St, T01905-27569. Another historic location with extremely well-kept beer and a very homely atmosphere.

The Fleece, The Cross, Bretforton, near Evesham, T01386-831173. This place is a definite must for fans of ale and history. It's a 15th-century National Trust property, kept in its original condition with three open fires and beamed ceilings. Among the delights it offers are 15 different types of fruit beer and a large orchard to drink in. Really idyllic.

Horn and Trumpet, 12 Angel St, T01905-29593. Very popular with the locals, this place isn't your typical inner city pub.
Oliver's Cafe Bar, 36 Bellevue Terr, Great Malvern, T01684-562272. Friendly local bar really more for young people who want to get funky with the odd live DJ.
The Pheasant Inn, 25 New St, T01905-29635. Probably the oldest building you'll ever have a drink in, this is a stunning 15th-century structure which used to be famous for cock-fighting.
RSVP, The Cross, T01905-729211. A tasteful conversion of a lovely Georgian church, serves food and has a big screen.
Swan with Two Nicks, 28 New St, T01905-28190. Extremely picturesque, one of the best places in Worcester to chill.
Unicorn Inn, 2 Bellevue Terr, Malvern, T01684-574152. Probably one of Malvern's best known taverns, featuring a superb range of real ales, it's much visited by out of towners, but also has an extremely loyal local following.

Entertainment

Worcester *p577*

Music

Huntingdon Hall, Crowngate, T01905-23428 www.huntingdonhall.com A splendid building, complete with organ and stained glass, it also has comedy and spoken word events.
Keystones Café Bar, 1 Copenhagen St, T01905-731437. If you prefer your music a bit more modern, this is an excellent bar and restaurant underneath the street and even has a fragment of 13th-century archway on the dance-floor. Local bands play every Thu from 2100-0000, and they're not half bad.
Worcester Cathedral, 10a College Green, T01905-28854. Some of the best music in the country can be heard here, and not just from the choir. It's an outstanding acoustic and orchestral works played here will have never sounded better.

Theatre

Worcester Swan Theatre, The Moors, T01905-27322. A charming city theatre, putting on the usual diet of thrillers and pantos, but a reasonably professional company if you like that sort of thing.

Festivals

May-Jun Hay-on Wye annual literary festival, www.hayfestival.com for further details.
Aug The Three Choirs Festival (mid-Aug), probably one of the most prestigious musical festivals in the world and even though Worcester shares it with Hereford and Gloucester, it's definitely worth catching it. Festival Administrator, 6 Edgar St, T01905-616200.
Nov Worcester City Christmas Fayre (28 Nov-1 Dec), an extremely successful Victorian themed street market which takes place every year and attracts thousands. Stallholders get all dressed up in Victorian costume and there's plenty to distract the kids while you hunt down some Victorian bargains.

Shopping

Worcester *p577*

In Mealcheapen St you'll find **F Durrant and Son**, T01905-25247, a stockist of country and sporting stuff, including shotguns. The proprietor will give you advice about huntin', shootin' and fishin' in the area. Just round the corner you'll come to **Reindeer Court** a superb covered market featuring some very special places like **The Worcester Antiques Centre**, T01905-610680, which is an Aladin's cave of affordable and not so affordable antiques from every period. Nearby is one of Worcester's smartest modern jewellers **Rock Lobster** 21 Reindeer Ct, T01905-729022, which looks minimal on the outside, but the prices certainly aren't. There are some other excellent clothes shops round here, like **Dare**, but you should save your pennies until you get to Friar St which features a range of very tempting places like **Emporio** and **Lynne Craig**, **Nicholas Smith** (men's formal wear) and **Birties of Worcester**.
Finally, whatever you do, don't forget the shopping opportunities afforded by **Royal Worcester Visitor Centre** (see page 579). But if you're not into buying porcelain that's quite that expensive, you could always try **G.R. Pratley and Sons**, Shambles, T01905-22678, which is a shop featuring a huge amount of china, glass and earthenware – as well as tribal rugs and country furniture.

Hay-on-Wye *p585, map p586*

Books

Addyman Books, 36 Lion St, T01497-821136, specialist in modern first editions and literature.

C. Arden Bookseller, Radnor House, Church St, T01497-820471, antiquarian and out of print books sold, very good for horticultural and landscaping interests.

Hay Cinema Bookshop, Castle St, T01497-820071, www.haycinemabookshop.co.uk. The largest shop, huge and rambling, bewildering variety of books.

Haybooks Ltd, Grove House, High Town, www.haybooks.com, the best place to search for old and out of print books in Britain.

Hay-on-Wye Booksellers, 13/14 High Town, T01497-820875, www.books-on-wye.co.uk, with a good general stock.

Mark Westwood Books, T01497-820068, publish a very useful summary and map guide leaflet to 38 different booksellers.

Marijana Dworski Books, 21 Broad St, www.balkanbooks.com, specializing in books on Eastern Europe and books on minority and unusual languages.

Richard Booth's bookshop, T01497-820322, claiming to be the world's largest second-hand bookstore, has a fine blue frontage in the middle of Hay with tiles outside depicting domesticated livestock and a mustachioed man, apparently not a caricature of the King himself.

Around Hereford *p582*

The Old Chapel Gallery, East St, Pembridge T01544-388842, displays an eclectic range of handicrafts and artworks by local artists and craftsfolk with an upstairs gallery given over to temporary exhibitions.

Activities and tours

Worcester *p577*

Bowling

Worcester Tenpin Bowling, Everoak Trading Estate, Bromyard Rd, St John's, T01905-420425.

Cricket

Worcestershire County Cricket Club, New Rd, T01905-748474, www.wccc.co.uk

Fishing

Bransford Game Fishery and Fisherman's Lodge, Hill End Farm, Station Rd, Bransford, T01905-830548, info@fishermensfeathers.com.

Quad biking

Peachley Quad Trekking, Peachley La, Lower Broadheath, WR2 6QR, T01905-641309.

Racing

Worcester Racecourse, Pitchcroft Grandstand Rd, T0870-2202772, http://worcester-racecourse.co.uk

Tennis

Cripple Gate Park Tennis Courts Cripplegate Park New Rd, WR2 4QG, T01905-722311, gredfern@cityofworcester.gov.uk.

Hereford *p582, map p583*

Boating

Cathedral Cruises, Hereford, T01432-358957. Mar-Oct, for 40-min riverboat trips on the Wye. **Hay-on-Wye Canoe Hire**, 15 Castle St, Hay-on-Wye, T01497-820604. Single kayak or Canadian canoes.

Racing

Hereford Racecourse, Roman Rd, T01432-273560. 16 race meetings a year.

Walking

Guided Walks of Hereford by **Guild of Guides**, T01432-356270. £2, May-Sep, departing TIC Mon-Sat 1100 and Sun 1430. Haunting and Horror Walk on Wed from Jul-Sep 1915.

Wye Valley and the Forest of Dean *p587, map p588*

Cycling

Pedalbikeaway, The Colliery New Road, Cannop, Forest of Dean, T01549-860065.

Boating

Wye Valley Canoe Centre, The Boat House, Glasbury-on-Wye, T01497-847213, www.wyevalleycanoes.co.uk Hire out single kayak or Canadian canoes. **Paddles and Pedals**, T01497-820604. Canoe hire at Symonds Yat West. **Wye Dean Canoe Centre**, Symonds Yat East, T01600-890129. Have a public launch site at Kerne Bridge. **Ferries**: **The Saracens Head**, Symonds Yat East,T01600-890435, and **Ye Old Ferrie Inn**, Symonds Yat West, T01600-890232. **Kingfisher Cruises**, Symonds Yat East, 30-min cruise trips up and down the river.

Riding

Tregoyd Mountain Riders, T01497-847351. Horse riding and pony trekking.

Walking

Ordnance Survey Outdoor Leisure 14 map.

Directory

Worcester *p577*
Hospitals Newtown Hospital and Eye Unit, Newtown Rd, T01905-763333. Worcestershire Royal Hospital, Charles Hastings Way, T01905- 763333. **Library** Foregate St, T01905-765312. Worcestershire Library and History Centre, Trinity St, T01905-765922. **Police** Castle St, T08457-444888. **Post office** 8-10 Foregate St, T0845-722 3344.

Shropshire

→ *Colour map 4, grid B2*

Shropshire remains one of England's proud-to-be-undiscovered corners. Like Herefordshire, its relatively low population density and tenacity to traditional farming have resulted in one of the least spoiled of England's rural landscapes. Shrewsbury is its county town, variously pronounced 'Shrozebury' or 'Shroosbury', a well-to-do castellated market town in a lovely position on the River Severn. A string of very attractive little towns run south parallel to the border with Wales on the A49 south of Shrewsbury: Church Stretton for hillwalkers, Ludlow for antique collectors and gourmands, and on into Leominster and Hereford. The Severn Valley from Shrewsbury embraces the unassuming delights of Much Wenlock and then the well-packaged tourist attractions at Ironbridge, 'birthplace of the Industrial Revolution', before heading on to Worcester and Gloucester. Quiet old towns, hillwalking, nature reserves and industrial heritage are the county's forte as far as visitors are concerned. In fact whatever Shropshire does, whether it's food, farming or family fun, it still does it well, beautifully backward and happily isolated from the rest of the UK. ▸▸ *For Sleeping, Eating and other listings, see pages 602-604.*

Ins and outs

Getting there There are hourly **trains** from London Euston, changing either at Crewe or Wolverhampton, taking around 3 hours depending on the connection. Shrewsbury is also linked by **rail** to the north and Birmingham.

Shrewsbury is most easily reached from the south on the M54 from Junction 11 on the M6. It's about 3 hours 30 minutes from London. Regular **National Express,** T08705-808080, services run from London, Birmingham, Liverpool and elsewhere, arriving at the **bus** station a few hundred yards from the **train** station.

Getting around The town itself is easily negotiated on **foot**. The surrounding countryside really needs a **car,** although a network of local buses to places like Much Wenlock are run by **Arriva Midlands North,** T0845-6012491, and several other companies (NB no buses to Ironbridge on Sun). **Traveline,** T0870-6082608.
Information **Shrewsbury TIC** ⓘ *The Music Hall, The Square, T01743-281200, www.shrewsburytourism.co.uk, Oct-Apr Mon-Sat 1000-1700, May-Sept Mon-Sat 0930-1730, Sun 1000-1600.* Accommodation booking £1 fee.

Shrewsbury

The county town of Shropshire, Shrewsbury makes up for the lack of a medieval cathedral with a variety of smaller examples of ecclesiastical architecture, quite an impressive old castle and a picturesque situation. Almost an island in a loop of the Severn river, this market town has been a fortified site since at least the fifth century. Visitors arriving by train still have to make their way beneath the castle walls up into the centre. Ignored by the Luftwaffe in the Second World War, many of the Tudor half-timbered buildings still survive. One of the best examples, Rowley's House, is now an excellent local history museum full of remarkable Roman finds. Other sights worth seeking out include three remarkable churches – St Mary's, the ancient Abbey of the Holy Cross, and St Chad's. It's the unhurried pace and quiet atmosphere of this famously unpronounceable place that make it such a good base for exploring one of England's most lovely lost corners.

From the station, a few steps away the steep **Castle Gate** heads up into the heart of the town. The Castle itself dates largely from the 14th century, with a few 18th-century alterations, and contains the **Shropshire Regimental Museum** ⓘ *Castle St, T01743-358516, www.shrewsbury-museums.com, Mid-Feb to Mar Wed-Sat 1000-1600, Apr-May Tue-Sat 1000-1700, Jun-Aug daily 1000-1600, £2,* One of the largest of its kind in the country, the museum contains the usual collection of military memorabilia, weapons, uniforms, china and medals, but on an impressive scale, while the Norman motte is worth climbing for views over the town.

A couple of hundred yards beyond the castle, off Castle St on the left, the soaring 200-ft spire of **St Mary's Church** ⓘ *T01743-357006, Mon-Fri 1000-1700, Sat 1000-1600, Apr-Oct also Sun,* dominates the old part of town. The closest the town comes to a cathedral, set in a pretty little close, the church displays a satisfying mix of Norman and Gothic architectural styles and contains a remarkable Tree of Jesse in the beautiful east window, imported from old St Chad's. Much of the other glass is also very fine, including a variety of French medieval craftsmanship.

Next on the left a few yards up Pride Hill, the continuation of Castle St, **Butcher Row** is a particularly well-preserved street of half-timbered Tudor houses, with the

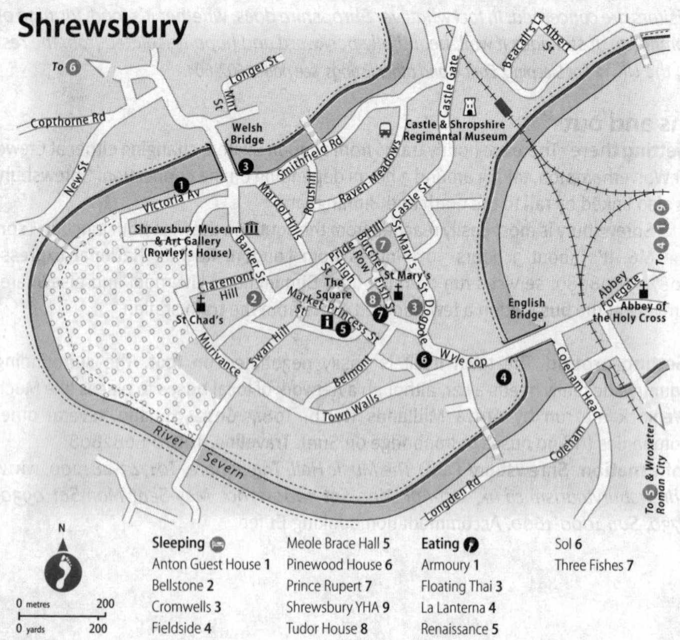

Walks in Shropshire

- **The Long Mynd**: 4 miles there and back. Start: Church Stretton. A fairly steep climb up rocky paths to the top of Shropshire's great ridge overlooking Wales. OS Map: Explorer 217, Landranger 137
- **The Stiperstones**: 4 miles there and back. Start: The Bog, 6 miles north of Bishop's Castle. A walk up to the eerie Devil's Chair with views into Wales and Shropshire. OS Map: Explorer 216, Landranger 137
- **Downton**: 5 mile circle. Start: Downton on the Rock, 7 miles by road west of Ludlow. Riverside walks along the Teme and woodland paths past the ruins of Victorian industry. OS Map: Explorer 203, Landranger 148
- **The Wrekin**: 2 miles there and back. Start: Little Wenlock, 6 miles north of Much Wenlock. Popular climb up a volcanic plug for distant views of Shrewsbury and the Severn. OS Map Explorer 242, Landranger 127
- **Titterstone Clee Hill**: 2 miles there and back. Start: Bitterley, 3 miles east of Ludlow. A short climb up to a superb viewpoint overlooking Ludlow in the distance. OS Map: Explorer 203, Landranger 137.

Abbot's House on the corner of Fish St an especially grand example. Two more – **Owen's Mansion** and **Ireland's Mansion** – can be seen a little further up Pride Hill where it joins the High St leading into the Square, the centre of town and home to the TIC in the late Geogian Music Hall. The Old Market Hall here is also Elizabethan.

A hundred yards north of the Square, down Barker St, the **Shrewsbury Museum and Art Gallery** ⓘ *T01743-361196, http://shrewsburymuseums.com, Apr-Oct Tue-Sat 1000-1700, Mon and Sun 1000-1600, Nov-Mar Tue-Sat 1000-1600, free.* in Rowley's House is well worth seeking out. Originally a warehouse for wool, built in the late Elizabethan era, the next door building was the first in the town to be made of brick. As well as many Roman finds from Wroxeter (see below) – including a mirror and the inscription over the town gate – and a medieval section, there's a highly rated Art Gallery with regular temporary exhibitions on local themes. A similar distance west of the Square, up Claremont Hill, **St Chad's** is a very fine Georgian round church in a spectacular position overlooking the river with a prominent spire and elegant neoclassical portico. Apparently the building of it caused riots in protest at the demolition of part of the old town walls. Beyond the church, a spacious public park slopes down to the riverbank. From St Chad's, a charming walk down Murivance and Town Walls circles the town following the course of the river downstream to **English Bridge**, a venerable old stone structure and good viewpoint. Over the bridge, a hundred yards up Abbey Foregate, the **Abbey of the Holy Cross** ⓘ *T01743-232723, Apr-Oct daily 1000-1730, Nov-Mar 1030-1500*, is a masterful Victorian improvement on a Norman foundation. Founded in 1083, the Abbey survived the dissolution thanks to its use by the laity as their local place of worship. Its greatest claim to fame these days is as the real-life home of Ellis Peter's fictional 'Brother Cadfael'.

An interesting day trip can be made to **Wroxeter Roman City** ⓘ *T01743-761330, 29 Mar-30 Sep daily 1000-1800, 1-31 Oct daily 1000-1700, 1 Nov-31 Mar daily 1000-1600*. On the evidence still standing today, 'City' seems a bit of an exaggeration, but 5 miles southeast of Shrewsbury, there are some fairly impressive remains of a place called Viroconium that once housed some 6000 souls, the fourth largest town in Roman Britain and part of Emperor Hadrian's fortification of his empire. The site of the baths and a large dividing wall can be seen, as well as a small museum of finds, although the best are in Rowley's House (see above). There's also a working **vineyard** ⓘ *Wroxeter, T01743-761888*, here which you can look round.

Church Stretton, The Long Mynd and Wenlock Edge

South of Shrewsbury, the best walking country in Shropshire can be found around the small Victorian resort town of Church Stretton, easily reached on the train. The Long Mynd is a 7-mile ridge of rounded hills just to the west of Church Stretton. Lonely walks lead up to heights of 1700 ft through bracken, heather and gorse, the most famous of which is the **Burway**. The **Port Way** runs along the top of the ridge, providing fantastic views into Wales and inland England almost as far as Birmingham. Deep secret valleys run down the Long Mynd's eastern slopes, accessible from villages like Little Stretton, Minton Batch and Priors Holt. Worth seeking out are the 20 or so acres of mixed deciduous woodland at **Old Rectory Wood**, just outside Church Stretton to the west. Details of all walks are available from Church Stretton **tourist information** ⓘ *T01694-723133, Easter-Oct.*

Six miles west of the Long Mynd, the **Stiperstones** are another belt of high land, very different in character. Much of the area surrounding the Devil's Chair, a strange rock formation on the summit with ghoulish associations, is a National Nature Reserve. The Romans mined lead in these hills, an industry that thrived until the mid-19th century. White calcite waste tips from the mines can still be seen near **Snailbeach**. One old shaft has been preserved near **The Bog**, a village to the east of the Stiperstones themselves.

East of Church Stretton, **Wenlock Edge** is a long limestone escarpment running northeast from Craven Arms to Much Wenlock, overlooking Ape Dale to the west towards the Long Mynd. Halfway along it stands the empty, unfurnished but unaltered **Wilderhope Manor** ⓘ *(NT), Longville, near Much Wenlock, T01694-771363, Apr-Sept Wed, Sat 1400-1630, Oct-Mar Sat 1400-1630, £1,* an Elizabethan manor house in a beautiful position on the Edge, with wide views and scope for lovely walks in the surrounding woods.

At the northern end, **Much Wenlock** is a gem of a town with a very helpful TIC, T01952-727679, and friendly locals. Narrow streets clamber away from the fine timbered Guildhall and the one main street. Nearby, the 12th-century Priory Ruins contain rare carvings and some well-kept topiary in the gardens.

Two miles east of the town, **Benthall Hall** ⓘ *T01952-882159, Apr-Sep Wed, Sun, bank holidays 1330-1730, £3.60,* at Broseley is a delightful 16th-century stone built manor house on the edge of the Severn Gorge. Still the home of the Benthall family, the interior features an impressive carved-oak staircase and elaborate plasterwork. Carefully tended old gardens lead down to a venerable little church dating back to the Restoration.

At the southern end of Wenlock Edge, near Craven Arms, **Stokesay Castle** ⓘ *(EH), T01588-672544, Apr-Sep daily 1000-1800, Oct daily 1000-1700, Nov-Mar Wed-Sun 1000-1600, £4.50, concessions £3.40, under-16s £2.30,* is one of the best-preserved 13th-century fortified manor houses in the country. The timber-framed Jacobean gatehouse is worth a look in itself, giving onto a grassy courtyard and the little old castle. Built in the 1280s by one of the richest wool merchants in the country, Lawrence of Ludlow, the whole place has been beautifully restored by English Heritage and occupies an idyllic position in the valley. The most remarkable survival is the Great Hall with its arched timber roof and an ornate carved-wood Elizabethan fireplace in the solar or great chamber.

About 8 miles west of Craven Arms towards the Welsh border, **Bishop's Castle** is a little border town and once the tiniest borough in England. Its Georgian town hall reflects this status, the dinky centrepiece of a town that could almost be a caricature of olde worlde charm, with its crooked-angled half-timbered buildings, ancient brewery and rolling hills all around.

Severn Gorge and Ironbridge

East of Much Wenlock, the **Severn Gorge** plunges down from a glut of museums at the **World Heritage Site** at **Ironbridge** to the gorge-side town of Bridgnorth. In Ironbridge, the first iron bridge in the world is still well worth a look after all these years. The result of three generations' worth of the Darby family's expertise in iron-smelting, it was erected in 1779. Now a well-preserved footbridge crossing the steep-sided gorge from the Victorian high street of the town, it forms the centrepiece of a pretty comprehensive celebration of the Industrial Revolution in Britain. An exhibition on the history of the bridge is housed in the original Tollhouse on the south side, over the bridge from the main drag of Ironbridge itself. The **Museum of the Gorge** ⓘ *T01952-432166, www.ironbridge.ws, daily 1000-1700, Passport tickets to all 10 museums, £12.95, under-16s and concessions £8.25, family £40*, a short walk west on the north bank, traces the history of the whole gorge in an 1830s warehouse, a highlight being the 40-ft scale model of the landscape in 1796. Up the road north from here in Coalbrookdale is the **Museum of Iron and Darby Houses**, on the site of Abraham Darby I's original blast furnace of 1709, with which he succeeded in smelting iron with coke rather than charcoal. The **Museum of Iron** offers a glimpse of the Great Exhibition of 1851 and also 'Enginuity', the new Coalbrookdale Interactive Technology Centre where visitors are encouraged to try out the principles of engineering for themselves. Beyond Ironbridge is the **Jackfield Tile Museum**, Ironbridge (currently closed for restoration, check T01952-882030) once a world centre for the decorative tile industry with a huge collection of tiles from the Victorian era on display, and also the **Coalport China Museum**, craft workshops in restored kiln workings, and the Tar Tunnel, where a source of natural bitumen was discovered some 200 years ago.

In Bridgnorth, perched on high above the river, you can ride up the 111-ft sandstone cliffs on the steepest funicular in the world, the **Bridgnorth Cliff Funicular Railway** ⓘ *Castle Terr, High Town and Underhill St, Low Town, Bridgnorth, T01746-762052, Apr-Oct Mon-Sat 0800-2000, Sun 1200-2000, Nov-Mar Mon-Sat 0800-1800, Sun 1200-1800.*

Ludlow

The jewel in Shropshire's crown, Ludlow is a very picturesque hill town perched on the banks of the river Teme. Heavily fortified by the Normans under Roger Montgomery, the castle is still the main event, although just wandering around the town is also a joy. Ludlow **tourist information** ⓘ *Castle St, T01584-875053, www.ludlow.org.uk, daily 1000-1700 (-1600 on Sat), closed Sun in Jan-Mar.*

Ludlow castle ⓘ *T01584-873355, www.lc.com, Apr-Sep 1000-1700 (-1900 in Aug), Oct-Mar 1000-1600, £3.50, concessions £3, under-16s £1, free audio guide*, was slighted by Parliamentarians during the Civil War, but not as badly as many others. The superb views from the top of the Norman keep, the Great Hall, where Milton's *Comus* was first performed, and an unusual round royal chapel are some of the highlights of a visit. The castle has a long and troubled history at the centre of centuries of border clashes. Eventually it became the HQ of the Marcher barons, the seat of the Council of Marches established in 1475 to govern Wales. Many unfortunate Princes of Wales were associated with the place, including Arthur, elder brother of Henry VIII – married aged 14 to Catherine of Aragon but dead in his bed here soon after – and Edward, briefly Edward V before being deposed and possibly murdered by his uncle Richard III. The place is haunted by Marion de la Bruere, who inadvertently let enemies in through the gates with her lover. She stabbed him with his own sword and then threw herself from the Pendower Tower. Regular events are now staged within the castle walls, the best during the Ludlow festival in June and July.

A few hundred yards from the fateful castle gates, across Castle Square (scene of lively markets most days of the week), the neoclassical **Butter Cross** is the centre of town. Behind it, the **Church of St Lawrence** well deserves its status as 'Cathedral of the Marches'. Evidence of the prosperity brought to the town by the wool trade, it contains a wealth of wonderful medieval glass, ancient tombs and royal misericords.

 From the Butter Cross, **Broad Street** slopes down to the river, surely one of the most delightful streetscapes in the country. Before reaching the river at Ludford Bridge, with its lovely views of the river, it passes through the **Broad Gate**, the sole survivor of the town's seven medieval gates.

Sleeping

Shrewsbury *p598, map p598*

B **Prince Rupert**, Butcher Row, T01743-499955, F357306. The smartest hotel in the centre of town, in a cunningly refurbished old house on the corner of Butcher Row and Pride Hill.

C **Meole Brace Hall**, Meole Brace, Shrewsbury, T01743-235566, www.meolebracehall.co.uk. ETC Silver Award, AGA Cook of the Year. About a 20-min walk, on the outskirts.

C **Tudor House**, 2 Fish St, T01743-351735. A good and central B&B.

D **Anton Guest House**, 1 Canon St, Monkmoor, Shrewsbury, T01743-359275, www.antonhouse.supernet.com. A reasonable budget option not far from the centre.

D **The Bellstone**, Bellstone, Shrewsbury, T01743-242100. Good value budget hotel in the centre of town with a brasserie attached.

D **Cromwells Hotel**, 11 Dogpole, T01743-361440, www.cromwellsinn.co.uk. Opposite the Guildhall, reasonably priced and interesting food, and about to undergo substantial refurbishment.

D **Fieldside**, 38 London Rd, T01743-353143, F354687. Further out, but very comfortable.

D **Pinewood House**, Shelton Park, The Mount, T01743-364200. A mile or so northwest of town, a 20-min walk, a B&B in a converted Victorian coach house.

F **Shrewsbury YHA**, the Woodlands, Abbey Foregate, T01743-360179. Has 54 beds in a Victorian ironmaster's house about a mile east of the train station.

Around Shrewsbury

A-B **Soulton Hall**, near Wem, T01939-232786, F234097. Grand Elizabethan house with a family atmosphere, 4 rooms in the house, 23 in coachhouse. £107 for 4-poster bed in the Cedar Lodge at the side of the walled garden.

C **Upper Brompton Farm**, Cross Houses, 4 miles south of Shrewsbury, T01743-761629, www.upperbromptonfarm.com A highly rated B&B on a working farm.

D **Burlton Inn**, Burlton, T01939-270284. Does good home-cooked food on the road to Ellesmere.

Church Stretton, Long Mynd and Wenlock Edge *p600*

B **Stretton Hall Hotel**, All Stretton, T01694-723224, www.strettonhall.co.uk £90 a double in a fine country manor house a short distance from Church Stretton.

C **Belvedere Guest House**, Burway Rd, Church Stretton, T01694-722232. One of the better guesthouses in Church Stretton (which has more than enough to go round), standing in its own gardens and handy for walks on the Long Mynd.

C **Willowfield Country Guesthouse**, Lower Wood, All Stretton, near Church Stretton, T01694-751471. A peaceful, dignified place with candlelit dinners in the Elizabethan dining room and its own gardens.

C **Three Tuns**, Salop St, Bishop's Castle, T01588-638797. Self-catering rooms (minimum 3-night stays) in the town's oldest pub.

C **Wenlock Edge Inn**, Hill Top, near Much Wenlock, T01746-785678, www.wenlockedgeinn.co.uk. 2 doubles and a twin, £70 for the 3-bed room. Superbly positioned pub with acclaimed grub and comfortable rooms.

D **Brook House Farm**, T01694-771308. Wall under Heywood, 5 miles east of Church Stretton beneath Wenlock Edge, is a stone-built non-smoking farmhouse B&B with great views and gardens, as well as self-catering cottages.

D **The Talbot Inn**, High St, Much Wenlock, T01952-727077. Fine pub grub in a beamed and welcoming village-style pub.

F **Stokes Barn Bunkhouse**, Much Wenlock, T01952-727293. Superb views, windy camping and cosy bunk-ups.

F **YHA Wilderhope Manor**, Longville in the Dale, T01694-771363. Has 4 dormitories, one 6-bed room and 1 4-bed in the National Trust's untouched Elizabethan manor house on Wenlock Edge.

Ironbridge *p600*
C **Thorpe House**, Coalport, T01952-586789. Offers 4 rooms in a Victorian house near the river, a little over a mile east of the bridge itself.
D **Woodlands Farm Guest House**, Beech Rd, Ironbridge, T01952-432741. Even closer to the bridge, a farm house on the edge of the gorge in 4 acres of its own grounds.
F **Ironbridge Gorge YHA**, High St, Coalport, T01952-588755. Has 160 beds in mainly 2-6 bedded rooms, spread over 2 sites at the Coalport China Museum.

Ludlow *p601*
A **Dinham Hall**, Dinham, T01584-876464, www.dinhamhall.co.uk. A grand 18th-century hotel beneath the castle walls with a good reputation for its food.
A **Overton Grange**, Hereford Rd, near Ludlow, T01584-873524. Another top-end option, a bit stuffy but also with an ambitious and accomplished menu, a short distance out of town towards Hereford on the B4361.
B **Mr Underhill's at Dinham Weir**, Dinham Bridge, T01584-874431. A charming restaurant with rooms on the river, a Michelin star for the food and a short bracing walk up into town.
B **Number Twenty Eight**, 28 Lower Broad St, T0800-0815000, www.no28.co.uk. 6 period townhouses below the Broad Gate, close to the river. A distinctly superior B&B.
C **Eight Dinham** 8 Dinham, T01584-875661. Refined B&B in an elegant period house close to the castle.
C **The Charlton Arms**, Ludford Bridge, T01584-872813. Family-run pub overlooking the Teme rapids, close to the old town bridge.
C **Seifton Court**, Culmington, near Ludlow, T01584-861214. A very comfortable 16th-century farmhouse nestling in Corvedale, 6 miles north up the B4365.
D **Church Inn**, Buttercross, T01584-872174, www.thechurchinn.com. A cheerful freehouse, tucked away behind the Buttermarket bang in the middle of town, which has reasonable rooms and does very filling, moderately priced meals in a jolly congenial atmosphere.
D **The Wheatsheaf Inn**, Lower Broad St, T01584-872980. At the bottom of Broad St, a family-run pub with clean, comfortable rooms.

Eating

Shrewsbury *p598, map p598*
£££ **Drapers Restaurant & Brasserie**, St Mary's Pl, T01743-344679. Another in a similar style.
£££ **Floating Thai Restaurant**, Welsh Bridge, T01743-243123. As its name suggests, exotic food in watery surroundings, evenings only.
£££ **La Lanterna**, The Old Vestry, St Julians, T01743-233552. A popular old-school Italian trattoria.
£££ **Renaissance**, 29a Princess St, T01743-354289. Occupies grand Georgian dining rooms and uses fresh local produce.
£££ **Sol**, 82 Wyle Cop, T01743-340560. Local produce expertly but rather too expensively prepared. Widely regarded as the best restaurant in Shrewsbury.
££ **The Armoury**, Victoria Quay, Victoria Av, T01743-340525, does modern British food in a converted warehouse restaurant-bar over-looking the river. Book for the weekend.
££ **The Riverside Inn**, T01952-510900, does rooms (C) and some good British food on an attractive stretch of the river Severn.
££**Three Fishes**, Fish St, T01743-344793. Worth seeking out for its excellent real ales in a fine Tudor building in the middle of town, as well as reasonably priced bar meals.

Church Stretton, Long Mynd and Wenlock Edge *p600*
££ **Three Tuns**, Salop St, Bishop's Castle, T01588-638797. Very old pub with its own brewery (granted a licence in the mid 17th century) with quiet self-catering rooms available in an annexe.
££ **Royal Oak**, Cardington, near Church Stretton, T01694-771266. Tables outside and wholesome meals for lunch and supper, close to Cardingmill Valley (NT).
££ **Horseshoe Inn**, Bridges, near Ratlinghope, T01588-650260. With self-catering accommodation and good food next to the river Onny.

Ludlow *p601*
£££ **Hibiscus**, 17 Corve St, T01584-872325, is another, also highly rated for its kitchen. Both need to be booked.
£££ **Merchant House**, Lower Corve St, T01584-875438. The original and best, about

££40 a head for some top-notch tucker, because of its Jacobean surroundings.

££ **Koo**, 127 Old St, T01584-878462, is a small, reasonably priced (about £20 a head) Japanese restaurant that has won the hearts of the locals.

££ **Aragon's Restaurant**, 5 Church St, T01584-873282, is a café-restaurant that does filling sandwiches, soups, pastas and pizzas all day.

££ **Ego Café Bar**, Quality Sq, T01584 878000, is a wine bar with decent enough food and a friendly atmosphere.

££ **Roebuck**, T01584-711230, in Brimfield, 4 miles south of Ludlow, also has a formidable reputation for its food.

££ **The Unicorn**, Corve St, T01584-873555, does above-average pub food in a cosy, beamed old place.

For pub grub, see also **The Charlton Arms, Church Inn** and The **Wheatsheaf Inn** in Sleeping above.

Festivals

Jun **Ludlow Festival**. Takes over the castle with theatre performances, music events in the town and an atmopshere of good-natured bonhommie.

Staffordshire

→ *Colour map 4, grid A/B3*

East of Shropshire and west of Derbyshire, Staffordshire is another Midland through-county that suffers by comparison. It lacks the landscape and the historical associations that draw people to its immediate neighbours. Even so, Stoke-on-Trent, can boast some world-class industrial heritage and an optimistic forward-looking attitude. The city is in fact six separate towns – Tunstall, Burslem, Hanley (the city centre), Stoke, Fenton and Longton – and is consequently known as 'The Potteries'. These places were powerhouses of the Industrial Revolution, producing most of the famous chinas of the Victorian era on a mass scale using secret Chinese recipes. Fifteen miles south down the M6 sits Stafford, the county town but not a place many choose to linger over very long. They're more likely to head for the cathedral town of Lichfield, another 20 miles or so southeast across Cannock Chase, or to the UK's most popular theme park at Alton Towers, 15 miles east of Stoke-on-Trent. ▸▸ *For Sleeping, Eating and other listings, see page 606.*

Ins and outs

Getting there With **Virgin Trains,** T08457-222333, operating one of their main routes from London to Manchester via Crewe and Stafford, you can be assured of trains every 30 minutes for most of the day. **Central Trains,** T08700-006060, run a local service from Birmingham and the West Midlands on a very regular basis. Handily situated just off the M6, Stoke-on-Trent is more or less slap bang in the middle of the country, so is easily accessible by **road** from all directions. From London take the M1 to Leicester and then the A50 takes you right into Stoke. Also the M40 from London will take you to Birmingham and you can get onto the M6 via the M42 and M5. Just after Newcastle-under-Lyme you turn right on to the A50 approaching Stoke from the west. From the southwest the M5 connects with the M6 outside Birmingham. From the north the M6 or the A1 will connect with the A50 for a fairly trouble-free journey.

Getting around With plenty of parking and a far from pedestrianized centre Stoke-on-Trent and its surroundings are ideal for those with **cars.** The centre of the city is Hanley, even though there's also an area called Stoke. The town museum is situated in this area, though there are visitors' centres and factory shops attached to most of the functioning Pottery concerns. Stoke-on-Trent does, however, benefit from having an excellent **bus** service. First, T01782-207999, have a Fareday ticket, priced £3.00 for an adult and £5.00 for a family (2 adults and 3 children), which you can buy on any **PMT** bus, and is valid for 1 day's unlimited travel on the local **First Network**. For further bus information and a handy journey planner visit www.ukbus.co.uk

Information Stoke-on-Trent TIC ⓘ *Quadrant Rd, Hanley, Stoke-on-Trent, T01782-236000, F01782-236005, Mon-Sat 0915-1715*. Comprehensive, helpful and conveniently situated in the Potteries Shopping Centre in Hanley. **Stafford TIC** ⓘ *Market St, Stafford, T01785-619619, Mon-Fri 0930-1700, Sat 1000-1700*.

The Potteries

As their name suggests, the Potteries – aka Stoke-on-Trent – are best known for being a world centre of ceramics, home to such luminaries as Royal Doulton, Spode and Wedgwood. These businesses still dominate the daily life of Stoke-on-Trent, the city of six towns. Dickens described it as 'opulent', Arnold Bennett immortalized it as 'Knype' in his 'Five Towns' books such as Clayhanger and more recently Robbie Williams and Anthea Turner both spent their early lives imbibing the rich cultural mix and still flourishing nightlife of the city, which no doubt helped at least one of them on their way to international stardom. The manufacture of pottery in this area goes back to Roman times, but it wasn't until the coming of the Trent-Mersey Canal and the development of local coal-fields in the 18th and early 19th centuries, that the place really took off, with the names listed above as well as quite a few others setting up factories which were soon generating handsome profits. An early exemplar of the truism 'where there's muck, there's brass', Stoke paid the price for this prosperity with legendary levels of pollution and some of the worst working conditions to be found in the country – a fact commemorated in one of the contemporary museums by a special 'child labour exhibit'. These days the urban landscape isn't quite so grimy and the famous bottle-kilns associated with Stoke – many of which are still standing – don't belch filthy smoke 24/7. Meanwhile kids aren't pressed into labour before they reach their teens, but are more likely to be found pressing their parents into taking them to Alton Towers, the nation's favourite theme park which lies a few miles east of Stoke.

Most visitors to Stoke-on-Trent will want to head straight for its 'cultural quarter' and **The Potteries Museum and Art Gallery** ⓘ *Bethesda St, Hanley, T01782-232323, Nov-Feb Mon-Sat 1000-1600, Sun 1300–1600 (except Christmas-New Year), Mar-Oct Mon-Sat 1000-1700, Sun 1400-1700, tours, book in advance via Visitor Desk – available during opening hours only, free*. Pick of the bunch, museum-wise, with the largest collection of pottery in the world, as well as an original Spitfire fighter plane from the Second World War, which was designed by local lad Reginald Mitchell. Commemorating local lads of a different industrial background, there's also the Coal Sculpture which is a memorial to the two local colliers who died on picket duty during the 1984 miner's strike.

While there's an excellent narrative of the town's association with pottery in the town museum, an even better one can be found in the **Gladstone Pottery Museum** ⓘ *Uttoxeter Rd, Longton, T01782-319232, daily 1000-1700, except Christmas to New Year, £4.95, child £3.50, concessions £3.95, family £14*, which is the only authentic reproduction of a Victorian pottery factory in the world and comes complete with cobbled yard and bottle-shaped oven-kilns. As befits a town that plays host to Royal Doulton, there's even a new exhibit at the Gladstone Museum called 'Flushed with Pride' which charts the history of the toilet. There's also a tearoom and gift shop.

For lovers of industrial history the **Etruria Industrial Museum** ⓘ *Lower Bedford St, Etruria, T01782-233144, car park is on Kiln Down Rd, off Etruria Vale Rd, Sat-Wed 1200-1630, except Christmas to New Year, closed weekends Jan-Mar. £1.50 child/concessions £1*, is Britain's sole surviving steam-powered potter's mill. Built in 1857 to grind materials for the pottery industry it's a great hands-on exhibit offering a superb insight into how it all worked back in the days when there were many others like it.

Seven miles north of Stoke-on-Trent, **Biddulph Grange** ⓘ *(NT), Biddulph, T01782-517999. Apr-Oct Wed-Fri 1200-1730, Sat, Sun 1100-1730, Nov-Dec Sat, Sun 1200-1600, £4.50, under-16s £2.40, family £11.50, Nov-Dec free*, has been fairly recently restored. This Victorian fantasy garden features a variety of different 'rooms' in different styles from around the world, planted appropriately to their provenance. Highlights include the Egyptian Court, imitation Great Wall of China and the rockeries.

Visit **The Wedgwood Story** ⓘ *Wedgwood, Barlaston, T01782-204218, daily Mon-Fri 0900-1700, Sat and Sun 1000-1600,* the working factory and see what it takes to call a cup a Wedgwood. Also a shop selling seconds.

Twenty miles east of Stoke-on-Trent, **Alton Towers** ⓘ *T08705-204060. Daily from 16 Mar-3rd Nov, daily 0930-2000 or dusk if earlier www.altontowers.com*, is the UK's most famous theme park. Thrill rides galore on Europe's big flying rollercoaster. Also Nemesis and Oblivion - real screamers. Don't miss the ice illusion show.

Near Stafford, the county town that has suffered thanks to the M6, the **Shugborough Estate** ⓘ *(NT) Milford, T01889-881388, Apr-Sep daily 1100-1700*, is the 900-acre ancestral home of Lord Lichfield. Nearby, the **National Forest** ⓘ *T01283-551211*, is a 200-square mile forest that impinges on three counties, with lovely woodland and walks.

Stafford ⓘ *Greengate St, Stafford, T01785-619619, Mon-Sat 1000-1700*, the county town, is an undistinguished market town closely associated with Sir Izaak Walton, the *Compleat Angler*. Its main attraction is the Ancient High House, the tallest timber framed townhouse in England. Built in 1595 and refurbished with Elizabethan period rooms.

South of Stafford, **Lichfield** is an 18th-century looking market town with a surprisingly grand sandstone cathedral with three spires but little else to recommend it except a rather staid atmosphere. Its most famous inhabitant was Dr Johnson, the 18th-century man of letters, who was born and educated here, although he spent most of his life in London, passing through in later life on his way to Wales with his patrons the Thrales. Erasmus Darwin, Charles Darwin's grandfather, also lived here.

Sleeping

The Potteries *p605*

B Garth Hotel, Wolverhampton Rd, Stafford, T01785-256124, www.corushotels.co.uk. A couple of miles south of Stafford itself, on the A449, this hotel that grew out of an old pub and now has 60 rooms.

B The Little Barrow Hotel, Beacon St, Lichfield, T01543-414500, www.tlbh.co.uk. 5-min walk uphill from the cathedral, a small (24 beds) family-run hotel that was once a sweet shop.

C Express Holiday Inn, Stanley Matthews Way, Trentham Lakes, Stoke-on-Trent, T01782-377000. Does a reasonable chain job.

C Manor House, near Denstone, Uttoxeter, T01889-590415. 3 miles away from Alton Towers is this ancient Tudor manor house B&B, very welcoming with 3 double rooms (en-suite bathrooms), each with 4-poster beds.

D Slab Bridge Cottage, Little Onn, Church Eaton, T01785-840220. A Victorian cottage on the Shropshire Union Canal, with 2 bedrooms with en-suite bathroom and offering boat trips too.

Eating and drinking

The Potteries *p605*

£££ Julians, 21 High St, Stafford, T01785-851200, do acceptable bistro fare for lunch and supper in the middle of the county town (about £25 a head).

££ The Olive Tree, 34 Tamworth St, Lichfield, T01543-263363, off the High St, does a Mediterranean menu in a buzzy and friendly atmosphere (about £12 a head).

££ The Queen's Head, Lichfield, T01543-410932, does a huge variety of different cheeses to go with its very fine real ales.

££ Scales Inn, Market St, Lichfield, T01543-441930 is a good pub with a welcoming, cosy atmosphere.

££ Stafford Arms, Railway St, Stafford, T01785-253313, close to the train station, pulls a very good pint of real ale. With bedrooms.

The Northwest

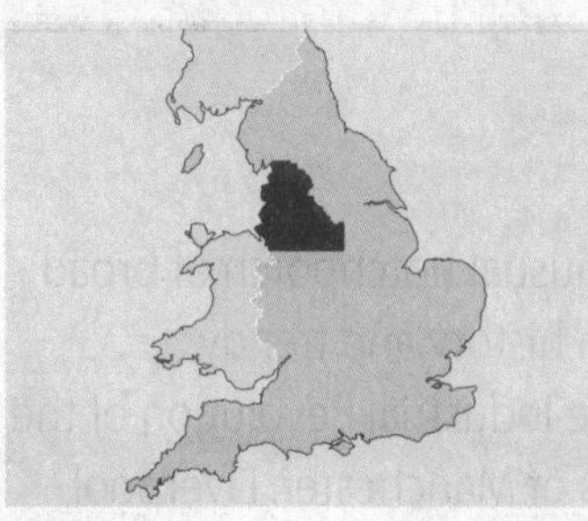

Footprint features

Introduction

The northwest of England is an unusual hotchpotch of broad plains, industrial cities, Pre-Roman history and trendy post-industrial chic. Shaped by the Industrial Revolution of the 18th and 19th centuries, the areas of Manchester, Liverpool and Lancashire were central to the development of industry in England. The bubble burst though and in the late 19th century the Northwest became synonymous with dark, desolate mills and urban decay.

These days though things have moved on. Manchester and Liverpool are lively cities much aided by the 2002 Commonwealth Games which allowed the almost total redevelopment of Manchester city centre and the creation of new museums like the Imperial War Museum of the North. They are two of the country's hot spots for nightlife, but that's not to say that there's nothing to do round here during the day. The Peak District National Park is the jewel of the region, curving around the spine of the Pennines with scenic views and wonderful walking country within an hour's journey of the city. The Cheshire Plain to the southwest is lush pasture, countryside with a depth of history like the Roman town of Chester, an ideal stop-over on the way to the Lake District.

One thing's for sure, this region has finally shrugged off the ghosts of the past, rejoicing in its heritage with an eye on the future. Whether looking over the hills of the Peak District or drinking beer in a canalside bar, take a moment to consider whether it really is all that grim up north.

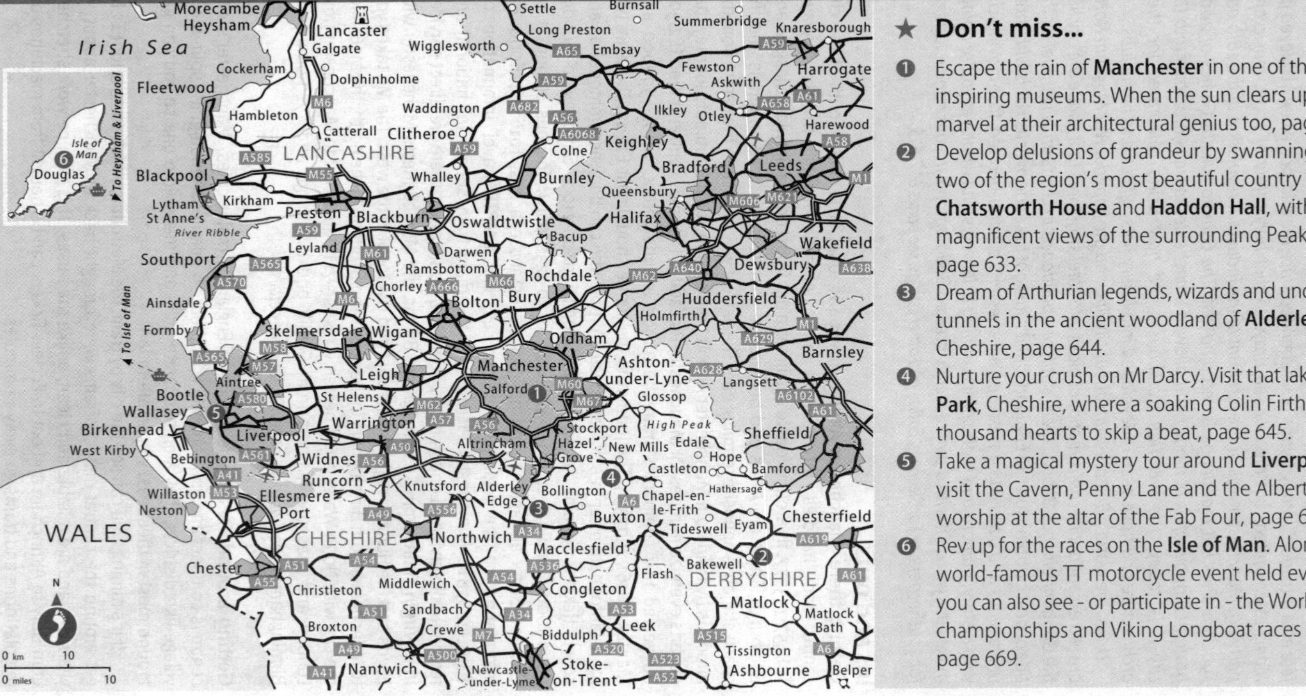

★ Don't miss...

1. Escape the rain of **Manchester** in one of the city's inspiring museums. When the sun clears up the rain, marvel at their architectural genius too, page 610.
2. Develop delusions of grandeur by swanning about in two of the region's most beautiful country houses, **Chatsworth House** and **Haddon Hall**, with magnificent views of the surrounding Peak District, page 633.
3. Dream of Arthurian legends, wizards and underground tunnels in the ancient woodland of **Alderley Edge**, Cheshire, page 644.
4. Nurture your crush on Mr Darcy. Visit that lake at **Lyme Park**, Cheshire, where a soaking Colin Firth caused a thousand hearts to skip a beat, page 645.
5. Take a magical mystery tour around **Liverpool** and visit the Cavern, Penny Lane and the Albert Dock to worship at the altar of the Fab Four, page 648.
6. Rev up for the races on the **Isle of Man**. Alongside the world-famous TT motorcycle event held every May, you can also see - or participate in - the World Tin Bath championships and Viking Longboat races in August, page 669.

Manchester

→ Colour map 6, grid B3

Manchester, said French footballer Eric Cantona, is a city in love with "le football, la fête et la musique". Many things have changed since the mid-90s when he played for Manchester United, but the city still prays to that holy trinity of sport, music and partying. Manchester was at the forefront of the industrial revolution of the 18th and 19th centuries but that image is receding fast. The Commonwealth Games of 2002 brought a huge influx of money and allowed Manchester to transform itself into the city it is today; the Victorian workhouses are now being celebrated for their architecture and have been redeveloped into luxury flats, offices and nightclubs.

Urbis, the world's first museum about city life, and the Imperial War Museum North are two exceptionally confrontational glass and steel structures that shape the city like the Guggenheim has Bilbao. There's stiff competition from Leeds and Liverpool for the title of best clubbing town in England, but it's just got the edge over its rivals with three universities and a thriving gay scene. Manchester's a warm-hearted, fast-moving city with history, humour and high-spirits running in its veins. But whatever you're doing, make sure you do it with a pint of locally brewed Boddington's in your hand – lager is for southerners. ➤ *For Sleeping, Eating and other listings, see pages 617-625.*

Ins and outs

Getting there **Manchester Airport**, T0161-4893000, is 12 miles south of the city centre and handles international and domestic flights. **British Airways**, T08457-733377, fly around four to five times a day from London Gatwick, Glasgow and Edinburgh, There are ATMs and bureaux de change in all three terminals and the coach station is opposite terminal one. The easiest way to get into the centre from the airport is by train from Manchester Airport train station. It's a 20-minute journey that departs every 20 minutes for **Manchester Piccadilly**, the city's central station (£2.30). Suggested taxi companies from the airport include **Airtax**, T0161-4999000 and **Mantax**, T0161-2303333. The journey to the centre should cost £12-13. There are two tourist information centres at Manchester Airport who can book accommodation and coach tickets: Terminal 1, T4363344, Mon-Fri 0800-2100, Saturday to Sunday 0800-1800; Terminal 2, T0161-4896412, 0730-1230 daily. The **bus** station is on Chorlton St for all regional and national buses and coaches, T0161-2426000. For information on the regional bus services, call **GMPTE** travel information on T0161-2287811. Manchester Piccadilly is the main train station for national and regional **rail** services, London is 2½ hours to 4 hours away, there are direct services from **Virgin Trains** from Euston station. By **car**, the M62 connects Manchester with Leeds and the Humber region to the east and Liverpool to the west. The M6 takes you to Manchester from Birmingham in the south and Scotland in the north; the M56 links the city with North Wales and Chester. It takes 3½ hours to get to Manchester from London and Glasgow, 3 hours from Cardiff and Edinburgh and 1½ hours from Birmingham. ➤ *See Transport, page 625, for more details.*

Getting around Despite being one of England's major cities, Manchester's city centre is compact and you can **walk** it in about 20 minutes. Although it's split into 8 village-like districts, they aren't separate units and merge into one so you can get around most of them easily in an afternoon.

If it's raining, you can see the city by **tram**, the **Metrolink**, which costs about £1 to get around the central district. Trams were brought back to Manchester about 10 years ago and are reliable and clean, unlike the buses. This tram network stretches from Bury to Altrincham and out to Eccles. Tickets can be bought from machines on the platforms and trams go every 12 minutes.

24 hour party people

If you've only got 24 hours to spend in Manchester, use it well to soak up the culture of the city – but bring an umbrella, so you don't soak up the rain too.

Start your day with a designer coffee in the Triangle centre in the Millennium Quarter before moving on to take in the independent record shops and boutiques of the Northern Quarter. Have lunch in a bar on Oldham Street then jump on the Metrolink and get out to Salford Quays for the afternoon. Make the most of the Imperial War Museum of the North and Lowry art gallery here, Manchester's dazzling new museums, which display different aspects of this diverse city. A curry in Rusholme should see you right for dinner so you can then head towards Deansgate Locks for a beer or two before going clubbing in one of the many waterside bars. Have a kebab and wave to the milkman on the way home.

Getting from Manchester Piccadilly to the other areas is easy by foot, but the station also has a free shuttlebus service lined up for you. Immediately outside the station the buses 1 and 2 take you around the city linking the four stations every 10 minutes and more frequently during rush-hour. The number 1 goes to Victoria Station (for the MEN arena and Urbis) via Chinatown and Kendals department store on Deansgate before heading back to Piccadilly; the number 2 takes you down to Oxford Road and Deansgate stations via the Town Hall and then back to Piccadilly. The service runs from 0700-1900.

Orientation Beside Piccadilly station is the bohemian **Northern Quarter**. Across the road from Piccadilly station running mainly along Canal Street is the **Gay Village**. The centre of Manchester just off St Peter's Square has **Chinatown**. **Peter's Fields** is the main business and conference area, also containing the Bridgewater Hall, the city's premier classical music venue. **Manchester University** is mainly on Oxford Road. **Castlefield** to the southwest sits on the canal network. **Deansgate Locks**, just a totter in high heels away, is also on the canal network. Up by Victoria station in the north is the **Millennium Quarter**, redeveloped since the IRA bomb of 1996. **Rusholme**, the Indian district in the south of Manchester, is also known as the curry mile. Just out of Manchester to the southwest is **Salford Quays**, the old industrial port area which has also been redeveloped. The home of Manchester United, **Old Trafford**, is just across the Manchester Ship Canal from here, and here you'll also find the Imperial War Museum of the North and The Lowry, an art gallery, theatre, cinema and discount shopping outlet.

Information The main **tourist office** ⓘ *town hall extension on Lloyds St at St Peter's Square, daily Mon-Sat 1000-1730, Sun 1100-1600 except 25 and 26 Dec and 1 Jan, T0161-2343157, www.manchester.gov.uk/visitorcentre*, can arrange accommodation, city walking tours, theatre and coach tickets and car hire. **Salford Quays TIC** ⓘ *1 the Quays, T0161-8488601, Mon-Sat 0830-1630, Sun 1000-1600*, provides information about Old Trafford, The Lowry and the Imperial War Museum of the North.

The websites www.destinationmanchester.com and www.manchester.com provide useful, up-to-date listings about the area. Your best bet if you've come to Manchester for a short break is to pick up a copy of **Citylife**, the city's glossy listings magazine which is in the mould of London's Time Out. It's published fortnightly on a Tue and is good for all things young, fun and Mancunian, www.citylife.co.uk. The **Manchester Evening News** is the regional daily newspaper with listings, and The **Metro** is a free daily commuter paper with digested national news and local listings.

Manchester

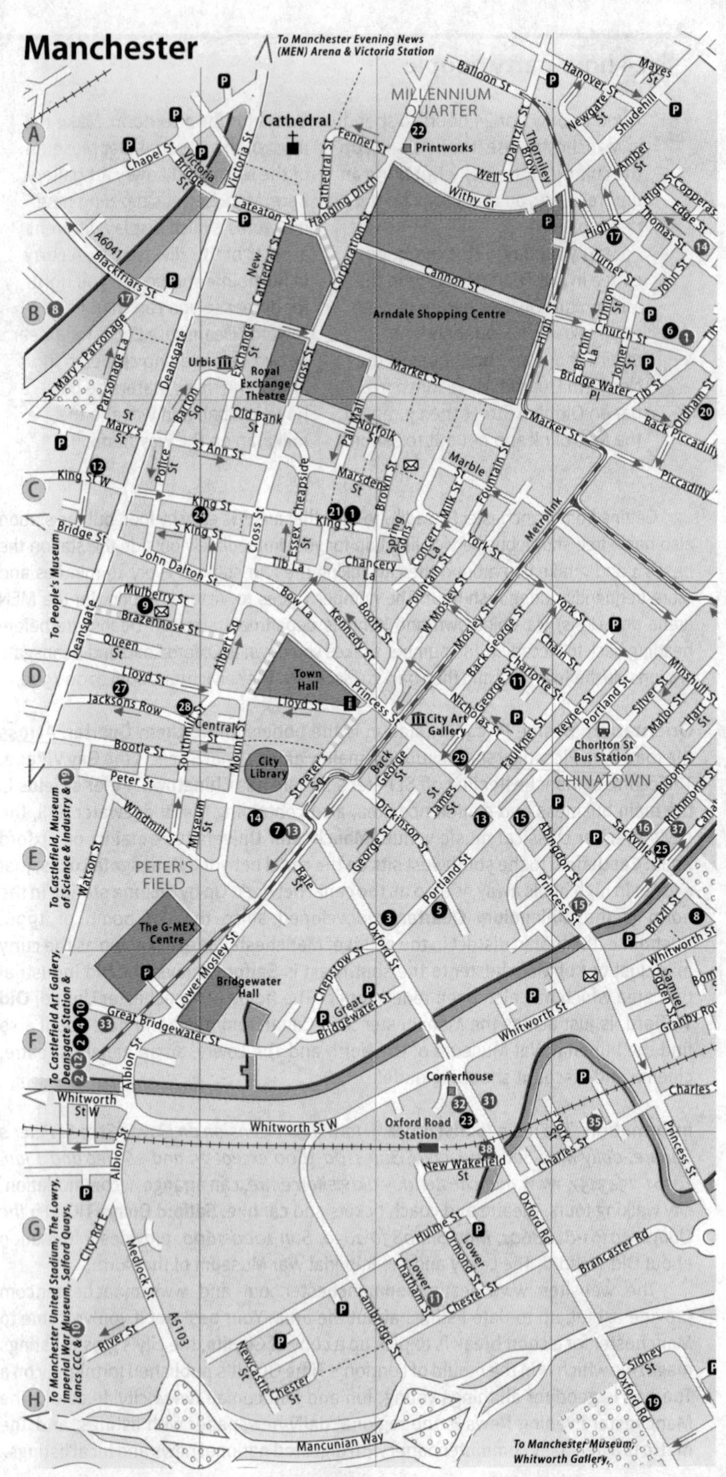
To Manchester Evening News (MEN) Arena & Victoria Station
Cathedral
MILLENNIUM QUARTER
Printworks
Arndale Shopping Centre
Urbis
Royal Exchange Theatre
Town Hall
City Art Gallery
City Library
Chorlton St Bus Station
CHINATOWN
PETER'S FIELD
The G-MEX Centre
Bridgewater Hall
Cornerhouse
Oxford Road Station
To People's Museum
To Castlefield, Museum of Science & Industry & 19
To Castlefield Art Gallery, Deansgate Station & 2 12 2 4 10
To Manchester United Stadium, The Lowry, Imperial War Museum, Salford Quays, Lancs CCC & 10
To Manchester Museum, Whitworth Gallery,
Deansgate
Market St
Piccadilly
King St
Princess St
Oxford St
Oxford Rd
Portland St
Mosley St
Whitworth St
Whitworth St W
Great Bridgewater St
Mancunian Way
Metrolink

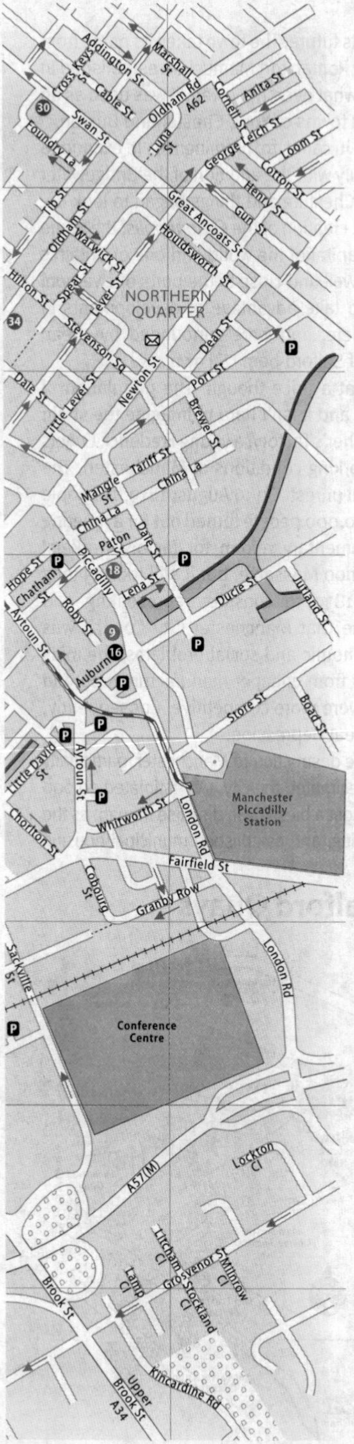

Addington St
Marshall St
Cross Keys St
Cable St
Oldham Rd A62
Cornell St
Anita St
Swan St
Foundry La
Luna St
George Leigh St
Loom St
Cotton St
Henry St
Gun St
Tib St
Great Ancoats St
Oldham St
Warwick St
Houldsworth St
Hilton St
Spear St
Lever St
NORTHERN QUARTER
Stevenson Sq
Dean St
Dale St
Newton St
Port St
Little Lever St
Brewer St
Tariff St
China La
Mangle St
China La
Paton St
Dale St
Hope St
Chatham St
Piccadilly
Lena St
Ducie St
Jutland St
Roby St
Aytoun St
Auburn St
Store St
Boad St
Little David St
Aytoun St
Manchester Piccadilly Station
Whitworth St
London Rd
Chorlton St
Fairfield St
Cobourg St
Granby Row
Sackville St
London Rd
Conference Centre
Lockton Cl
A57(M)
Litcham Cl
Grosvenor St
Milnrow Cl
Lamp Cl
Stockland Cl
Brook St
Kincardine Rd
Upper Brook St A34

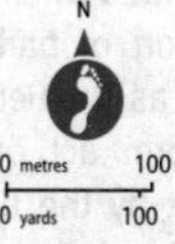

Sleeping
Britannia Sachs 1 *B4*
Castlefield 2 *F1*
Eleven Didsbury Park 3 *H5*
Elton Bank 4 *H4*
Etrop Grange 5 *H1*
Grafton 6 *H4*
Imperial 7 *H4*
The Lowry 8 *B1*
Malmaison Manchester 9 *D5*
Manchester Backpackers 10 *H1*
Manchester Student Village 11 *G3*
Manchester YHA 12 *F1*
Midland 13 *E2*
Millstone 14 *B4*
New Union 15 *E4*
Rembrandt 16 *E4*
Renaissance 17 *B1*
Rossetti 18 *D5*
Walkabout Inn 19 *E1*

Eating
39 Steps 1 *C2*
Atlas 2 *F1*
Beaujolais 3 *E3*
Dimitri's 4 *F1*
Don Antonio 5 *E3*
Earth Vegetarian Café 6 *B4*
French Restaurant 7 *E2*
Gaia 8 *E4*
Jowata 10 *F1*
Kailash 11 *D3*
Koreana 12 *C1*
Little Yang Sing 13 *E3*
Livebait 14 *E2*
El Machos Cantinas 15 *E3*
Malmaison Brasserie 16 *D5*
Market 17 *B4*
Monsoon Nights 18 *H4*
On the Eighth Day 19 *H4*
Café Pop 20 *C4*
Le Petit Blanc Brasserie 21 *C2*
Printworks 22 *A3*
Pure Space 23 *F3*
Reform 24 *C1*
Sarasota 25 *E4*
Shere Khan 26 *H4*
Simply Heathcote's 27 *D1*
Tampopo 28 *D1*
Yang Sing 29 *D3*

Pubs & bars
The Band on the Wall 30 *A5*
Copperface Jacks 31 *F3*
Cornerhouse 32 *F3*
Deansgate Locks 33 *F1*
Dry 34 *B5*
Lass O'Gowrie 35 *F4*
Night & Day Café 36 *B4*
Prague V 37 *E4*

History

Manchester's past is perhaps not as bright as its future. The town takes its name from the oldest part of its history, the turf and timber Roman fort Mamucium established in AD 79 in the area now called Castlefield. Somewhat overshadowed, it was used as an intermediate port between the more important towns of York, Chester and Buxton.

The city had to wait a long time before it came to prominence. It expanded considerably as a market town in the 18th century with the addition of the Bridgewater canal which connected the town with much of Cheshire and things began to look up. This canal infrastructure was instrumental in the creation of the *Cottonopolis*, the name given to Manchester as it became the cotton capital of the world and one of Britain's leading industrial cities. Located on the River Irwell and close to the ports of Liverpool and Chester, the city was perfectly situated to take advantage of developments in textile manufacture. Mills sprang up everywhere, and were surrounded by cheap terraced housing as depicted in the paintings of Salford-born LS Lowry.

This new-found sense of purpose came at a price though. The population of 76,000 in 1801 had grown to 316,000 by 1851, and it isn't hard to imagine the strain that this put on the city (while working in his father's factory, a young Frederick Engels was one of many writers who criticized the working conditions of Manchester). The rapid industrialization led to social and political unrest. On 16 August 1819, 11 people were killed and a total of 400 wounded when 50,000 people turned out for a meeting held in St Peter's Field in support of parliamentary reform for factory workers' conditions. The disaster is known as The Peterloo Massacre, but it still took 13 long years for the parliamentary reform act of 1832 to consider representing and supporting the underclasses. But by the time that Manchester City Council was established in 1853 to deal with the city's economic and social problems, the mills were in decline. Manchester was under threat from cheaper manufacturers abroad and by 1870 German and American factories were more competitive. Consequently, slum areas persisted and the city suffered a great depression.

The Second World War also brought immense destruction to Manchester, particularly in December of 1940 when the Christmas blitz decimated the city. (An estimated 30,000 houses were damaged by the shelling.) It was almost a blessing in disguise though, as the rebuilding programme eliminated the slum housing, and established municipal housing areas. (These have not been such a great success in recent years though, as areas like Moss Side are almost synonymous with violence and crime.)

More recently, destruction has come in the form of an IRA bomb in 1996 which disabled Market Street and principally the Arndale Centre, in an attack which has cost millions to rebuild. Still, it wasn't all in vain: it allowed Marks and Spencers to rebuild their Market Street store as the biggest Marks and Sparks in the world. After a failed Olympic bid in 2000, hosting the Commonwealth Games in 2002 prompted almost an entire redevelopment of the Piccadilly and Salford Quays areas and a host of sprightly new attractions. Manchester United, despite being the least supported locally of the city's two premiership sides, is still the single biggest moneyspinner of the city.

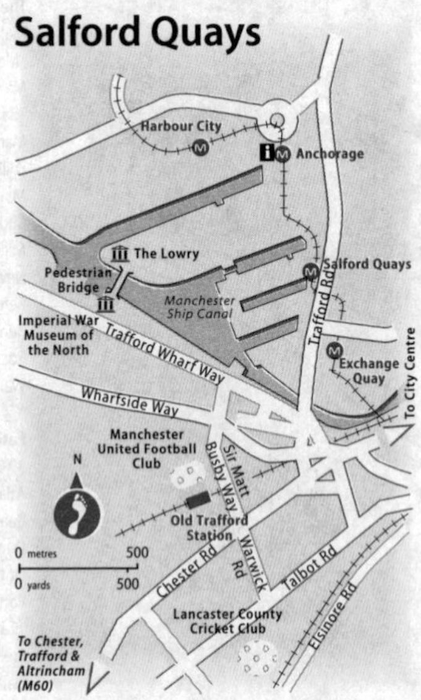

Humble beginnings

The Red Devils has a history of flamboyant players from George Best to clothes horse and media icon David Beckham. It wasn't always this way though, as they started out in 1878 as a local works football team, Newton Heath Lancashire and Yorkshire Railway. They joined the fledgling football league in 1892 and soon ran into financial difficulty. But a chance encounter by the captain's dog and local brewery owner John Henry Davies found a saviour for the soon-to-be red devils. He invested in the club and in 1902 they were renamed Manchester United. A move to Old Trafford in 1910, owned by Davies's Manchester Brewery Company, came not a minute too soon. Two days previously the old wooden Bank Street stand blew over in high winds. It was a good omen for the club as by the end of their first full season at Old Trafford, Manchester United were the new league champions.

Sights

Salford Quays

Not so long ago, the Quays area was a bit shabby and run-down, a relic of the industrial period that was still in use and that you'd only recommend visiting to your worst enemy. Now though, it's the place to be seen at, with an art gallery and museum that have been instrumental in Manchester's reinvention as a city of dynamism and culture. It's also spitting distance from Manchester's main claim to fame, the home turf of Manchester United at Old Trafford. Salford Quays is about a mile and a half to the southwest of the city centre and easily reached by Metrolink from Harbour City and Old Trafford tram stops.

Tickets to see Man United play are like gold dust even if you are a member, but you can console yourself with a look round the changing rooms and down on to the pitch at the **Manchester United Museum and Tour** ⓘ *North Stand, Old Trafford, Sir Matt Busby Way, T0161-8688631, www.manutd.com, Mon-Sun 0930-1700, closed on match days and the day before champions' league games, museum, £5.50, concessions £3.75, combined museum and tour £8.50, £5.75 concessions*. There's a lot to see here, from Busby's babes to glittering trophies, Best, Beckham and boots and plenty of stats and history for the die-hard fan.

Just one stop away on the Metrolink will take you to Harbour City and the Quays itself. It's a tough call, but of the two museums here, **The Lowry** ⓘ *Pier 8, T0161-8762000, www.thelowry.com, Mon-Wed 1100-1700, Thu-Fri 1100-1930, Sat 1000-1930, Sun 1100-1700, free, except for special exhibitions*, is probably the best, although you can easily visit this and the Imperial War Museum of the North (see below) in an afternoon. Salford's most illustrious son painted scenes of Manchester and the surrounding area in the first half of the 20th century and his depiction of the workers with eyes red-rimmed from the dust and malnourished children speak more about the city than any of the museums. He's more famous for his paintings of stick people pouring into the factory gates, and while there are a number of them on display, the individual portraits show another side to him, as do his views across the city to the Peak District. The Lowry exhibition is permanent and there are also rotating exhibitions by local and national artists, two theatres, a café, a restaurant and beautiful views across the quays.

Across the bridge from The Lowry you can see the stunning **Imperial War Museum of the North** ⓘ *Trafford Wharf, T0161-8364000, www.iwm.org.uk, daily 1000-1800* all year round, closed 24-26 Dec, free, arcing across the sky. The building itself, designed by the architect Daniel Libeskind and opened in 2002, is as much a draw as what's inside. He decided to represent conflict on the three planes of air, water and land with the three shards of glass and steel which divide your view here, and it certainly works as a confrontational structure. Manchester was decimated by bombs in the Second World War and, with the Imperial War Museum miles away in London, it's been a long-standing travesty that those in the north couldn't access this part of the nation's history, but now it's the Londoners who will feel left out. The focus of the museum is on the way that war shapes people's lives over a variety of different conflict situations and it contains thought-provoking and state-of-the-art exhibits.

St Peter's Square and around

Step outside the TIC and you'll be faced with the **Town Hall** and **Manchester City Library** ⓘ *T0161-2341900, Mon-Thu 1000-2000, Fri-Sat 1000-1700*, beside it. The town hall is one of the city's original Victorian buildings with a clear connection to the Cottonopolis days. It was built in the style of a medieval Flemish cloth hall, which gives the square a European feel, and has murals inside it by Ford Madox Brown. Manchester Library is the central library for the university and the city's other citizens and has a beautiful frescoed ceiling inside as well as archives for Manchester and an extensive music library.

Across the road on Mosley Street is the **City Art Gallery** ⓘ *T0161-2358888, www.cityartgalleries.org.uk, Tue-Sun 1000-1700, free*. It underwent a recent £35 million facelift and shows a wide variety of art from the Pre-Raphaelites to the Renaissance, Turner, Constable and a range of 20th-century art. The gallery seems to go on forever and has an unmissable interactive gallery where you can learn about inspirations for paintings.

Oxford Road and around

Peter Street running alongside the Library turns into Oxford Road. This is the main student area in Manchester and consequently has some good bars and clubs as well as a number of art galleries and university facilities. Oxford Road station is the main way to reach this area if you don't fancy a walk, but it's not far from St Peter's Square at all. All buses except the no. 47 will take you down Oxford Road.

Just outside the station is the avant-garde **Cornerhouse** ⓘ *70 Oxford Rd, T0161-2001500, www.cornerhouse.org, galleries Tue-Sat 1100-1800, Sun 1400-1800, closed Mon, free*, containing three galleries, three cinemas, two cafés, a bookshop and a bar. It's just about the best place in Manchester for foreign cinema and has varied exhibitions of modern art. The bar looks out on to Oxford Road and serves a host of foreign bottled beers for you to swig while watching passers-by. For cinema, see page 623.

Further down Oxford Road is **Manchester Museum** ⓘ *T0161-2752634, www.museum.man.ac.uk, Mon-Sat 1000-1700, Sun 1100-1600, free, virtually every bus going in this direction goes past it, and there's a bus every 3 mins*, at the University of Manchester. It's a traditional museum that's good for children, with its anthropological and natural history exhibits and gallery of live frogs, lizards and snakes. Manchester doesn't have a zoo, so this is the next best thing. They also have a range of well-preserved mummies.

Opposite the Manchester Royal Infirmary you'll find the city's most traditional art gallery, the **Whitworth Gallery** ⓘ *T0161-2757450, www.whitworth.man.ac.uk Mon-Sat 1000-1700, Sun 1400-1700, free. About 10 mins further down Oxford Rd from Manchester Museum, but you'll need to drive or take the bus, it's too far to walk.* Founded in 1889, it's the university's art gallery and specializes in watercolours, textiles and wallpaper. It also has a large collection of Turners and, as you will come to expect from a quick tour of Manchester's galleries, there's some modern art and sculpture in there too.

Castlefield

Castlefield, the oldest part of Manchester, has a couple of exceptional older museums that are particularly family-friendly, but after dark it's one of the main party areas with classy bars overlooking the canals. The Roman fort of Mamucium was situated here 2000 years ago and in later years the canals and railways helped to drive the industrial revolution. It became Britain's first urban heritage park in the 1980s and retains many original Victorian buildings like an 1830s warehouse down towards the river. Take the train to Deansgate station and then take a left to find Castlefield; otherwise try the GMEX Metrolink stop.

It's no surprise given this area's industrial heritage that the **Museum of Science and Industry** ⓘ *Liverpool Rd, T0161-8322244, 8321830, www.msim.org.uk, daily 1000-1700, free, turn left out of Deansgate Station*, is here. It tells of Manchester's industrial history and even offers you the chance to smell the Victorian sewers, reconstructed of course. Housed partly in old Victorian buildings, look out for the excellent air and space gallery with a host of aviational and astronomical models and interactive features. Big budget scientific exhibitions change over regularly and there's often a surcharge to enter them.

The **People's Museum** ⓘ *T0161-8396061, Tue-Sun 1100-1630, free on Fri, all other days £1*, around the corner at The Pumphouse on Bridge Street, tells the story of the ordinary people involved in industry from the beginning right through to today, including the rise of trade unions and the Suffragette movement which began close by in Lancashire. There are a lot of trade union banners and it's an interesting look at how England's social fabric has developed over the years.

Closer to the station in Knott Mill is **Castlefield Art Gallery** ⓘ *2 Hewitt St, T0161-8328034, www.castlefieldgallery.co.uk, Wed-Sun 1300-1800 except Thu 1300-2000, closed Sat-Tue, free*, Manchester's leading left of field art space – and that's saying something – with very modern and challenging exhibitions.

The Millennium Quarter

Up in the north of the city is the newly named Millennium Quarter, a substantially redeveloped area around Victoria station, reachable by train and Metrolink. The first thing you'll see as you pitch up at the station is the massive **Manchester Evening News** (MEN) **Arena**, a huge stadium which hosts all manner of things from Manchester Storm ice hockey team on a Sunday to touring rock and pop acts. Directly across from this is **Chetham's**, Manchester's top classical music academy, and **Urbis** ⓘ *Cathedral Gardens, T0161-9079099, www.urbis.org.uk, daily 1000-1800, Sat 1000-2000, £5, £3.50 concessions*. The immense £30 million 'glass-skinned' building has caused controversy in the city as another of the bright, new attractions built around the time of the 2002 Commonwealth Games. It's all about urban living, something that Manchester knows a lot about, and looks broadly at how the concept has developed through other countries and scenarios. The self-conscious modernity of the building is its real draw though, with a great glass elevator and exhibits that don't just involve you but use your participation to continually develop the way that it portrays city life.

Sleeping

The tourist information centre have further information on B&Bs in and around Manchester, T0161-2343157. Accommodation in the centre of Manchester is expensive and generally business-orientated. There are a few nice retreats though, and down Canal St there are a couple of characterful gay hotels. The YHA is very good but expensive and your best bet for B&Bs is to look a little further out of town on Oxford Rd. For a charge of £2.50 the TIC can secure 10% discounted rates on featured places. Make sure that you get in early with your bookings though, as when Manchester United are at home there's scarcely a bed to be found.

A The Lowry Hotel, 50 Dearman's Pl, Chapel Wharf, T0161-8274000, enquiries@thelowryhotel.com. Manchester's first 5-star hotel and one of only two in the Northwest area is the most exclusive and expensive place to stay. It's a Rocco Forte hotel with all that you'd expect of a top new modern hotel, including a Marco Pierre White restaurant (which doesn't quite live up to the hype) and a great location. They even organize shopping and spa breaks for you here, and you'll be seriously pampered.

A The Midland Hotel, Peter St, T0161-2363333, F9324100. This stately Edwardian hotel, now run by Crowne Plaza, is one of the most imposing buildings in the city. Decorative marbled halls, huge 4-poster beds, a gym and an excellent French restaurant are some of the attractions. It's seen some rock stars in its time and is the height of luxury.

A Renaissance Manchester, Blackfriars St, T0161-8316000, manchester.sales@renaissancehotels.com. Large luxury modern hotel as close as you can get to the best of Manchester's cultural attractions like the Royal Exchange, the MEN arena and Salford Quays, not to mention restaurants and shopping areas. Classy business-style accommodation.

A-B Malmaison Manchester, T0161-2781000, manchester@malmaison.com. Right in the middle of the not-so-exclusive Piccadilly area, opposite the station, this is a seriously chic, light and airy place to stay. Minimalist without being distant or pretentious. A gym, spa and brasserie and the additional attraction of a CD library for guests, all of which makes up for the fact that it's in a bit of a dodgy area.

A-B The Rossetti Hotel, 107 Piccadilly, T0161-2477744. Newly opened boutique hotel across the road from *Malmaison* with a young and hip vibe, ideal for weekenders. There's a warm and welcoming glow about the place, funky cushions, an Italian café/restaurant and a jazz lounge downstairs.

C Britannia Sachs Hotel, Tib St, T0161-2281234, F2369202. Although it has 223 rooms and a swimming pool, this place is unfortunately a bit garish and cheap looking inside and out. Still, it's really central and just the place if you're looking for a fight on the doorstep if you're returning late from anywhere.

D The Castlefield Hotel, Liverpool Rd, T0161-8327073, info@castlefield-hotel.co.uk. A classy modern hotel with a restaurant, bar and gym and friendly staff all overlooking the canal. There's even a running track hidden underneath the hotel, alongside basketball and squash courts and a swimming pool, making it one of the largest gyms in the Northwest.

D Walkabout Inn Hotel, 13 Quay St, T0161-8174800, F8174804. A small hotel attached to a bar and restaurant and an acceptable cheaper option without moving from this prime location. Good if you're after a lively night.

D-E Manchester Student Village, Lower Chatham St, T0161-2361776, info@thesv.com. Double rooms and cheaper and plainer singles around the corner from Oxford Rd station and the bars and clubs around it. Room quality ranges from passable to bog-standard. There are a number of cheaper and smaller hotels and B&Bs to the south of the city.

E Elton Bank Hotel, 62 Platt La, Rusholme, T0161-2253388, F2256688. A small and friendly family-run hotel by the University sports grounds. Fairly average accommodation but not far from the city centre as well as the Indian and Middle-Eastern delights of Rusholme itself.

E The Grafton Hotel, 56 Grafton St, beside the University off Oxford Rd, T0161-2733092, F2743653. A medium-sized friendly family-run B&B within walking distance of the city and its restaurants.

E The Imperial, 157 Hathersage Rd, Rusholme, 10 mins by bus from the city centre, T0161-2256500, F2256500. It sounds like a restaurant but isn't. The small hotel offers B&B and an evening meal if you want it and is fairly hectic.

E Manchester YHA, Potato Wharf, 5 mins from Deansgate train station, T0161-8399960, manchester@yha.org.uk. Accommodation here isn't all that cheap, but you get what you pay for. Light, airy, clean and spacious, this newish big hostel is right on the canalside in Castlefield and staff are really friendly. Breakfast is included in the price.

E **The Millstone Hotel**, 67 Thomas St, T0161-8390213, F8390213. A coaching inn dating back to 1700. It's recently been refurbished and is a bargain price for its location in the heart of the shabby-retro-chic of the Northern Quarter. Expect standard pub/B&B treatment and a number of locals sitting in the corner of the bar.

E **The New Union Hotel**, at the junction of Princess St and Canal St, T0161-2281492, F2280341. Not posh or classy, but a gay-friendly hotel with plenty of atmosphere and loud blaring music. A good value option and they serve breakfast on your return from your all-night partying.

E **Rembrandt Hotel**, 33 Sackville St, T0161-2361311, rembrandthotel@aol.com. Right in the thick of the action and very popular. If you head down to the bar you might catch the resident drag queen on the karaoke machine – this is not a place where you'll get much sleep either, but is maximum camp fun.

Manchester outskirts

A **Eleven Didsbury Park**, 11 Didsbury Park, Didsbury Village, T0161-4487711, www.elevendidsburypark.com. A classic contemporary townhouse hotel with minimalist design, polished floorboards and funky armchairs. A little different from staying in the beating heart of town but without compromising the style.

B/C **Etrop Grange**, Thorley La, Manchester Airport, T0161-4990500, etropgrange@corushotels.com. A beautiful big Georgian country house hotel with an award-winning restaurant and 4-poster beds as well as lovely grounds. Great if you're coming from the airport and looking for somewhere close by and romantic. They'll even pick you up from the airport in a Jag! It's not very Mancunian though, and is a bit of a way from the city centre.

E **Manchester Backpackers Hotel**, 64 Cromwell St, Stretford, T0161-8659296, www.manchesterback packershostel .co.uk, This small hostel is in a characterful terraced Victorian house with dorm and private rooms, a kitchen and TV lounge. A train ride from the centre but close to Stretford station.

Eating

You won't go hungry in Manchester, a place with all the culinary variety you'd expect of a multicultural modern city. Chinatown and Rusholme have excellent Chinese and Indian restaurants respectively, and you can find some top modern English restaurants in the centre of town around King St. Budget student grub is served up in the Northern Quarter and around Oxford Rd and if you're looking for a drink, they're also the places to check out. There's just about a pub on every corner, or if not a trendy new wine bar.

Manchester *p610, map p612*

£££ **39 Steps**, 39 South King St, Deansgate, T0161-8332432. Serving gourmet fish Mon-Sat in Manchester's finest and most recommended seafood restaurant, this is a classy, upmarket place to eat. Booking essential.

£££ **French Restaurant**, Midland Hotel, Peter St, T0161-2363333. The hotel itself is now owned by Crowne Plaza and has an impressive Edwardian interior. The most exclusive Fench restaurant in Manchester, but be warned, it is usually booked up weeks in advance here.

£££ **Koreana Restaurant**, 40A King St West, T0161-8324330. One of the leading Asian restaurants outside Chinatown. The Korean barbecue is a particular speciality.

£££-££ **Livebait**, 22 Lloyd St, T0161-8174110. Another of the city's snazzy fish restaurants, serving shellfish, including whelks, as well as tuna and swordfish. It's certainly not jellied eels and the place has got a young professional buzz about it.

£££-££ **Yang Sing**, 34 Princess St, Chinatown, T0161-2362200. Looks like nothing from the outside, but has been rated by food critic Jonathan Meades as "not only the finest Chinese restaurant in Britain, but one of the finest restaurants in Britain, full stop", and it offers a superb range of delicacies and dim-sum. It's not actually that pricey especially if you go for a lunchtime special.

££ **Beaujolais Restaurant**, 70 Portland St, T0161-2369626. A small French restaurant with impeccable service.

££ El Machos Cantinas, 103 Portland St, T0161-2369626. A lively and friendly Mexican restaurant.

££ Gaia, Sackville St. A fashionable mixed restaurant-bar venue with dim lights, comfortable sofas and European food. It's another place to spot Manchester's actors and musicians and has a young, funky vibe. Downstairs there are DJs on a Fri night. Open daily till 2300 for food.

££ Hard Rock Café, Printworks shopping complex, Millennium Quarter, T0161-8316700. For dining in a lively atmosphere.

££ Kailash, 34 Charlotte St, T0161-2361085. Nepalese restaurant serving gently spicy curries and other delicacies.

££ Le Petit Blanc Brasserie, 55 King St, T0161-8321000. Not far away from St Peter's Sq and another French special, it's another of Raymond Blanc's exclusive and stylish modern dining rooms offering French dishes with an Asian and Mediterranean twist.

££ Little Yang Sing, 17 George St, T0161-2287722. Great Asian dining.

££ Malmaison Brasserie, T0161-2781000, a French restaurant with minimalist surroundings in keeping with its relaxed and fashionable hotel on Piccadilly.

££ Market Restaurant at 104 High St, T0161-8343743, is a small family-run restaurant specializing in English food, especially puddings, serving freshly made food at decent prices. Open Wed-Sat.

££ Monsoon Nights, 108 Wilmslow Rd,Rusholme, T0161-2246669. Sophisticated curry house with marble floors.

££ Nandos, Printworks shopping complex, Millennium Quarter, T0161-3858181. A cheap and cheerful chain establishment, for cocktails and Mexican food.

££ Norwegian Blue, Printworks shopping complex, Millennium Quarter, T0161-8391451. A bar-café serving pan-European food like teriyaki prawns.

££ Pure Space, 11-13 New Wakefield St by Oxford Rd station, T0161- 2364899. An arty, minimalist place to eat with stripped wooden floorboards and wholesome bar food. It turns into a trendy club later in the evening and has a fresh feel to it. They've even got a roof-garden and modern art on the walls.

££ The Reform, King St, T0161-8399966. A relatively new restaurant serving contemporary English food. An intimate, plush, red velvety dining room attracts local celebrities, including Coronation St stars and footballers.

££ Ristorante Don Antonio, 52 Portland St, T0161-2360258. A charming family-owned Italian restaurant with reasonably priced à la carte and set menus.

££ Sarasota, 46 Canal St, T0161-2363766, With a rooftop bar serving British fusion cuisine, this is also very fashionable and friendly. This being Manchester, the roof can come back on if the weather's not behaving, and you get a great view of the canals.

££ Shere Khan, 52 Wilmslow Rd, Rusholme, T0161 256 2624. Has impeccable service, the milky drink *lassie* and balti specials.

££ Simply Heathcote's Jackson's Row, Deansgate, T0161-8353536. 'Celebrity chef' Paul Heathcote is famous for his northwest English cuisine, so expect black pudding, pies and hotpots, all in a modern, classy restaurant.

££ Tampopo, 16 Albert Sq, T0161-8191966. A well-priced, minimalist pan-Asian restaurant with specials from Thailand, Singapore, Japan and Malaysia.

££ Wagamama, Printworks shopping complex, Millennium Quarter, T0161-8395916. The best of the lot with large bowls of juicy noodles and reasonable prices.

£ Dimitri's, Campfield Arcade by Deansgate station, T0161-8393319. It has a small Mediterranean-based menu and has long been a favourite with locals, especially on a Fri and Sat evening when it serves up jazz along with the *dolmades*. Book in advance for weekends.

£ Grinch, 5 Chapel Walks just off Cross St, T0161-9073210. A friendly, intimate and very good value wine bar and restaurant with twisted metal light fittings and particularly good Italian and European food. It's got an even cheaper pre-theatre menu.

£ Jowata, Campfield Arcade by Deansgate station. An intimate restaurant serving traditional pan-African cuisine and wine and a variety of vegetarian dishes. It's a friendly and fairly casual dining experience with superb food. Open Tue-Sat, 1800-2430, credit cards not accepted.

Cafés

Atlas, 376 Deansgate, T0161-8342124, by Deansgate station, overlooking the canal. The delicious wholesome home-made food is served until 1430 daily and then it turns into a clubby bar later, open till 0200. Most of the other bars around Deansgate Station serve café-style lunches.

Café Pop, 34-36 Oldham St, T0161-2379688. It's a really cheap and fun greasy spoon place serving student grub like toasties, baked potatoes and vegetarian food. Prices are very low, and there's a retro boutique in the basement and a hairdressers called *Barberella*.

Earth Vegetarian Café, 16-20 Turner St, T0161- 8341996. Another good veggie place with changing daily menus, a more subdued atmosphere (not difficult) and very cheap organic food. Closed Sun.

On The Eighth Day, 107-111 Oxford Rd, T0161-2731850. It's a vegetarian co-operative café and store which has been running since the 1970s. An authentic hippy hang-out complete with buddhist chants soundtrack.

Pubs, bars and clubs

Manchester really comes alive after dark with clubs and bars of every description. The city's huge student population makes it a lively place to be, coupled with the distinct musical heritage of the place that brought you the likes of New Order, the Happy Mondays, Oasis and Badly Drawn Boy. The train service between Piccadilly and Oxford Rd and Deansgate means that it's easy to bar and club hop.

In general, bars in Manchester are open until around 0200 at the weekends and 1100-1200 during the week, longer if they are hosting events. **Canal St**, a short street packed with fashionable clubs and bars spilling out on to the streets, is well known for being one of the top gay attractions of England. This popularity gives it more of a mixed atmosphere at the weekend, but not during the week. **Oldham St** is one of the best places to sip a foreign beer in a trendy bar. **Deansgate Locks** is the place to go if your idea of a good night is dressing to the nines and sipping killer cocktails in bar-clubs surrounded by designer-clad beauties. It's the newest area to go out in and attracts a fashion-conscious, celeb crowd. Just follow the music from the train station to find the bars tucked away under the railway arches.

The Band on the Wall, 25 Swan St, T0161-8341786. Showcase live world music acts and have various clubby nights.

Cornerhouse Bar, 70 Oxford St, T0161-2001500. Opposite you as you walk out of the station. Shiny chrome surfaces and continental beers, attracting an older, more cultured group of people than some of the other bars round here.

Dry Bar, 28 Oldham St, T0161-2369840, in the early Nineties, then owned by Factory Records and New Order. They went bust and you're not likely to see Shaun Ryder propping up the bar these days, but it's still fairly hip and has a club atmosphere at the weekends.

Fat Cat Cafe Bar, Arch 8, Deansgate Locks, Whitworth St West, T0161- 8398243. Plays jazz and anything going.

The Lass O'Gowrie, 36 Charles St, T0161-2736932. A more traditional pub popular with students.

Manto, 46 Canal St, T0161 236 2667. A popular venue for which you won't have to pay to get in.

Night and Day Café, 26 Oldham St, T0161-2364597, a daytime café serving Mexican dishes and a night-time bar. A laid-back vibe – more designer jeans and trainers than high heels and fake tan. The Twisted Nerve label, home of Badly Drawn Boy, hold a regular night here.

Revolution, 88-94 Oxford St, T0161-2375377. A successful vodka bar, with others now in Liverpool, London and Deansgate Locks. The music is loud and clubby, attracting professionals and students.

Revolution, Deansgate Locks, Whitworth St West, T0161 8397558. A little less scruffy than the Oxford Rd venue, again with bottled beers and vodka shots with sherbet dip and refresher flavours.

Via Fossa, 28 Canal St, T0161 2366523. Popular haunt. Free to get in.

Soundtrack to the city

In the late 1980s, Factory Records and New Order decided that there were no clubs in Manchester that catered for their tastes. So they came up with one of their own. The Hacienda was a popular haunt with the musical sense to book Madonna for her first UK appearance. An explosion of local talent followed and with the crossover of the dance music and indie music scenes, 'Madchester' took off. People all over the country started laying claim to Mancunian blood and the university was massively oversubscribed with students wanting to spend their three years partying. You could spot Mancunian music a mile off with the swirling Hammond organ of the Inspiral Carpets right through to the swagger of the Stone Roses and the Happy Mondays who dominated the charts. The scene, like The Hacienda, boomed and then bust, but not without laying the foundations of the new local and national independent music scene.

Recommended listening
- Love Will Tear Us Apart – Joy Division
- This Is How It Feels – The Inspiral Carpets
- Blue Monday – New Order
- How Soon Is Now – The Smiths
- WFL – Happy Mondays
  Come Home – James
- The Only One I Know – The Charlatans
- Getting Away With It – Electronic
- Waterfall – Stone Roses
- Supersonic – Oasis

Clubs

Many of the bars mentioned above have music and dancing. Manchester hasn't got all that many warehouse-sized venues but is peppered with smaller bars and intimate clubs which all have different characters and various types of music depending on the night.

Oxford Rd is the place to come for Northern Soul and indie music as you'd expect from the nearby student population. **Deansgate Locks** is a little more dressy than some and most of the bars mentioned previously have dancing later on.

Attic, above *The Thirsty Scholar*, 50 New Wakefield St beside Oxford Rd station, T0161-2366071. The best Northern Soul venue in town Thu-Sat. You'll not be allowed in in a baseball cap or football shirt, but other than that it's pretty relaxed.

The Brickhouse, arch 66 off Deansgate, T0161-2364418, has been running for a lot longer than most, with Motown and soul anthems.

Citrus at 2 Mount St, T0161-8341344, near the town hall is open until 0100 and plays funky house. You have to pay an entry fee after 2400 but it's essentially a late bar with a small dance floor.

The Contact Theatre, T0161- 2740600, hosts club nights on Fri and Sat and a few gay nights which are similarly cool, just after the *Academy* on Oxford Rd.

Fat Cat, in the Locks itself, T0161-8398243, has a mixture of disco and jazz.

Fifth Avenue, 121 Princess St, T0161-2362754, is your typical student night with cheap drinks, sticky floors and no pretentions whatsoever.

Jabez Clegg at 2 Portsmouth St just off Oxford Rd, T0161-2728612. Plays house and chart music in a dressed-down environment and is really popular.

The Manchester Academy, Oxford Rd, T0161-2752930. Hosts indie nights during the week and is right next door to the Student Union. Trainers essential.

North, on the corner of Tib St and Church St, T0161-8391989. Plays funky house and garage in a more chilled-out atmosphere. Open till 0400 on Sat night/Sun morning.

The Paradise Factory, also on Princess St, T0161-2735422, is the city's most well-known gay club on a Sat with 3 floors of dance and all sorts. During the week it's open for student nights. People come from all over the north for the weekends here.

Po Na Na souk bar, 42 Charles St off Oxford Rd, T0161-2726044, has world music, jazz, hip-hop and all sorts in what feels like a dimly lit romantic boudoir.

The Ritz, Whitworth St West, T0161-2364355. Wed nights are 70s heaven at the long-running and perennially popular *Love Train* night. Prepare for the very dressed up and men with fake tans and medallions. It's a bit dodgier on other nights with student nights and a bit of rock and heavy metal.

Sankey's Soap, Beehive Mill, Jersey St, T0161-6619668. Set in an old mill, it's head and shoulders above the rest for house and dance music. It's a place for high heels and short skirts rather than the scruffy student look, so make an effort and don't wear sportswear or you won't be allowed in. They have various touring top named DJs on a regular basis.

Slice, 5 Cooper St near the town hall, T0161-2366007, have a night called *Tiger Lounge* on Sat where they play 60s tunes, movie soundtracks and mix Motown gems with rock and roll. It attracts the same kind of crowd as *Café Pop* in the Northern Quarter.

Sofa Central, again on Princess St, T0161-2737336, is another venue for R'n'B and soul, fairly trendy with leather sofas and a bar feel.

Entertainment

There's all sorts to keep you amused in Manchester if you like drama, from massive multiplexes to small theatre companies and West End shows. Listings here are for venues in the centre of the city.

Theatre

Contact Theatre just after the *Academy* on Oxford Rd, T0161-2740600, F2740640, www.contact-theatre.org.uk, is a state-of-the-art theatre and shows contemporary and innovative productions. It's a short bus ride from Oxford Rd on bus numbers 40-9 and also hosts R'n'B, gay and hip-hop club nights.

Library Theatre, T0161-2367110, www.libtheatreco.org.uk. Underneath the Central Library at St Peter's Sq is this intimate and classy theatre showing small productions for the more literary minded.

The Lowry, Salford Quays, T0161-8762000, www.thelowry.com. Houses both the **Lyric** and the **Quays** theatres, showing touring productions and small plays from Zulu dancers to Shakespeare.

The Opera House, Quay St, T0161-2422509, shows mainly touring dramas and West End musicals.

The Palace Theatre on Oxford St. Does the same drama and musicals with the addition of some ballet and opera.

Royal Exchange, T0161-8339833, www.royalexchange.co.uk. Described by Tom Courtenay as "a smaller world inside a greater one", the intimate theatre puts on superb productions from Oscar Wilde to Shakespeare and is highly recommended. They also have a bookshop, craft shops and a café and restaurant inside the complex. Beg, borrow or steal a ticket for a show here – they're worth it.

Cinema

The Cornerhouse cinema, 70 Oxford Rd, T0161-2001500, has 3 screens that show the best of foreign and independent films. The **Filmworks** at the The Printworks, Exchange Sq in the Millennium Quarter is expensive but has more screens than you can count, showing mainstream cinema, T08700-102030. Also at the Printworks is the **IMAX** showing 3D films, T08700-102030. Back in the centre of Manchester, **The Odeon** on Oxford St, T0161-2369778, has 7 screens and shows all new releases and mainstream cinema.

Comedy

The Comedy Store, Arches 3 and 4, Deansgate Locks opposite Deansgate Station, T08705-932932, attracts big names and is open Wed-Sat. Check *Citylife* or www. thecomedystore.co.uk for who's on when. **Jongleurs/Bar Risa**, 40 Chorlton St just off Canal St, is open Fri-Sat from 1930 and costs a flat rate of £12. It also attracts national and international funnymen and women for a mixed audience. *Bar Risa* has more of a gay vibe with a downstairs disco and also serves food.

Live music

Music of every description from unsigned, unwashed indie bands to operatic divas can be found in Manchester. There are immense stadium gigs at the MEN arena right through to chamber music at the RNCM by talented classical performers.

The Bridgewater Hall, an impressive glass building on Lower Mosely St near the GMEX tram stop, T0161-9079000, www.bridgewater-hall.co.uk, is the home of Manchester Camerata and the Halle Orchestra. Expect nothing but the best in this venue with superb acoustics and a serene environment. Outside is a huge Japanese touchstone or *ishinki*. Stroking it traditionally means that you'll return one day. There are also guided tours taking you backstage and around the building, £3.

Manchester Academy, 296 Oxford Rd, T2752930. For rock, pop and indie.

Manchester Apollo, Stockport Rd, T0161-2422560. Holding around 200-300 sweaty bodies for the latest rock and pop acts.

MEN Arena, T0870-1535353, www.men-arena.com. A huge 1000-seater place for screaming teens coming to see the latest pop idol, and screaming mums coming to see the likes of Tom Jones on tour.

RNCM, 124 Oxford Rd, T0161-9075200, showcases a wide range of musical talent from brass bands to chamber music of the highest standard in an intimate atmosphere. There are touring artists here as well as talented students.

Activities and tours

Cricket

Lancashire County Cricket Club, Old Trafford, Old Trafford Metrolink, T0161-2824000, www.lccc.co.uk. Tickets are available for 1 day and test matches during the season.

Football

There are 8 professional football teams in the Greater Manchester area, and every single one is dwarfed by the commercial might of **Manchester United**, see page 615 for contact details and tour information.

Manchester City, T0161-2323000, www.mcfc.co.uk, are in the middle of moving from their Maine Rd stadium by Moss Side to the new Commonwealth Games stadium, Eastlands, in a more desirable, redeveloped part of town. Their popularity in the city means that tickets are similarly difficult to get hold of. Lower division strugglers

Stockport County, T0161-2868888, play about 7 miles away at Edgerley Park near Stockport station. If you want to see good northern football, have a meat pie and watch a game untainted by the big bucks, tickets are usually available up to kick-off, Sat afternoons and Tue evenings, £14-16 adult, £4 child, £9 student.

Swimming

Manchester Aquatics Centre, All Saints' Campus, Booth St East, off Oxford Rd, is a Commonwealth games swimming pool open to the public in a striking building with 3 pools and flumes. Mon-Fri 0630-2200, Sat 0700-1800, Sun 0700-2000, £1.50.

Shopping

The **Northern Quarter** has an amazing array of boutiques and record shops. **Affleck's Palace**, T0161-8342039, at the end of Tib St is a labyrinthine 6 floors of clothes, knick-knacks, kitsch, fetish gear and fortune tellers. Mon-Sat 1000-1730, closed Sun. Across the road at 18 Oldham St is Manchester's best record shop, **Vinyl Exchange**, T0161-2281122. It's heaven for music lovers looking to buy or sell rarities, second-hand CDs or vinyl; anything goes really. Across the road are a number of dance music specialists. You'll certainly find what you're looking for, if not a local artist leafing through the record sleeves next to you. For designer labels and more high-street shopping, **King Street** is upmarket with DKNY and Armani stores amongst others. **The Triangle** in the Millennium Quarter is a fashionable shopping centre designed just for these top of the range brands and is full of well-coiffeured and perfumed women.

Transport

Bus

National Express, T08705-808080, run 11 services a day from Chorlton St bus station to and from **London Victoria** (5 hrs). They go 12 times a day to **Birmingham** (3 hrs), 6 times to **Edinburgh** (7 hrs), 6 times to **Gatwick airport** (7 hrs 10 mins via Birmingham and Heathrow) and 12 times to **Heathrow** (5 hrs 30 mins). Services to **Liverpool** are hourly (1 hr) and there are 7 daily services to **Stansted airport** (6 hrs 30 mins).
Stagecoach, T01772-884488, run the X61 hourly to **Blackpool**, (1 hr 30 mins) and there is a Transpeak, T01773-536336, service to **Nottingham** (3 hrs) through the **Peak District** via Buxton (1 hr), Matlock and Bakewell. **Eurolines**, T08705-143219, www.gobycoach.com, also run to major European cities via London.

Car

Easycar NCP car park, Chatham St, www.easycar.com, T09063-333333. **Hertz**, Auburn St across from Piccadilly Station, T08708-484848 (closed Sun), www.hertz.com. **Sixt Kenning**, Manchester Airport Terminals 1, 2 and 3, T4892666, www.e-sixt.co.uk.

Train

Virgin Trains are the main service to and from Manchester, T0870-0101127, www.virgintrains.co.uk. They go hourly to **London Euston** from Manchester Piccadilly, Mon-Sat until 2000, taking 3 hrs. Trains to **Birmingham** go regularly, take 1 hr and to **Liverpool** it takes 1 hr. From Manchester Piccadilly you can also get to **Glasgow** in 4 hrs. **National Rail Enquiries**, T08457-484950.

Directory

Internet Debenhams, Market St, T0161-8328666, £1 for 30 mins, **Easy Everything**, 8 Exchange Sq, T0161-8329200, £1 for 45 mins. **Manchester YHA**, Potato Wharf, T0161-8399960. **Post office** Spring Gardens off Market St, Piccadilly. **Hospital** Manchester Royal Infirmary, Oxford Rd, T0161-2361234. **Pharmacy** Boots, Market St, Moss Chemists at the top of Oxford St opposite Thomas Cook. **Police station** Bootle St behind the library, T0161-8725050.

The Peak District

→ *Colour map 6, grid B/C3*

At the southern end of the Pennine Hills between Manchester and Sheffield sits the Peak District National Park, an oasis in the heart of the Northwest's built-up areas. In 1932 the ninth Duke of Devonshire, the biggest private landowner in the Peak District, set his gamekeepers on trespassers venturing here on his grouse moors on Kinder Scout and sparked off a furore. Five of them were subsequently jailed for up to 6 months, but it was this trespass and the resulting outrage which brought about the existence of this and Britain's 10 other national parks. Nowadays of course, you're free to roam over the 555 square miles of moorland, dales, rocky cliffs and skyline-shattering tors which sit between six counties. Its proximity to the metropolitan areas of the Midlands and the Northwest as well as its beauty have made it the world's second-most visited national park after Mount Fuji.

The spa town Buxton is a nexus in the area, the source of the natural mineral water which is still the lifeblood of the town. Presiding over the southeast of the Peak District, the immense pile of Chatsworth House, home of the Duke and Duchess of Devonshire, welcomes visitors and is surrounded by a number of characterful stone villages. The Peak District is primarily walking territory though, and Dovedale, Edale and the High Peak are the places to exercise your legs, with views to delight all from the hardy to the picnic-loving day tripper. ▸▸ *For Sleeping, Eating and other listings, see pages 635-640.*

The Peak District

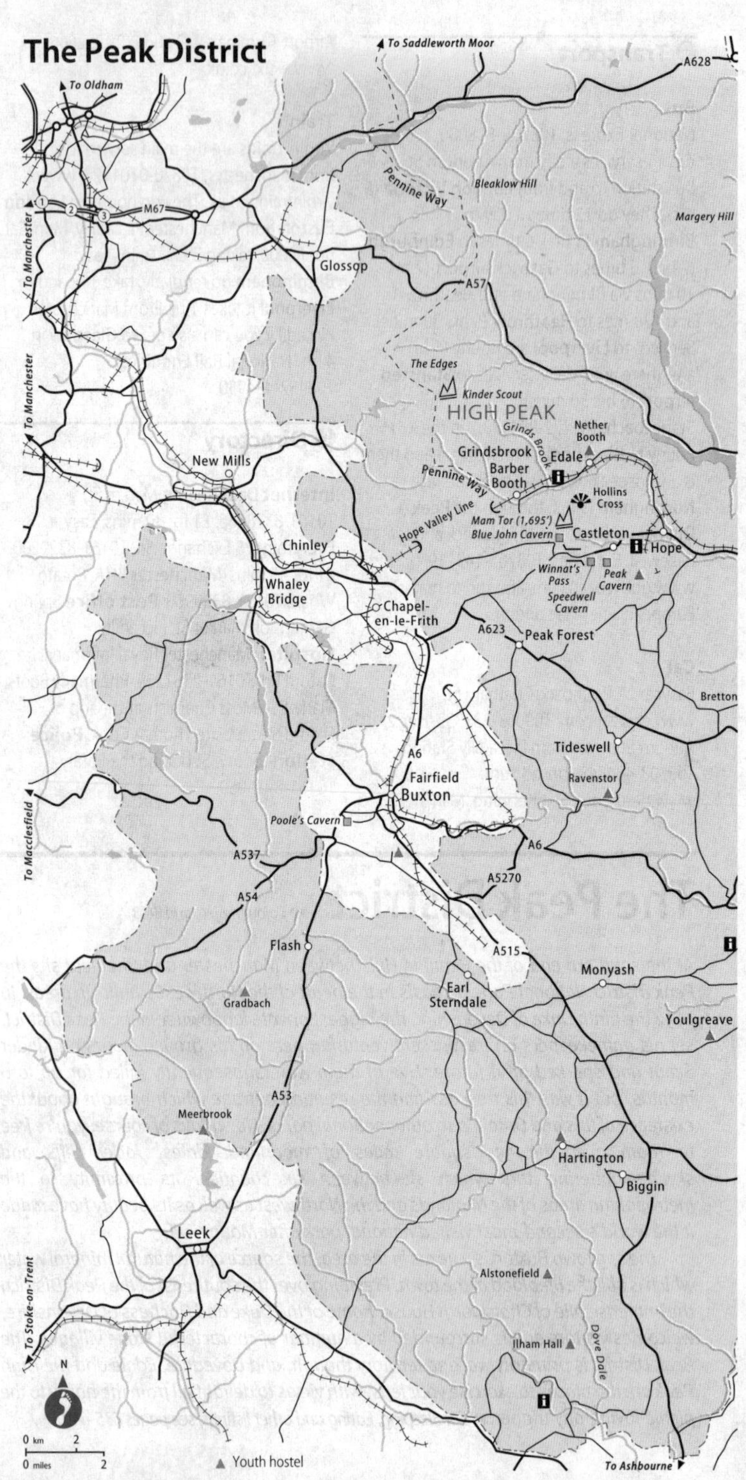

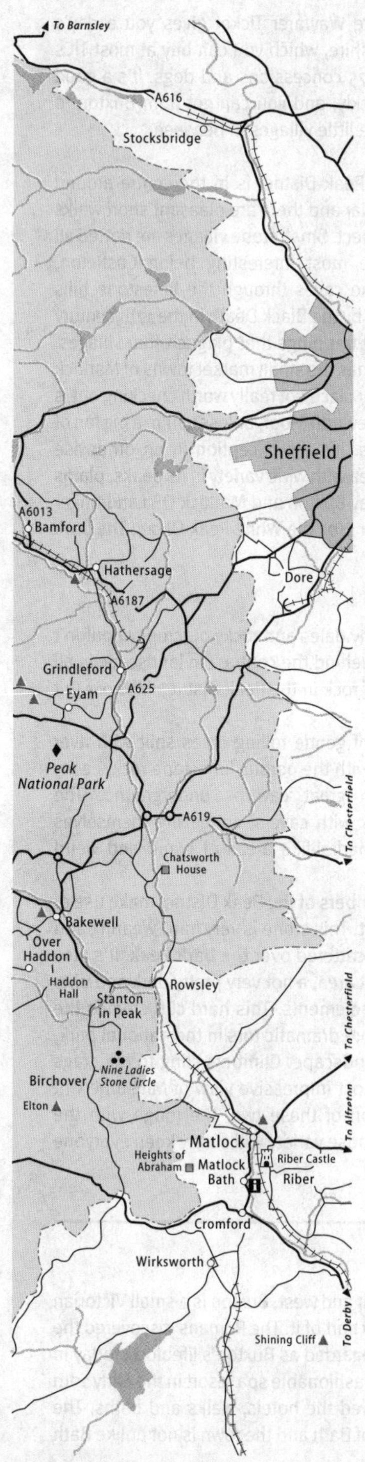

Ins and outs

Getting there Manchester airport, T0161-4893000, is the closest international and domestic airport, about 25 miles away by road, and has daily flights from the UK and abroad. You can get to the Peak District from here on the regular **train** service changing at Manchester Piccadilly for Buxton. Macclesfield is on the London Euston-Manchester intercity **rail** route, from where you can easily reach Buxton. Trains go several times a day. The Peak District, well-served by the **Hope Valley** train line (see Getting around, below) is also accessible from Chesterfield, Derby and Sheffield. **National Rail Enquiries**, T08457-484950. Situated between Manchester, Sheffield and Derby, the **road** access here is good. The Peak District is linked to Manchester and Derby by the A6, Chesterfield by the A619 and Sheffield by the A625. **National Express**, T08705-808080, run a coach service from London via Derby, Loughborough and Leicester into Buxton.

Getting around The public transport network in the Peak District is not too bad at all, especially considering that all the locals have cars to get around in. The **bus** and **train** services are especially useful if you're doing a non-circular walk. If you're driving, be aware that the 500,000 drivers a year that this area attracts have an enormous environmental impact on the scenery, so toll roads (costing £3) are to be introduced in certain areas including the Upper Derwent Rd in the north. By **train** there's the **Hope Valley line** which runs from Manchester to Sheffield calling at New Mills, Chinley, Edale, Hope, Bamford, Hathersage, Grindleford and Dore. Trains run a couple of times an hour in both directions with the last train at around 2200. From Manchester Piccadilly it takes just over an hour to get to Sheffield, costing £10.90 single, and it takes 45 minutes to New Mills Central. From Buxton, you need to take a train to New Mills to join the Hope Valley Line, a service that runs at least 3 times an hour and takes 30 minutes, £8.20. The Derbyshire Wayfarer Ticket gives you a day's unlimited travel on **buses** and **trains** in Derbyshire, which you can buy at most TICs and bus travel offices for £7.50 adult and £3.75 concessions and dogs. It's a good idea if you want to cover a lot of ground quickly, and you can get from Buxton to Sheffield on this service easily, taking in all the little villages in between.

Orientation The major **walking** area in the Peak District is in the centre around Edale. Dovedale in the south is also very popular and there are pleasant short walks to be had all over the national park as you'd expect. Small stone villages are dotted all over the place, with the most interesting being Castleton, complete with labyrinthine caves through the limestone hills and Eyam, a village struck by the Black Death in the 17th century which has avoided tourist trappings that plague other villages. The southeast of the park has the small market towns of Matlock and Bakewell, and the only place not really worth checking out is the northern area of Saddleworth Moor, unless you're a big fan of bleak, misty barren areas. It's the exception in an otherwise geologically interesting area with wide variety in its peaks, plains and sunny dales. For **maps** try: Ordnance Survey Buxton and Matlock OS Landranger 119; Sheffield and Huddersfield OS Landranger 110; The White Peak OL 24; The Dark Peak Explorer OL1.

The Ordnance Survey Explorer OL24 1:25,000 map, covering the White Peak area is the company's best selling map – 1/3 of the population of England live within an hour's drive of the area.

Geology

Wind-blown boggy moors, hay meadows, sunny dales and rocky outcrops shouldn't really exist together, but they do. The reason behind the contrast in landscape is all down to the interactions between two types of rock in the Peak District: Millstone Grit and Limestone.

The White Peak is a limestone plateau of gentle rolling dales split with river valleys. The softer landscape is underpinned with the porous limestone rock, easily dissolved by the slightly acidic rain into great caverns underground. The subterranean passages in this area are thick with cavers, squeezing themselves through the skinny tunnels in search of cathedral-like areas of grand and weird natural phenomena.

High above these mad pot-holers, the climbers of the Peak District make use of the other geological feature, the **Millstone Grit**. This stone is very hard-wearing and you can see examples of the old millstones scattered over **the Dark Peak**. It's also used in many of the churches of the northwest area, a not very pretty dark and dirty stone, but one which wears well against the elements. This hard cliff creates the rocky outcrops and splintered faces of the more dramatic tors in the national park, the Edges, which are unique in the British landscape. Climbers cling to the crags here and the aspect of Kinder Scout is the most impressive view of Millstone Grit that you'll see in the Peaks. The conjunction of these two, the rough with the smooth, makes for very interesting scenery whose variety will surely keep everyone happy in one way or another.

Buxton

Enclosed by the national park to the south, east and west, Buxton is a small Victorian town central to the district although not strictly part of it. The Romans discovered the mineral springs here in AD 78 which are still regarded as Buxton's lifeblood today in the form of Buxton Mineral Water. It became a fashionable spa resort in the early 19th century when the Duke of Devonshire improved the hotels, walks and baths. The Georgian style Crescent was built in imitation of Bath and the town is not unlike Bath in its feel – but without the hordes of tourists, and unfortunately without any surviving baths to look round. Buxton really comes alive in the summer with the Buxton Festival which draws artists and enthusiasts from miles around for an excellent week of musical enjoyment.

Ins and outs

Getting there Regular intercity **trains** run from London Euston to Manchester and there are connecting services to Buxton from Macclesfield and Stockport en route, which take roughly 30 minutes. Buxton is only an hour's drive from Manchester, Nottingham, Sheffield and Derby. **National Express,** T08705-808080, have a daily coach service to Buxton from London via Derby, Leicester and Loughborough. The local bus network runs through the Peak District via Buxton between Manchester, Derby and Nottingham and also from Sheffield, Stoke-on-Trent, Ashbourne and Macclesfield. **Traveline,** T0870-6082608.

Information **Buxton TIC** ⓘ *in the old hall just beside The Crescent 0930-1700 daily. T01298-25106, www.highpeak.gov.uk, www.peakdistrict-tourism.gov.uk,* and contains informative displays and exhibitions by local artists and craftsmen. They can book accommodation and are the main TIC for the Peak District.

The Crescent, undeniably Buxton's most dominant architectural presence and built in 1780-84, intended to rival the famous Royal Crescent in Bath. It's now a listed building undergoing massive refurbishment by English Heritage. Directly opposite is a small fountain, **St Anne's Well**, a public pump built by the eighth Duke of Devonshire to let the people of Buxton have a free supply of their famous water. It comes out of the pump at 28 degrees centigrade and usually has a stream of locals standing beside it filling containers. Next to that is the **Pump Room** where once visitors took the thermal waters; it is now used to display the work of local artists. Behind that you've got **The Slopes,** public gardens on a bit of a hill with a view of the cobblestone town from one side and the shadow of the Peaks on the other.

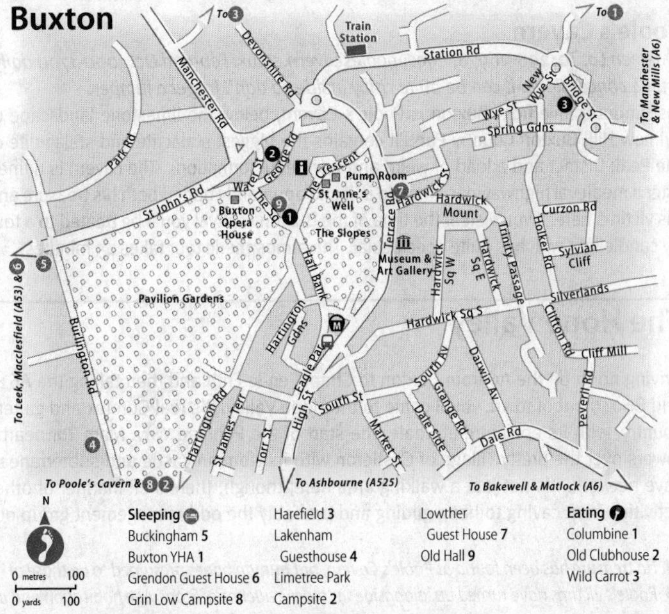

Sleeping
Buckingham 5
Buxton YHA 1
Grendon Guest House 6
Grin Low Campsite 8
Harefield 3
Lakenham Guesthouse 4
Limetree Park Campsite 2
Lowther Guest House 7
Old Hall 9

Eating
Columbine 1
Old Clubhouse 2
Wild Carrot 3

Walks around the northwest

- **The Pennine Way**: The Peak District. Start: Edale and head for south for Mam Tor or north for Kinder Scout. OS Landranger 110.
- **The Way of the Gull**: Isle of Man, 90 miles. Start Peel. Head out along the shoreline round ths island. OS Landranger 95.
- **The Roman Walls**: Chester. A 40-minute tour of the town and the best way to get your bearings.
- **The Grindsbrook Path**: The Peak District. A well-worn walking trail that eventually turns into the Pennine Way. OS Landranger 110.
- **The Ribble Valley Sculpture Trail**: Brungerley Park by Clitheroe, in Lancashire.

Directly next door to the TIC is the **Old Hall,** Buxton's oldest building dating from 1573 and now a hotel. Mary Queen of Scots stayed here when she visited the town to take the waters in a bid to alleviate her rheumatism. Walking past this, you come to **Buxton Opera House,** the town's main attraction, designed by Frank Matcham in 1903. It's immensely popular in the summer as it holds the spectacular **Buxton Opera Festival** and also the **International Gilbert and Sullivan Festival,** both of which bring the town alive, www.buxtonfestival.co.uk. **The Pavilion Gardens** beside it are classic Victorian landscaping.

If it's raining, or even if it isn't, the **Museum and Art Gallery** ⓘ *T01298-24658, F79394, Tue-Fri 0930-1730, Sat 0930-1700, Sun 1030- 1700, ground floor free, first floor £1 adults, 50p concessions*, on Terrace Rd is well worth a visit. Downstairs there's an exhibition tracing the contemporary multiculturalism of the region through individuals' life stories, from miners to farmers and refugees, and upstairs is an award-winning history of human life in the Peak District from the Stone Age to the present day.

Poole's Cavern

ⓘ *Green La, T01298-26978, info@poolescavern.co.uk. Feb-end Oct 1000-1700 daily. £5, £4 concessions. It can be quite chilly inside so don't forget a jumper.*
Just under a mile from Buxton is Poole's Cavern, below the limestone landscape of Grinlow Hill, Buxton Country Park. It contains the biggest stalactite and stalagmite of the Peak District and a load of weird and wonderful formations. The cavern is named after a medieval highwayman who hid in it and apparently buried both his treasure and his victims here. If you visit at the time of the Buxton Festival you'll be treated to a tour by candlelight which is quite spectacular. The atmospheric tour takes 45 minutes.

The Hope Valley

Driving north on the A6 from Buxton to Chapel-en-le-Frith and then taking the A623 and B6049 out of town, you'll come to the Hope Valley. It's real Goretex and gaiters country, with its epicentre at Edale, the start of the Pennine Way. Mam Tor nearby towers over the pretty village of Castleton with its Norman castle and subterranean cave network. It's not just a walking area here, though; there's all manner of other activities from caving to hang-gliding and probably the odd management group out

No treasure has been found at Poole's Cavern, but human bones presumed to be those of Poole's victims have turned up, alongside far older evidence of Stone Age habitation and a

on team-building exercises. A little further on is the small village of Eyam, whose fame as the plague village of the 17th century that submitted itself to voluntary quarantine to stop the spread of disease, is out of all proportion to its size.

Castleton

This beautiful, if touristy, village in the heart of the Peak District has underground caves, a Norman castle and the dramatic entrance through Winnat's Pass, a steep descent of 1300 ft. The pass is rocky, treacherous and with a heart-stopping view. To put it in context, if you were to drive down it on a bike, you'd be in Sheffield before you had to start pedalling. The area was heavily mined for lead and the mineral **Blue John**, found nowhere else in the world, and the resulting caves and caverns are now top tourist attractions, taking you deep into the middle of the earth, while the stone now twinkles in the window of every single tourist shop in the village. The area is a great base for walking and outdoor activities too and the caverns are worth visiting if you need to shelter from the rain.

The name of the naturally occurring blue and yellow stone comes from a corruption of the French 'bleu et jaune'.

Getting there The Manchester-Sheffield train stops at Hope and Edale where linking buses take you into Castleton. There is a small **national park information centre** ⓘ *just by the roundabout in the middle of the village, T/F01433-620679, castleton@peakdistrict-npa.gov.uk, Easter-Oct 1000-1730 daily, Nov-Easter 1000-1700 Sat-Sun only.*

Put the brakes on as you come to the bottom of Winnat's Pass and you'll find the best of the four underground caves in Castleton. The **Speedwell Cavern** ⓘ *T01433-620512, www.speedwellcavern.co.uk, daily except Christmas Day, 0930-1700 high season, 1000-1530 low season, £5.75, concessions £4.75, take a jumper, it's cold and damp down there*, takes you down through an airlock and on to a boat to explore the underground world. The guides are fun and informative and you can see where the miners carved out claustrophobic tunnels as well as the natural caves and stalactites and stalagmites.

Further into the village you'll find the **Peak Cavern** ⓘ *T01433-620285, www.devilsarse.com, Apr-Oct daily 1000-1700, Nov-Mar weekends only, 1000-1700, £5.25, concessions £4.25*, trumpeting about its alternative name, *The Devil's Arse*, where you walk into the limestone gorge below Peveril Castle on an hour-long tour.

Overlooking Castleton is all 1695 ft of **Mam Tor**. Meaning "mother mountain", it's known locally as the 'shivering mountain', because it is composed of crumbling layers of gritstone and shale which produce frequent, small landslips. It's an easy walk up because it has a stepped footpath, ideal if you're not a true walker. The views from the top show the limestone quarries, not too pretty, but try and imagine it 5000 years ago when it was a Bronze Age fort. You'll also see flocks of hang-gliders taking off and enjoying the scenery.

There's more of the same, without the attention-seeking name, at **Treak Cliff Cavern** ⓘ *T01433-620571, www.bluejohnstone.com, Mar-Oct 1000-1700, Nov-Feb 1000-1600*. And also **Blue John Cavern** ⓘ *T620638, www.bluejohn.gemsoft.co.uk, £6, £4.50 concessions*, which has a 45-min tour of the caves.

Peveril Castle ⓘ *T01433-620613, Apr-Oct daily 1000-1800, Nov-Mar Wed-Sun only 1000-1600, £2.40, £1.80 concessions*, overlooks Castleton, a Norman Castle given by William the Conqueror to William Peverel, his illegitimate son. It has a fantastic view and is a lovely spot for a picnic but unfortunately you have to pay to walk round it as it's owned by English Heritage. There's nothing to see but spacious views and the ruins.

The murder at Winnat's Pass

In the 18th-century, the nearby town of Peak Forest had the status of a southern Gretna Green, where couples could marry without living in the parish. In the mid-1770s, a young and affluent couple, Alan and Clara, decided to elope there. Stopping in Castleton on the way to Peak Forest, they rested in one of the village's many coaching inns, their wealth and status as out-of-towners clear to all present. Their conversation was overheard by six miners at a nearby table. The next day their bodies were discovered scattered across Winnat's Pass, robbed of all possessions. The miners were suspected of their murder, but no conclusive proof was ever found. In a spooky turn of events, each of the six miners was found dead in unpleasant or unexplained circumstances during the following year.

Edale

A pleasant walk from the centre of Castleton to Hollin's Cross will take you to Edale. It's also reachable by train on the Hope Valley line from Hope station and, as the beginning of the **Pennine Way**, is undoubtedly the most popular place to walk in the Peaks. The Way stretches from here through the High Peak, into the Yorkshire Dales beyond, into the Cheviot Hills and ends right up in the Scottish Borders. Opened in 1965 as the UK's first long distance path, it's a walk of 289 miles (463 km) up the backbone of England from Edale to Kirk Yetholm in the Scottish borders. It takes at least two weeks of solid walking across moorland and is a truly rewarding hike, but you need to be prepared for it. The high rainfall in the upland area and possibility of heatwaves make it unpredictable as far as the weather is concerned and you need to know how to use a map and compass. The best time of year to go is in the summer between late May and September. A number of walkers' books are available about the route, including Wainwright's *Pennine Way Companion*.

A nice afternoon's walk can be had up the glacial valley to the top of the dominant plateau of **Kinder Scout**. It takes about two hours to reach its commanding views at the top on the **Grindsbrook path**, a well-worn walking trail that turns into the Pennine Way a little later. It is nose-to-tail most of the way on a sunny Sunday here though as people from everywhere from Sheffield to Manchester forsake the city for the dramatic scenery. It's a well-marked trail and you can't get lost; just take the path behind the *Old Nag's Head* pub and walk up alongside the river.

Eyam

Pronounced *eem*, don't be surprised if you can't find anywhere to park in this small village or if you're assailed by hordes of schoolchildren waving clipboards at you on a weekday. Eyam is famous for being the plague village where from 1665-6 the villagers underwent a voluntary quarantine to protect others from catching the Black Death, see box, and primary schoolchildren know the story better than anyone. It's a pretty place to explore and there are lovely walks to be had in this area.

The best place to begin your exploration of Eyam is the **Eyam museum** ① *T01433-631371, Easter-Oct Tue-Sun 1000-1630, closed Mon, £1.75, £1.25 concessions*, at the top of the village. It explores the early history of plague in the village in detail with a strong anecdotal focus on how it affected individuals. Downstairs is a smaller display about the silk and cotton industries alongside mining and quarrying which make up the more recent history.

From the museum you can walk into town where you'll find the **Plague cottages**, pretty, residential stone cottages with plaques on the outside walls with gruesome death tallies. The medieval **Eyam Parish Church** is also just off the main road and has a small exhibition inside about the plague. It has a far older history than this though, with a Saxon font and a Saxon cross in the graveyard outside. Don't be shy about looking round, it's all trampled by schoolchildren on a daily basis as they hurdle gravestones in search of plague victims. From the church there's a pleasant walk (1 km) across the fields to **Mompesson's well** on the outskirts of the village.

Back in the centre of the village is the recently opened **Eyam Hall and Craft Centre** ⓘ *T01433-631976, www.eyamhall.co.uk, Tue-Sun 1030-1700, closed Mon, Christmas and New Year. House and gardens, Jun-Sep Wed, Thu, Sun 1100-1600, £4.25, child £3.25.* The hall is a 17th-century farmhouse with lovely gardens and a less emotive history.

Bakewell

The best thing about Bakewell, roughly 5 miles from Eyam, is its major claim to fame – the delicious almond pastry cakes, Bakewell pudding, which came about when someone tried to bake a Christmas cake and got it all wrong. Originally an old Saxon market town, it's now a large village or small town, easily reached from Buxton or Chesterfield, with a small shopping centre, public gardens and a river running through it under a stone bridge. But the major sights in the area, Haddon Hall and Chatsworth House, just outside the town, are what often bring people here.

Information The **tourist information centre** ⓘ *Old Market Hall, T01629-813227, F814782, www.peakdistrict.org, 0930-1730 daily*, in the centre of town has information on accommodation.

Two miles south of Bakewell on the A6, **Haddon Hall** ⓘ *T01629-812855, www.haddonhall.co.uk, Mar-Sep daily 1030-1700, Oct Thu-Sun 1030-1630, £7.25, £6.25 concessions, children £3.75*, is a real delight in an idyllic setting. It's a beautiful medieval hall with Tudor additions set high on the hill with views of the surrounding area and a babbling offshoot of the River Wye passing under a stone bridge. Owned by the Manners family for 800 years, the walled gardens are very romantic and inside the hall you can walk round the Tudor bedrooms and the medieval chapel with its original heraldic wall paintings pretending to be a lord or lady taking some exercise in the long gallery. It's a quintessentially English scene and totally unmissable on a lovely day and compared with its neighbour, Chatsworth House, Haddon Hall is much more intimate and manageable in size.

Chatsworth House and Gardens ⓘ *T01246-582204, www.chatsworth.org, house and garden, Mar-Dec daily 1100-1730, £8.50, £6.50 concessions, children £3, garden only, £5, £3.50 concessions, children £2, farmyard and adventure playground, Mar-Dec daily, 1100-1730, £3.90, park open year round, free, leave plenty of time to explore this palatial residence, which could easily take all day and wear some comfortable shoes*, eight miles north of Bakewell, is a huge 16th-century country estate known as the Palace of the Peak. The 105-acre garden is 450 years old and contains a maze, cottage gardens, five miles of wooded walks with rare trees and shrubs and a 200 m cascading waterfall. There's also a brilliant adventure playground up amid the trees and a working farmyard for children. The Duke and Duchess of Devonshire still live here and are actively involved in its upkeep. There are hundreds of richly decorated rooms, historic paintings and sculptures including works by Holbein, Rembrandt and Gainsborough. The Orangery in the gardens has some lovely craft shops and a café.

The duchess lists her occupation as 'housewife' in reference to her devotion to the place, a look inside reveals why.

"Greater love hath no man than this: that he lay down his life for his fellow man"

In September 1665, a small box of cloth was delivered from London to a tailor's assistant George Viccars in Eyam. The material was damp when he got it so he spread it out to dry. Within days Viccars fell ill and died, becoming the first of Eyam's victims of the Bubonic Plague.

In the following months, the plague took hold in the village and those who could fled to the moorland around in desperation to escape. Anxious to avoid further contagion, Eyam's rector William Mompesson consulted the villagers and asked them to quarantine themselves. The villagers agreed. Mompesson arranged with the Earl of Devonshire at Chatsworth House that food and medication should be left at two points on the edge of the village, the boundary stone to the south and what is now called Mompesson's well to the north. To pay for these items the villagers left money in the holes drilled into the stone, which were filled with vinegar to prevent infection. Thinking that the plague was an airborne infection – actually carried by fleas, so they weren't too far off – church services were suspended and open air sermons were conducted in Cucklett Delph, a valley nearby. There were also no public funerals for the same reason, and families buried their own. One lady, Mrs Hancock of Riley was in the sad situation of having to bury her husband and six children in an eight-day period.

In October 1666 the plague ended. A village that had previously numbered 350 in 76 families in 1665 was left with only 270 people. The selfless act of the villagers is remembered each year on Plague Sunday, the last Sunday in August, with a service at Cucklett Delph.

Matlock and Matlock Bath

Matlock is one of the larger towns in the Peak District. Surrounded by hills, and overlooked by a folly, Riber Castle, it's reasonably picturesque with a few good places to stay and eat but little in the way of tourist attractions - the real treasures lie outside the town. Matlock Bath, on the other hand, a couple of miles down the road, has plenty of child-friendly attractions – a cable car to a cave-riddled tourist centre, a Gulliver's Kingdom and an aquarium. Although its setting is undoubtedly striking, in a gorge with the River Derwent running through, these days it is awash with chip shops, amusement arcades and tacky trinket shops. In summer it becomes a haven for motorbikers attracted by the challenging, sweeping Derbyshire roads.

Getting there Regular **train** services go to Matlock and Matlock Bath from Derby. The **Transpeak bus** service runs every 2 hours between Nottingham and Manchester, calling at Derby, Belper, Matlock, Bakewell, Buxton and Manchester. **Traveline,** T0870-6082608. **National Express,** T08705- 808080, also run a daily coach service to Matlock from London Victoria. By **car,** Matlock is 25 miles north of Derby on the A6, 10 miles southwest of Chesterfield on the A632 and 8 miles west of Alfreton on the A632.

Information Matlock TIC ⓘ *Crown Sq, T01629-583388, www.derbyshire dales. gov.uk* and also at **Matlock Bath** ⓘ *The Pavilion, T01629-55082, 0930-1730 daily.*

The Edwardian spa town became less popular towards the end of the 19th century and there's not much left to see of the actual spa today. On a rainy day, you could visit the **Aquarium** ⓘ *T01629-583624, F760793, 110 North Pde, Easter-Oct 1000-1730, Nov-Apr weekends 1000-1700, closed during the week, £1.80*, found in the old Matlock Bath Hydro, complete with a marble staircase and thermal pool which now comforts the aches and pains of the koi carp rather than the people of the town.

Also in Matlock Bath is the **Peak Mining Museum and Temple Mine** ⓘ *The Pavilion, T01629-583834, www.peakmines.co.uk, museum, Easter-Oct daily 1000-1700, Nov-Apr daily 1100-1500, temple mine: daily Easter-Oct 1200-1600, Nov-Apr only weekends, 1200-1600, museum or mine, £2.50, £1.50 concessions, joint museum and mine ticket £4, £2.50 concessions*, with hands-on exhibits and a maze of twisting tunnels. It's a real insight into the industry which has shaped so much of the area.

Dips in the ground and shafts beside the road over the countryside round here are air holes and access points for the miners.

Riber Castle ⓘ *free*, at the top of the hill is a ruined 19th-century castle built and designed by local textile designer John Smedley who founded Matlock's hydros. It has been unoccupied for many years, hence its romantic and ruined appearance. Take a walk up the hill to see it for yourself.

A couple of miles to the south of Matlock Bath is **The Heights of Abraham** ⓘ *T01629-582365, www.heights-of-abraham.co.uk, Feb daily 1000-1630, Mar Sat-Sun only, 1000-1630, Apr-Nov daily 1000-1700, £7.50, £6.20 concessions, children £5.20*, where cable cars take you up above the Derwent River Valley to a limestone cliff. At the top you can go underground into the show caves and find out more about the mining history of the area. There's also an adventure playground for children and the view is breathtaking. Really it's a fully organized and commercial take on the countryside which you can see just as well by going for a walk independently, although the cable cars are fun.

Walks around Matlock

The TIC has six free leaflets on walks around Matlock town, all of which take a couple of hours, are relatively easy going and a highly recommended insight into the area and its heritage. They include the three and a half mile **Cuckoostone Walk**, a circular walk taking you from Chesterfield Road up to the Matlock moor area with views of Riber Castle, and **The Wellfield Walk** which takes you up to Lumsdale, one of the oldest industrial valleys in England and the wishing stone. (If you walk round it three times and leave some money on it, your dreams *will* come true.) There are a number of other walks around the area and the tourist office in Matlock provides comprehensive information on them, as does the YHA.

Nine Ladies ⓘ *3 miles northwest of Matlock, look for signs pointing to Stanton-in-Peak, Stanton Lees or Birchover*, on Stanton Moor is a Bronze Age stone circle enclosed by a small circular bank beside a wood, unfortunately under threat from quarrying in this area. The 3-4,000 year old burial ground of Stanton Moor is dotted about with over 70 cairns and is an atmospheric and peaceful grove particularly first thing in the morning when there are fewer dog walkers around. Folklore has it that the circle is made of people who were turned to stone as punishment for dancing on the Sabbath, with the 'fiddler', a few yards away, turned into the King stone.

Sleeping

Buxton *p628, map p629*
Buxton is encircled by some slabs of Victorian architecture, grand hotels that look like they'd be more at home in Brighton than the wilds of Derbyshire. There's also a number of homely B&Bs in stone cottages dotted about the town. Book all accommodation in advance in the summer – rooms fill up quickly during the opera season.

C Biggin Hall, Biggin-by-Hartington, 11 miles from Buxton, T01298-84451, www.

bigginhall.co.uk. A fabulously romantic 17th-century pile which boasts air so pure that it supposedly soothes asthmatics and insomniacs. The bedrooms are stunning, huge low-beamed affairs with 4-poster beds and antiques, as well as log fires in the sitting rooms and a library. There's also traditional farmhouse cooking.

C The Old Hall Hotel, centrally located on the Square back in Buxton itself, T01298-22841, www.oldhallhotel buxton .co.uk. This is where Mary Queen of Scots is said to have stayed and is the oldest hotel in Buxton. It's proud of its history and is a traditional old hotel offering bed and breakfast and rooms with 4-poster beds and wood-pannelled walls.

C-D Buckingham Hotel, 1 Burlington Rd, T01298-70481, frontdesk@bucking hamhotel.co.uk. A small and leafy hotel with friendly 'free spirited' staff and a homely, laid-back atmosphere. It's fairly upmarket with a plush bar and dining room.

D Lakenham Guesthouse, 11 Burlington Rd, T01298-79209. One of many such places overlooking Pavilion Gardens, it's a small family-run place with period furniture and antiques.

E Barms Farm, a mile north of Buxton at Fairfield, T01298-77723, F78692. The pick of the bed and breakfasts round here. The good value but luxury rooms are light and airy in this non-smoking country farmhouse.

E Fernydale Farm, just 5 miles from Buxton at Earl Sterndale, T01298-83236, F83605. Bed and hearty breakfasts are on offer at this pretty white stone cottage on a small working farm. From Buxton, take the A515 to Ashbourne for about 3 miles and it is signposted from there.

E Grendon Guest House, Bishops La off St John's Rd, T01298-78831, www. grendonguesthouse.co.uk. An Edwardian house with gardens and views across the hills. It's on a bit of a hill, like most of Buxton, and you'll be well looked after.

E Harefield, 15 Marlborough Rd, T01298-24029, www.harefield1. freeserve.co.uk. A quiet and spacious Victorian home with a croquet lawn, run by fun-loving hosts. It's only a little walk from the town centre with gardens that meet the moors and a real log fire.

E Lowther Guest House, Hardwick Sq West, T01298-71479. A little cheaper, this is a small and homely place. Easter-Oct.

F Buxton YHA, Sherbrook Lodge, T/F01298-22287, buxton@yha.org.uk. It's in wooded grounds 1½ miles from the station. Open from 1700.

Camping

Grin Low, by Poole's Cavern, T01298-77735; **Limetree Park**, T01298-22988.

Castleton *p631*

Most places in Castleton itself are unpretentious, walker-friendly and reasonably priced.

C The Castle Hotel, Castle St, T01433-620578. Really an old pub in the centre of the village, this is the only luxury accommodation here, 6 of its rooms containing jacuzzis, perfect after a long walk, and 4-poster beds. It is 350 years old, has wholesome pub food and welcomes walkers.

E Causeway House is one of many stone cottage B&Bs on the road out from the village towards Hope, T01433-623291.

E Cryer House B&B, is a charming homely small stone house with a cottage garden right next door to the Castle Hotel, T01433-620244.

F Castleton YHA, Castle St, T01433-620235, castleton @yha.org.uk. Hostel contained in a large stone farmhouse with a drying room, internet access, games rooms and information about local walks. They can also provide information about activities in the area like hang-gliding and pot-holing and are really friendly.

Camping

F Losehill Caravan Club Site, T01433-620636.

Edale *p632*

There are a number of stone cottages with the odd room let out as B&B accommodation in Edale.

E Brookfield, Barber Booth, Edale, T01433-670227.

E Mam Tor House, Edale, T01433-670253 Walker-friendly and homely.

E Stonecroft Grindsbrook, Edale, T01433-670262. They're all walker-friendly and homely places to stay.

F Edale YHA, Rowland Cote, Nether Booth on the wooded hillside of the Kinder plateau, T01433-670302, edale@yha.org.uk, is particularly good for activities and activity groups. In the middle of a network of footpaths.

Camping

There are also numerous farms who will let you pitch your tent in a field for a small price. No mod cons here, but at least it's cheap.

Ollerbrook Farm, T01433-670235. Owned by Mr Thornley.

Upper Booth Farm, T01433-670250. Ask for Mrs Hodgson.

Waterside Farm, T01433-670215. Ask for Mrs Cooper.

Eyam *p632*

E The Old Rose and Crown, on the main road, T01433-630858. The only place to stay in Eyam village. A charming white stone cottage, formerly the old village inn, now a B&B with lovely views of the area and 4 rooms.

F Bretton YHA, 2 miles from Eyam, T01433-631856, bookings T01629-592707, a small remote stone farmhouse with 18 beds.

F Eyam YHA, Hawkhill Rd, just out of town, T01433-630335, eyam@yha.org.uk An eccentric turreted Victorian building just up the road from the village with 60 beds, open from 1700. They also have crazy golf.

Bakewell *p633*

There are a number of B&Bs in and around Bakewell, generally family-run stone cottages.

C-D Rutland Arms Hotel, T01629-812812, F812309. A grand old establishment in the centre of Bakewell, which has played host to Wordsworth, Coleridge and Turner in the past, this is the home of the original Bakewell Pudding. It's the only hotel in the centre of Bakewell and has a welcoming restaurant serving traditional English food.

D Haddon House Farm, Haddon Rd just out of Bakewell, T01629-814024, www.haddon-house.co.uk. Quiet, spacious and a touch of romance with 2 luxurious double rooms.

E Bene-Dorme, The Avenue, T01629-813292. A badly named but friendly and traditional B&B close to town.

E Bourne House, The Park, Haddon Rd, T01629-813274. A former manse and fairly upmarket. Overlooks the park and the riverside.

E Croft Cottage, Coombs Rd, T01629-814101. A gorgeous 17th-century stone cottage with a luxury private suite in the converted barn. Comfortable and welcoming.

E Melbourne House, Buxton Rd, T01629-815357. A private Georgian house offering a variety of home-cooked breakfasts and a warm welcome.

Camping

F Chatsworth Park Caravan Club Site, T01246-582226 (Mar-Dec). In an old walled garden.

F Haddon Grove Farm, near Over Haddon on Monyash Rd, 4 miles west of town, T01629-812343. For camping.

Matlock *p633*

There are a lot of B&Bs in Matlock and the surrounding area for a reasonable price and which cater especially for walkers. There's also a small number of Victorian hotels in Matlock Bath which used to attract guests who came to the town for the water, and some still do.

A Riber Hall, Riber, Matlock, T01629-582795, www.riber-hall.co.uk. An exceptional historic country house in a tranquil upmarket setting, with period furniture and exquisite detail, where you'll receive first class treatment.

In Matlock Bath you can still take to the healing water – but only if you stay at

C-D The New Bath Hotel, New Bath Rd, T0870-4008119, www.heritage- hotels.com. The Victorian hotel has indoor and outdoor pools and 5 acres of grounds, and is run by the Forte Hotel Group.

D Hogkinson's Hotel, 150 South Pde, Matlock Bath, T01629-582170, enquiries@hodgkinsons-hotel.co.uk. A place with a dash of Victorian elegance, terraced gardens and a restaurant.

D-E Robertswood Guesthouse, Farley Hill, Matlock, T/F01629-55642, www.robertswood.com. An 8-bedroomed Victorian stone house with views and just a short walk from the centre of Matlock.

D **The Temple Hotel**, Temple Walk, Matlock Bath, T01629-583911, www.templehotel.co.uk. Another historic stone building with comfortable accommodation and a bar with real ale on tap. Lord Byron wooed one of his mistresses here and the restaurant is named after him. It's comfortable and friendly, but if Byron were around today, he'd probably stay at the more exclusive *New Bath Hotel* instead.
E **Farley Farm**, a little further on into Farley itself, T01629-582533. A gorgeous working country farm with log fires, a relaxing atmosphere and home cooking, perfect for indulging those countryside fantasies.
E **Fountain Villa**, 86 North Pde, Matlock Bath, T01629-56195, enquiries@fountainvilla.co.uk. A Georgian townhouse overlooking the Derwent river and with period interiors.
E **Glendon**, Knowleston Pl, Matlock, T01629-584732. A Georgian B&B by the river with 4 rooms and a relaxed atmosphere.
E **Jackson Tor Hotel**, 76 Jackson Rd, Matlock, T/F01629-582348, www.jacksontorhotel@uk2.net. B&B in a walker-friendly family-run hotel who especially cater for groups. Some lovely views of the countryside and its rolling hills.
E **Middlehills Farm**, by Grange Hill in Matlock, T01629-650368. Cheap and quirky stone farmhouse with home-baked bread and genial hosts. You can also make friends with a potbellied pig.
E **The Old Museum Guesthouse**, 172 South Pde, Matlock Bath, T/F01629-57783. In the centre of town this place has 3 en-suite rooms with 4-poster beds also with views over the river.
E **The Old Sunday School**, New St, Matlock, T/F01629-583347. If you want something a little different from your usual B&B try this converted ex-chapel with, despite its history, a friendly home-from-home atmosphere.
F **Matlock YHA**, 40 Bank Rd, T01629-582983, T0870-7705690, matlock@yha.org.uk. With charming laid-back staff, this medium-sized hostel used to be the Hydropathic Hospital. Has loads of information on the area as well as a bar. They also have information on inter-hostel walking trails which are a really good way to see around the Peak District as they're only between 9 and 17 miles apart.

Camping
F **Middle Hills Farm**, Grange Hill, Matlock, T01629-650368, l.lomas@btinternet.com. Camping and caravan site with toilets and showers and half a mile from the nearest pub. You can also camp at
F **Wayside Farm** on Matlock Moor, T01629-582967, wilder and with few mod cons.

Eating

Buxton *p628, map p629*
There are a few pubs where you can grab a cheap meal in Buxton and several tearoom mainly suited to day trippers.
££ **The Buckingham Hotel** 1 Burlington Rd, T01298-70481. Traditional English carvery menu most nights of the week, smoked salmon starters and a range of fish and vegetarian dishes too. Grilled chicken with goats' cheese and avocado, fillet steak and roast lamb are typical in a small but not unimaginative restaurant.
££ **Columbine Restaurant**, 7 Hall Bank, T01298-78752, is the town's best restaurant. Very reasonably priced for fresh local produce, there's a range of meat and fish dishes including venison in Guinness, and friendly service in a classy restaurant. Closed Sun and Tue Nov-Apr.
££ **The Old Clubhouse**, Water St, T01298-70117, is a traditional warm pub with an open fire serving pub grub. It also has a garden for the summer months.
££ **Old Hall Hotel** on the Square just across from the Opera House, T01298-22841, serving English Sunday lunch style roasts within its historic wood-panelled walls. They have a pre- and post-theatre menu and accommodation, see above. Vegetarians can get a feed at
£ **The Wild Carrot**, 5 Bridge St, T01298-22843, a small licensed cafe with home-cooked food. Open Wed-Sun. There's also a wholefood shop downstairs, open Mon-Sat.

Edale *p632*
£ **The Old Nag's Head**, Grindsbrook, Booth, T01433-670291, is a famous walkers' pub with a garden to the rear and special walkers' meals that are high in carbohydrates.

Bakewell *p633*
There are two particularly good bakeries to try in the town itself.

£ **The Bakewell Tart Shop and Coffee House**, Matlock St, T01629-814692, has a delicious variety of tarts from traditional to lemon and treacle with a small teashop inside.

£ **The Old Original Bakewell Pudding Shop**, The Square, T01629-812193. Less wide-ranging but with freshly baked bread and a licensed restaurant.

Matlock *p634*
Matlock has a lot of pubs and you'll easily find something to eat here, although characteristically for the area, it's more walkers' carbo-laden food than nouvelle cuisine.

Entertainment

Buxton *p628, map p629*
Buxton Opera House, T01298-72190, www.buxton-opera.co.uk. There are regular shows here throughout the year of various genres from book adaptations and poetry readings to opera, ballet and newly commissioned plays including *The Full Monty*. The Old Hall Hotel contains **The Pauper's Pit Theatre**, with more fringe productions.

The Buxton Buzz Comedy Club on the first Fri in the month upstairs at the *Old Clubhouse* from 2030. On the last Thu in each month **Club Acoustic Concerts** are also held upstairs in the Old Clubhouse, T01298-25954.

Activities and tours

Buxton *p628, map p629*
Pony trekking
Northfield Farm Riding and Trekking Centre in Flash, just outside Buxton, have rides by the hr or the day for all abilities. T01298-22543, F27849. A 2-hr trek costs £19 and it's £37 for a full day.

Walking
Free guided walks These run from the Hope Valley Line stations at different dates throughout the year. There's a good 9-mile walk from **Bamford to Edale**, or an easier 7-mile walk around **Hathersage**. All the walks start and finish at a railway station in good time for your train home. Further information on these walks and others can be found on a 24 hr information line, T0161-2426296.

Organized tours **Peak Tracks** run themed walking holidays and weekend breaks searching out the best of the area's historic houses, wildlife and scenery in walks that promise not to exceed 10 miles per weekend. A weekend costs £180 including hotel accommodation, T01663-732996, www.peaktracks.com.

Peakland Walking Trails Ideal forthe more experienced walker and based in Tideswell, Derbyshire, this company organizes self-guided tours and offers year-round weekend walking tours with an experienced guide from £165 including accommodation in Tideswell, T01298-872801, www.walkingholidays.org.uk.

Themed tours
Peak Premier Travel Tours, T01629-636877, run full- and half-day tours around the Peak District, including mystery tours of the area's country pubs. They also do pick ups or drop offs for one way walks in the region.

Edale *p632*
Riding
Ladybooth Trekking Centre, T01433-670205. Full and half-day treks through the Peak District, and lessons for beginners. A 2½-hr ride over the moors costs £18.

Bakewell *p633*
Bus tours
From the end of Mar to mid-Oct, the 211 bus takes a mini-tour of the attractions in the Bakewell area. It goes 6 times a day on the hour to **Haddon Hall**, the Peak Rail Station at Rowsley and **Chatsworth House** before returning to Bakewell Sq.

Matlock *p634*
Outdoor activities
Derwent Pursuits, Cromford Mill, Mill La, Cromford just outside Matlock, T01629-824179, info@derwent-pursuits.com. A range of courses from a full day to weeks where you can make the most of the

outdoors with orienteering, caving, climbing and abseiling. It's one of the few places where you can have a go without committing yourself to a full all-action week.
YHA. Provide information on outdoor pursuits in the area.

Transport

Hope Valley *p630*
Buses go from Castleton to **Bakewell** 5 times a day and 6 times a day to **Buxton**. The village is 3 miles from the nearest station in Hope, see Hope Valley Railway page 627. The no. 200 bus runs from Castleton bus station to **Edale** station hourly from 0853 and takes 20 mins. There's also a service from Castleton to **Bakewell** via **Buxton**, the 173 bus which takes 50 mins and runs every 2 hrs.

Buxton *p628, map p629*
Peak Cycle Hire in Hayfield, just outside Buxton on the A624, hire out bikes and have information on cycle trails throughout the Peak District, T01663-746222.

Cheshire

→ *Colour map 6, grid C2*

Contained within Cheshire's boundaries, which stretch from North Wales to Manchester and Derbyshire, are an inordinate number of country houses, medieval hunting estates and the small town of Prestbury, housing more millionaires per head than any other town in England. Small wonder that a lot of Cheshire's residents have delusions of grandeur – this is an upmarket area with a very desirable postcode. Chester, the much-visited Roman city with fantastic shopping and museums, is worth a visit, as is the lush countryside that the wealthy landowners liked so much. Cheshire is a serious bit of posh amid the metropolitan areas of the Northwest and its residents wouldn't want you to forget it. ▸▸ *For Sleeping, Eating and other listings, see pages 645-648.*

History

The teapot-shaped county bordered by Wales, Merseyside, Manchester, Shropshire and Derbyshire has a breadth and depth of both history and landscape. With wild hilly moorland in the east through to the western fertile plain and grassland in the south, Cheshire has a long history as an agricultural county. For nearly 500 years until 1830 it was a County Palatine, a little kingdom ruled by the Earl of Chester independently of the King. The county town Chester is a walled Roman town but there is also evidence of Stone Age occupation here. Thriving through the Middle Ages with bustling market towns, its forests popular hunting grounds for the Earl of Chester and many kings (James I was the last known king to hunt here), the county was decimated by plague in 1349.

But the real changes came with salt mining in the 18th and 19th centuries. The manufacturing industries coupled with canal infrastructure brought wealth to Cheshire. In 1847 the first chemical works opened up in Widnes and the northwest of the county still has an immense mineral oil industry today. The northeast by contrast benefited from the cotton industry of Manchester and the many mill towns were prosperous until the late 19th century, when overseas competition hit it hard. Liverpool took over from Chester as the area's major port serving Ireland and the county's fortunes changed again. Its shape has changed over the years as you might imagine, and the most recent change has been the loss of the Wirral peninsula in the north to Merseyside.

These days, Cheshire retains many small historic market towns while accommodating some of the urban sprawl of Merseyside and Manchester, and the far less picturesque but immensely valuable chemical works still brings in the money in Runcorn.

Chester

Chester is a walled Roman city on the Welsh borders and the Romans still rule the roost here today. Don't be surprised if you see the odd centurion or two sitting around having a coffee in one of the many cafés in the centre of town – as you'll realize within five minutes of being here, tourism is the main industry. Despite the Roman theme, your first impressions are likely to be of the beautiful black and white Tudor-style architecture, particularly the Rows, the half-timbered shopping precincts unique to Chester. While browsing the many shops, your ears will be assailed by any number of regional accents, buskers and odd gabble of Welsh – the language still thrives a couple of miles away across the border. Walking around the walls, taking a boat trip on the Dee and enjoying the historic pubs after a shopping spree around the Rows are some of the best ways to spend your day here.

Ins and outs

Getting there Chester is well-linked by **motorways, rail** and **bus** routes to the rest of England, Scotland and Wales although public transport around Cheshire as a whole is less user-friendly. **Manchester Airport** is 40 minutes away on the M56 and M53 from Chester for international and domestic flights, T0161-4898000. **Liverpool John Lennon Airport** in Liverpool is also 40 minutes away by road T0151-2884000. There are high speed *rail* services run from London Euston and Paddington to Crewe and Chester, also from Glasgow on the West Coast Main Line. It's also easy to get here from Manchester's Piccadilly and Oxford Road stations and Birmingham New Street. The station is a 15-minute walk from the centre. Chester is well-linked with the M53 and M56 for getting to and from Liverpool and Manchester. The **bus** station is on Delamere Street for all regional and national buses. Be warned that the local buses in this area aren't particularly direct or reliable. You can get to North Wales from here by bus and around Cheshire, but you'll need to check the timetables closely. **National Express**, T08705-808080, run coach services around England, Wales and Scotland and **Cheshire Traveline** has further information on local buses, T01244-602666.

Getting around It only takes 20 minutes to walk from one side of Chester to the other and going by foot is your only option as the centre of town is pedestrianized. Naturally, there are plenty of well-signposted car parks, mainly to the north of the town and a number of park and ride options at the far edges of the city.

Information Just outside the city walls to the southwest of the city is the excellent **Chester Visitor Centre** ⓘ *Vicar's La overlooking the amphitheatre, T01244-402111, www.chestertourism.com, Apr-Sep Mon-Sat 0900-1730, Sun 1000-1600, Oct-Mar Mon-Sat 1000-1700, Sun 1000-1600*. There you can book accommodation for a £3 charge, which will give you a 10% discount. Upstairs is an excellent historical exhibition and the chance to do some brass rubbing and candlemaking. The **TIC** ⓘ *in the town hall on Northgate St, T402111. Apr-Sep Mon-Sat 0900-1730, Sun 1000-1600, Oct-Mar 1000-1700*, books accommodation, walking tours and coach tickets.

History

Archaeologists have found evidence of human occupation in Chester since the Stone Age, but it really came to power as a trading settlement for the Romans from AD 1 until 410. The Romans named it Deva, after the goddess of the river Dee and it was one of the finest strategic outposts in England because of its proximity to the Welsh borders and its harbour. Roman relics are scattered around the city today, with a half-excavated amphitheatre which would have sat around 6000 people and the Grosvenor Museum containing the greatest number of Roman tombstones to be found outside Rome. They were discovered underpinning the city walls in the 19th century. In the 13th and 14th centuries it was developed as a port, mainly for trade with Ireland and was a military base for incursions against the Welsh. The Rows date back to around this time, half-timbered galleries on two levels which were named after the merchants trading on each one, for example Pepper Alley, Fish Shambles and Ironmongers' Row. Those that remain today are mainly Victorian reconstructions in the derided "mock-Tudor" style but which are unique in England and in some the medieval vaulted undercrofts remain.

Chester suffered greatly in the Civil War of 1642-6 when it chose to support the wrong side. Cromwell's men besieged the city for two years until starvation forced it to surrender; it had the last laugh though when Charles II came to the throne in 1660, bringing the wealthy back to his loyal town.

Today Chester remains a historic town and has yet to become a museum town. It prides itself on its history but also houses many businesses and still operates as a modern town. However, of late, shopping outlets like the Trafford Centre in Manchester and Cheshire Oaks in Ellesmere Port have stifled smaller shops, which

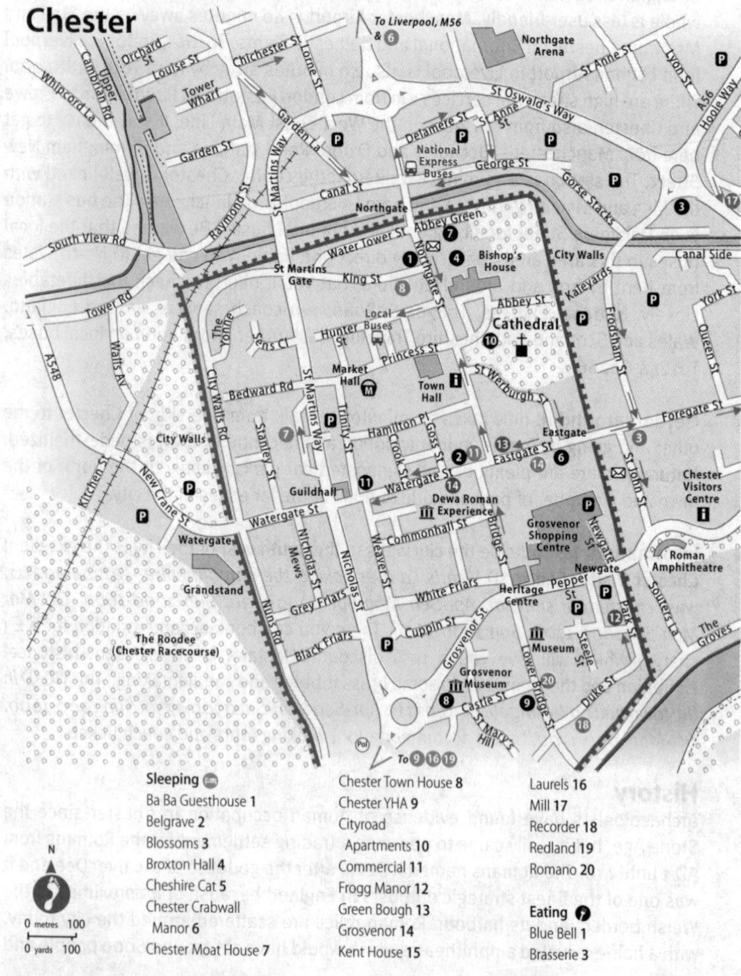

are quietly closing down along the Rows. For those living in the small market towns in Wales and Cheshire though, it's still a place to come to find the best variety of shops in one place.

Starting at the TIC at the town hall, walk under the 14th-century archway to the left of the cathedral into Abbey Square and through the northwest corner to find the **city wall**. Walking along the wall away from town will take you to the **Northgate** with its canals and locks behind it.

> *On the River Dee you can hire rowing boats and pedalos from the bankside in summer. They cost around £5 an hour.*

This is the beginning of a 40-minute walk into town which takes in most of the sights of Chester. To your left here the **cathedral** ⓘ *Daily 0730-1830, £2 donation,* stands where there has always been a church since AD 907. The cloisters are very atmospheric and it has a very good information trail including a manuscript of Handel's *Messiah* which he practised here en route to Ireland.

Next, the **Eastgate,** once the main entrance to the city is now a bridge over the main shopping street, Eastgate Street, with the second most photographed clock in England after Big Ben, commemorating 60 years of Queen Victoria's reign. Walking on, you reach **Newgate** from which there is a view over the **Roman amphitheatre** to the left, and the Chester visitor centre beyond it. It's not that impressive and has only been half excavated, but held between six and seven thousand spectators in its day. Beyond it is **Grosvenor Park**, a local beauty spot and ideal for a picnic.

Just beyond Newgate is the river, reached easily if you go down **the wishing steps**. Folklore has it that if you run up and down and then up again without drawing breath, your wish will come true. There aren't all that many of them, but they're uneven in depth which makes it a tricky one and may have you looking for a casualty ward if you're not careful.

Walking from here into town along the walls will take you to the Southgate, known locally as **Bridgegate** as it's opposite the 14th-century bridge out of town. Continuing round on the walls for a further 10 minutes will take you to the **Roodee racecourse** ⓘ *T01244-304600*, Britain's oldest. There are racing festivals on at various points throughout the summer and the horses, unusually, run anti-clockwise. Otherwise, from Bridgegate you can head straight up the street into town to shop in the Rows. A number of the shops have interesting histories, for example **The Bear at the Billet**, just by Bridgegate on the left, Chester's oldest timber-frame house, and on Bridge Street Row, **Booklands** bookshop which has a beautiful vaulted medieval crypt.

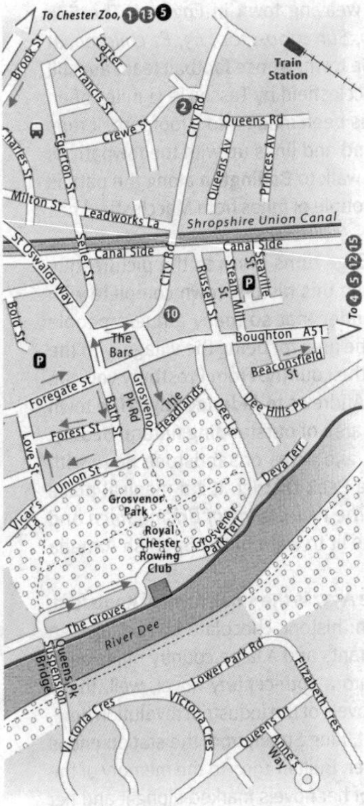

Elliot's **4**
Franc's Brasserie **5**
Grosvenor Hotel Brasserie **6**
La Boheme **2**
Mediterranean **7**
Pastarazzi **8**
Pizza Express **9**
Refectory **10**
Samsi Takitori **11**

Pubs & bars
Albion Inn **12**
Boot Inn **13**
Watergate's **14**

The **Grosvenor Museum** ⓘ *daily Mon-Sat 1030-1700, Sun 1400-1700, free,* is a bit dusty but has some interesting exhibits if you want to find out more about the town's history. Bringing the history alive more successfully is the **Deva Roman Experience** ⓘ *T01244-343407, F347737, daily 0900-1700*, a museum with lots of hands-on features on Pierpoint Lane, just off Bridge Street.

Around Cheshire

Ellesmere Port ⓘ *T0151-3555017, Apr-Oct daily 1000-1700, Nov-Mar Sat-Wed 1100-1600, £2.50, child £2*, seven miles away, has a popular **Boat Museum** on South Pier Road. It shows you just how important messing about on the river has been in this area over the years and is actually very interesting. It's only a 10-minute walk from the Ellesmere Port railway station.

The borough of **Macclesfield** in north Cheshire is the largest district in the county, comprising Alderley Edge, Knutsford, Poynton and Wilmslow, and is easily the most affluent. Accessible on the London-Manchester intercity rail link or from the M6, 'Macc' (as it's known to residents) is primarily known for its 18th and 19th century silk industry. At that time it was the greatest silk weaving town in England. The **Silk Museum** ⓘ *T01625-613210, Mon-Sat 1100-1700, Sun 1300-1700, £3, £2 children*, at the heritage centre on Roe St tells the story of the town, whose football team are still known as the Silkmen. Starting at the top of Macclesfield by Tescos is 11 miles of an old railway line, the **Middlewood Way**, which has been made into a footpath. It runs parallel to the Macclesfield Canal along grassland and links up with the towpath as an ideal place for a Sunday walk or bike ride. A walk to **Bollington** along the path is easy and rewarding as this little country town a couple of miles from Macclesfield has some nice old pubs.

The B5087 from Macclesfield to Alderley Edge turns north to the picturesque village of **Prestbury**. The river Bollin runs through this historic town complete with half-timbered Tudor buildings, and it's no wonder that so many affluent people have chosen to live around here. It's known in the area for being the village with the most millionaires per mile in the county, if not the country. From Prestbury you can wiggle round the village roads past Mottram St Andrews to **Alderley Edge.** The town itself is nothing special, but just before it is an area of outstanding natural beauty. Take your time to stop for a walk to the **Edge**, 250 acres of sandstone ridge with views out over the Cheshire Plain as far as the Peak District. It's a magical place which inspired Alan Garner's children's book, *The Weirdstone of Brisingamen* and with bronze age remains and a beacon that was lit to warn of the Spanish Armada adding to the romance.

A couple of miles west of Macclesfield on the A537 is the small town of **Knutsford**. It's all that you would expect of a Cheshire town: historic chocolate box cottages, a plethora of antiques shops and exclusive restaurants and a large country mansion in the background. If it feels like you've walked into a 19th-century novel, well, that's because you have. Elizabeth Gaskell based her novels of the industrial revolution here, including *Cranford*. The view from the main street, King Street, from the station end is dominated by the GMT, or **Gaskell Memorial Tower**. Built in 1907 to the memory of the novelist, it's quite an ugly thing with the names of her novels marked along it and her bust incorporated into it too. Next to it is the architecturally more interesting *Belle Epoque* restaurant, formerly the civic centre, which is one of a number of eccentric Italianate buildings in Knutsford. **RH Watt**, a Manchester glovemaker, brought back these ideals of architecture from his travels through southern Europe. Drury Lane at the

The name 'Knutsford' is said to relate to an occasion when King Canute (Knut) forded the river here.

end of King Street, has a number of examples of his buildings, including the Ruskin Rooms, after the painter who inspired Watt, now offices.

The Heritage Centre ⓘ *1330-1600 Mon-Fri, 1200-1600 Sat, 1400-1630 Sun, free,* just beside *Jumpers* was a 19th-century smithy and has a permanent exhibition about the town upstairs, including a video of its unusual Mayday parade. They have plenty of information about historic trails round the town and cheerfully answer all enquiries.

Following the blue heritage plaques down the street, you will finally come to the entrance to **Tatton Park** ⓘ *T534400, www.tattonpark.org.uk, park, Mar-Sep Mon-Sun 1000-1900, £3.60 for cars, free for walkers, mansion, gardens, Tudor old hall and farm, Tue-Sun (call to check times), £3, child £2.* The home of the Egerton family, this National Trust property has 1000 acres of land as well as a Georgian mansion, Japanese gardens and the Tudor old hall, which takes you through 450 years of history from the 15th century to the 1950s. On a nice day, a walk in the park is superb – and free – and you can see herds of red deer up close, as well as numerous birds. It's just a shame that Manchester Airport is so close, as the jet engines shatter your calm every now and again. Be warned: a walk from the gates to the hall itself is pretty exhausting and you really need a car or at least a bike to reach it.

Take the A523 from Macclesfield to Hazel Grove and then the A6 to High Lane and you'll find **Lyme Park** ⓘ *T01663-762023, hall and gardens, Apr-Oct Fri-Tue 1300-1700, £5.50, park, Apr-Oct daily 0800-2030, Nov-Mar 0800-1800, free for walkers, £3.50 per car, you can also reach the park by train and a short walk from Disley station.* In the borough of Stockport, it's the largest country house in Cheshire. With Ionic pillars, Greek marbles and an Elizabethan drawing room, the 16th-century house itself is very grand and not surprisingly frequently used as a backdrop for period dramas, including the BBC adaptation of *Pride and Prejudice*, where a dripping Colin Firth, as Mr Darcy, took a swim in the lake. Walks around the grounds along a number of well-marked trails are free and worth the effort. From the car park you can easily walk to **The Cage**, the folly at the top of the nearest hill from where the ladies of the house used to watch the hunt. You can see the Peak District from the top of the hill and the many red and fallow deer across the estate. More gruesomely, the lower part of the cage was used to jail poachers.

Sleeping

Chester *p641, map p642*

There are plenty of places to stay in Chester to suit every budget, which is atypical of Cheshire in general, so it's a good place to base yourself if you're exploring this area. Around the station are a huge number of guesthouses and hotels of a similar standard. Hoole Rd is also good for budget B&Bs, as is Hough Green on the opposite side of town.

A **Chester Moat House**, Trinity St, T01244-899988, F316118. A little less individual with a country hotel feel, but younger and with a great spa complex.

A **The Grosvenor Hotel** on Eastgate, T01244-324024. Bang in the centre of town and very plush, this place is owned by the Duke of Westminster and one of the two 5-star hotels in the Northwest. It is grand and traditional with leather armchairs and 4-poster beds.

B **Chester Crabwall Manor**, Parkgate Rd, Mollington, T01244-851666, www.marstonhotels.com. A country manor retreat set in private grounds with a swimming pool and elegant individually designed rooms.

C **Frogg Manor**, Nantwich Rd in Broxton, a short drive from Chester, T01829-782629, F782459. Flounces and frills and an overdose of romance in this eccentric place with mad 1930s and 40s-style bedrooms.

C **The Green Bough Hotel**, 60 Hoole Rd, T01244-326241, greenboughhotel@cwcom.net. A boutique-style hotel with 4-poster beds and luxurious fabrics in elegant, Georgian-inspired rooms. There's also a restaurant here, *The Olive Tree*, and antique furniture.

D Blossoms Hotel, St Johns St just off Eastgate, T01244-323186, F346433. Traditional and reasonably priced hotel but not particularly exciting. Has a restaurant and decent-sized rooms.

D The Broxton Hall Hotel, Whitchurch Rd, Broxton, T01829-782321, reservations @broxtonhall.co.uk. A stunning black and white 17th-century hall with landscaped gardens, fishing, riding and log fires.

D Hotel Romano, in the centre at 51 Lower Bridge St, T01244-325091, F315628. A slightly cheaper Georgian townhouse hotel with excellent service and very close to 2 Italian restaurants.

D Mill Hotel, Milton St near the station, T01244-350035, www.millhotel.com A new, modern hotel that used to be an old corn mill. Now with state-of-the-art gym and spa complex.

D Redland Hotel, 64 Hough Green, only a mile from the city centre, T01244-671024, F681309. A Victorian ambience with wood-panelled walls and period furnishings.

E Cheshire Cat, Whitchurch Rd, Christleton, T01244-332200, F336415. Slightly out of town, a country hotel with 14 rooms and a homely feel.

E Chester Town House, 23 King St, T01244-350021. A comfortable, 17th-century guesthouse with a family feel to it.

E Recorder Hotel right in the centre of Chester at 19 City Walls, overlooking the river Dee, T01244-326580, www.recorder hotel.co.uk. A stately guesthouse with individually designed bedrooms (12 guest rooms named after the signs of the zodiac), it also has romantic 4-poster and Victorian beds and the location is perfect.

E Belgrave Hotel, 61 City Rd, T01244-312138, F324951. A traditional family-run hotel about 10 mins from the centre and close to the station.

E Ba Ba Guest House, 65 Hoole Rd, T01244-315047, www.babaguesthouse.co.uk. An elegant Victorian townhouse, it's one of the most friendly and welcoming B&Bs in town.

E Commercial Hotel, St Peter's Churchyard, T01244-320749, F348318. A country hotel-style place with ivy growing up the walls and an individual service with 6 rooms and a relaxed atmosphere.

E Laurels, 14 Selkirk Rd, Curzon Park, T01244-679682, howell@ellisroberts. freeserve.co.uk. More of a family home with good value rooms and within walking distance of the racecourse and city centre.

E Kent House 147 Boughton, T01244-324171, kent-house@turner10101. freeserve.co.uk. Very friendly, a Georgian family home open for B&B, with 2 4-poster rooms and a smaller twin room, offering big breakfasts.

F Chester YHA, Hough Green House, 40 Hough Green, T01244-680056, chester @yha.org.uk. A Victorian house with a laundry, internet and kitchen facilities. It's bigger than it looks with around 100 beds and offers evening meals.

F Cityroad Apartments, 18 City Rd, T01244-313651 daytime, www.chesterooms.com. Very basic student room-style accommodation plus an optional breakfast. Even cheaper than the YHA.

Knutsford *p644*

C The Cross Keys Hotel on King St offers accommodation in the stables of the former 18th-century coaching inn with plenty of character and wooden beams and no horses, T01565-750404, F750510.

D Beech House, Toft Rd, T01565-634891. A family-run guesthouse in walking distance from the station.

D Tattondale Farm, T01565-654692, a working farm in the grounds of Tatton Park itself.

Eating

Chester *p641, map p642*

£££ Blue Bell restaurant, 65 Northgate St, T01244-317758. Excellent and highly recommended. Serves local produce in a medieval inn with a great wine list. Very relaxed and friendly.

£££ The Brasserie at the *Grosvenor Hotel* on Eastgate, T01244-324024, is more upmarket, serving French food in an elegant restaurant. You can also pop in here for afternoon tea, less expensive and more traditionally English.

£££ Pastarazzi, 29 Grosvenor St, T01244-400029. It's worth booking a table here if you like Italian food. An immense wine list and Grade II listed medieval building complete the classy dining experience.

££ **The Brasserie**, Brookdale Pl just off Frodsham St across the canal, T01244-322288, looks like an identikit pub from the outside but serves fantastic British and Mediterranean cooking in a trendy minimalist environment, blowing the cobwebs from most of Chester's older establishments.

££ **Elliot's**, T01244-329932, at 2 Abbey Green just off Northgate St beyond the town hall serves delicious organic and vegetarian food.

££ **The Mediterranean Restaurant** in Rufus Court just around the corner, T01244-320004, is particularly good for fish and has the atmosphere of a Greek taverna.

££ **Samsi Takitori**, 70 Watergate St at the other end of town, T01244-344883. For traditional Japanese dining.

££ **Franc's Brasserie** at the Dene Hotel, Hoole Rd, T01244-321165. A French brasserie specializing in asparagus in the summer months in a friendly café-style restaurant.

££ **La Boheme**, 58 Watergate St, T01244-313721, is an unusual fusion of Swedish and French cuisine, very good value and served in an elegant minimalist restaurant.

££ **Pizza Express** has the usual and occasional jazz sessions, 52-54 Lower Bridge St, T01244-350625.

£ **The Refectory** in Chester Cathedral is a very cheap and wholesome affair, seated on benches in what feels like a school canteen but with much nicer home-made snacks, T01244-313156.

Knutsford *p644*

There are a lot of upmarket places to dine here on King St alongside a number of pubs with reasonable lunches.

££ **Belle Epoque**, an award-winning French restauraunt with starched white tablecloths and an air of exclusivity.

£ **Goostrey cake and coffee shop**. Does lovely home-made cakes and rolls if you fancy a picnic in the park.

Pubs, bars and clubs

Chester *p641, map p642*

One of the best ways of soaking up the atmosphere is still a lunch in one of the many low-beamed pubs, although occasionally they're a little too tourist-orientated with their spurious tales of ghosts and the like. Most stop serving lunch after 1400.

The Albion Inn is a great stopping point along the walls just after Newgate but only if you're also 'hostile to kids' as it proclaims itself to be. It serves outstanding pub grub and has a warming log fire in winter.

The Boot Inn, is the oldest surviving pub in Chester, with traditional decor and oak beams and pub lunches. 14 roundheads were killed in the back room.

Watergate's Wine Bar on Watergate St is recommended, a candlelit crypt dating from 1120 with nooks and crannies to sit in and a friendly, young and trendy atmosphere.

Activities and tours

Chester *p641, map p642*

Guided walks

Guided walks around town can be arranged through the tourist office, some with guides dressed in full Roman gear leading children whooping around the streets and there's also a brilliant ghost hunter tour (every Thu, Fri and Sat from outside the town hall at 1930, Jun-Oct). This takes you past a number of pubs where spirits have been spotted over the years by those drinking too much of the same, and along the walls where a centurion is supposed to roam. Contact the TIC for further details.

Transport

Chester *p641, map p642*

Bus

Long distance There are 10 National Express coach services daily to **London** (6 hrs), 8 to **Birmingham** (2 hrs), 6 to **Cardiff** (5 hrs), 8 to **Gatwick** (8 hrs), 8 to **Liverpool** (1 hr), 6 to **Manchester** and **Manchester airport** (1 hr). For **Edinburgh** there are 4 services a day (11 hrs) and buses run to **Glasgow** twice daily (7 hrs).

Car

Avis 128 Brook St, T311463, Budget, The Bridgegate, Lower Bridge St, T313431, Hertz, Trafford St, T374705, Europcar, 143 Brook St, T312893, Eurodollar, Sealand Industrial Estate, T390008.

Train

Central Trains, www.centraltrains.co.uk, run from Chester to **Birmingham** (2 hrs) and **London Euston** (4 hrs). First Northwestern run the stopping service from Chester to **Manchester** via **Knutsford** (1 hr 15 mins) and various services into Wales including to **Holyhead** for the boat to **Dublin** (1 hr 30 mins).

Knutsford *p644*

Bus

Buses also go to **Macclesfield** hourly from here, for further information call T534850.

Car

Knutsford is on the old Liverpool-London road, the A50, and is 10 miles from Manchester Airport, 37 miles from Liverpool and 15 miles from Manchester.

Train

Trains to **Manchester** go hourly, just after the ½ hr and to **Chester** in the opposite direction just before it.

Liverpool

→ *Colour map 6, grid C1*

Liverpool's trying hard to shrug off its image as a city full of scallies, shell suits and curly perms, not least by winning the title of European Capital of Culture for 2008. Built around the docks and the River Mersey, it's a small city with the vibrant blend of cultures that its history as a major port has produced. There's an exceptional modern art scene nestled in a town with its fair share of rough areas, as well as museums, the Albert Dock and, of course, the Beatles. You could be forgiven for thinking that Liverpool has stood still after the demise of the four cheeky scousers: through the Cavern Quarter to the Albert Dock you'll find tours and trips to satisfy the worst of Beatlemaniacs. The overdose of Beatles culture can be righted with a trip to the Ropewalks area, throbbing with clubs and bars and not a shell suit in sight. Perfect for a hard day's night. ▸▸ *For Sleeping, Eating and other listings, see pages 655-660.*

Ins and outs

Getting there The newly renamed **Liverpool John Lennon Airport,** T0151-2884000, is 7 miles southeast of the city centre in Speke. There are now budget easyJet flights to destinations including Paris and Barcelona from here as well as services to Ireland. The airport has currency exchange facilities and ATMs in the main terminal. The express bus 500 is the only way to reach the centre of Liverpool by public transport as there's no train station. **Train** connections to London, Manchester and other major cities are at **Liverpool Lime Street station,** well-signposted just north of the centre of town. **National Express,** T08705-808080, services run from Norton Street to all major UK cities and towns from the station north of Liverpool Lime Street station. By **car,** Liverpool is 35 miles from Manchester on the M62 and M60, 215 miles from London and 102 miles from Birmingham on the M6. From the M6 follow the M56 or M62. The main **ferry** terminal, for ferries to the Isle of Man and Ireland, is at Pier Head to the west, within walking distance of the centre. The **Seacat** service, T0870-5523523, connects Liverpool with Dublin in 4 hours and the **Isle of Man Steam Packet** service, T08705-523523 (UK), T1800-551743 (Ireland), connects with Douglas, and **Norse Merchant Ferries** links with Dublin and Belfast, T0870-6004321. ▸▸ *See Transport, page 659, for more details.*

Getting around Finding your way around Liverpool isn't too difficult. It's a manageable size and you can orientate yourself easily by looking up to the Radio City tower, St John's Beacon, which has the TIC in Queen Square below it, or looking out towards the Royal Liver building and the docks. The Pier Head and the Albert Dock are a 15 minute walk from the TIC, or 2 minutes in a taxi or a bus, running also from Queen Square bus station. The **smart bus** network extends all over the city, taking you down to the Albert Dock on the no.1 from the Queen Square bus station.

Information The **main TIC** ⓘ *in Queen Sq, T0906-6806886, askme@visitliverpool.com, Mon, Wed-Sat 0900-1730, Tue 1000-1730, Sun 1030-1630*, they can book transport and accommodation for you. Blue badge walking tours also leave from outside at various pre-arranged times. There is a smaller TIC inside the **Albert Dock** ⓘ *T0906-6806886, www.albertdock.com, 1000-1730 daily*, again with an accommodation booking service.

The local newspapers *The Daily Post* and *Liverpool Echo* provide the regional news for Liverpool and Merseyside. The *Metro* appears at stations in the morning, a freebie for commuters with club and event listings inside. The official tourism websites are www.visitliverpool.com and www.makeitmerseyside.org.

History

On the Mersey estuary three miles from the Irish sea, Liverpool has a long tradition of seafaring. Founded in the 10th century, the small community became a town in 1207 when King John granted it a charter and it grew slowly through the Middle Ages as a fishing port. The first dock was built in Liverpool in 1715 and it soon outranked London. As with Manchester, Liverpool really came to power in the 18th century as a result of trade. It was officially made a city as the growing population and industry drew in workers from all over the country and the town expanded along the docks. Irish, Welsh and Scots were attracted by the economic opportunities or came as refugees from the poverty in their own areas.

By 1830 and the introduction of the railways, Liverpool was linked with Manchester and its growing cotton trade. With the Cheshire salt fields to the south and the coal fields of Lancashire to the north, the transport network of the Mersey was a vital link in the trade of the Northwest. Its location also made trade possible with the West Indies and the Americas and it became the most important port in the empire during this period. This status was, however, underpinned with a darker history. Liverpool was also Europe's main slave port, trading goods from Merseyside for slaves in West Africa.

From 1845-48 the Potato Famine in Ireland brought in more immigrants than ever before, many hoping for a passage to America. A large proportion stayed in Liverpool, unable to afford the boat over and the city has a rich Irish heritage today.

After the Second World War the city fell into decline as both an export and a passenger port. Trade slowed down and unemployment was rife as airlines began to replace boats. But the city soon became famous for another reason besides workers' strikes. In the 1960s, Allan Ginsberg described the city as "the cultural centre of the universe" and with good reason. The place was buzzing with music and talent. In that same year, the Beatles put Liverpool firmly on the map. The city has also produced two prime ministers amid myriad entertainers and sportsmen and its contribution to England's pop culture has been assured with sitcoms, singers and footballers aplenty.

More recently, EU grants and the opening of several car manufacturing plants in the region have repaired some of the problems, but not all. The loss of the city's major trade, replaced by cheap air travel, hit Liverpool hard and has still to be countered.

24 hours in Liverpool

Begin your day with a greasy fry-up in Ye Cracke off Hardman St, an old Lennon hang-out that's popular with students. Then head for the Walker Gallery to spend your morning in the city's best and most extensive art gallery.

From there you can wander down to the Cavern Quarter to snoop around the street that was swinging in the Sixties, and then jump on a bus to the Albert Dock for lunch in one of its waterside cafés or restaurants.

Spend the afternoon looking round the Tate Modern and The Beatles Story before heading to Hope Street for a smart dinner. Round off your day in the Ropewalks, which has enough trendy bars and clubs to see you through till morning.

Albert Dock

The Albert Dock, once the main quayside for the influential port in the 19th century, is now the city's main tourist attraction. You'll no longer see sacks of spices and exotic produce in the complex but some impressive museums telling the story of the city, from the slave trade through to the Beatles, amid cafés and a few touristy shops.

Just before you enter the Albert Dock along the Wapping Road that runs parallel to the dock, you'll see two modern sculptures, both bright yellow. One is the **Yellow Submarine**, cheery and recognizable from the cartoon, welcoming you to the city's biggest and best Beatles museum, The Beatles Story, inside the dock. The other is **SuperLambBanana**. It's basically a giant 18 ft yellow lamb morphing into a banana, the work of Japanese artist Taro Chiezo. It's a weird sight, set against the background of disused 19th-century warehouses, and it's one of many modern street sculptures you'll see in the city.

The entry point to the Albert Dock at Britannia Pavilion blasts a selection of Beatles' hits at you – it's the unmissable **Beatles Story** ⓘ *T0151-7091963, www.beatlesstory.com, daily 1000-1800, £7.95, £5.45 concessions*. Walk through mocked up streets of Liverpool and Hamburg, including a fake Cavern, and check out Lennon's white 'Imagine' piano. This is the city's finest tribute to the Fab Four from beginning to end. Set in the basement vaults it's a must if you're a fan. You'll be singing harmonies all day long and you can visit the gift shop stuffed full of memorabilia if you don't fancy paying the entry fee.

Walking through the docks around the square to the right, you'll find the small TIC in the Atlantic Pavilion. On Hartley Quay the **Merseyside Maritime Museum** incorporates the **HM Customs and Excise Museum** and the **Museum of Liverpool Life** ⓘ *All museums T0151-4784499, daily 1000-1700, free*. The customs museum on the ground floor has plenty of interactive features allowing you to experience a-day-in-the-life-of a customs officer while the Museum of Liverpool Life is housed on the other side of the Canning Dock with displays about the personality of Merseyside as well as a history of the city and its workers. The real gem here is in the basement of the Merseyside Maritime Museum itself. If you don't have time to visit any other attraction in Liverpool, make sure you don't miss the deeply moving **Transatlantic Slavery Gallery**. The exhibition, opened by Maya Angelou in 1992, explores this area of history in a personal and affecting way.

Tate Liverpool ⓘ *T0151-7027400, www.tate.org.uk/liverpool, Tue-Sun 1000-1800, closed Mon except bank holidays, free with a charge for special exhibitions*, is the original Tate Modern, with four floors of modern art and regular exhibitions by major international artists including exhibitions touring from the London Tate

“” At the top of the Liver Insurance Building are the Liver Birds, one of the city's symbols. Local legend says that if they fly away, the city will cease to exist...

Modern. There's something about it that doesn't work quite so well – the building has nothing of Bankside Power Station's buzz, and the low ceilings make it feel a little flat – they do host some interesting artist talks though.

Pier Head

From the Albert Dock you can take a walk along the Mersey on the **Riverside Walk** to Pier Head. It only takes a few minutes and you'll walk past one of Liverpool's most famous buildings, the **Liver Insurance Building** (pronounced like 'driver' rather than 'river'). It was built in 1910 as one of the world's first multi-storey reinforced concrete buildings and its clock, 'The Great George', has the largest face of any of Britain's clocks. Before it was brought to Liverpool, one of them was used as a dinner table to seat 40 people. At the top of the building are the Liver Birds, one of the city's symbols. The mythical species of bird owe their creation to an ancient corporation seal of the town which originally featured an eagle. Over the centuries it began to look more like a cormorant until it became the figure it is today. Local legend says that if they fly away, the city will cease to exist.

Pier Head is along the dock past the Liver Building, the home of **Mersey Ferries** ⓘ *Heritage cruises Mon-Fri 1000-1500, Sat-Sun 1000-1800, T0151-3301444, www.merseyferries.co.uk, £3.75, concessions £2.70*. Too many people warble the old 'ferree cross the mersee' song for it really to be worth mentioning, but that's exactly what you can do from here, take a 50-minute tour of the river. Liverpool grew up as a city around this port and the opportunities that it brought the people and the area have shaped it. It's the best way to see the city from the murky Mersey and takes you through 850 years of the city's history.

Cavern Quarter

More like a tiny fraction than a quarter with its three small streets, this area has had a disproportionately huge impact on the city as a whole. It's the home of the Cavern Club where the Beatles first found fame, providing more photo opportunities than anywhere else in the city. You can slink your arm around a young bronze John Lennon on Mathew Street as he lounges against a wall covered in names. This wall of fame celebrates the bands who have rocked the Cavern since 1957 from the glass-shattering voice of Cilla Black to the more recent sneer of Oasis. **The Cavern Club** opposite is a dingy little bar and club that's still going strong, see Live music, page 658.

Nothing to do with the moptops is the intimate **View Two Gallery** ⓘ *Thu-Sat 1200-1600, free*, three floors of modern art in a townhouse on Mathew Street. It's got wooden floorboards, white space and a particularly good gallery on the third floor. A calm environment away from the blatant tourism of the street below.

The end of Stanley Street leads on to Victoria Street with some upmarket bars and restaurants which are worth visiting later on in the evening. From Mathew Street you can also traverse **Cavern Walks** to the pedestrian precinct, a small indoor shopping centre with designer shops and a couple of cafés nestled around a bronze group of Beatles.

Liverpool

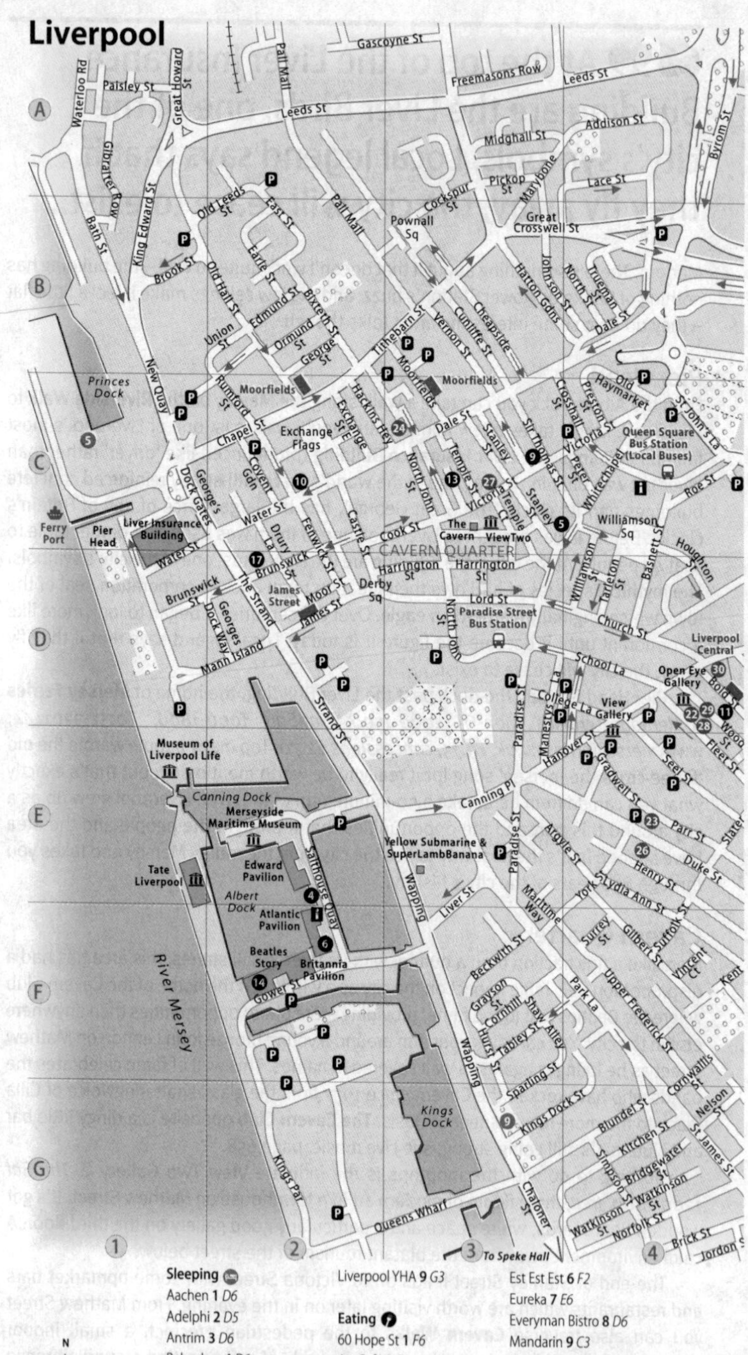

Sleeping
Aachen 1 *D6*
Adelphi 2 *D5*
Antrim 3 *D6*
Belvedere 4 *D6*
Crowne Plaza Liverpool 5 *C1*
Embassie 6 *G6*
Feathers 7 *E6*
International Inn 8 *E6*
Liverpool YHA 9 *G3*

Eating
60 Hope St 1 *F6*
Art Café 2 *E5*
Bechers Brook 3 *F6*
Blue Bar & Grill 4 *E2*
Café Eros 5 *C3*
Café Number Seven 12 *F6*
Est Est Est 6 *F2*
Eureka 7 *E6*
Everyman Bistro 8 *D6*
Mandarin 9 *C3*
Newz Brasserie 10 *C2*
Norwegian Blue 11 *D4*
Pacific Bar & Grill 13 *C3*
Pan-American Club 14 *F2*
Philharmonic 19 *E6*

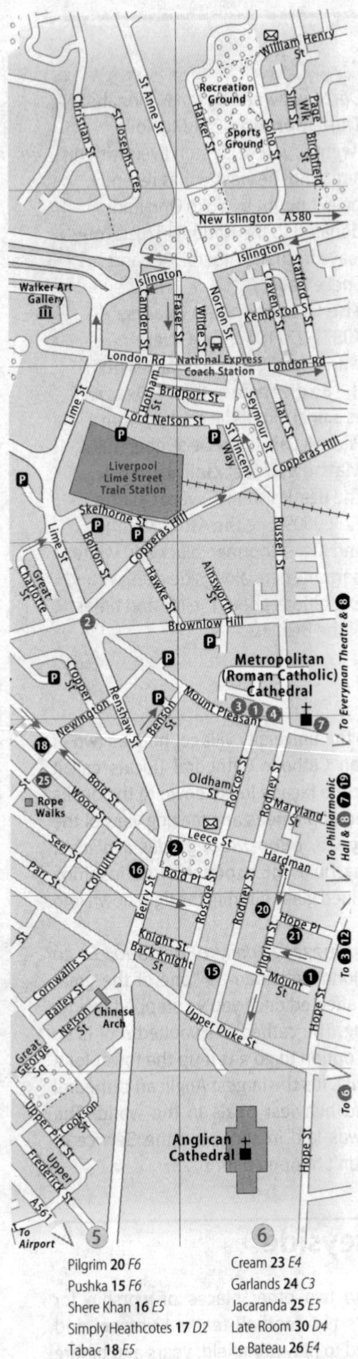

Pilgrim **20** *F6*
Pushka **15** *F6*
Shere Khan **16** *E5*
Simply Heathcotes **17** *D2*
Tabac **18** *E5*
Ye Cracke **21** *F6*

Pubs & bars
Baa Bar **22** *D4*
Cream **23** *E4*
Garlands **24** *C3*
Jacaranda **25** *E5*
Late Room **30** *D4*
Le Bateau **26** *E4*
Living Room & Mosquito **27** *C3*
Modo **28** *D4*
Revolution **29** *D4*

Walker Art Gallery

ⓘ *T0151-4784199, www.walkerartgallery.org.uk, Mon-Sat 1000-1700, Sun 1200-1700, free.* Adjacent to Liverpool Lime Street station on William Brown Street stands the grand **Walker Art Gallery**. Unlike most of Liverpool's art galleries, the Walker has a varied collection of paintings and sculptures dating from before 1950, including masterpieces by Rembrandt and a selection of impressionist paintings. There's only a small collection of modern art here, but that's pretty special too, with David Hockney hanging beside Gilbert and George. It's the city's biggest and most varied collection and one of the institutions that drove Liverpool's bid to be the European Capital of Culture in 2008.

Around Hanover Street

From the outside, the Gostins Building on Hanover Street looks like so many of those around it – a little dishevelled and ramshackle office block – but inside it's a treasure trove. The ground floor houses **The View Gallery** ⓘ *T0151-7097273, Mon-Fri 1000-1700, Sat 1200-1600, Sun closed, free*, View Two's big brother and a former furniture showroom. It's a private art gallery with quirky pieces of furniture and contemporary paintings going back far into the building. The modern paintings, predominantly by professional artists from the Northwest, are very interesting, particularly the owner's own politically slanted photo-collages. It's got all the atmosphere that the Tate Liverpool is crying out for – and you're likely to get a personal tour and a glass of wine too.

Just off Concert Square on Wood Street in the very centre of Liverpool is the **Open Eye Gallery** ⓘ *T0151-7099460, www.openeye.org.uk, Tue-Fri 1030-1730, Sat 1030-1700, closed Sun and Mon, free*. It was developed to exhibit photography, film and video and has survived being flooded, burnt out and prosecuted for obscenity to become one of the best photo and new media galleries in England.

Magical Mystery Tour

In 1960 four local Scouse lads changed the face of music forever. Hailing from Liverpool, John, Paul, George and Pete Best, soon to be replaced by Ringo Starr, spent the 60s singing about the places they'd remember all their lives, from Strawberry Fields to Penny Lane. Some places have changed and some remain the same, but here's a few of the places you can visit:

The Beatles Story, Albert Dock, T7091963. They've got the white Imagine piano on loan from George Michael in this museum, as well as a complete history of the band from Hamburg to the present day.

20 Forthlin Road, Speke, T427 7231. Paul McCartney's childhood home and the kitchen where he and Lennon wrote *Love Me Do*. Now owned by the National Trust. **Mendips**, 251 Menlove Avenue, where Lennon lived with his aunt until he was 23, has recently been bought by Yoko Ono and donated to the National Trust. Tours leave from the Albert Dock and Speke Hall.

The Cavern, Cavern Quarter, T0871-2221957. The Cavern witnessed 300 performances from the Beatles here in the 1960s as well as a final gig of the century from Paul McCartney in December 1999.

Mathew Street Gallery, above The Beatles shop, Cavern Quarter, T2360009. See the Astrid Kirchherr and Klaus Voorman black and white portraits here alongside displays and exhibitions about the life and times of the Beatles.

The cathedrals

Finally, the Hope Street area which leads up to the university village, houses two of Liverpool's landmarks. At one end, the Roman Catholic Cathedral (locals call it *Paddy's wigwam*) with its spiky crown and concrete façade looks down to the docks and at the other the tower of the Anglican cathedral provides an amazing view of the city. The **Metropolitan Cathedral** ⓘ *T0151-7099222, 0800-1800, guides available, donations encouraged*, is a distinctive building built 1962-1967 with an inspiring theatrical feel inside with Mondrian-inspired stained glass filtering the light down into the centre point.

The Anglican Cathedral ⓘ *T0151-7096271, F7027292, daily 0800-1800, £2.50 donations encouraged*, was described by Sir John Betjeman as "one of the great buildings of the world" and it's hard not to feel affected once you've stepped inside. The sheer volume of space inside is astounding. The cathedral's vaulted roof is so high that you feel swallowed up and there's an option to go 331 ft up the tower for a view of the city (*costing £2 adults, £1 concessions*). It's the largest Anglican cathedral in Europe and the bells have the highest and heaviest peals in the world. The Foundation stone for the Anglican Cathedral was laid in 1904, but the Service of Dedication and Thanksgiving for Completion didn't happen until 1978.

Around Liverpool and Merseyside

Saturdays bring another kind of pilgrimage to two other places of worship for Liverpudlians: Goodison and Anfield. The city's two **football teams** Liverpool and Everton have an interesting history. Everton used to play at Anfield, years ago before rent disputes caused them to move to another stadium, and Liverpool FC were created to play in the empty stadium they left behind.

The fans are rivals but, unusually, derby games see them standing in mixed supporters stands because they all get along. Recent years have seen Liverpool nurturing many of England's most influential players from John Barnes to Steve MacManaman and Michael Owen, while Everton lag a little behind. You can visit the Kop and the bulging trophy cabinets at **Anfield** ⓘ *Anfield Rd, 3 miles south of the city centre, T0151-2606677, www.liverpoolfc.net. The museum is open daily 1000-1700, £5, children £3. Tour and museum daily £8.50, concessions £5.50. Take a 17B, 17C, 17D or 217 bus from Queen Sq bus station.*

Speke Hall ⓘ *T0151-4277321, www.spekehall.org.uk, Tue-Sun 1100-1700, £5, child £3*, is a beautiful half-timbered Tudor mansion house dating from 1490, surrounded by a maze and some gorgeous woodland walks just eight miles to the south of the city centre. Actors dress up in Tudor gear for tours if you're after something atmospheric. Speke Hall is owned by the National Trust who more recently purchased another significant Liverpudlian property – **20 Forthlin Road** ⓘ *Allerton, Mar-Oct Wed-Sat, Nov-Dec Sat only*, the house where Paul McCartney grew up and where he and John Lennon used to practise riffs in the kitchen. It's the only original Beatles house that you can see round and can only be reached by minibus from Speke Hall or the Albert Dock.

Port Sunlight ⓘ *The Heritage Centre, on Greendale Rd, Port Sunlight, Wirral, T0151-6446466, daily 1000-1600*. A picturesque 19th-century village just outside Bebington on the Wirral Peninsula. It was originally created for the workers of Lever's soap factory by William Hesketh Lever. It's now a conservation area with landscaped gardens, primarily a tourist attraction as a 19th-century village stuck in time, all the more strange for being so close to the metropolis of Liverpool.

Sleeping

The tourist office book beds for free around Merseyside on 0845 6011125, www.visitliverpool.com.

A **Crowne Plaza Liverpool**, Princess Dock, Pier Head, T0151-2438000, F2438111. The only hotel in this price bracket, the Crowne Plaza is down on the waterfront with all that you'd expect from the chain of stylish modern hotels.

B-C **The Adelphi Hotel**, Ranelagh Pl, T0151-7097200, F7080743. This Liverpool landmark featured in a fly-on-the-wall documentary series *Hotel*. A massive Victorian hotel based on an oceanliner layout. It used to be the poshest hotel in the city, but the fame that the series brought has made it feel a little ridiculous.

D **Aachen Hotel**, 89-91 Mount Pleasant, T0151-7093633, F7091126. Recently voted the best small hotel in Liverpool. It's a small, central, friendly place with a huge all-you-can-eat breakfast.

D **Antrim Hotel**, 73 Mount Pleasant. Plenty of rooms.

D **Belvedere Hotel** at 83 Mount Pleasant, both small family-run hotels close to the city's attractions, T0151-7095239, F7097169. Is a bit smaller with only 9 rooms and is more of a guesthouse

D **Feathers Hotel**, 117-125 Mount Pleasant, T0151-7099655, F7093838. A fairly classy atmosphere and friendly service. They've got a bar and restaurant too.

E **Liverpool YHA**, Wapping, T0151-7098888, liverpool@yha.org.uk. Very close to Albert Dock this is a big purpose-built hostel with a restaurant, laundry, games room. Perfectly situated for most attractions.

F **Embassie Hostel**, 1 Falkner Sq, out of town to the south past Chinatown, T0151-7071089, www.embassie.com. It's the cheapest place to stay in Liverpool, a Georgian townhouse with relaxed and friendly atmosphere.

F **International Inn**, 4 South Hunter St off Hardman St (just off Hope St), T0151-7098135, info@internationalinn.co.uk. Set in a Victorian warehouse this place is friendly, more centrally located and very modern in design.

Around Liverpool and Merseyside

The Sefton Park area has a number of guest houses and hotels 3 miles south of the city centre towards Speke.

C **The Park Lane Hotel**, 23 Aigburth Dr, T0151-7274574, F7268091. Overlooks the park and has plenty of character with a popular Italian restaurant, see Eating. Really the nicest and most romantic place to stay in Liverpool, it's an 18th-century hotel where some rooms have 4-poster beds.

D Blenheim Lodge, 37 Aigburth Dr, T0151-7277380, F7275833. A private guesthouse which was once the house of Stu Sutcliffe, the Beatle who never was.

E Holme-Leigh B&B, 93 Woodcroft Rd, T0151-7342216/7269980. Another friendly Victorian family-run guesthouse close to Sefton Park.

E Redcroft Guest House, 12 Parkfield Rd, T0151-7273723. A good value comfortable Victorian guesthouse, very close to Sefton Park and not far from the city centre.

E Regent Maritime Hotel, 56-68 Regent Rd, Bootle, T0151-9224090, www.regentmaritimehotel.co.uk. About 2 miles away on the dock from Pier Head in Bootle. It's a very reasonable B&B/small hotel with internet facilities in each room. There are some large split-level bedrooms and a bar and restaurant.

Eating

Liverpool has food from Asia and Europe right through to traditional hotpot and cheap hangover brunches for that Sunday morning feeling. Many of the bars are cafés during the day and you'll find a trendy corner in the Ropewalks somewhere to watch the beautiful people if that's what you're after. Chinatown's Nelson St is lined with Chinese restaurants and the Albert Dock caters for tourists during the day with cheap cafés and the more selective crowd in its underground industrial vaults in the evening. The most fashionable and new restaurants are clustered around Victoria St with their minimalist interiors and soft leather armchairs and Hope St just off the Ropewalks has some exclusive places to eat too.

££ 60 Hope Street, T0151-7076060. Down the road towards the Anglican cathedral is a modern restaurant in a Georgian townhouse. It serves pancetta-wrapped kidneys and grilled sea bass upstairs and has a cheaper bistro in the same style with steak and chips and good chocolate brownies downstairs. Fairly exclusive but not snooty. Closed Sun.

££ Bechers Brook, Hope St, T0151-7070005. A classy modern restaurant, serving award-winning British cuisine like venison cutlet, beef and lobster. There's a cheaper lunch and pre-theatre menu. You'll need to make a reservation as the locals love it too. No hurdling required and no horses will be harmed in the making of meals.

££ Blue Bar and Grill in the Edward Pavilion at Albert Dock, T0151-7097097. Your best bet for spotting Liverpool FC's superstar players and maybe the odd cast member of Brookside. It's known as a footballer hang-out, a basement bar-club with a relaxed lounge atmosphere serving tapas and Portuguese food.

££ Est Est Est Another of the Italian restaurant's chain. Have dinner here and there'll be enough money left over to move to the *Blue Bar* for celeb-spotting.

££ Eureka, 7 Myrtle Pde, T0151-7097225, is a really popular place with the locals, it's a Greek restaurant that's cheap, cheerful and complete with chirpy Greek pop soundtrack.

££ Everyman Bistro under the Everyman Theatre on Hope St, T0151-7089545, is an arty option, serving French food in a contemporary restaurant.

££ Mandarin Restaurant, 73-79 and 40 Victoria St, T0151-2279011. Delicious Cantonese and Peking food – the best in Liverpool – in the centre of town.

££ Newz Brasserie, down towards Pier Head and the Albert Dock at 18 Water St, T0151-2362025. A mixture of a coffee lounge, bar and deli during the day and a delicious eaterie in the evening. The tablecloths are starched, the food is French and it's altogether a pretty glamorous affair.

££ Norwegian Blue is more central in Concert Sq, a funky modernist bar-café with interesting global cuisine to share like Tempura Shrimp and Mini Lobster Tails as well as burgers and sandwiches. The dance anthems get turned up really loud later on and then from 0230-0600 it's open as a chillout haven.

££ Pacific Bar and Grill, 11 Temple St off Victoria St, T0151-2360270. At the upper end of the price bracket on a Fri and Sat night, serves modern cuisine in dimly lit stylish surroundings with a bit of background jazz.

££ The Pan-American Club Britannia Pavilion, Albert Dock, T0151-7091156, has (Scouse accents notwithstanding) got a real New York atmosphere, fashionable with stone floor, burgers and steak-style food and dimly lit booths.

££ The Shere Khan, 17-19 Berry St, T0151-7096099, is one of the 5 Shere Khans in the Northwest and this one has a difference: the interior. The restaurant has the feel of a brasserie with a modern and contemporary design but thankfully still serves the highly-rated Indian food. Open to 0100 Fri and Sat.

££ Simply Heathcotes, 25 The Strand, Beetham Plaza (across from the Albert Dock), T0151-2363536. Serves up celebrity chef Paul Heathcote's trademark no-nonsense northwest cuisine in a select and stylish environment.

££ Tabac, 126 Bold St, T0151-7099502, is one of the city's award-winning trendy options with home-made soup and reasonably priced Sunday roasts with a twist just at the bottom of this price category.

£ Ye Cracke on Rice St near Hardman St. It's a very cheap pub with cozy snugs and value greasy-spoon meals.

£ The Philharmonic at 36 Hope St. It was built in 1900 in imitation of the gentlemen's club. There are a lot of pubs in Liverpool, but nowhere else will you find William Morris wallpaper, Art Nouveau tiling and marble urinals.

£ The Pilgrim on Pilgrim St off Hardman St is literally the cheapest place in Liverpool for Sunday brunch and a good old greasy fry-up. Relax in the Beatles-painted booths and tuck into an unhealthy brekkie.

Cafés

Art Cafe, 9-13 Berry St, just off Bold St. This amazingly cheap café exhibits local and recent Liverpool graduates contemporary artwork and does a good line in herbal teas and cheap muffins. Down-to-earth prices and a happy vibe.

Cafe Number Seven, 7 Falkner St, T0151-7099633. Just off Hope St, this is the city's best arty veggie option. It's minimalist, casual and art-studenty, serving things like home-made spicy parsnip soup and marmalade crumble cake. 0800-1900 Mon-Fri.

Café Eros, the Conservation Centre, Whitechapel, uses the feel and white space of an art gallery well, T4784994. It's good for Sunday brunch 1000-1600, and is open every day for expensive sandwiches and more reasonable tea and scones.

Pushka, 16 Rodney St, T0151-7088698, is a funky little European café serving Euro food with vegetarian options in a friendly, young atmosphere. It's just down the hill from Hope St towards the Ropeworks.

Around Liverpool and Merseyside

££ The Other Place, 141-3 Allerton Rd, T0151-7241234. It's particularly famed for its chips and serves modern British food. Staff are very friendly and it's a good place to rest your feet from the busy street. Closed Mon, lunch only Sun.

££ Park Lane Hotel, Sefton Park, 23 Aigburth St, T0151-7274754, has the fine dining Italian restaurant *D'Amicis* with a lovely view over the park. If it's raining, you can move indoors amid the Tuscan-style murals.

Pubs, bars and clubs

Liverpudlians are proud of their nightlife and concentrated in a small area you can find everything you could want from cozy pubs to sophisticated bars and trend-setting clubs. Bold Street was the original rope walk, the area providing the rope for the city's shipping trade. It's now a cosmopolitan strip, nothing remotely ropey about it, and the streets are jumping on Fri and Sat nights.

Baa Bar, 43-45 Fleet St, T0151-7070610, Liverpool's original trendy bar with some bargain drink offers and 2 floors of dancey, funky music.

Babycream, Atlantic Pavilion, Albert Dock, open 0800-0200, free. A spin-off bar-club of *Cream*, see below.

The Cavern Club 8-10 Mathew St, 0151 236 1964. Has live music most nights, see live music listings below. You'll also find a host of basement bars here, many with Beatles pictures on the walls or some other tacky connection. You won't hear much Scouse spoken in this area as these bars cater overwhelmingly for tourists.

Cream, Wolstenholme Sq, off Slater St in the centre of the Ropeworks, T0151-7091693, www.cream.co.uk, entrance fee £10-15, NUS discount. Open every Sat 2200-0400. A massive dance music venue with many spin-offs including a record label. The resident DJs are the best in the UK and it's always packed out on a Sat with clubbers looking for a good time. If you're a serious clubber, no doubt you've already been to one of Cream's paler imitations somewhere around the country.

G-bar, 1-7 Eberle St, T0151-2581230. Has a kitschy crowd: gay, straight and everything in between, all dressed up to the nines. Downstairs from *The Living Room*, at 15 Victoria St.

Garlands at 8-10 Eberle St, T0151-7078385. It's a riot of colour and attitude, a mixed gay and straight crowd dressed flamboyantly and out for a good time. It's an antidote to big warehouse clubs, broken down into smaller rooms, and the sort of place you expect to see a drag queen or two. Sat night's the night to go. £10 entry.

Jacaranda, on Slater St, T0151-7078281, is a relaxed low-key cellar bar with murals painted by Lennon and Sutcliffe. It's popular with the students and not as pretentious as most of the clubbier bars.

The Late Room, Bold St, T0151-7072333, a late night lounge bar. It's got a relaxed atmosphere and has a comedy club too.

Le Bateau, 62 Duke St, 0151 709 6508. They play underground hits, electronic, funk, and soul for an art student crowd.

Modo, 23-25 Fleet St, T0151-7098832. Attracts a mixture of young professionals and students.

Revolution, 18 Wood St, T0151-7071933, serves vodka in a million different flavours.

Entertainment

Cinema and theatre

The Everyman Theatre, 5-9 Hope St, T0151-7094776. A top venue for anything from small touring productions, classic theatre and Shakespeare to new plays, poetry and comedy.

The FACT Centre, Wood St, T0151-7092663, www.fact.co.uk. A newish addition to Liverpool's arts scene. Catering for Film and Creative Technology, the centre is a leading agency for the support and development of film, video and new media projects and is painfully cutting edge. Inside the complex there's an independent cinema, *The Picturehouse*, galleries, internet and a bar.

The Liverpool Playhouse, Williamson Sq, T0151-7094776, www.everymanplayhouse.com This is a more grown-up theatre, at the Shakespeare end and not so experimental but attracting big name actors and touring productions.

Odeon Cinema, London Rd up by Lime St Station, T08705-50007. Is your best bet, for new releases and mainstream films.

The Philharmonic Hall, Hope St, T0151-7093789, info@liverpoolphil.com. An unusual Art-Deco hall showing classic films, music and comedy. There's also a regular programme of classical music here with the Royal Philharmonic, see live music listings.

The Unity Theatre, 1 Hope Pl, T0151-7094988. An intimate space with a varied programme of dance, music and film.

Comedy clubs

From the city that gave the world Ken Dodd, Liverpool's comedy scene is surprisingly not bad at all.

Rawhide comedy club at the Albert Dock, T0151-7260077, www.rawhidecomedy.com. Hosts TV comedians and international rib ticklers. It's held on Fri and Sat nights at *Baby Blue* on Albert Dock.

The Royal Court Theatre, T0151-7094321, is another of the city's comedy venues with touring stand-ups and a variety of acts. Touring stand-ups and TV comedians can often be also found at the theatre venues as listed above.

Live music

Blundell Street, 57 Blundell St, the Albert Dock, T0151-7095779, www.blundellstreet.co.uk. A kind of lounge bar/easy listening music venue with an authentic 50s vibe, skilfully circumventing the kitsch image of the genre with small candlelit booths and a classy atmosphere. There are live acts here most nights for you to listen to while sipping cocktails, and they serve food too. Tue-Sat.

The Cavern, Mathew St, T0151-2221957. Has live music most days of varying quality with a stone floor and a slightly grotty feel. There's a lot of wannabees here and it doesn't really live up to its image as the first step on the ladder to fame.

The Picket, 24 Hardman St, T0151-7085318. Liverpool's favourite live music venue where you're most likely to catch the next big thing. They have a wide range of performers from the latest chart sensations to young breakthrough indie bands and Peruvian banjo players.

The Royal Liverpool Philharmonic, Hope St, T0151-7093789, info@ liverpoolphil.com Home to the city's orchestra, the Phil, have a regular programme of classical music and a Schumann festival in Jan and Feb each year. If you want to hear classical music, this is the best place, and it's a quirky hall with its Art Deco design.

Activities and tours

Football

You're very unlikely to be able to get tickets for either of Liverpool's premiership sides, but you can visit both stadiums and check out the trophies, stadia and see behind the scenes. See page 655. Turn up at Goodison Park for Everton on a match day and you might be lucky, T0151-3302300, www.evertonfc.com.

Horse-racing

The Grand National takes place every year on the second Sat in Apr at Aintree, a 15-min train ride from the city centre. If you're into racing but in Liverpool at the wrong time, the racecourse has a Grand National simulator and racecourse tours too. Ormskirk Rd, T0151-5232600 for grand national, T0151-5222929 for Aintree racecourse in general, T0151-5222921 for the **Grand National Experience**, £7, £4 concessions.

Tours

Magical Mystery Tours run 2-hr trips in vintage buses showing where the Fab Four grew up with landmarks including John Lennon's childhood home on Penny Lane and Strawberry Fields before finishing at the Cavern. Daily tours from the Albert Dock at 1400 and 1500 and Queen Sq outside the TIC at 1340 and 1440, T0151-2369091, F2368081, £10.95.

Liverpool Ducks, T0151-7087799, enquiries@liverpoolducks.co.uk. Odd yellow vehicles taking you from Atlantic Pavilion in the Albert Dock around the city's waterfront, city and dock areas. It's not the yellow submarine, but it's not far off. . Tickets cost £9.95 for adults, £7.95 concessions, for which you get an hr long land and sea tour. Tours run mid Feb-Christmas daily 1030-1800, approximately every hr.

Festivals

Aug **Creamfields**. The dance music festivalis hosted by Cream every year on the Aug Bank Holiday weekend and is regularly voted the best dance event in the UK. T0151-7091693, www.cream.co.uk; tickets cost around £45 and sell out fast.

Aug **International Beatle Week** runs from 22-27 Aug and is the biggest celebration of Beatles music in the world, with numerous sound- and look-alike bands, T0871-2221963. It incorporates the **Mathew St Festival**, a free music festival with over 200 bands playing from 24-26 Aug.

Shopping

Shopping in Liverpool is not as varied or interesting as Leeds or Manchester as it's dominated by high street stores, but there are a few little places where you can find something unique, and that doesn't just mean Beatles memorabilia.

The Beatles Shop, 31 Mathew St, T0151-2368066, www.thebeatleshop@ aol.com. Has the largest selection of Beatles stuff in the world next to rare records and a jukebox.

Bluecoat Arts Centre, just off the Ropewalks on School La, T0151-7075297. Good for picking up contemporary crafts and design.

Cavern Walks, on Mathew St has a number of small clothes shops selling designer and clubby gear.

Transport

Bus

National Express, T08705-808080, have regular services to major towns and cities in Britain from the Norton St Coach Station. **London Victoria** 12 times daily (5 hrs), **Birmingham** 12 times daily (3 hrs), **Manchester** 19 times daily (1 hrs 30 mins), **Blackpool** 8 times daily (1 hr 45 mins), **Edinburgh** 7 times daily (8 hrs).

Car

Skydrive UK, South Terminal Lennon Airport, T0151-4480000, F4481044; **Avis**, 113 Mulberry St, T0151-7094737; **Easycar**, NCP car park Paradise St, www.easycar.com.

Taxis

Mersey Cabs, T0151-2982222, T2072222 or the ranks up by Lime St station, on Whitechapel or Clayton Sq.

Train

From Liverpool Lime St you can reach most major UK destinations, including **Manchester**, (1 hr), **Birmingham** (1 hr 30 mins) and **London Euston**, (3-4 hrs), on Virgin trains, www.virgintrains.com National Rail Enquiries, T08457-484950.

Directory

Internet STA Travel, £2 per hr, Bold St, 0930-1730 Mon-Fri, 1000-1730 Thu, 1100-1700 Sat shut Sun; **Planet Electra Internet Cafe**, £3 per hr students, £4 per hr non-students, London Rd, T7080303. **Post offices** The Lyceum, Bold St and 23-33 Whitechapel. **Hospitals** Royal Liverpool University Hospital, Prescot St, T0151-7062000. **Chemists** Moss Chemists, 68-70 London Rd. **Police** just off Clayton Sq on Church St, T0151-7096010.

Lancashire

→ *Colour map 6, grid B2-3*

Lancashire is a diverse mix of the constituent parts of the North of England. To the north, the county borders Cumbria with stunning views, lakes, mountains and moors; in the south, Manchester spreads into the dark mill towns of Preston, Blackburn and Burnley. The county town of Lancaster in the northwest is historic and beautiful with wide cobbled streets and country pubs. The working castle in the town is the final destination of the Pendle Witch Tour, tracing the steps of 10 witches from the eastern part of the county who were condemned to hang during the 17th century. This eastern part of the country borders Yorkshire where the Lancashire forests meet the dales.

Lancashire in general is not well-visited by tourists. The southernmost towns are not geared up for mass tourism but the northern and eastern countryside is great walking country and you'll receive a warm Lancastrian welcome in the small stone villages. There is, however, one spot in the county that gets more than its fair share of attention: the Las Vegas of the North, Blackpool. It's a traditional seaside resort that has got out of hand with its largest rollercoaster in Europe and its Golden Mile of arcades and flashing lights. If Elvis had ever performed in England, it's unlikely that he would have held court in the ballroom here amid the kiss-me-quick hats, but then there are more than enough Elvis impersonators on each of the three piers to make up for that. ▸▸ *For Sleeping, Eating and other listings, see pages 666-669.*

Ins and outs

Getting around The best and easiest way of exploring the region, particularly the charming country villages, is by **car**. Local **buses** run in Lancashire but are not always as frequent or regular as necessary. **Train** services between major towns in Lancashire, however, are very regular every day except Sun and coach connections from Liverpool and Manchester to Blackpool are reliable, going every hour or more frequently. Manchester and Liverpool are the main coach, bus and air transport hubs in the Northwest, including Lancashire. ▸▸ *See Transport, page 668, for more details.*

Blackpool

In reality, Blackpool is better described as the Bognor Regis of the North than the Vegas of the North. The town has got the biggest glitterball in the world, weighing 4.5 tonnes and a host of claims to fame including the Pleasure Beach, a huge park with amusement arcades and rollercoasters. The Blackpool Illuminations run from 30 August to 3 November, a swathe of neon lights along the promenade overlooking the seven miles of yellow sand, lighting up the many chip shops, gypsy fortune tellers and candy floss stalls along the Golden Mile. Tacky, bold, brash and particularly nasty on a hot summer bank holiday Monday, you can still have a good time here if you like rollercoasters and don't mind paying over the odds for the tourist attractions.

Ins and outs

Getting there The station is walking distance from the centre of town on Talbot Road and has links with Scotland on **Virgin Trains,** T08457-222333, www.virgin.com/trains, with the northeast of England on the **Transpennine Express,** and with Preston and Manchester with **First North Western** trains. Blackpool is easily reached by **car** from Manchester on the M61, M6 and M55, Leeds on the M62, M6 and M55 and the rest of Lancashire on the M6 and M55. **National Express,** T08705-808080, run regular coach services from Manchester and Liverpool. The coach stop is on Lonsdale Rd in summer and Talbot Rd during the winter season.

Information Blackpool TIC ⓘ *1 Clifton St near the North Pier, T01253-478222, tic@blackpool.gov.uk, www.blackpool.gov.uk, www.blackpooltourism.co.uk, Mon-Fri 0900-1700.* They can book accommodation and tickets into the main tourist attractions are discounted here. There is also a smaller TIC on the promenade between the North and Central Piers ⓘ *Mon-Fri 0915-1700, Sun 1015-1530.* They can also book accommodation and offer discounted entry to the attractions.

Safety Blackpool is perennially busy with groups of young people thronging the promenade. Pickpockets are a problem in the town, particularly in the summer, and you should ensure that parked cars are locked with no valuables on display as break-ins are frequent. The beach is popular in the summer too and you should always take care in the water with regard to tides. In a coastal emergency call 999 and ask for the coastguard.

Sights

The 518 ft of **Blackpool Tower** ⓘ *Bank Hey St, T01253-292029, www.theblackpool tower.co.uk, daily until Nov 3, 1000-2300, £11.50, child £7.50, £8.50 adults and children after 1900*, contains a family-orientated circus, souvenir stalls and the Tower Ballroom. It might well be one of Blackpool's most famous features but it's a very pricey trip up to the top to look over the sand and grey sea. **The Pleasure Beach** ⓘ *Ocean Boulevard, T0870-444558, www.blackpoolpleasurebeach.co.uk, weekends only Jan-Mar 2, daily from 23 Mar-Nov 3, times subject to change, 1-day wristband costs £26, individual rides £1-5*,is the real attraction in Blackpool with huge rollercoasters overlooking the sea and the southernmost end of the town. Admission into the park is free and you can either pay per ride or per day. The **Big One** is Europe's tallest and fastest rollercoaster at 235 ft high and 87 mph, a massive structure that is closed on windy days. There are lots of other white-knuckle rides as well as arcades, candy floss stalls, cafés and tacky musical shows. **Blackpool Sandcastle** ⓘ *South Promenade, T01253-343602, www.black pool-sandcastle.co.uk, daily 0900-1730* , is for a family day

According to Bill Bryson (Notes from a Small Island), Blackpool consumes more chips per capita than anywhere else on the planet.

out, a swimming pool complex with twisting wild water rides, chutes, saunas and sun loungers. Altogether much healthier than paddling or swimming in the sea.

You cannot consider yourself a true English seaside town unless you've got at least one **pier**. Blackpool, true to form, has gone over the top and has three. When they were first built in the 19th century there were only two, the North and the South, now there is also the Central Pier. The North was considered more prestigious and the working classes generally frequented the South. There isn't much to pick between them all now, except that you have to pay 25p to visit the North Pier, which has a short tram ride on it to take you to the end. All three piers are garish and have more arcades and stalls than is strictly necessary; the Central Pier also has a big wheel and other rides amid the Blackpool rock stalls. Alongside the promenade it is possible to take pony and trap rides along the **Golden Mile**. Unlike other tourist resorts that view the end of August as the end of the season, Blackpool takes it as a cue to begin enticing visitors back to the town. The Illuminations, famed in 1879 for being like "artificial sunshine" and now for being an immense gaudy display of neon and plastic, are switched on at the end of August and carry on until the beginning of November. Just outside Blackpool, the **Zoo** ⓘ *East Park Dr, T01253-830830, www.blackpoolzoo.org.uk, daily 1000-1630. £7.95, child £5.75, free bus 21 from outside the Tower goes to the zoo and it can easily be reached by car just 2 miles from the seafront*, was recently voted one of the UK's top five zoos and has a particular speciality in the Gorilla Mountain as well as over 400 animals in captivity here including dolphins, orang-utans and elephants. It's fairly spacious as British zoos go.

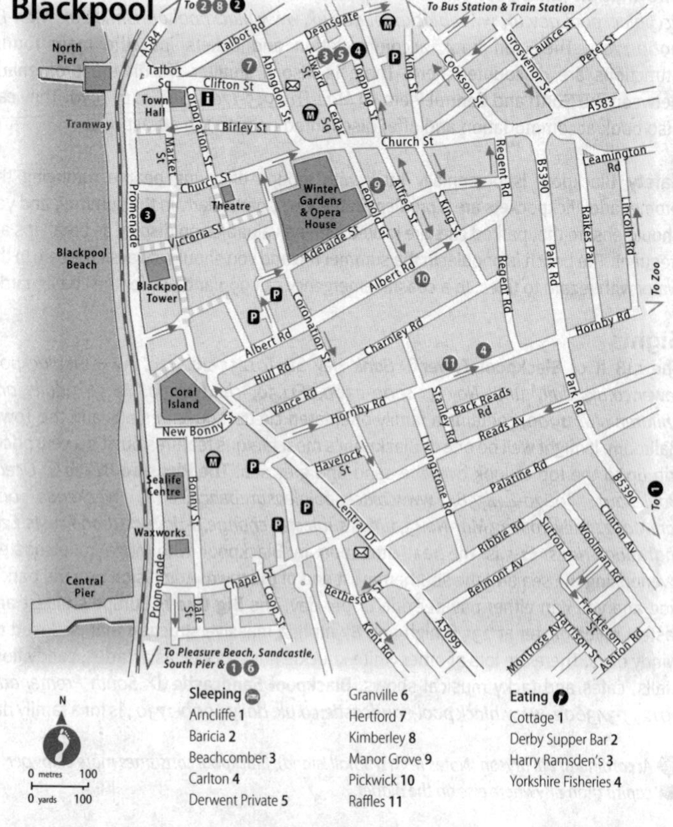

Lancaster

Lancaster is the historic county town of Lancashire and was recently granted city status. The main feature of the town is its Norman castle, used today as a court and prison. It has held some notorious inmates in its time including the Pendle witches and the Birmingham Six. The town centre is compact and charming with wide cobbled streets and cosy traditional pubs. All in all the city is a pleasant place to stop on the way to or from the Lakes, just south of the Cumbrian border.

Ins and outs

Information Guided walks ⓘ *leave from the castle gates at 1930 on Thu evenings in Aug and Sep, T01524-792089, www.catwalks-lancaster.co.uk, £3, 50p children*, around Lancaster telling of ghosts and murderers, pubs, the Pendle witch trail and the town's history. **Lancaster TIC** ⓘ *29 Castle Hill, T01524-32878, www.lancaster.gov.uk, 1000-1700 daily*. The TIC has further information on other walks around the city through the year including Halloween walks and torchlit Old Calendar walks and can book accommodation.

Sights

Lancaster Castle ⓘ *Lancaster Castle, Castle Hill, T01524-64998, F847914, daily mid Mar-Dec 1000-1700, guided tours leave half hourly from 1030-1600, £4, £2.50 concessions, entrance through the back of the castle, not through the imposing John of Gaunt gate, the main entrance for the prison*, is the dominant building in Lancaster and has been since it was built in 1093. The hill on which it stands was used as a fort by the Romans around AD 79 and in 1093 a Norman baron, Roger of Poitou, built a motte and bailey castle here. Fifty years later that was replaced by a stone keep, some of which survives today. The castle is currently a fully working castle that you cannot walk round independently. There are around 250 inmates detained in the prison and the courthouse is still in regular use. Tours of the castle, an hour-long trail around the courts, the oldest parts of the castle, the old cells and hanging corner are well worth taking.

Lancaster Priory ⓘ *Lancaster Priory, Castle Hill, T01524-65338, www.priory.lancaster.ac.uk, daily 1000-1630*, is adjacent to the castle and was originally a Benedictine priory in 1094. It is now a parish church and contains carved stones and crosses from the 9th-11th centuries. There is a refectory inside the church serving teas and coffees. To the rear of the church on the hill are the remains of the old Roman baths.

In the centre of town and originally home to one of the witch hunters, Thomas Covell, the **Judges' Lodgings** ⓘ *Judges' Lodgings, Church St, T01524-32808, www.bringinghistoryalive.co.uk, free*, is a beautiful Grade I listed Georgian building. It has also been home to the chief jailor and afterwards became the residence of judges visiting the Assize courts. Inside the house is a Museum of Childhood with dolls, toys and games from the 18th century, a large collection of Lancaster's delicate Gillow furniture and a portrait collection depicting the town's connections with the slave trade.

In the former customs house of Lancaster, the **Lancaster Maritime Museum** ⓘ *Lancaster Maritime Museum, Custom House, St George's Quay, T01524-64637, F841692, daily Easter-Oct 1100-1700, Nov-Easter 1230-1600*, explores the history of Lancaster as a port, the Lancaster canal, fishing and the nearby Morecambe Bay. The exhibitions are brought alive with audio-visual stimuli, smells, sounds and reconstructions and provide an interesting history of the city's development.

Outside Lancaster

Overlooking the city to the south, the commanding Ashton Memorial Folly **Williamson Park** ⓘ *Williamson Park off Wyresdale Rd, T01524-33318, www.williamsonpark.com, daily all year long with theatre and special events throughout the year, free, signposted from junctions 33 and 34 of the M6 and from the city centre*, is visible from some distance. The ornate Victorian dome was commissioned by Lord Ashton, who made his fortune producing oilcloth and linoleum, as a tribute to his late wife. The 54-acre park itself is full of woodland walkways, terraced paths and water fountains.

Carnforth Station ⓘ *Carnforth Station and Railway Trust, Carnforth Station, T01524-732805, carnforth.station@virgin.net*, to the north of Lancaster on the M6 and A6 has found a special place in English romantic mythology. It was originally an important junction linking the London-Glasgow and Carnforth-Leeds railway but is more commonly known as the film set for David Lean's film *Brief Encounter* starring Celia Johnson and Trevor Howard. There is a trail around the station so you can follow the camera positions. The station has undergone extensive renovation after falling into disuse and you can now use it to reach stations in the Lakes and Lancaster as well as a location to conduct brief affairs yourself. There is also a history centre opening here in late 2003, a collection of advertising posters from 1845-1945 and a tribute to David Lean.

The Ribble Valley

The east of Lancashire is an undiscovered gem with wonderful walking trails around the Forest of Bowland, charming stone cottages and country pubs. With more of the feel of rural Yorkshire, it all seems a lot further away from the old industrial towns of south Lancashire than it really is. Pendle Hill dominates the area with the town of Clitheroe and its 12th-century castle. The area is well known in the county as the home of the Pendle Witches, hung in 1612 at Lancaster Castle. From Clitheroe you can follow their path around the district. Alongside the River Ribble around Clitheroe you can also follow geology and sculpture trails in the open countryside. The Forest of Bowland is another beautiful area with many walking and cycle trails.

Ins and outs

Getting there The town of Clitheroe is 7 miles north of Blackburn on the A666/A59. There is a **train** station in Clitheroe with a regular service to Blackburn and Manchester every day but Sun. Local **buses** run to the town from Preston, Bury, Skipton in Yorkshire and Manchester. By far the most convenient way to explore this area of Lancashire is by car, which allows you to reach the more out-of-the-way spots. » *See Transport, page 669, for more details.*

Information The **main TIC** is in Clitheroe ⓘ *14 Market Pl, T01200-425566, Mon-Sat 0900-1700*.

Clitheroe

Clitheroe is a small country town presided over by a 12th-century **Norman castle** with an unusual hole in the wall of its keep. The town has an array of pubs and a few places to stay as well as a charming arts and crafts gallery in a refurbished railway building.

Climb up the steep and winding path around the formal garden and you will reach the castle keep of **Clitheroe Castle** ⓘ *Daily until 2200, free*. It was built in 1186 by Robert De Lacy to protect his estate and is made of limestone and sandstone. There's a great view of Pendle Hill from 35 m above the limestone bed as well as the surrounding rural area.

Housed in one of the Georgian stone buildings in the courtyard behind the castle, the **castle museum** ⓘ *T0120-0424635, www.ribblevalley.co.uk, Easter-Oct daily 1100-1630, Nov-mid Dec Sat-Sun 1100-1630, closed Jan, weekends only Feb, Mar-Easter Sat-Wed 1100-1630*, has displays on local history, including the Pendle witches, geology and a sound system to provide an authentic experience of life in an Edwardian kitchen. Upstairs is a reconstructed 18th-century lead mine with whistling and coughing miners to keep you company.

Modern arts and crafts are on display at the **Platform Gallery** ⓘ *Station Rd, Clitheroe, T0120-443071, platform.gallery@ribblevalley.gov.uk, Mon-Sat 1000-1630, free*, in a refurbished railway building next door to the train station. The changing exhibitions feature ceramics, sculpture, design, paintings and felt work in an intimate quirky space. The contemporary crafts are mainly produced by local artists based in the Northwest.

Forest of Bowland

Just 8 miles from Clitheroe, the **Bowland Wild Boar Park** ⓘ *Bowland Wild Boar Park, Chipping, Preston, T01995-61554, www.wildboarpark.co.uk, Easter-end Oct daily 1030-1730, weekends 1030-1730 at all other times. 2 miles from Chipping village on the Chipping to Dunsop Bridge road in the Forest of Bowland*, is 65 acres of woodland with wild boars, longhorn cows and deer roaming freely. In the spring you can hand-feed the lambs and it's a great area for picnics.

The farm sells wild boar meat, pork and dry cured bacon, so don't get too friendly with the inhabitants.

Walking trails around Clitheroe

Pendle Witches Trail The TIC in Clitheroe sells guides to the Pendle Witches Trail around the area. It is a 45-mile route that traces the path taken by the 10 convicted witches from the Pendle area to their final destination at Lancaster Castle. Begin at **Pendle Heritage Centre**, Park Hill, Barrowford, Nelson, T01282-661701. It's a 17th-century hall with a video about the witches which will start you off. The trail continues via a number of small country towns and Clitheroe to Lancaster Castle, contact TIC for further details.

Geology trail Salthill Quarry near to Clitheroe has provided the town with limestone for the last 300 years and was reclaimed in 1980 as a geology trail. The limestone rocks here date back to 300 million years ago when Britain lay at the equator. The route along the trail is punctuated with signboards telling you about the rocks and the creatures that lived in the basin like corals and sponges. The trail starts and ends at the Salthill industrial estate just off Lincoln Way just on the edge of Clitheroe town and has well-marked footpaths throughout.

Ribble Valley Sculpture Trail Brungerley Park just outside Clitheroe on the B6478 towards Waddington takes you across a part of the Ribble Way from Brungerley Bridge to Crosshill Quarry following sculptures based around the natural environment. The entrance is marked from the road and the artists have made the most of natural features like hollow tree trunks and fungus to create an interesting trail.

The Ribble Way The Ribble Way is a 70-mile long path along the River Ribble from its source to the estuary. You can pick up the trail at various locations and it takes you through limestone gorges, marshland and moorland. The best map to take for the area is the OS Explorer OSL41 Forest of Bowland and Ribblesdale and further information about the path can be found at the Clitheroe TIC.

The Pendle Witches

In 1612 under the reign of Protestant King James I, the greatest number of witches ever caught were found in the Pendle area and hung at Lancaster Castle. James was obsessed with witchcraft and the Catholic area of Lancashire was seen as a hotbed for this kind of heresy.

The Pendle witchcraft trials centred on two peasant families headed by two old crones, Demdike and Chattox. They were believed to have magic powers, and their daughters and sons likewise, using them to do harm and to consort with the devil. Many locals testified to their evil-doings and, most remarkably of all, the witches confessed to their crimes unlike in other trials of the time. One of the witches, the wonderfully named Alice Nutter, was convicted on the evidence of a nine-year-old child. Her grave is in nearby Newchurch where the graveyard has an eye of God in it to prevent her evil harming others.

Witchcraft was also practised in this time in a healing capacity and local people were paranoid about the existence of witches. Growing bluebells in your garden was said to be a sign of witchcraft, as witches used the flowers to lure fairies to their houses so that they could pick their brains.

Today, the only remaining evidence about the Pendle witches is the transcript of the court proceedings and many stories have been created in the region to fill in the missing background.

Sleeping

Blackpool *p661*
There are no 5-star hotels in Blackpool and although there are an enormous number of bed and breakfasts in the town, the majority conform to the stereotype of grotty rooms, greasy breakfasts and over-bearing landladies. Beware also of stag nights and hen parties in your guesthouse or hotel. These are the best of the rest.

C **Carlton Hotel**, 107 Hornby Rd, T01253-621347. Small well-kept 3-star hotel in central Blackpool, with en suite bathrooms and a seaside atmosphere. Pets welcome.

D **The Derwent Private Hotel**, 42 Palatine Rd, T01253-620004. 11-bedroomed small family hotel with en suite bathrooms and welcoming friendly hosts. Dinner is available for £7 as well as B&B.

D **The Granville Hotel**, 12 Station Rd, T01253-343012. Pleasant small hotel catering particularly for families and groups with en suite bathrooms, a licensed bar and home-cooked meals.

D **Hertford Hotel**, 18 Lord St, T01253-292931. Small friendly hotel close to the centre of town and the main attractions.

D **The Kimberley**, 25 Gynn St, T01253-352264. Comfortable frilly B&B with en suite bathrooms and no stag or hen parties in a slightly quieter part of town.

D-E **Baricia Hotel**, 40-2 Egerton Rd, T01253-623130. Family-run small B&B hotel close to the station. Cosy rooms, en suite bathrooms also available.

D-E **Beachcomber Hotel**, 78 Reads Av, T01253-621622, beachcomber@euphony.net. Family guesthouse with small rooms, a restaurant and car park.

D-E **Manor Grove Hotel**, 24 Leopold Grove, T01253-625577. Friendly hotel/guesthouse with cosy rooms, standard B&B and an evening meal if required.

E **Pickwick Hotel**, 93 Albert Rd, T01253-624229. Fun, family hotel with a large bar, pool table and darts. Close to the centre of town and popular with groups.

E **Raffles Hotel**, 73-5 Hornby Rd, T01253-294713, raffleshotelblackpool.co.uk. Smart very English hotel with full English breakfast, top service and as much elegance as you can find in Blackpool. Friendly and pleasant.

F Arncliffe Hotel, 24 Osborne Rd, South Shore, T01253-345209, arncliffe.hotel@virgin.net. Small, licensed family-run hotel catering for families and couples and no, repeat no, stag or hen parties. Small cosy rooms and B&B, discounted tickets for Blackpool's attractions also on sale here.

Lancaster *p663*

Lancaster is a great place to base yourself if you are touring the Northwest or for a stop on the way to the Lake District.

B Royal Kings Arms, Market St, T01524-32451, F841698, www.menzies-hotels.co.uk. A 3-star period hotel on one of Lancaster's wide cobbled streets, the King's Arms is modern, relaxed and welcoming. Charles Dickens stayed here in 1854 and 1862 and although much of the interior has been modernized, the stained-glass windows and features like the Minstrel's Gallery remain.

D The Farmer's Arms Hotel, Penny St, T01524-36368, farmersarmslancaster@btinternet.com. Small family-run hotel priding itself on creating a comfortable, relaxed Northern atmosphere.

D Greenbank Farmhouse, Abbeystead, T/F01524-792063, www.greenbankfarmhouse.co.uk. Stone farmhouse just outside Lancaster in the rolling countryside, 15 mins from the city centre at junction 3 of the M6. Well-kept grounds, good location for walking and fishing and a wonderful personal touch.

D Railton Hotel, 2 Station Rd, T01524-388364, F388364. Reasonably priced B&B close to the station with basic facilities and en suite rooms.

D Shakespeare Hotel, 96 St Leonardgate, T01524-841041. Popular and award-winning bed and breakfast on the outskirts of town with top-class service.

E Castle Hill House, 27 St Mary's Pde, Castle Hill, T01524-849137, gsutclif@aol.com.uk. Terraced Victorian B&B in the centre of Lancaster beside the castle with quiet and comfortable rooms.

Ribble Valley *p664*

A-C Mitton Hall Country House Hotel, Mitton Rd, Whalley, near Clitheroe, T01254-826544, www.mittonhall.com. Grand and beautiful old country house with historic interior, large fireplace, lovingly decorated with antlers, and antique furniture. There are 4-poster beds for the ultimate in romance and luxury; golfing, fishing and executive breaks also catered for.

C Hotel Don Dino, 78-82 Whalley Rd, Clitheroe, T01200-424450. Not the mafia hang-out its name would suggest, a hotel attached to the local Italian restaurant with clean, modern rooms, full English breakfast, all en suite.

C Old Post House Hotel, 44-8 King St, Clitheroe, T01200-422025, www.posthousehotel.co.uk. Family-run townhouse in the centre of Clitheroe town with cosy and charming décor and friendly service. Recommended.

D Brooklands, 9 Pendle Rd, Clitheroe, T/F01200-422797, kenandjean@tesco.net. Warm homely 3-bedroomed Victorian B&B on the outskirts of Clitheroe near to the train station. Rooms are large, comfortable and en suite.

D The Brown Leaves Country Hotel, Longsight Rd, Copster Green, Blackburn, T01524-249523. Just outside the town of Clitheroe, a small award-winning hotel combining rustic charm and modern convenience. Landscaped gardens and great views of the Ribble Valley countryside, well-kept and professional.

D Lower Standen Farm, Whalley Rd, Clitheroe, T01200-424176. 16th-century farmhouse a mile from the town centre with warm and personal service. Good if you're planning on lots of walking in the area. All rooms en suite.

D Petre Lodge, Northcote Rd, Langho near Clitheroe, T01254-245506, www.petrelodge.co.uk. Large stone cottage-style hotel on the edge of the Ribble Valley a short drive from Clitheroe. B&B with the option of evening meals, quality service and upmarket decor.

For an explanation of the sleeping and eating price codes used in this guide, see the inside front cover. Other relevant information is provided in the Essentials chapter, page 40.

D **Station Hotel**, King St, Clitheroe, T01200-443205. Standard B&B above a stone pub in the centre of Clitheroe, home-made bar meals and evening meal by arrangement.

Eating

Blackpool *p661*

If you're looking for gourmet dinners and elegant restaurants, you took a wrong turning somewhere.

Fish and chip shops

There is very little difference between the shops below apart from Harry Ramsden's, the fish and chip shop chain offering a proper sit down meal and a hiked-up price for the privilege. For all others you should be able to eat for around £5 a head.

£ **The Cottage**, 31 Newhouse Rd, T01253-694010.

£ **Derby Supper Bar**, 273 Dickson Rd, T01253-625312.

£ **Fish Inn**, Balmoral Rd, T01253-341033.

£ **Gynn Supper Bar**, 301 Dickinson Rd, T01253-354130.

£ **Harry Ramsden's**, 60 Promenade, T393529.

£ **Seniors**, 106 Normoss Rd, T01253-393529.

£ **Yorkshire Fisheries**, 16 Topping St, T01253-627739.

Lancaster*p663*

Lancaster is a university town and has a number of pubs, snack bars and fast food placesto eat out.

£££ **The Castle Restaurant**, *Royal Kings Arms Hotel*, Market St. Large wine list, good service and traditional English food served in this historic hotel overlooked by a minstrel's gallery. The best place to eat out in Lancaster.

££ **Pizza Margherita**, 2 Moor La, T01524-36333, is a large, airy and bright Italian restaurant operating as a café, bar and restaurant. It's the classiest of the Italian restaurants in the town.

£ **The Old John O'Gaunt** at 53 Market St Particularly recommended is this quaint and charming pubwith stained-glass windows, snugs, stuffed birds and pictures of jazz legends on the walls. They serve traditional pub food and real ale and boast of having *strange staff*. You'll have to find out what that means yourself.

£ **The Sun**, Church St, is another traditional pub serving home-cooked food in a warm and cosy atmosphere.

Ribble Valley *p664*

££ **Browns Bistro**, 10 York St, Clitheroe, T01200-426928. Romantic, intimate French restaurant with an intimate atmosphere on the edge of Clitheroe. Open for evening meals through the week and lunch on Fri, closed on Sun.

££ **Hotel Don Dino**, 78-82 Whalley Rd, Clitheroe, T01200-424450. High class Italian food served in a warm and friendly environment showing fans of identikit chains what they're missing out on.

££ **Penny Black Restaurant**, 44-48 King St, Clitheroe, T01200-422025. Traditional English restaurant and coffee house serving lunches 1200-1400 and evening meals 1900-2100. Ideal for a roast on a Sun in a relaxed, upmarket atmosphere or pan-fried lamb, grilled gammon and other meat dishes during the week.

£ **The Apricot Meringue**, 15 King St, Clitheroe, T01200-426933. Elegant teashop just off the high street serving high tea, home-made cakes and vegetarian dishes.

£ **Bashall Barn**, Bashall Town, Clitheroe, T01200-428964. On the road out of Clitheroe towards Bashall, this dairy barn has been converted into a café, craft workshop and walking centre serving home-cooked snacks out in the country. A cheerful place for a stop while you're walking in the area and a good rain shelter.

£ **Halfpenny's of Clitheroe**, Old Toll House, 1-5 Parson La, Clitheroe, T01200-424478. Listed building housing a traditional English teashop serving sandwiches, roasts, cream teas and pastries. Welcoming and homely.

Transport

Lancaster*p663*

Bus

By bus there are twice-hourly services to **Preston** (1 hr 10 mins), **Blackpool** (1 hr 15 mins) and **Kendal** (1 hr 20 mins), **Windermere** (1 hr 30 mins) and **Keswick** (2 hrs 30 mins) in the Lake District.

Train
From Lancaster there are regular train services to **Preston** (25 mins) where you can change to get to **Liverpool** (1 hr), **Manchester** (45 mins) and **London** (2 hrs 40 mins). You can also reach **Carnforth** (10 mins) by rail.

Ribble Valley *p664*
From Clitheroe it is easy to reach the Yorkshire Dales by road and towns to the south of Lancashire.

Bicycle
The Ribble Valley area has a number of cycle trails through the countryside. The only cycle hire in the area is at Pedal Power, Waddington Rd, Clitheroe, T01200-422066. Mon-Fri 0900-1730, Sat 0900-1630, closed Sun. They can advise on nearby cycle routes through the Forest of Bowland and the Ribble Valley.

Bus
Local buses run to **Accrington** (35 mins), **Manchester** (1 hr 25 mins), **Blackburn** (35 mins), **Bolton** (1 hr 15 mins) and **Preston** (35 mins). For further information about rail and bus services in the region, T01200-429832.

Train
There are regular trains to **Blackburn** (20 mins), **Blackpool** (1 hr 15 mins) and **Manchester** (1 hr 15 mins).

Directory

Blackpool *p661*
Banks Birley St, Corporation St and Victoria St have branches of all the high street banks. **Medical facilities** **Victoria Hospital**, Whinney Heys Rd, T01253-300000. **Late Night Chemist**: **Lloyds Pharmacy**, Talbot Rd, open until 2100, T01253-627932. **Police** Bonny St, turn left opposite the central pier, T01253-293933. **Post office** Abingdon St.

The Isle of Man

→ *Colour map 7*

The Isle of Man is a place of its own in many different ways. It's a self-governing kingdom, an island a mere 33 miles long and 13 miles wide, 60 miles off the Lancashire coast in the Irish Sea. It's classified as a 'crown dependency', neither belonging to the UK nor the EU, with its own parliament, laws, traditions, stamps, currency and language. Everyone in the country speaks English, however, and English money is accepted.

But, like the Bee Gees who hail from this part of the world, the island is often unfairly stereotyped and ridiculed when it should be celebrated for retaining its eccentricity. Perhaps the island is stuck behind in the fifties, a haven for tax dogers, while the rest of the UK is hip, modern and trail-blazing. Perhaps the kudos of being the venue for the world's most prestigious motorcycle race is somewhat marred by the fact that it also holds the World Tin Bath Championships. But forget all the criticisms and accolades for a moment and take the time to look at the scenery. There are grouse moors and mountains, wide romantic beaches and leafy woodland dells, ruined castles and an ancient stone circle. The scenery is a microcosm of the British Isles and glorious sunsets in Port Erin and Peel emphasize this natural isolation. ▸▸ *For Sleeping, Eating and other listings, see pages 674-.*

History
The Isle of Man has been inhabited by hunter-gatherers from 8000-4500 BC and has a rich and varied political and cultural history. In slightly more recent times the Celts lived here, an era of myths and legends backed up by archaeological evidence found on St Patrick's Isle in Peel and a number of beautiful carved stone crosses. The Isle of Man was never ruled by the Romans or the Anglo-Saxons around this time and was Christianized during the 5th and 6th centuries by Irish monks. Around the year 800, the Norwegian Vikings appeared and settled on the island, a good base for raiding

and trading around the Irish Sea. The Kingdom of the Sudreys was established in the 970s, consisting of the Isle of Man and the Western Isles of Scotland, ruled over by the Tynwald, the Viking age parliament established on the Isle of Man which still exists today and is the oldest continuous national parliament in the world.

The Kingdom of the Sudreys was under threat from the Scots and finally dissolved in 1265 with the death of Norse King Magnus III in Castletown. The Scots ruled the island briefly at this point until 1290 when England took over. Between 1290 and 1333 it came under English and Scots rule alternately until finally the battle between the two powers at Hallidon Hill resolved the issue: the Isle of Man was to be kept under the sovereignty of the English Crown and ruled by English noblemen.

Tourism became popular in the 19th century and reached a peak in 1899 attracting a combination of working class people from Scotland and the North of England as well as the wealthier classes. In the next few years the advent of the motor car and motor car racing on the Isle of Man began to bring even more enthusiasts over as the sport was less regulated on the island than on the stricter mainland. The Isle of Man did not escape the Depression in the 1930s, and the country's lead, copper and zinc mines were abandoned. With the Second World War, the island was again involved in war as a prisoner of war camp and internment centre. It was said at the time that the only casualties on the island during this time were a rabbit and a frog, killed by a German jettisoning his bombs! Since the Second World War the island has seen political, social and economic changes but still governs itself, albeit with close connections to Westminster.

Isle of Man

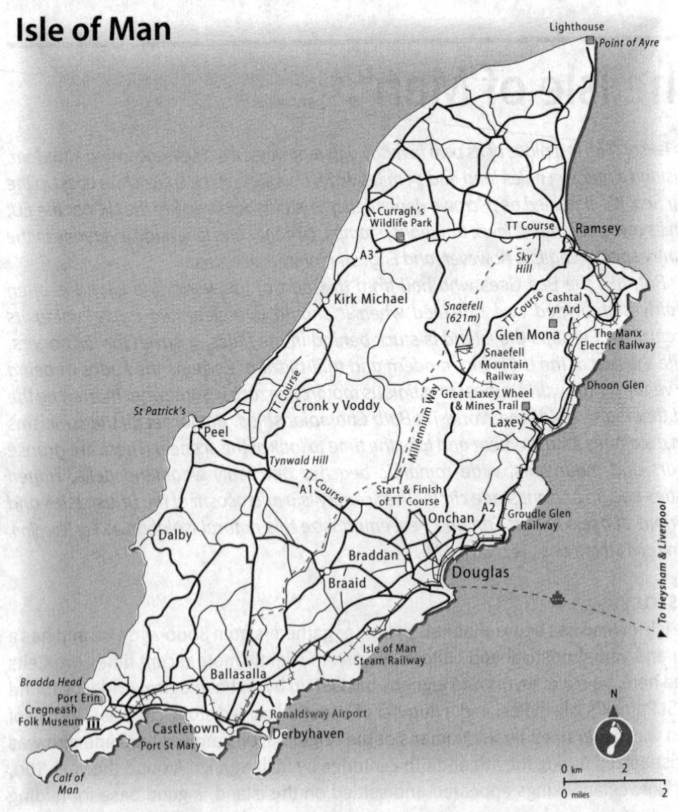

Ins and outs

Getting there **Flights** to **Ronaldsway Airport,** T01624-821600, in the southeast of the island are available on **Manx Airlines,** T08457-256256 (UK only), T01260-1588 (Republic of Ireland), www.manx-airlines.com, (from £65 for a return flight from Birmingham, Dublin, Glasgow, Jersey, Leeds-Bradford, Liverpool, London Heathrow, London Luton, Manchester and Southampton). **British European** also fly to the Isle of Man, T08705-676676, www.british-european.com (return flights from London City, Bristol and Belfast cost from £68.60). The small airport is well served by local buses into Douglas and there are a number of car hire operatives. **The Isle of Man Steam Packet Company** run **ferry** crossings across the rough stretch of the Irish Sea from Heysham and Liverpool into Douglas taking around 2 hours 30 mins, T08705-523523 (UK), T1800-551743 (Republic of Ireland) www.steampacket.com (return from £21 for a foot passenger day trip and from £73-185 for a car plus one passenger). Booking in advance for cheaper deals is recommended. ▸▸ *See Transport, page 677, for more details.*

Getting around

The Isle of Man is blessed with some unconventional and quaint forms of transport, many with a Victorian heritage, T01624-662525 for timetable enquiries for all. The ferry company also offers island explorer deals including free unlimited travel on all the island's public transport from £28 per adult for a day, £14 children. In the south of the country from Douglas to Castletown, Port St Mary and Port Erin there is a **rail** link with old steam trains that inspired the *Thomas the Tank Engine stories.* From Douglas to Laxey and Ramsey in the north there is an electric railway link and it is possible to reach the top of the island's highest mountain Snaefell by the Snaefell Mountain Railway. *It is easy to get around the island on the reasonably-priced bus service which serves all towns. However, hiring a car is one of the best ways of exploring the island, especially if you want to discover the glens. The centre of the Isle of Man is only barely reachable by road and is mainly uninhabited. Beware of motorcyclists – even outside the TT season there are more around than you would expect. Bike hire is available in Douglas and Ramsey for exploring the island in a more leisurely fashion. Surprisingly, you cannot hire a motorbike on the Isle of Man due to license restrictions.*

Douglas

The Victorian seaside resort of Douglas is the administrative and banking capital of the island as well as being its main hub for hotels and shops. A yellow sand beach lies at the foot of a sweeping promenade still busy with 19th-century horse-drawn trams. It isn't as pretty as any of the island's other towns but it's the most developed and has many restaurants and hotels.

Information Douglas TIC ⓘ *Sea Terminal Building, Douglas, T01624-686766, www.visitisleofman.com, Summer 1000-1900 daily, Oct-May Mon-Thu 0900-1730, Fri 0900-1700,* is the central information point for the island. **The Story of Mann Heritage Pass** is available from the TIC and each individual attraction included on it. For £10 adults get admission to four of the following sites: The Old House of Keys, Castle Rushen, The Nautical Museum, Rushen Abbey, Cregneash Folk Museum, Peel Castle, The House of Manannan, The Great Laxey Wheel, The Grove Rural Life Museum. Children and family tickets also available and the adult saving is £5.25 overall.

The **Manx Museum** ⓘ *The Manx Museum, Douglas, T01624-648000, Mon-Sat year round, free,* contains the National Art Gallery, Geology, Archaeology, Social History and TT race displays. It also has some beautiful glass beads believed to belong to a Viking noblewoman found at Peel Castle. Allow a couple of hours to explore the museum thoroughly. The best place in Douglas to escape the rain and entertain children with fairy folklore and multimedia displays.

Just 2 miles out of the town past the suburb of Onchan is the **Groudle Glen Railway** ⓘ *T01624-670453, the glen is 2 miles along the coast road from Douglas to Laxey, trains run at half hourly intervals on Sun 5 May-29 Sep 1100-1630, and on Wed evenings 3 Jul-14 Aug 1900-2100, fares cost £2.50, £1.50 children*, a late Victorian narrow gauge railway service that takes you down through beautiful woodland and beach scenery to Sea Lion Rocks.

Around the island

CastletownAn hour by bus from Douglas, **Castletown**, a large village with a beach and pretty harbour in the south of the island, is dominated by the large **Castle Rushen** ⓘ *The Quay. 29 Mar-Oct 1000-1700 daily, £4.25, £2.25 children*, which dates back to the 12th century. The limestone fortress was the home of the former Kings and Lords of Mann, including the last Norse monarch, King Magnus in 1265. Having been an administrative centre, prison and law court amongst other things in the past, it is now a fabulous museum. Walking around the walls and down to the dungeons is also well worth it. The long and turbulent history of the Isle of Man's political independence is explored in the **Old House of Keys** ⓘ *Old House of Keys, Parliament Sq, T01624-648000, 29 Mar-Oct daily 1000-1700, guided presentations run on the hour, £3, £1.50 children*. It has been restored to its 1866 glory as the parliament house and debating chamber.

Port St Mary and **Port Erin**, charming neighbouring coastal towns at the south of the island, are often called the sisters of the south. Port St Mary is a quaint and pretty place with a small harbour and beach that's perfect for rockpooling. A walk along the coast beside the palm trees for about five minutes takes you to **Chapel Beach**, a sandy stretch just a little out of the way. Along the coast in the other direction will take you to the cliffs and the **Chasms**, dramatic vertical rifts in the rocks. Not far from the town is the **Cregneash Folk Museum** ⓘ *Cregneash Village Folk Museum, Cregneash, Port St Mary, T01624-648000, 29 Mar-Oct, 1000-1700 daily, £3, £1.50 children*, which represents the way that crofters lived and worked in the 19th century. From Port Erin, just 8 miles from Port St Mary on the west coast, a walk up **Bradda Head** is worth doing on a nice day where you'll find the perfect place to watch the sun set. **Erin Arts Centre** ⓘ *Victoria Sq, T01624-835858, open year round Tue-Fri 1300-1630, prices for various events differ*, acts as a small art gallery to display local work and a venue for opera, touring shows and theatre. Daily boat trips from Port Erin take you to the bird sanctuary of **Calf Island**, a 616-acre islet off the southern tip of the Isle of Man ⓘ *Calf Island Cruises, Raglan Pier, T01624-832339, Apr-Oct weather permitting, 1015, 1130 and 1300.*

Peel is also known as the Sunset City for its beautiful west coast views across the sandy beach and historic castle.

These days, **Peel** is the main fishing town of the island and has a **Kipper Museum** to prove it. ⓘ *Mill Rd, T01624-843622. Apr-Oct Mon-Fri 1000-1700*. But Peel is also one of the oldest cathedral cities in the British Isles, dating back to the 6th century. Its narrow winding streets are historic and pretty if you overlook the ugly power station and chimney to the top of the town. The unmissable **House of Manannan** ⓘ *Mill Rd, T01624-648000, open all year 1000-1700, £5, child £2.50*, is a multimedia feast of Viking, Celtic and Manx history with sights, sounds, talking waterfalls and excellent short films bringing each period alive. **Peel Castle** stands on the St Patrick's Isle, used as a fortress since the Celtic Iron Age and a former Viking stronghold. The crumbling sandstone walls enclose an 11th-century church and round tower, **St Germain's Cathedral** ⓘ *St Patrick's Isle, T01624-648000, 29 Mar-Oct 1000-1700 daily, £3, £1.50 children* and the ruins of the later apartments of the Lords of Mann. The island used to be completely cut off from the mainland at high tide but when the causeway was built to link the island a small sandy beach, Fenella's Beach, was created naturally on one side. On the road from Peel to

The three legs of Man

The three legs of Man aren't a representation of a genetic mutation or its fairy heritage but a symbol of the island's independence. The symbol is displayed on houses, tourist attractions and flags all over the island and the Latin legend beneath it translates as "Whichever way you throw me I stand". Many nations have risen to the challenge from the Vikings to the English but it remains self-governing, with the Tynwald parliament the oldest continuous parliament in the world.

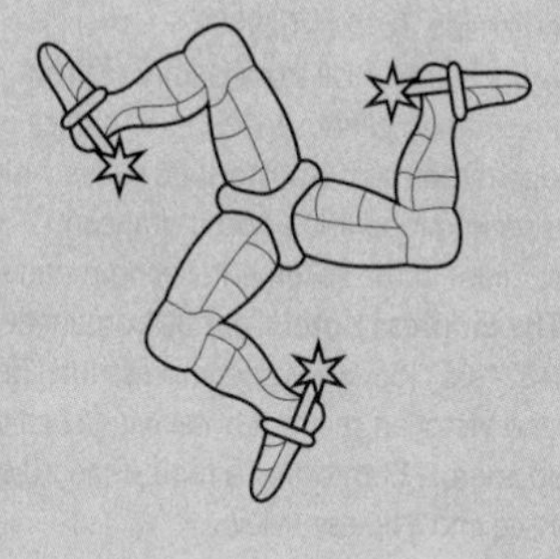

Douglas, the **Tynwald Hill** is the site of the oldest continuous parliament in the world. The name derives from the Norse word *Thing-voeller* meaning Parliament Fields, and the site is a small circular area of stepped grass crowned with a flag.

The mountain of **Snaefell** is one of the highlights of the Isle of Man. At 2036 ft Snaefell means "Snow Mountain" and it is said that from the top of the mountain you can see the six kingdoms: England, Ireland, Scotland, Wales, Mann and the Kingdom of Heaven. You can reach the top by walking all the way, taking the tram halfway and walking the rest or by taking the 100-year-old **mountain railway** ⓘ *Laxey Station, T01624-663366, 20 Apr-29 Sep, fares from Laxey to the summit return £6, 1 child free per fee-paying adult, all others £3*, all the way to the top. There's a small café at the top to rest yourself or commiserate when all you can see is a large blanket of mist. The megalithic standing stones at **Cashtal yn Ard** are thought to mark a burial ground and stand in an eerie part of the country. Follow the A2 road from Laxey north past Dhoon Glen and then take the next right after Glen Mona. The standing stones are on the left-hand side of the road.

The Millennium Way In 1979 to commemorate 100 years of the Tynwald parliament, the Millennium Way was established as the first long distance footpath in the island. It is based on the Royal Way recorded by the monks of Rushen in the 14th century and takes in both historical and natural points of interest in its 28 miles. It can be walked by an experienced hiker in one day or you can split it into three legs. Starting from the main road to Kirk Michael from Ramsey, approximately 1 mile from Ramsey Town Square, the route climbs up towards Sky Hill, site of the 1079 battle between the Norse King Godred and the Manx which the Scandinavians won. The way continues down around the stream at the foot of Snaefell and finishes at Castletown after traversing the countryside and Norse landmarks between. Maps and close descriptions of the walk can be found at the TIC.

The Way of the Gull A coastpath runs 90 miles along the northern shore from Peel right around the island, marked with a sign with the silhouette of a gull. It takes about four days to complete. The walk follows a disused railway line from Peel to the beach at the bottom of Glen Trunk at Orrisdale. From there it follows the beach past the lighthouse at the Point of Ayre through to Ramsey, down to Douglas and beyond to Castletown. From here the Chasms at Port St Mary are visited, vertical rifts in the cliffs, providing excellent views of the Calf of Man. The walk finishes at Contrary Head where the tide divides, one part flowing southwest to the Calf and the other northeast to Jerby. A full description and further information is available from the TIC.

Sleeping

Douglas *p671*

A-D Admiral House Hotel, 12 Loch Promenade, T01624-629551, www.admiralhouse .com Luxury seafront hotel with excellent service and a choice of modern rooms or 4-poster-bed suites. Also a bar serving food and a Mediterranean restaurant in the basement. Recommended.

C The Empress Hotel, Central Promenade, T01624-661155, www.theempresshotel.net. Grand Victorian seafront hotel with a health club, marble bathrooms, a high standard of service and a fine sea view.

C Sefton Hotel, Harris Promenade, T01624-645500, www.seftonhotel.co.im. Large spacious and classy seafront hotel with leisure club, cycle hire and library. The restaurant serves Manx specials and rooms are comfortable with sofas and fridges. Relaxing, hospitable and luxurious.

C-D Mount Murray Hotel and Country Club, Santon, T01624-661111, www.mountmurray.com. Just out of Douglas, the island's most luxurious timbered hotel with a full health complex, golf course and acres of beautiful scenery.

D Claremont Hotel, 18-19 Loch Promenade, T01624-698800, www.sleepwellhotels.com. Young, modern seafront hotel with 28 luxury rooms, modern pine-floored designer bar and restaurant serving Mediterranean and French food.

D The Wellbeck Hotel, Mona Dr, off Central Promenade, T01624-675663, www.wellbeckhotel.com. Small traditional family-run relaxed hotel-guesthouse just off the promenade with bar, restaurant and gym.

E Allerton Guest House, 29 Hutchinson Sq, T01624-675587, www.allerton.ttfans.com. Small family B&B in the centre of town overlooking sunny garden square. Very good value.

E Hydro Hotel, Queen's Promenade, T01624-676870, F663883. Large traditional Victorian hotel with a cosy bistro and great view of the seafront.

E The Savoy Hotel, Central Promenade, T01624-676454, T621695. Small family-run traditional English seaside hotel. Open the door and you're practically on the beach.

Camping

F Glen Dhoo Campsite, Glen Dhoo Farm, T01624-621254. Medium-sized campsite to the north of Douglas open all year round, £3.95 per person per night. Follow the A18 out of Douglas to the north to Hillberry and Glen Dhoo farm.

Around the Island *p672*

D Ballacallin House, Dalby, T01624-841100. A little out of town, Ballacallin House is a large old whitewashed Manx farmhouse with wonderful views, 4-poster beds and a lounge bar and restaurant.

D Falcon's Nest Hotel, The Promenade, Port Erin, T01624-834077, www.falconsnest.co.uk. Pleasant family-run hotel just off the promenade with cosy rooms and mod cons. It's above a traditional Manx pub serving local ale in the glow of an open fire. Very friendly.

D The George Hotel, The Parade, T01624-822533, Castletown. Central large traditional Georgian hotel with a classy ambience.

D The Grand Island Hotel, Bride Rd, Ramsey, T01624-812455, www.hotel-selection.co.uk Large traditional Georgian hotel with three acres of ground in Ramsey with sea views and a restaurant.

D The Grosvenor Hotel, The Promenade, Port Erin, T01624-834124, www.thegrosvenorhotel.com. Stylish and attractive small Victorian seafront hotel with views of Bradda Head.

D Ocean Castle Hotel, The Promenade, Port Erin, T01624-836399, hotel@oceancastle.co.uk. Excellent sea view from this traditional Victorian seaside hotel. They also have self-catering apartments. 1950s bistro-style restaurant serves Manx food. Eat-as-much-as-you-like Sunday lunch is served in the carvery from 1200-1430.

D The River House, Ramsey, T/F01624-816412. Small charming Georgian house with a true English country feel, en suite bathrooms and exemplary service.

D-E Rowany Cottier, Spaldrick near Port Erin, T01624-832287, F835685. Spacious, elegant house with a large garden and extensive Manx breakfast menu. Family-run with high quality service.

E Albert Hotel, Athol St, Port St Mary, T01624-832118. Pub-hotel B&B accommodation on the outskirts of Port St Mary.
E Ballaquinney Farm, Ronague near Castletown, T01624-824125. Manx farmhouse B&B with evening meals in the countryside near to Castletown.
E Ballashloague Farm, Main Rd, Glen Mona, T01624- 861750. Secluded Edwardian farmhouse halfway between Ramsey and Laxey with a farmhouse breakfast and good walking nearby.
E Beachcroft Guest House, Beach Rd, Port St Mary, T01624-834521, crompton @beachcroft1.fsnet.co.uk. Secluded family-run guesthouse with lovely views of the surrounding countryside.
E Mr and Mrs Brookes, Cronk Moar, Truggan Rd, Port St Mary, T01624-834612. Private bed and breakfast near the coast.
E The Creek Inn, East Quay, Peel, T01624-842216. Self-catering accommodation in the small, cosy central pub.
E The Fernleigh, Marine Parade, Peel, T01624-842435. Comfortable small hotel with a family feel offering B&B.
E The Merchant's House, 18 Castle St, Peel, T01624-842541. Georgian merchant's house with a walled garden with B&B accommodation.
E The Waldick Hotel, Promenade, Peel, T/F01624-842410. Friendly family-run hotel on the promenade in Peel overlooking the beach.
F Peel Campsite, T01624-842341, ptc@mcb.net. Large campsite open from Apr-Nov, £3.50 per person per night.

Eating

Douglas *p671*

At the lower end of this price bracket the **£££ Waterfront Restaurant**, North Quay, T01624-673222, is very good value for money. It's run by television chef Kevin Woodford and is warm and friendly. With a menu of traditional Manx-English food like sausage and mash with red onion gravy, Dover sole and Manx rarebit and a classy atmosphere, it's the best restaurant in Douglas by some way.
££ La Brasserie, Empress Hotel, Central Promenade, T01624-661155. French restaurant inside the *Empress Hotel* which is a copy of an authentic French Brasserie near the Gare du Nord in Paris. Various menus available including a Sunday roast in a stylish and traditional restaurant.
££ Copperfield's Olde Teashoppe, 24 Castle St, T01624-613650. Unusual Edwardian period teashop serving cream teas and restaurant food including filled Yorkshire puddings, burgers and lasagne and local Manx produce. At the lower end of this price bracket, open 0900-1730 Mon-Sat.
££ Greens Vegetarian Restaurant, Steam Railway Station, North Quay, T01624-629129. Small relaxed vegetarian restaurant-café next to the historic railway station.
££ La Nuova Cucina, 54 Bucks Rd, T01624-623959. One of many Italian restaurants, this time the oldest in Douglas with daily specials and à la carte menu. Intimate and homely.
££ La Piazza, Loch Promenade, T01624-672136. First floor stylish wooden-floored Italian restaurant open for lunch and evening meals Mon-Sat.
££ La Posada, Admiral House Hotel, 12 Loch Promenade, T01624-629551. Basement restaurant specializing in Spanish and Mediterranean food in a warm cantina-style atmosphere.
££ Scotts Bistro, 7 John St, T01624-623764. Smart warm bistro inside the oldest house in Douglas. The bistro specializes in jacket potatoes and other home cooking and has a decent wine list. In the summer you can eat outside in the courtyard. Recommended.
£ Curry Express Indian Takeaway, The Crescent, Central Promenade, T01624-677002. Cheap, cheerful and as speedy as they can be. Open daily.
£ Laughing Buddha, Prospect Hill, T01624-673367. Located towards Onchan, specializes in Peking food for lunch, dinner and takeaways. Closed Sun.

For an explanation of the sleeping and eating price codes used in this guide, see the inside front cover. Other relevant information is provided in the Essentials chapter, page 40.

Around the island *p672*

££ The Garrison, Bank St, Castletown. Atmospheric wine and tapas bar in one of Castletown's historic stone houses. Tapas dishes cost around £3.

££ The Marine Hotel, The Promenade, Peel, T01624-842337. Large pub with a bar and restaurant serving home-cooked food and real ale. If you want the true Manx experience, ask for a kipper dish.

££ The Port Bistro, The Quay, Port St Mary, T01624-832064. Fairly expensive fine food bistro with an intimate atmosphere, specializing in locally caught seafood specials, grills, poultry with a long wine list.

££ The Whitehouse, Tynwald Rd, Peel, T01624-842252. Manx farmhouse-pub with home cooking, bar snacks and meals and a large range of guest beers as well as the local Okell's brew.

£ BarLogo, 39 Parliament St, Ramsey, T01624-813557. One of the Isle of Man's only young, fresh, continental café bars with bar snacks, Mediterranean food and a large range of cocktails.

£ The Creek Inn, East Quay, Peel, T01624-842216. Friendly pub with hot and cold food served throughout the day. The seafood is particularly good.

£ Food For Thought, 2 Victoria Buildings, Parliament St, Ramsey, T01624-816763. Inexpensive café serving chicken, steak and seafood for lunch and dinner. Open late on Fri-Sat, closed Sun-Mon.

£ The Old Bakery Café and Restaurant, 31 Malew St, T01624-823092, Castletown. Comfortable and traditional Manx teashop and restaurant in the centre of the town.

£ Seaview Inn, The Grand Island Hotel, Bride Road, Ramsey, T01624-812455. Bar meals available for lunch and dinner with great sea views and at very reasonable prices. Three course meals from £6.95.

£ Timm's Bistro, 5 East St, Ramsey, T01624-817967. Friendly bistro serving Manx food, specializing in seafood. Open Tue-Sat 12-1400, 1900-2200, Sun 1200-1700, closed Mon.

Activities and tours

Cycling

The Isle of Man has calm country roads that are well suited to cycling, although you should make sure you keep clear of the TT fortnight at the end of May and beginning of June if you want a relaxing experience. The TIC provides a pamphlet on cycling around the island including six one-day trails of differing levels around the glens and pretty seaside villages.

Eurocycles, 8a Victoria Rd (off Broadway), Douglas, T01624-624909. £10 per day.

Pedal Power, 5 Willow Terr, Douglas, T01624-662026, F842472. £8 per day, £35 per week.

Fishing

For a list of fishing locations, call the TIC, T01624-686766. They also provide a pamphlet on fishing in the country.

Sea, river and reservoir fishing are on offer on the island. All anglers must get a licence, available from the TIC at the Sea Terminal in Douglas. River fishing runs until the end of Sep, reservoir fishing until the end of Oct and salmon and sea trout fishing is mainly in late summer and autumn. Freshwater fishing is mainly for salmon, brown and rainbow trout and the occasional sea trout. There is a daily bag limit of 6 fish, of which no more than two may be salmon and sea trout, and angling is only allowed between 0600 or sunrise and 30 minutes after sunset or 2230. Douglas Harbour has breakwater and pier fishing for coalfish, plaice, flounder, wrasse, pollack and conger eels.

Pony trekking

Stables are a way out of town and can only be reached by car. Prices vary according to where you go and how long for and start from £15 an hr.

Abbeylands Equestrian Centre, Abbeylands, Braddan, T01624-676717.

Ballahimmin Riding School and pony trekking centre, Ballahimmin Farm off Little London Rd, Cronk y Voddy, T01624-878547/482990.

GGH Equitation Centre, Ballacallin Beg near Braaid, Marown, T01624-851574/851450.

Pennybridge Stables, Main Rd, Kirk Michael, T01624- 878859. For experienced riders only.

Sailing and windsurfing

The TIC has a pamphlet detailing all sea-going activities on the island. The Isle of Man is an ideal place for sailing

and windsurfing whether you're experienced or a novice. The harbours are picturesque and there are 6 sailing clubs. Derbyhaven is a popular spot for windsurfers, contact **Manx Marine Limited**, Yacht Chandlers, 35 North Quay, Douglas, T01624-674842,for further details.
Douglas Bay Yacht Club, Trafalgar House, South Quay, Douglas, T01624-621823.
Isle of Man Yacht Club, Club House, Lime St, Port St Mary, T01624-832088.
Manx Sailing and Cruising Club, North Quay, Ramsey, T01624-813494.
Manx Yachting Association, MA McMahon, T01624-621823.

Tours

Film location tours of the scenery shown in *Waking Ned* and *The George Best Story* as well as others including TT tours, Manx Castles and Celtic Cross tours can be arranged with **Motion Enterprises,** T07624-471300, www.motionenterprises.com.

TT motorcycle race

The international Tourist Trophy (TT) motorcycle race has been held on the Isle of Man since 1904 and is one of the world's most famous motorsport events. Every year on the last week in May and first week in Jun the island comes alive with passionate fans watching the contenders fly by. The circuit is 37.73 miles long and leading riders can make speeds of 120 mph/200 kmph. If you're planning to watch, accommodation is hard to come by and you are advised to book in advance, www.iomtt.com.

Walking

The island has some idyllic scenery to walk through on a number of marked long distance footpaths (see TIC pamphlet). The undulating countryside has sand dunes, marshland, mountains and meadows of wild flowers to delight all comers.

Festivals

Apr Isle of Man Food and Drink Festival. Celebration of Manx food from smoked kippers to cream teas.
May TT Festival Fortnight. World famous Tourist Trophy motorcycle event lasting 2 weeks.
Jun Isle of Music Festival. Festival celebrating the best of the island's music.
Jun Manx National Week. Celebration of Manx culture, language and customs.
Jul Tynwald Day. The national day of the Isle of Man.
Jul International Cycling Festival. 5 days of cycling around the island's roads.
Aug Manx Grand Prix. Grand Prix event around the island.
Aug World Tin Bath Championship. In essence, it's 1 person per tin bath racing against another across the harbour at Peel to see if anyone can stay afloat long enough to reach the finish line.
Aug World Championship Viking Longboat Races. Viking longboat races remembering a portion of the island's history.

Transport

Douglas *p671*

Douglas is well connected with the island by all manner of public transport.

Bus

Bus numbers 4,5,6,8 and 10 run to **Peel** from the bus station on North Quay; buses 1 and 2 run to **Port St Mary**, **Port Erin** and **Castletown**.

Car

Athol Garage, Ronaldsway Airport, Ballasalla, T01624-822481. **E B Christian & Co**, Airport Garage, Ballasalla, T01624-822126. **Hertz**, Ronaldsway Airport, Ballasalla, T01624-823760, www.hertz.co.uk. **Mylchreests Car Rental**, Ronaldsway Airport, T01624-823533, F825587.

Taxi

Laxey Cabs, T07624-432343.

Train

The **Electric Railway** runs from the Derby Castle stop at the far end of the promenade to **Ramsey**, and **Laxey**, stopping in **Groudle Glen** and changing at Laxey for the Snaefell Mountain Railway.

Directory

Douglas *p671*
Internet Feegan's Lounge, 22 Duke St, T01624-679280, www.feegan.com, £1 per 15 mins, open 0900-1900 Mon-Fri, 0900-1700 Sat, closed Sun. **Medical facilities** Boots, 14-22 Strand St, T01624-616120. **G.J.Maley**, 15 Strand St, T01624-676341. **Hemensley Pharmacy**, 1 Windsor Rd, T01624-675162. **Palatine Group Practice**, Palatine Health Centre, 2 Hailwood Court, Governor's Hill, T01624-67544. **Noble's Hospital**, Westmoreland Rd, T642642.
Police Glencrutchery Rd, T631212.
Weather check T0900-6243300.

Yorkshire

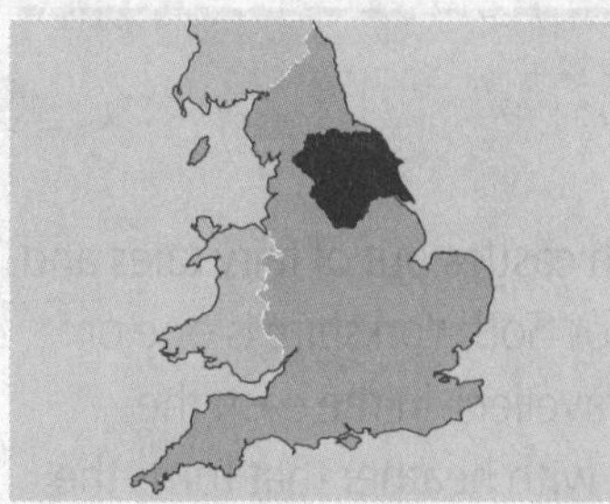

Footprint features

Introduction

Ruggedly beautiful, and filled with castles out of fairy tales and monuments to man's reverence for God, Yorkshire is one of the richest regions of Britain for travellers. In the east, the rolling hills of the moors are thick with heather that turns the horizon pink in the summertime and nearly black in the winter. Here, villages like Lealholm make you stop in sheer wonder that something so perfectly pretty can exist in this modern age. The breathtaking views of the moors crashing into the sea on sheer cliffs that drop hundreds of feet to the icy waters is broken up by fishing villages like Whitby, with its gothic edge and homely centre, and little nooks like Robin Hood's Bay, with its smugglers history and tiny cottages.

In the west, the craggy rocks of the dales seem to defy anything to grow upon their sharp edges, and yet the heather persists, against the odds. Here walkers follow trails to picturesque waterfalls, and then retreat to soak their feet in the fabled waters of gorgeous Harrogate. At the centre of it all, the soaring towers of York's historic cathedral is juxtaposed by the busy modern nightlife in Leeds and Sheffield, where the beat never stops.

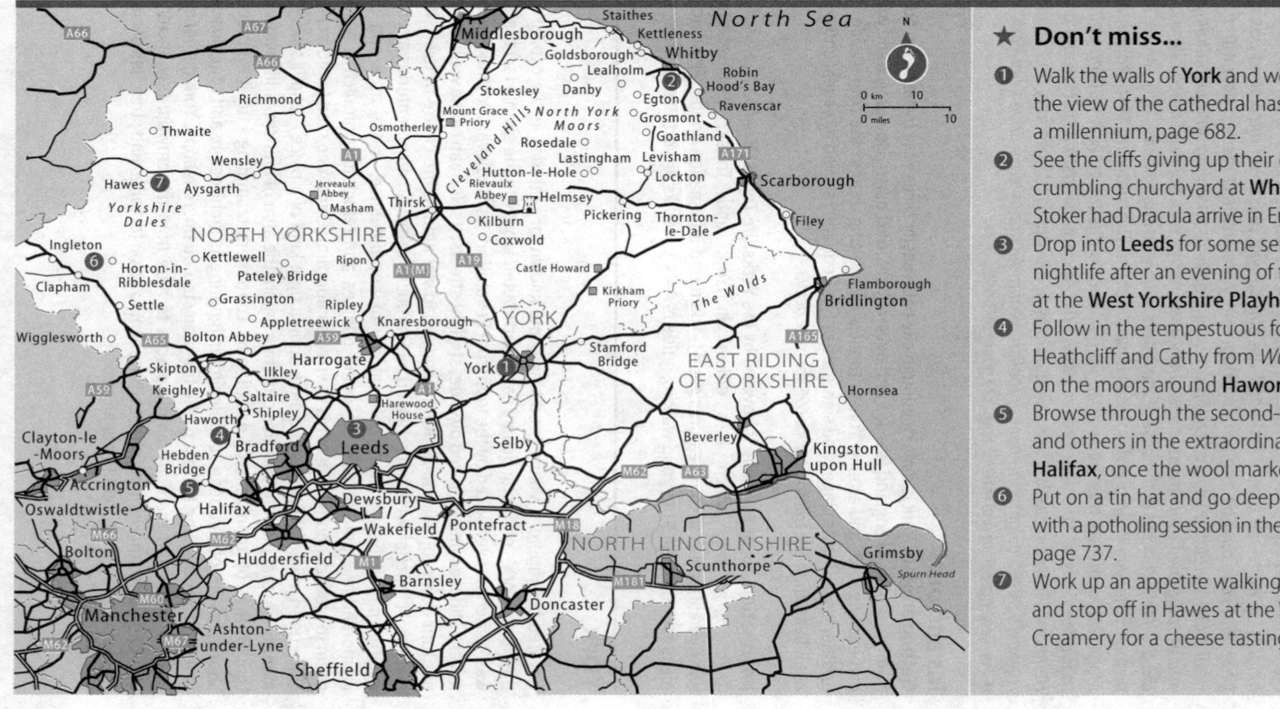

★ Don't miss...

1. Walk the walls of **York** and wonder how much the view of the cathedral has changed in half a millennium, page 682.
2. See the cliffs giving up their dead in the crumbling churchyard at **Whitby**, where Bram Stoker had Dracula arrive in England, page 707.
3. Drop into **Leeds** for some serious student nightlife after an evening of top-class theatre at the **West Yorkshire Playhouse**, page 724.
4. Follow in the tempestuous footsteps of Heathcliff and Cathy from *Wuthering Heights* on the moors around **Haworth**, page 730.
5. Browse through the second-hand bookshops and others in the extraordinary Piece Hall in **Halifax**, once the wool market, page 731.
6. Put on a tin hat and go deep underground with a potholing session in the **Yorkshire Dales**, page 737.
7. Work up an appetite walking in **Wensleydale** and stop off in Hawes at the Wensleydale Creamery for a cheese tasting, page 747.

York and Central Yorkshire

➔ *Colour map 6, grid B5*

Picture perfect and bearing a glossy sheen, the city of York juts out of the rolling hills of the Yorkshire Moors like a real life version of Oz's Emerald City. The awe-inspiring heights of Walter de Grey's cathedral are still so well preserved after hundreds of years that you could be forgiven for wondering if the architect made a deal with the devil that his building should stand forever. But for all its charming antique buildings and winding medieval streets, the countryside around York holds as much allure as the city itself. York sits at the base of the moors, where so many shades of green are to be found that you'll run out of words to describe them. The sprawling North Yorkshire Moors National Park was made to wander in, and so it is traced with walking paths that offer views to take your breath away. Tucked away amidst all that beauty are Helmsley's Norman castle, the ancient abbeys at Rievaulx and Rosedale, and Castle Howard's spectacular monument to foolish wealth. All are an easy drive from York.

⏩ *For Sleeping, Eating and other listings, see pages 693-696.*

Ins and outs

Getting around York is a major enough city to be easily accessible by **train** and **bus** from most parts of England (see Ins and outs for York, next page). However, while you can easily get to, and around York without a car, getting around the countryside is another issue. Most villages and sights are only infrequently served by **coach**, and not at all by train. ⏩ *See Transport, page 696, for more details.*

Information All of Yorkshire is covered by the **Yorkshire Tourist Board** ⓘ *T01904-707070*, which has offices in York and Thirsk. Its website, www.yorkshirevisitor.com, features good background information on the region and ideas for walks. Another good walking guide is AA's *50 Walks in North Yorkshire*.

York

Coveted by emperors, Vikings and kings, and known for centuries as the capital of the North, York's enduring beauty can be attributed largely to the simple fact that it was somehow overlooked by the Industrial Revolution. Its medieval alleyways were never bulldozed and replaced by wide, straight streets. Its Norman castle walls were not torn down to make room for a handy roadway around the centre of town. Its medieval churches were not replaced by Starbucks cafés. So now, centuries after it left the national stage as a political city of any influence, it sits as a sort of memorandum from the past. Its grand edifices and ferociously protective walls seem to state defiantly, 'Once this town was important. Once men died to protect it. Once upon a time...' For this is a once upon a time kind of a place – and it's worth mentioning that modern York lies prostrate before the altar of tourism. Still, overrun though it is by trainloads of day-tripping Londoners cramming into its antique shops, hordes of European schoolchildren ignoring its architecture and coachloads of Americans queuing in front of the too-many too-quaint teashops, York demands to be visited. And there are ample places to hide from the crowds: tiny ancient churches, dark and winding streets that seem to go on for miles and stretches of city wall where you'll be completely alone.

Ins and outs

Getting there York is on the east coast mainline, and is served by **GNER, Virgin Trains** and **Arriva**. From London King's Cross, **trains** to York run every 30 minutes; the journey takes approximately 2 hours. Trains arrive at York Station, at the edge of the city walls across the River Ouse about a 15-minute walk from the centre of town. By **car**, York is 20 minutes drive from the M1/M62 motorway. **Coaches** and regional **buses** pick up and drop off passengers about 200 yds north of the train station on Rougier St, near Lendal Bridge, although many coach services also drop passengers off at the train station itself. **National Express**, T08705-808080. ▸▸ *See Transport, page 696, for more details.*

Getting around This is a tiny city, best handled on **foot. Taxis** are plentiful when it all gets to be a bit too much, but you can easily walk from one city wall clear across town to the other in about 15 minhutes. With all of its pedestrianized sections and its strictly limited parking, driving takes longer and is more difficult than walking. City bus routes are operated by **First York**, T01904-622992. This is such a tourist town that the most common vehicle on the tangled streets of York seems to be the tour bus. There are dozens to choose from, and you can find brochures for most of them in the tourist office if you fancy adding to the road congestion. On the other hand, there are equally as many guided walks about, and these are often more interesting and hands-on. Some of the best are led by the **York Association of Voluntary Guides** ⓘ *T01904-640780, www.york.touristguides*, which generally meet daily in Exhibition Square.

Information York's tourist offices are the biggest and best in Yorkshire. **Main** TIC ⓘ *Exhibition Square in front of Bootham Gate. Apr-Jun, Sep, Oct Mon-Sat 0900-1800, Sun 0930-1800, Jul-Aug daily 0900-1900, Nov-Mar Mon-Sat 0900-1700, Sun 0930-1500*. There's also a convenient branch located in **York Station** ⓘ *T01904-621756, Apr-Oct Mon-Sat 0900-1700, Sun 1000-1700, Nov-Feb Mon-Sat 1900-1700, Sun 1000-1600, Mar Mon-Sat 0930-1730, Sun 1000-1700*. The **York Tourism Information Centre** publishes a free guide on York, which you can receive by phoning or emailing **tic@york-tourism.co.uk**, or at **www.visityork.org**

History

Nobody knows exactly who it was that first chose to settle in the sheltered, marshy area between the rivers Ouse and Foss at the edge of the Yorkshire Moors, but it was the Romans who first put York on the map. The site where the city now stands was once a critical part of Roman England. While conquering the north of England, Roman soldiers camped where York is now, and found the site to be so well located for defence purposes that they built a permanent fort there and named it Eboracum – believed to be a slightly uncreative name meaning 'the place of the yew trees'. A century later, Eboracum was a thriving Roman village, home to 6000 soldiers and the de facto headquarters for all troops in northern England. While very little remains of the structures that housed the troops, extensive Roman artefacts have been discovered that give a clear indication that, as early as AD 180, York was a substantial, bustling city. Streets like Stonegate and Petergate are believed to follow the routes of the Roman streets once known as Via Praetoria and Via Principalis.

Saxon invaders were the next to take over the area, and they, too, valued York, making it the capital of the regional state of Deira. They renamed it Eoforwic, and promptly began adding onto the Roman structures and battlements. In 625, King Edwin of Northumbria married Princess Aethelburga, a Christian. As there were no churches in the area at the time in which to hold the ceremony, the king ordered one built, and a plain, wooden chapel was built on the site of what is now the Minster. Saxons were followed by Vikings, who found the city offered a handy base to use while raping and pillaging the countryside. They modified the Saxon name to sound more familiar, calling it Jorvik. Viking street names remain the same – in fact, as it is in York, the term 'gate' was used to mean 'street' in Viking dialects.

William the Conquerer also made York his military headquarters. Normans rebuilt the city in stone, using the old Viking structures as a foundation for their architecture. This medieval period of construction is responsible for much of the city's appearance today, and most of its religious structures. Work began on the current Minster in 1220, and continued for more than 200 years. Dozens of churches and abbeys were built in the city during this time, and many of them survive today

As the inescapable tour guides tell their charges at the beginning of virtually every foray through town: in York the streets are called gates, the gates are called bars and

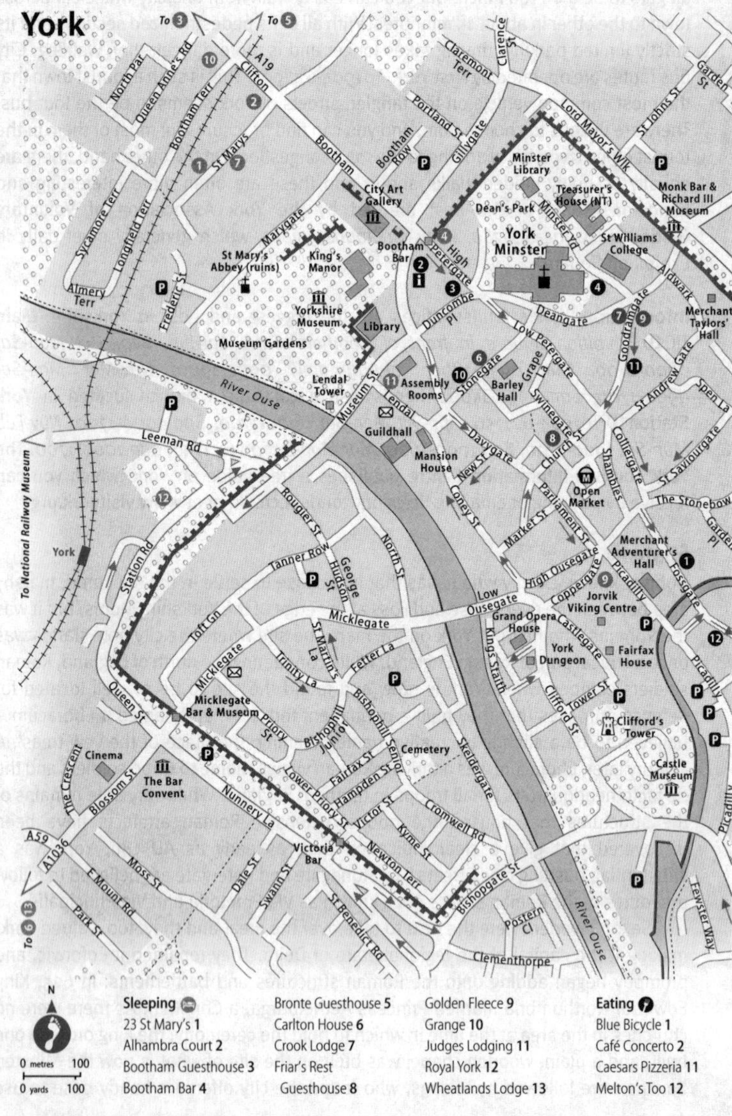

the bars are called pubs. Sure it's silly, but once you've got that down, it all makes a little more sense. The most significant sights in York are all contained within its rambling city walls, but the streets wind and wander in a quaint but confusing fashion that all but guarantees that you'll spend some of your time here lost. But that's fine, really, as that might be the moment when you stumble across a beautiful piece of history all your own.

Bootham Bar

A good place to start any walk through town is at Bootham Bar, the oldest of the four city gateways, dating, in part, from the 11th century, although most of it was built over the subsequent two centuries. It offers entrance to the city via High Petergate. This is the only of the four gates that sits on the site of one of the original entrances to the old Roman fortress. It bears the Stuart coat of arms, and still has its original wooden portcullis.

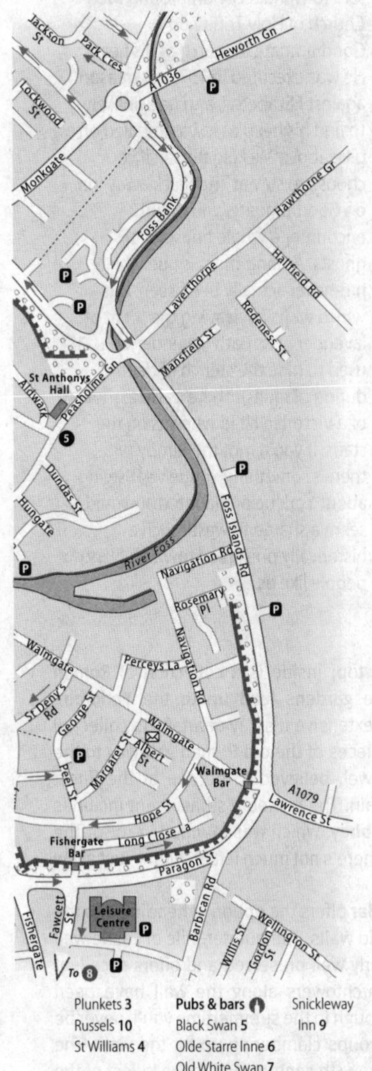

Just adjacent to the bar is the city's main tourist office in the De Grey rooms, while across the busy intersection from the gate is **Exhibition Square**, with its unimpressive fountain and a chunk of the old walls. This is where you'll find the **City Art Gallery** ⓘ *Exhibition Sq, daily 1000-1700, £2*, and its small but varied collection of continental works including pieces by Bacchiacca (*Agony in the Garden*), Domenichino (*Monsignor Agucchi*) and Bellotto (*View in Lucca*).

Next to the gallery is the **King's Manor**, which once formed part of the abbot's lodging of **St Mary's Abbey**, which lies in ruins not far away. Sections of the manor date from 1270, although most of it is was built in the late 1400s. After the Dissolution it was taken over by the Lord President of the Council of the North, after which it was used as a royal headquarters in Yorkshire. During its time the manor was visited by James I, Charles I and Henry VIII. It's now used by the University of York and only its courtyard and a few rooms are open to the public.

Museum Gardens

Just a short distance down St Leonard's Place from the Manor, past the endless queues waiting for tour buses, is the lovely green space of the Museum Gardens, where a cluster of ruins sit in various stages of decay. To the right of the entrance are the remains of **St Leonard's Hospital**, which was founded in the 12th century. Nearby stands the **Multangular Tower**, which has a

Spooksville

"We have travelled extensively working on research projects across the globe and nowhere have we found more ghosts than in historic York." So said Jason Karl, president of the Ghost Research Foundation International, when in 2002, he named York the most haunted city in Europe. The city was so proud of this award that it promptly put out a press release, which only slightly had a 'See? We *told* you we had ghosts' ring about it. In fact, reports of apparitions scaring the bejesus out of living folk go back hundreds of years here. Not just ghosts but *battalions* of spooks. A plumber's apprentice working in the Treasurer's House in 1953 reported seeing an entire Roman legion, led by a centurion on horseback, marching through the basement. His detailed description of their uniforms was first used to discredit him – such uniforms had never been heard of by archaeologists – and then to back him up, when descriptions of uniforms matching those he'd seen were actually found. King's Manor is haunted by a monk, thought to be from the adjacent St Mary's Abbey, and by a lady in a green Tudor dress, who holds a bouquet of roses. Patrons in the Old Starre Inn, on Stonegate, have heard the groans of Cavaliers, whose wounded were brought to the stables behind the inn during the Civil War. There's also an old woman ghost who climbs the stairs there, and two spectral black cats. A decapitated Thomas Percy is said to wander blindly around the Church of Holy Trinity on Goodramgate in search of his head. He was executed in 1572 for treason against Elizabeth I, and he's unlikely to find his head as it was impaled on a pike above Mickelgate Bar. If you choose to stay at The Snickleway Inn on Goodramgate, you might encounter a whole houseful of ghosts. Among them is one which has never actually been seen, but which wafts by, leaving the scent of lavender in its path (lavender was used to hide the stench of death during plagues). There's also a ghost of a Victorian child who sits on the stairs. If you're not the jumpy type, there's something vaguely satisfying about York being haunted. It would seem a shame to waste such a historically preserved town on living people like us.

fourth-century Roman base and a medieval top; inside is a collection of Roman coffins unearthed in and around York. The gardens lead up to the **Yorkshire** Museum ⓘ *Daily 1000-1700, £4.50*, with its extensive display of artefacts collected in the region. Included in the collection are pieces of the old Roman gateway to the city, Viking artefacts and the Middleham Jewel, believed to be one of the finest examples of medieval jewellery found in Britain. The museum's basement includes the original fireplace and walls of **St Mary's Abbey**, which was founded in 1080. The rest of the craggy abbey ruins are nearby, but there's not much left of them – just a few sections of the old walls and a row of apses.

Entering the city walls through **Bootham Bar** offers the option of heading into the town centre or of taking a wander down the old walls. The quarter-mile of castle wall between Bootham and **Monk Bar** is particularly well preserved and offers excellent views of the city and its cathedral. The watchtowers along the wall have been converted to resting points with benches, although in the summertime you'll never be allowed to rest for a second between tour groups clambering up for the view. The imposing and gloomy Monk Bar dates from the 14th century, and is the tallest of the city's old gates. All four gates have their original portcullises, but Monk Bar is the only one in full working order. Inside it is the particularly cheesy **Richard III** Museum ⓘ *Daily 1000-1600, £1.80*, one of several pseudo-museums in town with virtually no artefacts. The gate is a magnificent building, though, with tiny cells and precarious stairways between the levels that give an excellent indication of what it must have been like for those who lived and worked here 600 years ago.

The Minster

ⓘ *T01904-557216, www.yorkminster.org. Opening times vary each month and for different areas of the building. You can pick up a helpful diagram of the building at the front desk, where you can also make a donation to the building's maintenance and repair. Be warned, though, that if you plan on visiting the entire building, fees are charged to enter the crypt, the Chapter House and the central tower. You can easily spend £10 without ever leaving the building.*

If you walk into town through Bootham Bar down High Petergate, you're essentially following in Roman footsteps on a route they called Via Principalis. The street curves a short distance past restaurants, pubs and shops and leads directly to where the extraordinary **York Minster** soars above low-slung York. The single most important historic building in all of Yorkshire, and the largest medieval cathedral in Britain, its pale towers are 200 ft tall and can be seen from miles away. Not bad for a church that was started as little more than a quickly built place in which to baptise a king. Its name is actually a misnomer: it is called a 'minster', which comes from the Latin *monasterium*, but it never served as a monastery. It stands on the site of the old Roman military headquarters, and impressive remains from Roman and Norman times have been found in its foundations. One of the most significant of the Roman finds stands to the right of the Minster in the form of the incongruously simple Roman column, which was unearthed in the Minster's basement and re-erected nearby in 1971, on the city's 1900th birthday. Historians believe the column was part of a huge Roman hall (the *Principia*) that once stood where the Minster is now.

A church has stood on this site for 1300 years. The earliest known church on this plot of soil was a wooden structure built in 627 for the baptism of King Edwin of Northumbria. It was later replaced in stone, but that building was destroyed in William the Conqueror's 'Harrying of the North'. The Norman archbishop Thomas of Bayeux oversaw the reconstruction that began in 1080, and the remains of that building can still be seen in the foundation and the crypt. The current Minster was begun in 1220, when Archbishop Walter de Grey ordered a church built to rival Canterbury's cathedral. Construction took 250 years, which explains why the building contains so many architectural styles – over and over again, the construction process outlived the designers. The south transept was the first section completed in 1240, and the north transept the second in 1260. By the time the nave was completed in 1345, de Grey was long dead. The choir was completed in 1405 and the towers in 1480, bringing construction, at last, to an end.

The crowning glory of York Minster is its glass. The most beautiful example is the heart-shaped **West Window,** which was created in 1338. The oldest glass is to be found in the second bay window in the northern aisle of the nave. Created in 1155, it contains the oldest stained glass in the country. While in the nave, take note of the ceiling which, while made of wood (it was built in 1840 to replace the previous roof destroyed by fire), has been painted to resemble stone. Throughout the rest of the Minster, the roof is actual stone.

At the cathedral's crossing is the north transept's **Five Sisters Window**, which gets its name from its five thin 50-ft tall panes. Near the window a vestibule leads to the **Chapter House** (£1.50). Built in the 13th century, it contains some of the finest decorated stonework in the country. Unusually, the vaulted wooden roof of the octagonal Chapter House stands without the support of a central column.

Back in the Cathedral, the window directly opposite the Five Sisters is the elaborate **Rose Window**, which was built to mark the marriage of Henry VII and Elizabeth of York in 1486. Also in the crossing is de Grey's own austere tomb, sadly dusty and lightly draped in cobwebs.

In the centre of the crossing, the **Choir** is separated from the **Nave** by a fascinating stone rood screen. Dating to the late 15th century, it features life-size statues of all the English kings (up to that date) except for Henry VI. At the end of the east aisle is the most impressive window in the Minster: the remarkable and awe-inspiring **East Window**, which, at 78 ft by 31 ft, is recognized as the world's largest medieval stained-glass window. Created around 1405 by John Thornton, its themes are varied, and include the beginning and the end of the world, with the upper panels telling the story of the Old Testament, and the lower panels the grim predictions of Revelations. Unfortunately, if understandably, visitors are kept so far from the window that, without binoculars, it's virtually impossible to make those scenes out. It's all a lovely, massive blur. A display nearby contains sketches of some of what you're missing, including strange interpretations of the Bible, with scenes of Adam and Eve being handed apples by a creature that is half-snake/half-woman and inexplicably winged. Another shows a drunken Noah being glared at by his family, while a third shows his ark populated by a handful of people and a whippet.

In the south transept are stairs down to the foundations or **undercroft** (£3.50) which has been converted into one of the most fascinating museums in all of Yorkshire. The space under the church was excavated in the 1960s during restoration work. While the work was underway, archaeologists uncovered extensive Roman and Norman relics that have been preserved here. Also found were the original foundations of the Roman fort, as well as extensive sculpture and stonework from the original Norman church. All are well displayed and arranged. Some sections – with Norman tombs for babies – are quite moving. From the undercroft you can visit the treasury, with silver plate pilfered from de Grey's tomb, and the cold and gloomy crypt, which contains interesting remnants of the 1080 church. A small doorway in the crypt opens onto the base of a pillar that was once part of the guardhouse of the original Roman camp.

Finally, before leaving the church, if you're not afraid of heights you can climb to the top of the **central tower** (£3) for bird's eye views of the city.

Around the Minster

The large green park through an arched gateway directly beside the Minster is **Dean's Park**, which makes a pleasant space for a picnic on sunny afternoons. The arched architectural fragments along its far edge are part of a Norman archbishop's palace, and if you follow the path that cuts through the park you'll reach the 13th-century chapel that holds the **York Minster Library** ⓘ *Mon-Fri 0900-1700*. It's here that you'll find the baptismal records for one of York's most famous sons, Guy Fawkes. Continuing through the park (and following the signs) is the **Treasurer's** House ⓘ *1030-1700, £3.80*, just outside the Minster grounds. The 17th-century building looks startlingly modern compared to its more ancient neighbours, but it's excellently preserved and has lovely gardens. It is most popular with lovers of period furnishings, as it is outfitted appropriately to its age, and there are regular tours of the interior. For those for whom a chair is a chair, the gardens out front are free.

On the other side of the Minster from Dean's Park is one of the oldest buildings in York. **St William's College** ⓘ *Mon-Sat 1000-1700, Sun 1230-1700*, is a half-timbered building that dates to 1467. Its name refers back to when it served as a school for the Minster's chantry priests. At other times it has been the Royal Mint and the king's printers. Today it holds an upscale restaurant, as well as a visitors' centre for the Minster. Three of its rooms are open to the public when they're not in use, as is its courtyard.

Stonegate

The streets around the Minster are sprawling shopping lanes, filled with tourist boutiques, tourist restaurants and tourist pubs. The most impressive of these streets is Stonegate, surely the most photographed street in all of York. This medieval lane made of the same stone as the Minster traces its history back to Roman times when it was called Via Praetoria. Today it is lined with antique jewellery shops and boutiques selling sweaters made of Yorkshire wool, alongside the usual suspects like *Crabtree & Evelyn*. Day and night it is packed with tourists, not least because it makes a handy cut-through from the Minster area down to Lendal Street along the river. Despite the constant throngs, it is still charming in its medieval completeness. This is also the street where Guy Fawkes' parents lived (look for the plaque). Sneaking down the little medieval pedestrian alleys – called (delightfully) snickleways or ginnels – that lead off of it can be rewarding. One ginnel leads to a rare fragment of a Norman house, while others lead to pubs and teashops. Look for the little red devil that squats on the wall outside No 33. Little figures like this one, high on the walls, once served as adverts or signs for the shops underneath them. This is one of the most unusual in York, and is believed to have served as a sign for a printworks once located here – printer's assistants were once called 'printers' devils'. Another intriguing figure can be seen at the head of Stonegate, at the intersection of High Petergate, where Minerva lounges on a stack of books up by the street signs. She marks the site of where a 19th-century bookseller operated out of a corner shop. The snickleway beside the red devil is known as **Coffee Yard**, and, at 70 m, is one of the longest in York. It's also one of the most used cut-throughs by locals, as it connects Stonegate with Grape Lane, with its pleasant restaurants, cafés and quality shops.

Lendal Street

If you're not carried away by the lure of ginnels, from Stonegate you can wander down to Lendal Street toward **St Helen's Square** where there is usually a hubbub with local street musicians entertaining the crowds. This is where you'll find the famed **Betty's** tearoom where it is still, evidently, 1945. People queue for hours through much of the day for a pricey cuppa here, but it's worth noting that before 1030 you can usually waltz right in for a breakfast scone. At one corner of the square, kind of tucked away, is the small but lovely 13th-century **St Helen's church**. The front of the church is sort of a trip through the ages, as the base is 13th-century, the capital 15th-century and the bowl 12th-century. Lendal turns into a wide shopping lane from here, with all the usual high street names, so unless you're in the market for some clothes, head back into the medieval town centre where Low Petergate leads to Goodramgate.

The Shambles

If you aren't lost by the time you stumble onto the Shambles, just at the edge of King's Square at the southern end of Goodramgate, you will be shortly. The narrow, crowded shopping lanes that run off of this street are generally overrated in terms of the shops they hold, but absolutely unmatchable in sheer historic charm. So old is this section of town, that it is the only street in York mentioned by name in the *Domesday Book* of 1086, which also lists the half-brother of William the Conquerer as owning a stall on the Shambles. While most of the stores today are the sadly predictable hocus-pocus magick shoppes or tepid stationery stores or sellers of Scottish/Irish/Yorkshire woollens, the streets are lined with wonderfully photogenic ancient timber-framed buildings. Once the city's butchers' quarter, it's easy to imagine what it must have been like to come here for a bit of meat for dinner when it was a teeming, stinking pit. The sharp-eyed will notice that some buildings still have old meat hooks hanging from their exterior walls. The similarly overrated, but no less charming **Newgate Market** is at one end of the Shambles as well, but you're unlikely to find anything to take home from it aside from a snapshot. Near the Shambles is York's most whimsically named street – **Whip-ma-Whap-ma-Gate**. Don't believe any explanations given to you by locals as to the derivation of the name; the sad truth is, nobody remembers anymore. It is one of history's curiosities.

Around the castle

The Shambles are a short stroll from the castle section of town, such as it is. This is the more modern section of York, with shopping centres and vast car parks. **Coppergate,** once the busiest street in Viking York, is no less crowded now that it is an über-high street. It tries to part you from your money over and over again throughout its length. Buskers sing sad songs outside unattractive buildings, and it's all more than a little depressing. At the end of the street is the much-hyped **Jorvik Viking Centre** ⓘ *T01904-543403, www.jorvik-viking-centre.co.uk, daily Apr-Oct 0900-1900, Nov-Mar 0900-1730, £6.50.* Now, the people of York are so damn proud of this place that it seems churlish not to marvel at it, but to be honest, this one's mostly for the kids. The centre is largely a recreation of a Viking village – which would be fine in itself, but they've turned it into a kind of carnival ride, which is just strange. You sit in a ferris wheel seat as you're motored smoothly past plastic blacksmiths and marketers of the Viking era. The selling point is the fact that the faces of the 'people' in the museum were based on Viking skulls found in the area, so this is probably what the early inhabitants did look like. Along with sights there are smells and sounds as well, but, all-in-all, you're unlikely to learn anything here that you didn't know already.

Not far from the Viking centre on Fossgate is the **Merchant Adventurers' Hall**, a gorgeous timber-framed hall once owned by the region's leading businessmen and wool traders. Its sheer beauty and historic completion are the primary reasons for sticking your head in the door. Nearby on Castlegate is the **Fairfax** House ⓘ *T01904-655543, Mon-Thu, Sat 1100-1700, Sun 1330-1700*, another one of those lovely historic houses restored with period furnishings. This one is Georgian and has the added attraction of containing the 18th-century art collection of chocolate magnate Noel Terry.

As for the **Castle** itself, aside from the city walls, all that's left is the sad-looking and sparse keep called **Clifford's Tower**, which stands ignobly on its mound in the centre of a modern car park. This version was built in the mid-1200s. The old Norman keep was destroyed quite infamously in 1109 during a pogrom in which 150 Jews were hidden there to protect them from an anti-Semitic mob, which then surrounded the building and waited to kill them. Forced to choose between starvation and murder, the Jews committed mass suicide by setting their own prison aflame. Fascinating and dark though its history is, there's little here now of any interest. Across the parking lot, though, is the wonderfully eccentric **Castle Museum** ⓘ *T01904-653611, www.york castlemuseum.org.uk, Apr-Oct Mon-Sat 0930-1730, Sun 1030-1730, Nov-Mar Mon-Sat 0930-1600, Sun 1030-1600*, with its bizarre and extensive collection of artefacts through the ages. These were amassed by one mysterious man, a Dr Kirk from nearby Pickering, who decided 80 years ago that somebody should protect the pieces of the area's heritage or all would be lost. So he gathered everything he could, including pieces belonging to his patients who handed them over instead of cash for treatment. The museum is actually located in an old debtors' prison, and includes a little bit of everything, from the ancient to the just-a-few- years-ago. His recreation of a medieval York street is quite magnificent, and some of the pieces he found – including a Viking helmet found in excavations on Coppergate – are truly impressive.

Elsewhere in York

One of the least visited of the city's bars is **Walmgate Bar** (which is located far from the action at the end of Fossgate), and more's the pity as it is the only gate in the country to retain its barbican. The 14th-century walls still bear the scars from the Civil

War battles that took place here in 1644. The last gate, **Micklegate Bar**, was once the most important of the four, as it oversaw the main road to York from London. It also once served as a prison for the wealthy. Today it holds another one of those pointless museums-without-artefacts, designed more to amuse than to educate.

Past Micklegate Bar and the York train station, is one of the best museums in the country. The **National Railway Museum** ⓘ *Leeman Rd, T01904-621261, daily 1000-1800, free*, is a vast, exhaustive, extraordinary facility detailing the history and engineering of train travel in Britain. The enormous museum contains more than 50 locomotives dating back to the early 1800s, all still in working order, along with gorgeously restored railcars that date back to the 1700s, some splendid and rich, others definitely second class. There's memorabilia galore, with posters, charts, adverts and bits and pieces of train history sure to have trainspotters refusing ever to leave.

Around York

Within an hour's drive of York the countryside changes, as the flat farmland gives way to the rolling hills of the moors. Between the city and the hills are a series of charming villages, reminders of wealth past and ancient edifices.

Castle Howard

ⓘ *T01653-648444, www.castlehoward.co.uk, Feb-Nov, house 1100-1600, grounds 1000-1630. House and grounds inclusive, £9, concessions £8, under 16s £6; gardens and grounds only, £6, under 16s £4. Off the A64, 11 miles northeast of York, well-signposted.*

In 1772, Horace Walpole wrote of Castle Howard: "Nobody... had informed me that I should at one view see a palace, a town, a fortified city, temples on high places, woods worthy of being each a metropolis of the Druids, vales connected to hills by other woods, the noblest lawn in the world fenced by half the horizon, and a mausoleum that would tempt one to be buried alive; in short I have seen gigantic places before, but never a sublime one." While that might be overstating it a little, it is *only* a little. This fantastic building among the farmland about 15 miles north of York has an irresistible lure to anybody who followed breathlessly the trials and tribulations of the upper classes in the series *Brideshead Revisited*. The extraordinary manor house that served as a backdrop to that 1970s programme was Castle Howard. With its domed roof and Grecian-style statues, this vast building stands as proof that some people have more money than sense. Not a castle at all, but a mansion with ambition, the Baroque building was designed in 1699 by Sir John Vanbrugh and Nicholas Hawksmoor for Charles Howard, the third Earl of Carlisle. Vanbrugh, who was not an architect, designed and oversaw the construction of the main house until its completion in 1712, and was working on the rest of the building when he died in 1726. Vanbrugh's lack of construction and design experience has led many experts to speculate that Hawksmoor had much influence on the design of the building. Nobody knows precisely what Howard was thinking when he chose Vanbrugh to design his home, although some speculate that he simply liked his fellow nobleman personally. But amateur though he was, Vanbrugh obviously had a knack, as Hawksmoor later agreed to work with him on Blenheim Palace.

The sheer length of time it took to complete the structure affected its design. While the central building is elaborate, with a large dome, rooftop statues, and fussy detail, the house's two wings are in slightly different styles. The west wing, in particular, completed in the late 1700s, is much simpler in style than the main building, reflecting changes in architectural tastes over the course of that century. But the dominance of the central structure means that you barely notice the lack of

Walks in Yorkshire

- **Haworth Moor**: 11 miles one-way. Start: Haworth. A bracing climb up on to the moors past Wuthering Heights and down through the wooded valley of Hebden Water to Hebden Bridge. OS Maps: Outdoor Leisure 21
- **Bolton Abbey**: 6 miles there and back. Start: Bolton Abbey, 5 miles east of Skipton. A gentle riverside walk up the Wharfe valley to find the Strid Wood Nature Trail. OS Maps: Outdoor Leisure 2
- **Leeds and Liverpool Canal**: 4 miles there and back. Start: Gargrave, 4 miles west of Skipton. Another gentle stroll along an attractive stretch of canal from Gargrave to Bank Newton. OS Maps: Outdoor Leisure 2
- **Stoodley Pike**: 4 miles there and back. Start: Hebden Bridge. A stiff walk up to the monument and viewpoint overlooking the town. OS Maps: Outdoor Leisure 21
- **Robin Hood's Bay**: 7 miles there and back. Start: Robin Hood's Bay, 5 miles south of Whitby. A coastal fossil-rich clifftop walk south along part of the Cleveland Way to Ravenscar. OS Maps: Outdoor Leisure 27
- **Wheeldale Moor**: 6 miles there and back. Start: Goathland, 8 miles south west of Whitby. A walk up onto the moors past Mallyan Spout waterfall to find the remains of a Roman road called Wade's Causeway. OS Maps: Outdoor Leisure 27
- **Rye Dale**: 8 miles there and back. Start: Helmsley. Past Duncombe Park and up the lovely Rye Dale towards Rievaulx Abbey. OS Maps: Outdoor Leisure 26
- **Whernside**: 5 miles there and back. Start: Chapel Le Dale. A well-trodden but enjoyable hike up to the top of the highest peak in Yorshire Dales, 2419ft high. OS Maps: Outdoor Leisure 2
- **Littondale**: 4 miles there and back. Start: Halton Gill. A secluded moorland walk up onto the hill of above one of the Dales' more peaceful valleys. OS Maps: Outdoor Leisure 2

perfect balance in the wings. The inside of the building is, if anything, even more over the top than the exterior, filled as it is with paintings by Rubens and Van Dyck, along with so many Chippendale chairs sitting below friezes and plasterwork frills that the mind boggles. The word 'gaudy' doesn't just come to mind, it leaps into the cerebellum. Not all of the building is open to visitors, as members of the Howard family still live here, but there's enough to be seen to satisfy.

The thousand acres of **grounds** are better, really, than the house. Even before you reach the building you drive through one unnecessary-but-beautiful archway after another. In the front of the house, a huge fountain gushes amidst statuary and perfectly manicured hedges. Peacocks saunter across the grounds and glower at visitors from the shade of trees. Vanbrugh's excess is here again in the form of man-made lakes that glitter in the distance, and the pointlessly lovely **Temple to the Four Winds** that lures you to take the necessary hike to find it. Then there's the family **mausoleum,** which towers impressively. The extensive walled gardens have a way of keeping horticultural types absorbed for hours. When it all becomes too much, as it likely will, you can take a seat in the house's teashop and rest your feet for the duration of a cream tea. If the kids are getting tetchy about all the adult stuff, take them down to the children's playground by the lake, or wander the nature trails. This is the Disneyland of manor houses.

Kirkham Priory

ⓘ *Apr-Oct 1000-1800, £1.70, off the A64, 5 miles southwest of Malton.* Just a few miles from Castle Howard, the scant remains of this Augustinian priory attracts few visitors, and that's a shame if only because while there's not much left of the building itself, the setting is spectacular. The 14th-century ruins sit in a green valley beside the slow-moving River Derwent. It is one of the most peaceful, naturally gorgeous locations of any of England's old abbeys.

Thirsk

The bustling town of Thirsk, 23 miles north of York, once home to the world's most famous veterinarian, is a trifle disappointing in quite a few ways. James Herriot's village idyll is not the good-sized town, with traffic and impatient drivers, modern buildings and high street shops that you see before you. You'll find no stone cottages, sheep or lowing cattle here. There's a hint of the old medieval Thirsk in the large, colourful **market place**, but it all gets lost in the traffic jams. There are a few Georgian homes on and around Kirkgate, near the market. The moderately interesting **Thirsk Museum** ⓘ *16 Kirkgate, www.thirskmuseum.org Easter-Oct 1000-1600 Mon-Wed, Fri, Sat. £1.50*, does its best to make up for the modern look of the town by telling you what it looked like back when it was charming. But just about everybody who comes here breezes past that museum and heads to the nearby **World of James Herriot museum** ⓘ *23 Kirkgate, www.worldofjamesheriot.org, Easter-Sep 1000-1800 daily, Oct-Easter 1100-1600 daily, £4.50.* The vast size of the car parks near this facility give a good idea of what people are here for. Thirsk claims rightful ownership to being the town that Herriott called 'Darrowby' in his books, and it was here that the author, whose real name was Alf Wight, worked as a veterinarian. The museum – inside his animal surgery, 'Skeldale House' – is dedicated to his life and practice. The years of work, and £1.4 million in cash, that went into creating this ode to Alf paid off, though, as the museum is an entertaining and painstaking recreation of living quarters for the 1940s and 50s and sets of the TV series *All Creatures Great and Small*. Along with a peek at how Wight might have lived, there are also displays on veterinary work past and present. Interactive exhibits examine horse dentistry, as well as the strength needed to calve a cow.

Sleeping

York *p682, map p684*

York is a tourist town, so hotels abound, and B&Bs even more so. While accommodation is scattered about, Bootham and Clifton streets have the highest concentration, and is a particularly good place to go hunting for a room if you've arrived without reservations. The tourist office in the train station will also book a room for you.

A The Grange Hotel, 1 Clifton, T01904-644744, www.grangehotel.co.uk. This grand old building has large, gorgeous rooms with all the modern amenities along with a friendly staff and some of the best restaurants in York. It's well located in easy walking distance of the city centre.

B Judges Lodging Hotel, 9 Lendal, T01904-638733, www.judges-lodging.co.uk. A short stroll from the Minster in a listed Georgian townhouse on the tourist track. Many of its rooms have 4-poster beds.

B Royal York Hotel, Station Rd, T01904-653681, www.principalhotels.co.uk. Makes, if nothing else, a lovely view, with three acres of landscaped gardens. It is designed to pamper in historic elegance.

C Alhambra Court Hotel, 31 St Mary's, Bootham, T01904-628474, www.alhambra courthotel.co.uk. Well-appointed rooms with period furnishings within walking distance of the centre.

C Bootham Bar Hotel, 4 High Petergate, T01904-658516, www.booth ambarhotel.com. This period building is tantalizingly close to the Minster but has only a handful of rooms, some of which share a bathroom.

C Wheatlands Lodge Hotel, 75-85 Scarcroft Rd, T01904-654318, wheatlodge@aol.com. A large, friendly facility near the train station with all the modern conveniences, along with a pleasant bar and handy restaurant.
D 23 St Mary's, 23 St Mary's, T01904-622738. A sweet, centrally located hotel near St Mary's Abbey - family owned.
D Bootham Guesthouse, 56 Bootham Cres, T01904-672123, F672123. A friendly, quiet place tucked inside a period building, walking distance from the centre, with cheery owners and massive breakfasts.
D Bronte Guesthouse, 22 Grosvenor Terr, T01904-621066, F653434. In a period building with charming rooms with en suite bathroom, walking distance from the centre.
D Carlton House Hotel, 134 The Mount, T01904-622265, www.carltonhouse.co.uk. An elegant Georgian house with modern accoutrements 5 mins from the centre.
D Crook Lodge, 26 St Mary's, T01904-655614, www.crooklodge.co.uk. Historic building with 7 rooms (bathroom en suite) 500 yds from the centre.
D Friar's Rest Guesthouse, 81 Fulford Rd, T01904-629823, www.friarsrest.co.uk. Has 7 rooms (bathroom en suite) in an historic monastery 10 mins' walk from the centre.
D The Golden Fleece, 16 Pavement, T01904-627151, goldenfleece@fibbers.co.uk. A few lovely rooms in a historic pub, it's also extraordinarily well located with views of the Minster and the Shambles. Best of all, every inch of the place is said to be haunted.

Eating

York *p682, map p684*
It seems like the only thing there's more of than churches in York is restaurants. Choose carefully from the ranks, and you can have a very good meal here.
£££ Blue Bicycle, 34 Fossgate, T01904-673990. The fantastic serves fabulous gourmet dishes with a seafood emphasis in a gorgeous building that once served as a brothel. Don't even think about going if you haven't booked, though.
£££ The Grange Hotel 1 Clifton, T01904-644744. Modern European dishes in an unashamedly posh atmosphere. Prices are unsurprisingly steep at both restaurants.
££ Melton's Too, 25 Walmgate, T01904-634 341. A good option for an excellent dinner or just an afternoon nibble, offers modern dishes in a 1690s building.
££ Rubicon, 5 Little Stonegate, T01904-676076. Rubicon is a modern, elegant and cool vegetarian restaurant. The bustling atmosphere here is all business, the food is creative and international in scope.
££ Russells Restaurant 34 Stonegate, 01904 641432. Dinner for two around £30. There's almost always a crowd gathered round the big plate-glass windows out front of this place on touristy Stonegate, watching the carvers cutting enormous legs of beef and lamb on to large plates. This place packs 'em in, night after night, for meaty meals from carving stations.
££ St Williams Restaurant, College St, T01904- 634830. Offers modern British cuisine in the grand setting of one of York's most historic buildings right next to the Minster.
£ Caesars Pizzeria & Ristorante 27-9 Goodramgate, T01904-670914. Inauspiciously located at the foot of the Minster, this casual Italian may be filled with tourists, but the food is good traditional fare and the atmosphere is laid back.
£ Café Concerto, 27 High Petergate, T01904-610 478. Creative fusion cuisine at a reasonable price in this sunny café, although it's even better for a piece of cake and a cup of coffee in the afternoon.
£ The Patio, 13 Swinegate Court East, T01904-627879. This breezy, cheery restaurant has as many tables outdoors as in, and its menu is basic reliable food, with an emphasis on English dishes and a wide array of salads and sandwiches for lunch. Very near the Minster, often crowded.
£ Plunkets, 9 High Petergate, T01904-637722. Offers American dishes with a southwestern flavour at moderate prices, although booking is essential at weekends.

For an explanation of the sleeping and eating price codes used in this guide, see the inside front cover. Other relevant information is provided in the Essentials chapter, page 40.

Pubs, bars and clubs

York *p682, map p684*
Some of York's pubs are almost too historic and quaint. You feel like it's a put on.
The Black Swan, Peasholme Green, T01904-686911, is one of these. In a distinguished medieval timber-frame house, the pub dates back to 1417. Understandably, it is believed to be haunted, so look out for a filmy but beautiful girl staring anxiously into the fireplace.
Blue Bell pub on Fossgate. For friendly locals head to this tiny and adorable pub where two dinky rooms surround the little bar. The amiable staff will look out for you, and there are occasional (and challenging) pub quizzes on Sun nights.
The Olde Starre Inne, 40 Stonegate, T01904-623063. The sign for this pub is one of the easiest to spot in town, as it stretches clear across Stonegate. The sign itself dates from 1733, while the tavern preceded it by a couple of hundred years. Despite its spot on the tourist path, this is a lovely boozer with lots of wood panelling, open fireplaces and etched glass.
The Old White Swan, Goodramgate, T01904-540911. One of the largest pubs in town, spread over a warren of nine medieval, timber-framed buildings. Its lunches are particularly good.
The Roman Bath, St Sampson's Square, T01904 620 455. An ancient pub with a modern interior and enough noise and nonsense to scare any ghost back to the tomb. Generally, this place is tourist hell, and not particularly pleasant in any way except that in 1930, during renovations, Roman baths were discovered in its cellar. The baths are so well preserved that footprint indentations from its centurion users can be seen along with the insignia of a Roman legion.
Snickleway Inn, also on Goodramgate T01904-656138. When you enter its historically perfect rooms of this sweetly named 15th-century pub, with open fireplaces and a real sense of history, it won't seem surprising that this is believed to be one of the most haunted pubs in York.

Entertainment

York *p682, map p684*
Cinema
City Screen, 13-17 Coney St, T01904-541155, has transformed York's cinema life to include art-house films in a riverside setting with a posh café and bar packing them in every night.
Odeon, Blossom St, T01425-954742. For mainstream films.

Theatre
Grand Opera House, Cumberland St, T01904-671818. Has a variety of productions including ballet, theatre, musicals and opera.
Theatre Royal, St Leonard's Pl, T01904-623568. This is where the locals go for musicals, pantos and mainstream theatre.

Shopping

York *p682, map p684*
In many ways, this whole town is one big shopping centre. Major shopping streets include **Stonegate**, with its antique jewellery shops, toyshops, and woollens, **Coppergate**, with its high-street shops for clothing, **Lendal St** with its department stores and chain bookstores. Less high profile but more interesting are the designer clothing boutiques and quality art stores on **Grape Lane** and **Swine Gate**. For more touristy shops you can join the crowds in **The Shambles** and nearby **Newgate Market**.

Activities and tours

York *p682, map p684*
One of the best-known horse racing tracks in the country,
York Racecourse, T01904-620911, is just outside of town. By road, the A64 and A1036 will get you there. On race days, a shuttle bus runs every 20 mins from York Station. York Racecourse dates back to 1731.

Festivals

York *p682, map p684*
Jul York's **Early Music Festival**, which is held each Jul, is justifiably famous, and historically based musical groups travel here from all over the world to perform.

Jul York Mystery Plays, T01904-551800 are held every 4 years in the Museum Gardens, with the next one set for summer 2004.
Aug Tote Ebor Festival at the racetrack attracts more than 80,000 fans every year.

Transport

York *p682, map p684*

Bus
National Express, T08705-808080, run direct services from **London Victoria** (5 hrs), **Birmingham** 1 daily (3 hrs), **Manchester** 2 daily (3 hrs), **Leeds** (1 hr), **Sheffield** 1 daily (2 hrs 30 mins).

Car
Europcar, York Station, T01904-656161; Practical Car and Van Rental, 5 mins' walk from the station on Rougier St, T01904-624277.

Taxi
Castle Cars, 22 Fetter La, T01904-611511; Station Taxis, Station Rd, T01904-623332.

Train
Virgin Trains, run services to York from **London King's Cross** (2 hrs) and **Birmingham New Street** (2 hrs 30 mins). Arriva run direct services from **Manchester Piccadilly** (1 hr 30 mins), **Leeds** (30 mins), **Sheffield** (1 hr 15 mins).

Around York *p691*

Bus
There's National Express, T08705-808080, bus service to **Thirsk** from York (2 buses a day), and local bus service to nearby towns like **Kilburn**, **Coxwold** and **Helmsley** Mon, Fri and Sat. Buses stop at the market place.

Train
The train station (with trains to York and Middlesbrough) is just west of town on the A61 – there's a shuttle service to the centre of town National Rail Enquiries T08457-484950.

Directory

York *p682, map p684*

Internet Internet Exchange, 13 Stonegate, T01904-638808. **Hospital** York District Hospital, Wigginton Rd, T01904-631313.

North York Moors

→ *Colour map 6, grid A4/5*

The stark beauty of the moors never fails to impress. Were there no signs at all telling you that you had reached them, you would still know that you were there. The view changes from emerald green farmland to the dark, almost black-green, hue of the heather. In summer, when it is in flower, the vista is tinted dark pink as far as the eye can see. At the farthest points of the North York Moors, you can drive for miles without seeing anything but roaming sheep, which, occasionally, you must shoo from the road in order to continue on your way. The villages here tend to be small and quaint, and in the middle of nowhere. The names of villages – Goathland and Hutton-le-Dale – reflect the languages of centuries of invaders and there is a comfortable sense here that little has changed, or will change, as the decades go by. ▸▸ *For Sleeping, Eating and other listings, see pages 704-705.*

Ins and outs

Getting there and around The **Moorsbus,** T01439-770657, www.moorsbus.net, connects many of the towns, in its brief operating season, otherwise a car is absolutely necessary to get to the smaller villages. Run by the National Park Authority, and intended to make the very limited transport through the region more convenient, the Moorsbus runs throughout the North York Moors in the high season. The service is very limited, operating only Sun and bank holidays from Apr-Oct, and daily from late Jul-1 Sep. Still, it is helpful if you can arrange your schedule around it. You can pick up timetables in all area tourist offices. The routes are from Helmsley to Sutton Bank, Osmotherley, Rieveaulx, Coxwold and Kilburn; Pickering to Hutton le Hole and Castleton; Danby to Rosedale Abbey and Dalby Forest; and Helmsley to Pickering. There's also long-distance service to Beverley, Darlington, Hartlepool, Hull, Middlesbrough, Northallerton, Redcar, Saltburn, Scarborough, Stockton, Thirsk and York. ▸▸ *See Transport, page 705, for more details.*

Information Helmsley TIC ⓘ *in the town hall, T01439-770173, Easter-Oct 0930-1700 daily, Nov-Easter 1000-1600 Sat, Sun*, is helpful for all your questions about how to get around, things to see in the area and where to stay. It sells information, maps and guides for walks in the moors and the Cleveland Way.

North York Moors National Park (West)

Osmotherley

The little stone village of Osmotherley sits with medieval charm about 10 miles north of Thirsk. Once an agrarian centre, it is now best known to ramblers who wander by it while hiking the ambitious Cleveland Way. Even if you're more into four-wheel transport, it's worth a visit, both for its sheer cuteness and for its mysterious stone table. According to lore, John Wesley preached from atop this rock, although there's not much to back that up. There's also an old market cross nearby to glance at before you head for the Mount Grace Priory nearby. Well-marked walks from here include one to the priory (about 2 miles), or you can try your legs at the stretch of the **Cleveland Way** walk to the 982-ft summit of **Scarth Wood Moor** and on to **Cod Beck Reservoir** about 3 miles away. Of course, if you think that's for wimps, you can get on the **Lyke Wake Walk**, which stretches for 42 exhausting miles across the rolling moors to the white cliffs of **Ravenscar** on the coast (see page 711).

Most people choose the short route to **Mount Grace Priory** ⓘ *Apr-Sep 1000-1800 daily, Oct 100-1700 daily, Nov-Mar 1000-1300, 1400-1600 Wed-Sun, £3*, (which can be reached either by foot or car, just off the A19), and for good reason. Its simple structure and lovely setting make it a uniquely beautiful place. Historians consider it to be the most important and best-preserved Carthusian ruin in Britain, and its modest structure stands in stark contrast to the more spectacular Cistercian ruins, such as Rievaulx (see page 699). Built in 1398, its simple design is explained by the equally simple life led by Carthusian monks, who lived lives of solitude – having taken vows of silence – unlike the communal Cistercians. Rather than living in grand shared houses, each Carthusian monk was given his own stone hut and a garden to tend, with a handsome church (the tower of which still remains) in the middle of the large grounds. Despite their proximity to one another, they lived in isolation – even their little homes were hidden from one another by tall stone walls. While most of the huts lie in ruins, one has been reconstructed to give an idea of their size and appearance. There's also a herb garden, landscaped to fit the monks' descriptions of their own gardens. There's an on-site information centre and gift shop.

Coxwold

The sweet little village of Coxwold, with its quaint stone buildings and flowering window boxes, has been attracting tourists for as long as the writer Laurence Sterne has been dead. Sterne, author of *The Life and Opinions of Tristam Shandy*, served as vicar at the church of St Michael's from 1760 until he died in 1768, and is buried in the churchyard. While the tombstone standing above his grave is damaged, there's another stone on the porch from his first grave in London. Sterne's story is a strange one. Educated as a vicar, his writings made him a star. *Tristam Shandy* was published in 1760, and after that he was a famous figure on the London scene.

Further volumes of the tale only made him more famous. When he died in London of pleurisy in 1768, he was buried there. But controversy arose immediately as rumours circulated that his grave had been vandalized and his body stolen along with hundreds of others, and sold for medical research. The story circulated for centuries, and so, in 1969, his body was exhumed. When the coffin was removed from the grave, authorities found a mixture of bones and five skulls inside. One of the skulls was determined to be Sterne's, and it, along with the bones, was taken to Coxwold for reburial. Exactly what happened to Sterne, and whose heads that were buried with his, is not known for certain. The most likely explanation is that the graverobbers took the body before the headstone was carved, and did not know that they had stolen a famous man. Upon figuring out just what they'd done, they hurriedly refilled his coffin with whatever body parts they could find.

Along with the curiosity of Sterne's grave, Coxwold also offers the charms of **St Michael's Church**, with its unusual octagonal tower and medieval stained-glass windows. Up the road is Sterne's home, **Shandy Hall** ⓘ *T01347-868465, house, May-Sep Wed 1400-1630, Sun 1430-1630, gardens, May-Sep, daily except Sat 1100-1630, house and garden £4.50, child £1.75, garden only £2.50, child £1.25,* which has been converted into a museum to his life, filled with books and memorabilia. The aptly named home was where Sterne lived when he wrote the controversial *Tristam Shandy*, and his travel tales *A Sentimental Journey through France and Italy*.

You can meet other tourists for a beer and some lunch at the comely Fauconburg Arms pub on Main Street. It is named, by the way, after the husband of Oliver Cromwell's daughter Mary. The happy couple lived in a house at nearby **Newburgh Priory**, which was once a monastery founded in 1150. According to lore, Mary brought her father's body back to her house at the priory after it was exhumed from Westminster Abbey in retaliation for Cromwell's leadership role in the Civil War. This story maintains that she brought only the body, and not the head (in order to conceal his identity), and then buried the parts she had at the priory. There's nothing much to back the story up, but it's a colourful tale nonetheless.

Byland Abbey

ⓘ *2 miles south of A170 between Thirsk and Helmsley. Apr-Sep 1000-1800 daily, Oct 1000-1700 daily, £1.80.*

There's not much left of the 12th-century Byland Abbey, but what remains looks like a Gothic sculpture. An arc of stone that once held a huge stained-glass window scoops the sky, and a single turret points up, as if indicating the direction of heaven. Surrounded by miles of nothing, the image is striking. For historians, its biggest attraction is the large section of cream-coloured medieval floor tile that remains in the chapel, continually threatened by the grass that tries to overgrow it. There's also a well-preserved walkway, believed to have been used by lay workers who served the cloistered monks.

Helmsley

Teetering at the edge of the North York Moors, Helmsley is a picture-perfect village, complete with flowering window boxes, stone cottages, arched bridges across streams, picturesque churchyards and the ruins of a Norman castle, in short, this town is a travel photo waiting to happen. Luckily, you're saved from the tooth-hurting cloyness of non-stop charm by the intercession of hundreds upon hundreds of tourists, and – that sure indication that a town is overrun – coach parking areas. There's a handy public car park in the central **town square**, which is an excellent starting base for an exploratory wander. The square is surrounded by shops (there's a useful tourist office in the town hall) and is the scene of the weekly market each Friday. The cross at the centre of the square marks the start of the **Cleveland**

Way ⓘ *For information on the Cleveland Way, ask at the Helmsley tourist office (see page 697) or contact The Cleveland Way Project, T01439-770657.* The famed walking path that starts at Helmsley and crosses the North York Moors, the Cleveland Hills and the coastal cliffs before ending in Scarborough.

Beyond the square the town's medieval lanes are lined with twee shops likely to warm the heart of any grandmother. If you're looking for pink hand-knitted jumpers or garden gnomes, you'll be in heaven. Just past the shops, the stark ruins of **Helmsley Castle** ⓘ *Apr-Sep 1000-1800 daily, Nov-Mar 1000-1300, 1400-1600 Wed-Sun. £2.40*, overlook the town from a well-tended green field. While not a great deal is left of this Norman castle, what remains is quite evocative. You enter via a wooden bridge over the moat, past remnants of the walls. The one standing tower makes for a dramatic photo, while more recent 15th-century structures are also intact, and you can wander through them at will.

At the edge of Helmsley is the 18th-century manor house **Duncombe Park** ⓘ *T01439-770213, May-Oct Sun-Thu 1100-1730, house £6, gardens £3, nature preserve £2*. Built in 1713, the vast building sits on impressive grounds overlooking Helmsley Castle and the River Rye. The current home of Lord and Lady Feversham, direct descendants of the Duncombe family who first ordered the house built in 1713, the house is filled with furnishings impressively authentic to the age of the structure. But the 35 acres of landscaped gardens, and 450 acres of woodland in the house's nature preserve, are even more impressive. There's a spectacular view of Helmsley below.

Nunington Hall ⓘ *Jun-Aug 1330-1700 Tue-Sun, Sep, Oct, Apr, May 1330-1630 Wed-Sun, £5*, a grand 16th- and 17th-century manor house at the edge of the Rye is most famous for its Carlisle Collection, a series of miniature rooms, all exquisitely filled with period furniture. The grand old house also features a sweeping staircase and lofty entrance hall. It's surrounded by lovely gardens and woods, and the whole place is said to be haunted, although you're more likely to see tourists than ghosts.

Rievaulx Abbey

ⓘ *T01439-798228. Apr-Sep 1000-1800 daily, Jul-Aug 0930-1800 daily, Oct, Feb 1000-1700 daily, Nov-Mar 1000-1600 daily. £3.60 (Terrace £3.40). There is a well-signposted walking path from Helmsley to Rievaulx (about 3 miles), otherwise you can take the Moorsbus, T01439-770657 in season, or drive the brief distance following the clear signs that lead you there.*

Several miles from Helmsley, just inside the North York Moors, are the remains of one of the most spectacular abbeys in all of England. Once the most important Cistercian abbey in the country, Rievaulx was founded in 1132 by French Cisctercians seeking to expand their sect into Britain. Its biggest period of growth came under the rule of its third abbot, St Aelred about 20 years later, when construction first began on most of the buildings that remain now. Aelred was the most famous monk of his day, and he is considered by some to have been the greatest religious writer in England during the Middle Ages. For several hundred years, Rievaulx was an enormous working abbey, with farmland, fisheries, textiles and mining operations run by lay workers. At its peak, Rievaulx was home to 140 choir monks and 500 lay brothers and lay servants. From the 13th century on, however, the population in the abbey declined, as political changes made it difficult for the abbey to prosper. By the time Rievaulx was suppressed in 1538, only 22 monks still lived on the grounds.

The ruins of Rievaulx are impressively complete, and the look of the place – with the jagged arched walls juxtaposed against green wooded hills – is breathtaking. Enough is left of the buildings to give an awe-inspiring indication of how magnificent it all must have been when it was complete. In particular, the spectacular **nave**, where arch within symmetrical arch still stand, is vast and towering. Signs tucked into the grass and mounted on the walls show where the chapel stood, and what the various rooms that remain once were. Little is left of the cloister, but the Chapter House still holds a shrine to the first abbot. There's also a well-preserved **refectory**, considered one of the finest ever built by the Cistercians. Even the monks' **dormitory** and **latrine** remain.

The on-site **visitors' centre** offers more information about Rievaulx, as well as a few sandwiches and drinks. The little village around the abbey – with medieval stone houses – is simultaneously charming and forbidding, the latter, perhaps, simply because of the rural isolation of the place.

On the wooded hill above Rievaulx, are the terraced woodlands that once made up some of the gardens of Duncombe Park. The **Rievaulx Terrace and Temple** is separate from the abbey (and requires a separate entrance fee), divided by thick woods. The grass-covered terraces and woods were designed in the mid-1700s to offer a bird's eye view of the abbey, as it still does today. There are two elaborate 'temples' on the terrace, with period furnishings and paintings. There is also an ongoing display on landscape design.

North York Moors National Park (East)

Hutton-le-Hole

Hutton-le-Hole is undeniably precious, with perfect stone cottages and colourful gardens framing a quiet stream with grassy banks upon which lovers woo and children gambol. Pesky sheep wander the streets at will, stealing a nibble through fence posts, and snoozing in the shade of garden walls. But everybody knows about this place, so it's packed to the gills with tourists and in such a little village, the crowds can be downright oppressive. The locals who run the *Barn Hotel and Tearoom* and the *Crown* pub try to keep up, but are quickly overwhelmed and then submerged in the waves of hungry and thirsty travellers. As these are the only options for food and drink, it would not be a bad decision to see Hutton-le-Hole and then go eat somewhere else. Still, it's charming, and worth a quick wander. Its proximity to Helmsley, just 8 miles away, is probably as responsible for its popularity as are its pretty gardens. Along with the sheer charm of the place, the **Ryedale Folk Museum** ⓘ *T01751-417367, daily 1000-1630, £3.50, child £2, family £9*, is the biggest draw in town. This two-acre museum is respected for its efforts to recreate and preserve historic rural life. Inside you can watch metal being hammered in a 16th-century blacksmith's shop, and glass being blown in a glass furnace. There's a traditional herb farm, a Tudor cottage, craft workshops, and that's just the start. The museum's gift shop has information on the area and on local walks for amblers.

> *If you want to get the most popular and adorable moors village out of the way first, start here.*

Lastingham

After only a mile or so of sheep and moors and winding narrow roads, the tiny hilltop village of Lastingham appears with its stern stone houses whose gloomy aspect is successfully lightened by the colour spilling from lush gardens and windowboxes. In the summer, moors sheep wander down the curving roads and graze lazily in the picturesque churchyard around the parish church. In fact, one tends to inadvertently herd the docile creatures while seeking out the more interesting gravestones. (In revenge, you can eat them for lunch at the pleasant *Blacksmiths Arms* pub directly opposite.) Lastingham is tiny enough and far enough off the beaten track to be one of those rare lovely Yorkshire villages not overrun with day-tripping tourists. Along with the almost clichéd perfection of the town, the main attraction here is **St Mary's Church**, which holds the distinction of having one of the oldest crypts in the country. The small sanctuary is pleasant, if somewhat ordinary because of repeated renovations over the centuries, but the crypt is simply extraordinary. Bede mentioned a monastery at Lastingham in 731 in his *History of the English Church and People*, and it's believed that the first monastery was founded here more than a hundred years before that. It was started by a bishop named Cedd, who later died in Lastingham of the plague in 664, and was buried here. This made the church a regular stopping point for pilgrims. Vikings destroyed much of the church in the ninth century, but it was rebuilt a century later as a shrine to St Cedd (who, by then, had been beatified). All of the crypt that doesn't date from the 600s was built then. (The crypt is thought to be the only one in England with an apse (rounded end) together with a chancel, nave and side aisles.) The four Norman columns supporting the vault have bases that appear to be of pre-Conquest workmanship. Historians believe that the crypt has not been changed since the time of William the Conquerer. Best of all, access is free, and it's not unusual to have the whole place to yourself.

Rosedale

It's best to approach Rosedale from the north, as from that direction you top a high hill with an extraordinary view of rolling moors that extends for miles. From a distance the old mining village is obscured by trees, and thus it appears suddenly in front of you as you drive up. It's a less charming and more gangly town than Lastingham or Hutton-le-Hole, where nature seems to be taking over; no sheep wander its streets keeping the grass tidy, houses are hidden away behind thick foliage. Built as it is on the side of a steep hill, in places its streets are precipitously vertical, and the signs telling you where to find **Rosedale Abbey** are hard to see, and difficult to understand. If you do successfully find your way to the town – which took its deceptive name from a long-gone Cistercian monastery – you'll find there's not much there except for the beautiful countryside. The remains of the abbey were largely scavenged to build **St Lawrence's** parish church. Still, the crowds pour in to Rosedale village on summertime weekends, mostly just to sit around the *Milburn Arms*, a busy pub (and rather overpriced inn) with a good view. Others are here to head out on one of several **walks** that pass by the area. A particularly daunting one follows the route of the old moorland railway that once carried ore mined from the nearby hills. The train line is now a popular pathway offering extraordinary views. Bear in mind, of course, that the sweeping views are directly proportional to the steepness of the path. You can join the walk at **Hill Cottages**, about a mile or so north of Rosedale Abbey (there are a few fairly unhelpful signs virtually ensuring that you will get lost, so OS Landranger 100 map is recommended). A full walk around the head of the valley covers 10 largely uphill miles and takes several hours. Along with the pub, there are a few small inns in town, as well as the inevitable *Abbey Tea Room*, and a caravan site down by the river ⓘ *T01751-417272*.

Pickering

One of the biggest market towns in the moors, Pickering, like Helmsley, is a hub of sorts. Although it's a rather charmless town, it offers lots of places to stay, impressive castle ruins, and, of course, the fabulous **North Yorkshire Moors Railway**. It makes a good base for wandering the eastern moors by car, foot or via the episodic Moorsbus or the romantic steam railway. There's usually parking places to be found in the centre of town, although if that fails there are car parks down near the railyard. Near the centre of the hillside town is the gloomy **Church of St Peter and St Paul**. The church features a Norman font, and is famous (or infamous) for the 15th-century wall paintings in its nave, which were painted over in the 19th century by an overly anxious vicar who feared they would arouse passion and idolatry among his parishioners. Later restored, they tell biblical and historical tales, but hardly arouse passion or idolatry. Further up the hill from the church are the solid stone walls of **Pickering Castle** ⓘ *Apr-Sep 1000-1800 daily, Oct 1000-1300, 1400-1700 daily, Nov-Mar 1000-1300, 1400-1600 Wed-Sun, £2.50.*

Once a splendid royal home used primarily as a hunting lodge, the castle dates back to William the Conquerer, although most of what remains was built in the 12th century. The motte (a man-made hill on which the keep was built) was ordered built by William himself, in order that he could defend the castle from attacks coming from the surrounding territory. His 11th-century defences make for excellent 21st-century views – from the top you can see for miles. Aside from the walls and the motte, there's not much left of the castle, but what remains is impressive. The restored castle chapel was built in 1227, and features an exhibition on the history of the structure, including the fact that Richard II was held captive here after his abduction.

You can see the steam from the undeniably pretty **North Yorkshire Moors Railway** engines from the top of the castle's motte ⓘ *T01751-472508, www.northyorkshire moorsrailway.com, £10 for an all-day adult pass, £5 child, £8.50 seniors, £25 for a family of 4*. A short walk downhill takes you to the quaint station, which, right down to the advertisement posters on the walls, has been restored to look as it did in 1937. This is what most people are in Pickering to see, and if you come across no tourists elsewhere in town, you will surely find plenty on the colourful train platform, where the crowd surges forward to see the old engines pull in, puffing mightily, in an utterly authentic swirling cloud of steam and cinders. The train takes an 18-mile journey from Pickering to Grosmont, stopping along the way at Levisham Station in the scenic Newton Dale Valley, then at Newton Dale Halt and Goathland Station. The train is particularly popular with walkers, as a variety of paths pass near those stations, so you can easily leave the train at one stop and walk to the next. The whole enterprise is a labour of love, since most of the workers on the trains and in the stations are volunteers. Even the old carriages, with their wooden fittings, were restored by volunteers working in their spare time. The train follows one of the oldest lines in England; trains travelled this route from 1835 to 1965. After being closed down, the line was reopened as a private operation in 1973. Days and times of operation vary from month to month, although service is hourly during the summer. Timetables can be picked up at the station or at any TIC in the area.

In a fine Regency building behind the train station, the **Beck Isle Museum of Rural Life** has a series of rooms devoted to different aspects of historical life in the area. One room is a cobblers, another a barber's shop, and so forth. Further examples, including a blacksmith's forge and wheelwright, are located in outbuildings. Or you could just taste a little rural life of your own at the **Moorland Trout Lake** next to the station, where, in a kind of circular food chain, you can either catch fish to eat, or throw food for the fish to eat. You can hire tackle and bait, as well as fish food, on-site.

Thornton-le-Dale

Just two miles from Pickering, the village of Thornton-le-Dale would have you believe it's the 'prettiest village in Yorkshire'. Unfortunately, that's just not the case. It's pretty enough, but when it comes to sheer sweetness and beauty, Lastingham and Lealholm leave it in the dust. Still, it's worth a look. Its stone houses and old market cross are attractive, and it has interesting long houses. The man-made streams that babble down the main roads are a remnant of its past as a milltown. The old stocks have place of honour next to the cross in the village centre. Just across the street from the cross are **Lady Lumley's Almshouses**, a series of 12 structures built in 1670, and still used as housing. The old **forge** has been converted into a twee gift shop, and its old pharmacy into a modern chemist. Inevitably there's a glut of teashops here, all of which you can give a miss without any guilt. Its main claim to fame is its one thatch-roofed cottage, which tourists crowd to photograph.

Dalby Forest

Just outside Thornton-le-Dale, the Dalby Forest begins. A favourite with hikers, the thick expanse of wilderness includes a number of paths. The most popular walks pass near the car park at **Low Stain Dale**; the best known of these is the **Bridestones Trail** which features many of the mysterious sandstone boulders that appear throughout the moors, and whose origin is not really known. There are a number of well-marked paths to choose, but if you'd rather drive, there's a nine-mile toll road through the forest (£4, road open 0700-2100 daily) that ends near the town of Hackness. Whichever way you travel, it's a good idea to visit the visitors' centre, at **Low Dalby** ⓘ *T01751-460295, www.forestry.gov.uk, May-Sep 1000-1700 daily, Oct and Apr 1000-1600 daily, closed winter*, where you can get information on trails, wildlife and the history of the forest.

Levisham and Lockton

Just at the edge of the Dalby Forest, you can pick up the North Yorkshire Moors Railway at Levisham Station, which is about a mile outside the pretty flower-strewn village of Levisham. A popular **walk** passes through here as well, heading to the equally charming town of Lockton about a mile away, where there is a handy **youth hostel**, T01751-460376. (Be aware that it is a very long mile, as the two villages are separated by a deep gorge.) Both villages are so old that they are mentioned in the *Domesday Book*. For many people though, the longest walk they will take is the short walk from the station to the *Horseshoe Inn*, T01741-460240, which does an excellent lunch. It has a few rooms as well although, if you haven't booked in advance, you'll have to be satisfied with a meal. Still, few things in life are more pleasant than sitting in front of the *Horseshoe* on a sunny day watching the weary walkers stride by.

Hole of Horcum

This extraordinary gorge just off the A169 north of Levisham is so breathtaking that local officials had a car park built opposite it to stop motorists running one another off the road as they gazed at it. A deep, heather-covered indentation in the hills, much lore surrounds the Hole, which is also called the Devil's Punchbowl. Legend holds, for instance, that a giant named Wade scooped the Hole when he grabbed a handful of dirt to throw at his wife during one of their rows. The clod missed her, and fell a mile away, forming the hill known as **Blakey Topping**. The view from the edge is stunning, also a number of paths lead down into the depths of the valley, and across to the nearby hills.

Goathland

If you feel like you've seen this place before – with its plain stone houses, bright red roofs and close-cropped village green – you probably have. The town of Goathland stands in for the imaginary 'Aidensfield' in the popular television series *Heartbeat*.

The town's name sounds like 'Goatland' but it's actually a corruption of the word *gaut*, which meant 'gorge'. 'Sheepland' might be a more appropriate name, since farmers have grazing rights to the whole town, and sheep wander freely, grazing on the wide lawns, keeping the village green sheared down nearly to dirt, and nibbling naughtily at flowers in people's gardens. While the town is distinctive – all stone cottages with unusual red roofs – most of the attraction lies in natural wonders at the edge of the village. Carved by the movement of water, Goathland is surrounded by natural water features, including several waterfalls. The best of the bunch is the impressive 70-ft **Mallyan Spout**, which can be reached by a footpath that starts next to the *Mallyan Spout Hotel*, T01947-896486, not a bad place to stay the night, or just to have a lazy drink. You can also pick up the **North Yorkshire Moors Railway** here, and take a ride courtesy of steam power. From Goathland you can also hike up to the tiny village of **Beck Hole**, accessible only by foot. The mini-village features an equally small pub, the **Birch Hall Inn**, which is highly rated by pub experts. It also serves as a store and sandwich shop, and its home-baked pies are legendary.

Around Grosmont

Several miles of lovely moorland northeast of Goathland, the village of Grosmont bustles in the summertime, with traffic from trains, coaches and the Moorsbus unloading crowds of walkers attracted to the excellent walking paths in the area. But, aside from the **North Yorkshire Moors train** station, where the steam engines are lined up at the end of every day (Grosmont is the terminus), there's not much to see in the town itself. Built to house workers on the old Pickering-Whitby train line, the town is plain and utilitarian. Similarly, the nearby towns of **Egton** and **Danby** are popular primarily for their lovely natural settings, and as stops for walkers making their way down one of the many moors paths. Egton, and it's neighbour **Egton Bridge**, has historic religious attraction as well. Known as 'the village missed by the Reformation' Egton Bridge remained a staunchly Catholic stronghold throughout the suppression of Catholicism. It was the birthplace of Father Nicholas Postgate, who carried on a secret Catholic ministry in the town, and was arrested in 1678 for illegally baptizing a child. After his trial in York, the 80-year-old priest was hanged, drawn and quartered. The Egton Bridge **Church of St Hedda** holds a number of Postgate's belongings. On a walking path midway between Egton and Egton Bridge is the **Mass House**, which still has a tiny chapel secreted away in its loft, where once-banned Catholic masses were held. The loft, which is accessible only by a hidden passageway, had been forgotten until it was discovered in the mid-19th century.

Lealholm

Despite other claims to the contrary, it is entirely possible that this is the prettiest village in Yorkshire. A few miles northeast of Grosmont on a narrow country lane, the town appears as the road dips down into a small valley. Thick green trees surround the cottages gathered at the edge of the shallow River Esk. There really is nothing here at all, except for the rare simple beauty of the place. The river is crossed downstream by a bridge of peach-tinged stone, while a short stroll away a stepping stone bridge in the same subtle pastel hue offers a more amusing way to cross from one bank to the other. Nearby, you might see a child being taught to fish by his grandfather, and residents catching up on their gardening may pass you with arms filled with plant cuttings. You get the feeling that the quiet here is constant. Three or four buildings make up the centre of town; there's a little antiques shop and the *Shepherd's Inn*, which has a few rooms, acres of chintz and a good restaurant. Across the bridge, *Cameron's Inn* has a charming restaurant and tearoom with views over the river.

Virtually all of the houses in this farming village have the same enigmatic symbol above their doors, and some bear the inscription, "Ancient Society of Shepherds".

Sleeping

Helmsley *p698*

If you're looking to stay in Helmsley, there is no shortage of accommodation, as long as you don't mind the B&B variety. Many B&Bs line Ashdale Rd (just up Bondgate from the square). If you prefer a hotel, there are fewer options, though one of the best is the slightly expensive **B Black Swan** on Market Pl, T01439-770466, which has lovely gardens, pub and restaurant.

For an explanation of the sleeping and eating price codes used in this guide, see the inside front cover. Other relevant information is provided in the Essentials chapter, page 40.

C **Feversham Arms**, just behind the old church, 1 High St, T01439- 770766. There is an excellent bar and restaurant as well, and serves modern European cuisine.

Hutton-le-Hole *p700*
This is a tiny village, and there are few options if you're determined to stay here.
D **Barn Hotel**, T01751-417311, is usually booked months in advance in the summertime.
D **Hammer and Hand**, T01751-417300. A lovely B&B, make sure to book. Alternatively ask at the folk museum for more advice on B&Bs in the area.

Pickering *p701*
In the summer, accommodation in Pickering can get booked up quickly, so, if you haven't booked ahead, be prepared to do a little searching. The **TIC** near the Eastgate car park has helpful lists of B&B availability, T01751-473791. Apr-Oct 0930-1800 Mon-Sat, 0930-1700 Sun; Nov-Mar 1000-1630 Mon-Sat.
C **Forest and Vale Hotel**, Malton Rd, T01751-472722, www.forestand valehotel.co.uk. An 18th-century manor house a little way out of town.
D **The Black Swan**, 18 Birdgate, T01751-472286, F472928. An 18th-century coaching inn with 4-poster beds and a good restaurant downstairs.
D **Crossways Hotel**, 134 Eastgate, T01741-472804, F472804. Has a good location and is a lovely Victorian building.
D **The White Swan** T01751-472288, www.white-swan.co.uk. Among the better hotels in town, this is a charming, old inn located right on the marketplace.

Transport

North York Moors National Park (West) *p697*
Bus
You can get to Coxwold by (relatively infrequent) bus from York - Mon, Fri and Sat only). There is also a seasonal **Moorsbus**, T01439-770657, www.moors bus.net, that runs a regular service daily to towns and significant sites in the area between Jul and 1 Sep (see also page 696), and on Sun and bank holidays from Mar-Oct.

Car
Coxwold is off the A170 five miles east of Thirsk, or off the A19 down a series of winding country road

Helmsley *p698*
Bus
There is a bus service between Helmsley and other nearby towns including York and Scarborough, T0870-6082608, as well as the **Moorsbus** T01439-770657 (see page 696) which runs regular service from late Jul to early Sep.

Coastal Yorkshire

→ *Colour map 6, grids A5-B6*

From the edge of the moors you can look into the distance and see the deep blue – almost midnight blue – of the North Sea. The black-purple hills roll right to the edge of land, and the sudden appearance of the flat expanse of sea is almost startling. Here the atmosphere changes drastically from the straightforward farm communities to the wry humour of the wayfarers who make their living at sea. Mysterious moors stones give way to mischievous whalebone sculptures. The shrieking of gulls replaces the vibrato of sheep. Gentle hills are truncated by threatening cliffs. Similarly, the stolid stone villages of the moors disappear, and colourful towns like Scarborough, with its creams and yellows, Whitby, with its blue and russet hues, and Robin Hood's Bay, with its vivid red rooftops, gleam. This is a different Yorkshire in many ways, but the seaside promenades, rock candy and silly hats are also accompanied by ancient ruins of castles and abbeys that tell the tale of the history of this land. ▸▸ *For Sleeping, Eating and other listings, see pages 717-721.*

Dracula's town

The Irish author Bram Stoker was searching for a hit when he visited Whitby on holiday in 1893. He was working with Sir Henry Irving at the time, running the London Lyceum Theatre, and he longed to write a play that would bring attention to the theatre and to himself. Instead, of course, he ended up writing a novel that has continued to attract readers – and filmmakers – for more than a century. Staying at No 6 Royal Crescent, Stoker was taken by the dark beauty of the town and its ruins. Searching for a villain, he discovered the name 'Dracula' while reading in the old Subscription Library near where Pier Road meets Khyber Pass. He based the Count's shipwreck arrival in Whitby – wherein his vessel crashes into the rocks near the pier – on an actual shipwreck that occurred here in 1885. He would later have one of the characters in the novel describe the abbey he could see from his own window as "a most noble ruin, of immense size, and full of beautiful and romantic bits". He placed the novel's heroines Mina and Lucy, as well as Count Dracula's attorney, in houses on East Crescent. And describes the town in detail, as Mina races down the western cliff, across the bridge, up Church Street, then climbs the stairs to the churchyard in her bid to save her friend. While there is certainly a kind of cult of Dracula in Whitby, and visitors could be forgiven for thinking the town cultivates this, in fact, the reverse is true. The town is not gloomy because Stoker based Dracula here. The feel of the place hasn't changed in centuries and it seems entirely probable that if he had not based a horror novel here, somebody else would have.

Ins and outs

Getting around It's relatively difficult to travel around here by **train**, as only Scarborough and Whitby have stations. Trains to Scarborough run from Hull every 2 hours, and from York every 45 minutes. There are four trains daily to Whitby from Danby, Grosmont and Middlesbrough.

A series of coastal **roads** skirt the ocean and connect to one another, the A174 in the north, the A171 in the centre and the A165 in the south. Keep an eye out for signs, as many towns along the coast have only one entrance road and if you miss it, you've missed it. There are regular **buses** between Scarborough and Helmsley, Hull, Leeds, Milton, Middlesbrough, Pickering, Robin Hood's Bay and Whitby. **Traveline**, T0870-6082608. For information on the periodic Moorsbus service, see page 696. ▸▸ *See Transport, page 720, for more details.*

The coast to Whitby

Staithes

The northernmost village on the Yorkshire coast, little Staithes clings tenaciously to the edge of the land. It's easy to miss the turnoff from the A174, so keep an eye out for the signs, and don't be put off by the first somewhat grim view of the town. After you park in the public car park and walk down the cliff to the town, you'll understand why you came this far. (Don't make the mistake of driving into the town; the signs are true – you really can't park down there, and you don't even want to think about trying to turn a car around on its claustrophobically narrow streets.) It's a wonder this weatherbeaten town still exists, considering the strength of the storms that regularly slam against it. But it's a good thing that it hangs on, as Staithes is probably the most historically authentic fishing village in the region. In fact, it has changed little since Captain James Cook came here as a boy to bide his time before he could take to the sea. While some coastal towns are fairy tale pretty, Staithes is rugged, yet not without charm. Set against the backdrop of the cliff known as **Cowbar Nab**, the village is divided down the middle by a deep gorge, and on either side are stone houses – some on the side of the steep divide seem to defy gravity – with red tiled roofs. Everywhere are fishing nets and lobster pots drying in the sun. Fishing and crabbing are still the main business here, and the small harbour is filled with bobbing, workaday boats – this is no yacht harbour. While the town has a look of unchanging completeness about it, in fact, many of its buildings have washed away over the years. The colourful *Cod and Lobster* pub has blown away three times. The drapers' shop near the pub, where James Cook worked as a lad, was destroyed by the weather in 1745 – the building now on the site (marked by a plaque) is a replacement.

To learn more about Captain Cook, head to the High Street for the **Captain Cook and Staithes Heritage Centre** ⓘ *Daily 1000-1730, £1.75*, which not only tells the story of his life, but includes a recreation of an 18th-century Staithes street, complete with shops. Otherwise, there's not much to do here except to wander around and take in the sights and sounds. Just north of town you can hike up the **Boulby Cliffs**, which tower at 650 ft, making them the highest on the coast. Or you can follow the cars with surfboards sticking out the windows to the nearby beaches said to offer some of the best waves in England.

Kettleness and Goldsborough

The barren strip of rocky coast at Kettleness is often overlooked by travellers, and, in fairness, there's not much here except an amazing view. Once the site of massive alum mines, the clifftops here are empty of foliage, and only the tiny village, and massive flocks of seabirds, provide signs of life. It would seem you'd need wings to live here, and, in fact, the entire village was destroyed in a landslide in 1829 – the villagers were plucked from the sea by ships. Today the towering brown cliffs make for devastatingly stark photos, and a fascinating hike. Half a mile from Kettleness, the town of Goldsborough stands on the site of a fourth-century Roman signal station. The road known as **Wade's Causeway** was once a Roman road. Still, this one is mainly for history buffs, as there's not much to see here now save for a grass-covered mound off the road between Kettleness and Goldsborough.

Whitby

Erstwhile home to both Bram Stoker and Captain Cook, Whitby is a town with two distinct personalities. The waterfront promenade with novelty shops, candy floss and fish and chip shops is one Whitby, while the other is manifested in the grim clifftop church and the skeletal abbey which loom above the town like an admonishment. This is one of the most interesting towns in all of Britain, a beautiful and paradoxical place. For centuries, Whitby was cut off from the rest of the country by its isolated location at the foot of cliffs. By the 18th century, however, it had become a prosperous major port and a northern leader in shipbuilding, fishing and whaling. Its wealth lasted through the 19th century and is demonstrated in the row of fine Georgian houses on the top of the west cliff, built by and for successful shipbuilders. Most of the town, though, is more modest, with the whitewashed cottages and humble shops built for fishermen making up the most common structures.

Ins and outs

Getting there Whitby is on the Esk Valley line and **trains** run once daily to Middlesbrough (1 hour 30 minutes) from the station on the harbour near the town centre. Getting there from London King's Cross involves two changes at Darlington and Middlesbrough (4 hours 45 minutes).

Whitby is on the A174, and is well signposted. There are large **car** parks next to the train station. You can catch most buses at the bus station, next to the train station. ➤ *See Transport, page 720, for more details.*

Getting around The River Esk divides the town as it flows out to sea. This provides a handy geographical division of the town's two personalities: Whitby Abbey stands on the east cliff above the oldest section of Whitby, while a statue of Cook and a massive arch of whalebones dominate the more modern west side. The town is quite small, and best handled on foot. There are a very few local buses, with a stop near the train station, but these are only useful if you're going out of town, as walking is simply the best way to get around.

Information Whitby TIC ⓘ *corner of Langborne Rd and New Quay, near the bus station. T01947-602674, May-Sep 0930-1800 daily, Oct-Apr 1000-1230, 1300-1630 daily.* It offers maps, information on tours and an accommodation booking service.

Eastern Whitby

As you cross the swing bridge toward eastern Whitby, looking out to sea the two piers on either side of the river reach out into the water like pincers, with a small lighthouse in the centre of each. Cobblestone streets that twist and turn up the eastern cliffside are flanked on either side by tourist-orientated shops, restaurants and pubs. Because there was limited space at the base of the cliffs, buildings were constructed very close together and they crowd up the steep sides of the hills, connected by medieval pedestrian alleyways (called ginnels) and stone staircases. **Church St** is the main route on this side, and it is filled with jewellery shops peddling Whitby jet – the famed glossy black stone (actually fossilized wood) that was so fashionable among the funereal set in Victorian times – antique stores and clothing shops. Tiny **Grape Lane**, which branches off to the right, has buildings dating back to the 17th and 18th centuries. About midway down its short length is a former bank building with a single bottle-glass window that stretches the length of the building, the result of window tax evasion. Nearby is the former home of Captain John Walker, a ship owner under whom Captain Cook served his apprenticeship from 1746-49. The house has been converted into the **Captain Cook Memorial Museum** ⓘ *T01947-601900, www.cookmuseum whitby.co.uk, Apr-Oct 0945-1700 daily, Mar 1100-1500 Sat, Sun, £2.80, concessions from £1.80*, and contains a number of pieces of memorabilia, although some of it is only distantly related to Cook's life.

The cobbled area at the intersection of Church and Grape streets was once the Tollgate where, until 1540, the abbot of Whitby gathered his dues. The **Salt Pan Well Steps** leading off of Church St climb up to the old ropery which once made rigging for shipbuilders. Following the path to the **Boulby Bank** (once used by monks from the abbey to move goods down to the seafront) and past the old **Seamen's Hospital** leads to a gallery with wide views across the town and harbour. Nearby is **Elbow Terrace**, which once held a busy smuggler's tunnel, long ago filled in and replaced with houses. Back at the top of Church Street is the curved base of the famous **199 steps** up to the Gothic **St Mary's Church**. Bram Stoker memorialized the steps in his novel *Dracula*, in which Mina, in a frantic effort to save Lucy, rushes up the steps to the churchyard above. Climbing to the top is the equivalent of climbing an 11-storey building, so most people don't rush up; they creep, pausing to take in the view and grab a breath along the way. It's easy to see why the steps struck Stoker: they were originally built for pallbearers carrying coffins up to the churchyard at the top. It must have been a spectacularly dark sight, the black-clad people silently carrying a body up the long stairway as the church bell tolled. At night, the gloomy old church is lit by spotlights aimed up from the ground – the architectural equivalent of the old campground trick of holding a torch under your chin to cast scary shadows on your face. Local youths have discovered that if they stand in front of the lights and stretch their arms out to either side they can cast giant shadows that look, from the town, like moving crosses on the walls of the church – it's funny, in a scary way. The windswept churchyard reaches to the very edge of the high seafront cliff and is almost too gloomy to be real, with long grass bending in the constant wind past the blackened tombstones. Hollywood could not create a spookier looking place. The Romanesque church dates back to the 12th century (although it has been altered many times since then), and the inside is even more strange than the outside. In the 18th century, the chapel was filled with wooden galleries and high-backed box pews that fill every inch of space. Some have the names of families painted distinctively on the side. One is labelled 'For strangers only'. The three-level pulpit is undoubtedly a matter of necessity: it has to be high in order for the vicar to be seen from the high-walled pews.

Through the churchyard to the back is a lane leading to the **abbey** ⓘ *T01947-603568, Apr-Sep 1000-1800, Oct 1000-1700, Nov-Mar 1000-1600, £3.80, child £1.90, family £9.50. If the stairs are a problem, there is a car park at the top of the cliff behind the abbey, follow the brown signs off the A171*, which is directly behind St Mary's. Over the years, **Whitby Abbey** has been one of the most photographed ruins in the country, and it is an astonishingly bleak combination of terrain and architecture that can be seen from miles away. An abbey has stood here since the seventh century, when the Northumbrian king, Osway, first founded a monastery, unusually, one that was for both men and women, on this site. The abbey flourished under the leadership of the abbess Hild, later St Hild, and grew to be a religious centre in Anglo-Saxon society. It's believed that the monastery was destroyed by the Danes in the ninth century (the only remains of this first abbey are a handful of gravestones near the nave). The abbey was not rebuilt until after the Norman Conquest, when a knight named Reinfrid, who fought on the side of William the Conquerer at the Battle of Hastings, decided to rebuild it. The Benedictine abbey he founded here lasted until Henry VIII suppressed the country's monasteries. The land was sold to a wealthy family in the 17th century, who demolished much of the abbey and built the large manor house adjacent that is now the abbey's visitors' centre. It is believed that the only reason the abbey ruins still stand is because its distinctive outline was an important navigation point for ships. The most impressive part of the structure that still remains is the 13th-century choir, with its soaring east wall and banks of arched windows. In the grass inside the choir are deep markings showing where the original church ended in a rounded apse. The 13th-century north transept stands at the site of the church's crossing, and still has a medieval inscription carved into its northern arcade column crediting a monk with carving a long lost altar.

The first known poem in English, 'The Song of Creation', was written here by a monk named Caedmon.

Western Whitby

The western side of the town is mostly a 19th-century development, created when Whitby became a popular seaside resort, and the mood of holiday frivolity couldn't be more different from the town's east side. Along the waterfront all the usual noisy arcades, chip shops and 'kiss me quick' hats are present and accounted for. Further down Pier Rd is the more serious attraction of the **Whitby Lifeboat Museum** ⓘ *T01947-602001/606094, Easter-Oct daily 1000-1600 (subject to weather), donations requested*, which has an interesting exhibition on the death-defying work of lifeboat crews. Up above on West Cliff are elegant houses and Georgian crescents as well as the much-photographed whalebone arch and statue of Captain Cook. Not far from here, at the **Royal Crescent** on West Cliff, No 6 was the house where Stoker stayed in Whitby (it's marked with a plaque). Down below, heading away from the sea via Baxtergate is the *Tap and Spile* pub, which once had a river frontage and sat above the entrance to a smuggler's tunnel. Goods were brought into the pub from the river and carried through the tunnel underneath the nearby cottages to a pub (at the site of the restaurant now called *The Smuggler's Café*) where they were distributed. A short distance down Bagdale Street is the impressive Tudor manor house **Bagdale Hall**. Now a hotel and restaurant, the building still has many of its original fittings and the massive fireplaces that once provided all the building's heat. Further up Bagdale, behind Broomfield Terrace, is **Victoria Spa**, a circular building with a lantern roof that was popular in the 19th century for its medicinal waters. Nearby, at Pannett Park, is the unique **Whitby Museum** ⓘ *May-Sep 0930-1730 Mon-Sat, 1400-1700 Sun, Oct-Apr 1030-1300 Mon, Tue, 1030-1600 Wed-Sat, 1400-1600 Sun, £2,* a wonderful, old-fashioned place in which some objects are still explained in script on yellowing notecards. Much of the museum is devoted to the city's heritage among seafarers and whalers. There's still more Cook memorabilia here, including objects his crew brought back from their trips, alongside some unusual fossils – including some from the Jurassic period – that had been discovered in the area.

Whitby to Scarborough

Robin Hood's Bay

One of those rare towns that lives up to its fairy tale name, Robin Hood's Bay huddles on the side of sheer cliffs as if it's trying to hide from view. It fails completely, of course, betrayed by its roguish beauty and lovely setting. There's not much in the way of traditional sights here – no museums or castles – its just a peaceful and pretty place in which to wander and get lost on its tangled staircases emerging, suddenly, on the windswept headland. Its trademark bright red rooftops seem to stack one on top of each other as the whitewashed stone cottages are built on nearly perpendicular rocks that reach inexorably for the sea. The Bay, as locals call it, does less fishing and more tourism these days, and only a few boats are tied up at the water's edge. The name is one of the many mysteries of the town; nobody knows where it comes from, although legends abound. The least fanciful story is that the Merry Men fled here at some point, and the green one disguised himself as a fisherman until the heat was off. There's a car park at the top of the hill, and all visitors are required to park there and walk down the steep cobblestone road to the town below; ignore this rule at your peril, as these roads were built for horse-pulled carts, not for Vauxhall Astras. There's one street in the village, its edges sprinkled with a few art shops, one or two souvenir shops and a couple of tiny pubs and restaurants. The rest of the houses are reached by a series of stone staircases. There's no harbour, and houses are built all the way to the water's edge. *The Bay Hotel*, which stands closest to the sea, famously had its windows smashed by the prow of a boat that got too close. The writer Leo Walmsley lived at No 8 King St from 1894 to 1913, and based a series of novels in the fictional fishing village of 'Bramblewick', which acted as a stand-in for Robin Hood's Bay. Known for its history as a haven for smugglers, it is said that, in the 18th century, everybody in the town was so complicit in the crimes that goods could be passed from one house to the next, through windows and tunnels, all the way from the harbour to the top of the road. When a cottage on Chapel St was renovated in the 1980s, the owners found a pit under the floorboards big enough to hold four casks of brandy.

For sun worshippers, there's a sandy **beach** to one side of the town, and a rocky strip of coast on the other. When the tide is out, this is said to be a good place to find fossils.

Ravenscar

A few miles south of Robin Hood's Bay, some of the best views on the coastline can be had at the ill-fated 'town' of Ravenscar. On red-stone cliffs that soar hundreds of feet above the dark blue sea, the gorgeous view stretches for miles. The area looks like a flat, grassy park, until you study it further and notice that it is arranged like a cul-de-sac. In fact, a developer named John Septimus Bland planned to turn the area into a resort town, and laid out the roads, put in a drainage system and built a couple of shops and houses before realising it was a terrible idea. The perch is too high, the route down to the sea too precarious, and the competition from Whitby and Scarborough too intense for it ever to have worked. He dropped the idea, and the abandoned development now provides handy parking spaces from which to stroll to the isolated *Raven Hall Hotel*, T01723-870353, which once acted as George III's hideaway when the mental demons were acting up. The views from the hotel, where the cliffs reach 800 ft high, are extraordinary.

Scarborough

Scarborough is one of those towns that looks best from afar: from a distance it glows like a cream-coloured mirage against the backdrop of dark blue sea and green hills. Up close, it's somewhat more tacky, particularly along the waterfront, where casinos, arcades and souvenir shops fight for space with hamburger stands and candy shops. Above it all, the ancient fortifications of Scarborough Castle bristle anachronistically. The castle might be the only attraction here, were it not for a woman named Elizabeth Farrow, who, upon drinking a glass of local spring water in 1620, and noting its mineral taste, pronounced it medicinal. Over the subsequent years, thousands poured into the town to take 'the cure', and the town was built up to cater to them. By the time Queen Victoria took the throne, Scarborough was one of the country's most popular resort towns among the moneyed classes.

Ins and outs

Getting there The **train** station is conveniently located in the centre of town at the top of the hill on Westborough. Trains leave daily for Hull (1 hour 20 minutes), Leeds (1 hour 30 minutes) and York (1 hour). You can get to Scarborough from London King's Cross by way of York (3 hours). If you're driving down the coast, Scarborough is on the A165. If you're driving in from Central Yorkshire it's on the A170. **Coaches** and **buses** arrive at the train station including the **Yorkshire Coastliner**, T01653-692556, services which connect Leeds and York with the coast, and **National Express**, T08705-808080, buses from London and York. **Traveline**, T0870-6082608. ➡ *See Transport, page 720, for more details.*

Getting around Scarborough is sprawling, but walkable, if you've got the time. If you prefer to ride, there is a handy park-and-ride bus system that will shuttle you to major sights in town – look for the signs near any of the 12 car parks in the town centre. This is a better option than attempting to drive from one sight to another, as traffic is congested, parking is competitive (lots often fill up early) and the general frustration of trying to find a streetside parking place can take the fun out of the day.

Information There are two TICs in Scarborough. The **main office** ⓘ *Pavilion House on Valley Bridge Rd, T01723-373333. May-Sep 0930-1800 daily, Oct-Apr 1000-1630 daily just across the road from the train station.* There's another office on the waterfront ⓘ *Sandside, Easter-Oct only (no phone enquiries).*

Sights

Along the waterfront the amusements are quite obvious. The **North Bay** offers the most places to spend your money with its water slides, games and miniature North Bay Railway. At the far north end, the **Sea Life Centre** ⓘ *T01723-376125, daily 1000-1600, £6.95, concessions £5.95, child £4.75,* has hands-on aquatic exhibits with aquariums filled with sealife and rockpools. All along the waterfront are carnival rides and games rooms, as well as myriad opportunities for ocean cruises and speedboat rides. On the curve of the headland, there's nothing but sea views – an acknowledgement of the power of the sea that prevents any development here. On the other side, the beaches on the **South Bay** are wider and more popular than are those on the north. Here, too, are more silly seaside amusements, but there are also grown-up options in the form of the lush **South Cliff Gardens** to which a hydraulic lift ascends (Jul and Aug only), offering great views of the town and sea. From the gardens you can branch out across the clifftop neighbourhoods to explore the city's lovely Victorian architecture. For fans of Victoriana, the house known as **Wood End** ⓘ *The Crescent, Jun-Sep 1000-1700 Tue-Sun, Oct-May 1100-1600 Wed, Sat, Sun,* is now a museum dedicated to that time. It was once the holiday home of the Sitwell family, famed as writers and philosophers.Of all the buildings in Scarborough, the single most beautiful is the rambling, turreted structure that stands commandingly at the top of the cliff. Still called the Grand Hotel, it was a

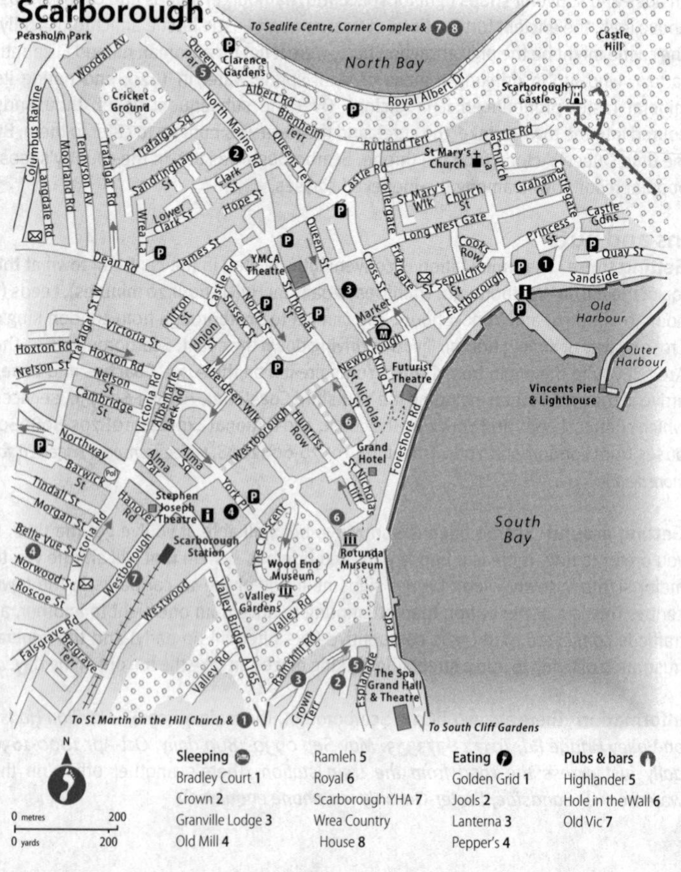

favourite haunt of the rich and famous after its construction in 1867, but today it offers a humbling lesson in faded glory, as it is now an inexpensive lodging.

Virtually all of the city's museums are at this end of town. The unique round Georgian building on Vernon Road that holds the **Rotunda Museum** ⓘ *Jun-Sep 1000-1700 Tue-Sun, Oct-Apr 1100-1600 Tue, Sat, Sun, a £2 ticket known as a Museum S Pass, can be purchased at any of Scarborough's museums, and provides entrance to all of them*, is hard to miss. The best museum in town, the Rotunda holds interesting archaeological remains that have been discovered in the area, including the 3500-year-old body that has come to be known as Gristhorpe Man. He was discovered buried in the trunk of a hollowed oak tree. The museum also has the only information you're likely to find on the Scarborough Fair, which first appeared on the scene when Henry III was king. On Albion Road, the church of **St Martin on the Hill** is home to a collection of pre-Raphaelite art. The pulpit features panels by Rossetti, while other pieces are by Burne-Jones and William Morris.

According to local lore, King Richard III so loved the views from **Scarborough Castle** ⓘ *T01723-372451, Apr-Sep 1000-1800 daily, Oct 1000-1700 daily, Nov-Mar 1000-1600 daily, £2.80, concessions £2.10, child £1.40, family £7.00*, that his ghost still returns here today. For nearly 900 years, the castle's rambling ruins have dominated the northern headland, but use of the site as a fortress has been traced back much further than a millennium. Archaeological digs have uncovered items from the Bronze and Iron ages. The Romans used it as a signalling station in the fourth century. The structure that remains dates from 1136, when it was built by William de Gros to replace a wooden fort. Henry II later took the castle for himself – even as he was destroying similar structures around the country as he asserted his authority over the territory – because he saw it as virtually impossible to invade. He was right. Although the castle was repeatedly besieged, it was never taken by force. Still, its isolation was also ultimately its weakness: in 1645 Hugh Chomley's Royalist troops held out for months under attack by John Meldrum's Scottish army, until their food stocks ran out. Even then they fought on until they became too weak to continue. They were allowed to surrender with honour – many of the survivors were so malnourished they had to be carried out of the garrison. Today the barbican, walls and three-storey keep gives an idea of the vastness of the structure that once stood here.

Richard III had a good eye – the sweeping view from the walls is extraordinary.

Just down the street from the castle entrance the gothic **St Mary's Church** dates back to 1180, making it nearly as old as the castle that overshadows it. Its shady graveyard contains the tomb of the least known of the Brontë sisters – Anne – who died in Scarborough in 1849.

Scarborough to Hull

Filey

About 8 miles south of Scarborough, Filey is one of the most underrated towns on the coast. This is somewhat understandable, considering that it lacks Scarborough's glitz and Whitby's fame, but with its long expanse of dark sand beach, Edwardian architecture and a general sense of decorum that eludes other seaside towns, Filey has much to offer. Its natural setting, surrounded by dark stone cliffs and green hills, is its primary charm and its **beach** is undeniably the best on the coast, stretching for miles down as far as Flamborough Head to the south. Just north is **Filey Brigg**, with its pleasant nature trails that wander through the hills and down to the shore. For information on **walks** in the area stop in at the **Visitors' Centre** ⓘ *John St, T01723-518000, May-Sep 1000-1700 daily, Oct-Apr 1000-1500 Sat, Sun.*

Bempton Cliffs, Flamborough Head

The sheer white cliffs at Bempton, on the B1229 off the A165, plunge hundreds of feet straight down into the chill waters of the North Sea and seem the most inhospitable of places in which to live, but in the summer, thousands of seabirds call them home. The Bempton Cliffs RSPB nature reserve was set up to protect the cliffs and to allow safe vantage points for watching the birds in action. From a series of viewing stations along the clifftops you can watch big white gannets wheeling through the skies in search of supper. Between May and early July this is the best place in the country to see impossibly adorable puffins, with their colourful beaks and penguin-like bodies. They nest here in the spring and early summer, but by August their young have grown large enough to head out to their winter grounds. Other birds to be seen include kittiwakes, guillemots and razorbills. Helpful displays help amateurs separate one from another, but binoculars are necessary for a good view. Just south of the Bempton Cliffs, the cliffs at Flamborough Head offer equally spectacular views of chalky white rock and deep blue sea. The lighthouse at Flamborough village dates back to the 1700s. You're not allowed to go inside, but it still makes a lovely photograph.

Bridlington

The last of the coastal resort towns in more ways than one, poor Bridlington pales in comparison to its northern neighbours. It's unfair really, considering that the town has stood on this spot for nearly a millennium, but it peaked in the Edwardian years and it's all been downhill ever since, it seems. Today the seafront is its only selling point, particularly its sandy beach, but Filey's beach is better, and Scarborough's seaside amusements make Bridlington's look tattered. Still, it's less crowded than Scarborough, and, as it specializes in attracting families with children, it offers clean, wholesome fun. There are plenty of amusements and candy shops and little stores with bad souvenirs. But really, unless you live nearby and need a place to take the kids for the day, there's little to bring you here.

Hornsea to Spurn Head

Below Bridlington the coastline becomes more empty and forbidding. Hornsea is the last village of any size, and it is known primarily for the eponymous **pottery** that is made here. If you're a fan, there's a factory on the main road, the B1242, which is open for tours and has a **shop** ⓘ *0930-1800 daily*. Near the village is the vast, freshwater **Hornsea Mere**, the largest lake in Yorkshire. It is another RSPB bird sanctuary, and is home to flocks of herons. South of Hornsea is mile after mile of empty beach. About 7 miles down the road near Aldbrough, is **Burton Constable** Hall ⓘ *T01964-562400, Mar-Oct 1300-1700 Mon-Thu, Sat, Sun, £6*, a manor house that dates back to Elizabethan times. The lovely building – which was altered in the 18th century – has been fitted with period furnishings and is open to the public most afternoons. Among its 'decorations' are paintings by Renoir, Pissarro and Gainsborough. Its vast grounds were landscaped by Capability Brown.

The end of the Yorkshire coast comes at **Spurn Head**, a thin spit of beach that reaches out into the sea, then curves back as if it has changed its mind. It is now a Yorkshire Wildlife Trust nature reserve, and is reached down a toll road from the village of Easington on the B1445. Except for a few animal lovers, you'll often have the whole thing to yourself; well, that is, you and the seals, floating butterflies and seabirds that live protected lives there.

Hull

The area just inland from the south Yorkshire coast is a flat, undistinguished land known as the Wolds. Its miles of farmland are dotted with villages – most of them unspectacular – and there are few features here to convince tourists to take their right foot off of the accelerator pedal. In fact Hull itself – which is much better suited to its truncated nickname than by its rarely used full name of Kingston-upon-Hull – is certainly not a tourism hub. It sits at the mouth of the River Humber, an old port city with a reputation as a town of tough guys – and a good place to get beaten up if you stray into the wrong pub at the wrong time. Only recently it was voted Britain's 'crappest town'. Hull was England's biggest port for centuries, and is still a busy seaport, although these days some of its major docks have been renovated into expensive flats and shining modern shopping malls.

Ins and outs

Getting there The **train** station is on busy Ferensway Street on the west side of town. There are regular trains to Leeds (1 hour 30 minutes), London King's Cross (3 hours, with trains every 30 minutes), Scarborough (1 hour 20 minutes) and York (1 hour 15 minutes).

From the north, the A1079 and the A165 both go to Hull. It is about 10 miles south of Beverley and 45 miles southeast of York. There is a convenient central **car** park at the Princes Quay shopping centre – it's well signposted. The **bus** station is just to the north of the train station, and served by **National Express,** T08705-808080, coaches. If you're driving from the west, Hull is on the A63. From the east it's on the A1033.

P&O North Sea Ferries, King George Dock, Hedon Rd, T08705-202020, from Rotterdam and Zeebrugge arrive at the ferry port on the eastern side of town, and there are shuttlebuses from the dock to the town centre. ⏩ *See Transport, page 720, for more details.*

Getting around Hull is a busy city with a useful bus system. There is a park and ride scheme from Walton Street and Anlaby Road (signposted on main routes into the city) with shuttles every 3 mins from Mon-Sat. Fare £1. Otherwise you can catch buses near the train station and the bus station, or from main streets in the city centre. Once you're in the city centre, you can walk to the main sights in the old city and along the waterfront. But a good map is necessary, and the tourist office can offer guidance and directions to get you started.

Information Hull TIC ⓘ *Queen Victoria Sq, T01482-223559, www.hullcc.gov.uk 0900-1800 Mon-Sat, 1100-1500 Sun.* You can pick up information and maps available and the office also offers very good guided tours for £2.50.

Sights

Princes Quay in particular is now the town's shopping pride and joy – a sparkling modern shopping mall, it has all the high street shops on several levels. Nearby on the waterfront is **The Deep** ⓘ *Tower St, T01482-381000, www.thedeep.co.uk, 1000-1700 daily, £6, children £4, families £18,* the city's gleaming new aquarium. It's a massive and absorbing place with every imaginable form of sealife.The town's maritime history dates back to the 13th century, and you can learn absolutely everything there is to know about that at the **Town Docks Museum** ⓘ *T01482-613902, 1000-1700 Mon-Sat, 1330-430 Sun, free,* on Queen Victoria Square near the Princes Quay. Appropriately located in the old town Docks Office, the well-designed museum traces the seafaring side of Hull back to the days of Edward I. It also goes into some detail on Hull's whaling history, including hundreds of pieces of (now politically incorrect) whaling technology and memorabilia. There are elaborate whalebone carvings made by sailors, and massive equipment used to handle the giant mammals. It's all quite fascinating if you're not squeamish. Along with the sea you often get those whose artistic soul is struck by the ocean, and Hull was once home to Philip Larkin, who didn't like it much, and before then the 17th-century poet

Andrew Marvell who did. Marvell, like most people who grew up in Hull at the time, attended the **Old Grammar School** ⓘ *1000-1700 Sat, 1330-1630 Sun, and all school holidays, free*, a 16th-century red-brick building off Trinity House Lane that is now a museum. The school concentrates on historical Hull, and has a good interactive exhibit aimed at children.Not far from the school is the city's traditional market area, with its indoor **market hall** ⓘ *0730-1700 Mon-Sat*, and on Tuesdays, Fridays and Saturdays a colourful outdoor market is open adjacent to the indoor version. Both of these are mostly for locals, with an emphasis on life's necessities, but they're worth a wander, and you never know what you'll find. Not far from the markets down Trinity House Lane the handsome **Holy Trinity Church** makes for a pretty picture, and a few blocks past the Old Grammar School is the small, cobblestone area that makes up old Hull. While there's not much to it (German bombs destroyed much of historic Hull during the Second World War), you can peek in at the wrought-iron staircase and ornate stucco work of the **Maister House** ⓘ *(NT), 160 High St, T01482-324114*, a restored, 18th-century home now owned by the National Trust. Further along is the **Wilberforce House** ⓘ *25 High St, T01482-613902, 1000-1700 Mon-Sat, 1330-1630 Sun, free*, the former home of William Wilberforce, who was the leading campaigner for abolition of slavery in the British Empire. The Jacobean house is now a monument to the anti-slavery movement and includes a small but interesting collection of memorabilia and information on Wilberforce's work. Behind the house on the waterfront you can climb onto a restored fishing boat, the **Arctic** Corsair ⓘ *T01482-613902 for a free tour that gives you an idea of what it was like for those who lived and worked on the sea.*

Beverley

It's easy to see that this bustling, mid-sized town 10 miles north of Hull was once a market centre for the region, and though the streets have been widened, and the old shopfronts replaced with modern high street façades, you can still see how the streets once curved around to a broad open-air market.

Ins and outs

Getting there The **train** station is near Station Square near the Minster, and coaches stop just around the corner in the square. Trains leave hourly for Hull, where you can catch connecting services to London, Leeds, York and Scarborough.

Information **Beverley TIC** ⓘ *34 Butcher Row, T01482-391672, 0930-1730 Mon-Fri, 1000-1700 Sat, 1000-1400 Sun (closed Sun from Sep-May).*

Sights

Today, aside from the interesting layout of the town, and the lovely minster, Beverley manages not to *feel* historic – quite a feat for a town in which 350 buildings are listed. This town – the childhood home of Mary Wollstonecraft (1759-97) – still feels like a modern town, and so things like the old **North Bar** – the only of the city's medieval gates still standing – come as something of a surprise. While not as elaborate as York's gates, the gate at the busy corner of Hengate and North Bar, is quite pretty, and gives you some idea of how very much the town has changed since its 14th-century construction. Heading down North Bar toward the centre, the church of **St** Mary's ⓘ *Apr-Sep 0915-1200, 1330-1730 Mon-Fri, 1000-1730 Sat, 1400-1700 Sun, Oct-Mar 0915-1200, 1300-1615 Mon-Fri, 0915-1200, 1300-1615 Sat, free*, the lesser of the town's two churches, is small but exquisitely detailed. Because it has been altered repeatedly over the years, it is hard to date it by just looking at it, but its oldest section – the south porch – dates back to the 14th century, while most of it was built before the 15th century. Inside you may quickly develop a pain in you staring up at its painted ceilings, with portraits of every king from Sigebert to He Everywhere are wall carvings, most with a musical theme. The town was known for its minstrels, whose work provided much of the financing for the decoration inside the church – thus there are carvings of lutes, horns and drums. Finding the cute little 'Pilgrim's Rabbit' carving (we'll not give away its hiding place) is part of the fun of coming here.

Most people who come to Beverley are drawn by its **Minster** ⓘ *Mar-Apr, Sep and Oct 0900-1700 Mon-Sat, 1400-1600 Sun, May-Aug 0900-1800 Mon-Sat, 1400-1600 Sun, Nov-Feb 0900-1600 Mon-Sat, £2 donation requested*, which is on the other side of the town centre from **St Mary's**. You can't really miss it, as its twin towers are the tallest structures in the city. Once a humble chapel, it became a monastery in the eighth century, under the leadership of a monk called John of Beverley. His body still lies under the nave, and after he was canonized, pilgrims made regular journeys to the church to worship and to donate money. Kings from Athelstan to Henry V credited their pilgrimages here with victories in battle, and so they showered the church with gifts. All of this funded constant expansions until the church grew to its current jaw-dropping size. The west front, which dates from the early 15th century, is considered by many to be the most beautiful part of the building. Inside, the Saxon sanctuary chair was built in the 10th century. The 16th-century oak choir is one of the most perfectly preserved in the country. The Percy Tomb on the north side of the altar – believed to be the tomb of Lady Idoine Percy (who died in 1365) – is a masterpiece of medieval art. Behind the minster, on Friars Lane, are a few buildings that were once part of the Dominican friary founded in 1240. The Beverley friary is namedropped by Chaucer in his *Canterbury Tales*. Some of the buildings are now used as a youth hostel, that generally allows curious members of the public to have a wander.

Sleeping

Staithes *p706*
Most accommodation in town is in B&Bs, although several of the restaurants and pubs also rent out rooms. One of the best is the **D Black Lion**, T01947-841132.

Whitby *p707*
Most accommodation in Whitby is in the form of guesthouses and B&Bs, although there are a few small hotels. B&Bs are clustered on the West Cliff, and rooms here are generally quite affordable.

D Bagdale Hall Hotel, 1 Bagdale St, T01947-602958. A beautiful Tudor mansion, Bagdale has 6 bedrooms with en suite bathrooms, some with 4-poster beds, and one of the best restaurants in town.

D Saxonville Hotel, Ladysmith Av, T01947-602631, www.saxonville.co.uk. On the West Cliff overlooking the town, Saxonville has 22 well-appointed rooms.

D Stakesby Manor Hotel, High Stakesby, T01947-602773. With 13 comfortable rooms in a converted Georgian manor house with extensive grounds, Stakesby overlooks both Whitby and the moors.

D The White House Hotel, Upgang La, T01947-600469. A favourite with golfers, this 2-star hotel overlooks Whitby Golf Course and Sandsend Bay.

E Cliffemount Hotel, Runswick Bay, T01947-840103. This 1920s hotel perches on the cliff above town and offers panoramic views of the countryside. Most of its rooms have en suite bathrooms, many have sea views.

E The Grove, 36 Bagdale, T01947-603551. This family-run guesthouse offers 7 rooms in a lovely building near the town centre.

E The Old Ford, 1 Briggsworth, T01947-810704. 3 rooms in a charming cottage in a bucolic setting at the edge of the River Esk.

F Whitby YHA, East Cliff, T01947-602878. This excellent hostel has a spectacular location beside the abbey at the top of the east cliff overlooking Whitby, the sea and the moors. Most beds in dorms.

...e, but the most ...ation is the self-catering ...get a list from the tourist ...online at ...ods-bay.co.uk.

...otel, at the top of the hill, ...0205. A grand Victorian structure with ...eeping views of the sea, and a popular bar.

E Bay Hotel, sits right at the water's edge, and offers lovely views, T01947-880278.

E Boathouse Bistro, at the foot of the cliff, T01947-880099. Has one of the best restaurants in town, and rents out a few comfortable rooms, as well as the pretty Little House, a tiny self-catering cottage.

F YHA hostel, in an old corn mill on the path from Robin Hood's Bay to Boggle Hole, a mile down the coast, T08707-705704.

Scarborough *p711, map p712*

Most restaurants are atop the north and south cliffs, and there are quite a few B&Bs clustered in the area around the train station.

B The Crown, The Esplanade, T01723-357424, www.scarboroughhotel.com. The most elegant hotel in Scarborough, this is a lovely 19th-century building with excellent views, outstanding facilities and fabulous indoor swimming pool surrounded by statues.

B The Royal Hotel, St Nicholas St, T01723-364333, F500618. A beautiful Regency building overlooking the South Bay and with a gorgeous central lobby.

C Wrea Head Country House Hotel, Barmoor La, Scalby, just outside Scarborough, T01723-3788311, F355936. A stunning place offering peace and beauty on 11 acres of secluded woodlands.

D Bradley Court Hotel, 7-9 Filey Rd, T01723-360476, F376661. A frilly, white period building, but excellent value for money, and has a quality restaurant.

E Granville Lodge Hotel, Belmont Rd, T01723-367668, www.granville.scarborough.co.uk. With an excellent location on the South Cliff, this place has 37 rooms overlooking the city.

E The Old Mill Hotel, Mill St, off Victoria Rd, T01723-372735, www.windmill-hotel.co.uk. Surely the most unique hotel in Scarborough offering, as the name implies, 11 rooms inside an 18th-century windmill near the centre of Scarborough.

E The Ramleh Hotel, 135 Queen's Pde, T01723-365745. Many of the rooms have views across the North Bay. There's a handy licensed bar downstairs and good restaurant.

F Scarborough YHA, Burniston Rd, Scalby Mills, T01723-361176. Located in a picturesque old watermill outside the town centre on the A165 and conveniently perched at the edge of the popular Cleveland Way walking path.

Hull *p714*

Because this isn't a tourism hub, it's fairly easy to find a room here, whether you've booked or not. Most are personality-free chain hotels, however.

C Posthouse, Hull Marina, Castle St, T0870-4009043. One of the best hotels in the city, with a view of the river and a good restaurant.

C Ramada Jarvis Grange Park La, Willerby, T01482-656488 F01482-644848. A pleasant place on landscaped grounds with 102 rooms and a useful bar and grill as well as an enormous indoor swimming pool.

D Comfort Inn, 11 Anlaby Rd, T01482 323 299. A basic chain hotel, but it's handily located near the train station.

D Clyde House Hotel, 13 John St, T01482-214981. A pleasant, well located B&B.

Beverley *p716*

C Beverley Arms, North Bar Within, T01482-869241. Offers historic luxury in one of the pricier places in town.

C Manor House, Northlands, Walkington, T01482-881645. Rural luxury just outside of town.

D Windmill Inn, 53 Lairgate, T01482-862817. In town, there are a dozen acceptable room with a handy pub downstairs.

E Burton Lodge Hotel, Brandesburton, Driffield, T01964-542847, F544771. Cheaper rural pleasures are to be had at this country house on rambling grounds.

E YHA, Friars La, T01482-881751, has the best setting in town, in a 13th century Dominican friary.

Eating

Whitby *p707*
There are only a handful of quality restaurants in Whitby.
££ Bagdale Hall, 1 Bagdale St, T01947-602958. Offers excellent traditional European cuisine in a gorgeous historic setting at surprisingly reasonable prices.
££ Grapevine 2 Grape La, T01947-820275. Has Spanish-orientated cuisine at affordable prices; the emphasis on tapas.
££ Green's, 13 Bridge St, T01947-600284.The kitchen offers creative modern cuisine using local fish and game. Booking is essential at weekends.
££ Huntsman Inn in the tiny village of Aislaby (about 15 mins' drive away) is highly rated for its excellent affordable cuisine.
£ Magpie Café, 14 Pier Rd, T01947-602058. This has to be one of the world's largest fish and chips shops. Unfortunately, the queues are enormous in the high season, and the wait can exceed 45 mins.
£ White Horse & Griffin Church St, T01947 604 857. Probably the best bet in town for good pub grub and atmosphere.

Robin Hood's Bay *p710*
There's not much choice in this tiny village, but you can still get a good pint of ale and a hearty meal. All the pubs and restaurants are on the main street.
£ The Old Chapel bookshop Vegetarians can grab a guilt-free lunch here, a veggie café and coffeeshop.
£ Boathouse Bistro For a proper seafood meal, head here, by the water's edge.

Scarborough *p711, map p712*
Most dining options in Scarborough are of the lowest common denominator variety - cheap seafront chippies, tattered cafés and pizza places abound. But if you look around there are a few options for slightly more upscale dining.
££ Jools, 36 North Marine Rd, T01723-377800. Goes for more traditional British dining in a somewhat twee Victorian setting.
££ Lanterna, 33 Queen St, T01723-3636161. Offers excellent Italian cuisine in a formal setting.
££ Peppers, 11 York Pl, T01723-500642. Offers fusion cuisine that cross-pollinates food from around the globe - mixing, for example, rare salt beef with fennel and Thai dressing.
£ Golden Grid, 4 Sandside, is said by fans to offer the best fish and chips in town.

Hull *p714*
££ Cerutti's, 10 Nelson St, T01482-328501. Hull's best-known restaurant offers excellent seafood at relatively reasonable cost near the waterfront.
££ Pier Luigi, 84 Princes Av, T01482-342357. Fans of pasta crowd to get into this place with its well-prepared Italian food and friendly atmosphere.
£ Hitchcock's, 1 Bishop La, T01482-320233. With its all-you-can-eat buffet, this is also an affordable vegetarian restaurant.

Beverley *p716*
Food is a bit of a difficult one here, for some reason. There are pubs and teashops galore, but finding a decent restaurant is tricky.
££ Cerutti's 2, Station Sq, T01482-866700. A sister to the restaurant of the same name in Hull, which offers seafood dishes in rich sauces.

Pubs, bars and clubs

Whitby *p707*
The best pubs in town are on Church St on the east bank of the river.
The Black Horse is a traditional pub,
The Duke of York, near the 199 steps, offers excellent views and good food, and
Middle Earth has regular music nights and outside seating in the summer.

Robin Hood's Bay *p710*
The Bay Horse pub is popular in the evening, and you can get a good pub meal there as well.
The Dolphin pub can get wonderfully raucous on weekend nights.

Scarborough *p711, map p712*
The Highlander, The Esplanade, next to *The Crown Hotel*, is a traditional pub with a sunny beer garden, and a massive variety of whiskys.

The Hole in the Wall, Vernon Rd, is a small pub with an excellent selection of ale.
The Old Vic, 79 Westborough, has been welcoming tourists to town for decades. It also has the odd claim to fame of being located in the building in which the actor Charles Laughton was born.

Hull *p714*
You can grab a pint in the old town at the **Ye Olde Black Boy**, 150 High St,
Green Bricks, 9 Humber Dock St, also specializes in real ale and is by the waterside.

Beverley *p716*
The Tap & Spile on Flemingate behind the Minster is a local favourite.
The White Horse, near St Mary's on Hengate is an old-fashioned pub with music nights.

Entertainment

Scarborough *p711, map p712*
Theatres and live music
Scarborough's summer theatre scene has been renowned for years.
Corner Complex, in the North Bay, T01723-362079. Variety shows and kids disco parties are the speciality.
Futurist Theatre, Foreshore Rd, T01723-365789. For more crowd pleasers – of the *Bjorn Again* ilk.
Peasholm Park. For free brass band concerts on summer afternoons.
Spa Complex in the South Bay, T01723-376774. From May-Sep you can catch crowd pleasers, orchestra performances and musicals virtually every night at the Spa Theatre here.
Stephen Joseph Theatre on Westborough, T01723-37054. High quality performances – often with casts from London theatre – is to be had at Sir Alan Ayckbourn's theatre here, where most of his plays premier.
YMCA Theatre, St Thomas St, T01723-506750. Theatre groups put on performances here.

Hull *p714*
Hull Truck Theatre Company, Spring St, T01482-323638, has made quite a name for itself over the years, and its performances are often ground-breaking, and well worth catching if your visit coincides with one.

Festivals

Whitby *p707*
Aug Regatta. Features beautiful boats and a fireworks show over the harbour.
Aug Whitby Folk Week. When the town fills with singers, bands, dancers, storytellers and artists, and music can be heard on every streetcorner.
Nov Goth Weekend. If you feel besieged by Marilyn Manson lookalikes, it might be as Goths hit the town a couple of times each year – usually in Nov and Apr – to parade their black lipstick and pay homage to Bram Stoker.

Hull *p714*
Oct **Hull Fair**. The most popular local event is a massive event that fills the town with carnival rides and candyfloss for a solid week in early Oct.
Nov **Hull Literature Festival**. Much smaller but well-respected. Runs for 2 weeks.

Transport

Whitby *p707*
Bus
Yorkshire Coastliner, T01653-692556, services connect **Leeds** and **York** with the coast. National Express, T08705-808080, buses from **London** (7 hrs 45 mins) and **York** (2 hrs) arrive on Langborne Rd, around the corner from the train station. **Traveline**, T0870-6082608.

Scarborough to Hull *p713*
Train and bus
Trains run from Filey Station to Bridlington, Hull and Scarborough. There's also an hourly bus service connecting Filey with Bridlington and Scarborough.

Hull *p714*
Car
Budget, 70 Manchester St, T01482-323862; Thrifty, 2-4 Cleveland St, T01482-219561.

Taxi
City Cabs, 243 Walton St, T01482-501501; Hull Cab Company, 6 Woodhall St, T01482-588533.

Directory

Hull *p714*
Internet: **The Cyber Café**, St Margaret's Church, Shannon Rd Long hill Estate, T01482-795040; **MIJ Internet Express**, 327a Beverley Rd, T01482-474422. **Medical facilities Hull and East Yorkshire Hospital**, Hedon Rd, T01482- 376215.

South and West Yorkshire

→ *Colour map 4 grid B3/4*

At the edge of the Pennines and the Yorkshire Dales, West Yorkshire is a hilly evocative country where miles of farmland are broken up by the busy college town of Leeds, with its non-stop nightlife and funky, laid-back atmosphere. This is where Brontë country begins, the area that inspired the dark Gothic tales that have led generations to wonder just what is so romantic about the heather on the hill. Thousands of tourists each year descend upon the town of Haworth seeking more understanding of the famed family and its doomed daughters. The old spa town of Harrogate has hardly changed at all in the last century, except to change the signs from welcoming the upper class to welcoming the business class. Similarly, South Yorkshire is marked by miles of rolling green hills, with rich farmland and horse pastures. The old steel town of Sheffield is the fitting centre of this region, with its steep hilly streets, old millstreams and wonderfully gloomy architecture. **» *For Sleeping, Eating and other listings, see pages 732-737.***

Sheffield

The unofficial capital of South Yorkshire, Sheffield has gone from feast to famine over the course of the last century. Once the affluent industrial centre of the country, its modern, and largely unattractive appearance is a result of the fact that it was nearly obliterated by German bombs during the Second World War. Reconstruction after the war was hurried and paid little attention to aesthetics, and the city developed a sterile and ugly appearance, so much so that it acquired the local motto of 'the city that Hitler built on his way home'. Still, it has some remnants of its old beauty, in dark, red-brick Victorian buildings, that dot its hilly streets.

The city had just finished rebuilding when the steel industry that had made it such a target in the first place, shifted from the first to the third world. After that, Sheffield lost its point. Thousands of jobs disappeared in the 1970s and 80s, and the city became synonymous with poverty. To claw its way out of recession, Sheffield diversified its business base and embraced tourism and the arts. These days it is a city in transition, with a vibrant nightlife and music scene and a burgeoning arts movement. Its attempts to expand its economy have not been as successful, though, and it still struggles to reach financial stability. Its biggest attractions are its modern museums and the grand buildings that survived the war.

Ins and outs

Getting there Sheffield's **train** station is about 15 minutes' walk east of the centre of town near Sheaf Square. There is a regular service to Leeds (1 hour), London (King's Cross 2 hours 30 minutes) and York (1 hour). Sheffield is on the A57 from the east or west and on the A629 from the north, and the A61 from the south. The Sheffield Interchange bus station is on Pond St, and here you can catch **National Express,** T08705-808080, services to London (4 hours 30 minutes) Leeds, (1 hour), York (2 hours 30 minutes), Manchester (3 hours), Liverpool (3 hours) and many other cities. **Traveline,** T0870-6082608. ▸▸ *See Transport, page 736, for more details.*

Getting around Sheffield is a big, bustling city, and walking is generally not an option, particularly because many of its museums are on the outskirts of the city. You can walk the city centre, however, and a good place to start is at the tourist office on Tudor Square (see below), which is just a few minutes' walk from both the train and bus stations. Local public transport includes numerous buses and the handy **Supertram,** T0114-2728282. Most buses depart from the High St. Fare and timetable information are available at the **Travel Information Centre** in the

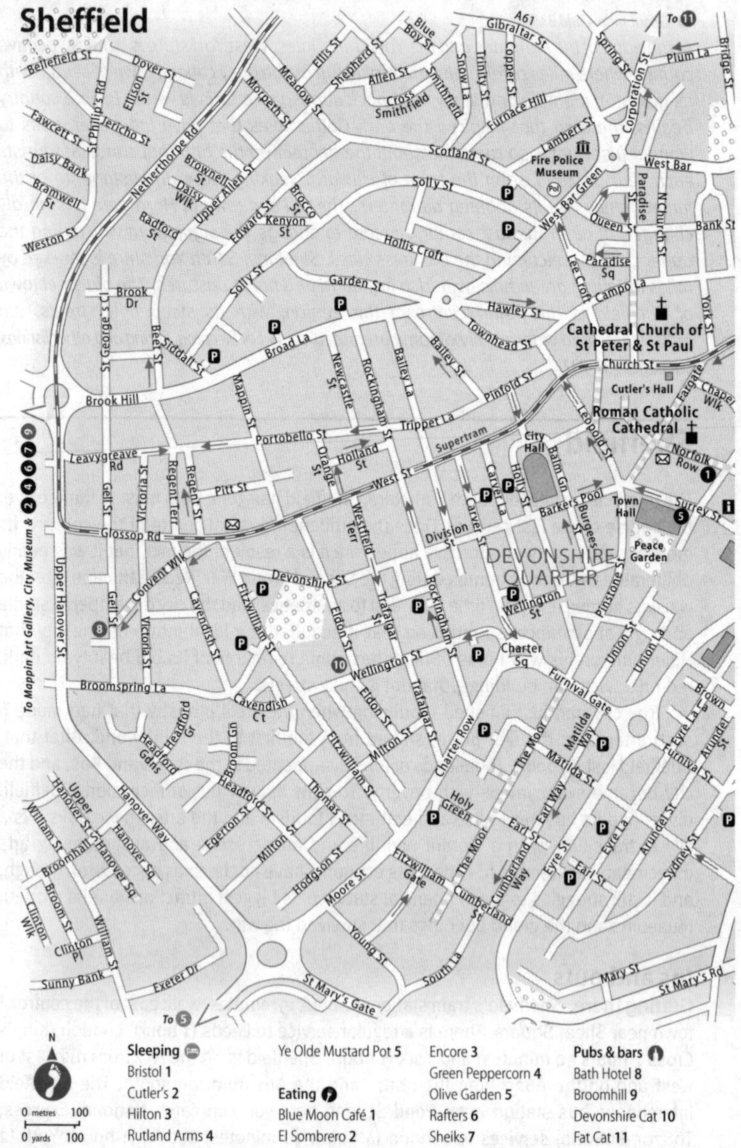

Interchange. 0800-1730 Mon-Fri, 0830-1700 Sat, 0900-1700 Sun. A one-day pass is £4.95 and allows unlimited travel throughout the area, while a day pass for the Supertram is £1.90.

Information **Sheffield TIC** ⓘ *Tudor Sq, T0114-2211900, www.sheffieldcity.co.uk, 0930-1715 Mon-Fri, 0930-1615 Sat.* It can, and will, bury you in maps, brochures and guides.

Sights

Winning the gold star for 'most improved part of Sheffield' – and the obvious place to start any tour – is the **Cultural Industries Quarter**. This is the newly renovated section of town near the train station filled with trendy nightclubs and art galleries, as well as the offices of IT companies that have opened here over the last few years. One of the best of the galleries in this area is the **Site Gallery** ⓘ *Brown Street, 1100-1800 Tue-Fri 1100-1730 Sat, free*, with its acclaimed collection of photography.More art collections worth your attention can be found in the centre of town. The **Graves Art Gallery** ⓘ *T0114-2782600, 1000-1700 Mon-Sat, free*, is on the top floor of the City Library on a rather grim section of Surrey Street. It has a surprisingly solid collection of works by European artists including pieces by Matisse, Turner and Nash in a modern setting. The library is located near the Gothic-Victorian **Town Hall** on Pinstone Street, which gets its distinctive dark look from the Derbyshire stone from which it is made. The green space in front of the town hall is the **Peace Garden**, with its fountains and summertime flowers.

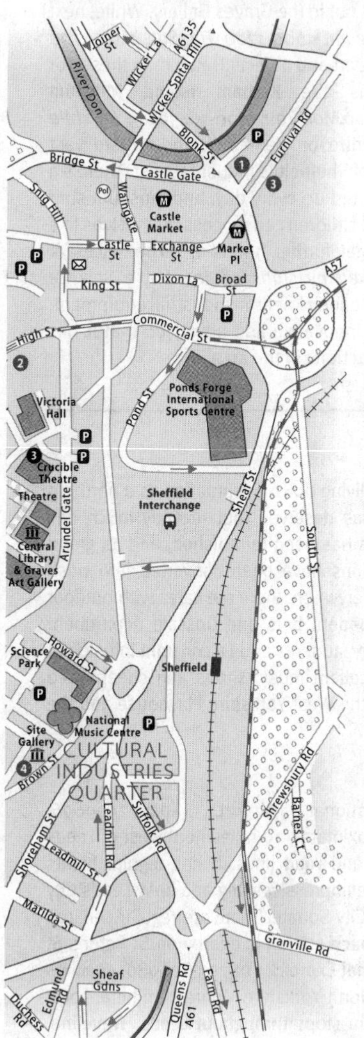

If you head south down Division Street from the town centre you enter the **Devonshire Quarter,** which is the hippest shopping section of Sheffield. This is where the students from Sheffield University stock up on their flares and CDs. There's a café culture here that you won't find elsewhere in town, and it's a great place to sit outside and sip a cappuccino, while looking as cool as possible.

If you head north from the town centre, the area around the medieval **Church of St Peter and St Paul** marks the centre of old Sheffield. Although much altered over the years, the church dates back to the 15th century. Its Lady Chapel contains the tomb of the sixth Earl of Shrewsbury, who served as the keeper of

Mary, Queen of Scots, when she was imprisoned in Sheffield from 1570-84. If you head east on Church Street from here, you reach **Castle Market** and the very scant remains of **Sheffield Castle**, where she was held. There is next to nothing to see here, though, as the ruins are all but gone. Across from the church is the old **Cutler's** Hall ⓘ *T0114-2728456*. Sheffield was once the centre of the cutlery industry, and this 1832 building was their headquarters. It is much more fabulous on the inside than on the outside, and there is an extraordinary collection of silver here, but you have to call ahead in order to see it.

There are yet more art museums to the west of the town centre. The **Mappin Art Gallery** ⓘ *closed for redevelopment until Autumn 2005*, is in Weston Park, and houses much of the city's art collection that is not in the Graves Gallery. While, next door, the **City Museum** ⓘ *Gallery and museum, 1000-1700 Tue-Sat, 1100-1700 Sun, free*, holds more cutlery and locally made art and objects.Better than these, for those really interested in Sheffield, is the **Kelham Island Museum** ⓘ *T0114-2722106, www.simt.co.uk, 1000-1600 Mon-Thu, 1100-1645 Sun, £3, child £2, family £8*, a mile north of the city centre on Kelham Island, where vast exhibitions display objects that tell the story of Sheffield's industrial past. There's a 12,000 horsepower steam engine that is started up every day, and museum staff show how steel was pounded into shape, and children can process themselves like steel in the interactive exhibits. Kids can get further hands-on experiences at **Magma** ⓘ *1000-1700 daily, £6, well marked by signs off the M1*, a science adventure centre where little ones can get up to their knees in industrial equipment, musical devices and more. This place is so innovative and advanced that it has quickly become one of the most popular attractions in the area.

Leeds

The cultural centre of Yorkshire, Leeds is still living down a reputation as a northern industrial town. For years that reputation was deserved, but recently much has changed. Over the last decade, central Leeds has been refurbished, and its grand Victorian buildings restored. Industrial sections have been converted into posh modern shopping and residential arcades. Everywhere there are cafés with outdoor tables (in defiance of the weather), cool, modern bars and upscale department stores. The presence of thousands of university students adds a constant infusion of youth – along with crowded nightclubs, excellent music shops and cheap used clothing stores – while the many museums, the West Yorkshire Playhouse and the Opera North provide an acclaimed art sector.

Ins and outs

Getting there Leeds/Bradford International **Airport**, T0113-2509696, www.lbia.co.uk/contact/index.shtml, is approximately 10 miles northwest of Leeds City centre and has a variety of **train**, **bus** and **road** links. It has regular flights throughout Britain and to western Europe. The impressively big and busy Leeds City **train** station is in the town centre in front of City Square. There are regular services from several major UK cities. The **bus** and **coach** station is nearby on St Peter's St behind Kirkgate Market. You can catch **National Express**, T08705-808080, coaches as well as regional services to York and the North Yorkshire Moors from here. Local buses also set out from here, as well as from stops throughout Leeds. **Traveline,** T0870-6082608. The **Metro Travel Centre** at the bus station can get you going in the right direction (Mon-Fri 0830-1730, Sat 0900-1630) and advise you which travel card will work for you. **Metroline,** T0113-2457676, 0800-2000 daily, has free bus travel advice for the confused and lost. ►► *See Transport, page 736, for more details.*

Getting around Leeds has an extensive **bus** system, but most of the sights are in the compact city centre, and few tourists ever need the buses, unless they're going to the few far-flung sights. The **train** station makes an easy starting point for a walking tour, but buses can be caught on St Peter St, a short walk from the train station. The tourist office has helpful maps and information about transport. Taxis are plentiful and affordable, and there's a rank adjacent to the train station.

Information Leeds TIC ⓘ *inside the train station, T0113-2425242, 0930-1800 Mon-Sat, 1000-1600 Sun*. A large and helpful tourist office which can weigh you down with free maps, brochures, guides and advice.

Central Leeds

The area around the train station provides the best examples of Leeds' massive Victorian architecture. From the second you step out of the station you are surrounded by the statues and overly elaborate bronze gas lamps that the Victorians so loved. The area directly in front of the station is the recently renovated **City Square,** at an intersection of several busy streets. Recent renovations have pedestrianized the square and added new cafés with views of 19th-century statues, which include the Black Prince on horseback and Joseph Priestley, James Watt, John Harrison and Dean Hook. The Gothic church on the east side of the square is the **Mill Hill Chapel** where Priestley was minister in the mid-1700s. The obvious next stop on any wander around central Leeds is down Park Row, past a row of well-restored 19th-century office buildings then continuing up The Headrow to the domineering **Leeds Town Hall**, just a few blocks away. The enormous 19th-century building has every imaginable decoration – stone lions, a clocktower, sculptures and columns. Architect Cuthbert Brodrick used everything in his bag of architectural tricks on this one. Next door to the Town Hall, the **City Art Gallery** ⓘ *Mon-Sat 1000-1700, Wed 1000-2000, Sun 1300-1700, free*, is the biggest and best art collection in the north of England. It has a clear British emphasis with a constantly changing display of selections from its vast permanent collection of mostly 19th- and 20th-century art including works by Courbet, Sisley, Constable and Crome. Particularly notable is its collection of works by Henry Moore (who studied at the Leeds School of Art). The adjacent **Henry Moore Institute** ⓘ *Mon-Sat 1000-1700, Wed 1000-2000, Sun 1300-1700, free*, features more works and information on the sculptor and changing exhibitions of sculptures by other artists. The institute also features a study of the art of sculpture and a library.

East of here, **Briggate** is a pedestrianized lane of shops and businesses in 19th-century buildings with all the filigree, stained glass and marble you could dream of. This section of town has been elegantly restored, and best of all is the frilly arcade of the **Victoria Quarter** where *Harvey Nichols* has planted its northern flag – along with other expensive shops – to the eternal joy of local ladies who lunch. While its clothes are a draw, as in London, its posh café – with its odd mixture of low-cal dishes and high-cal desserts – is the biggest attraction for many visitors. Also on Briggate, **St John's Church** is a lovely, Gothic structure built in 1632. Its screen, pews and pulpit are all original. More shopping calls for your attention from **Kirkgate Market** across Vicar Lane from Harvey Nics. Marketers have been peddling wares here since medieval times. The current market is the largest in Yorkshire and is set up in a lovely Edwardian building (every day except Wed and Sun). Beyond Vicar Lane, Eastgate continues to Quarry Hill Mount to the acclaimed **West Yorkshire Playhouse**. Known for its quality productions, if there's a show on here while you're in town, it is worthwhile to try to catch it. Follow Vicar Lane down to Duncan Street to reach the vast **Corn Exchange** (open daily). Yet another market, this one has an emphasis on the needs of the university crowd, with its hand-made jewellery, art, antique clothes and CDs. Just behind the exchange is one of Leeds' trendiest neighbourhoods. The **Exchange Quarter** is filled with cool cafés, upscale restaurants, arty stores and hip bars.

On the water

The once grim industrial section of Leeds along the Leeds-Liverpool Canal was a symbol for urban blight. Today, however, it stands as a shining tribute to renewal and renovation, as the formerly empty and decrepit old warehouses and brownfield sites have been converted into expensive loft flats, and along with those have come the Siamese triplets of such developments, expensive restaurants, open-air cafés and trendy bars. A waterside footpath connects pricey apartment complexes with dozens of entertainment options, all close to the town centre. **Granary Wharf**, for instance, is just a few minutes' stroll from the train station, and is filled with art shops. It's worth visiting just for its Gothic-style architecture alone, if not for its popular weekend market. Much further along the canals at Armouries Way and Crown Point Road stands one of Leeds' best museums, the **Royal Armouries** ⓘ *T0113-2201940, www.armouries.org.uk, 1000-1700 daily, £4.90.* Designed to hold the armour and weaponry from the Tower of London, it has been cleverly expanded into an interactive museum with a educational collection that spans 3,000 years. There are excellent displays, costumed demonstrations, dramatic interpretations and live action events daily, along with well-made films and hands-on technology. It is almost impossible not to learn something here.

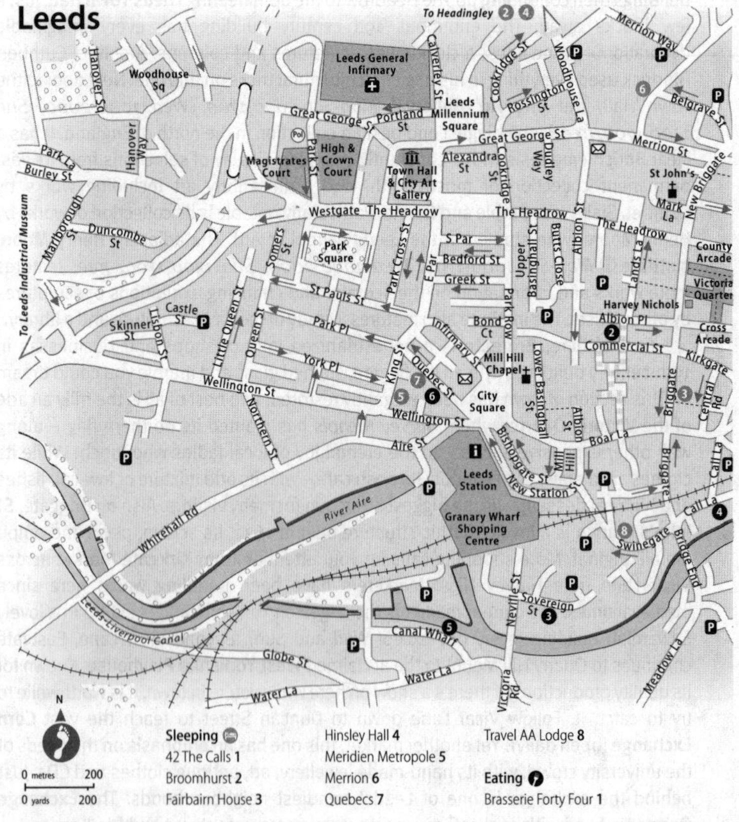

Yorkshire South & West Yorkshire

In the suburbs

Two educational museums lie on the fringes of Leeds. The **Leeds Industrial Museum** ⓘ *Armley Mills, Canal Rd, T0113-2637861, Tue-Sat 1000-1700, Sun 1300-1700, £2, concessions £1, child 50p, 2 miles west of Leeds City centre off the A65, from the centre take bus 5A, 14, 66 or 67,* has an unpromising name, but actually offers an interesting look at the city's past. The museum is located in a 17th-century mill, and it tells the tale of the development of industry in Leeds, and in Britain as a whole. It delves into the development of the textile industry, and has hands-on exhibits and a century-old steam locomotive. The **Thackray Medical Museum** ⓘ *Beckett St, T0113-2457082, Tue-Sun and bank holidays 1000-1700, last admission 1500, £4.40, concessions £3.60, child £3.30, just off the A64 to the east of the city centre, from the town centre take bus 5A, 13, 17, 41, 42, 43, 40 and 88,* is an enormously amusing place, with an entertaining display on the history of medical technology. Clearly designed to make medicine more interesting than frightening, it still has a serious bent and can get a bit grotesque at times. But it's all in the spirit of fun, and kids have a great time here.

East of Leeds

Just a couple of miles outside the city centre off the A65, the walls of **Kirstall Abbey** stand gloomily in a large green park on the River Aire. Considered the best preserved of all the Cistercian houses in the north of England, Kirkstall was founded in 1152 by monks from Fountains Abbey looking for a place of their own. It has stood empty for nearly 500 years since Henry VIII shut it down, and so it is astonishing how intact it remains. Its **church** is particularly interesting, even with its collapsed tower. The Norman **chapter house** is nearly perfect, in defiance of time, while the 13th-century **abbot's lodging** is simply beautiful. The 12th-century **gatehouse** has been restored and turned into the **Abbey House Museum**, and is mostly devoted to Victoriana, with toys and games and reconstructed Victorian streets with an eye for detail in its shops, cottages and homes. ⓘ *Dawn to dusk daily, free, from central Leeds take bus 732, 733, 734, 735 or 736.*

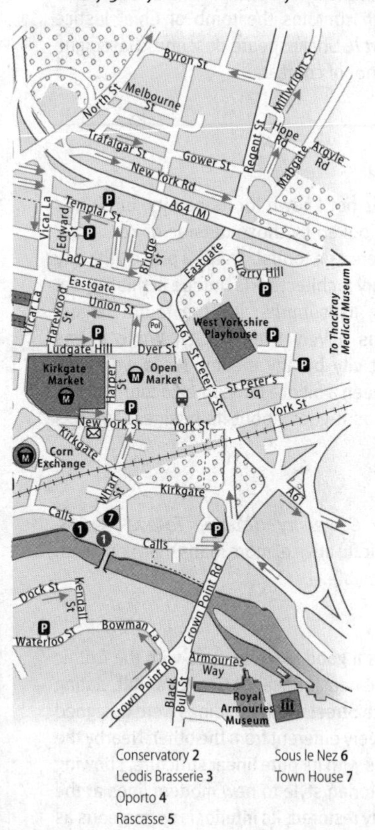

About 4 miles off the A63, **Temple Newsam** ⓘ *T0113-2647321, Apr-Oct Tue-Sat 1000-1700, Sun 1300-1700, Nov, Dec and Mar Tue-Sat 1000-1600, Sun 1200-1600, £2.00, concessions £1, children 50p,* holds the decorative art collection of the Leeds City Art Galleries. The Jacobean house is a bit of an artwork itself, and inspired 'templestowe' in Scott's *Ivanhoe*. Inside, the impressive collection includes pottery, silver and furniture from the 16th-18th centuries. The house sits on farmland, with seven gardens and park laid out by the ever-busy Capability Brown. It's a popular and picturesque place for a picnic on a sunny summer day.

A few miles further east from here still more art from the Leeds City Art Galleries is on display in **Lotherton Hall** ⓘ *To113-2813259, Mar-Oct Tue-Sat 1000-1700, Sun 1300-1700; Nov and Dec 1000-1600, Sun 1200-1600, £2, concessions £1.00, child 50p,* which holds silver, porcelain, jewellery, period furniture and mostly minor paintings. The entire contents were once the belongings of one wealthy family. Much like Temple Newsam, the house is surrounded by lovely grounds, gardens and a deer park.

North of Leeds

About seven miles north of central Leeds is the model village of **Harewood** and the mansion known as **Harewood House** ⓘ *To113-2181010, www.harewood.org, Apr-Oct 1100-1630 daily, Nov-Mar 1100-1630 Sat and Sun, £8, grounds and bird garden only £6.25*. The house was built from 1759-72 by a superteam of designers, landscapers and architects assembled by the respected Yorkshire architect John Carr. The building was designed by Carr and modified and finished by Robert Adam, the gardens were created by Capability Brown and the furniture by Thomas Chippendale (who was born not far from here in Otley). Even when the building was remodelled 100 years later, it was by the best of the best – Sir Charles Barry (who designed the Houses of Parliament) remodelled the façade and added the third storey. The art inside is an astonishing collection that includes works by Titian, Tintoretto, Bellini, El Greco and Turner. Outside is an extensive bird garden with acres devoted to hundreds of species of exotic birds. Also on the grounds are the ruins of Harewood Castle and Harewood Church. In a bit of literary trivia, the church contains the tomb of Chief Justice Gascoigne, who died in 1419. In *Henry IV, Part II*, Shakespeare describes Gascoigne committing the future King Henry V for contempt of court.

Bradford

Another northern industrial town, Bradford is not known for its beauty, but it has some attractive sections that are often overlooked by those outside of Yorkshire, most of whom would never think of coming here as a tourist. That's a pity, as the city has a lot to offer. Some of its early 20th-century architecture is unique in this region. But this is a very modern town. Including its suburbs, it's the fourth largest metropolitan area in England, and remains a very lived-in city. While it has interesting tourist sights, it is not a tourist city by any means. It's a workaday modernized industrial community, that has been a bit of a latecomer to tourism. But if you don't mind the town hurrying by you as it goes about its business, there's much to be seen here.

Ins and outs

Information Bradford TIC ⓘ *City Hall on Centenary Square, To1274-753678, Mon-Fri 0900-1730, Sat 0900-1700*. Offers helpful advice, more maps than you need, and more brochures than you might think possible.

Sights

The City Hall precinct on the inner ring road is a good place to start, with the Gothic **City Hall** built in the late 19th century, and the neoclassical **St George's Hall**, dating from 1853 and dominating the corner of Bridge Street. Both buildings were designed by the same architecture firm, and yet each is very different from the other. Nearby the creamy columns of the **Alhambra Theatre** lures with its pure linear structure, showing the transition of architectural mores from Victorian style to new modern lines at the time of its construction in 1914. Now beautifully restored, its interior is as gorgeous as its exterior. From the front of the theatre you can see the excellent **National Museum**

of Photography, Film and Television ⓘ *T01274-202030, www.nmpft.org.uk, Tue-Sun and public holidays 1000-1800, free*, the main reason why many tourists make their way to Bradford. Opened in 1983, it holds the largest cinema in Britain, where there are daily IMAX screenings. The ground floor holds the Kodak Gallery, which traces the history of photography, using the film company's private collection as illustrations. The rambling museum holds room after room of exhibitions on cameras and equipment, the art of film photography and the history of television. Amateur photographers will be in heaven. You can spend hours here, so it's lucky there's a café for sustenance, and a shop filled with prints, movie posters and clever souvenirs. Another themed museum is the **Colour Museum** ⓘ *Providence St, off Westgate, T01274-390955, Tue-Sat 1000-1600, £1.75*, which is an unusual facility dedicated to the history, development and technology of colour. It makes for an interesting and informative visit in which everybody is guaranteed to learn something.

Heading back to the city centre, the Gothic **Wool Exchange** on Market Street – once again by Lockwood and Mawson, who designed the City Hall – is one of few indications you'll find around town that Bradford was once the world's largest producer of worsted cloth and wool production. The old exchange has been beautifully renovated and converted into a shopping and dining mall. Above the exchange, the tower of the beautiful **Bradford Cathedral** stands on nearby Stott Hill. The 14th-century building was much altered during the 20th century, but still contains a 15th-century font cover and 19th-century stained glass in the Lady Chapel. Opposite the Wool Exchange stands the **Peace Museum** ⓘ *10 Piece Hall Yard, T01274-7754009, www.peacemuseum.org.uk, Wed-Fri 1100-1500, free*, a one-of-a-kind facility with informative displays devoted to world leaders who espouse non-violence, tactics by which violence can be avoided, and conflict resolution. This worthy facility has an outreach element that offers tutorials on peace.

There are several museums at the edge of Bradford that can warrant a visit. The **Bradford Industrial Museum** ⓘ *Moorside Rd, Eccleshill, T01274-631756, Tue-Sat 1000-1700, Sun 1200-1700, free*, for example, has an outstanding display on the city's industrial past. Built inside a converted 19th-century worsted spinning mill, the museum also features a recreated industrial neighbourhood with mill stables and shire horses, a mill owner's house and worker cottages. There are horse-pulled-bus rides and daily demonstrations of spinning techniques, and on Wednesdays, steam looming machinery is fired up and operated.Further out on Market Street, 4 miles west of the town centre, is the former parsonage where Charlotte, Branwell, Emily and Anne Brontë were born. Now a small museum, the **Brontë Birthplace** ⓘ *72 Market St, T01274-830849, www.brontebirthplace.org.uk, Apr-Sep 1200-1600 Tue-Sun, £2.50, child £1.00*, is not the best of the Brontë sites in the region, but it does feature memorabilia related to the famous writing family, and is notable simply because it was once their family home.

Saltaire

Just at the edge of Bradford off the A650, Saltaire is a fascinating model village designed by a 19th-century mill tycoon (Sir Titus Salt) who sought to create the perfect industrial world. When Salt moved his mills from Bradford to the countryside, he decided that industrial didn't have to mean 'ugly', and so he created a village based on the architecture of Italy, which he loved. He built terraced housing with an Italian Renaissance look. He chose the countryside so that workers would breathe fresh air, rather than pollution. Today, sadly, Bradford's sprawl has wrapped around Saltaire, so the fresh country breezes are no more but still, it's an extraordinary place.

Ins and outs Trains run to Saltaire from Bradford's Forster Square, as does bus 679. Alternatively, you can take the **Apollo Waterbus** ⓘ *T01274-595914, www.apollocanalcruisers.co.uk. £1.25-£5*, down the river to Hirst Wood and Shipley, through the lock.

 Information **Saltaire TIC** ① *2 Victoria Rd, T01274-774993*. To get the most of the town, take one of the guided walks on offer: Saturdau, Sunday and public holidays 1100, 1400. £2.

Sights

The massive **mill** is designed like an overgrown Italian palazzo, but don't be fooled by its beauty as this was a workhorse of a building. It once contained more than 1200 looms. Today, somewhat unsurprisingly, it's an upscale shopping centre filled mostly with art boutiques. Its largest tenant is the **1853 Gallery**, which is devoted to the works of David Hockney, the artist born in nearby Bradford. Around the mill, Salt built up the community for his workers in houses of different sizes based on the position of the worker who lived there, schools, hospitals and baths. Today it's a pretty and perfectly organized town – too perfectly organized, in fact. It's almost eerily unblemished. Appropriately enough, the man who's vision this all was, had himself buried at the centre of his town: Salt is in the mausoleum by the United Reform Church (which was built in 1859 by Lockwood and Mason, who designed many of Bradford's most impressive buildings).

Just outside of the town centre, follow the signs across the Leeds-Liverpool Canal along Victoria Rd to **Shipley Glen** ① *May-Sep daily, Oct-Apr Sat and Sun only, 50p*, where a Victorian funicular tram travels up the hill to a funfair.

Haworth

Whatever Haworth once was, today it is Brontë country. The little village at the edge of the Pennines has long ago had its way of life subsumed by the world's seemingly limitless curiosity about these reclusive, rural sisters who wrote tales of repressed passions on heather-strewn moors. In 1820, when Anne, Emily and Charlotte were still small, their father moved them and their three other siblings from the edge of Bradford where they'd been born, to this stony village at the edge of miles of hills and sweeping vistas. Here they would grow up, and all of them would see their work affected by the stark, dramatic countryside around them. It seems that every street they once walked on, and every building they ever entered, has been turned into some sort of Brontë memorial, but the biggest is the **Brontë Parsonage Museum** ① *T01253-642323, www.bronte.org.uk, daily Apr-Sep 1000-1730, Oct-Mar 1100-1700, £4.80, concessions £3.50, child £1.50*, at the top of the main street. Located in the simple house in which they grew up, the displays inside tell the family's sad tale. The house is filled with pictures of the children and the furniture remains the same as it did when they lived here. There are extensive original documents written by the girls, starting when they were children and working up to their successful novels. This is a good museum, but crowded in the high season. Also popular is the **parish church** adjacent, in which all of the family, except Anne (who is buried in Scarborough, see page 713) are entombed in the family vault. Nearby is the **Sunday school** where the sisters taught when they weren't writing, down the road is the pharmacist where their brother Branwell bought the opium to which he was addicted. This has been converted into a souvenir shop, and the *Black Bull Inn*, where he often drank himself into a stupor, is still open for business.

The countryside around Haworth is beautiful, and there are numerous **walks** along the paths that so inspired the Brontës. The tourist office ① *2 West La, at the top of Main Street, T01535-642329, 0930-1730 daily*, will give you maps and directions. The most interesting of the walks is the one to **Top Withens**, a ruined, gloomy building out in the hills that many determinedly believe was the model for *Wuthering Heights*. Aside from the desolate nature of the countryside there, the windswept hills and the

The poet Ted Hughes grew up near Haworth, and wrote about walking in the footsteps of the Brontës, as so many do here every year.

heather, there is no reason to think so, according to Brontë scholars, who say the buildings – do not now and never did look the way Emily described them in her book. Further along, though, is **Ponden Hall**, which could well have been the building she called Thrushcross Grange in her novel.

Hebden Bridge and Heptonstall

A few miles south of Haworth, the A646 dips into the valley of the River Calder, and the Pennine Way walking path crosses the road by the stark **Stoodley Pike obelisk**, which makes for sweeping photographs. Nearby sit the twin tiny mill towns of **Hebden Bridge** and **Heptonstall**. In the 19th century, when these were bustling towns producing enormous amounts of textiles, the mills in Hebden Bridge ran constantly, while the workers lived up the hill in Heptonstall. The mills were long ago silenced, and these are now quiet villages, but the two towns are still connected by a path that once was used by packhorses moving fabric and wool. Hebden Bridge still has a rare working clog mill that is open to visitors. The sight of it groaning into life offers an interesting perspective on how life must have once been in this section of Yorkshire when hundreds of such mills ran non-stop. Heptonstall is a handsome village, much less crowded with tourists than Haworth (as the Brontë's never came here). At its centre is an old ruined church, as well as a slightly newer (18th-century) Wesleyan chapel. But its main draw is the grave in the newer of its two churchyards in which the American poet Sylvia Plath lies buried. Her husband, Ted Hughes, was born in nearby Mytholmroyd, and grew up in and around Heptonstall. He frequently wrote about the towns, not the least in the poem *Heptonstall Churchyard*.

Halifax

One of the biggest towns that grew out of the worsted wool trade that dominated this section of Yorkshire for hundreds of years, Halifax clings for dear life to a hillside leading down into the Hebble valley. Over the years, its importance waned with the Yorkshire wool industry; but today its most interesting sites are virtually all tied to the textile industry in which it once had such success.

Information The **tourist information office** ⓘ *inside Piece Hall, T01422-368725 Apr-Sep 1000-1700 Mon-Sat, 1100-1700 Sun, Oct-Mar 0930-1630 Mon-Sat, 1000-1600 Sun*, can help you book a room or find good local walks.

Sights

The biggest memorial to that time is the central colonnaded **Piece Hall** ⓘ *T01422-349422*, which was built in 1779 as a trading market for the wool industry. The only surviving cloth hall in Yorkshire (and it was very nearly torn down in the 1970s) its sheer size – covering 10,000 sq yds – is a good indication of just how enormous that industry was at the time of its construction. These days it holds dozens of art shops and clothing boutiques, as well as the TIC and the **Pre-industrial Museum**, which tells the story of the rise and fall of the Yorkshire wool and cloth industry. There's also a colourful open-air market in the hall's vast courtyard on Fridays and Saturdays. Next to the hall, the **Industrial Museum** tells the story of what happened next. Among the displays is the 17th-century blade which armed the town's own version of the guillotine, called a 'gibbet'. So ferocious was the town's anti-crime bent – and so enthusiastic its use of the gibbet – that criminals used to joke darkly "From Hull, hell and Halifax, good Lord deliver us". A reconstructed gibbet stands in **Gibbet Street**, where the real device once did its bloody work. The jagged spire that juts up behind the Piece Hall is the only surviving part of the 19th-century **Square Church**, which long ago burned down. The nearby 17th-century **Square Chapel** has been converted into an arts centre, and is the site of regular performances by touring international dance and theatrical groups.

The town has a number of strikingly beautiful 15th- and 16th-century houses, which reflect the rise of the yeoman class of clothiers, who took in the wool from several workers, and thus grew in wealth. Among the most beautiful of these houses is the half-timber **Shibden Hall** ⓘ *Lister's Rd, T01422-352246, Mar-Nov 1000-1700 Mon-Sat, 1200-1700 Sun, Dec-Feb 1000-1600 Mon-Sat, 1200-1600 Sun, £3.50, child £2.50, family £10,* off the A58 about a mile north of the town centre. The large 15th-century house stands in a gorgeous park above a lake and has been converted into a museum filled with period furniture and late 16th-century paintings. Some of the outbuildings have been converted into the **Folk Museum of West Yorkshire,** including a brewhouse and dairy, period agricultural equipment and craft workshops. At the time of writing, the house was undergoing restorations that were expected to continue throughout 2003. While the house is scheduled to remain open to the public, some disruption is to be expected.

Sleeping

Sheffield *p721, map p723*

B Sheffield Marriott, Kenwood Rd, T0114-2583811. Located in a handsome old buildings on landscaped grounds, and has all the luxuries and essentials.

B Bristol, Blonk St, T0114-2204000. Bustling and efficient this place caters to the business crowd, with all the extras that implies.

B Cutlers, George St, T0114-2739939. Well located right at the centre of the action.

C Hilton, Victoria Quays, T0114-2525500. With a location on the canals and great views, and with all of its usual luxuries – not a bad choice.

D Ye Olde Mustard Pot, Mortimer Rd, T01226-761155. A 17th-century inn offering good inexpensive accommodation just at the edge of town.

D Rutland Arms, 86 Brown St, T0114-2729003. A few basic rooms at a good price in a Victorian building above a pub.

Leeds *p724, map p727*

With its universities and busy business centre, Leeds has plenty of places to stay, from lush expensive modern properties, to low-cost B&Bs. Most expensive places are in the town centre, while most B&Bs are in the Headingley neighbourhood, which is easily accessible by bus.

A 42 The Calls, 42 The Calls, T0113-2440099, www.42thecalls.co.uk. If the name is the same as the address, you can almost guarantee it's going to be trendy and expensive. Fits the bill on both counts. A modern boutique hotel in a historic townhouse overlooking the waterfront, this is the hottest hotel in town. Weekend packages can make this place slightly more affordable.

A Meridien Metropole, King St, T0113-2450841, F2341430. In a terracotta building in the city centre, the *Meridien* is one of the loveliest hotels in town.

A Quebecs, 9 Quebec St, T0113-2448989, www.etontownhouse.com. Another of Leeds' posh boutique hotels in a fabulous Gothic building with 45 luxurious rooms and suites.

B Merrion Hotel, Wade La, T0113-2439191, F2423527. Slightly less pricey and well located in the town centre. Also has a handy bar and restaurant.

C Travel AA Lodge, Blayds Ct, Blayds Yard, off Swinegate, T08700-850950, F0113-2445793. It's hotel-by-numbers, but it's centrally located, clean and basic accommodation.

D Broomhurst Hotel, 12 Chapel La, Headingley, T0113-2786836, F2307099. Victorian building in a leafy street just over a mile from the city centre in the pleasant Headingley neighbourhood.

D Fairbairn House, 2 Lower Briggate, T0113-2436454, F2434241. This grand Victorian edifice is owned by the University of Leeds. It's well located, pleasant, quiet and good value for money.

D Hinsley Hall, 62 Headingley La, T0113-2618000, F2242406. This extraordinary 19th-century manor house is worth a visit in its own right. Owned by the Diocese of Leeds, it sits on tranquil grounds 2 miles from the city centre.

Bradford *p728*

Most accommodation is near the town centre, but there are many good B&Bs in the small towns nearby or in Haworth.

B Midland Hotel, Forster Sq, T01274-735735. The height of Victorian luxury and conveniently located near the train station.

B Quality Victoria Hotel, Bridge St, T01274-728706. Equally lush and designed by the same slick team that did the trendy *42 The Calls* in Leeds.

C Jarvis Bankfield Hotel, Bradford Rd, Bingley, just outside of town, T01274-567123. Less central but equally deluxe it's located in a gorgeous manor house with 103 elegant rooms where you can rest in style.

D Ivy Guest House, 3 Melbourne Pl, T01274-727060. Provides affordable, nice enough accommodation in the city centre.

D New Beehive Inn, 169 Westgate, T01274-721784. A charming, gaslit inn with Edwardian character and, more importantly, cheap rooms.

Haworth *p730*

There are plenty of B&Bs in town, but they book up quickly, even in the low season, so plan well in advance. You can get a full list from the tourist office.

C Weavers, 15 West La, T01535-643822. The most upscale guesthouse in town, it's a lane of old weavers' cottages that have been converted into guestrooms, filled with antiques.

D The Apothecary, 86 Main St, T01535-643642. There are excellent views from the windows of this charming guesthouse in the centre of the village.

E Old White Lion Hotel, Main St, T01535-642313. A picturesque, rambling old inn right next to the parsonage. It has 2 charming old bars and a handy restaurant.

E Heather Cottage, 25 Main St, T01535-644511. A small guesthouse with pleasant tearooms.

Halifax *p731*

There are quite a few charming hotels in Halifax, and even more featureless but handy chains.

D Hobbit Hotel, Hob La, Norland, T01422-832202, F835381. One of the most entertaining hotels in town has been an inn for more than 100 years, since a series of delvers' cottages were converted for that purpose. Today it has a penchant for 4-posters, and occasional 'medieval nights' in its restaurant, which serves fine food.

D Ploughcroft Cottage, 53 Ploughcroft La, just a few miles out of Halifax, T01422-341205. 3 18th-century crofters cottages at the top of the hill overlooking Halifax.

D Shibden Mill Inn, Shibden, T01422-365840, F362971. So attractive and elegant that it is a favourite choice for weddings. It also has an excellent restaurant.

D Windmill Court Hotel, Ogden, T01422-244941, F240719. A few miles outside of Halifax, the country house atmosphere here is very pleasant.

E Heathleigh Guest House, 124 Skircoat Rd, T01422-323957. An attractive 19th-century house offering good value for money and a beautiful setting.

Eating

Sheffield *p721, map p723*

There's plenty to choose from these days in Sheffield when it comes to dining, although it's not as well-known for its culinary offerings as Leeds.

££ El Sombrero, 27 Regent Terr, T0114-272 9587. Casual Mexican fare, popular.

££ Encore, in the Crucible Theatre on Tudor Sq, T0114-275 0724. Modern British food with a pre-theatre bent, a reasonable choice.

££ Green Peppercorn, 352 Meadowhead, T0114-2745202. Join the trendy crowd for a fusion meal.

££ Olive Garden, Surrey St, T0114-2728886. A central option.

££ Rafters, 220 Oakbrook Rd, T0114-2304819. More upmarket and formal.

££ Sheiks, 274 Glossop Rd, T0114-2750555. Good Lebanese food in a popular local favourite.

£ **Blue Moon Café**, Norfolk Row, T0114-2763443. Provides a good, solid vegetarian meal.

Leeds *p724, map p727*

In recent years Leeds' restaurant and café scene has been transformed from fish-and-chips to fusion and Beaujolais Nouveau. The best element is that here you get London food at Leeds prices – even many of the top restaurants here price most main courses below £15.

£££ **Brasserie Forty Four**, in the posh 44 The Calls Hotel, T0113-2343232, was recently listed as the best brasserie in Leeds by the *Good Food Guide*, its trendy atmosphere and French-style food are unbeaten here. Prices are correspondingly high.

£££ **Leodis Brasserie**, Victoria Mill, Sovereign St, T0113-2421010. Another highly rated place. Located in an old mill it offers beautiful views along with English and French food.

££ **Fourth Floor Café** at *Harvey Nichols*, Briggate, T0113 -2048000. One of the hottest places in town, it packs in shoppers and non-shoppers for light lunches and traditional British dinners.

££ **Oporto**, 31-33 Call La, T0113-2454444. Less trendy, but just as good, *Oporto* offers casual fusion meals combining European and Asian cooking techniques in the Exchange Quarter, or come later in the evening where drinks are served until 0200.

££ **Rascasse**, Canal Wharf, Water La, T0113-2446611. A stylish, modern waterfront restaurant with Anglo-French cooking.

££ **Sous le Nez**, The Basement, Quebec House, Quebec St, T0113-2440108. Another highly rated restaurant that serves expertly crafted seafood to a trendy crowd.

£ **Harry Ramsden's**, White Cross, Guiseley, T01943-879531, Standing for the old-style Leeds restaurants, this place has been selling fish and chips many consider to be the best in town, for decades. It's in the 'burbs though, but you can find your way there on buses 732, 733, 734 or 736. Expect to queue.

Cafés

The Conservatory, Albion Pl, T0113-2051911. It's a cellar bar where you can have an excellent breakfast or lunch, or just sip a coffee in its refined atmosphere.

Harvey Nichols Espresso Bar, Victoria Quarter, T0113-2048000. Serves impressively expensive morning coffee, lunches, snacks and afternoon tea.

Town House, Assembly St, T0113-2194000. Similarly flexible place which has good coffee and equally good beer along with light meals during the day, and turns itself into a remarkably hip bar at night. If you want the feel of a private club without the bother of joining one, head here.

Bradford *p728*

Bradford's curry restaurants are legion and renowned. If you don't fancy curry, however, you might be in a bit of trouble, as there's not much to choose from.

££ **Bombay Brasserie**, Simes St, T01274-737564, which offers elegant versions of gourmet curry-based dishes in a lovely setting.

££ **Ramada Jarvis**, Bradford Rd, a few miles outside town, T01274-567123. The Jarvis has an elegant restaurant with a consistently good menu.

£ **Kashmir**, 27 Morley St, T01274-726513. Established and renowned for its good food at reasonable prices.

£ **Ring O'Bells**, 212 Hilltop Rd, T01274-832296, for an excellent pub meal.

Haworth *p730*

This is a very small village, so your choice is going to be quite limited. Pubs are the best option for lunch.

£ **The Black Bull** on Main St is a popular choice for lunch or a pint. It was a favourite of Branwell Brontë's as well.

£ **The Old White Lion** has two pubs inside as well as a restaurant that can get quite crowded at lunchtime.

£ **Weavers** on West La. For a slightly more sophisticated meal. Book ahead.

For an explanation of the sleeping and eating price codes used in this guide, see the inside front cover. Other relevant information is provided in the Essentials chapter, page 40.

Halifax *p731*
The most picturesque pubs and restaurants in Halifax tend to be in the Sowerby Bridge section, where many hotels are also located.
££ The Puzzle Hall Inn, Hollins Mill La, Sowerby Bridge, T01422-835547, is a friendly pub with a good selection of real ales and occasional evening entertainment.
£ The Hobbit, Hob La, Sowerby Bridge, T01422-832202, has a large busy restaurant/pub with views of the town. A great place to sit outside.
£ The Navigation Inn Chapel La, Sowerby Bridge, T01422-831636, is a lovely pub for riverside drinking if you don't mind maritime themes, excellently located next to the Calder and Hebble.
£ The Brown Cow, 565 Gibbet St, T01422-361640, is a great traditional pub in an old building with good ale.One of the best pubs in Halifax.

Pubs, bars and clubs

Sheffield *p721, map p723*
Bath Hotel, 66 Victoria St, off Glossop Rd. Head here for a good pint of real ale.
Broomhill, 484 Glossop Rd, which has great music playing virtually whenever its doors are open.
The Fat Cat, 23 Alma St, is a great but tiny pub, a very local joint quite a way out from the centre on Kelham Island.
Devonshire Cat, closer in on Devonshire Green. Popular local

Clubs
This is the city that created Pulp, Human League, Def Leppard and Heaven 17. Sheffield's music and nightclub scene is legendary. You're spoiled for choice, so it's a good idea to pick up the *Sheffield Telegraph* or the local music mag, *The Sandman*, which is free from pubs, restaurants and cafés around town, and gives you more guidance about just what's going on.
Area 51, 14 Matilda St. A warehouse converted into an unbeatable nightclub.
The Boardwalk, Snig Hill, T0114-2799090. For live music.
Leadmill, 6-7 Leadmill Rd, T0114-2754500. A wicked little underground venue with Playstations in a nook at the back. The best place to hear a band.
Republic 112 Arundel St, T0114- 2766777, which is in an old factory. Great for dancing.

Leeds *p724, map p727*
One thing you're unlikely to hear somebody say in Leeds on a Fri night is, 'There's nothing to do here.' This town lounges all day and parties all night, in proper college town fashion.
The Ship on Ship Inn Yard off Briggate, For a real pub scene you'll need to head over here where you can get a very nice pint or a bit of pub grub.
Victoria on Great George St. The only place for frilly Victorian pub life.
The Vine, 11 The Headrow, T0113-2031820, is a traditional Bass pub that acts as sort of a pub/club combination. Its regular disco nights put paid to the idea of it being a normal pub, however.
Whitelocks on Turk's Head Yard. Only slightly older and more famous is this nearby pub which is known for its traditional pub decor and enormous crowds.

Clubs
Creation, 55 Cockridge St, T0113-2800100, There's a mix of touring international and local bands here.
The Elbow Room, 64 Call La, T0113-2457011, for quality jazz acts.
Milo, 10-12 Call La. Ranks as one of the most unpretentious bars in town. Depending on the night, you can catch a quality local band, dance to DJ-spun tunes or sit gabbing lazily with your friends.
Norman, 36 Call La. At the other end of the spectrum here, it's all glitz and some glamour and claims to have been voted one of the 100 best bars in the world.
The Observatory is a unique Victorian building with a domed ceiling and two levels of bars and dancing. Its interior balcony allows you to be above it all. It's quite popular with the student population.
Velvet, 11 Hirst's Yard. If you've got the look, go on to dance the night away here, a place that brags about its 'rigorous door policy'.

Bradford *p728*
After dinner you can grab a drink in one of the town's many pubs.
Chicago Rock Café, Great Horton Rd. Popular with students at nearby Bradford

University for its food, crowds and occasional band nights.

The Fighting Cock on Preston St features real ales.

Love Apple, Great Horton Rd. Popular student joint.

The New Beehive, on Westgate is a friendly place for a drink or a meal.

The Peel on Richmond Rd is known for its good food, as well as its laid-back atmosphere.

Entertainment

Sheffield *p721, map p723*

There are several theatres in Sheffield, all under the Sheffield Theatres Trust. The **Crucible**, **Crucible Studio** and **Lyceum** theatres are all located around Tudor Square, and hold acclaimed performance by nationally known theatre groups and classical music on a regular basis. T0114-2496000, www.sheffieldtheatres. co.uk

Leeds *p724, map p727*

Theatre

Grand Theatre and Opera House, 46 New Briggate, T0113-2226222. This is where *Opera North* puts on a regular season of professional performances, as does the *Northern Ballet Theatre*.

Leeds Town Hall, The Headrow, T0113-2476962. Classical music is produced frequently here in this glorious venue.

West Yorkshire Playhouse, Quarry Hill Mount, T0113-2137700. The best-known theatrical group in town, which puts on a range of highly rated performances in its two theatres.

Festivals

Leeds *p724, map p727*

Aug Reading/Leeds Music Festival. Packs in hundreds of thousands of people in a field outside of town for a four-day rock concert each Aug bank holiday weekend.

Aug West Indian Carnival. A sort of Notting Hill Carnival of the North.

Oct International film festival. This gets the local film buffs lining up for tickets for an annual basis.

Transport

Sheffield *p721, map p723*

Car

Europcar, NCP Car Park, Matilda Way, T0114-2768802; **Sixt Kenning**, 198a Gibraltar St, T0114-2766050; **Thrifty**, Parkway Av, T0114-2443366.

Taxi

Abbey Taxis Ltd, 20 Bedford St, T0114-2751111; **Central Cab Company**, 240 Woodbourn Rd, T0114-2769869; **Sheffield Taxi Services Ltd**, 20 Bedford St, T0114-2558888.

Leeds *p724, map p727*

Bus

Long distance National Express, 08705-808080, serve Leeds from **London Victoria** (4 hrs 30 mins) almost hourly throughout the day, also services from **Manchester** (1 hr 30 mins), **York** (1 hr), **Birmingham** (3 hrs 30 mins), **Sheffield** (1 hr) as well as many other destinations.

Car

Avis, Roseville Rd, T0113-2439771 and at the airport, T0113-2503880; **Europcar**, Aspley House, 78 Wellington St, T0113-2376855.

Taxi

A Metro Cars Private Hire, 66a New Briggate, T0113-2444031; **New Headingley Cars**, 1 Royal Park Rd, T0800-0155454.

Train

It's served by regular GNER trains from **London King's Cross** (2 hrs 20 mins) as well as from **Birmingham** (2 hrs), **Liverpool** (2 hrs), **Manchester** (1 hr), **Sheffield** (1 hr) and **York** (25 mins).

Haworth *p730*

Bus

Haworth is located off the A6063, and it is well signposted. From Bradford there are regular buses throughout the day, including buses 663, 664, 665 and 699.

Train

Best of all, though, is the **Keighley and Worth Valley Railway**, T01535-647777, which runs a steam-engine train from

Keighley to Oxenhope, stopping at Haworth. You can catch trains to Keighley from Leeds and Bradford and then switch to the steam train. Services run daily in the summer, and Sat and Sun Sep-Jun. £5-£8.

Directory

Sheffield *p721, map p723*
Hospitals The Royal Hallamshire Hospital, Glossop Rd, T0114-2711900.
Internet: Bar Matrix, 4 Charter Sq, T0114-2754100; **Havana Internet Cafe**, 32-34 Division St, T0114-2495452; **Refresh Cafe**, 198 Whitham Rd, T0114-2667979.

Leeds *p724, map p727*
Hospitals Leeds General Infirmary, Great George St, T0113-2432799.

The Yorkshire Dales → *Colour map 6, grids A2/3-B3*

The western equivalent of the North York Moors, the Yorkshire Dales are just as beautiful and, if anything, even more dramatic. Seeing one without taking in the other is like hearing half the story. The word 'dale' comes from the Viking word for valley – and while the moors are marked by gently rolling hills layered one upon another, the dales are more rugged, the hills steeper and more frequent, culminating in the three peaks of Pen-y-ghent, Ingleborough and Whernside. Amidst it all are the charming villages of Wensleydale, the arrogant beauty of Harrogate and the history of Ripon and Richmond. *» For Sleeping, Eating and other listings, see pages 748-751.*

Ins and outs

Getting there The best **rail** access into the Dales is via the **Settle to Carlisle Railway**, which offers glorious views into the bargain. There are connections to the line from Skipton and Leeds, www.settle-carlisle.co.uk.

From Leeds, the A65 provides easy entry to the Dales, heading through Ilkley and on to Skipton. From York, the A59 heads through Harrogate and on to Skipton. Once in the Dales, however, the most scenic route is on the small country **roads** that wind and sprawl across the empty miles. The dales are well covered by **bus** service, especially in the summer, although service is patchy on Sun and some holidays. **Traveline**, T0870-6082608. If you're travelling by bus, the **Dales Explorer** bus timetable is absolutely essential. You can pick one up at any tourist information office in the region.

South Dales

Ilkley

Heading into the dales from Leeds on the A65, the charming town of Ilkley is the first of any size that you come to. This allows the town to call itself 'the gateway to the dales' and, well, fair enough. One of several spa towns, the town's grand buildings owe their existence to Ilkley's 19th-century popularity among the upper classes (not much has changed) as a place to retreat for rest and 'healing' waters. Its best-known building is the dark grey **Manor House** ⓘ *T01943-700066, 1100-1700 Wed-Sat, 1300-1600 Sun*. Built between the 15th and 17th centuries, it is reached through a stone archway from Church Street. It's been converted into a museum that traces the history of the village back to prehistoric times.

Ins and outs Ilkley is connected to Leeds and Bradford by **train** and **bus**, both of which arrive at the central station.

Information You can get walking maps from the **TIC** ⓘ *opposite the train station on Station Rd, T01943-602319, 0930-1730 Mon-Sat, 1300-1700 Sun.*

Ilkley Moor

The countryside around Ilkley is fantastically dark and beautiful. The miles of heather on the Ilkley Moor are broken up by a number of ancient stone circles and hilltop crags. Unsurprisingly, there are many well-marked walks around the village, with two particular favourites: one to the **White Wells** – a whitewashed stone cottage built in 1756 around a moorland spring favoured by the infirm for its health-giving properties, and the other to the **Cow and Calf Rocks**, craggy hilltops that offer views that stretch for miles.

Skipton

Just a few miles from Ilkley, the bigger town of Skipton is a bustling place whose name, which means 'Sheeptown', rather gives away what the main business here once was.

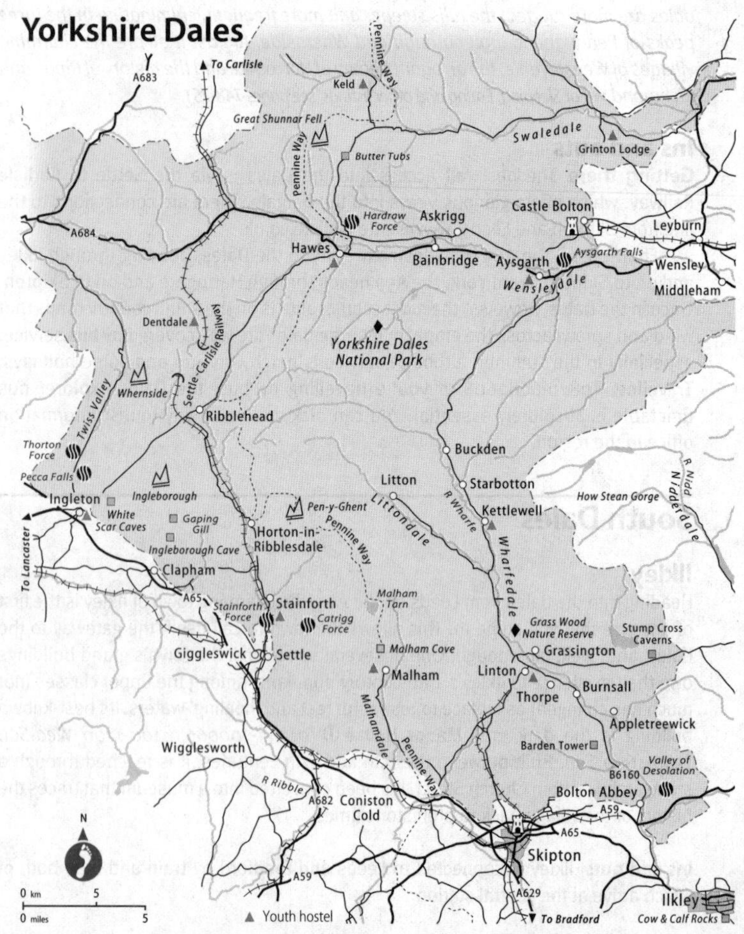

Ins and outs Skipton is a transport hub in the South Dales, so there is train service to Skipton Station from Leeds, Bradford, Keighley, Carlisle, Lancaster and Morecambe. The station is near the centre on Broughton Rd. You can also connect to the Settle-Carlisle Railway, www.settle-carlisle.co.uk, directly from here. The bus station is on Keighley Rd, where many B&Bs are also clustered, at the bottom of the High St. There is regular **National Express**, T08705-808080, coach service from London, as well as regional buses from Bradford and Keighley, Leeds, Ilkley, Harrogate and York. **Traveline,** T0870-6082608.

Information Skipton TIC ⓘ *Coach St, T01756-793809, www.skiptononline.co.uk, Mon-Sat 1000-1700, Sun 1130-1400 1530-1700*. Has information on local B&Bs, good local walks, history and more.

Sights

Today it could be called Castletown as the well-preserved **Skipton Castle** ⓘ *Mar-Sep Mon-Sat 1000-1800, Sun 1200-1800, Oct-Feb Mon-Sat 1000-1600, Sun 1200-1600, £4.40, child £2.20, family £11.90*, is one of the town's biggest tourist draws. A castle has stood on this site since 1090, although most of the current structure was built in medieval times. The thick 14th-century walls have endured more than time. They have survived a three-year siege by Parliamentarians during the Civil War. So sturdy was the squat little fortification with its rounded battlements (in places, its walls are 12 ft thick), that Cromwell ordered the roof to be removed, as it had survived one bombardment after another. When the castle's owner, Lady Anne Clifford, later asked to replace the roof, he allowed her to do so, as long as it was not strong enough to withstand cannon fire. Today the buildings are so complete that you cannot help but get the feel for what life was like for the villagers who worked and lived in its shadow, and under its protection.

In front of the castle, at the top of the high street stands the **Church of the Holy Trinity** ⓘ *Summer 0900-1630 daily, winter 0900-dusk daily, £1 donation requested*, which also was restored by the resourceful Lady Anne, and contains the Clifford family tombs with heraldic decoration, a 15th-century roof and an elaborate 16th-century chancel screen.

From here, if you turn left, you'll come to the old town, where medieval Skipton had its centre. The canals, and stone buildings here cry out for photos

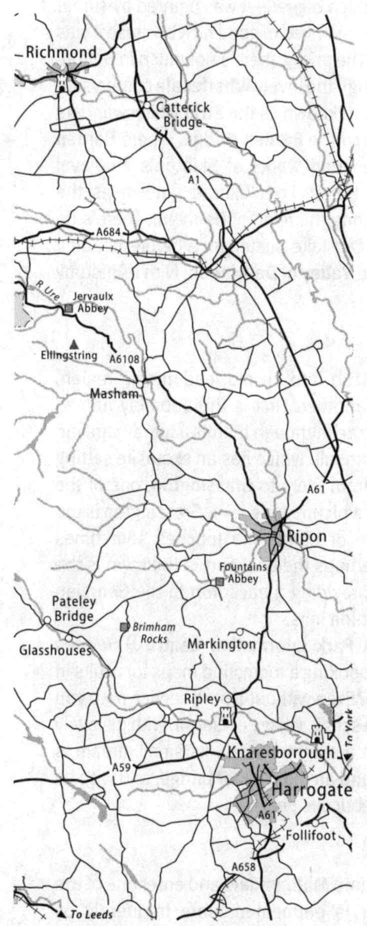

to be taken, in particular those around the **High Corn Mill**, the watermill that has been here so long it is mentioned in the *Domesday Book*. It still works, although it's now a shopping centre (naturally) rather than an operating mill. Below the castle and the old town, Skipton is still an old market town, as it has been for centuries. Its four weekly **market days** – Monday, Wednesday, Friday and Saturday – are events that bring in people from throughout the area to shop, drink and mingle. Its Christmastime markets are particularly colourful and busy. Further down the High Street the old town hall has converted its first floor into the **Craven Museum** ⓘ *T01756-706407, Apr-Sep Mon and Wed-Sat 1000-1700, Sun 1400-1700, Oct-Mar Mon and Wed-Fri 1330-1700, Sat 1000-1600, free*, which is packed with lots of interesting folk history, archaeological finds and geological displays from the area around Skipton, which is known as Craven.

Bolton Abbey

This is another one of those towns that has taken its name from an old monastery. In this case, unlike in some towns, at least the abbey ruins still exist. In fact, the scant remains of the **Bolton Priory** are the primary attraction here. The priory once formed part of a wide-ranging Augustinian network of churches and monasteries throughout the region. The building was started in 1150, and stood complete until the Dissolution when it was abandoned. The ruins were once much bigger – it was painted by Turner – but now all that remains is the nave, which has survived in good nick because it was used as the parish church for years. Aside from the priory, there's not much in Bolton, except the beginnings of a variety of **walks** through the lovely **Wharfedale** countryside and along the riverbanks. You can follow the path known as the **Strid** which wanders from the abbey for 4 miles alongside the river to the **Barden Bridge**, where **Barden Tower** stands as a further monument to the good works of Skipton's medieval conservationist, Lady Anne. It was used by Henry, Lord Clifford (known as the 'Shepherd Lord') for his alchemical studies during the reign of Henry VII. There's no gold here, but there *is* a tearoom where you can take sustenance before heading back, or you can continue on to the aptly named **Valley of Desolation**, with its gloomy beauty and waterfalls.

Grassington and around

Heading north from Bolton Abbey on the B6160 into an old lead-mining region, there's one tiny charming dales village after another. First is the adorably named village of **Appletreewick**, which is nothing but cute (although there's a handy caravan park here), following on is the tiny village of **Burnsall**, which has an exquisite setting along a burbling stream. It's just a few miles from there to **Grassington**, one of the bigger villages in the dales. Built on the edge of a picturesque river, Grassington is too big to be really pretty, but it has a mixture of handsome touches sometimes overshadowed by a rather high twee factor. Perhaps the best part of the town is the setting, with the **Grass Wood nature reserve** providing a backdrop to the Georgian houses at the centre, the cobbled streets and olde inns.

Grassington also has the main **National Park Information Centre** ⓘ *Hebden Road, T01746-752774*, where you can get help booking a room, find maps for walks in the area and explore the history of Wharfedale. Even without a park service map you can drive the few miles from Grassington to the scenic village of **Linton**, with its lovely parks. This is a fantastic place for a picnic on a summer's day. Its small stream is crossed by both an ancient packhorse bridge and an old clapper bridge, and with its perfect 12th-century church, it is the picture of bucolic peace.

Around Malham Village

Due west of Linton you cross from Wharfedale into **Malhamdale** and enter one of the prettiest regions of the dales. The heather is permeated more frequently by limestone here, as this is a rocky region of striking high stone cliffs. It's a favourite with walkers, and the **Pennine Way** wanders through here, bringing a steady stream of ramblers. The biggest and busiest hub for these backpack toters is Malham Village. In the summertime, you simply cannot move for the walkers in this tiny village with its quaint stone cottages. In fact, by some estimates, half a million people a year make their way here. That means that, unless you are using this town as a setting off point yourself, there's too much of a crush here for it to actually be pleasant. If you're walking, there's a handy car park where you can leave your car and set off, and there's a **National Park Information Centre** ⓘ *T01729-830363, Easter-Oct daily 1000-1700, Nov-Easter Sat, Sun 1000-1600*, stocked with maps and advice on where to stop off on a multiple-day hike. The main attraction here, aside from the pub meals and comfy B&B rooms is the proximity to nearby walking trails. Walking north on a well-marked path you can travel about a mile to the absolutely stunning **Malham Cove**, the misnamed geological formation along the Mid-Craven Faultline created by movement of the earth's plates, it is a massive limestone amphitheatre that towers hundreds of feet above the beautiful surrounding countryside. Another walk will take you to the glacial **Malham Tarn**, a lake protected as a nature reserve and inhabited by crowds of birds and animals.

Settle

Heading just a few miles west from Malhamdale to Settle, you cross over into the dark, dramatic moors of **Ribblesdale**. Settle is the biggest village in this area, and the terminus of the gorgeous Settle-Carlisle rail line, which passes through some of the most consistently beautiful countryside in Britain. As Malham does in Malhamdale, Settle makes a popular base for walkers in Ribblesdale. With the added attraction of the railroad, this small town can get quite crowded as well in the summer. And, similarly, there's not much here save for B&Bs and pubs. Walkers usually head directly to the TIC in the town hall on Cheapside off the market, T01729-825192, 1000-1700 daily, to pick up maps and to get guidance from staff on the best walks around the village. The well-signposted train station is a few minutes' walk from the tourist office and the town centre.

For walkers, there is plenty to see around Settle; Ribblesdale is dotted with charming villages. The village with the best name in all of the dales, **Giggleswick**, is less than a mile away on the opposite bank of the River Ribble. Happily, it is just as adorable as its name, with a river gurgling past, green moors all around, and old stone buildings on its tree-shaded streets. The old town school was built in 1512, while the small domed chapel is more beautiful inside than out. Just across the bridge from Giggleswick there's a smooth, easy footpath along the river from Settle to the tiny village of **Stainforth** with its charming pubs. Around the village, the **Stainforth Force** creates natural swimming holes, and there's an old packhorse bridge nearby which makes for an irresistible Kodak moment. If you've picked up a map of area walks, you may also be drawn to hike to **Catrigg Force**, a small but beautiful waterfall just east of Stainforth.

Horton-in-Ribblesdale

Along with Settle, the old quarry town of Horton-in-Ribblesdale is one of the most popular stops for walkers in the Dales. Many of the deep carvings around the village were scratched into the stone when the Settle-Carlisle Railway was being built in the late 1800s. The deep cuts and rocky hills make the area around here one of the most unusual you're likely to see in the North. The very industry that once made this town ugly and utilitarian has, over time, created extraordinary vistas. You can get lunch and tourist information at the *Peny-y-Ghent Café*, which is also a **National Park Information Centre** ⓘ *T01729-860333. May-Sep Mon, Wed-Fri 0900-1800, Sat and Sun 0800-1800. Oct-Apr Mon and Wed 0900-1800.* This is where hikers planning to tackle the famed **Three Peaks Walk** often gather beforehand for information, advice and camaraderie. The three peaks in question are the mountains **Pen-y-Ghent** (2273 ft) to the east, **Ingleborough** (2373 ft) and the highest point in Yorkshire **Whernside** (2419 ft). The walk is a gruelling path around all three that takes 12 hours and covers more than 25 miles. It is only for fit and experienced hikers. Most hikers register at the *Pen-y-Ghent Café* when they head out for the path, and check in when they return, as a safety precaution. Getting lost or getting hurt are possibilities up there, and you want somebody to know that you're missing. Each April dozens of true fanatics race over all three of the hills in the mad dash known as the **Three Peaks Race**. The fastest runners complete the whole circuit in three hours.

Clapham

Famed for its caves, the attractive little village of Clapham is a few miles due west from Horton-in-Ribblesdale at the foot of the Ingleborough. There's a car park at one end of the little town, where you're well advised to leave your wheels and strike out on foot like everybody else. Aside from climbers headed up the peak, the main draw here is in the other direction, down into the **Ingleborough Cave** ⓘ *Mar-Oct 1000-1700 daily, Nov-Feb 1030-dusk Sat, Sun, £4.50*. There's an easy footpath that travels the mile from town to the cave entrance, and you can get a map showing the way, along with other useful information, at the **National Park Information Centre** ⓘ *next to the car park, T01524-251418. Summer 1000-1600 daily, winter 1000-1600 Sat, Sun*. The cave is extraordinary, filled with dark chambers and passages. The ceiling and floor are lined with dangerous looking stalactites and stalagmites that glitter like daggers.

Heading up another mile or so past the cave, you'll come to **Gaping Gill**, a cavern that plummets more than 300 ft down, with a waterfall that rushes over the edge. Along with the spectacular view, there are also ruins on the summit of an Iron Age fort, with standing walls and foundations of circular huts that have been dated to the first century BC.

Ingleton

The furthest west point in the dales, the charming village of Ingleton straddles the junction of two picturesque streams in a ravine crossed by a 19th-century railway viaduct. Although the town is lovely, as with other dales villages, most people who come here aren't here to see the village. They're just fuelling up for one of the nearby hikes. Before setting out, get maps and information at the Ingleton TIC by the car park on Main St, T01524-241049. You can also get help on accommodation here as well. The most popular hike is the one and a half mile walk to the **White Scar Caves** which are, if anything, more spectacular than the Ingleborough Cave. An internal waterfall provides a constant rumble that grows to a roar as you get closer to it. A series of walkways have been erected to make the tour through the depths safer, but it's still a cave, so there's a section where the walls are only about a foot apart, and another where they're less than 5 ft high. A tour here is not for the unfit. At the centre of the cave is the massive **Battlefield Cavern** ⓘ *T01524-241244, 1000-1700 daily, £6.25*, 300 ft long and 100 ft high. All tours into the cave are guided, and it's not cheap, but it's well worth it.

The other popular walk from Ingleton is the **Falls Walk** which climbs more than 2 miles up the gorgeous **Twiss Valley**, with viewing stations to take in the breathtaking scenery of the **Pecca Falls** and **Thornton Force**. There's a farm at the top of the walk where you can get something to eat and drink, and then a different path takes you back for a fresh perspective on it all.

East Dales

Litton to Kettlewell

Heading east from the Three Peaks, you enter **Littondale**, where more small villages and good walks can be found. In the little stone village of Litton there's a very small but useful **National Park Information Point** inside the post office where you can get maps and guidance. Litton makes a good base for climbing Pen-y-Ghent, but be aware that the villages here are so tiny that it gets harder to find accommodation or restaurants, so either bring your own tent and provisions, or drive back to one of the larger villages at the end of the day. Just beyond Litton the countryside is particularly beautiful, with rolling hills and deep valleys. The village of **Starbotton** is so tiny that if you blink you will indeed miss it, but that would be a shame as its *Fox and Hounds* pub with its stone floors, large fireplace that all but heats the place itself, and good food, is legendary.

A few miles down the road is another tiny village, **Buckden**, which is home to a handful of useful B&Bs as well as a **National Park Information Point** located inside the Riverside Gallery at the centre of town. By the time you get to the village of **Kettlewell** you're back in Wharfedale. This makes a particularly good base for exploring the countryside, as the town is more beautiful and less busy than places like Grassington. There's a very small **National Park Information Point** inside the *Over and Under* outdoor shop, where you can get supplies as well as maps and information. There are a handful of B&Bs in town, a **campsite** north of town at Fold Farm, T01756-760886, as well as a couple of good pubs in the town centre.

Pateley Bridge

Heading into the eastern Dales, the focus remains on rural walks, gorgeous countryside and charming villages like little Pateley Bridge. Small this village may be, but it's extremely important for walkers interested in taking in the scenery. You don't have to go far, a short stroll takes you up to the ruins of the church of **St Cuthbert** perched overlooking it all from a nearby hilltop. The ruins are striking – a compelling combination of dark and beautiful – and the view of the surrounding moors is simply spectacular. But that's not enough for most visitors, so it's handy that the TIC, 18 High St, T01423-711147, Easter-Oct only, has maps, information, advice and guidance for those interested in striking out. Before you head off, staff in hand, stop in at the **Nidderdale Museum** ⓘ *Apr-Oct 1400-1700 daily, Nov-Mar 1400-1700 Sat, Sun, £1.50*, which can help you brush up on local history, complete with a recreated 18th-century village street.

The best walks start a short drive from the town centre. For instance, the **Stump Cross Caverns** ⓘ *Apr-Oct 1000-1800 daily, Nov-Mar 1000-1600 Sat, Sun, £4.50*, with spectacular caverns and stalactites are about five miles west of Pateley Bridge.Or you could drive 5 miles east of town to the legendary **Brimham Rocks**, a walk that takes you over hundreds of acres upon which thousands of these mysterious boulders sprout like weeds. The overall landscape is strange and beautiful, with stones incongruously towering over green moors. If you head a few miles north from Patelely Bridge you'll reach **How Stean Gorge** ⓘ *1000-1700 daily, £2.50*, with its deep ravine and spooky caves.

Harrogate

Most people reach Harrogate from the west, which is unfortunate, as coming at it from the northwest is particularly beautiful (with the added attraction of stopping to take a photo of the sign for the wonderfully named nearby village of **Glasshouses**). The best known town in the Dales, everything Harrogate has it owes to water. A specific kind of water that rises from Tewit Well, to be precise. The sulphur springs were discovered in 1571 and the rest is history. In the spa boom of the 18th and 19th centuries, Harrogate soon rose to the top, and the town bloomed around the springs in an explosion of austere and grand architecture, befitting the class of those who flocked to the town to drink the water, soak in the water, be electrified in the water, and all the other strange things they did back then in the name of 'health'. Agatha Christie took the waters here while considering divorcing her husband during her disappearance in 1926.

Ins and outs

Getting there The train station is on Station Parade near the town centre. There are regular trains from Leeds and York. Harrogate is on the A59 from Skipton and the A61 from Leeds. It's well located for access to the Dales. The bus station is just down the street from the train station, with local and regional services. » *See Transport, page 751, for more details.*

Information Harrogate TIC ⓘ *inside the Royal Baths on Crescent Rd, T01423-537300, May-Sep Mon-Sat 0900-1800, Sun 1200-1500, Oct-Apr Mon-Fri 0900-1715, Sat 0900-1230*. They can help you book guided tours of the town and offer guidance on accommodation and good restaurants in town.

Sights

So well-preserved is the town that you can walk in the footsteps of 19th-century society starting at the **Royal Baths Assembly Rooms** ⓘ *Crescent Road, T01423-556746*. Plunge right in by taking a bath yourself. Just around the corner from the baths is the **Royal Pump Room** ⓘ *Crown Place, Apr-Oct Mon-Sat 1000-1700, Sun 1400-1700, Nov-Mar Mon-Sat 1000-1600, Sun 1400-1600, £2*. It stands over the well that provides sulphurous water for the baths, and has been converted to include an interesting museum. The big building that stands across from the baths is the 19th-century **Royal Hall**, where those in town for the waters would catch ballets and symphonies in the evening. Down the road from the Pump Room, the **Mercer Art Gallery,** just a short distance away on Swan Road, is in the oldest pump building in town.

The beautiful parkland that stretches across town is called (wonderfully) **The Stray**, and has decorated Harrogate for hundreds of years, exactly as it does today. Other historic gardens are nearby at the gorgeous **Valley Gardens** and the showy **Harlow Carr Botanical Gardens** which combine to give the town its deserved reputation as the horticultural centre of the North. There's also the **Museum of Gardening** ⓘ *£4.50 in summer, £3 in winter*, located inside the Harlow Carr space.

Knaresborough

A worthwhile daytrip from Harrogate, Knaresborough – just four miles away – may well be one of the most underrated cities in England. Sitting as it does in the shadow of its famous neighbour, it's not well known despite its dramatic location above the River Nidd, its well-preserved townhouses, traditional pubs and colourful gardens. Even the railroad viaduct that crosses the ravine makes for an extraordinary view. Along with the lovely setting, Knaresborough has a modest **castle** ruin in a most picturesque location, towering above it all on a desolate hilltop. The remains of the Norman castle are mostly limited to its keep, but it's worth a visit if only because of its historic importance, which is well documented in the **Old Court House** Museum ⓘ *Castle Yard, Easter-Sep 1030-1700 daily, £2*. Best of all, you're given freedom to wander the dark old tunnels that run under the castle.On the river bank is the strange **Chapel of Our Lady of the Crag,** a mysterious shrine carved into the rocks – apparently around 1400 – that contains the figure of a knight. Across the river from the castle in the **Dropping Well Estate** is a mysterious cave that was once home to the famed 15th-century prophet known as Mother Shipton. She is said to have predicted many of the events of the subsequent 500 years, from the Great Fire of London to the phenomenon of world wars. **Mother Shipton's Cave** ⓘ *Easter-Oct 0930-1745 daily, Nov-Easter 1000-1645 daily, £3.95*, is filled with strange memorabilia and spooks the punters. It's located very near the other punter puller, the quite cool **Petrifying Well**, where the natural lime-rich waters turn everything they touch to stone. People have been putting objects here for years – from clothing to toys – and they are petrified in weeks.

Ripley

Just a few miles north from Knaresborough the little town of Ripley is another of those strangely compelling 'model villages' on the lines of Saltaire (see page 729). This one was designed by Sir William Amcotts Ingilby in the 1820s, based on the traditional designs of Alsace-Lorraine villages, apparently on a whim. It's just the look of the place, with its vivid flower gardens, European square and shops selling your basic Yorkshire woollens and lavender soaps, that are its main attractions. But the best part is **Ripley Castle**, which stands above it all, as if in disbelief. The fairly well-preserved castle has a 15th-century gatehouse, a 16th-century tower and a nifty man-made lake. Parts of the castle are stocked with armour, memorabilia and period furnishings. Like most of the castles in these parts, it has a Cromwell connection, as he spent his first night here after the battle of Marston Moor. From the castle, near the bridge, you'll come across the old **All Saints' church**, where the walls are still nicked and dented from musket balls. According to local lore, the damage happened when Royalist soldiers were executed against the wall after Marston Moor.

Fountains Abbey

ⓘ *Abbey and gardens, Apr-Sep 1000-1900 daily, Oct, Feb, Mar 1000-1700 daily, Nov-Jan 1000-1700 Sun-Thu, £4.50.*

It's difficult to decide what's more beautiful, the remains of the Cistercian abbey or the wooded setting in the valley of the River Skell. Surrounded by the water gardens known as **Studley Royal**, which were designed in the 19th century to compliment that rambling, jagged ruins of the abbey, the whole scene is simply extraordinary, equalled only by the hillside ruins at Rievaulx (see page 699). Fountains Abbey was founded by a rebellious group of Benedictines from York in 1132, but was taken over by the Cistercians within three years. Over the next century it grew into the most successful of the Cistercian monasteries in England, and that is reflected in the size of the ruins that remain today, growing out of the hillside in castle-like proportions of stone turrets and archways. Unlike many other Yorkshire abbeys, the ruins here are very substantial, including much of the **nave**, and the pointed **arcade** towering above Norman piers. The filigree remains of the **Chapel of the Nine Altars** gives some idea of how extraordinary this building must have been when complete. The **dormitory** where the lay workers slept is still largely intact, and it's clear that it was once massive, as it would have needed to be in order to house the hundreds of workers who lived and worked here, alongside the monks. On the south side of the ruins, the old **warming rooms** can be seen, along with the massive fireplaces which gave the rooms their names. The enormous tower that hovers over all the ruins was added in the 16th century, but remains the only later addition of any substance amidst the 12th-century ruins. The building by the entrance is **Fountains Hall**, built in the 17th century by Sir Richard Gresham, who bought the property on which the abbey stood after the Dissolution, and cannibalized much of the stone for his home from the old abbey. Luckily, the next owner of the property, John Aislabie, was more sympathetic to the old building. He stopped the destruction of the abbey, and designed the stunning gardens that now surround it, with a mixture of flowers, woods, deer parks and lakes.

 The most unusual of the features designed by Aislabie is the water gardens that include ponds, cascades and lakes, all integrated perfectly into the wild, wooded landscape. Scattered around the grounds are the more affected addition of garden buildings (so popular in the 17th century) including the 'Temple of Piety' and a banquet house. One building that does work is the 19th-century **St Mary's Church** which includes an approach through an avenue of limes that frame the view of the abbey from the church. Despite the occasional wrong note hit by enthusiastic owners over the years, the combined effect of ruins and gardens is breathtaking.

Ripon

The pretty town of Ripon sit a few miles from Fountains Abbey and about 11 miles north of Harrogate. For more than 1,300 years, its main draw has been its small but exquisite **cathedral** ⓘ *0800-1830 daily, £2 donation requested.* From the outside, it looks much like any other parish church, but inside the architecture dates back to its foundation by St Wilfrid in 672. Even a decade before then, though, there was a monastery on this site, mentioned by the ancient historian Bede in his writings of that time. The labyrinthine crypt, with its arched passageways and mysterious shadows has been dated to that period, and is, without question, the most extraordinary part of the building. A number of relics, including the Ripon jewel (discovered in 1976 and dated back to the building's earliest years) are on display down here. The Danes destroyed the rest of that first building in the ninth century. The chapel was built in the 11th century, and much of the rest of the building dates from the 12th century, although the twin towers at either side are 13th-century structures. There are regular chamber concerts here, usually on Monday evenings, and the Ripon Cathedral Choir is justifiably famous, and any chance to catch one of their performances should be grabbed. There's also an annual celebration in honour of St Wilfrid, as a procession moves regally down the streets in his name on St Wilfred's Feast the Sunday before the first Monday in August.

There's really not much else in Ripon, although if you happen to be in town at around 2100 you'll catch the charming and historic **Wakeman ceremony**, in which a horn is blown from each of the central market square's four corners, and in front of the **Wakeman's House** on one side of the market. This dates back to 886, when Alfred the Great first granted the town a charter, and presented Ripon with an ox's horn for the setting of its nightly watch. The person who blew the horn nightly was the wakeman, and, until 1637, a wakeman always lived in a house on the square.

Masham

After the cathedrals, abbeys and castles of the rest of Yorkshire, Masham, about eight miles north of Ripon, has a bit of an air of 'and now for something completely different'. For this is beertown, pure and simple. In fact, beer lovers make pilgrimages here to see for themselves the mecca of **Theakston's** breweries. Tours of the large breweries tell you the current ways and means of beer brewing, along with the history of brewers' mysterious recipes and rules. The tours include a free pint at the end, and if that just leaves you wanting more, there's an on-site pub ⓘ *T01765 684 333 Apr-Nov 1030-1730 daily, £4.* There's also an independent micro-brewer in town, the **Black Sheep Brewery** ⓘ *1030-1730 Mon, Sun, 1030-2300 Tue-Sat, £3.75,* which offers tours of the microbrewery process.

Jerveaulx Abbey and Middleham Castle

Just north of Masham, at the beginning of Wensleydale, the barely-there ruins of the Cistercian **Jerveaulx Abbey** ⓘ *Dawn-dusk daily, £1.50 donation requested,* are located more or less in the middle of nowhere. There's not much left of this monastery, which is now privately owned, but the setting is lovely, and the fact that it all feels so abandoned and forgotten is part of the attraction.

Northeast Dales

Wensley and around

Just north of Middleham, the old farming community of **Leyburn** is another charming village with busy markets, cobbled streets, and lots of 18th-century buildings. Many people come here just to stop for lunch at the cosy **Golden Lion inn** on the marketplace, and to watch the rural world go by. Similarly adorable is the little village of **Wensley**, just a mile or so away. The town after which the dale is named, Wensley has a lovely 15th-century bridge and a parish church that dates from the 13th century. Inside the church of the **Holy Trinity** the 16th-century choir stalls are elaborately carved with poppies, and it has a 14th-century brass relief of a priest.

A mile or so west of Wensley are the 14th-century ruins of **Castle Bolton** ⓘ *T01969-623981, Mar-Oct 1000-1700 daily, £4*. The starkly beautiful surroundings and the cold thick walls of the castle were once the only view that Mary, Queen of Scots, had, as she was held prisoner here for months in 1658. A few parts of the ruins have been restored – in particular, the great hall and the castle gardens – but the best part of it all are the sweeping views of the rolling Wensleydale hills from the top of the battlements.

Aysgarth and Askrigg

The hilltop village of **Aysgarth** is blessed with a gorgeous setting at the edge of the River Ure, which streams by on its limestone bed and then tumbles over impossibly picturesque **waterfalls**. In the summer, the little village fills with walkers, parking their cars, picking up maps at the **National Park information centre** ⓘ *T01969-663424*, and striking up the surrounding hills. The paths are well marked, both the **Upper Falls** and the **Lower Falls** are a short walk from the town centre through thick woods. And the views are extraordinary. A few miles west is the village of Askrigg, which may look familiar if you watched the TV series of the James Herriott book *All Creatures Great and Small*, which was filmed here and around. Aside from looking for buildings you recognize, there are walks from here to the ruggedly beautiful **Whitfield Force** and **Mill Gill Force**, each well marked and fairly short – neither is more than a mile from the town centre. The jewel-like town of **Bainbridge** is just a couple of miles southwest of Askrigg, and has a historic nightly ceremony in which a horn is sounded on the village green at 2100, to call travellers in from the surrounding moors. The haunting horn sound is extremely evocative, and if you hear it without getting goosepimples, you're harder than most. The best place to be when the horn sounds is the 15th-century coaching inn, the *Rose & Crown Hotel*, T01969-650 225, which has a magnificent pub, and a few pleasant rooms.

Hawes

The little mountain town of Hawes is an unlikely tourist hub. It is home to just 1,300 souls, isn't particularly pretty and is primarily a centre of business and shopping for nearby farmers. But it is also surrounded by hills and waterfalls that act like flame to a moth for hikers. At 800 ft, Hawes claims to be the highest market town in Yorkshire, and its weekly market on Tuesday is crammed with cheeses and locally made jams and fresh butter. The **Wensleydale Creamery** on Gayle Lane is a regular stop for visitors stocking up before heading home. Cheese has been made in Hawes since the Cistercians started making it here in the 12th century, and it is sold everywhere in town. Most people are here to walk, however, and the closest, and easiest walk, takes you from the '*Green Dragon*' pub, where you pay 70p to enter the path up to the somewhat disappointing and small **Hadraw Force**. More difficult walks head up to the **Great Shunner Fell**, or to the natural wells known as the **Butter Tubs**. Before you head out, stop by the **National Park information centre** for maps and advice. It is located inside the surprisingly good **Hawes Ropemakers Museum** ① *T01969-667450, Jul-Oct 0900-1730 Mon-Fri, 1000-1730 Sat, Nov-Jun 0900-1730 Mon-Fri, free*, which offers free demonstrations on the local skill of ropemaking.

Richmond

Just at the edge of the furthest eastern border of the dales, and about eight miles from Castle Bolton, the splendid castle town of Richmond provides a fitting ending to the dales, with its market square, Georgian architecture and bright gardens.

Information TIC ① *Friary Gardens on Victoria Rd, T01748-850252, Apr-Sep 0930-1730 daily, Oct-Mar 0930-1630 Mon-Sat.* In addition to providing maps and advice for walks in the area, it will also help you find B&B accommodation in the rural area around Richmond.

Sights At the centre of it all is the 11th-century **castle** ① *Apr-Oct 1000-1800 daily, Nov-Mar 1000-1300, 1400-1600 daily, £2.70*, which stands guard from a steep precipice above the river. Lore connects this castle to England's most famous mythical king, as King Arthur is said to lie in a nearby cave, waiting for the time when England needs him again. Unlike many Yorkshire castles, the gloomy walls of Richmond Castle still hold many of its original Norman buildings including its gatehouse, keep (one of very few surviving Norman keeps in the country, and perhaps the eldest) and curtain wall. Along with all of this you get dramatic views from the sheer cliffs atop which it stands.

Like the castle, Richmond retains many of its original features as well. The town's streets are still cobbled and its narrow Medieval alleyways still wander confusingly in a spiderweb of walkways and streets. The desanctified 12th-century **Holy Trinity church** now holds the **Green Howards Museum** ① *1000-1600 Mon-Sat, £2*, which tells the story of North Yorkshire's Green Howards regiment. Also of interest is the small but perfectly formed **Theatre Royal** ① *1430-1545 Mon-Sat, £1.50*. Built in 1788, it is England's oldest theatre, only re-opened to the public in 1963 after sitting derelict for a century, which is difficult to believe when you see its exquisite Georgian interior. The little **museum** at the back of the theatre is all good fun, with hands-on access to stage sets and costumes.

At the edge of Richmond stand the ruins of **Easby Abbey** ① *Dawn to dusk daily, free*, which was founded in 1152, and once was home to hundreds of Premonstratensian canons. Access to the site is free, and there is an easy, well-marked path here from the town centre. And there are few sights more beautiful than the jagged ruins of this abbey at sunset.

Sleeping

Skipton *p738*

C Hanover International Hotel, Keighley Rd, T01756-700100, www.hanover-international.co.uk. The biggest hotel in town, it has all the necessary luxuries along the Leeds-Liverpool Canal.

D Coniston Hall Hotel, Coniston Cold, T01756-748080, www.conistonhall.co.uk. Set in acres of private parkland is a sprawling, beautiful hotel with its own lake and promises of "shooting, fishing, archery, corporate activities".

D Maypole Cottage, Blackburn House Farm, Thorpe, T01756-720 609. A detached old stable converted to form private self-catering accommodation which can be rented by the week.

D Highfield Hotel, 58 Keighley Rd, T01756-793182. This small and centrally located hotel is very handy and affordable.

E Craven Heifer Inn, Grassington Rd, just outside Skipton, T01756-792521, www.cravenheifer.co.uk. A grand old barn that has been converted into a rural guesthouse with a good bar and restaurant.

E Skipton Park Guest 'Otel, 2 Salisbury St, T01756-700640. Friendly and cheap best describes this place.

Bolton Abbey *p740*

L-A The Devonshire Arms, T02756-710441. The ancestral home of the Duke and Duchess of Devonshire, it's a gorgeous manor house just south of Bolton Abbey, filled with antiques.

Around Malham Village *p740*

Because Malham is so very popular, you will need to book ahead if you plan to use it as a base for your travels. In general, though, especially if you arrive without booking in advance, you're better off trying any of the nearby villages, which are less crowded, book up less quickly and are slightly less expensive.

C Riverhouse Hotel, on the main road, T01729-830315. A Victorian country house that's been converted into a decent hotel with a good restaurant.

D Miresfield Farm, by the National Park office, T01729-830414. Lovely and friendly, this is one of the best places to stay.

E The Buck Inn, a traditional country inn with basic rooms and a good pub downstairs.

Camping

F Youth Hostel T01729-830321. Very popular.

Townhead Farm, T01729-830287. Camping space by the cove.

Settle *p741*

For those making Settle their base, there are plenty of B&Bs and inns to choose from. 2 reliable options on the market square are:

C Golden Lion, T01729-822203 and

C Royal Oak, T01729-822561.

D Yorkshire Rose, Duke St, T01729-822032. A small and friendly place, out of the town centre.

E Penmar Court Guest House, T01729-823258. Again outside the town and affordable and handy.

D Plough Inn, in nearby Wigglesworth, T01729-840243, F840243. Offers lovely views and a fine restaurant.

D Husbands Barn, in Stainsforth, T01728-822240. A stone farmhouse and B&B.

F Stainforth Youth Hostel, T01729-823577.

Horton-in-Ribblesdale *p741*

If you're planning to make Horton-in-Ribblesdale your base, you'd best book well in advance, as rooms are few and they get snatched up early.

D Crown Hotel, T017239-860238. Decent rooms, as well as good food and a convivial evening atmosphere as everyone relaxes over a few drinks after an exhausting day. There's also the somewhat more upscale

D Rowe House, on the Ribblehead Rd near the station, T01729-860373.

Camping

E Holme Farm, T01729-860281. A tents-only campsite just outside of town.

Ingleton *p742*

There's quite a bit of accommodation to choose from, although booking ahead in the summer is essential.

D Bridge End Guest House, Mill La, T01424-241413. Handy and attractive.

D Ingleborough View, Main St, T01424-241523. Pretty and popular.

D Moorgarth Hall, New Rd, T01524-241946. Handsome building outside of town which has good views of the surrounding countryside.

Camping

Moorgaarth Farm, T01524-241428.About a mile outside of town.

Stacksteads Farm, T01524-241386. Also has a bunkhouse barn.

Harrogate *p743*

Harrogate is filled with hotels and B&Bs for every budget. The best areas to troll for a room are on King's Rd and Franklin Rd, where they stand shoulder to shoulder.

A Rudding Park Hotel, Rudding Park, Follifoot, T01423-871350, www.ruddingpark.com. A converted manor house just outside of town on the A661, one of the most elegant hotels in the area. It also has an excellent restaurant and gorgeous bar.

B The Imperial, Prospect Pl, T01423-565071. One of the town's grande dames, perfectly located and absolutely gorgeous. Worth the money if you can swing it.

D Alexander Guest House, 88 Franklin Rd, T01423-503348. A grand Victorian building on a quiet street.

D Ascot House Hotel, 53 King's Rd, T01423-531005, www.ascothouse.com. For much of the glamour at less of the price, try this rambling, turreted house on lovely grounds and has a fabulous bar.

D Cedar Court Hotel, Queen Building, Park Parade, T01423-858585, www.cedarcourt hotels.co.uk. Wonderfully noble, this place dates back to 1671 and claims to be the town's first hotel. It's beautifully restored and offers affordable luxury.

D Fountains Hotel, 27 King's Rd, T01423-430483. Friendly and family-run and offering basic comfort at a reasonable price.

D Hob Green Hotel, Markington, T01423-770031, F771589. About 5 miles north of Harrogate on vast, beautiful grounds with wonderful views and period furnishings, as well as an excellent restaurant.

Richmond *p748*

There's quite a few options when it comes to accommodation in Richmond.

C King's Head Hotel Market Pl, T01748-850220, www.kingshead richmond.co.uk, One of the most beautiful, a Georgian building stocked with antiques. Its pub and restaurant are among the best in town.

D Bridge House Hotel, Catterick Bridge, T01748-818331, Pretty hotel at the edge of the water, and offers gorgeous views. It also has a good bar and two restaurants.

D The Old Brewery Guesthouse, 29 The Green, T01748-833460, is, as the name implies, a converted old brewery just below the castle.

D Willance House, 24 Bridge St, T01748-824467 Dating from the 17th-century, this lovely guesthouse, but only has a couple of rooms.

Eating

Skipton *p738*

There are plenty of places catering for tourists in the centre of Skipton.

££ Le Caveau, 86 High St. One of the nicest options, with modern European cooking in an elegant atmosphere.

£ Bizzie Lizzies, Swadford St, which locals swear is the best fish and chips in town.

£ Wooly Sheep Inn, which has a good selection of beer and a not-bad selection of pub food.

Settle *p741*

Most of the inns in town also have good restaurants:

£ The Golden Lion, **The Royal Oak** and **The Plough Inn** included.

£ Ye Olde Naked Man Café, However, everybody is drawn to this place, which has good food and a wonderful sign to take somebody's picture in front of.

Harrogate *p743*

You can't swing a cat without hitting a restaurant, pub or teahouse in Harrogate.

££ Clock Tower, Rudding Park, T01423-871350. Good modern British cuisine, or you can just sip a drink in its very nice bar.

££ Court's, 1 Crown Pl, T01423-536336. The posh environs are ideal for sipping a glass of wine.

££ Courtyard, 1 Montpellier Mews, T01423-530708. For an upscale modern European meal.

££ Drum and Monkey, 5 Montpellier Gardens, T01423-502650, provides outstanding fish and chips, with a similar historic pedigree.

Tearooms

You will never have a better chance to stuff yourself with scones.

Betty's, 1 Parliament St, T01423-502746, has stood on this spot for 80 years. Tea and scones for 2 about £10. The best tea place in town, by popular acclaim.

Garden Room Restaurant in the Botanical gardens, T01423-505604. For slightly smaller crowds and a better view, you can get an excellent cream tea or lunch here.

Richmond *p748*

There are dozens of pubs in Richmond, where you can get a pint of real ale and a good meal. The most obvious choices are those on the market square. Several of the hotels listed have good restaurants and pubs.

£ The Restaurant on the Green on Bridge St, which offers good food in a pleasant atmosphere.

£ The Unicorn on Newbiggin. One of the best pubs, a little way out from the castle, and therefore not as crowded as some of the closer places.

Festivals

Harrogate *p743*

Apr **Flower Show**. Each Apr and Sep there are massive flower shows in the town's sprawling gardens that draw in garden lovers from all over the country and abroad.

Jul **Great Yorkshire Show**. Brings in thousands for a few days of arts, crafts and entertainment..

Sep **The Northern Antiques Fair** is the place to go for antiquarians.

Transport

Harrogate *p743*

Bus

National Express, T08705-808080. Buses drop off and pick up on Victoria Av, near the library. **Traveline**, T0870-6082608.

Clapham *p742*

Train

There's a train station in Clapham with trains to Leeds and Skipton, but it's a mile south of the village.

The North

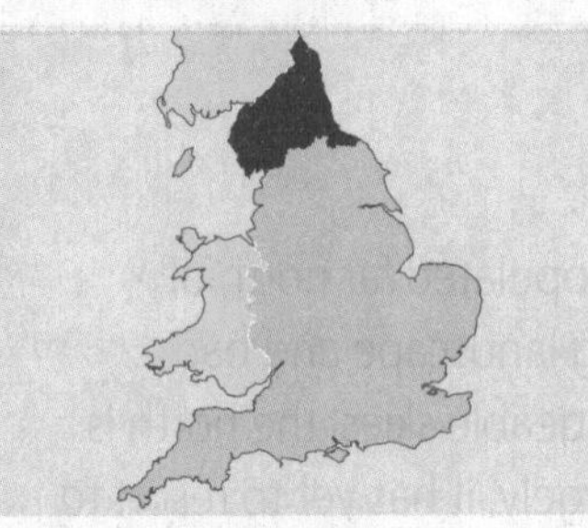

Footprint features

Introduction

First impressions of the sparsely populated far north of England are likely to involve its big landscape and bad weather. Spread wide under changeable skies, the north is hard-bitten but open-hearted. Largely, it has yet to resort to the more cynical trappings of commercialized mass tourism. Sadly though, that's no longer entirely true of its most popular destination, the Lake District. This mountainous little bit of Cumbria off the M6 has been pulling in the punters for centuries not without good reason. Here, the landscape celebrated by the Romantic poets still stirs the soul, but the roads winding through it are often terribly overcrowded. The rest of Cumbria offers more peaceful touring, hiking and strolling, especially around the rivers Eden and Lune.

To the north, Carlisle broods on its troubled history close to the Scottish border and makes a good base for exploration of the country's longest Roman landmark, Hadrian's Wall. At the other end of the wall, the city of Newcastle upon Tyne is the largest in the north and is reinventing itself as a happening European cultural centre, with close ferry links to Scandinavia. To its south, Durham rests on its laurels as the 'land of the Prince Bishops', boasting one of the most spectacular pieces of old architecture in the UK, its hilltop Norman cathedral. Further north than all these, one of the least spoiled or hyped counties in England, Northumberland seems determined to keep it that way. Sometimes chilly and bleak, it also rains less often here than almost anywhere else. Mile upon mile of deserted beaches are holiday heaven around Alnwick, while the crowds still flock to the Holy Island of Lindisfarne, near to the doughty border town of Berwick-upon-Tweed. It sits on the northern edge of the Northumberland National Park as a big treat for serious ramblers.

★ Don't miss...

1. Visit **Blackwell**, a renovated Arts and Crafts villa overlooking peaceful Lake Windermere, page 762.
2. Eat Kendal Mint Cake on top of **The Calf** in the Howgills after hiking up past Cautley Spout in the Lune valley, page 770.
3. Explore the history of the Border Reivers before checking out the remains of the Roman answer to the problem in the shape of **Hadrian's Wall**, page 784.
4. Blink in astonishment at the transformation of **Newcastle Gateshead's** Quayside district, complete with its 'blinking bridge' across the Tyne, page 787.
5. Amble around **Alnwick** and see what the Duchess of Northumberland has been up to in her castle garden, page 804.
6. Take a train trip on the spectacular **Leeds-Settle-Carlisle railway**, stopping at **Kirkby Stephen** to find the oldest known representation of the devil in human form, page 770.

Cumbria and the Lake District

→ Colour map 7, grid C2

The north by northwestern corner of England comes as quite a surprise. Cumbria embraces the wildest and most spectacular scenery in England. The M6 motorway slices through on its way to Glasgow and even traffic hurtling along this high road gets a taste of the region's bleak beauty. Rising suddenly from sea level to about 3000 ft, the Lake District National Park is no more than 100 miles in circumference but contains 64 lakes, at least 15 of them impressive in their scale, brooded over by about 200 mountains over 2000 ft. Windermere is the largest (although no more than 10 miles in length), most accessible and most famous of the lakes, surrounded by a softer landscape than most. Lonely Wastwater is the most extreme, and then there's quiet Ullswater, breezy Bassenthwaite, picturesque Derwent Water and glassy Coniston Water among other much smaller but equally individual pools and tarns. The Lake District may be the most attractive and popular of England's National Parks but unfortunately it knows it only too well. Motorists have been jamming up the narrow mountain roads since the 1920s in the rush to enjoy some of the most extraordinary scenery in the country and locals can sometimes be offhand in their hospitality. And then there's the problem of protecting the prize asset itself, the natural environment, from the stamping crowds and avaricious landlords. Recently awarded the first ever Green Globe, inaugurated at the Rio Summit, for being a shining example of sustainable tourism, the conflicting demands of visitors, locals and the natural environment are more carefully monitored and balanced here than anywhere else in the UK. But even now, when large tracts are in the care of the National Trust, and its livelihood seems to depend solely on being admired, the Lake District is not entirely tame. Some of its peaks still earn the respect of veteran mountaineers and hillwalkers relish mapping out fresh challenges across their flanks. Meanwhile, on the lakesides, anyone and everyone can still appreciate the beauty, if not the solitude, that so captivated the Wordsworths 200 years ago. To the east of the M6, lonelier fells roll off towards County Durham, studded by sturdy pockets of civilization, small market towns like Sedbergh, Kirkby Stephen and Appleby-in-Westmorland. Westmorland was the old county that bordered Lancashire to the north until the 1970s but its name lives on throughout the southern part of the new region, wonderful walking country usually soft underfoot. Cumberland, its grim northern neighbour, also included the mining communities on the coast and the border country up to Hadrian's Wall and Carlisle, now the county town of Cumbria. ▸▸ *For Sleeping, Eating and other listings see pages 775-784.*

Ins and outs

Getting there **Oxenholme**, a couple of miles west of Kendal, is the mainline station for the Lakes, for hourly **Virgin Trains**, T0870-0101127, from London (3-4 hours depending on connections), Carlisle, Preston, Birmingham and the West Country and Manchester. From Oxenholme a branch line run by **First North Western** runs hourly the 5 minutes into **Kendal** (although it can often be quicker to catch the bus rather than wait for a connection) and on for another 20 minutes calling at **Burneside** and **Staveley** (for summer bus services to Kentmere) to **Windermere**. **First North Western** also run the line from Barrow-in-Furness along the Cumbrian coast. ▸▸ *For further details, see Transport page 784.*

Road Only too accessible by car from the M6 motorway, most traffic from the south uses Junction 36 (5 hours' drive from London) and the dual carriageway A590 for Barrow-in-Furness to reach the Lakes. As the A591 the same road bypasses Kendal after 6 miles (which can also be reached on the winding A684 from Junction 37), and reaches **Windermere**, seven miles from Kendal. From Windermere, the centre of the Lake District, the lovely A592 runs north over Kirkstone Pass to **Patterdale**, beside Ullswater and finally reaching **Penrith** (26 miles); and south down the eastern shore of Lake Windermere to **Newby Bridge** (9 miles) where it joins the A590 on its way to **Ulverston**, **Barrow-in-Furness** and the **Cumbrian Coast**. From Windermere again, the A591 continues northwest along the northeastern shore of the lake to **Ambleside** (4 miles), past Rydal Water to **Grasmere** (8 miles) and on past Thirlmere to **Keswick** (25 miles). From Ambleside, the A593 heads southwest to **Coniston Water** (10 miles) and **Broughton-in-Furness** (19 miles). Three busy branch roads within five miles of Ambleside head south to **Hawkshead**, north to **Langdale**, and west over the steep and narrow Wrynose and Hardknott Passes to **Eskdale**, **Wastwater**, and **Ravenglass** on the Cumbrian Coast. The **Northern Lakes** are most easily reached from Penrith and Junction 40 on the M6, from where the dual-carriageway A66 runs the 17 miles to **Keswick**. From Keswick, the A66 continues to **Cockermouth** (13 miles) near the Cumbrian Coast, with the B5289 making a loop south round Derwent Water via Borrowdale, Buttermere, and Crummock Water and then on to Cockermouth (about 25 miles).

National Express, T08705-808080, coach 570 leaves London Victoria daily at 1100 calling at **Kendal** (arrives 1815), **Windermere** (1837), **Ambleside** (1850), **Keswick** (1920) and **Whitehaven** (2015). Standard return to Kendal costs about £35. The quickest coach journey to the Lakes from London is the overnight National Express coach 588 to Glasgow and Inverness via **Penrith**, leaving London Victoria at 2300 and arriving at 0505. National Express also run two direct coaches to **Carlisle** daily at 0930 and 2230 (6 hours 35 minutes).

Getting around

While a **car** is undeniably still the most convenient way of getting around Lakeland, the roads are so busy and twisted, especially in summer, that driving can be exhausting. That said, short of hiring expensive minicabs, many of the most remote corners are really only accessible with your own transport. Motorbikes are popular even though the roads are dangerous and weather far from ideal for two-wheeled touring. The same applies to cycling, although mountain-biking is still increasing in popularity. With enough time, easily the best way to explore is on foot, and luckily the local bus network is just about comprehensive enough to make this a practical alternative, especially if you want to avoid circular walks.

All the main towns are connected by regular bus services, except on Sun. **Kendal**, **Windermere**, **Ambleside**, **Keswick**, **Hawkshead** and **Coniston** are all connected by at least one bus in any two hours between Monday and Saturday throughout the year. Summer timetables usually operate between 25 March and 26 October. They include: from Kendal, the **Coniston Rambler** to Coniston via Windermere, Ambleside and Hawkshead, hourly Monday to Saturday with **Stagecoach** in Cumbria 505; **Lakeslink** to Windermere, Ambleside, Grasmere and Keswick, hourly daily with **Stagecoach** in Cumbria 555/556. Less frequent routes of particular interest to walkers include Route 541, Monday to Saturday, four buses daily between Kendal, Crook, Underbarrow, Crosthwaite and Windermere; Route 516, the **Langdale Rambler**, six buses daily between Ambleside, Elterwater and Dungeon Ghyll; Route 517, the **Kirkstone Ramber**, three buses on Saturday and Sunday (daily 21 July-31 August) summer only between Bowness, Windermere, Troutbeck, Kirkstone Pass, and Patterdale; Route 525, **the Mountain Goat**, four buses daily July, August, September from Hawkshead to Grizedale. Other places

The Lake District

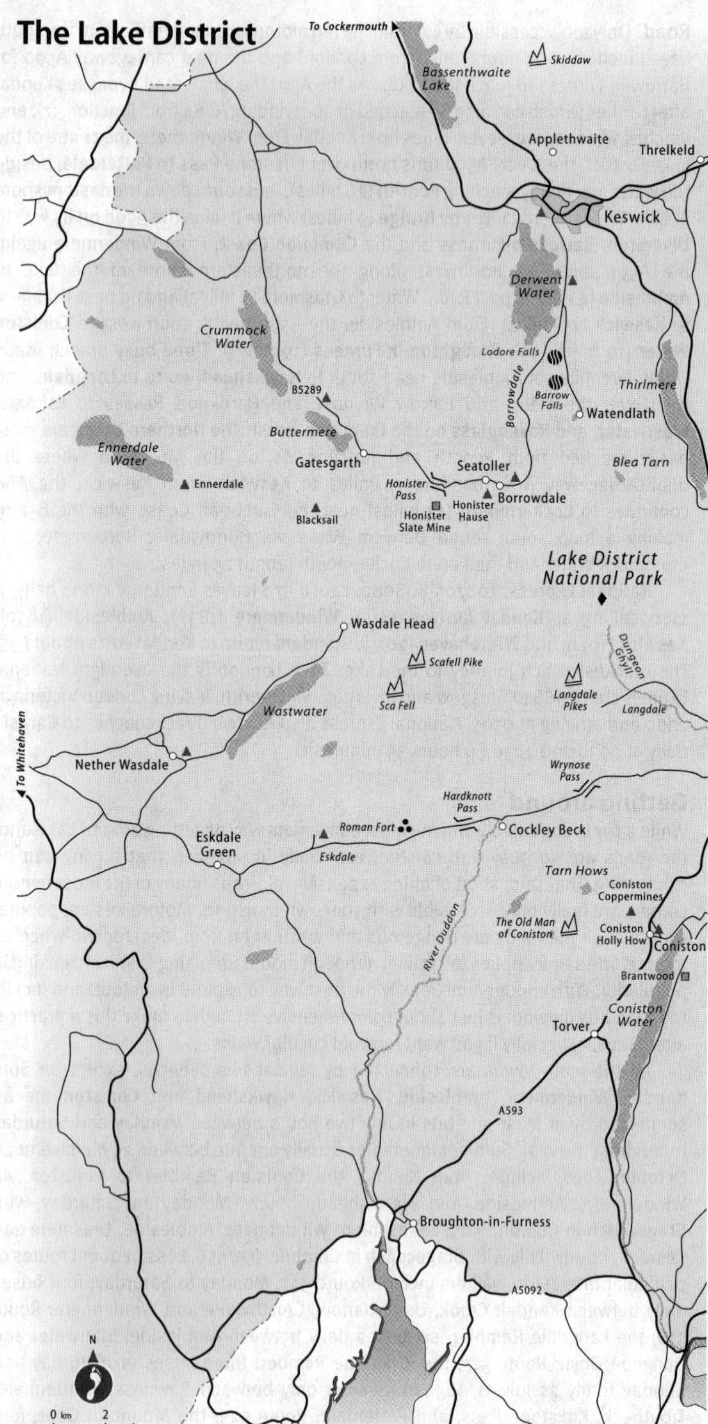

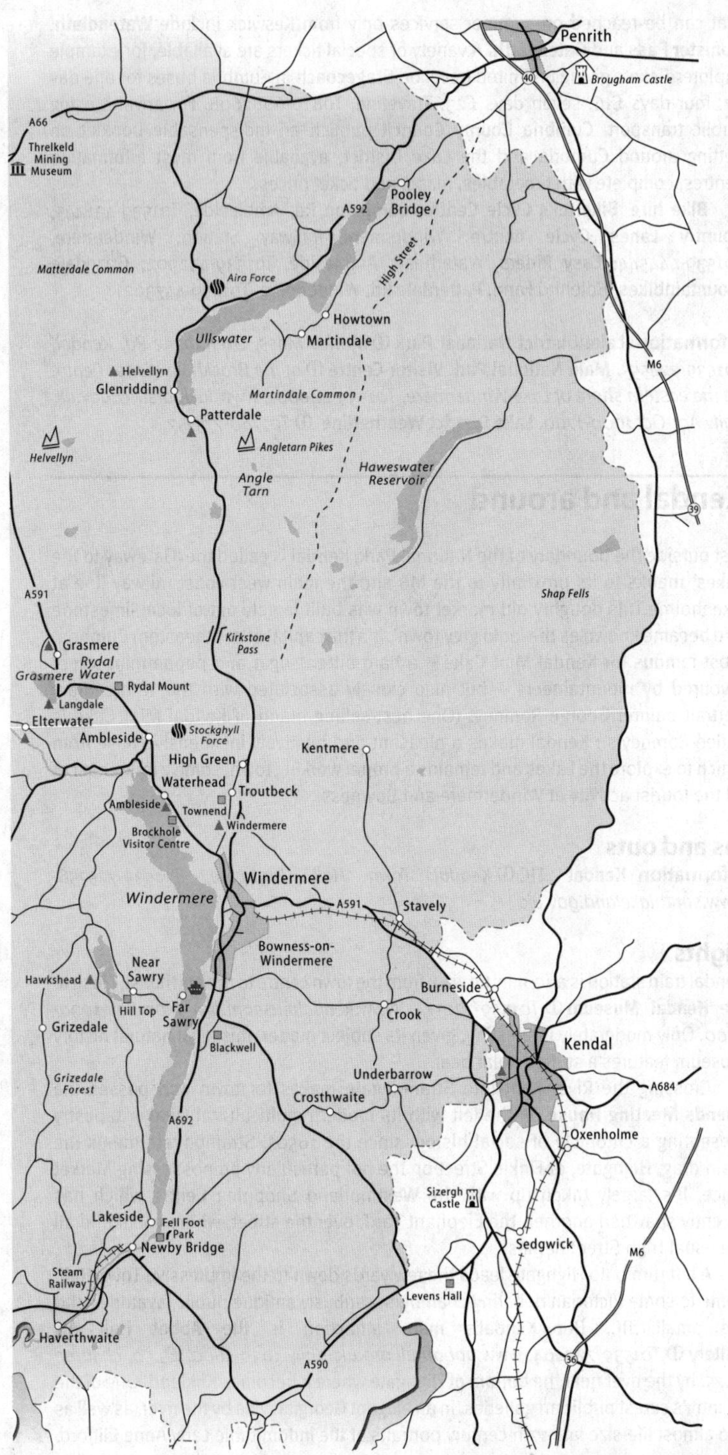
Penrith
Brougham Castle
40
A66
Threlkeld Mining Museum
Pooley Bridge
A592
High Street
Matterdale Common
Aira Force
Howtown
Ullswater
Martindale
M6
Helvellyn
Glenridding
Martindale Common
Patterdale
Angletarn Pikes
Helvellyn
Haweswater Reservoir
Angle Tarn
39
A591
Shap Fells
Kirkstone Pass
Grasmere
Rydal Water
Grasmere
Rydal Mount
Langdale
Elterwater
Stockghyll Force
Ambleside
Kentmere
High Green
Waterhead
Troutbeck
Ambleside
Townend
Windermere
Brockhole Visitor Centre
Windermere
Windermere
A591
Stavely
Bowness-on-Windermere
Near Sawry
Hawkshead
Burneside
Hill Top
Far Sawry
Crook
Grizedale
Blackwell
Kendal
Grizedale Forest
Underbarrow
A684
Crosthwaite
A692
Oxenholme
Sizergh Castle
Lakeside
Fell Foot Park
Sedgwick
Newby Bridge
M6
Steam Railway
Levens Hall
Haverthwaite
A590
36

 that can be reached on summer services only from Keswick include **Watendlath**, **Honister Pass** and **Gatesgarth**. A variety of special tickets are available, for example Explorer Tickets giving unlimited travel on **Stagecoach** in Cumbria buses for one day £7, four days £16, seven days £23. **Traveline,** T0870-6082608. For anyone using public transport, **Cumbria County Council** publish an indispensable booklet on getting around Cumbria and the Lake District, available from most information centres, complete with timetables, maps, and ticket prices.

Bike hire Biketreks Cycle Centre, Compston Rd, Ambleside, T01539-431245; **Country Lanes Cycle Centre,** Windermere Railway Station, Windermere, T01539-444544; **Easy Riders,** Waterhead, Ambleside, T01539-432902; **Grizedale Mountainbikes,** Holehird Farm, Patterdale Rd, Windermere, T01539-447302.

Information Lake District National Park ⓘ *Murley Moss, Oxenholme Rd, Kendal, T01539-724555.* **Main National Park Visitor Centre** ⓘ *at the Brockhole Visitor Centre on the eastern shore of Lake Windermere, T01539-446601, www.lake-district.gov.uk, daily Apr-Oct 1000-1700.* **Lake District Weatherline** ⓘ *T01768-775757.*

Kendal and around

Just outside the boundary of the National Park, Kendal is called the 'Gateway to the Lakes' thanks to its proximity to the M6 and the main west coast railway line at Oxenholme.This doughty old market town was built largely out of local limestone and became known as the 'auld grey town'. It's the capital of southeastern Cumbria, most famous for Kendal Mint Cake – a hard-bitten sugar and peppermint sweet favoured by mountaineers – but also closely associated with the 18th-century portrait painter George Romney. (One best-selling brand of Kendal Mint Cake is called Romney's.) Kendal makes a pleasant and relatively inexpensive base from which to explore the Lakes and remains a proper working town, some 7 miles east of all the tourist activity at Windermere and Bowness.

Ins and outs

Information Kendal TIC ⓘ *Kendal Town Hall, Highgate, T01539-725758, www.southlakeland.gov.uk.*

Sights

Kendal train station is a 10-minute walk from the town centre to the northeast, close to the **Kendal Museum** ⓘ *T01539-721374, www.kendalmuseum.org Mon-Sat 1030-1600.* Only moderately interesting, given its subject matter, this local natural history museum features a stuffed polar bear.

Crossing the River Kent into Stramongate makes for town and passes the **Friends Meeting House** on the left with its modern multicultural Quaker tapestry presenting a chronicle of social history since the 1650s. Stramongate meets the main drag, Highgate, at Finkle Street on the not particularly prepossessing Market Place. It's largely taken up with the Westmorland Shopping Centre which has recently spawned another, the Elephant Yard, over the street, where you'll find all the usual High Street names.

A left turn onto Highgate leads the few yards down to the impressive **Town Hall,** home to some Victorian debating chambers, seriously antique public lavatories and the small TIC. But Kendal's main attraction is the **Abbot Hall Art Gallery** ⓘ *T01539-722464, www.abbothall.org.uk, daily 1030-1600, £3.50, children £1.75,* by the river near the bottom of Highgate where it becomes Kirkland. One of the country's cutest public art galleries, in an elegant Georgian villa by the river, as well as two almost life-size late-17th-century portraits of the indomitable Lady Anne Clifford,

Walks in the Lake District

- **Coniston**: 11 miles one-way. Start: Coniston village. From Coniston to Langdale along part of the Cumbria Way, through farmland and woods and up to the Dungeon Ghyll Hotel at the feet of Langdale Pikes. OS Maps: Outdoor Leisure 6
- **Ennerdale**: 12 miles one-way. Start: Ennerdale Bridge. A hike into the heart of the Lakes through Ennerdale to Seatoller and Borrowdale, past lonely Ennerdale Water and beneath Green Gable. Part of the Coast-to-Coast walk. OS Maps: Outdoor Leisure 4
- **Harter Fell**: 8 miles there and back. Start: Kentmere. Quite a stiff climb up alongside the river Kent to a peak of the eastern lakes overlooking Haweswater Reservoir. OS Maps: Outdoor Leisure 7
- **Great Gable**: 6 miles there and back. Start: Wasdale Head. A climb up for views down Wast Water from the top of the 2949ft Great Gable via Sty Head. OS Maps: Outdoor Leisure 6
- **Blea Tarn**: 6 miles there and back. Start: Watendlath. A fairly gentle stroll up Borrowdale to the tranquility of the little Blea Tarn. OS Maps: Outdoor Leisure 4

it holds works by local man George Romney, as well as Lakeland scenes by Turner, Ruskin and contemporary art by Lucien Freud and Bridget Riley.

Next door to the Abbot Hall, the **Museum of Lakeland Life** ⓘ *T01539-722464, www.lakelandmuseum.org.uk, daily 1030-1600, £3.50, children £1.75*, features recreated traditional Lakeland farmhouse rooms, as well as a reconstruction of Arthur 'Swallows and Amazons' Ransome's study. From here, a riverside walk leads either to **Kendal Parish church** with its Strickland tombs and memorials to local girl Catherine Parr, lucky enough to have been widowed instead of executed by Henry VIII, or over a footbridge up to the hardly spectacular ruins of her birthplace, **Kendal Castle**, but in a fine position overlooking the town and Abbot Hall from the opposite bank of the river.

Back on Highgate, the **Brewery Arts Centre** ⓘ *T01539-725133, www.breweryarts.co.uk*, is a gardenside arts centre with interesting contemporary art exhibitions and theatre shows, with a good café and reputable restaurant.

Outside Kendal

Sizergh Castle ⓘ *(NT), T01539-5600700, Apr-Oct Mon-Thu, Sun 1330-1730, £5, children £2.50, family £12.50*, has been the Strickland family home for over 700 years. A medieval castle redeveloped in the Elizabethan period with an exceptional carved-wood interior, the highlight is the Inlaid Chamber and an outstanding limestone rock garden.

World-famous yew and box topiary, which takes six weeks of clipping each year to maintain, can be seen in the gardens of **Levens Hall** ⓘ *T01539-560321 www.levenshall.co.uk, Apr-Oct Mon-Thu, Sun 1000-1700 (house 1200-1700 last admission 1630)*. Laid out in the French style in the late 17th century, the owners of Levens never followed the fashion for Capability Brown landscape and they benefit today. The gardens surround an Elizabethan mansion, home to the Bagot family, that was built around a 13th-century pele tower. Bagot goats with their distinctive horns wander around in the deer park.

Windermere and Bowness-on-Windermere

Windermere, just up the hill on the eastern side of the lake that gave it its name, and neighbouring Bowness, on the shore of the lake itself, are the centre of day tripping Lakeland but hardly typical of the region as a whole. Windermere is quite an attractive jumble of Victorian villas and guesthouses that sprang up after the coming of the railway (fiercely resisted by one William Wordsworth) in the mid-19th century. Bowness-on-Windermere is the Lake District's superbly tacky party prom, a shoreline riddled with cheap and cheerful souvenir shops, heaving with tourists throughout the season and the launch point for cruises on the lake. The landscape visible from this unholy pair is not the most dramatic the Lakes have to offer but very pretty all the same, with low rolling green hills sloping down to a lake often bathed in a cool grey mist.

Ins and outs

Information Windermere TIC ⓘ *Victoria St, T01539-446499, www.lakelandgateway.info, daily 0900-1700, Jul-Aug, 0900-1830*. **Bowness Bay National Park Information Centre** ⓘ *Glebe Rd, T01539-442895, Apr-Oct daily 0930-1730*.

There aren't really many sights as such in Windermere, although the **Lakeland Plastics** kitchen shop could almost count as one. Instead the crowds head down into Bowness-on-Windermere to queue up for the **World of Beatrix Potter** ⓘ *T01539-488444, www.hop-skip-jump.com, Apr-Oct 1000-1730, Nov-Mar 1000-1630, £3.75, children £2.50*, in the Old Laundry. This see-hear-and-smell show is really only for kids and insatiable fans of Potter, featuring a variety of vaguely threatening much larger-than-life-size characters from the books, including Peter Rabbit and Jemima Puddle-Duck in her 'woodland glade'.

The Lake

The main event here remains Lake Windermere itself. Cruises can be taken in some style from the **Windermere Steamboat Museum** ⓘ *Rayrigg Rd, T01539-445565, www.steamboat.co.uk, Apr-Oct daily 1000-1700, £3.50, £5 for cruises*. The Museum is worth a look to appreciate that Bowness has long been the way it is today, the sheer variety of different launches and pleasure boats on display a testament to the enduring lure of the lake. That's as powerful as it ever was, and there are any number of different ways to enjoy it. **Boat hire** is available at Bowness Pier, from where *Windermere Lake Cruises* also run trips to **Waterhead** ⓘ *near Ambleside, single £4.20, return £6.20*, at the top of the lake and **Lakeside** ⓘ *see below, at the southern end, single £4.30, return £6.40*. Combined tickets are available with the **Aquarium of the Lakes** in Lakeside and the Lakeside-Haverthwaite steam railway, as well as Freedom of the Lake tickets (round the lake from any pier) costing £11, valid for 24 hours. A ferry runs across to **Ferry House**, from where it's a long steep climb up to Beatrix Potter's study house at Hill Top in Near Sawrey (see page 767).

South of Windermere and Bowness

Just over a mile south of Bowness, just off the A5074 on the B5360, **Blackwell** ⓘ *T01539-446139, www.blackwell.org.uk, daily 1000-1700 (-1600 in Feb, Mar, Nov, Dec, closed Jan-mid-Feb), £4.50, concessions £2.50, family £12*, is an immaculate Arts and Crafts house built for the Manchester brewer Sir Edward Holt in a beautiful position looking towards Coniston Old Man in the last two years of the 19th century. Restored and reopened by the Lakeland Arts Trust in 2001, it now represents one of the finest examples extant of the design movement founded by William Morris in pursuit of locally sourced materials, skills and inspiration. Designed by Mackay

Stone love

Thrown over most of the northern moors and fells is a slippery net of dry stone walls. They're probably longer in total than the Great Wall of China and even though not visible from space, are one of the most immediately striking features of the north of England. Local variations aside, most are built without mortar, resting on shallow trenches filled with parallel lines of square footing stones, in turn filled with 'heartings' of smaller irregularly shaped rocks. Most were built in the early 19th century, when labour was cheap, and although they require a lot of maintenance today, often the dedicated work of national park volunteers, it's remarkable how many are still standing and in good repair. Coping stones are sometimes placed along the top of the wall to stop sheep jumping over them. Other features of the walls are stoups (posts with holes for bars), hogg holes (for yearling sheep or hogs to pass through), step stiles and squeeze stiles. Even smaller holes at ground level are likely to be rabbit smoots, designed to catch unwary rabbits in a covered pit on the other side.

Hugh Baillie Scott, it must indeed have made a very welcoming and informal second home away from Victorian Manchester, although the slightly precious atmosphere today hardly evokes the lively family home it might once have been.

Seven miles south of Bowness, **Fell Foot Park** is a Victorian lakeside pleasure garden restored by the National Trust at the southern end of Lake Windermere. The gardens are at their best in spring or autumn, and there's a tearoom with rowing boat hire in season (Apr-Oct). Round the corner on the opposite side of the lake, beyond Newby Bridge in Lakeside, the **Aquarium of the Lakes** ⓘ *T01539-530153, www.aquariumofthelakes.co.uk, daily 0900- 1800 (-1700 Nov-Mar, last admission 1 hr before closing)*, is a good wet-weather attraction, a very comprehensive freshwater aquarium tracing a local river from its source to the sea. Here's the chance to see what ducks get up to while they're underwater, meet an otter or come face to face with a fearsome pike.

The **Lakeside and Haverthwaite Steam Railway** ⓘ *T01539-531594, May-Oct, £4.10 return*, runs 20-minute trips up the Leven Valley from Lakeside, with combined steam and boat trips on the Victorian gondola *MV Tern*.

Ambleside

Five miles north of Windermere, beyond the Lake District's main visitor centre at Brockhole and the small village of Troutbeck, Ambleside is the other half of Lakeland's pulsating heart and not very aptly named: this is where the tough get going. None of the ambling lazy pleasures of Bowness and Windermere here. This is a serious hiker town with a fairly forbidding grey-stone look to go with. That said, Ambleside does have a polite and rather sedate side, best appreciated down by the lake where it becomes Waterhead, and has a vaguely bohemian atmosphere in its pubs and cafés. Part of the reason for the town's cachet with hikers is that it's within (serious) walking distance of Windermere station and several strenuous, rewarding climbs can be made right out of the town centre itself.

Ins and outs

Information Ambleside TIC ⓘ *Central Buildings, Market Cross, T01539-432582, www.amblesideonline.co.uk, daily 0900-1700.* **Waterhead National Park Information Centre** ⓘ *near Ambleside, T01539-432729, daily Apr-Oct 1000-1700.*

Sights

Just out of Windermere on the road to Ambleside, a right turn at Troutbeck Bridge leads the mile up the valley to **Troutbeck**. Just before the village itself, which is the starting point for walks up to viewpoints overlooking Ambleside, the National Trust has preserved a 17th-century yeoman's house at **Townend** ⓘ *Townend (NT), T01539-432628, Apr-Oct Tue-Fri, Sun 1300-1700 (or dusk if earlier), £3, children £1.50, family £7.50.* A remarkable survival, the sturdy whitewashed stone and slate house contains furniture, books and woodwork from the period, very little altered after some 400 years' occupation by the Browne family.

Back on the main A591, half way between Windermere and Ambleside, the **National Park's main visitor centre** ⓘ *Brockhole, T01539-446601, www.lake-district.gov.uk, daily Apr-Oct 1000-1700,* is surrounded by lakeside gardens and contains the latest interactive wizardry to elucidate and entertain visitors about the National Park, including a three-dimensional model of the central massif and a gift shop.

Just before Waterhead, the **Stagshaw Garden** ⓘ *(NT), T01539-446027, Apr-Oct daily 1000-1830, £1.50,* is a small and little-known woodland garden particularly impressive in the spring, when the azaleas and camellias are in bloom, with walks leading up through the **Skelghyll Woods** to **Jenkins Crag** (half a mile) where there are great views down the length of Lake Windermere.

Ambleside itself is introduced by **Waterhead**, at the head of the lake, with a Youth Hostel and landing stages for the steamer services and boat hire, about a mile from the centre of the town. A left turn here leads past the attractive lakeside gardens of Borrans Park to the site of the Roman Fort called **Galava**. Little remains of it now except marks in the ground, but its strategic position on the banks of the river Rothay is easy to appreciate.

The A561 becomes Lake Road as it heads into town, round the one-way system and up to the Market Cross, passing **Zeffirelli's Cinema**, an unusual combination of pizzeria and two-screen cinema. Nearby, and equally unconventional, is **Homes of Football** ⓘ *100 Lake Rd, T01539-434440, www.homesoffootball.co.uk, daily 1000-1700, Jun-Aug 1000-1900, free*, an exhibition of offbeat photographs of football grounds great and small around the country, focusing on the people that inhabit them, both fans and players.

Since the renovation of the old bus station, the centre of town has moved away from the gloomy Market Place into the open area called **Market Cross**, surrounded by shops and cafés that almost manage an Alpine buzz. The rivulet of Stock Ghyll flows into town from the east here, crossed by the Bridge House, apparently built to evade land tax. Further up Rydal Road, the **Armitt Museum** ⓘ *T01539-431212, www.armitt.com, daily 1000-1700 (last admission 1630), £2.50, concessions £1.80, families £5.60*, is the town's interesting local history museum, with finds from Galava Roman Fort and displays on the 19th-century writers and artists that once made Ambleside such a vibrant place: Charlotte Mason, Beatrix Potter, and the Collingwoods. Founded in 1912, the museum is named after Mary Louisa Armitt who gave her library to the town.

Walks

Walks around Ambleside range from the short stroll up to **Stockghyll Force**, under a mile, to the climb up alongside **The Struggle**, the road that heads up to the *Kirkstone Inn* on Kirkstone Pass (4 miles) over to Ullswater. More serious is the delightful hike over to **High Green** above Troutbeck and up on to the Roman road called **High Street** that runs along the high ridge between Ullswater and Haweswater all the way to Brougham Castle near Penrith (about 15 miles). Details of this walk and many others from the TIC.

West of Ambleside to Wastwater

Beyond the Langdale Valley, the tortuous **Wrynose Pass** climbs up to Cockley Beck at the head of the Duddon Valley before the even steeper **Hardknott Pass** beneath Sca Fell. The road runs by **Hardknott Roman Fort**, an awe-inspiring spot for a legionary outpost overlooking beautiful Eskdale (see page 774). From Eskdale Green a tiny road runs round to **Nether Wasdale** at the foot of **Wastwater**, the deepest, most remote and mysterious of the Lakes, with precipitous scree slopes on its southern side. A difficult road runs along its northern shore all the way to **Wasdale Head**, the most isolated settlement in the entire region. The pub here is suitably serious (many of its customers have walked miles to reach it) and the little church is a moving place too.

Grasmere

Four miles up the road from Ambleside, Grasmere is an undeniably pretty stone-built village five minutes' walk from its own little lake. And it's also the most popular in the Lakes thanks to one William Wordsworth and his younger sister Dorothy, whose homes at Dove Cottage, in the village itself, and at Rydal Mount, on the road up from Ambleside, have been preserved as shrines to the spirit of Lakeland. Although it always becomes very busy with day-trippers in summer, and occasionally dismissive in its attitude to tourists, Grasmere still makes a good base for serious walkers, with wonderful trails west leading up Sour Milk Gill to Easdale Tarn, the Langdale Pikes and over to Borrowdale; or east on to the flanks of Helvellyn, the Lake District's most famous mountain.

Ins and outs

Information Grasmere National Park Information Centre ① *Red Bank Rd, T01539-435245, Apr-Oct daily 0930-1700.*

First stop from Ambleside on the Wordsworth trail is **Rydal Mount** ① *T01539-433002. Mar-Oct daily 0930-1700, Nov-Feb Mon, Wed-Sun 1000-1600, £4, concessions £3, children £1.50.* The Wordsworths moved into this comfortable whitewashed stone house in 1813 and lived here until 1850. Still owned by their descendants, highlights include the attic room where Wordsworth worked once he was Poet Laureate (although not where he did his best work), the cosy dining room and airy library adding up to an evocative insight into the early Victorian literary life and one of Lakeland's better wet-weather options. The sloping garden was designed and much loved by the great man himself, and his original plantings have been respected. The main road skirts the shoreline of **Rydal Water** on its way into Grasmere. The best views of the small lake are not from this road though but from the fells above, reached on the Grasmere-Eltwater road.

Fans thirsting for more information on the poet, his sister and famous friends will want to press on to **Dove Cottage** ① *T01539-435544, www.wordsworth.org.uk, daily 0930-1650 (museum -1730), £5.80, children £2.60, concessions £4.50.* They lived here from 1799-1808 and the enormously enthusiastic 20-minute guided tours every half hour fill in much of the information missing at Rydal Mount. Coleridge stayed with them here and the eight-room cottage has been restored to look pretty much as it might have done at the turn of the 19th century. Ticket price includes a modern art gallery and the Wordsworth Museum, packed with memorabilia and trivia related to the influential Lakeland literary circle. Weather-permitting, the garden is included on the tour too. Also in Grasmere, the **Heaton Cooper Studio** ⓘ *T01539-435280, www.heatoncooper.co.uk*, is a permanent celebration of the work of remarkable landscape artist William Heaton Cooper.

A very minor road heads round the little Grasmere lake itself and then climbs steeply up to Elterwater, a charming village on the main hiker's trail up the **Langdale Valley**. Possibly the most popular area with walkers and climbers in the central Lake District, the Langdale Valley can become almost as busy as Grasmere down below.

Hawkshead and Coniston

West of Ambleside, or reached by ferry across Lake Windermere, Hawkshead and Coniston are relatively quieter and less frequented villages. Hawkshead is an attractive place, sitting at the top of tiny Esthwaite Water, below the heights Near Sawrey (where Beatrix Potter's Hill Top House is the main attraction) and Far Sawrey (for the ferry to Bowness). Coniston is set some way back from Coniston Water itself, a more sedate version of Ambleside, but equally popular with hikers wanting to tackle the Coniston Old Man looming above the village.

Ins and outs

Information Hawkshead National Park Information Centre ⓘ *Main Car Park, T01539-436525.* **Coniston National Park Information Centre** ⓘ *Main Car Park, T01539-441533.*

Sights

As Grasmere is to William Wordsworth, so Coniston is to John Ruskin (1819-1900), and it's not too fanciful to think that the differences in the two villages says something about the difference between the two men. Ruskin was inspired by the works of Turner and Wordsworth to find a place of his own in the Lake District. Instead of Rydal Mount, with its cosy situation, he settled at **Brantwood** ⓘ *T01539-441396, www.brantwood.org.uk, mid-Mar to early Nov daily 1100-1730, mid-Nov to early Mar Wed-Sun 1100-1730, £4.75, concessions £3.50, children £1, family £10*. He famously described it as "little more than a hut" when he arrived, but the breathtaking beauty of its position ensured that he perservered until he was inhabiting the fairly grand house it is today. Some way along the eastern shore of the lake, best reached on the splendid steam yacht *Gondola* from Coniston itself, Brantwood is one of the most remarkable houses in the Lake District. Quite apart from the wealth of information on Ruskin's life and work, the place was lived in recently enough for it to remain powerfully redolent of his character. A meticulous genius, many of his ideas are now taken for granted: the dignity of labour, the Welfare State, and the National Trust amongst many others. Visitors can wander the house at will, looking into his drawing room with his piano (well-trained fingers are welcomed to try it), his study, and his extraordinary dining room with its seven-arched picture window symbolic of the Seven Lamps of Architecture: truth, beauty, memory, life, obedience, power and sacrifice. The gardens also command magnificent views over the lake.

In Coniston itself, the **Ruskin Museum** ⓘ *T01539-441164, www.ruskinmuseum.com, Easter to mid-Nov daily 1000-1730, mid-Nov to Easter Wed-Sun 1030-1530, £2.50, concessions £2*, gives an inspiring insight into the man and his works, including his attempts to improve the local economy and ideas on art and life. Ruskin is buried in the churchyard.

The other man to have left his mark on Coniston was Donald Campbell, who died on the lake attempting to beat his own waterspeed record in 1967. The *Sun Inn* contains a collection of memorabilia associated with his repeated attempts to improve the world waterspeed record first set by his father Malcolm.

Hawkshead is often trumpeted as the 'prettiest village in the Lake District', a claim that could well be justified thanks to the measures that have been taken to keep it that way. Consequently the whole place has an unreal atmosphere: traffic-free, overpriced and often overcrowded. Hawkshead also boasts the **Beatrix Potter Gallery** ⓘ *(NT), T01539-436355, Apr-Oct Mon-Wed, Sat, Sun 1030-1630, £3, children £1.50, entry by timed ticket*, in the tiny house that was once her husband's law office, little altered since his day, putting on changing displays of her original artwork for her stories.

In Near Sawrey, **Hill Top** ⓘ *(NT), T01539-436269. Apr-Oct Mon-Wed, Sat, Sun 1100-1630 (1030-1730 Jun-Aug), £4.50, children £1, family £10, advance booking advisable*, was the house where Beatrix Potter wrote many of her best-loved stories, and has been kept exactly as she left it, complete with her furniture and china. Mrs Tiggywinkle would feel quite at home here, but she'd have to join the queue like everyone else, unless she'd been a sensible little hedgehog and booked ahead.

South of Hawkshead stretch the 9000 green acres of **Grizedale Forest**, home to the Grizedale sculpture trail, where over 60 contemporary artists have transformed bits of the wood with startling responses to the natural environment since the 1970s.

Keswick and around

Keswick is the capital of the Northern Lakes, a lively market town with few pretensions and very popular with fell walkers. The business end of the Lake District, at the head of lovely Derwent Water on the River Greta, Keswick retains the atmosphere of a hard-working Cumbrian town and makes a good base for exploring Borrowdale, Watendlath and Buttermere. It also has a variety of fairly half-baked attractions to kill time if the weather's bad. Scafell Pike, the highest mountain in England, is usually tackled from here or from Langdale. To the north, Skiddaw presents a worthwhile challenge, overlooking peaceful Bassenthwaite Lake.

Information

Keswick TIC ⓘ *Moot Hall, T01768-772645, www.keswick.org, daily Apr-Oct 0930-1700, Nov-Mar 0930-1630*. **Seatoller Barn National Park Information** Centre ⓘ *Borrowdale, T01768-777294*.

Sights

The centre of Keswick is the **Moot Hall**, home to the National Park Information Centre, where the most comprehensive array of leaflets on the Northern Lakes is available. Top of the range of Keswick's attractions is the **Cumberland Pencil Museum** ⓘ *T01768-773626, www.pencils.co.uk, daily 0930-1630* , an unusual and intriguing insight into the history of the humble pencil. The industry in the town as a whole was killed off by technological advances, but one factory remains, manufacturing high-quality graphite Derwent pencils. Somehow inevitably, the museum boasts the world's largest pencil. Kids though would probably be happier looking into the **Cars of the Stars Motor Museum** ⓘ *Standish St, T01768-773757, www.carsofthestars.com, daily 1000-1700*, featuring original and replicas of various celebrity motor vehicles, from Chitty Chitty Bang Bang, via Herbie, to Knightrider's Kitt.

The local **history museum** ⓘ *Keswick Museum and Art Gallery, T01768-773263, daily Easter-Oct 1000-1600, £1*, charts the town's mining past with a variety of interesting displays on Lakeland themes, a scale model of the area and the famous 'Musical Stones', an extraordinary sort of stone glockenspiel played by four men.

Around Keswick

Most people come to Keswick to walk and opportunities abound all around the town. To the north the conifer-clad flanks of Skiddaw beckon, overlooking peaceful Bassenthwaite Lake. Nestling beneath the mountain, **Mirehouse** ⓘ *T01768-772287, Apr-Oct Wed, Sun 1400-1630, gardens Apr-Oct daily 1000-1730, house and gardens £4, children £2, family £11.75, gardens only £2, children £1*, is a doughty old lakeside mansion with some fine furniture and a happy family-home atmosphere. Thomas Carlyle and Alfred, Lord Tennyson used to visit here. The piano is played in the living room in summer. The gardens feature a poetry walk and adventure playground and there's a tea-room too.

Three miles east of Keswick off the A66 the **Threlkeld Mining Museum** ⓘ *Threlkeld Quarry and Mining Museum, 3 miles west of Keswick, T01768-779747, Mar-Oct daily 1000-1700, museum £3, children £1.50, mine tour £4, children £2*, is one of the best places to get to grips with the Lake District's industrial heritage. As well as a huge variety of different mining implements, large and small, tours of the workings are given by experienced guides and there's even a chance to pan for gold.

Another more spectacular mine tour is at the **Honister Slate Mine** ⓘ *T01768-777230, www.honister-slate-mine.co.uk, mine tours daily 1030, 1230, 1530 (and 1400, 1700 in summer), £7, children £4, family £20*, on Honister Pass above Borrowdale, nine miles from Keswick, where the Westmorland Green Slate has been mined for centuries.

South of Keswick, the B5289 skirts Derwent Water and heads up into **Borrowdale**, many people's favourite Lakeland valley. Sights on the way include the famous **Falls of Lodore**, a waterfall praised to the skies by Robert Southey; the **Barrow Falls**, on the road up to Watendlath, another popular beauty spot, with trails up on to the hills overlooking the mystical little Blea Tarn; and the **Bowdler Stone**, an enormous erratic boulder on top of which people climb around. The village of Borrowdale itself is often mobbed with tourists pausing before making the steep ascent up **Honister Pass** beyond Seatoller. After three miles the road descends to **Buttermere** and **Crummock Water**, a pair of the most windswept lakes in the district.

Ullswater

The second largest and most northeasterly of the lakes, Ullswater has a special kind of menacing charm that was much appreciated by Wordsworth. Even though roads run down either shore, it often seems unnaturally quiet here. Relatively one of the least congested of the lakes, the road from Pooley Bridge to Glenridding is the most impressive approach by road to Helvellyn (3116 ft), the mountain climbers' favourite challenge.

Ins and outs

Information Glenridding National Park Information Centre ⓘ *Ullswater, T01768-482414*.
Pooley Bridge National Park Information Centre ⓘ *The Square, T01768-486530*.

Sights

From Pooley Bridge a tiny road runs along the southern shore of the lake to Howtown and then to **Martindale** with its lonely chapel and then on to Dale Head Farm. From Howtown a lovely walk leads up on to **Martindale Common. Angle Tarn**, beneath the twin Angletarn Pikes, is one of the most picturesque mountain pools or tarns in the Lake District, with its oddly irregular shape, small islands and popularity with the local herds of red deer.

Three miles before Glenridding, **Aira Force** is an impressive 70 ft waterfall that tumbles down the south face of **Matterdale Common** (where Wordsworth is supposed to have seen his host of nodding daffodils) to the north of the lake. The beck is said to be haunted by the ghost of Sir Eglamore, who made the mistake of waking his somnambulist lover as she wandered around their trysting place mourning his absence. It's a short walk up from the car park on the A5091.

The Lune and Eden Valleys

Much less visited than the more dramatic Lake District on the other side of the M6, the valleys of the Lune and the Eden are a lovely pair, embracing one of the most charming forgotten corners of the country. The Lune rises on the Shap Fells in the western Lake District, flowing south through beautiful Borrowdale and down the western flank of the rolling Howgill Fells. It passes below the mountain town of Sedbergh, through doughty little Kirkby Lonsdale and on to the sea at Lancaster. The Eden rises in Mallerstang and flows north past Kirkby Stephen, round the northern edge of the Howgills, through Appleby-in-Westmorland, around Penrith and on to meet the sea beyond Carlisle in the Solway Firth. As well as the wonderful walking country on the fells above, it's the small towns like Kirkby Lonsdale, Sedbergh, Kirkby Stephen, and Appleby-in-Westmorland that make a holiday here so rewarding. Among the most unspoiled in the country, almost untouched by 19th-century heavy industry or 20th-century development, they have so far also managed to resist the worst excesses of 21st-century commercialization. Penrith sits on the northeastern edge of the Lake District on the M6, a convenient and businesslike market town but not much else. To its northwest, reached along a spectacular road, Alston is a high, riverside old town near the meeting of three counties

Ins and outs

Getting there The Leeds-Settle-Carlisle **railway**, one of the most scenic in England, is run by **Arriva Train Northern**, T01729-822007. Useful stations are Appleby, Kirkby Stephen, and Garsdale (near Sedbergh). Kirkby Stephen station is a mile and a half south of the town itself, on the A685. Garsdale is the closest station to Sedbergh, but the town is most easily reached by bus from Kirkby Stephen, the next stop up the line towards Carlisle, or from Oxenholme mainline station near Kendal. Penrith (about 4 hours from London Euston via Preston) is the on the same line as Oxenholme, a useful stop for Ullswater and the northeastern Lake District.

Both valleys are surprisingly easily reached off the M6 **motorway** from the south. From the east the A66 dual carriageway follows an old packhorse route, roaring across the North Pennines from Scotch Corner, near Richmond in North Yorkshire, to Penrith via Appleby. The A685 and then A683 are scenic roads south of the A66 at Brough passing through Kirkby Stephen, Sedbergh and Kirkby Lonsdale. **Stagecoach Darlington** run the 564 three times a day Monday-Saturday from Kendal and Oxenholme mainline station to Sedbergh, Kirkby Stephen, Brough and Darlington. More frequent buses link Brough with Appleby and Penrith (also on the West Coast Main Line).

Getting around The local **bus** network is reliable but not frequent. Unfortunately a car is really the only convenient way to explore the area. **Cycling** is a workable option in the summer, but the big roads can be intimidating.

Information **Kirkby Lonsdale TIC** ⓘ *Main St, T01524-271437*. **Appleby TIC** ⓘ *Moot Hall, Boroughgate, T01768-351117, www.applebytown.org.uk, Apr-Oct daily 1000-1700, Nov-Mar Fri, Sat 1000-1500. Also try www.appleby.uk.net.* **Kirkby Stephen TIC** ⓘ *Market Square, T01768-371199, www.visiteden.co.uk Easter-Oct daily*

 1000-1700, Nov-Mar Mon-Sat 1000-1300. **Yorkshire Dales National Park and TIC** ⓘ *72 Main St, Sedbergh, T01539-620125.* **Penrith TIC** ⓘ *Penrith Museum, T01768-867466, Easter-Oct daily 0930-1700, Nov-Easter Mon-Sat 0930-1600.* **Alston TIC** ⓘ *Town Hall, T01434-3882244. Easter-Oct daily 0930-1700, Nov-Easter Mon, Wed-Sat 0930-1200.*

Kirkby Lonsdale

Just over the Lancashire border, five miles east of Junction 36 on the M6, Kirkby Lonsdale is a delightfully sturdy little 18th-century town clustered round its old market place above the River Lune. Turner sketched the hills around and John Ruskin thought the area one of the loveliest in England. Ruskin's View is a good viewpoint from the churchyard and the church itself has some striking Norman stonework inside and out. A 13-mile walk from the town west to Arnside Moss called **The Limestone Link** is the subject of a well-written leaflet guide available free from the TIC. It passes over the 15th-century **Devil's Bridge**. The A683 up the Lune Valley towards Sedbergh (11 miles) makes for a beautiful drive.

Sedbergh

Sedbergh is another very attractive place, a mountain market town at the meeting point of four valleys and four rivers. Very popular with hikers, it's also the parkland seat of an ancient and hearty public school (past pupils include Will Carling, the former English rugby team captain.) Each year the school stages a gruelling run to the top of **Winder Fell** that looms over the town and provides more superb views. Hidden away up Garsdale in the valley of the River Dee, 5 miles southeast of Sedbergh, is the small village of **Dent**. Once a centre of the local knitting industry – wonderful Herdwick wool sweaters – it's still a popular corner with woolly ramblers, in the far northwest of the Yorkshire Dales National Park, and accessible on the Leeds-Settle-Carlisle railway. The station is a four-mile walk from the village, in the lea of **Widdale Fell**.

Three miles north of Sedbergh, **Cautley Spout** is a waterfall that drops some 250 yds down a rocky natural amphitheatre beneath the Calf. It's a stiff but rewarding hour-long walk up from the *Cross Keys* temperance hotel. **The Calf** is the 2219 ft peak of the beautiful Howgill Fells. Much softer in look and on the legs than the Lake District, these fells were the favourite of A. Wainwright, whose meticulously handwritten, illustrated and mapped walking guides reintroduced the joys of hillwalking to a generation in the late 1960s and early 70s.

Kirkby Stephen

The lovely A683 continues for another 14 miles up to Kirkby Stephen, an important staging post on Wainwright's popular **Coast-to-Coast** walk. Strung out along the main road, this solid-looking town is still very much the working centre of its region, yet to have its character completely altered by the demands of tourism. On the main Market Square a Georgian loggia stands in front of the impressive church, which contains a mysterious eighth-century Anglo-Danish relic called the **Loki Stone**. The only one of its type in England, it's a remarkable survival, apparently the earliest known depiction of the devil in human form – the troublemaking Norse god Loki in horns and chains.

The source of the river Eden lies some 10 miles south up the Mallerstang valley via Outhgill on the B6259. The river is already a significant obstacle as it flows past the east side of the town. Three miles down this mysterious and lonely valley road are the ruins of little **Pendragon Castle**. On a small mound beside the river, this was supposedly where King's Arthur's father Uther was poisoned. Like the castles at Brough, Appleby and Brougham, it was restored in the 17th century by the indefatigable wandering medievalist Lady Anne Clifford. Since then it has become a very quiet and picturesque ruin.

Appleby-in- Westmorland

Tucked into a loop in the river 12 miles northwest of Kirkby, Appleby-in- Westmorland is a delightful old red stone riverside town, solid and castellated. Once the county town of Westmorland, it's a sort of mini-Edinburgh with its **castle** (closed for redevelopment at time of writing) at the top of its cobbled main street, Boroughgate, columns at either end marking the extent of the market and battered old church behind a colonnade at the bottom. The church, like the castle, was restored by Lady Anne Clifford, and contains one of the oldest organ cases in the country, as well as the memorial chapel to the great woman herself. The draped effigy of her mother was apparently carved by the same hand as that of Elizabeth I in Westminster Abbey.

Penrith

Sitting next to junction 40 on the M6, Penrith is a fairly unprepossessing market town on the main west coast railway line that makes a useful launch pad for Ullswater and the northeastern Lakes. There's not a huge amount to see in the town, apart from the small Penrith Museum, T01768-867466, and the ruined castle, but its specialist shops make for some rewarding browsing. Southeast of town, however, **Brougham Castle** ⓘ *(EH), T01768-862488, Apr-Sep daily 1000-1800, Oct daily 1000-1700, £2.20, children £1.70, concessions £1.10,* is beautifully situated on the banks of the River Eamont. The castle was involved in border disputes throughout its early history, and the ruin was taken in hand by Lady Anne Clifford in the late 17th century. Today it remains one of the most impressive examples of her restorations.

Alston

Northwest of Penrith, the A686 heads up on to the North Pennines via the village of **Melmerby** (famous for its organic bakery) affording spectacular views over the Lakeland hills and Eden Valley before it reaches **Alston**, the highest market town in England. It's a serious stone-built old-fashioned place in the middle of nowhere on the South Tyne River and the Pennine Way, close to the meeting of Cumbria, Northumberland and County Durham.

The Cumbrian coast: Grange-over-Sands to Cockermouth

Between the Lakeland mountains and the Irish Sea, the Cumbrian Coast is a strange, embattled, but in places very beautiful region, largely overlooked by many Lakeland tourists. Most immediately attractive and accessible are its southern fringes, known as the Furness Peninsulas. This broken, heavily indented coastline spreads out into the sandflats of Morecambe Bay around the shipbuilding and gas-terminal port of Barrow-in-Furness, defined by the silted estuaries of the rivers Kent, Leven and Duddon. Grange-over-Sands is the main town on the smaller eastern peninsula, the traditional landing point of the route over the sands once used by the monks and nuns of Cartmel Priory. The village of Cartmel is still the main attraction, along with the famous gardens at Holker Hall. The larger promontory to the west boasts the lively market town of Ulverston before petering out at with industrial sprawl of Barrow at its tip. The port does draw in a few visitors with its interesting dockside museum, some superb nature reserves and small boat trips out to Piel Island and its ruined castle. Broughton-in-Furness is a dignified little town that sits at the root of the peninsula near the mouth of the Duddon. The coast road and railway then sneak round the bulk of Black Combe, with its extraordinary panoramic views, and head north, past pretty Ravenglass, where Eskdale meets the sea. Beyond St Bees Head, the dramatic starting point for Wainwright's Coast-to-Coast walk, Whitehaven introduces the abandoned industrial wasteland

and marshes of the northern stretches of the coast. Inland, Cockermouth is a gritty but fine Georgian-looking town on the edge of the northwestern Lakes.

Ins and outs

Getting there The Furness Line from Lancaster to Carlisle also runs right round the coast, calling at Grange-over-Sands, Ulverston, Barrow-in-Furness, Ravenglass, Seascale, St Bees, Whitehaven, and Maryport, among other places. From Junction 36 on the M6 the A590 leads to Ulverston and Barrow-in-Furness. Off this big **road**, the A595 is reached via the A5092 and runs all the way round the coast back to Carlisle at the top of the M6. **National Express**, T08705-808080, run **coaches** to Kendal from where the X35 runs to Ulverston and Barrow-in-Furness. Cartmel can be reached by bus from Grange-over-Sands.

Getting around Once again, a **car** is easily the most convenient way of exploring the coast, although the **train** and **bus** service is significantly more reliable and regular than elsewhere in Cumbria.

Information Grange-over-Sands TIC ⓘ Victoria Hall, Main St, T01539-534026. **Barrow-in-Furness TIC** ⓘ *Town Square, T01229-894784, www.barrowtourism.co.uk.* **Ulverston TIC** ⓘ *Coronation Hall, T01229-587120. Mon-Sat 0900-1700, www.lakelandgateway.info.* **Cockermouth TIC** ⓘ *01900-822634.*

Grange-over-Sands

Grange-over-Sands is a solid-looking Victorian seaside town with a breezy prom overlooking Morecambe Bay. Otherwise there's not much to keep visitors here long. Some will no doubt want to head off on foot on the 33-mile **Cistercian Way** to Piel Island via Cartmel and Ulverston that starts here. Its first leg heads up through the yew tree woods of Eggerslack onto Hampsfell, with wide-reaching views of the muddy bay. Grange was also once the landing point of the short-cut over the sands from Lancaster to the Lake District taken by the monks of Cartmel and Furness Abbeys.

Cartmel, a couple of miles west, just inland, is the most popular and also one of the most attractive little villages in these parts, clustered around the remains of its 12th-century **priory** ⓘ *(NT), Cartmel Priory Gatehouse, Cavendish St, T01539-536874. Easter-Oct Wed-Sun 1000-1600, Nov-Mar Sat, Sun 1000-1600.* The church survived the Dissolution, thanks to also being the place of worship for the parish, and is still a very fine building indeed. Restored by the Preston family of Holker Hall in the 17th century, its bell tower sits at an angle to the main church. Inside, highlights include the stained glass, medieval chancel, Jacobean screen and carved choir stalls. The gatehouse of the priory is also still standing, thanks to being a grammar school in the 17th and 18th centuries, and is now in the care of the National Trust, containing displays on the history of the village, priory and the peninsula.

Five miles west of Grange on the B5277, the main part of **Holker Hall** ⓘ *T01539-558328, www.holker-hall.co.uk, Apr-Oct Mon-Fri, Sun 1000-1800, £7.25, children £4.50*, was built in the 1870s for William Cavendish, the Seventh Duke of Devonshire, and represents Victorian country house style at its best. Still the home of Lord and Lady Cavendish, the interior of the house is warm and welcoming, decorated with an impressive variety of antiques and Old Masters, but it's the gardens that have made the house famous. Vaguely Italianate in style, they feature a limestone cascade, sunken garden and a fountain, as well as the **Lakeland Motor Museum** ⓘ *T01539-558509, www.lakelandmotormuseum.co.uk, open same hours as hall, inclusive tickets available*, where a variety of veteran vehicles share space with an exhibition devoted to Donald Campbell, the waterspeed recordbreaker. The **garden festival** held in the first week of June is one of the most prestigious in the country.

Ulverston

From Holker Hall, the shifting sands of the Leven estuary can be crossed on foot with the guidance of Mr Raymond Porter, T01229-580935. It's a wonderful and bracing way to reach Ulverston or Conishead Priory on the opposite bank. Ulverston is a delightful old market town, complete with cobbled streets, ancient alleys and a vigorous local life. It's the homebase of experimental community theatre group **Welfare State International** ⓘ *Lanternhouse, the Ellers, T01229-581127,* who organize an extraordinary lantern procession through the town early each September. But the most famous performer associated with the town remains Arthur Jefferson, aka Stan Laurel. He was born here and went on to find success in Hollywood, a career lovingly charted for fans at the exhaustive **Laurel and Hardy Museum** ⓘ *4c Upper Brook St, T01229-582292. Daily (but closed Jan) 1000-1630, £2.50, £5 family.* The town is overlooked from the north by the monument to the founder of the Royal Geographical Society, Sir John Barrow, on Hoad Hill, which commands fine views. The other great man associated with Ulverston is George Fox, who founded Quakerism at Swarthmoor Hall to the south of the town. The **Cumbria Way** is a long-distance footpath that runs from here to Carlisle for 70 miles.

Two miles south of the town, **Conishead Priory** ⓘ *Priory Rd, near Ulverston, T01229-584029, Apr-Oct Sat, Sun 1400-1700, Mon-Fri by appointment,* was designed by the son of James Wyatt for Thomas Bradyll in the early 19th century on the site of a 12th-century convent. Its architecture is an extraordinary combination of neo-Elizabethan and neo-Gothic, still being restored by the Buddhist Manjushri Mahayana Buddhist Centre, who have built a temple housing an 8-ft Buddha in the gardens. They offer accommodation, courses and retreats as well as light refreshments.

Barrow-in- Furness

At the end of the peninsula, Barrow-in-Furness was developed in the mid-19th century by William Cavendish of Holker Hall as a port for iron ore and then steel. It became one of the main shipbuilding yards in the country and now relies on the handling of nuclear fuel and gas for most of its income. The town's main attraction is the **Dock Museum** ⓘ *T01229-894444, Apr-Oct Tue-Fri 1000-1700, Sat, Sun 1100-1700, Nov-Mar Wed-Fri 1030-1600, Sat, Sun 1100-1630, free,* with models of the ships that have been constructed here, and interesting displays on the development of the town.

Just before Barrow-in-Furness, **Furness Abbey** ⓘ *T01229-823420, Apr-Sep daily 1000-1800, Oct daily 1000-1700, Nov-Mar Wed-Sun 1000-1600, £2.80, concessions £2.10, children £1.40,* was founded in the early 12th century by Savigniac monks and enlarged shortly afterwards by the Cistercians. Once one of the most important monasteries in the north of England, its situation today hardly bears comparison with its more famous cousins in Yorkshire, but enough has survived to give a good impression of the life led by the monks before the Dissolution. The other main draw from Barrow is the 14th-century **Piel Castle** ⓘ *T01229-835809,* now in ruins, built to defend Furness Abbey from the Scots. It sits lonely and remote on Piel Island, reachable by an erratic small-boat ferry from Roa Island. On the island, which was given to the people of Barrow by the Duke of Buccleuch in memory of their dead in the First World War, the *Ship Inn* provides hearty refreshments.

Off the A590 to Barrow, clearly signposted, the **South Lakes Wild Animal Park** ⓘ *T01229-466086, www.wildanimalpark.co.uk, daily 1000-1630, tiger feeding daily 1430-1500, £7, children £5, winter £5, children £3,* claims to be Europe's top tiger sanctuary. Thanks to some cunning landscape design, animals as diverse as kangaroos, monkeys, rhinos, lions, apes and giraffes appear to be wandering free over about 17 acres. Recent arrivals, the only ones in England, are the spectacled bears. The tiger feeding each afternoon is very popular.

Around Black Combe

Just within the National Park, at the top of the peninsula, **Broughton-in-Furness** is an old stone-built town with an attractive market square where the fish slabs, stocks and obelisk celebrating the coronation of George III still survive. From here the A593 runs up into the Lake District and Coniston Water, a small road branching off left up the relatively unexplored valley of the river Lickie with lovely walks above Broughton Mills.

Just before Duddon Bridge, on the main A595 coast road, another small road leads north up the Duddon Valley to **Ulpha**. A favourite of Wordsworth's, the rolling fells embracing the Duddon Valley remain surprisingly undiscovered compared to much of the Lake District. The coast road continues through Whicham, from where an easy path leads up to the **Black Combe**, rising to 1970 ft and providing one of the most spectacular views in the country from its heathery summit. On a clear day the panorama includes the Isle of Man and Ireland beyond to the west, as well as the main peaks of the Lake District to the east.

Eskdale

Ten miles further up the coast, **Ravenglass** ⓘ *T01229-717171, www.ravenglass-railway.co.uk, Apr-Oct daily, Nov-Dec and Mar Sat, Sun, phone for running times, £7.40, children £3.70, concessions £6.90*, is a little village sitting at the bottom of Eskdale. From here the road climbs up the valley of the Esk and into the Lakes via Hardknott and Wrynose passes, the only road eastwards and hence often jammed. (The only other way back into the Lakes is all the way round to the north via Cockermouth and Keswick). The valley of the Mite, next door to the Esk, carries a miniature railway seven miles from Ravenglass to Boot, originally built to carry iron ore, and known as **La'al Ratty**. It's a big hit with kids.

More family fun is on offer at **Muncaster Castle** ⓘ *Muncaster Castle, T01229-717614, www.muncaster.co.uk, Mar-Oct Gardens and Owl Centre daily 1030-1800 (or dusk if earlier), castle Mon-Fri, Sun 1030-1800 (or dusk if earlier) £5.50, children £3.50, family £16.50, castle and gardens £7.80, children £5, family £21*, home of the **World Owl Centre**, the largest collection of the wise birds in the world, and there's also the opportunity of taking an interactive wand tour of the castle's interior, still home to the Pennington family after 800 years.

Surprisingly enough perhaps, one of the most popular attractions on this stretch of coast is the **Sellafield Visitor Centre** ⓘ *Seascale, T01946-727027, www.sparkingreaction.info, www.bnfl.com, Apr-Oct daily 1000-1800, Nov-Mar daily 1000-1600, free.* Since September 11 2001 there have been no regular tours of this nuclear reprocessing facility for security reasons, but visits can still be arranged with two months notice in writing. Visitors on spec will have to make do with BNFL's PR exhibition and displays on the nuclear reprocessing plant that caused enough controversy to force a change of name (Windscale sounded just too ominous) in the 1980s. Calder Hall, nearby, was the first nuclear power station to be commissioned in Britain, and Sellafield was originally designed to cope with its spent rods. It now handles a large amount of other nuclear waste, from as far away as Japan.

St Bees Head and Whitehaven

Somehow Sellafield and its heavy industrial buildings set the bleak and sadly unprepossessing tone for the rest of the Cumbrian Coast to the north. The relatively dramatic cliffs of St Bees Head are a glorious exception, popular with puffins and seals, and there's an excellent little overhanging cave system at **Fleswick Beach**. This is close to the start of Wainwright's Coast-to-Coast walk to Robin Hood's Bay on the North Yorkshire coast. **Kangol** ⓘ *T01946-818260, www.kangol.com*, recently one of the most fashionable names in headgear, has a factory shop at the otherwise unattractive village of **Cleator**, 5 miles west of the headland.

Round the corner from St Bees, the relatively large town of Whitehaven developed on a grid plan by the Lowther family, was heavily involved in the 18th-century sugar, rum and slave trade. Their Georgian church of St James's survives at the top of the town on Queen Street, but much of the rest of the town has suffered badly since. It has recently had a facelift on its harbourfront though, including attractions such as **The Beacon** ⓘ *T01946-592302, www.copelandbc.gov.uk, Easter-Oct Tue-Sun 1000-1730, Nov-Mar Tue- Sun 1000-1630, last admittance 45 mins before closing*, the town's local history museum, including a Met Office gallery, the story of the town's mining heritage, and the founder of the US navy, privateer John Paul Jones's attempted attack on the the town, as well as the *Whitehaven Quest*, an information pack detailing 10 historical trails round the area. **The Rum** Story ⓘ *T01946-592933, www.rumstory.co.uk, Oct-Mar daily 1000-1600, Apr-Sep daily 1000-1700, £4.50, £2.95 under-14s*, in the new Historic Harbour development, tells some of the story of the town's slaving history, with dummies in dioramas, spiced up with stories of the rum trade thanks to its location in Jefferson's late-18th-century shop and bonded warehouses.

Cockermouth

Thirteen miles northeast of Whitehaven and seven miles inland, Cockermouth is a hard-bitten but good-looking farming town. Its main visitor attraction is the National Trust's **Wordsworth House** ⓘ *Main St, T01900-824805*, where Dorothy and William were born. Their large house has been filled with a few momentoes, but it's not the most engaging of stops on the Wordsworth trail. Monthly changing exhibitions by accomplished local artists can be seen at the impressive Georgian home of the **Castlegate House Gallery** ⓘ *T01900- 822149, www.castlegatehouse.co.uk*.

Maryport

Maryport, the last town of much importance on the coast, with a dinky little harbour, can boast the **Lake District Coast Aquarium** ⓘ *T01900-817760, www.lakedistrict-coastaquarium.co.uk, Apr-Oct daily 1000-1700, Oct-Mar 1000-1600, £4.50, children £2.95*, and the **Senouse Roman Museum** ⓘ *The Battery, Sea Brows, T01900-816168, Oct-Mar Fri, Sat, Sun 1030-1600, Apr-Jun Tue, Thu-Sun 1000-1700, Jul-Oct daily 1000-1700, £2.50, children 75p*, with its altar stones, household gods, mysterious Serpent Stone and observation tower, next to the site of Alauna Roman fort at the end of Hadrian's Wall.

Sleeping

The Lake District is packed with self-catering options, from mansions to bothies. Endless different campsites are on offer, details from the local tourist office. Freerange camping is not exactly encouraged, but if done carefully on National Trust land (most of the central range) without disturbing the environment in any way at all, no one's likely to mind. The other option is one of the 25 Youth Hostels. They usually need to be booked well in advance and many are not open in winter, so it's best to ring first. Facilities also vary quite widely. More basic still, but in the most glorious positions, are the range of YHA Camping Barns. There are at least 10 dotted around the Lake District, many within walking distance of each other, but they too need to booked ahead some time in advance especially in high season. Not all are open all year. Contact **Lakeland Barns Booking Office**, Moot Hall, Market Sq, Keswick, CA12 4JR, T01768-772645.

Camping barns (no. of beds): **Blake Beck** (12), **Catbells** (12), **Cragg** (8), **Dinah Hoggus** (12), **Fell End** (12), **High Gillerthwaite** (14), **Hudscales** (12), **St John's-in-the-Vale** (8), **Swallow** (18), **Swirral** (8). Cost £4 per person per night.

Kendal and around *p760*

C Lakeland Natural, Queen's Rd, T01539-733011. Provides non-smoking, vegetarian accommodation in an elegant Victorian home within beautiful gardens. There are numerous B&Bs, details from the TIC.
D The Glen, Oxenholme, T01539-726386, www.glen-kendal.co.uk, a small friendly guesthouse on outskirts of town. Above Oxenholme station, close to the pub.
D Hill Crest Bed & Breakfast, 98 Windermere Rd, T01539-727851, family-run with good views from the front room to Shap and en suite bathrooms.
F Kendal YHA, 118 Highgate, T01539-724066. With 54 beds in the middle of town close the Brewery Arts Centre.

Outside Kendal *p761*

C Burrow Hall Country Guest House, Plantation Bridge, Staveley, T01539-821711, www.burrowhall.co.uk. 2 miles outside Kendal, an old Lakeland house, tastefully furnished in peaceful countryside, £50.
C Heaves Hotel, near Levens Hall, Sedgwick, T01539-560269, www.heaveshotel.co.uk. Has 13 very good-value rooms in a superb country house hotel in the old manor house of Heaves. Recommended.
D Garnett House Farm, ¼ mile from Burneside station, 2 miles out of Kendal towards Windermere, T01539-724542, www.garnetthousefarm.co.uk. A 15th-century farmhouse on a working farm with some rooms en suite.
D Hollowgate Farm, 8 miles north of Kendal towards Shap, on the A6, T01539-823258. Working farmhouse off the A6.

Windermere *p762*

L Gilpin Lodge, Crook Rd, Windermere, T01539-488818, www.gilpin-lodge.co.uk. With very friendly service, not overly formal, there's a small country house atmosphere at this hotel with top-notch food at around £45 a head.
L Miller Howe, Rayrigg Rd, Windermere, T01539-442536, www.millerhowe.com. The smart option in Windermere, a 'luxury hotel' with a reputation for its excellent food. Great views over fells and lake.
A Holbeck Ghyll, Holbeck La, between Windermere and Ambleside, T01539-432375, www.holbeckghyll.com. A romantic country house hotel with superb views and thoroughly competent kitchen.
C The Coppice Guest House, Brook Rd, Windermere, T01539-488501, www.thecoppice.co.uk Guesthouse with quality food, all home prepared and leisure club membership included in the price. Well-behaved pets welcome. Non smoking.
D Almaria Guest House, 17 Broad St, Windermere, T01539- 443026. Offers friendly hospitality and comfortable accommodation.
C The Cottage Guest House, Elleray Rd, Windermere, T01539-444796, www.thecottageguesthouse.com. A family-run guesthouse, most rooms have en suite bathrooms. Close to station.
D Aspen Cottage Guest House, 6 Havelock Rd, Windermere, T01539-443946. Quiet and fairly centrally located, one of the least expensive options in town.
D Green Gables Guest House, 37 Broad St, Windermere, T01539-443886, www.lakespages.co.uk. Another family-run guesthouse in the town with lounge bar, most rooms have en suite bathrooms.
D Villa Lodge Hotel, 25 Cross St, Windermere, T01539-443318, www.villa-lodge.co.uk. A fully licensed hotel.
F Windermere YHA, Bridge La, Troutbeck, T01539- 443543. With 69 beds in a panoramic position above the town, good for gentle walks through the woods.

Ambleside *p763*

A Ambleside Salutation Hotel, Lake Rd, Ambleside, T01539-432244, www.hotelambleside.uk.com. Right in the middle of Ambleside, a large hotel with 42 rooms.
A Rothay Manor Hotel, Ambleside, T01539-433605. Traditional Ambleside hotel with good restaurant and fairly comfortable rooms.
B Wasdale Head Inn Wasdale Head, T01946-726229. Venerable walkers and climbers pub with a serious atmosphere and comfortable rooms.
C Claremont House, Compston Rd, Ambleside, T01539-433448, www.claremontambleside.co.uk. Family-run, friendly, 8 rooms most with en suite bathrooms.

C Elder Grove Hotel, Lake Rd, Ambleside, T01539-432504, www.eldergrove.co.uk. Victorian house with 10 rooms, car park, non-smoking.

C Freshfields Guest House, Wansfell Rd, Ambleside, T01539-434469, www.freshfieldsguesthouse.co.uk. Spacious, 3 well-appointed rooms with en suite bathrooms, non-smoking, no children or pets. Off-road parking. Between Ambleside and Waterhead.

C Lingmell House, Wasdale Head, T01946-726261. Booking well ahead advised for this charming B&B in remote Wasdale.

C Meadowbank Guesthouse, Rydal Rd, Ambleside, T01539-432710. Set in its own grounds with views of fells.

C Riverside, Under Loughrigg, at the other end of Ambleside, T01539-432395, www.riverside-at-ambleside.co.uk, £68 5-room family-run B&B overlooking river. 10 mins from the centre.

D Walmar Hotel, Lake Rd, Ambleside, T01539-432454, www.walmar-ambleside.co.uk. Victorian house with off-street parking, family-run, 8 rooms with en suite bathrooms.

F Ambleside YHA, Waterhead, Ambleside, T01539-432304. With 245 beds in 43 2-5-bedded rooms and 16 6-8 bedded rooms, near the landing stages for the lakes.

F Elterwater YHA, Elterwater, near Ambleside, T01539-437245. With 45 beds in the last village in Langdale, very popular with climbers.

F Langdale YHA, High Close, Loughrigg, near Ambleside, T01539-432304. With 96 beds in a Victorian mansion owned by the National Trust, lower than the other Langdale hostel.

F Wastwater YHA, Wasdale Hall, Wasdale, T01946-726222 with 50 beds in an imposing National Trust property on the edge of Wastwater. One of the most dramatically situated youth hostels in the Lakes.

Grasmere *p765*

A Gold Rill Hotel, Red Bank Rd, Grasmere, T01539-435486, www.gold-rill.com. Awards for hospitality and its restaurant at this hotel with 25 rooms, 8 with lake views. A couple of min's walk from village.

A The Grasmere Hotel, Broadgate, Grasmere, T01539-435277, www.grasmerehotel.co.uk. Quiet location with 13 rooms, Victorian house renowned for quality of its food.

A Lancrigg Country House Hotel, Easedale Rd, T01539-435317, www.lancrigg.co.uk. Snuggled into the Easedale valley, with a particularly good vegetarian restaurant.

A Michael's Nook, Grasmere, T01539-435496. Michelin-starred cuisine at this Victorian country house hotel. Dress smart.

A Oak Bank Hotel, Broadgate, Grasmere, T01539-435217, www.lakedistricthotel.co.uk. Good cooking, quite fancy, family-orientated.

A Red Lion Hotel, Grasmere, T01539-435456. Coaching inn at the centre of the village.

B Bridge House Hotel, Church Bridge, Grasmere, T01539-435425, www.bridgehousegrasmere.co.uk. Family-owned hotel beside the River Rothay with peaceful woodland gardens.

B Moss Grove Hotel, Grasmere T01539-435211 www.mossgrove.co.uk. £84 Some 4-poster beds with balconies, conservatory, sauna, free use of nearby indoor pool in the Wordsworth.

B Old Dungeon Ghyll Hotel, Great Langdale, T01534-937272, www.odg.co.uk. Basic but practical enough, the classic Lakeland mountaineer's pub, with 14 bedrooms and the hiker's bar in a magnificent position beneath the Langdale Pikes.

B Traveller's Rest Inn, Grasmere on the outskirts on the A591, T0800-0199740. 16th-century inn at foot of Helvellyn, real fires, home-cooked food.

C Dunmail House, Keswick Rd, Grasmere, T01539-435256, www.dunmailhouse.freeserve.co.uk. Small, friendly family-run guesthouse with 3 doubles, no pets or under-10s.

C The Harwood, Red Lion Sq, Grasmere, T01539-435248, www.harwoodhotel.co.uk. Small, traditionally built, family-run quiet guesthouse in the centre of the village with 7 rooms.

C How Foot Lodge, Townend, Grasmere, T01539-435366, www.howfoot.co.uk. Victorian country guest house, close to lake, 6 spacious bedrooms with nice views.

F **Grasmere Butterlip How YHA**, Easedale Rd, Grasmere, T01539-435316. With 82 beds close to the heart of the village and very popular with walkers.
F **Grasmere Thorney How YHA**, Easdale Rd, Grasmere T01539-435316. With 53 beds, smaller and more secluded than the other Grasmere hostel, also a favourite with ramblers.

Hawkshead and Coniston *p766*
B **Coniston Lodge Hotel**, Station Rd, Coniston, T01539-441201, www.coniston-lodge.com Award-winning 6-room hotel with superb cooking, set back from the village.
B **Sun Inn Hotel**, Coniston, T01539-441248, www.thesunconiston.com. Family-run hotel with views of the fells, good food and ales, 10 rooms with en suite bathrooms.
B **Waterhead Hotel**, Coniston, T01539-441244 www.pofr.com. A 21-room hotel lying in its own grounds with private jetty and rowing boats. Owned by the Post Office Fellowship of Remembrance.
C **Arrowfield Country Guest House**, 1½ miles towards Torver, T01539-441741. A 5-bedroomed Victorian house in a quiet location, lovely views, log fires and delicious breakfast.
C **Beech Tree Guest House**, 150 yds from the centre of Coniston, T01539-441717. An 18th-century house with its own gardens, 8 double rooms, 4 with en suite bathrooms.
C **Queen's Head Hotel**, Hawkshead T01539-436271. Just off the Square, 16th-century, village centre inn with beams and loads of charm. Great food, children welcome.
F **Coniston Coppermines YHA**, Coniston, T01539-441261 with 28 beds in a beautiful mountain setting above Coniston village, ideal for the taking on the Coniston Old Man.
F **Coniston Holly How YHA**, Far End, Coniston T01539-441323. With 60 beds and within walking distance of the village.
F **Hawkshead YHA**, Hawkshead, T01539-436293. With 109 beds in a Regency mansion overlooking Esthwaite Water, popular with families.

Keswick and around *p767*
L **Underscar Manor**, Applethwaite, T01768-775000. Reputable, expensive restaurant and stunning lake views from this Italianate Victorian mansion.
A **Lyzzick Hall**, Under Skiddaw, T01768-772277. More superb views and a beautiful garden at this old manor house hotel with a swimming pool.
C **Acorn House Hotel**, Ambleside Rd, Keswick, T01768-772553, www.acornhousehotel.co.uk. A comfortable Georgian house near the town centre with colourful gardens, non-smoking.
C **Charnwood**, 6 Eskin St, Keswick, T01768-774111. Popular and roomy Victorian guesthouse near the middle of the town.
C **Chaucer House Hotel**, Derwentwater Pl, Keswick, T01768-772318. An informal Victorian house, a few mins' walk from both town and lake, with fresh home-made food.
C **Dale Head Hall Lakeside Hotel**, Lake Thirlmere, T01768-772478, www.dale-head-hall.co.uk. With award-winning food and informal comfort on Lake Thirlmere.
C **Greystones Hotel**, Ambleside Rd, Keswick, T01768-773108. Small, well-appointed guesthouse within walking distance of both town centre and lake.
C **Hazeldene Hotel**, The Heads, Keswick, T01768-772106. Views over the fells on the outskirts of town, family-run, and good food.
F **Borrowdale YHA**, Longthwaite, Borrowdale, T01768-777257. With 88 beds in 2,4,6 and 8-bedded rooms, a cedarwood cabin beside the river.
F **Buttermere YHA**, Buttermere, T01768-770245. With 70 beds in an old farmhouse at the foot of Honister Pass.
F **Derwentwater YHA**, Barrow House, Borrowdale, near Keswick, T01768-777246. With 88 beds, in an 18th-century mansion overlooking the lake.
F **Ennerdale YHA**, Cat Crag, Ennerdale, T01946-861237. With 24 beds, basic facilities at the head of the lake.
F **Honister Hause YHA**, Seatoller, near Keswick, T01768-777267. With 26 beds, high up on Honister Pass, within strenuous walking distance of the highest summits in the Lakes.
F **Keswick YHA**, Station Rd, Keswick, T01768-772484. With 91 beds close to the river and the centre of town.
F **Thirlmere YHA**, Old School, Stanah Cross, near Keswick, T01768-773224. With 28 beds in an old schoolhouse.

Ullswater *p768*
L Sharrow Bay Country House Hotel, T01768-486301. A 4-star hotel on the lake shore with a solid and traditional Michelin-starred restaurant. 26 bedrooms in 4 different locations near the lake.
A Glenridding Hotel, T01768-482228, www.glenriddinghotel.co.uk Surrounded by mountains and the lake, warm friendly atmosphere, with a swimming pool.
A Howtown Hotel, Howtown, on Ullswater, T01768-486514, www.howtownhotel.co.uk. Traditional, old-fashioned and rather friendly hotel in a fabulous position on the southern shore of the Lake. £58 per person for dinner, B&B. Recommended.
C Netherdene Guest House, Troutbeck, T01768- 483475, www.netherdene.co.uk. Traditional Lakeland country house, great views, rooms with en suite facilities.
C Whitbarow Farm, T01768-483366. Hilltop position, good views, good hearty breakfast.
C White Lion, Patterdale, T01768-482214. About a mile from the end of Ullswater, a very popular pub with walkers.
F Helvellyn YHA, Greenside, Glenridding, T01768-482269. With 64 beds at 900 ft, base camp for the mountain above Ullswater.
F Patterdale YHA, Patterdale, T01768-482394. With 82 beds in a Scandinavian-looking building.
F Skiddaw House YHA, Bassenthwaite, near Keswick T01697-478325. With 20 beds in the middle of nowhere beneath the summit of Skiddaw.

Camping
Camping Barn, Swirral, on the Helvyllyn Range, near the routes to Striding Edge and Ullswater. Sleeps 8.

The Lune and Eden Valleys *p769*
B Augill Castle, South Stainmore, near Kirkby Stephen, T01768-341937, www.stayinacastle.com. Wonderfully converted old castle with friendly hosts, fluffy towels in the bathrooms and happy breakfast atmosphere in the old dining room. Recommended.
B The Black Swan Hotel, Ravenstonedale, near Kirkby Stephen, T01539-623204, www.blackswanhotel.com. Privately owned, comfortable hotel in a Victorian building in the middle of a quiet village. Recommended.
B Hipping Hall, Cowan Bridge, Kirkby Lonsdale, T01524-271187. Very pleasant country house hotel just outside Kirkby Lonsdale, good for exploring the Lune Valley.
B Royal Oak, Bongate, Appleby, T01768-351463. The best bet for staying above a pub, does good and imaginative pub food freshly prepared daily. Recommended.
B Tufton Arms Hotel, Market Sq, Appleby, T01768-351593. Rambling old hotel right in the middle of town, with good value lunchtime snacks, comfortable rooms and conservatory restaurant.
C Old Hall Farmhouse, Bongate, Appleby, T01768-351773. A smaller B&B operation on the outskirts of town.
D Bongate House, Bongate, Appleby, T01768-351245. A large family-run guesthouse in a fine Georgian building on the northern edge of town.
D Croglin Castle Hotel, South Rd, Kirkby Stephen, T01768-371389. Decent pub hotel with good food, convenient for the station.
D Ing Hill Lodge, Mallerstang Dale, near Kirkby Stephen, T01768-371153. Georgian house with a warm welcome in a beautiful position not far from Pendragon Castle.
D The Manor House, Mellbecks, Kirkby Stephen, T01768-372757. An 18th-century B&B with Aga-cooked breakfasts, open Apr-Dec.
F Bents Camping Barn T01768-371760 or T01539-623681. £4 per person per night, £48 for sole use, with 12 beds. A 17th-century barn on the edge of the Howgill Fells, 5 miles from Kirkby Stephen railway station, on the Coast to Coast walk.
F Dentdale YHA, Cowgill, Dent, near Sedbergh, T01539-625251. An old shooting lodge a couple of miles from Dent station, with 38 beds in 2 8-bedded, 1 10-bedded and 1 12-bedded room.
F Kirkby Stephen YHA, Market St, Kirkby Stephen, T01768-371793. Right in the middle of town, a mile and a half from the station, in a converted chapel with 44 beds in 2, 4, 6, and 8 bedded rooms.

The Cumbrian coast *p771*
A Bay Horse Hotel, Canal Foot, Ulverston, T01229-583972, www.thebayhorsehotel.co.uk. Overlooks the estuary and has a confidently ambitious but quite expensive restaurant (about £40 a head).

A **Netherwood**, Lindale Rd, Grange-over-Sands, T01539-532552. Another grand old country house, Victorian, with views over Morecambe Bay.

B **Graythwaite Manor**, Fernhill Rd, Grange-over-Sands, T01539- 532001, www.graythwaitemanor.co.uk. A dignified old place with beautiful gardens.

B **Winder Hall Country House**, Lorton, near Cockermouth, T01900-85107. An ancient manor house hotel with a lovely garden.

B **Aynsome Manor Hotel**, Cartmel, T01539-536653. A small family-run country house hotel, cosy and wood-panelled with glorious views from the garden and good food in the quiet restaurant.

C **Brookhouse Inn**, T01946-723288, www.brookhouseinn.co.uk, on the Eskdale Green to Hard Knott Road is a popular choice with walkers.

C **Burnmoor Inn**, Boot, T0845-1306224, www.burnmoor.co.uk In the village itself, with decent-sized rooms.

C **Cavendish Arms**, Cartmel, T01539-536240. An old locals' pub with character in the middle of the village, fine real ales (including their own brew) and a back garden.

C **Church Walk House**, Church Walk, Ulverston, T01229-582211. A charming, central B&B.

C **Dale View B&B**, Boot, T01946-723236. B&B in the old Post Office.

C **Holly House Hotel**, Main St, Ravenglass, T01229-717230. A centrally located hotel with reasonable food.

C **Masons Arms**, Strawberry Bank, Cartmel Fell, T01539-568486, www. masonarms.co.uk. A very popular own-brew pub with comfortable good value rooms, reliable food and views all around.

C **Penny Hill Farm**, T01946-723274. Small B&B a mile up the valley towards Hardknott.

D **Ross Garth Guest House**, Main St, Ravenglass, T01229-717275. Has comfortable rooms, also in the middle of the village.

F **Eskdale YHA**, T01946-723219. The local youth hostel.

Camping

Hollins Farm Campsite, at the other end of the Esk valley, in Boot, T01946-723253. Idyllic pitches for about £5 a night. **Turner Hall Farm**, Seathwaite, Duddon Valley, T01229-716420. Camping for about £5 a night per pitch.

Eating

Kendal and around *p760*

£££ **Moon**, 129 Highgate, T01539-729254. A long-standing local favourite doing modern European cooking in a civilized environment (about £30 a head).

££ **Déjà Vu**, 124 Stricklandgate, T01539-724843. A small French restaurant doing vegetarian and Spanish evenings as well, with starters at about £5, mains around £11. Booking essential at the weekends.

££ **Eastern Balti**, 22 Wildman St, T01539-724074. Kendal's first Balti House, doing fine Indian cooking in elegant surroundings with a comprehensive vegetarian menu, and a takeaway service.

££ **Paulo Gianni's**, 21a Stramongate, T01539-725858. Popular local Italian with good pizzas and pasta as well as daily specials of Mediterranean food.

££ **Shang Thai**, 54 Stramongate, T01539-720387. The only Thai restaurant in Kendal, very laid-back and reasonably priced (about £15 a head).

Windermere *p762*

££ **Jericho's**, Birch St, T01539-4442522. Well-prepared modern British food in the middle of town (about £12 main courses).

££ **Jambo**, Victoria St, close to the station, Windermere, T01539-443429. Freshly prepared British food (mains about £13) with friendly service and fine wines.

££ **Oregano**, 4 High St, T01539-444954. Don't only do Italian food but what they do they do well (mains about £12).

££ **Postilion Restaurant**, Ash St, Bowness-on-Windermere, T01539-445852. A traditional British and continental restaurant, its home-made food £14 for 3 courses, with fine wine selection.

££ **Porthole Eating House**, Bowness-on-Windermere, T01539-442793. Another popular, traditional Lakeland restaurant.

£ **Oriental Kitchen** T01539-445110. A sensible Chinese restaurant with take-away service.

Ambleside *p765*

£££ Sheila's Cottage, The Slack, Ambleside, T01539-433079. Simple English food for around £25 a head.

££ Glass House, Rydal Rd, T01539-432137. Modern imaginative menu and décor in a lovely setting, unfussy and reasonably priced at around £20 a head.

££ Lucy's on a Plate, Church St, Ambleside, T01539-431191. Café by day (bacon and goat's cheese rösti £6), and other eclectic fare, 'tickled trout' £13.

££ The Queen's Head, Townhead, Troutbeck, T01539-432174. A 17th-century inn with excellent food.

££ Zeffirelli's, Compston Rd, Ambleside, T01539-433845. Wholesome wholefood pizzeria unusually enough with a 2-screen cinema attached, right in the village centre.

£ Apple Pie, Rydal Rd, Ambleside, T01539-433679. Excellent home-made cakes, breads and sandwiches in this popular little café.

£ The Jade Garden, Compston Rd, T01539-431888. Convenient Chinese, close to the centre of town.

£ Lucy 4, 2 St Mary's La, T01539-434666. A tapas wine bar.

£ Mr Dodds Restaurant, Rydal Rd, Ambleside, T01539-432134. Morning coffee, lunch or evening menu, vegetarian dishes, pizza to eat in or take-away.

£ Spice of Bengal, 3 Kelsick Rd, Ambleside, T01539-431250. Reliable Indian, also doing takeaways.

Grasmere *p765*

£££ Michael's Nook Hotel, see above, T01539-435496. Expensive gourmet option, about £50 a head, dress smart and booking essential.

££ Cumbria Carvery, Stock La, Grasmere, T01539-435005. Daytime canteen and nighttime table service for some decent English food, about £15 a head.

££ Jumble Room Café, Grasmere, T01539-435188. A cheerful place for filling British food.

££ Rowan Tree, Church Bridge, Stock La, Grasmere, T01539-435528. About £20 for a 3-course vegetarian meal just off the main road. Booking weekends advisable.

Hawkshead and around *p766*

£ Seasons, The Square, Hawkshead T015394 36490 is a traditional Lakeland café restaurant, open on summer evenings.

Keswick and around *p767*

££ Golden Hills, 70 Main St, T01768-773165. An eat-in or take away Chinese restaurant favoured by locals.

££ Luca's Greta Bridge, High Hill, T01768 774621. Popular local Italian restaurant, family- owned and run, with home-made pizzas and pastas, as well as steaks, fish and vegetarian menu (about £20 a head).

££ Morrel's, 34 Lake Rd, T01768-772666. Well-respected traditional British restaurant on the road down to the theatre, (starters £5), braised oxtail (£12.50) and plenty of vegetarians. Weekend booking essential.

The Lune and Eden Valleys *p769*

£ Costas Tapas Bar, 9 Queen St, Penrith, T01768-866987. Delivers a shot of sunny Spain in the centre of town, with authentic snacks.

£ Croglin Castle Hotel, Kirkby Stephen, T01768-371389. Does a very good modern British menu in the evenings, and for lunch on Fri, Sat and Sun.

£ Hoagy's Bistro, High Wiend, Appleby, T01768- 352368. Quiet and friendly with a varied menu served evenings only.

£ Riverside Fish and Chips, Sands, Appleby, T01768-351464. Serves up the national dish for lunch and supper to eat-in or take-away beside the River Eden.

£ Royal Oak, Bongate, Appleby, T01768-351463. Does good and imaginative pub food freshly prepared daily.

£ Ruhm Gallery and Café, 15 Victoria Rd, Penrith, T01768-867453. Has well-filled sandwiches and freshly ground coffee next to a small contemporary art and craft gallery.

£ Sorrel and Thyme, Kirkby Lonsdale, T01524-272772. Cheerful, bright and friendly café serving up macaroni cheese, chicken and bacon salads, and picnic bags, each for about £5.50, as well as rarebits.

The Cumbrian coast *p771*

£££ Zest Low Rd, on the outskirts of Whitehaven, T01946-692848. A newish brasserie with an accomplished modern British menu, meals ranging in price from £15 to £25 a head.

££ Quince and Medlar, 13 Castlegate, Cockermouth, T01900-823579. A candlelit top- class vegetarian restaurant.

Pubs, bars and clubs

Kendal and around *p760*

£ Bar 99, 99 Highgate, T01539-722123. A lively wine bar with a good atmosphere but no food.

Ambleside *p765*

£ Golden Rule, Smithy Brow, Ambleside, T01539-432257. A very good pub popular with walkers and pulling some fine real ales. No hot food but great pork pies.

The Lune and Eden Valleys *p769*

£ Sun Inn, Dent, T01539-625208. A cosy, beamed pub with reliable food and its own-brew ales.

The Cumbrian coast *p771*

£ Blacksmith's Arms, Broughton Mills, just outside Broughton in the lovely Lickie Valley, T01229-716824. A locals' pub hidden away, with a very ancient interior and a barman with a poor attitude to strangers but reliable food.

Entertainment

Keswick *p767*

Alhambra Cinema, St John's St, with interesting screenings of mainstream and arthouse films by the Keswick Film Club, T01768-772398, www.keswickfilmclub.org.

Theatre by the Lake, Lakeside, Keswick T01768-774411, www.theatrebythelake.com. Middle-scale touring productions at one of the most prettily situated theatres in the UK.

Activities

Ballooning

High Adventure, RM Travel, Rayrigg Rd, Bowness-on-Windermere T01539- 446588;

Lakeland Balloons, Lytham St Anne's, T01253-736869;

Virgin Balloons, from Fell Foot Park and Hawkshead, T08705-228483;

Pleasure in Leisure, Tirobeck, 10 Keldwyth Park, Windermere, T01539-442324.

Blacksmithing

One-day blacksmithing courses are run by **Steve Hopps** at 'Sandbed', Fell End, Ravenstonedale, near Kirkby Stephen T01539-623327. £70 by appointment to forge your own piece of wrought iron work.

Boating

Among the plethora of companies offering watersport activities of all kinds (canoes, kayaks, windsurfers, dinghies).

Adventure Company UK, Denton House, Penrith Rd, Keswick, T01768-775351.

The British Small Boatbuilders Association, 56 Braycourt Av, Walton-on-Thames, Surrey, T01932-224 910, publish a fine little guide to small boating and traditional boatbuilders in the UK as a whole. It's called *The Quiet Adventure*.

Coniston Boating Centre, Lake Rd, Coniston, T01539-441366, day boats for hire.

Coniston Launch, T01539-436216, www.conistonlaunch.co.uk also operate trips right round the lake.

Hedley Outdoor Pursuits, The Spit, Glenridding, Ullswater T01768-4894033.

Howtown Outdoor Activity Centre, Ullswater, T01768-486508.

Keswick Launch, trips on Derwentwater on Annie Mellor, an open-decked wooden launch, T01768-772263. Daily sailings mid-Mar to Nov.

National Trust Steam Yacht Gondola, Coniston to Brantwood T01539-463850. Round-trip £4.80. Apr-Oct 5 sailings daily 1100, 1200, 1400, 1500, 1600 from Coniston. The National Trust also operates a free bus service on Sun Apr-Oct between Hawkshead, Tarn Hows and Coniston.

Nichol End Marine, Portinscale, Keswick, T01768-773082, www. boatspecialists.co.uk For windsurfer, kayak, dinghy, rowing boat and motorboat hire.

Caving

Paul Ramsden, Sun Lea, Joss La, Sedbergh, T01539-620828. Introductory caving trips for individuals and groups.

Cycling

The **Cumbria Cycleway** runs through Kirkby Lonsdale, Sedbergh, Garsdale, Kirkby Stephen and Appleby. Details from TICs. The **Yorkshire Dales Cycleway** passes through Dent.

Ambleside Mountain Bikes, Ghyllside Cycles, The Slack, Ambleside, T01539-433592.
Askew Cycles, Old Brewery, Wildman St, Kendal, T01539-728057.
The Croft Mountain Bike Hire (Easter-Oct only), The Campsite, North Lonsdale Rd, Hawkshead, T01539-436374.
Gone Mountain Biking, Kinniside Portinscale, Keswick T01768-780812, www.gonemountain biking.co.uk. Bike hire and organized trips.
Grizedale Mountain Bikes, Grizedale Forest, Old Hall Car Park, near Hawkshead, T01229-860369.
Keswick Mountain Bikes, Southey Hill, Keswick T01768-775202.
Lakeland Pedlar, Bicycle Centre and Wholefood Café, Henderson Yard, Keswick, T01768-775752.
Millennium Cycles, Bankside Barn, Crook Rd, Staveley, T01539-821167.
Summitreks, 14 Yewdale Rd, Coniston, T01539-441212.

Dry stone walling
Contact the **British Trust for Conservation Volunteers**, Brockhole, Windermere, T01539-443098, if you'd like to lend a hand maintaining the Lake Districts crumbling enclosure walls, footpaths, plant trees or cut back rhododendrons.

Fishing
Permits for fishing in respective areas of the Lake District can be obtained from Ambleside, Kendal and Windermere TICs, as well as **Carlson's Fishing Tackle Shop**, Kirkland, Kendal, T01539-724867, or **Kendal Sports**, 30 Stramongate, Kendal, T01539-721554, and **Fishing Hut**, The Boulevard, Windermere Rd, Grange-over-Sands, T01539-532854. These places can also provide maps and other useful information showing where fishing is allowed. Or consult www.lakedistrictfishing.net. Around the Lune Valley, day permits from **Pigneys**, Appleby, T01768-351240, or in Kirkby Lonsdale from TIC. In Kirkby Stephen from **WAS Kilvington**, Market Sq, T01768-371495. In Sedbergh, tickets from the TIC. Mar-Aug £10 day.

Horse riding
Hipshow Riding Stables, Hipshow Farm, Mealbank, near Kendal, T01539-728221.
Lakeland Equestrian, Wynlass Beck Stables, Windermere, T01539-443811.
Park Foot Trekking Centre, Howtown, Pooley Bridge, T01768- 486696.
Rookin House Farm, Troutbeck, T01768-483561.
Spoon Hall Riding School, Coniston, T01539-441391.

Hound trailing
Racing hound dogs over the hills along a pre-scented trail takes place Apr-Oct. With binoculars in hand it makes a great spectactor sport. For details of events contact the **Houndtrailing Association**, T01768-483686, www. houndtrailing.org.uk

Parachuting
Cark Airfield, Moor La, Flookburgh, T01539-558672.

Paragliding
Lakeland Leisure Paragliding, Coppermine Valley, Coniston, T01539-441825.
Lakes Paragliding Centre, Greyber, Maulds Meaburn, Penrith, T01931-715050.
Phoenix Paragliding, Denton House, Penrith Rd, Keswick T01768-773767, www.phoenixparagliding.com.

Rock climbing
Howtown Outdoor Activity Centre, Ullswater, T01768-486508.
Mere Mountains, Windermere, T01539-488002.

Walking
The **National Park Authority** publishes a free annual Events and Parklife magazine (available from most TICs) with details of guided walks and other events throughout the year. Walking tours for individuals in groups are also organized by the **Brathay Exploration Group Trust**, Brathay Hall, Ambleside, T01539-433942; **Cumbria Outdoors**, Hawsend Centre, Portinscale, Keswick, T01768-772816; **Lake District Fell Guides**, Park Cottage, 44 Sedbergh Rd, Kendal, T01539-723007; and **Lakeland Walking Holidays**, Keswick, T01768-773610.

Long-distance paths across the Lake District include the 70-mile Cumbria Way from Ulverston to Carlisle, and the first part of Wainwright's Coast-to-Coast walk from St Bee's Head to Robin Hood Bay.

The area around the Lune and Eden Valleys abounds in way-marked walks, a selection below, but many of the fells are open access too. The **Alternative Pennine Way** runs through Kirkby Stephen and Appleby, more interesting than the National Trail, details from Kirkby TIC; the **Eden Way** long distance walk begins at Rockcliffe Marsh and ends at Mallerstang along the course of the river; **Westmorland Heritage Walk** traces the boundaries of the old county, passing through Kirkby Lonsdale, Sedbergh, Mallerstang and Appleby; **Lady Anne's Way** runs for 100 miles from Skipton to Penrith along the route ridden by the elderly Lady Anne as she restored her 6 castles; **Dales Way** (from Ilkley to Bowness-on-Windermere) passes through Sedbergh, Dent and Lea Yeat (Guide from Kirkby Lonsdale or Sedbergh TIC).

Festivals

Windermere *p762*
Sep Bowness Theatre Festival. Hosted by the Old Laundry each year from mid-Sep to Oct, www.oldlaundrytheatre.com or find details from the *The World of Beatrix Potter*, which usually features some top names in performance, with poetry readings, films and interesting talks.

The Lune and Eden Valleys *p769*
Jun Appleby Horse Fair. Is a traditional Gypsy horse fair. See the ponies being washed in the Eden ready for sale.

Transport

The Lune and Eden Valleys *p769*
Traveline, T0870-6082608.
Cycle hire from **Stephen McWirter**, Station Yard, Kirkby Stephen, T01768-372442.

Hadrian's Wall

→ *Colour map 7, grid B2-5*

Built by the Romans and their slaves, Hadrian's Wall marked the northern boundary of their empire in the second and third centuries AD and was their most impressive engineering achievement in Northern Europe. Strategic considerations at the time of its construction mean that the route it takes still commands some of the best views between Carlisle and Newcastle. Carlisle advertises itself as a 'great border city' with some justification. This strategic town near the mouth of the River Eden was continually at the centre of border disputes right up to the rebellion of Bonnie Prince Charlie in 1745. Today it's the county town of Cumbria and still a fairly forbidding place despite a clutch of attractions worth an afternoon of anyone's time: the cathedral, castle and local museum and art gallery called Tullies House. Stretching away to the east of Carlisle and really the best reason for a visit to the city, the World Heritage Site of Hadrian's Wall is a crumbling relic, 73 miles long, still standing up to 6 of its original 10 ft in some places, hugging the high ground all the way to Newcastle. The most complete remains of forts are at Birdoswald, Housesteads and Chesters, with a superb stretch of the wall itself near Walltown Crags. Hexham is a good-looking Abbey town close to the wall above the river Tyne. Further east, Newcastle upon Tyne is the most vigorous city in the North, thanks to its wealth of new developments and optimistic, forward-looking spirit born out of industrial decline. ▸▸ *For Sleeping, Eating and other listings see pages 792-796.*

Ins and outs

Getting there Carlisle is on the main eastcoast **train** line to Glasgow from London Euston. A branch line runs to Brampton, Haltwhistle, Reburn, Haydon Bridge, Hexham and Newcastle. The Leeds-Settle-Carlisle railway is easily the most scenic route to the city, www.settle-carslisle.co.uk. **Virgin Trains** serve Carlisle direct from London Euston (3 hours 40 minutes) or more frequently with a change at Preston (4 hours 30 minutes). Carlisle is at the top of the M6 **motorway**, a little over 300 miles from London, about five hours' drive. Hadrian's Wall is easily reached along the impressive A69 to Newcastle upon Tyne (46 miles to the east). Most of the major Roman sites are reached along the B6318, a minor road following the course of the one built by General Wade to suppress the Scots under Oliver Cromwell. **National Express**, T08705-808080, run two **coaches** to Carlisle from London Victoria at 0930 and 1030 arriving at 1610 and 1745 respectively, as well as a nightcoach leaving at 2230 arriving at 0505. Coaches also run from Carlisle to Leeds, Manchester and Birmingham, T08705-143219. ➡ *For further details, see Transport page 796.*

Getting around The centre of **Carlisle** is easily small enough to be explored on **foot**. **Buses** to Hadrian's Wall leave from Warwick Road and the bus station on Lonsdale Street. **Hadrian's Wall Bus** run by **Stagecoach** in Cumbria, T01434-322002, www.hadrians-wall.org, May to September links Carlisle with Hexham, Haltwhistle, Brampton and most of the main Roman sites. By **train**, the Tyne Valley Line to Newcastle from Carlisle calls at Brampton, Haltwhistle, Bardon Mill and Haydon Bridge.

Information Carlisle Visitor Centre ⓘ *Old Town Hall, T01228-625600, www.historic-carlisle.org.uk, Apr, Sep, Oct Mon-Sat 0930-1700, may also open Sun 1030-1600, Jun, Jul, Aug Mon-Sat 0930-1730, Sun 1030-1600*. For cycle routes, bike hire and accommodation. **Haltwhistle TIC** ⓘ *Railway Station, Sation Rd, T01434-322002, ppen all year*. **Hexham TIC** ⓘ *Wentworth Car Park, T01434-652220, open all year.*

Carlisle

From Court Square in front of the train station, the round towers of the 19th-century **Citadel**, modelled on a gate erected by Henry VIII, make an imposing entrance to the town centre down English Street. A further 100 yds down, this pedestrianized area opens out into the market square. The cross from which Bonnie Prince Charlie proclaimed his father king still stands, as does the Elizabethan town hall, now home to the helpful Carlisle Visitor Centre. Next door is the **Guildhall** ⓘ *T01228 534781*, which has a small museum on the history of the building, dating from 1405.

To the left of the Guildhall, Castle Street heads down past the cathedral to the Tullie House Museum, and then over the new Irishgate footbridge or under the subway to the castle itself. **Carlisle cathedral** ⓘ *T01228-48151, Mon-Sat 0730-1815, Sun 0730-1700, Prior's Kitchen, T01228-543251, open until 1630 Mon-Sat in summer, in the medieval undercroft of the Fratry,* is largely a 19th-century concoction although a fair amount of the medieval building survives. Built out of distinctive red sandstone, highlights of the interior include the East Window with its 14th-century stained glass images of the Last Judgement in the tracery lights, and the Brougham Triptych: a carved Flemish altarpiece depicting the Passion in St Wilfrid's Chapel. The choir has a 14th-century barrel-vaulted ceiling and beautifully carved capitals on its columns representing the labours of the months of the year. The choir stalls provide more fine examples of medieval carving. Early 16th-century paintings in the north and south aisles on the back of the choir stalls tell the stories of St Cuthbert and St Anthony. There's also a gift shop in the cathedral and good value food in the atmospheric vaults of the Prior's Kitchen.

Just down the road from the cathedral, the **Tullie House Museum** ⓘ *Castle St, T01228-534781, www.tulliehouse.co.uk, Apr-Oct Mon-Sat 1000-1700 (-1800 Jul and Aug), Sun 1200-1700 (1100-1800 Jul and Aug), Nov-Mar Mon-Sat 1000-1600, Sun 1200-1600, £5.20, concessions £3.60, children £2.60, family £14.50*, is an award-winning local history museum and art gallery. Vivid and imaginative interactive displays trace the history of the city from the Romans to the present day, a place where visitors are encouraged to 'come face to face with the people who lived, loved, fought and died for this part of Britain over the last ten thousand years'. As well as a reconstruction of part of Hadrian's Wall, there's a particularly strong section on the Border Reivers, the lawless families that terrorized this part of Britain for centuries.

Carlisle Castle ⓘ *(EH), T01228-591922, Apr-Sep daily 0930-1800, Oct daily 1000-1700, Nov-Mar daily 1000-1600, £3.20, concessions £2.40, children £1.60*, was built on the site of a Roman fort, between the natural barriers of the rivers Eden and Caldew, to defend the western end of the border with Scotland. Many of the remains still standing today, including the massive keep, date from the 12th century, constructed under the orders of Henry I. The keep contains an exhibition on the last time the castle saw action, when it served as the prison for captured Jacobites after Charles Stuart's unsuccessful attempt on the throne in 1747. The castle is also home to the military museum of the King's Own Royal Border Regiment and the **Cumbria Record Office** ⓘ *T01228-607285*, if you want to track down your Cumbrian ancestors. Great views from the castle walls.

Hadrian's Wall

Hadrian's Wall was built by order of the Emperor Hadrian following his visit to Britain in AD122. It was planned as a continuous wall with a mile castle every Roman mile, with two turrets between each castle, running some 80 miles from Maia (Bowness-on-Solway) past Luguvalium (Carlisle) to Segedunum (Newcastle upon Tyne). A new 81-mile National Trail now follows its entire length, through some of the bleakest landscape in Britain. The wall itself survives most visibly east of Birdoswald and west of Chesters along the military road built by General Wade, now the B6318.

At **Birdoswald** ⓘ *Roman Fort, T01697-747602, Mar-Oct daily 1000-1730 (last admission 1700), Nov-Feb exterior only, £3, concessions £2.50, children £1.75, family £7.75,* the remains include a unique drill hall or basilica as well as the outline of granary buildings, at what was once a large fort designed for 1000 legionaries. The masonry of the fort's west gate is particularly impressive. There's also an interactive visitor centre.

Close to the old village of Brampton, just before Birdoswald, the **Banks East Turret** and **Pike Hill Signal Tower** are both well preserved. They can be reached beyond the atmospheric remains of a 12th-century **Lanercost Augustinian priory** ⓘ *(EH), T01697-73030, Apr-Sep daily 1000-1800, Oct daily 1000-1700, £2.20, concessions £1.70, children £1.10.* One mile from Birdoswald, the milecastle at **Poltross Burn**, Gilsland is in an exceptionally good state of repair.

At **Greenhead**, 'Gateway to Hadrian's Wall', the A69 becomes a spectacular road as it enters Northumberland, with distant views north and south over apparently endless wastes. The 400-m-long section of the wall at **Walltown Crags** is one of the most impressive: here it's still at least 7 ft wide and 5 ft high in places as it clings to the precipitous edge of the crags, including the remains of a turret.

Close to the Walltown Crags is the entertaining **Roman Army Museum** ⓘ *T01697-747485, www.vindolanda.com, daily mid-Feb to mid-Nov 1000-1700 (-1600 Feb, Nov, -1730 Apr, Sep, -1800 May, Jun, -1830 Jul, Aug), £3.30, concessions £2.90, children £2.20, £6 with Vindolanda*, ideal for a rainy day. Exhibits include a Roman Army recruitment video, an Eagle's Eye View from a chopper along the wall, as well as some real Roman pottery amid the replicas of legionaries' uniforms and weaponry.

At Once Brewed, the **Northumberland National Park Centre** ⓘ *Visitor Centre T01434-344396, Mar-May, Sep-Oct daily 0930-1700, Jun-Aug daily 0930-1800*, provides information and walking leaflets on this central and most popular section of the wall. Within walking distance of the centre is **Vindolanda** ⓘ *T01434-344277, www.vindolanda.com Daily mid-Feb to mid-Nov 1000-1700 (-1600 Feb, Nov, -1730 Apr, Sep, -1800 May, Jun, -1830 Jul, Aug), £4.10, concessions £3.70, children £2.70*, a recently excavated little civilian settlement, as well as an open-air museum featuring a reconstructed Roman Temple, Shop, House and Croft.

Two and a half miles northeast of Bardon Mill on the B6318, **Houseteads Roman Fort** ⓘ *(EH and NT), T01434-344363, Apr-Sep daily 0930-1800, Oct daily 1000-1700, Nov-Mar daily 1000-1600, £3.10, concessions £2.30, children £1.60*, is the most complete of its type to survive in the UK. Four gates, the commandant's house, barracks, granaries, hospital and latrines can all be clearly discerned. Superb views from the site too.

Signposted off the A69 between Bardon Mill and Haydon Bridge is the Allen Banks Car Park. This provides access to an extensive stretch of National Trust ornamental and historic woodland, formerly the **Ridley Hall estate**, along the banks of the River Allen, a tributary of the Tyne. Walks lead past abandoned 19th-century summerhouses to the medieval **Pele Tower** of Staward Peel, standing on a promontory above the gorge.

Half a mile west of Chollerford on the B6318, is one of the best-preserved examples of a **cavalry fort** ⓘ *(EH), T01434-681379, Apr-Sep daily 0930-1800, Oct daily 1000-1700, Nov-Mar daily 1000-1600, £3.10, concessions £2.30, children £1.60*, featuring the remains of the baracks, bath-house and HQ. In a beautiful riverside setting, it overlooks the remains of the bridge that carried the wall over the Tyne. The **Clayton Collection** of the altars and sculptures found along the wall is also here.

Twenty miles west of Newcastle, **Hexham** is a dignified old town on the River Tyne blessed with a remarkable Abbey Church. The best approach by car is from the north and the A69, over an impressive bridge across the Tyne. The train station is on this side of town too, along with the Tynedale Retail Park, T01434-607788, full of discount high street stores. It's a short walk uphill beyond this eyesore into the town, up cobbled Hallgate (past the TIC) from the Safeway's car park. The first sight as such is the **Old Gaol**, the oldest recorded one of its type in England, purpose-built in 1332. It now contains the interesting **Border History Museum** ⓘ *T01434-652349. Apr-Oct daily 0930-1600, Nov, Feb, Mar Mon, Tue, Sat 0930-1600, £2, children £1, family £5*, where you can 'listen to the medieval punishment commentary, hear about cross border marriages in 1587 and find out what a Pele tower is'. Next up is the **Moot Hall** (which sometimes holds craft fairs, contact TIC for details) with a gateway into the main Market Place, with the **Abbey Church** ⓘ *Hexham Abbey, T01434-602031, Oct-Apr daily 0930-1700, May-Sep 0930-1900*, on its far side, and an attractive public park behind. Founded in 674, the ruddy stoned old building dominates the town and contains rare Roman and Saxon carvings. One of the more remarkable commemorates a Roman standard bearer called Flavinus of the Cavalry Regiment of Petriana stationed on the wall, who died aged 25 during the first century AD. The Saxon Crypt of St Wilfrid also survives, open at 1100 and 1530 daily.

Newcastle and Gateshead

As Nottingham is to the East Midlands, so Newcastle upon Tyne is to the Northeast: on the up and up. In quite a spectacular position above the Tyne River, the once coal-blackened and grimey hub has become an upbeat weekending destination with twenty-somethings thanks to injections of European and lottery cash, a vigorous nightlife and the energy of its citizens, known as Geordies. First impressions are still unlikely to be very favourable: apart from its dramatic multilevel river crossings, including the famous mini prototype of Sydney Harbour bridge, the city is a mess of roundabouts, big roads and building sites. That said, it doesn't take long to discover what all the excitement is about: the opening of the Gateshead Millennium Bridge and Baltic Centre for Contemporary Art has confirmed the boom along the riverside in Newcastle and its fiercely competitive neighbour on the south bank, Gateshead,

Newcastle upon Tyne

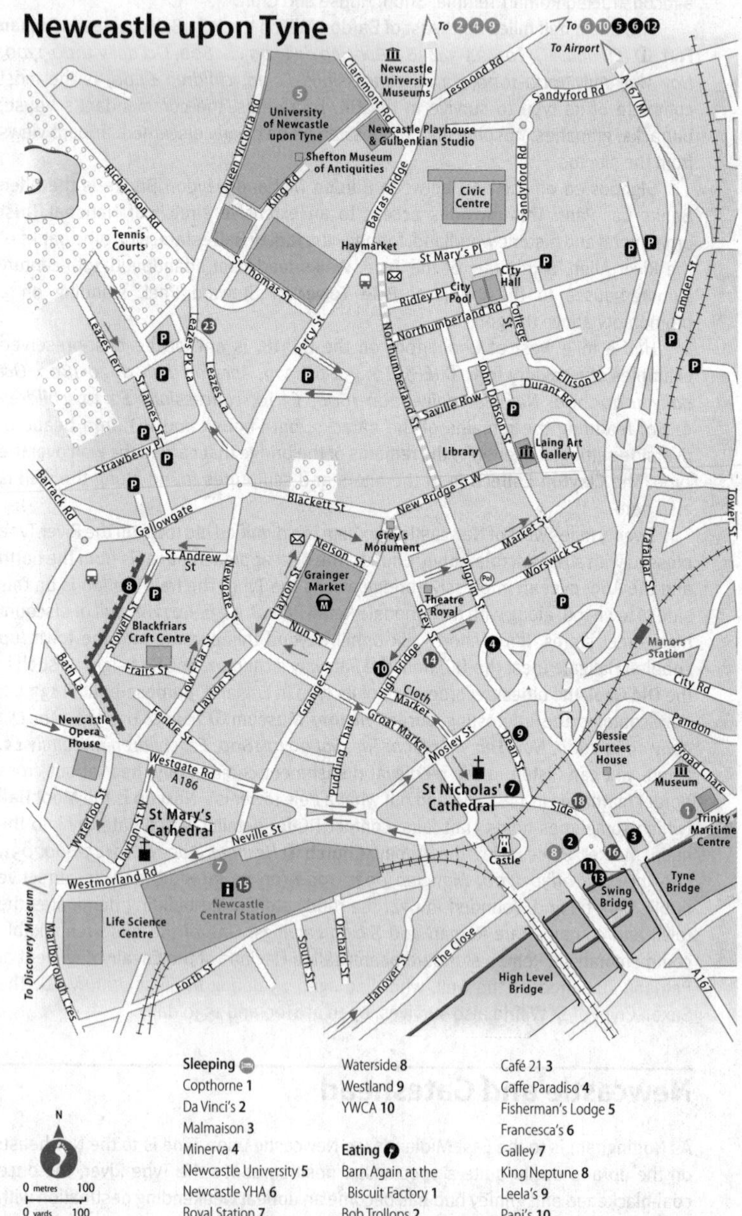

Sleeping
Copthorne 1
Da Vinci's 2
Malmaison 3
Minerva 4
Newcastle University 5
Newcastle YHA 6
Royal Station 7
Waterside 8
Westland 9
YWCA 10

Eating
Barn Again at the Biscuit Factory 1
Bob Trollops 2
Café 21 3
Caffe Paradiso 4
Fisherman's Lodge 5
Francesca's 6
Galley 7
King Neptune 8
Leela's 9
Pani's 10

that's been underway for the last few years. The Quayside was at the centre of the 'Newcastle Gateshead Buzzin' bid to be European Capital of Culture in 2008. It may be the latest addition to Newcastle's attractions, but even the older parts of the city centre have been caught up in the wave of optimism sweeping the region. Some say it all started with the Angel of the North, a giant gliderman sculpture perched above the A1. The rusty red steel thing sings in the wind, a potent symbol of this once heavily industrialized corner of the UK's vibrant hope for a less gritty future.

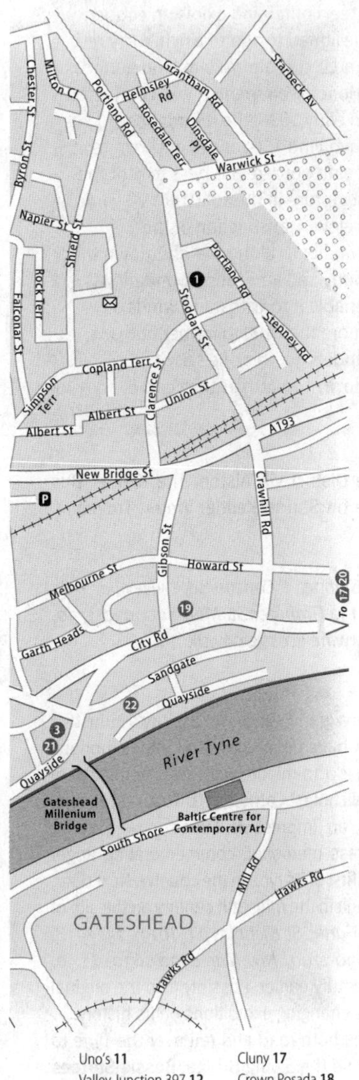

Uno's **11**
Valley Junction 397 **12**
Vujon **13**

Pubs & bars
Barluga **14**
Centurion **15**
Chase **16**
Cluny **17**
Crown Posada **18**
Egypt Cottage **19**
Free Trade Inn **20**
Pitcher and Piano **21**
Stereo **22**
Trent House Soul Bar **23**

Ins and outs

Getting there Newcastle **airport**, T0191-2144444, www.newcastleairport.com, is 6 miles northwest of the city centre at Woolsington, with a 25-min metro link into the city centre. Direct flights to destinations all over Europe. **Ferries** dock and depart from the International Ferry Terminal, Royal Quays, North Shields (seven miles east of Newcastle upon Tyne). **Fjord Line,** T0191-2961313, www.fjordline.com, operates car ferries to Bergen, Stavanger, and Haugesund in Norway. **DFDS Seaways,** T08705-333000, www.dfdsseaways.co.uk, sail to Kristiansand in Norway, Gothenberg in Sweden and Amsterdam in Holland. Bus 327 runs out to the terminal from Central Station, Gallowgate and the Youth Hostel prior to ferries' departure. The Percy Main Metro station is a 20-min walk from the terminal. Newcastle upon Tyne is a main stop on the London-York-Edinburgh **rail** line. London King's Cross (3 hours 30 mins to 4 hours), Edinburgh (1 hour 40 minutes).

Newcastle is on the A1, about 275 miles north of London, usually reached in six hours on that road, sometimes less on the M1 via Leeds. **National Express,** T08705-808080, run **coaches** to most major towns and cities in the UK from Newcastle. Service 425 runs five times a day and once a night to London, taking about 7 hours.

Getting around Although the areas of most interest to visitors are within **walking** distance of each other, the Newcastle Metro can be very useful for reaching Jesmond, the student district to the north of the universities. Regular **buses** operated by **Arriva Northumbria,** run to Hexham and Carlisle from the Haymarket bus station. The scenic route 888 run by **Wright Bros,** T0191-2778000,

Rusty redeeming angel

Standing on top of a disused coalmine just off the A1 south of Gateshead, the Angel of the North has become the symbol of the northeast's regeneration. It's the largest sculpture in Britain, a giant steel man with huge glider-like wings for arms. The artist, Antony Gormley has commented on the poetic resonance of its position, above a place where men once worked in the dark. He has said that 'the effect of the piece is in the alertness, the awareness of space and the gesture of the wings – they are not flat, they're about 3.5 degrees forward and give a sense of embrace'. Commissioned by Gateshead Council in 1994, the sculpture stands taller than four double decker buses, with its stiff outstretched wings almost as long as a jumbo's. It was made in three parts, of a special weather resistant steel containing oxidising copper, designed to age to a rich, rusty red, and it cost almost a million pounds. Money well spent, it was completed in early 1998, the foundations involving 150 tonnes of concrete being poured into piles to root the sculpture in the solid rock 20 yards below. Transmission of the windloads along the ribs, down the body and into these foundations enable it to withstand winds of more than 100 miles per hour. As angels go, this one's as down-to-earth as they come.

connects Newcastle with Keswick in the Lake District via Alston. The **Kielder Bus Service** 714 run by Arriva is a summer service on Sun to Keilder Water. **Traveline,** T0870-6082608.

Information Newcastle TIC ⓘ *Central Station Concourse, Neville St, T0191-2778000, Mon-Sat 0930-1700*. Also ⓘ *132 Grainger St. Mon-Sat 0930-1730, Thu - 1930, Easter-Sep also Sun 1000-1600, www.newcastle.gov.uk.*

Sights

Newcastle **Central Station** is quite a sight in itself: a grand survival of the city's industrial heyday, with lavish Victorian waiting rooms that have been converted into salubrious bars. Its main entrance is on Neville Street, which is a 10-minute walk away from most of the city's main sights. A right turn leads past **St Nicholas' Cathedral** ⓘ *T0191-2321939* , formerly the Anglican parish church but with an impressive lantern tower, some interesting stained glass and a 15th-century brass memorial, commemorating Roger Thornton, thrice mayor of Newcastle, possibly the first of its type in the country. Next door, tucked beneath a railway arch, stands the keep built in the mid-12th century on the site of the Norman 'new' **castle** ⓘ *Castle Keep, Castle Garth, St Nicholas St, T0191-2327938, www.castlekeep-newcastle.org Apr-Oct daily 0930-1700, Nov-Mar 0930-1630, £1.50, 50p concessions*, that gave the city its name a century earlier. Possibly also the original end point of Hadrian's Wall, the keep now stages changing exhibitions on its history.

From the castle the **High Level Bridge** takes both road and rail over the Tyne to Gateshead. Staying on the north bank, just above the Swing Bridge, **Bessie Surtees House** ⓘ *Access on the Quayside, T0191-2691227, Mon-Fri 1000-1600, free*, consists of two buildings surviving from Tudor and Jacobean Newcastle. Now the regional offices of English Heritage, once the homes of wealthy merchants, they contain 17th-century panelling, fireplaces and plaster ceilings. History includes the 18th-century love story and elopement of Bessie Surtees.

Northern accents

Although parodied by southerners as a succession of by gums, by 'eck and such like, the way people speak 'up North' is very finely differentiated. Within the space of any 20 square miles there are likely to be several different words for even the most common features of the local landscape. In Lancashire for example they call the hills 'fells', unlike the 'moors' of Yorkshire. Generally agreed upon across the region though are a 'beck' or stream, 'force' or waterfall, 'gill' or ravine, and 'tarn' or pond among many others mainly of Scandinavian origin. A law unto themselves are the Geordies. Regularly voted the most trustworthy telephone accent in the British Isles, Geordie is the native tongue of the citizens of Newcastle upon Tyne. Apparently the name, diminutive for George, dates back to the city's refusal to rise with the Northumbrian Jacobites in 1715 in support of the Old Pretender, would-be James III, against the new Hanoverian King George I. At its broadest, the accent can be quite incomprehensible to non-Geordies. Its peppered with 'Alreet' meaning Alright, and 'But' or 'Mon' used willy nilly at the end of sentences. A 'gadgie with a bottle of dog' translates as an old man with a bottle of Newcastle Brown Ale. Good luck trying to understand him.

From the Swing Bridge downstream to the new **Gateshead Millennium Bridge**, both banks of the Tyne have become the epicentre of 'Newcastle Gateshead', their wealth of new developments really 'buzzin'. The **Tyne Bridge**, symbol of the city, was completed in 1928 and looks beautiful at night. It's taken 70 years for it to be upstaged by the Gateshead Millennium Bridge half a mile upstream. The world's only tilting bridge, designed to look like a blinking eye, it too is impressively lit at night throwing patterns across the river. The footbridge leads over the river to the massive contemporary visual art space in the converted Baltic Flour Mill. The **Baltic Centre for Contemporary Art** ⓘ *South Shore Rd, Gateshead, T0191-4781810, www.balticmill.com, Mon-Sat 1000-1900, Thu 1000-2200*, houses temporary exhibtions and provides studio space for artists. Definitely worth a look with its restaurants, cafés, bar, bookshop, and library, it's the north's answer to Tate Modern in London, although without the permanent collection of modern art.

Also on the Gateshead side of the river, across Baltic Square, Sir Norman Foster's glassy facility for all kinds of live music, **The Sage Gateshead** ⓘ *T0191-4434555*, was still under construction at time of writing. It promises to be a major regional centre for music-making of all kinds, with an auditorium seating 1670 and home to the Northern Sinfonia and Folkworks, the founding partners in the project. Information on the new developments and their attractions can be found at the **Gateshead Quays Visitor Centre** ⓘ *T0191-4775380, www.gateshead.gov.uk, www.gateshead-quays.com, Mon-Thu 0830-1700, Fri 0830-1630, Sat 1000-1700, Sun 1100-1700*. Displays on the redevelopment at the TIC on the Gateshead side of the Tyne Bridge.

Back on the Newcastle bank, the **Quayside** is home to the exciting Live Theatre (see entertainment, below) as well as a glinting array of new restaurants and bars. Round the corner, anyone interested in Newcastle's maritime heritage may want to take a guided tour of **Trinity House** ⓘ *Broadchare, T0191-2328226, Fri at 1300*. For £3.50 you get an hour-long tour of the ancient building of the Guild of Master Mariners covering its role in the education of seamen down the ages, including Captain Cook, and a look inside the chapel.

A walk up into town from the Quayside beneath the Tyne Bridge heads up busy Side and Dean Streets into Grey Street, a remarkably unspoiled curving Victorian greystone street that leads up to the centre of Newcastle at **Grey's Monument**. The statue was put up when Earl Grey was Prime Minister, in honour of the Reform Act of 1832. From around the same time is the **Theatre Royal** ⓘ *Grey St, T0870-9055060, www.theatre-royal-newcastle.co.uk, Mon-Sat 0900-2000*, with its lovely Victorian auditorium by Frank Matcham, the place to see touring opera, ballet, theatre and various spectacles for the family. There's a restaurant, tours, poetry and discussions and tearoom.

A short walk down New Bridge Street, the **Laing Art Gallery** ⓘ *Higham Pl, T0191-2327734, Mon-Sat 1000-1700, Sun 1400-1700, free*, is the grand Victorian repository of the city's art collection, including the 'Art on Tyneside' permanent collection, silver, glass and costume collections and the Proctor and Gamble Children's Gallery.

A good 15-minute walk further north, some other museums worth a look are all part of Newcastle University. The **Shefton Museum of Antiquities** ⓘ *The Quadrangle, University of Newcastle, T0191-2228996, www.ncl.ac.uk/shefton-museum, Mon-Fri 1000-1600, free*, is the major archaeological museum of the region, including artefacts found at Hadrian's Wall and a model of the thing itself. The **Greek Museum** ⓘ *Hatton Gallery, The Quadrangle, University of Newcastle, T0191-2226057*, holds fine art exhibitions and also has a permanent collection of antiquities. The **Hancock Museum** ⓘ *Claremont Rd, T0191-2227418*, is the region's finest natural history museum with permanent displays on 'The Living Planet' and 'The Land of the Pharaohs'.

Two other attractions close to the train station are the new **Life Science** Centre ⓘ *Times Sq, Scotswood Rd, T0191-2438223, www.centre-for-life.co.uk, Mon-Sat 1000-1800, Sun 1100-1800, £6.95, children £4.50, family £19.95*, which promises 3-4 hours of entertainment, with motion rides, interactive touch-tellies and games broadly based on the subject that was once called biology. Great for kids, and adults who wouldn't recognize a double helix if it bit them, it's based around a cutting-edge life science research institute. The place becomes an open-air ice rink in winter.

North of the University, the Jesmond district is home to most of the cheaper accommodation and has a lively student atmosphere.

A 100 yards west, the **Discovery Museum** ⓘ *Blandford Sq, T0191-2326789, Mon-Sat 1000-1700, Sun 1400-1700, free*, is a recently refurbished interactive museum telling the story of Newcastle from the Romans to the present day. Filled with reconstructions, it offers the chance to re-enact the tales of its characters and includes the Turbina Display – built on the Tyne, she was the first ship to be powered by steam turbines and was the fastest of her time. In the Science Maze, there are hands-on demonstrations of scientific and engineering principles, including the waterpower inventions of celebrated Georgie William Armstrong.

Sleeping

Carlisle *p785*

L Farlam Hall, near Brampton, T01697-746234, www.farlamhall.co.uk. A Victorian country house hotel with amazing terraced gardens and very good walks round about.

B Beaumont Hotel Beaumont St, Hexham T01434-602331. Right in the middle of town and close to the abbey, with comfortable guest rooms.

B Number Thirty One, 31 Howard Pl, Carlisle, T01228-597080, www.number31.freeservers.com. 3 rooms in an elegant and tastefully decorated Victorian townhouse in the middle of the town. Book well ahead.

C Angus Hotel, 14 Scotland Rd, Stanwix, T01228- 523546. 11 comfortable and quiet rooms with en suite bathrooms on the edge of the town over the river.

C **Broomshaw Hill Farm**, a mile outside Haltwhistle, T01434-320866, www.broomshaw.co.uk. Farmhouse B&B near the wall.
D **Langleigh House**, 6 Howard Pl, Carlisle, T01228-530440, www.langleighhouse .co.uk. Comfortable and roomy B&B in a pleasant part of town.
D **West Close House**, Hextol Terrace, Hexham, T01434-603307, www.smoothound.co.uk/hotels/westclose. A non-smoking fairly central 1920s guesthouse off Allendale Rd, a 10-min walk east of the Abbey.
F **Carlisle YHA**, Old Brewery Residences, Bridge La, Caldewgate, Carlisle, T01228-597352. With 56 beds in single bedrooms, a university hall of residence.
F **Greenhead YHA**, Greenhead, near Brampton, T01697-747401. With 40 beds in a converted Methodist chapel close to Hadrian's Wall.
F **Once Brewed YHA**, Military Rd, Bardon Mill, T01434- 344360. With 90 beds mainly in 4-bedded rooms, close to Vindolanda.

Newcastle *p787, map p789*
A **Copthorne Hotel**, The Close, Quayside, T0191-2220333, www.milleniumhotels .com A new building with 156 rather characterless and functional rooms, has full leisure club including spa, gym, solarium, swimming pool.
A **Malmaison**, 104 Quayside, T0191-2455000, www.malmaison.com. Some weekend special offers.
Creamy natural walls, crisp white sheets, rich royal spreads and throws, this place is only 5 years old. Chicly developed from old co-op warehouse with modern rooms. French restaurant with view onto river. Eggs benedict, wild mushrooms polenta, thyme roasted sea bass are on offer in the restaurant.
B **Royal Station Hotel**, Neville St, T0191-2320781, www.cairnhotelgroup.com. A massive but beautiful Victorian building right beside the station. All the rooms are different, some with flowery décor, most currently under refurbishment. Restaurant also under refurbishment. The newly remodelled bar is a bit trendy with peachy walls and wooden floors all stripped to look 'clean'.
B-C **The Waterside**, 48-52 Sandhill, T0191-2300111, www.watersidehotel.com A standard but acceptable 3-star hotel, the rooms are not exactly modern and not exactly antique. Breakfast not included in the price: £10.50 English breakfast, £6.50 continental breakfast.
C **Da Vinci's Hotel**, 73 Osbourne Rd, Jesmond, T0191-2815284, www.davin cis.co.uk. A clean and comfortable place in the Jesmond district with a decent Italian restaurant attached.
C **Westland Hotel**, 27 Osbourne Av, T0191-2810412, www.westland-hotel.co.uk (cheaper rooms without bathroom available). A 14-bedroom hotel in a large double-fronted Victorian house, 20 mins' walk into town. It's family run, provides TV, and hairdryers and refurbishment is underway. Good value, comfortable and clean.
D **Minerva Hotel**, 105 Osborne Rd, Jesmond, T0191-2810190, F2870119. Breakfast included. A fairly ordinary B&B on 3 floors with rooms facing the road or a back yard. Comfortable but nothing special about building.
E **Newcastle University Student Halls of Residence**, T0191-2226296. Offers student rooms in the summer vacation, as does the **University of Northumbria**, T0191-2274204.
E **YWCA**, Jesmond House, Clayton Rd, T0191-2811233, F2120070. Hostel building, built in 1985. No rooms with bathrooms. Weekend deal £106.68 incl breakast and dinner.
F **Newcastle YHA**, 107 Jesmond Rd, T0191-2812570, F2818779. Has 60 beds in a large townhouse, divided into 2-bedded rooms and dormitories. It also offers single rooms in University of Newcastle halls of residence for £15 a night in Jul, Aug.

Eating

Carlisle *p785*
££ **Almond's Bistro**, 16 Scotland Rd, Stanwix, Carlisle, T01228-523546, open until 2100 Mon-Sat. English and continental food served in the evenings (steak about £9) with internet access thrown in. Next door to the Angus Hotel.

££ Bunter's Coffee Shop, 10 Hallgate, Hexham, T01434-605907. Cheap, cheerful, colourful and bright café opposite the Old Gaol that transforms itself into the Athena Greek Restaurant at night (about £15 a head).
££ The Lemon Lounge, 18 Fisher St, Carlisle, T01228-546363. Mediterranean food in a cheerful atmosphere with a bar area attached (about £17 a head).
£ Fat Cat's Coffee House, Hallgate, Hexham. A good value coffee and lunch stop behind the Old Gaol.
£ Milecastle, Military Rd, near Haltwhistle, T01434- 320682. An isolated and welcoming real ale pub with very decent pub grub, both at the bar, and in more sophisticated style in the restaurant.
£ Valley Connection 301, Market Pl, Hexham, T01434-601234. The latest in a popular and innovative local chain of curry houses. The first, in Corbridge (T01434-633434) is based in the old station house and runs a 'Package to India' popular with groups on a night out from Newcastle.
£ Wallace Arms, Rowfoot, south of Haltwhistle off the A69 towards Alston, T01434-321872. A lovely old pub with excellent food and fine real ales.

Newcastle *p787, map p789*
Newcastle is blessed with a wide variety of very decent places to eat out. It's no surprise that the Quayside comes out top of the pops.
£££ Bob Trollops, 32 Sandhill, T0191-2611037. An incongruous 17th-century timber-framed building surviving amid Quayside's redevelopment, home to a characterful vegan/vegetarian restaurant and bar.
£££ Café 21, 19-21 Queen St, Princes Wharf, Quayside, T0191-2220755. Generally regarded as one of the best restaurants in the city with its bistro-style fusion menu. A meal here could cost anything from £10-£30 or more.
£££ Fisherman's Lodge, Jesmond Dene, T0191-2813281. In Heaton Park, a lakeside setting and wooded seclusion as well as serious cuisine make this one of the city's grandest dining experiences (about £30 a head).
£££ Leela's, 20 Dean St, T0191-2301261. A recommended South Indian restaurant with top-rate vegetarian options and affable staff. More expensive than the average curry house though (about £25 a head).
££ Caffe Paradiso, 1 Market La, T0191-2211240. Live piano music to enhance the atmosphere of this cerebral and reflective restaurant and bar (about £20 a head).
££ Francesca's, Manor House Rd, T0191-2816586. A friendly local Italian, very reasonably priced at about £15 a head.
££ King Neptune, 34-36 Stowell St, T0191-2320868. The best bet in Newcastle's Chinatown.
££ Pani's, 61-65 High Bridge, T0191-2324366. A much-loved and authentic Italian café-restaurant, near Grey St.
££ Uno's, 18 Sandhill, Quayside, T0191-2615264. Another popular choice for Italian food and surprisingly affordable (£10 mains) given the celebrity cult that's grown up around it. Booking advisable.
££ Vujon, 29 Queen St, T0191-2210601. A reliable and friendly curry house (about £15 a head).
£ The Galley In the wee small hours, this 24-hour chippy also on Dean St called might come in useful.
Elsewhere £££ Barn Again at the Biscuit Factory, Stoddard St, Shieldfield, T0191-2303338. Offers an innovative menu attached to a warehouse art gallery (about £30 a head).
££ Valley Junction 397, The Old Station, Archbold Terr, T0191-2816397. An unusual and exceptional curry house in a converted junction box and railway carriage.

Pubs, bars and clubs

Newcastle *p787, map p789*
This is an activity that Newcastle takes seriously, and there are any number of different places to enjoy it.
Barluga, 35 Grey St, T0191-2302306. Mood lighting, sweet soul music and soft, soft furnishings.
The Centurion, Central Station, Neville St, T0191-2616611. A drink in the splendour that was once the station's first-class waiting room (amazing Victorian tiling and murals) is

a good place to start. Again the Quayside is the place to continue.

Chase, 13 Sandhill, T0191-2450055. This 70s-themed designer bar is still one of the city's most striking pre-club warm-up destinations. Has a beer garden beneath the Tyne Bridge. Spot the footballer but do not disturb.

The Cluny, 36 Lime St, T0191-2304474. A 15-min walk from the centre, a huge converted warehouse that's become a live-music venue and riverside art gallery of some note.

The Crown Posada, 31 The Side, T0191-2321269. An unreconstructed boozer with Victorian stained-glass windows, also in the shadow of the Tyne Bridge.

Egypt Cottage, 117 City Rd, T0191-2320218, A little further afield, this bar once made a kind of musical history as the local for the cult TV show The Tube, which happened next door.

Free Trade Inn, St Lawrence Rd, T0191-2655764. Has a large beer gardens with fabulous views over the city from a bog-standard boozer doing great sandwiches.

Nice at the Playrooms, Low Friar St, T0191-2302186. Saturday here is one of the most popular and happening garage and house nights in the city.

The Pitcher and Piano, 108 Quayside, T0191-2324110, In pole position on the waterfront, with its huge windows overlooking the Tyne and Gateshead Millennium Bridge with a vibrant mix at the bar.

Reverb at Scotland Yard for techno and good atmosphere. Look out for flyers in specialist clothes shops.

Revolution, Collingwood St, T0191-2616998. Close to the Bigg Market and a massive hit with locals at weekends.

Stereo, Sandgate, Quayside, T0191-2300303. At the other extreme is this place, currently one of the hippest bars in the city, with its funky furnishings and fishfinger sandwiches.

Stone Love at Foundation, 57-59 Melbourne St, T0191-2618985. Favoured by Indie rockers and glamour pusses. Thursday night's the night.

Trent House Soul Bar, 1-2 Leazes La, T0191-2612154. A little underground style bar with a tangible air of multicultural cool.

World Headquarters, 9 Marlborough Cres, T0191-2618648. Sweaty and lively.

Entertainment

Newcastle *p787, map p789*

Cinema

Side Cinema, Courtesy of Side Gallery, 5/9 Side, T0191-2610066. Small cinema showing art and good independent films.

Tyneside Cinema, 10 Pilgrim St, T0191-2321507, www.tynecine.org. For the film buff, showcase for London Film Festival tours.

Live music

The Cluny Warehouse, Lime St, near Byker Bridge, T0191-2304474. Good beer, staff and great for alternative music. Monthly jazz from big jazz stars and plenty of gigs from up and coming local bands.

Newcastle Opera House, Westgate Rd, T0191-2320899, www. newcastle operahouse.org. Capacity of 1100. Live mainstream rock, folk, pop and jazz venue.

Telewest Arena, Arena Way, T0191-2605000, www.telewestarena.co.uk. Booking on T0870-7078000, www.telewestarena.co.uk, for any big gigs.

Tut and Shive, 52 Clayton St West, T0191-2616998.

Trillions, Princess Sq, T0191-2321619. Has quality local rock/metal/ska/whatever bands on most nights.

Theatre

Live Theatre, 27 Broad Chare, Quayside, T0191-2321232, www.live.org.uk. Café live run by *Café 21*. Small city centre venue for new plays, music, dance and new writing, often with touring productions by national companies.

Newcastle Playhouse and Gulbenkian Studio, Barras Bridge, T0191-2305151, www.northernstage.com. Middle-scale innovative classic and contemporary drama by the resident *Northern Stage Company* as well as touring productions. With non-smoking bar.

Theatre Royal, Grey St, T0870-9055060. Plays host to major touring companies like the *RSC* and *National Theatre* as well as ballet, opera and dance.

Activities and tours

Newcastle *p787, map p789*

Football

Newcastle United, St James' Park, T0191-2611571, www.nufc.co.uk.

Bowling alleys

Megabowl, Metro Centre, Gateshead T0191-4600444.

Newcastle Bowl, Westgate Rd, T0191-2730236 16-lane alley.

Sightseeing cruises

Tyne Leisure Line Ltd, T0191-2966740, www.tyneleisureline.co.uk. Run 3-hr sightseeing cruises on the Tyne departing from Sidney St, North Shields, a few hundred yard downriver of the Millennium Bridge.

Transport

Newcastle *p787, map p789*

Bus

Long distance National Express, T08705-808080, serve Newcastle from most major UK cities, including: **Manchester** (5 hrs), **York** (2 hrs 30 mins), **London** (6 hrs 40 mins), **Durham** (30 mins), **Leeds** (2 hrs 30 mins) and **Edinburgh** (3 hrs).

Car

Argyle Garage Ltd, Coquet St, T0191-2322905; **MD Jowetts Ltd**, 8a Marlborough Cres, T0191-2325735; **Hutton Hire Service**, 133 Sandyford Rd, T0191-2811920.

Taxi

ABC Taxis, 1-3 Cross St, T0191-2323636; **Central Taxis**, Prudhoe St, Haymarket, T0191-2716363; **Noda Taxis**, Central Station, Neville St, T0191-2221888.

Train

GNER serve Newcastle from **London King's Cross** frequently throughout the day (3 hrs 30 mins). There are also direct services from **Birmingham** (3 hrs 45 mins), **Leeds** (1 hr 20 mins), **York** (1 hr), **Edinburgh** (1 hr 40 mins) and **Durham** (10 mins). For services from **Liverpool** and **Manchester**, change at Leeds.

Directory

Newcastle *p787, map p789*

Internet Internet Exchange, 26-30 Market St, T0191-2301280. **Post office** St Marys Pl, T0845-7223344. C.L.E.O, 23 Newbiggin Hall Centre, T0191-2862694. **Hospitals** The Royal Victoria Infirmary, Queen Victoria Rd, T0191-2325131. **Police** Newcastle City Centre Police Station, Market St, T0191-2146555.

County Durham

→ *Colour map 7, grid B4-5*

Until relatively recently, County Durham was synonymous with mining: limestone and lead in the west and coal on the coast. Most of the coal pits were closed down in the 1970s and early 80s, often with terrible consequences for the local communities. Some have recovered since, especially along the coast, which has been given a thorough clean-up. The western part of the county stretches into the Pennines towards Cumbria and the valleys of the Wear and the Tees lure in hillwalkers and ramblers. Barnard Castle is the market town at the heart of the area, with the magnificent ruined fortification and an interesting stately home at Bowes, its main attractions. Although the highlight of a visit to the county is still Durham itself, once you've seen the cathedral you've pretty much seen the city. There are signs that the venerable old place has begun to wake up to the fact, though: the new visitor centre in Millennium Place pulls out all the stops in an attempt to showcase the other attractions of the city and its county. ▸▸ *For Sleeping, Eating and other listings see pages 801-802.*

Walks in County Durham

- **Cronkley Fell**: 7 miles there and back. Start: Forest-in-Teesdale, 15 miles west of Barnard Castle. A climb up into the lower regions of Mickle Fell in the Lune Forest to a wonderful nature reserve. OS Maps: Outdoor Leisure 31
- **High Force**: 6 miles there and back. Start: Holwick, 12 miles west of Barnard Castle. A walk along part of the Pennine Way alongside the Tees to the famous waterfall High Force. OS Maps: Outdoor Leisure 31
- **Hunderthwaite Moor**: 4 miles there and back. Start: Kelton, 10 miles west of Barnard Castle. A gentle stoll on to the moors overlooking the Selset and Balderhead Reservoirs. OS Maps: Outdoor Leisure 31
- **Hamsterley Forest**: 3 mile circle. Start: Redford, 12 miles north of Barnard Castle. Forest walks and nature trails in a well-managed beauty spot. OS Maps: Outdoor Leisure 31
- **Easington Colliery**: 4 miles there and back. Start: Easington Colliery. A breezy beach and low clifftop walk along the renovated east coast. OS Maps: Explorer 308

Durham

Durham presents passing train travellers with a wonderful spectacle: stacked up half a mile away on a ridge in a tight loop of the River Wear, its massive cathedral towers up behind the castle, a grey-brown stone fantasy of a place. Visually it's unlikely to disappoint day-trippers either, although there's not a huge amount more to do than wander over the river on to the 'peninsula' and up to the cathedral, enjoying the compact and cobbled centre of this university town. The recent opening of the Gala centre in Millennium Place beside Millburngate Bridge is supposed to address that problem with a state-of-the-art visitor centre, theatre, cinema, library and café complex. Chances are that it will provide an entertaining night out following the mandatory appreciation of what is arguably the most impressive Romanesque cathedral in Europe. After soaking up the atmosphere of this mighty achievement of the Norman church, the tour of the castle might come as a bit of a disappointment. Archaeologists are well served by the university's museum close by though, while the Oriental Museum, a mile to the south on the main campus, is another unusual attraction. Otherwise Durham makes a reasonable base from which to explore the hillwalking delights of Weardale and Teesdale in the Pennine hills to the west.

Ins and outs

Getting there GNER run about 17 express west coast **trains** to Durham from London King's Cross daily, taking about 2½-3 hours. Durham is just off the A1 (M) linking it to north and south, about 260 miles from London, a journey that usually takes about 5 hours. From the west, the A68 'holiday route' crosses Northumberland and Border Country. **National Express**, T08705-808080, service 425 runs five times a day to Durham from London Victoria, including a nightbus, leaving at 0830, 1230, 1500, 1730 and 2330. The journey takes just over 6 hours. Durham is also connected by coach to Newcastle and York. »» *For further details, see Transport page 802.*

Getting around The medieval centre of Durham can easily be negotiated on foot. All the main sights are located within half a square mile on the peninsula of the river Wear. In fact, Durham pioneered congestion charging in Britain with its £2 charge for cars using the town centre from Monday to Saturday 1000-1600. The paypoint is next to St Nicholas' church at the entrance to the market place. Durham Cathedral Bus no 40 runs from the Coach Park and train station to the cathedral via the Market Place, every 20 minutes Monday to Friday 0805-1725, Saturday 0905-1725, Sunday 0945-1645. Local buses run out to the university campus and Durham Art Gallery. **Traveline,** T0870-6082608.

Information Durham TIC ⓘ *Millennium Pl, T0191-3843720, www.durhamtourism.co.uk, Mon-Sat 0930-1730, Sun 1100-1600.* All the usual tourist information services, and during the season the visitor centre shows a short film about St Cuthbert called the 'Sacred Journey', on a giant screen.

History

A Saxon monastery was founded where Durham Cathedral now stands in 998. It was built around the church containing the body of St Cuthbert brought here three years earlier. He actually died in 687 but the miraculously preserved corpse of this father of the Celtic Church had been carried around the north for more than a century by monks from his monastery at Lindisfarne, fleeing Danish raiders in the ninth century. Apparently they found the sacred spot by following a dun cow. (The grey-brown ruminant is commemorated by a carving near the cathedral's east end and Dun Cow Lane.) A few years after the Conquest, the Norman emissary to Durham was slaughtered on arrival. When the Normans came back, their revenge was brutal, William himself overseeing the 'Harrying of the North', only complete in 1075. Walcher of Lorraine replaced the monastery with a Benedictine institution with monks borrowed from Monkwearmouth on the coast. Work started on the cathedral that stands today in 1093 and was all but complete – barring the towers – by 1140. Its first bishop, William of St Calais, introduced the French style in its architecture. He was the first of the so-called Prince Bishops, clerics with almost as many powers as the King, who ruled this virtual buffer-state between England and Scotland until the modern period. In the 19th century, Durham County became famous for its surrounding coal fields until the closure of most pits in the late 20th century.

From the station, on high ground in the west of the city, after taking a moment to enjoy the view it's a 15-minute walk downhill over the river to the cathedral. The most direct route is also the best, heading down North Road past the bus station to pedestrianized Framwelgate Bridge. From here there are more fine views of the castle walls up above, before the steep climb up to the Market Place via Silver Street. As well as the grand Town Hall and Victorian covered market, the Market Place boasts a fine statue of Neptune, God of the Sea. The spire of **St Nicholas Church** at the entrance to Market Place is a useful landmark.

A right turn from here leads up Saddler Street towards the heart of the peninsula. Down to the left, Elvet Bridge slopes off across the river again to the Elvet district, the city's administrative centre with its classiest hotels, *The Royal* and the *Three Tuns*. Cobbled Owengate on the right again climbs the short distance up to Palace Green, the wide open lawn dividing cathedral and castle at the top of the hill.

Cathedral

ⓘ *T0191-3864266, www.durham cathedral.co.uk, Mon-Sat 0930-dusk (varies, phone for details), Sun 1230-dusk (varies, phone for details). The Cathedral's Treasures of St Cuthbert: Mon-Sat 1000-1630, Sun 1400-1630. £2.50, concessions £2.00, children 70p, family £6. Tower: Apr-Sep Mon-Sat 1000-1600 (last entry 1540), Oct-Mar Mon-Sat 1000-1500 (last entry 1440). £2.50, children £1.50, family £7. Monk's Dormitory: Apr-Sep Mon-Sat 1000-1530, Sun 1230-1515. £1, concessions 30p. Guided tours: mid-Apr-Sep Sat 1100, 1430 (also 1815 and Sun 1700 mid-Jul, Aug), late Jul-Sep Mon-Fri 1100, 1430. £3.50, concessions £2.50, children free.*

Durham Cathedral is the most superb Norman survival in England, a fact recognized by its designation as a World Heritage Site, but its striking position, remarkable state of preservation and sheer size are what make first impressions so immediately rewarding. A powerful statement of the authority of the Norman Conquest, this is still a place with presence. On the north door, the main entrance, hangs a replica (the original is in the Treasures of St Cuthbert Museum in the cloisters) of the Sanctuary Knocker, used by criminals and exiles seeking safe haven and passage to the coast.

Once inside, the eye is drawn down the long nave toward the round east window by the huge columns supporting the vault of the nave: this was the first church in Europe to be rib-vaulted throughout, its piers alternately rounded or clustered, the round ones decorated with geometric patterns. Approaching the high altar they spiral up towards heaven. Highlights of the interior, apart from the overall impression, include the **Galilee Chapel** at the west end, which contains the tomb of the Venerable Bede, (his *Ecclesiastical History of the English People*, written in the eighth century, long set the benchmark for early histories of the country); the tombs of the powerful **Neville family**; **Prior Castell's Clock**, an early-16th-century clock restored in 1938; the **Bishops Throne** in the choir, that of Prince Bishop Hatfield (1345-1381); the **Miners Memorial** in the nave; and beyond the Frosterley Marble Bar, marking the limit of

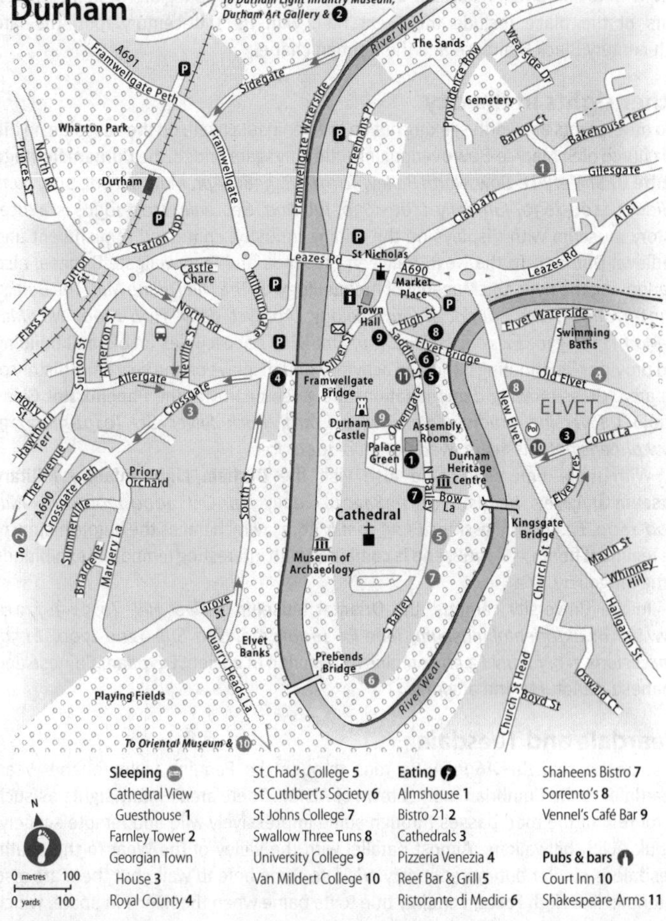

 women's permitted access to the monastic church, the **shrine of St Cuthbert** himself in the Chapel of Nine Altars. The shrine was demolished during the Reformation, and the saint now lies buried beneath a marble slab. South of the main body of the cathedral, the original monastic buildings clustered around the cloisters, built in the early 15th century. The monk's dormitory with its fine timber roof can be seen, although more interesting perhaps are the **Treasures of St Cuthbert**, a revamped exhibition of the cathedral's valuables, including a piece of the saint's coffin and some of the relics found inside. Look out too for the original **Sanctuary Knocker** and some extraordinary illuminated manuscripts. Finally, the views from the top of the **tower** on a fine day are well worth the modest charge.

Castle

Opposite the north side of the cathedral, a couple of hundred yards away across Palace Green, the **castle** ⓘ *T0191- 3743800, www.durhamcastle.com, Jul-Sep daily 1000- 1230, 1400-1630, Oct-Jun Mon, Wed, Sat, Sun 1400-1600, guided tours for about 40 mins. £3.50, children £2.50, concessions £3*, was started in the early 1070s, a key element in William the Conqueror's subjugation of the north. Although the arch of the gateway is original, additions and renovations to the whole castle were undertaken in the 19th century when it became the first college of the university. Like Oxford and Cambridge, **Durham University** operates a collegiate system. Guided tours of the place include the Great Hall, with its 14th-century roof, the late 17th-century Black Staircase and the Norman chapel.

Other sights in the city

Two other sights are worth seeking out on the peninsula itself: on the east side, in the old church of St Mary-le-Bow overlooking little Kingsgate bridge, the **Durham Heritage Centre** ⓘ *St Mary-Le-Bow, North Bailey, T0191-3845589. Apr, May, Oct Sat, Sun, bank holidays 1400-1630, Jun daily 1400-1630, Jul, Aug, Sep daily 1100-1630*, is a local history museum with displays on the mining industry, crime and punishment and medieval Durham. To the west, between Prebends and Framwellgate Bridges, also overlooking the river, the **Museum of Archaeology** ⓘ *The Old Fulling Mill, The Banks, T0191-3743623, www.dur.ac.uk/archaeology, Apr-Oct daily 1100-1600, Nov-Mar Fri-Mon 1130-1530, £1, concessions 50p, family £2.50*, occupies an old mill building and provides illuminating hands-on activities and displays on the very early history of the area. Glass-blowing demonstrations are given nearby at the **Phoenix Hot Glass Studio** ⓘ *Riverside Studios, 1-2 Fowlers Yard, Back Silver St, T0191-3847773, www.phoenixhotglass.com, Wed-Sat 1100-1600, free.*

With more time you could also visit the **Durham Light Infantry Military Museum** ⓘ *Aykley Heads, T0191-3842214, daily Apr-Oct 1000-1700, Nov-Mar 1000-1600, £2.50, concessions £1.25, family £6.25*, which traces the heroic history of the regiment from 1758-1968, and is combined with interesting temporary exhibitions in the art gallery.

In the University campus, the **Oriental Museum** ⓘ *Elvet Hill, T0191-3477911, www.dur.ac.uk/oriental.museum, Mon-Fri 1000-1700, Sat, Sun 1200-1700, £1.50, concessions 75p, family £3.50.*contains a collection of ancient Egyptian, Chinese and Japanese sculptures and artworks.

Weardale and Teesdale

West of the city, the A690/A689 runs through the Pennine valley of the Wear, Weardale, to the Cumbrian market town of Alston. There aren't many sights as such en route, but the road passes through some impressively wild and remote scenery, popular with hillwalkers. Almost parallel with the valley of the Wear to the south, Teesdale is similar but more touristy. Visitors come here to walk, but there are also waterfalls like **High Force**, certainly true to its name when the river's in spate, which draw in the punters. **Barnard Castle** ⓘ *T01833-638212, Apr-Sep daily 1000-1800, Oct daily 1000-1700, Nov-Mar Wed-Sun 1000-1600 (closed 1300-1400 all year), £2.50, concessions £1.90, children £1.30*, is the heart of the area, a fairly attractive market town dominated by the ruined fortification beside the Tees. Once one of the largest in England, it was the principal seat of the powerful Baliol family, who often held the balance of power between England and Scotland. The romantic ruins overlook the river, surrounded by acres of gardens, including a 'sensory' one.

A mile or so west of Barnard Castle, on the edge of town, the **Bowes Museum** ⓘ *T01833-690606, www.bowesmuseum.org.uk, daily 1100-1700. £5, £4 concessions, children free*, is housed in a Victorian French chateau purpose-built to show off the fine art collection of industrialist John Bowes. Antique furniture and ceramics surround an important array of Old Masters, including two Canalettos.

Beaches near Durham

East of Durham the black coal mining coast that featured to memorable effect in the cult Michael Caine film *Get Carter* has been so thoroughly cleaned up that locals hardly recognize it. The beaches around Easington Colliery now make for refreshing breezy walks but the area round about remains sadly depressed.

Sleeping

Durham *p797, map p799*

A **Royal County Hotel**, Old Elvet, T0191-3866821, www.marriotthotels.co.uk/xvudm. The first 'smart' option, conveniently situated but with a very corporate atmosphere.

B **Swallow Three Tuns**, New Elvet, T0191-3864326, www.swallowthreetuns.ntb.org.uk. A fully refurbished 16th-century coaching inn, comfortable but slightly characterless if less formal than the Marriot, with a good reputation for its food.

C **Cathedral View Guesthouse**, Claypath, 212 Gilesgate, T0191-3869566, www.cathedralview.com. True to its name from a couple of its rooms at l east, this is a comfortable B&B close to Millennium Place.

C **Farnley Tower**, The Avenue, T0191-3750011, www.farnleytower.co.uk. There is indeed a tower, but that's not the main feature of this friendly B&B, which provides comfortable accommodation on the western edge of the city.

C **The Georgian Town House**, 10 Crossgate, T0191- 3868070. Attractive building about 5 mins' walk from the market place, some rooms with views of the cathedral.

D **University of Durham Halls of Residence** late Mar-late Apr, Jul-Sep. B&B from £20 per person. For location try the **University College**, Palace Green, T0191-3743863, in the castle itself, or **St Johns College**, 3 South Bailey, T0191-3743598, next to the cathedral, or **St Cuthbert's Society**, 12 South Bailey, T0191-3743464, on the river in the crux of the bend, and **St Chad's College**, 18 North Bailey, T0191-3743364. Just outside the city, on the main university campus, **Van Mildert College**, Mill Hill La, T0191-3743900, is more modern and marginally more comfortable with a good canteen.

Eating

Durham *p797, map p799*

Thanks to the student population, there's no shortage of places to eat a lot very cheaply in Durham. Finding anywhere that sets its culinary sights a bit higher can be challenging.

££ **The Almshouse**, T0191-3861054. A very polite tearoom on Palace Green bang in the middle of town.

££ **Bistro 21**, Aykley Heads House, Aykely Heads, T0191-3844354. Probably the best mid-range option. It does good value English food in a cosy place, with set lunches for

For an explanation of the sleeping and eating price codes used in this guide, see the inside front cover. Other relevant information is provided in the Essentials chapter, page 40.

about £12, but it's some way from the centre, near the Durham Art Gallery and Light Infantry Museum.

££ Cathedrals, Court La, T0191-3709632. The former Durham city police station converted into a large airy restaurant with a bar on the ground floor and a bistro and restaurant above (about £15 for 3 courses).

££ Sorrento's, 16 Elvet Bridge, T0191-3864618. A reliable Italian restaurant, of the kind Durham does well.

££ Vennel's Café Bar, Saddler St, behind Waterstone's bookshop, up a little alleyway, is a popular and busy wholefood café.

£ Pizzeria Venezia, 4 Framwellgate Bridge, T0191-384 6777. Even more mobbed, an authentic family-run Italian.

£ The Reef Bar and Grill, Saddler St. A dive bar popular with law students but does very good Belgian beers and chips.

£ Ristorante di Medici, 21 Elvet Bridge, T0191-3861310. Another Italian joint doing pizza or pasta deals for £3, popular with students.

£ Shaheens Bistro, The Old Post Office, 48 North Bailey, T01913-860960. An accomplished and friendly Indian restaurant.

Pubs, bars and clubs

Durham *p797, map p799*

The Court Inn, Elvet, has a cult following with sporty students because of its filling grub.

Shakespeare Arms, Saddler St, T0191-3869709. An unbeatably authentic traditional locals' pub with very good beer.

Entertainment

Durham *p797, map p799*

Gala Theatre, Millennium Pl, T0191-3324041, www.galadurham.co.uk. Regular touring theatre productions.

Shopping

Durham *p797, map p799*

The Durham Indoor Market has almost 100 different stalls in a Victorian building on Market Place, T0191-3846153.

Farmer's markets every 3rd Thu of the month 0930-1530.

Mugwump, 37 Saddler St, stocks interesting gifts and costumes, one of a strip of shops on Elvet Bridge worth a browse.

Town Hall Craft Fairs every 4th Sat of the month, 0930-1630.

Activities and tours

Durham *p797, map p799*

Boating

Brown's Boathouse, Elvet Bridge, T0191-3863779. Apr-Oct daily. £2.50 an hr. Punts and rowing boats for hire on the River Wear. Great views from the river of cathedral and castle. Also 1-hr cruises on board the **Prince Bishop**, T0191-3869525. £3.50, children £1.50.

Transport

Durham *p797, map p799*

Bicycle

Specialist Cycles, within Meadowfield and District Soc, Frederick St South, Meadowfield, T0191-3783753.

Car

Enterprise Rent-a-Car Ltd, Enterprise Premises, Darlington Rd, Nevilles Cross, T0191-3868666; **S Jennings**, High St, Carrville, T0191-3846655.

Taxi

Direct Taxis, The Warehouse, Rennys La, T0191-3862002; **Pratts Taxis**, Maven House, Frankland La, T0191-3860700.

Directory

Durham *p797, map p799*

Internet Saints Bar, Chop House and Internet Café, Back Silver St, T0191-3867700.
Post office: 33 Silver St, T0845-7223344.
Hospitals **University Hospital**, Lancaster Rd, T0191-3332300. **Police** Durham Police HQ, Aykley Heads, T0191-3864929.

Northumberland

→ Colour map 7, grid A-B4

North of Newcastle and also embracing the best bits of Hadrian's Wall, the wilds of Northumberland are a remote haven for naturalists, historians and hikers. Still the least densely populated of English counties, from Alnwick to Berwick, the coast plunges in and out of the North Sea around rocky headlands, ruined castles and windswept fishing villages. Offshore, the Farne Islands support an extraordinary variety of seabirds, while Holy Island provided sanctuary for the early Celtic Christian church in the seventh century. Alnwick itself was recently voted by Country Life readers the most desirable town in the UK in which to live, going some way towards explaining the popularity of green wellies, working dogs and conservative attitudes throughout the county. Its castle is still the ancestral home of the Duke of Northumberland, and the gardens recently given a multimillion pound Millennium makeover by the Duchess. On the border with Scotland, Berwick-upon-Tweed has an embattled charm born of its deeply disputed history. Inland, much of the rest of the county is taken up with the Northumberland National Park, an ancient granite plug surrounded by mile upon mile of the kind of carboniferous limestone that forms the bedrock of Ireland. Recent campaigns by conservationists have encouraged the return of indigenous wild flowers and grasses across many parts of this beautiful moorland. ▸▸ *For Sleeping, Eating and other listings see pages 809-811.*

Alnwick and the coast

Walking or driving along anywhere between Alnwick and Berwick is a rare pleasure: few cars, fewer walkers and miles of superb empty beaches, though swimming and sunbathing are perhaps only for the hardiest. The coast unfolds a landscape of spectacular beauty, dotted with the country's finest selection of castles and home to a wide variety of birds and wild flowers. The long swathes of sand are punctuated by rocky promontories and quiet fishing villages that are gradually turning into quiet resorts and retirement homes as the fish disappear and, though not picturesque, they get on with the job as unobtrusively as possible. Out to sea, the Farne Islands promise prolific birdlife while across the causeway on Holy Island lies the bleak outpost that produced the vigorous flower of early English Christianity.

Ins and outs

Getting there Intercity and local **rail** services run along the mainline Edinburgh to London route, fast trains calling four times a day at Alnmouth, about 5 miles from Alnwick itself. Berwick (30 minutes), Newcastle (40 minutes) and Edinburgh (40 minutes). Newcastle has frequent trains from London (4 hours). **National Rail Enquiries,** T08457-484950. The A1 runs between Newcastle and Berwick while the scenic route hugs the coast more closely. Newcastle to Alnwick takes 45 minutes and Alnwick to Berwick the same again. To the southwest, the B3642 runs down to Rothbury, Hexham and The Wall and the B6346. **National Express,** T08705-808080, service X18 runs between Newcastle and Berwick, making a stop at Alnwick, also calling at Warkworth and Alnmouth for connections to the train.

Getting around **Arriva,** T0191-2123000, run a good if infrequent network of local buses along the coast. **Cycling** is very popular locally, and there are cycle routes in abundance along the flattish coast.

 Information Alnwick TIC ⓘ *The Shambles opposite the market place, T01665-510665, 0900-1700 Mon-Sat, 1000-1600 Sun.* **Northumbria Tourist Board** ⓘ *www.ntb.org.uk*, has a wealth of tourist and orientation information.

Alnwick

This charming town quite simply has it all: a magnificent castle, cobbled streets, a breezy local welcome, spectacular views over the Cheviot Hills and bright, clean air. Though small enough to easily find your way around, Alnwick (pronounced Annick) wears its rich historical grandeur with grace yet is far enough away to avoid overcrowding even in high season. Elizabeth I felt sufficiently uncomfortable about the wealth of the Dukes of Northumberland and their distant estates centred round Alnwick that for many years the earl was forbidden to visit his lands on pain of death. Stroll round the market place and take in the characteristically ambitious new gardens laid out for the millenium when the sun shines, or lose yourself in the castle's palatial interior and enjoy the fast, good natured banter in one of the town's many pubs when the sharp northeasterlies blow through and you cannot help but notice the strong, almost feudal sense of pride and independence.

Sights

The **Castle** ⓘ *T01665-510777, daily end Mar-end Oct, 1100-1700 (last admission 1615), £7.50, £6.50 concessions, children free*, like its town, comes complete in medieval splendour with all the trimmings: imposing gatehouse, majestic lions and cobbled courtyards. It has been in the Percy family since 1309 and in active military use for the following 250 years, playing an important part in the incessant border wars. In the 18th century, the first duke – they had been humble earls until then – undertook the first of several rounds of restoration thereby making it into one of the grandest statelys on the circuit. After Windsor it is the largest inhabited castle in the country and there is certainly a luxurious if not royal feeling of grandeur about the place. Lofty state rooms with Adam interiors are hung with paintings by Canaletto, Van Dyck and Titian, high windows overlook a Capability Brown landscape, elegant cabinets overflow with Meissen in the dining room while the library boasts one of the finest collections of books in the country. Watch out for Harry Potter fans on pilgrimage to locations used in the film.

The **Alnwick Gardens** ⓘ *£4, concessions £3.50, children 16 and under, free but must be accompanied by an adult*, reopened in 2002 after a £7 million redig, were masterminded by the current Duchess. A monumental cascade takes centre stage, its fountains periodically erupting in great bursts while paths meander along the carefully planted beds in the walled garden above. The huge scale might initially seem stark but given time, the garden should grow into its own, delighting rather than overpowering the senses.

Book lovers and train enthusiasts will find rich pickings at **Barter** Books ⓘ *T01665-604888, www.barterbooks.co.uk 0900-1900 daily*, housed in the former Alnwick Station. Starting off in what was the ticket and parcel office, the bookshop has expanded down the platforms and through the waiting rooms, until it now covers over one-quarter of the whole station site. Over 8000 sq ft, 350,000 books, three miles of shelving and a model train that runs round the lot. Cakes, tea and coffee for the sore of foot or eye.

Coast from Alnwick

Alnmouth and Warkworth

The town's port at Alnmouth has a picturesque harbour which had a bustling trade with Norway, Holland and London during its heyday in the 18th century. Now it sits happily at the mouth of the River Aln welcoming holiday makers, walkers, hardy swimmers and cream tea enthusiasts with colourful warmth. A must for the die-hard bucket and spade brigade.

A 5-mile walk south along a beautiful stretch of sand will bring you to the small town of Warkworth, dominated by a particularly impressive **castle** ⓘ *T01665-711423, Apr-Sep daily 1000-1800, Oct 1000-1700, Nov-Mar 1000-1600 (closed 1300-1400), £3.20, concessions £2.50, child £1.70, family £7.70*, dating from the 14th century, proud on a hill above a bend in the River Coquet. Also owned by the Percy family, it's understandable that even they were unable to keep up two such establishments so close to each other. The unrestored ruins here, however, give a good idea of how a purely military castle gradually changed into a fortified house: note particularly the enormous fireplaces and spartan bed chambers. Its dramatic setting is put to good use in Shakespeare's *Henry IV*. It is also possible to visit **Warkworth Hermitage**, a mile up the river. Dating from the late 15th century, some say it was founded by a murderer atoning for the death of his brother, others by a warrior who was mourning the loss of his sweetheart. **Warkworth Church** also has a good interior despite its troubled early life: burnt to the ground by invading Scots as early as the 12th century, it was rebuilt and though it has a mixture of Norman, Gothic and Jacobean elements, they contribute to a pleasing whole.

Dunstanburgh Castle ⓘ *(EH), T01665-576231, Apr-Oct 1000-1800 daily, Nov-Mar 1000-1600 Wed-Sun, £2.20, children £1.10*. The ruins of this 14th-century castle sitting high above the waves on a rocky outcrop are among the most evocative and romantically positioned of any in the country. Built by John of Gaunt, it was fortified during The Wars of the Roses only to fall into disuse thereafter. Although only the gatehouse and some of the walls remain, the 30-minute walk up to the castle from Craster and the longer stretches beyond along the Bays of Embleton and Beadnell are richly rewarding whatever the weather. In fact, dark clouds and rain suit Dunstanburgh as diamonds would the Ritz. Golfers can admire the castle from the greens of the nearby course.

Bamburgh

Bamburgh's village green complete with pub, hotel, butcher, church, baker et al is quintessentially English and its pedigree is impeccable. In Anglo-Saxon times, it was the royal capital of the Kingdom of Northumbria and looking up at the **castle** ⓘ *T01668-214515, Apr-Oct 1100-1700 daily, £5, children £2*, its Norman keep still standing proud and its high walls crowning a magnificent natural fortress, you'll see why. The panoramic view from the top is knockout, sweeping in most of the coastline and a good deal of the beautiful country inland, though the chilly interior has little of interest except the comprehensive collection of **Victorian kitchenware** in its bare scullery.The village also comes with a towering Victorian heroine in the shape of **Grace Darling**, the brave daughter of a lighthouse keeper who rowed across stormy seas to save nine people from a sinking steamboat in 1838. The house of her birth has a small **museum** ⓘ *T01573-223333, free*.

Farne Islands

ⓘ *(NT), trips to the islands can be made throughout the year from nearby Seahouses, though the best 'birding' is to be had during the breeding season from May-Jul. T01655-721297, www.farne-islands.com, or the TIC near the pier T01655-721099 for other operators. £8, children £6 for a 1 hr 30 min tour. Landings all year round on Inner Farne and Staple Island (at captain's discretion in bad weather) an additional £4 for adults and £2 for children. Deep sea fishing and diving also available.*

These bare islands beloved of birds and hermits are one of the few places in the world where visitors can get so close to such a variety of breeding seabirds. As many as 28 species crowd on to the inhospitable rocks some 4 miles off the mainland, their numbers including an estimated 70,000 puffins, half a million fulmar as well as 3000-odd grey seals. Guillemots, razorbills, cormorants and shags jostle for space with oyster catchers and eider duck, known locally as Cuddy duck, after St Cuthbert who spent his dying days here in 687. A chapel commemorates the community of monks who lived here until Henry VIII's Dissolution when the tower on the island was briefly used as a government fort.

Lindisfarne

Low-lying Holy Island is a strange mixture: the beautiful isolated setting, the picturesque ruins of the priory and the island's legacy of inspired artistry sit at odds with the concerned, almost apologetic air and limp handshake characteristic of contemporary Christianity and the inevitable tourist trappings. Linger a while, however, and wander round when the crowds return to the mainland with the high tide and the island's graceful inspiration may return.

St Aidan established the first community here in the seventh century hoping that the isolated position would provide protection and inspiration for his monks. Invited by King Oswald of Northumbria, he arrived from Iona in 635 making the island a base for active conversion of first the northeast and then farther afield. It became a place of considerable scholarship, encouraging literacy and a flourishing of the arts. The Benedictine monks of Lindisfarne produced wonderful illuminated texts of which the Lindisfarne Gospels, with their interlaced patterns of intricate birds and animals are the most outstandingly beautiful. Dedicated to St. Cuthbert, the island's most famous hermit and reluctant abbot, they left with the monks who feared renewed attack in 875 and are now in the British Museum.

The Priory ⓘ *T01289-389200, www.lindisfarne.org.uk, daily, all year, 1000-1600, 1800 from Apr-Sep and 1700 in Oct, 1600 Nov-Mar, £3, children £1.75,* whose splendid Romanesque ruins stand today, was built in the late 11th century and run by a handful of monks from Durham as a branch house until 1537. The nave of the church is particularly impressive with the stark outline of its one remaining arch, monumental columns and towering west window. The **Visitor Centre** ⓘ *T01289-389244, Apr-Oct 1200-2000 daily, longer when tide suits, £4,* has a strong display and good introduction to the island's history while the 12th-century Parish Church of St Mary is also well worth a visit. Lindisfarne Castle, largely built with stone from the abandoned Priory in 1550, followed the local pattern of brief active service and lengthy decline until it was restored by Lutyens in 1903. It has a small walled garden by Gertrude Jekyll.

Berwick-upon-Tweed

→ *Colour map 7, grid A4*

Berwick's graceful bridges and elegant high street belie its tempestuous border past, at the height of which the town changed hands between Scots and English no less than 13 times, making it apparently second only to Jerusalem as the most fought over city worldwide. Its famous walls have stood the test of time, however, and the oldest of the three bridges, finished in 1624, was certainly built with law and order in mind. A traveller in 1799 remarked, "The sixth pillar separates Berwick from the county of Durham. The battlements at this pillar, higher than the others, are always covered with sods as a guide to constables and others in the execution of warrants for the apprehension of delinquents." Walking across today you may be hissed at by a swan dallying on The Tweed but otherwise passage should be uneventful, leaving you to enjoy the fine views and the prospect of a warm welcome on the other side.

Ins and outs

Getting there The A1 runs up the coast from Alnwick (30 minutes) and the south, passing through Berwick on its way to Edinburgh (1 hour). The A6105 takes you east to Kelso and Jedburgh. Intercity **train** services on the mainline Edinburgh (1 hour) to London

(4 hours 30 minutes) route stop frequently, local services are good to the north and south but you are poorly served if you're coming from Carlisle and the west. **National Express**, T08705-808080, **coach** from London (10 hours) also calls at Newcastle (2 hours) and Alnwick, before heading north to Edinburgh (1 hour 30 minutes).

Getting around **Arriva**, T0191-2123000, run local services to the south. Cycling is very popular locally, with cycle routes in abundance along the flattish coast.

Information **Berwick TIC** ⓘ *106 Marygate, T01289-330733. 0900-1700 Mon-Fri, 1000-1700 Sat.* Try **www.berwickonline.org.uk** for comprehensive local information, **www.northumberland.gov.uk** for the bigger picture.

Though nothing remains of the medieval walls begun by Edward II, the town's fine Elizabethan **walls** ⓘ *guided tours 1115 Mon-Sat, 1430 Sun*, were the most sophisticated that the 16th century could muster, built to an Italian design with protection from light artillery and gunfire in mind. However, as the Border Wars gradually became less ferocious, little dent was made in the 12 ft thick walls and you can still walk almost all the way round (1hr 30 mins). The medieval castle faired less well, though more from builders than soldiers, for the Border Bridge, the Parish Church and the Barracks are all built with its stone and it was finally demolished to make way for the 19th-century railway station.

The **Barracks** ⓘ *T01289-304493, daily 1000-1600 (1700, Oct, 1800 Apr-Sep), closed Mon-Tue Nov-Mar, £2.80*, designed by Vanbrugh, were the first purpose-built in England in answer to the people's protests at having soliders billeted on them. They now house a number of exhibitions including the Berwick Borough Art Gallery which includes paintings by Degas and Japanese 'Arita' pottery on loan from the Burrell collection in Glasgow.

Around Berwick

The rich, fertile countryside surrounding the town is worth exploring. It makes a modest contribution to the county's castle tally with **Norham** overlooking the Tweed 6 miles to the west, T01289-382329, and a smaller 14th century number, T01890-820332, in the pretty village of **Etal**, 12 miles to the south. Between the two, **Heatherslaw** is notable for its unusually healthy mixture of the industrial and agricultural: a **Light Railway** ⓘ *T01890-820244. £3.70, child £2.20, Mill, T01890-820338, Apr-Oct 1000-1800,* carries children and dedicated enthusiasts on the hour from 1030-1530, while the restored mill on the River Till still churns out flour, making delicious cakes and scones for the hungry. **Lady Waterford Hall** ⓘ *T01890-820524, Apr-Oct 1030-1730, £1.50,* in Ford has a remarkable schoolhouse commissioned by an enlightened Victorian marchioness, Louisa Anne, decorated with Biblical murals, featuring local people, flora and fauna.

Central Northumberland

Some of the most dramatic and beautiful moorland in the country stretches unspoilt from Hadrian's Wall in the south to the wide expanse of Kielder Water and the prominent peak of The Cheviot in the north. The return to less intense farming over the past 20 years has allowed many of the faltering species of wild flowers to return to strength, speckling the hillside with colour in May and June. The walking is exhilarating and inspiring whether you tackle the challenges of the famed Pennine Way or opt for something more gentle around Wooler or Rothbury. The paths are well-kept and clearly signed but a large scale Landranger Map or one of the more detailed walking guides is indispensable for a longer tramp. For the indoor bound,

 Chillingham and Cragside are well worth a visit, their wonderful gardens offering nature close at hand rather than the wilder scenery elsewhere.

Ins and outs

Getting there The A69 runs east-west along the south side of the park while the A697 borders the east going up to Wooler from Morpeth and the A68 comes from Jedburgh and the north. Minor B **roads** criss-cross the park but look out for the signs indicating military or MOD activity. **Bus** services are limited although the **National Express**, T08705-808080, coach from Newcastle to Edinburgh runs twice a day with stops at Otterburn, Byrness, Jedburgh and Melrose.

Getting around Walking is highly recommended for those without transport as the scenery is unparalleled and long waits likely at the infrequent bus stops. However, local service includes postbus from Hexham to Bellingham and **Arriva**, T0191-2123000, service 880. Also Newcastle to Rothbury via Morpeth once a day.

Information Ingram National Park TIC ⓘ *T01665-578248.* **Rothbury TIC** ⓘ *T01669-620887.* **Otterburn TIC** ⓘ *T01830-520093.* **Wooler TIC** ⓘ *T01668-282123.* Online at www.nnpa.org.uk, for more details on guided walks and other events throughout the year, and www.kielder.org

The National Park

Nearly 400 square miles of empty moorland, bog and rushing water make up the park, lying in isolated splendour on both sides of the border. Contested and viciously fought over in the Middle Ages, few villages prospered and those inhabitants who did not leave tended towards the more hospitable and easily defendable lowland areas. Aspiring romantics and the outward bound will find inspiration and challenges a plenty. The **Pennine Way** ⓘ *www.thepennineway.co.uk, includes details of accommodation and luggage taxi*, follows the border south from Kirk Yetholm, skirting the summit of The Cheviot, turning south at Byrness and proceeding down through Bellingham to Hadrian's Wall. **St Cuthbert's Way** ⓘ *www.stcuthbertsway.fsnet.co.uk*, follows the monk's 65-mile journey from Melrose Abbey in Scotland to Holy Island. For the less steely limbed, the 2-hour walk from **Bellingham up to Hareshaw Linn** has wonderful views as does the walk up to **Yavering Bell from Wooler** while getting to the top of **The Cheviot** and back will take about 4 hours all in, but do check with the Wooler TIC ⓘ *T01668-282123*, for weather conditions as low cloud and mist swoop down with unexpected speed.

The beautiful country around the wide open expanse of **Kielder Water** can seem bleak and austere in poor weather and is prone to intense midge activity from May to September making walks tough going unless there is a stiff wind or copious repellent to hand. The **Border Forest Park**, however, breaks up the moorland and offers riding as well as pleasing variety to the eye and as the most capacious man-made lake in Europe, the Water itself has the full range of fishing, boating, and other watersports available at **Leaplish Waterside Park** ⓘ *T01434-250312, www.kielder.org*.

Bellingham is a pretty town standing on the North Tyne river and makes a good base for touring the surrounding country. You'll find thorough descriptions of good walks, and cheap guides for sale, at www. shepherdswalks.co.uk, T01670-774675, while www.birdwatchnorthumbria.co.uk arranges birding for the novice watcher. The post-walk bath will undoubtedly benefit from the plant oils and organic herbs that go into the handmade goodies from **The Natural Soap Shop** ⓘ *T01434-220548*. The 12th-century **church** here is particularly fine with its stone roof consisting of hexagonal ribs overlaid with stone slabs. Medievalists may want to visit the **Percy Cross Memorial** commemorating the Battle of Otterburn (1338) where Harry Hotspur fought a moonlit battle against a Scots raiding party led by Earl Douglas.

To the east, **Rothbury** is unremarkable except for the Victorian mansion of **Cragside** ⓘ *(NT), T01669-620333, 1030-1900 Apr-Oct, house only in the afternoon, closed Sun*, built by the pioneering engineer Lord Armstrong who used it as a place to test his engineering theories, giving the house a worldwide first in the hydro-electric light stakes. The Terraced Garden contains an Orchard House and restored 19th-century clock tower.

Wooler is a good base for walking but otherwise unrewarding although **Chillingham Castle** ⓘ *T01668-215359, www.chillinghamcastle.com, daily 1200-1700 Jul and Aug, Wed-Mon May, Jun and Sep, £4.50, children free*, to the southeast is delightful. Dating from the 12th century, it has been in the hands of the Grey family since 1245 and been lovingly and imaginatively restored by its current owners. An impressive, eclectic collection complements garden, state rooms, dungeons and torture chamber. The handsome **Chillingham Wild Cattle** ⓘ *T01668-215250, Apr-Oct 1000-1200, 1400-1700 Wed-Sun, afternoons only*, roam in the park where they have done so for the past 700 years, isolated from other herds and rarely touched by human hand. Their remarkable endurance and nobility may be due to the fact that the fittest and strongest bull becomes 'King' and the leader of the herd. He remains so for just as long as no other bull can successfully challenge him in combat, and has the pleasure of siring all the calves that are born, thus ensuring only the best available blood is carried forward. Winner, as they say, takes all.

Sleeping

Alnwick and the coast *p804*

C **The White Swan**, Bondgate Within, T01665-602109. The dining room here has been kitted out with the ceiling, stained glass and panelling from the *Titanic's* sister ship, the *Olympic* though the rooms upstairs are very much au style touristique.

D-E **The Georgian Guest House**, Hotspur St, T01665-602398, GeorgianGuestHouse@eggconnect.net Very good value accommodation close to the castle.

Self-catering

Holiday cottages available for week bookings in summer, weekends Nov to mid-Mar from the Duke of Northumberland's Estate Office, T01665-510777.

Coast from Alnwick *p804*

A **Waren House**, in Budle Bay, T01668-214581, www.warenhousehotel.co.uk For the full country house hit.

C **The Warkworth House Hotel**, Bridge St, Warkworth, T01665-711276, www.warkworthhousehotel.co.uk. Comfortable and welcoming.

C-D **The Blue Bell** in Belford, T01668-213543, www.bluebellhotel.com Less grand but welcoming and comfortable. Handy for Holy Island and the Farnes without being in Seahouses which is a large bonus.

D **Burton Hall** in Bamburgh, T01668-214213. A good B&B.

D **The Famous Schooner**, Alnmouth, T01665-830287. Jolly and hospitable.

D **The Lindisfarne Hotel**, T01289-389273, The one to go for if you want to stay on Lindisfarne.

Berwick-on-Tweed *p806*

A **Marshall Meadows Country House Hotel**, just outside Berwick, T01289-331133, www.marshallmeadows.co.uk. Caters to the well-heeled with a Victorian manor house, croquet lawn and fishing. Restaurant and bar.

C **The Cobbledyard Hotel,** 40 Walkergate, T01289-308407. More modest, though friendly.

C **The King's Arms Hotel** in Hide Hill, Berwick, T01289-307454. 20 individually furnished rooms in an old coaching inn which has a warm welcome.

For an explanation of the sleeping and eating price codes used in this guide, see the inside front cover. Other relevant information is provided in the Essentials chapter, page 40.

D **Clovelly House** in West St, T01289-392952. Popular B&B.

D The Estate House, T01890-820668, theestatehouse@supanet.com, offering dinner and a bed.

D Ford & Etal Estate, T01890-820647 hayfarm@talk21.com.

D Ladythorne House in Cheswick, T01289-387382, www.ladythorneguesthouse.freeserve.co.uk. A stylish B&B option.

D Mill Lane Apartments at 2 Palace St East, T01289-304492 have flats for the self-catering.

Central Northumberland *p807*

B Otterburn Tower Hotel, T01830-520620, www.otterburntower.co.uk. Pull the stops out at an old country house with 3 stars, known for its food, with 17 bedrooms.

C The Percy Arms Hotel, Otterburn, T01830-520261. As it sounds, an old-fashioned charmer on the edge of the National Park.

B Riverdale Hall Country House Hotel, Bellingham, near Hexham, T01434-220254. Decent rooms with a good fish and game restaurant. Self-catering also a possibility.

C The Tankerville Arms Hotel, Cottage Rd, Wooler, T01668-281581, www.tankervillehotel.co.uk A similar style and offers fishin', shootin' and even huntin' though covers its back with a good vegetarian menu.

D Bridgeford Farm, Bellingham, T01434-220940.

D Mrs J A Scott, Kielder. A contender for national best, wowing visitors year in year out with her hospitality and breakfasts, T01434-250254.

D Lee Farm B&B, near Rothbury has a warm heart, T01665-570257, www.leefarm.co.uk.

E The New Moorhouse, T01665-574638, www.newmoorhouse.co.uk. A definite cosy option.

Self-catering

C Ridd Cottage, sleeps 6 from £500 a week and has been well-kitted out, T0191-2533714, www.northumberlandcottageholidays.co.uk.

D Chillingham Castle, T01668-215359. If you want to indulge in a bit of medieval fancy then book a suite here.

D Conheath Farm Cottages sleep 5 from £230 per week upwards, T01434-220250, www.conheath.co.uk.

D Dunns Houses, Bellingham, T01830-520677, www.northumberlandfarmholidays.co.uk Pets welcome, stable facilities for horses and has fishing.

Eating

Alnwick and the coast *p804*

Alnwick's drawbacks are few but chief among them is the limited range of good places to eat. Some visitors might also find the approach to Sat nights overenthusiastic or downright basic depending on preference.

££ The Wine Cellar Café Bar, in Bondgate Within, T01665-605264, has light meals.

£ Tanners Arms in Hotspur St for standard bar fare.

Coast from Alnwick *p804*

££ Blue Bell, Belford, T01668-214581, have good bar food as well as à la carte.

££ Waren House, Budle Bay T01668-214581, is more upmarket and good if expensive.

£ The Jolly Fisherman, Craster, T01665-576218. Great for some of the local kippers.

£ Royal Victoria Hotel in Bamburgh, T01668-214431. The standard fare at the .

£ The Ship in delightful Low Newton by the Sea is a good stop off for coastal walkers and beachcombers.

Berwick-upon-Tweed *p806*

££ Foxton's Restaurant and Bar, Hide Hill, T01289-303939, acceptable Mediterranean food.

££ St Magnus Restaurant, 25 Main St, T01289- 302925, reasonable meals.

££ Tillmouth Park, T01890-882255. Impressive though confidently priced.

£ The Market Shop in the High St. Great if the sun is shining and you fancy a picnic.

£ Barrels Ale House, Bridge St, T01289-308013, good, no-frills menu.

£ The Black Bull, in Etal, T01890-820200. Popular and impressive.

£ Cannons, 11 Castlegate. For fish and chips.

Central Northumberland *p807*
Most of the villages in the area sport at least one if not two pubs with food improving steadily albeit from a lowly threshold. As elsewhere in the county, gourmets should head for the smarter hotels (see above) or pack rocket and parmesan with their wellies.
££ The Blackcock Inn, Falstone, T01434-240200, will stoke you up for walking or wind you down in the evening.
££ The Cheviot Hotel, Bellingham, T01434-220696. Perfect for a hearty steak or lasagne.
££ The Coquet Vale Hotel, Rothbury, T01669-620305. For good filling fare.

Entertainment

Alnwick and the coast *p804*
Alnwick Playhouse, Bondgate Without, T01665-510785, www.alnwickplayhouse.co.uk, has a variety of performances, good concerts, interesting exhibitions of local work and panto in season.

Berwick-upon-Tweed *p806*
The Maltings Theatre and Arts Centre, T01289-330999,
www.maltingsberwick.co.uk, has an eclectic mix of film, drama, music and exhibitions.
www.berwickonline.org.uk, and www.northumberlandtoday.co.uk, have comprehensive listings for the area as does the local press.

Festivals

Alnwick and the coast *p804*
The town has 3 major annual events.
Jun Alnwick Fair The week-long festival begins on the last Sun.
Aug The Alnwick International Music **Festival** features traditional musicians and folk dancers from around the world and begins on the first Sat
Nov The Northumberland Gathering, a day of traditional music competitions and events is held.

Berwick-upon-Tweed *p806*
Aug Given the town's history, the **Berwick Military Tattoo** in the last weekend in Aug is the chief highlight.

Activities and tours

Alnwick and the coast *p804*
Boating
Sea trips and general information can be had from the TIC and The Estate Office T01665-510777.

Fishing
Fishermen will find inspiration at **The House of Hardy**, 4 miles to the south on the A1, T01665-510027, and, appropriately kitted out, will find fly, sea and coarse fishing available. 0900-1700 Mon-Sat. The River Aln has some fishing while the River Coquet to the south is stocked and managed by the **Northumberland Anglers Federation**, T01670-787663.

Walking
Walkers not tempted by the bigger challenges of The Cheviot and surrounding hills should head for Hulne Park on the outskirts of town but check with The Estate Office for opening times.

Shopping

Berwick-on-Tweed *p806*
There is a **market** in Marygate on Wed and Sat, and a **farmers' market** on the last Sun of each month.
Bridge Street Bookshop at no 41, has an excellent local history and literature range.

Central Northumberland [illegible]

Most eating venues in the area [illegible] one or two pubs will [illegible] the [illegible] the [illegible] for the [illegible] and [illegible] the [illegible]

The Blackcock Inn, Falstone [illegible] will [illegible] walking [illegible]

The Cheviot Hotel, Bellingham [illegible]

The Queen's Head Hotel [illegible]

Entertainment

Alnwick and the coast

Alnwick Playhouse [illegible] (T [illegible]) [illegible]

Berwick-upon-Tweed

The Maltings Theatre and Arts Centre

T [illegible]

[illegible] film, drama, music and exhibitions [illegible]

Festivals

Alnwick and the coast

[illegible]

Aug: The Alnwick International Music Festival [illegible] from around the world [illegible]

Nov: The Northumberland Gold [illegible] day of traditional music, song and dance, is held.

Berwick-upon-Tweed

Aug: [illegible] Military Tattoo [illegible]

Activities and tours

Alnwick and the coast

Boating

[illegible]

Fishing

[illegible] House of Hardy [illegible] south on the A1 (T 01665 510027) [illegible] Northumberland Anglers Federation [illegible]

Walking

Walks [illegible] the Cheviot [illegible]

Shopping

Berwick-upon-Tweed

[illegible] market [illegible] farmers' market [illegible]

Bridge Street Books [illegible] local history and [illegible]

Background

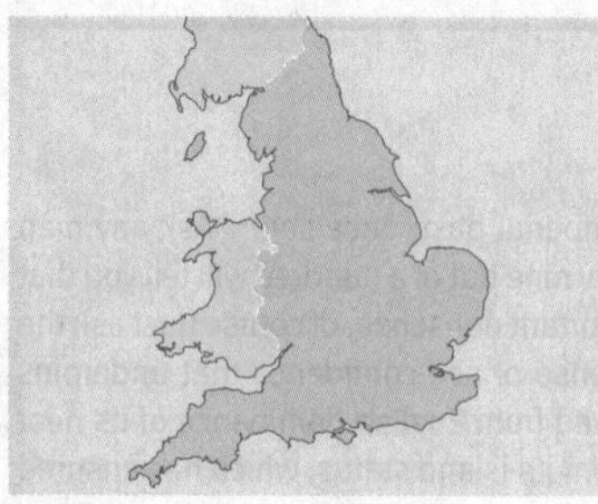

History

Cecil Rhodes, one of the icons of Britain's imperial past, once said: "Ask any man what nationality he would rather be, and ninety nine out of a hundred will tell you that they would prefer to be Englishmen." Self important nonsense, of course (just ask the Scots, Welsh or French), but it reflected a sense of self-confidence that underpins much of English history. Much of this is derived from English dominance of its near neighbours, Wales and Scotland, and also from its island status, which has ensured its borders are easier to defend. That is not to say that these shores have not been breached. Indeed, to the English, invasions are a source of some ambivalence. Only two have been 'formally' successful (the Romans in AD 43 and the Normans in 1066), but many others have tried – the Spanish in 1588, and the Germans in 1940 to name but two. Indeed, resistance to attempted invasions are among the nation's proudest moments. Nevertheless, while England may pride itself on repelling the foreign hordes, it has consistently received, and generally welcomed, immigrants. The English are a colourful mix of Celts from the Danube, Saxons from northern Europe, Scandinavian Vikings, Jews, Afro-Caribbeans, those from the Asian Subcontinent and more recently, refugees from civil wars in Africa and the Balkans. Naturally, throughout England's history, there has been some resistance, talk of being 'swamped', of foreigners taking 'our' jobs and not fitting in. In time, however, all groups have been assimilated, such that in a generation or two it is sometimes they who complain about the arrival of new people from abroad. After all, England, and later Britain, has had Danish, Norman, French, Welsh, Scottish, Dutch and German sovereigns. And the current monarch, Elizabeth II, who speaks the Queen's English with such clarity, is of course from the House of Saxe-Coburg-Gotha (codename Windsor) and married to a Greek. Like so many of her subjects, she represents an immigrant family that has adapted to the culture and changed their name to boot. And, in that respect, she is quintessentially English.

Early settlement

The human colonization of Europe took place during the Ice Age, when Britain was still linked to mainland Europe. Human remains, from *homo erectus* (800,000 years ago) to our more immediate ancestors, *homo sapiens* (40,000 years ago), have been found in Boxgrove on the south coast and Swanscombe, Kent, now the bastion of middle-class respectability, but then the home of hirsute creatures wielding clubs. The remains of exotic wildlife, such as elephants, hippopotami, giant beavers and sharks have all been uncovered in the more hospitable lowlands of southeast England. The Neolithic age witnessed bands of hunters wandering the country in search of food, and it wasn't until some 6000 years ago, long after the seas had finally swallowed up England's link to mainland Europe, that Stone Age hunters began to settle. Clearings were formed, crops grown, homes built and stone tombs erected to house the dead. Wayland's Smithy, just off the Ridgeway to the west of Wantage, is one of the most impressive of a clutch of Neolithic and early Bronze Age settlements to be found scattered around the Marlborough Downs; West Kennet, Wiltshire, is one of the largest.

Bronze Age folk lived in thatched roundhouses, and immigrant groups such as the Beaker Folk (so-called because of the distinctive beakers found in their barrows and tumuli in Wiltshire) brought new and relatively sophisticated knowledge of bronze metalwork. They also transported huge bluestones to Stonehenge (from Pembrokeshire in South Wales) which formed the second stage of the building of the megalithic structure. Stonehenge was built over three stages from the early Bronze Age in around 2500 BC through to 1500 BC in the late Bronze Age. The purpose of the monuments is still disputed (although its links with the summer solstice are surely more than coincidence), but they are undoubtedly the work of a society of spiritual and some technological sophistication.

The Iron Age

The Celts were new settlers from Central Europe, a striking people, tall, fair-haired and blue-eyed. They began to arrive around 800 BC, easily achieving supremacy over the existing (primitive) residents. They settled in farmsteads and villages, caring for livestock and working the patchworks of fields that they established. Although much of England had already been cleared of its ancient forest by then (historians have recently suggested that the population of Iron Age Britain – the Iron Age ran from about 1500 BC through to the arrival of the Romans in the first century AD – was almost as large as the population under Elizabeth I), there was still ample woodland in which to hunt boar and other wildlife. Aside from the farmsteads, large hill-forts dotted the countryside: Danebury in Hampshire and Maiden Castle in Dorset, the capital of the large Durotriges tribe, are notable examples which survive to this day. Such forts, sometimes built with up to eight lines of defence against attack, were arranged in 'streets' and housed workshops, granaries and shrines as well as extensive accommodation. As the centuries passed small tribes merged to form larger regional tribes: the Iceni flourished in East Anglia, the Catuvellauni lived around present-day London and the Brigantes in the north. At the head of each tribe was the king, and below him lay three-tiers of society. The nobles were the warriors, relied upon to defend the land. The druids, the Celts' priests, teachers and administrators, were also drawn from the noble's class, and reinforced the role of the supernatural in their human sacrifices, charms and incantations. The masses, as ever, propped up the whole structure. While Celtic society demonstrated some skilled metalwork and hardy farming, violence and death were ever-present. Not only were there tribal skirmishes between warriors painted in bright blue woad, but the druids practised human sacrifice.

The Romans

Tales of the extent of England's natural resources, not to mention the ferocity of its warriors, would have reached Roman ears long before they began to invade her shores. At first these sorties were tentative. Under Julius Caesar (in 55 and 54 BC), the Romans landed briefly, struck deals with one or two local chiefs and returned to Gaul. In AD 43, however, Emperor Claudius determined to annex the island for himself, partly for its metal deposits, and partly to finally rout the remaining Belgae who had retreated to England after their recent defeats in Gaul. Therefore the 40,000 Romans who arrived at Richborough in Kent ensured that any resistance from the beleaguered Belgae was cursory. For the most part, in fact, the local Kings were open to negotiation and where that failed, to a combination of threats and rewards. There were exceptions: Caractacus, the King of the Catuvellauni, resisted for nine years, and was eventually pardoned such was the Romans' admiration for his courage and tenacity. Later, Boudicca, Queen of the Iceni and to this day a potent symbol of British courage and tenacity, led an army against the Romans in East Anglia. She managed to lay waste to the Roman strongholds of Colchester and London, before finally taking her own life by means of poison when all seemed lost (probably somewhere around present-day St Pancras Station in London). However, while her fortitude and success was a dent to the image of Roman invincibility, she had not always been a die-hard rebel. Her husband the King had been happy to co-operate with the Roman invaders and it was only when a newly arrived Governor tried to make slaves of the Iceni people, in the process killing the King and having her daughters raped before her eyes, that Boudicca turned rebel.

Despite the occasional hiccup, and the occasional dagger-happy governor, Britannia, as the Romans named the island, became a largely peaceful place. What had worked elsewhere across their dominions also seemed to work here, as the Empire began to reproduce its tried and tested systems. Towns emerged, bigger, grander and altogether more sophisticated than those devised by the Celts; road networks spread across the country; water systems were created, and trade with the rest of the Empire flourished. As the decades passed, a Romano-British society began to be established. Towns such as Bath, with its fabulous spa (still in existence today), Chichester, Colchester, St Albans and London grew to be major Roman towns. Local bigwigs adopted the Roman tradition of building villas in the countryside – Fishbourne Palace in Sussex, Woodchester in Gloucestershire and Rockbourne in Hampshire, all of which retain some of their fine mosaics, attest to this. Tribes in the northern lowlands and highlands such as the Scots (originally from Ireland) and the Picts (from Scotland) were an occasional irritation, such that in the second century the Roman Emperor Hadrian was prompted to build a wall from the Solway to the Tyne. Hadrian's Wall is still largely intact today. Although the 8 foot thick, 15 foot high wall clearly served a military purpose, it soon also became a magnet for trade, with the several forts along its length serving as much as a customs posts as military fortifications. Towards the end of the Roman occupation (the last legions left in AD 409) several forts were built along England's south and east coasts, as raids on its cities by German pirates became frequent. The remains of one such fort are still visible in Richborough, Kent, while the Roman wall around Londinium is still visible at various points.

The Dark Ages

It was only when the Roman Empire began experiencing trouble closer to home near Rome, and the legions were called away, that the Roman presence in Britain began to diminish. As the Romans left, so the Germanic migrants such as the Saxons and the Angles became more frequent intruders, and when Rome was finally sacked in AD 410, and the last two legions had left, England welcomed a new arrival.

The newcomers were a motley crew: predominantly Saxons from the mouth of the Rhine, Angles from Germany and Jutes from Denmark. These tribes settled across much of England, with the names of a number of modern English counties bearing this out. The South Saxons settled in Sussex, the east Saxons in Essex, and the West Saxons in Wessex (a name no longer used on maps, but recently revived by the Prince Edward, Earl of Wessex). The new immigrants did not, however, manage to spread to the western extremities of the island. A small proportion of Romano-British society had fled to Devon and Cornwall and remained loyal to the banner of Ambrosius Aurelianus, an aristocrat of Roman descent. There Ambrosius and his followers built an earthen barrier from Wiltshire to Berkshire which succeeded in keeping out the Saxon hordes. Ambrosius' successor, according to legend, was Arthur, he of the Round Table and the castle of Camelot. The true genesis of Arthur and the Arthurian legend is still something of a mystery. The Welsh have claimed him for their own (with some justification), the 12th century Frenchman Chretien de Troyes is credited with the Round Table and Camelot story but actual historical records throw little light on the matter. There is some evidence of a courageous and noble warrior in the southwest of England who fought 12 (victorious) battles against the Saxons. In further support of this, Cornwall, in the southwest tip of Britain, remained a Celtic stronghold, relatively untroubled by the Saxon invaders until well into the 9th century. Some say that Arthur was born at Tintagel, a Cornish coastal settlement and a rare but fine relic of an early sixth-century royal centre. Whatever the true facts of Arthur's life and death, his legend lives on. Successive poets have made the Arthurian tales of love and heroism their own, from Edmund Spenser with his *Faerie Queene* through to Tennyson's *Morte D'Arthur*. Composers such as Parry and Elgar have exploited the story and the Pre-Raphaelite painters of the 19th century repeatedly used the tale for artistic inspiration. More recently, comedians such as Monty Python have capitalised on the enduring strength of the Arthurian legend with their film *Monty Python and the Holy Grail*. Those seeking a taste of Camelot today should consider a visit to Cadbury Castle in Somerset; for Avalon take the road to Glastonbury, and for the Round Table look no further than Winchester castle (where there is indeed a Round Table, probably built for Edward I). Regardless of the historical accuracy of the tales, there is no doubt some truth to be found, and plenty of embellishment to be enjoyed.

Anglo-Saxon England continued to take shape through the sixth and seventh centuries. The towns tended to be abandoned in favour of a more rural life, and although some urban centres did emerge (Southampton and Ipswich, for example), even London saw the population shift to outside its city walls. Meanwhile, archaeological digs of the burial mounds at Sutton Hoo in East Anglia give some insight into seventh-century life. The ship and the wealth of precious objects from all over Europe that were uncovered – French coins, Byzantine plates – indicate that trade was widespread, while the sheer opulence of the items and the amount of armour suggest that this was the burial site of an Anglo-Saxon king (probably King Raedwald).

Gradually, three kingdoms began to emerge across England – Northumbria in the north, Mercia in what we now call the Midlands, and Wessex in the south. In 597, another crucial event in England's history took place: St Augustine was consecrated Bishop of the English and given permission to build a cathedral at Canterbury. Christianity was not new to England (the three previous centuries had known Celtic Christianity) but at the Synod of Whitby in 664, it was decided to follow the Church of Rome, and move away from the Christianity advocated by Celtic missionaries such as St Aidan, the founder of the monastery on Lindisfarne. Such a decision was to define English Christianity for the next nine hundred years or so, until Henry VIII's rejection of papal authority in the sixteenth century. The seventh and eighth century not only saw the shaping of the spiritual heart of the country, but also the emergence of a fine literary tradition, including the illuminated Lindisfarne gospels (the *monastery was Romanised by St Cuthbert after the Synod), the poems of Caedmon and the Ecclesiastical History of the English Peopl*e by a monk from Jarrow, the Venerable Bede.

While Northumbria had dominated the seventh century, and Mercia the eighth, the ninth century saw the supremacy of Wessex. As Anglo-Saxon influence was spreading, England was visited by one of the age's most advanced and belligerent forces, the Danish and Norwegian Vikings ('viking' means plundering). This 'great heathen host', colonisers of Iceland and Greenland, and early discoverers of America, brought with them skilled metalwork, advanced and adventurous seafaring skills, exotic goods such as amber and furs and lyrical tales told in their poetry sagas. They also brought with them death and destruction. As Alcuin of York observed after a raid on the city in 793: "Never before has such an atrocity been seen ...the church of St Cuthbert is spattered with the blood of the priests of God, stripped of all its furnishings, exposed to the plundering of pagans." In time, the Vikings destroyed the Saxon kingdoms in the north and east, and the raids turned to invasion and settlement.

The rampaging Vikings were threatening to overthrow even the Saxon kingdoms of the south and west until the arrival of Alfred, King of Wessex, in 878. This Saxon king is best known for burning the cakes of an old lady in Somerset, but his achievements are of much more lasting importance. Not only did he co-ordinate resistance to the Vikings, and force them to confine their interests to the northeast of England (a region then known as Danelaw), but he also built over the ruins of Roman London to re-establish the city as the hub of country. He constructed a fleet, which helped divert later Danish invaders towards Normandy for easier game. He repaired pillaged churches, brought over foreign scholars, founded schools for the nobility, translated Bede and began the compilation of the Anglo-Saxon Chronicle, a forerunner to the Domesday Book of 1086.

By the time of his death in 900, Alfred had been proclaimed king of all England not under Danelaw. Alfred's epithet, 'the Great' was only accorded him several hundred years later, when historians saw the significance of his reign to the formation of an English state. However, when the fledgling state envisioned by this act was finally realised is open to debate. Certainly the early Anglo-Saxon settlers have long been seen as the fathers of the English nation, but when this nation came into being is unclear. Some might argue that it preceded Alfred, when at the dawn of the ninth century, Egbert, King of Wessex, subdued the Celts in Devon and Cornwall, defeated the Mercians in battle, and so nominally became the first King of England (even though subsequent Viking invasions to disrupted the hegemony). Others trace it back to 886 when Alfred captured London and made peace with the Danes, as the treaty made mention of "all the English race". Or was it one of Alfred's grandsons? Athelstan introduced a single currency and by 937 had succeeded in commanding respect as a single king from a land populated by Norsemen, Danes and Saxons from Northumbria, Wessex and Mercia. His successor, Edmund, was accepted by both the Saxon and Danish settlers and proclaimed the first King of the English. Certainly after Edmund's reign, even though the country now called England was ruled by Kings from many countries in Europe, and there were several disputed successions, it was never again divided between competing monarchs.

The ensuing decades saw England's population grow, and the English and the Danes learning, for the most part, to co-exist in relative harmony. The English shires and counties began to take shape, and local justice was implemented by a royal appointee. Ethelred the Unready, so called because of his clear unsuitability to rule anything, anywhere, lost his throne to the Viking Cnut when his ill-judged tax regime tested even the heartiest of Saxon loyalists. Even under King Cnut (he who tried to stop the advance of the waves), when England was part of a Danish Empire that also incorporated Norway, the country thrived in relative peace. King Cnut changed very little, and employed Anglo-Saxons, such as Earl Godwine (father to Harold II, who lost an eye, his life and his throne at the Battle of Hastings), as advisers. Cities such as Winchester, Ipswich and Southampton grew as important centres, and London continued to prosper. York, or Jorvik, became the second largest city, a thriving Viking settlement busy with textile production, glassworks and metallurgy, and conducted a healthy trade with Ireland and Scandinavia.

Medieval England

Cnut's sons allowed the Danish Empire to collapse, so in 1042 Edward the Confessor (son of Ethelred the Unready) became king of an independent England. A religious recluse, Edward's greatest achievement was to build a palace on Thorney island in London with a church, the West Minster, nearby. Both are still in existence today and are better known as the Palace of Westminster and Westminster Abbey. Edward died childless in 1066 and the succession was initially won by Harold Godwinson, Earl of Wessex. However King Harold's accession was not undisputed. While Harold was up at Stamford Bridge near York defeating his brother Tostig and another claimant to the throne, the Norwegian King Harald Hadrada, he received word of another invasion, this time from France in the form of William the Bastard of Normandy. The English king marched his exhausted battle-weary army swiftly south to meet the Normans, who had landed at Pevensey Bay. The historic Battle of Hastings ensued, fought on a field near the coastal town of Battle, on 14th October 1066. It famously saw not only Harold killed, shot through the eye by an arrow, but also the death of about half of England's noblemen and came to be known by the Normans as 'senlac', or 'the lake of blood'.

So William the Bastard became William the Conqueror. A domineering, temperamental and tremendously strong man, he ruled England with uncompromising efficiency. Any resistance to William, mainly centring round York and Ely, was dealt with swiftly and without mercy. The few remaining English nobles were deprived of their lands, which William then bestowed on his followers. As William of Malmesbury wrote a few decades later: "It is the habitation of strangers and the dominion of foreigners. There is today no Englishman who is either earl, bishop or abbot." The feudal system was formalized and strengthened, a sheriff represented the king in every shire and, to ensure that every penny was eked out of his subjects, a thorough survey was conducted of all the manors in England. This survey, which came to be known as the Domesday Book, has left historians with a remarkable picture of 11th-century England. It tells us that in 1086, half the cultivated land was owned by only 170 barons, of which fewer than five were English, and that the church owned over one third of the country. By 1087, William had established a new England, one whose Norman legacy remains to this day in every aspect of our lives from our surnames to our architecture to the fact that the monarch still uses Norman French when formally passing parliamentary legislation.

Having secured England as his own, William set about fortifying his position. Some 90 castles were built during his reign and it was under William that the wooden motte and bailey castle was replaced by stone buildings. The most notable is the White Tower, part of the Tower of London, but others such Corfe in Dorset, Arundel in Sussex (one of a number along the south coast), Hedingham (Essex) and Warwick Castle in the Midlands are among those that still stand in some form of ruin or repair. These strongholds became the administrative centres and often the focal point of a town. They served to oversee and defend a baron's lands, acted as a home for the local magnate, as a store for winter fuel and food and accommodation for the local servants and horses.

William also reorganized the church, placing his own supporters in key posts and making his own choice, Lanfranc, Archbishop of Canterbury. Norman churches and cathedrals were built in the new Romanesque style. Two particularly good examples can be found at Iffley village near Oxford and at Ely Cathedral. The status of the church grew, as it formed both the spiritual and often secular hub of the community. Saints days dotted the calendar, and religious relics drew worshippers on pilgrimages. Chaucer's Canterbury Tales are told by pilgrims on their way from London to Canterbury to pay homage to the murdered Archbishop of Canterbury, Thomas à Becket. It is alleged by Edward Grim that in 1170 Henry II's henchmen severed the crown of Becket's head "so that the blood white with the brain and the brain red with blood, dyed the surface of the virgin mother Church with the life and death of the confessor and martyr in the colours of the lily and the rose."

The church also served as a valuable centre for education in the country. Every cathedral provided a school, and around the beginning of the 13th century both Oxford and Cambridge Universities emerged from the schools set up by local orders. Benedictine, Carthusian, Franciscan and Cistercian orders built and maintained monasteries and nunneries, farming the land around while promoting a holiness and level of education not always in evidence among the parish priests. In areas such as Yorkshire, where the Cistercians were particularly strong, several monasteries existed relatively close by each other. The ruins of Jervaulx, Byland, Fountains and Rievaulx Abbey in North Yorkshire give some idea of the layout of a monastery – the church, the refectory, kitchen, infirmary, dormitory and library, all set among a series of cloisters (Fountains and Rievaulx are particularly spectacular).

Meanwhile trade flourished, as England began to establish itself as one of the foremost trading nations in Europe. Agriculture dominated the medieval economy, with the hamlets and villages sustained by the fields around them and each family owning two or three strips. London continued to grow, as, according to William fitz Stephen, "from every nation under heaven merchants delight to bring their trade by sea". The East Anglian wool trade became the foremost business in the southeast, if not the country, such that Norwich became England's second city after London. Towns such as Saffron Walden in Essex, and the size and majesty of some of the region's churches reflect the wealth that the cloth trade afforded the area.

England, along with the rest of Europe and much of the world, also endured the Black Death, the bubonic plague of 1348-9 that wiped out whole communities and just under a half of the country's population. Plague outbreaks in 1361 and 1369 further decimated population levels. Wages rose steadily, and the worker began to enjoy his new-found position of (relative) autonomy. The Peasant's Revolt of 1381 led by Wat Tyler and Jack Straw was a show of strength made by an emboldened workforce. The fact that Wat Tyler was executed by the Mayor of London after being guaranteed safe passage merely goes to show that the medieval feudal order ultimately prevailed.

The politics of medieval England followed the predictable course of family feuds leading to dynastic struggles and civil wars; expansionist ambitions triumphantly achieved and then rudely interrupted or tragically lost; and an eclectic mix of wise and successful policies or glamorous disasters and ignominious defeats. When William the Conqueror's second son, Henry I, died childless in 1135 there was civil war between two of William's grandchildren, Stephen and Matilda, when the castles, according to the English Chronicle, were filled "with devils and evil men". It was Stephen who ultimately triumphed to become king in 1135.

During the course of the 12th century a sense of political autonomy was slowly but steadily growing among the body of royal advisers and it was these figures who would eventually emerge as a parliament. Matters came to a head under King John whose insensitive, bullish threats against the barons led to what is considered to be one of the greatest watersheds in English constitutional history. The Magna Carta, foisted on the king by aggrieved barons and signed at Runnymede in Berkshire in 1215, attempted to outline what the monarch was and was not allowed to do. In short, it established the principle that the monarch was not above the common law but subject to it. Later that century, in 1264 when the commoner Simon de Montfort won the Battle of Lewes, England briefly flirted with republicanism as a parliament of knights and noblemen presumed to discuss the fate of the country's King and Prince (Henry III and Edward I to be).

This was also an era of almost continuous conflict with France. The Angevin dynasty, as Henry II and his Plantagenet successors came to be known, hailed from Anjou in France. With the lands from his marriage to Eleanor of Aquitaine, Henry II controlled more of France than his supposed feudal overlord, the King of France, as well as most of England and Wales. For the next three hundred or so years, England and France were involved in battles over the empire, culminating in the 100 Years' War (1337-1453) and the attempts by Edward III and his successors to realize their claim to the French throne. The later medieval period was taken up with the Wars of the Roses, a 30-year war between the house of Lancaster, whose emblem was a red rose, and the house of York, whose emblem was a white rose. It was only in 1485, after the infamous reign of Richard III (York) made famous in the Shakespeare play of the same name, that the war was resolved by the quiet determination of Tudor King Henry VII.

Reformation and Renaissance

In the wake of the Wars of the Roses came one of the strongest dynasties of the early modern period. The Tudors were of Welsh origin, but in the language of the Roses, Henry Tudor, who plucked the crown from the thorn hedge at Bosworth Field in 1485, was a Lancastrian. And a particularly wise one at that, for one of his first acts was to marry Elizabeth of York, and so unite the two houses – the Tudor Rose (a red and white rose, one of the earliest examples of propagandist design) still decorates many ceilings and doorways of Tudor buildings. Henry VII's reign, however, was largely uneventful, certainly compared to those of his successors, and marked only by the peace and security he brought to England, both militarily and financially. So when his son Henry VIII succeeded to the throne, he had at his disposal a broadly united England and full coffers with which to posture abroad, a bountiful wealth of which he took full advantage. This was the era of Renaissance man, when the French and English kings and the Habsburg ruler, Maximillian I, were young virile men vying to assert their diplomatic, and if necessary, military might in Europe. In 1520 Henry and Francis I of France met in the Field of the Cloth of Gold to negotiate, a meeting so outrageously opulent (Henry arrived at the tented city with an entourage of 5000), that it has gone down in history. This was at least a peaceful encounter, whereas the Battle of the Spurs in 1513 (which helped establish Henry's military skill), and later broadsides in the 1540s incurred significant human and financial costs (the Mary Rose, now on view in Portsmouth, sank as it left port to engage with the French navy in 1545). After all, the English still held Calais, and enduring dreams of once again extending the kingdom across the Channel.

One of the defining features of the Tudor dynasty was the religious rollercoaster that England endured through the 16th century. Desperate for a male heir and clearly besotted with his pregnant mistress Anne Boleyn, in 1532 Henry VIII was determined to divorce the ageing Catherine of Aragon and marry her. The Pope, however, would not annul Henry's marriage to Catherine, so in 1534 Henry engineered the Break with Rome, rejecting papal authority and declaring himself head of the church in England. And so was born the Anglican church, the Church of England. Nevertheless, although this followed hard on the heels of the emergence of the Lutheran (Protestant) church in Germany, England could not be said to have fully embraced the Protestant cause, but more to have developed a form of English Catholicism. Indeed Henry's motives were as much economic and political as spiritual. For with the break came the opportunity for him to claim all the monasteries and their lands as his own. The Dissolution of the Monasteries, as it came to be known, was an enormous boost to the royal coffers (much in need due to several costly and ineffectual forays abroad), allowing Henry to exploit the enormous wealth of the church. Monasteries and abbeys were torn down and their lands sold off or given to deserving followers; in some cases the buildings remained but were put to other purposes or simply fell into ruin (Henry himself took possession of Hatfield House in Hertfordshire, previously the grand residence of the Bishop of Ely) and churches were stripped of their more extravagant iconography.

After Henry VIII's death in 1547, England wavered in its religious direction. The child king Edward VI (he was nine when he came to the throne, 16 when he died) and his 'protectors' Somerset and Northumberland, departed from the Catholic way, introducing two new Prayer Books whose sympathies undoubtedly lay with the Protestant side. Edward soon died, however, and Mary I, daughter of Catherine of Aragon and a devout Catholic herself, set about restoring the 'true faith' to England, encouraged by her long absent husband, Philip II of Spain. Her methods were simple and direct, causing the death of over 400 heretics in five years, most notably the Oxford martyrs Cranmer, Latimer and Ridley, who were burnt at the stake in what is now Broad Street. (Her attacks on the heretics earned her the epithet 'Bloody Mary'; yet another piece of effective Protestant propaganda from the later 16th century.)

When Mary I died in 1558, the country's religious direction hung in the balance. Elizabeth I adopted a wise course. Although she didn't pursue her Protestant religious convictions with the aggressive zeal displayed by her elder sister, she observed enough of a Protestant line to prompt the Pope to excommunicate her in 1570. Elizabeth maintained that she did not want to make 'windows into men's souls', and it was only when a Catholic rebellion threatened, as with the Rising of the Northern Earls in 1569 or the Armada in 1588, that she was punitive of her Catholic subjects. (Jesuit priests were another irritation for the establishment – pursued by the government, many Catholic nobles hid them in 'Priest holes' in their houses.) By 1603, when James I (James VI of Scotland) came to the throne, it could safely be said the monarch sat firmly at the head of a Protestant Church of England.

The Early Modern period was also the age of the playwrights Marlowe and Shakespeare, and the emergence of the Elizabethan theatre. In 1576 James Burbage opened The Theatre in Shoreditch, London, which was later moved outside the City's jurisdiction to south of the Thames near the brothels and the bear-baiting pits on Bankside, and renamed the Globe. The Tudor monarchs built palaces by the hatful: Bridewell, Richmond, Nonsuch and Hampton Court were among the 55 new residences built by Henry VIII alone (Hampton Court was initially commissioned by Henry's chief adviser Thomas Wolsey). As the court had to move with the monarch, these palaces and great houses needed to be large enough to accommodate both courtiers and the royal household. These 'progresses' around the country by the monarch and the royal household were one way of maintaining a visible presence – Elizabeth I would ride through the countryside either in a carriage or in a litter. She added the wily trick of inviting herself to the grand homes of her rich courtiers and staying a while, thereby keeping their wealth, and so their power, in check. Great houses were built, such as Loseley Park near Guildford, Chatsworth in Derbyshire (one of Elizabeth I's favourites) and Burghley House in Lincolnshire (built by Elizabeth's adviser, William Cecil Lord Burghley). Some, such as Hardwick Hall in Derbyshire, were 'more glass than wall', while whole or half-timbered houses like Rufford Old Hall and Speke Hall in Lancashire were typical of the period. In central London, both Henry VIII (and later James I) extended the palace at Westminster, where Inigo Jones built the magnificent Banqueting Hall in which many Jacobean feasts were held. In the arts, Hans Holbein was employed by Henry to promote the grandeur of the Tudor dynasty in his portraiture; Elizabeth continued the practice, commissioning a number of portraits brimming with allegorical significance that spoke of her magnificence. Later, Charles I accumulated one of the greatest art collections in Europe, and welcomed Anthony van Dyke as his court painter. Although during Elizabeth's reign some significant explorations to the New World took place, with Raleigh and Drake attacking the Spanish Indies, and bold attempts at founding a settlement in the Americas, by Elizabeth's death in 1603, England had no permanent settlement overseas. Over the next two and a half centuries, however, England and Britain would become the most powerful, and widespread, imperialists in the world, with an Empire stretching to across the globe.

Life for ordinary people in Tudor England, however, was considerably less lavish. Over the course of the 16th century prices rose hugely in excess of wages, and the growing practice of enclosure hurt the land worker further still. Not only did he lose some of the common land (the landowners often pinched some in the process of enclosing), but if the landowner then changed from arable to livestock, there were fewer job opportunities. With the growth in unemployment, so the poor became an increasing feature of daily life. Under Elizabeth some attempt was made to provide for the 'deserving' poor – those who were considered genuinely in need – but the others were readily dismissed as rogues. There were as many as 24 categories – cranks, foisters, vagrants and vagabonds (often branded as such with a 'V' upon the forehead), Abraham men or Tom O'Bedlams (who pretended to be mad), and a host of other conceits that consigned them to the stocks, lashings or even hangings. For those with some economic stability, albeit a limited one, the year revolved around the demands of the seasons. Towns held market days – a focal point for local trade, travelling fairs or troops of actors might pass through the local town, and on May Day there was dancing round the maypole. Some pastimes were less quaint. 'Football', wrote a Puritan in 1583, 'is more like a friendly fight than a game! Sometimes necks are broken – or backs, legs or arms. Noses gush with blood'. Cudgel-play involved belting your opponent with a wooden stick until he bled, and grand meetings such as the Cotswold Games, to which all and sundry would travel, included stick-fighting and shin-kicking. Animals, naturally, fared even worse, with cock-fighting and bear-baiting common.

Revolution and Restoration

The Stuart dynasty began inauspiciously. On his progression down to London from Scotland James VI of Scotland, now James I of England, was so generous with his knighthoods that he devalued the honour's status (sirloin is supposed to be a reference to his enthusiasm to knight anything, even a piece of meat). and when he first addressed Parliament his accent, the fact that his tongue was too big for his mouth and his propensity to dribble, caused consternation among his English subjects. Nevertheless, despite his penchant for extravagant masques and elegant young men in tights such as George Villiers, 1st Duke of Buckingham, James restored some control to royal expenditure after the expensive wars of Elizabeth's reign, and earned himself the ambiguous title of 'the wisest fool in Christendom'.

Regrettably, however, he did produce Charles I, an arrogant and impatient man whose reign was sharply curtailed by the executioner's axe. Charles was impatient of parliament, who ever since Elizabeth's reign had made growing demands of their monarchs. After all, they were the principal collectors and payers of tax, and yet they had no say in the disastrous and costly foreign policies pursued by their kings. In addition, the members of the House of Commons wished for more say in the choice of advisers made by the king – again with a view to avoiding costly policies that would ultimately hurt their pockets. Charles, however, was impervious to their demands, considering them to be both impertinent (he believed in the Divine Right of Kings, whereby he was answerable only to God) and unjustified. In 1629 he dismissed parliament, and resorted to a series of outdated laws to raise the funds he needed. When financial desperation forced him to recall parliament in 1640, he was met with a barrage of demands. And when he broke into the House of Commons to arrest some of its members, the Speaker nailed his colours to the Parliamentary mast: "I have neither eyes to see nor ears to hear except that which this house commands me". This sounded the death knell for the monarch's authority over parliament, and Civil War seemed inevitable.

The English Civil War of the 1640s was a revolutionary period in England – "the world turn'd upside down" as an anti-radical pamphlet of the time described it. Families were split in two, some supporting the Parliamentarians (the Roundheads, so called because their hair was closer cropped than the longhaired Cavaliers, or 'swaggerers'), and others remaining loyal to the King (the Cavaliers), with brother fighting brother, and families never speaking again. The battles themselves (many in Buckinghamshire and Oxfordshire), saw the emergence of the first truly organised and trained army, the New Model Army, under the leadership of Oliver Cromwell. This Cambridgeshire MP, who went on to lead the English Republic, was a strong-willed man of Puritan beliefs, and was notorious for his less than glamorous look – the expression 'warts and all' derives from Cromwell's directions to his portrait painter. "That sloven...hath no ornament in his speech", spoke one Buckinghamshire MP, "but that sloven, I say, if we should ever come to a breach with the king, in such a case, I say, that sloven will be the greatest man in England." Indeed, when the crown finally fell, along with Charles I's head in 1649 ("there was much scrabbling for the king's blood"), it was Oliver Cromwell who succeeded as Lord Protector.

Cromwell's rule was not particularly distinguished. His puritanical streak ensured that some traditional religious practices were outlawed and entertainment was frowned upon – the celebration of Christmas was 'banned', many alehouses were closed, actors were "whipped till their bodies be bloody" and bear-baiting was banned not, some say, because it was cruel to bears, but because humans enjoyed it. Radicalism and non-conformism, however, flourished, although without the approval of the Protectorate. The Levellers, a quasi-political sect of Puritans, demanded universal suffrage and religious tolerance and were a foretaste of later radical thinkers. They were imprisoned in and finally shot down outside St John the Baptist church in Burford, Oxfordshire – the bullet-holes and some graffiti remain visible – and they are still celebrated today by socialist radicals. The Diggers believed that the land belonged to everyone, and so began farming where they chose. To his credit, Cromwell did allow the Jews to return to England – they had officially been expelled in 1290. All sorts of other non-conformist groups emerged, all broadly under the Puritan banner – Millenarians, Baptists, Muggletonians, Independents, Seekers, Calvinists, Presbyterians and Fifth Monarchists. George Fox formed the 'Children of Light', later to become the Quakers; while the Ranters shocked contemporaries with their liberal attitudes to dancing, smoking, drinking and sharing sexual partners. Of more lasting consequence was Cromwell's attempted suppression of Ireland, and particularly his laying waste to Drogheda and Wexford, attacks that left thousands dead. Of all the British or English injustices against the Irish (and to Republican eyes there are many), the Cromwellian abuses still serve as one of the most potent rallying cries.

It is indicative of the ambivalence with which many of the English, including some Parliamentarians, viewed the Protectorate that it was a cause for celebration when Charles I' son was invited to take the throne in 1660. Diarist Samuel Pepys recorded that in London "at night there were more bonfires than ever. Bells were rung and the King's health was drunk", and England could once again rest easy in the comfort blanket of the monarchy. Cromwell's head was exhumed and placed upon the top of Westminster Hall, there to remain for a further 25 years. The first years of Charles II's reign were not uneventful. In 1664 the bubonic plague once again spread throughout the country. Outbreaks of plague were not uncommon, but only the Black Death of the 14th century matched the ferocity of this visitation. Aided by hot weather and the narrow, dirty streets, whole towns and villages were wiped out, and cities such as London lost almost half its population over the next 18 months. Bells were rung through the streets of London once again, this time by corpse-bearers, and accompanied by the cry 'Bring out your dead' Charles moved the court to Oxford to avoid its ravages, but others were less fortunate. In the small village of Eyam in Derbyshire, the disease arrived with a flea trapped in a parcel from a tailor in London (the county was largely free of the disease when the first casualty in the village was recorded). Instead of a mass exodus of the village, the vicar and residents decided to protect their neighbouring communities by closing off Eyam to all and sundry. No one was allowed to leave, and food and supplies were left on boundary stones at the edge of the village. It was a brave act, through which only a few members of the village survived.

Hard on the heels of the Great Plague was the Great Fire of London in 1666, a fire that began in a bakery in the city, but that ended up destroying much of the capital and driving the inhabitants either to the high ground of Hampstead or onto the river. In the aftermath of this Charles considered several plans for the rebuilding of the city. Some favoured a grid system, but the traders and dealers of the Square Mile could not afford to stand idly by while Charles pondered, and so the pre-fire city street pattern was largely re-established. One lesson had been learnt, however – out went the timber-framed houses that had burnt so readily, and architects favoured brick or stone buildings. Furthermore, one of the greatest English architects of all time left his mark on the city. In the weeks that followed, as the embers died on the city's streets, Sir Christopher Wren could be seen pacing and measuring any number of his magnificent churches. Greatest of all was St Paul's Cathedral, a Protestant church to match the grandeur of the Catholic St Peter's in Rome. It dominated the London skyline in the 18th century (it wasn't completed until 1710) in a manner unimaginable today, but it is the smaller Wren churches pricking the City's skyline that also bear witness to his genius. He designed 25 in as many years, and is also responsible for the Royal Observatory, Greenwich, Greenwich Hospital and the Sheldonian Theatre in Oxford.

As both an astronomer as well as an architect, Wren was invited to join the Royal Society, a club founded by Charles II whereby a number of intellectuals were brought together to discuss the 'Advancement of Natural Science'. The diarists Samuel Pepys and John Evelyn, physicist Robert Boyle, philosopher John Locke and Sir Isaac Newton were among its members. England's first scientific journal was produced, and with the help of Newton's advanced telescope and Robert Hooke's extensive use of the microscope, scientific understanding grew. Meanwhile Charles was also a great patron of the arts. Theatres reopened, palaces were refurbished and parks laid out. He played pall mall, an Italian version of croquet, in the park alongside St James's Palace in London. Milton wrote both Paradise Lost and *Paradise Regained*, Dryden polished off *The Pilgrim's Progress*, and when in 1679 the Ashmolean Museum was founded it could claim to be the first museum in the country. After the austerity of Cromwell's Protectorate, some semblance of vitality and colour was returning to English society.

Cromwell had made adultery a capital offence, a law that would challenge the population of any society, but would certainly have seen the early demise of Charles II. Charles had several illegitimate sons, but none by his wife Catherine of Braganza, so when he died his brother James assumed the throne. James II was a Catholic, set upon restoring the faith to England, so when he fathered a boy in 1688, several of the powerbrokers of the time invited the Protestant (and Dutch) William of Orange, married to James's daughter Mary, to take the throne. Despite some resistance in Scotland, and a battle at the Boyne in Ireland in 1690 still provocatively celebrated in Northern Ireland today, the Glorious Revolution was largely bloodless. William and Mary had to sign a Bill of Rights confirming the rights and authority of Parliament (for instance, parliament had to be called every year, not on the monarch's whim), and although the Crown retained significant powers, parliament ensured that it would play an ever-present role in government.

Enlightenment

The 18th century was largely the domain of the German monarchs. After the brief reigns of James's daughters Mary II and Anne, Britain (since the Act of Union with Scotland in 1707, it now was Britain under the symbolic flag, the Union Jack) was ruled by the Georges from Hanover. Over the next 100 years Britain emerged as the greatest power in the world. Her dominance of the seas was emphasised by the threefold increase in her trading fleet over the course of the century while her colonial possessions extended to several West Indian Islands, bases in India such as Bombay and Calcutta, and in time control of Canada was wrested from the French. Trade flourished, as the colonies absorbed some 40% of British produce, and she grew fat on the wealth created by the slave trade. Bristol and Liverpool were particular beneficiaries of this as the ports bulged with goods exchanged for slaves in the West Indies or Americas. Furthermore, while the 13 colonies were lost to American Independence in 1782, in 1770 Captain Cook raised the Union Jack at Botany Bay to claim Australia. The country's population also grew almost two-fold by 1800, by which time London could claim to be the largest city in the world. With the growth in towns came a more urban-based existence, even for those with wealth. Spa towns developed – Buxton, Tunbridge Wells, and of course Bath, became favoured venues. Town planning shifted from the narrow streets of Tudor and Stuart England to bold brick terraces in squares and crescents – witness the work of John Wood, senior and junior, designers of the Royal Crescent and Circus in Bath. Towns also built their own theatres and assembly rooms for dancing; coffee houses, clubs and race-meetings became favourite meeting places for an increasingly open society.

This was also the age of enlightenment. Grand piles were erected by those who benefited from the new found wealth. Blenheim Palace, later the birthplace of Winston Churchill, was built as a royal reward to the Duke of Marlborough, and was so colossal as to prompt Alexander Pope to write "tis a house but not a dwelling". Other houses such as Castle Howard, Chiswick House or Stourhead all reflected the English interest in the Baroque and Palladian styles, influences brought to this country by the growing popularity among the wealthy for doing the 'Grand Tour' of Europe. While Continental styles were fashionable in England, the exchange of ideas and influence wasn't simply one-way. Lancelot 'Capability' Brown, a self-taught landscape gardener, revolutionised the private gardens and parks of the landed gentry and royalty. Uprooting the formal gardens so favoured by the French, and by-passing the classical allusions introduced by William Kent (his masterpiece still exists at Rousham in Oxfordshire), Brown introduced sweeping lawns, lakes, and clumps of trees, usually covering hundreds or thousands of acres. British artists also earned reputations abroad. Portraits by Joshua Reynolds and Thomas Gainsborough captured the aspirations of the wealthy, as did the equine portraits by George Stubbs, and the world of music celebrated works by George Frederick Handel ('Zadok the Priest' from the Messiah, has been sung at every English coronation since the accession of George II in 1727), and welcomed residences from Haydn and Mozart. The century saw the publication of Pope's *Rape of the Lock*, Defoe's *Robinson Crusoe*, Johnson's *Dictionary* and the first edition of the *Encyclopaedia Britannica*. Chippendale produced wonders with wood, Wedgwood with clay, and the first cast-iron bridge was erected at Coalbrookdale. Meanwhile many sports established administrative centres that still exist today. The MCC was founded in 1787, over 30 years after the Jockey Club and the Royal and Ancient Golf Club in St Andrews. Equally long-lasting, but for many more spiritually uplifting, was the work of John Wesley, who travelled the land preaching twice a day 'to promote vital practical religion' and established the Methodist Church. Furthermore, although Britain was firmly immersed in the slave trade, in 1772 it was determined that a slave became free on entering Britain – Olaudah Equiano fought for the abolition from England having achieved his own freedom. This was consistent with the country's healthy tradition for political debate and protest – whether economic theories as proposed by Adam Smith or political philosophies explored by Thomas Paine, Edmund Burke and Mary Wollstonecraft. In the early 19th century reformer Jeremy Bentham and anti-establishment radicals William Cobbett and Robert Owen were among those who articulated the increasing popular discontent over the lack of parliamentary and labour reform.

The period saw the emergence of an urban society. In Tudor and Stuart times England had remained a largely rural economy, but with the scientific revolution came industrial innovations that boosted the economy. While the Industrial Revolution as we now know it was yet to fully take off, the country's manufacturing and industrial base grew decade by decade, burgeoned by new inventions and better communications. Textile production was aided by inventions such as John Kay's flying shuttle and James Hargreaves's spinning jenny, and James Watt's steam engine provided a more efficient source of power. Stephenson's Rocket speeded communications, while the rivers and new canals linked the major ports of England – Hull, Bristol, Liverpool and London. Improved (private) roads called turnpikes allowed for goods and people to travel around the country with greater efficiency and speed: carriages, and later the canal network, improved communications enormously. Journeys that at the beginning of the century took three days, say from London to York, could by 1800 be completed in 24 hours. Home industry was slowly replaced by factories and workshops, as villages became towns and towns became cities billowing unhealthy smoke. Towns such as Birmingham, Sheffield, Leeds, Derby and Manchester became the home to small steel-making and metalworking industries. In agriculture new machinery revolutionised farming techniques, and increased yield. The smaller landowners were bought out by the large landowners, so rendering more labourers without the security of their own patch of land. Many agricultural labourers, therefore, moved to the towns in search of work, further inflating the growing urban population. The peak of worker exploitation and misery was yet to come, but such were the conditions by the end of the 18th century that protests and uprisings were not unheard of. The Luddites broke machines in factories across Nottingham, Leicester, Lancashire, Cheshire and Yorkshire as a protest against the replacement of workers with new technology, and by 1829 such protests had spread throughout the country. Added to this were concerns over low wages, but the employers and authorities response was unsympathetic: hundreds were sent to prison and hundreds more transported to the Australian colonies. In 1834 some farm labourers in the village of Tolpuddle in Dorset were transported for trying to organise a union, a court ruling that earned them martyr status in labour history, such that they are celebrated to this day.

England of the 18th century inspired various responses from abroad. Much of British society was the source of admiration – the strength of the social structure, reiterated through the education system, was envied by countries such as France, not least as their revolution took hold in the latter part of the century. Meanwhile Britain's imperial expansion provoked mixed responses. It became the source of friction and brief wars with France, as the two European powers sought to assert their ascendancy over trading posts in places as far afield as Jamaica, Canada and India. Indeed, as the new century dawned, Britain found itself at war with Napoleonic France, as the Emperor tried to expand his empire within Europe and beyond, and threatened an invasion of Britain. Meanwhile, those from colonial stock began to resent the rule of their mother country, most notably in America, where the colonists fought for independence, finally achieving their goal in 1783.

Industry and Empire

The accession of Victoria to the throne in 1837 signalled the beginning of a golden age for Britain, one in which her wealth and influence grew further still and her pre-eminence throughout the world was assured. The Empire expanded into Africa and established a firmer and more lucrative grip on Asia, such that by 1900 it spread so far and wide across the globe that the 'sun never set on the British Empire'. In fact, despite the abolition of slavery in the colonies in 1833 (£20 million had to be paid to compensate the slave owners), her trading outlets were as healthy as ever. The Great Exhibition of 1851, laid out in a sparkling Crystal Palace in Hyde Park in London, displayed the triumph and achievements of 'the workshop of the world'. The thousands of exhibits included the latest agricultural and industrial technology, as well as fine arts and exhibits from abroad (the Chinese stand was particularly popular). It attracted millions, and was considered by Victoria "the happiest, proudest day of my life", on account of her beloved husband's (Albert) significant contribution in its organization.

Seaside resorts became reachable for a day trip – the Observer reported in 1856 one beach to be "so crowded with ladies and gentlemen that it is difficult to walk through the throng" and the water to be "black with bathers". Blackpool (its famous tower was built in 1894), Scarborough and Broadstairs were among the most popular venues, where the beaches were dotted with donkey rides and Punch and Judy shows and lined by promenades to give walkers the sea air. Business was good enough to encourage Thomas Cook to start a travel business; by the end of the century he was offering holidays in the Holy Land and Egypt. Music-halls were popular evening venues, as was the pub, where "the adult male population gathered every evening, to sip its half-pints,... and to discuss local events, wrangle over politics or farming methods, or to sing a few songs". The upper classes would shoot on the estate or, as the century drew to a close, enjoy a spot of motoring; for others it might simply be 'ratting' or going to the local fair or the travelling circus. This was also a blossoming age of children's stories, whether Rudyard Kipling's *Jungle Book*, Robert Louis Stephenson's *Treasure Island*, Anna Sewell's *Black Beauty* or Lewis Carroll's *Alice's Adventures in Wonderland*. Towards the end of the century Sherlock Holmes, the ultimate sleuth, began to prowl the streets of London, while Bernard Shaw's and Oscar Wilde's plays dominated the theatres of the West End of London.

Inventions transformed life across the country with the railway, the telephone, the automobile and the postal service allowing for the quicker and freer movement of people and information. Double-decker buses were introduced into towns in the 1850s, the electric tram in the '80s, and the underground in London in the 1860's. The iron and steel industry benefited from new inventions that revolutionized production, fuelled by the extensive coal mines of the north of England and south Wales. Many feats of engineering and architecture still exist today – bridges, such as the Clifton Suspension Bridge near Bristol, railway stations, such as St Pancras in London, seaside piers, countless school buildings, and much of the railway network. Despite the rapid industrialisation across the country, agricultural also enjoyed a boom from the 1850s. The growing urban population needed feeding, and so farmers made huge profits. Farm labourers, however, reaped little reward, and many still sought work in the cities as new farm machinery, such as the steam-powered thresher, took their jobs. In medicine anaesthetics, antiseptics and vaccinations began to reduce unnecessary infections and pain, while Florence Nightingale gave nurses a professional and respected role in society.

As the industrial revolution took hold, cotton mills spread across Lancashire and woollen mills in Yorkshire. Towns such as Manchester underwent a rapid transformation, tripling in population in the space of 30 years. The Prime Minister, Benjamin Disraeli described it as a "modern Athens" as it grew and adapted as a textile centre. Factories and warehouses sprang up alongside the canals and railways; municipal buildings were built to cope with the civil and commercial administration of a growing town. With the lively business came the lively mind – the Manchester Guardian newspaper (now the Guardian) was born here in 1821, as was the first lending library and many radical political and educational movements. But there was the less glamorous side too. Smoke hung over the city, slum areas developed, such as 'Little Ireland', and the rivers were open sewers. The middle-classes moved out to the surrounding villages, and the town began to swelter in its own smoke-riddled population boom.

As Manchester's growth illustrated, all these symbols of wealth and power hid a harsher side to Victorian Britain, those Victorian values that people are less keen to remember. This was an age of extreme poverty for some, where slums and back-to-backs lined the streets beneath unhealthy clouds of soot. Open drains emptied into the rivers which in turn fed the water-pumps. In Leeds (where row upon row of back-to-back houses still exist) the River Aire supplied the city's drinking-water. The river was 'fed' by 'the contents of about 200 water-closets..., the draining from dunghills, the Infirmary,... slaughter houses, chemical soap, gas, dung, ... pig manure, old urine wash' to name but a few of its colourful ingredients. Children (who made up 25% of the nation's labour force) worked 14-hour days down the mines, up the chimneys or in the cotton mills, and the factory owners paid their workers in tokens to ensure that the workers had to spend their earnings in the factory owner's shop. Industrial injuries were commonplace, not least because the exhausted workers often fell asleep at their machines and physical abuse by the foremen was standard practice. Being sent to the workhouse was a common fate for orphans or those who needed support rather than further punishment. With such poor standards of public health, it is unsurprising that cholera epidemics swept the country (in 1846-49 50,000 people died). There were several people and organizations that fought for the dispossessed. The Earl of Shaftesbury argued for factory reform and the protection of women and children in the mines; William Booth, a Methodist minister, set up the Salvation Army to provide shelter for the destitute; Dr Barnardo founded homes for children; Elizabeth Fry campaigned for prison Reform and the American philanthropist George Peabody gave money to build 'model dwellings'. It's worth noting that both Marx and Engels knew England well, and Marx saw Britain, not Russia, as ripe for the workers' revolution.

Indeed, as the century wore on the workers, whether urban or rural, began to flex their collective muscles. Following the limited concessions of the 1832 Reform Act, a group of radicals known as the Chartists produced the People's Charter demanding the right to vote for all men, secret ballots and the end to restrictions on who could become an MP. Parliament refused to listen, but by the end of the century almost all the demands had been introduced. Nevertheless the movement served as a precursor of the trade union movement, which grew in strength and authority, such that towards the end of the century strikes were successfully forcing changes upon the employers. In 1900 the union movement spawned its own political party in Westminster, The Labour Party. With the dawn of a new political era came the death of another. When Victoria died in 1901 aged 81, Britain was no longer the leading power in the world. Both America and Germany had industrialised, and were rapidly overtaking Britain as the Globe's foremeost manufacturers. The Empire was proving increasingly difficult to control, with war in South Africa reflecting an increasing restlessness among the Empire's subjects.

Two World Wars

The first half of the 20th century, of course, was dominated by two wars, both against Germany, and featured the French as allies, a turn around in English foreign policy. England itself remained largely untouched by the Great War, save for the devastation it caused to families as their young went off to the killing fields of northern France. The four years of slaughter cost Britain some 900,000 men, a result, in many people's eyes, of an army of 'lions led by donkeys'. The poetry that emerged from the likes of Siegfried Sassoon, Rupert Brooke and Wilfred Owen during this period is one of the few bright features of the 'war to end all wars'. As if to add insult to injury, a flu epidemic in 1919 killed more people than did the war itself. The call-up of the nation's young men also allowed the nation's women to demonstrate their worth, as they kept the nations industrial and agricultural output afloat. This strengthened the suffragette movement's demands for universal suffrage (it was finally achieved in 1928), although one leading suffragette's assessment that: "The Great War is God's vengeance on the people who held women in subjection", made too much of the link.

Some distraction from the war was to be found in Ireland, where Britain still ruled the roost, with support from the loyalist Protestant community (mainly in the north of the island), and tremendous resentment from the nationalist majority. The nationalists were particularly frustrated by the British delay on home rule on account of the Great War, and had life faith that it would be achieved anyway, and so rose up against the British. The Easter Rising of 1916, led by Patrick Pearse, was fiercely suppressed by the British, and the sixteen leaders executed. Such repression backfired – while in the short term the 'Irish Question' was manageable, it created martyrs and pushed many nationalists to support the more extreme policies of Sinn Fein, and ultimately the Irish Republican Army (IRA). In 1921 the island was divided into the Unionists in the Protestant north (which remained within the United Kingdom) and the Republicans in the Cathoic south (now Eire), a situation that still remains to this day. The IRA's terrorist acts, and others perpetrated by unionist paramilitaries, have plagued both Northern Ireland and mainland Britain since the 1970s, and involved attacks on politicians (the Conservative Government were bombed in their Brighton hotel at their party Conference in 1984), the military and civilians. It is only now, following the Good Friday Agreement of 1998, that there is some hope for a peaceful solution.

Following the war, Ramsay Macdonald, albeit briefly, led the first Labour Government, and in 1926 a General Strike across the country demonstrated the power of the unions. However, the strike only lasted a week, and the miners were left to continue their strike alone. The Jarrow Crusade some 10 years later is equally famous in the history of the trade union movement, but also achieved little. The 200 or so shipbuilders who marched 300 miles south from the northeastern town on the River Tyne to London earned much support and praise along the way, and represented a brave and courageous stand on behalf of the unemployed, but gained little for them or their region. Following the Wall Street Crash in 1929 and Depression in America, Europe had also suffered from the slump in world trade, and unemployment remained very high in some areas (it had been 75% in Jarrow). Not everyone, of course, was affected by the depression, and for those in work the 1930s was a good time, as prices fell and the standard of living rose. While the old industries of the north – coal mines, textile mills, shipyards and iron and steel foundries all saw a fall in trade, the southeast enjoyed growing job opportunities for the young in the so-called 'new industries' of car manufacturing, electrical and chemical goods. Art Deco factories such as the Hoover Building in West London bear witness to the growing wealth of such industries. Tourism flourished, as seaside resorts such as Blackpool and Brighton became increasing popular. The number of motor cars in the country doubled from 1 million in 1930 to 2 million in 1939, although the towns and cities were still busy with horse and carts and electric trams. The cinemas were popular venues for films and as the source of news, and even though 1936 saw the first public broadcast by the BBC (the first in the world), it wasn't until after the war that television began to threaten the popularity of the cinema. Meanwhile in the same year King Edward VIII abdicated in order to marry the American divorcee Wallace Simpson causing a constitutional crisis that was only resolved when his brother took the throne as George VI.

With the outbreak of the Second World War in 1939, England once again faced the prospect of invasion. Hitler failed to invade with an army, but first his bombers and later his V1 and V2 rockets devastated many of the country's cities. The Blitz of 1940-41 was largely centred on London, but not exclusively so. Cities such as Coventry, Liverpool and Manchester suffered tremendous damage, with hundreds killed and wounded on any given night. Families were torn apart not only by death and conscription, but also by evacuation, whereby children were despatched to the country or abroad to live with families that they had never met before in surroundings they had never experienced. Many would subsequently lose one or both parents in the course of the war, and never return to their urban past. In the cities Anderson shelters were erected in the gardens and Morrison shelters doubled as tables in the kitchens. Air raids became less frequent when Hitler turned his attention towards Russia, but austerity measures such as rationing still ensured a grim existence at home. Furthermore, when the unmanned rockets (the 'doodlebug') began landing on the cities in 1944 people once again looked skyward in fear and trepidation. When the war finally ended in 1945 street parties sprung up throughout the towns and cities, although the constraints of rationing continued for many years to come.

Post-War England

However, some hope of relief was provided by one of the most influential series of reforms in the country's history – the formation of the Welfare State. The Labour Government swept into power on a landslide, (the Conservative Churchill was revered as a wartime leader, but the British electorate was not going to get sentimental), promising to tackle the five great 'evils' facing the country – squalor, disease, want, idleness and ignorance. Not only were a number of industries such as steel, coal, gas, electricity and the railways nationalised, but education and health received huge boosts from central government. The school leaving age was raised to 15, and health care, from hospitals to opticians and dentistry were paid for by the government out of the taxes collected. In addition, a pension scheme was established for the older generation.

The war had also destroyed millions of homes across the country, causing an unprecedented housing shortage. The problem was initially tackled by 'prefab' houses, almost a 'kit' that could be erected with relative speed and ease to provide emergency housing. During the course of the 1950s, however, a number of new towns emerged such as Corby, Harlow, Peterlee, Swindon and Milton Keynes, while modern housing estates were built on the outskirts of existing towns. When rationing finally ended in 1954, the British economy picked up, with machines taking over many of the jobs previously done by manual labourers, and all sorts of new domestic goods changing life at home – television, fridges, and telephones became increasingly commonplace. Meanwhile American rock 'n' roll was absorbing the country's youth, with teddy boys, their hair slicked back with Brylcreem and wearing winkle picker shoes would listen to Elvis Presley or Buddy Holly on the jukebox in the cafés, or home-grown talent such as Tommy Steel or Cliff Richard. By 1959 Prime Minister Harold Macmillan was confident enough to tell the people "You've never had it so good".

The 1950s and 60s saw a new wave of immigration, this time in the aftermath of Empire. In 1947 India had become the first British colony to win Independence – in the next two decades Britain lost most of its overseas possessions. At the same time, immigration from Commonwealth countries grew, especially from the Caribbean and South Asia. Labour shortages in Britain meant government incentives to draw workers to Britain, and although immigration numbers reached 30,000 a year in the 1960s (most settling in the poorer areas of the inner cities), and racial tensions could sometimes lead to riots, emigration still outpaced immigration.

Meanwhile, in the 1960s England become the fashion centre for the western world. *Time* magazine reported that London 'swings, it is the scene'. Bands such as the Who, the Rolling Stones and the Small Faces earned huge followings, but it was the Beatles that took the world by storm. From a basement club in Liverpool emerged four Liverpudlians who were to revolutionise popular music and challenge America's dominance of the music scene. Pirate radio stations blossomed, many of them broadcasting from the Channel. Alongside the youth revolution, and partly contributing to it, was the production in 1961 of the contraceptive pill. This gave women far greater autonomy, and so helped to create the sexual revolution, a more liberal view of sexual morality that horrified the older generation, but was enthusiastically embraced by the 'love and peace' generation of hippies. Carnaby Street and the King's Road in London became the fashion focus of the country and beyond, the mini-skirt a fashion classic, and the model Twiggy a cultural icon. The growth in youth politics and influence, and the increase in teenage population was also reflected in the opening of seven new universities, such as Sussex, East Anglia and Warwick.

The 1970s and early 1980s were partly defined by the number of strikes, and the power of the Trade unions. Conservative Prime Minister Edward Heath's government was brought down by a miner's strike, but not before he ensured Britain joined the European Union, some 16 years after its inception in 1957. When Margaret Thatcher became the country's first female Prime Minister in 1979, she set about a rigorous economic policy designed to, among other things, take on the unions and restore Britain's 'self-confidence and her self-respect', or as she more alarmingly had it, 'put the Great back into Britain'. The result was harsh for many. Britain's manufacturing base was severely hit, both in the north and the south, but while new technology and service industries reappeared in the south, the north struggled to fill the employment gap. A north-south divide was becoming more accentuated, and an 'underclass' of unemployed and homeless were beginning to fill the cities' shop doorways and underpasses. The high unemployment led to inner city riots in Brixton, London, Toxteth, Liverpool and St Paul's, Bristol, all areas where black and Asian youths felt discriminated against by both employers and police. Meanwhile the City of London, the square mile of the capital that still broadly follows the lines of its Roman walls, became the financial capital of Europe, if not the world – in the 1980s there were more foreign banks located here than anywhere else in the world. Thatcher's period in office only came to an end when she was brought down by her own party, concerned by her increasingly isolated and intransigent position over Europe, and her obstinacy over a local tax, the Poll Tax. Indeed, while the Conservative Party retained power for another seven years until 1997, their constant squabbling over Europe and some high profile sexual and financial misdemeanours among their members meant that the moderniser Tony Blair led a Labour government to electoral victory in 1997 after 18 years in opposition.

The issue of how completely to embrace the European union and the single currency still plagues all the major parties, while the Channel Tunnel ensures the free movement of people and goods between Britain and the Continent. Britain therefore maintains an uneasy relationship with its neighbours across the channel, most recently demonstrated by the difference of opinion over how far to go in order to disarm Iraq. Whichever side you take on this particular issue, it is symbolic of the history of English, and British, foreign relations – fractious mistrust of France, and friendly bonhomie with America (despite the late 18th century blip). And while almost all political parties have emphasised the need for Britain to be at the 'heart of Europe', it quite clearly cannot fully embrace the idea. It is an island geographically detached from the continent, with an island mentality. The Labour government has pushed through constitutional change to give Wales its own Assembly and Scotland its own Parliament. Although these devolved institutions are fairly limited in their powers (compared with Westminster), the political map of Britain has changed once again, and it will be interesting to see what devolution means for the English. While the Scottish, Welsh and (Northern) Irish have a fairly clear identity (helped, no doubt, by a dislike of the English), the English identity seems to rest on the idea that it is there to be 'discarded and challenged'. Read any analysis of what it means to be English, and it will produce a confusion of images and stereotypes – from the *People* newspaper's survey (in 1951) conclusion that the English were a unified but dull people, to a people 'conceived in irony', and countless other stereotypes involving cricket on village greens, mediocre (at best), stodgy food, an ironic sense of humour, obstinacy and courage.

Whatever makes up this 'nation of shopkeepers' as Napoleon called the English, it is once again experiencing massive changes. There are countless languages in common usage throughout the country, and some parts of cities have fewer whites than blacks or Asians. It all sounds very familiar – the assimilation of immigrants and their language and culture, which in time creates a new England. Indeed, what with the talk of a single European currency, increasing independence for the home nations, and an urban traffic system barely faster than the horse, Britannia seems to be returning to its Roman past.

Culture

Architecture

Stonehenge proves that architecture has been practised in England with considerable professionalism for at least the last 4000 years. The most famous exceedingly old building in the country, whatever its purpose or origins, stands out from the majority of more recent vernacular buildings though in its refusal to use local building materials. Many of its stones were shipped in from Wales, and others were dragged 20 miles to the site. In general, the sheer variety of different building types in England pre-1800 can largely be explained by the variety of its geology. People built with whatever was immediately to hand: stone, wood or clay bricks.

The Romans introduced architecture as we now know it and several of their monuments remain – although don't go looking for anything on the scale of the Pont du Gard or Colosseum. Most impressive perhaps are the leisure facilities they created for themselves at Bath. Interesting examples of their skill in military engineering survive at Richborough in Kent, Colchester in Essex, Portchester Castle near Portsmouth and in the north along sections of Hadrian's Wall. The luxurious mosaic flooring of their villas can still be seen at Fishbourne, Chedworth and Lullingstone.

The Saxons built mainly in wood and hence less of their handiwork survives. Later Saxon churches were built of stone, though, some of them in imitation of timber construction. Venerable examples can be seen at Breamore in Hampshire, Earls Barton in Northamptonshire and Barton upon Humber in Yorkshire. St Albans Cathedral gives a good idea of the way the Saxons sometimes made use of Roman materials. Even so, English architecture proper still only really begins with the Normans in the 11th century.

With the Normans, we're talking Romanesque churches and square castle keeps for the most part, since most of their houses have either been demolished or adapted down the centuries beyond recognition. Two exceptions are the Jew's House in Lincoln and Moyse's House in Bury St Edmunds, both still in good states of repair. As church builders, Durham Cathedral is probably their most spectacular achievement, its heavy round columns and rounded arches typical of their style. The repetition of the semicircular arch, sometimes elaborately decorated with fabulous carvings and chevron zig-zags, is their hallmark. Gloucester Cathedral furnishes another particularly impressive example. On a more intimate scale, Romsey Abbey and the Hospital of St Cross in Hampshire, the small churches of Kilpeck in Herefordshire and Barfreston in Kent are worth seeking out. Unadulterated Norman castles can be found at Rochester or Castle Hedingham, Richmond or Bolton, as well as those forming the core of later fortifications, as in the Tower of London. In all of them the walls are several feet thick and often protects a central baron's hall – bedroom, living room and dining room all in one, warmed by a hearth fire.

From some time around the middle of the 12th century, throughout the Middle Ages, until the beginning of the modern period in the 16th century, Gothic held sway over ecclesiastical architecture. Pointed arches replaced round, windows featured increasingly elaborate tracery, and eventually the most fantastic fan-vaulted ceilings blossomed over naves and chancels. This continental style allowed builders to escape the restrictive width-to-height ration of Romanesque and aspire heavenwards. The most famous example of Early Gothic in England is undoubtedly Salisbury Cathedral. Unlike many other cathedrals, which adapted Norman edifices, it was built from scratch between 1220 and 1260. The distinguishing characteristic of Early Gothic is the slender lancet window, usually grouped in three or fives, those in the centre the tallest. Later the whole group would be framed beneath one arch. Other important examples of the style include the east end of Canterbury Cathedral, much of Lincoln Cathedral and the west front of Wells Cathedral.

In the early 14th century, the Decorated style of Gothic introduced more elaborate carving and extravagant window tracery. This style was one of enlargement and alteration and was itself quite rapidly superceded by the Perpendicular and so survives only in parts of greater wholes: the cloisters of Norwich Cathedral, the Lady Chapel and Chapter House of Wells Cathedral, the Octagon at Ely and the choir of Bristol are all good examples. The Perpendicular style is the most famous and dominant form of Gothic in England, achieving its full impact towards the middle of the 15th century but still informing architectural decisions as late as 1570. As its name suggests, it emphasised the vertical, but also widened windows, replaced decorative tracery with simple stone strips, and raised roofs. The most famous examples are probably King's College Chapel, Cambridge, and St George's Chapel in Windsor Castle, but there are countless others, especially in the wool rich parish churches of East Anglia, the Cotswolds and Somerset. Think Lavenham, Clare, Northleach, or Thaxted.

Until the Dissolution of the Monasteries by Henry VIII in the 1530s, the great abbeys of England were also triumphs of Gothic architecture. Apart from those whose churches survived thanks to being turned over to the parish – Shrewsbury, Abbey Dore, Cartmel and Minster-in-Sheppey to name a few – many only remain as evocative ruins: Rievaulx, Bolton and Fountains in Yorkshire are the most visited, but almost every county contains a carefully preserved handful of these forlorn and romantic monastic shells, their roofs open to the sky. Their remote situations, away from the main towns and villages, also often adds to their desolate charm. All follow much the same pattern: a square cloister joined to the south wall of the church (complete monastic cloisters are still extant at Norwich and Gloucester), as well as a dormitory, dining hall and storage barns.

While churches were built across England throughout the Middle Ages, there was little development in castle-building. The formidable fortifications that had secured the country for the Normans became a threat to the security of the monarchy itself. By order of the Crown, castles could only be constructed in Wales and in the north. Bodiam Castle in Sussex is one of the very few distinctively medieval castles in the south, a wonderful ruin still surrounded by its spring-fed moat beneath towering walls. Instead, domestic architecture in the Middle Ages is represented in a wealth of moated manor houses like Ightam Mote, near Sevenoaks in Kent, small castles like Stokesay in Shropshire and great barns like those at Bradford-on-Avon near Bath or Hales Hall in Norfolk which is one of the earliest brick-built buildings in the country. From the 15th century onwards, the variety of building materials available began to make itself felt. Stone was still used where it was plentiful – the Cotswolds and parts of the North mainly – but timber and brick were often more convenient. The black-and-white villages of Herefordshire are some of the most notable examples of half-timbered construction in the country, although many other counties can boast their fair share: Long Melford in Suffolk and Chiddingstone in Kent for example.

With the Tudors we're at the beginning of the Modern period and the extraordinary flowering of architectural talent in the 17th century. Hampton Court Palace, just outside London, is a splendid essay in the transition from mellow red brick to stone-fronted neo-classicism. Other essential destinations for an appreciation of Tudor and Elizabethan architecture are Penshurst Place or Knole, in Kent, Longleat in Wiltshire and Hardwick Hall in Derbyshire. Jacobean architecture can be seen at its grandest at Audley End in Essex or Blickling Hall in Norfolk. The end of Gothic was spelled during the English Renaissance by an increasing interest in the classics, including the architecture of the Ancient World. In the court of Kings James I, Inigo Jones introduced Palladianism, with its concern for correct proportion and classical symmetry, in the early 17th century, the finest surviving example of his work being the Banqueting House in Whitehall. Before the revival of Palladianism in the early 18th century, we are entering the Golden Age of the Architect in Britain, when the Baroque was given an English twist in the hands of Sir Christopher Wren and others, such as his pupil Nicholas Hawksmoor and the playwright John Vanbrugh.

Wren's most spectacular work remains St Paul's Cathedral in the City of London, but he was also responsible for 25 smaller City churches, various bits of Oxford and Cambridge, and the Fountain Court of Hampton Court Palace. Hawksmoor is justly famous for his monumental City churches and parts of the

Royal Naval College in Greenwich. Vanbrugh designed the staggering pile of a place that is Blenheim Palace. This was just the beginning of the great age of the country house, when the wealth of Empire was poured into vast estates surrounding houses that often looked to Greece and Rome for inspiration. The 18th century passion for Palladianism saw whole villages and hills removed as landscape architects like William Kent, 'Capability' Brown and Humphrey Repton went to work creating lakes, vistas and gardens in imitation of classical scenes. The banker Henry Hoare created a perfect little Virgilian idyll for himself at Stourhead in Wiltshire. The great name in interiors at this time was Robert Adam, whose work at Kedleston, Audley End and Harewood is exceptionally well-preserved.

Neo-classicism, variously interpreted by the likes of John Nash, Sir John Soane and Decimus Burton, continued to dominate the scene pretty much until the Gothic Revival in the 19th century. The greatest of these three was the manic-depressive Sir John Soane (1757-1837). Few architects before or since have handled the play of daylight inside buildings so well. Luckily, Soane's own truly fantastic house which was also his personal museum has survived inside three customised Georgian terraced houses in Lincoln Inn's Fields, London. The Sir John Soane Museum is an architectural sonnet.

The Gothic Revival was a major new departure, inspired in part by the writings of John Ruskin (who lived at Brantwood in the Lake District) and taken to its greatest heights by architects like Augustus Pugin (the Palace of Westminster) and George Gilbert Scott (St Pancras Station), paving the way for the medievalist fantasies of the pre-Raphaelites, and the Arts and Crafts movement led by the socialist William Morris. One of the best examples of this fin de siècle style has recently been beautifully renovated in the Lake District, at Blackwell near Windermere.

In the 20th century, the period after First World War gave birth to Art Deco, influenced by America and the jazz age with its sweeping curves and clean lines. The De La Ware Pavilion in Bexhill-on-Sea near Brighton is the most famous example. After the Second World War, Brutalism was imported from the continent where Le Corbusier was making bold statements about the modernist architectural idiom. Some notable examples of work under his influence in England include the Hayward Gallery, London and the Trellick Tower in west London, designed by Erno Goldfinger, whose own house can be seen visited in Hampstead. James Stirling, also influenced by Le Corbusier, Richard Rogers and Norman Foster are the big three British architects that have an international reputation. Stirling designed the Clore Gallery extension to Tate Britain in London; Rogers designed the Millennium Dome in Greenwich and the Lloyds Building in the City; Foster has been responsible for Stansted Airport, Canary Wharf station on the Jubilee Line, the Sainsbury Centre in Norwich and the Great Court at the British Museum. Other signs of the renaissance in architecture are the Millennium Wheel and Millennium Bridge on the Thames in London. Outside London, lottery-funded millennium projects have provided a spate of opportunities for contemporary architects, many seized upon with alacrity and flair: the National Space Centre in Leicester, the Imperial War Museum in Leeds and the Eden Project near St Austell to name but a few.

Literature

Literature is the art for which England is most celebrated. And since its language has become one of the most widely spoken and understood on the planet, it's also the most accessible. The British tourist industry capitalises on a clutch of the greats around the country. Top of the trails is of course Shakespeare's, who has a whole 'country' named after him round his birthplace in Stratford-upon-Avon. Although the staging of his works really does achieve new heights here thanks to the Royal

 Shakespeare Company, audiences of *As You Like It* are unlikely to be much the wiser for a visit to the Forest of Arden nearby although there's plenty about the man, whoever he was, in the town. Down in the south and west, Thomas Hardy and Jane Austen duke it out as the most-mentioned: Hardy also has his own 'country', its capital being Dorchester in Dorset with its borders stretching up to Oxford in the north and Bournemouth on the coast. Even though the gloomy down-trodden Wessex of his novels is hardly recognisable amid the properous commuter counties of today, his trail remains one of the more genuine because of the thoroughness of his fictionalised geography for the area. Austen rules the roost in Hampshire and in Bath, where a couple of her immaculately written novels of middle class manners are partly set. Kent deserves and really does need Charles Dickens to boost its appeal. He was born and lived out his last years in the north of the county, although his fans are also well served in London. In the north of England, the literary tours opt either for the Wordsworths, William and his sister Dorothy, as well as their poet friends Coleridge and Southey, in the Lake District, or the novelist Brontë Sisters, Charlotte, Emily and Anne in Haworth, Yorkshire. Doomed Emily's *Wuthering Heights* remains required reading for visitors to the West Yorkshire Moors, but Charlotte's nicer novels – *Jane Eyre*, *Villette* – hardly refer to the place. The Lakes, however, could really almost have been summoned up by Wordsworth and Co. A reading of their poetry is also highly recommended for visitors to the Exmoor Coast and the Wye Valley.

But what of the 20th and 21st centuries? The tourist trails go a bit cold as the writing becomes more contemporary, although the southwest furnishes a few pickings. Here there's John 'French Lieutenant's Woman' Fowles in Lyme Regis, Agatha Christie in Torquay, and Daphne Du Maurier further west in Fowey. Elsewhere, and from the earlier part of the 20th century there's the grim visionary DH Lawrence near Nottingham and depressed deb Virginia Woolf in Sussex. On a broader canvas, Anthony Powell's *Dance To The Music Of Time* is an epic series of 12 novels following a few upper class family histories through several generations in England from the 1920s onwards. Mid-century there's the classic English humourist PG Wodehouse (think Surrey and golf for the most part); Evelyn Waugh and his neo-Catholic novels of upper class of mores laced with Somerset sadness; another major Catholic voice is Graham Greene, one of his most site-specific novels being the smalltime gangster scene of *Brighton Rock*; and there's that acute observer of middle class angst EM Forster, one of his masterpieces, *Howard's End*, being set in Shropshire and London. In the later 20th century, England has steadily become more of a springboard than a subject for novelists, many native writers choosing to find their inspiration overseas. That said, rafts of English 'outsiders' have continued to focus on aspects of contemporary life: Bill Bryson with his riotously successful *Notes from a Small Island*; more ambitiously there's Hanif Kureishi's *London Kills Me*; Kazio Ishiguro's *The Remains of the Day*; and Vikram Seth's *An Equal Music*, looking at the life of a chamber musician. The literary scene in the 80s and 90s seemed to belong to Martin Amis, before he headed for America; Julian Barnes and Salman Rushdie. Women writers of a particulary English bent include Angela Carter, Jeanette Winterson and AS Byatt, each examining in very different ways what it's like to be female in modern England. Less highbrow, Joanna Trollope's 'aga' sagas on life in the Shires have been enormously popular, as has the comic Wimbledon writer Nigel Williams describing suburban middle age crises. Tougher nuts on the contemporary scene include Graham Swift, his *Last Orders* taking a close look at the East End and *Fenland* doing the same for Cambridgeshire. One promising young London writer is Courttia Newland, whose stories in *Society Within* give voice to a group of black youth on a London housing estate.

London

Almost every English writer, as well as many writers in English, have been touched by London at some time in their lives. For centuries the city has been the place they have looked for both inspiration and a livelihood. In the late 14th century, the 'father of English literature', court poet Geoffrey Chaucer (1342-1400), started his pilgrims on the road from Southwark for his jaunty *Canterbury Tales*. Two centuries or so later, next door on Bankside, one William Shakespeare (1564-1616) was writing plays for the Globe theatre. A delightful replica of the theatre can now be seen in all its reconstructed glory close to the original site thanks to Hollywood film director Sam Wanamaker. Across the river, in the 17th century, the old cathedral of St Paul's had one of England's most intelligent poets, John Donne (1572-1631), for its Dean, while London found a vivacious, self-regarding observer and commentator in the diarist Samuel Pepys (1633-1703). He watched the cathedral and city go up in smoke in the Great Fire of 1666 from the steeple of All Hallows church next to the Tower of London. At the turn of the 18th century, Daniel 'Robinson Crusoe' Defoe (1660-1731) was making a name for himself as a journalist and spy. In his 'Journal of the Plague Year' he describes the panic and the body count with a creative flair that few modern correspondents would dare emulate. In 1726 he completed *A Tour through the Whole Island of Great Britain*, a guidebook in three volumes that gives an invaluable insight into the state of the nation at the time, describing the city as 'out of all shape, uncompact and unequal'. No change there then. The really big name in London during the 18th century, though, was Dr Samuel Johnson (1709-84) whose house just off Fleet St has been preserved. England's first true 'man of letters', his ground-breaking Dictionary and lengthy poems and miscellanies are now less popular than the image we have of the man and his Cheshire Cheese companions – the poet Oliver Goldsmith, Edmund Burke and Edward Gibbon among others – largely thanks to the efforts of his indefatigable young biographer James Boswell (1740-95). Infinitely quotable (way ahead of his time with his soundbites), he recorded Johnson remarking that "When a man is tired of London, he is tired of life, for there is in London all that life can afford". Boswell's own *London Journal* bears out the truth of the observation with energetic descriptions of his social climbing and sexual exploits in St James Park. Meanwhile, William Blake (1757-1827), England's greatest visionary poet and artist, was greeting visitors to his house in Lambeth sitting in the nude with his wife, also naked. Naturism may not have caught on just then, but Nature itself became all the rage. William Wordsworth (1770-1850), loved the Lakes of course (see the North below), but also wrote of the city from Westminster Bridge that "Earth has nothing to show more fair..." As the 19th century gathered steam, London seemed far from fair to the likes of Shelley (1792-1822) who wrote that "Hell is a city much like London"; Dickens (1812-70), who captured the law's interminable delay in *Bleak House* and whose home off the Grays Inn Rd is now a museum; and Marx (1818-83), who lodged with his family in Dean St, Soho, while penning *Das Kapital* in the British Museum. Keats (1795-1821) did his best work in Hampstead, where his house can be visited; Byron (1788-1824) lived in Albany, Piccadilly, before his marriage; George Eliot (1819-80) wrote *Middlemarch* in St John's Wood; and Henry James (1843-1916) *A Portrait of a Lady* in Bolton St, Piccadilly. *The Golden Bowl* contains much vivid description of the London of his day. The Anglo-Irish flooded into the capital during the fin de siecle: after his marriage the celebrated wit Oscar Wilde (1856-1900) lived at 34 Tite St, Chelsea; before becoming a bearded sage, George Bernard Shaw (1856-1950) lodged in Fitzrovia as a young man; a dandified WB Yeats (1865-1939) strolled near his home on Primrose Hill. In the early years of the 20th century, TS Eliot (1888-1965) worked in a bank in the City. Bloomsbury gave its name to the group that included Virginia Woolf (1882-1941). Contemporary London writers include Peter Ackroyd, Ian Sinclair, Martin Amis, Jeanette Winterson, Ian McEwan, Maureen Duffy, Michael Moorcock and Hanif Kureishi. And a younger generation like Nick Hornby, Will Self, Tim Lott, and Graham Swift.

Southeast

The unavoidable name on the literary tourist trail in Kent is Charles Dickens. His study at Broadstairs is a well-preserved shrine with wonderful sea views, while his writing chalet can be seen in Rochester, one of various places around here that fuelled his formidable descriptive prose: the Cooling marshes, Gravesend and Chatham are others. Further inland, Sissinghurst Castle was the home of novelist, poet and member of the Bloomsbury set, Vita Sackville-West (1892-1962). The garden that she designed and planted with her husband Harold Nicolson is one of the National Trust's most popular properties. She was brought up at Knole in Sevenoaks and was also an inspiration to the other big name in the Southeast, Virginia Woolf lived with her husband at Monks House in Rodmell, Sussex, close to her sister Vanessa Bell's farmhouse at Charleston on the South Downs, before drowning herself in 1941. Both houses are open to the public in summer. One of the few of her contemporaries that she ever had much time for was Henry James. He lived in his later years at Lamb House, Rye (now a museum). Further inland again, Ashdown Forest is famous for being the fictional home of AA Milne's Winnie the Pooh. The bridge where that bear of very little brain liked to race floating sticks now groans with Pooh-stick players young and old each summer. Just to the north, Chartwell was home to the prolific historian Winston Churchill (1874-1965), also famous for being Prime Minister during Second World War. He liked to write standing up. Or dictating from his bed. Equally celebrated in his own day was the Elizabethan courtier, soldier and poet Sir Philip Sidney (1554-86) who lived at Penshurst Place in the Weald of Kent where he wrote a Defence of Poesy and his celebration of courtly love Astrophil and Stella.

South and southwest

Oxford educated some of the leading lights of the English literary canon, including Sir Philip Sidney and John Donne, and later Shelley, and in Victorian times the poet and public school inspector Matthew Arnold (1822-1888), John Ruskin (1819-1900), Charles Luttwidge Dodgson aka Lewis Carroll (1832-98), and Oscar Wilde. In the 20th century the university harboured those friendly rivals JRR Tolkien (1892-1973) and CS Lewis (1898-1978), both now with tourist trails in the city in their honour after the success of the rollicking blockbuster film version of *The Lord of the Rings* and the weepie *Shadowlands* about CS Lewis' tragic affair with an American writer. On a similar note to the latter, the last days of novelist Dame Iris Murdoch (1919-99) as she succumbed to Alzheimers with husband John Bayley by her side have also received the movie treatment in Iris starring Judi Dench and Jim Broadbent. In Hampshire the village of Selborne has become a place of pilgrimage for devoted naturalists seeking out the small 18th-century home of Gilbert White whose vivid *Natural History of Selborne* set an early benchmark in nature notes. In the Chilterns, one unlikely find is John Milton's Cottage where the blind old Parliamentarian poet came up with *Paradise Lost*. The big name in the south of England though remains Jane Austen (1775-1817), whose house in Chawton, near Alton in Hampshire, can be visited. Bath is the other big Austen destination, thanks to its role in *Persuasion* and *Northanger Abbey* and the fact that the novelist lived in the city for some time. Bath was also a favourite of Tobias Smollett, Henry Fielding and the playwright Sheridan and featured in Charles Dickens' *Pickwick Papers*. Although the epicentre of Thomas Hardy Country is Dorchester, most consistently described in *The Mayor of Casterbridge*, many more rewarding destinations for his fans lie round about: Rainbarrow Hill on Egdon heath, memorably described in *The Return of the Native*; Stonehenge for *Tess of the d'Urbervilles* and Oxford, called Christminster in *Jude the Obscure*. Further southwest, at Nether Stowey in Somerset, Samuel Taylor Coleridge (1772-1834) wrote *The Rime of the Ancient Mariner* after taking a stroll along the coast with the Wordsworths, and also *Kubla Khan* after taking a lot of opium. Inspired by the south Cornish coast, Daphne du Maurier (1907-89) wrote classics like *Rebecca* and *Jamaica Inn*.

The Midlands and East Anglia

Bestriding the middle of the country like a colossus is Shakespeare. Many of the attractions at Stratford-upon-Avon provide excellent insights into the Elizabethan world, and the whole experience is spiced up by the suspicion that he may not have been a Stratford man at all. Elsewhere in the Midlands, on a much less well-trodden tourist trail, DH Lawrence (1885-1930) hailed from Nottinghamshire, and his novels set in the pit towns and grand houses around here remain among his most popular, especially *Sons and Lovers*. Lord Byron (1788-1824) lived for a while at Newstead Abbey which preserves his memory by offering visitors to dress like the poet. East Anglia was the home of the nature poet John Clare and later the Cambridge society poet Rupert Brooke. The latter's trail around Grantchester is still surprisingly fresh. The professor of German literature at the University of East Anglia, WG Sebald, more recently brought a morbid, erudite and searching curiosity to the Suffolk coast in *The Rings of Saturn*.

Yorkshire and the North

The Brontë Sisters have Yorkshire pretty much sewn up around Haworth, near Keighley. Anne, the least well-known of the peculiar threesome, remained true to her roots with the *Tenant of Wildfell Hall*. More accessible perhaps is the nature poetry of Ted Hughes (1930-2000), who lived near Mytholmroyd close to Hebden Bridge with the poet Sylvia Plath. His urban contemporary in Hull was Philip Larkin (1922-85), the true voice of England's quiet despair. On the other side of the country, in Liverpool, poets like Roger McGough and Brian Patten were much more cheerful in the face of urban blight. More recently, the novelist Jonathan Coe has wittily caricatured the collapse of a landed northern family in his novel *What a Carve Up*.

Theatre

The first public theatre in the country, simply called The Theatre, was erected in Shoreditch, London, by James Burbage in 1576. Before then, theatre companies had no fixed abode unless they were attached to the court or a great house. Strolling players in the Middle Ages would perform morality plays on temporary stages around the country, some of which, like The Mysteries, have recently been thrillingly revived.

The most perennially popular playwright in the English language, William Shakespeare (1564-1616) wrote and acted in his plays in the late 16th and early 17th centuries. The Elizabethan and Jacobean theatre was characterised by a boom in talent that also included the likes of Christopher Marlowe and Ben Jonson. Many of these dramatists were lucky enough to have a stake in their troupes, allowing them to make a living. Shakespeare's actual identity has fuelled much scholarly controversy but it's generally agreed that he was born in Stratford-upon-Avon. He worked with several different companies including the Lord Chamberlain's Men and King James I's own company, as well as possibly being part-owner of the Globe and Blackfriars playhouses. The reconstructed Globe Theatre on Bankside in London is close to the original site and gives a superb idea of what these Elizabethan playhouse were like: thatched, round and open to the sky. These were spaces where both a mannered declamatory style and more intimated soliloquys could equally work their magic over an audience stacked up to the rafters and milling around in 'the pit'.

In 1642, during the Civil War, Parliament shut down the theatres in England and executed King Charles I. On the continent though, his son Charles II was developing a taste for the play and on his Restoration to the throne in 1660, he presided over an astonishing recrudescence of the theatrical arts. This time, though, they looked not to Shakespeare, but to French dramatists and Italian designers and for the first time in England, women, not boys, took the female parts. Some, like Nell Gwynne, became favourites at court. Theatre in France was beginning to be more preoccupied with the mechanics of scenery and spectacle and English theatres like the Theatre Royal Drury Lane were constructed in imitation of those in Paris. The plays themselves were often masques in which costume and scene changes were as important as acting and plot, although in the hands of Restoration dramatists such as William Congreve and William Wycherley, highly polished wit became a hallmark of the English theatre.

Although the theatres were still licensed and controlled by the state, the 18th century saw the first stirring of a truly popular theatre once again. Theatre in England during the 18th century was dominated by an actor of genius, David Garrick (1717-1779), who was also a manager and playwright. Garrick developed a more naturalistic stage manner than many of his predecessors and his performances were enormously influential in society. He established the audience in the seated stalls, and kept himself and his actors behind the Proscenium arch that still dominates many a West End theatre. Plays increasingly more ordinary subject matter, such as in She Stoops to Conquer by Oliver Goldsmith (1730-1734), and *The School for Scandal* by Richard Brinsley Sheridan.

During the 19th century, the Industrial Revolution changed the way people lived and worked and it changed the face of theatre as well. Gas lighting was first introduced in 1817. Arc-lighting followed and, by the end of the century, electrical lighting made its appearance on stage. The necessity of controlling lighting effects made it imperative, once and for all, that the actors retreat behind the proscenium (until the reappearance of open stages and theatre in the round in the 20th century). It has been suggested that the poor quality of lighting contributed to the growth of 'melodrama' in the mid-19th century in which character and plot were strictly subsidiary to spectacular scenic effects and action. Only with the arrival of playwrights like Henrik Ibsen (1828-1906), whose first run of *Ghosts* on the Haymarket was attacked by a crowd outraged at its obscenity, and later with George Bernard Shaw (1856-1950), did serious drama engage audiences attentions.

In the 20th century, various different theatrical movements vied for ascendancy, from realism, naturalism, symbolism, surrealism, and impressionism to anti-realism, as artists struggled to connect with their audiences in a meaningful way. At the same time, the theatre developed very popular forms of entertainment called musicals. In order to compete with the cinema, scenery once again became the key to success. Even so, the witty plays of Noel Coward were still very popular in the mid-20th century as theatre embraced changes moving from the uncertainties of 1945 through to a post-Thatcher Cool Britannia at the end of the 90s. In 1954 British theatre's putative renaissance was heralded by a production of Samuel Becket's *Waiting for Godot* at the Arts Theatre and Tennessee Williams *A Streetcar Named Desire.* Critics like Kenneth Tynan fanned the flames, while playwrights like Christopher Fry, Terence Rattigan and the young Harold Pinter were dip on the scene. The first English writer to really run with the zeitgeist two years later at the Royal Court Theatre was John Osborne, with *Look Back in Anger*. This was followed by a spate of innovative plays that shook the Establishment, like Shelagh Delaney's *A Taste of Honey*, Peter Brook's ground-breaking production of *A Midsummer Night's Dream*, Joe Orton's *Loot*, and Joan Littlewood's Theatre Workshop production of *Oh, What a Lovely War!* The National Theatre was established in 1967. Writers like Edward Bond (*Saved*), Arnold Wesker, Howard Brenton, David Edgar and David Hare established a reputation for powerful and provocative subject matter and socialist agendas.

More recently, the English theatre, especially in the regions, has suffered from chronic underfunding while London milked the tourist dollar with a slew of tatty musicals. Audiences began to dry up, for reasons not unrelated to the mediocrity of many of the productions. A mini renaissance in the theatre after the Millennium has been largely attributed to the presence of Hollywood stars (Nicole Kidman, Kathleen Turner, and Paul Newman to name a few), but can also be put down to the consistent efforts over several years of directors like Sam Mendes at the Donmar Warehouse and Stephen Daldry at the Royal Court. Both have carved out successful careers in film too. A large part of the history of post-war British theatre has been about rocking the boat. It is to be hoped that it still can.

Music

Classical music

English music like all the other arts took root and form initially in sacred rites. Great court composers like the Catholics William Byrd and Thomas Tallis transcended sectarian boundaries even in the reign of Elizabeth I. Latin church music excelled in England in the 16th century with works such as Cantiones sacrae by William Byrd conveying a message both personal and religious with enormous musical poignancy. Henry Purcell (1659-1695) wrote prolifically under Charles II and then turned his talents to secular works and lifted English music theatre to new heights after the Reformation. With the Glorious Revolution and William of Orange – British taste concentrated on the magical and fantastic (for instance, the role of the witches) notably the magestic opera *Dido and Aeneas*. One of the greatest English composers, Edward William Elgar, was born in Worcester 1857. In his cello concerto in E minor we hear something profound about a man's attitude to life. Other English composers that have made their mark almost as brilliantly are Ralph Vaughan Williams and later Benjamin Britten and Peter Maxwell Davies. Meanwhile English classical musicians have often reached the pinnacle of their art: wonderful pianists like Solomon and Murray Perahia; cellists like Jacqueline du Pré and Steven Isserlis; the accompanist Gerald Moore; Dennis Brain, outstanding on the horn; Nigel Kennedy – a kooky but talented violinist from the Malverns, like Elgar himself; and a string of great conductors from Sir John Barbirolli (Italian born, but who lived all his life in England – except for a short spell in NYC and founded the Hallé Orchestra, establishing it as one of the finest; Sir Thomas Beecham, founder of the London Philharmonic and Royal Philharmonic Orchestras; Sir Malcolm Sargent, founder of the Proms); Sir Colin Davis (now LSO, but long and renowned carrier at Covent Garden, Berlioz cycle); right up to Sir Simon Rattle (who established Birmingham Symphony Orchestra and now conducts the Berlin Philarmonic). England has also produced its fare share of great opera singers: Kathleen Ferrier; Dame Felicity Lott; and Dame Janet Baker, Robert Tear and Peter Pears (Benjamin Britten's partner). And its orchestras continue to amaze and delight despite severe funding problems: the London Philharmonic is noteworthy because of their lineage, embracing Haitink and Tennstedt. Their cello, strings and their sound overall is very classical and pure. The Philharmonia and the London Philharmonic share the residency at the Royal Festival Hall in London. The London Sinfonia is a highly skilled chamber orchestra with repertoire of interpretive performances of modern composers and experimental music.

Rock and pop

Maybe Larkin didn't quite get his dates quite right, "Sexual intercourse began/ In nineteen sixty-three", 'Annus Mirabilis 1967', but it's impossible to think of the 1960s without thinking of the youth revolution: from the mods to the hippies and beyond. Everyone was young and exploring the limits of mind expanding drugs and 'free love'. And it was all channeled through music: pure, unadulterated, hard, frothing, undulating gyrating music. In fact this sub-culture had been brewing in England for two decades before the 60s. During and after World War II, American music flooded into the country and became all the rage. Jazz and big bands filled the dance halls. In the 1950s, when Macmillan declared that 'we'd never had it so good', the new sense of prosperity inspired a group of Savile Row tailors to knock up a new-look Edwardian suit: narrow trousers, fancy waistcoats, long jackets with narrow lapels. Gents may not have warmed to it, but the 'spivs' and other London gangster types, working classes on the make from south London, took it to their hearts. The Teddy Boy was born. For this act of subversion, appropriating the dress of the upper class and making it their own, the Teds deserve the honour of being hailed as the first true dissident youth movement in England. They took to American rock n' roll instantly. In the mid-1950s Elvis Presley and Bill Haley entered the British charts and the middle classes joined in. Since then the country has seen the same rebellion over and over again, wearing different clothes.

What about the music? Skiffle is arguably where it all started – English folk music with rockabilly overtones: think Lonny Donnegan and the Shadows. Long before the Beatles, Tin Pan Alley was churning out off the peg songs, with artists like rocker Tommy Steele keeping one foot firmly in the Music Hall. Cliff Richard and Donovan were the anaemic English Elvis and Dylan respectively. In the 1950s the influx of American GIs to Soho pubs and clubs, with their taste for soul and rock music, had engendered a cross-fertilization of the music scene that eventually created two huge movements: the Mods and the Rockers. Fashion and mobility characterized them as much as the music did. The Mods rode scooters, had short hair, and looked tidy in their short jackets, mohair and tonic suits. See them in the film *Quadrophenia* starring The Who. With their scooters laden with mirrors and target decals, the look created customised status and individuality. They liked not only The Who, but also The Small Faces and Rod Stewart as well as black soul music. Their drug of choice was amphetamine (speed). Later Mods went on to become skinheads and liked ska. Meanwhile, the Merseybeat scene featuring bands like Jerry and the Pacemakers was well under way. American rock and roll records arriving by sea landed first in Liverpool. Local bands honed their skills in The Cavern nightclub, also fuelled by speed, as well as in Hamburg, in sweaty dive bar clubs, wearing leather jackets. Easily the most famous product of this rocker scene were the Beatles. When their manager Brian Epstein insisted that they put on neat suits (loathed by Lennon) the cross-fertilization was complete. The Rolling Stones were also heavily influenced by America, both rock and roll and jazz-influenced blues. Keith Richards was obsessed with Chuck Berry (covering *Come On* as their first single) while Brian Jones (the original founder later swept aside by the Glimmer Twins Jagger and Richards) called himself Elmo Lewis after Elmore James. He had named the band after a Muddy Waters song. Towards the end of the decade, the gravity had shifted firmly to Swinging London. A heady cocktail of Mary Quant, the mini skirt, the pill, louche aristocrats and drugs on the King's Road and Carnaby Street – *Dedicated Follower of Fashion*, by The Kinks – gave this period its upbeat, optimistic appeal. But it had its dark side. The 1960s also witnessed infamous summer bank holiday riots, although apparently less scary in reality than the press pretended. The Mods would ride down to Brighton on their scooters, to take the sea air away from London, and the Rockers would go along too for a fight. These rockers rode motorbikes like British-made Triumphs, liked leather, denim, grew their hair long and preferred beer and dope to speed. The all-time English rock hit was recorded by Johnny Kidd and the Pirates: *Shakin' all over*. When rock went dark and heavy, the rockers turned to the Rolling Stones, the Beatles and Led Zeppelin. By 1968 though, it was the summer of love and all had changed – Mods and Rockers dispersed and some of both became hippies. Peace and love were the words. Also, by the end of the decade, psychedelia and LSD had made the sound more introverted and druggy. Her Majesty the Queen even remarked that The Beatles are "getting awfully strange these days". The Rolling Stones dabbled in the occult and Brian Jones drowned in his swimming pool. Jimi Hendrix overdosed in the Cumberland Hotel. Also worthy of mention around this time were the English crooners: the likes of Englebert Humperdink, Dusty Springfield and Petula Clark.

The 1970s are a much-maligned, misrepresented decade, caricatured by John Lydon's "never trust a hippy". He was taking a swipe at the overblown self indulgence of psychedelic rock like Pink Floyd and the "concept album". The Stones still managed (albeit in the South of France) to produce one of their best records Exile on Main Street. Punk rock was a reaction not just to the stagnating music scene, but to control shifting away from the kids to the businessmen. It was a reaction to the politic climate of the time too, with a Labour government in power, Denis Healey doing deals with the IMF, the three-day week, powercuts, strikes, and rubbish on the streets. The Clash wrote *London's Burning* (with boredom now). The Sex Pistols (home base Sex, the shop owned by Malcolm MacLaren and Vivien Westwood on the King's Road) epitomised a makeshift, do-it-yourself, art school feel – anarchic, yet still subliminally strangely patriotic. In the song *God Save the Queen* on Anarchy in the UK, "she ain't no human being" they say, yet "we love our queen". The Pistols were allegedly deliberately and fraudulently kept off the No 1 spot during the Silver Jubilee in 1977 by a Rod Stewart tune. Punk was also heavily influenced by Jamaican reggae imports and the scene shifted to Ladbroke Grove. This phase of the movement was epitomised by The Clash cover of *Police and Thieves* by Junior Marvin. Other great punk bands include The Buzzcocks, The Slits, The Damned and also Siouxsie and the Banshees, one of the few female-fronted punk bands, cool but hyper-emotional. Some English bands, also punk in inspiration, expressed not screaming anarchy, but gave intelligent voice to socialist agendas. Most prominent were the Gang of Four, middle class ex-students of the Marxist art historian TJ Clark from the university of Leeds. Their music rebelled against personal lives becoming public – prestructured for them by the consumer and entertainment industries. And glam rock was born in this decade too. Think platform shoes, glitter and flare etc. Some (like Slade) ridiculous, some (like Roxy Music) inspired. Roxy Music's biggest hit, *Love is the drug*, with legendary band members like the Brians Ferry and Eno. With their stylish artwork using exotic and extravagant urban women, they paved the way for the break-down of a readymade notions of sexual identity. Brian Eno went on to produce the Irish band U2 and play an important role in the development of 'ambient' music, becoming a soundscape artist in his own right. This was the decade that gave us David Bowie, T Rex and Mark Bolan, Nick Drake, and The Incredible String Band.

After punk, in the late 70s and early 80s, came the "New Wave", with bands like The Boomtown Rats (fronted by Bob Geldof, who went on to organise Liveaid), Elvis Costello and the Attractions, The Stranglers, and the best of these groups The Jam (fronted by Paul Weller). Very English and post-Mod, the Jam were also heavily politicised, expressing the frustrations of growing up in suburban Woking and with the class system (Eton Rifles), although they occasionally slipped into English pastoral (*English Rose*). Meanwhile another Malcolm McLaren-conceived band – Bow Wow Wow – further encouraged teenage delinquency, being fronted by a 15-year-old Burmese girl brought up in London who became the focus of media mayhem about the exploitation of child nymphets. The furore was capitalised upon by the New Romantics (foppish, gender bending again) including the likes of Boy George (at clubs like Taboo and The Blitz), ABC, Duran Duran, Adam Ant, Depeche Mode, and Spandau Ballet. Also in the early 80s, humanoid electro-synth bands appeared like The Human League, Gary Numan, Ultravox, and Orchestral Manoeuvres In The Dark (OMD). And more serious synth-based sounds issued from the likes of the The Cure, also riding the gender-bending train in the shape of lipstick wearing frontman Robert Smith, and Echo and the Bunnymen from Liverpool.

In the mid-80s, the arrival of the next great English indie rock band, paving the way for the likes of Oasis and Blur in the Britpop boom, was The Smiths. Their sound was characterised by the jangly, indie guitars of Johnny Marr and the literate, melancholia of Morrissey's lyrics – arguing the merits of Keats and Yeats on one side, Wilde on the other for example. They were based in Manchester ("so much to answer for" in a song about the Moors murderers) and the forerunners of another spectacular explosion of talent from the run-down industrial north. The rave scene of the late 80s kicked off in Manchester (or Madchester), important for the club dance scene (the most famous being The Hacienda), as well as indie bands like the Joy Division, the Fall, the Happy Mondays, and Stone Roses. Ecstasy became the drug of choice at big outdoor parties, with car-loads of wide-eyed loved-up funsters racing around the M25 in search of the buzz. The villagers got angry and farmers quietly trousered big cheques. The early 90s saw the birth of Britpop, a manufactured British guitar-based sound, a head-to-head clash between Oasis (swaggering Mancunian louts...What's The Story Morning Glory LP) and Blur (Damon Albarn an Essex art school student...Park Life LP). This is the strain of current pop that has degenerated into Popstars and Pop Idols, with TV gameshow-manufactured stars like Hearsay, Will Young and Gareth Gates. Really it's glorified karaoke, singing other people's songs rather badly but proves the power of TV (as if it were necessary) to shape popular tastes. Some hope may lie in the re-kindling the spirit of spontaneous independents like Tricky, Massive Attack, and Portishead, as well as the Orb, with their sample-based trip hop, dub and drug sound – progenitors of the Trance, Techno, and raves that inspired a generation dedicated to the weekend. Meanwhile in the clubs, the drum and bass explosion continues, started in London by the likes of LTJ Bukem and Goldie, with artists like Aphex Twin and Squarepusher crafting distinctively British, surprisingly un-American break beats.

Film

The British film industry has famously been in terminal decline pretty much since the invention of the medium. It only takes a brief look through history to see that this sorry reputation hardly tells the whole story. Although there has never been a studio industry on the scale of Hollywood, Bollywood, France or Italy, the country can still lay claim to nurturing some of the great names in cinema. For directors, look to Alfred Hitchcock, Carol Reed, Powell and Pressburger, David Lean, Richard Attenborough, and more recently to Ridley Scott, Mike Leigh, Sam Mendes and Stephen Daldry. For actors, see Cary Grant, Deborah Kerr, Vivien Leigh, Elizabeth Taylor, Alec Guinness, Dirk Bogarde, Peter O'Toole and Michael Caine, as well as a host of more contemporary lights such as Hugh Grant, Kate Winslett and Ralph Fiennes. Either list could be almost indefinitely extended, although it would soon become obvious that not many of them have ever found much work near home. When they have, the landscape and cities of England itself have sometimes provided glorious locations. David Lean insisted on shooting *Great Expectations* (1946) on the Cooling marshes near Dickens' home, Gads Hill in Kent. Powell and Pressburger's peculiar story of the glueman, *A Canterbury Tale*, was shot on location near the cathedral and in the countryside around, while their astonishing *Matter of Life and Death* was partly filmed on the Norfolk beaches. For his strange gangster pic *Cul-de-Sac* (1966), Roman Polanski headed for Lindisfarne Castle on Holy Island off the coast of Northumberland. Robert Bolt's *A Man for All Seasons* (1966) about the trials and tribulations of Sir Thomas More was one of the very few films ever to have been allowed access to Hampton Court Palace. Hardy Country was memorably committed to celluloid in *Far from the Madding Crowd* (1967), shot around the rolling hills of Devizes and Shaftesbury. *Anne of a Thousand Days* (1969) made use of Anne Boleyn's actual childhood home, Hever Castle in the Weald of Kent. Similarly, the film adaptation of John Fowles' *French Lieutenant's Woman* (1981) insisted on using modern day Lyme Regis in Dorset. Peter Greenaway's meticulous *Draughtsman's Contract* (1982) was filmed almost entirely at Groombridge Place near Tunbridge Wells. *A Fish Called Wanda* (1988) made memorable use of

Heathrow Airport. Other London locations were used for the spate of gangster capers that included Guy Ritchie's *Lock, Stock and Two Smoking Barrels* (1998). Stanley Kubrick made London gangsters look both hip and ridiculous when he banned his own film, *A Clockwork Orange* (1971), from being screened in Britain. Parts of it were shot in the basement of the Barbican Centre (as it was being built); other parts in the mean streets of the East End.

The best way of discovering the myths behind the movies is to explore the locations yourself. The possibilities are endless. Films like Merchant Ivory's *Howards End* (1992) are so stuffed with beautifully appointed location shots that they deserve an entire chapter to themselves: Roast beef at Simpson's-in-the-Strand; shopping at Fortnum and Mason's; a conversation by Admiralty Arch; a train to St Pancras; St James Court Hotel in Buckingham Gate doubling as a flat; and a hero's down-at-heel digs in Park Street in Southwark (home to Borough Market the best food market in London), all these locations feature in this Oscar-winning Merchant Ivory film which starred Helena Bonham Carter, Anthony Hopkins, Vanessa Redgrave, Sam West, and Oscar-winner Emma Thompson. Young female romantics will probably find the journey to the Travel Bookshop (13 Blenheim Crescent, W11) a greater thrill. It's here that the shy Portobello bookshop owner, Hugh Grant, accidentally spills fruit juice over browsing superstar, Julia Roberts, in Roger Michell's *Notting Hill* (1999). But the area has never quite recovered its bohemian cool, made famous by Hanif Kureshi's drug-dealing hero Clint (Justin Chadwick) in the 1991 film, *London Kills Me*. Beyond the capital, *Four Weddings and a Funera*l (1994) made use of the stately home at Luton Hoo, while in that disastrous box office flop *Heaven's Gate*, Oxford stands in for Harvard. *The Madness of George III* (1994) used location at Arundel Castle in Sussex and Wilton House in Wiltshire. *The Remains of the Day* (1993) headed for Dyrham Park, near Bath and shot the interiors at Corsham Court nearby. Few directors will be able to top Kubrick's *Full Metal Jacket* (1987). Perhaps only Kubrick had the nerve to recreate the Vietnam War in the derelict Beckton Gas Works just beyond Docklands on the north bank of the Thames. Matthew Modine and his lads blew up so much of the property, and left so many of the old derelict office buildings unsafe, that the area had to be sealed off from the public. In more recent years, on a smaller scale, the Samuel L Jackson thriller *51st State* (2001) was shot in Liverpool, and Michael Winterbottom's *24 Hour Party People* (2002), starring the British TV comic Steve Coogan, charted the spectacular rise and fall of Manchester's infamous Hacienda nightclub and was shot entirely on location in Manchester.

Books

Contemporary fiction

Amis, Martin, *Money* (2000) Penguin. Scabrous dissection of the 80s.

Ballard, JG, *Crash* (1995), Vintage. Erotic tales of automania.

Boyd, William, *Armadillo* (1999), Penguin. Entertaining thriller about a loss adjuster in London.

Byatt, AS, *The Virgin in the Garden* (1994), Vintage. Baroque Elizabethan and contemporary relationship problems.

Coe, Jonathan, *What a Carve Up* (2001), Penguin. Very funny story of in-fighting among a landed northern family in decline.

Kureishi, Hanif, *The Buddha of Suburbia* (1993), Faber and Faber. An immigrant perspective on modern London.

McEwan, Ian, *Enduring* Love, (1998), Vintage. Psychological thriller about obsession.

Winterson, Jeanette, *Oranges are not the Only Fruit* (1991), Vintage. Awakening sexuality in the north.

Literature classics

Austen, Jane, *Pride and Prejudice* (1994), Penguin. Early 19th-century middle class marriages.

Brontë, Emily, *Wuthering Heights* (2003), Penguin. Desperate romance on the Yorkshire Moors.
Conrad, Joseph, *The Secret Agent* (2004), Oxford World's Classics. Early 20th century conspiracy thriller, set in and around Greenwich and Soho.
Dickens, Charles, *Bleak House* (2003), Penguin. London-set novel about being caught in chancery.
Eliot, George, *Middlemarch* (1998), Oxford World's Classics. Early 19th-century middle class manners.
Fielding, Henry, *Joseph Andrews* (1999), Penguin. 18th century picaresque novel.
Hardy, Thomas, *Mayor of Casterbridge* (1994), Penguin. Reformed man comes unstuck again in rural Wessex.
James, Henry, *The Golden Bowl* (2000), Wordsworth Editions Ltd. Late 19th-century London society novel.
Madox Ford, Ford, *Last Post* (2002), Penguin. Early 20th-century soldiers' fortunes.
Waugh, Evelyn, *Men at Arms* (2001), Penguin. Mid 20th-century soldiers' fortunes.
Woolf, Virginia, *The Waves* (2000), Penguin. Early 20th-century middle class ennuie.

History

Black, Jeremy, *A New History of England* (2000), Sutton Publishing. Straightforward and brief background history.
Davies, Norman, *The Isles* (2000), Papermac. Gripping and highly Eurocentric history of Britain.
Hill, Christopher, *The World Turned Upside Down* (1991), Penguin. Story of the sects that flourished around the time of the Civil War, or The English Revolution, by the same author.
Hobsbawm, E, *Industry and Empire* (1999), Penguin. Classic socio-economic history of the industrial revolution.
Schama, Simon, *History of Britain* (2000), BBC Consumer Publishing. Well-illustrated gazetteer of the popular TV series.

Nature and wildlife

Non-fiction

Hoskins, WG, *The Making of the English Landscape* (1991), Penguin. Classic textbook on how the country came to look the way it does.
Mabey, Richard, *Food for Free* (1999), Collins. Entertaining information on edible things growing wild in the English countryside.
White, Gilbert, *The Natural History of Selborne* (1996), Wordsworth Editions Ltd. An 18th-century naturalist's close observation of a corner of Hampshire.

Fiction

Adams, Richard, *Watership Down* (1993), Puffin. Talking rabbits in peril in Berkshire.
Grahame, Kenneth, *Wind in the Willows* (1991), Penguin. Toad, Rattie and Mole tell tall tales on the banks of the Thames.
Maxwell, Gavin, *Ring of Bright Water* (2001) Puffin. Days in the life of an otter in Devon.
Potter, Beatrix, *The Tale of Peter Rabbit* (1992), Puffin. Beautifully illustrated rabbit dodges the gardener Mr McGregor.
Williamson, Henry, *Tarka the Otter* (1995) Puffin. A tale of an otter's life in Devon, as seen through its own eyes.

Travel and general interest

Armitage, Simon, *All Points North* (1999), Penguin. Entertaining observations on his home area by a popular poet.
Bryson, Bill, *Notes from a Small Island* (1996), Black Swan. One bluff Anglophile American's journey round the country.
Danziger, Nick, *Danziger's Britain: A Journey into the Abyss* (1996), HarperCollins. Travels among the underclass created by Thatcher's government.
Deakin, Roger, *Waterlog* (2000), Vintage. Lively journal of a swim through England.
Raban, Jonathan, *Coasting* (1995), Picador. Round the coast in a boat with a sardonic commentator at the tiller.
Sebald, WG, *Rings of Saturn* (2002), Vintage. Extraordinary account of a resonant walk along the Suffolk Coast.

Footnotes

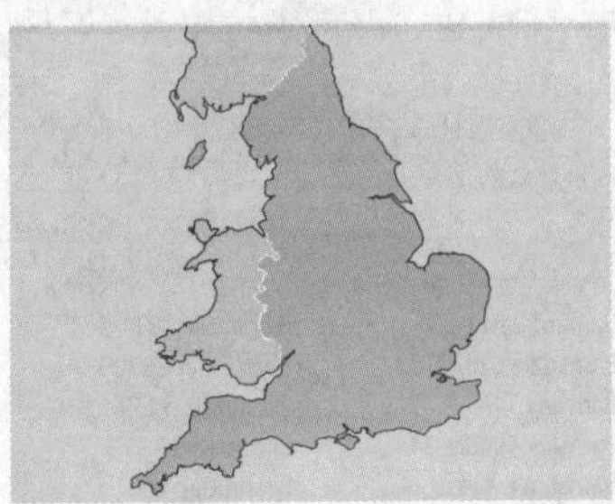

Index

D

E

F

S

T

Y

Z

Map index

Map symbols

Administration

- Capital city
- Other city/town

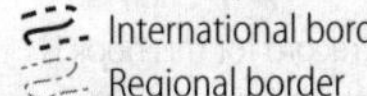

- International border
- Regional border
- Disputed border

Roads and travel

- Motorway
- Main road
- Minor road
- 4WD track
- Footpath
- Railway with station
- Airport
- Bus station
- Metro station
- Cable car
- Funicular
- Ferry

Water features

- River, canal
- Lake, ocean
- Seasonal marshland
- Beach, sand bank
- Waterfall

Topographical features

- Contours (approx)
- Mountain
- Volcano
- Mountain pass
- Escarpment
- Gorge
- Glacier
- Salt flat
- Rocks

Cities and towns

- Main through route
- Main street
- Minor street
- Pedestrianized street
- Tunnel
- One way street
- Steps
- Bridge
- Fortified wall
- Park, garden, stadium
- Sleeping
- Eating
- Bars & clubs
- Entertainment
- Building
- Sight
- Cathedral, church
- Chinese temple
- Hindu temple
- Meru
- Mosque
- Stupa
- Synagogue
- Tourist office
- Museum
- Post office
- Police
- Bank
- Internet
- Telephone
- Market
- Hospital
- Parking
- Petrol
- Golf
- Detail map
- Related map

Other symbols

- Archaeological site
- National park, wildlife reserve
- Viewing point
- Campsite
- Refuge, lodge
- Castle
- Diving
- Deciduous/coniferous/palm trees
- Hide
- Vineyard
- Distillery
- Shipwreck
- Historic battlefield

Credits

Footprint credits

Text editors: Davina Rungasamy, Sarah Thorowgood
Map editor: Sarah Sorensen
Picture editor: Claire Benison

Publisher: Patrick Dawson
Editorial: Alan Murphy, Sophie Blacksell, Claire Boobbyer, Felicity Laughton
Cartography: Robert Lunn, Claire Benison, Kevin Feeney
Series development: Rachel Fielding
Design: Mytton Williams and Rosemary Dawson (brand)
Advertising: Debbie Wylde
Finance and administration: Sharon Hughes, Elizabeth Taylor

Photography credits

Front cover: Alamy – Angel of the North, Gateshead.
Back cover: Robert Harding – fish and chips.
Inside colour section: Photo Library, Pictures Colour Library, British Museum Press Office, Alamy, National Trust, English Heritage, Britain on View, Cornish Picture Library.

Print

Manufactured in Italy by LegoPrint
Pulp from sustainable forests

Footprint feedback

We try as hard as we can to make each Footprint guide as up to date as possible but, of course, things always change. If you want to let us know about your experiences – good, bad or ugly – then don't delay, go to **www.footprintbooks.com** and send in your comments.

Publishing information

Footprint England
2nd edition

April 2004

ISBN 1 903471 91 5
CIP DATA: A catalogue record for this book is available from the British Library

Published by Footprint

6 Riverside Court
Lower Bristol Road
Bath BA2 3DZ, UK
T +44 (0)1225 469141
F +44 (0)1225 469461
discover@footprintbooks.com
www.footprintbooks.com

Distributed in the USA by

Publishers Group West

Neither the black and white nor colour maps are intended to have any political significance.

Every effort has been made to ensure that the facts in this guidebook are accurate. However, travellers should still obtain advice from consulates, airlines etc about travel and visa requirements before travelling. The authors and publishers cannot accept responsibility for any loss, injury or inconvenience however caused.

Acknowledgements

Charlie Godfrey-Faussett would like to thank the many people who have helped with this book, especially Steve Watson, Siam Chowkwanyun, Jason Gathorne-Hardy, Rowland Trafford-Roberts, Rupert John Gale, Keith Coventry, Lizzie Taylor, Jessica Greenman, Peter Oswald, John Ford, Clare de Jong, Hugh Simpson, Alice Lucas-Tooth, Matthew Brett, Tim Clark, Nicky Mist, Jessica Purcell, James Christopher, Nick Barton, Fi Godfrey-Faussett, Caro Taverne, Arthur Tewungwa, David Butler, and most of all Addie Godfrey-Faussett.

Thanks also to the following for their useful listings contributions: Charlotte Aston, Jonathan Cailes, Richard Fuller, Jessica Lumley, Gavin Stewart, Ben Townsend and Purni Morell for the Essentials chapter.

And to the whole Footprint editorial team, for giving up the secrets of Bath's underworld and especially Alan Murphy for his unfailing enthusiasm for the weird (manifested specifically in the book's boxes and festivals section), Claire Boobbyer for her Kentish know-how and Stef Lambe for her constant support and help.

Contributors

Alex Studholme (Bristol, Wells, Glastonbury, Exeter, Leicester and Norwich), returns to his native land from more esoteric pursuits. The author of *The Origins of Om Manipadme Hum* (SUNY Press 2002), he discovers his spiritual home really lies, not in Tibet, but in the green fields and ancient monuments of England's west country.

After spending years as a freelance investigative journalist in the US, **Christi Daugherty** (Yorkshire chapter), pitched it all in and moved to England, where she now works as a travel writer and editor-for-hire. In recent years she has co-written and edited travel guides to Boston and New Orleans, as well as European destinations. Her work has also appeared in *The Washington Post*, the *Dallas Morning News* and the *Financial Times*.

Laura Dixon (Northwest chapter), was born on the south coast, grew up in Kent and spent the majority of her adolescence attempting teenage rebellion in south Manchester. Having lived in London, Oxford and Surrey, she now lives in Bath and occasionally pines for the swagger, music and rain of the north. She is the author of *Footprint Reykjavik* and a contributor to the *Footprint Scotland Handbook*.

Max Carlish (Birmingham, Coventry, Warwick and Kenilworth, Stratford-upon-Avon, Leamington, Worcester and the Malverns), is a lecturer in film and TV at the University of Central England in Birmingham. He has contributed to magazines *Esquire* and *The Idler* and has made documentaries for the BBC, Channel 4 and Channel 5.

Andrew White (History) is a freelance editor and writer.

Ben Joliffe (St Ives, Land's End and the Lizard and Northumberland), writes about food, travel and the modern life of the soul. He lives in Somerset.

Chris Moore (Brighton, South Downs and Coast) is a London-based writer working for bbci who sporadically enjoys the charms of his East Sussex roots.

Complete title listing

Footprint publishes travel guides to over 150 destinations worldwide. Each guide is packed with practical, concise and colourful information for everybody from first-time travellers to travel aficionados. The list is growing fast and current titles are noted below.
Available from all good bookshops and online

www.footprintbooks.com

(P) denotes pocket guide

Latin America and Caribbean
Argentina
Barbados (P)
Bolivia
Brazil
Caribbean Islands
Central America & Mexico
Chile
Colombia
Costa Rica
Cuba
Cusco & the Inca Trail
Dominican Republic
Ecuador & Galápagos
Guatemala
Havana (P)
Mexico
Nicaragua
Peru
Rio de Janeiro
South American Handbook
Venezuela

North America
Vancouver (P)
New York (P)
Western Canada

Africa
Cape Town (P)
East Africa
Libya
Marrakech & the High Atlas
Marrakech (P)
Morocco
Namibia
South Africa
Tunisia
Uganda

Middle East
Egypt
Israel
Jordan
Syria & Lebanon

Australasia
Australia
East Coast Australia
New Zealand
Sydney (P)
West Coast Australia

Asia
Bali
Bangkok & the Beaches
Cambodia
Goa
Hong Kong (P)
India
Indian Himalaya
Indonesia
Laos
Malaysia
Nepal
Pakistan
Rajasthan & Gujarat
Singapore
South India
Sri Lanka
Sumatra
Thailand
Tibet
Vietnam

Europe
Andalucía
Barcelona
Barcelona (P)
Berlin (P)
Bilbao (P)
Bologna (P)
Britain
Copenhagen (P)
Croatia
Dublin
Dublin (P)
Edinburgh
Edinburgh (P)
England
Glasgow
Glasgow (P)
Ireland
Lisbon (P)
London
London (P)
Madrid (P)
Naples (P)
Northern Spain
Paris (P)
Reykjavík (P)
Scotland
Scotland Highlands & Islands
Seville (P)
Spain
Tallinn (P)
Turin (P)
Turkey
Valencia (P)
Verona (P)

Also available
Traveller's Handbook (WEXAS)
Traveller's Healthbook (WEXAS)
Traveller's Internet Guide (WEXAS)

England

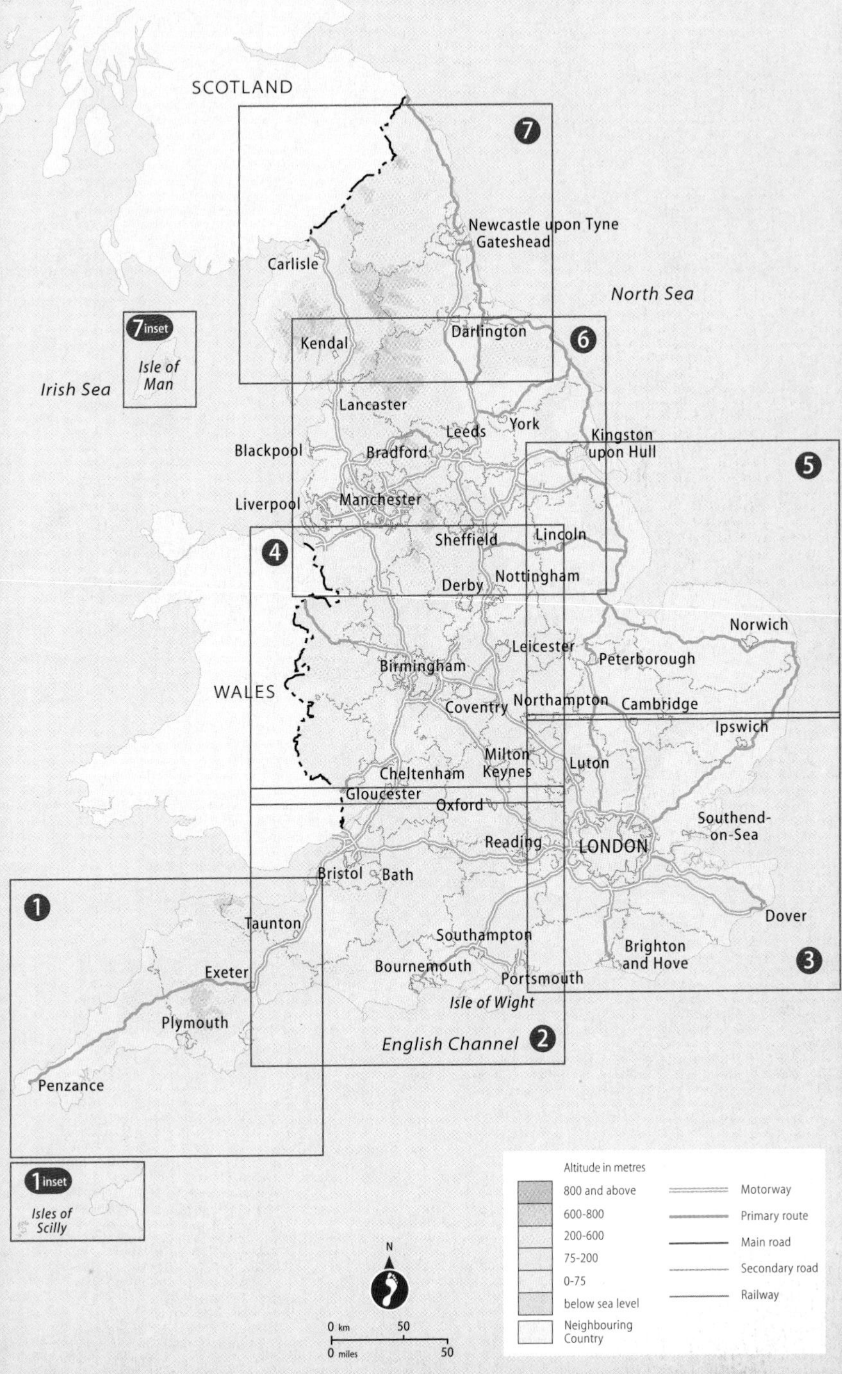

SCOTLAND
WALES
Irish Sea
North Sea
English Channel
7
6
5
4
3
2
1
7 inset
Isle of Man
1 inset
Isles of Scilly
Carlisle
Newcastle upon Tyne
Gateshead
Darlington
Kendal
Lancaster
York
Leeds
Kingston upon Hull
Blackpool
Bradford
Liverpool
Manchester
Sheffield
Lincoln
Derby
Nottingham
Norwich
Leicester
Peterborough
Birmingham
Coventry
Northampton
Cambridge
Ipswich
Milton Keynes
Luton
Cheltenham
Gloucester
Oxford
Southend-on-Sea
Reading
LONDON
Bristol
Bath
Taunton
Dover
Southampton
Exeter
Bournemouth
Portsmouth
Brighton and Hove
Isle of Wight
Plymouth
Penzance
N
0 km 50
0 miles 50
Altitude in metres
800 and above
600-800
200-600
75-200
0-75
below sea level
Neighbouring Country
Motorway
Primary route
Main road
Secondary road
Railway

Map 1

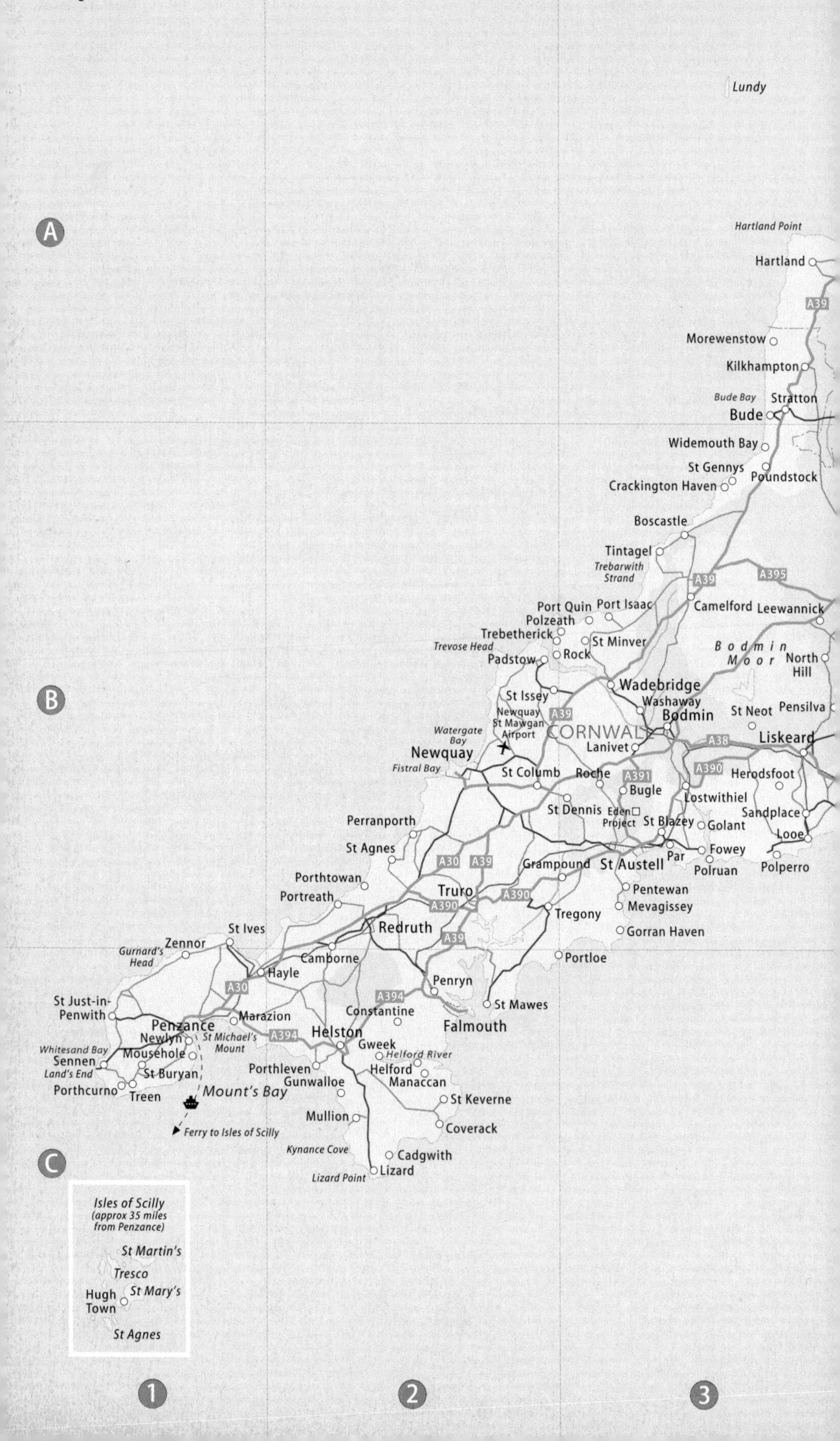

Lundy
A
Hartland Point
Hartland
A39
Morewenstow
Kilkhampton
Bude Bay
Stratton
Bude
Widemouth Bay
St Gennys
Poundstock
Crackington Haven
Boscastle
Tintagel
Trebarwith Strand
A39
A395
Port Quin
Port Isaac
Camelford
Leewannick
Polzeath
Trebetherick
St Minver
Trevose Head
Padstow
Rock
Bodmin Moor
North Hill
B
St Issey
Wadebridge
Washaway
Newquay St Mawgan Airport
A39
Bodmin
St Neot
Pensilva
Watergate Bay
CORNWALL
A38
Liskeard
Newquay
Lanivet
Fistral Bay
St Columb
Roche
A391
A390
Herodsfoot
Bugle
Lostwithiel
St Dennis
Eden Project
St Blazey
Golant
Sandplace
Perranporth
Looe
St Agnes
A30
A39
Grampound
St Austell
Par
Fowey
Polruan
Polperro
Porthtowan
Truro
A390
Pentewan
Portreath
A390
Mevagissey
Tregony
St Ives
Redruth
A39
Gorran Haven
Zennor
Gurnard's Head
Camborne
Portloe
Hayle
A30
Penryn
St Just-in-Penwith
A394
Constantine
St Mawes
Penzance
Marazion
Falmouth
Newlyn
St Michael's Mount
A394
Helston
Gweek
Whitesand Bay
Mousehole
Helford River
Sennen
Land's End
St Buryan
Porthleven
Helford
Manaccan
Porthcurno
Treen
Gunwalloe
Mount's Bay
St Keverne
Mullion
Coverack
Ferry to Isles of Scilly
Kynance Cove
Cadgwith
C
Lizard
Lizard Point
Isles of Scilly (approx 35 miles from Penzance)
St Martin's
Tresco
Hugh Town
St Mary's
St Agnes
1
2
3

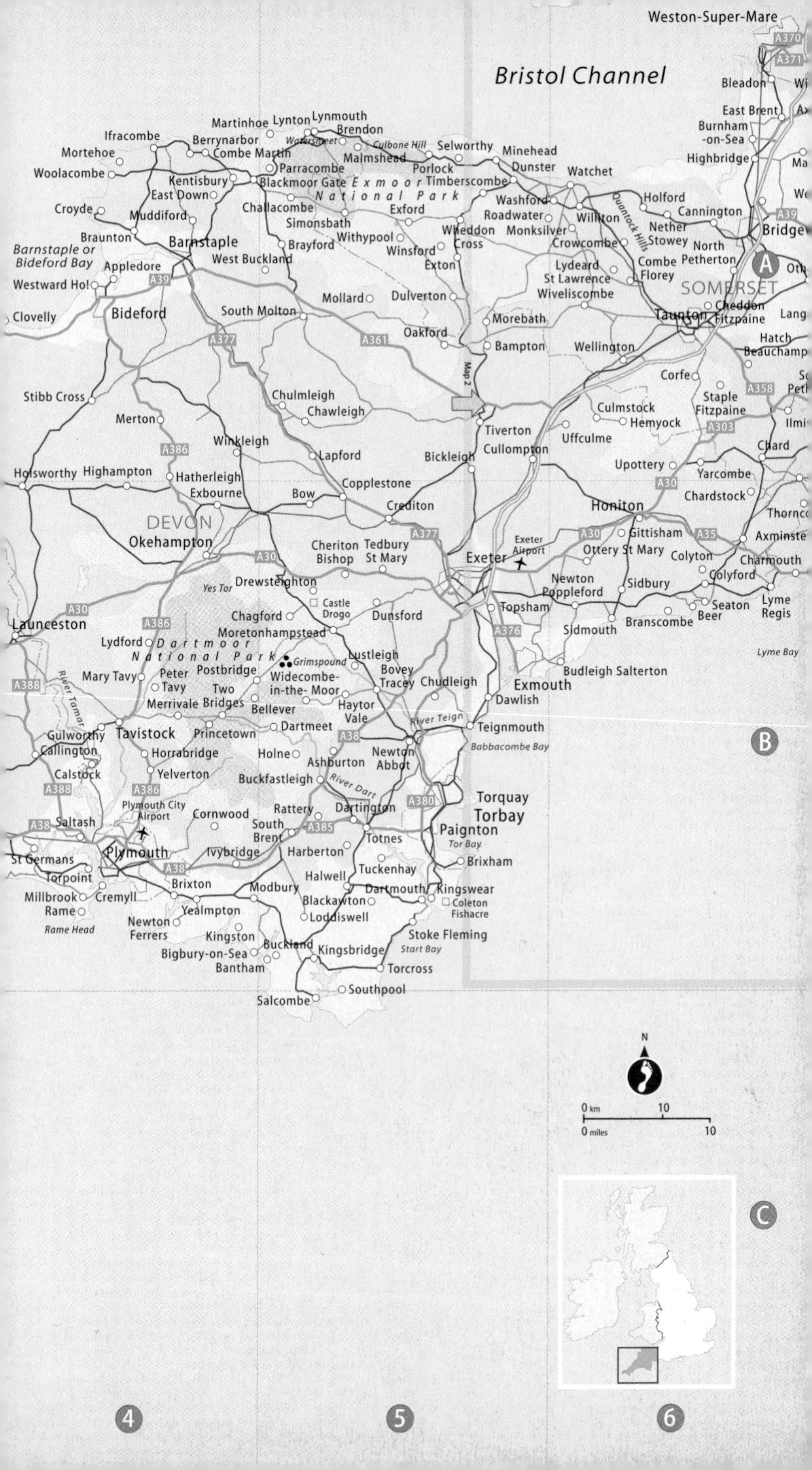

Weston-Super-Mare
A370
A371
Bristol Channel
Bleadon
East Brent
Burnham-on-Sea
Highbridge
Martinhoe
Lynton
Lynmouth
Brendon
Watersmeet
Culbone Hill
Selworthy
Minehead
Ifracombe
Berrynarbor
Combe Martin
Malmshead
Porlock
Dunster
Watchet
Mortehoe
Parracombe
Woolacombe
Kentisbury
Blackmoor Gate
Exmoor National Park
Timberscombe
East Down
Challacombe
Washford
Holford
Croyde
Muddiford
Exford
Roadwater
Williton
Cannington
Simonsbath
Quantock Hills
A39
Braunton
Withypool
Wheddon Cross
Monksilver
Nether Stowey
Bridge
Barnstaple or Bideford Bay
Barnstaple
Brayford
Winsford
Crowcombe
North Petherton
A
West Buckland
Exton
Lydeard St Lawrence
Combe Florey
Appledore
A39
Westward Ho!
SOMERSET
Mollard
Dulverton
Wiveliscombe
Cheddon Fitzpaine
Clovelly
Bideford
South Molton
Taunton
Morebath
A377
A361
Oakford
Bampton
Wellington
Hatch Beauchamp
Map 2
Corfe
Stibb Cross
Chulmleigh
Staple Fitzpaine
A358
Chawleigh
Culmstock
Hemyock
Merton
Tiverton
A303
A386
Winkleigh
Cullompton
Uffculme
Chard
Lapford
Bickleigh
Upottery
Holsworthy
Highampton
Hatherleigh
Yarcombe
Copplestone
A30
Exbourne
Bow
Chardstock
Crediton
Honiton
DEVON
A377
A30
Gittisham
A35
Axminster
Okehampton
Cheriton Bishop
Tedbury St Mary
Exeter
Exeter Airport
Ottery St Mary
Colyton
Charmouth
A30
Yes Tor
Drewsteighton
Colyford
Newton Poppleford
Sidbury
Castle Drogo
Seaton
Lyme Regis
A30
Chagford
Dunsford
Topsham
Beer
Launceston
A386
Moretonhampstead
Branscombe
Sidmouth
A376
Lydford
Dartmoor National Park
Lustleigh
Lyme Bay
Grimspound
Bovey Tracey
Budleigh Salterton
Mary Tavy
Peter Tavy
Postbridge
Widecombe-in-the-Moor
Chudleigh
A388
River Tamar
Two Bridges
Exmouth
Merrivale
Haytor Vale
Dawlish
Bellever
River Teign
Gulworthy
Tavistock
Princetown
Dartmeet
Teignmouth
A38
Callington
Babbacombe Bay
B
Horrabridge
Holne
Newton Abbot
Ashburton
Calstock
Yelverton
Buckfastleigh
River Dart
A388
A386
Torquay
Torbay
Plymouth City Airport
Cornwood
Rattery
Dartington
A380
A38
Saltash
South Brent
A385
Paignton
Totnes
Tor Bay
St Germans
Plymouth
Ivybridge
Harberton
Brixham
A38
Torpoint
Tuckenhay
Brixton
Halwell
Millbrook
Cremyll
Modbury
Dartmouth
Kingswear
Rame
Yealmpton
Blackawton
Coleton Fishacre
Rame Head
Newton Ferrers
Loddiswell
Kingston
Stoke Fleming
Bigbury-on-Sea
Buckland
Kingsbridge
Start Bay
Bantham
Torcross
Southpool
Salcombe
N
0 km
10
0 miles
10
C
4
5
6

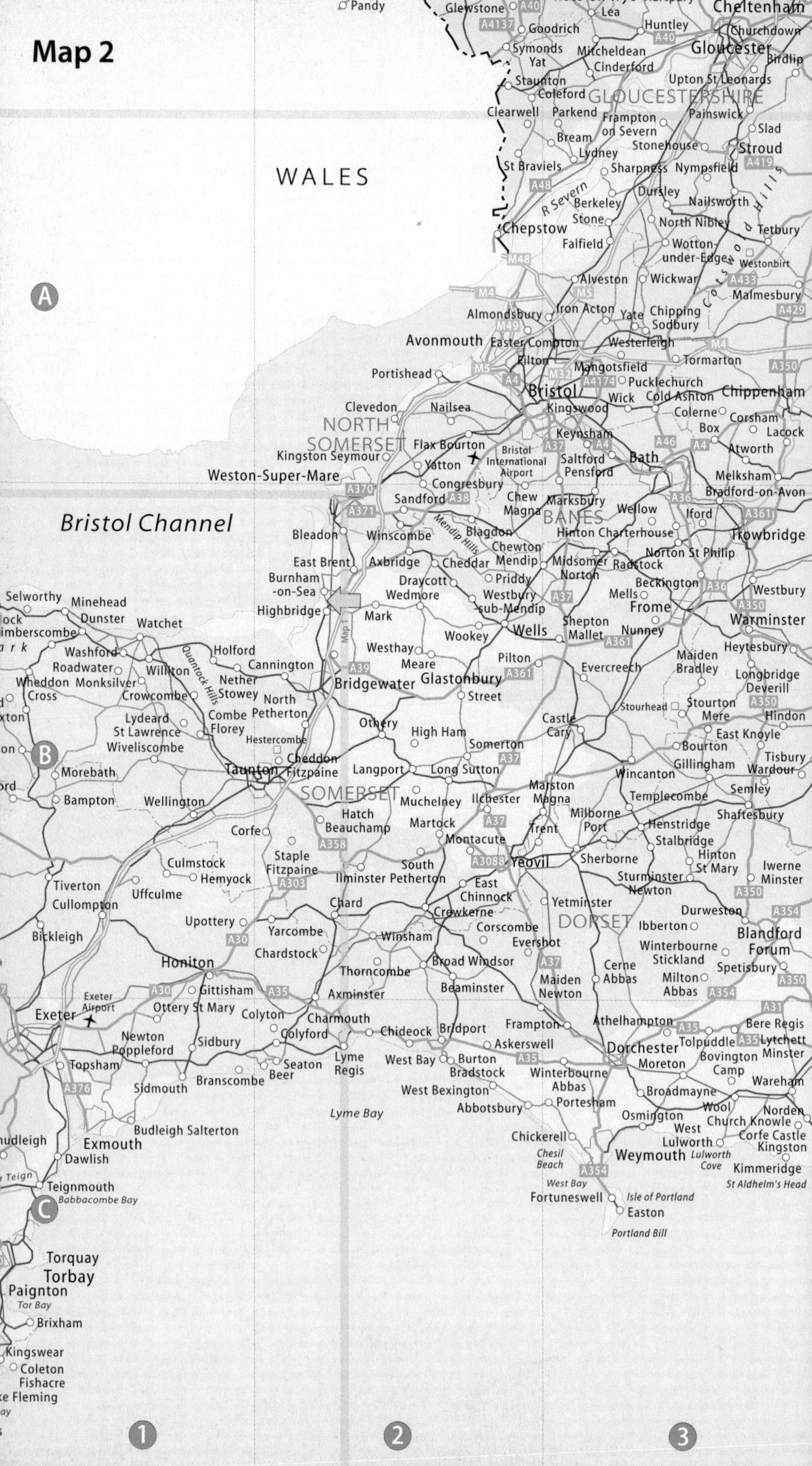

Map 2
WALES
Bristol Channel
GLOUCESTERSHIRE
NORTH SOMERSET
BANES
SOMERSET
DORSET
A
B
C
1
2
3
Pandy
Glewstone
Lea
Cheltenham
Goodrich
Huntley
Churchdown
Symonds Yat
Mitcheldean
Gloucester
Birdlip
Cinderford
Staunton
Upton St Leonards
Coleford
Clearwell
Parkend
Frampton on Severn
Painswick
Slad
Bream
Stonehouse
Stroud
Lydney
St Braviels
Sharpness
Nympsfield
R Severn
Berkeley
Dursley
Nailsworth
Stone
Chepstow
North Nibley
Tetbury
Falfield
Wotton-under-Edge
Westonbirt
Alveston
Wickwar
Malmesbury
Almondsbury
Iron Acton
Yate
Chipping Sodbury
Avonmouth
Easter Compton
Westerleigh
Filton
Tormarton
Portishead
Mangotsfield
Pucklechurch
Bristol
Wick
Cold Ashton
Chippenham
Clevedon
Nailsea
Kingswood
Colerne
Corsham
Box
Lacock
Keynsham
Kingston Seymour
Flax Bourton
Bristol International Airport
Saltford
Bath
Atworth
Yatton
Pensford
Melksham
Weston-Super-Mare
Congresbury
Bradford-on-Avon
Sandford
Chew Magna
Marksbury
Wellow
Iford
Bleadon
Winscombe
Mendip Hills
Blagdon
Hinton Charterhouse
Trowbridge
Chewton Mendip
Norton St Philip
East Brent
Axbridge
Cheddar
Midsomer Norton
Radstock
Burnham-on-Sea
Draycott
Priddy
Beckington
Westbury
Wedmore
Westbury-sub-Mendip
Mells
Frome
Highbridge
Mark
Shepton Mallet
Warminster
Selworthy
Minehead
Dunster
Watchet
Wookey
Wells
Nunney
Westhay
Heytesbury
Holford
Meare
Pilton
Maiden Bradley
Washford
Roadwater
Cannington
Williton
Quantock Hills
Evercreech
Longbridge Deverill
Wheddon Cross
Monksilver
Nether Stowey
Bridgewater
Glastonbury
Crowcombe
North Petherton
Street
Stourhead
Stourton
Mere
Lydeard St Lawrence
Combe Florey
Othery
Castle Cary
Hindon
High Ham
East Knoyle
Wiveliscombe
Hestercombe
Somerton
Bourton
Tisbury
Cheddon Fitzpaine
Langport
Long Sutton
Gillingham
Wardour
Morebath
Taunton
Wincanton
Semley
Marston Magna
Bampton
Wellington
Muchelney
Ilchester
Templecombe
Shaftesbury
Hatch Beauchamp
Milborne Port
Corfe
Martock
Trent
Henstridge
Montacute
Stalbridge
Staple Fitzpaine
Hinton St Mary
Culmstock
South Petherton
Yeovil
Sherborne
Iwerne Minster
Hemyock
Ilminster
East Chinnock
Sturminster Newton
Tiverton
Ufculme
Cullompton
Chard
Yetminster
Crewkerne
Durweston
Upottery
Yarcombe
Corscombe
Ibberton
Blandford Forum
Bickleigh
Winsham
Evershot
Winterbourne Stickland
Chardstock
Broad Windsor
Cerne Abbas
Spetisbury
Honiton
Thorncombe
Maiden Newton
Milton Abbas
Gittisham
Beaminster
Exeter Airport
Axminster
Ottery St Mary
Colyton
Charmouth
Athelhampton
Bere Regis
Exeter
Frampton
Newton Poppleford
Chideock
Bridport
Tolpuddle
Lytchett Minster
Colyford
Askerswell
Sidbury
Dorchester
Bovington Camp
Topsham
Lyme Regis
Seaton
West Bay
Burton Bradstock
Moreton
Beer
Winterbourne Abbas
Wareham
Branscombe
Sidmouth
West Bexington
Broadmayne
Abbotsbury
Portesham
Wool
Norden
Lyme Bay
Osmington
Church Knowle
West Lulworth
Corfe Castle
Budleigh Salterton
Chickerell
Kingston
Exmouth
Chesil Beach
Weymouth
Lulworth Cove
Dawlish
Kimmeridge
Teign
Teignmouth
West Bay
St Aldhelm's Head
Babbacombe Bay
Fortuneswell
Isle of Portland
Easton
Portland Bill
Torquay
Torbay
Paignton
Tor Bay
Brixham
Kingswear
Coleton Fishacre
Map 1
A40
A4137
A48
M48
M4
M5
M49
M32
A4174
A4
A37
A46
A370
A371
A38
A36
A361
A39
A350
A419
A433
A429
A303
A358
A3088
A30
A35
A354
A376
A31

Brockhampton
Lower Slaughter
Bledington
Charlbury
BUCKINGHAMSHIRE
Whitchurch
Wing
Buzzard
Dunstab
Great Rissington
Bourton-on-the-Water
A436
A40
A34
A41
Waddesdon
A418
Ivinghoe
Whips
Leafield
Woodstock
Northleach
Great Barrington
Ramsden
Islip
Aylesbury
Aldbury
Chedworth
A40
Swinbrook
Bladon
Kidlington
Stanton St John
Long Crendon
Stone
Aston Clinton
Tring
North Cerney
Sapperton
Burford
Minster Lovell
Witney
Eynsham
Wytham
A40
M40
Map 4
Bibury
Aldsworth
Stanton Harcourt
Oxford
Wendover
Winstone
Barnsley
Coln-St-Aldwyns
Carterton
Princes Risborough
Berkhamsted
A429
OXFORDSHIRE
A4142
Thame
A413
Chesham
Meysey Hampton
Fairford
Bampton
Northmoor
Great Milton
Tetsworth
Great Missenden
Cumnor
Nuneham Courtenay
Chiltern Hills
A4010
Amersham
Cirencester
Kelmscott
Aston
Standlake
Wootton
Stadhampton
Little Missenden
Kemble
South Cerney
Lechlade on Thames
Buckland
A420
Abingdon
Chalgrove
West Wycombe
Chalfont St Giles
Buscot
Kingston Bagpuize
Sutton Courtenay
Dorchester
Watlington
Ashton Keynes
A419
Faringdon
Highworth
East Hanney
Appleford
Fingest
High Wycombe
A355
Cricklade
Northend
Lane End
Shrivenham
Uffington
Steventon
Didcot
Benson
Turville
A
Minety
A420
Wantage
A34
Wallingford
Nettlebed
Stonor
Marlow
A404
M40
Ardington
Hurley
Swindon
Ashbury
Moulsford
Woodcote
Henley-on-Thames
Cookham
Maidenhead
Slough
Wanborough
East Ilsley
Streatley
Goring
Bray
Eton
Baydon
Lambourn
Lower Basildon
Mapledurham
M4
Lyneham
A34
Windsor
River Thames
Great Shefford
Yattendon
Reading
Hilmarton
Aldbourne
A346
Ramsbury
M3
Hermitage
Theale
Egham
Calne
Cherhill
Axford
Bracknell
Ascot
Avebury
Froxfield
Hungerford
Thatcham
Sunningdale
Bishops Cannings
Marlborough
Little Bedwyn
Newbury
Wokingham
M3
River Kennet
Aldermaston
Crowthorne
Windlesham
Wootton Rivers
Kennet and Avon Canal
Burghclere
Sandhurst
Chobham
Devizes
Highclere
Silchester
Camberley
WILTSHIRE
Pewsey
Burbage
A339
Hartley Wintney
Woking
A33
A338
Kingsclere
Sherborne St John
Bisley
Urchfont
Upavon
Collingbourne Kingston
Hurstbourne Tarrant
Market Lavington
Everleigh
Hook
Fleet
Farnborough
Basingstoke
M3
Guildford
Ludgershall
A34
Overton
Aldershot
Netheravon
Tidworth
Hurstbourne Priors
Map 3
Farnham
Weyhill
Whitchurch
Salisbury Plain
Thruxton
Andover
Herriard
A303
A303
A3
Stonehenge
HAMPSHIRE
Godalming
Codford St Mary
Amesbury
Middle Wallop
Sutton Scotney
Preston Candover
Alton
A31
Wylye
Stapleford
Headley
Hindhead
Stockbridge
A34
Great Wishford
New Alresford
Selborne
Chiddingfold
Teffont Magna
King's Somborne
Crawley
Haslemere
Wilton
A3
Salisbury
Liphook
Compton
Winchester
A31
Cheriton
B
Chamberlayne
A36
Bramdean
Liss
Northchapel
Fovant
Coombe Bissett
Bishopstone
Whiteparish
Hursley
Alvediston
Nunton
M3
Twyford
West Meon
A272
Midhurst
Petworth
Downton
Petersfield
Redlynch
Romsey
Southampton International Airport
Warnford
Whitsbury
Eastleigh
Meonstoke
South Harting
WEST SUSSEX
Breamore
West Wellow
Droxford
Cocking
Hambledon
Fordingbridge
M27
Southampton
Bishop's Waltham
Compton
Cranborne
North Gorley
on
Minstead
Horndean
Singleton
A3(M)
Knowlton
Ibsley
Ashurst
Hamble-le-Rice
Wickham
Lyndhurst
Havant
Slindon
Witchampton
Ringwood
A31
New Forest
Hythe
Southampton Water
Cosham
A27
Chichester
Brockenhurst
Fareham
Emsworth
Wimborne Minster
A338
Beaulieu
Fawley
Bournemouth International Airport
Burley
Portsmouth
Bucklers Hard
Exbury
Sway
Boldre
Gosport
South Hayling
Bognor Regis
Sopley
Cowes
Southsea
New Milton
Lymington
The Solent
East Wittering
Fishbourne
Ryde
Christchurch
Selsey
Keyhaven
Newtown
Seaview
Poole
Bournemouth
Milford-on-Sea
Selsey Bill
St Helens
Poole Harbour
Yarmouth
Newport
Bembridge
Brownsea Island
Poole Bay
Freshwater
Brading
Carisbrooke
Isle of Purbeck
Studland Bay
Totland
Studland
Shorwell
Sandown
The Needles
Godshill
Brighstone
ISLE OF WIGHT
Shanklin
Swanage
Isle of Wight
Durlston Head
Chale
Ventnor
Worth Matravers
St Catherine's Point
C
English Channel
N
0 km
10
0 miles
10
4
5
6

Map 3
Wellingborough
Higham Ferrers
Rushden
Water
Great Staughton
Oakington
Waterbeach
Barrow
Lolworth
Elsworth
Bottisham
Newmarket
Bozeat
Sharnbrook
St Neots
Map 5
Eltisley
Cambridge
Cambridge Airport
Lidgate
Dullingham
Castle Ashby
Thurleigh
Caxton
Yardley Hastings
Milton Ernest
Abbotsley
Grantchester
Trumpington
Wickhambrook
Horton
Lavendon
Renhold
Roxton
Gamlingay
Bedford
Orwell
Sawston
Thurlow
Olney
Sandy
Shepreth
Linton
Cardington
Cockayne Hatley
Kempston
Elstow
Biggleswade
Duxford
Haverhill
Clare
Newport Pagnell
Steeple Morden
Great Chesterford
Saffron Walden
Steeple Bumpstead
Ridgewell
Wolverton
BEDFORDSHIRE
Ampthill
Clophill
Shefford
Ashwell
Royston
Great Yeldham
Milton Keynes
Stotfold
Arlesey
Baldock
Wendens Ambo
Barkway
Newport
Finchingfield
Flitwick
Map 4
Shillington
Letchworth
Buckland
HERTFORDSHIRE
Thaxted
Woburn
Hitchin
Buntingford
Great Bardfield
Padbury
Braughing
Winslow
Stewkley
Stevenage
Stansted Airport
Great Dunmow
Braintree
Leighton Buzzard
Luton
Luton Airport
Knebworth
Standon
Bishop's Stortford
Hatfield Forest
High Roding
Wing
Dunstable
Whitwell
Much Hadham
Waddesdon
Ivinghoe
Kimpton
Whipsnade
Harpenden
Ware
Leaden Roding
Great Waltham
Aylesbury
Hertford
Stone
Tring
Aldbury
Redbourn
Welwyn Garden City
Sawbridgeworth
ESSEX
Aston Clinton
Hemel Hempstead
St Albans
Hatfield
Harlow
Wendover
Princes Risborough
Berkhampsted
Moreton
Chelmsford
Great Baddow
Chesham
Great Missenden
Kings Langley
Potters Bar
Cheshunt
Epping
Chipping Ongar
Ingatestone
Amersham
Watford
Stock
Little Missenden
Waltham Abbey
West Wycombe
Chenies
Enfield
Barnet
Rettendon
Billericay
Chalfont St Giles
Fingest
High Wycombe
Rickmansworth
Chigwell
Wickford
Brentwood
Turville
Lane End
Beaconsfield
Gerrards Cross
Harrow
GREATER LONDON
Basildon
South Benfleet
Marlow
Hurley
Barking
Dagenham
Rainham
Cookham
Uxbridge
Maidenhead
Slough
Iver
City of London
City Airport
Westminster
Bray
Eton
Grays
Cliffe
Tilbury
Windsor
River Thames
Hounslow
LONDON
Heathrow Airport
Richmond
Merton
Dartford
Egham
Staines
Sunbury
Kingston upon Thames
Bracknell
Ascot
Bromley
Swanley
Rochester
Sunningdale
Farningham
Chatham
Wokingham
Meopham
Crowthorne
Chertsey
Sutton
Sandhurst
Windlesham
Croydon
Orpington
Eynsford
Wouldham
Chobham
Weybridge
Camberley
Epsom
Purley
Biggin Hill
Snodland
Hartley Wintney
Woking
Wisley
Bisley
Banstead
Warlingham
Wrotham
River Wey
Leatherhead
Farnborough
Caterham
Westerham
Maidstone
Sevenoaks
Fleet
East Clandon
Oxted
Mereworth
Aldershot
Guildford
SURREY
Loose
Shere
Dorking
Reigate
Redhill
Godstone
Crockham Hill
Yalding
Low Weald
Farnham
Chiddingstone
Leigh
Hildenborough
Tonbridge
Outwood
Hever
Holmbury St Mary
Marden
Penshurst
Gatwick Airport
Godalming
East Grinstead
Southborough
Royal Tunbridge Wells
Goudhurst
Ockley
Capel
Horley
Charlwood
Headley
Hindhead
Cranleigh
Crawley
Cranbrook
Selborne
Chiddingfold
Rudgwick
Haslemere
High Weald
Crowborough
Liphook
Horsham
Ashdown Forest
Hawkhurst
Liss
Northchapel
Map 2
Billingshurst
Maresfield
Haywards Heath
Cowfold
Petersfield
Midhurst
Petworth
West Grinstead
Burgess Hill
Uckfield
South Harting
WEST SUSSEX
Fittleworth
Heathfield
EAST SUSSEX
Cocking
Hurstpierpoint
Low Weald
Battle
Compton
Storrington
Ditchling
Singleton
Amberley
Washington
Ninfield
South Downs
Lewes
Slindon
Arundel
Findon
Glynde
Hailsham
Chichester
West Firle
Brighton and Hove
Emsworth
Worthing
Bexhill
Alfriston
Pevensey
Shoreham-by-Sea
Rottingdean
Littlehampton
Newhaven
Peacehaven
Eastbourne
Bognor Regis
Seaford
East Wittering
English Channel
East Dean
Beachy Head
Selsey
Selsey Bill
A
B
C
1
2
3

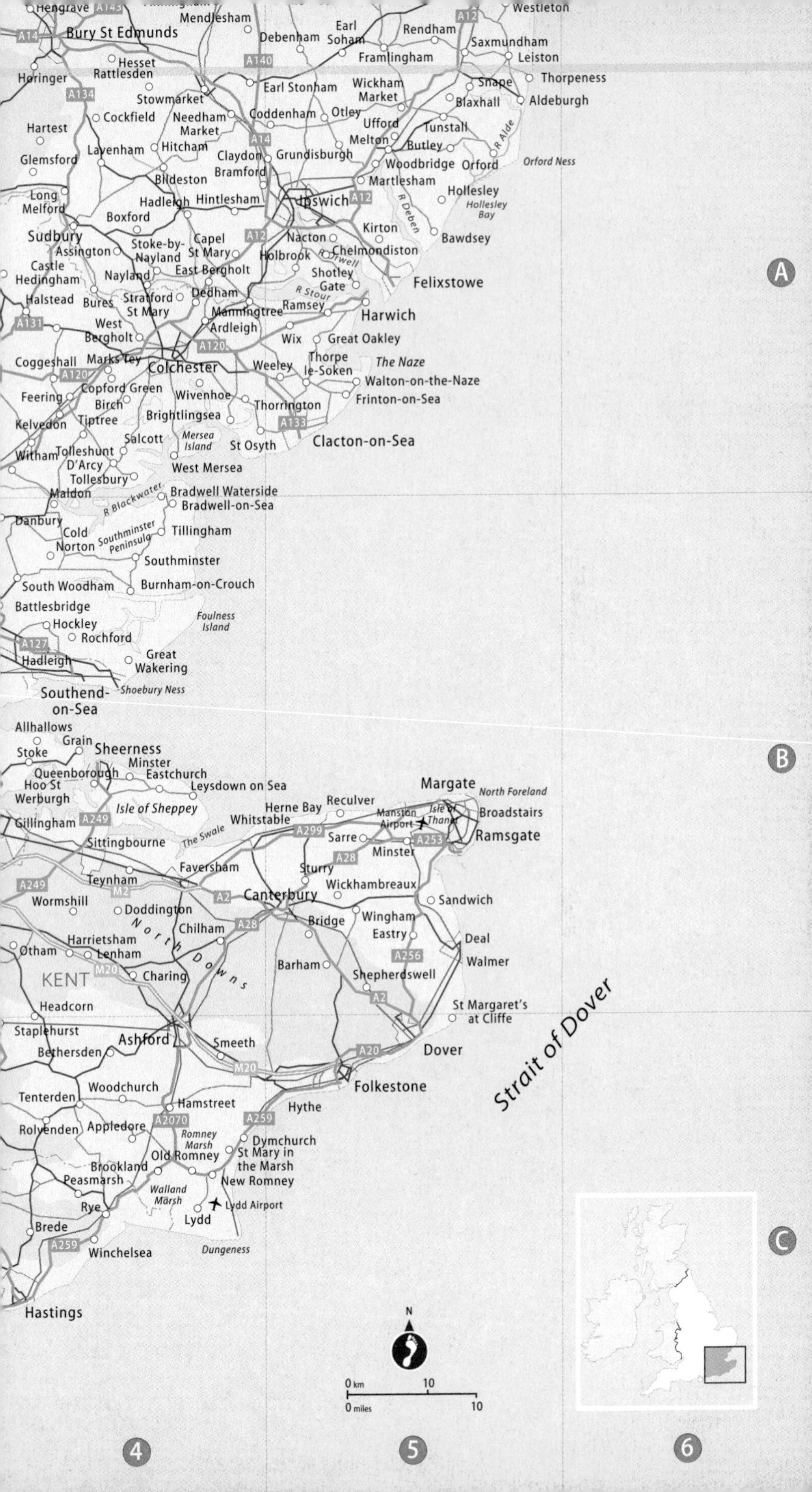
Hengrave
Mendlesham
Westleton
Bury St Edmunds
Debenham
Earl Soham
Rendham
Saxmundham
Hesset
Framlingham
Leiston
Horinger
Rattlesden
Earl Stonham
Wickham Market
Snape
Thorpeness
Stowmarket
Blaxhall
Aldeburgh
Cockfield
Needham Market
Coddenham
Otley
Hartest
Ufford
Tunstall
R Alde
Melton
Butley
Glemsford
Lavenham
Hitcham
Claydon
Grundisburgh
Woodbridge
Orford
Orford Ness
Bramford
Martlesham
Bildeston
Long Melford
Hadleigh
Hintlesham
Ipswich
Hollesley
Hollesley Bay
Boxford
R Deben
Kirton
Sudbury
Capel St Mary
Nacton
Bawdsey
Assington
Stoke-by-Nayland
Chelmondiston
Castle Hedingham
Holbrook
R Orwell
Nayland
East Bergholt
Shotley Gate
Felixstowe
Halstead
Bures
Stratford St Mary
Dedham
R Stour
Ramsey
Manningtree
Harwich
West Bergholt
Ardleigh
Wix
Great Oakley
Thorpe le-Soken
Coggeshall
Marks Tey
Colchester
Weeley
The Naze
Walton-on-the-Naze
Feering
Copford Green
Wivenhoe
Frinton-on-Sea
Birch
Thorrington
Kelvedon
Tiptree
Brightlingsea
Salcott
Mersea Island
St Osyth
Clacton-on-Sea
Witham
Tolleshunt D'Arcy
West Mersea
Tollesbury
Maldon
R Blackwater
Bradwell Waterside
Bradwell-on-Sea
Danbury
Cold Norton
Southminster Peninsula
Tillingham
Southminster
South Woodham
Burnham-on-Crouch
Battlesbridge
Foulness Island
Hockley
Rochford
Hadleigh
Great Wakering
Southend-on-Sea
Shoebury Ness
Allhallows
Grain
Stoke
Sheerness
Minster
Queenborough
Eastchurch
Hoo St Werburgh
Leysdown on Sea
Margate
North Foreland
Reculver
Herne Bay
Isle of Sheppey
Manston Airport
Isle of Thanet
Broadstairs
Gillingham
Whitstable
The Swale
Sarre
Ramsgate
Sittingbourne
Minster
Sturry
Faversham
Teynham
Wickhambreaux
Canterbury
Sandwich
Wormshill
Doddington
North Downs
Chilham
Bridge
Wingham
Eastry
Deal
Harrietsham
Otham
Lenham
Barham
Walmer
KENT
Charing
Shepherdswell
Headcorn
St Margaret's at Cliffe
Strait of Dover
Staplehurst
Ashford
Smeeth
Bethersden
Dover
Folkestone
Woodchurch
Tenterden
Hamstreet
Hythe
Rolvenden
Appledore
Romney Marsh
Dymchurch
St Mary in the Marsh
Old Romney
Brookland
New Romney
Peasmarsh
Walland Marsh
Lydd Airport
Rye
Lydd
Brede
Dungeness
Winchelsea
Hastings
A14
A143
A12
A140
A134
A131
A120
A133
A127
A249
A299
A253
A28
M2
A2
A256
M20
A20
A259
A2070
N
0 km
10
0 miles
10
A
B
C
4
5
6

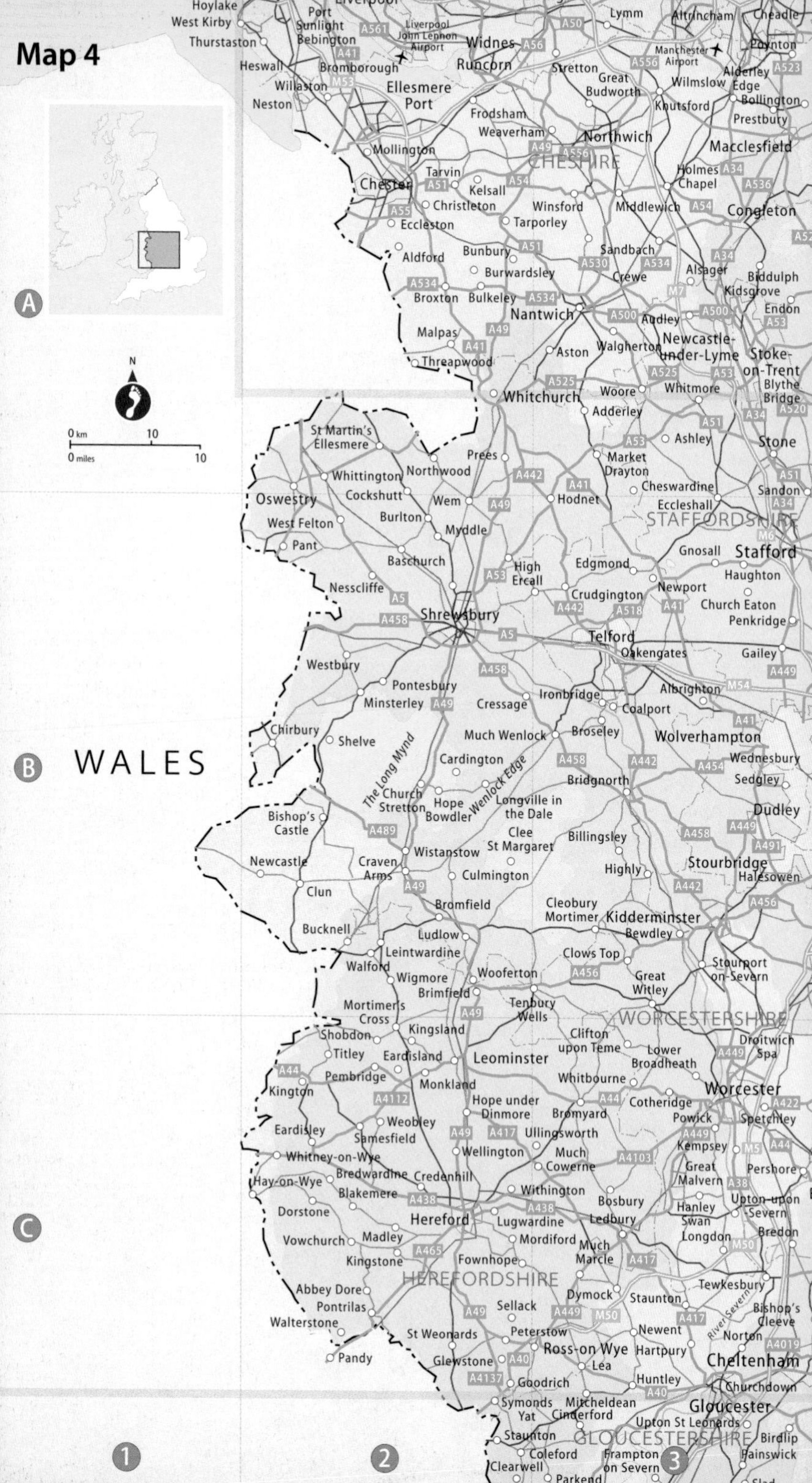

Map 4
A
B
C
1
2
3
N
0 km
10
0 miles
10
WALES
CHESHIRE
STAFFORDSHIRE
WORCESTERSHIRE
HEREFORDSHIRE
GLOUCESTERSHIRE
Hoylake
West Kirby
Thurstaston
Heswall
Willaston
Neston
Port Sunlight
Bebington
Bromborough
Liverpool John Lennon Airport
Widnes
Runcorn
Ellesmere Port
Lymm
Altrincham
Cheadle
Manchester Airport
Poynton
Stretton
Great Budworth
Wilmslow
Alderley Edge
Knutsford
Bollington
Prestbury
Frodsham
Weaverham
Northwich
Macclesfield
Mollington
Chester
Tarvin
Kelsall
Christleton
Eccleston
Winsford
Tarporley
Middlewich
Holmes Chapel
Congleton
Aldford
Bunbury
Sandbach
Burwardsley
Crewe
Alsager
Biddulph
Kidsgrove
Broxton
Bulkeley
Nantwich
Audley
Endon
Malpas
Aston
Walgherton
Newcastle-under-Lyme
Stoke-on-Trent
Threapwood
Whitchurch
Woore
Whitmore
Blythe Bridge
Adderley
St Martin's
Ellesmere
Prees
Ashley
Stone
Market Drayton
Whittington
Northwood
Cheswardine
Sandon
Oswestry
Cockshutt
Wem
Hodnet
Eccleshall
West Felton
Burlton
Myddle
Pant
Baschurch
High Ercall
Edgmond
Gnosall
Stafford
Haughton
Nesscliffe
Crudgington
Newport
Church Eaton
Shrewsbury
Penkridge
Telford
Oakengates
Gailey
Westbury
Pontesbury
Albrighton
Minsterley
Cressage
Ironbridge
Coalport
Chirbury
Much Wenlock
Broseley
Wolverhampton
Shelve
The Long Mynd
Wenlock Edge
Cardington
Wednesbury
Sedgley
Bridgnorth
Church Stretton
Hope Bowdler
Longville in the Dale
Dudley
Bishop's Castle
Clee St Margaret
Billingsley
Newcastle
Wistanstow
Craven Arms
Culmington
Highly
Stourbridge
Halesowen
Clun
Bromfield
Cleobury Mortimer
Kidderminster
Bucknell
Ludlow
Bewdley
Leintwardine
Clows Top
Walford
Wigmore
Wooferton
Stourport on-Severn
Brimfield
Great Witley
Mortimer's Cross
Tenbury Wells
Shobdon
Kingsland
Clifton upon Teme
Droitwich Spa
Titley
Eardisland
Leominster
Lower Broadheath
Pembridge
Kington
Monkland
Whitbourne
Worcester
Hope under Dinmore
Cotheridge
Bromyard
Powick
Spetchley
Weobley
Eardisley
Samesfield
Ullingswood
Kempsey
Wellington
Much Cowarne
Whitney-on-Wye
Bredwardine
Credenhill
Great Malvern
Pershore
Hay-on-Wye
Blakemere
Withington
Bosbury
Upton-upon-Severn
Dorstone
Hereford
Lugwardine
Ledbury
Hanley Swan
Vowchurch
Madley
Mordiford
Longdon
Bredon
Much Marcle
Kingstone
Fownhope
Tewkesbury
Abbey Dore
Dymock
Staunton
Pontrilas
Sellack
Bishop's Cleeve
Walterstone
River Severn
St Weonards
Peterstow
Newent
Norton
Ross-on Wye
Hartpury
Pandy
Lea
Cheltenham
Glewstone
Goodrich
Huntley
Churchdown
Symonds Yat
Mitcheldean
Cinderford
Gloucester
Upton St Leonards
Staunton
Birdlip
Coleford
Frampton on Severn
Painswick
Clearwell
Parkend
Slad
Forest
A561
A41
M53
A50
A56
A556
A523
A49
A34
A536
A51
A54
A55
A530
A534
A52
M7
A500
A53
A525
A520
A442
M6
A5
A458
A518
M54
A449
A454
A489
A491
A456
A4112
A417
A4103
M5
A438
A465
A422
M50
A40
A4019
A4137

High Peak
Sheffield
Sheffield City Airport
Gainsborough
Marple
Edale
New Mills
Hope
Bamford
Castleton
Hathersage
Whaley Bridge
Chapel-en-le-Frith
Eyam
Blyth
Beckingham
Hayton
Willingham by Stow
Worksop
Retford
Marton
Sturton by Stow
Newton on Trent
Saxilby
Dronfield
Buxton
Tideswell
DERBYSHIRE
Chesterfield
Bolsover
Cuckney
Tuxford
Harby
Market Warsop
Shirebrook
Ollerton
Thorpe on the Hill
Branston
Bakewell
Flash
NOTTINGHAMSHIRE
Mansfield Woodhouse
Pleasley
Clay Cross
Kneesall
Carlton-on-Trent
Collingham
Harmston
Hartington
Matlock
Mansfield
Sherwood Forest
Matlock Bath
Sutton in Ashfield
Caunton
Navenby
Leek
Alfreton
Kirklington
Newark-on-Trent
Whatstandwell
Kirkby in Ashfield
Leadenham
Wirksworth
Southwell
Beckingham
Tissington
Ripley
Ambergate
Lowdham
Caythorpe
Ashbourne
Belper
Heanor
Eastwood
Arnold
Flintham
Honington
Mayfield
Duffield
Cheadle
Ilkeston
Nottingham
Bingham
Bottesford
Barkston
Denstone
Brailsford
Quarndon
Upper Tean
Stapleford
Radcliffe on Trent
Sedgebrook
Derby
Beeston
Belvoir
Grantham
Long Eaton
Keyworth
Croxton Kerrial
Great Ponton
Uttoxeter
Chellaston
Upper Broughton
Draycott in the Clay
Tutbury
Castle Donnington
Willoughby-on-the-Wolds
Melbourne
East Midlands Airport
Colsterworth
Abbotts Bromley
Saxelbye
Milford
Burton upon Trent
Swadlincote
Wymeswold
Saxby
Yoxall
Shepshed
Loughborough
Melton Mowbray
Castle Bytham
Ashby-de-la-Zouch
LEICESTERSHIRE
Stretton
Mountsorrel
Rearsby
Cannock
Coalville
Map 5
Empingham
Lichfield
Anstey
Oakham
Rutland Water
Groby
Manton
Normanton
Leicester
Billesdon
East Norton
Preston
Ketton
Brownhills
Tamworth
Oadby
Wigston
Walsall
Uppingham
Duddington
Great Glen
Sutton Coldfield
Kibworth Harcourt
Cottingham
Rockingham
Hinckley
Birmingham
Nuneaton
Market Harborough
Corby
Weldon
Brigstock
Bedworth
Husbands Bosworth
Birmingham International Airport
Lutterworth
Desborough
Rushton
Geddington
Ansty
Rothwell
Boughton
Pailton
Swinford
Welford
Allesley
Coventry
Kettering
Brinklow
Solihull
Knowle
Binley
Thornby
Burton Latimer
Brandon
Rugby
Lamport
Kenilworth
Crick
Packwood
Dunchurch
Cottlesbrooke
Brixworth
Bromsgrove
Baddesley Clinton
NORTHAMPTONSHIRE
Wellingborough
Higham
Royal Leamington Spa
Rushden
Redditch
Lowsonford
Warwick
Althorp
Ufton
Daventry
Wootton Wawen
Northampton
Earls Barton
Coughton
WARWICKSHIRE
Southam
Bozeat
Castle Ashby
Alcester
Alveston
Bishop's Itchington
Yardley Hastings
Map 3
Horton
Lavendon
Shottery
Stratford-on-Avon
Blisworth
River Avon
Farnborough
Stoke Bruerne
Olney
Harvington
Norton
Long Marston
Towcester
Edgehill
Sulgrave
Kempston
Evesham
Bretforton
Upper Tysoe
Silverstone
Mickleton
Hidcote
Shipston-on-Stour
Middleton Cheney
Newport Pagnell
Vale of Evesham
BEDFORD
Willersey
Chipping Camden
Wolverton
Broadway
Banbury
Brackley
Milton Keynes
Buckland
Paxford
Swalcliffe
Stanton
Batsford
Addebury
Aynho
Buckingham
Stanway
Moreton-in-Marsh
Snowshill
Deddington
Croughton
Woburn
Padbury
Winchcombe
Bourton-on-the-Hill
Chipping Norton
Steeple Ashton
Great Tew
Guiting Power
Stow-on-the-Wold
Winslow
Stewkley
Leighton Buzzard
Upper Slaughter
Bicester
BUCKINGHAMSHIRE
Brockhampton
Bledington
Lower Slaughter
Wing
Great Rissington
Charlbury
Whitchurch
Dunstable
Bourton-on-the-Water
Waddesdon
Ivinghoe
Cotswold Hills
Northleach
Great Barrington
Leafield
Woodstock
Ramsden
Aylesbury
Aldbury
Swinbrook
Islip
Tring
Chedworth
Bladon
Stone
Burford
Witney
Kidlington
Stanton St John
Long Crendon
North Cerney
Sapperton
Eynsham
Wendover
Aldsworth
Minster Lovell
Stanton Harcourt
Bibury
Berkhamsted
Barnsley
Oxford
Princes Risborough
Coln-St-
Carterton
A
B
C
4
5
6

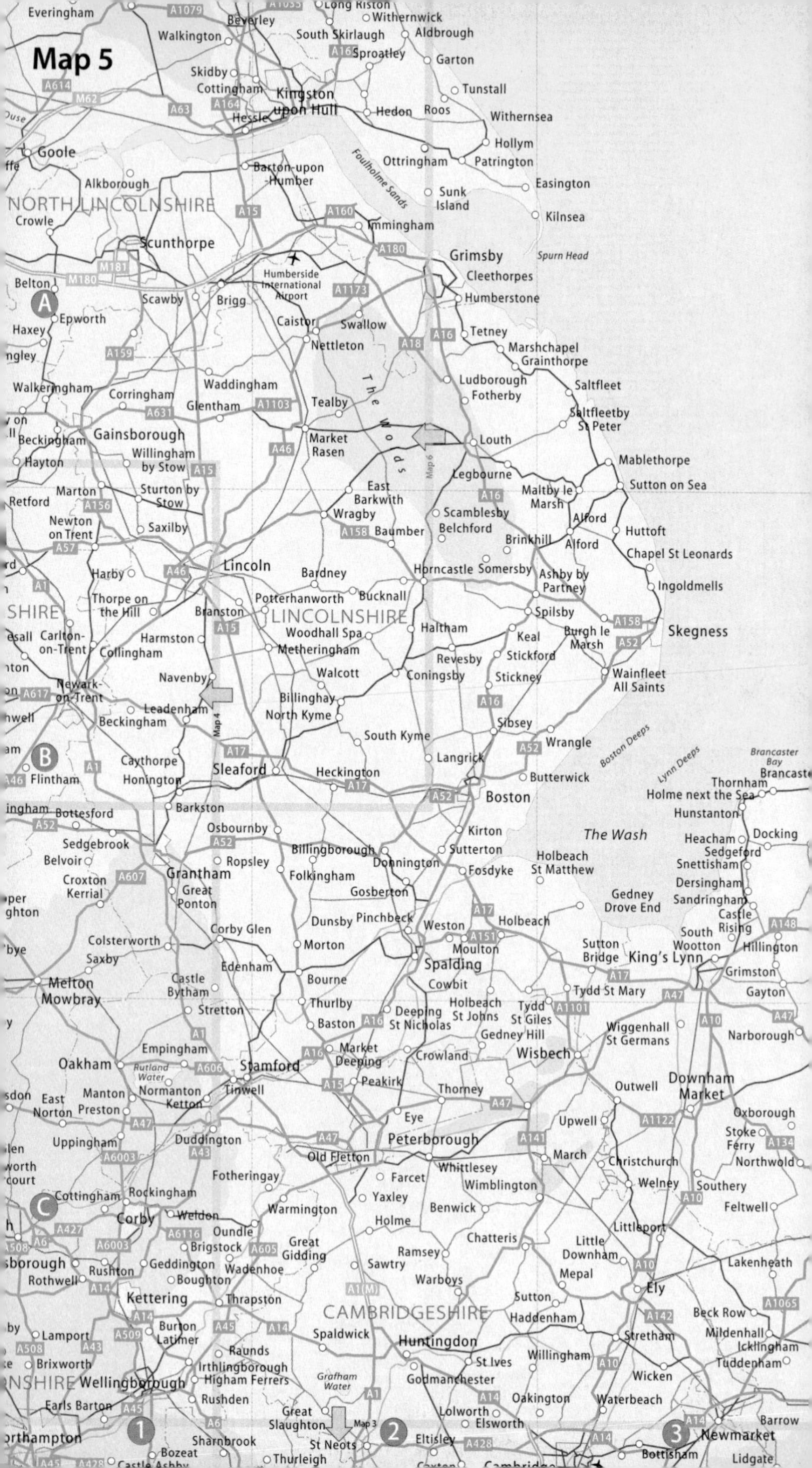

Map 5
Everingham
Beverley
Long Riston
Withernwick
Walkington
South Skirlaugh
Aldbrough
Sproatley
Garton
Skidby
Cottingham
Kingston upon Hull
Tunstall
Hessle
Hedon
Roos
Withernsea
Goole
Hollym
Ottringham
Patrington
Barton-upon-Humber
Foulholme Sands
Alkborough
Sunk Island
Easington
NORTH LINCOLNSHIRE
Crowle
Kilnsea
Immingham
Scunthorpe
Grimsby
Spurn Head
Humberside International Airport
Cleethorpes
Belton
Scawby
Brigg
Humberstone
Epworth
Caistor
Swallow
Haxey
Nettleton
Tetney
Marshchapel
Grainthorpe
The Wolds
Ludborough
Waddingham
Saltfleet
Walkeringham
Corringham
Fotherby
Glentham
Tealby
Saltfleetby St Peter
Beckingham
Gainsborough
Market Rasen
Louth
Hayton
Willingham by Stow
Mablethorpe
Legbourne
Marton
Sturton by Stow
East Barkwith
Maltby le Marsh
Sutton on Sea
Retford
Newton on Trent
Saxilby
Wragby
Scamblesby
Alford
Baumber
Belchford
Huttoft
Brinkhill
Chapel St Leonards
Lincoln
Harby
Bardney
Horncastle
Somersby
Ashby by Partney
Ingoldmells
Thorpe on the Hill
Potterhanworth
Bucknall
Branston
LINCOLNSHIRE
Spilsby
Skegness
Carlton-on-Trent
Harmston
Woodhall Spa
Haltham
Keal
Burgh le Marsh
Collingham
Metheringham
Revesby
Stickford
Walcott
Coningsby
Stickney
Wainfleet All Saints
Navenby
Newark-on-Trent
Billinghay
Leadenham
North Kyme
Beckingham
Sibsey
South Kyme
Wrangle
Boston Deeps
Brancaster Bay
Brancaster
Flintham
Caythorpe
Langrick
Lynn Deeps
Honington
Sleaford
Heckington
Butterwick
Thornham
Holme next the Sea
Boston
Barkston
Bottesford
Hunstanton
Osbournby
Kirton
The Wash
Sedgebrook
Heacham
Docking
Billingborough
Sutterton
Sedgeford
Belvoir
Ropsley
Donnington
Holbeach St Matthew
Snettisham
Croxton Kerrial
Grantham
Folkingham
Fosdyke
Dersingham
Great Ponton
Gosberton
Gedney Drove End
Sandringham
Castle Rising
Dunsby
Pinchbeck
Holbeach
Corby Glen
Weston
South Wootton
Colsterworth
Morton
Moulton
Sutton Bridge
King's Lynn
Hillington
Saxby
Spalding
Edenham
Grimston
Melton Mowbray
Castle Bytham
Bourne
Cowbit
Tydd St Mary
Gayton
Thurlby
Holbeach St Johns
Tydd St Giles
Stretton
Deeping St Nicholas
Baston
Wiggenhall St Germans
Narborough
Gedney Hill
Empingham
Market Deeping
Crowland
Wisbech
Oakham
Rutland Water
Stamford
Peakirk
Outwell
Downham Market
Manton
Normanton
Tinwell
Ketton
Thorney
East Norton
Preston
Eye
Upwell
Oxborough
Stoke Ferry
Uppingham
Duddington
Peterborough
Old Fletton
Whittlesey
March
Christchurch
Northwold
Fotheringay
Farcet
Wimblington
Welney
Southery
Cottingham
Rockingham
Yaxley
Warmington
Benwick
Feltwell
Corby
Weldon
Oundle
Holme
Littleport
Brigstock
Great Gidding
Chatteris
Little Downham
Ramsey
Rushton
Geddington
Sawtry
Lakenheath
Rothwell
Wadenhoe
Mepal
Boughton
Warboys
Ely
Kettering
Thrapston
CAMBRIDGESHIRE
Sutton
Haddenham
Beck Row
Burton Latimer
Mildenhall
Lamport
Spaldwick
Huntingdon
Stretham
Icklingham
Raunds
Willingham
Brixworth
Irthlingborough
St Ives
Tuddenham
Higham Ferrers
Grafham Water
Wicken
Wellingborough
Godmanchester
Rushden
Oakington
Waterbeach
Earls Barton
Great Staughton
Lolworth
Elsworth
Barrow
Sharnbrook
Map 3
Newmarket
Eltisley
Bozeat
St Neots
Bottisham
Thurleigh
Lidgate
Map 4
Map 6

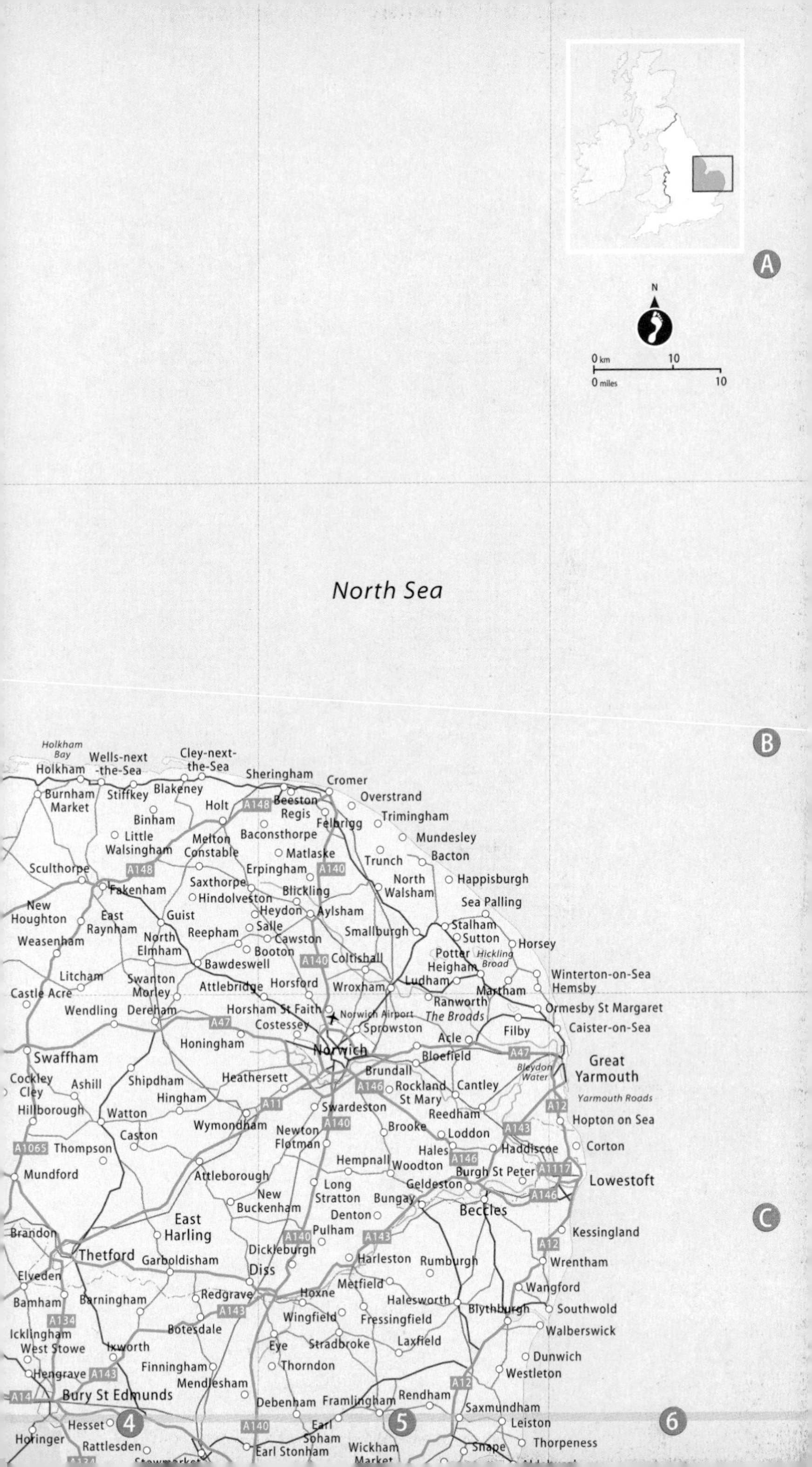

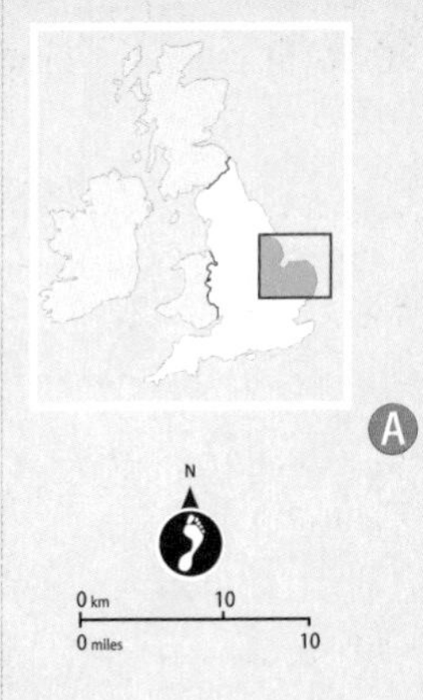

A

N

0 km 10
0 miles 10

North Sea

B

Holkham Bay
Wells-next -the-Sea
Cley-next- the-Sea
Holkham
Sheringham
Cromer
Burnham Market
Stiffkey
Blakeney
Beeston Regis
Overstrand
Holt
A148
Felbrigg
Trimingham
Binham
Baconsthorpe
Little Walsingham
Melton Constable
Mundesley
Matlaske
Sculthorpe
A148
Erpingham
A140
Trunch
Bacton
Fakenham
Saxthorpe
North Walsham
Happisburgh
New Houghton
Hindolveston
Blickling
East Raynham
Guist
Heydon
Aylsham
Sea Palling
Weasenham
North Elmham
Reepham
Salle
Cawston
Smallburgh
Stalham
Sutton
Booton
Horsey
Litcham
Bawdeswell
A140
Coltishall
Potter Heigham
Hickling Broad
Winterton-on-Sea
Hemsby
Castle Acre
Swanton Morley
Attlebridge
Horsford
Wroxham
Ludham
Martham
Wendling
Dereham
Horsham St Faith
Norwich Airport
Ranworth
The Broads
Ormesby St Margaret
A47
Costessey
Sprowston
Filby
Caister-on-Sea
Swaffham
Honingham
Norwich
Acle
Bloefield
A47
Bleydon Water
Great Yarmouth
Cockley Cley
Ashill
Shipdham
Heathersett
Brundall
Rockland St Mary
Cantley
Yarmouth Roads
Hilborough
Hingham
A146
A11
Swardeston
Reedham
A12
Hopton on Sea
Watton
Wymondham
A140
Brooke
Loddon
A143
Caston
Newton Flotman
Hales
Haddiscoe
Corton
A1065
Thompson
A146
Hempnall
Woodton
Burgh St Peter
A1117
Mundford
Attleborough
Geldeston
Lowestoft
Long Stratton
Bungay
A146
New Buckenham
Beccles
East Harling
Denton
C
Brandon
A140
Pulham
A143
Kessingland
Thetford
Garboldisham
Dickleburgh
A12
Diss
Harleston
Rumburgh
Wrentham
Elveden
Metfield
Wangford
Bamham
Barningham
Redgrave
Hoxne
Halesworth
Blythburgh
Southwold
A134
A143
Wingfield
Fressingfield
Icklingham
Botesdale
Walberswick
West Stowe
Ixworth
Eye
Stradbroke
Laxfield
Dunwich
Finningham
Thorndon
Westleton
Hengrave
A143
A12
Mendlesham
A14
Bury St Edmunds
Debenham
Framlingham
Rendham
Saxmundham
Hesset
4
A140
Earl Soham
5
Leiston
6
Horringer
Rattlesden
Earl Stonham
Wickham Market
Snape
Thorpeness

Map 6
Derwent Water
Glenridding
Ullswater
Martindale
Thirlmere
Patterdale
Helvellyn
Haweswater
Shap
M6
CUMBRIA
A66
Brough
North Stainmore
Barnard Castle
Bowes
A67
A685
Winton
Kirkby Stephen
A66
Grasmere
Dungeon Ghyll
Grasmere
Rydal Water
Scafell Pike
Elterwater
Ambleside
Kentmere
Troutbeck
Tebay
A685
Ravenstonedale
Scotch Corner
Richmond
Keld
Boot
Hawkshead
Windermere
Staveley
Grayrigg
Reeth
Thwaite
Muker
Feetham
Bowness-on-Windermere
Coniston Water
Crook
Kendal
Sedburgh
Grizedale
Windermere
Underbarrow
River Kent
Oxenholme
Dent
Hawes
Askrigg
Bainbridge
Redmire
Leyburn
Wensley
Aysgarth
West Witton
East Witton
Broughton in Furness
Newby Bridge
Levens
Sedgwick
River Lune
Middleton
A590
Heversham
Masham
A595
Millom
Ulverston
Lindale
Cartmel
Holker
Kirkby Lonsdale
Yorkshire Dales
NORTH YORKSHIRE
Map 7
A590
Bardsea
Grange-over-Sands
Burton-in-Kendal
A65
Horton-in-Ribblesdale
Buckden
Litton
Kettlewell
Middlesmoor
Warton
Borwick
A687
Ingleton
Ramsgill
Aldingham
Carnforth
A683
Clapham
Austwick
Starbotton
Barrow-in-Furness
Bolton-le-Sands
Hornby
Stainforth
Conistone
Pateley Bridge
Morecambe
Claughton
Giggleswick
Grassington
Settle
Threshfield
Burnsall
Summerbridge
Heysham
Lancaster
Long Preston
Linton
Malham
Appletreewick
A65
M6
Overton
Galgate
Wigglesworth
Rylstone
Glasson
Blubberhouses
Embsay
Bolton Abbey
Fewston
Dolphinholme
A682
A65
Cockerham
A59
Skipton
Addingham
Fleetwood
Askwith
Pilling
Silsden
Ilkley
Otley
Ferry to Isle of Man
Cleveleys
Hambleton
Waddington
A56
A629
Thornton
River Wyre
Catterall
A682
A6068
Guiseley
Clitheroe
Keighley
LANCASHIRE
A59
Barrowford
Colne
Bingley
Yeadon
Poulton-le-Fylde
Nelson
Blackpool
A585
Whalley
Brierfield
Haworth
Shipley
M55
Padiham
A629
Wrea Green
Kirkham
Burnley
Oxenhope
Bradford
Blackpool Airport
Fulwood
Rishton
Clayton-le-Moors
Lytham St Anne's
Freckleton
Preston
Blackburn
Accrington
Hebden Bridge
Queensbury
M606
A59
Oswaldtwistle
Halifax
River Ribble
Longton
Haslingden
Withnell
Bacup
Todmorden
Brighouse
Tarleton
Banks
Leyland
Darwen
Rawtenstall
Mirfield
A565
A666
Elland
Eccleston
Ramsbottom
Southport
Chorley
Whitworth
Littleborough
M61
A640
A570
Rufford
M62
Adlington
M66
Huddersfield
Slaithwaite
A59
M6
Burscough Bridge
Parbold
Rochdale
Kirkburton
Ainsdale
Horwich
Denshaw
Standish
Meltham
Bolton
Bury
A629
Shaw
Marsden
Ormskirk
Royton
Denby Dale
Great Altcar
Wigan
Formby
Skelmersdale
Farnworth
A59
Oldham
Holmfirth
A565
Hindley
Middleton
Lees
Dunford Bridge
Maghull
M58
Atherton
Mossley
Rainford
M60
M57
Ashton-under-Lyne
Leigh
A628
Crosby
Aintree
Manchester
Langsett
Kirkby
Billinge
Litherland
Ferry to Isle of Man
Salford
St Helens
A580
Bootle
A580
Knowsley
M67
Hollingworth
Peak
Wallasey
M62
Birkenhead
Glossop
Prescot
M60
Hoylake
Liverpool
Warrington
A57
A56
Stockport
Marple
High Peak
Port Sunlight
Lymm
Altrincham
Cheadle
Hazel Grove
New Mills
Edale
Kirby
A561
Liverpool John Lennon Airport
A50
Bebington
Widnes
Thurstaston
A56
Manchester Airport
A6
Bamford
A41
Poynton
Map 4
Castleton
Heswall
Runcorn
A556
Bromborough
Stretton
A523
Hope
Whaley Bridge
Chapel-en-le-Frith
Willaston
Great Budworth
Wilmslow
Alderley Edge
Hathersage
Ellesmere Port
M53
Knutsford
Eyam
Neston
Frodsham
Bollington
A623
Prestbury
Buxton
Weaverham
Tideswell
Northwich
A6
A49
A556
Macclesfield
Mollington
C
Tarvin
CHESHIRE
Holmes Chapel
A34
DERBYSHIRE
Chester
Kelsall
A54
A51
A536
Flash
Bakewell
WALES
Christleton
Winsford
Middlewich
A54
A55
A53
A515
Tarporley
Congleton
Eccleston
Hartington
A523
Bunbury
Sandbach
Aldford
A51
A34
A530
A534
Alsager
Biddulph
Leek
A515
Burwardsley
Crewe
Kidsgrove
Wirksworth
A534
M6
Broxton
Bulkeley
A534
A520
Endon
Nantwich
A500
A500
A523
Tissington
Audley
A53
0 km
10
0 miles
10
A49
Malpas
Newcastle-under-Lyme
A41
Aston
Walgherton
Stoke-on-Trent
A52
Ashbourne
Threapwood
A525
Mayfield
A53
Cheadle
A52
A525
Whitmore
Denstone
Whitchurch
Woore
Adderley
A520
A34
Blythe
Upper Tean

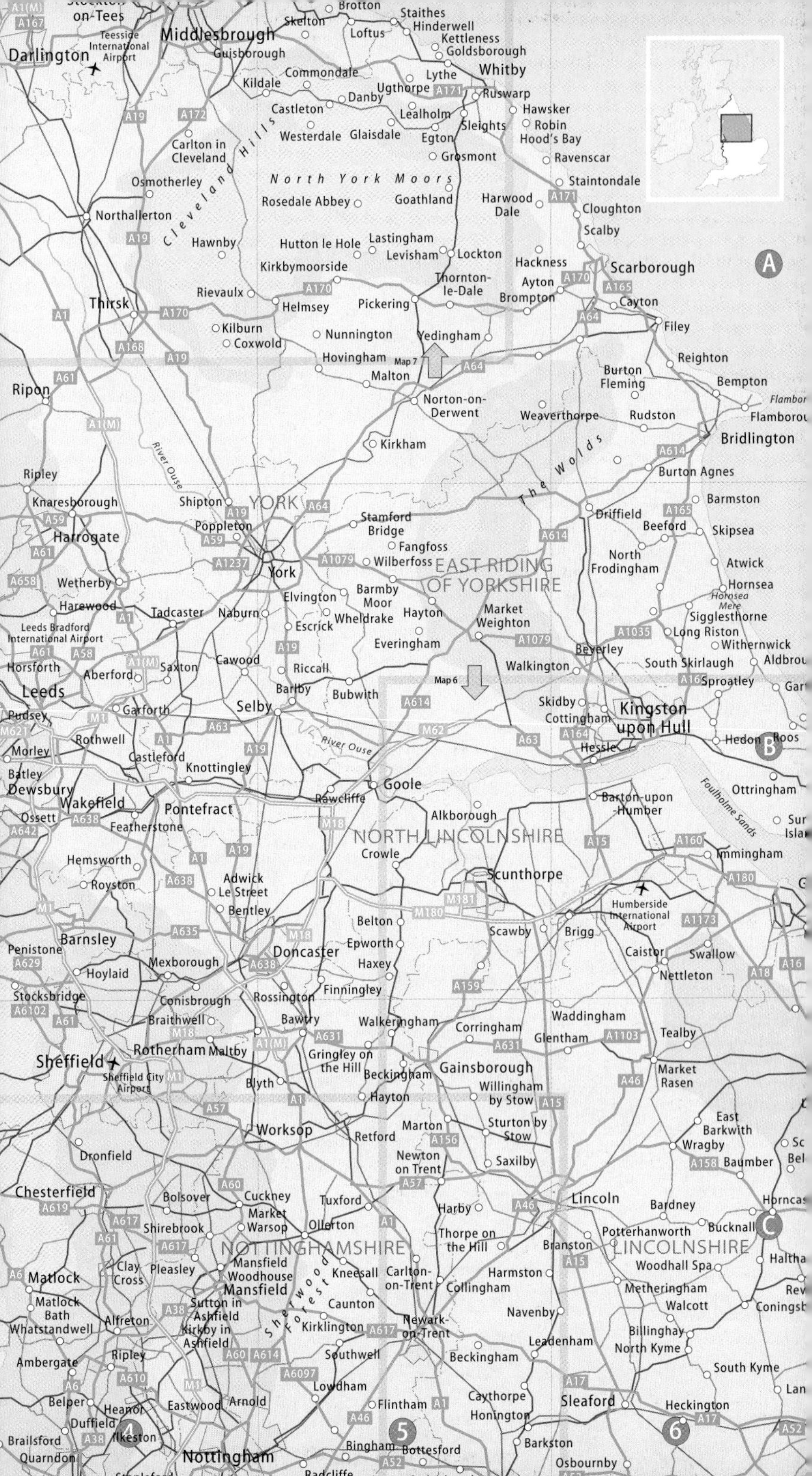

Brotton
Staithes
on-Tees
Skelton
Hinderwell
Middlesbrough
Teesside International Airport
Loftus
Kettleness
Darlington
Guisborough
Goldsborough
Commondale
Lythe
Whitby
Kildale
Danby
Ugthorpe
Ruswarp
Castleton
Lealholm
Hawsker
Sleights
Robin Hood's Bay
Westerdale
Glaisdale
Egton
Carlton in Cleveland
Grosmont
Ravenscar
Cleveland Hills
North York Moors
Osmotherley
Staintondale
Rosedale Abbey
Goathland
Harwood Dale
Cloughton
Northallerton
Scalby
Hawnby
Hutton le Hole
Lastingham
Levisham
Lockton
Hackness
Scarborough
Kirkbymoorside
Thornton-le-Dale
Ayton
Rievaulx
Helmsey
Pickering
Brompton
Cayton
Thirsk
Filey
Kilburn
Nunnington
Yedingham
Coxwold
Hovingham
Map 7
Reighton
Malton
Burton Fleming
Bempton
Ripon
Norton-on-Derwent
Weaverthorpe
Rudston
Bridlington
Kirkham
River Ouse
The Wolds
Burton Agnes
Ripley
Barmston
Knaresborough
Shipton
YORK
Driffield
Stamford Bridge
Beeford
Skipsea
Harrogate
Poppleton
Fangfoss
North Frodingham
Wilberfoss
York
EAST RIDING OF YORKSHIRE
Atwick
Wetherby
Hornsea
Hornsea Mere
Elvington
Barmby Moor
Harewood
Tadcaster
Naburn
Market Weighton
Sigglesthorne
Hayton
Wheldrake
Leeds Bradford International Airport
Escrick
Long Riston
Everingham
Withernwick
Cawood
Beverley
Horsforth
Saxton
Riccall
Walkington
South Skirlaugh
Aberford
Map 6
Sproatley
Barlby
Bubwith
Leeds
Skidby
Selby
Garforth
Kingston upon Hull
Cottingham
Pudsey
Rothwell
Hedon
Roos
Morley
Castleford
River Ouse
Hessle
Batley
Knottingley
Goole
Ottringham
Dewsbury
Foulholme Sands
Wakefield
Pontefract
Rawcliffe
Barton-upon-Humber
Ossett
Alkborough
Featherstone
NORTH LINCOLNSHIRE
Crowle
Immingham
Hemsworth
Scunthorpe
Adwick Le Street
Royston
Humberside International Airport
Bentley
Belton
Scawby
Brigg
Barnsley
Epworth
Caistor
Swallow
Penistone
Doncaster
Haxey
Mexborough
Nettleton
Hoylaid
Finningley
Stocksbridge
Conisbrough
Rossington
Waddingham
Braithwell
Bawtry
Walkeringham
Corringham
Tealby
Glentham
Rotherham
Maltby
Gringley on the Hill
Sheffield
Market Rasen
Sheffield City Airport
Beckingham
Gainsborough
Blyth
Willingham by Stow
Hayton
Marton
Sturton by Stow
East Barkwith
Worksop
Retford
Wragby
Dronfield
Newton on Trent
Saxilby
Baumber
Chesterfield
Tuxford
Lincoln
Bolsover
Cuckney
Harby
Bardney
Market Warsop
Ollerton
Shirebrook
Potterhanworth
Bucknall
Thorpe on the Hill
Branston
NOTTINGHAMSHIRE
LINCOLNSHIRE
Clay Cross
Pleasley
Mansfield Woodhouse
Woodhall Spa
Matlock
Kneesall
Carlton-on-Trent
Harmston
Mansfield
Collingham
Metheringham
Matlock Bath
Sutton in Ashfield
Sherwood Forest
Caunton
Walcott
Navenby
Alfreton
Whatstandwell
Kirkby in Ashfield
Kirklington
Newark-on-Trent
Billinghay
Leadenham
North Kyme
Ripley
Southwell
Ambergate
Beckingham
South Kyme
Lowdham
Belper
Heanor
Arnold
Caythorpe
Sleaford
Eastwood
Flintham
Heckington
Duffield
Honington
Ilkeston
Brailsford
Bingham
Bottesford
Barkston
Quarndon
Nottingham
Osbournby
Radcliffe
A
B
C
4
5
6

Map 7

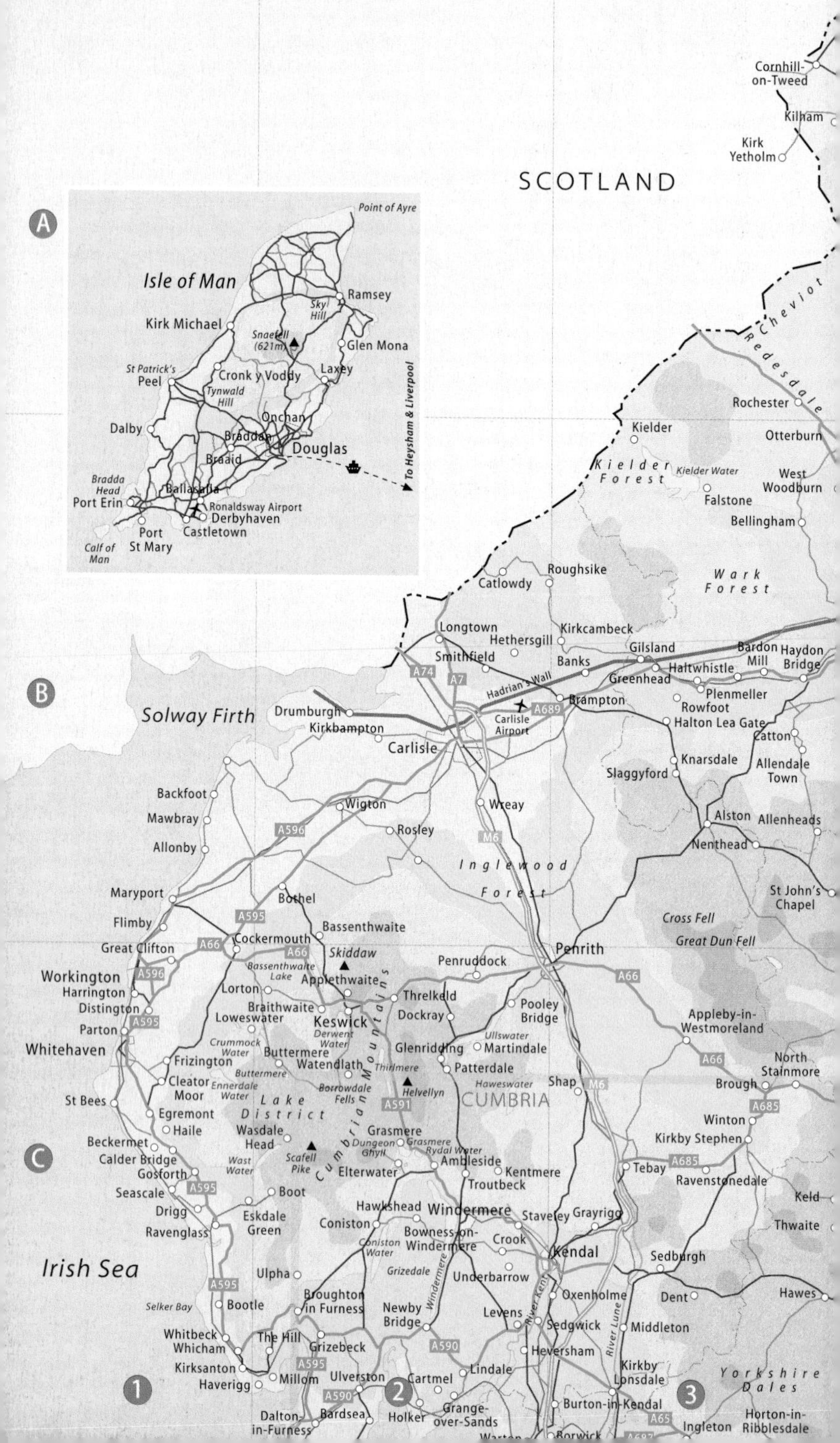

SCOTLAND

Cornhill-on-Tweed
Kilham
Kirk Yetholm

A

Isle of Man
Point of Ayre
Ramsey
Sky Hill
Kirk Michael
Snaefell (621m)
Glen Mona
St Patrick's Peel
Cronk y Voddy
Laxey
Tynwald Hill
Onchan
Dalby
Braddan
Douglas
To Heysham & Liverpool
Braaid
Bradda Head
Ballasalla
Port Erin
Ronaldsway Airport
Derbyhaven
Port St Mary
Castletown
Calf of Man

Cheviot
Redesdale
Rochester
Kielder
Otterburn
Kielder Forest
Kielder Water
West Woodburn
Falstone
Bellingham
Roughsike
Catlowdy
Wark Forest
Longtown
Kirkcambeck
Hethersgill
Gilsland
Bardon Mill
Haydon Bridge
Smithfield
Banks
Haltwhistle
Greenhead
Hadrian's Wall
Plenmeller
Brampton
Rowfoot

B

Solway Firth
Drumburgh
Kirkbampton
Carlisle
Carlisle Airport
Halton Lea Gate
Catton
Knarsdale
Allendale Town
Slaggyford
Backfoot
Wigton
Wreay
Alston
Allenheads
Mawbray
Rosley
Nenthead
Allonby
Inglewood Forest
Maryport
Bothel
St John's Chapel
Cross Fell
Flimby
Bassenthwaite
Great Dun Fell
Great Clifton
Cockermouth
Skiddaw
Penrith
Workington
Bassenthwaite Lake
Applethwaite
Penruddock
Harrington
Lorton
Threlkeld
Distington
Braithwaite
Pooley Bridge
Appleby-in-Westmoreland
Parton
Loweswater
Keswick
Dockray
Whitehaven
Derwent Water
Crummock Water
Buttermere
Glenridding
Ullswater
Martindale
North Stainmore
Frizington
Watendlath
Thirlmere
Patterdale
Cleator Moor
Ennerdale Water
Buttermere
Borrowdale Fells
Helvellyn
Haweswater
Shap
Brough
St Bees
Lake District
Cumbrian Mountains
CUMBRIA
Egremont
Winton
Haile
Grasmere
Kirkby Stephen
Wasdale Head
Dungeon Ghyll
Grasmere
Rydal Water
Beckermet

C

Calder Bridge
Scafell Pike
Ambleside
Tebay
Gosforth
Wast Water
Elterwater
Kentmere
Ravenstonedale
Seascale
Troutbeck
Boot
Keld
Drigg
Hawkshead
Windermere
Staveley
Grayrigg
Ravenglass
Eskdale Green
Coniston
Thwaite
Bowness-on-Windermere
Crook
Coniston Water
Kendal
Sedburgh
Irish Sea
Ulpha
Grizedale
Underbarrow
Windermere
Hawes
Selker Bay
Bootle
Broughton in Furness
Newby Bridge
Oxenholme
Dent
Levens
River Kent
River Lune
Sedgwick
Middleton
Whitbeck
Whicham
The Hill
Grizebeck
Heversham
Kirksanton
Lindale
Kirkby Lonsdale
Yorkshire Dales
Haverigg
Millom
Ulverston
Cartmel
Burton-in-Kendal
Dalton-in-Furness
Bardsea
Holker
Grange-over-Sands
Ingleton
Horton-in-Ribblesdale

A7
A74
A689
A596
M6
A595
A66
A591
A685
A590
A65

1
2
3

Berwick-upon-Tweed
Tweedmouth
Norham
Cheswick
Grindon
Ancroft
Holy Island
Holy Island
Duddo
Bowsden
Farne Islands
Crookham
Ford
Lowick
Ross
Bamburgh
Flodden
Milfield
Doddington
Seahouses
Kirknewton
Beadnell
Akeld
Chillingham
Wooler
Ellingham
High Newton-by-the-Sea
The Cheviot Hills
North Charlton
Embleton
Eglingham
Craster
Wooperton
Howick
Rennington
Longhoughton
Glanton
Alnwick
Boulmer
Lesbury
Alnmouth
Edlingham
Warkworth
Snitter
Amble
Holystone
Newton on the Moor
Rothbury
Rothbury Forest
Broomhill
Hepple
Longhorsley
Widdrington
Cresswell
Elsdon
Ellington
West Woodburn
Ashington
Newbiggin-by-the-Sea
Kirkwhelpington
Morpeth
Ridsdale
Cambois
NORTHUMBERLAND
Bedlington
Blyth
Belsay
Cramlington
Seaton Sluice
Newcastle International Airport
Whitley Bay
Chollerford
Ponteland
Humshaugh
Hadrian's Wall
Newcastle upon Tyne
Tynemouth
South Shields
Corbridge
Ryton
Gateshead
Hexham
Prudhoe
Blaydon
Whitburn
Riding Mill
Whickham
Rowlands Gill
Sunderland
Slaley
Whittonstall
Washington
Stanley
Houghton-le-Spring
Ryhope
Consett
Chester-le-Street
Seaham
Anfield Plain
Blanchland
Hetton-Le-Hole
North Sea
Durham
Easington
Peterlee
Eastgate
Stanhope
Brandon
Wolsingham
Tow Law
Westgate
Crook
Frosterley
Hartlepool
Willington
DURHAM
Spennymoor
Bishop Auckland
Woodland
Redcar
Newton Aycliffe
Marske-by-the-Sea
Billingham
Saltburn-by-the-Sea
Staindrop
Stockton-on-Tees
Brotton
Staithes
Skelton
Barnard Castle
Hinderwell
Map 6
Loftus
Darlington
Middlesbrough
Kettleness
Teesside International Airport
Bowes
Goldsborough
Guisborough
Whitby
Lythe
Commondale
Kildale
Ugthorpe
Danby
Ruswarp
Castleton
Lealholm
Scotch Corner
Sleights
Westerdale
Glaisdale
Egton
Richmond
Carlton in Cleveland
Grosmont
Reeth
Osmotherley
North York Moors
Cleveland Hills
Muker
Feetham
Rosedale Abbey
Goathland
Harwood Dale
Northallerton
Askrigg
Redmire
Leyburn
Hawnby
Hutton le Hole
Lastingham
Bainbridge
Levisham
Lockton
Wensley
Aysgarth
West Witton
Kirkbymoorside
Thornton-le-Dale
East Witton
Rievaulx
Helmsey
Pickering
Thirsk
Masham
NORTH YORKSHIRE
Kilburn
Nunnington
Yedingham
Buckden
Coxwold
Hovingham
Middlesmoor
Malton
Litton
A1
A1068
A696
A189
A68
A19
A69
A1231
A1018
A693
A167
A691
A690
A1(M)
A689
A688
A6072
A67
A66(M)
A66
A171
A172
A170
A168
A61
A64
A
B
C
4
6
N
0 km
10
0 miles
10